Drawing on the unique resources of the *Oxford English Dictionary*, *Stone the Crows* features over 6,000 slang words and expressions, from the British **beer goggles**, through the American **cockamamie**, to the Australian **giggle-house**. This fascinating collection contains old favourites as well as the very latest slang terms. In addition to the A–Z entries, the book contains a comprehensive thematic index, details of origins, dates of first printed use, and thousands of illustrative quotations from famous names including John Lennon and Woody Allen. Lively and entertaining, *Stone the Crows* is sure to provide a stonking good read for all.

Blue funk
Bunny-boiler
Cow-spanker
Futz
Happy as Larry
Monkey-man
Off one's rocker
Q.B.I.
Phoney baloney
Shonky
Safe
Toad-stabber
Trustafarian
Waffle stomper
Wingding
Zazzy

Stone the Crows

Stone the Crows

Oxford Dictionary of Modern Slang

Second Edition

John Ayto
John Simpson

OXFORD
UNIVERSITY PRESS

OXFORD
UNIVERSITY PRESS

Great Clarendon Street, Oxford OX2 6DP

Oxford University Press is a department of the University of Oxford.
It furthers the University's objective of excellence in research, scholarship,
and education by publishing worldwide in

Oxford New York

Auckland Cape Town Dar es Salaam Hong Kong
Karachi Kuala Lumpur Madrid Melbourne Mexico City Nairobi
New Delhi Shangai Taipei Toronto

With offices in

Argentina Austria Brazil Chile Czech Republic France Greece
Guatemala Hungary Italy Japan Poland Portugal
Singapore South Korea Switzerland Thailand Turkey Ukraine Vietnam

Oxford is a registered trade mark of Oxford University Press
in the UK and in certain other countries

Published in the United States
by Oxford University Press Inc., New York

British Library Cataloguing in Publication Data

Data available

Library of Congress Cataloging in Publication Data

Data available

Typeset by SPI Publisher Services, Pondicherry, India
Printed in Great Britain
on acid-free paper by
Clays Ltd., St Ives plc

ISBN 978-0-19-954370-0

1

Contents

The body and its functions
People and society
Animals
Sustenance and intoxication
Articles and substances
Money, commerce, and employment
Behaviour, attitudes, and emotions
Thought and communication
The arts, entertainment, and the media
Time and tide
Location and movement
Abstract qualities and states

Preface
to Second Edition

A year, to paraphrase Harold Wilson, is a long time in slang. Sixteen years have now passed since the publication of the first edition of the *Oxford Dictionary of Modern Slang*, and it is more than high time it was refreshed.

Over that period, thousands of new slang words and expressions have flooded into the English language, most of them only to be flushed summarily away, but many tenacious enough to make at least some sort of semi-permanent impression on the language. It may seem to many that the late 20th and early 21st centuries have been a golden age for English slang, in variety, inventiveness, and not least quantity. That could well be the case (although as far as quantity is concerned, reliable statistics are hard to obtain in this field). If it is, to what can we attribute it? Numerous factors must play a part, among which the most salient are probably the much wider acceptance accorded nowadays to colloquial or informal language (of which slang forms a part) than was the case a quarter of a century ago, and the higher profile enjoyed by all facets of youth culture, from which a significant proportion of new slang emerges. The deconstruction of deferential hierarchies has had inevitable linguistic consequences: contexts in which relatively formal language was once de rigueur now happily embrace colloquialism. Media outlets, broadcast and print, and other electronic communications both contribute to and promulgate the trend, which has headed firmly in the tabloid direction (it would once have been unthinkable, for instance, to hear *gun down* on a BBC news bulletin). Fear of fuddy-duddiness facilitates the spread of youth slang beyond its original enclaves. The most powerful driving force in this area over the past twenty years has been hip-hop culture. Originating among the African American and Hispanic populations of New York City in the late 1970s, and comprising elements such as rap music, graffiti art, and break-dancing, its vocabulary was not slow to cross the Atlantic, where it melded with Afro-Caribbean and South African elements and items of existing British urban slang to form the new cool-speak. Probably its best-known 21st-century representative was *bling-bling* (or simply *bling*), which duly made the cross-over to general usage, but it had already been preceded there by many others, such as *crew*, *phat*, and *tag*.

The perennial questions about what to include and what to leave out are always more acute in the case of slang, with its reputation for ephemerality (unless one is misguided enough to steer towards that lexicographic mirage, the comprehensive slang dictionary). In the present case the editors have adhered to the policy of the first edition of the *Oxford Dictionary of Modern Slang*, as set out in the Introduction: to cover slang of the 20th century which is included in the *Oxford English Dictionary*. Its publication followed closely on that of the second edition of the *OED*; this new edition takes the story forwards by including the slang items which appear in the ongoing online third edition of the *OED*. It also plugs a few gaps in the coverage of its original version, particularly from other, non-British varieties of English—most notably American and Australian. In all, around a thousand additional items—new words, and new meanings of existing words—have found their way into this edition, from *ace boon coon* to *gay* 'foolish, lame', from *tombstoning* to *wag*, from *chuddies* to *knobhead*. A feature included for the first time is a thematic index, which enables the user to track down slang expressions in a particular subject area, and also to gain an impression of those areas of human existence that are the most prolific engenderers of slang.

As in the first edition, a date is given against each word and meaning included, representing the earliest written or printed example of it in the *OED*'s files. Thanks to the ongoing work of revising the *OED*, the editors have been able to antedate several items from the original edition (often by a considerable margin: for example, *meat-head* 'stupid person' from 1945 to 1863, and *organ* as a euphemism for 'penis' from 1903 to 1833). But there is still much evidence out there waiting to be uncovered, and as before, we would be delighted to hear from anyone who can provide a reliably dated earlier attestation for any item in the dictionary.

Introduction

to First Edition

S lang is a colourful, alternative vocabulary. It bristles with humour, vituperation, prejudice, informality: the slang of English is English with its sleeves rolled up, its shirt-tails dangling, and its shoes covered in mud. This dictionary presents a panoramic view of twentieth-century English slang—from Britain, North America, Australia, and elsewhere in the English-speaking world— from World War I until the present day.

The *Oxford English Dictionary* identifies three types of slang. The first to which the term 'slang' was applied, in the mid-eighteenth century, was 'the special vocabulary used by any set of persons of a low and disreputable character', the thieves' cant or patter of earlier centuries. This vein of slang thrives today in the vocabulary of the underworld, street gangs, drug-trafficking. But soon after the mid-eighteenth century, the meaning of 'slang' broadened to include 'the special vocabulary or phraseology of a particular calling or profession': printers' slang, costermongers' slang, even the slang vocabulary of doctors and lawyers. Both of these types of slang served many purposes, but the predominant one was as a private vocabulary binding together members of a subculture or social group, conferring upon them an individuality distinct from the rest of the community. Finally, in the early years of the nineteenth century, the term 'slang' came to be applied much more generally to any 'language of a highly colloquial type, considered as below the level of standard educated speech, and consisting either of new words or of current words employed in some new special sense'. Today slang covers all three of these areas: not all colloquial or informal vocabulary is slang, but all slang is colloquial or informal.

The *Oxford Dictionary of Modern Slang* contains the slang of the twentieth century which is included in the twenty-volume *Oxford English Dictionary*. Some minor terms have been omitted, when it was clear that they had not obtained a substantial foothold in the language. But in addition, a further five hundred or so slang words, or slang meanings of words, have been included which are currently in preparation for the *OED* but which have not yet been published there.

The vocabulary of slang changes rapidly: what is new and exciting for one generation is old-fashioned for the next. Old slang often either drifts into obsolescence or becomes accepted into the standard language, losing its eccentric colour. Slang items from the nineteenth century and earlier that have remained in the nether regions of the English language to the present day are included in the dictionary, but those that have proved upwardly mobile— including ones which originated in the twentieth century—are not. *Flapper*, for instance, started life in the late nineteenth century as a slang term for a young unconventional or lively woman, but subsequently moved into the general language as a specific term for such a young woman of the 1920s, so it finds no place in this book. Similarly, the use of *gay* in the sense 'homosexual' has its roots firmly in slang (of the 1930s), but is now widely accepted as standard terminology, so it too is not included. Many words take the opposite course: *arse*, for example, was the normal word for 'buttocks' in the Old and Middle English period; only thereafter did it begin to be perceived as 'rude', and to slip into that area of the language regarded as 'slang'.

The pace of change in the usage of slang is curious in its own right, and was an aspect which we wanted to highlight in this dictionary. As a result, each slang word or meaning is supplied with the date at which it is first recorded as entering the English language. In addition, multiple slang senses for any word are ordered chronologically in each entry, with the earliest first and the most recent last. These datings are taken in the main from the full *OED*, though occasionally earlier attestations are taken from other sources (notably the *Australian National Dictionary* and the Oxford English Dictionary department's own unpublished files). These are predominantly based on printed sources, and it is commonly argued that slang vocabulary lives for many years an underground existence before it comes to be written down, and that therefore these earliest dates do not necessarily reflect the real picture. Other dictionaries—and in particular Eric Partridge's *Dictionary of Slang and Unconventional English*—supply approximate dates at which a word or sense is thought to have come into use. Such a system is perfectly respectable, but suffers in turn from the charge of subjectivity: it is likely that some dates are too cautious and others too adventurous. In choosing to supply the earliest dates available to us from the printed record, we hope that the dictionary represents a checklist of what is actually known for certain about each slang term, and also that readers who come across earlier attestations—which do in many cases certainly exist—will alert us to them so that we will be able to correct this aspect of the heritage of English in subsequent editions. As well as this, we should be delighted to receive notification (particularly from published sources) of items which have not been included in the present edition, but which might merit inclusion at a later date.

It should also be noted that in the case of words (like *arse*) which began life as standard terms but later came to be regarded as slang, we have generally given the date of the first recorded occurrence of the term in the relevant sense, regardless of its level of usage.

On occasions, slang can be offensive, because it singles out a particular group of people in an insulting or condescending way, or because it breaks taboos about permissible objects of reference in everyday speech. The English language is not always politically correct. But it would have been improper to censor the contents of this dictionary on such grounds, and indeed the tradition of the lexicography of slang in English has required that such language be included. Prejudicial or coarse vocabulary has been labelled accordingly. Our view has been that however regrettable this aspect of English may be, its inclusion in a dictionary of slang does not sanction its use, but simply records the facts as far as they are available.

Each entry in the dictionary consists at its barest of a headword, part of speech, definition, and period of usage. The great majority of the entries are also supplied with at least one illustrative example of the term in context, from a published source. These examples are not usually the first recorded use, but represent typical later examples from throughout the present century, and attempt to give some impression of the flavour of the word illustrated. These citations are normally extracted from the full *Oxford English Dictionary*, to which the reader is referred for more comprehensive bibliographical and other information. Occasionally citations are taken from other sources, most often from the files of the *OED*.

Many entries also contain labels indicating the region, social group, or discipline within which a word is prevalent. It is therefore possible to trace a word's development from, say, the slang of service personnel in World War I, through changes of meaning as it was taken up in North America or Australia, to a modern sense restricted to the vocabulary of a particular 'calling or profession'. The genealogy of slang presented in this way often reveals a surprisingly tortuous and humorous or idiosyncratic development.

Derivations or etymologies are not supplied when they are self-evident. On the other hand, popular misconceptions are typically alluded to, if only to be dismissed. Similarly, pronunciations are given (in the International Phonetic Alphabet) only in cases of ambiguity or other difficulty.

Pronunciation symbols

Consonants

b	but	l	leg	t	top	θ	thin
d	dog	m	man	v	voice	ð	this
f	few	n	no	w	we	ŋ	ring
g	get	p	pen	z	zoo	x	loch
h	he	r	red	ʃ	she	tʃ	chip
j	yes	s	sit	ʒ	decision	dʒ	jar
k	cat						

Vowels

æ	cat	ɒ	hot	aɪ	my	ɪə	near
a:	arm	ɔ:	saw	aʊ	how	ɔɪ	boy
e	bed	ʌ	run	eɪ	day	ʊə	poor
ɜ:	her	ʊ	put	əʊ	no	aɪə	fire
ɪ	sit	u:	too	eə	hair	aʊə	sour
ɪ:	see	ə	ago				

(ə) signifies the indeterminate sound as in garden, carnal, and rhythm.

(r) at the end of a word indicates an r that is sounded when a word beginning with a vowel follows, as in *clutter up* and *an acre of land*.

The main or primary stress of a word is shown by ' preceding the relevant syllable; any secondary stress in words of three or more syllables is shown by ˌ preceding the relevant syllable.

Principal abbreviations

a. (in dates)	before
Austral	Australian (English)
attrib	attributive
b.	born
Brit	British (English)
c. (in dates)	about
cap	capital(s)
cent.	century
cf.	compare
comb form	combining form
compar.	comparative
conj	conjunction
derog	derogatory
esp.	especially
fig.	figurative
int	interjection
intr.	intransitive
N Amer	North American (English)
NZ	New Zealand (English)
obs.	obsolete
OE	Old English
orig	originally
perh.	perhaps
phr.	phrase
pl.	plural
prep	preposition
prob.	probably
pron	pronoun
refl	reflexive
S Afr	South African (English)
sing.	singular
spec.	specifically
superl.	superlative
trans.	transitive
transf.	in transferred sense
US	United States (English)
usu.	usually

abaht /ə'ba:t/ prep (Used in writing to represent) a Cockney or other British dialect pronunciation of *about*. 1898–. G. B. SHAW Wot abaht them! Waw, theyre eah (1901).

Abdul noun Applied, usu. dismissively, to a Turkish man or Arab, often specifically a Turkish soldier, esp. in World War I. 1916–. G. BERRIE I'd give a quid to be planted somewhere where I could watch some Abdul go in (1949). [From the Arabic male forename.]

Abo /'æbəʊ/ adjective and noun Also **abo.** Austral, now mainly derog (An) Aboriginal. 1908–. BULLETIN (Sydney): The idea of better housing for the abos (1933). [Shortened from *aboriginal*.]

abso-bloody-lutely adverb Used as a considerably more emphatic version of 'absolutely'. 1935–. E. WEEKLEY A crude example of this persisting instinct [to 'add body and content to words'] is offered by the contemporary *abso-bloody-lutely* (1935). Other infixed forms of the word are **abso-blessed-lutely,** the now dated **abso-bally-lutely,** the equally euphemistic **abso-blooming-lutely** (A. J. LERNER Oh so loverly sittin' abso-bloomin'-lutely still! I would never budge 'til Spring crept over me windersill (1956)), and **abso-fucking-lutely.**

Abyssinia noun jocular Used when taking leave of someone. 1934–. L. P. HARTLEY Goodbye, dear, cheerio, Abyssinia (1949). [A use of *Abyssinia*, former name of Ethiopia, based on its supposed resemblance to a casual pronunciation of *I'll be seeing you*, an expression of farewell.]

Acapulco gold noun A high grade of marijuana, typically brownish- or greenish-gold in colour, originally grown around Acapulco, a seaside resort on the west coast of Mexico. Also **Acapulco.** 1965–.

acca noun Also **acker** Austral An academic. 1977–. SUN (Melbourne) Ackers up from the university, who read Saturday's 'Sydney Morning Herald' (it used to be the 'Guardian') at half time (1984). [Shortening.]

accident noun **1** An unintentional act of urinating or defecating. 1899–. NATION Then a new child had, as Mabel calls it, 'an accident'. She may have been afraid of asking to go out (1926). **2** A child whose conception was not planned. 1932–. M. DRABBLE I had two, and then Gabriel was an accident (1967).

according adjective Dependent on circumstances; esp. in phr. *that's according*, that depends. 1863–. CARIBBEAN QUARTERLY I do take a drink, but it is according (1971).

[Elliptical use of *according to . . .*; cf. French *c'est selon*.]

account noun **on account** Because. 1936–. P. G. WODEHOUSE I was feeling kind of down, on account that tooth of mine was giving me the devil (1936). [Conjunctional use abbreviated from the phrase *on account of the fact that*.]

AC/DC adjective Also **AC-DC.** euphemistic, orig US Of a person: bisexual. 1960–. K. MILLETT You can also tell *Time* Magazine you're bisexual, be AC-DC in the international edition (1974). [From the abbreviations *A.C.* 'alternating current' and *D.C.* 'direct current,' suggesting contrasting options.]

ace noun **1** US A dollar, or a one-dollar bill. 1925–. **2 aces** US Someone or something outstandingly good. 1931–. AMERICAN SPEECH That broad (female) is aces with me (1943). **3 ace in the hole** mainly N Amer **a** A high-value card or trump card concealed up one's sleeve. 1915–. **b** An advantage so far concealed. 1933–. NEW YORK TIMES AM's ace in the hole may be the $213 million net operating loss carryforward it still has left (1984). adjective **4** orig US Outstandingly good. 1936–. GUARDIAN The ace byliners found their stories on the back page (1961). verb trans., US **5a: to ace it** to achieve high marks in an examination, etc.; hence generally, to achieve complete success. 1959–. NEW YORKER Our tradition is 'Give us a few seconds and we'll ace it' (1986). **b** To achieve high marks in (an examination, etc.). 1962–.

ace boon coon noun African-American A best friend. 1962–. SEATTLE TIMES My 10 good friends, my ace boon coons, my real dogs, they're all dead or locked up except me (1991).

ace-face noun An exceptionally fashionable mod. 1980–.

acher noun Austral = ACRE.

acid noun **1 to put the acid on** (someone) Austral To exert pressure on (a person) for a loan, a favour, etc. 1906–. **P. WHITE** And a woman like that, married to such a sawney bastard, she wouldn't wait for 'em to put the acid on 'er (1966). **2 to come the acid** to speak in a caustic or sarcastic manner. 1925–. **H. CECIL** Why come the old acid? Not even a 'sit down, old man—' (1953). **3** orig US The hallucinogenic drug LSD. 1966–. **J. LENNON** I was influenced by acid and got psychedelic, like the whole generation (1970). [In sense 3, short for *lysergic acid diethylamide*.]

acid head noun Someone who habitually takes the drug LSD. 1966–.

acid trip noun A hallucinatory experience induced by taking the drug LSD. 1967–.

ackamarackus noun Also **ackamaracka**. **the old ackamarackus** orig US A specious, characteristically involved tale that seeks to convince by bluff; nonsense, malarkey. 1934–. [Of unknown origin.]

ack emma orig military, now dated. adverb **1** Ante meridiem; in the morning. 1898–. **D. L. SAYERS** Some damned thing at the Yard, I suppose. At three ack emma! (1927). noun **2** (in the RAF) An air mechanic. 1930–. Compare *pip emma* at PIP² noun. [From the former military communications code-names for the letters *a* and *m*.]

acker¹ noun Also **akka, akker**. orig services' **1** military A piastre, especially an Egyptian piastre (a coin of low denomination). 1937–. **2** Money, cash; coins or banknotes; usu. in pl. 1939–. **H. R. F. KEATING** I can't offer a great deal in the way of ackers. Though you'd get your ten per cent, old man (1965). [Prob. from Arabic *fakka* small change, coins; apparently first used among British and allied troops in Egypt.]

acker² noun = ACCA.

acre noun Also **acher**. Austral The buttocks. 1965–. **F. HARDY** Wiping between his toes and falling on his acre (1971). [Euphemistic, from *acre* measure of area, from the notion of a large expanse of buttocks; the spelling *acher* perh. inspired by the notion of a 'pain in the arse'.]

across prep **to get across** to annoy, get on the wrong side of (someone). 1926–.

act verb **1 to act up** to behave or function abnormally, often in order to impress. 1903–. noun **2 to put on an act** to talk or behave for display only; act insincerely. 1934–. **M. DICKENS** This girl's not naturally like that. She's putting on an act (1946). **3 to get into the act** orig US To become a participant; involve oneself in some (successful, fashionable, etc.) venture or activity; also **to get** (or **be**) **in on the act**. 1947–. **SPECTATOR** President Chamoun got back into the act by announcing that they would not be asked to withdraw from the Lebanon (1958). **4 a hard** (or **tough**) **act to follow** orig US An outstanding performance; something or someone difficult to rival. 1975–. **P. F. BOLLER** It was not easy being the second President of the United States; George Washington was a hard act to follow (1981). **5 to get one's act together** orig US To (re-) organize effectively one's (muddled or disorganized) life, business, etc. 1976–. **TIMES** We need to get our act together. . . . Users have been divided so far and are being picked off by the publishers one by one (1984).

action noun orig US **1** Activity of a desirable, exciting, or noteworthy sort, esp. gambling. 1933–. **D. RUNYON** He is well established as a high player in New Orleans, and Chicago, and Los Angeles, and wherever there is any action in the way of card-playing, or crap-shooting (1933). **2 where the action is** the centre of significant, fashionable, or exciting activity. 1964–. **C. SAGAN** We [i.e. mankind] are in the galactic boondocks, where the action isn't (1973). **3 a piece (share,** etc.) **of the action** involvement in a (potentially) profitable activity. 1966–.

actual adjective Brit Denoting the genuine or authentic thing, in phr. *your actual*. 1966–. **TIMES** There won't be any room for your actual horny-handed sons of toil in the TUC; there'll be too many sharp-suited managers (1976).

Adam noun orig US The hallucinogenic drug MDMA (methylenedioxymethamphetamine), associated in the UK with the acid house culture; = ECSTASY noun. 1985–. **OBSERVER** 'Ecstasy'—also known as 'MDMA' or 'Adam'—has been reported on sale in Bath, Bristol and Cardiff (1988). [Prob. a reversal and partial respelling of the chemical name MDMA, perh. influenced by the first Adam's connections with Paradise.]

Adam-and-Eve verb trans. Rhyming slang for 'believe'. 1925–. **E. A. THORNE** A baby! Would you Adam-and-Eve it! (1956).

adjectival adjective = ADJECTIVE adjective. 1910–. **G. MITCHELL** Beresford told him to take his adjectival charity elsewhere (1959).

adjective adjective Euphemistically substituted for an expletive adjective (e.g. *bloody*). 1851–. IDLER To know where the adjective blazes they are going (1894).

admin noun Administrative functions or duties, or the department of an organization that deals with these. 1942–. W. BUCHAN A mass of practical details—sheer 'admin' (1961). [Short for *administration*.]

Adrian Quist adjective Also **Adrian**. Austral Drunk. 1978–. SYDNEY MORNING HERALD They didn't look particularly decorous . . . collapsed, Adrian Quist, as the racing men say, under the hedge (1982). [Rhyming slang for *pissed*; from the name of the Australian tennis player Adrian Quist (1913–91).]

adult adjective euphemistic, orig US Sexually explicit, esp. in a pornographic way. 1958–. TAMPA (Florida) TRIBUNE Rentals for adult videos outstrip purchases by 12 to 1 (1984). [From the unsuitability of such material for children.]

aerial ping-pong noun jocular Austral Australian Rules football. 1964–. BULLETIN (Sydney) In Europe . . . cycling is about the same mad preoccupation as aerial ping pong is to the Melbourne crowds (1985). [From the frequent exchange of high kicks in the game.]

Afghanistanism noun US Preoccupation (esp. of journalists) with events in far distant countries, as a diversion from controversial issues at home. 1961–. [From the name of *Afghanistan* thought of as typifying a far-away country + *-ism*.]

after noun Abbreviation of 'afternoon'. Cf. ARVO noun. 1890–. J. MULGAN Boss wants us to get the hay in up top this after (1939).

afterthought noun The youngest child in a family, esp. one born considerably later than the other children. 1914–. G. MCINNES Terence was the youngest child . . . ('I'm a little afterthought') (1965). [From the supposition that the birth of such a child was not envisaged when the older children were conceived.]

ag adjective mainly N Amer Abbreviation of 'agricultural'. 1918–. RIDGE CITIZEN (Johnston, S. Carolina): Feed, seed, fertilizers, farm supplies and ag chemicals are manufactured and purchased for farmer members (1974).

aggro noun Also **agro**. Brit **1** Deliberate trouble-making or harassment (esp. formerly by skinhead gangs), violence, trouble. 1969–. M. GEE He had to stop the titters with a bit of aggro . . . , a bit of knuckles and a bit of razor (1981). **2** Annoyance, inconvenience. 1969–.

[Abbreviation of *aggr*(*avation* or *aggr*(*ession* + *-o*.]

agricultural adjective Of a cricket stroke: ungraceful, clumsy. 1937–. TIMES Keith . . . took an agricultural swing at Wardle and was bowled (1955). [From the unsophisticated strokeplay associated with village cricket.]

aid noun **what's this** (or **that**) **in aid of?** what is the meaning or purpose of this?, what is this all about? 1935–. M. INNES He couldn't quite make out what Olivia's questions and speculations were in aid of (1956). [From the phrase *in aid of* in support of 1837–.]

ain't[1] verb Contracted form of 'are not', also used for 'am not' and 'is not'. It is characteristic of the working-class dialects of London and other areas, and was formerly also found in British upper-class speech. 1778–. DICKENS 'You seem to have a good sister.' 'She ain't half bad' (1865).

ain't[2] verb Contracted form of 'have not' and 'has not'. 1845–. DIALECT NOTES He ain't got sense enough to carry guts to a bear (1914).

air noun **1a**: **(up) in the air** of a person: in doubt, uncertain; of an idea or theory: speculative, hypothetical. 1752–. J. GALSWORTHY Keep him in the air; I don't want to see him yet. . . . Keep him hankering (1910). **b: up in the air** orig US Explosively angry. 1906–. E. WALLACE Abiboo, who is a strict Musselman, got up in the air because Bones suggested he might have been once a guinea-pig (1928). **2 to give** (someone) (or **get**) **the air** US To dismiss or reject (someone) (or be dismissed or rejected). 1900–. P. G. WODEHOUSE Surely you don't intend to give the poor blighter the permanent air on account of a trifling lovers' tiff? (1934).

airhead noun mainly US A silly or foolish person. 1980–. DAILY TELEGRAPH One can imagine the media barons when they saw that these entertainment-world 'airheads' (the current preferred term) had concocted an irresponsibly tendentious account from these very press reports (1984).

aka abbrev orig US Abbreviation of 'also known as' (introducing a pseudonym, nickname, etc.). 1955–. TIMES He is perhaps a shade too comfortable and not enough of a cad as Johnson, aka Ramirez, the outlaw (1982).

akka noun Also **akker** = ACKER[1].

alec noun Also **aleck**. Austral A stupid person. 1944–. A. SEYMOUR He looked such a big aleck, marching along as though he'd won both wars single-handed (1962). [Short for *smart alec* bumptious person.]

Alf noun Austral A derogatory term for the type of the uneducated and unthinkingly conservative Australian. 1960–. J. SPENCER See man, the thing is that all the oldies and the alfs are in it together to stop the really creative people like you and me from making it (1966). [From the proper name *Alf*, shortening of *Alfred*.]

alive adjective **alive and well (and living in . . .)**, etc.; alive and active, flourishing (at the place named), esp. despite suggestions to the contrary. 1966–. TIME The last English eccentric is alive and well and living comfortably in Oakland (1977). [Prob. orig a graffito.]

alky /ˈælkɪ/ noun Also **alchy, alki(e).** orig and mainly US **1** (Illicit) alcoholic liquor. 1844–. R. & J. PATERSON All they [i.e. bootleggers] need is a shack and a can of alky (1970). **2** A drunkard or alcoholic. 1929–. CITY LIMITS Nazi sympathizers, alkies, junkies, and the unemployed (1986). [Abbrev. of *alc(ohol* and (sense 2) *alc(oholic* + -*y*.]

all adverb Very. 1932–. DAILY TELEGRAPH You can spoof politics, sports, business—but when it comes to religion, they get all upset (1991).

alley noun **to be (right) up (someone's) alley** to be suited or congenial to a person; be up a person's street. 1931–. D. CARNEGIE Bridge will be in a cinch for you. It is right up your alley (1936).

alley cat noun US A disreputable or immoral frequenter of city streets, esp. a prostitute. 1941–. [From the reputation of stray cats for street wisdom, thieving, quarrelsomeness, slyness, etc.]

all-fired adjective and adverb mainly US Infernal(ly), extreme(ly). 1837–. M. M. ATWATER Tell him to get all-fired busy on it (1935). [Prob. a euphemistic alteration of *hell-fired*.]

all-firedly adverb mainly US Extremely, excessively. 1833–. H. DE SELINCOURT I'm most all-firedly sorry about it (1924). [From ALL-FIRED adjective + -*ly*.]

alligator noun **1** dated US A person who is a fan of jazz or swing music (but does not play it). 1936–. **2 see you later, alligator (in a while, crocodile)** jocular (used when taking leave of someone). 1957–. [In sense 1, origin unknown. In sense 2, prob. from sense 1; first recorded as the title of a song by

R. C. Guidry (1957) which was popularized by Bill Haley and the Comets.]

all in adjective Exhausted. 1903–. M. LASKI You look all in. . . . Been doing too much, that's what it is (1952).

all-overish adjective dated Having a general and indefinite sense of illness pervading the body. 1832–1929. [As ALL-OVERS noun.]

all-overs noun mainly US **the all-overs** a feeling of nervousness or unease, or sometimes annoyance. 1870–. L. CRAIG It gives me the all-overs to have a gun pointed in my ribs (1951). [From the notion of a feeling affecting the whole body.]

all-right adjective attrib Used to indicate approval. 1953–. M. PROCTER He seemed an all-right bloke to me (1962). [From the phrase *all right* satisfactory.]

all there adjective Sane, mentally alert. 1864–.

Ally Pally noun A nickname for Alexandra Palace in Muswell Hill, North London, the original headquarters of BBC Television. 1949–. S. BRETT Back in Ally Pally days . . . you were just a technical boffin with all the sound recording stuff (1979). [Rhyming abbreviation of *Alexandra Palace*.]

altogether noun **the altogether** the nude; esp. in phr. *in the altogether*. 1894–. N. BALCHIN Should I get a kick out of just seeing a girl in the altogether? (1947). [From the notion of being 'altogether' or 'completely' naked.]

amber fluid noun Austral Beer. Also **amber liquid, amber nectar.** 1959–. NORTHERN TERRITORY NEWS (Darwin): There'll be 360 meat pies and 30 kilos of snags [= sausages] to demolish, washed down with 40 cartons of amber fluid (1980).

ambidextrous adjective euphemistic, orig US = AMBISEXTROUS. 1966–. [From earlier sense, able to use right and left hands equally well.]

ambisextrous adjective jocular Sexually attracted by or attractive to persons of either sex; bisexual. 1929–. SPECTATOR She avoids ever producing her ambi-sextrous young publisher (1960). [Blend of *ambidextrous* and *sex*.]

ambulance-chaser noun derog, orig US A lawyer who specializes in actions for personal injuries. 1897–. [From the reputation of such lawyers for attending the site of road, rail, etc. accidents, or visiting

Alf   alive   alky   all   alley   alley cat   all-fired   all in

hospitals afterwards, in order to persuade the victims to sue for damages.]

Amerika noun Also **Amerikkka.** derog, orig US American society viewed as racist, fascist, or oppressive, esp. by African-American consciousness. 1969-. BLACK PANTHER The political situation which exists here in Nazi Amerikkka (1973). So **Amerik(kk)an,** adjective [From German *Amerika* America; variant form *Amerikkka* with the initial letters of *K*u *K*lux *K*lan.]

amidships adverb Of the striking of a blow: in the abdomen. 1937-. TIMES Buss hit him painfully amidships and he had to leave the field (1961). [From earlier sense, in the middle of a ship, implying the most crucial or vulnerable part.]

ammo noun Ammunition, esp. for small arms. 1917-. R. CAMPBELL And we'll hand in our Ammo and Guns As we handed them in once before (1946). [Short for *ammunition*.]

amped adjective orig US Excited, agitated, or energetic (as if) from consumption of amphetamines or other stimulants; usu. followed by *up*. 1972-. Hence **amp** verb trans. To cause to become amped; usu. followed by *up*. 1979-. [Shortened from *amphetamine*.]

ampster noun Also **amster.** Austral The accomplice of a showman or trickster, 'planted' in the audience to start the buying of tickets, goods, etc. 1941-. H. PORTER A shady Soho club patronised by dips, amsters, off-duty prostitutes (1975). [Perh. short for *Amsterdam*, rhyming slang for 'ram' = a trickster's accomplice.]

amscray verb intr To go away hastily. 1931-. M. BISHOP I told that . . . daddy bastard to amscray (1988). [Pig Latin for *scram*.]

anchors noun Brakes. 1936-. PRIESTLEY & WISDOM There is more to it . . . than just putting on the brakes—or, to use the colourful language of the sporting motorist, 'clapping on the anchors' (1965).

and how int orig US Used to reinforce or emphasize a statement. 1865-. LISTENER 'Alas,' wrote Harrington, 'all earthly things do fail to mortals in enjoyment.' And how (1965).

Andrew noun **the Andrew** the Royal Navy. 1867-. G. FREEMAN That's 'ow it is in the Andrew. . . . That's what we call the navy (1955). [Short for earlier *Andrew Millar* or *Miller*, reputedly a notorious member of a pressgang.]

angel noun **1** orig US A financial backer of an enterprise, esp. one who supports a

theatrical production. 1891-. P. G. WODEHOUSE Ike hasn't any of his own money in the thing. . . . The angel is the long fellow you see jumping around (1921). **2** RAF, mainly World War II. Height; spec. a height of 1,000 feet. Usu. in pl. 1943-. P. BRENNAN We climbed into the sun, Woody advising us to get as much angels as possible (1943). verb trans. **3** mainly US To finance or back (an enterprise, esp. a theatrical production). 1929-. NEWSWEEK Last week . . . Aunt Anita agreed to angel a new Manhattan morning tabloid (1949). [In sense 2, perh. from the notion of the altitude at which angels live.]

angel dust noun orig US The depressant drug phencyclidine, used as a hallucinogen. 1973-. J. WAMBAUGH My nephew was arrested because he was holding this angel dust for somebody else (1978).

animal noun A person or thing of a particular kind; esp. in the phr. *there is no such animal.* 1922-. TIMES REVIEW OF INDUSTRY Computer makers would therefore have us believe that there is no such animal as a typical programmer (1963).

ankle verb intr. dated To **walk, go.** 1926-32. P. G. WODEHOUSE Ankling into the hospital and eating my grapes with that woman's kisses hot upon your lips (1932).

ankle-biter noun Austral A young child. 1981-. SYDNEY MORNING HERALD Travelling overseas with an ankle-biter has its advantages. It keeps you out of museums, cathedrals and temples and shows you the raw side of life: playgrounds, supermarkets, laundrettes and public toilets (1984). [From children's height and sporadic outbursts of violence.]

Anno Domini noun jocular Advanced or advancing age. 1885-. E. V. LUCAS When the time came for A. to take the bat he was unable to do so. *Anno Domini* asserted itself (1906).

anorak noun derog Brit Someone obsessively involved with something (e.g. a hobby) that is generally regarded as boring or unfashionable. 1991-. EMPIRE Any schoolboy or classics anorak will tell you that the old sheet-wearer was around a good 400 years before boring old monotheism (1993). [From the stereotypical wearing of anoraks by certain types of hobbyist (e.g. train-spotters).] Hence **anoraky** adjective derog Brit 1992-.

ant noun **to have ants in one's pants** orig US To fidget constantly, esp. because of extreme agitation, excitement, nervousness, etc.; to be impatient or restless. 1940-. E. MCLEOD Once

Amerika amidships ammo amped ampster ant

again I'm ready too soon. My friend . . . takes me to task. . . . 'You've always got ants in your pants' (1954).

antsy adjective mainly US Agitated, impatient, restless; also, sexually eager. 1838–. W. A. NOLEN Her husband got antsy and asked me to have Tom Lewis see her in consultation (1972). [From *ants*, pl. of *ant* (cf. the phr. *to have ants in one's pants* at ANT noun).]

any pron **to be not having any** to want no part in something; to turn down a proposition or to reject an overture of friendship. Also, more positively, to refuse to tolerate a situation. 1902–. A. L. ROWSE Lady Mary Hastings was thought of for promotion to the bed of Ivan the Terrible. She was not having any (1955).

A-OK adverb mainly US (orig astronaut.) In perfect order or condition; excellent, fine. 1961–. DAILY TELEGRAPH The blood sample proved A-OK, but a following ultrasound scan showed a discrepancy in the size of the foetus (1978). [Abbreviation of 'all (systems) OK': see O.K. adjective.]

A1 adjective Excellent, first-rate. 1837–. [From the designation applied in Lloyd's Register to ships in first-class condition.]

ape noun **to go ape** orig US To go crazy; to become excited, violent, sexually aggressive, etc.; to display strong enthusiasm or appreciation; also, to malfunction. 1955–. D. B. HUGHES I go ape over Johnny Mathis (1963). [From the frenzied, panic-stricken behaviour (including defecation) of monkeys and apes when captured and caged.]

ape-shit noun **to go ape-shit** orig US = to go ape (see APE noun). 1955–. SUNDAY TIMES Some parents would have gone apeshit. I think my parents were just sad (1989).

apple¹ noun **(to be) apples** Austral and NZ (To be) fine or satisfactory. 1943–. T. A. G. HUNGERFORD How's it going, Wally? Everything apples? (1952). [Short for *apples and rice* (or *spice*), rhyming slang for 'nice'.] See also BIG APPLE noun.

Apple² noun orig US = BIG APPLE (1938).

apple-polisher noun orig and mainly US A person who curries favour; a toady. 1928–. E. A. MCCOURT The apple-polishers in the front row laughed with forced heartiness (1947). [From

the practice of American schoolchildren presenting their teacher with a shiny apple, in order to gain favour.] So **apple-polishing,** noun. 1935–.

apples and pears noun Brit Rhyming slang for 'stairs'. Also **apples.** 1857–. C. MACKENZIE I soon shoved him down the Apples-and-pears (1914).

applesauce noun US Nonsense; often used as an interjection to deflate or reject flattery. 1919–. [Cf. earlier theatrical slang sense, silly comedy.]

arb noun Short for 'arbitrageur', a person who trades in securities, commodities, etc., hoping to profit from price differentials in various markets. 1983–. DAILY TELEGRAPH He has intervened in several British bid battles . . . , but only as a genuine 'arb'; taking a position after the bid, and betting on being able to sell out higher up (1986).

'arf noun, adjective, and adverb Also **arf.** (Used in writing to represent) a Cockney or other British dialectal pronunciation of *half*. 1854–. G. B. SHAW Here! Mister! arf a mo! steady on! (1903).

Argie noun Brit Short for 'Argentinian' and 'Argentine'. Frequently in the context of the Anglo-Argentinian conflict over sovereignty of the Falkland Islands (1982). 1982–. SUNDAY TELEGRAPH Small boys still play at Argies and Commandos (1986).

argy-bargy orig Scottish. **1** noun Contentious argument, wrangling; an instance of this. 1887–. J. B. PRIESTLEY 'Aving a proper argy-bargy in 'ere, aren't you? Losing your tempers too (1948). verb **2** intr. To engage in such disputation. 1888–. [Earlier, *argle-bargle*, a reduplication prob. formed on *argue* (perh. influenced by *haggle*).]

arm noun **1 as long as one's arm** very long. 1846–. M. ALLINGHAM Jock has a record as long as your arm (1938). **2 under the arm** inferior, poor, bad. 1937–. NEW STATESMAN All that's under the arm (i.e. no good) (1963). **3 an arm and a leg** Brit An exorbitant amount of money. 1956–.

arm candy noun orig US A physically attractive companion, esp. one escorting a more celebrated or influential person at a social event. 1992–. Cf. EYE CANDY noun.

> "Avin a proper argy-bargy in 'ere aren't you?"

artist

GUARDIAN It's true, a number of people did think that he was arm candy. But in fact he's the love of my life (1999).

armpit noun mainly US Used (esp. in the formula **the armpit of . . .**) to designate a place or part considered disgusting or contemptible; a place that 'stinks'. 1968–. WASHINGTON POST Your alma mater is still the armpit of the universe (1986). [From the offensive smell of an unwashed armpit.]

arrow noun darts A dart. 1946–. MORECAMBE GUARDIAN Best individual scores: B. Lilly (Royal) 180 in three arrows; B. Norris (Smugglers) 180 in three arrows (1976).

arse noun 1 The buttocks, posterior. OE–. 2 **arse over tip** (or **tit**) head over heels. 1922–. W. S. MAUGHAM I'm pretty nimble on my feet, but I nearly come arse over tip two or three times (1932). 3 **my arse** I don't believe it or agree! 1933–. WILCOX & RANTZEN 'I think we should both be pleased that she's made this friendly gesture— even if it is a little eccentric.' 'Eccentric my arse,' he said, shocking me into silence (1981). 4 A stupid or contemptible person; a fool. 1968–. C. PHILLIPS I got two eyes in me head which is more than I can say for the arse who umpired the game last year (1985). verb 5 **to arse about** (or **around**) to fool around, mess about. 1664–. A. WESKER Don't arse around Ronnie, the men want their tea (1960). 6 **to arse up** mainly Brit to make a mess of, bungle. 1979–. SUNDAY HERALD When Daft Punk and Air both arsed up their new album . . . , it was left to Basement Jaxx and newcomers Royksopp to assume their vacant thrones (2001). See also *kiss* (a person's) *arse* at KISS, SMART-ARSE adjective, noun, and verb, and cf. ASS noun.

arse-bandit noun derog A sodomite; also, a male homosexual. 1967–. PRIVATE EYE The Chief Rabbi . . . is very sound in . . . things like cracking down on the arsebandits (1989).

arsed adjective mainly Brit and Irish English Willing to make the required effort; bothered; mainly in such negative phr. as *can't be arsed to do something*. 1988–. MINX If you weren't really bothered about that bloke, you wouldn't be sufficiently arsed to cop off with him in the first place (2000).

-arsed adjective Having buttocks of the stated type, size, etc. OE–. See also HALF-ARSED adjective, SMART-ARSED adjective.

arse-end noun The rear part or end. 1880–.

arsehole noun 1 The anus. 1400–. 2 **arsehole of the universe** an unpleasant or godforsaken place. 1950–. D. THOMAS This arsehole of the universe . . . this . . . fond sad Wales (1950). 3 A stupid or obnoxious person. 1981–. BLITZ I was on the Farringdon Road, and some arsehole decided to cut across (1989). Cf. ASSHOLE noun.

arseholed adjective Extremely drunk. 1982–. DJ I'd been . . . utterly arseholed from Gatwick to Bangkok . . . ; straight into a drinking contest with some Thai bloke (2001). [Perh. from the earlier phr. *as pissed as arseholes*.]

arse-licking adjective and noun Toadying. 1912–. P. SCOTT I can't go up and ask Were you my brother's C.O.? . . . it'd look like arse-licking (1958). Hence (as a back-formation) **arse-lick,** verb intr. 1990–. Also **arse-licker,** noun A sycophant, toady; an obsequious hanger-on. 1967–. FRENDZ Maybe we should have been talking with Henry Ford rather than this professional arse-licker (1971).

arsey adjective 1 Austral Lucky. 1953–. 2 Brit Bad-tempered, uncooperative; also, arrogant, pretentious. 1989–. OFF LICENCE NEWS We get the odd arsey customer but you just have to grit your teeth and get on with it (1998). [In sense 1, cf. TIN-ARSED.]

arsy-versy adverb With the backward part in front; the wrong way round; perversely, preposterously. 1539–. S. BECKETT Like Dante's damned, with their faces arsy-versy (1957). [From ARSE noun + Latin *versus*, past participle of *vertere* to turn, assimilated to reduplicated compounds like *hurly-burly*, etc., on the model of *vice versa*.]

artic /aːtɪk/ noun Short for *articulated lorry* (*vehicle*, etc.), a lorry or similar vehicle made of two separate but connected sections. 1951–. D. RUTHERFORD To see a woman at the wheel of a big artic was surprising (1977).

article noun 1 Now mainly jocular derog A person, esp. of the stated type. 1811–. M. K. JOSEPH Listen, you sloppy article, who was on guard from twelve to two last night? (1957). 2 euphemistic A chamber-pot. 1922–. J. CANNAN How could he be so rude, she asked, when he said 'pot' instead of 'bedroom article' (1958).

artist noun A person devoted to or unusually proficient in the stated (reprehensible) activity. 1890–. D. M. DAVIN A real artist for the booze, isn't he? (1949); M. SAYLE Education, if he [i.e. the Australian worker] thinks of it at all, seems to him a childish trick whereby the 'bullshit artist' seeks to curry favour with the boss and thus get a better job (1960). See also PISS ARTIST noun.

armpit   arrow   arse   arse-bandit   arsed   -arsed

arty-farty adjective Pretentiously artistic. Also **artsy-fartsy.** 1967–. BARR & YORK In dress, one wants to look tidy, reassuring and appropriate (Sloane), not visual and arty-farty (1982). [Modelled on *arty-crafty* adjective.]

arvo /ˈɑːvəʊ/ noun Austral Afternoon. 1927–. C. MCGREGOR For most people life begins at five o'clock on Friday arvo. (1980). [Representing a voiced pronunciation of *af-* of *afternoon* + the Australian colloquial suffix *-o*.]

as adverb **as and when** when possible, eventually. 1965–. CUSTOM CAR We hope to be half-inching a J72 in the near future, so more on that as and when (1977).

ash-can noun US services' A depth charge. 1919–. G. JENKINS 'I give it five minutes before the ash-cans come.' . . . Waiting for a depth-charge attack is probably as bad as the attack itself (1959). [From its shape, like that of a dustbin (US *ash-can*).]

ask verb **1 to ask for it** to act in such a way as to bring trouble upon oneself, to give provocation. 1909–. M. INNES 'The damned scoundrels!' . . . The girl was philosophical. 'I asked for it, all right' (1946). **2 ask me another** I do not know (the answer to your question). 1910–. I. COMPTON-BURNETT 'Devoted?' said Josephine, raising her brows. 'Ask me another. I am not in a position to give you an account of their feelings' (1933). **3 if you ask me** in my opinion. 1910–. PUNCH If you ask me, a little of that sort of thing would brighten up the trade wonderfully (1932). [In sense 1, substituting for *to ask for trouble*.]

asparagus-bed noun military, mainly World War II An anti-tank obstacle consisting of an array of strong metal bars set in concrete at an angle of 45 degrees. Also **asparagus.** 1939–. [From the resemblance of the bars to asparagus growing thickly in a bed.]

ass noun mainly US **1** = ARSE noun 1. 1860–. **2 to drag** (also **haul, tear**) **ass** to move fast, hurry; to leave. 1918–. L. ERDRICH Well, all I can say is he better drag ass to get here, that Gerry (1984). **3** Sexual gratification. Also, a woman or women regarded as an object providing this. 1942–. J. UPDIKE Then he comes back from the Army and all he cares about is chasing ass (1960). See also **piece of ass** at PIECE noun **4 to work (run, etc.) one's ass off** to work (run, etc.) very hard, to the point of exhaustion. 1946–. MELODY MAKER You want to . . . retire to your bedroom and practise your ass off for a year till you become competent enough to try it (1984). **5 one's ass** one's self or person. Usually with *get* and an adverb (phr), as a

synonym for 'go'. 1958–. LANGUAGE Get your ass in here, Harry! The party's started! (1972). **6 to have one's ass in a sling** US To be in trouble. 1960–. S. F. X. DEAN Gonna get my ass in some sling if I miss that plane (1982). **7 up your ass!** an exclamation of contemptuous rejection. 1965–. [Vulgar and dialectal spelling and pronunciation of ARSE noun] See also *break* (a person's) *ass* at BREAK verb, *chew* (a person's) *ass* at CHEW verb, SMART-ASS adjective, noun, and verb.

ass-backwards adverb and adjective Also **ass-backward.** orig and mainly US Backwards, back to front, the wrong way round; in a way contrary to what is usual, expected, or logical. 1937–. R. GUTWILLIG I think you're going at this ass-backwards (1958). [Cf. BACK-ASSWARDS, BASS-ACKWARDS.]

-assed adjective mainly US = -ARSED adjective. 1932–. R. I. MCDAVID The Navy name for a lady marine, i.e., Broad-assed marine (1963).

asshole noun mainly US = ARSEHOLE noun. 1935–. R. SCHOENSTEIN ET AL. Two distinct kinds of Nerds are indigenous to America today: the asshole with a high IQ and the asshole with a low one (1981).

ass-kiss verb trans. mainly US To flatter, truckle to. 1984–. S. BELLOW If it could have been done by ass-kissing his patrons and patronesses, B.B. would have dried away a good many tears (1984). [Back-formation from ASS-KISSING adjective and noun]

ass-kissing adjective and noun mainly US Toadying. 1974–. ROLLING STONE Glossy fringe publishing, T-shirt peddling and political ass kissing (1977). So **ass-kisser,** noun A toady. 1978–. See also *kiss* (a person's) *ass* at KISS verb.

ass-licking adjective and noun mainly US = ARSE-LICKING adjective and noun. 1970–. So **ass-licker,** noun A toady. 1939–.

ATS /æts/ pl. noun Also **A.T.S., Ats.** Members of the Auxiliary Territorial Service, a British army corps consisting of women (1938–48) (singular forms **AT, A.T., At**). 1941–. J. BETJEMAN As beefy ATS Without their hats Come shooting through the bridge (1958). [Acronym from *A.T.S.*, abbreviation of *Auxiliary Territorial Service*.]

attaboy int Also **at-a-boy, ata boy.** orig US An exclamation expressing encouragement or admiration. 1909–. AUDEN & ISHERWOOD Chin up! Kiss me! Atta Boy! Dance till dawn among the ruins of a burning Troy (1936). [Said to represent careless pronunciation of *that's the boy!*]

arty-farty arvo as ash-can ask asparagus-bed

attagirl int orig US Used in place of *attaboy* when addressing a girl or woman. 1924–.

attitude noun orig US Truculent temperament or demeanour. 1962–. WASHINGTON POST Customers with an attitude, and who needs them? (1993) [From the use of the earlier sense, (demeanour arising from) a set of opinions, with negative connotations (as in *I don't like your attitude*).]

attract verb trans. euphemistic To steal. 1891–. E. CAMBRIDGE He 'attracted' some timber and built a boathouse (1933).

attrit verb trans. military orig US To wear down or erode (resources, morale, etc.) by unrelenting attack. Also **attrite**. 1956–. NEWSWEEK His defense was designed to attrit us . . . Every American you kill, it's another family protesting the war (1991). [Back-formation from *attrition*.]

auction noun **all over the auction** Austral Everywhere. 1930–. N. SHUTE You'd be surprised at the number of letters that there are—all over the auction (1960).

Aunt Edna noun Used of a typical theatre-goer of conservative taste. 1953–. N. F. SIMPSON The author . . . leans forward . . . to make simultaneous overtures of sumptuous impropriety to every Aunt Edna in the house (1958). [Coined by Terence Rattigan (1911–77), British playwright.]

Aunt Emma noun Used in croquet of a typically unenterprising player (or play). 1960–. CROQUET He played too much 'Aunt Emma' (1967).

Aunt Fanny noun Used in various phrases expressing negation or disbelief, esp. *my Aunt Fanny*. 1945–. G. CARR 'Agree my Aunt Fanny,' retorted the other loudly (1954).

auntie noun Used sarcastically as or before the name of an institution considered to be conservative in style or approach; spec. (Brit) the BBC or (Austral) the Australian Broadcasting Corporation. 1958–. J. CANAAN I saw about Uncle Edmund in auntie *Times* (1958); LISTENER The BBC needs to be braver and sometimes is. So let there be a faint hurrah as Auntie goes over the top (1962). [From the notion of an aunt as a comfortable and conventional figure.]

Aunt Sally noun used in cricket, now dated A wicketkeeper. 1898–1927. OBSERVER A 'keeper' . . . who combines batsmanship with all the 'Aunt Sally's' excellencies (1927). [From the notion that a bowler 'aims' the ball at

the wicketkeeper in the same way as people aim balls at a fairground Aunt Sally, a dummy typically in the shape of an old woman smoking a clay pipe.]

au reservoir int A joking substitution for 'au revoir'. 1853–. Cf. OLIVE OIL int.

Aussie noun **1** An Australian. 1917–. S. HOPE Most Aussies, contrary to popular belief, are town-dwellers (1957). **2** Austral Australia. 1917–. AUSTRALIAN 'Cheers from A Sunburnt Country!' the advertisement trumpets. 'Toast your Pommie mates with a gift from good old Aussie' (1974). adjective **3** Australian. 1918–. I. L. IDRIESS Fred Colson, a cheerful Aussie bushman (1931). [Abbreviation of *Australia(n)*.] Cf. OZZIE noun and adjective.

awesome adjective mainly N Amer Wonderful, great. 1980–. MAKING MUSIC I just know it'd be an awesome band (1986). [Trivialization of earlier sense 'staggering, remarkable, prodigious'.] So **awesomely**, adverb mainly N Amer Used as an intensifier. 1977–.

awful adverb Very. 1818–. R. D. PAINE A prairie town called Follansbee that looks awful good to me (1923). [From the adjective *awful*.]

AWOL /ˈeɪwɒl/ adjective orig US military Acronym for 'absent without leave'. 1921–. WODEHOUSE Nothing sticks the gaffe into your chatelaine more than a guest being constantly A.W.O.L. (1949).

A.W.O. Loose adjective US military = AWOL. 1920–. [Adapted from *AWOL*.]

axe noun Jazz and Rock Music A musical instrument; formerly esp. a saxophone, now usually a guitar. 1955–. ROLLING STONE While Keith bashes madly on the drums . . . Pete Townsend disposes of his axe with good natured dispatch (1969). [Perh. from such expressions as Swing that axe, man]

axeman noun Jazz and Rock Music A guitarist, esp. one who plays in a band or group. 1976–. WASHINGTON POST He learned guitar from Fats Domino's axeman, Walter (Papoose) Nelson (1985).

Aztec hop noun jocular Diarrhoea suffered by foreign holidaymakers in Mexico. Also **Aztec revenge, Aztec two-step**. 1962–. J. WAMBAUGH So long, Puerto Vallarta! With his luck he'd die of Aztec Revenge anyway, first time he had a Bibb lettuce salad (1978). [*Aztec* name of a former native American people of Mexico.] Cf. MONTEZUMA'S REVENGE noun.

attagirl attitude attract attrit auction auntie

Bb

b noun Also **B.** euphemistic Abbreviation of 'bugger' (or 'bastard') (sometimes printed **b-**). 1851–. N. STREATFEILD Can't 'elp bein' sorry for the poor old B (1952).

bab noun Austral and NZ = BABBLER noun. 1936–. BULLETIN (Sydney) The bab's present rate for cooking for more than seven is £14 4s. 11d. (1959).

babbler noun Austral and NZ A cook. esp. one who works in a sheep station, army camp, etc. 1919–. WEEKLY NEWS (Auckland): We worked it out that the old babbler made 112,000 rock cakes during those four months (1963). [Short for BABBLING BROOK noun.]

babbling brook noun Austral and NZ = BABBLER noun. 1919–. SUNDAY MAIL (Brisbane): Local good cooks asked for the recipe, but minds boggled at the quantities the army's babbling-brook recited for their benefit (1981). [Rhyming slang for 'cook'.]

babe noun orig US An attractive young woman. 1915–. Popularized by the 1992 film *Wayne's World*. [Prob. from earlier *babe* sweetheart.]

babelicious adjective orig US Very sexually attractive. 1991–. Popularized by the 1992 film *Wayne's World*. [Blend of BABE noun and *delicious*.]

baby bonus noun Canadian Family allowance. 1945–. GLOBE & MAIL (Toronto) Extra tax on rich to be eliminated; baby bonus to rise (1976).

Babylon noun African-American or African-Caribbean English, mainly Jamaican, contemptuous or dismissive. Anything which represents the degenerate or oppressive state of white culture; *esp.* the police or a policeman, (white) society or the Establishment. 1943–. G. SLOVO My father him work as a labourer for thirty years in Babylon (1986). [Earlier applied to any great luxurious city, as Rome or London, after the Biblical city.]

baby's head noun A steak (and kidney) pudding. 1905–. K. GILES He went to the counter and ordered kidney soup and a baby's head and chips (1967). [Perh. from the round shape and pallid appearance of the pudding in its basin.]

baby-snatcher noun jocular A person who enters into an amorous relationship with a much younger member of the opposite sex. 1911–. V. SACKVILLE-WEST You don't imagine that he really cared about that baby-snatcher? Good gracious me, he was a year old when her daughter was born (1930). Hence **baby-snatch**, verb intr., **baby-snatching,** noun.

baccy noun Also **backy, backey, bakky.** Tobacco. 1821–. G. ORWELL Dere's sixpennorth o' good baccy here! (1933) [Shortening of *tobacco* + -y.]

bach /bætʃ/ verb intr. Also **batch.** N Amer, Austral, and NZ Usu. of a man: to live as a bachelor; to live alone and do one's own cooking and housekeeping. Also with *it*. 1870–. D. IRELAND How are you getting on, batching? Are you going to get married again? (1971). [From *bach* noun abbrev. of 'bachelor' *US*. 1858–1904.]

back-asswards adverb N Amer, jocular = ASS-BACKWARDS. 1951–. U.S. NEWS & WORLD REPORT 'You can't do this thing back-asswards,' says Whitley Bruner, a former CIA station chief in Iraq (2002). Hence **back-assward** adjective N Amer, jocular [A humorous Spoonerization of *ass-backwards*.] Cf. BASS-ACKWARDS.

back burner noun **on the back burner** orig US Of an issue, etc.: in the state of being (temporarily) relegated or postponed; out of the forefront of attention; deferred, pending. 1963–. TIMES He had misgivings about the GM bid for BL because under its global strategy Britain had been put on the 'backburner' for the last decade (1986). [From the use of the rearmost ring, hotplate, etc. on a cooking stove for simmering rather than boiling.] Cf. FRONT BURNER noun.

backhander noun A tip or bribe made surreptitiously, a secret payment. 1960–. LISTENER A bit of a backhander and, boy, you're in (1968). [From the notion of concealing payment by making it with the hand reversed; cf. the earlier sense, blow with the back of the hand, and *back-handed* indirect, ambiguous, devious (as in 'a back-handed compliment').]

back of (or **o'**) **Bourke** /bɜːk/ phr Austral (In or characteristic of) remote inland country; the 'back of beyond'. 1898–. CANBERRA TIMES One of the customers whose accent was decidedly back o'Bourke complained that she had mixed up his order (1981). [From *Bourke*, a town in the extreme west of New South Wales.]

back passage noun euphemistic The rectum. 1960–. P. FALCONER As she sucked, so her fingers reached his back passage. Uninvited, she positioned two fingers at the entrance of his arsehole, and crudely thrust into him (1993).

backroom boy noun A person engaged in (secret) research. 1943–. TIMES The man most responsible for the development of the rocket projectile . . . is Group Captain John D'Arcy Bakercarr . . . whose 'backroom boys' at the Ministry of Aircraft Production have worked unremittingly with him (1944). [From the notion of a secluded room at the rear of a premises where secret work is carried out; cf. LORD BEAVERBROOK in LISTENER Now who is responsible for this work of development on which so much depends? To whom must the praise be given? To the boys in the back rooms. They do not sit in the limelight. But they are the men who do the work (1941).]

back-seat driver noun derog One who criticizes or attempts to direct without responsibility; one who controls affairs from a subordinate position. 1955–. TIMES [He] replied that it was contrary to democracy for elected members to consult 'pressure groups' and 'back-seat-drivers' (1955). [From the earlier sense, a passenger in the rear seat of a car who gives unsolicited directions to the driver.]

backside noun euphemistic The buttocks. *c.*1500–. GENTLEMAN'S MAGAZINE He shall fall on his back-side (1827). [From earlier sense, rear part.]

backyarder noun Brit, now dated A person who keeps chickens in his backyard; a small poultry-keeper. 1922–42.

bacon noun US The police. 1974–. [Suggested by *pig* police officer.]

bad adjective **1 in bad** orig US Out of favour (*with*, etc.), in bad odour. 1911–. K. AMIS This ought to put me nicely in bad with the Neddies (1953). **2** orig and mainly US, esp. jazz and African-American English Extremely good; of a musical performance or player: going to the limits of free improvisation; of a lover: extravagantly loving. 1928–. TIME Adds longtime Fan Carolyn Collins: 'Oh man, I don't think he's changed. He got quiet for a while but he's still cool-blooded. He's still bad.' Bad as the best and as cool as they come, Smokey is remarkably low key for a soul master (1980).

baddy noun orig US A bad person, esp. a villain in a play, film, etc.; usu. used in the pl. 1937–. EUROPEAN His thin legs seem to shuffle at the sight of a linebacker, as if they were Tintin's running away from the baddies (1991). [From *bad* + -*y.*]

bad hair day noun orig US A day on which everything seems to go wrong; a period in which one feels unusually agitated, stressed, or dissatisfied. 1991–. I apologise for all the hostility, but I think you'll understand. I'm having a bad hair day (1995). [From earlier sense, day on which one's hair is particularly unmanageable.]

bad mouth noun Also **bad-mouth.** orig US **1** Esp. among African-American speakers: a curse or spell. 1835–. H. M. HYATT I have known of people that have had the record of saying that they could put a bad mouth on you (1970). **2** Evil or slanderous talk; malicious gossip; severe criticism. 1970–. FORTUNE The bad-mouth went out over the CB network. Every accident was blamed on the anti-skid brake (1979). [Translation of *da na ma* in the Vai language of southern Liberia and Sierra Leone, or of some similar expression in various other African or W. Indian languages.]

bad-mouth verb trans. orig US To abuse (someone) verbally; to criticize, slander, or gossip maliciously about (a person or thing). 1941–. P. BOOTH But now Jo-Anne was a bitter enemy who could be relied on to bad-mouth her at every opportunity (1986). [From BAD MOUTH noun.]

bad news noun Something or someone unpleasant, unlucky, or undesirable. 1926–. D. GRAY Milly these days was plain bad news. Her fascination had evaporated (1974).

bag noun **1** derog, orig US A woman, esp. one who is unattractive or elderly; esp. in phr. *old bag*. 1924–. M. DICKENS I've never really known a pretty girl like you. At the training college they were all bags (1961). **2** orig US A person's preoccupation, speciality, or preferred activity; a distinctive style or category; esp. a characteristic manner of playing jazz or similar music. 1960–. SUNDAY TIMES His bag is paper sculpture (1966). See also BAGS noun. verb trans. **3 to bag school** US To play truant. Also **to bag it.** 1934–. PHILADELPHIA BULLETIN Threatening him with castor oil, when he seemed set to bag school, never did any good (1948). **4** Austral To criticize, disparage. 1975–. AUSTRALIAN It pains me to report that Choice, journal of the Australian Consumers' Association, bags Vegemite for having too much salt in it (1981).

bagel noun US, derog and offensive A Jew. 1955–. [From the Jewish origins of the bagel, a ring-shaped bun.]

bag job noun US An illegal search of a suspect's property by agents of the Federal Bureau of Investigation, esp. for the purpose of copying or stealing incriminating documents. 1971–.

bag lady noun orig US A homeless woman, often elderly, who carries her possessions in shopping bags. 1972–. M. AMIS They even had a couple of black-clad bagladies sitting silently on straight chairs by the door (1984).

bagman noun orig and mainly US One who collects or administers the collection of money obtained by racketeering and other dishonest means. 1928–. NATIONAL TIMES (Australia): The money is always paid in cash, by personal contact in a pub or a car. The police 'bag man' will call once a month to collect (1973). [From the bag supposedly carried to hold the money collected; cf. the earlier sense, a commercial traveller.]

bags noun **1** Trousers. 1853–. D. L. SAYERS Just brush my bags down, will you, old man? (1927). **2 bags of mystery** sausages. 1864–. JOHN O' LONDON'S The bags of mystery or links of love are sausages (1962). **3** A lot; plenty. 1917–. A. WESKER We 'ad bags o' fun, bags o' it (1962). adverb **4** Much; lots. 1919–. J. B. MORTON It's not gay, this life, but it might be bags worse (1919). [Plural of bag noun: in sense 1, from the garment's loose fit; in sense 2, from the uncertain nature of the ingredients.]

bags I phr Also **bags, I bags.** A formula used (orig by children) to assert a claim to an article, or the right to act in a certain way, on the grounds that one is the first to speak up. 1866–. A. A. MILNE Bags I all the presents (1921); LISTENER I bags be Anthony Wedgwood Benn (1968). [From bag verb, to secure, get hold of.]

bagsy verb trans. Brit, orig children's To assert a claim or right to (something) by using the expression 'bagsy'; to demand as one's due for being first to claim. 1979–. C. AHERNE ET AL.

Mam. I think I'll do chicken. *Antony.* Bagsey me breast (1998). [From BAGS I.]

bail bandit noun Brit Someone who commits a crime while on bail awaiting trial. 1991–.

bait noun = BATE.

bakky noun = BACCY.

balderdash noun Nonsense. 1674–. ECONOMIST In May, the development corporation wrote giving notice that it would end the management agreement, which, it claimed, the council itself had repudiated by conducting its survey. That is balderdash, says the council (1988). [Cf. earlier sense, froth; ultimate origin unknown.]

ball¹ verb trans. **1 to ball** (something) **up** orig US To bring (something) into a state of entanglement, confusion, or difficulty. 1885–. J. DRUMMOND These electrical devices are always getting balled up (1959). **2 to ball the jack** US To travel fast, to hurry. c.1925–. J. H. STREET They think as soon as you die you go balling-the-jack to God (1941). [From *ball* noun, spherical object.]

ball² verb intr. N Amer To enjoy oneself, to have a wonderful time; also **to ball it up.** 1942–. K. ORVIS A so-called friend invites you . . . to a coloured joint—to ball it up for the night (1962). [From *ball* noun, dance, with reference to the phrase *to have a ball*, to enjoy oneself.]

ball³ verb trans. and intr. orig US Esp. of a man: to have sexual intercourse (with). 1955–. G. VIDAL And you can tell all the world about those chicks that you ball (1978). [Perh. an extension of BALL² verb, influenced by BALLS noun 1.]

ball and chain noun jocular A man's wife. 1921–. EASTERN EYE Attractive Arabian Yemeni male . . . seeking a pretty Sunni Muslim female (18–30) that is pleasing to my eyes and heart for the intention of marriage, not the traditional classic old ball and chain routine (1996). [From the 'ball and chain' attached to a convict's leg to prevent escape, alluding to a wife's restriction of her husband's freedom.]

ball-breaker noun orig US **1** A difficult, boring, or exasperating job, problem, or situation. 1954–. **2** A person who sets difficult work or problems; a hard

bags of mystery
sausages

bagel bag job bag lady bagman bags bags I

taskmaster. 1970–. N. ARMSTRONG ET AL. The quality control inspector is a sort of nitpicker. We're the most unwanted people (1970). **3** A dominating woman, one who destroys the self-confidence of a man. 1975–. I. SHAW Tom told me about that wife of his. A real ball-breaker, isn't she? (1977). [From BALLS noun 1.] Hence **ball-breaking,** adjective 1976–.

ball-buster noun orig US = BALL-BREAKER noun. 1954–. M. FRENCH A woman who blames men or male society for anything, who complains, is seen as a . . . castrator, an Amazon, a ballbuster (1980). [From BALLS noun 1.] Hence **ball-busting,** adjective. 1944–.

ballocking, ballock-naked, ballocks variants of BOLLOCKING noun, BOLLOCK-NAKED adjective, BOLLOCKS noun.

ballpark noun **1 in the (right) ballpark** orig and mainly US Plausibly accurate, within reasonable bounds. 1968–. SLR CAMERA This basic filtration, though, has very often saved me a test strip because it's got me into the right ball park filter-wise (1978). adjective **2** attrib Approximate, within a reasonable range of accuracy. 1967–. NEW YORKER How many times per week do you have sexual relations? On the average—just a ballpark figure (1984). [From *ballpark* noun, broad area of approximation, similarity, etc., figurative extension of the earlier sense, a baseball stadium.]

balls noun **1** Testicles. *a.*1325–. D. H. LAWRENCE She . . . gathered his balls in her hand (1928). **2** Nonsense; frequently as an interjection. 1889–. A. WILSON 'Look here! this is awful balls,' said John (1956); L. COOPER Fanciful? Balls! It's what happens (1960). **3 to make a balls of** to muddle, to do badly. 1889–. S. BECKETT I've made a balls of the fly (1958). Cf. BALLS-UP noun. **4 to get or have** (someone) **by the balls** to have (someone) completely in one's power. 1950–. HARPER'S As you can see, I'm one of the fortunate few who has Blue Cross by the balls (1993). **5** mainly US Courage, determination; (manly) power or strength; masculinity. 1958–. M. AMIS Just keeping a handhold and staying where you are, . . . even that takes tons of balls (1984). Cf. BALLSY adjective. verb trans. **6 to balls** (something) **up** to do (something) badly, to make a mess of (something). 1947–. S. PRICE The public would laugh fit to bust if someone really ballsed-up the Civil Service (1961). Cf. BALL¹ verb. [Plural of *ball* noun; in sense 1, from their approximately spherical shape.]

balls-aching adjective Causing annoyance, revulsion, or boredom;

extremely irritating or tedious. 1912–. R. M. WILSON I don't quite know why I bother with all this ballsaching fire and semi-satire (1989). Hence **balls-achingly,** adverb. 1972–. [From BALLS noun 1.]

balls-up noun A confusion, a muddle, a mess. 1939–. R. FULLER Stuart Blackledge made a ballsup of the valuation (1956). Cf. BALLS noun 3 and verb.

ballsy adjective mainly US Courageous, plucky; determined, spirited; also, powerful, aggressive, masculine. 1959–. E. LEONARD The old man was showing off . . . he knew his way around. Ballsy little eighty-year-old guy (1983). [From BALLS noun 4.]

bally adjective and adverb Brit, euphemistic = BLOODY adjective and adverb, used as a vague intensive of general application. 1885–. C. ORR I . . . talked gaily about the bally old war (1919). Cf. *abso-bally-lutely* at ABSO-BLOODY-LUTELY adverb.

ballyhoo noun orig US Excessive noise, fuss, publicity, etc. ECONOMIST The event was surrounded by the sort of ballyhoo you might expect if Toyota had taken over GM itself (1988). [From an earlier application to a fairground showman's touting speech; ultimate origin unknown.]

balmy adjective = BARMY.

baloney noun and int Also **boloney** orig US Nonsense; rubbish. 1928–. J. BRAINE All that baloney about going upstairs to play a harp or downstairs to roast (1959). [Commonly regarded as from *Bologna* (*sausage*) but the connection remains conjectural.]

bamboozle verb trans. To confuse, bewilder. 1712–. E. GASKELL He fairly bamboozles me. He is two chaps (1854). [From earlier sense, deceive, trick; ultimately prob. of cant origin; cf. obs. *bam* hoax.]

Banana-bender noun Austral, jocular = BANANALANDER. 1976–.

Bananaland noun Austral, jocular Queensland. 1893–. [From the abundance of bananas grown in the state.] Hence **Bananalander,** noun. 1887–. K. DENTON I c'n tell a bananalander any time. I c'n pickem. You come from Queensland 'n' I *know* it! (1968).

bananas adjective Crazy, mad, wild (with excitement, anger, frustration, etc.); esp. in phr. *to go* (also *drive*) *bananas.* 1968–. J. KRANTZ Jesus, thought Lester, his first movie star and she turns out to be a bit bananas (1978). [Perh. from obs *banana oil* nonsense.]

ball-buster ballocking, ballock-naked, ballocks balls

bang¹ adverb **1 bang goes** Indicating that something is spoiled, ruined or lost. 1868–. T. E. LAWRENCE I am afraid I have to drive from here to Urfa (Edessa) which is going to cost me about £7: so bang goes my proposed purchases in Damascus (1909). **2 bang to rights** of a criminal: (caught) red-handed. Also **banged to rights**. 1904–. F. NORMAN One night a screw looked through his spy hole and captured him bang to rights (1958). **3 bang on** Precise, exact. 1936–. SPECTATOR As a realistic tale of low life in London, it is bang on (1958). noun **4** US Excitement, pleasure; a 'kick'. 1931–. J. D. SALINGER I hate the movies like poison, but I get a bang imitating them (1951). **5** An act of sexual intercourse. 1937–. J. UPDIKE I bet she even gives him a bang now and then (1968). verb trans. and intr. **6** To have sexual intercourse (with). 1937–. J. KEROUAC He rushes from Marylou to Camille . . . and bangs her once (1957). **7 to bang on** Used to denote insistent or repetitious talk about a particular subject. CAR So if you bang on now about how wonderful these cars were, don't be surprised by the odd hollow laugh from your more mature patrons (1990).

bang² noun US Cannabis. Also, a 'shot' (of cocaine, etc.). 1929–. K. ORVIS He . . . talked me into sampling a bang (1962). [Variant of *bhang* cannabis, often treated as if a slang sense of BANG¹ noun.]

banger noun **1** A kiss, esp. a violent one. 1898–. H. HOBSON 'Here—give us a banger first.' Honeypuss . . . obediently offered him her lips (1959). **2** A sausage. 1919–. M. DICKENS The chap had bought him tea and bangers and mash (1949). **3** An old motor vehicle, esp. one which runs noisily; usu. in phr. *old banger*. 1962–. TIMES It is true though that one misses out on one's husband's early years of struggle: the rented flats, . . . the third-hand old bangers, the terrifying overdraft (1985). [In sense 2, prob. from the explosive noises made by frying sausages.]

banjax verb trans. Anglo-Irish To batter or destroy (a person or thing); to ruin; to confound, stymie. 1939–. T. WOGAN I am out to banjax the bookies (1979). So **banjaxed,** adjective Ruined, stymied. 1939–. NATURE My sense of enlightenment was somewhat tempered by the banjaxed mood in which I found myself (1974). [Origin unknown; perh. orig Dublin slang.]

banker's ramp noun Brit A conspiracy by bankers to engineer a financial crisis in order to damage the standing of a government to which they are inimical. 1931–. Cf. RAMP noun.

bar noun Brit dated A pound; esp. in phr. *half a bar*, ten shillings. 1911–58. [Prob. from earlier sense, ingot (of gold, etc.).]

barbie noun Austral A barbecue. 1976–. AGE (Melbourne): On-site tucker . . . ranges from barbecued chicken to 'spaget marinara' ('suitable for the barbie on the building site') (1983). [Abbreviation.]

Barcoo salute noun Austral A gesture with which one brushes flies from one's face, considered to be typical of Australians. 1973–. SYDNEY MORNING HERALD The Barcoo salute . . . is also the feature of Australia most often commented on by overseas visitors (1974). [From *Barcoo* river and district in Queensland.]

barf orig and mainly US, verb intr. **1** To vomit or retch. 1960–. CHICAGO SUN-TIMES If you are Princess Diana, you have to stay home and do needlepoint until all danger of barfing in public is past (1982). noun **2** An attack of vomiting; vomit, sick. 1966–. Hence **barfy** adjective N Amer Nauseating, disgusting; redolent or reminiscent of vomit. Also: liable to vomit, nauseated. 1957–. TORONTO STAR It's hard enough dealing with kids in the car, let alone barfy kids (2000). [Origin unknown; perh. imitative.]

barking adjective Brit Crazy, mad. Also as adverb, esp emphatically in **barking mad**, utterly mad. 1968–. R. INGRAMS It was considered perfectly in order for a man who was clearly barking mad to sit for many years dispensing justice to his fellow citizens (1984). [From the image of barking like a mad or uncontrollable dog.]

barmpot noun Brit, orig and mainly northern dialect A witless person, a fool. 1951–. T. & P. MORRIS Thus a harmless schizophrenic will be classified by the staff as a 'barmpot' and by the prisoners as a 'nutter' (1963). [From earlier sense, pot for storing barm or yeast; prob. influenced by BARMY.]

barmy adjective Also **balmy** Slightly mad, foolish. 1891–. DAILY MAIL Teachers' unions called the idea 'barmy' even though European pupils often extend their school week to include Saturday morning (1991). [From earlier sense, flighty; ultimately from *barm* froth + *-y*; the spelling *balmy* (used especially in the US) results from confusion with *balmy* pleasantly mild.] Also **barmy** (or **balmy**) **in** (or **on**) **the crumpet** dated = BARMY. 1891–. H. G. WELLS I heard my aunt admit that one of the Stuart Durgan ladies did look a bit 'balmy on the crumpet' (1909). [From *crumpet* head.]

bang   banger   banjax   banker's ramp   bar   barf

barnet noun Brit **1** The hair. 1931–. F. NORMAN They send you to a doss house, so that you can get lice in your barnet (1962). **2** The head. 1969–. G. SIMS 'Use your barnet!' Domino said (1969). [Short for *Barnet fair*, rhyming slang for 'hair,' from the name of the London borough of *Barnet*.]

barney noun A noisy dispute or altercation. 1864–. ENCOUNTER There was a right barney at the other end of the shop (1958). [Origin unknown.]

barrel verb intr. orig and mainly US To move or travel rapidly, esp. in a motor vehicle. 1930–.

bash noun **1 on the bash: a** Scottish and NZ On a drinking bout. 1919–. KELSO CHRONICLE The village tailor . . . had an unfortunate weakness for getting terribly 'on the bash' perhaps twice a year (1924). **b** Brit Soliciting as a prostitute. 1936–. STREETWALKER From the hours you keep . . . I'd say you were on the bash (1959). **2** An attempt; esp. in phrase *to have a bash (at)*. 1948–. I. MURDOCH Come on . . . have a bash. You can translate the first word anyway (1957). **3** orig US A good time; a spree; a party. 1948–. SUNDAY TIMES He and Lloyd Webber go for the truly megabash, with 1,000–1,500 guests, sometimes a sit-down dinner, vast decorated venues and an upmarket guest list (1991). verb trans. **4 to bash up** to beat (someone) repeatedly; to thrash or batter. 1954–. I. & P. OPIE 'Hand it over—or else'— 'I'll bash you up' (the most usual suggestion) (1959). **5 to bash (someone's) ear** To talk inordinately to; to harangue. 1962–. DAILY TELEGRAPH Mr. Wigg bashes the ear as once he bashed the square (1962). [Cf. EAR-BASH.]

basher noun Brit, orig services' A person with the stated duties, occupation, etc. 1942–. GEN One of the cookhouse bashers that came off at five (1945). [From the notion of using, repairing, etc. a particular implement in a robust or careless way.] Cf. BIBLE-BASHER noun.

bashing noun Brit, services' Arduous work, esp. of the specified sort. 1940–. G. KERSH Poor old Gerald done fourteen drills that week, plus a nice basinful of spud-bashing (1946).

basinful noun An excessive amount, (more than) enough. 1935–. NEWS CHRONICLE I've had a basinful of bowler-hat and furled-umbrella parts (1960).

basket noun Euphemistic alteration of *bastard*. 1936–. J. GILLESPIE He's a nice old basket really (1958).

basket case noun orig US military **1** Someone (esp. a soldier) who has lost all four limbs. 1919–. M. PUZO 'Hunchbacks are not as good as anyone else?' I asked . . . 'No . . . nor are guys with one eye, basket cases and . . . chickenshit guys' (1978). **2** A person who is no longer able to cope emotionally or mentally; something no longer functional. 1967–. [From the notion of a person not able to support himself physically.]

bass-ackwards adverb and adjective N Amer, jocular = ASS-BACKWARDS. 1930–. MACUSER Organizers and calendar programs take a bass-ackwards approach to time management by reacting to your busy schedule, rather than allowing you to manage how your time is used (1994). [A humorous Spoonerization of *ass-backwards*.] Cf. BACK-ASSWARDS.

bastard noun **1** Used as a term of abuse, esp. for a man or boy. 1830–. H. G. WELLS Serve the cocky little bastard right (1940). **2** A fellow, chap. 1919–. K. WEATHERLY 'You're not a bad bastard, Hunter,' he said, 'in spite of your lousy cooking' (1968). **3** Something bad or annoying. 1938–. J. MACLAREN-ROSS This bastard of a bump on the back of my head (1961). [From the earlier sense, one born out of wedlock.]

bat[1] noun **1 (to have) bats in the belfry** (to be) crazy or eccentric. *c*.1901–. BLACKWOOD'S MAGAZINE The sahib had bats in his belfry, and must be humoured (1928). Cf. BATS adjective, BATTY adjective. **2 (to go) like a bat out of hell** (to go) very quickly. 1921–. I. FLEMING The motor cyclist . . . had gone like a bat out of hell towards Baker Street (1961).

bat[2] noun A rate of stroke or speed, pace. 1824–. J. WELCOME We turned on to the main . . . road and started going a hell of a bat across the Cotswolds (1961). [From the earlier sense, a blow or stroke with a bat, club, etc.]

bat[3] noun Also **batt**. orig US A spree or binge. 1848–. E. WAUGH Why don't you switch to rum? It's much better for you . . . When did you start on this bat? (1942). [Of obscure origin; cf. BATTER noun.]

bat verb **to bat a thousand** US to be or have been completely successful or right. 1920–. [From the notion of a perfect batting average in baseball.]

batch variant of BACH verb.

bate noun Also **bait** Brit dated A fit of anger or bad temper. 1857–. OBSERVER 'Lenny Henry will be back at half time,' the voice on the Tannoy assures us, as the 'funny' man stalks off off the pitch in something of a bate (1996). [From *bait* harass, persecute.] Hence **batey** adjective Also **baity** dated Angry. 1921–.

bats

P. H. JOHNSON I'd better roll the damned thing in or Mater will be batey (1954).

bats adjective Mad, dotty. 1919–. E. BOWEN You're completely bats (1938). [From the phrase *bats in the belfry* (see BAT¹ noun.)]

batter noun A spree, debauch; esp. in phr. *on the batter*. 1839–. J. OSBORNE Have you been on the batter, you old gubbins! (1957). [Of obscure origin; cf. BAT³ noun.]

battleaxe noun derog, orig US A domineering woman. 1896–. C. BROOKE-ROSE Do I look like a female novelist? I thought they were all battle-axes (1957).

batty adjective Mad, dotty. 1903–. BRITISH WEEKLY He's a bit batty every now and anon (1926). [From the phrase *bats in the belfry* (see BAT¹ noun).]

batty noun orig Caribbean The buttocks. 1935–. A. LEVY The second one him run off with a young girl with a big batty and wiggle-wiggle hips (1999). [From a Caribbean pronunciation of *botty* bottom.]

batty boy noun Also **batty bwoy.** orig Caribbean = BATTYMAN. 1992–.

battyman noun orig Caribbean A homosexual man. 1967–. L. ROSS For me, this pretty man was the ultimate looker, and I laughed privately when male friends called him a 'battyman' because he wore lace (2000). [From BATTY noun + *man*; cf. BUM-BOY.]

bawl verb **to bawl (someone) out** orig US To reprove or reprimand (someone) loudly or severely. 1899–. L. A. G. STRONG He bawled him out. Gave him such a tongue lashing as the louse will remember to his dying day (1942). Hence **bawl-out** noun US A strong reprimand. 1915–. J. BLACK I . . . don't want to . . . give myself a bawl-out in front of the woman (1926).

Bay City noun San Francisco. 1879–. R. CHANDLER They put Dad in charge of the Bureau of Records and Identification, which in Bay City is about the size of a tea-bag (1940). [From San Francisco Bay.]

bazongas noun pl. US Also **bazoongas, bazonkas.** Humorous alterations of BAZOOKAS. 1972–.

bazookas noun pl. A woman's breasts; applied esp. to large breasts. 1963–. [From earlier sense, portable rocket launcher, but presumably suggested mainly by BAZOOMS.]

bazooms /bəˈzuːmz/ noun pl. orig US A woman's breasts. 1955–. E. LEONARD Another case of Bio-Energetic Breast

Cream . . . for South Beach bazooms (1983). [Jocular alteration of *bosoms*.]

beach bum noun A person, esp. a youth, who hangs about on beaches. 1962–. OBSERVER He is the reverse of the popular image of a 'surfie' as a beach bum (1963).

beak noun Brit, dated **1** A magistrate or justice of the peace. 1838–. E. WALFORD We hope and trust [they] were brought before the 'beak' and duly punished (1879). **2** schoolboys' A schoolmaster, esp. a headmaster. 1888–. J. BETJEMAN Comparing bruises, other boys could show Far worse ones that the beaks and prefects made (1960). [Prob. from thieves' cant, though derivation from *beak* = bird's bill cannot be entirely discounted.]

beam noun **1** The (width of the) hips or buttocks; esp. in phr. *broad in the beam*. 1929–. MRS. HICKS-BEACH A cast-off of Jim's. He's grown too broad in the beam for it (1944). **2 to be on the beam** to be on the right track, right, sane. So **to be off (the) beam.** 1941–. OBSERVER Hugh Burden, as Barnaby, was right on the beam from the start (1948). [In sense 2, from an earlier sense, to be on the course indicated by a radio beam.]

Beamer noun orig US A BMW car. 1982–. [Fancifully elaborated acronym.]

bean noun **1 (to know) how many beans make five** to be knowledgeable or not easily fooled. 1830–. A. GILBERT Mr. Crook knew how many beans make five (1958). **2** orig US The head. 1908–. R. D. PAINE If these Dutchmen get nasty, bang their blighted beans together (1923). **3** Any money at all. 1928–. D. L. SAYERS None of the Fentimans ever had a bean, as I believe one says nowadays (1928). See also *full of beans* at FULL adjective, *to give* (a person) *beans* at GIVE verb, *a hill of beans* at HILL noun, *not to know beans* at KNOW verb, OLD BEAN noun, *to spill the beans* at SPILL verb. verb trans. **4** mainly US To hit on the head. 1910–. C. MORLEY She was beaned by a copy of *A Girl of the Limberlost* that fell from the third floor (1939). [In sense 3, from the earlier sense, a guinea or sovereign.]

bean-eater noun **1** US A native, inhabitant or representative of Boston, Massachusetts. 1867–. WASHINGTON POST The brothers crack wise in Hah-vahd Yahd beaneater accents (1999). **2** orig and mainly US A person of Latin American (esp. Mexican) origin. 1919–. [In sense 1, cf. BEAN TOWN.]

beaner noun US **1** An impressive or excellent thing; an oustanding example of

bats batter battleaxe batty batty boy battyman

bee

its kind. 1911–. **2** derog and offensive A Mexican (or Mexican-American) person. 1969–. R. THOMAS You know how the beaners are when it comes to time (1983). [In sense 2, cf. BEAN-EATER 2.]

beanery noun US A cheap restaurant (orig one where beans were served). 1887–. E. HEMINGWAY Inside the door of the beanery Scripps O'Neil looked around him (1933).

beano noun A festive entertainment frequently ending in rowdyism. 1914–. LISTENER Dear-heart, I fear we will have to make a token appearance at the beano those thrusting young String-Along's are giving tonight (1967). [Abbreviation (orig among printers) of *beanfeast* festive occasion.]

beanpole noun A very tall thin person. 1837–. [From earlier sense, stick up which a bean plant is grown.]

Bean Town noun US Boston, Massachusetts. 1901–. R. LUDLUM He's what they call a functioning alcoholic, something of a character in Bean Town's shadier districts (1990). [From the inhabitants' legendary liking for beans.]

bear noun orig and mainly US A policeman. 1975–. DAILY PROVINCE (Victoria, British Columbia). The Bear in the Air will be staying up there (1977). [Short for SMOKEY BEAR noun.] See also *to feed the bears* at FEED verb.

beard noun orig US Someone of the opposite sex who accompanies or acts as partner to a gay person so as to conceal or distract attention from their homosexuality. 1971–. [From the notion of a beard as a disguise; cf. earlier slang sense, person who places bets on behalf of another in order to conceal their identity.]

beardie noun Also **beardy**. A bearded person. 1941–. SPECTATOR There were more than forty thousand of us—weirdies and beardies, colonels and conchies, Communists and Liberals (1960). [From *beard* noun + *-ie, -y*.]

beast noun prisoners' A sex offender. 1989–. DAILY TELEGRAPH The arrival of a police van at a prison might often be accompanied by comments such as 'a couple of beasts for you', with the result that the prisoners are immediately identified (1989).

beat verb trans. **1 to beat the Dutch** = to beat the band. 1775–1939. **2 to beat it** orig US to go away. 1878–. J. WYNDHAM Fedor had not waited once the plane was down. He had switched off the lights, and beat it (1951). **3 to beat**

the band to exceed, surpass, or beat everything. 1897–. A. CHRISTIE Well, if that doesn't beat the band! (1923). **4 to beat it up** to have rowdy fun, typically resulting in breakages. 1933–. DAILY TELEGRAPH What sort of noise did the neighbours complain about? Did the Purdoms and their friends beat it up a little in the evenings? (1958). **5 to beat** (something or someone) **up** of a pilot: to fly low over or 'buzz' (e.g. an airfield) in a threatening manner. 1940–. T. RATTIGAN I put the old Wimpey into a dive and beat him up—you know, pulled out only a few feet above his head and stooged round him (1942). **6 to beat one's** (or **the**) **meat** orig US To masturbate. Cf. MEAT noun. 1967–. J. O'FAOLAIN What did people do in a place like this? Beat their meat probably (1980). adjective **7** Exhausted; esp. in phr. *dead beat*. 1832–. P. FRANKAU I was too beat and hazy to take anything in (1954). [In sense 3, from the earlier sense, to drown the noise made by the band.]

beat-up adjective mainly US Worn out, shabby, showing signs of over-use. 1946–. W. R. BURNETT The girl was sitting once more in the beat-up leather chair (1953).

beaut /bjuːt/ Also (now rare) **bute**. mainly US, Austral, and NZ. noun **1** A beautiful or outstanding person or thing. 1866–. K. WEATHERLY The bushie grabbed a plate and headed for the camp oven. 'You beaut,' he said. 'Coffee'll do' (1968). adjective **2** Wonderful, great. 1952–. N. SHUTE It's been a beaut evening (1957). [Abbreviation of *beauty*.]

beaver noun **1** The female genitals or pubic area. 1922–. **2** US A girl or woman, esp. one who is sexually attractive. 1968–. adjective **3** Of pornographic pictures, films, etc.: featuring the female genitals and pubic area. 1969–. LISTENER Like the beaver mags, . . . television has only a limited number of shots with which to titillate the viewer (1976). [From earlier colloquial sense, beard; ultimate origin unknown.]

bedroom eyes noun Eyes or a look suggestive of sexual desire. 1947–. J. POTTER George's wife had blue bedroom eyes (1967).

bee¹ noun **to put the bee on** dated mainly US **a** To quash, put an end to; to beat. 1918–. P. G. WODEHOUSE The old boy . . . got the idea that I was off my rocker and put the bee on the proceedings (1927). **b** To ask for a loan from, to borrow money from. 1929–. J. CURTIS If a bloke had come up and put the bee on him all the handout would have been . . . a lousy tanner (1936).

beanery beano beanpole Bean Town bear beard

bee² noun A respelling of the letter B, used euphemistically for 'bloody'; so **bee aitch,** bloody hell; **bee eff,** bloody fool. 1926–. M. CECIL 'Your mother's relations,' he muttered, 'bee effs, every one of 'em' (1960).

Beeb noun Abbreviation of 'BBC' = British Broadcasting Corporation; often with *the.* 1967–. TIMES The licence fee the 'Beeb' is asking for is a shade less than the 18p a day for a popular newspaper (1985). Cf. AUNTIE noun.

beef noun **1 beef to the heel(s)** of a person: massive, brawny. 1867–. **2** orig US A protest, (ground for) complaint, grievance. 1899–. DAILY EXPRESS The beef is, Why should every battle we fight have to be a 'Battle of Britain?' (1945). verb **3** intr. orig US To complain, grumble, protest. 1888–. H. CROOME Stop beefing, Frank. You'll be seeing her again soon enough (1957). **4** trans. US To knock down. 1926–. A. HYDER 'Yo' kills niggers?' 'Like flies,' Charley assured her. 'You want me to beef a few for you?' (1934). **5 to beef** (something) **up** to strengthen; to add vigour, power, or importance to. 1941–. NEW SCIENTIST The Defense Department has spent $50 billion building and beefing up the non-nuclear elements of the armed forces (1966). [In sense 4, from the earlier sense, to slaughter (an ox, etc.) for beef.]

beefcake noun orig US (A display of) sturdy masculine physique. 1949–. GUARDIAN The other poster . . . shows Albert Finney in a beefcake pose with his shirt slit to the navel (1963). [Humorously, after CHEESECAKE noun.]

beer belly noun **1** A paunch developed by drinking large quantities of beer. 1942–. ROLLING STONE Woods pauses to tuck his shirt between a beer belly and a silver belt buckle (1969). **2** A person with a beer belly. 1972–.

beer goggles noun pl. orig US An alcohol-induced effect on one's vision, whereby one finds others more sexually attractive. 1987–. INDEPENDENT Never go out there wearing beer goggles. Otherwise you end up going to bed with Madonna and waking up with Hilda Ogden (1992).

beer gut noun = BEER BELLY noun 1. 1976–. LOS ANGELES TIMES Fregosi took to wearing the jacket . . . when he began to develop a beer gut while trying to play for the Mets (1986).

beer-off noun Brit An off-licence. 1939–. A. SILLITOE Bill . . . had called at the beer-off by the street-end (1958).

beer-up noun A beer-drinking session; a binge. 1919–. E. TAYLOR Does you good to have a bit of a beer-up now and then (1945).

bees and honey noun Rhyming slang for 'money'. 1892–. J. ASHFORD D'you reckon we'd waste good bees and honey on a slump like you for nothing (1960).

bee's knees noun dated, orig US Something outstandingly good. 1923–. D. POTTER As you'd all know, we get a lot of blokes from round here nowadays as do reach Universities. And they think they be the bee's knees (1967). [A *bee's knee* was formerly the type of anything small or insignificant, though this sense appears to be a separate development.]

bees and honey rhyming slang for 'money'

beetle verb intr. To make one's way hurriedly; to scuttle. 1948–. N. COWARD There was . . . a terrible scene . . . and Freda beetled off to America (1952). [From earlier slang sense, move like a beetle.]

beetle-crusher noun A boot or foot, esp. a big one. Also **beetle-squasher.** 1860–. A. GILBERT He looked down . . . at his own enormous beetle-crushers in bright tan Oxfords (1958).

beezer noun The nose. 1915–. P. G. WODEHOUSE It is virtually impossible to write a novel of suspense without getting a certain amount of ink on the beezer (1960). [Origin unknown.]

beggar noun Brit, often mildly derog Applied to a person (typically a man or boy) of the stated sort. 1833–. N. STONE In the old days, I played squash reasonably well, but gave it up on reaching age 41, when my small boy was born—it is a dangerous sport for over-weight middle-aged chaps who smoke too much, and I have a duty to see the little beggar through until his first divorce (1992). [From earlier sense, mendicant, partly as a euphemistic substitute for *bugger*.]

begorra /bɪˈɡɒrə/ int Also **begarra, begorrah.** Anglo-Irish Alteration of the expletive 'by God!' 1839–. Cf. BEJESUS int.

behind noun euphemistic The buttocks, posterior. a.1830–. G. B. SHAW You can say 'If

I catch you doing that again I will . . . smack your behind' (1928).

bejabers /brˈdʒeɪbəz/ int Also **bejabbers** /-ˈæ-/. mainly Anglo-Irish = BEJESUS int. 1890–. [Variant of earlier *be jappers*, alteration of *by Jesus*.]

bejesus /brˈdʒiːzəs/ int Also (mainly Anglo-Irish) **bejasus** /-ˈdʒeɪzəs/. Alteration of the expletive 'by Jesus!' Also as noun in phr. *to beat the bejesus out of*, to give a good hiding to. 1908–. J. TEY I know men who'd beat bejasus out of you for that (1949). Cf. BEGORRA *int*.

bell noun **to give** (someone) **a bell** to telephone (someone), 'give (someone) a ring'. 1982–. G. F. NEWMAN I was going to give you a bell. But I thought it best to give the phone a miss (1986).

bell end noun Brit The glans of the penis. 1997–.

bells and whistles noun pl. Attractive additional features or trimmings, esp. on a computer. 1977–. [Prob. after their use on a fairground organ.]

belly-ache verb intr. orig US To complain querulously or unreasonably; to whine, grizzle. 1888–. E. CALDWELL I reckon there's enough to complain about these days if a fellow wants to belly-ache some (1933). [From *bellyache* noun, pain in the stomach.] So **belly-acher,** noun. 1930–.

belly button noun The navel. 1877–. J. B. PRIESTLEY If you'd ever gone to school with your belly-button knockin' against your backbone (1946).

bellyful noun An excessive amount; as much as one can bear. 1687–. SPORTS QUARTERLY I have had a bellyful of trouble over the years, with white cops in particular (1992).

belly-laugh noun A deep unrestrained laugh. 1921–. E. LINKLATER He laughed, deep belly-laughs (1931).

belly up verb intr. US To make a bold approach; orig. applied literally to walking up to something (e.g. a bar) and standing with one's stomach against it; usu. followed by *to*. 1907–. WALL STREET JOURNAL Only a handful of FDIC-administered institutions have been allowed to belly up to its [i.e. the Federal Reserve's] window (1989).

belt verb **1** trans. To hit; to attack. 1838–. **2** intr. orig dialect and US To hurry, to rush. 1890–. NEW STATESMAN Cor, we used to belt along that road (1962). **3 to belt out** to sing, play,

or speak with great vigour. 1953–. J. STEINBECK One of the finest jazz combos I ever heard was belting out pure ecstasy (1959). **4 to belt up** to be quiet, shut up. 1949–. LISTENER May we hope that Hamilton will do a service to art by belting up and going back to school? (1969). noun **5** A heavy blow or stroke. 1899–. L. A. G. STRONG He'd give Moo a belt in the puss (1953). [In sense 1, from earlier sense, to hit with a belt.]

beltway bandit noun US A company or individual, esp. one formerly employed by various US government agencies, hired by a company to assist in securing government contracts for companies in the private sector. 1978–. [From the location of many such companies on the beltway (ring road) surrounding Washington.]

bench-warmer noun US A person who sits idle on a bench, esp. a substitute in a sports team; also, any lazy or ineffectual person. 1892–. LOS ANGELES TIMES He thought about leaving after the 1984 season, his third straight year as a bench-warmer (1986).

bend verb trans. **1** To use for a wrongful or crooked purpose; to steal; to lose (a contest, etc.) deliberately. 1864–. OBSERVER There are honest landladies in districts like Victoria who let a flat to someone they think is an ordinary girl, who then proceeds to 'bend' it: uses it for prostitution (1958). noun **2 on the** (or **a**) **bend** on a (drinking) spree. 1887–. L. A. G. STRONG Been on the bend, 'aven't you? (1936). **3 round the bend** crazy, insane. 1929–. J. I. M. STEWART Right round the bend . . . I mean . . . as mad as a hatter (1955). [In sense 1, revival of an earlier sense 'to pervert from the right purpose or use'.] See also *to catch* (someone) *bending* at CATCH verb.

bender noun **1** orig US A leg or knee. 1849–. A. S. M. HUTCHINSON They say family prayers there with the servants every night, all down on their benders (1925). **2** orig US A bout of drinking; a violent party. 1846–. BULLETIN (Sydney): Being on a strenuous bender, he had forgotten to sign a cheque (1933). [In sense 2, cf. obsolete *bend* verb, to have a bout of hard drinking.]

Benjamin noun US A one-hundred-dollar bill. Also more generally (in pl.): large sums of money. 1994–. GQ You've made the Benjamins. Now you need a billfold to hold them (1999). [From *Benjamin* Franklin (1706–90), US statesman, whose portrait appears on US $100 bills.]

benji noun US = BENJAMIN. 1985–. VILLAGE VOICE Watch kids who can barely afford food put down a benji for a pair of Nikes (1998).

bejabers bejesus bell bell end bells and whistles

benny¹ noun US An overcoat. 1903–. [Apparently a shortening of obsolete *benjamin* overcoat, perh. from the name of a tailor.]

benny² noun orig US A benzedrine tablet. 1955–. The benny was starting to wear out and I was hot, thirsty and exhausted (1967). [Abbrev. of *benzedrine*.]

bent adjective **1** orig US Dishonest, criminal, crooked. 1914–. SUNDAY PICTORIAL A 'bent screw' . . . a crooked warder who is prepared to traffic with a prisoner (1948). **2** orig US Illegal; stolen. 1930–. P. WILDEBLOOD He had got a short sentence for receiving stolen goods, which he swore he had not known to be 'bent' (1955). **3** Of things: out of order, spoiled. Of persons: eccentric, perverted; spec. homosexual. 1930–. F. RAPHAEL 'Great thing about gay people . . .' 'Gay?' Tessa said. 'Bent, queer, you know. Homosexual' (1960).

berk /bɜːk/ noun Also **birk, burk(e).** A fool. 1936–. J. OSBORNE The Tories were burglars, berks and bloodlusters (1959). [Abbrev. of BERKELEY HUNT noun or *Berkshire Hunt.*]

Berkeley Hunt /ˈbaːklɪ ˈhʌnt/ noun A fool. Also **Berkeley.** 1937–. A. BRACEY Lane's face cleared. 'Tell us, chum!' 'And spoil the nice surprise! Not bloody likely!' 'You always was a berkeley,' said Lane cheerfully (1940). [Rhyming slang for 'cunt'; from the name of a celebrated hunt in Gloucestershire; now largely replaced by BERK noun.]

berry noun **1** US A dollar; Brit a pound. Usu. in pl. 1918–. J. DOS PASSOS He had what was left of the three hundred berries Hedwig coughed up (1936). **2 the berries** dated An excellent person or thing; the cat's whiskers. 1925–6.

best girl noun orig US A girlfriend or female lover. 1887–. SATURDAY REVIEW To pluck a bouquet for his best girl (1944).

bet verb trans. **1 to bet one's life** (or **boots, bottom dollar**) to stake everything or all one's resources (on the truth of an assertion). 1852–. P. FRANK He would bet his bottom dollar . . . that his target would be one of those bases (1957). **2** In forms (*I, you,* etc.) **betcha, betcher,** representing colloquial pronunciation of *bet you* or *your* (*life*). 1922–. J. LUDWIG Your tea's cold, I betcha (1962).

Betsy noun orig US Also **Bessy, Betsey,** and with lower-case initial. A gun or pistol; spec. one's favourite gun; frequently **old Betsy.** 1856–. J. P. CARSTAIRS 'You've noticed I'm toting a Betsy.' 'Betsy?' 'Equalizer, rod, gat, iron' (1965).

[Var. of *Betty*, diminutive of *Bet*, abbreviation of *Elizabeth*.]

Betty noun US A (young attractive) woman. 1989–. [From the female personal name *Betty*.]

Betty Martin noun (**all**) **my eye and Betty Martin** = (all) my eye (see EYE noun). 1781–. W. DE LA MARE You might be suggesting that both shape and scarecrow too were all my eye and Betty Martin (1930).

bevvy Also **bevie, bevy.** Brit noun **1** A drink, esp. beer. 1889–. P. ALLINGHAM 'I think this calls for a bevvy,' I said, and we walked off to the nearest pub together (1934). verb intr. **2** To drink. 1934–. F. SHAW ET AL. Ard cases who could bevvy by the jug (1966). So **bevvied,** adjective Drunk. 1960–. L. LANE The Scouser's favourite excuse for an act of hooliganism is *I wuz bevvied* (1966). [From *bev(erage)* noun + *-y*.]

BF noun orig Brit services' Also **B.F.** Abbreviation of 'bloody fool'. 1925–. C. DAY LEWIS You really are a B.F., Arthur (1939).

B-girl noun US A woman employed to encourage buyers to buy drinks at a bar. 1936–. F. ARCHER If I stand here, I'm a waitress, see? If I sit down, I'm a B-girl, and this joint doesn't pay for that kind of protection (1964). [Abbreviation of *bar-girl*.]

bi /baɪ/ adjective and noun Abbreviation of 'bisexual'. 1966–. LISTENER Some were gay, many apparently bi, and a few were so hard that they would be given a wide berth in a Gorbals pub (1983). See also BI-GUY noun.

Bible-banger noun mainly Austral and NZ = BIBLE-POUNDER noun. 1942–. Also **-basher.** Hence **Bible-banging, -bashing,** adjective and noun.

Bible-pounder noun often derog One who expounds or follows the Bible in a vigorous and aggressive manner, esp. a clergyman. Also **-puncher, -thumper.** 1890–. A. L. ROWSE It's always the Bible-thumpers who are the greatest hypocrites (1942). Hence **Bible-pounding, -punching, -thumping,** adjective and noun. 1951–.

biddy noun mainly derog A woman. 1785–. C. P. SNOW I believe she's the bloodiest awful specimen of a party biddy (1960). [Abbreviation of the female forename *Bridget*.]

biff verb **1** trans. To hit, strike. 1888–. A. BARON Where'd you get that bruise on your forehead? Girl friend been biffing you with the old rolling pin? (1950). **2** trans. and intr. Austral and NZ To throw. 1941–. NEW ZEALAND LISTENER 'All I can do is biff.' 'Then just biff—as hard as you can. You're a natural [at putting the shot]' (1964). noun **3** A blow, whack. 1889–. [Imitative.]

bifter noun Brit and Irish English (orig Liverpool) A cigarette, esp. (outside Liverpool) a marijuana cigarette. 1989–. GUARDIAN The completed bifter burns at 0.3cm per minute and is 15cm long. You are the last in line for the spliff (2002). [Origin unknown.]

big adjective **1 big on** orig US Liking, enthusiastic about. 1867–. C. MCFADDEN He said he'd had amazing results just acting out his anger with his patients. He was also big on video feedback . . . , role-playing . . . and Japanese hot tubs (1977). **2** Fashionable, up-to-date. 1970–. DAILY TELEGRAPH A bale of soft material, patterned in that modernismus which was so big in the Thirties, and now survives chiefly in British Rail (1970).

big verb trans. **to big (someone) up** Brit to praise someone, to boost their reputation or self-esteem. 1992–. G. MALKANI I in't makin all this up just to big Samira up, she honestly really is into her political shit (2006).

Big A noun = BIG APPLE. 1980–.

Big Apple noun orig US New York City. 1928–. UNITED STATES **1980/81** (Penguin Travel Guides): Many Broadway-bound shows play Chicago before heading for the Big Apple (1979). [Apparently from earlier obs. US slang *big apple* important person, big shot (cf. *top banana* big shot); in early use mainly applied specifically to the top New York City racetracks; adopted into jazz musicians' slang in the 1930s, and often applied specifically to Harlem; revived and popularized in 1971 by Charles Gillett, president of the New York Convention and Visitors Bureau, as part of a publicity campaign for the city.]

Big Bang noun The deregulation of the London Stock Exchange on 27 October 1986, when a number of complex changes in trading practices were put into effect simultaneously. 1983–. [From the earlier senses, creation of the universe in one cataclysmic explosion, hence any sudden forceful beginning.]

big boy noun orig US = BIG SHOT noun; frequently used as an ironical form of address. 1918–. J. B. PRIESTLEY 'Am I right, sir?' 'You sure are, big boy' (1939).

big bucks noun orig US Large amounts of money. 1970–. FORBES They could afford big

bucks for advertising and theater rentals and still come out way ahead (1975).

big bug noun orig and mainly US Often derog = BIG SHOT noun. 1827–. E. WAUGH He seems to have been quite a big bug under the Emperor. Ran the army for him (1932).

big C noun euphemistic Cancer. 1968–. TIME John Wayne . . . accepted the news with true grit. 'I've licked the big C before,' he said (1979).

big cheese noun orig US = BIG SHOT noun. 1934–. J. MASTERS 'Where's the manager?' 'The manager?' 'The Bara Sahib. The Big Cheese. The Boss.' 'The Brigadier is out' (1961). [From earlier sense of *cheese*, the right or excellent thing, prob. from Urdu *chīz* thing.]

Big D noun US Dallas, Texas. 1930–. N. MAILER They found her vagina in North Carolina and part of her gashole in hometown Big D (1967).

big daddy noun orig US = BIG SHOT noun. 1948–. SPECTATOR Mr. Francis Williams, journalism's Big Daddy (1958).

big deal noun orig US Used ironically to indicate that one is not impressed. 1951–. S. HARVESTER So, I can charge an evening's entertainment to business expenses. Oh, big deal. Carry on (1966).

Big Ditch noun US The North Atlantic Ocean. 1909–.

big E noun An unceremonious dismissal or rejection, the 'push'. 1982–. [From the first letter of *elbow*: see *to get* (or *give someone) the elbow* at ELBOW noun 2.]

Big Easy noun US New Orleans, Louisiana. 1970–. [Apparently coined by James Conaway as the title of a novel, and popularized by the 1986 film based on this.]

big enchilada noun orig US = BIG SHOT noun. 1973–.

big fish noun orig US = BIG SHOT noun. 1836–. NEW SCIENTIST What with being a writer and a T.V. personality and a sort of know-all pundit A.L.W. was quite a big fish (1991).

biggie noun **1** orig US = BIG SHOT noun. 1931–. MELODY MAKER It's time for me to be a biggie . . . My aim now is to get . . . on to the front page (1969). **2** pl. A children's word or euphemism for 'excrement'. 1953–. A. WILSON He's a bit erratic where he does his biggies, now he's a grown-up parrot (1967). [From *big* adjective + *-ie*.]

big girl's blouse noun Brit An ineffectual male. 1983–.

bifter big Big A Big Apple Big Bang big daddy

big gun noun = BIG SHOT noun. 1834–.
B. KIMENYE Mrs Lutaya's set absolutely refused to accept this high-handed ruling, preferring to remain large fish in their own small pond, rather than compete with the big guns of Gumbi and Male villages (1966). [Variant of earlier *great gun* in same sense.]

big hair noun orig US Long hair teased and lacquered into a large bouffant. 1988–. SUNDAY TIMES Big hair, make-up, shiny pink leotards with contrasting tights are out (1993).

big house noun orig US A prison. 1916–. D. HUME You'll land yourself in the big house for fourteen years (1942). [From earlier sense, workhouse.]

big mouth noun derog orig and mainly US A very talkative or boastful person; also, loquacity, boastful talk. 1889–. E. COXHEAD He was a big mouth. He picked up strangers . . . and told them the story of his life (1951). Hence **big-mouthed,** adjective Loquacious or boastful. 1914–.

big noise noun orig US = BIG SHOT noun. 1911–. M. KENNEDY Say you don't want him. You're the big noise here (1957).

big one noun orig US A thousand dollars or a thousand-dollar bill. 1935–. M. TORGOV I'd have to cough up two hundred and fifty big ones, right? I haven't got that kind of bread lying around (1990). [From earlier more general sense, large-denomination bill.]

big pond noun = POND. 1833–.

Big PX noun US military The USA as a place of easily available consumer goods and home comforts. 1962–. [From PX, the name applied to shops on US military bases.]

Big Q noun US San Quentin Prison, California. 1961–.

big shot noun orig and mainly US A person of high rank or importance. 1929–. NEW STATESMAN On arrival I was asked to dine with Thomas Lamont, along with a number of big-shots in the American newspaper world (1960). [Variant of earlier *great shot* in same sense.]

big sleep noun orig US Death. 1938–. [Popularized by the name of the novel *The Big Sleep* (1938) by Raymond Chandler, and prob. coined by Chandler himself.]

big time noun orig US The highest level of success. 1910–. CRESCENDO Scores of drummers who hit the big time play Premier (1966). Hence **big-time** adjective orig US Of the best kind or the highest rank. 1914–. AMERICAN SPEECH

Big-time gangsters, racketeers, and the criminal aristocrats do not use narcotics (1936). Also **big-time** adverb orig US To the maximum extent. 1957–. WASHINGTON POST 'Everybody is turning the heat up on our organization big-time,' he told a rally of more than 2,000 people in Louisville (1993).

Big Town noun US New York City. 1902–.

bi-guy noun A bisexual male. 1973–. GAY NEWS Good looking bi-guy, 30s . . . wants friendship with similar couple (1977). Cf. BI adjective and noun.

big wheel noun orig and mainly US = BIG SHOT noun. 1942–. M. DICKENS He was evidently quite a big wheel at the studio (1958). [Figurative use of *big wheel* Ferris wheel.]

bigwig noun mainly jocular = BIG SHOT noun. a.1731–. L. DEIGHTON He was there to give the Cubans some advice when they purged some of the bigwigs in 1970 (1984). [From the large wigs formerly worn by men of high rank or importance.]

bike noun **1 to get off one's bike** Austral and NZ (Usu. in negative contexts) to get rattled, to get annoyed. 1939–. **2 on your bike!** go away!, push off!; now also with the implication that the person addressed should go and look for work. The latter implication was popularized by a speech given by Employment Secretary Norman Tebbit at the Conservative Party Conference in 1981, in which he pointed out that his father had not rioted in the 1930s when unemployed, but 'got on his bike and looked for work'. 1967–. TIMES 'On your bike, Khomeini,' the crowd shouted outside the Iranian Embassy during the siege (1981).

bikie noun Austral and NZ A motor-cyclist; spec. a member of a gang of motor-cyclists, usually leather-jacketed, with a reputation for violent or rowdy behaviour. 1967–. [From BIKE noun + -*ie*.]

bilge noun Nonsense, rubbish, 'rot'. 1908–. A. S. M. HUTCHINSON They didn't talk any of this bilge about us fighting in England (1921). [From the earlier senses, (the foul matter which collects in) the bottom of a ship's hull.]

bill noun Brit The police force; a policeman. Frequently preceded by *the*. 1969–. BRITISH JOURNAL OF PHOTOGRAPHY There wasn't going to be no questions asked in the House about some working-class kid getting hisself duffed up by the bill (1979). [Short for OLD BILL noun.]

big gun big hair big house big mouth big noise

bim¹ noun US A girl, woman; a whore. 1925–. J. T. FARRELL Studs Lonigan copped off a bim whose old man is lousy with dough (1935). [Abbreviation of BIMBO noun.]

bim² noun = BUM¹ noun 1. 1935–. C. DAY LEWIS He slid gracefully down it on his bim (1948).

bimbette noun orig US A bimbo, esp. an adolescent or teenage one. 1982–. TIME Serious actresses, itching to play something more demanding than bimbette and stand-by wives, love divine masochist roles (1982). [From BIMB(O noun + diminutive -ette.]

bimbo noun orig US **1** mainly derog A fellow, chap. 1919–. R. CHANDLER There's a thousand berries on that bimbo. A bank stick-up, ain't he? (1936). **2a** A young woman considered sexually attractive but of limited intelligence. 1927–. W. ALLEN Sure, a guy can meet all the bimbos he wants. But the really brainy women—they're not so easy to find (1976). **b** A woman; esp. a prostitute. 1929–. DETECTIVE FICTION WEEKLY We found Durken and Frenchy LaSeur, seated at a table . . . with a pair of blonde bimboes beside them (1937). [Italian, = little child, baby.]

bin noun **the bin** short for LOONY BIN noun. 1938–. L. A. G. STRONG The chaps who certified you and popped you in the bin (1942).

bind verb dated, mainly services' **1** trans. To bore, weary. 1929–. **2** intr. derog To complain. 1943–. N. SHUTE Eddy's been binding to Vic about you (1959).

binder noun **1** dated mainly services' **a** A boring person or thing. 1930–. **b** derog A complainer. 1944–. **2** pl. Brakes. 1942–. AMERICAN SPEECH Most often used in referring to emergency stops. 'Hit the binders!' (1962). [In sense 1, from BIND verb.]

bindle noun N Amer **1** A bundle containing clothes and possessions; esp. a bedding-roll carried by a tramp. 1900–. J. STEINBECK George unslung his bindle and dropped it gently on the bank (1937). **2** Any package or bundle; spec. one containing narcotics. 1916–. DIALECT NOTES *Bindle*, a package containing either morphine or cocaine. 'Give me a bindle of snow' (1923). [Prob. an alteration of *bundle* noun, but cf. Scottish *bindle* noun, cord or rope that binds something.]

bindle-man noun N Amer A tramp who carries a bindle. Also **bindle-stiff**. 1900–.

binge noun **1** A heavy drinking-bout; hence, a period of self-indulgence (e.g. in eating or shopping). 1854–. P. G. WODEHOUSE Eh?

What about our Monte Carlo binge? (1928). verb intr. **2** To have a binge. 1910–. SUCCESSFUL SLIMMING You fall into the trap of fasting for two days, then bingeing for three—obviously a self-defeating exercise (1989). [Special use of British dialect *binge* verb, to soak (a wooden vessel).] Hence **binged** adjective dated Drunk. 1916–. SUNDAY AT HOME One man was so binged in drink and so enchained by the craving for it (1925).

binghi /ˈbɪŋɡɪ/ noun Also **Binghi**. Austral, derog An Aboriginal. Often attributive. 1902–. M. DURACK Before long every white family in Broome had acquired a mission educated 'binghi' couple (1964). [From Aboriginal (Awabakal and neighbouring languages) *biŋay*, (elder) brother.]

bingy /ˈbɪndʒɪ/ noun Also **bingee, bingie, bingey, binjy**. Austral The stomach, belly. 1832–. AUSTRALASIAN POST Plenty tucker here. Just look at those binjies! (1963). [From Aboriginal (Dharuk) *bindi*.]

binman noun A dustman or refuse collector. c.1966–. DAILY TELEGRAPH Another common request was for . . . a waste-disposal system that would eliminate the need for bin men (1986).

bins noun pl., Brit Glasses, spectacles. 1981–. (first recorded in print in 1981, but other evidence (e.g. obs. Cockney rhyming slang *Errol Flynns* spectacles) suggests much earlier use). J. MCVICAR Frank gives me the once-over and pushes the bins back tight on my eyes. If George saw my minces, he might pull the deal (1992). [Shortening of *binoculars*.]

bint noun mainly derog A girl or woman; girl-friend. 1855–. (The term was in common use among British servicemen in Egypt and neighbouring countries in the wars of 1914–18 and 1939–45.) K. AMIS As the R. A. F. friend would have put it, you could never tell with these foreign bints (1958). [From Arabic *bint* daughter.]

bionic adjective Outstandingly gifted or competent. 1976–. HORSE AND HOUND Bionic couple required as groom/gardener and housekeeper (1976). [From the earlier sense, having artificial body parts; inspired by the 1970s US television series *The Six Million Dollar Man*, featuring a bionic man with superhuman powers.]

bippy noun orig US **you bet your (sweet) bippy** be assured, certainly. 1968–. H. WHITTEMORE You bet your bippy we're taking a position. [A nonsense formation orig. used in the US television comedy programme *Rowan and Martin's Laugh-In* (1968–71).]

bird noun **1** A man, fellow. 1852–. J. B. PRIESTLEY He's one of them queer birds that aren't human until they're properly pickled (1939). **2** Esp. in the phrases *to get the bird, give* (someone) *the bird:* **a** orig theatrical A show of disapproval by an audience, esp. in the form of hissing. 1884–. P. G. WODEHOUSE Would a Rudge audience have given me the bird a few years ago? (1928). **b** Dismissal, the sack. 1924–. P. KEMP She gave him the bird—finally and for good. So he came to Spain to forget his broken heart (1957). **3** A girl or woman; girl-friend. 1915–. NEWS CHRONICLE Hundreds more geezers were taking their birds to 'The Hostage' and 'Make me an Offer' (1960). **4** A prison sentence; prison. 1924–. LISTENER Having done his bird, as imprisonment is called in the best circles (1953). **5** An aeroplane. Also, a guided missile, rocket, or space-craft. 1933–. A. SHEPARD I really enjoy looking at a bird that is getting ready to go (1962). **6** **(strictly) for the birds** orig and mainly US Trivial, worthless; appealing only to gullible people 1951–. LISTENER Our answer, at that age, would have been that Stanley Matthews was for the birds. Football was just not mobile enough (1963). [In sense 2, short for earlier *the big bird*; in sense 3, a use paralleled by Middle and early Modern English *bird* maiden, girl; in sense 4, short for BIRD-LIME noun.]

bird-lime noun Rhyming slang for 'time'; often spec. a term of imprisonment. 1857–. RADIO TIMES In the past Charley's done his 'birdlime' but he was given time off for good behaviour (1962).

birl noun Austral = BURL noun.

biscuit noun **1 to take the biscuit** = to take the cake (see CAKE noun). 1907–. LISTENER For the sheerest idiocy, it's the comparative 'as contemporary as . . . ' that takes the biscuit (1961). **2** military A square brown palliasse or mattress. 1915–35.

biscuit-shooter noun US, dated A waitress or (occasionally) waiter. 1893–1927.

bish noun A mistake, blunder. 1937–. B. GOOLDEN She . . . suddenly realised she'd made an [*sic*] complete bish (1956). [Of unknown origin.]

bit noun **1a: a bit of fluff (goods, muslin, mutton, skirt, stuff)** a woman or girl. 1847–. J. I. M. STEWART They mustn't quarrel over a bit of skirt (1977). **b** A woman or girl (perh. short for *a bit of fluff, goods*, etc.). 1923–. B. GOOLDEN If I want a common little bit for a best girl that's my look-out, too (1953). **2** A prison sentence. 1871–. J. H. SMYTH The only question was how much of a bit Lucky would get (1951). **3 a (little) bit of all right** something or someone highly satisfactory; esp. applied to a pretty or obliging woman. 1898–. M. DICKENS 'What's she like?' . . . 'The daughter? Bit of all right, from her pictures' (1956). **4** orig US jazz and bop musicians' An aggregate of features, way of behaving, etc. characteristic of a particular activity, lifestyle, etc. 1958–. GANDALF'S GARDEN I was originally on the jazz scene and in a terrible state. You know, doing the whole bit, being on the phoney junky trip which nearly every jazz musician was on (1969).

bitch noun **1** Something outstandingly difficult or unpleasant. 1814–. T. E. LAWRENCE 'She,' says the incarnate sailor, stroking the gangway of the *Iron Duke*, 'can be a perfect bitch in a cross-sea' (1931). **2** A malicious or spiteful woman. 1913–. E. WAUGH Mrs Cecil Chesterton was a bitch and a liar. I think you inoffensively make that clear (1962). verb **3** trans. To spoil, bungle. 1823–. R. DANIEL But for a squall bitching his escape route . . . he would be in France (1960). **4** intr. orig US To speak scathingly, complain, grumble. 1930–. B. CRUMP Couples bitching at each other is human nature (1961). **5** trans. To be spiteful or unfair to. 1934–. G. GREENE She said 'I thought you were never coming. I bitched you so' (1948). Hence **bitchy,** adjective Malicious, catty. 1947–. [In sense 2, from the earlier meaning, lewd or sensual woman; in all senses, ultimately from *bitch*, female dog.]

bitching adjective orig and mainly US **1** Unpleasant, hellish, despicable. 1928–. M. RAVENHILL Fuck the bitching world and let's be . . . beautiful (1997). **2** Great, excellent, wonderful; very attractive or appealing, fashionable. 1957–. LANE & CRAWFORD Tommy is like such a hunk, I just can't stand it! Like, he's just so bitchin' (1982). Cf. BAD adjective 2, WICKED adjective.

bitch slap noun US A stinging slap or blow, esp. one delivered to humiliate

biscuit-shooter

a waitress or waiter

someone regarded as inferior. 1987–. Hence **bitch-slap** verb trans. US 1991–. ENTERTAINMENT WEEKLY [He] claims he merely 'bitch-slapped' the producer three times ('A little bitch slap don't hurt nobody') (1997).

bite verb trans. **1 to bite someone's ear** to borrow money from (someone). 1879–. P. G. WODEHOUSE His principal source of income . . . was derived from biting the ear of a rich uncle (1925). **2** Austral To cadge or borrow (money, etc.) from. 1919–. L. GLASSOP Can I bite you for a few quid, Lucky? (1949). noun **3 to put the bite on** orig and mainly US To borrow money from; also, to threaten, to blackmail, to extort money from. 1933–. S. RANSOME Everybody keeps putting the bite on me for money I haven't got (1950).

bitsy adjective mainly US = BITTY adjective. 1905–. Cf. ITSY-BITSY. W. GOLDING A bitsy village with reed thatch and wrought-iron work (1959). [From *bit* or BITTY + *-sy*.]

bitty adjective US Tiny. 1905–. Cf. ITTY-BITTY. R. CHANDLER That toy . . . It's just a little bitty gun, a butterfly gun (1940). [From earlier sense, consisting of little bits.]

bivvy noun **1** army A temporary shelter for troops; a small tent. 1916–. **2** mountaineers' A night spent in the open air without a tent; an open-air encampment. 1961–. AMERICAN ALPINE JOURNAL This was the real stuff, one of the typical miserable alpine bivvies that you read about in the American Alpine Journal (2003). verb intr., orig military **3** To camp with little or no shelter. 1943–. **4 to bivvy up** anglers' To use a small tent for shelter while fishing, esp. for several days. 1992–. [From *biv(ouac* + *-y*.]

bizzo noun Austral A thing that is unnamed, or that one does not wish to name. 1969–. G. MORLEY Sheilas sitting down against the wall, legs up in the air, showing their bizzos (1972). [From *bus(iness* + *-o*.]

blabbermouth noun orig US A speaker who reveals too much; an indiscreet person. 1936–. D. KARP No, Burney isn't a blabbermouth. He tells you a lot less than he knows (1956). [From *blabber* one who blabs + *mouth*.]

black noun **1 to put the black on** to blackmail. 1924–. J. B. PRIESTLEY Got a lovely pub . . . and yet wants to start putting the black on people! (1951). **2** orig services' A serious mistake or blunder; esp. in phr. *to put up a black*, to make a blunder. 1939–. N. SHUTE Probably I should have to . . . leave Government service altogether, having put up such a black as that (1948). verb trans. **3** To blackmail. 1928–.

G. SIMS He . . . took naughty photos of them and then blacked them (1964).

black bomber noun An amphetamine tablet. 1963–.

black tar noun An exceptionally pure form of heroin originating in Mexico. 1986–. ECONOMIST What makes black tar heroin unique is that it has a single, foreign source—Mexico— and finds its way into Mexican-American distribution networks, often via illegal immigrants (1986).

black velvet noun Austral and NZ offensive A black-skinned or coloured woman, esp. as the sexual partner of a white man; such women collectively. 1899–. G. CASEY Did you see the girls, when you were out there? . . . The sort of black velvet that sometimes makes me wish I wasn't a policeman (1958).

bladder noun mainly US A newspaper, esp. a poor one. 1936–. OBSERVER The news of your return has caused hardly a ripple in the daily bladders (1973). [Cf. BLAT noun.]

bladdered adjective Brit Very drunk. 1992–. OBSERVER Friends say she and 'Hooky' enjoy hitting the clubs together, getting 'bladdered', and generally acting like soppy teenagers in each other's company (1995). [From the notion of a full bladder.]

blag noun **1** Robbery (with violence); theft. 1885–. OBSERVER The top screwing teams, the ones who went in for the really big blags, violent robberies (1960). verb trans. **2** To rob (with violence); to steal. 1933–. So **blagger,** noun A robber. 1938–. [Origin unknown.]

blag verb Brit **1** trans. To obtain or achieve by persuasive talk or plausible deception. 1934–. MIRROR It was the biggest night in the British music calendar and yours truly blagged an invite (2001). **2** intr. To talk persuasively, if disingenuously, in an attempt to obtain or achieve something. 1991–. So **blagger** noun A bluffer, scrounger, or cadger. 1963–. [Origin uncertain; perh. from BLAG noun.]

blah Also **bla, blaa.** orig US. noun **1** Meaningless, insincere, or pretentious talk or writing; nonsense, bunkum. Also used as a derisive interjection. 1918–. E. H. CLEMENTS A good deal of blah about waste of public money (1958). verb intr. **2** To talk or write 'blah'. Also **blah-blah.** 1924–. [Imitative.]

blah adjective **1** Obs Mad. 1924–8. **2** Dull, unexciting; pretentious. 1937–. J. VERNEY One of those blah sneery voices like a butler in a film (1959). [Cf. BLAH noun.]

bite bitsy bitty bivvy bizzo blabbermouth black

blahs noun orig and mainly US Depression, despondency, low spirits; usu. *the blahs*. 1969–. DETROIT FREE PRESS A good haircut, maybe some streaking to lift the winter blahs (1978). [From BLAH adjective 2, perh. influenced by *blues*.]

blank verb trans. Brit To ignore (a person), esp. intentionally; to cold-shoulder. 1977–. SELECT As Alex wanders inside to bid the local support band a polite hello he is blanked outrageously (1991).

blanket noun **on the blanket** applied to supporters of the Irish Republican cause held in the Maze prison (near Belfast) and elsewhere, who wore blankets instead of prison clothes as a protest against being treated as criminals rather than as political prisoners. 1977–. M. WALLACE The first prisoner had gone 'on the blanket' in September 1976, refusing to wear prison clothing (1982).

blast noun A party, esp. one that is very noisy or wild. 1959–.

blast verb trans. and intr. mainly US To smoke (marijuana). 1959–. Cf. BLASTED adjective.

blasted adjective mainly US Under the influence of drugs or alcohol, intoxicated. 1972–. J. CARROL Den O'Coole forced his way to the bar . . . He was already blasted (1978).

blat noun Also **blatt**. orig US A (popular) newspaper. 1932–. TIMES An otherwise bald and unconvincing interview on the telly or column in the blats (1986). [From German *Blatt* leaf, newspaper.]

blatherskite noun mainly US (orig Brit dialect) Also **bletherskate**. **1** A noisy, talkative person, esp. one who talks utter rubbish. *c.*1650–. **2** Foolish talk, nonsense. 1825–. C. WILSON For Nietzsche . . . there is no such thing as abstract knowledge; there is only useful knowledge and unprofitable blatherskite (1956). [From *blather*, *blether* foolish chatter + *skite*, corrupt use of *skate*, the fish (in Scottish used contemptuously).]

bleeder noun A very stupid, unpleasant, or contemptible person; also used more or less inoffensively, preceded by *little*, *poor*, etc. 1887–. A. BARON She'll kill the poor little bleeder (1952).

bleeding adjective and adverb A substitute for BLOODY adjective and adverb 1858–. TIMES Why don't you bleeding do something about it? (1967).

blerry adjective Also **blerrie, blirry**. S Afr = BLOODY adjective 1. 1920–. C. LASSALLE Do you

boys call this blerry muck breakfast (1986). [S Afr alteration of BLOODY adjective.] Cf. PLURRY adjective.

blighter noun Brit A contemptible or unpleasant person; also *loosely*, a person, fellow. 1896–. J. I. M. STEWART 'What we have to contrive,' he said, 'is fair shares . . . for each of the little blighters' (1957). [From *blight* + *-er*.]

Blighty noun Also **blighty**. Brit army **1** dated Britain, home. (Used by soldiers serving abroad.) 1915–. J. R. ACKERLEY I was not happy in Blighty (1968). **2** In World War I applied to a wound that secured return to Britain; mainly attrib 1916–. W. J. LOCKE Mo says he's blistering glad you're out of it and safe in your perishing bed with a Blighty one (1918). [Contracted form, originating in the Indian army, of Hindustani *bilāyatī*, *wilāyatī* foreign, European.]

blimey int Also **bli' me, blime**. Brit An expression of surprise, contempt, etc. 1889–. J. JOYCE Blimey it makes me kind of bleeding cry (1922). [Contraction of (*God*) *blind me!*] Cf. *cor blimey* at COR int and GORBLIMEY int, noun, and adjective.

blind adjective **1** Drunk. 1630–. W. S. MAUGHAM On the night he arrived in London he would get blind, he hadn't been drunk for twenty years (1930). noun **2** Brit A heavy drinking- bout; a binge; esp. in phr. *on a blind*, 1917–. J. B. PRIESTLEY I'm not off on a blind, if that's what you're worrying about (1943). verb intr. **3** To go blindly or heedlessly; to drive very fast. 1923–. DAILY EXPRESS By recreation I do not mean blinding along the Brighton road at fifty miles an hour (1928). **4** To use profane or indecent language, to swear; esp. in phr. *to eff and blind*. 1943–. [In sense 1, short for *blind drunk*; in sense 4, from the use of *blind* in imprecations such as *blind me!*]

blinder noun Brit Something excellent, esp. an excellent performance in a sport. 1950–. D. STOREY You played a blinder . . . It was the best game I ever saw (1960). [From the notion of being 'dazzlingly' good.]

bling-bling Also **bling**. noun orig US Ostentatious jewellery or other flashy personal adornment. Hence: wealth; conspicuous consumption 1999–. [Prob. suggesting the visual effect of light reflected off precious stones or metal.]

bliss verb intr. **to bliss out** US To reach a state of ecstasy. Chiefly **blissed out** adjective, in such a state; **blissing out** noun. 1973–. NEW YORKER Long-haired Westerners . . . blissing out or

blahs blank blanket blast blast blasted blat

freaking out in the streets (1986). [Modelled on *to freak out* (see FREAK verb).]

blister dated Brit. noun **1** A person, esp. an annoying one. 1806–. P. G. WODEHOUSE Women are a wash-out. I see no future for the sex, Bertie. Blisters, all of them (1930). **2** A summons. 1903–. F. SARGESON He'd been paying off a few bob every time he had a few to spare . . . And then he gets a blister! (1947). verb trans. **3** To serve with a summons. 1909–.

blithered adjective Austral Drunk. 1911–. BULLETIN (Sydney) A Mildura settler was making home one night in the dusk slightly blithered (1944). [From *blither* talk nonsense.]

blivit noun Also **blivet.** US, mainly jocular Something useless, unnecessary, annoying, etc.; a thingamajig. 1967–. AVIATION WEEK & SPACE TECHNOLOGY Refueling of helicopters . . . surfaced as an alternative to air dropping blivits (1980). [Origin unknown; cf. *blip, widget,* and the occurrence of *bl-* as an initial sound in words expressing inconsequence, rejection, etc.]

blob noun **1** cricket A batsman's score of no runs, a 'duck'. Hence generally, a foolish error, blunder. 1889–. B. HAMILTON A cricketer . . . may make a string of blobs, and then hit a couple of hundreds (1958). **2** mainly Austral A fool. 1916–. LISTENER If you could only see what a pathetic blob you look in your leotard and tights you'd never do another class (1983).

block noun The head; esp. in phr. *to knock someone's block off,* to strike someone powerfully on the head. 1928–. So **off one's block** angry, insane. 1925–. Also **to lose or do (in) one's block** mainly Austral and NZ To become angry, excited, or anxious. 1907–. H. G. WELLS Many suggestions were made, from 'Knock his little block off', to 'Give him more love' (1939).

block-busting adjective and noun US Introducing African-American residents into traditionally white areas. 1959–. NATION The block-busting real-estate men show homes in integrated districts only to prospective Negro buyers (1961). Hence **block-buster,** noun. 1967–. [From *block* noun, quadrangular division of buildings, etc. bounded by four streets.]

blocker noun Brit A bowler hat. 1934–. F. SHAW Foremen traditionally wore bowler-hats, or 'blockers' (1966).

blog noun An Internet website containing an eclectic and frequently updated assortment of items of interest to its author.

1999–. [Shortening of *weblog*.] So **blogger,** noun.

bloke noun **1** A man, fellow. 1851–. A. BLEASDALE Do you know I followed a bloke to court one morning . . . and sat there and watched while he . . . pleaded guilty to the offences I was still following him for? (1983). **2** Naval The commander of a ship. 1914–. [Shelta.] Hence **blokeish,** adjective Also **blokish,** Brit Applied to positive behaviour associated with men, esp. straightforwardness, bluffness, and lack of affectation. 1957–. SUNDAY TIMES The Mayles then popped up in a restaurant in Provence, Lindsay Duncan all cutesy and John Thaw all blokeish ('When you're ready, maestro!') (1993).

blokie noun Also **blokey.** now mainly Brit = BLOKE noun 1. 1841–.

blood noun orig and mainly US (in African-American usage) A black person; also, esp. as a form of address, a (close) male friend. 1965–. Q Sounds like there's a lot of politics going on, blood (1997). E. CONLON I swear, Officer, I did not touch another woman, I was sniffin' coke with my bloods all night! (2004). [Prob. shortening of *blood brother*.]

blood wagon noun An ambulance. 1922–. S. MOSS Out came the 'blood wagon' and to the ambulance station in the paddock I went (1957).

bloody adjective **1** Expressing annoyance or antipathy, or as an intensive; attrib. 1785–. LANDFALL You mind your own bloody business (1950). **2** Bad, unpleasant, deplorable; predic. 1934–. A. HECKSTALL-SMITH Why go out of your way to be bloody about Archie when I'm trying to help him? (1954). adverb **3** As an intensive. 1676–. E. TAYLOR You bloody know you didn't (1951).

blooey adjective Also **blooie.** US Awry, amiss; usu. in phr. *to go blooey.* 1920–. J. UPDIKE A clear image suddenly in the water wavering like a blooey television set (1961). [Origin unknown.]

bloomer noun orig Austral A blunder. 1889–. ECONOMIST 'The Times' . . . has this week made a bloomer about a president (1959). [From *blooming error*.]

blooming adjective and adverb euphemistic = BLOODY adjective and adverb, used as a vague intensive of general application. 1882–. SCOTSMAN You asks me no bloomin' imper'int questions, an' I tells yer no bloomin' lies (1885). [From the notion of something being at full bloom, and hence at its extreme point.]

blister blithered blivit blob block block-busting

blooper

blooper noun orig and mainly US A blunder. 1947–. DAILY TELEGRAPH The Administration had made a 'blooper' over the custom of allowing members of Congress to provide constituents with guided tours of the White House (1961). [From the earlier sense, a radio set that causes interference in neighbouring sets, prob. influenced by BLOOMER noun.]

blotto adjective Intoxicated, drunk. 1917–. P. G. WODEHOUSE Did you ever see a blotto butler before? (1951). [Obscurely from *blot*.]

blow verb **1** trans. To expose, betray, inform on. 1575–. E. WALLACE This officer 'blew' the raid to Tommy (1925). **2 to blow the gaff** to let out a secret; to reveal a plot. 1812–. B. FORBES It's my hunch you were primarily responsible for blowing the whole gaff (1986). **3 blow me tight!** used for expressing great surprise. 1819–. P. MACDONALD 'Blow me *tight!*' said Sergeant Guilfoil. For things were certainly happening in Farnley (1933). **4** trans. **a** To get through (money) in a lavish manner; to squander. 1874–. ECONOMIST He will probably feel able to blow with a clear conscience the £2,000 (1957). **b: to blow in** mainly US To spend, squander. Also *absol.* 1886–. F. SARGESON Then he'd go to town and blow his money in, usually at the races (1946). **5** trans. US To treat (someone) *to*. 1889–. A. MILLER Tell Dad, we want to blow him to a good meal (1949). **6** intr. orig US To go away, leave hurriedly. 1912–. E. LINKLATER 'And what's happened to Rocco?' . . . 'He's blown. He's gone up north' (1937). **7 to blow** (someone) **away: a** To kill, esp. by shooting or explosion. Orig Southern US dialect, but given wider currency during the Vietnam War. 1913–. GUARDIAN A gunman smiled as he shot dead a young policeman after being jilted by his girlfriend, the Old Bailey was told yesterday. 'I blew your copper away because my girlfriend blew me away,' Mark Gaynor . . . told officers later (1991). **b** orig US To have an overwhelming effect on someone's mind. 1975–. **8** trans. To stimulate (someone's) penis orally. Also intr., to practise fellatio. 1933–. P. ROTH 'I want you to come in my mouth,' and so she blew me (1969). Cf. BLOW JOB noun. **9 to blow one's stack** orig US To lose one's temper. 1947–. W. H. CANAWAY I ain't whingeing, honest . . . I'm sorry I blew me stack (1979). **10 to blow** (a person's) **mind** to induce hallucinatory experiences in (a person) by means of drugs, esp. LSD; hence transf, to produce in (a person) a pleasurable (or shocking) sensation. 1966–. SAN FRANCISCO CHRONICLE Because when the Red Sox rallied to beat the Minneapolis Twins . . . Boston fans

blew their minds (1967). noun **11** orig US Cocaine for inhaling. 1971–.

blower noun The telephone. 1922–. J. WYNDHAM I'd of said the old girl was *always* listenin' when there was anyone on the blower (1957).

blow job noun orig US An act of performing fellatio or cunnilingus. 1961–. P. BOOTH Turning the other cheek was for girls who hadn't had to give blow jobs to tramps in exchange for a few pieces of candy (1986). Cf. BLOW verb 7.

BLT noun US Abbreviation of 'bacon, lettuce, and tomato'; a sandwich filled with this. 1952–. US AIR He eats at his desk every day, sometimes dining on such delicacies as a hot dog or a BLT (1989).

bludge verb **1** intr. To act as a prostitute's pimp. 1919–. **2** intr. Austral and NZ To shirk responsibility or hard work; to impose *on*. 1931–. R. LAWLER I won't bludge. I'll get a job or something (1957). **3** trans. Austral and NZ To cadge or scrounge. 1944–. R. CORNISH We cleaned the house, painted the wall . . . bludged some furniture (1975). noun **4** An easy job or assignment; a period of loafing. 1943–. [Back-formation from BLUDGER noun.]

bludger noun **1** A prostitute's pimp. 1898–. OBSERVER They are strikingly different to the white prostitutes who ply their trade for coloured bludgers (1960). **2** Austral and NZ A parasite or hanger-on; a loafer. Now often in weakened sense. 1900–. COURIER-MAIL (Brisbane): Surely if one is willing to give a good day's work for a good day's pay one should be given a chance to earn. I'm no bludger (1969). [Shortened from *bludgeoner* noun, someone armed with a bludgeon.]

blue noun Austral and NZ **1** A nickname for a red-haired person. 1932–. **2a** A mistake or blunder. 1941–. B. CRUMP Trouble with you blokes is you won't admit when you've made a blue (1961). **b** An argument; a fight or brawl. 1943–. N. COLOTTA When you get into a blue do yer pull knives? (1957).

blue verb trans. To spend recklessly; to squander. 1846–. W. DE LA MARE She had taken a holiday and just blued some of her savings (1930). [Perh. a variant of BLOW verb.]

blue funk noun dated derog A state of extreme fear or terror. 1861–.

blue murder noun A loud and alarming noise; a great din or commotion; **to cry (yell, etc.) blue murder,** to shout desperately, as if being attacked. 1859–. A. GILBERT Corpses don't yell blue murder (1959).

bluey noun **1** Austral A blanket, esp. as used by travellers in the bush. 1891–. S. CAMPION To bed they went, wrapped as before in their blueys on the rain-loud verandah (1941). **2** Austral and NZ A summons. 1909–. N. Z. E. F. TIMES That speed cop, who gave me my last bluey on point duty (1942). **3** Austral and NZ A nickname for a red-haired person. 1918–. **4** services' An airmail letter-form available free of charge to service personnel stationed abroad and to their correspondents at home. 1990–. TIMES Blueys . . . are being distributed to post offices by the defence ministry (1991). [In senses 1, 2, and 4, from their colour.] See also *to hump one's bluey* at HUMP verb.

blunt noun orig US A cigar whose wrapper has been emptied of tobacco and filled with marijuana. 1988–. [From *Phillis Blunt*, the name of a popular US brand of cigar.]

bo noun mainly US Used as a term of address to a male. 1825–. JUDGE The man who tells the bootblack 'Keep the change, bo' (1919). [Prob. a shortening of *boy*.]

boat noun Brit The face. 1958–. R. COOK We've seen the new boat of the proletariat, all gleaming eyes (1962). [Short for BOAT-RACE noun.]

boatie noun mainly Austral and NZ A boating enthusiast; one who sails a boat, esp. for pleasure. 1962–. SOUTH CHINA MORNING POST Yachties, boaties and junk owners will have to dig deeper into their pockets following the Government's increase in pleasure boat mooring charges (1985).

boat-race noun Brit Rhyming slang for 'face'. 1958–.

bobby-dazzler noun orig dialect A remarkable or excellent person or thing. 1866–. J. BRAINE By God, you're what my old Nanny used to call a bobby-dazzler in that dress (1959). Cf. RUBY-DAZZLER noun.

bobsy-die noun NZ A fuss; usu. in phr. *to kick up bobsy-die*. 1952–. T. MCLEAN By generally kicking up bobsy-die (1960). [From earlier *Bob's-a-dying* fuss, commotion.]

Boche /bɒʃ/ derog noun **1** A German, esp. a German soldier, or Germans collectively. 1914–. E. F. DAVIES If the Boche wanted a rough-house he could rely on Pickering to give it to him (1952). adjective German. 1917–. [French slang, orig = rascal: applied to Germans in World War 1.]

bod noun Brit A person. 1933–. P. SHARP To join a station you have to get these cards signed by odd bods all over the place (1955). [Abbreviation of *body* noun.]

bodacious /bəˈdeɪʃəs/ adjective US orig dialect Remarkable, noteworthy. 1845–. [Perh. a variant of English dialect *boldacious*, a blend of *bold* and *audacious*.]

bodger adjective Austral Inferior, worthless, false. 1945–. F. J. HARDY This entailed the addition of as many more 'bodger' votes as possible (1950). [From *bodge* verb, to patch or mend clumsily.]

bodgie noun Austral and NZ Applied to the Australasian equivalent of the Teddy-boy. 1950–. Cf. WIDGIE. NEW ZEALAND LISTENER Every psychologist who has talked with bodgies will know that fear of an uncertain future is one of the factors in youthful misconduct (1958). [Perhaps from *bodger* inferior, worthless + *-ie*.]

boff noun mainly Brit A scientist or technical expert, esp. one involved in (secret) research. 1984–. BUSINESS TIMES (South Africa) The technical boffs are poring over their charts to see if there is another 20 points of profit still to come (2000). [Shortened from *boffin*.]

boff verb trans. and intr. To have sex (with). 1937–. OBSERVER They're the only two decent-looking people on Brookside: who on earth else would they want to boff (1996)? [From earlier sense, hit hard.]

boffo adjective US, orig theatre Extremely entertaining or successful. Hence, very impressive or effective; excellent. 1943–. US NEWS & WORLD REPORT The Mall of America hopes to thrive as a boffo regional entertainment center (1989). [Alteration of *buffo* comic, burlesque.]

boffola noun US A hearty laugh; a very funny joke. 1946–. [From BOFFO adjective.]

bog noun Brit A lavatory. a.1789–. NEW LEFT REVIEW Toilet paper in the bogs (1960). [Short for *bog-house* noun, of uncertain origin.]

bogan noun Austral and NZ An uncouth, stupid, or square person. 1988–. [Origin uncertain; prob. connected in some way with the name of the *Bogan* River in rural western New South Wales.]

bogart verb trans. **1** US (mainly in African-American usage) To force, coerce; to bully, intimidate. 1966–. D. COYLE A lot of top dogs would have tried to bogart me back into the game (1993). **2** orig and mainly US To

bluey blunt bo boat boatie boat-race Boche bod

appropriate (a marijuana cigarette) greedily or selfishly. Hence more generally, to take or use most of; to steal. 1968–. s. CISMEROS While I ran out to reload the machines, someone had bogarted my table, the window booth next to the jukebox (1991). [From the name of Humphrey *Bogart* (1899–1957), US film actor: in sense 1, from the tough-guy roles he often played; in sense 2, from his enthusiastic on- (and off-)screen smoking.]

boggle verb **the mind** (or **the imagination**) **boggles** the mind is overwhelmed or stupefied; *boggle* also used transitively, in phr. *boggle the* (or *someone's*) *mind*. 1971–. L. SANTE The mind boggles at the spectacle of garrote artists weeping at a song about shame ... ear-chewers remembering their white-haired mothers (1991). [Prob. a back-formation from MIND-BOGGLING adjective.]

bog standard adjective mainly Brit Ordinary, basic, standard; without extra features or modification; unexceptional or uninspired. 1968–. EMPIRE A bog-standard biography with a cheap *Psycho* sales gimmick, you can't help thinking Perkins deserved better (1995). [Origin uncertain: perh. from *box standard*, applied (orig) to cycles and other vehicles as they emerged (in their box) from the factory, with no subsequent alteration or customization (although that is not recorded before 1983), influenced by BOG noun.]

bog-trotter noun derog An Irish person. 1682–.

bogy[1] noun Also **bogey. 1** A detective; a policeman. 1924–. J. CURTIS One of the bogies from Vine Street reckernizes me (1936). **2** A piece of dried nasal mucus. 1937–. D. PINNER He ... removed wax from ears, bogeys from nose, blackheads from chin (1967).

bogy[2] Also **bogey.** Austral verb intr. **1** To bathe. 1788–. SMOKE SIGNAL (Palm Island): 'Bogey' with plenty of soap and water *every day* (1974). noun **2** A bathe. 1847–. F. D. DAVISON They went down for a bogey on hot days (1946). **3** A bathing-place; a bath. 1941–. [From Aboriginal (Dharuk) *bu-gi*.]

bohunk /ˈbəʊhʌŋk/ noun N Amer A Hungarian; an immigrant from central or south-eastern Europe, esp. one of inferior class; hence, a low rough fellow, a lout. 1903–. J. DOS PASSOS Bohunk and polak kids put stones in their snowballs (1930). [Apparently

from *Bo(hemian)* + *-hunk*, alteration of *Hung (arian)*.]

boiled adjective Intoxicated, drunk. Also in phr. *as drunk as a boiled owl*. 1886–. H. PENTECOST He's boiled to the ears (1940).

boiler noun orig Austral An unattractive (old) woman; often in phr. *old boiler*. 1965–. I-D You get a lot of dodgy boilers fronting acts, but here was a woman who didn't need to wear mini-skirts to attract attention (1993). [From the notion of a boiling fowl being older and tougher than a young chicken.]

boko noun The nose. Also (US) **boke.** 1859–. P. G. WODEHOUSE For a moment he debated within himself the advisability of dotting the speaker one on the boko, but he decided against this (1961). [Origin unknown.]

bog standard
applied to cycles as they emerged from the factory

bollix noun **1** A mess, confusion. 1935–. verb trans. Also **bollux 2** To bungle, make a mess of, confuse; also with *up*. 1937–. J. STEINBECK He'd made a mess of things. He wondered if he'd bollixed up the breaks (1952). [Alteration of BOLLOCKS noun.]

bollock verb trans. Also **ballock.** To reprimand or tell off severely. Often **bollocking,** noun A severe reprimand. 1938–. TIMES LITERARY SUPPLEMENT Sir John French, CIGS, came down for open day at 'The Shop', gave everyone a bollocking for slackness and indiscipline, and shortly afterwards retired the Commandant (1978). [From BOLLOCK(s noun.]

bollock-naked adjective Also **ballock-naked.** Stark naked. 1922–.

bollocks noun Also **ballocks. 1** The testicles. 1744–. LANDFALL Fine specimen of a lad, my Monty. All bollocks and beef (1968). **2** Nonsense, rubbish. Often as int. 1919–. IT It's really a load of bollocks (1969). [*Bollock*, variant of *ballock*, from late Old English *bealluc*, testicle; related to *ball* noun, spherical object.]

Bolly noun Brit Bollinger champagne. 1982–. STANDARD A special bottle of bolly (1982). [Shortening.]

bolshy adjective Also **bolshie.** Uncooperative, recalcitrant; truculent. 1918–. D. CLARK You can stop looking so bolshie, because I think you've done what you did well enough (1969). [From earlier sense, Bolshevik.]

boggle bog standard bog-trotter bogy bohunk

boob

BOLTOP Acronym based on *better on lips than on paper* (on envelopes or at the bottom of a letter, next to an X for a kiss); first recorded in 1989, but in use much earlier. DAILY TELEGRAPH During the war there were soldiers who marked their letters to wives and sweethearts BOLTOP (1989).

bomb noun **1** Austral and NZ An old car. 1953–. M. SHADBOLT The car . . . wasn't much more than an old bomb (1965). **2** Brit A large sum of money. 1958–. A. E. LINDOP I might flog it for a bomb in me old age (1969). **3** = BOMBER noun 1. 1960–. E. WYMARK First they simply smoke marijuana . . . They refer to the smokes as sticks or bombs, depending on their size (1967). **4** US A bad failure, esp. a theatrical one. 1961–. verb intr. **5** Orig US To fail. Also with *out*. 1963–. TV TIMES (Australia): Everyone had expected it to be [good], so when it bombed it was a shock (1968).

bombed adjective Under the influence of drink or drugs. Often with *out*. 1959–. A. LURIE I was bombed out—didn't know what I was doing (1984).

bomber noun **1** US A (large) marijuana cigarette. 1952–. J. KEROUAC Victor proceeded to roll the biggest bomber anybody ever saw (1957). **2** A barbiturate drug. 1962–. K. NICHOLSON I was planning to go back on bombers today (1966).

bombo noun Austral Cheap wine, often fortified. 1942–. S. GORE He done in the whole issue on sheilas and bombo (1968). [Prob. from *bomb* something of explosive effect + -*o*, but cf. obs. *bumbo* drink concocted from rum, sugar, water, and nutmeg.]

bona adjective Good, excellent; attractive. 1846–. GUARDIAN Bona puddings. Brilliant beer and proper wine (2001). [From Polari, from Italian *buona* good or Spanish *buena* good.]

bonce noun Brit The head. 1889–. L. DEIGHTON This threat . . . [is] going to be forever hanging over your bonce like Damocles' chopper (1962). [From earlier sense, large playing-marble.]

bone-head noun orig US A stupid person. Also as adjective. 1908–. J. & W. HAWKINS The best of us have made a bonehead mistake or two (1958). Hence **bone-headed**, adjective 1903–.

boner noun orig US **1** A blunder. 1912–. SPECTATOR This Government has made about every boner possible (1960). **2** An erection of the penis. 1962–. [From *bone* + -*er*; cf. BONE-HEAD noun.]

bone up verb intr. orig US To learn more about a topic by diligent study; usu. followed by *on*. 1887–. DAILY TELEGRAPH Mr Robert Powell, . . . who is on the set as technical adviser but who wastes no opportunity to bone up on his hobby—Romanesque architecture (1968).

bonk noun **1** (A sudden attack of) fatigue or light-headedness sometimes experienced by especially racing cyclists; usu. preceded by *the*. 1952–. WATSON & GRAY The British call this attack of nauseous weakness the 'Bonk' (1978). **2** An act of sexual intercourse. 1984–. verb intr. and trans. **3** To have sexual intercourse (with). 1975–. DAILY TELEGRAPH Fiona . . . has become so frustrated that she has been bonking the chairman of the neighbouring constituency's Conservative association (1986). [In sense 1, origin unknown; in sense 2, from verb; in sense 3, from earlier sense, to hit resoundingly or with a thud.]

bonkbuster noun mainly Brit A book or film characterized by frequent sexual encounters between the characters. 1988–. D. BROOKS We have these high-toned sex journals in the finer bookstores, but old-fashioned Harold Robbins-style bonkbusters are déclassé (2000). [Blend of BONK noun 2 and *blockbuster* noun.]

bonkers adjective Mad, crazy. 1957–. SIMPSON & GALTON By half-past three he'll be raving bonkers (1961). [Origin unknown.]

bonzer adjective Also **bonza, bonser,** etc. Austral, dated Excellent, extremely good. 1904–. V. PALMER 'A bonzer night!' she said with drowsy enthusiasm (1934). [Perh. formed in word play on French *bon* good, influenced by *bonanza*.]

boo[1] noun orig US Marijuana. 1959–. PLAYBOY Where's the fun in . . . inhaling carbon-monoxide fumes, when you could be toking refreshing essence of boo smoke (1985). [Origin unknown.]

boo[2] noun US (orig in African-American usage) esp. among teenagers A girlfriend or boyfriend. Also as a form of address. 1988–. T. N. BAKER But, datz still my boo, and shhhit, ya'll know what dey say, 'Love is blinda than a muthafucka' (2004). [Perh. an alteration of *beau* boyfriend, male admirer.]

boob noun orig US **1** Prison. 1908–. COAST TO COAST Seeing Don get chucked out of the Ballarat and carted off to the boob (1941). **2** A fool, simpleton. 1909–. G. B. SHAW You gave it away, like the boobs you are, to the Pentland Forth Syndicate (1930). **3** mainly Brit An embarrassing mistake. 1934–. P. MOLONEY Newspapers have I

BOLTOP bomb bombed bomber bombo bonce

read in every town And many a boob and misprint I have seen (1966). verb intr. **4** mainly Brit To make an embarrassing mistake. 1935–. N. SHUTE If I boob on this one it'll mean the finish of the business (1951). [Shortened from *booby*; in sense 1, short for BOOBY-HATCH noun.]

boobies noun pl. orig US The breasts. 1934–. GUARDIAN The characters were constantly referring to her large bosom (even descending to calling them 'big boobies') (1968). [Prob. alteration of dialect *bubby* noun, breast.] Cf. BOOBS noun.

boo-boo noun orig US A mistake. 1954–. O. MILLS My fault, I'm afraid. I've just made what the Yanks call a boo-boo (1967). [Prob. reduplication of BOOB noun.]

boobs noun pl. orig US The breasts. 1949–. DAILY MIRROR If people insist on talking about her boobs, she would rather they called them boobs, which is a way-out word, . . . rather than breasts (1968). [Prob. shortened from BOOBIES noun.]

boob tube noun **1** orig and mainly US Television. 1966–. M. FRENCH I sit and watch the stupid boob tube (1977). **2** A woman's close-fitting strapless top. 1978–. MY WEEKLY Now the rush around to find . . . a variety of tops from waterproofs to 'boob-tubes' (1986). [In sense 1, from BOOB noun 2 + TUBE noun 2; in sense 2, from BOOB(s noun + *tube* noun.]

booby-hatch noun **1** US A lock-up or gaol. 1859–. **2** orig and mainly US A lunatic asylum. 1923–. P. G. WODEHOUSE What, tell people you're me and I'm you. Sure we could, if you don't mind being put in the booby-hatch (1936). [Cf. earlier sense, hatch on a boat which lifts off in one piece.]

boodle orig US. noun **1** Money acquired or spent illegally or immorally, esp. in connection with the obtaining or holding of public offices; the material means or gains of bribery and corruption; also, money in general. 1883–. J. JOYCE Ready to decamp with whatever boodle they could (1922). verb trans. and intr. **2** To bribe. 1904–. [From earlier sense, crowd, pack, lot.]

boofhead noun Austral A fool. 1945–. AUSTRALIAN Mr Hayden . . . described the former ALP secretary as a boofhead (1983). [Perh. from obs. *bufflehead* fool; popularized by a comic-strip character of that name created by R. B. Clark in 1939 and running in the *Sydney Daily Mirror* 1941–70.]

booger noun US = BUGGER noun 1, 3. 1770–. LONGMAN DICTIONARY OF CONTEMPORARY ENGLISH You wouldn't want to meet him in a dark alley—he's a mean-looking booger (1995). [From a dialectal pronunciation of *bugger*.]

boogie noun US, derog An African-American. 1923–. E. HEMINGWAY I seen that big boogie there mopping it up (1937). [Perh. alteration of *bogy*.]

book noun **to get** or **do the book** US To suffer the maximum penalty. 1928–. [Cf. colloquial *to throw the book at* to inflict the maximum penalty on.]

boom box noun orig US = GHETTO BLASTER noun. 1981–. WASHINGTON POST How about a law against playing 'boom boxes' in public places? (1985).

boomer noun Austral **1** A very large kangaroo. 1830–. **2** Something exceptionally large, great, etc. of its kind. 1843–. T. RONAN Fights you're talking about! Well, I just seen a boomer! (1956). [From earlier British dialect sense, anything very large of its kind.]

boondock noun US Rough or isolated country; usu. in pl. 1944–. SPECTATOR Those who have been feeling the public pulse out in the boondocks report a good deal of unrest (1965). [From Tagalog *bundok* mountain.]

boondoggle US. noun **1** A trivial, useless, or unnecessary undertaking; wasteful expenditure. 1935–. NEW YORK REVIEW OF BOOKS (*heading*): Nixon and the arms race: the bomber boondoggle (1969). verb intr. **2** To engage in trifling or frivolous work. 1937–. [Origin unknown.]

boong /buŋ/ noun Austral, derog An (Australian) Aboriginal; a native of New Guinea; also, any coloured person. 1924–. TIMES He is trying to lead Australians away from what he calls the 'poor old bloody boong' mentality (1969). [From Aboriginal (Wemba Wemba dialect of Wemba) *beŋ* man, human being.]

boonies noun US Rough or isolated country. 1956–. [From BOON(DOCK noun + *-ies*.]

boot noun **1 to give** (a person) **(the order of) the boot** to give (someone) the sack. also **to get the boot.** 1888–. **2** US A recruit at a boot camp. 1915–. AMERICAN SPEECH It is taught to the 'boot' before he leaves boot camp (1963). **3 to put the boot in** to kick (in a brutal manner); also fig. 1916–. GUARDIAN When he's lying there some cow in the front row puts the boot in (1964). **4** derog An African-American person. 1957–. H. SIMMONS A lot of paddy studs still didn't know that boots were human (1962).

bottle

boot camp noun US A centre for the initial training of American naval or Marine recruits. 1944–.

booty noun orig US **1** Sexual intercourse; a person (esp. a woman) regarded as an object of sexual ambition or desire. 1926–. **2** Buttocks. 1959– (but prob. in use much earlier). NEW YORK TIMES This is a woman's best part . . . A skirt has to scoop under the booty (1999). [Prob. an alteration of BOTTY noun.]

booty bandit noun US, prisoners' A homosexual man; (also) a man who commits male rape. 1962–.

bootylicious adjective orig US Very sexually attractive. 1994–. [From BOOTY noun + de(licious).]

booze verb intr. **1** To drink alcohol, esp. to excess. 1768–. noun **2** Drinking, a drunken spree; esp. in phr. *on the booze*. 1850–. J. CARY If I didn't you'd go on the booze and say it was all my fault (1959). **3** Alcoholic drink. 1859–. T. S. ELIOT We're gona sit here and drink this booze (1932). [Variant of earlier *bouse, bowse*, from Middle Dutch *būsen* to drink to excess.]

boozed adjective Drunk; sometimes followed by *up*. 1850–.

boozer noun **1** A (heavy) drinker. *a.*1819–. **2** Brit A pub. 1895–. P. MOLONEY The boozer on the corner (1966). [From BOOZE verb + *-er.*]

boozeroo noun NZ An alcohol-drinking session. 1943–. LANDFALL The Saturday night boozeroo in the Sydenham side-street with the keg in the kitchen-sink (1952). [From BOOZE noun 2 + *-eroo.*]

booze-up noun A drinking bout. 1897–. J. BRAINE The traditional lunchtime booze-up (1957).

bo-peep noun Austral and NZ A look. 1941–. LANDFALL Take a bo-peep at old Lionel (1969). [Extension of *peep*, after *bo-peep* noun, nursery game.]

boracic adjective Brit Penniless. 1959–. D. RAYMOND 'He's boracic,' said someone. 'He's out grafting' (1984). [Short for *boracic lint*, rhyming slang for 'skint'.]

borak /ˈbɒræk/ noun Also **borac(k), borax.** Austral and NZ Nonsense, humbug; banter; esp. in phr. *to poke (the) borak*, to make or poke fun. 1845–. X. HERBERT The old boy had been poking borak at him about anthropology (1975). [From Aboriginal (Wathawurung) *burag*.]

Bork verb trans. US To defame or vilify (someone) systematically, esp. in the mass media, usu. with the aim of preventing his or her appointment to public office. 1987–. NEW YORK TIMES REVIEW OF BOOKS This powerful force . . . that now goes around 'Borking' politically incorrect nominees (1993). [From the name of Robert H. *Bork* (b. 1927), a judge whose nomination to the US Supreme Court in 1987 was rejected following a large amount of unfavourable publicity for his allegedly illiberal and extreme views.]

bosh noun and int Nonsense. 1850–. W. GADDIS A lot of bosh, of course, . . . but it gives these fool scientists something to do (1952). [From Turkish *boş* empty.] Hence **bosher,** noun Someone who talks nonsense. 1913–.

bosh-shot noun = BOSS-SHOT noun. 1939–. G. ORWELL The Nazis chop people's heads off . . . and sometimes the executioner makes a bosh shot (1939). [Alteration of *boss-shot*, after BOSH noun.]

bosker adjective Austral and NZ, dated Good, excellent, delightful. 1905–. F. SARGESON It turned out a bosker day (1943). [Origin unknown.]

boss adjective orig and mainly US Excellent, wonderful. 1961–. M. AMIS I have to tell you right off that Martina Twain is a real boss chick by anyone's standards (1984). [From earlier attrib sense of *boss* noun, (of persons) master, chief.]

boss-eyed adjective Cross-eyed or having only one eye. 1860–. I. & P. OPIE It is unlucky for a cross-eyed woman to look at you . . . When somebody who is boss-eyed goes by you spit on the ground (1959). [Origin uncertain; cf. Brit dialect *boss* to bungle.]

boss-shot noun An unsuccessful attempt. 1912–. [From earlier sense, badly aimed shot (apparently from the notion of a shot fired by a boss-eyed person).]

bot Austral and NZ. noun **1** A sponger, cadger. 1916–. J. H. FINGLETON One of . . . the officials was berating Pressmen . . . as a 'lot of bots who wanted everything for nothing' (1960). verb intr. **2** To sponge, cadge. 1934–. [From the parasitic habits of the bot-fly.]

bottle noun **1** A collection or share of money. 1893–. J. B. PRIESTLEY Knocker brought out some money . . . 'Not much bottle. A nicker, half a bar' (1939). **2** naval A reprimand. 1938–. **3** Brit Courage, guts. 1958–. S. DYER The government is losing its bottle and is using 'concern for the environment' as something of an excuse to renege on promises and punish the motorist (1991). **4 on the bottle** addicted to alcoholic drink. 1967– DAILY MIRROR Watch that daily tipple,

boot camp booty booty bandit bootylicious booze

ladies. You could end up on the bottle (1976). verb **5** intr. To collect money. 1934–. **6** trans. naval To reprimand. 1946–. **7 to bottle out** Brit To lose one's nerve, to chicken out. 1979–. TIMES Why did Ken Livingstone 'bottle out' and vote to set a legal GLC rate? (1985). [In sense 3, prob. from obs. slang *no bottle* no good, useless, but often popularly associated with the rhyming slang term *bottle and glass* arse, and other similar expressions, perh. with the connotation (in the phr. 'to lose one's bottle') of the temporary incontinence associated with extreme fear.]

bottled adjective Drunk, intoxicated. 1927–. J. B. PRIESTLEY The guv'nor must be good an' bottled (1939).

bottle-o(h) noun Austral and NZ A collector of empty bottles. 1898–. D. WHITTINGTON 'What do you do for a living?' 'I'm the local bottle-O' (1967). [From *bottle* + *o* int.]

bottler noun and adjective Austral and NZ (Something or someone) excellent. 1855–. G. SLATTER Congratulations boy, a glorious try, a real bottler, you won the game (1959). [Origin unknown.]

botty noun The buttocks. 1874–. R. FIRBANK De time de scorpion bit her botty (1924). [From *bott(om* + -*y*.]

bourgie adjective mainly US (orig in African-American usage) **1** bourgeois, middle-class (orig used derogatorily of African-Americans). 1967–. noun **2** A bourgeois person, esp. an African-American. 1980–. [From *bourg(eois* + -*ie*.]

bovver noun Brit Trouble, disturbance, or fighting, esp. as caused by skinhead gangs. 1969–. DANIEL & MCGUIRE Around the Collinwood there was about twenty on average but with bovver there was sometimes more than that (1972). [Representing a Cockney pronunciation of *bother*.]

bovver boot noun Brit A heavy boot with toe-cap and laces, of a kind characteristically worn by skinheads. 1969–.

bovver boy noun Brit A hooligan; spec. one of a gang of skinhead youths. 1970–. LISTENER Mr Hanna is the nearest thing *Newsnight* has to a bovver boy, but that is not to say that he is a vulgar or crude person (1983).

bowler-hat verb trans. Brit To retire (a person) compulsorily, esp. to demobilize (an officer). 1953–. [From the earlier phr. *to be given one's bowler*; from the bowler hat

formerly worn by many British male civilians.]

box noun **1** orig US A safe. 1904–. **2** A coffin. 1925–. **3** orig and mainly US The female genitals. 1942–. R. DREWE I've seen some great tits and some of the bushiest boxes you could imagine (1983). **4 the box** television; a television set. Cf. GOGGLE-BOX noun. 1958–. E. HUMPHREYS I saw one of your plays, Dicky. On the old box (1963). [In sense 4, from the earlier sense, gramophone or radio set.]

boy noun dated Champagne; often as *the boy*. 1882–1929. MELODY MAKER Lord Delamere came up to them with a foaming magnum of champagne and said, 'Well, boys! you've given us a glorious time! What do you say to a beaker of ''the boy''?' (1929) [Origin unknown.]

bozo noun orig and mainly US A fool, clot. 1920–. ENCOUNTER Frank, the grey bozo behind the counter (1961). [Origin unknown.]

bracelet noun A handcuff. 1816–. F. FORSYTH Letting him run sticks in my craw. He should be on a flight Stateside—in bracelets (1989).

Bradbury noun Brit, dated A pound note. 1917–26. G. FRANKAU Cynthia had decided to 'risk a couple of Bradbury's each way' (1926). [From the name of John Swanwick *Bradbury*, Secretary to the Treasury 1913–19.]

Bradshaw verb intr. RAF To follow a railway line in flying. 1946. [From the name of 'Bradshaw's Railway Guide', former British railway timetable orig issued by George Bradshaw (1801–53), printer and engraver.]

Brahms and Liszt /ˌbrɑːmz ənd ˈlɪst/ adjective Brit Drunk, intoxicated. Also **Brahms.** Cf. MOZART AND LISZT adjective. 1978–. P. S. Do you remember the first time you got . . . a bit Brahms? . . . My five cousins took me out round the pubs and I got ill on Pernod and blackcurrant (1989). [Rhyming slang for PISSED adjective 1; arbitrary use of the names of two composers, Johannes *Brahms* (1833–97) and Franz *Liszt* (1811–86).]

brainiac adjective mainly N Amer **1** Highly intelligent. 1976–. noun **2** A very intelligent person; an expert. 1982–. TORONTO STAR They're . . . math brainiacs, born and/or raised with the potential to move beyond the frontiers of knowledge (1994). [From *Brainiac*, the name of a super-intelligent character in Superman comic strips from 1956, from *brain* + *man)iac*.]

brannigan noun N Amer **1** dated A state of intoxication; hence, a drinking bout or spree. 1903–. G. ADE Those who would enjoy the wolfish Satisfaction of shoveling it in each Morning must forego the simple Delights of acquiring a Brannigan the Night before (1918). **2** A brawl or fracas; a violent argument. 1941–. TORONTO STAR It hadn't exactly been a brawl to rank with the most homeric barroom brannigans in which Simon had ever participated (1955). [Origin uncertain; perh. from the surname *Brannigan*.]

brass noun **1** Money. 1597–. B. T. BRADFORD She was obviously a relation of the Bells who were local gentry, posh folk with pots and pots of brass (1986). **2** orig US Senior officers in the armed forces; esp. in phr. *the big* (or *top*) *brass*. 1899–. A. C. CLARKE The general was unaware of his *faux pas*. The assembled brass thought for a while (1959). Cf. BRASS-HAT noun. **3** A prostitute. 1934–. F. NORMAN His old woman who was a brass on the game (1958). verb **4 to brass off** orig services' To reprimand severely. 1943–. V. CANNING After I'd brassed you off for pinching my parking space (1964). **5 to brass up** to pay. 1898–. P. G. WODEHOUSE What did he soak him? Five quid? . . . And Gussie brassed up and was free? (1949). [In sense 2, from the brass or gold insignia on officers' caps; in sense 3, short for *brass nail*, rhyming slang for 'tail'.] See also *to part brass-rags* at PART verb.

brassed off adjective orig services' Fed up. 1941–. P. BRENNAN ET AL. Very tired and brassed off, we bundled our kit on our shoulders (1943).

brass-hat noun Brit An officer of high rank in the armed services. 1893–. A. MACLEAN The German brass-hats in Norway may well be making a decision as to whether or not to try to stop us again (1984). [From the brass or gold insignia on officers' caps.] Cf. BRASS noun 2.

brassic adjective Brit Penniless. 1982–. M. BLAKE And he's got to front us the cash. I've been brassic for weeks (2001). [Contraction of BORACIC adjective.]

brass monkey noun Used allusively in referring to extremely cold weather; esp. in phr. *cold enough to freeze the balls off a brass monkey*. 1928–. GUARDIAN Brass monkey weather (1973).

brass neck noun Audacity, effrontery. 1984–. GUARDIAN You can only marvel at the brass neck of Rupert Murdoch's *Sun*. Yesterday it launched its Politicians' Complaints Commission, a watchdog—well the *Sun* is nothing if not barking—to scrutinise the performance of MPs and others (1992).

brass razoo noun Austral = RAZOO².

brat pack noun orig US A group of young Hollywood film stars of the mid-1980s popularly regarded as enjoying a rowdy, fun-loving lifestyle; hence, any precocious and aggressive clique. 1985–. CITY LIMITS Andie . . . is torn between desire for rich kid Blane . . . and contempt for his brat pack lifestyle (1986). Also **brat packer,** noun A member of a brat pack. 1985–. [Punningly after *rat-pack*, itself applied earlier to a brash Hollywood set including Frank Sinatra.]

bread noun orig US Money. 1939–. DOWN BEAT If I had bread (Dizzy's basic synonym for loot) I'd certainly start a big band again (1952).

bread-basket noun **1** The stomach. 1753–. **2** A large bomb containing smaller bombs. 1940–4.

breadhead noun orig US A person who is motivated by or obsessed with making money; a materialist. 1969–. SCOTLAND ON SUNDAY Even Dylan knew he was a brand, an industry. He presented it as: 'I'm not in it for the money, I'm not a bread head,' but he had the finest lawyers working for him (2001). [From BREAD noun + HEAD noun 3.]

break verb **1 to break** (someone) **up** orig and mainly US, orig theatrical To cause (someone) to laugh uncontrollably. 1895–. M. WOLFF It . . . breaks me up. I can't help but laugh (1956). **2** intr. orig US To happen, occur. 1914–. J. CURTIS Everything'll break good (1936). **3 break it down** Austral and NZ Stop it, come off it. 1941–. J. R. COLE 'Break it down!' Wood shouted from the telephone. 'I can't hear a thing' (1949). **4 to break** (someone's) **ass** US To beat (someone) up. 1949–. H. ROBBINS 'Come on, kid,' he said. 'Let's break their asses!' (1949). **5** int Citizens' Band, mainly US Used to request permission to interrupt a conversation on a particular channel, to offer access to a channel, and to signify termination of transmission. 1973–. PARADE Break, Channel 10. I'm calling that blue truck with Ohio plates, westbound (1975). Cf. BREAKER noun.

breaker noun orig US A Citizens' Band radio user; esp one who interrupts a conversation in order to begin transmitting. 1963–. TRUCK & DRIVER Brian's currently searching for a CB buff to set up shop in the cafe to repair broken sets and sell replacement ones to passing breakers (1985). [From the action of *breaking* into the conversation of others; cf. BREAK verb 4.]

breeze noun **1 to hit, split,** or **take the breeze** to leave. 1910–. D. RUNYON And with this

brannigan brass brassed off brass-hat brat pack

she takes the breeze and I return to the other room (1931). **2 to get, have,** or **put the breeze up** to get or put the wind up (see WIND noun). 1925–. D. BALLANTYNE She was only making out she hadn't seen you so's you wouldn't get the breeze up (1948). **3** orig US Something easy to achieve, handle, etc.; a 'cinch'. 1928–. S. CARPENTER All in all, the test was a breeze (1962). See also *to shoot the breeze* at SHOOT verb.

breezer noun Austral A fart. 1973–. G. MURNANE Barry Launder has ordered every boy to write in his composition at the picnic I let a breezer in my pants or else be bashed to smithereens after school (1974).

brewer's droop noun orig Austral Temporary impotence as a result of drinking excessive amounts of alcohol (esp. beer). 1970–. M. KNOPFLER I'm not surprised to see you here— you've got smokers cough from smoking, brewer's droop from drinking beer (1982).

brewer's goitre noun Austral (The condition of having) a large paunch as a result of beer-drinking. 1953–. M. POWELL The condition is known as 'brewers goitre', and it eventually leads to 'brewers droop'. Well, I knew Australia had a small population, but surely not for this reason (1976). [Transferred use of *goitre*, swelling of the neck resulting from enlargement of the thyroid gland.]

brick noun Someone reliable or dependable; a sterling fellow. 1840–. [From the strength and solidity of a brick.]

brick verb **to brick it** to be extremely anxious or apprehensive. 1989–. BOSTON GLOBE Both Thomas (38.9 percent) and Dumars (37.9) are bricking it big time (1991). [A euphemistic adaptation of *to shit bricks* (see SHIT verb 5).]

brickie noun Also **bricky.** A bricklayer. 1880–. ECONOMIST Something to help the brickie with corners (1964).

bride noun A girl, woman, esp. a girlfriend. 1935–. LISTENER This load of squaddies . . . ain't got any brides with them (1964).

brief noun Brit An accused person's solicitor or barrister. 1977–. P. WHALLEY Fair sang your praises he did. Said I could tell you things I wouldn't tell my own brief (1986). [From

earlier sense, legal case given to a barrister to argue in court.]

brill adjective Wonderful, marvellous. 1981–. GUARDIAN It may have been an awful night . . . but the meat and potato pies were brill (1983). [Abbreviation of *brilliant* adjective.]

bring verb **to bring home the bacon** to succeed in an undertaking; to achieve success. 1924–. P. LARKIN The College takes a number of fellows like him to keep up the tone . . . but they look to us to bring home t'bacon (1946).

bristols noun Brit The breasts. 1961–. R. COOK These slag birds used to go trotting upstairs . . . arses wagging and bristols going (1962). [Short for *Bristol Cities*, rhyming slang for 'titties'; from the name of *Bristol City* Football Club.]

Britney Spears
rhyming slang
for 'beers'

Britney Spears noun pl. Brit Also **Britneys.** Rhyming slang for 'beers'. 1999–. INDEPENDENT Nick Leeson was spotted in a Leicester Square pub, chugging Britneys . . . with three of his old muckers from Barings over the weekend (1999). [From the name of *Britney Spears* (b. 1982), US pop singer.]

bro noun **1** A brother. a.1666–. N. BLAKE I must . . . report to my bro on the sinister bloke we've just chased off (1940). **2** orig US A male friend; mainly as a form of address. 1957–. BEBO.COM Hey bro xxx how u gettin on in AMerica (2007). **3** orig and mainly African American A man. 1970–. [Shortening.]

broad noun orig and mainly US A woman; spec. a prostitute. 1914–. E. LINKLATER Slummock . . . had got into a jam with a broad; no ordinary broad, but a Coastguard's broad (1931). [Cf. obs. US *broadwife* female slave separated from her husband, from *abroad* + *wife*.]

broads noun pl. dated Playing-cards. 1789–. F. D. SHARPE They . . . were also playing the Broads on the train (1938).

broadsman noun dated A card-sharper. 1860–. F. D. SHARPE Broadsmen, or three-card sharpers, kept the Flying Squad busy in its early days (1938). [From BROADS noun + *man.*]

broke adjective **to go for broke** orig US To make strenuous efforts; to go all out. 1951–.

GUARDIAN The enemy is 'going all out—...he is going for broke' (1968).

brolly noun Brit **1** An umbrella. 1874–.
2 A parachute. 1934–. J. M. B. BEARD I was floating still and peacefully with my 'brolly' canopy billowing above my hand (1940). [Abbreviation and alteration of *umbrella* noun.]

bromo noun (A dose of) a sedative drug containing a bromide mixture. 1916–.
ENCOUNTER For God's sake take a Bromo! (1961). [Short for *Bromo-seltzer* proprietary name for such a drug.]

bronc noun orig and mainly US A bronco, a horse. 1893–. [Abbreviation of *bronco* noun.]

Bronx cheer noun US A derisive noise made by blowing through closed lips; a raspberry. 1929–. P. G. WODEHOUSE She told me...that she was through...No explanations. Just gave me the Bronx Cheer and beat it (1932). [From *Bronx* the name of a borough of New York City.]

bronze noun Austral The buttocks. Also **bronza, bronzo**. 1959–. L. RYAN Go and sit on your bronze while we give scabs your jobs (1975). [From earlier sense, anus.]

brothel-creepers noun pl. Suede or soft-soled shoes. 1954–. G. SMITH Poncing about the place in those brothel-creepers of his (1954). Cf. CREEPERS noun pl.

brother noun African-American A (fellow) African-American man. 1910–.

brown bomber noun Austral In New South Wales, a traffic warden or 'parking cop'. 1953–. [From the colour of their uniforms until 1975.]

brown bread adjective Brit Dead. 1973–. [Rhyming slang.]

browned off adjective Brit Bored, fed up, disgusted. 1938–. OBSERVER Medical boards were always being begged by browned-off invalids to pass them fit for active service (1958).

Brownie point noun orig US A notional credit for an achievement; favour in the eyes of another, esp. gained by sycophantic or servile behaviour. 1963–. TIMES EDUCATIONAL SUPPLEMENT Those who took part in extra activities would get a Brownie point, he said, but classroom effectiveness would be the prime test of a teacher's success (1986). [Prob. a development from BROWN-NOSE verb, but popularly associated with *Brownie* member of the junior Girl Guides and hence often spelled with a capital *B*.]

brown job noun orig RAF A soldier; also collectively, the Army. 1943–. ECONOMIST General Delacombe was a pretty undiplomatic brown-job (1963). [From the British Army's khaki uniforms.]

brown-nose orig US. noun **1** A sycophant. 1939–. M. PUGH It was part of the tradition to hate a Highland laird or be a brown-nose (1969). verb trans. and intr. **2** To curry favour (with); to flatter. 1939–. J. SYMONS If you don't...get cracking on a few little jobs for this paper instead of spending your time brown-nosing Mr. Fairfield, you [etc.] (1960). So **brown-noser**, noun. 1950–. [From the equation of servility with licking, etc. someone's anus.]

brown sugar noun A drug consisting of heroin diluted with caffeine and strychnine. 1974–.

brush noun Austral and NZ often derog Girls, young women. 1941–. SUN-HERALD (Sydney): He [was] intrigued by the younger men's comments about the beautiful 'brush' (women) eager to be entertained by visiting trainers (1984). [Perh. from the female pubic hair.]

B.S. noun mainly N Amer Abbreviation of 'bullshit'. 1912–. J. GOULET Shit...you can't be around a project like this for two years without picking up some of that B.S. (1975).

bub noun US Used as a term of address to a man. 1839–. CHICAGO STAR Hey bub—can I get a squint at yer uppers? (1948) [Perh. representing a childish pronunciation of *brother*, or from German *Bube* boy.]

bubble-and-squeak noun Brit, derog A Greek person. Also **bubble**. 1938–. R. COOK All the best Anglo-Saxon grafters come from mine [i.e. my school], and the Bubbles and the Indians from the other (1962). [Rhyming slang for 'Greek'.]

bubblehead noun orig US An empty-headed or stupid person; a fool. 1952–. TIME But Jack is not a Hollywood bubblehead...He sometimes thinks before he says his lines. Or anyway he thinks he thinks, which for an actor amounts to the same thing (1988). Hence **bubbleheaded,** adjective. 1966–. [Cf. AIRHEAD noun. In early use apparently often applied to Henry A. Wallace, US Vice-President 1941-5.]

buck[1] noun orig and mainly US A dollar. 1856–. A. BARON 'What did you do before the war?' 'Anythin' fer a buck' (1953). [Origin unknown.]

buck[2] noun Also **bukh** dated Talk, conversation; spec boastful talk, insolence; esp. in phr. *old buck*. 1895–. PENGUIN NEW WRITING

brolly bromo bronc Bronx cheer brown bomber

Nah then, none o' yer ol' buck, Ernie (1941). [From Hindustani *bak*, Hindi *buk buk*.]

buck adjective US Belonging to the lowest grade of a particular military rank. 1918–. TIMES From general officer to buck private (1962). [Prob. from *buck* male.]

Buck House noun jocular Buckingham Palace, the British sovereign's residence in London. 1922–. R. JEFFRIES Come on in—the door's wide open and this isn't Buck House (1962).

Buckley's noun Austral and NZ In full **Buckley's chance** (or **hope**, etc.): a forlorn hope, no chance at all. 1895–. D. NILAND You reckon I haven't got Buckley's? (1955). [Origin obscure; perh. from the name of William Buckley, a celebrated 19th-century Australian escaped convict known as the 'wild white man'.]

bucko Nautical adjective **1** Swaggering, blustering, bullying; esp. in phr. *bucko mate*. 1883–. noun **2** A swaggering or domineering fellow. 1899–. BLACKWOOD'S MAGAZINE A great big bucko of a man (1927). [From *buck* noun, male animal + -*o*.]

buckshee adjective and adverb Brit Free of charge. 1916–. C. BARRETT The Chief of Staff . . . snapped 'Want a buckshee trip, eh?' (1942). [Alteration of *baksheesh* noun, ult. of Persian origin.]

buer noun Brit, orig northern dialect and tramps' slang A woman; often used with an implication of promiscuity. 1807–1938. G. GREENE 'Christ,' the boy said, 'won't anybody stop that buer's mouth?' (1938) [Origin unknown.]

buff noun The naked skin; now mainly in the phr. *in the buff* naked and *to the buff* so as to be naked. 1654–. ROLLING STONE The girls call themselves the Groupies and claim they recorded their song in the buff (1969). [From earlier sense, buffalo-skin (leather).]

buff adjective Attractively fit and muscular in appearance; physically attractive. 1982–. SUNDAY TELEGRAPH (Sydney) [In] many films he got naked and looked buff as a male model (2000). [Origin uncertain; prob. related to *buff* to polish.]

buffalo verb trans. N Amer To overpower, overawe, or constrain by superior force or influence; to outwit, perplex. 1903–. E. A. MCCOURT Jerry Potts himself would have been buffaloed (1947). [From *buffalo* noun.]

buffer noun Brit A silly or incompetent old man; often in phr. *old buffer*. 1749–. LONDON REVIEW OF BOOKS I take my stand beside the other old buffers here (1979). [Prob. from obs. *buff* verb, imitative of the sound of a soft body being struck, or from obs. *buff* verb, to stutter.]

bufu noun US A male homosexual. 1982–. [Prob. from *butt-fucker*.]

bug noun Brit, schoolboys' A boy; usu. with defining word. 1909–. J. RAE You're new, Curlew, and new bugs should be seen and not heard (1960).

bug verb intr. mainly US To get *out*; to make *off*; to leave quickly; to scram. 1953–. F. MANNING (Victoria, British Columbia). He also said that Canada is not 'bugging out' of NATO (1969). GUARDIAN If you happen to be a worker, a homosexual, a woman, a Hispanic, you can bug off. Bush is playing to ITT, IBM, ATT, Dow Chemical, GM (1992). [Origin uncertain.]

bugger noun **1a** A despicable or unpleasant man. 1719–. LISTENER Come and sit on my other side. Otherwise they will put me beside that bugger Oparin (1969). **b** A fellow; usu. with defining word. 1854–. F. MANNING Not when there are two poor buggers dead, and five more not much better (1929). **2 not to give** or **care a bugger** not to care at all. 1922–. F. RAPHAEL It'd be a wonderful thing to have a magazine that didn't give a bugger what it said about anyone (1960). **3** Something unpleasant or undesirable; a great nuisance. 1936–. PENGUIN NEW WRITING Drilling before breakfast's a bugger, believe me (1942). **4 bugger-all** nothing. 1937–. I. JEFFERIES 'What did they offer to give you?' 'Bugger-all' (1961). verb **5** trans. Used like *damn* in various exclamations. 1794–. S. BECKETT I'll be buggered if I can understand how it could have been anything else (1953); D. PINNER Bugger me, he thought, looking at the grin on his watch, it's three o'clock! (1967). **6 to bugger off** to go away. 1922–. PRIVATE EYE Let's go up to palace, pick up O.B.E.'s and bugger off 'ome like (1969). **7** trans. To mess *up*; to ruin, spoil. In passive, to be tired out. 1923–. A. WILSON No hippos in their natural lovely setting of the Severn or beavers buggering up the Broads (1961); H. C. RAE He was so utterly buggered that he had no hunger left (1968). **8** With *about* and *around*: **a** intr. To mess about and waste time. 1929–. J. WAINWRIGHT Let's not bugger around being polite (1968). **b** trans. To cause difficulties for. 1957–. M. KENNEDY Do I then have to be buggered about by a lot of professors and critics (1957). [From

buck Buck House Buckley's bucko buckshee buer

bum

earlier sense, one who practises anal intercourse.]

buggery noun Hell, perdition. 1898–. COAST TO COAST 'Pipe down, Rymill!' 'Go to *buggery*, Rymill!' (1961). [From earlier sense, anal intercourse.]

bughouse noun **1** orig US A lunatic asylum. 1902–. N. MARSH You're bigger bloody fools than anybody outside a bughouse (1940). **2** A tatty or second-rate theatre or cinema. 1946–. J. OSBORNE If there's nothing else on, I still go . . . to the bug house round the corner (1957). Cf. FLEA PIT noun. adjective **3** mainly US Crazy; very eccentric. 1895–. SAPPER For a moment I thought he'd gone bughouse (1930). [In sense 1, cf. *bug* person obsessed with an idea; in sense 2, from *bug* insect.]

bug-hunter noun jocular An entomologist. 1889–. So **bug-hunting**, noun.

builder's bum noun mainly Brit (The sight of) the buttocks, and esp. the cleft between their cheeks, as revealed by a low waistline, esp. when someone bends over. 1988–. [From the alleged propensity of building labourers to make such involuntary revelations.]

bulge noun dated, orig US The advantage or upper hand; the superior position; usu. with *the*; esp. in phr. *to have the bulge on*, to have the advantage over. 1841–1963. P. G. WODEHOUSE The Assyrians had the bulge on him (1963).

bull noun **1** US A policeman. 1893–. J. LONDON I noticed the bull, a strapping policeman in a grey suit . . . I never dreamed that bull was after me (1909). **2** orig US Trivial, insincere, or untruthful talk or writing; nonsense. 1914–. G. GIBSON I have never heard such a line of bull in all my life (1946). **3** orig services' Unnecessary or routine tasks or ceremonial; excessive discipline or spit-and-polish. 1941–. ECONOMIST The drudgery and 'bull' in an MP's life (1958). Cf. BULLSHIT noun. verb trans. **3** services' To polish (equipment, etc.) in order to meet excessive standards of neatness. 1957–. [In sense 2, from earlier sense, ludicrously contradictory statement.]

bull and cow noun Rhyming slang for 'row'. 1859–. A. GILBERT The murder might have been the result of a private bull-and-cow (1961).

bulldagger noun US derog (mainly in African-American usage) A lesbian with masculine tendencies. 1938–. [Variant of BULL-DYKER noun (an intermediate form was *bull-digger* (a.1929)).]

bull dust noun orig US, now Austral Rubbish, nonsense. 1943–. J. HAMILTON I'm not in the mood for your bulldust. Where have you been all night? (1967). [Euphemistic alteration of BULLSHIT noun, based on earlier *bull dust* fine powdery dirt or dust.]

bull-dyke noun A lesbian with masculine tendencies. Also **bull-dike(r), -dyker.** 1926–. J. RECHY On the dance-floor, too, lesbians—the masculine ones, the bulldikes—dance with hugely effeminate queens (1964). [Cf. DYKE noun.]

bullet noun **1** Notice to quit, the sack. With *the*. 1841–. CRESCENDO It was only the boss's inherent good nature that saved me from the bullet (1967). **2** pl. Beans or peas. 1929–.

bull-fiddle noun US A double bass or cello. 1880–. Hence **bull-fiddler**, noun US 1933–. W. C. HANDY As usual the bull-fiddler sawed away in G (1957).

bull-ring noun Army A military training-ground. 1928–. E. DE MAUNY Drawing equipment at the Q.M., drilling on the bull-ring (1949). [From earlier sense, bullfight arena, with reference to BULL noun 2.]

bullshit noun **1** Rubbish, nonsense; = BULL noun 1. *c*.1915–. P. ROTH I swear to you, this is not bullshit or a screen memory, these are the very words these women use (1969). **2** = BULL noun 2. 1930–. R. HOGGART The world of special parades in the Services, of 'blanco and bullshit' (1957). verb trans. and intr. **3** To talk nonsense (to); also, to bluff *one's way through* (something) by talking nonsense. 1942–. E. POUND Wot are the books ov the bible? Name 'em, don't bullshit *me* (1949). [From *bull* + SHIT noun.]

bullshitter noun One who exaggerates or talks nonsense, esp. to bluff or impress. 1941–. J. LENNON He is a bullshitter. But he made us credible with intellectuals (1970). [From BULLSHIT verb + *-er*.]

bull's wool noun Also **bullswool**. Austral and NZ = BULL noun 1. 1933–. I. CROSS That last bit was all bulls-wool of course, but I had to be careful (1957). [Euphemistic alteration of BULLSHIT noun.]

bum[1] noun mainly Brit The buttocks, bottom. 1387–. LOOKS Begin with a warm-up and concentrate on your bum and thighs, and work on your boobs and tum as well when you turn the poster over (1989). [Origin unknown.]

bum[2] orig and mainly US. verb **1** intr. To wander *around*; to loaf. 1863–. MANCHESTER GUARDIAN WEEKLY The unshaven months he spent bumming around

New York (1950). **2** trans. To beg; to obtain by begging; to cadge. 1863–. L. A. G. STRONG An odd sort of bloke . . . bummed a light and a fill of tobacco off me (1941). noun **3** A lazy and dissolute person; a habitual loafer or tramp. 1864–. PUNCH The bums in the dosshouse have reached bottom (1958). [Prob. short for obs. *bummer* noun, idler, loafer.]

bum adjective orig US Of low quality. 1859–. A. POWELL This is a bum party (1931). [Cf. BUM² noun.] See also BUM STEER noun.

bumbershoot noun orig and mainly US An umbrella. 1896–. LEAR'S The oversized bumbershoot lets you dodge raindrops with ease and flair (1992). [From *bumber*, a humorous alteration of *umbr-* (as in *umbrella*) + *shoot*, perh. a respelling of *-chute* (as in *parachute*).]

bum-boy noun A young male homosexual, esp. a prostitute. 1937–. D. THOMAS A ringed and dainty gesture copied from some famous cosmopolitan bumboy (1938). [From BUM¹ noun.]

bumf /bʌmf/ noun Brit Also **bumph**. Toilet paper; hence (esp. somewhat contemptuously), paper, documents collectively. 1889–. M. K. JOSEPH Matthews is bringing the bumf . . . He says be sure and type it on Army Form A2 (1957). [Short for older *bumfodder*: see BUM¹ noun.]

bum fluff noun Brit The incipient growth of hair on the face of an adolescent boy. 1961–. NEW MUSICAL EXPRESS You must be a pretty crap Satan if you can only appeal to bumfluff-faced adolescent, social inadequates out to shock their mums (1995).

bum-freezer noun mainly Brit A short coat, jacket, or the like. Also (dated) **bumperisher, -shaver, -starver**. 1889–. H. SPRING A nice little Eton suit—what Greg inevitably called my bum-freezer (1955).

bummer¹ noun US An idler or loafer. 1855–. [Cf. BUM² verb, perh. after German *Bummler*.]

bummer² noun orig and mainly US An unpleasant or depressing experience, esp. one induced by a hallucinogenic drug; a disappointment, failure. Freq. in phr. *to be a bummer*. 1967–. N. MAILER It was a bummer. Hitchhiking over to the nuthouse, the whole day got lost (1979). [From BUM adjective + *-er*.]

bump noun The action of thrusting forward the abdomen or hips in a dance. 1943–. Cf. GRIND noun 5. [From earlier sense, (sound of) a heavy blow.]

bumper noun Austral and NZ A cigarette end. 1899–. SOUTHERLY He patted the bare mattress . . . where a bumper had burned a hole sometime in the past (1967). [Apparently blend of *butt* and *stump* + *-er*.]

bump off verb trans. orig US To murder. Also **bump**. 1910–. E. WAUGH They had two shots at bumping me off yesterday (1932).

bum rap noun mainly US A false charge, an undeserved punishment. 1927–. Cf. RAP² noun.

bum's rush noun Forcible ejection. With *the*. 1925–. E. LINKLATER I told him I'd give him the bum's rush if he tried to pull that stuff on me (1959). [From BUM² noun.]

bum steer noun False or poor information or advice. 1924–.

bum-sucker noun Brit An obsequious person; a toady, sycophant. 1877–. G. ORWELL The lords of property and their hired liars and bumsuckers (1943). [From BUM¹ noun.] Hence **bum-suck** verb intr. Brit 1930–. L. COOPER He bumsucked to all the rich men (1960).

bun¹ noun **1 to do one's bun** NZ To lose one's temper. 1944–. **2 a bun in the oven** a child conceived. 1951–. A. SILLITOE Brenda on the tub, up the stick, with a bun in the oven (1958). **3** In pl., US The buttocks. 1960–. E. LEONARD She saw . . . a white band below his hips, sexy, really nice buns (1985).

bun² noun A drunken condition, esp. in phr. *to get, have, tie a bun on*, to get drunk. 1901–54. [Origin unknown.]

bunce noun Money; extra profit or gain, bonus. 1719–. C. DRUMMOND They take the place for a fee and pocket any bunce (1968). [Origin unknown; perh. an alteration of *bonus*.]

bunch of fives noun A fist; hence, a punch. 1825–. B. W. ALDISS My only regret was that I had not given Wally a bunch of fives in the mush while I had the chance (1971). [From the five fingers.]

bunco US. noun **1** A swindle perpetrated by means of card-sharping or some form of confidence trick. Also **banco, bunko**. 1872–. SPECTATOR The bunco-artists from the lunatic fringe of the Democratic party (1963). verb trans. **2** To swindle or cheat. Also **bunko**. 1875–. [Said to be from Spanish *banco* a card-game similar to monte.]

bundle noun orig US A large amount of money. 1903–. GUARDIAN This is not the world's fastest dish, since it requires home-made stock.

bum   bumbershoot   bum-boy   bumf   bum fluff

business

Nor is it the cheapest, since porcini cost a bundle (1992). [From earlier sense, roll of banknotes.]

bung Brit. verb trans. **1** To bribe; to pay; to tip. 1950–. J. BURKE Don't forget the solicitors . . . They'll want bunging (1967). noun **2** A bribe. 1958–. J. ASHFORD What's the matter? Not being offered enough bung? (1966). [Origin unknown.]

bung adjective Austral and NZ Dead; bankrupt; ruined, useless. Also in phr. *to go bung*, to die; to fail; to go bankrupt. 1882–. L. MACFARLANE We were bung, completely down and out (1948). [From Aboriginal (Jagara) *baŋ*.]

bung-ho int Also **bung-o**. An exclamation used at parting or as a drinking toast. 1925–. D. L. SAYERS 'Dry Martini,' said Wimsey . . . 'Bung-ho!' (1928).

bunk noun **1 to do a bunk** to make an escape; to depart hurriedly. *c*.1870–. G. B. SHAW If my legs would support me I'd just do a bunk straight for the ship (1921). verb intr. **2** To leave, esp. to be absent from school without permission; often followed by *off*. 1877–. TIME OUT A lot of kids here bunk off, as all kids do. The rate here is about 18% (1973). [Origin unknown.]

bunny-boiler noun derog, mainly Brit A jealous or obsessive woman whose behaviour in pursuit of a former or intended partner is considered desperate or dangerous. 1990–. M. BEAUMONT Hey up, I thought, a bunny-boiler—either she's after an autograph or she wants to take Rebecca home and bury her under the floorboards (2002). [Inspired by the film *Fatal Attraction* (1987), in which a character played by Glenn Close kills and boils a pet rabbit belonging to the daughter of her former lover.]

bupkis noun US Nothing at all. 1942–. [Yiddish, literally 'beans'.]

buppie noun orig US A Black city-dwelling professional person who is (or attempts to be) upwardly mobile; a Black yuppie. 1984–. INDEPENDENT Derek Boland—the . . . rap singer Derek B—was present as a representative of 'buppies' (black yuppies) (1988). [Acronym formed on Black urban (or upwardly-mobile) professional, after YUPPIE noun.]

burk(e) variant of BERK noun.

burl noun Also **birl** Austral An attempt, a go; esp. in phr. *to give it a burl*. 1917–. D. M. DAVIN I thought I'd give it a burl. And I made it, got clean away (1947). [From earlier Scottish sense, spin, whirl.]

burn verb **1** trans. To swindle or cheat (someone). 1808–. J. BLACK If you'd burnt Shorty for his end of that coin, you'd have been here just the same (1926). **2** trans. To smoke (tobacco). 1929–. **3** intr. Of a car, etc.: to travel at speed. 1942–. SUNDAY MAIL (Brisbane): In burns a police car . . . Out jumps a senior sergeant (1972). noun **4** A smoke; tobacco, esp. a cigarette; **to have a burn** to smoke a cigarette. 1941–. A. THORNE Rolling cigarettes for 'a quiet burn' (1956). **5** A race, ride, or drive in a car, etc. at high speed. 1966–. ROLLING STONE The nonstop, trans-Texas burn was 800 miles and Aykroyd took it in 16 hours (1977).

buroo /bəˈruː, bruː/ noun Also **brew, broo, b'roo**. dated, mainly Scottish The employment exchange; hence, unemployment benefit; esp. in phr. *on the buroo*, receiving such benefit. 1934–. [Representing regional (esp. Scottish) pronunciation of *bureau*, in 'Labour Bureau'.]

burton noun Also **Burton**. **to go for a burton** Brit Of a pilot: to be killed; of a person or thing: to be missing, ruined, destroyed. 1941–. E. ROBERTS I can see those flowers going for a burton (1946). [Origin unknown; perh. connected with *Burton* type of beer from Burton-on-Trent.]

bus noun dated **1** An aircraft, esp. an old or dilapidated one. 1910–. J. BUCHAN Got here last night after a clinkin' journey, with the bus [i.e. an aeroplane] behavin' like a lamb (1924). **2** A car, esp. an old or dilapidated one. 1921–. J. GASH 'I gave him a lift to the station.' 'Did he survive?' She's always pulling my leg about my old bus (1977).

bush noun (A bushy growth of) pubic hair. 1922–. A. POWELL He insisted on taking a cutting from my bush—said he always did after having anyone for the first time (1973).

bushed adjective N Amer Tired, exhausted. 1870–. 'CASTLE' & BAILEY You thought you'd reached the end then—completely bushed, with not another ounce left in you (1958). [From earlier sense, 'lost in the bush'.]

bushwa /ˈbʊʃwɑː/ noun Also **booshwa(h), bushwha, bushwah**. N Amer Rubbish, nonsense. 1920–. J. R. MACDONALD If you're a detective, what was all that bushwa about Hollywood and Sunset Boulevard? (1959). [Apparently a euphemistic alteration of BULLSHIT noun.]

business noun Sexual services bought from a prostitute. 1983–. J. AYTO Prostitutes' use of *business* both to designate their profession

bung bung-ho bunk bunny-boiler bupkis burl

and as a shorthand euphemism for their services—as in 'You want business, love?' (1993).

bust verb trans. **1** To break into or raid (a house, etc.). 1859–. **2** To dismiss, demote; to arrest, jail. 1918–. w. R. BURNETT Roy showed his [police] badge. 'You'll get busted for this,' shouted the man (1953). noun **3** A police raid or arrest. 1938–. w. BURROUGHS Provident junkies . . . keep stashes against a bust (1959).

buster noun mainly US A riotous fellow; a 'mate', chap (esp. as a friendly or slightly disrespectful form of address). 1850–. A. SHEPARD 'OK, Buster,' I said to myself, 'you volunteered for this thing' (1962). [Dialectal variant of *burster*.]

busy noun Brit A detective. 1904–. M. ALLINGHAM I don't know 'ow long we've got before the busies come trampin' in (1948). [From *busy* adjective.]

butch adjective and noun orig US (Typical of) a tough youth or man, or a lesbian of masculine appearance or behaviour. 1941–. NEW STATESMAN One of the femmes, secure in the loving protection of her butch (1966). [Perh. short for *butcher*.]

butcher's noun **1** Brit A look. 1936–. K. AMIS Have a butcher's at the *News of the World* (1960). **2 to be** or **go butcher's** Austral and NZ To become angry. 1941–. [Short for *butcher's hook*: in sense 1, rhyming slang for 'look'; in sense 2, rhyming slang for 'crook' = angry.]

butt noun mainly US The buttocks. 1860–. [Recorded since the late Middle Ages in non-slang use.]

butter-and-egg man noun US
A wealthy unsophisticated man who spends money freely. 1926–. ANTIOCH REVIEW The 'butter-and-egg' man who startles the foreign lecturer with blunt questions (1948).

butterbar noun US military A second lieutenant. 1973–. [From *butterbars* two golden bars worn as a badge of rank by a second lieutenant, from their yellow colour (not recorded before 1983 but apparently extant in the mid-1960s).]

butter-boy noun Brit A new taxi driver. 1939–. C. RAY [The] owner-driver . . . is called a 'butter-boy' when he first appears on the rank, taking the butter from the older hands' bread, they say (1960).

buttinsky noun Also **buttinski**. orig US Someone who butts in; an intruder. 1902–. P. G. WODEHOUSE It is never pleasant for a man of sensibility to find himself regarded as a buttinski (1960). [Humorously from *butt in* + *-sky, -ski*, final element in many Slavic names.]

button verb trans. **to button (up)** one's lip, face to be silent. 1836–. Also **to button it.**
1980–. HARPERS AND QUEEN I laugh involuntarily, and am met with an impatient glare. I hastily button my lip (1992).

buy the farm

to crash an aircraft, usu. fatally

buy verb trans. **1** To suffer (some mishap or reverse); spec to be wounded; to get killed, to die; to be destroyed. Often with *it*. 1825–. R. LEHMANN He'd lived in London before the war, but the whole street where he'd hung out had bought it in the blitz (1953). **2 to buy the farm** US orig services' Also **to buy the ranch: a** To crash an aircraft, usu. fatally. 1955–. ECONOMIST These demonstrations cost money and lives. A number of commercial test pilots have 'bought the farm' while doing demonstrations (1988). **b** To be killed (in action), hence more generally, to die. 1958–. [In sense 2, explained as referring to government compensation paid to a farmer when a military aircraft crashes on his farm.]

buzz noun A telephone call. 1930–. G. USHER Shall I give him a buzz? (1959).

buzz off verb intr. To go away quickly. 1914–. MORECAMBE GUARDIAN When a 79-year-old motorist was asked to move his car he told a police sergeant to 'buzz off' (1976).

cabbage noun dated, mainly N Amer Money. 1926-. OBSERVER The white, crinkle, cabbage, poppy, lolly, in other words cash (1960). [From the notion of being green and crisp, like a dollar bill.]

cabbaged adjective Brit (Insensible as a result of being) extremely drunk or high on drugs. 1991-. COLLIN & GODFREY The influx of MDA 'Snowballs' resulted in squatting rows of cabbaged clubbers clinging separately onto walls (1997). [Perh. from *cabbage* person of impaired mental activity.]

caboodle noun orig US In phr. *the whole* (*kit and*) *caboodle* everything, 'the whole lot'. *a*.1848-. STRAND MAGAZINE Actually, the whole caboodle, sold, not pawned, produced seventy, not fifty—hundred and twenty in all (1923). LISTENER The whole kit and caboodle of us were then investigated by the FBI to see how many subversives there were among us (1969). [Alteration of earlier *boodle* crowd, pack, lot, of unknown origin.]

Caesar noun medical (A case of) Caesarian section. 1952-. GUARDIAN One Roman Catholic doctor . . . will awaken this convenient custodian of his conscience with the words: 'I'm doing a fourth Caesar' (1964).

caff noun Brit A café. 1931-. SUNDAY TIMES MAGAZINE In 1979 . . . the *Sunday Times Magazine* ran a fearful article predicting the demise of the working man's caff (1991).

cag Also **kagg.** nautical. noun 1 An argument. 1916-. verb intr. 2 To argue, to nag. 1919-. N. SHUTE I'm not going to worry you, or cag about this any more (1932). [Cf. obs. Brit dialect *caggy* ill-natured.]

cahoots noun in cahoots orig US Acting as a group, usu. conspiratorially. 1862-. A. UPFIELD She was in cahoots with a doctor (1953). [From earlier *in cahoot*; ultimate origin unknown.]

cake noun to take the cake to carry off the honours, rank first; often used ironically or as an expression of surprise. 1847-. G. HEYER I've met some kill-joys in my time, but you fairly take the cake (1938). Cf. *to take the biscuit* at BISCUIT noun and see also *piece of cake* at PIECE noun.

cake-hole noun Brit A person's mouth. 1943-. I. & P. OPIE Shut your cake-hole (1959).

camel jockey noun US derog An Arab. 1965-. OBSERVER The British papers quickly followed the American lead. Although none quite sank to the level of 'Camel jockeys killed your kids' . . . the British tabloids were not far

behind (1996). [From the use of the camel as a method of transport (and allegedly as a vehicle for sexual gratification) in the Middle East.]

can noun 1 US The lavatory. 1900-. J. D. SALINGER She kept on saying . . . corny . . . things, like calling the can the 'little girls' room' (1951). 2 orig US Prison. 1912-. 20TH CENTURY I'll stand by my man Though he's in the can (1961). 3 orig and mainly US The buttocks. 1930-. J. MCCORMICK A toilet bowl in the corner with a scratched metal lid that freezes your can when you sit on it (1965). verb trans. 4 orig US To stop doing (something). 1906-. E. FERRARS 'Can that bloody row, can't you?' he grunted (1953).

cancer stick noun A cigarette. 1959-.

canned adjective Drunk, intoxicated. 1914-. J. J. CONNINGTON Being rather canned, he sticks the candle on the table, and forgets all about it (1926).

canned Willie noun Also **corned Willie.** US services' Corned beef or corned-beef hash. 1902-.

canoodle verb intr. orig US To kiss and cuddle. 1859-. H. WALPOLE She's in there . . . I'm off on some business of my own for an hour or two, so you can canoodle as much as you damned well please (1921). [Origin unknown.]

Canuck /kəˈnʌk/ N Amer (in US, sometimes derog) noun 1 A Canadian; spec. a French Canadian. 1849-. 2 The French-Canadian patois. 1904-. H. GOLD Bon jour, Grack, tu viens enfin? That's Canuck for you ain't been a son to your ma (1965). adjective 3 Canadian. 1862-. T. E. LAWRENCE The three Canuck priests (1910). [Apparently from the first syllable of *Canada*.]

caper noun An activity, occupation. Also, a 'game', dodge, racket. 1839-. J. BURKE I know your caper. The kidney punch and the rabbit clout (1964).

cabbage cabbaged caboodle Caesar caff cag can

capisce /kəˈpiːʃ/ verb intr. To understand; often used interrogatively: Do you understand? 1904–. G. BAXT Nobody . . . gets a look at this thing until I'm good and ready. *Capisce?* (1966) [From Italian *capisce*, 3rd person present sing. of *capire* to understand.]

Captain Cook noun Austral A look. 1932–. D. O'GRADY Got a Captain Cook at your dossier— it's thicker than your frickin' head (1974). [Rhyming slang; from the name of James Cook (1728–79), British navigator and explorer.]

card noun dated An eccentric, amusing, clever, audacious, etc. person. 1853–. W. B. JOHNSON That old Witch-Hammer was really quite a card (1942). [Prob. from such expressions as *sure card*, *good card*, etc., orig applied to playing cards, *transf.* to people.]

cardy noun Also **cardi(e)**. Abbreviation of 'cardigan'. 1968–. J. MILNE He wore his yellow cardy with the leather buttons (1986).

cark verb Also **kark**. orig Austral **1** intr. To die. 1977–. **2 to cark it** to die. 1982–. SUNDAY MAIL (Brisbane) He turns nasty and binds her, then locks her in a shed and leaves a gas-powered lawn mower running. Will she cark it from the carbon monoxide fumes (1991)? [Perh. from Austral *cark* caw, from the association of crows with death.]

carney adjective Also **carny**. Artful, sly. 1881–. E. BLISHEN Macbeth was pretty carney in the way he handled Banquo (1955). [From obs. dialect *carn(e)y* verb, to wheedle.]

carpet verb trans. **1** To reprimand. 1840–. J. KELMAN It was a while since he had been carpeted (1989). noun **2 on the carpet** orig US Being reprimanded. 1900–. SKETCH His manager had just had him on the carpet, pointing out that his work had been getting steadily bad for the last few months (1936). **3** criminals' Three months' imprisonment. 1903–. J. CURTIS Long enough to've been in Wandsworth and done a carpet (1936). **4** The female pubic hair or external genitalia (used esp. in the context of cunnilingus). 1981–. [In sense 3, short for *carpet-bag*, rhyming slang for obs. *drag* three months' imprisonment.]

carpet muncher noun derog and offensive A lesbian. 1992–. Cf. RUG MUNCHER noun. [From CARPET noun 4.]

carry verb intr. **to carry on: a** To behave, esp. to speak, strangely or over-excitedly. 1828–. R. L. STEVENSON There was Adams in the middle, gone luny again, and carrying on about copra like a born fool (1892). **b** To flirt or have a love

affair. Often with *with*. 1856–. W. S. MAUGHAM It was impossible that she could be 'carrying on' with Lord George (1930). Hence **carry-on,** noun Fuss, to-do, excitement. 1890–. P. BULL We were all engaged in a radio version of Hamlet . . . I had never realized the incredible carry-on connected with these productions (1959).

cars(e)y variant of KARZY noun.

cart verb trans. **1** To carry or transport (something heavy or cumbersome) over a long distance or with considerable effort. 1881–. B. TRAPIDO We carted home a great quantity of accumulated litter from our desks in a plaid blanket (1982). **2** dated To put (someone) in difficulties; to cause to feel let down. 1889–. HANSARD Many had lived in camp according to the promised scale of pay, with the result that they lived beyond their means. To use an Army expression, 'They were properly carted' (1948). noun **3 in the cart** in serious trouble or difficulty. 1889–. J. B. HOBBS We made 238, which was enough practically to put South Africa hopelessly in the cart (1928).

carve verb trans. **1** To slash (a person) with a knife or razor. Usu. with *up*. 1929–. G. GREENE They just meant to carve him up, but a razor slipped (1938). **2 to carve up** to cheat, swindle. 1933–. H. PINTER Then after that, you know what they did? They carved me up. Carved me up. It was all arranged, it was all worked out (1959).

carve-up noun A sharing-out, esp. of spoils, often in a dishonest way. 1935–. TIMES Is the selection of justices of the peace in Britain . . . a 'political carve-up', as alleged by some of the more vociferous of the system's opponents? (1963). [From *to carve up* (see CARVE verb 2).]

case noun dated orig and mainly US An infatuation. So **to have a case on,** to be infatuated with or enamoured of. 1852–1951. STORY-TELLER By the end of the second year the girls were saying that Salesby *had* quite *a case on* Chips (1931).

case verb trans. orig US To reconnoitre (a house, etc.), esp. with a view to robbery. 1915–. M. GAIR What he was doing was casing the gaff; or, in police terms, 'loitering with intent to commit a felony' (1957).

caser noun dated A five-shilling coin, a crown; US a dollar. 1849–1967. [Yiddish; from Hebrew *kesef* silver.]

cash verb intr. **to cash in** to die. Also trans. with *checks* or *chips* as object. 1884–. D. VARADAY Because of the size of the dead animal, at first

capisce   Captain Cook   card   cardy   cark   carney

Charlie

I thought it to be buffalo. 'Poor Bill or Phyl, cashed in?' (1966).

cat¹ noun **1 not a cat (in hell)'s chance** no chance at all. 1796–. GUARDIAN One seaman said the union had not 'a cat in hell's chance' of beating the Government as well as the shipowners (1966). **2** orig US An expert in, or one expertly appreciative of, jazz. 1932–. WOMAN'S OWN 'It's got beat and a lot of excitement,' said one teenage 'cat' I talked to (1958). **3** A 'regular guy', fellow, man. 1957–. C. MACINNES The coloured cats saw I had an ally, and melted (1959).

cat² noun Brit Abbreviation of 'catalytic converter'. Also as adjective, fitted with one. 1988–. PERFORMANCE CAR If I remove the cat, could I use leaded petrol or will it damage the engine? (1989).

catbird seat noun US A superior or advantageous position. With *the.* 1942–. P. G. WODEHOUSE 'If we swing it, we'll be sitting pretty.' 'In the catbird seat' (1958). [From *catbird* noun, an American thrush.]

catch verb trans. **to catch (someone) bending** to catch (someone) at a disadvantage. 1910–. A. WILSON He then goes off singing 'My word, if I catch you bending, my word, if I catch you bending' (1967).

cat-house noun A brothel. 1931–. G. ORWELL He's took her abroad an' sold her to one o' dem flash cat-houses in Parrus (1935). [Cf. obs. *cat* noun, prostitute.]

cat's whiskers noun orig US An excellent person or thing. 1923–. Also **cat's meow** 1921–, **cat's pyjamas** 1922–, **cat's nuts** 1928–. TIMES Lord Montgomery . . . holds that to label anything the 'cat's whiskers' is to confer on it the highest honour (1958).

caulk noun nautical A short sleep or nap. 1917–. H. C. BAILEY 'Having a caulk' where he sat and . . . he woke at eight (1942). [From obs. *caulk* verb, to sleep, perh. from a comparison between closing the eyes and stopping up a ship's seams.]

cellie noun Also **celly.** prisoners', mainly N Amer A cellmate. 1967–. [From *cell* + *-ie.*]

century noun US A hundred dollars. 1859–. R. CHANDLER He . . . arranged five century notes like a tight poker hand (1964).

cert noun Something considered certain to happen or succeed, esp. a horse considered certain to win a race; esp. in phr. *a dead cert.* 1889–. AUDEN & ISHERWOOD We'll be able to start

tomorrow for a cert (1936). [Abbreviation of *certain, certainty.*]

cha var. of CHAR noun.

chair noun US The electric chair. 1900–. J. J. FARNOL I've left papers—proofs, 'n' it'ud be the chair for yours—savvy? (1917).

chalkie noun Also **chalky.** Austral A teacher. 1945–. L. CLANCY After I was taken on as a staff member I used to drink with a group of 'chalkies', as they like to call themselves (1979). [From teachers' use of chalk for writing on blackboards.]

champ noun orig US Abbreviation of 'champion'. 1868–. GLOBE & MAIL (Toronto): US Open champ Gay Brewer . . . had a 75 at Spyglass in the first round (1968).

champers /ˈʃæmpəz/ noun Brit Champagne. 1955–. M. AINSWORTH Champers or something with gin in it? (1959). [From first syllable of *champagne* + *-ers.*]

chancer noun One who takes chances or does risky things. Also, one who trades on people's credulity; one who tries it on. 1884–. J. MILNE If you're a detective where's your warrant card? I don't think you're a detective at all. You're just a chancer (1986). [From *chance* verb + *-er.*]

chapess noun Brit jocular A woman. 1966–. INDEPENDENT There are plenty of leisure interest groups catering for the brighter than average, from the Conan Doyle Society to the Sundial Society, from the Queen's English Society to the Society for Psychical Research—all packed with brights chaps and chapesses eager to discuss matters of mutual interest with a view to forming a lasting relationship (1996). [From *chap* + female suffix *-ess.*]

char noun Also **cha.** Brit Tea. 1919–. H. SPRING I thought of the thousands of cups o' char that batmen had produced at such moments as this (1955). [From Chinese *cha.*]

charge noun **1** US A dose or injection of a drug; marijuana, esp. a marijuana cigarette. 1929–. MELODY MAKER Club promoters are worried that the hippies could close them down by smoking charge on the premises (1969). **2** orig US A thrill, kick. 1951–. NEW YORK TIMES MAGAZINE It seems to me that people get a bigger charge out of their grandchildren than they did from their own offspring (1963).

Charlie Also **Charley.** noun **1** pl. A woman's breasts. 1874–. P. WILDEBLOOD Carrying her famous bosom before her like the tray of an usherette she was disconcerted to hear . . . a nasal cry of:

cat   catbird seat   catch   cat-house   cat's whiskers

'Coo, look at them charlies!' (1957). **2** A fool, esp. in phr. *a proper* (or *right*) *Charlie*. 1946–. SIMPSON & GALTON I felt a right Charlie coming through the customs in this lot (1961). **3** US Black English A white man. Also **Mr. Charlie.** 1960–. GUARDIAN Stokely Carmichael was there promising 'Mr. Charlie's' doomsday (1967). **4** US services' The North Vietnamese and Vietcong; esp. a North Vietnamese or Vietcong soldier. 1965–. NEW STATESMAN Friendly forces have made contact with Charlie and a fire fight followed (1966). adjective **5** Afraid, cowardly; esp. in phr. *to turn Charlie*. 1954–. F. NORMAN I was dead charlie and little fairies were having a right game in my guts (1958). [In sense 4, short for VICTOR CHARLIE noun.]

Charley-horse noun Also **charley-horse.** N Amer Stiffness or cramp in the arm or leg, esp. in baseball players. 1888–. GLOBE & MAIL (Toronto): Rookie centre Gordon Judges departed in the second half suffering a severe charley horse in his left thigh (1968). [Origin uncertain.]

chase verb **to chase the dragon** to take heroin by inhalation. 1961–. R. LEWIS There's this myth among the kids that if they inhale the burned skag it isn't going to hurt them. Chasing the dragon, they call it (1985). [From the resemblance between the movements of the burning heroin and the undulations of a dragon's tail.]

chaser noun US An amorous pursuer of women. 1894–. S. GREENLEE The women thought him an eligible bachelor, if a bit of a chaser (1969).

chassis noun jocular The body of a person or animal. 1930–. P. G. WODEHOUSE 'Did he seem very fond of her?' 'Couldn't take his eyes off the chassis' (1930). [From earlier sense, frame of a car.]

chat verb trans. Brit To talk to, esp. flirtatiously or with an ulterior motive; often with *up*. 1898–. SUNDAY EXPRESS He saw a pretty girl . . . smiling at him. He smiled right back. 'I like chatting the birds,' he said (1963); K. AMIS I must have spent a bit of time chatting them up (1966).

chav noun In Britain (orig the south of England): a young person of a type characterized by brash or loutish behaviour and the wearing of designer-style clothes, esp. sportswear; usu. with connotations of lower-class status. 1998–. SUNDAY TIMES Older children desire nothing more than to dress, talk and behave like chavs, that is, a youth tribe that prides itself on council-estate chic—man-made

fabrics, fake labels and lots of eight-carat gold: think Vicky Pollard in Little Britain (2004). [Prob. either from Romani *čhavo* unmarried Romani male, male Romani child, or shortened from CHAVVY noun (the notion that it is connected with *Chatham*, the name of a Kent town associated in the popular imagination with chav culture, is almost certainly a post hoc rationalization).]

chavette noun Brit A female chav. 2000–. DAILY RECORD (Glasgow) How's this for a door policy at 2 Die 4 @ CubaCuba, on a Saturday night? No beer boys, chavers, chavettes, Lacoste, kickers, YSL, Hilfiger, Ben Sherman or moustaches (2000). [From CHAV noun + -*ette.*]

chavvy noun Brit A baby, child. 1886–. J. J. CONNOLLY Most will end up fucked-up one way or another—the girls with more chavvies than they can handle or love and the geezers doing hard time (2000). [From Angloromani *chavvy* child, ultimately from Sanskrit *śāva* the young of any animal.]

chavvy adjective Brit Like, characteristic of, or being a chav. 1999–. STUFF The horribly chavvy gold version has also been replaced by a pink model (2005). [From CHAV noun + -*y.*]

cheap adjective **as cheap as chips** Brit, Austral, and NZ extremely cheap. 1850–. TIME OUT The Indoor Market looks like it hasn't altered in twenty years, but Turkish slippers and suitcases are as cheap as chips (2004).

cheap Charlie noun US, mainly military A mean person. 1965–. [From *cheap* adjective mean.]

cheapie noun **1** Also **cheapy.** Something cheap; a thing of little value or of poor quality; spec a film, book, etc., produced on a low budget. 1898–. GUARDIAN It identified insurance shares as a cheapy a couple of years back (1983). adjective **2** Rather cheap, and often of inferior quality. 1898–. [From *cheap* adjective + -*ie*, -*y.*]

cheapo adjective **1** Inexpensive, and often of inferior quality. 1967–. BARR & YORK Cheapo fun dangly earrings (1982). noun **2** = CHEAPIE noun. 1975–. LISTENER They want to see if you're wearing a Timex cheapo or a Rolex that's worth stealing (1985). [From *cheap* adjective + -*o.*]

cheapskate noun Also **cheap skate.** mainly US A mean or contemptible person. 1896–. J. PORTER They were hardened women of the world and knew a cheap skate when they saw one (1973). [From *cheap* adjective, mean + SKATE noun 2.]

Charley-horse chase chaser chassis chat chav

cheaters noun US Spectacles, glasses. 1921–. R. CHANDLER The eyes behind the rimless cheaters flashed (1949).

cheese verb trans. dated, orig thieves' To stop, give up, leave off; esp. in phr. *cheese it!* 1812–. P. G. WODEHOUSE He had been clearing away the breakfast things, but at the sound of the young master's voice cheesed it courteously (1923). [Origin unknown.] See also BIG CHEESE noun, HARD CHEESE noun.

cheesecake noun orig US A display of sexually attractive females, esp. in photographs. 1934–. J. WAIN She had a sexy slouch like a Hollywood cheesecake queen (1958). Cf. BEEFCAKE noun.

cheesed off adjective Brit Fed up, disgruntled. Also **cheesed.** 1941–. A. BARON Whenever I'm cheesed off I just open it and start reading (1948). [Origin unknown.]

cheesy adjective Also **cheesey.** Inferior, second-rate, cheap and nasty. 1896–. R. MACAULAY Hare and rabbit fur are just utterly revolting and cheesey (1930).

Chelsea tractor noun Brit derog or humorous A four-wheel-drive or off-road vehicle which is used predominantly in urban areas. 1994–. METRO I find it difficult to believe someone of his intelligence would consider buying a 4×4, aka 'Chelsea Tractor' (2005). [From the supposed abundance of such vehicles in the wealthy middle-class London district of Chelsea.]

chemmy noun Also **shemmy** The card-game chemin-de-fer. 1923–. PUNCH How to behave when a . . . bingo-club or a chemmy-party . . . is visited by the police (1962). [Abbreviation and alteration of *chemin-de-fer*.]

cherry noun orig US **1** Virginity; esp. in phr. *to lose one's cherry*; similarly, *to take* (etc.) *a cherry.* 1928–. R. H. RIMMER The day I lost my cherry didn't amount to much, anyway (1975). **2** A virgin. 1935–. M. RICHLER Gin excites them. Horseback riding gives them hot pants too. Cherries are trouble, but married ones miss it something terrible (1959).

chesty adjective US Arrogant. 1900–. A. LOMAX George was a little bit chesty, because all the girls around were making eyes at him (1950). [From the notion of sticking out one's chest with pride.]

chew verb trans. **1 to chew the rag** or **fat** to discuss a matter, esp. at length; to grumble. 1885–. J. TEY We had that paper in the pantry last Friday and chewed the rag over it for hours (1948). **2 to chew** (someone) **out** US, orig

services' To reprimand (someone) severely. 1937–. GUARDIAN Gen Schwarzkopf also has a small personal office he sometimes uses for private discussions. It has also been used to chew out officers whose performance does not please him (1991). **3 to chew** (someone's) **ass** US To reprimand (someone) severely. 1946–. BLACK PANTHER Maybe if he saw it, some pig might . . . get his ass chewed (1973).

chewy noun Also **chewie** Austral Chewing gum. 1924–. MCDONALD & HARDING The easiest to prepare, cheap as mud to buy, and the slowest to eat, is a couple of pieces of chewy (1976).

Chi /ʃaɪ/ noun Chicago, Illinois. 1895–. [Abbreviation.]

chiack /ˈtʃaɪæk/ verb intr. and trans. Also **chyack.** Austral and NZ = CHI-HIKE verb. 1853–. K. S. PRICHARD The rowdy bodgie youths kept seats near this group, chiacking the buxom, brassy-haired waitress as she rushed around with a tray-load of dishes and lively back-chat (1967).

chib noun, now mainly Scottish A knife, used as a weapon. 1929–. I. WELSH The Yank, the boy likes, jist wouldnae hand ower the wallet, even when Begbie pulled the chib (1993). [Prob. a variant of CHIV(E) noun.]

chick noun orig US A girl; a young woman. 1927–. IT Jackie, always a 'with-it chick' (1971).

chicken verb intr. orig US To back down or fail to act through fear or lack of nerve. Usu. with *out.* 1943–. ECONOMIST Nobody can trust the others not to chicken out if they take the first plunge (1965). [From *chicken* noun, cowardly person.]

chicken colonel noun US A US officer of the rank of full colonel. 1948–. E. HEMINGWAY Maybe they treat me well because I'm a chicken colonel on the winning side (1950). [From a colonel's insignia of a silver eagle.]

chicken-feed noun orig US Something of little importance, esp. a trifling sum of money. 1937–. NEW REVIEW In peacetime, officers in the British Army were men of independent means to whom their Army pay was chicken-feed (1941). [From earlier sense, food for chickens.]

chicken ranch noun US A brothel. 1973–. S. KING Someone finally found a way to clean up the dope in Boston's Combat Zone and the chicken-ranch business in Times Square (1990). [Claimed to be from the name of an actual brothel in La Grange, Texas, which was the subject of the musical *The Best Little Whorehouse in Texas.*]

cheaters   cheese   cheesecake   cheesed off   chicken

chickenshit noun orig US **1** Something worthless, insignificant, or contemptible. 1929–. **2** Petty detail, esp. petty military regulations. **3** A despicable person, esp. a coward. 1947–. adjective **4** Contemptible, worthless. 1934–. **5** Cowardly, scared. 1945–. C. BERNSTEIN In her [Betsey Wright's] own words, she was for long 'too chickenshit' to discuss his [Bill Clinton's] behaviour with Hillary (2007).

chicklet noun Also **chiclet**. US A (sexually attractive) young woman. 1922–. [From CHICK noun + diminutive suffix -*let*, punningly after *Chiclets*, name of a brand of chewing gum.]

chief noun **too many chiefs and not enough Indians** denoting (disorganization due to) an excess of managerial staff and not enough ordinary workers. 1988–. NATIONAL TRUST MAGAZINE The way the National Trust has grown, I can't help feeling that there are too many Chiefs and not enough Indians (1992).

chiefy noun services' A person in charge; one's superior; spec. in the R.A.F., a flight sergeant. 1942–. M. K. JOSEPH The chiefy who done him out of his stripes (1957). [From *chief* noun + -*y*.]

chi-hike /tʃaɪhaɪk/ verb intr. and trans. Also **chi-ike**. To shout derisively (at); tease; barrack. 1874–. SPECTATOR Half a dozen chi-iking louts (1962). [From obs. *chi-hike* a shout of salutation.]

chili-eater noun US derog A Mexican. 1911–.

chill verb **to chill out** mainly US To become less tense, relax. 1982–. SKI The fat one whistles, waves madly and rudely ignores my fatherly admonitions to chill out (1989).

chin noun orig and mainly US A talk, conversation; spec. insolent talk, cheek. 1877–. NEW YORKER We'd like to have a little chin with you right now (1952). Cf. CHIN-WAG noun and verb.

china noun Also **China**. Brit A friend. 1925–. NEW STATESMAN I have my hands full with his china who is a big geezer of about 14 stone (1965). [Short for *china-plate*, rhyming slang for 'mate'.]

Chinaman's chance noun mainly US A negligible prospect. 1914–. F. YERBY You haven't a Chinaman's chance of raising that money in Boston (1951).

chin chin int Brit Used as a drinking toast, a greeting, etc. 1795–. P. JONES Two glasses appeared, with ice tinkling in the Scotch. Paul raised his, smiling. 'Chin chin' (1967).

Chink noun derog and offensive A Chinese person. 1901–. We used to have a couple staying with us. Chinks, they were, medical students (1969). [Irregularly from *China*.]

Chinkey noun Also **Chinkie, Chinky.** derog and offensive = CHINK noun. 1879–. N. MAILER A certain Chinkie (1959). [As CHINK noun + -*ie*, -*y*.]

chin-wag noun **1** A chat, talk. 1879–. verb intr. **2** To talk, chatter. 1920–. A. BARON Didn't he send her down to the village to chinwag with the Indian chiefs? (1954).

chicklet
a (sexually
attractive
young woman)

chippy noun Also **chippie. 1** dated orig US Usu. derog A (promiscuous) young woman; a prostitute. 1886–. TIMES LITERARY SUPPLEMENT Opal and other 'chippies' at Moll's 'sporting house' (1938). **2** orig naval A carpenter. 1916–. A. WESKER I'll work as a chippy on the Colonel's farm (1960). **3** Brit A fish-and-chip shop. 1961–. LISTENER In the industrial towns the housewife . . . found that time, labour, and money were saved by the chippie (1965). [From *chip* noun + -*y*, -*ie*.]

chips noun pl. **1 to pass** (or **hand**) **in one's chips** US To die. 1879–. **2 to have had one's chips.** To be beaten, finished, killed, etc. 1959–. TECHNOLOGY The St. Albans lot will have had their chips by this time next week (1961).

Chips noun mainly naval (A nickname for) a carpenter. 1785–.

chisel verb trans. To defraud, cheat. 1808–. Hence **chiseller,** noun A swindler, cheat. 1918–. E. HYAMS Harry was easy with all men because they were all equal as chisellers (1949).

chism variant of JISM noun.

chiv(e) /tʃɪv/ criminals'. noun **1** A knife. 1673–. verb trans. **2** To knife; also, to slash with a razor. 1725–. TIMES Three of Heaton's pals threatened to 'chiv' him (1955). [Origin unknown.]

49

chronic

chiv(v)y /tʃɪvɪ/ noun Also **chivey**. The face. 1889–. A. WILSON I can't keep this look of modest pride on my chivvy forever (1958). [Short for *Chevy Chase*, rhyming slang for 'face'.]

chivvy /tʃɪvɪ/ verb trans. Also **chivey**. = CHIV(E verb. 1959–. K. HOPKINS He got chivvied at Brighton races (1960).

chizz noun Also **chiz**. Brit A swindle; a nuisance. 1953–. E. PARTRIDGE 'What a chizz!' What a nuisance (1961). [From CHISEL verb.]

chocker adjective Also **chocka, chokker**. Brit orig naval Fed up, disgusted. 1942–. F. NORMAN I'm a little chocker of this place (1958). [Short for *chock-a-block* adjective, full up.]

choco /tʃɒkəʊ/ noun Also **chocko**. Austral A militiaman or conscripted soldier. 1918–. G. DUTTON You are all volunteers. Your country called you and you came. Not a chocko amongst you (1968). [Short for *chocolate soldier*.]

choked adjective Extremely disappointed or disgusted. 1950–. OZ My governor is going to be choked when I take the day off. He's going to be double choked if I enjoy myself (1969).

choky /tʃəʊkɪ/ noun Also **chokey**. Brit Prison. 1873–. F. DONALDSON I'll buck you up when I get home . . . that's to say if I'm not arrested and shoved in chokey (1982). [Orig Anglo-Indian, from Hindi *caukī* shed.]

choof verb intr. Also **chuff**. Austral To go, walk. 1947–. B. HARDY 'If my presence is going to cause trouble,' I said, 'I'd rather not be here, so I think I'll choof off' (1979). [From *chuff* puff as a steam-train does.]

chook /tʃʊk/ noun Austral and NZ A chicken or other domestic fowl. Also **chookie, -y, chucky, -ie**. 1855–. COAST TO COAST His been wild-eyed, scraggy long-legged chooks, few in number, sneaking into the kitchen after scraps (1969). [Cf. Brit dialect *chuck* chicken.]

choom /tʃʊm, tʃuːm/ noun Austral and NZ An Englishman; an Englishman. 1916–. BULLETIN (Sydney): He wasn't a choom; he came straight from Brisbane and had been born and reared in Sydney (1935). [Variant of *chum* noun.]

chop¹ noun **not much chop** Austral and NZ Not up to much, of no or little value. 1847–. A. BUZO They've improved a lot, these clubs. Twenty years ago they weren't much chop, just a place to go when you wanted to go out on the grog (1973). [From Anglo- Indian *first* (*second*) *chop* first (or other) rank or quality, from Hindi *chhāp* impression, print, stamp, brand, etc.]

chop² noun **1** Austral and NZ One's share; esp. in phr. *to be in for one's chop*. 1919–. D. H. CRICK Tell him his quid today'll be worth ten bob tomorrow, so he better get in for his chop (1966). **2** Brit Being killed; also, being brought to a sudden end; dismissal from a post. Preceded by *the*; often in phr. *to get the chop*. 1945–. INK The Anglo-Italian tournament . . . must be due for the chop (1971).

chop-chop adverb and int Quickly; be quick! 1834–. [Pidgin English, from Chinese *k'wâi-k'wâi*.]

chopper noun **1** US A machine-gun or -gunner. 1929–. I. FLEMING There was a mixture of single shots and bursts from the chopper (1962). **2** pl. orig US Teeth, esp. (a set of) false teeth. 1940–. SUN A set of false choppers were once found in the grounds of Buckingham Palace, after a Royal Garden Party (1965). **3** orig US A helicopter. 1951–. **4** orig US A motor-cycle, esp. one with high handlebars. 1965–. ECONOMIST An Evel Knievel doll on the notorious chopper motor bike (1977). **5** A penis. 1973–.

chopsocky adjective **1** characteristic of a genre of film featuring violent action involving martial arts, esp. kung fu. 1978–. noun **2** A chopsocky film. 1982–. [A punning alteration of *chop suey*, alluding to SOCK¹ verb 1.]

chow noun **1** derog mainly Austral A Chinese person. 1864–. P. WHITE Like one of the Chinese beans the Chow had given them at Christmas (1970). **2** Food or a meal. 1886–. LANDFALL That night at chow time, Rankin called along to Tiny (1958). [Short for *chow-chow*, a medley or assortment, from Pidgin English (Indian and Chinese).]

Chrisake Also **Chrissake, Chris(s)akes**. mainly US Used in oaths and imprecations; usu. preceded by *for*. 1933–. M. PROCTER For Chrissake gimme a cigarette. [Representing a casual pronunciation of *Christ's sake*.]

Christer /kraɪstə(r)/ noun US derog An overpious or sanctimonious person. 1924–. J. PHILIPS I'm a Christer and a do-gooder . . . I wasn't welcome (1966). [From *Christ* + *-er*.]

chromo /krəʊməʊ/ noun Austral A prostitute. 1883–. J. IGGULDEN Some rotten poxy bitch of a chromo dubbed them in (1960). [Abbreviation of *chromolithograph* noun, a picture lithographed in colours, with reference to the 'painted' face of the prostitute.]

chronic adjective Of low quality; bad; unsatisfactory. 1904–. SCOTSMAN 'The weather is

chivvy chizz chocker choco choked chopsocky

chronic,' says a Seaforth Highlander (1915). [From earlier senses, continuous, persistent.]

chubby-chaser noun orig US A man who is sexually attracted to fat women (or, if homosexual, to fat men). 1975–.

chuck verb **1 to chuck it** to stop, desist. 1888–. G. K. CHESTERTON But the souls of Christian people . . . Chuck it, Smith! (1915). **2 to chuck off** Austral and NZ To speak sarcastically, sneer, jeer. 1901–. A. E. MANNING Your friends 'chuck off' at you for being a 'goodie-goodie' (1958). noun **3** Dismissal. Preceded by *the*. 1892–. ARGOSY When they gave me the chuck, you married me out of hand (1930).

chuddies noun pl. Indian English Underpants, knickers. 1995–. GUARDIAN The Bhangramuffin with the cheeky grin and the catchphrase 'Kiss my chuddies' (1999). [Origin uncertain; perh. an alteration of Hindi *chadar* square piece of cloth, shawl.]

chuff noun The buttocks or anus. 1945–. B. MASON Get up off your chuff and say hullo to a gentleman (1980). [Origin unknown.]

chuff verb intr. = CHOOF verb intr.

chuffed adjective Brit, orig services' **1** Pleased, satisfied. 1957–. CRESCENDO I cannot express too much just how 'chuffed' I am with the drums (1967). **2** Displeased, disgruntled. 1960–. C. DALE Don't let on they're after you, see, or she'll be dead chuffed, see? She don't like the law (1964). [In sense 1, prob. from Brit dialect *chuff* pleased; in sense 2, perh. from Brit dialect *chuff* surly.]

chuffing adjective and adverb Brit Used as an intensifier. 1980–. WIRE To which you may reply, 'It's all just your chuffin' problem, mate!' (2001) [Euphemistic alteration of FUCKING adjective and adverb.]

chug orig US. verb trans. **1** To drink, esp. in large gulps without pausing. 1958–. DIVA She pauses to chug her customary, lurid alcopop in celebration (2004). **2** noun = CHUGALUG noun. 1958–. [Shortening of CHUGALUG verb and noun.]

chugalug orig US. noun **1** The drinking of a glass of beer, etc. at a single swallow. c.1936–. verb trans. **2** To drink in large gulps without pausing. 1945–. YAHOO! INTERNET LIFE Check your e-mail while you chugalug milk from the carton (2000). [From *chug-a-lug* in imitative of the sound of drinking in large gulps.]

chugger noun Brit derog A person who solicits charitable donations in the street. 2002–. GUARDIAN I counted all the people who

accosted me. There was a busker . . . and no fewer than three 'chuggers' (2002). [Blend of *charity* and *mugger*.]

chummy noun Brit Police A prisoner; a person accused or detained. 1948–. D. CLARK We could get Chummy into the dock and pleading guilty, but we'd not get a verdict (1969). [Cf. earlier sense, friend.]

chump noun **1** The head. 1864–. V. NABOKOV Think how unpleasant it is to have your chump lopped off (1960). **2 off one's chump** mad, crazy. 1877–. A. WILSON The chap Beard seems to be off his chump. He's evacuated all the wallabies (1961).

chunder verb intr. Also **chunda**. Austral To be sick, vomit. 1950–. PRIVATE EYE Many's the time we've chundered in the same bucket (1970). [Prob. from rhyming slang *Chunder Loo* for 'spew', after a cartoon figure *Chunder Loo of Akin Foo* orig drawn by Norman Lindsay (1879–1969) and appearing in advertisements for Cobra boot polish in the Sydney *Bulletin* between 1909 and 1920.]

chuppie noun Also **chuppy** orig and mainly N Amer A Chinese yuppie. 1988–. GUARDIAN A backlash has built up in Vancouver . . . against the 'Chuppies' (Chinese urban professionals) in the long established community (1989). [From *Ch(inese)* + YUPPIE noun.]

churning noun orig US The practice or result of buying and selling a client's investments, etc. simply to generate additional profit for the broker. 1953–. BOND BUYER The churning of corporate bank accounts on or near tax dates typically pushes the funds rate higher (1983).

chutty noun Also **chuddy**. Austral and NZ Chewing gum. 1941–. N. HILLIARD 'Better have some chuddy,' said Tom (1960). [Origin unknown.]

chutzpah /ˈxʊtspə/ noun Also **chutzpa, chutzbah**. Brazen impudence, shameless audacity, cheek. 1892–. O. HESKY The sheer *chutzpa*—the impudence—of defecting . . . right in front of his own eyes (1967). [Yiddish.]

cig noun Abbreviation of 'cigarette' and 'cigar'. a.1889–. J. FRASER Greens on the slate, never beer. Never cigs, either (1969).

cigarette roll noun US A parachute jump in which the parachute fails to open. 1962–.

cigger noun Austral A cigarette. 1922–. R. HALL Last night as we enjoyed a quiet cigger, The stars reflecting open life outback (1973).

chubby-chaser chuck chuddies chuff chugalug

ciggy noun A cigarette. 1962–. SCOTTISH DAILY MAIL What had been 'fags' became 'ciggies' because The Beatles always talked of ciggies (1968). [From *cig(arette* + *-y*.]

Circus noun The British Secret Service. 1963–. J. LE CARRÉ In your day the Circus ran itself by regions . . . Control sat in heaven and held the strings (1974). [From its address at Cambridge Circus, London.]

cits noun US services', dated Civilian clothes. 1829–1930. CHICAGO TRIBUNE They were in full dress uniform. Later they were joined by Maj. Judson of the engineers in 'cits' (1907). [From *cit* civilian (shortening of *citizen*).]

city noun US Used as a suffix or final element designating a person, situation, etc., as described by the preceding noun or adjective. 1960–. ROLLING STONE When I learned I could do that just by being honest, whole vistas of trouble opened up. I get on a talk show. I get talking and *whoa*! Trouble city! (1979). [Cf. -VILLE.]

civvies noun pl. services' Civilian clothes. 1889–. DAILY TELEGRAPH Young men exchange their uniforms for 'civvies' (1946). [From *civ(ilian* + pl. of *-y*.]

civvy adjective services' Civilian, non-military. 1915–. DAILY EXPRESS Civvy cigarettes are dearer now (1945). [From *civ(ilian* + *-y*.]

Civvy Street noun services' Civilian life. 1943–. J. BRAINE Dick was in splendid shape, sampling every delight Civvy Street had to offer (1959).

Claire Rayners noun Brit Trainers (i.e. training shoes). 1997–. [Rhyming slang; from the name of the British journalist and agony aunt *Claire Rayner* (b. 1931).]

clam verb intr. mainly US To shut *up*; be silent. Also **to clam up on,** to refuse to talk to (someone). 1916–. J. M. KAYE I didn't mean to pry, but there's no need . . . to clam up on me (1959). [From the notion of the clam taciturnly but firmly closing its shell.]

clam noun US An American dollar. 1886–. WASHINGTON POST You get your privacy, mostly, and you're out just a few hundred clams (2002). [Origin uncertain.]

clanger noun A mistake, esp. one that attracts attention; phr. *to drop a clanger*, to make such a mistake. 1948–. NEW STATESMAN Mr Macmillan is the kind of Premier who enjoys covering up for any Cabinet colleague that drops a clanger (1958); DAILY MAIL I have boobed dreadfully, old boy. Apparently a carnation with

gongs is a terrible clanger (1959). [From *clang* verb + *-er*.]

clap noun Venereal disease, esp. gonorrhoea. 1587–. A. DIMENT Rocky Kilmarry is about as good for you as a dose of clap (1967). [Old French *clapoir* venereal bubo.]

clapped out adjective Brit Worn out (esp. of machinery, etc.); exhausted. 1946–. DAILY EXPRESS The clapped-out car handed in for replacement (1960). [From *clap* verb, to hit + *-ed*.]

clappers noun **like the clappers** Brit Very fast or hard. 1948–. J. BRAINE I've got to work like the clappers this morning (1959). [From *clapper* noun, tongue of a bell.]

clean verb **1 to clean out** to deprive of money. 1812–. BIG COMIC FORTNIGHTLY Oh no! There's been a bank raid! I've been cleaned out! (1989). **2 to clean up** mainly US **a** trans. To acquire as gain or profit. 1831–. 20TH CENTURY A concerted drive to ensure that this 25-year-old veteran cleans up another £16 million (1960). **b** intr. To make a large profit. 1929–. J. STEINBECK It's the fastest-selling novelty I've ever handled. Little Wonder is cleaning up with it (1947). adjective **3** Free from suspicion of criminal or treacherous intent or involvement; not carrying incriminating material, such as drugs or weapons. 1926–. M. PUZO They'll frisk me when I meet them so I'll have to be clean then, but figure out a way you can get a weapon to me (1969). **4** Free from or cured of addiction to drugs. 1953–. TIMES Only one-tenth of heroin addicts are ever completely 'clean again' (1970).

cleaners noun **to take (someone) to the cleaners: a** To take away all or most of someone's money, esp. by fraud. 1949–. GUARDIAN Many a gilded youth . . . has been 'taken to the cleaners' once too often at midnight parties (1961). **b** To criticize someone strongly. 1963–. LISTENER I hoped Mr Carr might round on Mr Cousins and start taking the apprenticeship system to the cleaners (1963).

clean-skin noun orig Austral A person with a clean police record. 1907–. SUN-HERALD (Sydney): Cameron's death was . . . ordered because the drug gang had no further use for the former 'clean skin' they had recruited and it was feared he would give evidence against them (1984). [From earlier sense, unbranded animal.]

clean-up noun orig US A profit; an exceptional financial success; also, a robbery or its proceeds. 1878–. K. TENNANT He was now a hundred pounds in debt; but that, for Alec, was

ciggy Circus cits city civvies civvy Civvy Street

practically no debt at all; one good clean-up, and he would be clear (1946).

clever Dick noun mainly ironical One who is or purports to be smart or knowing. Also **clever-boots, clever-clogs, clever-sticks.** 1847–. I. & P. OPIE There is bound to be some clever-dick who has hidden in a coal-hole and refuses to show himself (1969); LISTENER On each double-spread billing page it is three columns to the populars and eight for the clever-clogs (1983).

click verb intr. To become clear or understandable; to fall into place. 1939–. A. BURGESS Then the name clicked, because somebody in the town had talked about Everett (1960).

click noun variant of KLICK noun.

clickety click noun Brit Sixty-six; used mainly in the game of bingo and its forerunners. 1919–. DAILY TELEGRAPH Clickety click, 66; Gates of Heaven, No. 7 (1962). [Rhyming slang.]

cliner noun Also **clinah** Austral dated A girlfriend or female lover. 1895–1947. A. W. UPFIELD I 'elped to get 'is clinah out of quod for what she and 'im did for me (1928). [Prob. from German *kleine* little.]

clink[1] noun Prison. 1836–. K. TENNANT They'll only dock my pay or shove me in clink (1946). [From the name of a former prison in Southwark, London.]

clink[2] noun US mainly baseball A mistake or error. Cf. CLINKER noun 2. 1968–. WASHINGTON NEWS Ed Brinkman, the shortstop, merely yelled, 'clink' (1968). [Transferred use of *clink* noun, sharp ringing sound.]

clinker noun 1 Brit Something or someone excellent or outstanding. 1836–. W. HOLTBY By God she could ride. A clinker across country (1936). 2 orig and mainly US A mistake or error (esp. in Baseball), a failure; spec. a film, song, etc. with little or nothing to commend it. Cf. CLANGER noun. 1934–. VIDEO WORLD There are countless Grade Z horror clinkers that provide unintentional amusement because of the ineptitude with which they are made (1986). [From *clink* verb + *-er*.]

clip verb trans. orig US To swindle; to rob, steal. 1927–. H. WAUGH I'm not holding still like some people while their buddy-buddy pals clip them for nine thousand bucks (1968).

clip-joint noun orig US A bar, club, etc. charging exorbitant prices. 1933–. DAILY TELEGRAPH The 'clip joints' specialise in luring customers inside, by means of attractive showcards and insistent 'hostesses', and then fleecing them (1964).

clippie noun Also **clippy.** Brit A bus-conductress. 1941–. G. USHER An ex-clippie on a local bus (1959). [From *clip* verb (referring to the clipping of tickets) + *-ie, -y.*]

clit noun Abbreviation of 'clitoris'. 1958–. GAY TIMES Now available . . . Set of 4 clit stimulators (1990).

clitty noun A clitoris. 1873–. [From *clit(oris* noun + *-y.*]

clobber noun Brit 1 Clothes. 1879–. OBSERVER To pay for the kiddies' clobber (1959). 2 Equipment; gear; rubbish. 1890–. LANCET Every cellar stockroom . . . is packed tight with fantastic collections of clobber and junk (1965). [Origin unknown.]

clobber verb trans. 1 To defeat heavily. 1949–. BACK STREET HEROES The Welsh revenge is the way they clobber us in rugby (1987). 2 To hit repeatedly; beat up. 1951–. O. MILLS He must have seen me clobber Leeming when he dived for the brief-case (1959). 3 To reprimand or criticize severely. 1956–. WALLIS & BLAIR The Press sure clobbered Roger Law . . . Don't know why I got off so easy (1956). 4 To deal severely or oppressively with. 1969–. DAILY TELEGRAPH Butlin's is heavily clobbered by the increase in Selective Employment Tax (1969). [Origin unknown.]

clock noun 1 Brit The face. 1923–. J. I. M. STEWART His clock was still the affable Brigadier's, but you felt now that if you passed a sponge over it there'd be something quite different underneath (1961). 2 A punch (on the face). 1959–. J. MACLAREN-ROSS It was my turn to administer the anaesthetic—by a final clock in the jaw (1961). verb trans. 3 To punch in the face; to hit. 1941–. P. H. JOHNSON I should have clocked Dorothy, as the saying goes, more times than I care to count (1959). 4 orig US To watch or observe; to look at, notice. 1942–. SUNDAY EXPRESS MAGAZINE Our waiter . . . was so busy clocking him that he spilt a bottle of precious appleade over the table cloth (1986).

clod noun 1 A thick-headed or doltish person. 1605–. 2 A copper coin; usu. in pl. 1925–. A. BURGESS He began to search for coppers. 'Lend us a couple of clods,' he said to his twin (1960). [From earlier sense, lump; cf. CLOT noun, of which *clod* is a variant.]

clodhopper noun 1 A boorish or clumsy person. 1824–. CUMMINGS & VOLKMAN The drive for success . . . would turn a son, especially, into a *cafone* (clodhopper, fool) (1990). 2 A large heavy shoe; usu. in pl. 1836–. TIMES These high-technology developments are far removed from the customised clodhoppers which are the ancestors of today's lightweight sports shoes (1991). [From earlier sense, one who walks over ploughed land, a ploughman or other agricultural worker.]

clodpoll noun Also **clodpole**. A fool. 1601–. TIMES LITERARY SUPPLEMENT The former editor of the *Far Eastern Economic Review* is worried . . . that his book will fall into the hands of clodpoles (1986). [From CLOD noun + *poll* noun, head.]

clogger noun Brit A soccer player who tackles heavily, usu. fouling his opponent. 1970–.

clonk verb trans. To hit. 1949–. SPECTATOR I have never been able to pick up a hammer without clonking myself one (1960). [From earlier sense, to make the sound of a hard blow.]

closet noun **to come out of the closet** to admit something openly, esp. one's homosexuality. 1963–. LITERARY REVIEW Old Cheever, crowding seventy, has gone Gay. Old Cheever has come out of the closet (1985).

closet queen noun A secret male homosexual. 1967–. MAIL ON SUNDAY His colleagues' retort is that Jimmy is a closet queen because he doesn't live with a woman (1984).

clot noun Brit A fool. 1942–. P. MORTIMER Jolly bad luck, what a clot she is (1958). [From earlier sense, lump.]

cloth-ears noun (A person with) a poor sense of hearing. 1912–. NEW STATESMAN I've told you once, cloth-ears (1965). Hence **cloth-eared**, adjective 1965–.

clout noun orig US Power of effective action, esp. in politics or business; influence, weight. 1958–. INK France and other countries have large agricultural surpluses and farmers with electoral 'clout' (1971). [From earlier sense, heavy blow.]

club noun **in the (pudding) club** pregnant. 1936–. J. N. SMITH When the doctor told me I was in the club I told him he was daft—that I'd never—well, you know (1969).

cluck noun US A fool; esp. in phr. *dumb cluck*. 1904–. S. RANSOME Showing ourselves up as a fine pair of clucks (1950). [From earlier sense, sound made by a hen.]

clunk variant of KLUNK noun.

clusterfuck noun mainly US **1** A sexual orgy. 1965–. **2** orig military (in the Vietnam war) A botched undertaking, esp. a disorganized or chaotic military operation. 1969–.

cob noun Brit **to have** (or **get**) **a cob on** to be annoyed, to get angry. 1937–. R. GORDON 'Don't you blokes go without me,' he added threateningly. 'I'll get a cob on if you don't wait' (1953). [Origin unknown.]

cobber Austral and NZ noun **1** A companion, a mate, a friend. 1893–. M. SHADBOLT Jack was my cobber in the timber mill (1959). verb intr. **2 to cobber up** to make friends with. 1918–. B. PEARSON It's natural for a young chap to cobber up with chaps his own age (1963). [Perh. from Brit dialect *cob* verb, to take a liking to.]

cobblers noun pl. Brit **1** Testicles. 1936–. J. CURTIS Well, they got us by the cobblers (1936). **2** Nonsense, rubbish. 1955–. MELODY MAKER Geno Washington says Grapefruit's recent attack on the Maryland Club, Glasgow, was 'a load of cobblers' (1968). [Short for *cobbler's* (or *cobblers'*) *awls*, rhyming slang for 'balls'.]

cock noun **1** The penis. 1618–. LANDFALL 'She had her hand on his cock.' 'There's no need to be crude' (1969). **2** Brit Used as a form of address to a man. 1837–. G. MELLY Smarten yourself up a bit, cock, before we go on! (1965). **3** An unfounded statement, nonsense. 1937–. N. SHUTE I've never heard such cock in all my life (1948). verb trans. **4 to cock** (something) **up** to make a mess of (something), bungle. 1948–. G. SWIFT I'm sorry I messed up your classes, sir. I'm sorry I cocked things up for you (1983). Hence **cock-up,** noun A muddle, mess-up. 1948–. J. PORTER George turned the local boys in it and you've never seen such a cock-up in your life! (1964). [In sense 3, from earlier sense, fictitious narrative, short for *cock-and-bull story*.]

cockamamie /ˈkɒkəˌmeɪmɪ/ adjective Also **cockamamy, -manie, -many.** US Ridiculous, incredible. 1960–. E. MCBAIN You marched into the precinct with a tight dress and a cockamamie bunch of alibis (1962). [From earlier *cockamamie* noun, decal, transfer, alteration of *decalcomania* noun, transfer or the printing of transfers.]

cockatoo noun **1** Austral and NZ A small farmer. 1845–. O. DUFF The most they [i.e. sheep-farmers] can hope for is an uneasy truce with dairymen . . . or an alliance with Labour to control the 'cockatoos' (1941). **2** Austral A lookout or sentinel acting on behalf of people engaged on some illegal activity. 1934–. TELEGRAPH (Brisbane): They watched Foster (the 'cockatoo' or spy) point out our punters who had laid a large bet (1966). [From earlier

clodpoll clogger clonk closet closet queen clot club

cocker

sense, a convict serving a sentence in Cockatoo Island on Sydney Harbour.]

cocker noun Brit = COCK noun 2. 1888–. A. WESKER It was good of you to help us cocker (1960).

cock-eye Bob noun Also **cock-eyed Bob.** Austral A cyclone or thunderstorm. 1894–.

cock-eyed adjective orig US Drunk. 1926–. E. LINKLATER You wouldn't have have asked me to marry you if you hadn't been cock-eyed at the time (1934). [From earlier sense, squint-eyed.]

cockrag noun Austral A loincloth, esp. as worn by an aboriginal. 1964–. NGABIDJ & SHAW Wallambain threw away his woomera and cock rag and jumped in (1981). [From COCK noun 1 + rag.]

cocksman noun orig and mainly US A man who is promiscuous, esp. one considered to be exceptionally virile or sexually skilled. a.1896–. J. DOS PASSOS Research proves R.L. S. to have been a great cocksman (1932).

cock-stand noun An erection of the penis. 1867–. A. WILSON Marcus . . . found, as his eyes took in the young man's flirtatious glance, that he was beginning a cock-stand (1967).

cocksucker noun Someone who performs fellatio; often used as a term of abuse. 1891–. J. BALDWIN If it wasn't for the spooks couldn't a damn one of you white cock suckers *ever* get laid (1962). So **cock-sucking,** adjective 1923–.

cock-teaser noun derog A sexually provocative woman who evades or refuses intercourse. 1891–. Hence **cock-tease,** verb trans. 1957–; **cock-teasing,** adjective 1968–. T. E. B. CLARKE The sixth commandment hadn't been broken in his manor since a Polish farm labourer strangled a cock-teasing Sunday hiker (1968). Cf. PRICK-TEASER noun.

cocky noun Austral and NZ = COCKATOO noun 1 1871–. B. CRUMP The cocky had a sheep-run in the foothills of the Coromandel Ranges (1960).

cocoa verb intr. Also **coco.** Brit **I should cocoa** mainly ironic Rhyming slang for 'I should say so'. 1936–. O. NORTON What me? . . . I should coco. Sheila'd think I was off my head (1967). [Prob. fanciful use of *cocoa* noun, chocolate drink.]

coconut noun Also **coconut head** derog A black person who seeks to integrate with whites. 1988–. DAILY TELEGRAPH Mrs Boateng, former member of Lambeth council's social services committee, has been banned from Brent's Black Section for two years after being branded a 'coconut' (1988). [From the notion of the coconut's brown exterior and white interior.]

cod noun Also **cod's, cods.** Brit Abbreviation of CODSWALLOP noun. 1963–. M. TRIPP If you think its all a load of cod's why the hell waste a pound? (1970).

codger noun An old man, esp. one with strange habits; usu. in phr. *old codger.* 1756–. WINDSOR MAGAZINE A certain sedate and Britishly respectable old codger (1904). [Perh. a variant of *cadger* sponger.]

codswallop noun Brit Nonsense. 1963–. A. PRIOR All that stuff about mutual respect between police and criminal was a load of old codswallop (1966). [Origin unknown, despite popular theories of a Mr Cod and his beer.]

coconut a black person who seeks to integrate with whites

coffin-nail noun orig US A cigarette. 1888–. P. G. WODEHOUSE Most of these birds [i.e. invalids in a sanatorium] would give their soul for a coffin-nail (1928). [From the fatal effects of cigarette-smoking, perh. reinforced by the vaguely nail-like shape of cigarettes.]

coit noun Austral = QUOIT noun.

cojones /kəˈhəʊneɪs/ noun **1** Courage, guts. 1932–. GUARDIAN You have the cojones to ask me if I still got confidence in Britain? (1966). **2** The testicles. 1966–. [From Spanish, pl. of *cojón* testicle.]

coke orig US. noun **1** Abbreviation of 'cocaine'. 1908–. P. CAPON He started introducing her to drugs. . . . Reefers at first, and then . . . coke (1959). verb trans. **2** To drug (oneself) with cocaine; often with *up*. 1924–. N. BLAKE They let him coke himself up for the occasion (1954). Hence **cokey,** noun Also **cokie.** A cocaine addict. 1922–.

coldie noun Austral A glass, bottle, or can of cold beer. 1953–. OVERLAND Bet they're both downin' a few coldies (1976). [From *cold* + *-ie*.]

cold turkey noun orig US The sudden, complete, giving up of an addictive drug, esp. as a method of withdrawal. 1921–. K. ORVIS

cocker cock-eye Bob cock-eyed cockrag cocksman

I made one cold-turkey cure and it nearly killed me (1962). [From the notion of the simple abruptness of the withdrawal, with reference to a simple dish of cold turkey, without garnish.]

collar noun Criminals' and Police orig US An arrest. 1893–. NEW YORK REVIEW OF BOOKS The only guys that want to make a collar today are the guys who are looking for the overtime (1977). See also *to feel someone's collar* at FEEL verb.

combo /ˈkɒmbəʊ/ noun **1** Austral A white man who lives with an Aboriginal woman. Also **comboman**. 1896–. **2** US Combination, partnership. 1929–. AMERICAN SPEECH A woman in a supermarket was heard to exclaim enthusiastically, 'Me and Tide—some combo!' (1963). **3** orig US A small instrumental band, esp. playing jazz. 1935–. NEW YORK TIMES The Conspiracy is a chatty three-guitar combo that sings songs and makes jokes (1970). [From *comb(ination* + *-o*.]

come verb **1** intr. To have an orgasm. Also with *off*. *a*.1650–. D. H. LAWRENCE And when I'd come and really finished, then she'd start on her own account (1928). **2a** trans. To play the part of; behave like. 1837–. C. WATSON I never thought he'd come the old green-eyed monster (1962). **b: to come it over** or **with** (someone): to try and get the better of, esp. by trickery. 1827–. A. HUXLEY When he saw . . . that no attempt was being made to come it over him, he had begun to take an interest (1939). **3 come again?** orig US What did you say? 1884–. A. GILBERT Nurse Alexander startled them all by saying suddenly, 'No scones.' Crook turned. 'Come again, sugar?' (1956). **4 to come off it** usu. imper as an expression of disbelief or refusal to accept another's opinion, behaviour, etc. 1912–. LISTENER On which side was the preponderance of wealth, as of men and armaments? Do come off it, Mr. Mansfield (1969). **5 to come over** to suffer the onset of the stated symptoms. 1922–. N. F. SIMPSON There was nothing wrong with him . . . and then next day he came over funny at work (1960). noun **6** Ejaculated semen. 1923–. MISS LONDON His attitude to sex is ambivalent. 'Each night I had to clean the come off the back seat of the cab,' he remarks in reasonable disgust (1976).

come-on noun An enticement, inducement. 1902–. M. DICKENS They like the sound of foreign investments. It has that magic, millionaire ring to it, like foreign exchange. Just another come-on (1958).

Commie noun often derog Abbreviation of 'Communist'. 1940–. M. SPARK After all, one

might speak in that manner of the Wogs or the Commies (1965). Cf. COMMO noun.

Commo noun Austral and NZ, often derog Abbreviation of 'Communist'. 1941–. J. CLEARY I've been reading how the Commos have eliminated all the flies in China (1959).

common noun Short for 'common sense'. 1906–. H. PINTER You mutt. . . . Have a bit of common. They got departments for everything (1960).

Company noun US The Central Intelligence Agency; with *the*. 1967–. LISTENER Americans working (presumably) for 'the Company' . . . are privately scathing about the failure of positive vetters (1982).

compo noun Austral and NZ Compensation, esp. as paid for an injury received while working. 1941–. P. WHITE You got a bad hand. You see the doc. . . . You'll get compo of course (1961). [From *comp(ensation* + *-o*.]

con noun criminals' Abbreviation of 'convict' and 'conviction'. 1893–. F. NORMAN I had three really good friends among the cons (1958).

con verb trans. orig US **1** To deceive, dupe. 1892–. LISTENER This mild tale of a shy boy conned into giving a girl a fortune (1962). noun orig US **2** A confidence trickster. 1897–. **3** A swindle, fraud. 1901–. LISTENER The intellectual theoreticians of visual pop culture have succeeded . . . in pulling a con (1967). [Short for *confidence* (as in *confidence trick*).]

con artist noun orig US A confidence trickster. 1937–. Also **con merchant**. 1963–. SUNDAY TELEGRAPH Among the hundreds of thousands passing by each day are customers for prostitutes and drug dealers, mugs for con artists—an old, old New York tradition—and victims for street robbers (1991).

conchy /ˈkɒntʃɪ/ noun Also **conchie, conshy**. often derog Abbreviation of 'conscientious objector'. 1917–. LANDFALL The deal that is going on here is worse than the one the Conchies got (1951).

conk noun **1** The nose. 1812–. TIRESIAS We soon become familiar with the regulars: . . . the keen young one whose hat is too big; the lugubrious one with the Cyrano de Bergerac conk (1984). **2** The head. So **off one's conk**, off one's head, crazy. 1870–. H. PINTER Why are you getting on everybody's wick? Why are you driving that old lady off her conk? (1959). [Perh. a fig. application of *conch* type of shell.]

collar combo come come-on Commie Commo con

conk¹ verb intr. Formerly also **konk**. To break down, fail; to die, collapse, or lose consciousness; mainly with *out*. 1917–. M. HERZOG I told Lionel that rather than conk out next day on the slope, it seemed far better for me to go down (1952). [Origin unknown.]

conk² verb trans. Also **konk**. orig US, African-American To straighten (curly hair). 1944–. NEW YORKER He conked his hair to a sleek russet straightness (1992). [From *congolene*, the name of a chemical application for straightening hair.]

connect verb intr. US To meet someone in order to obtain drugs. 1938–. K. ORVIS If you're connecting from Frankie, he should have told you (1962).

connection noun Also **connexion**. orig US A supplier of narcotics; the action of supplying narcotics. 1934–. J. KEROUAC A couple of Negro characters whispered in my ear about tea. . . . The connection came in and motioned me to the cellar toilet (1957).

contract noun orig US An arrangement to kill someone, usu. for a fee; often in phr. *to put a contract (out) on* (someone), to arrange for (someone) to be killed by a hired assassin. 1940–. MACLEAN'S MAGAZINE Some policemen believe that a West End mobster named 'Lucky' has put a contract out for Savard (1976).

coo int An exclamation expressing surprise or incredulity. Also **coo-er**. 1911–. TIMES Coo, is that really the time! (1963).

cooee noun Also **cooey**. **within (a) cooee (of)** Austral and NZ Within hailing distance; within easy reach, near (to). 1836–. WEEKLY NEWS (Auckland): But nothing that Roux has achieved on this tour came within coo-ee of the effort of Gainsford (1965). [From Aboriginal (Dharuk) *guwi* a call used to communicate over distance.]

cook verb **1 to cook with gas** (or **electricity, radar**) orig US To succeed, to do very well; to act or think correctly. 1941–. K. ORVIS These Mounties cook with gas. With gas, brother—they're murder (1962). **2 what's cooking?** orig US What is happening or being prepared? 1942–. A. GILBERT What's cooking?. . . . Are you going to uncover the villain? (1956). **3** intr. orig US To play music with excitement, inspiration, etc. 1943–. CRESCENDO The band used to get up on the bandstand and *really* cook (1968).

cookie noun orig US **1** A woman; esp an attractive girl. 1920–. R. LONGRIGG I met a cookie I know. . . . She said you'd said *Faustus* was like

Oklahoma (1959). **2** A man; often with defining adjective. 1928–. W. R. BURNETT He's a real tough cookie and you know it (1953). **3 (that's) how** (or **the way**) **the cookie crumbles** (that is) how things turn out; the unalterable state of affairs. 1957–. P. G. WODEHOUSE Oh well, that's the way the cookie crumbles. You can't win 'em all (1961).

cookie-duster noun US jocular A moustache. 1934–.

cookie-pusher noun US A counter attendant; fig. a man leading a futile social life; spec a diplomat devoting more attention to protocol or social engagements than to his work. 1942–. ECONOMIST The popular image of the cookie-pusher in Foggy Bottom [i.e. the US State Department] (1962).

cool verb trans. **1** US To kill. 1930–. J. MORRIS He wasn't killed in any private fight. . . . He was cooled by a Chinese agent (1969). **2 to cool it** orig US To relax, calm down, take it easy. 1953–. CRESCENDO Cool it will you? I said once a *week*, there's no need to go stark raving mad (1968). adjective **3** orig US **a** orig jazz and bebop Restrained, relaxed, unemotional; hence excellent, marvellous; fashionable. 1947–. OBSERVER They got long, sloppy haircuts and wide knot ties and no-press suits with fat lapels. Very cool (1959). **b** All right, OK; satisfactory, acceptable, unproblematic; also, unconcerned *about* or content *with* something. 1952–. A. THOMAS I am 'laying another trip' on him but that's cool, he can deal with it (1984). KEO.CO.UK Blacks cool about centre quandary [headline]. The All Blacks are not concerned by the fact that they haven't settled on a centre combination (2007). WORLDTRIBUNE.COM Poll finds most of world is cool with China catching up with U.S. [headline] A new public opinion poll shows a majority of the American people do not see a danger in China's economic and military buildup (2007). noun **4** US A truce between gangs. 1958–. H. SALISBURY A 'cool' was negotiated by street club workers. But it was an uneasy truce, often broken (1959). **5** Composure, relaxedness. 1966–. LISTENER Professor Marcus keeps his cool when sex is being discussed; all the four-letter words are used without blanching (1967). Cf. SUPERCOOL adjective.

cooler noun orig US A prison or prison cell. 1884–. C. DICKSON I am not at a time of life when one enjoys being chucked in the cooler for telling truths (1943).

coon noun derog and offensive A black person. 1862–. OZ You might . . . deplore the way that the publicity was angled—poor old coon, he'll thank us in the end (1969). [Abbreviation of *racoon*.]

cootie noun A body louse. 1917–.
R. BUCKMINSTER FULLER The Publicitor's cheap brand of lacquer Only stuck to some cooties and fleas (1962). [Perh. from Malay *kutu* biting parasitic insect.]

cop verb trans. **1** To capture, arrest. 1704–.
2a To receive, suffer (something bad). 1884–.
A. CHRISTIE Yes, it looked bad, it did. Looked as though he might have copped one (1941). **b: to cop it** to get into trouble; to be punished; also, to die. 1909–. BLACKWOOD'S MAGAZINE Half of the beggars had copped it for good and all (1927).
3 to cop a feel to fondle someone in a sexual manner, esp. furtively. 1935– INDEPENDENT Pretending to be a dear old boy, he gets close enough to the court ladies to cop a feel (2001).
4 to cop out to withdraw; to give up an attempt; also, to go back on a promise.
1961–. NEW STATESMAN But Peacock and Co. . . . could not cop out at that early stage and announce that advertising on the BBC would be a bad thing (1986). noun **5 to cop off** Brit to succeed in striking up an amorous or sexual relationship; to have sex; often followed by *with*. 1986–. GUARDIAN Harry Potter kissing a girl? Harry Potter getting some osculatory action? Harry Potter . . . copping off? (2007). noun **6** A policeman, a 'copper'. 1859–.
L. DEIGHTON A police car with two cops in it cruised past very slowly (1983). **7** Brit A capture or arrest. 1886–. J. GUTHRIE The young man . . . glared round as if for some means of escape. . . . 'It's a fair cop!' said the young man (1935). **8 not much** (or **no**) **cop** Brit Of little or no value or use. 1902–. K. GILES The house . . . has never been much cop. People don't like living opposite a church or a graveyard (1970). [Perh. from obs. *cap* verb, to arrest, from Old French *caper* seize, from Latin *capere*; in sense 6, perh. short for COPPER noun.]

copacetic /kəʊpəˈsɛtɪk, -siːtɪk/ adjective Also **copasetic**. US Fine, excellent. 1919–. DOWN BEAT We hear two city cops chatting. 'Well, everything seems copasetic,' says one. 'Yeah, we might as well move on,' the other agrees (1969). [Origin unknown.]

cop-out noun A cowardly or feeble evasion. 1967–. WIN Isn't it a cop-out to secede from New York State but remain a part of the nation? (1969). [From *to cop out* (see COP verb 3).]

copper noun Brit A policeman. 1846–.
J. WAINWRIGHT And yet he was still Lennox; the man-hunter; the thief-taker; one of that very rare breed of men who are born coppers (1980). [Prob. from COP verb + *-er*.]

cop-shop noun A police station. 1941–.
M. DUFFY The blue light above the cop-shop door for once meant safety (1962).

cor int Brit Expressing surprise, alarm, exasperation, etc.; often in phr. *cor blimey*. 1931–. SIMPSON & GALTON Oh cor blimey, I don't understand you people! (1961). [Alteration of *god*.]

corker noun **1** An excellent or astonishing person or thing. 1882–. R. D. ABRAHAMS My girl's a corker (1969). **2** NZ Used attrib or as adjective Splendid, stunning. 1937–. D. W. BALLANTYNE The kids told Syd what a corker sixer it had been (1948). [From earlier sense, something that closes a discussion, from the notion of 'putting a cork in it'.]

corking adjective Strikingly large or splendid. 1895–. LADIES' HOME JOURNAL He . . . engaged me, at a corking fee, to come up and take this case (1926).

cornball noun orig US An unsophisticated person, (as if) from the country; a bumpkin. 1952–. MOVIE An expatriate cornball like Jerry Court (1962). [From earlier sense, sweet made of popped corn.]

corned adjective dated Drunk. 1785–1931. [From the use of grain in making beer and spirits.]

corned Willie noun US = CANNED WILLIE noun.

corn-fed adjective orig jazz Banal, provincial, commercial. 1929–. ARCHITECTURAL REVIEW Either way this is a rather negative formulation . . . useful to the critic defending Bauhaus to a cornfed audience of Ruskinians (1954). [Punningly from earlier sense 'fed on corn (i.e. maize)' and *corn* something hackneyed or banal.]

cornstalk noun Austral dated A native-born, non-Aboriginal Australian; hence, more specifically, someone from New South Wales. 1827–. S. HART 'Never say that to anyone in New South Wales, or you'll be laid out flat as a pancake!' he warned me . . . Couldn't the Cornstalks take a joke? (1957)

corp noun A corporal; often as a term of address. 1909–. F. D. SHARPE 'We are going to Hendon, aren't we, corp?' the corporal replied: 'Yes.' (1938).

cootie cop copacetic cop-out copper cop-shop cor

corpse verb trans. and intr. actors' To (cause to) laugh inadvertently on stage or to forget one's lines. 1873–. A. BENNETT *Mrs Brodribb*: When Max—. *Geoff*: Max (*He corpses*) (1972).

corpse-reviver noun A mixed drink, esp. one intended as a hangover cure. 1871–.

cosh noun **under the cosh** at one's mercy, helpless. 1958–. OBSERVER As for the Criminal Justice Act, it could be very useful to have all the villains under the cosh, as they expressed it. It made it much easier to get information (1960).

cossie /ˈkɒzɪ/ noun Also **cozzie**. Austral A swimsuit or pair of swimming trunks. 1926–. TIMES A girl in a cozzie with a dead animal draped over her shoulders is a powerful image (1981). [Diminutive of *costume*.]

Costa del Crime noun Brit, jocular The south-east coast of Spain, as used by several British criminals as a bolt-hole to escape British justice. 1984–. [*Costa* from Spanish, coast, with reference to the names of various holiday coastlines in Spain, e.g. *Costa Brava*.]

Costa Geriatrica /dʒɛrɪˈætrɪkə/ noun Brit, jocular A coastal area with a large residential population of old and retired people, esp. the south coast of England. 1977–. [After *Costa Brava*, etc., from Spanish *costa* coast + mock-Latin *geriatrica* of or for the elderly.]

cottage noun A public lavatory or urinal, as used by male homosexuals for assignations. 1966–. GUARDIAN Wakefield's answer to Danny La Rue trips out of a little hutch at the side of the stage labelled 'Ye Olde Camp Cottage' (1968).

cotton-picking adjective orig Southern US Used as term of disapproval or abuse. 1958–. J. PHILIPS You have to be a hero or out of your cotton-picking mind (1968).

couch potato noun derog, orig US Someone who spends leisure time as passively as possible (esp. watching TV or videos), eats junk food, and takes little or no exercise. 1979–. NEW MUSICAL EXPRESS [She] gave up opportunities in the world of modelling and in Tinseltown LA in order to stop her kids becoming couch potato video generation trash brains (1987). [From the notion of reclining like a vegetable on a *couch*; the use of *potato* apparently derives from the original Couch Potato club, founded by cartoonist Robert Armstrong, who represented the typical *boob-tuber* (see BOOB TUBE noun 1) as a vegetable 'tuber', the potato. The expression is said to have been coined by Tom Iacino.]

cough verb **1 to cough up** to hand (something) over; esp to pay up (money). 1894–. G. MOORE Now, then, old girl, cough up! I must have a few halfpence (1920). **2** intr. orig US To confess; to give information. 1901–. W. J. BURLEY Once he realized we had it on him he was ready to cough fast enough (1970).

counter-jumper noun dated, derog A shop assistant or shopkeeper. 1829–. J. BRAINE You'll not waste your time with bloody consumptive counter-jumpers! (1959). [From the notion of jumping over a counter to go from one part of the shop to another.]

cove noun now mainly Austral A fellow, chap. 1567–. ADVERTISER (Adelaide): You Aussie coves are just a bunch of drongoes (1969). [Origin unknown.]

cow noun **1** A woman, esp. a coarse or unpleasant one. 1696–. D. LESSING It's just that stupid cow her mother (1960). **2** Austral and NZ An unpleasant person, thing, situation, etc.; often used good-humouredly. 1864–. F. D. DAVISON Looking for work's a cow of a game! (1940).

cowabunga /kauəˈbʌŋgə/ int orig and mainly US An exclamation, orig of annoyance, but subsequently of exhilaration, delight, or satisfaction (esp. in surfing, as the surfer climbs or rides a wave). 1954–. TIME Shouting . . . 'cowabunga!' they climb a 12-ft. wall of water and 'take the drop' off its shoulder (1963). [Apparently coined by Eddie Kean, writer of the US television programme *The Howdy Doody Show* (1947–60); most recently adopted as a rallying-cry by the Teenage Mutant Ninja Turtles.]

cowboy noun derog **1** orig US A reckless or inconsiderate driver. 1942–. TRUCKIN' LIFE We have to weed out the cowboys. . . . We need the top professional drivers (1984). **2** An unscrupulous, incompetent, or reckless person in business, esp. an unqualified one. 1972–. PUNCH I started by ringing a few cowboys through the *Yellow Pages*, just to check on prices (1985). [From cowboys' reputation for boisterousness.]

cow-spanker noun Austral and NZ A dairy farmer or stockman. 1906–. WEEKLY NEWS (Auckland): The good old New Zealand cowspanker (1963).

cozzer noun Also **kozzer**. Brit A policeman. 1950–. GUARDIAN I grin at the picture of Frank opening the door . . . to a couple of kozzers asking him the name of the jibber who rang him on the day in question from the Cavendish Hotel

corpse corpse-reviver cosh cossie Costa del Crime

(1992). [Prob. a blend of COPPER noun and ROZZER noun.]

cozzpot noun Brit = COZZER noun. 1962–. J. ASHFORD The cozzpots ain't givin' me a chance (1969). [Perh. alteration of first syllable of COPPER noun + *pot* person of importance.]

crack noun **1** Anglo-Irish Enjoyment, fun; often in phr. *for the crack* for fun. *a*.1966–. SUNDAY TIMES They came to Lisdoonvarna only for 'the crack' . . . 'Crack' has several ingredients, of which two are merriment and mischief, but the word is really defiant of precise definition (1982). **2** orig US A potent hard crystalline form of cocaine broken into small pieces and inhaled or smoked. 1985–. US NEWS AND WORLD REPORT Crack . . . has rocketed from near obscurity to national villainy in the past six months (1986). [In sense 2, prob. from the cracking sound it makes when smoked or from the fact that it is cracked into small pieces.]

cracked adjective Crazy. 1692–. LISTENER I suppose all writers of children's classics have been cracked, or at least extremely weird (1968).

cracker noun **1** Brit = CRACKERJACK noun; spec. a (sexually) attractive person. 1914–. SHOOT! I've played in a few crackers in my time but it's hard to think of a more exciting tussle than the one we had at Anfield in 1985 (1988). **2** Austral and NZ The smallest imaginable amount of money; also, a pound (-note); mainly in negative contexts. 1934–. N. HILLIARD I've got nothing, Harry: not a cracker (1960).

cracker factory noun US A mental hospital. 1981–. [Cf. CRACKERS adjective.]

cracker jack Also **crackajack**. orig US. noun **1** Something or someone exceptionally fine, splendid, skilful, etc. 1895–. J. BUCHAN I've got a cracker jack of an editor (1933). adjective **2** Wonderful, splendid. 1910–. [A fanciful formation on *crack* verb or *cracker* noun.]

crackers adjective Brit Crazy. 1928–. DAILY TELEGRAPH Liberal Party is 'crackers', says Ld. Morrison of Lambeth (1959). [Cf. CRACKED adjective.]

crackhead noun orig US A person who habitually takes the drug crack. 1986–. OBSERVER Charlie and two fellow 'crackheads' took me to a vast housing estate in south London where crack is on sale for between £20 and £25 a deal (1988). [From CRACK noun + HEAD noun 3.]

crackling noun Women regarded as objects of sexual desire; **a bit of crackling**, an attractive woman. 1949–. P. DICKINSON 'You

know her?' 'I do, sir. Nice bit of crackling, she is' (1968). [From earlier sense, the crisp skin of roast pork.]

crackpot noun **1** An eccentric or impractical person. 1883–. J. CARY The public is used to grievance-mongers and despises 'em— they'll put him down for a crack-pot (1959). adjective **2** Crazy, unworkable. 1944–. G. JENKINS The High Command still thought it a crackpot idea (1959).

cracksman noun dated A housebreaker. 1812–. J. CONRAD 'Give it up—whatever it is,' he said in an admonishing tone, but not so kindly as if he were condescending to give good advice to a cracksman of repute (1907). [From obs. slang *crack* housebreaking + *man*.]

cradle-snatcher noun derog, orig US A person who has a sexual affair with a much younger person. 1925–. R. ERSKINE Crispin asked me to dance. 'Cradle-snatcher,' said Miranda nastily (1965). So **cradle-snatch,** verb 1938–.

crammer noun A school or similar institution that prepares pupils for exams by intensive study. 1931–. DAILY TELEGRAPH The spectre of January retakes at some smart London crammer (1986). [From *cram* verb, to prepare pupils in this way.]

cram-shop noun derog = CRAMMER noun. 1926–. J. CARY The young man . . . made Ella promise to play [the piano] with him every afternoon when he could escape from what he called his cram-shop (1946). [As CRAMMER noun.]

crank verb intr. To inject oneself with an illegal drug; often followed by *up*. 1971–. DAILY TELEGRAPH If . . . I continue to crank I will be dead within 18 months (1972).

crap verb **1** intr. To defecate. 1846–. A. BARON They'd crapped on the floor, in the same rooms they'd slept in (1953). **2** trans. US To talk nonsense to; to act or speak deceitfully to. 1930–. S. ELLIN I don't want you to crap me. . . . I want your honest opinion (1958). **3 to crap out** US To be unsuccessful, to lose; to fail; to withdraw from a game or other activity. 1933–. **4 to crap around** US To behave foolishly; to mess around. 1937–. S. KAUFFMANN Let's not crap around. Let's get to the business in hand (1952). noun **5** Excrement; defecation. 1898–. J. D. SALINGER There didn't look like there was anything in the park except dog crap (1951). **6** Rubbish, nonsense. 1898–. PUNCH And what a load of crap that was (1964). [Earlier noun senses 'chaff, refuse from fat-boiling'; ultimately from Dutch *krappe*. In sense 3,

cozzpot crack cracked cracker cracker factory crap

perh. from *crap(s)* a game of chance played with dice.]

crapper noun A lavatory. 1932–. c. HIMES Go to the crapper? What for? They weren't children, they didn't pee in bed (1969). [From CRAP verb + *-er*.]

crappy adjective orig US Rubbishy; inferior, worthless; disgusting. 1846–. WEEKLY GUARDIAN Rents as high as £52 a month 'for crappy quarters' (1970). [From CRAP noun + *-y*.]

crash verb 1 trans. orig US To enter without permission. 1922–. R. FULLER I hope you'll forgive me crashing your excellent party (1953). 2 intr. To sleep, esp. for a single night in an improvised bed; often with *out*. 1969–. GUARDIAN The homeless one was sure that someone would always offer him a place 'to crash' (1970).

crash pad noun A place to sleep, esp. for a single night or in an emergency. 1968–. GUARDIAN I have . . . lived 'underground', slept in 'crash pads' and taken my food on charity (1970).

crate noun orig services' An old aeroplane or other vehicle. 1928–. TIMES You must travel in an antiquated crate which goes puttering over Central Asia at about 90 miles an hour (1957).

crazy noun 1 orig US A mad or eccentric person. 1867–. GUARDIAN There's no leadership at all. All this is being done by the street crazies (1969). adjective 2 orig US jazz Excellent. 1953–. J. BALDWIN She laughed. 'Black Label [Scotch]?' 'Crazy' (1962). 3 **like crazy** orig US to the maximum extent. 1924–. PUNCH Here were all those guys consuming like crazy and having to be regularly restocked (1968). 4 **crazy like a fox** orig US Very cunning or shrewd. 1935–.

crazy house noun US A mental hospital. 1887–.

cream verb trans. orig US To beat or thrash; to defeat heavily, esp. in a sporting contest. 1929–. J. CARROLL Brady had pretended, for ambition's sake, to garner less power than Curley, and in the end Curley had creamed him (1978). [Perh. from the notion of 'creaming' butter and other foods by vigorous beating.]

crease verb 1 trans. mainly US **a** To tire out. 1909–. **b** To stun or kill. 1913–. D. WARNER Christ . . . you creased him. . . . It's a topping job (1962). 2 trans. and intr. To make or become

incapable through laughter; often with *up*. 1977–. TODAY On the set of Family Business he had the cast and crew creased up with laughter with his impersonations (1990). [In sense 1, from the notion of shooting a horse in the 'crest' or ridge of the neck.]

create verb intr. Brit To make a fuss or an angry scene. 1919–. M. HASTINGS What does he do but come aboard and start creating about the loss of time! (1959).

cred noun 1 Also **cred.** (with point). Financial credit. 1979–. **2000AD** Special talent for turning any object (cred card, drink cup) into lethal weapon in his hands (1990). 2 Credibility, reputation, or status amongst one's peers; = STREET CRED noun. 1981–. B. GELDOF 'Cred' was achieved by your rhetorical stance and no one had more credibility than the Clash (1986). [Abbreviation.]

creek noun **up the creek: a** In difficulties or trouble; spec. pregnant. 1941–. I. KEMP 'You okay?' asked Donovan. . . . 'I thought you were properly up the creek' (1969). **b** Crazy. 1960–.

creep noun orig US 1 An obnoxious or tiresome person. 1886–. PUNCH 'Maurice Thew School of Body-building'? That'll be that phoney creep upstairs (1966). 2 A stealthy robber; a sneak thief; esp. one who works in a brothel. 1914–. OBSERVER A creep is a highly expert thief. . . . He is so quiet that he can move about a house for hours without waking anybody (1960). 3 Stealthy robbery; petty thieving, esp. in a brothel. So **at** or **on the creep**, engaged in stealthy robbery. 1928–.

creepers noun pl. Shoes with soft soles. 1904–. E. BLISHEN Real up-to-the-minute yobo's thick-soled creepers (1955). Cf. BROTHEL-CREEPERS noun pl.

creep-house noun US A brothel or other place where prostitutes rob their clients. 1913–. Also **creep joint** 1921–. A. LOMAX Creep joints where they'd put the feelers on a guy's clothes (1950).

creeping Jesus noun An abject, sycophantic, or servile person; one who is hypocritically pious. *c*.1818–. R. CAMPBELL The Zulus naturally despise the creeping Jesus type who sucks up to them (1934).

crazy like a fox
very cunning or shrewd

crew noun orig US In hip-hop subculture: a group of rappers, breakdancers, graffiti artists, etc. working or performing together; also, more broadly, a person's friends, associates, or entourage. 1979–. UNITY As you can tell I have a major problem with townies as they give so much trouble to me and my crew just because we skate (1999).

crib noun mainly US A disreputable bar or brothel. Also **crib-house, -joint.** *c.*1857–. P. GAMMOND ET AL. Forced into the dives and crib-joints of the red-light district of New Orleans (1958).

crikey int An expression of astonishment. 1838–. J. RAE Crikey, I thought, he's tough (1960). [Euphemistic alteration of *Christ.*]

crim noun US and Austral Abbreviation of 'criminal'. 1909–. TELEGRAPH (Brisbane): (*headline*) Crims 'in turmoil' (1970).

Crimble noun Christmas. 1963–. J. LENNON Garry Crimble to you, Garry Crimble to you, Garry Bable, Dear Christmas, Happy Birthday, me too! (1963) [Humorous alteration of *Christmas* noun.]

Crimbo noun Christmas. 1928–. GQ A crisp £20 handed to the dustman just before Crimbo may seem like sheer profligacy (2001). [Humorous alteration of *Christmas* noun.]

crimp noun **to put a crimp in** or **into** US To thwart or block; to impair or interfere with. 1896–. NEW YORKER Finally, a giant black panther leaps upon me and devours my mind and heart. This puts a terrific crimp in my evening (1969).

crimper noun A hairdresser. 1968–. E. TREVOR He'd opened up as a crimper . . . decorating the salon and supervising the work himself (1968). [From *crimp* verb + *-er.*]

cripes int An expression of astonishment. 1910–. A. F. GRIMBLE The captain goggled at me for a second, 'Cripes!' he said (1952). [Euphemistic alteration of *Christ.*]

croak verb **1** intr. To die. 1812–. J. WELCOME Your old man has croaked and left you the lot (1961). **2** trans. To kill; to murder; to hang. 1823–. L. A. G. STRONG Who croaked Enameline? (1945).

croaker noun now mainly US A doctor, esp. a prison doctor. 1859–. MEZZROW & WOLFE The most he needed was some bicarbonate of soda and a physic, not a croaker (1946). [From CROAK verb, perh. with ironic reference to the sense 'kill' + *-er*; cf. also obs. slang *crocus* quack doctor,

perh. from the Latinized surname of Dr Helkiah Crooke, a 17th-century surgeon.]

crock noun **1** An old person, esp. one who is debilitated or an invalid; often in phr. *old crock.* 1876–. GUARDIAN Behind him at yesterday's launch . . . were enough old crocks to remind you that Major does come from a new generation (1992). **2** An old or worn-out vehicle. 1903–. H. G. WELLS I understand you want all of these out-of-date crocks of yours . . . to fly again (1935). Hence **crocked** adjective Hurt, damaged, disabled. 1900–. [In sense 1, from earlier meaning, old ewe.]

crocked adjective orig US Drunk. 1927–. GUARDIAN The curtain fell and the audience retired to get crocked (1970). [Perh. from *crock* verb, to collapse, disable.]

crock of shit noun US A pack of lies. 1945–. S. FALUDI A male editor assigned reporter Marilyn Goldstein a story on the women's movement with these instructions: 'Get out there and find an authority who'll say this is all a crock of shit' (1992). [From *crock* pot.]

cronk adjective Austral Out of order, unsound; fraudulent, dishonest. 1889–. J. LINDSAY Not that I believe in doing anything cronk (1958). [Prob. from Brit dialect *crank* adjective, infirm, sick; orig applied to fraudulently run horseraces.]

crook adjective Austral and NZ **1** Dishonest; illegal. 1898–. M. NEVILLE Accused him of some crook dealings (1954). **2** Bad, inferior, unsatisfactory. 1900–. J. O'GRADY When the mulga starts to die things are crook all right (1968). **3** Ill; injured. 1908–. A. J. HOLT I'm crook in the guts now (1946). **4** Angry; esp. in phrs. *to go crook (at, on), to be crook on.* 1910–. F. HARDY The landlords are crook on this (1967). [Shortened from *crooked* dishonest.]

crooked /krʊkt, ˈkrʊkɪd/ adjective **crooked on** or **about** Austral Angry about; hostile to. 1942–. A. SEYMOUR Now, if Alf was you he'd have a reason to be crooked on the world (1962). [From CROOK adjective.]

cropper noun **to come (fall, get) a cropper: a** To fall heavily. 1858–. TIMES I came a proper cropper, dearie, all black and blue I was (1963). **b** To fail badly. 1874–. T. RATTIGAN We bachelors welcome competition from married men. We so much enjoy watching them come the inevitable cropper (1951). [Perh. from phr. *neck and crop.*]

crow[1] noun derog A girl or woman, esp. one who is old or ugly; often in phr. *old crow.* 1925–. R. C. SHERRIFF MAYFIELD There's an old lady named Miss Fortescue . . . . *Ben (laughing)*

crew   crib   crikey   crim   Crimble   Crimbo   crimp

crow

Coo!—I know *that* old crow (1957). **See also** *to eat crow* at EAT verb, *stone the crows* at STONE verb.

crow² noun Also **cro.** Austral A prostitute. 1950–. B. HERBERT What are you, anyway? A Kings Cross crow. Every Yank in town's been rootin' you (1980). [Prob. an abbreviation of CHROMO noun.]

crown verb trans. To hit (someone) on the head. 1746–. O. MILLS 'Someone crowned me, I take it?' The sergeant nodded. 'With the poker from our own hearth' (1959).

crown jewels noun pl. The male genitalia, esp. the testicles. 1970–. J. MITCHELL This one's [i.e. a horse] a gelding. . . . He lost his crown jewels (1986). Cf. FAMILY JEWELS noun pl. 1.

crucial adjective Brit In enthusiastic commendation: great, excellent; essential. 1987–. LOOKS Yazz's crucial new video *Yazz—The Only Way Is Up* is a must for your Chrissie list, with all her best tracks (1989).

crud noun orig US **1** An unpleasant person or thing. 1940–. K. A. SADDLER Can't stand the man. A real crud (1966). **2** orig army A disease or illness. 1945–. F. SHAW ET AL. I got Bombay crud, I am suffering from looseness of the bowels (1966). **3** A deposit of unwanted impurities, grease, etc. 1950–. **4** Nonsense, rubbish. 1955–. T. STURGEON Would you say that . . . the writer of all this crud, believes . . . in what he writes? (1955). Hence **cruddy,** adjective orig US Dirty, unpleasant. 1949–. J. KIRKWOOD He had the largest collection of cruddy-looking suède shoes in the world (1960). See also CRUT noun. [Variant of *curd* noun.]

cruel verb trans. Austral To thwart, spoil. 1899–. I. HAMILTON I've got a good job and I don't want to cruel it while everything's going for me (1967). [From *cruel* adjective.]

cruet noun Austral The head. 1966–. R. BEILBY 'Where did he get it?' 'Through the cruet' (1977). [Origin uncertain; perh. connected with CRUMPET noun 1, and cf. Austral slang *crudget* head, recorded once, in 1941, origin unknown.]

cruise verb intr. and trans. orig US To walk or drive about (the streets, etc.) in search of a sexual (esp. homosexual) partner. 1903–. TIMES LITERARY SUPPLEMENT Male metropolitan homosexuals . . . who cruise compulsively (1984). Hence **cruiser,** noun A person who does this. 1903–.

crumb noun orig US An objectionable or unpleasant person. 1918–. WOMEN SPEAKING If a man doesn't like a girl's looks or personality, she's a . . . crumb (1970). [Prob. back-formation from *crumby, crummy* lousy, dirty, distasteful, of low quality, itself from *crumb* in the obs. slang sense, body-louse.]

crumbly noun Also **crumblie.** derog An old or senile person. 1976–. S. TOWNSEND At the end of the party Rick Lemon put 'White Christmas' by some old crumblie on the record deck (1984). [From *crumbly* adjective, with reference to the physical effects of old age.] Cf. WRINKLY noun.

crummy noun N Amer, dated A caboose or railway car on a goods train used by the train's crew or to transport workmen; also, a truck which transports loggers to and from the woods. 1926–. B. HUTCHISON Most of these men . . . travel perhaps forty miles to work in a 'crummy' (1957). [From *crummy,* variant of *crumby* adjective, full of or strewn with crumbs, lousy, in allusion to *crumb* noun in the obs. slang sense, body-louse (see CRUMB noun).]

crumpet noun **1** The head; esp. in phr. *balmy* or *barmy on* (or *in*) *the crumpet,* mad. 1891–. R. H. MORRIESON It's Madam Drac, gone right off her crumpet at last (1963). **2** Women (or occasionally men) regarded collectively as a means of sexual gratification. So **a bit** (or **piece**) **of crumpet,** a desirable woman (or man). 1936–. D. LAMBERT Ansell . . . watched the couples wistfully. 'Plenty of crumpet here, you know. Why don't you chance your arm?' (1969).

crunk adjective orig US Excellent or fun; (of a person) extremely energetic or excited, esp. as a result of listening to (hip-hop or rap) music. Often in *to get* (*it*) *crunk* and similar phrases. 1995–. PHILADELPHIA Get crunk with some raw hip-hop (2004). [Perh. a fanciful past participle of *crank* verb, or alternatively a blend of *crazy* adjective + *drunk* adjective.]

crush noun orig US A group or gang of people; spec. a body of troops; a unit of a regiment. 1904–31. OBSERVER The best recruiter is the man who is pleased with his 'crush' (1927).

crust noun Impudence, effrontery. 1900–. P. G. WODEHOUSE Actually having the crust to come barging in here! (1954). [From the notion of an insensitive outer covering.]

crusty noun Also **crustie.** Brit Any of a group of homeless and vagrant young people, usu. living by begging in cities, and characterized by rough clothes, matted, often dreadlocked hair, and an unkempt appearance. 1990–.

crow   crown   crown jewels   crucial   crud   crumbly

cut

[From the notion of being encrusted with dirt.]

crut noun US = CRUD noun 1, 4. 1937–. J. P. DONLEAVY Two years in Ireland, shrunken teat on the chest of the cold Atlantic. Land of crut (1955).

cube¹ noun dated An extremely conventional or conservative person. 1960–. G. BAGBY When I sang it to him . . . he told me I was a complete fool. Daisy Bell was for the cubes (1968). So **Cubesville,** noun A group or set of such persons. 1959–. [From the notion of being even more conventional than a 'square'.]

cube² noun A small partitioned space for working, sleeping, etc.; spec. an office compartment that is part of a larger open-plan workspace. 1937–. OREGONIAN She spends her days crunching numbers in a cube (2005). [Shortening of *cubicle* noun.]

cuckoo adjective orig US Mad, crazy. 1918–. M. GILBERT Never asked for references? . . . She must be cuckoo (1955). [From *cuckoo* noun, silly person.]

cuckoo house noun US A mental hospital. 1930–.

cuckoo's nest noun US A mental hospital. 1962–. [Popularized by the title of the novel *One Flew Over the Cuckoo's Nest* (1962) by Ken Kesey.]

cuffs noun pl. Handcuffs. 1861–. [Previously applied in the 17th century to iron wrist-fetters.] Also **cuff** verb trans. To handcuff. 1851–. WALL STREET JOURNAL It's very, very rare that you would arrest anyone, cuff them in public and take them from their offices (1989).

cugine noun US derog A young Italian-American man; also, a young man seeking induction into the Mafia. 1988–. [From Italian *cugino* cousin.]

culchie noun Anglo-Irish, mildly derog A simple country person; a provincial or rustic. 1958–. B. GELDOF We Dublin boys called the country pupils 'culchies', which they hated (1986). [Apparently an alteration of *Kilti(magh)*, the name of a country town in Co. Mayo.]

culture vulture noun derog A person eager to acquire culture. 1947–.

cunt noun coarse 1 The female external genitals, the vagina. *a.*1325–. H. MILLER O Tania, where now is that warm cunt of yours (1934). 2 A foolish or despicable person, female or male. 1929–. V. HENRIQUES 'What d'you think

you're doing, you silly cunt?' the driver shouts at her (1965). [Middle English *cunte, count(e)*, ultimately from Germanic *kuntōn.]

cunt-struck adjective coarse Infatuated with women. 1891–. F. SARGESON We were all helplessly and hopelessly c. . . . struck, a vulgar but forcibly accurate expression (1965).

curl verb trans. **to curl the mo** Austral To succeed brilliantly, to win. 1941–. So **curl-(kurl-) the-mo, curl-a-mo,** etc., attrib phrs., excellent, outstanding. COAST TO COAST 1967–8: He . . . lifts one of the brimming pilsener glasses: 'Come an' get it! It's curl-a-mo chico. Lead in the old pencil' (1969). [*Mo* prob. = moustache (see MO¹ noun), denoting self-satisfied twirling of the moustache.]

currant bun noun The sun; also applied since the 1980s to *The Sun* newspaper. 1938–. OBSERVER It was . . . the Currant Bun that won it for 'Tone' [i.e. Tony Blair] in June and luxuriated in its role of the UK's 'most politically influential paper' (2001). [Rhyming slang.]

curry noun **to give** (someone) **curry** Austral To make life difficult or 'hot' for (someone), esp. to abuse or scold angrily. 1936–. NATIONAL TIMES (Sydney): He used to play football, until he was sent down for giving curry to the ref (1984).

curse noun Menstruation; with *the*. 1930–. G. GREENE I forgot the damn pill and I haven't had the curse for six weeks (1969).

curtains noun The end; spec. death. 1912–. WALLIS & BLAIR If the Party ever got on to it . . . it would be curtains for Kurt (1956). [From the notion of the closing of the curtain at the end of a theatrical performance.]

cushty adjective Brit Good, wonderful; fine; brilliant. 1929–. J. SULLIVAN *Del.* No, no, no, everything's cushty! Yeah, no, no, no, you've got nothing to worry about! (1985) [From Romani *kushto, kushti* good, perh. influenced by CUSHY adjective.]

cushy adjective Of a post, job, etc.: easy and pleasant. 1915–. A. SILLITOE You were always on the lookout for a cushy billet (1970). [Anglo-Indian, from Hindustani *khūsh* pleasant.]

cut verb **1 to cut and run** orig nautical To run away. 1704–. HUTCHINSON'S PICTORIAL HISTORY OF THE WAR We anticipated a cut-and-run operation by a force consisting of two or three battleships (1945). **2 to cut the cackle** to stop talking (and get to the heart of the matter, the real business). 1889–. P. WYNDHAM LEWIS Cut the cackle, Arthur—I'm pressed for time! (1930). **3 to cut along** dated to go away, depart; often used in

crut cube cuckoo cuckoo house cuckoo's nest cuffs

the imperative to children and subordinates. 1902–. M. INNES 'And now you'd better cut along.' Captain Cox was a great believer in the moral effects of abrupt dismissals on the young (1949). **4 to cut the mustard** mainly US To come up to expectations, to meet requirements. 1907–. CITIZEN (Ottawa): What if it doesn't work out? What if I'm bored with it? What if I'm no good at all? What if I just can't cut the mustard? (1974). **5** trans. NZ To finish (esp. drink). 1945–. G. WILSON Here, drink it down. We must cut this bottle tonight (1952). See also HALF-CUT adjective.

Cuthbert noun dated Brit, derog A man who deliberately avoids military service; esp in World War I, one who did so by getting a job in a Government office or the Civil Service; a conscientious objector. 1917–35. J. CARY All you Cuthberts are fit for is to dodge responsibility at the cost of other people's lives (1933). [From the male personal name *Cuthbert*, used in a cartoon by 'Poy' in the London *Evening News*.]

cutie noun Also **cutey.** orig US An attractive young woman. 1917–. DAILY EXPRESS His sweetheart, a 'cabaret cutie' (1927). [From *cute* adjective + *-ie*.]

cutie-pie noun orig US A sexually attractive person. 1941–. G. DONALDSON He could see a flicker in the eyes of the local cutie-pies (1993).

cut-out noun A person acting as a middle-man, esp. in espionage. 1963–. E. AMBLER Through our cut-out I have made an offer for the shares (1969).

cuts noun Austral and NZ Corporal punishment, esp. of schoolchildren. 1915–. D. ADSETT If anyone was careless enough to use the wrong peg, their coat, hat and bag could be thrown to the floor without fear of getting the cuts (1963).

D noun Abbreviation of 'detective'. 1879–.
F. D. SHARPE They [i.e. crooks] very often know that
a man is a 'D', as they call us, without being
aware of his identity, because of the fact that he
happens to be on the lookout (1938). Cf.
DEE noun.

DA noun Abbreviation of DUCK'S ARSE noun.
1951–. M. DICKENS His hair, which was swept back
in the popular D.A. hair-cut into a little drake's
tail at the back (1961).

dabs noun pl. Brit Fingerprints. 1926–.
K. FARRER You'll get his photo and dabs by airmail
today (1957).

dad noun dated orig jazz = DADDY noun 3. 1959–.
TIME & TIDE *Sunset Strip* is real zoolie, dad (1960).

dad-blasted adjective US Expressing
annoyance or antipathy, or as an intensive.
1840–. Also **dad-blamed** 1883–, **dad-gasted**
1892–. [*dad* euphemistic alteration of *god*.]

daddy noun **1** The oldest or supreme
example; usu. followed by *of*. 1901–. W. GARNER
You graduate from taking little chances to
taking big ones. This one was the daddy of 'em
all (1969). **2** US An (older) male lover. 1926–.
H. WAUGH He wasn't pimping for her. . . . He's my
daddy and he plays it for five other girls (1970).
Cf. SUGAR DADDY noun **3** dated orig jazz Used as a
form of address, usu. to a male. 1927–. NEW
YORKER The bebop people have a language of
their own. They call each other Pops, Daddy,
and Dick (1948).

daddy-o noun dated orig jazz = DADDY noun 3.
1949–. TIME & TIDE The walls are crazy, . . . And the
scene uncool for you, Daddy-o (1960).

daffy adjective orig dialect Foolish, frivolous.
1884–. GUARDIAN One of those charming fusions
of the daffy benevolence of youth with the
guilelessness of middle aged PROs (1968). [From
dialect *daff* noun, simpleton + *-y*.]

dag noun Austral and NZ An eccentric or
noteworthy person; a character. 1875–.
D. M. DAVIN Gerald seemed to have become a bit
of a dag since the old days (1970). [From Brit
dialect *dag* noun, dare, challenge.] See also *to
rattle one's dags* at RATTLE verb.

dago /ˈdeɪɡəʊ/ noun derog **1** A foreigner, esp. a
Spaniard, Portuguese, or Italian. 1832–.
LISTENER England should have won. All that
stopped us was that the dagos [i.e. Paraguayans]
got more goals than us (1968). **2** The Spanish
or Italian language. 1900–. MRS M. WATTS They
were eternally being enjoined to say it in French,
say it in German, say it in dago! (1923). [From
Spanish *Diego* = James.]

dago red noun US Cheap red wine, esp.
Italian. 1906–. J. DOS PASSOS As we poured down
the dago red he would become mischievous
(1966).

daisy noun **1** mainly US An outstanding or
splendid specimen of anything. 1757–.
2 under the daisies dead and buried. 1866–.
S. VINES I think she's drinking herself under the
daisies, so to speak (1928). See also **to push
up (the) daisies** at PUSH verb. adjective **3** US Fine,
outstanding, splendid. 1886–. E. WALLACE I'll
introduce you to the daisiest night club in town
(1927).

daisy chain noun Sexual activity
involving three or more people. 1941–.
S. BELLOW You have to do more than take a little
gas, or slash the wrists. Pot? Zero! Daisy chains?
Nothing! Debauchery? A museum word (1964).

daisy roots noun Brit Rhyming slang for
'boots'. 1859–. GEN Your toes are poking out
of your daisy-roots (1943).

damage noun Cost, expense; esp. in phr.
what's the damage? how much is there to pay?
1755–. B. PYM You must let me know the damage
and I'll settle with you (1977).

dame noun US A woman. 1902–. J. CANNAN I've
never set eyes on the dame (1962).

damn noun **1** A negligible amount; in
phrs. *not worth a damn, not to care a damn, not
to give a damn*. 1760–. J. CARY It was
obvious . . . that he didn't give a damn—and so
they were enraged (1959). adjective **2 damn
all** nothing at all. 1922–. D. L. SAYERS I'll tell you
my story as shortly as I can, and you'll see I know
damn all about it (1926).

dancer noun dated criminals' A thief who
gains entry through upper-storey windows.
1864–.

dang adjective and adverb Also **danged.** mainly
US Expressing annoyance or antipathy, or as

an intensive. 1886–. w. a. fraser I was that danged near bushed, toward the last that I was feared I might go right on sleepin' (1910). [Euphemistic alteration of *damn* or *damned*.]

darky noun Also **darkie**. offensive A black person. 1840–. j. le carré Was it something about not taking the darkies on as conductors? (1983). [From *dark* + *-y*, *-ie*.]

darl noun Austral Used as a term of address, esp. to a female. 1930–. truckin' life Newcastle to Gosford is only a short run darl (1984). [Shortening of *darling*.]

date noun mainly jocular A foolish or comic person; esp. in phr. *soppy date*. 1914–. g. ingram A kid like that ought not to talk about love at her age, the soppy little date (1935). [From *date* fruit.]

date rape noun orig US The rape by a man of his partner on a date. 1983–.

dawg noun Representing a colloquial or dialectal pronunciation of *dog*. 1898–. o. lancaster Beaten copper reminders that a man's best friend is his dawg (beloved of the golf-playing classes) (1939).

daylights noun to beat, scare, etc. the (living) daylights out of (someone): to beat, scare (someone) severely. 1848–. illustrated london news I might have chuckled throughout 'The Suitor' if its chief actor did not happen to scare the living daylights out of me, as the current saying goes (1964). [From obs. slang *daylights* eyes.]

dead adverb **1** Utterly, completely. 1589–. d. lessing 'That's right,' said Charlie, 'you're dead right' (1963). **2 dead to rights** = bang to rights (see bang adverb). 1859–. a. a. fair We've got her this time dead-to-rights (1947). [From earlier sense, to the point of death.]

dead duck noun orig US An unsuccessful or useless person or thing. 1844–. a. gilbert Once a chap's proved innocent . . . he's a dead duck to the Press (1958).

dead-head verb intr. and trans. orig and mainly US To drive (an empty train, truck, taxi, etc.); to travel in (an empty vehicle). 1911–. people (Australia): Another fireman was deadheading in the cab with us and he took over for me (1970). [Cf. earlier sense, to gain admittance without payment, from *deadhead* noun, a person so admitted.]

dead president noun US A US banknote. 1944–. l. rainwater I want me a 1965 Cadillac and some dead presidents (money) in my pocket (1970). [From the portraits of various former statesmen printed on US banknotes.]

dead soldier noun orig US An empty bottle. 1917–.

dead-wood noun to get, have the dead-wood US To have someone at a disadvantage. 1851–. e. s. gardner Well, they've evidently got the dead-wood on you now, Perry. They know that you took Eva Martell to that rooming-house (1951). [From *dead wood* a pin in tenpin bowling that has been knocked down and lies in the alley in front of those remaining.]

deal verb intr. To peddle illegal drugs. 1958–.

deaner noun Also **deener, dener, diener**. dated, mainly Austral and NZ A shilling. 1839–. w. dick One thing about him, though, he knew how to make a deener on the side (1965). [Prob. alteration of *denier* former small French coin, hence small amount of money.]

death noun **1** like death warmed up very tired or ill. 1939–. j. pendower It damned near killed me. . . . I still feel like death warmed up (1964). adjective **2** US (in African-American usage) Excellent, impressive, outstanding. 1979–. e. l. sturz This looks like a death little workshop to me, run by . . . cool people (1983).

debag verb trans. Brit To remove (a person's) trousers, esp. as a joke. 1914–. b. nichols A number of us chased Sir Robert down the moonlit High Street in an endeavour to debag him (1958). [From *de-* + *bag*(s trousers).]

debs' delight noun mainly derog An elegant or attractive young man in high society. Also **debbies' delight**. 1934–. n. marsh Lord Robert half suspected his nephew Donald of being a Debs' Delight (1948).

deck noun **1** US A packet of narcotics; a small portion of a drug wrapped in paper. 1922–. c. himes When it's analysed, they'll find five or six half-chewed decks of heroin (1966). **2** orig airforce The ground. 1925–. n. shute She spun her Moth into the deck (1958). verb trans. **3** orig US To knock (someone) to the ground, esp. with a punch; to floor. 1953–.

> 'Lord Robert half suspected his nephew of being a Debs' Delight'

darky darl date date rape dawg daylights dead

dibs

G. V. HIGGINS Janet riled you enough so that you decided to deck Janet. Janet called the cops (1985).

dee noun A detective. 1882–. E. DE MAUNY You've got to look out, if the dees come (1949). [The first letter of *detective*.] Cf. D.

deep adjective **to go (in) off the deep end** to give way to emotion or anger. 1921–. T. PARKER I'm not going to do what I've done before, go off the deep end, nothing like that (1963). [From the notion of diving into the deepest part of a swimming pool.]

deep six noun Death, the grave. 1929–. S. PALMER My old lady went over the hill with my bank account before I was out of boot camp. I'd have given her the deep-six if I coulda got a furlough (1947). [Perh. from the custom of burial at sea, at a depth of six fathoms.]

deevy adjective Also **deevie**. dated Delightful, sweet, charming. 1900–42. V. M. SACKVILLE-WEST Tommy, you're going, aren't you? How too deevy! (1930). [Affected alteration of *divvy*, from first syllable of *divine* + -y.]

def adjective orig US Excellent, great, extremely 'cool'; often in **def jam** superb music. 1981–. SMASH HITS Like all good 'def' and 'baaaaad' rappers do, Sandra and 'Tim' really love their Mum (1988). [Origin uncertain; often said to be an abbreviation of *definite* or *definitive*, but perh. better explained as an alteration of DEATH adjective 2.]

dekko noun Also **decko**. Brit, orig army A look or glance. 1894–. OBSERVER Once I'd grabbed hold of the script and taken a good dekko at it, my worst fears were confirmed (1958). [From Hindustani *dekho*, imperative of *dekhnā* to look.]

Delhi belly noun mainly jocular An upset stomach accompanied by diarrhoea such as may be suffered by visitors to India. 1944–. [From the name of *Delhi* capital of India.]

demon noun Austral **1** A policeman. 1889–. K. GILES 'Tell the truth, Bert,' said the Australian, 'always help a demon in distress' (1967). **2** A detective. 1900–. SUNDAY MAIL MAGAZINE (Brisbane): To the Australian criminal a demon is a ... detective (1967). [From earlier sense, person of more than human energy, speed, skill, etc.]

de-pants verb trans. US = DEBAG verb. 1939–. J. MENO I got a flash of this kid ... on the wrestling team, who I once saw de-pants some

honors-class fag in the gym locker room (2004). [From *de-* + *pants* trousers.]

Derby kelly noun Also **Darby kelly**. Rhyming slang for 'belly'. Also **Derby kel**. 1906–. T. RATTIGAN Just that ride home. Cor, I still feel it down in the old derby kel (1942).

derry[1] noun Austral and NZ A feeling or attitude of hostility; an animus; a down; esp. in phr. *to have a derry on*, to be prejudiced against. 1883–. D. STUART And warfare, that's another thing Peter has a derry on (1974). [Prob. shortened from the refrain *derry down*, used jocularly for DOWN noun.]

derry[2] noun A derelict building. 1968–. GUARDIAN Mary ... lives with her husband, two Belgian boys, three girls, and a young Frenchman in a 'derry'—a deserted house—in Chelsea (1969). [From *derelict* + -y.]

des res /dez ˈrez/ noun estate-agents' A house or other dwelling presented as a highly desirable purchase. 1986–. TIMES The days of the 'des res' that clearly isn't are set to end for estate agents (1990). [Shortened from *desirable residence*.]

dex noun orig US = DEXIE noun. 1966–. HARPER'S Pops a dex or a bennie occasionally, especially during exam week (1971).

dexie noun Also **dexy**. orig US A tablet of the amphetamine drug Dexedrine, taken as a stimulant; also, the drug itself. 1956–. L. SANDERS I think he's on something. I'd guess Dexies (1969). [Abbreviation.]

dexter noun US = POINDEXTER noun. 1985–. D. GAINES On another coast—they'd be toners. Archenemies of jocks, dexters, rah-rahs, or socs for all eternity (1991). [Shortening.]

dial noun Brit A person's face. 1811–. L. A. G. STRONG You should have seen the solemn dials on all the Gardas and officials (1958). [From a supposed resemblance to the dial of a watch or clock; cf. CLOCK noun 1.]

diamond noun Brit, mainly London A stalwart or reliable person. 1990–. Also used as an adjective, esp. in phr. *diamond geezer*.

dibs noun **1** Money. 1812–. **2 to get, have dibs on** (something): US To have first claim to. 1932–. NEW YORKER Patterson took care to remember ... which upstream banks had dibs on which borrowers (1985). [Earlier sense, pebbles for game, also *dib-stones*, perh. from *dib* verb, to dab, pat.]

dee deep deep six deevy def dekko Delhi belly

dice noun **1 no dice** orig US (It is or was) useless, hopeless, unsuccessful, profitless, etc. 1931–. M. PUGH Nothing doing. I'm not going. No dice (1959). verb trans. **2** Austral To reject; to leave alone, abandon. 1943–. F. HARDY No bastard puts my daughter in the family way then dices her . . . and gets away with it (1963). [Verb from earlier sense, to gamble away by playing dice.]

dicey adjective orig airforce Risky. *a.*1944–. P. CAPON The river got a little dicey. I thought we'd wait for the moon (1959). [From *dice* (from the risk of gambling with dice) + -*y*.]

dick[1] noun The penis. 1891–. P. ROTH You might have thought that . . . my dick would have been the last thing on my mind (1969). [Pet form of the name *Richard*; cf. earlier sense, riding whip.]

dick[2] noun A detective; a policeman. 1908–. E. WALLACE They'd persuaded a couple of dicks— detectives—to watch the barriers (1924). [Perh. arbitrary contraction of *detective*.]

dicken int Also **dickin, dickon.** Austral and NZ An exclamation expressing disgust or disbelief. 1894–. NEW ZEALAND LISTENER 'You don't lie and cheat the way my mother does.' 'Ah, dicken' (1970). [Prob. variant of the exclamation *dickens* or the personal name *Dickens.*]

dick-head noun A stupid person. 1969–. A. BLEASDALE But I lost that job, it was alright, I deserved to lose it, I was a dickhead (1983). [From DICK[1] noun + *head* noun.]

Dickless Tracy noun jocular, orig US A female police officer. 1963–. [Punningly from DICK[1] noun and the name of *Dick Tracy*, US comic-strip detective introduced in 1931 by Chester Gould.]

dickwad noun orig and mainly US = DICKWEED noun. 1989–. HOTDOG Chill out, dickwad (2002). [From DICK[1] noun + *wad* noun.]

dickweed noun orig and mainly US A stupid, obnoxious, or contemptible man. 1984–. O. GOLDSMITH It would be a pleasure to wake that dickweed up early (1992). [From DICK[1] noun + *weed* noun.]

dicky adjective Also **dickey.** Brit Unsound, likely to collapse or fail. 1812–. [Perh. from phr. *as queer as Dick's hatband*.]

dicky-bird noun Also **dickey-bird.** Rhyming slang for 'word'; mainly in negative contexts. 1932–. A. DRAPER George didn't say a dicky bird when I ambled in (1970).

dicky dirt noun Brit A shirt. 1925–. [Rhyming slang, perh. suggested by *dicky* false shirt-front (1811).]

dicty adjective US **1** Conceited, snobbish. 1926–. **2** Elegant, stylish, high-class, 1959–. [Origin unknown.]

diddle verb now mainly US **1** trans. and intr. To have sex (with). 1879–. W. FAULKNER Just out of curiosity to find out . . . which of them was and wasn't her diddling her? (1940). **2** intr. and refl To masturbate. 1960–. K. MILLETT Paraphernalia with the scarf . . . . Supposed to diddle herself with it. Male fantasy of lonely chick masturbating in sad need of him (1974). [From earlier sense, to move jerkily from side to side.]

diddly-squat noun US A trivial amount or number; nothing. 1963–. Also **diddly-shit** 1964–, **diddly** 1964–. NEW YORK TIMES MAGAZINE This ballplayer would be shown fumbling on the guitar, prompting the veteran rock musician to say, 'Bo, you don't know diddly' (1990). SUNDAY TIMES MAGAZINE When it was all over, I got a huge free bag of ginseng. Lucy got diddly-squat. 'You see?' I told her smugly, as we walked back out on the street. 'Sometimes it pays to be a crybaby' (1997). [Alteration of DOODLY-SQUAT noun.]

didicoi noun Also **didakai, -kei, diddekai, diddicoy, didekei, -ki, -kie, -ky, didicoy, didikai, -koi, didycoy.** A gipsy. 1853–. [Romany.]

diesel dyke noun Also **diesel.** orig US A lesbian with aggressively masculine tendencies. 1958–. [From the stereotypically male associations of diesel engines, vehicles, etc.]

dif noun Also **diff.** Abbreviation of 'difference'. 1896–. H. CALVIN Here today gone tomorrow. What's the diff, duckie? (1967).

dig noun Austral and NZ Abbreviation of DIGGER noun 1916–. G. MCINNES Often they shouted at us . . . 'Howsit up in the dress circle, dig?' (1965).

dig verb orig US **1** trans. To understand, appreciate, like, admire. 1935–. NEW YORKER I just don't dig any of these guys. I don't understand their scenes (1969). **2** intr. To understand. 1936–. C. MACINNES Twist now—you dig? (1957). [Perh. from the earlier sense, to study hard at subject, from the notion of strenuous digging.]

digger noun An Australian or New Zealander; spec. in World Wars I and II, a soldier from Australia or New Zealand, esp.

a private. 1916–. R. FINLAYSON Put your bag under the seat, digger (1948). [From the earlier sense, one who digs for gold, from the high profile of such people in late 19th-century Australia.]

dike variant of DYKE[1,2] noun.

dill noun Austral and NZ A fool or simpleton; spec. one who is duped by a trickster. 1941–. TELEGRAPH (Brisbane): At the start he felt a bit of a dill in a wig and robes (1969). [Prob. back-formation from DILLY adjective.]

dilly adjective mainly Austral Foolish, stupid. 1905–. J. K. EWERS Cripes, it'd drive a bloke dilly! (1949). [Perh. blend of *daft* and *silly*; cf. obs. Brit dialect *dilly* cranky, queer.]

dilly noun orig US A remarkable or excellent person or thing. 1935–. DAILY COLONIST (Victoria, British Columbia): The new [oil] well . . . looks a dilly (1970). [From obs. *dilly* wonderful, from the first syllable of *delightful* or *delicious*.]

dime noun **a dime a dozen** N Amer So plentiful as to be worthless. Also **dime-a-dozen** attrib phr. 1930–. I. SHAW 'I thought you were too good looking just to be *nobody*.' 'A dime a dozen,' Wesley said. 'I'm just a seaman at heart' (1977).

dinah noun Brit dated A girlfriend or female lover. 1898–. J. R. WARE Is Mary your Dinah? (1909) [Alteration of DONA noun, prob. influenced by the female forename *Dinah*.]

dinero /dɪneərəʊ/ noun orig US Money, cash. 1856–. C. MACINNES You need a bit dinero? Five pounds do? (1959). [From Spanish *dinero*, penny, coin, money.]

ding noun Austral A party or celebration, esp. a wild one. 1956–. F. HARDY It appears that he had drunk fifteen of them there drinking horns of beer at a Commemoration Day ding (1967). [Perh. from DING-DONG noun or WINGDING noun.]

ding-a-ling noun **1** N Amer A crazy person; an eccentric or oddball. 1940–. J. CARROLL Hell, Pius—that dingaling—would never of given me my hat. Thank God for Pope John (1978). **2** The penis. 1972–. R. H. RIMMER My damned ding-a-ling was pointing my bathrobe into a tent (1975). [In sense 1 from earlier sense, prisoner driven mad by confinement.]

dingbat noun **1** pl. Austral and NZ, esp. in phr. *to have the dingbats*, *to be dingbats*, to be mad, stupid, eccentric; also, to have delirium tremens. 1911–. G. SLATTER Boozin' again! You'll end up with the dingbats, you will (1959). **2** US and Austral A stupid or eccentric person.

1915–. NEW YORK TIMES Miss Sternhagen's mother increases in giddiness, even to wearing what appears to be a feather in her hair. She is, in fact, a certifiable dingbat (1985). [Cf. earlier senses, money, thingumajig, tramp; perh. from *ding* to beat + *bat* hitting implement, or from *ding* sound of a bell + *bat* flying animal, with jocular reference to phr. *bats in the belfry*.]

ding-dong noun **1** A heated quarrel. 1922–. J. WYNDHAM You can't have a proper ding-dong with those quiet ones (1956). **2** A tumultuous party or gathering. 1936–. A. SMITH The sons and daughters . . . coming up for a ding-dong which went on till far into the night (1961). [From earlier sense, sound of bells.]

dinge noun US, derog A black person. Also as adjective, esp. with reference to a jazz style developed by black musicians. Also **dingy**. 1848–. E. HEMINGWAY That big dinge took him by surprise . . . the big black bastard (1933); V. BELLERBY The 'dinge' piano trill . . . instinctively holding the rich overtones of Negro speech (1958). [Back-formation from *dingy* adjective.]

dingleberry noun **1** orig US A piece of dried faecal matter attached to the hair around the anus. 1953–. **2** A stupid person, a fool. 1969–. RIGHTING WORDS Tell that dingleberry I'm not here (1990). **3** pl. The female breasts. 1980–. BRITISH JOURNAL OF PHOTOGRAPHY Daddy says knockers and jugs and bazooms and dingleberries. . . . And then he laughs and goes 'wuff! wuff!' (1980). [From the earlier US sense, a cranberry, *Vaccinium erythrocarpum*, of the south-eastern US. The origin of *dingle* is uncertain.]

dingo Austral noun **1** A coward or scoundrel. 1869–. T. RONAN Jim Campbell was a different proposition. He was a bloody dingo (1962). verb **2** intr. To retreat, back out, act in a cowardly or treacherous way. 1935–. E. LAMBERT 'Where is Allison?' 'He dingoed at the last minute' (1952). **3** trans. To back out of; to shirk. 1942–. J. CLEARY You ain't dingoing it, are you? You can't toss in the towel now (1952). [From the characteristics (cowardice, treachery, etc.) popularly attributed to the dingo in Australia.]

dingus noun US **1** dated An unnamed or unspecified thing. 1876–. D. HAMMETT Then you think the dingus is worth two million? (1929). **2** The penis. c.1888–. [From Dutch *dinges* thing.]

dink[1] noun US, military, derog A Vietnamese person. 1969–. GUARDIAN These are not

dike dill dilly dime dinah dinero ding dingbat

dink

people.... They are dinks and gooks and slant-eyed bastards (1970). [Origin unknown.]

dink² noun Also **Dink.** orig N Amer = DINKY noun. 1987–. CHICAGO TRIBUNE The DINKS . . . and empty-nesters now have a greater potential to travel off-season (1990). [See DINKY noun.]

dinkum adjective and adverb Austral and NZ Honest(ly), genuine(ly); esp. in phr. *fair dinkum*, fair and square, honest. 1890–. SUN (Melbourne): Fair dinkum, North's been waiting so long for its ship to come in, the pier's collapsed (1969). [From noun, (hard) work, of unknown origin.]

dinkum oil noun Austral and NZ The honest truth, true facts. Also **dinkum.** 1915–. J. H. FULLARTON Anyway there's no dinkum oil. Only latrinograms . . . it may be all hooey (1944).

dinky noun Also **dinkie**, and with capital letter. orig N Amer Either partner of a usu. professional working couple who have no children, characterized as affluent consumers with few domestic demands on their time and money. 1986–. [Acronym from the initial letters of *double* (also *dual*) *income, no kids*, after YUPPIE noun. The final *y* is sometimes interpreted as 'yet'.]

dinky-di(e) /-daɪ/ adjective and adverb Also **dinki-di.** Austral and NZ = DINKUM adjective. 1915–. AUSTRALIAN Sinister karate chopping Japanese battling with true-blue, dinki-di locals (1969).

dinner-pail noun **to hand, pass,** or **turn in one's dinner-pail** to die. 1905–. P. G. WODEHOUSE My godfather . . . recently turned in his dinner pail and went to reside with the morning stars (1964).

dinnyhayser noun Also **dinnyhazer.** Austral A knock-out blow. 1907–. W. W. AMMON Sometimes he let his dinnyhazer go with such viciousness that Stevie shook his head (1984). [Reputedly from the name of a boxer, *Dinny Hayes.*]

dino noun US = DYNO noun.

dip¹ noun **1** A pickpocket. 1859–. DAILY TELEGRAPH New Yorkers who have had their pockets picked . . . on the city's Underground . . . learned yesterday that the person responsible was probably a professional 'dip' (1970). verb **2 to dip (one's) wick** of a man, to have sex. 1958–.

dip² noun US A stupid, unremarkable, or contemptible person. 1932–. W. SPINRAD There were few distractions in Poughkeepsie. The girls were all airheads, and the boys were dips (1987). [Back-formation from DIPPY adjective.]

dippy adjective Mad, insane, crazy. 1903–. TIMES REVIEW OF INDUSTRY In past days the senile and the slightly dippy were clapped into institutions (1967). [Origin unknown.]

dipshit noun orig US A stupid, inept, or contemptible person. 1963–. R. STONE A cowboy isn't some dipshit with a ten-gallon hat and a dinner plate on his belt (2003). [Perh. from DIP² noun + SHIT noun 7.]

dipstick noun **1** The penis. 1980–. MALEDICTA I overheard in a cinema once the cry 'Keep your lipstick off my dipstick' (1980). **2** A stupid person; a fool, clot. 1981–. R. BLOUNT If I'd told the truth to that dipstick who played me, I would have just said, 'Sugar' (1990). [Transferred use of *dipstick*, rod for measuring depth of liquid, esp. engine oil. In sense 1, prob. reinforced by *to dip one's wick* (see DIP verb); in sense 2, prob. partly a euphemistic alteration of DIPSHIT noun.]

dirt noun **to do dirt (to)** orig US To harm or injure maliciously. 1893–. W. HAGGARD Dotties could do you dirt; they could remark . . . in public, that . . . you were living with the curate (1959).

dirty noun **1 to do the dirty on** Brit To play a mean trick on. 1914–. G. KERSH It took me to do the dirty on him (1942). adverb **2** (With adjectives expressing magnitude) very. 1920–. D. CLARK Time for a dirty great pint (1971).

dirty dog noun A (lecherous) scoundrel; a despicable man. 1928–. J. PORTER 'Bit of a dirty dog, our Gordon Pilley,' said Sergeant MacGregor with a smirk (1964).

dirty old man noun A lecherous older man. 1932–. D. CLARK A man of my age on the look out for a lovely young lass puts me into the dirty-old-man class (1971). Cf. DOM noun.

dis /dɪs/ adjective Abbreviation of 'disconnected'. Hence, broken, not working. 1925–. T. R. G. LYELL The poor old chap's brain's going dis (1931).

dis verb trans. Also **diss.** orig US (in African-American usage) **1** To put (someone) down, usu. verbally; to show disrespect for by insulting language or dismissive behaviour. 1980–. SKY MAGAZINE What is a Gas Face? That's the kind of face you pull if you're trying to kick it with some girl and she disses you (1990). noun **2** Failure to show respect; abuse, disparagement; an insult. 1986–. [Shortened from *disrespect* verb and noun.]

discombobulate verb trans. orig and mainly US To confuse, bewilder. 1916–. E. QUEEN

dink dinkum dinkum oil dinky dinky-di dino

I don't want you people to be in any way discombobulated (1970). [A variant of obs. US slang *discombobberate* to confuse (1838–1916), itself prob. a jocular alteration of *discompose* or *discomfit*.]

dish verb trans. **1** To defeat completely, ruin, do for. 1798–. T. HEALD This effectively dished Lady Antonia's chances of the same treatment (1983). **2 to dish it out** To deal out punishment; to fight hard. 1939–. noun **3** A sexually attractive person. 1929–. A. WILSON That man I've been talking to is rather a dish, but I'm sure he's a bottom-pincher (1958). [In sense 1, from the notion of food being *done*, and *dished* up.]

dishy adjective Brit Very attractive, esp. sexually. 1961–. J. GARDNER 'Mm, is *that* him?' said the girl, all velvet. 'He's dishy' (1964). [From DISH noun + *-y*.]

diss verb and noun = DIS verb and noun.

ditch verb trans. **1** To defeat, frustrate. 1899–. **2** To abandon, discard; to jilt. 1921–. P. KEMP Davis . . . was struggling to carry the heavy wireless set; I shouted to him to ditch it and save himself (1958). [From earlier sense, to throw into a ditch.]

ditsy adjective Also **ditzy.** orig US **1** = DICTY adjective; also, fussy, intricate. 1978–. NEW YORK TIMES They'll cook and clean for a week before a party and worry over the ditsy little touches, the table, the flowers, the matching guest towels (1981). **2** Esp. of a woman: stupid, scatterbrained, cute. 1980–. WASHINGTON POST Willie Scott . . . is a ditsy blond who sings at a Shanghai nightclub (1984). Hence (as a back-formation) **ditz,** noun A ditsy person. 1984–. [Origin uncertain; perh. an alteration of DICTY adjective.]

dive noun **1** orig US A disreputable nightclub; a drinking-den. 1871–. SPECTATOR The degenerate dives of Berlin (1958). **2** boxing, football, etc. An intentional fall taken to deceive an opponent or official; (in boxing), a feigned knock-out; broadly, a simulated failure. Often in phr. *to take a dive*. 1942–. CHICAGO SUN-TIMES 'Freddy took a dive six times,' Time quoted one investigator as saying of Furino's performance on the polygraph (1982).

divot noun US dated jocular A wig, hairpiece. 1934–. [From earlier sense, portion of turf removed.]

divvy¹ Also **divi.** noun **1** Abbreviation of 'dividend'. 1872–. G. CHAPMAN ET AL If you'll wait till Saturday I'm expecting a divvy from the Harpenden Building Society (1970). verb trans.

2 To share out; divide; often followed by *up*. 1877–. TIMES LITERARY SUPPLEMENT The problem of 'divvying-up' the spoils of automation (1957).

divvy² Also **divy.** Brit (Midlands and North). adjective **1** Foolish, idiotic; daft. 1975–. GUARDIAN The flight lieutenant must be from Liverpool. . . . Divy is that city's word for moronic, or worse (1981). noun **2** A foolish or half-witted person. 1989–. [Origin uncertain.]

dizz noun Also **diz.** US A foolish or eccentric person. 1963–. [Back-formation from *dizzy* foolish.]

DMs noun pl. Brit Abbreviation of *Doctor Marten's*, name of a brand of boot. 1993–. I. WELSH Skinhead haircut, green bomber-jaykit, nine-inch DMs. A stereotypical twat (1993).

do verb trans. **1** To cheat, swindle. 1641–. TIMES The disgruntled 'unchurched' . . . seem to think they are being 'done' by rigourists (1990). **2** To break into; to burgle or rob. 1774–. H. R. F. KEATING My Billy noticed the set in a shop-window. . . . He did the place that very night (1968). **3** To arrest; to charge; to convict. 1784–. GUARDIAN 'This is a murder charge. There is no certainty that you will be done for murder.' . . . He did not say that Kelly would only be done' for robbery and not murder (1963). **4** To defeat. 1841–. **5 to do** (someone) **over: a** To handle roughly; to beat up. 1866–. A. UPFIELD 'Done over properly, wasn't he?' 'From appearances, yes. Mitford must be a rough place' (1953). **b** To have sex with; to seduce. 1873–. JOHN O' LONDON'S A truly Moravian rape-scene in a ruined church, with Cesira and Rosetta both done over by a screeching pack of Moroccan *goums* (1961). **6** mainly Austral and NZ To spend completely; often followed by *in*. 1889–. V. PALMER Now he's done his money in (1930). **7 to do** (someone or something) **in: a** To ruin, do injury to; to kill. 1905–. LISTENER These were professional killers who 'did in' John Regan (1963). **b** To exhaust, wear out. 1917–. E. HILLARY For the first time I really feel a bit done in (1955). **8** To have sex with. Phr. **to do** (it), to have sex. 1913–. V. CANNING Some service-man . . . did your mother in Cyprus . . . and then . . . made an honest woman of her (1967). **9 to do it** to urinate or defecate. Cf. DOING noun 3. 1922–. H. GOLD It's so easy, boy, after you do it once. Before that it's hard. You do it in your pants (1956). **10** To beat up or kill. 1954–. ENCOUNTER I . . . told him . . . I'd do him if I ever saw his face again (1959). **11** orig US To take (a drug); to smoke (marijuana). 1971–. NEW YORKER Their lives . . . involve . . . smoking (tobacco, marijuana, cloves), drinking (everything), and doing drugs—mainly cocaine (1985). noun

12 A hairdo. 1966–. OBSERVER Missed gigs, drunken antics and that beehive 'do (2007).

13 Also **doo** mainly *childrens'* Excrement, esp. canine; esp. in phr. *doggy('s) do*. 1974–. SOUNDS He adopts a facial expression when discussing punks of a man reluctantly handling doggy's do (1977).

dob verb trans. **to dob** (someone) **in** Austral To betray, inform against. 1955–. PUNCH Those Canberra wowsers have really dobbed us in this time (1964). [Fig. use of Brit dialect *dob* to put down, throw down.]

dock noun **in** (or **out of,** etc.) **dock in** hospital, undergoing treatment; (of a vehicle) laid up for repairs. 1785–. NEWS CHRONICLE He's just out of dock after the old appendix (1960).

doctor noun **1** nautical A ship's cook; US and Austral a cook in a camp. 1821–. R. S. CLOSE Hey doctor! What about something to eat? (1945). **2 to go for the doctor** Austral To make an all-out effort. 1949–. D. STIVENS There were three of the bastards and they went for the doctor. But I had time to get on my guard (1951).

go for the doctor

to make an all-out effort

doddle noun Brit Something very easy to do. 1937–. M. WOOD If the climb had reached any level of difficulty higher than Moderate, which is the Climbers' Club's polite way of labelling a gumshoe doddle, we'd have died (1966). [Perh. from the verb *doddle* walk unsteadily.]

dodge verb trans. **1 to dodge the column** to shirk one's duty; to avoid work. 1919–. H. SPRING My father, so great an expert in dodging any column he didn't see the point of joining (1955). **2 to dodge Pompey** Brit naval to avoid work on board ship. 1929–. **3** Austral To steal (an animal). 1965–. T. RONAN For every poddy that's up in the Coronet breakaways there's a dozen blokes trying to dodge it off (1965). Cf. PODDY-DODGE verb. [In sense 2, cf. POMPEY noun Portsmouth; in sense 3, from earlier Austral sense, to drive (sheep or cattle).]

dodger noun Austral and services' A sandwich; bread, food. 1897–. N. CULOTTA Smack us in the eye with another hunk o' dodger (1957). [From US *dodger* hard-baked corn-cake; cf. N. Eng. dialect *dodge* lump.]

dodger adjective Austral Good, excellent. 1941–. D. STIVENS Instead of having to risk a knock on the Pearly Gates everything was dodger

(1953). [Perh. from DODGER noun, but cf. SNODGER noun.]

dodgy adjective Awkward, unreliable, tricky. 1898–. H. PINTER It'd be a bit dodgy driving tonight (1960). [From earlier sense, full of dodges, evasive.]

doer noun Austral and NZ An eccentric, a character; esp. in phr. *hard doer*, a hard case. *a.*1885–. S. H. COURTIER Laurie could have been joking. He was that kind of doer, you know (1959). [Prob. from the notion of being an active person.]

dog noun **1** US and Austral An informer; a traitor. Often in phr. *to turn dog on*, to betray. 1846–. K. TENNANT Old Sharkey turned dog on us, didn't he, Bet? Said he'd get me for abduction (1941). **2 to put on the dog** orig US to put on airs. 1865–. J. T. FARRELL They were all trying to put on the dog, show that they were lace-curtain Irish, and lived in steam-heat (1934). **3** pl. The feet. 1924–. J. STEINBECK We ain't gonna walk no eight miles ... to-night. My dogs is burned up (1939). **4** US Something poor or mediocre; a failure. 1936–. NEW YORKER Audiences are in a mess. ... They don't know what they want. ... So many movies are *dogs* (1970). **5** A horse that is slow, difficult to handle, etc. 1944–. T. RATTIGAN Is it going to be dry at Newbury? ... Walled Garden's a dog on heavy going (1955). verb intr. **6** orig and mainly US With *it*. To act lazily or half-heartedly (i.e. like a dog); to shirk or avoid responsibility, risk, etc.; to slack, idle. 1905–. A. ALVAREZ Most guys playing for that kind of money will dog it, but Doyle's got no fear (1983).

dog and bone noun Brit Rhyming slang for '(tele)phone'. Also **dog.** 1961–. [Cf. earlier US *switch and bone* in same sense.]

dog-and-pony show noun Also **dog-and-pony** US **1** Orig, a small circus or travelling show; hence, a small-scale or poor-quality entertainment or service. 1914–. **2** An elaborate occasion or display designed to attract people's attention. 1953–. ST LOUIS (Missouri) POST-DISPATCH The FAA delayed several American Airlines flights on Jan. 3 for several hours. The fact of the matter is, it's nothing more than a dog-and-pony show to give us the sense of security (2002). Hence **dog-and-pony** adjective US Of, like, being,

dob   dock   doctor   doddle   dodge   dodger   dodgy

doing

or participating in a dog-and-pony show. 1943–. [From the limited range of animal participants in such a show.]

dog-box noun Austral A compartment in a railway carriage without a corridor. 1905–. E. O. SCHLUNKE We had to get out of our sleepers into dog-boxes and found we still had over a hundred miles to go (1958). [From earlier sense, compartment in a railway van for conveying dogs.]

dog-end noun A cigarette butt. 1935–. P. WILDEBLOOD The ensuing 'dog-ends' are unpicked, re-rolled and smoked again (1955).

dogface noun US A soldier, esp. an infantryman, in the US army. 1941–.

dogging noun Brit The practice of gathering with other people in a public place, esp. a car park, to watch or engage in exhibitionist sexual activity. 1986–. SUN My husband is into swinging, dogging, sex with strangers—you name it, he wants it (2007). [Prob. from *dog* pursue closely.]

doggo adverb **to lie doggo** to lie motionless or hidden. 1893–. F. MACLEAN Lying doggo with an expression of angelic innocence when he came to see if she was in bed and asleep (1955). [Prob. from DOG noun.]

doggone adjective and adverb US Damned. 1851–. E. CALDWELL When I get a load of it, I'll know dog-gone well my ship has come in (1933). [Prob. from *dog on it = God damn it*.]

doggy Also **doggie**. adjective **1** Dashing, stylish, smart. 1889–. A. J. WORRALL I like your tie, it is very doggy (1932). noun **2** orig services' An officer's servant or assistant. 1909–. A. GRIMBLE My function would be to act as doggie—that is, clerical assistant and odd-job man—to . . . the District Officer (1952).

dog-house noun **1** jazz A double-bass. 1923–. **2 in the dog-house** orig US In disgrace, out of favour. 1932–. P. H. JOHNSON He'd been getting bad grades, he was in the dog-house as it was (1963).

dog-robber noun **1** A navy or army officer's orderly. 1863–. **2** pl. Civilian clothes worn by a naval officer on shore leave. 1898–. M. DICKENS Then he . . . changed into dog robbers and went into the town to get drunk (1958).

dog's age noun orig US A long time. 1836–. M. DE LA ROCHE She hasn't laid an offering on the altar of Jalna for a dog's age (1933).

dogsbody noun orig nautical A junior person, esp. one to whom a variety of menial tasks is given; a drudge, a general utility person. 1922–. LISTENER I was a sort of general dogsbody to begin with—assistant stage-manager, and what have you (1967). [Cf. earlier nautical slang sense, dried peas boiled in a cloth.]

dog's bollocks noun Brit Something or someone outstanding in their field; the best. c.1986–. TIMES Before Tony Blair's speech, a chap near me growled: "E thinks 'e's the dog's bollocks.' Well, he's entitled to. It was a commanding speech: a real dog's bollocks of an oration (1995). [Perh. from the notion of being outstanding, from the prominence of the testicles in the male of certain breeds of dog, but cf. earlier *the cat's nuts, the cat's balls*, and similar expressions denoting excellence such as CAT'S WHISKERS noun and BEE'S KNEES noun; popularized by *Viz* magazine.]

dog's breakfast noun A mess. 1937–. TIMES He can't make head or tail of it. . . . It's a complete dog's breakfast (1959).

dog's dinner noun **1 like a dog's dinner** smartly or flashily (dressed, arranged, etc.). 1934–. J. TRENCH Tarting up my house and the gardens like a dog's dinner (1954). **2** = DOG'S BREAKFAST noun. 1971–. GUARDIAN The influential Georgian Group described the main frontage of the scheme as a dog's dinner yesterday (1985).

dog tag noun US An identity disc worn by service personnel. 1918–. PENGUIN NEW WRITING If I should die tomorrow, I suppose this is where my bones, if not my dog-tag, would lie for ever (1947).

dogwatch noun mainly US A night shift, esp. in a newspaper office; any late or early period of duty, or the staff employed on this. 1901–. TRUCKIN' LIFE Alan and Sue are the hosts and Neville looks after the shop on the dogwatch shift (1983). [From the earlier nautical sense, either of two short watches (4–6 or 6–8 p.m.).]

doing noun **1** A scolding; a thrashing, beating-up. 1880–. B. TURNER 'For God's sake, man! You'd get three years if you give him a doing,' she exclaimed (1968). **2** pl. Things needed; adjuncts; things whose names are not known. 1919–. G. GREENE Her skirt drawn up above her knees she waited for him with luxurious docility. . . . 'You've got the doings, haven't you?' (1938). **3** pl. euphemistic In phr. **to do one's doings,** to go to the lavatory; hence, excrement. 1967–. P. BEALE There's a

dog-box dog-end dogface dogging doggo doggone

lump of bird's doings on the windowsill (1984). Cf. *to do it* at DO verb 9.

doll noun A young woman, esp. an attractive one. 1846–. SCOPE (South Africa): You don't have to do it, doll (1971).

dollar noun dated, orig Brit Five shillings; esp. in phr. *half a dollar*, two shillings and sixpence. 1848–. H. SCANLON Could you lend me a dollar till tomorrow? (1925). [Prob. from the former exchange rate of five shillings to one US dollar, but there may be some connection with the use in Britain of Spanish dollar notes overstamped four shillings and nine pence in 1804.]

dolly-bird noun Brit An attractive and stylish young woman. Also **dolly.** 1964–. R. CRAWFORD You'll have to take . . . that dolly-bird you hide in Romford with you (1971).

DOM noun Abbreviation of DIRTY OLD MAN noun. 1959–. B. RODGERS DOMs should know better than to come to the tubs and fuck it up for the rest of us (1972).

dona /dəʊnə/ noun Also **donah.** Brit A woman; a man's sweetheart. 1873–. [From Spanish *doña* or Portuguese *dona* woman.]

doncher /dəʊntʃə(r)/ Also **doncha, dontcha, dontcher.** Representing a casual pronunciation of *don't you*. 1893–. L. J. CHIARAMONTE Why dontcha come around with us? (1969).

dong[1] Austral and NZ. verb trans. **1** To hit, punch. 1916–. P. WHITE 'I will dong you one,' shouted Hannah, 'before you tear this bloody fur' (1961). noun **2** A heavy blow. 1932–. [From earlier sense, sound of a large bell.]

dong[2] noun mainly US The penis. 1930–. P. ROTH I was wholly incapable of keeping my hands off my dong (1969). [Origin uncertain; perh. from *Dong*, name coined by Edward Lear (1877) for an imaginary creature with a luminous nose.]

donk noun dated A donkey. 1868–1957. R. CROMPTON Look out for the donk, you ole ass (1922).

donkey-lick verb trans. Austral To defeat easily, esp. in horse-racing. Also **donkey-wallop.** 1890–. NATIONAL TIMES (Australia): The Pommies . . . threw in a quartet of speedsters that had been donkey-licked by every cricketing nation around the world (1981). [*lick* defeat.]

Donnybrook noun Also **donnybrook.** A scene of uproar and disorder; a riotous or uproarious meeting; a heated argument.

1852–. ECONOMIST Imagine the Donnybrook there would be in France or Italy (1966). [From the name of *Donnybrook*, a suburb of Dublin, Ireland, once famous for its annual fair.]

doobie noun Also **dooby.** orig US Marijuana or a marijuana cigarette. 1967–. M. BRANT We'll all go down to Cassie's room to smoke a dooby (2002). [Origin uncertain; perh. connected with *dobby* household sprite, brownie.]

doobry noun Brit An unnamed or unspecified thing. 1990–. NEW STATESMAN I've got to go down to Sainsbury's to get the doobry for the loo and some petits fours for the dinner party (1996). [Prob. modelled on similar words beginning *do(o)-* (e.g. DOODAH noun 2).]

doodad noun mainly US A fancy article (of dress), a thingumajig; esp. a trivial or superfluous ornament. 1905–. D. ENEFER An open lacquered box with hair clips and other doodads (1966). [Origin unknown.]

doodah noun Also **do-da, dooda. 1** all of a doodah in a state of excitement; dithering. 1915–. P. G. WODEHOUSE Poor old Clarence was patently all of a doodah (1952). **2** = DOODAD noun. 1928–. H. CROOME They make little plastic doodahs to use in electrical machinery (1957). [From the refrain *doo-da(h)* of the plantation song 'Camptown Races'.]

doodle-bug noun A German flying bomb of World War II; a V-1. Also **doodle.** 1944–. T. PARKER I left school in 1944, just after the doodle-bugs finished (1969). [Cf. earlier sense, a tiger beetle, or the larva of this or various other insects.]

doodly-squat noun US A trivial amount or number; nothing. 1934–. Also **doodly** 1939–. [A fanciful formation.]

doo-doo noun orig and mainly N Amer **1** mainly childrens' Excrement. 1954–. **2** Nonsense, rubbish. 1954–. **3** Serving as a euphemistic substitute for *shit* in a range of idiomatic expressions. 1989–. FRONT What starts out as good, clean American fun, ends in tears, as they find out they're in deep doo-doo (2000). [A reduplication of DO noun 12.]

doofer noun Also **doofah. 1** Half a cigarette. 1937–. **2** A thing whose name is unknown or forgotten. 1945–. P. DICKINSON This is a very fancy doofer indeed. . . . It transmits along one wavelength and receives along another (1970). [Prob. alteration of *do for* in such phrases as *that will do for now*; cf. GOFER noun.]

doll dollar dolly-bird DOM dona doncher dong

dosh

doofus noun orig and mainly US A foolish or stupid person; an idiot. 1955–. L. BLOCK I feel sorry for Mapes, but he's sort of a doofus, isn't he? (2001). [Perh. an alteration of GOOFUS noun, perh. influenced by German *doof* stupid.]

doohickey noun Also **dohickey, doohicky.** orig and mainly US Any small object, esp. mechanical; a thingumajig. 1914–. A. LURIE Just unhitch that dohickey there with a wrench (1967). [From DOO(DAD noun + HICKEY noun.]

doojigger noun Also **do(-)jigger, doojigger.** US = DOOHICKEY noun 1927–. T. PYNCHON The extra little doojigger sort of coming out of the bell (1966). [From DOO(DAD noun + JIGGER noun.]

dooky noun Also **dookey, dookie, dukey.** orig and mainly US Excrement; hence, rubbish, trash. 1965–. P. BULLOCK Like we get dog dukey, put it in a bottle, throw it on them (1969). [Perh. an alteration of DOO-DOO noun.]

doolally adjective orig services' In full **doolally tap.** Deranged, mad. 1925–. J. CURTIS What's the matter with that bloke? Doolally? (1936). [Spoken form of *Deolali* (Marashtra, India), site of a British army camp + obs. *tap* malaria, from Persian *tap* fever, heat.]

Doolan noun Also **doolan.** NZ A Roman Catholic; an Irish Catholic. 1940–. D. M. DAVIN She'll have me a doolan yet, Father (1947). [Prob. from the Irish surname *Doolan*.]

door-step noun A thick slice of bread. 1885–. LISTENER Won't you slice me a doorstep please? (1969).

doover noun Also **doovah** Austral An unnamed or unspecified thing. 1941–. S. GORE They was humpin' along all these other doovers as well as the tucker (1968). [Origin uncertain; perh. representing a Yiddish pronunciation of Hebrew *davar* word, thing.]

doozer noun N Amer = DOOZY noun. 1930–. K. M. WELLS A storm was brewing. 'A real doozer,' I mumbled. 'A doozer' (1956). [See DOOZY adjective and noun.]

doozy orig and mainly N Amer. adjective 1 Remarkable, first-rate, stunning, 1903–. COURIER-MAIL (Brisbane): Swingers Saturday Night was doozy (1975). noun 2 Something of surprising size or excellence. 1916–. [Origin uncertain; perh. a variant of DAISY noun 1, first-rate example of anything.]

dope noun 1 orig dial A stupid person. 1851–. P. CAPON Silly dope, he can't go on dodging the court for ever (1959). 2 A narcotic drug. 1889–. TRUCKING INTERNATIONAL Police drugs squad . . . arrested the gang and seized 64 boxes of the 'best' Lebanese dope (1987). 3 A drug given to a horse or greyhound, or taken by an athlete, to affect performance. 1900–. 4 Information about a subject, esp. if not generally known. 1901–. A. CHRISTIE I shouldn't dream of denying it. You've obviously cabled to America and got all the dope (1945). verb 5a trans. To administer a drug to. 1889–. TIMES He had heard of greyhounds being doped, but not to make them run faster (1955). b intr. To take addictive drugs. 1909–. M. HONG KINGSTON I don't dope anymore. I've seen all there is to see on dope; the trips have been repeating themselves (1989). 6 to dope out to discover; to get the truth about. 1906–. N. MARSH Uncle James dopes it out that it's been Questing's idea to get this place on his own (1943). [Cf. earliest sense, any thick liquid used as a food or a lubricant.]

dopester noun orig US 1 One who collects information on, and forecasts the result of, sporting events, elections, etc. Cf. DOPE noun 4. 1907–. ECONOMIST The inside dopesters, squeezing the latest gossip about intra-party machinations out of politicians (1964). 2 One who sells, uses, or is addicted to, drugs. 1938–. [From DOPE noun + -ster.]

dopey adjective Also **dopy.** orig US Stupid, foolish. 1896–. H. GARNER That dopey foreman. He didn't bother to check with me (1963). [From DOPE noun + -y; orig sense prob., affected with a drug, sluggish, dozy.]

dork noun mainly US 1 The penis. 1964–. SPECTATOR A man with one leg and a vermilion bladder, violet stomach and testicles and a scarlet dork is seen putting it into another amputee (1984). 2 A fool; also as a general term of contempt. 1972–. ZIGZAG It will attract talentless dorks out for a taste of notoriety or a fast buck (1977). [Origin uncertain: perh. variant of *dirk* noun, influenced by DICK[1] noun.]

dose noun 1 (A bout of) a venereal infection. 1914–. B. TURNER She's riddled with pox. I know four blokes who've copped a dose from her (1968). 2 like a dose of salts Fast. 1837–. J. WAINWRIGHT If we don't hold 'em they'll go through this city like a dose of salts (1968). [In sense 2, from the sudden effect of aperient salts.]

dosh noun Money. 1953–. M. KENYON 'America! The money's in America!' . . . ''Tis true. The Yankees have the dosh all right' (1970). [Origin unknown.]

doofus doohickey doojigger dooky doolally Doolan

doss Brit verb intr. **1** To sleep, esp. roughly or in cheap lodgings; often with *down*. 1785–. DAILY EXPRESS If he wants to be on his way at daybreak he dosses down with his face to the east (1932). noun **2** A bed, esp. in cheap lodgings. Also with suffixed adverb. 1789–. E. BLYTON Only an old fellow who wants a doss-down somewhere (1956). [Prob. of same origin as obs. *doss* ornamental covering for a seat-back, etc., from Old French *dos*, ultimately from Latin *dorsum* back.]

dosser noun Brit A person who dosses. Also, = DOSS-HOUSE noun. 1866–. POLICE REVIEW The tipple of the down-and-out itinerant, the 'dosser' or 'scat' (1984). [From DOSS verb + *-er*.]

doss-house noun orig Brit A cheap lodging house, esp. for vagrants. 1888–.

dot verb trans. **1** To hit; esp. in phr. *to dot* (a person) *one*. 1895–. J. B. PRIESTLEY Any monkey tricks an' I'll dot yer one (1951). noun **2** pl. mainly jazz Originally, the notes on sheet music; hence, written or printed music. 1927–.

dothead noun US derog and offensive A person of South Asian origin or descent. 1982–. [From the tika mark or bindi on the forehead of some Hindu women.]

double O noun US An intense look. 1917–. R. A. HEINLEIN The cashier came over and leaned on my table, giving the seats on both sides of the booth a quick double-O (1957). [From the resemblance to a pair of staring eyes.]

double sawbuck noun US Also **double saw**. **1** Twenty dollars; a twenty-dollar note. 1850–. L. DUNCAN I learned quickly that a dollar-bill was a fish-skin; . . . a twenty a double-saw (1936). **2** A twenty-year prison sentence. 1945–. [Cf. SAWBUCK noun.]

double whammy noun See WHAMMY.

doubloons noun pl. Money. 1908–. P. BULL I . . . was anxious to lay my hands on anything that brought in the doubloons (1959). [From earlier sense, Spanish gold coin.]

douche-bag noun US An unattractive or boring person; also as a general term of contempt. 1967–. PUNCH 'Send them away!' she hissed. 'If they are found here, those douche-bags will incriminate us all' (1968). [From earlier sense, apparatus used for douching.]

dough noun orig US Money. 1851–. TIMES I'm going back to business and make myself a little dough (1955). [From earlier sense, mixture of flour and liquid.] Cf. BREAD noun.

doughboy noun US A US infantryman, esp. in World War I. 1867–. A. LOOS During World War I, she dressed as a doughboy in olive drab (1966). [Perh. from *doughboy* boiled flour dumpling, from a supposed resemblance to the large round buttons on US infantry uniforms in the Civil War.]

doughfoot noun US A soldier, esp. an ordinary infantryman, in the US army. 1943–. [Suggested by DOUGHBOY noun.]

Douglas noun Austral An axe; esp. in phr. *to swing Douglas*. 1905–. J. HACKSTON Sometimes on a Sunday morning exhibitions of axemanship . . . were given; right and wrong way to swing Douglas (1966). [Formerly a proprietary name in the US for axes, hatchets, etc., produced by the Douglas Axe Manufacturing Co., East Douglas, Mass.]

down noun **1 to have a down on** orig Austral To dislike, be badly disposed towards. 1828–. W. S. MAUGHAM She had a down on Lady Kastellan and didn't care what she said about her (1947). **2** orig US = DOWNER noun 2. Often in pl. 1969–. M. KAYE Tom needed money for drugs . . . pot, acid, speed, ups, downs (1972). [In sense 1, from obs. Brit criminals' slang *down* suspicion, alarm, discovery.]

downer noun **1 to have (or get) a downer on** = to have a down on (see DOWN noun). 1915–. S. SASSOON He asserted that I'd got 'a downer' on some N.C.O. (1936). **2** A depressant or tranquillizing drug, esp. a barbiturate. 1966–. DAILY TELEGRAPH Those that shoot dope are soon stoned and on the habit, junkies liable to write their own scripts and thieve your downers and perhaps your chinky (1983). **3** A depressing person or experience; a failure. 1970–. T. BARR The role of a downer should not be a downer to watch (1982). **4** A downward trend, esp. in business or the economy. 1976–. Cf. UPPER noun.

downie noun = DOWNER noun 2. 1966–.

down-low adjective (orig in African-American usage) **1** Secret, quiet, low-profile; spec. (of a man) secretly homosexual. 1991–. noun **2** on the down-low in secret; spec., secretly homosexual. 1992–.

dozy adjective Brit Stupid or lazy. 1924–. J. MACLAREN-ROSS What's funny, you dozy berk? (1961). [From earlier sense, sleepy.]

drack Also **drac**. Austral adjective **1** Dismal, dull. 1945–. G. DUTTON You blokes get on to some bloody drack subjects (1968). **2** Esp. of a woman: unattractive. 1953–. SYDNEY MORNING HERALD Mr Hardy said he would put aside his

doss dosser doss-house dot dothead double O

drip

memories . . . of meeting Raquel Welch ('A drac sort—not nearly as good looking in the flesh as you would expect') (1972). noun **3** Someone unattractive or unwelcome (esp. a woman or a policeman). 1960–. B. BEAVER I thought she was going to kiss it [my hand] or bite it like another silly drack I knew once did (1966). [Origin uncertain; sometimes said to derive from the name of the US film *Dracula's Daughter* (1936).]

drag verb **1 to drag the chain** Austral and NZ To go slowly; to fall behind the rest. 1912–. G. SLATTER Stop dragging the chain and have one with me (1959). **2** intr. orig US To draw on a cigarette, etc.; followed by *at* or *on*. 1919–. H. CROOME He lit one cigarette from the butt of another and dragged at it nervously (1957). **3** trans. dated To arrest. 1924–. E. WALLACE If you particularly want him dragged, you'll tell me what I can drag him on (1928). **4** intr. US To race a car; to take part in a drag race. 1950–. HOT ROD MAGAZINE There ought to be a place to drag in every city. . . . There would be no excuse to drag on the streets (1950). noun **5** Now mainly US A street, road; esp. in phr. *the main drag.* 1851–. J. P. CARSTAIRS We drove through . . . the main drag of Babaki (1965). **6** A boring or dreary person, duty, performance, etc. 1857–. C. MACINNES The whole thing was becoming something of a drag (1959). **7a** Women's clothes worn by men. 1870–. J. OSBORNE You would never have the fag Of dressing up in drag You'd be a woman at the weekend (1959). **b** A party at which these are worn. 1927–. **c** Clothes in general. 1959–. LISTENER Laurence Olivier, doing his Othello voice and attired painstakingly in Arab drag (1966). **8** US Influence, pull. 1896–. E. HEMINGWAY We had a big drag with the waiter because my old man drank whisky and it cost five francs, and that meant a good tip (1923). **9** A draw on a cigarette, etc. 1914–. COAST TO COAST 1961–2 We stopped beside a little trickle of water for ten minutes' break and a drag (1962). **10** A car. 1935–. OBSERVER A stately great drag . . . with a smart chauffeur at the wheel (1960). [In sense 7, from the (unaccustomed) length and weight of women's dresses.]

dragging noun Stealing from vehicles. 1812–1938.

draggy adjective orig US Tedious; uncongenial. 1922–. LISTENER I know it's draggy having the au pair feeding with us; but one has to be madly democratic if one wants to keep them (1967). [From DRAG noun 6 + -*y.*]

drag queen noun A male homosexual transvestite. 1941–.

drain noun **1 to go** (etc.) **down the drain** to be lost or wasted. 1925–. ANNUAL REGISTER It appeared that at least one donor country was realizing that aid could easily go down the drain (1961). **2 to laugh like a drain** to laugh loudly; guffaw. 1948–. K. NICHOLSON Old Hester would laugh like a drain if she could see us singing hymns over her (1966).

drape noun A suit of clothes; also, in pl., clothes. 1945–. M. SWAN He was a . . . man of thirty-two, wearing gaberdine drapes and a bow-tie (1957). [From earlier sense, cloth, drapery.]

drat Also (dated US) **drot**. int **1** Expressing (mild) annoyance. 1815–. verb trans. **2** Used in mild imprecations, as a euphemistic substitute for 'damn'. 1857–. Hence **dratted,** adjective Confounded. 1869–. [From archaic *'od rot*, euphemistic alteration of *God rot.*]

draw verb **to draw it mild** to be moderate in speech; not exaggerate. 1837–. [From the notion of drawing beer from the cask.]

dream-boat noun orig US An extremely attractive person or thing, esp. a member of the opposite sex. 1947–. T. RATTIGAN I thought you'd be quite old and staid and ordinary and, my God, look at you, a positive dream boat (1951).

dreamy adjective Delightful; marvellous. 1941–. M. DICKENS She said she had a date with a dreamy boy (1953).

drear noun A dreary person. 1958–. J. B. PRIESTLEY He was just a miserable little drear (1966). [Back-formation from *dreary* adjective.]

dreary noun = DREAR noun. 1925–. H. G. WELLS The parade of donnish and scholastic drearies (1936). [From *dreary* adjective.]

dreck noun Also **drek**. Rubbish, trash. 1922–. O. HESKY Meat better than the usual *drek* we get (1967). [From Yiddish *drek* filth, dregs, dung.]

drink noun **the drink** orig US The sea. 1941–. L. MEYNELL [He] had fished us out of the drink just . . . in time (1960). [From *big drink* sea, from earlier *drink* any body of water, including a river.]

drip noun **1** orig US Nonsense; flattery; sentimental drivel. 1919–. B. GRAY 'We'll have nothing of the sort,' interrupted Joy, putting a welcome stop to this drip (1946). **2** A stupid, dull, or ineffective person. 1932–. J. CANNAN Of all the wet drips! (1951). **3** orig naval A grumble, complaint. 1945–. GUARDIAN One of the accused,

drag   dragging   draggy   drag queen   drain   drape

drippy

Able Seaman Edward Kirkbride, said he remembered someone saying: 'I am going to have a drip (complaint)' (1970). verb intr. **4** naval To complain, grumble. 1942.

drippy adjective orig US Ineffectual; sloppily sentimental. 1952–. o. norton Men get so drippy when they're over-civilized, don't they? (1967). [From drip noun + -y.]

drive noun US A thrill; exhilaration, esp. resulting from the use of narcotics. 1931–. n. algren I like to see it hit. Heroin got the drive awright—but there's not a tingle to a ton (1949).

drongo /ˈdrɒŋgəʊ/ noun Austral and NZ A fool, simpleton. 1941–. advertiser (Adelaide): You Aussie coves are just a bunch of drongoes (1969). [Cf. earlier sense, bird of the family Dicruridae found in India, Africa, and Australia, from Malagasy *drongo*; perh. suggested by the use of the word as the name of an Australian racehorse of the 1920s that often finished last.]

'Men get so drippy when they're over-civilized, don't they?'

droob noun Also **drube**. Austral A hopeless-looking ineffectual person. 1933–. j. jost You're not normal boy . . . . You're a mug, a droob, a weak mess of shit! (1974). Hence **drooby**, adjective Austral 1972–. [Prob. from droop noun.]

droog noun A young ruffian; an accomplice or henchman of a gang-leader. 1962–. times literary supplement How long ago it seems since the *New York Times* referred to the spray-can droogs of the subways as 'little Picassos' (1984). [An adaptation of Russian *drug* friend, introduced by Anthony Burgess in *A Clockwork Orange*.]

drool noun orig US Nonsense, drivel. 1900–. n. freeling He switched the radio on—no short wave, and the medium band was filled with drool (1966). [From earlier sense, spittle.]

droop noun US An ineffectual or wet person. 1932–.

droopy drawers noun jocular An untidy, sloppy, or depressing woman or man. 1939–. a. gilbert The neighbours round about thought what bad luck on that charming Mr. Duncan having a droopy-drawers for a wife (1966). [*drawers* underpants.]

drop verb **1 to drop (down) to** or **on (to)** to become aware of. 1819–. r. braddon It was the

only place we *could* live—without being caught that is. Surprises me you never dropped to it, Mr Prime Minister, sir (1964). **2 to drop one's bundle** Austral and NZ To go to pieces, give up. 1897–. s. gore It started to rain, too. And at this, he really drops his bundle (1968). **3a: drop dead!** orig US An exclamation of intense scorn. 1934–. i. & p. opie The well-worn sentiments . . . . 'Do me a favour—drop dead' (1959). **b: drop-dead** orig and mainly US awe-inspiring(ly), amazing(ly). 1970–. new york times That's the other way of succeeding, to be drop-dead gorgeous (1993). **4** trans. To pass (counterfeit money, cheques, etc.). 1938–. l. black The known value of counterfeit fivers dropped is more than double that (1968). **5** trans. To take (a drug); esp. in phr. *to drop acid*. 1966–. s. bellow Some kids are dropping acid, stealing cars (1984). **6 to drop** (someone) **in it** to cause (someone) to be in trouble. 1991–. just seventeen Your mate reveals she's really dropped you in it with your folks today, but she's just winding you up. Had you going for a minute though (1996). noun **7 to get** (or **have**) **the drop on** orig US To get (have) a person at a disadvantage. 1883–. new yorker F.B.I. agents had been trying to 'crawl up through the belly of the plane either to get the drop on him [i.e. a hijacker] or to get a shot at him' (1970). **8** A dealer in stolen goods; a fence. 1915–. k. orvis You say you buy expensive jewels. You say you pay better prices than ordinary drops do (1962). **9a** A hiding-place for stolen or illicit goods. 1931–. k. orvis Employing an expensive West End brothel . . . as a heroin drop (1962). **b** A secret place where documents, etc. may be left or passed on by a spy. 1959–. i. fleming They had arranged an emergency meeting place and a postal 'drop' (1965). **10** A bribe. 1931–. g. orwell A half-penny's the usual drop (gift) (1933). [In sense 7, from earlier sense, to have the chance to shoot before one's opponent can do so.]

drop-in noun US Something easily done or acquired, esp. money. 1937–. [Perh. from the notion of a gullible person 'dropping into' a confidence trick.]

dropper noun One who passes counterfeit money, cheques, etc. 1938–. c. hare The functionary whose mission it is to put forged currency into circulation is known technically as a dropper (1959). [Cf. drop verb 4.]

drippy drive drongo droob droog drool droop drop

dropsy noun Money, esp. paid as a tip or bribe. 1930–. P. WILDEBLOOD A nice bit of dropsy to a copper usually does the trick (1955). [Jocular extension of *dropsy* excess of fluids in body tissue, from the notion of 'dropping' money into someone's hand; cf. DROP noun 9.]

drugger noun = DRUGGY noun. 1941–. H. R. F. KEATING Your precious Peacock . . . was nothing but a low-down little drugger (1968). [Cf. earlier sense, druggist.]

druggy adjective 1 Of or like narcotic drugs or their users; consisting of drug-takers. 1959–. TIMES I was enmeshed in a very druggy crowd at the time (1984). noun 2 Also **druggie**. A drug-addict. 1968–. WASHINGTON POST Sherlock Holmes fans . . . remember his portrayal as an angstridden druggie a few years back (1979). [Cf. earlier adjective sense, of medicinal drugs.]

drug-store cowboy noun US A swaggering fellow; a loafer, good-for-nothing; a person who is not a cowboy but is dressed as one. 1925–. P. FRANK She married . . . a marijuana-smoking drugstore cowboy (1957).

drum noun 1a A house, flat, etc.; a place where someone lives. 1846–. L. SOUTHWORTH They probably checked at the Probation office as soon as they left my drum (1966). b mainly US A nightclub, drinking-place, or brothel. 1859–. C. ROHAN Each one of these houses was that dreariest, dullest, loneliest and ugliest institution in the whole history of harlotry—the one-woman drum (1963). 2 Austral and NZ A swagman's pack. 1866–. BULLETIN (Sydney): I sees a bloke comin' along the road from Winton with 'is drum up (1933). See also **to hump one's drum** at HUMP verb. 3 Austral A piece of reliable information, esp. a racing tip. 1915–. D. O'GRADY Gave us the drum on where to get hold of the particular rifles we had our eyes on (1968). 4 A tin or can in which tea, etc., is made; so **drum-up**, a making of tea; the preparation of a meal. 1919–. verb 5 trans. Austral To provide with reliable information. Also with *up*. 1919–. D. NILAND Jesus, don't bite me, son. I was only gonna drum you (1969). 6 **to drum up** to make tea in a billy-can, etc.; also, to prepare a rough-and-ready meal. 1923–. G. ORWELL After getting to Bromley they had 'drummed up' on a horrible, paper-littered refuse dump (1935). 7a intr. To steal from an unoccupied house, room, etc. 1925–. OBSERVER They were both making a steady living at drumming (1962). b trans. To ring or knock on the door of (a house) to see if it is unoccupied before attempting a robbery; hence, to reconnoitre

with a view to robbery. 1933–. [In sense 1a, from earlier sense, a street.]

drummer noun 1 A thief, esp. one who robs an unoccupied house. 1856–. OBSERVER Nobody wanted to know the drummers, those squalid daytime operators who turn over empty semi-detached villas while the housewives are out shopping (1960). 2 Austral and NZ, dated The worst or slowest sheep-shearer in a team. 1897–. H. P. TRITTON It's not every man that is drummer in four sheds running (1959). 3 Austral and NZ, dated A swagman or tramp. 1898–1945. [In sense 2, perh. jocular use of obs. *drummer* commercial traveller; in sense 3, partly from DRUM noun 2, partly from *drummer* commercial traveller.]

drunk noun A drinking-bout; a period of drunkenness. 1779–. H. NIELSEN She was sleeping off a drunk in the bedroom (1966).

drunk tank noun N Amer A large prison cell for the detention of drunks. 1947–.

dry verb 1 intr. **a: to dry up** to stop talking; esp. in imperative. 1853–. F. SCOTT FITZGERALD 'Oh, dry up!' retorted Basil (1928). **b** theatre To forget one's lines; often with *up*. 1934–. M. SHULMAN 'O.K., Allan,' said the director into his microphone. 'If she fluffs badly or dries we'll go straight to Three' (1967). 2 **to dry out** intr. Of a drug addict, alcoholic, etc.: to undergo treatment to cure addiction. Also trans., to cure (a drug addict or alcoholic) in this way. 1967–. E. TIDYMAN By eight she had undergone . . . the drying-out procedure in private institutions (1970). noun 3 orig US Someone who opposes the sale and consumption of alcohol; a prohibitionist. 1888–. P. G. WODEHOUSE The woman who runs the school is a rabid Dry and won't let her staff so much as look at a snifter (1965). 4 Brit A Conservative politician who advocates individual responsibility, free trade, and economic stringency, and opposes high government spending. 1983–. SUNDAY TELEGRAPH For ten years the Tory party has been split between Wets and Dries (1987). Cf. WET noun.

dry bath noun A search of a prisoner who has been stripped naked. 1933–. NEW STATESMAN Two or three times a week the Heavy Mob rushed into our cells and gave us a 'dry bath' (1965).

dry fuck noun US A simulated act of sexual intercourse, without penetration, or an unsatisfactory or anticlimactic act of intercourse. 1971–. Hence **dry-fuck,** verb.

dropsy   drugger   druggy   drug-store cowboy   drum

D.T.

D.T. noun Also **D.T.'s** Abbreviation of 'delirium tremens'. 1858–. KESSEL & WALTON Delirium tremens—DTs—generally begins two to five days after stopping very heavy drinking (1969).

dub[1] noun criminals' A key, esp. one used for picking locks. a.1700–1923. [Cf. DUB[1] verb.]

dub[2] noun orig and mainly US An inexperienced or unskilful person. 1887–. O. NASH The unassuming dub Trying to pick up a Saturday game In the locker room of the club (1949). [Perh. related to obs. *dub* to beat flat, *dubbed* blunted, pointless.]

dub[1] verb **to dub up** to shut up or in. 1753–. F. NORMAN Everybody in the nick had already been dubbed up for the night (1958). [Cf. earlier sense, to open; perh. alteration of obs. *dup* to open, from *do up*.]

dub[2] verb intr. To pay up; contribute money; followed by *in* or *up*. 1823–. E. BLUNDEN Five or six boys 'dub in' for a pot of strawberry jam (1923). [Origin unknown.]

ducat noun Also **ducket(t)**. A ticket, esp. a railway-ticket or ticket of admission. 1871–. GUARDIAN My wife and I had a couple of ducketts to see the Marxes' Broadway musical, 'Animal Crackers' (1970). [Prob. from earlier sense, coin; perh. influenced by *docket* and *ticket*.]

duchess noun **1** dated A girl or woman, spec. one's mother or wife. 1895–1923. Cf. DUTCH noun. **2** A term of address to a woman. 1953–. L. FORRESTER Start talkin', Duchess. We're gonna toss what you got into the computer . . . and see what comes out (1967). [From earlier sense, woman of imposing demeanour or showy appearance.]

duck noun **1** Brit **a** A term of endearment. 1590–. A. SILLITOE Don't get like that, Ernie, duck (1979). **b: ducks.** A friendly form of address. 1936–. E. HYAMS Talked like you'e did, ducks (1958). Cf. DUCKY noun. **2** US An amphibious aircraft. 1938–42.

duck's arse noun Also **duck-arse, duck's ass, duck's anatomy, duck's behind**. A haircut with the hair on the back of the head shaped like a duck's tail. 1951–. N. COHN He looked like another sub-Elvis, smooth flesh and duck-ass hair (1969). Cf. DA noun.

duck's disease noun Also **ducks' disease, duck-disease**. A facetious expression for shortness of the legs. 1925–. B. MARSHALL Plinio, the barman with duck's disease, came running up (1960).

duck-shoving noun Austral and NZ The practice of taxi-drivers not waiting their turn in the rank, but touting for passengers; hence, manoeuvring for advantage, manipulative action. 1870–. SYDNEY MORNING HERALD This sniping and duck shoving between county councils and the Electricity Commission should also cease (1982). Hence **duck-shove,** verb intr. and trans.; **duck-shover,** noun.

duck soup noun orig and mainly US An easy task. 1912–. OGILVY & ANDERSON The number 307 comes out, in binary notation, to be 100110011 which would not have the convenience of 307 at the grocery store, but is duck soup for the Computer (1966).

duck-tail noun **1** = DUCK'S ARSE noun. 1955–. **2** S Afr A young hooligan or teddy-boy. 1959–. GUARDIAN He [i.e. Dr Verwoerd] described South Africa's overseas critics as 'the ducktails (Teddy boys) of the political world' (1960). [In sense 2, from the preferred hairstyle of teddy-boys.]

ducky Brit noun **1** Also **duckie**. A friendly form of address, or a term of endearment. 1819–. E. HYAMS I must have sounded disagreeable, because Matilda said, 'Don't be narky, ducky' (1958). Cf. DUCK noun 1. adjective **2** Sweet, pretty; fine, splendid. Mainly in affected or ironic use. 1897–. M. DICKENS I shall tell the tradesmen that you have no authority to give orders. . . . That's going to make you look just ducky, isn't it? (1958). [From DUCK noun + *-y*.]

dud noun **1** pl. Clothes. 1307–. W. KENNEDY Put her in new duds, high heels and silk stockin's (1979). **2** A counterfeit article. 1897–. **3** A futile or ineffectual person or thing. 1908–. R. GRAVES An expert on shell-fish, otherwise a dud (1951). **4** A shell, bomb, firework, etc. that fails to explode or ignite. 1915–. PUBLIC OPINION All the torpedoes they carry are duds (1923). adjective **5** Counterfeit. 1903–. **6** Useless, worthless, unsatisfactory, or futile. 1904–. TIMES LITERARY SUPPLEMENT The dud violinists rehearsing in the next room (1958). [Origin uncertain.]

dude noun US **1** A non-westerner or city-dweller who tours or stays in the west of the US, esp. a holiday-maker on a ranch. 1883–. H. CROY I'm going to put up the finest cattle barn in the state—that is, belonging to a real dirt farmer, not to one of them city dudes (1924). **2** A fellow; a guy; also (through African-American use) applied approvingly to a member of one's own circle or group. 1918–. M. AMIS I think my dog go bite one of them white dudes (1984). verb trans. and intr. **3 to dude up**

D.T. dub ducat duchess duck duck's arse ducky

orig US To dress (oneself) in one's smartest or most impressive clothes; usu. in phr. *duded up.* 1899–. GUARDIAN The two men, shaved and rested and all duded up (1960). [From earlier sense, fastidiously dressed man, dandy; prob. from German dialect *Dude* fool.]

duff¹ Brit noun **1** Something worthless or spurious; counterfeit money; smuggled goods. 1781–. G. INGRAM 'That's all duff,' he proceeded. The announcement that so much was rubbish, as it consisted of imitation jewellery [etc.] (1935). adjective **2** Counterfeit, spurious. 1889–. G. NETHERWOOD It was said by the erks that he once sold rock on Blackpool sands. This was just 'duff gen' (1944). **3** Broken, useless; of poor quality. 1956–. J. LYMINGTON I went down to the pub because the play was so duff (1965). [Perh. from *duff* dough (see DUFF² noun).]

duff² noun **up the duff** orig Austral Pregnant. 1941–. X. HERBERT Anyway, next thing she's up the duff. But to whom? (1975). [Prob. same word as Brit *duff* dough; cf. *in the pudding club* pregnant, at CLUB noun.]

duff verb trans. **1** Austral **a** To steal (cattle, sheep, etc.), often altering their brands. 1859–. H. C. BAKER Complaining to the police that his stock was being duffed (1978). **b** To pasture (stock) illegally on another's land. 1900–. **2** Brit Of a golfer: to mishit (a shot, a ball); also generally, to make a mess of. 1897–. SUNDAY EXPRESS The ninth provided Landale's crowning error, for he duffed two mashie shots (1927). **3 to duff (someone) up** to beat (someone) up. 1961–. R. LAIT They had been duffed up at the police station (1968). [Perh. back-formation from DUFFER noun.]

duffer noun **1** An inefficient, useless, or stupid person. 1842–. G. SMITH While the truly great . . . go unknighted there is no shortage of such accolades for the second-rate: duffers like Henry Newbolt and John Squire (1984). **2** Austral A person who steals stock, often altering their brands. 1844–. R. H. CONQUEST That veteran cattle-man . . . had been a bit of a duffer himself in his youth (1965). **3** Austral and NZ An unproductive mine, goldfield, or claim. 1855–. N. MILES I haven't had much luck on the last four 'duffers' I've sunk (1972). verb intr. **4** Austral and NZ Of a mine: to prove unproductive or become exhausted; usu. followed by *out.* 1880–. C. SIMPSON Billy's tin show must have duffered out by now (1952). [Perh. from Scots *doofart* stupid person, from *douf* spiritless.]

dug-out noun A person of outdated appearance or ideas; spec. a retired officer, etc. recalled to temporary military service. 1912–. P. KEMP The Assistant Provost Marshal . . . was a dug-out major of a famous cavalry regiment (1958). [From the notion of digging out something previously disposed of by burying; cf. earlier *dug-out* canoe made from a hollowed-out tree trunk, excavated shelter.]

dujie noun Also **duji.** US Heroin. 1959–. [Origin unknown.]

duke Also **dook.** verb trans. **1** dated To shake hands with. 1865–1929. D. RUNYON The old judge does himself proud, what with kissing Madame La Gimp's baby plenty, and duking the proud old Spanish nobleman (1929)–. noun **2** The hand or fist; usu. pl. 1874–. J. MITFORD The funeral men are always ready with dukes up to go to the offensive (1963). [Prob. short for *Duke of Yorks*, rhyming slang for *forks* fingers.]

dullsville noun and adjective Also **Dullsville.** orig US (Characteristic of) an imaginary town that is extremely dull or boring; hence, (in) a condition or environment of extreme dullness. 1960–. OXFORD TIMES January and February are traditionally 'dullsville' months in restaurants and pubs and clubs (1978). [From *dull* adjective + -VILLE.]

dumb-ass adjective US **1** Also **dumb-assed.** Stupid. 1957–. noun US **2** = DUMB-BELL noun. 1958–.

dumb-bell noun orig US A stupid person; a fool. 1920–. PUNCH A dumb-bell being the kind of person who writes to the manufacturer asking him to replace a gadget that has been lost, and then adds a postscript telling him not to bother as the missing gadget has just been found (1936). [After *dumb* stupid; cf. earlier sense, weighted bar used for exercise.]

dumb bunny noun = DUMB-BELL noun. 1922–.

dumb-butt noun US = DUMB-BELL noun. 1973–. [From *dumb* stupid + BUTT noun.]

dumb cluck noun Also **dumb-cluck.** orig US = DUMB-BELL noun. 1929–. O. MANNING For the last half-hour I've been telling these dumb clucks to find me a bloke who can speak English (1960). [Cf. CLUCK noun.]

dumb Dora noun A stupid girl or woman. 1922–. G. MCINNES They [i.e. hens] would then wait expectantly, heads cocked on one side with a sort of dumb-Dora inquisitive chuckle (1965). [From the female personal name *Dora*.]

dumb-dumb noun Also **dum-dum.** orig N Amer = DUMB-BELL noun 1970–. CALGARY HERALD

duff duffer dug-out dujie duke dumb bunny

Better they should employ some dumb-dumb (1970). [Reduplication of *dumb* stupid.]

dumbfuck noun US = DUMB-BELL noun. 1949–.

dumbhead noun mainly US = DUMB-BELL noun. 1887–. C. E. MULFORD Have I got to do *all* the thinking for this crowd of dumbheads? (1921). [From *dumb* stupid + *head*, after German *Dummkopf*, Dutch *domkop*.]

dumbo /ˈdʌmbəʊ/ noun orig US = DUMB-BELL noun. 1960–. S. TOWNSEND I am sharing a book with three dumbos who take half an hour to read one page (1984). [From *dumb* stupid + *-o*.]

dumbshit noun US = DUMB-BELL noun. 1961–. W. GIBSON 'Sorry, gentlemen, but this official warlord biz,' this dumbshit says (1986).

dummkopf /ˈdʊmkɒpf/ noun Also **dumkopf, dumbkopf**. orig US = DUMB-BELL noun. 1809–. LISTENER They may turn out . . . to have been fall guys, dumbkopfs, dupes of their own chicanery (1968). [German *Dummkopf* idiot, from *dumm* stupid + *Kopf* head; cf. DUMBHEAD noun.]

dummy noun **1** A stupid person. 1796–. SUNDAY EXPRESS MAGAZINE The emphasis at the school was all on rugby and the classics. Art was for dummies (1986). **2** A deaf-mute; a tramp or beggar who pretends to be deaf and dumb. 1874–. C. MCCULLERS But a dummy! . . . . 'Are there any other deaf-mute people here?' he asked (1940). **3** NZ The punishment cell in a prison. 1936–. O. BURTON The aggressor in this case was promptly led off and incarcerated in the 'dummy' (1945). verb intr. **4 to dummy up** US To refuse to talk or give information; to clam up. 1926–. K. ORVIS All right, dummy up, then (1962). [From *dumb* adjective + *-y*; cf. earliest sense, dumb person.]

dump noun **1** An act of defecating. 1942–. W. H. AUDEN To start the morning With a satisfactory Dump is a good omen All our adult days (1966). verb intr. **2 to dump on** (or **all over**) (a person): mainly US To criticize or abuse (someone); to get the better of. 1963–. WOMAN'S OWN One minute I'm with a woman who makes me feel like a man, the next I'm with someone who's dumping all over me (1985).

dunno /dʌˈnəʊ, dəˈnəʊ/ Also **dunna(w)**, etc. Representing a casual pronunciation of (*I*) *don't know*. 1842–. P. MOLONEY A sed 'Wharar thee whack?' 'A dunno,' she said back (1966).

dunny noun Also **dunnee**. Austral and NZ An outdoor earth-closet; hence, *broadly*, any lavatory. 1933–. PRIVATE EYE It seems a bit crook

for old bazza to spend the night in the dunnee! (1970). [From Brit dialect *dunnekin* privy, of unknown origin.]

dunt noun RAF, dated A jolt suffered by an airship as a result of rising or falling air currents. 1924–8. [From earlier sense, blow, stroke.]

durry noun Austral A cigarette. 1941–. N. MANNING *Steve*: (stubbing out his cigarette) Waste of a good durry! (1977). [Origin unknown.]

dust verb trans. **1** To hit, thrash. 1612–. TIME [Miners] dusted one of [the district leader's] lieutenants with an old shoe for trying to talk them back to work (1950). **2 to dust** (someone) **off** orig US To defeat or kill (someone). 1938–. TIMES They have always been dusted off in the inter-zone matches (1960). [In sense 1, perh. from the notion of striking in order to raise or remove dust; but cf. also Middle English *dust* verb to throw or hit violently, of uncertain origin.] Cf. DUST-UP noun.

dustbin noun Brit A gun-turret of an aircraft, esp. one beneath the fuselage. 1934–. [From its resemblance in shape to a dustbin for refuse.]

duster noun naval A flag or ensign. 1904–. PUNCH She's dipped her dingy duster in the spray of all the seas (1918). [From earlier sense, cloth for removing dust.] Cf. RED DUSTER noun.

dust-up noun A quarrel, fight, disturbance. 1897–. N. SHUTE He had a bit of a dust-up with one of his girl friends (1944). [Prob. from obs. slang *dust* noun, row, disturbance + *up*; cf. DUST verb 1.]

dusty adjective **not** (or **none**) **so dusty** Brit Fairly good. 1856–. J. B. PRIESTLEY 'You're a swell tonight all right!' . . . 'Not so dusty, Mar,' said Leonard (1929).

Dutch noun **1 to do a** (or **the**) **Dutch** (**act**) orig US To desert, escape, run away; also, to commit suicide. 1904–. M. A. DE FORD You can't face it . . . so you're doing the Dutch and leaving a confession (1958). **2 in Dutch** orig US In disfavour or trouble. 1912–. J. DOS PASSOS I plodded around . . . trying to explain my position and getting myself deeper in Dutch every time I opened my face (1968). See also *to beat the Dutch* at BEAT verb.

dutch noun dated, mainly Brit A wife, esp. orig a costermonger's wife; esp. in phr. *old dutch*. *a.*1889–. T. PYNCHON Time for closeting, gas logs, shawls against the cold night, snug with your

dumbfuck   dumbhead   dumbo   dumbshit   dump

young lady or old dutch (1973). [Abbreviation of DUCHESS noun 1.]

Dutching noun Brit The practice of sending food destined for the UK market for irradiation abroad (usu. in the Netherlands), to mask any bacterial contamination before it is put on sale. 1989–. [From *Dutch* adjective + *-ing*.]

Dutchy noun Also **Dutchee, Dutchie.** derog orig US A Dutch or German person. 1835–. [From *Dutch* noun + *-y*.]

dweeb noun US Someone held in contempt, esp. a swot or 'weed'; a nerd. 1982–. CHICAGO TRIBUNE Any community that can knowingly elect a dweeb like Edwin Eisendrath as alderman obviously has a precious sense of fun (1990). [Origin uncertain; perh. influenced by *dwarf* and *weed* feeble person.]

dyke¹ noun Also **dike.** A water-closet or urinal. 1923–. J. CLEARY I learned . . . to respect her privacy. And I don't mean just when she went to the dike (1967). [From earlier sense, ditch.]

dyke² noun Also **dike.** A lesbian; a masculine woman. 1942–. E. MCBAIN 'Was your wife a dyke?' 'No.' 'Are you a homosexual?' 'No' (1965). Cf. BULL-DYKE noun. [Origin unknown.] Hence **dikey,** adjective Like a lesbian. 1964–. J. MORRIS Helen's gone dikey in her old age (1969).

dynamite noun orig US A narcotic drug, esp. heroin. 1924–. M. CULPAN 'A little bit of horse? Some dynamite?' Horse was heroin; so was dynamite (1967). [From its explosive effect on the user.]

dyno noun Also **dino** US A vagrant, tramp. 1918–. [Apparently shortened from obs. vagrants' slang *dynamiter* sponger.]

Dutching Dutchy dweeb dyke dynamite dyno

E e

E noun = ECSTASY noun. 1989–. NEW MUSICAL EXPRESS 'People will dance to anything now,' muses Mal. 'I blame the E meself!' (1990). [Abbreviation.]

ear-bash verb trans. and intr. mainly Austral To talk inordinately (to); to harangue. 1944–. S. GORE Just like you hear 'em ear-bashin' each other in Parliament to this day (1968). Hence **ear-basher,** noun A chatterer; a bore. 1941–.

ear-biter noun dated, orig Austral Someone who is always trying to borrow money; a cadger. 1899–. P. G. WODEHOUSE Two things which rendered Oofy Prosser a difficult proposition for the ear-biter (1940). [From the phr. *to bite someone's ear* (see BITE verb).]

earful noun **1** As much as one is able to hear or can tolerate hearing. 1917–. F. SARGESON I tried to get an earful when I heard somebody out on the landing-place (1946). **2** A strong and often lengthy reprimand. 1945–. TIMES I used to put a bottle on the seat and if it rolled off when the pupil let his clutch out, he got an earful (1964). [From *ear* noun + *-ful*.]

earhole noun The ear. 1923–. JOHN O' LONDON'S Before you know it you'll be out on your earhole (1962).

early doors adverb Brit Early on; near the beginning. 1979–. Q That's why I put money into your little drugs operation . . . I knew early doors that Bones was holding you back (1997). [From earlier noun sense, the opening of a theatre's doors a relatively long time before the start of a performance, affording customers a wide choice of seats.]

earner noun A lucrative job or enterprise; esp. in phr. *a nice little earner*, a means of making easy and often illicit profits. 1970–. SUNDAY TELEGRAPH The family letting rooms on the quiet, or the person who has a 'nice little earner' on the side (1987).

earthly noun **no earthly, not an earthly** no chance whatever. 1899–. LISTENER Received standard, like the Liberals, won't stand an earthly (1965). [From such phrs. as *no earthly chance* (or *hope*, etc.).]

earwig verb intr. often jocular To eavesdrop. 1927–. GUARDIAN Anyway, apparently you sometimes get a Miss Millett 'earwigging' in a dark corner, so she was paraded before me for a formal introduction (1992).

easy-peasy adjective orig children's Childishly or ridiculously simple. 1976–. FAST FORWARD 'Easy peasy' we hear you cry. 'We'll wait until we hear the chart and then rush a postcard in,' we hear you cheatingly thinking to yourself (1990). [Arbitrary reduplication of *easy*.]

easy rider noun US **1** A sexually satisfying lover. 1912–. **2** A guitar. 1949–. [In sense 1, from the notion of 'riding' one's sexual partner; in sense 2, apparently from the guitar's curved outlines, suggestive of a voluptuous woman.]

eat verb trans. **1 to eat crow** US To be forced to do something extremely disagreeable and humiliating. 1877–. NEW YORKER I was going to apologize, eat crow, offer to kiss and make up (1970). **2** US To practise fellatio or cunnilingus on. 1927–. L. ALTHER 'Eat me,' he said, seizing my head with his hands and fitting my mouth around his cock and moving my head back and forth (1975). **3 could eat a horse** am/is/etc. extremely hungry. 1936–. C. GEORGE 'Shall I put the pasta on now?' 'Please do!' He leaned against the door-jamb, his hair brushing the lintel. 'I could eat a horse, Madame Chef' (1991). **4 to eat** someone **alive** to defeat comprehensively. 1939–. FUSION (US) At first, in solitaire play, most gamers will be eaten alive by the CPU, but once the learning curve is slammed, gamers will be performing tomahawk jams, alley oops and all them other 'phat' moves with elan (1995). **5 to eat pussy** of a man, to have sexual intercourse or perform cunnilingus. 1967–. [In sense 1, formerly also *to eat boiled crow*, from the notion of swallowing something unpalatable; in sense 5, cf. PUSSY noun 1.]

eats noun pl. Food. 1841–. J. P. DONLEAVY On the tables were eats the like of which I'm sure have never been seen on this isle (1955). [Pl. of earlier obs. *eat* food, from the verb *eat*.]

ecstasy noun orig US A powerful synthetic hallucinogenic drug, 3,4-methylene-dioxymethamphetamine, taken in capsule form, which induces feelings of euphoria. 1985–. SUNDAY TIMES Acid House (the music) and

Ecstasy (the drug) became inextricably bound together and the fans turned to it (1988). [From its effect on the user.]

edge noun US The condition of being drunk. 1920–. E. HEMINGWAY 'How do you feel?' . . . 'Swell. I've just got a good edge on' (1925).

edgy adjective orig US At the forefront of a trend; up-to-date, trendy, cutting-edge. 1976–. N. LAWSON Show Euro-cool by dolloping on some good and edgy and far more grown-up crème fraîche instead (1998).

eff verb **1** intr. To say 'fuck' or a similar expletive; esp. in phr. *to eff and blind*, to swear continuously. 1943–. A. WESKER He started effing and blinding and threw their books on the floor (1959). **2** trans. and intr. euphemistic = FUCK verb 2, 3, 4, 5, 1950–. K. AMIS You young people eff off (1958); D. SANDERSON You sure effed things up (1958). [Variant of *ef*, name of the letter F, euphemistically representing FUCK verb.] Hence effing, noun, adjective, and adverb 1944–. PRIVATE EYE The relatives get effing tough (1969).

egg noun **1** A person or thing of the stated sort. 1855–. P. G. WODEHOUSE She's a tough egg (1938). **2** Brit, dated In exclamations qualified by an adjective esp. **good egg** expressing enthusiastic approval and **tough egg** expressing commiseration. 1903–. H. E. BATES 'It seems there's a bar.' 'Good egg,' Pop said. 'That's something' (1959). **3** A bomb, a mine. 1917–. WAR ILLUSTRATED The Germans are thought to be using relays of U-boats. Even the smallest of these can carry up to a dozen 'eggs' (1939).

egg-beater noun US A helicopter. 1937–. [From the resemblance of the rotors to those of a mechanical egg-whisk.]

ego pron Brit schoolchildren's, dated I; used esp. in public schools in answer to the question *quis?* who?, esp. when claiming an object. 1913–. [From Latin *ego* I.] See QUIS? pron.

eight noun (**to have had**) **one over the eight** (to have had) too much to drink; to be drunk. 1925–. DAILY EXPRESS Luton magistrate: what does he mean by 'one over the eight'? ('A glass too many'?) (1928). [From the (fanciful) notion that eight pints of beer represents the maximum intake consistent with sobriety.]

eight ball noun **behind the eight ball** US At a disadvantage; snookered. 1934–. NEW YORK HERALD An attempt to describe what makes the drawings funny lands you behind the eight ball (1944). [From the disadvantage, in a variety of the game of pool, of having the black ball (numbered 8 and which one is penalized for touching) between the cue ball and the object ball.]

eighty-six US. noun **1** In restaurants and bars, an expression indicating that the supply of an item has run out, or that a customer is not to be served; also, a customer to be refused service. 1936–. G. FOWLER There was a bar in the Belasco building, . . . but Barrymore was known in that cubby as an 'eighty-six' (1944). **2 eighty-six on** enough of, no more of. 1981–. W. SAFIRE Eighty-six on etymologies for 'cocktail' (1981). verb trans. **3** To eject or debar (a person) from premises; to reject or abandon. 1959–. J. RECHY I'll have you eighty-sixed out of this bar (1963). [Prob. rhyming slang for NIX noun.]

ekker noun Brit, university or school Exercise. 1891–. WYKEHAMIST Whatever the supposed range of activities that qualify as ekker, the demands of the major games . . . usually over-ride all others (1970). [From first syllable of *exercise* + -ER.]

elbow noun **1 to bend, lift the** (or **one's**) **elbow** to drink to excess. 1823–. COAST TO COAST 1965–6 He's not much chop. Too fond of bending the elbow (1967). **2** Rejection, dismissal; esp. in phrs. *get the elbow*, *give* (someone) *the elbow*. 1971–. TUCKER'S LUCK ANNUAL 1984 You really think I should give her the elbow? . . . Tough, innit? She'll get over it, they always do! (1983).

el cheapo orig US. adjective **1** Of poor quality; very cheap. 1967–. 80 MICROCOMPUTING You could get away with an el cheapo cassette recorder for storage (1983). noun **2** A cheap or shoddy service or product. 1977–. [Jocular pseudo-Spanish.]

electric soup noun Brit Alcoholic drink. 1992–. OBSERVER Private Eye's 'Dear Bill' letters purportedly written by Denis to Bill Deedes, golfer, electric soup-drinking chum and former editor of the Daily Telegraph (1995).

> 'Show Euro-cool by dolloping on some good and edgy . . . crème fraîche instead.'

edge edgy eff egg egg-beater ego eight eight ball

elephant

elephant noun **1 to see, get a look at,** etc. **the elephant** US To see the world, or the bright lights of the big city; to get experience of life. 1844–. ⊤. ᴠ. ᴏʟsᴇɴ Saturdays some of the boys from the three big outfits come in to see the elephant (1960). **2** Brit army A dug-out with a semi-circular corrugated-iron lining. Also **elephant dug-out.** 1917–25. [In sense 1, from the notion of the elephant as an exotic animal seen only rarely, in zoos and circuses.]

elephant('s) trunk adjective Brit, dated Rhyming slang for 'drunk'. Also **elephants.** 1859–. ᴇᴠᴇɴɪɴɢ sᴛᴀɴᴅᴀʀᴅ He came home and found the artful dodger elephant trunk in the bread and butter (He found the lodger drunk in the gutter) (1931).

emma noun military Used for the letter *m* in telephone and code messages (cf. ᴀᴄᴋ ᴇᴍᴍᴀ adverb and ᴘɪᴘ² noun). 1891–.

empty nester noun mainly US Either member of a couple whose children have grown up and left home. 1962–. sᴜɴᴅᴀʏ ᴛɪᴍᴇs Builders . . . have ignored an increasingly important category of housebuyer—the busy, well-off executive couple who either have no children or whose children have grown up and left. Americans call them 'empty nesters' (1980).

end noun **1 the end: a** The limit of endurability. 1938–. ɢ. ꜰʀᴇᴇᴍᴀɴ Donald, you really are the absolute end (1959). **b** US mainly jazz The best, the ultimate. Also attrib 1950–. ɴᴇᴜʀᴏᴛɪᴄᴀ Senor this shit [i.e. narcotic] is the end! (1950); ɴᴜɢɢᴇᴛ I was blowing some jazz in the student lounge on this end Steinway (1963). **2 to get** (or **have**) **one's end away** Brit To succeed in having sexual intercourse; usu. used of a man. 1975–. ɢᴜᴀʀᴅɪᴀɴ They called him Grandad, asked him how his girlfriends were. 'Are you getting it?' they kept repeating. 'Getting your end away?' (1995).

endsville noun US Also **Endsville, Endville. 1** The best, the greatest. 1957–60. **2** A place or situation of no further hope; also, the ᴇɴᴅ noun a.1962–. ꜰ. sɪɴᴀᴛʀᴀ You can be the most artistically perfect performer in the world, but the audience is like a broad—if you're indifferent, endsville (1984). [From ᴇɴᴅ noun + -ᴠɪʟʟᴇ.]

enforcer noun orig US A strong-arm man, esp. in an underworld gang. 1934–. ᴛɪᴍᴇs An east London wholesaler was cleared at the Central Criminal Court yesterday of the gangland execution of an underworld 'enforcer' (1983).

eppie noun Also **eppy.** Brit A fit of temper; a tantrum. 1987–. ɢᴜᴀʀᴅɪᴀɴ Don't have an eppy, aged parent (1987). [From *epi(leptic fit* + -*ie.*]

equalizer noun orig US A revolver; also, a cosh or some other sort of weapon. 1931–. ɪ. ᴊᴇꜰꜰᴇʀɪᴇs He just thought anybody running about with a nasty look and an equalizer was a foreigner (1961). [From the notion that a powerful weapon reduces all its actual or potential victims to the same level.]

-er suffix Also **-ers.** Brit Used to make colloquial or jocular forms of words and names, with curtailment and often some distortion of the root, as in *soccer* (= Association Football) and *Johnners* (= (Brian) Johnston, British cricket commentator). 1892–. sᴜɴᴅᴀʏ ᴛɪᴍᴇs The twenties were the age of the 'er' at Repton. The changing-room was the chagger and a sensation a sensagger. A six at cricket was a criper (1963). [Apparently orig Rugby School slang, introduced into Oxford University in the mid-1870s.]

Erich noun Also **Eric** Brit, usu. derog A male German. 1985–. [From the German male forename *Erich.*]

'er indoors noun = ʜᴇʀ ɪɴᴅᴏᴏʀs noun.

erk noun Also **irk.** Brit **1** dated A naval rating. 1925. **2** A person of lowest rank in the R.A.F.; an aircraftman. 1928–. ᴘ. ʙʀᴇɴɴᴀɴ ᴇᴛ ᴀʟ. The erks came running up to tell us that . . . the 109 had been diving down (1943). **3** A disliked person. 1959–. [Origin unknown.]

ethno noun Austral An immigrant. 1976–. [From *ethn(ic* + -*o.*]

euchred adjective Austral Exhausted. 1932–. ᴊ. ᴍᴏʀʀɪsᴏɴ This man has worked hard in Australia for forty years, but he's euchred now . . . All he asks for is the old age pension (1973). [From earlier US sense, outwitted, orig. in the card game euchre.]

even Stephen adjective and adverb Also **even Steven.** Even(ly); spec. fairly shared. 1866–. ʀ. ʙʀᴀᴅʙᴜʀʏ It's a fifty-fifty fight. Even Steven (1955). [Rhyming phrase based on the male personal forename *Stephen, Steven.*]

ex noun A former husband, wife, or lover. 1929–. ʟᴀᴅɪᴇs' ʜᴏᴍᴇ ᴊᴏᴜʀɴᴀʟ His 'ex' also got away with every stick of furniture and household equipment (1971). [From earlier sense, one who formerly occupied a particular position, from the prefix *ex-.*]

excess verb trans. US, euphemistic To declare to be in excess of requirements, make redundant; also with *out.* 1976–. ɴᴇᴡ ʏᴏʀᴋ ᴛɪᴍᴇs

elephant elephant('s) trunk emma empty nester

Assistant principals, who are removed, or 'excessed', . . . ostensibly because of declining enrollment (1980).

ex-con noun Abbreviation of 'ex-convict'. 1907–. PUBLICATIONS OF THE AMERICAN DIALECT SOCIETY Better than fifty per cent of Pinkertons are ex-cons (1955).

exes /ˈeksɪz/ noun pl. Also **ex's, exs.** Abbreviation of 'expenses'. 1864–. K. GILES Their ten thousand bucks per year plus exes (1970).

eye noun **1 (all) my eye (and Betty Martin)** stuff and nonsense. 1768–. **2 my eye!** an expression of emphatic incredulity or denial. 1842–. W. FAULKNER 'How about Bigelow's Mill . . . that's a factory.' 'Factory my eye' (1929). **3** orig US **a: the eye** the Pinkerton Detective Agency. 1914–. **b** A detective, esp. a private one; a lookout man. 1936–. [In sense 3, from the Pinkerton trademark, an all-seeing eye.]

eyeball verb trans. and intr. US To look or stare (at). 1901–. LISTENER This movie is so richly risible that I advise all, in John Wayne's phrase, to go down to the Warner and eyeball it (1968). [From *eyeball* noun.]

eye-candy noun Something visually arresting but intellectually undemanding; someone who is very attractive to look at but may have little else to recommend him or her. 1986–. DAILY TELEGRAPH But *Baywatch*, we are told, is not just mildly salacious eye-candy (1997).

eyeful noun **1** A long steady look, esp. at something or someone remarkable, beautiful, etc.; esp. in phr. *to get an eyeful of* 1899–. N. BALCHIN He thought to himself this is a bit of all right and started right in to get an eye-full, see? (1947). **2** A visually striking person or thing; spec. a very beautiful woman. 1922–. A. GARVE You're both quite an eyeful (1960). [From earlier sense, as much as the eye can take in at once.]

Eyetie /ˈaɪtaɪ/ noun and adjective Also **Eyety, Eyetye, Eytie.** offensive (An) Italian. Also **Eyeto.** 1925–. E. H. CLEMENTS The Yugoslavians, the two Eyetyes, some West Germans (1958). [From *Eyetalian*, representing a non-standard or jocular pronunciation of *Italian*.]

eyewash noun Pretentious or insincere talk; nonsense. 1884–. ECONOMIST This does not mean that the proposals . . . are so much eyewash (1957). [From earlier sense, soothing lotion for the eyes.] Hence **eyewasher,** noun A person who talks eyewash. 1920–.; **eyewashing,** noun and adjective. 1937–.

excess ex-con exes eye eyeball eye-candy eyeful

fab adjective Wonderful, marvellous. 1961–. MEET THE BEATLES Most of the Merseyside groups produce sounds which are pretty fab (1963). [Abbreviation of *fabulous* adjective.]

face noun **1** dated A term of address. 1923–. D. SMITH Come on, face—don't get mopey (1938). **2** A person. 1945–. J. MORGAN Now this face was the ideal man for me to have a deal with (1967). See also *to shut one's face* at SHUT verb.

face-ache noun A mournful-looking person; also as a disparaging term of address. 1937–. SIMPSON & GALTON On a train . . . a carriageful of the most miserable-looking bunch of face-aches (1961). [Cf. earlier sense, neuralgia.]

face-fungus noun jocular A man's beard or other facial hair. 1907–. LISTENER Svengali . . . with his face-fungus and rolling eyes (1959). See also FUNGUS noun.

factory noun **1** Austral, dated A women's prison. 1806–1930. **2** A police station. 1891–. R. BUSBY Detectives relieved the tedium of observation duties by using the facilities of the local police stations, the 'factory' in the area they happened to be working (1987).

fade verb **1** intr. and trans. US To bet against (the player throwing the dice) in the game of craps. 1890–. noun **2 to do** (or **take**) **a fade** US To disappear, leave. 1949–. K. ORVIS Then, pal, we'll both do a fade (1962).

faff about verb intr. Also **faff around** Brit, orig dialect To behave in a foolishly time-wasting way. 1874–. N. COWARD The Welfare Officers appeared, . . . faffed about, used either too much initiative or too little, and retired in due course (1954). [Cf. obs. *faffle* in same sense, orig. meaning 'stutter', of imitative origin.]

fag[1] noun **1** A cigarette. 1888–. C. BARRETT Cobbers of the men in detention had hit upon an ingenious method of smuggling fags to them (1942). verb US **2** trans. To supply with

a cigarette. 1926–. W. FAULKNER 'Fag me again.' The corporal gave him another cigarette (1954). **3** intr. To smoke. 1940–. [Abbreviation of FAGEND noun; cf. obs. senses, cigarette end, cheap cigarette.]

fag[2] noun US Abbreviation of FAGGOT noun 2. 1923–. L. EGAN You can't tell the fags from outside looks (1964).

fag-end noun Brit A cigarette end. 1853–. A. HOLLINGHURST The flames showed up the hundreds of fag-ends that had unthinkingly been thrown in (1988). [From earlier sense, final unused portion of something; *fag* perh. ultimately from obs. *fag* verb, to droop, hang loose, perh. alteration of *flag* verb.]

faggot noun derog **1** orig dialect A woman. 1591–. SUNDAY MIRROR 'Urry up wi' that glass o' beer, you lazy faggot! (1969). **2** orig and mainly US A (male) homosexual. 1914–. H. KANE Duffy was no queen, no platinum-dyed freak, no screaming faggot (1962). [Cf. earlier sense, bunch of sticks.] Hence **faggoty,** adjective derog Characteristic of or being a homosexual. 1928–. A. BINKLEY Albie in his faggoty silk pajamas (1968).

faggy adjective = FAGGOTY adjective. 1967–. J. LE CARRÉ 'I had such a good time,' says Grant, with his quaint, rather faggy indignation (1986). [From FAG[2] noun + -y.]

fag hag noun A woman who consorts habitually with homosexual men. 1969–. A. MAUPIN Do you think I'm a fag hag? . . . Look at the symptoms. I hardly know any straight men anymore (1978). [Rhyming formation on FAG[2] noun + *hag* noun. Cf. the earlier US *fag-hag* woman who chain-smokes, from FAG[1] noun.]

fag tag noun US A loop at the collar of a man's shirt for hanging it up by. 1980–.

fain verb Brit, orig dialect Used by children as a truce-word in the expressions *fains* or *fain(s I, fain it, fainit(e)s* to request temporary withdrawal from a game and exemption from any penalty for so doing. 1870–. J. BETJEMAN 'I'd rather not.' 'Fains I.' 'It's up to you' (1948). [Variant of obs. *fen* to forbid, perh. an alteration of *fend* verb.]

fairy noun derog A male homosexual. 1895–. E. WAUGH Two girls stopped near our table and looked at us curiously. 'Come on,' said one to the other, 'we're wasting our time. They're only fairies' (1945).

fake verb trans. and intr. jazz To improvise. 1926–. SPOTLIGHT There was enough good music 'faked' in those days (1944).

farmer

fall verb intr. **1** criminals', dated To be arrested, convicted, or sent to prison. 1879–1938. s. WOOD A young Jew at Parkhurst who fell for three years at the game simply because he failed . . . of ascertaining the actual *locale* of the university of which he claimed to be an alumnus (1932). **2 to fall about** to laugh uncontrollably. 1967–. TIMES The thought of producing a book in that time is enough to make us fall about (1973). noun **3** criminals', dated An arrest, period of imprisonment. 1893–1935.

fall guy noun orig US **1** Someone who is easily tricked into doing something; a sucker. 1906–. S. BELLOW Perhaps he was foolish and unlucky, a fall guy, a dupe, a sucker (1956). **2** Someone who is set up to receive the blame or responsibility for another's crime or misdemeanour; a scapegoat. 1912–. SPECTATOR Ward began to hear from friends that he was being cast for the part of fall guy . . . by Profumo's friends (1963).

fall money noun criminals', dated Money set aside by a criminal for use if he should be arrested. 1893–1929.

falsies noun pl. orig US A padded bra; breast-pads. 1943–. M. DICKENS The secretary slouched in . . . her falsies pushing out her sweater like cardboard cones (1958). [From *false* adjective + *-ie*.]

family jewels noun pl. **1** orig US = CROWN JEWELS noun pl. 1946–. P. O'DONNELL 'E might be in 'ospital . . . . I'm not quite sure what spirits of salts does to the old family jewels (1965). **2** US (Information about) confidential and often illicit activities, esp. by the CIA. 1978–.

fan verb trans. **1** To hit, beat. 1785–. L. STEFFENS You wonder why we fan these damned bums, crooks, and strikers with the stick (1931). **2** To search (a person) quickly, to frisk. 1927–. E. WALLACE Legally no policeman has the right to 'fan' a prisoner until he gets into the police station (1927).

fancy Dan noun US A showy but ineffective worker or sportsman. 1943–. J. DEMPSEY The amateur and professional ranks today are cluttered with . . . 'fancy Dans' (1950).

fancy man noun derog A woman's lover, often adulterous. 1811–. B. NAUGHTON You won't get one husband in ten feels any thanks to the wife's fancy man for the happiness he brings to the marriage (1966).

fancy pants noun derog A showily dressed, conceited person, esp. a man. 1942–. M. HUNTER Some puffed-up fancy

pants . . . said something which made the barmaid laugh (1967).

fancy woman noun derog A man's mistress. Also **fancy girl, fancy piece**. 1812–. B. W. ALDISS What makes you think I want even to hear about it, or the series, knowing your fancy woman is in them both? (1980).

Fannie Mae noun US A nickname for the Federal National Mortgage Association, established by the US Government in 1938 and since 1970 a private corporation, which assists banks, trust companies, etc., in the distribution of funds for home mortgages and guarantees mortgage-backed securities. 1948–. [Acronym elaborated from the name of the association, after the female personal names *Fannie* and *Mae*.]

fanny[1] noun **1** mainly Brit The female genitals. 1879–. J. JOYCE Two lads in scoutsch breeches went through her . . . before she had a hint of a hair at her fanny to hide (1939). **2** orig and mainly US The buttocks, backside. 1928–. N. SHUTE I'd never be able to think of John and Jo again if we just sat tight on our fannies and did nothing (1960). [Origin unknown.]

fanny[2] noun **1** Glib talk, a tall story. 1933–. G. KERSH A Guardsman comes to Bill with some Fanny about needing some cash (1942). verb trans. **2** To deceive or persuade with glib talk. 1949–. A. PRIOR They could not fanny Norris into thinking they believed he might have been out to a woman (1965). [Origin unknown.]

fanny about verb intr. Also **fanny around** Brit To behave in a foolishly time-wasting way. 1971–. SUNDAY TIMES 'I don't want you bringing the ball out and fannying around with it the way you do at Arsenal', Jack Charlton once snapped at him (1993). [From FANNY[2] noun or perh. FANNY[1] noun.]

Fanny Adams noun Brit **1** naval **a** Tinned meat. 1889–. **b** Meat stew. 1962–. **2** Esp. in phr. *sweet Fanny Adams*, nothing at all. 1919–. J. R. COLE What do they do? Sweet Fanny Adams! [From the name of a young woman murdered *c*.1867; in sense 2, sometimes understood as a euphemism for (*sweet*) *fuck all* in the same sense.] See also SWEET F. A. noun.

fantabulous /fænˈtæbjʊləs/ adjective Indescribably wonderful. 1959–. SUNDAY EXPRESS (Johannesburg): Since the bust up of the fantabulous group, it's been George who's been doing most of the slogging (1971). [Blend of *fantastic* and *fabulous*.]

farmer noun nautical A sailor who has no duties at the wheel or on watch during the night. 1886–. P. A. EADDY I was a 'farmer' that night, . . . not having any wheel or look-out (1933).

far-out adjective orig US **1** Of jazz: of the latest or most progressive kind. 1954–. M. STEARNS There were too many choices in 'far-out' harmony (1956). **2** Excellent, splendid. 1954–. **3** Avant-garde, far-fetched. 1960–. SCIENCE JOURNAL Talking with computers, so much a far-out idea when this journal discussed IBM's work on it four years ago, now seems quite straightforward (1970).

fart verb intr. **1** To fool *about* or *around*; to waste time. 1900–. J. WAINWRIGHT Look! It's important. Stop farting around (1969). noun **2** A contemptible person. 1937–. INK Marty Feldman said to the judge as he left the witness stand, 'I don't think he even knew I was here, the boring old fart' (1971). [Cf. earlier sense, break wind.]

fash noun **1** Abbreviation of 'fashion'. 1895–. WASHINGTON POST Two heaps on the floor afforded a primer on kiddie fash ins and outs (1986). adjective **2** Abbreviation of 'fashionable'. 1977–. HAIR Flash and fash feeling for a successful new season style (1985).

fast one noun orig US A deceptive trick; usu. in phr. *to pull a fast one* to play such a trick. 1923–. A. GILBERT Mad to think they can pull a fast one . . . over the whole community (1958).

fat cat noun derog **1** orig and mainly US A wealthy and hence privileged person. 1928–. FLYING Those who view the business jet as a smoke-belching, profit-eating chariot of the fatcat (1971). **2** Austral A highly paid executive or official. 1973–. CANBERRA TIMES Staff of the National Library are by no means in the fat-cat class (1984).

fat chance noun A negligible prospect. 1906–. W. S. MAUGHAM Fat chance I've got of going to France now (1933).

fat-head noun A foolish person. 1842–. GUARDIAN When they [i.e. MPs] behave like fatheads, people are apt to notice (1991). [Back-formation from earlier *fat-headed* foolish.]

fat lot noun A negligible amount. 1892–. B. WRIGHT Fat lot of use it was me getting my posterior frozen for a whole night to do my host a favour (1967).

fat-mouth US. noun **1** Someone who talks extravagantly, a loudmouth. 1942–. J. HELLER Okay, fatmouth, out of the car (1961). verb mainly Black English **2a** intr. To talk excessively.

1970–. **b** trans. To cajole or sweet-talk. 1971–. B. MALAMUD I ain't asking you to fatmouth me, just as I am not interested in getting into any argument with you (1971).

fat show noun NZ = FAT CHANCE noun. 1948–. D. BALLANTYNE It would be corker if he could go outside with Carole Plowman . . . Fat show! (1948).

fatso noun jocular or derog = FATTY noun. 1944–. L. DEIGHTON I began to envy Fatso his sausage sandwiches (1962). [Prob. from *fat* adjective or the designation *Fats*.]

fatty noun jocular or derog A fat person; often used as a derisive nickname. 1797–. PETTICOAT Success stories connected with slimming are few and far between, so any fatties who might be reading this—take note of this tale! (1971). [From *fat* adjective + *-y*; cf. earlier *fatty* adjective.]

fave noun and adjective orig US Abbreviation of 'favourite', used esp. in show business. 1938–. SOUNDS I reckon 'Violation' has already found a place in my end-of-the-year-faves listing (1977).

fave rave adjective and noun orig US (Being) a special favourite piece of music, film, musician, etc. 1967–. TIMES The American fan magazine market, always at the ready to replace a current fave rave (1973).

favour noun **do me** (or **us**) **a favour** used ironically in rejecting a suggestion as impracticable, implausible, etc. 1963–. GUARDIAN Was she hoping to get engaged during the year of the tour? 'Good God, no, do us a favour' (1969).

feck verb intr. and trans. orig Irish English A euphemistic alteration of FUCK verb. 1987–. Hence **fecking** adjective and adverb 1963–. FRONT Let's just feckin eat 'em . . . roite here, roite now (2001).

Fed noun US A US federal official; spec. an FBI agent. 1916–. PUBLICATIONS OF THE AMERICAN DIALECT SOCIETY Anyway, the Feds got the letter where I sent him $400 (1955). [Abbreviation of *federal* adjective.]

feeb noun US A stupid or feeble-minded person. 1914–. E. FENWICK Sometimes I envy that pretty little feeb of his. Suppose if I played dumber I could get one too (1968). [Short for *feeble-minded* adjective.]

feed verb **1** trans. and intr. To tire or bore (someone). 1933–. M. MARPLES 'It's *feeding*, isn't it?' (i.e. calculated to make one *fed-up*) (1940). **2 to feed one's face** to eat excessively or impolitely. 1939–. L. ERDRICH I had a desperate

far-out   fart   fash   fast one   fat cat   fat chance

hungry craving. I kept pouring it in and feeding my face fast as I could (1984). **3 to feed the bears** orig and mainly US To receive a ticket or pay a fine for a traffic offence. 1975–. [In sense 3, cf. BEAR noun policeman.]

feel verb trans. **1** To fondle the genitals of; to grope; esp. followed by *up*. 1930–. M. RICHLER He literally bumped into Ziggy feeling up the prettiest girl at the party in a dark damp corner (1968). **2 to feel no pain** to be insensibly drunk. 1947–. B. SWEET-ESCOTT A vast quantity of vodka was drunk, and twice I saw senior Russian officers being carried out of the room evidently feeling no pain (1965). **3 to feel** (someone's) **collar** to arrest (someone). 1950–. DAILY TELEGRAPH Will old-timers be able to play dominoes or cribbage without the risk of having their collars felt? (1985). noun **4** An instance of fondling someone's genitals. 1932–. ZENO I gave her a feel, and she pulled away (1970).

feelthy /ˈfiːlθɪ/ adjective jocular Obscene, pornographic. 1933–. B. S. JOHNSON Maurie has a great collection of feelthy books down here—including a first edition of Cleland's *Fanny Hill, or the Memoirs of a Woman of Leisure* (1963). [Imitation of a foreign pronunciation of *filthy* adjective.]

feisty /ˈfaɪstɪ/ adjective US Aggressive, excitable, touchy. 1896–. J. POTTS He couldn't shake her loose—she hung on to his arm, feisty as a terrier (1968). [From *feist* fist, small dog + *-y*.]

felch verb trans. orig US Usu. of a male homosexual: to perform anilingus on (someone); spec., to suck out semen previously introduced into the rectum. 1972–. Hence **felching** noun 1989–. [Origin unknown.]

feller noun Representing a colloquial pronunciation of *fellow*, in modern usage usu. with the sense 'young man' or 'boyfriend'. 1825–. Also **fella** 1864–. PETTICOAT If we did walk into a pub alone and not one feller blinked an eyelid we'd probably think there was something wrong with us (1971). SUN The only thing I think could come close to the thrill [i.e. of bungee-jumping] would be to be a Page Seven Fella (1992).

feminazi noun N Amer derog A radical feminist. 1990–. MS I fight my way to my destination, finally arriving in a bad mood,

militant black woman, cranky feminazi (1994). [From *femi(nist* noun + *nazi* noun.]

femme /fem/ noun **1** Also **fem.** US A young woman. 1928–. AMERICAN SPEECH The organizer of a *Brush-off club* 'made up of mournful soldiers who were given the hemlock cup by femmes back home' (1944). **2** A lesbian who adopts a passive, feminine role. 1961–. NEW STATESMAN One of the femmes, secure in the loving protection of her butch (1966). Cf. BUTCH adjective and noun. [From French *femme* woman.]

fence verb trans. and intr. **1** To deal in or sell (stolen goods). 1610–. S. BELLOW After stealing your ring, he didn't even know how to fence it (1989). noun **2** A receiver of or dealer in stolen goods. *a*.1700–. B. REID She'd had a fence living in while I was away, and she'd flogged my expensive wedding presents (1984). **3 over the fence** Austral and NZ Objectionable, unacceptable, 1918–. SYDNEY MORNING HERALD Some publications which unduly emphasise sex were 'entirely over the fence', the Chief Secretary, Mr C. A. Kelly, said yesterday (1964).

fender bender
a usu. minor motor accident

fender-bender noun mainly US A usu. minor motor accident. 1966–. PLATE & DARVI A fender-bender at a busy intersection (1981). [N Amer *fender* vehicle's wing or mudguard.]

fetch verb **1 to fetch up** orig US to arrive eventually at the stated place. 1858–. LISTENER I grew used to bummelling around the Bond Street dealers and fetching up for tea at the National Gallery or the Tate (1971). **2** trans. To strike (a blow) against (someone). 1865–. PUNCH Fetch 'im [a donkey] a good whack 'ith your rumbereller! (1865). [In sense 1, from earlier sense, come to a stop.]

fiddle and flute noun Also **fiddle.** US dated A suit of clothes. 1919–68. [Rhyming slang.]

fiddley-did noun Austral, dated The sum of one pound; a pound note. Also **fiddley.** 1941–. R. BIELBY He would 'like to be home right now, putting a couple of fiddleydids on a little horse' (1977). [Rhyming slang for 'quid' (= pound).]

filbert noun dated The head. 1886–. G. CURTIS Get that into your old filbert (1936). [From earlier sense, hazel-nut; cf. NUT noun 1.]

feel feelthy feisty felch feller feminazi femme

fill

fill verb trans. **to fill (someone) in** to beat (someone) severely. 1948–. TIMES A naval rating accused of murdering . . . an antique dealer . . . was alleged to have . . . said: 'I filled in a chap and took his money' (1959).

filth noun criminals' The police; usu. with *the*. 1967–. J. WAINWRIGHT He's a big wheel in the filth, Mr Nolan. Y'know . . . assistant chief constable and all that (1979).

fin noun US A five-dollar bill; the sum of five dollars. 1925–. W. R. BURNETT Costs a fin just to check your hat (1953). [Short for FINNIP noun.]

finagle verb intr. US **1** To scheme, intrigue. 1922–. **2** trans. To manipulate, alter, or obtain by fraudulent or underhanded means. 1927–. WALL STREET JOURNAL The young president . . . already has finagled a $2 billion loan from the Japanese government (1989). [Alteration of British dialect *fainaigue* cheat, of unknown origin.]

financial adjective Austral and NZ Financially solvent; having money. 1899–. P. WHITE 'Shall I tell you, Alf,' he called, 'how us girls got to be financial?' (1961).

finger noun **1a** A police informer. 1914–. **b** One who supplies information or indicates victims to criminals. Also **fingerman**. 1926–. E. MCGIRR He was right to concentrate on Fall. There could have been the fingerman watching him (1968). **2** A pickpocket. 1925–. K. HOPKINS He's a finger, works in Fulham mostly. Small profits, quick returns (1960). **3 to put the finger on** orig US To inform against, to denounce to the police; to identify (a victim) to an assassin. 1926–. DAILY TELEGRAPH I have not heard of anyone who wants to put the finger on me (1971). **4 to pull** (or **get, take**) **one's finger out** to get a move on, get cracking. 1941–. TIMES (Duke of Edinburgh) I think it is about time we pulled our fingers out (1961). **5 to give** (someone) **the finger** orig US To make an obscene gesture with the middle finger raised as a sign of contempt; also fig, to show contempt for, betray. 1941–. J. MILLS Wayne drove past us slowly, grinning and giving us the finger. We waved back and gave him the finger but it was all very cheerful (1978). verb trans. **6** US To put the finger on (sense 3 above). 1930–. H. ROTH She . . . couldn't finger them for any crime (1954).

finito adjective Finished for the worse. 1945–. A. MAUPIN You tell your friend that she'd better report to me on Friday or she's out on her ass . . . Friday . . . After that, finito (1982). [From the past participle of Italian *finire* to finish.]

fink¹ US. noun **1** A despicable person, esp. one who behaves disloyally by informing on a colleague, being a blackleg, etc. 1903–. R. CHANDLER Now he's looking for the fink that turned him up eight years ago (1940); C. WILLIAMS Except for being a rat, a fink, a scab, a thug, and a goon, he's one of the sweetest guys you'll ever meet (1959). See also RAT FINK noun. **2** A detective. 1925–. verb intr. **3** To inform on. 1925–. ROLLING STONE The gang tries to sell their smack to a black hippie pusher who finks on them (1969). [Origin unknown.]

fink² verb Brit Representing a casual or nonstandard pronunciation of 'think'. 1888–. N. MARSH Makes you fink, don't it? (1962).

finnip noun Brit A five-pound note. Also US, five dollars. Also **fin, finny, fin(n)if(f), finnup, finuf**. 1839–. R. STOUT I . . . got out my wallet and extracted a finif (1966). [Said to represent a Yiddish pronunciation of German *fünf* five.]

firewater noun Any strong alcoholic drink (orig. represented as being a Native American usage; latterly mainly jocular). 1826–. P. ABLEMA I am not a teetotaller but I always use the firewater cautiously (1991).

fish¹ noun **1** mainly derog A person of the stated sort. 1750–. F. SCOTT FITZGERALD I'm tired of being nice to every poor fish in school (1920); LISTENER The old man is revealed as having been a very cold fish (1958). **2** nautical A torpedo. Cf. TIN FISH noun. 1928–. B. KNOX The Navy didn't like losing a torpedo. . . . Each 'fish' represented some £3,000 in cash (1967).

fish² noun US A dollar. 1917–. N. ALGREN Used to get fifteen fish for an exhibition of six-no-count (1949). [From earlier sense, counter used in gambling; ultimately from French *fiche* peg, counter.]

Fisher noun Brit, dated A one-pound note or other currency note. 1922–3. MOTOR CYCLING The Bench mulcted him of a couple of Fishers and warned him as to his future behaviour (1923). [From the name of Sir Warren Fisher, Permanent Secretary to the Treasury 1919–39; cf. BRADBURY noun.]

fish-skin noun US **1** dated A dollar bill. 1936–43. **2** A condom. 1936–.

fist-fucking noun orig US Insertion of the hand into someone's anus as a means of sexual gratification. 1972–. Hence **fist-fuck** verb trans. orig US 1978–.

fisting noun orig US = FIST-FUCKING noun. 1981–.

fill filth fin finagle financial finger finito fink

fit adjective Brit Sexually attractive, good-looking. 1985–. GLOUCESTER CITIZEN I would choose Gillian Anderson from the X-Files, because she's dead fit (2000).

fit verb trans. orig Austral To (attempt to) incriminate (a person), esp. by planting false evidence; to frame; often followed by *up*. 1882–. G. F. NEWMAN Danny James might have fitted him, Sneed thought, but immediately questioned how (1970); OBSERVER He says he was fitted up by the police, who used false evidence to get a conviction (1974). [From obs. Brit *fit* verb, to punish in a fitting manner.]

fit-up noun **1** theatrical A temporary stage set, piece of scenery, etc. Hence (in full **fit-up company**), a travelling company which carries makeshift scenery and props that can be set up temporarily. 1864–. DAILY TELEGRAPH Today there are some 40 off-Broadway houses. You might add another 40 off-off-Broadway clubs and fit-ups (1970). **2** An act of incriminating someone unjustly. 1985–. R. BUSBY We was fitted, you ratbag! . . . Nothing but a lousy fit-up! (1985). [In sense 2, from FIT verb.]

five-finger discount noun US, euphemistic, mainly CB users' The activity or proceeds of stealing or shoplifting. 1966–. LIEBERMAN & RHODES The perfect 'gift' for the 'midnight shopper' looking for a 'five-finger discount' (1976).

Five-O noun orig US A police officer or detective; the police. 1983–. SNOOP Muslims . . . are now the most likely victims of stop and search with a full beard being like a red rag to a bull for the Five-O to go Rambo on ya (2004). [From the name of the US television police drama series *Hawaii Five-O* (1970–82).]

five-to-two noun Brit, derog or offensive Rhyming slang for 'Jew'. 1914–. E. WAUGH They respect us. Your five-to-two is a judge of quality (1948).

fix orig US. noun **1** A bribe; bribery; an illicit arrangement (e.g. between politicians, or between policemen and criminals). 1929–. W. P. MCGIVERN He had come up through the ranks of a society that was founded on the fix (1953). **2** A dose of a narcotic drug. Also **fix-up**. 1934–. OXFORD MAIL A weird scene where the dope peddlers gather to beat up Johnny, who gets more into debt with each 'fix' (1958). verb intr. and trans. **3** To inject (oneself) with narcotics. 1938–. M. M. GLATT ET AL. At first I 'fixed' only once a week, then more often, and after about six months I was addicted (1967). **4 to fix (someone's) wagon** US To bring about

someone's downfall, to spoil someone's chances of success. 1951–. J. D. SALINGER What ever became of that stalwart bore Fortinbras? Who eventually fixed *his* wagon? (1959).

fizgig noun Austral A police informer. Also **phizgig**. 1895–. SUN-HERALD (Sydney): We described him as rather a big crim and also a 'fiz gig'—an interesting word that means a grass, an informer (1984). [Cf. earlier sense, silly or flirtatious young woman.] Cf. FIZZER[2] noun.

fizz noun Champagne. 1864–. V. M. COTTRELL A bottle of 'fizz' each (1942). [From its effervescence.]

fizz-boat noun NZ A motor boat, a speedboat. 1977–. METRO (Auckland): There are everyman's little fizz-boat to the great petrol guzzling twin 200 horsepower outboard motor driven racing machines (1984). [After the noise made by the engine.]

fizzer[1] noun **1** services' A charge-sheet; esp. in phr. *on a* (or *the*) *fizzer*. a.1935–. NEW SOCIETY Feeling I was on a fizzer (army talk for a disciplinary charge) (1966). **2** Austral A disappointing failure; a fiasco or wash-out. 1957–. FACTS ON FILE John Howard . . . ridiculed the prime minister's address as the biggest fizzer since Halley's Comet (1986). [In sense 2, from earlier sense, firework that fails to go off.]

fizzer[2] noun Austral A police informer. Also **fizz, phizzer**. 1943–. AUSTRALIAN SHORT STORIES 'See any drugs over there? . . . We catch twenty a week,' he lied. 'Mostly through fizzers' (1985). [From FIZGIG noun.]

flack noun **1** mainly US A publicity agent. 1946–. C. DRUMMOND They were booked to do ten matches in Mexico City; Bull, their flack, had lined up the opposition (1968). verb N Amer **2** intr. To act as a publicity agent (*for*); hence, to disseminate favourable publicity, etc.; to proselytize. 1966–. FORBES You could cite the country's poverty. . . . You might even fault the tourism board for not flacking hard enough (1984). **3** trans. To promote or speak in favour of; to disseminate (information, etc.) to this end. 1975–. [Origin unknown.]

fladge noun Also **fladj, flage**. Flagellation, esp. as a means of sexual gratification; pornographic literature concentrating on flagellation. 1958–. J. I. M. STEWART I have some damned odd fantasies when it comes to quiet half-hours with sex. Flage, and all that (1975). [Shortened from *flagellation*.]

flak-catcher noun orig US Someone employed to deal with hostile comment, etc., on behalf of a person or institution that

fit fit-up five-finger discount Five-O five-to-two

is thereby protected from attack. 1970–.
MELODY MAKER They defend themselves pretty well,
putting up their wittiest flak-catchers for
interview (1984). [From *flak* adverse criticism
+ *catcher*.]

flake noun mainly US A crazy or eccentric
person; also, a slow-witted or unreliable
person. 1968–. EASYRIDERS Gotta git rid of that
flake Bobby Joe. He's just too gutless for the big
time (1983). [Back-formation from FLAKY
adjective.]

flaky adjective orig US Liable to behave
eccentrically; crazy; also, feeble-minded,
stupid. 1964–. NEW YORKER People can choose
their own words to describe Qaddafi's mental
state—President Reagan called him 'flaky', and
later denied that he considered Qaddafi mentally
unbalanced (1986). [Perh. from the notion of
'flaking out' through exhaustion, the
influence of drugs, etc.]

flaming adjective and adverb Used to express
annoyance, or as a mild intensifier. 1895–.
PRIVATE EYE He's saved my life if he only flamin'
knew it (1969). [From the earlier sense,
burning hot.]

flaming onions noun dated, services' An
anti-aircraft projectile consisting of about
ten balls of fire shot upwards in succession;
also, anti-aircraft tracer fire. 1918–43. [From
its resemblance to a string of onions.]

flanker noun, orig military A trick, a swindle.
1923–. B. KNOX This bloke wasn't content wi' just
fiddling the h.p. He'd been workin' another
flanker (1962). [Perh. from the notion of
slipping past the side or 'flank' of someone.]

flannel Brit noun 1 Extravagant or
exaggerated talk; hot air, nonsense; also,
flattery. 1927–. DAILY TELEGRAPH This coupon will
bring you our 'all facts—no flannel' brochure
telling you all about us (1970). verb intr. and trans.
2 To talk flatteringly or evasively (to). 1941–.
J. BRAINE I managed to flannel him into the belief
that I approved of his particular brand of
efficiency (1957).

flannel-mouth noun US An empty talker;
a flatterer. 1933–.

flapdoodle noun Nonsense, rubbish.
1878–. DAILY TELEGRAPH It's the one form of theatre
which never calls for explanation or critical
flapdoodle (1987). [Origin unknown; cf.
earlier sense (1833–63) 'the stuff they feed
fools on' F. Marryat.]

flash verb intr. and refl 1 Of a man: to
indecently expose oneself briefly. 1846–.

G. VIDAL Men stared at me. Some leered. None,
thank God, flashed (1978). Cf. FLASHER noun. noun
2 The brief pleasurable sensation obtained by
injecting a narcotic drug. 1967–. OZ
More & more people started shooting it to get
the flash all the real hip suckers were talking
about (1971).

flasher noun A man who indecently
exposes himself. 1974–. A. POWELL He was
apparently a 'flasher', who had just exposed
himself (1976).

Flash Harry noun An ostentatious, loudly
dressed, and typically bad-mannered man.
1960–. TIMES Her flash-Harry boy-friend (1962).

flash mob noun A large group of people
who, by private arrangement, suddenly
gather at a particular place and perform an
arbitrary action. 2003–.

flat adjective US Penniless. 1833–. TIMES LITERARY
SUPPLEMENT Satisfying his desires freely when he
can, starving when he is 'flat' (1930). [From *flat*
broke.]

flat-foot noun orig US A policeman, a plainclothes man. 1913–. C. DAY LEWIS Suppose the
flatfeet got to hear of it? (1948). [From the
alleged flatness of policemen's feet.]

flat-head noun A fool, simpleton. 1862–.
NEW STATESMAN Gobbledygook is the defence of
the American intellectual aware of the hostile
mockery of the surrounding flatheads (1966).

flat-top noun 1 US An aircraft-carrier.
1943–. C. S. FORESTER Escort vessels and destroyers
and baby flat-tops were coming off the ways as
fast as America and England and Canada could
build them (1955). 2 A man's short flat
haircut. 1956–.

flatty noun Also **flattie**. A policeman.
1899–. P. G. WODEHOUSE 'You know Dobbs?' 'The
flatty?' 'Our village constable, yes' (1949). [Prob.
from FLAT-FOOT noun.]

flea-bag noun 1 A bed; also, a soldier's
sleeping-bag. 1839–. R. PERTWEE He snaked his
feet into his flea bag (1930). 2 A shabby or
unattractive place, person, etc. 1932–. E. DUNDY
God, how I hated Paris! Paris was one big
flea-bag (1958).

flea pit noun A shabby and allegedly
verminous cinema. 1937–.

fleas and itches noun Austral Films; the
cinema. 1967–. D. O'GRADY When not too tired,
a man was able to visit . . . the open-air fleas-n'
itches (1968). [Rhyming slang for *pictures*,

flake flaky flaming flaming onions flanker flat

with an allusion to the vermin infesting cheap cinemas.]

flick noun Brit **1** A film. 1926–. J. BRAINE Where shall we go this afternoon anyway? Tanbury and tea at the Raynton, then a flick? (1959). **2 the flicks** the cinema. 1931–. F. SWINNERTON He would take her to the theatre, the ballet, the flicks (1949). [Cf. FLICKERS noun.]

flickers noun pl. dated Films, the cinema. 1927–69. GISH & PINCHOT Mother, guess who we saw acting in 'flickers'? (1969). [From the flickering effect of early cinema films.]

flim noun Brit, dated A five-pound note. 1870–1954. N. BLAKE They . . . offer Bert . . . a flim for his boat (1954). [Short for obs. slang *flimsy* banknote, from the thin paper formerly used for such notes.]

flip noun **1** A flippant, foolish, or crazy person. 1942–. I. ROSS 'She's a flip . . . . Nuts,' he translated, 'Loony. Off her rocker' (1961). verb intr. **2** To become suddenly very enthusiastic, excited, angry, etc. Also **to flip one's lid, wig.** 1950–. B. CRUMP As he spoke one of the dogs sank his teeth into a tender part and the bull flipped his lid completely (1960); R. MACDONALD She's a phoney blonde . . . . I can't understand why he would flip over her (1969).

flipper noun A hand or arm. 1812–. G. BRACH Free our guests' flippers so they may drink to our health (1986). [From earlier sense, broad fin of a fish, etc.]

flipping adjective and adverb Brit, euphemistic Used to express annoyance, or as a mild intensifier. 1911–. GUARDIAN They wax indignant about pornography but when it comes to doing anything about it they are bone flipping lazy (1971). [From *flip* verb; euphemism for FUCKING adjective and adverb.]

flit noun US, derog A male homosexual. 1942–. J. D. SALINGER Sometimes it was hard to believe, the people he said were flits and lesbians (1951). [Perh. from the notion of light fluttering effeminate movements.]

flivver noun orig, US A cheap car or aircraft. 1910–. S. BELLOW He had driven a painted flivver (1956). [Origin unknown.]

floater noun **1** US A dead body found floating in water. 1890–. J. MITFORD Floaters . . . are another matter; a person who has been in the Bay for a week or more . . . will decompose more rapidly (1963). **2** A mistake, bloomer. 1913–. A. WILSON I've as good as said that we don't want your money . . . . Just the sort of floater I would make, babbling on (1967).

3 US An official order to leave a town or district; a sentence suspended on condition that the offender leaves the area. 1914–. J. STEINBECK There's a permanent order in the Sheriff's office . . . that if I . . . admit I'm your wife I'll get a floater out of the county and out of the state (1952). **4** prisoners' A book, newspaper, etc. passed surreptitiously from cell to cell. 1933–. F. NORMAN It's [i.e. a book] a floater so you can sling it if you think you are going to get a turn over (1958).

flog verb **1** trans. Brit, orig military To sell. 1919–. M. DRABBLE Let's go . . . and look at the ghastly thing that Martin flogged us (1967). **2** intr. and refl To proceed by violent or painful effort. 1925–. TIMES [Lorry drivers] are being encouraged to 'flog on' even in bad weather (1964).

floozie noun Also **floosie, floozy.** A (young) woman, esp. a disreputable one. 1911–. L. DEIGHTON Stinnes had reached that dangerous age when a man was only susceptible to an innocent cutie or to an experienced floozy (1984). [Origin uncertain; cf. *flossy* adjective, fancy, showy and dialect *floosy* adjective, fluffy.]

flop verb intr. **1** orig US To sleep. 1907–. W. A. GAPE Where the hell are you going to 'flop' tonight? (1936). noun **2** A soft or flabby person. 1909–. F. O'CONNOR She was a great flop of a woman (1936). **3** US A bed; a place to rest or sleep; also, a flop-house. 1910–. J. DOS PASSOS They couldn't find any-place that looked as if it would give them a flop for thirty-five cents (1930).

flop-house noun orig US A doss-house. 1923–.

flopperoo noun Also **floperoo.** N Amer A failure. 1936–. R. JEFFRIES His case was a real flopperoo (1970). [From *flop* verb, to fail + *-eroo* suffix.]

flowery noun Brit A prison cell. 1925–. T. CLAYTON Found aht on the Moor . . . that if you have a new play to read weekends in the flowery . . . you can kid yourself you're having a Saturday night aht (1970). [Short for *flowery dell*, rhyming slang for 'cell'.]

flub verb orig US. verb trans. and intr. **1** To botch, bungle. 1924–. TV TIMES (Brisbane): Sullivan twitches. He mumbles. He flubs (1969). noun **2** Something badly or clumsily done. 1952–. [Origin unknown.]

fluff noun See *a bit of fluff* at BIT noun 1a.

flick flickers flim flip flipper flipping flit flivver

flunk orig and mainly US. verb **1** intr. To fail utterly, back out; often followed by *out*. 1823–. SUNDAY TIMES (Johannesburg): Sinatra himself said: 'I've flunked out with women more often than not. Like most men, I don't understand them (1971). **2** trans. To fail (an examination candidate). 1843–. WORD STUDY For if English teachers had always based their grades in English on the moral probity of their students' private lives, they would have had to flunk such naughty boys as Christopher Marlowe . . . and . . . Edgar Allan Poe (1966). **3** intr. To fail an examination; often followed by *out*. 1848–. **4 to flunk out** to be dismissed from college, etc. after failing an examination. 1920–. READER'S DIGEST He flunked out of various high schools, not because he was too stupid (1951). **5** trans. To fail (an examination, course, etc.). 1924–. TIMES I was utterly, deeply, completely depressed and flunked my A levels (1970). noun **6** An instance of flunking. 1846–. TIME This time there were twice as many flunks (1948). [Cf. FUNK² noun and verb and obs. *flink* verb, to be a coward.]

flush adjective Well supplied with money. 1603–. [From earlier more general sense, plentifully supplied.]

flutter noun Brit A small bet. 1883–. DAILY TELEGRAPH The British are great gamblers . . . The human instinct to have a flutter is as strong in Britain as anywhere else (1991). [From earlier sense, an attempt, try.]

fly adjective Brit Knowing, clever, alert. 1811–. [Origin uncertain; perh. from *fly* verb.]

fly noun **there are no flies on** (someone) orig Austral or US There is no lack of alertness, astuteness, competence, or energy in (a person). 1888–. OBSERVER There are no flies on Benaud. If England start bowling their overs slowly, no one will have to draw his attention to it (1961). [Cf. earlier *there are no flies about* (someone), in same sense; perh. from the notion of cattle so active that flies will not settle on them.]

fly verb trans. **go fly a kite** mainly US Go away, clear off. 1942–.

fly boy noun US A member of the Air Force, esp. a pilot. 1946–. LIFE The generals are no full-throttle 'fly-boys' (1948).

fly-by-night noun **1** dated A person who runs away in order to evade creditors. 1823–. adjective **2** Ephemeral, unreliable. 1914–. GUARDIAN It is not all heart in the mini-cab world. Far too many are fly-by-night hustlers (1971).

[From such people's nocturnal departure; cf. earlier sense, one who flies by night.]

fly-flat noun criminals', dated A foolish or gullible person who considers him- or herself clever. 1864–. J. CARY 'I don't see why we should consider the speculators.' 'A lot of fly-flats who thought they could beat us at the game' (1938). [From FLY adjective + obs. slang *flat* noun, gullible person.]

flying boxcar noun US services' A large cumbersome aircraft. 1918–.

flying fortress noun A nickname for the Boeing B-17, an American long-range bomber developed in the late 1930s. 1937–. R.A.F. JOURNAL The company has doubled its production of Flying Fortresses since Pearl Harbour (1942).

fogy noun Also **fogey** derog A person with old-fashioned or reactionary ideas or habits; usu. in phr. *old fogy*. 1780–. SUCCESSFUL FARMING MAGAZINE N Sync and Britney Spears (for you old fogies, those are the latest music stars) (2004). Hence **fogyish** adjective derog Typical of a fogy; old-fashioned, stuffy. 1873–. [Related to obs. slang *fogram* old-fashioned person, of unknown origin.]

footer noun Brit, dated The game of football. 1863–. E. WAUGH I had to change for F-f-footer (1945). [From *foot* noun + -ER.]

footsie noun Also **footsy.** Amorous play with the feet; also fig. Also **footy, -ie** and reduplicated forms. 1935–. G. FOWLER I played footsie with her during Don Jose's first seduction by Carmen (1944); ECONOMIST Pakistan is . . . despite recent games of footsie with Peking, a staunchly anti-communist ally (1963). [Jocular diminutive of *foot* noun.]

footy noun Also **footie.** mainly Austral and NZ The game of football. 1906–. SOUTHERLY Evans . . . strides off with her to ask race-goers, cinema queues and footy fans to sign peace petitions (1967). [Diminutive of *football* noun.]

foozling noun mainly golf Bungling; inept play. 1927–. G. MCINNES The rest of the eighteen holes were a miserable exhibition of foozling, duffing, [etc.] (1965). [From obs. *foozle* to do clumsily, perh. related to German dialect *fuseln* to work hurriedly and badly, to work slowly.]

foreigner noun Brit, orig military Something done or made at work by an employee for personal benefit; a piece of work not declared to the relevant authorities; esp. in phr. *to do a foreigner*. 1943–. A. BLEASDALE We're

flunk flush flutter fly boy flying fortress fogy

both gettin' followed, for all we know, we're both goin' t'get prosecuted f'doin' a foreigner while we're on the dole (1983).

for it phr. orig services' In danger of getting into trouble, esp. of being punished. 1909–. WAR ILLUSTRATED If a bomb comes, one is 'for it' (1940).

form noun A criminal record. 1958–. M. UNDERWOOD He has form for false pretences, mostly small stuff (1960). [From horse-racing use: a horse's past performance as a race-guide.]

forty noun Austral, dated A sharper, swindler. 1876–. M. M. BENNETT Their numbers swelled with rowdies and 'forties'—gambling sharpers who travelled from shed to shed making five pounds by cheating for every five shillings they earned (1927). [Orig applied to the members of a Sydney gang, perh. with reference to the tale of Ali Baba and the Forty Thieves.]

forty-rod whisky noun orig US Cheap, fiery whisky. Also **forty rod**. 1863–. DAILY OKLAHOMAN (Oklahoma City): The mere possession of a few gills of forty rod is not counted as an ample offset to planned assassination (1948). [Prob. from obs. *forty-rod lightning* in same sense, supposedly from a jocular reputation for being lethal at forty rods (about 200 metres).]

four-by-two noun derog and offensive Rhyming slang for 'Jew'. 1936–. E. MCGIRR 'This Marx, was he a four by two?' demanded Quimple. 'Pardon?' 'A Jew, sir, a Jew' (1970).

four-eyes noun jocular A person who wears glasses; often as a term of address. 1874–. COURIER-MAIL (Brisbane): Aha, foureyes! You're nicked! (1988).

four-flusher noun US One who bluffs; a fraud or cheat. 1904–. L. A. G. STRONG You shouldn't let these four-flushers come it over you (1944). [From *four flush* flush in poker containing only four (instead of five) cards and so almost worthless, hence something not genuine.]

four-letter man noun Brit, euphemistic An obnoxious man. 1923–. I. MURDOCH Felix regarded Randall as a four-letter man of the first order (1962). [Prob. from the four letters of the word *shit*.]

fourpenny dark noun Austral Cheap wine (orig as served in a miniature mug with

a handle). 1955–. D. HEWETT You'd better watch your step with that fourpenny dark. It'll get you before you know it (1976). [From its price and colour.]

fourpenny one noun Brit A blow, hit; also, a scolding. 1936–. N. FREELING I think he got mad because he gave her a real four-penny one. I bet she has a real black eye (1964).

fowl noun naval A troublesome or undisciplined sailor. 1937–8. GIRALDUS I was a 'fowl' of the first water. I was always getting 'run-in', always in trouble and had no zeal for the Navy whatsoever (1938).

fox noun US An attractive young woman. 1963–. L. HAIRSTON Daddy, she was a real fox! (1964). So **foxy**, adjective US Of a woman: sexually attractive. 1913–. EASYRIDERS W/f [white female] . . . 21 years old and foxy, would like to hear from a gorgeous man with a terrific body (1983). See also *crazy like a fox* at CRAZY adjective.

> 'Felix regarded Randall as a four-letter man of the first order.'

fracture verb trans. US To impress, excite, amuse greatly. 1946–. CRESCENDO I know he fractured you the same as he did me (1966).

frag verb trans. US, military To throw a hand grenade at (one's superior officer, esp. one who is considered too eager for combat). So **fragging**, noun. 1970–. [Abbreviation of 'fragmentation (grenade)', as used by US troops in Vietnam.]

fraid cat noun Also **fraidy cat**. A timorous person; used mainly by children. c.1910–. M. CRICHTON 'You okay with the fence, Tim?' 'Sure.' 'Want some help?' 'Tim's a fraidy-cat,' Lex called (1991). [From *fraid* (reduced form of *afraid*) (+ -y).]

frail noun mainly US A woman. 1908–. K. PLATT A smaller soggy shape was huddled behind him. . . . An Angel and his frail challenging another night (1970). [From *frail* adjective; cf. *the frail sex* women.]

frame verb trans. **1 to frame up** US dated To pre-arrange surreptitiously and with intent to deceive; to fake the result of (a contest, etc.). 1906–. R. D. PAINE All I need is a little work with your catcher, to frame up signals and so on (1923). **2** orig US To concoct a false charge or evidence against. 1922–. R. BRADDON If they were prepared to lie about Marseille then obviously they intended to frame her (1956).

noun **3** US = FRAME-UP noun. 1914–. J. EVANS
He . . . wasn't a killer but just the victim of a
frame (1948).

frame-up noun orig US A conspiracy, esp.
to make an innocent person appear guilty.
1900–. IT While serving a six month
sentence . . . Ian learned a lot about frame ups,
about prison conditions (1971). [Cf. FRAME
verb 1, 2.]

frank noun orig US A frankfurter. 1925–.
WASHINGTON POST Safeway Skinless All Meat Franks.
2 lb. pkg. 99c (1968). [Shortening.]

frat¹ noun Also **frat.** US college (A member
of) a college fraternity. 1895–. PUNCH The only
Frank Lloyd Wright building on my campus was
a frat. house (1967). [Abbreviation of
'fraternity'.]

frat² noun A woman met by fratting;
also, = FRATTING noun. 1945–. G. COTTERELL Then,
take my frat I go with, what harm did she ever
do? (1949). [From FRAT verb.]

frat verb intr. Of British and American
occupying troops in West Germany after
World War II: to establish friendly and esp.
sexual relations with German women.
1945–. M. K. JOSEPH 'He was fratting, wasn't he?'
'Sure—dark piece, lives up the Ludwigstrasse'
(1957). Hence **fratting,** noun. 1945–. S. SPENDER
At the messes most of the conversation was
about 'fratting' (1946). **fratter,** noun One who
frats. 1949–. G. COTTERELL So he's married. . . . I bet
she doesn't know what a shameless old fratter
you were (1949). [Abbreviation of
'fraternize'.]

freak orig US. noun **1** A person with the
stated enthusiasm or interest. 1908–. P. BOOTH
Boy, are you exercise freaks into punishment
(1986). **2** A person who experiences
hallucinations; a drug addict. 1967–. INK An
ideological community of 25 freaks plus guru in
Copenhagen (1971). verb **3** intr. and trans. To
(cause to) experience hallucinations or
intense emotions, esp. from the use of
narcotics; usu. followed by *out.* 1965–. NATURE
One question asked the respondents how often
they had seen other people 'freak out', that is,
have intense, transient emotional upsets (1970).
4 intr. To adopt a wildly unconventional
lifestyle; usu. followed by *out.* 1967–. IT
Freedom to freak-out, yes; freedom to do your
own thing, sure (1968).

freakazoid noun orig US **1** A bizarre or
freakish person. 1984–. adjective **2** Bizarre,
freakish. 1990–. GUARDIAN The procession of
neurotic freakazoid flatmates that blighted my

early 20s (2005). [From *freak* noun + the suffix
-oid, with the addition of *-az-* (perh. suggested
by *schizoid* noun or SLEAZOID noun).]

freak-out noun An act of freaking out;
a hallucinatory or strong emotional
experience. 1966–. L. DEIGHTON That helicopter
trip is a futuristic freak-out (1968).

freckle noun Austral The anus. 1967–.
B. HUMPHRIES I too believed that the sun shone out
of Gough's freckle (1978).

freebase orig US. noun **1** Cocaine that has
been purified by heating with ether, and is
taken by inhaling the fumes or smoking the
residue. 1980–. verb intr. and trans. **2** To purify
(cocaine) for smoking or inhaling; to take
(the drug) in this form. 1980–. TIME The Los
Angeles say Pryor told them that the accident
occurred while he was 'free-basing' cocaine
(1980).

freebie Also **freebee, freeby.** orig US.
adjective **1** Free, without charge. 1942–. noun
2 Something that is provided free. 1946–.
E. LACY She'll write 'free' on the slip. . . . They
come in for the freebie and end up buying more
copies (1962). [Arbitrarily from *free* adjective.]

French noun **1** Fellatio. 1958–. T. PARKER
There's two things I won't let her do though,
that's French and sadism (1969). verb trans. and
intr. **2** To practise fellatio or cunnilingus (on).
1958–. W. YOUNG In England . . . we call . . . cunt-
licking Frenching (1965). [From the supposed
predilection of the French for oral sex.]

French blue noun A non-proprietary
mixture of amphetamine and a barbiturate.
1964–. J. WELCOME Some say French blues kill the
itch to drink. With me they didn't (1968).

French letter noun Also **french letter.**
mainly Brit A condom. *c.*1856–. J. R. ACKERLEY My
elder brother Peter was the accident. 'Your
father happened to have run out of french
letters that day' (1968). [*letter* perh. = hinderer,
from *let* hinder.]

Frenchy noun Also **Frenchie. 1** derog
A French person or French Canadian. 1883–.
MACLEAN'S I was constantly laughed at, pointed at
and corrected, as a stupid Frenchy (1966).
2 Also **frenchy.** = FRENCH LETTER noun. 1953–.
T. SHARPE You can't feel a thing with a Frenchie.
You get more thrill with the pill (1976). [From
earlier *Frenchy* adjective, French-like, from
French adjective + *-y.*]

fresh adjective orig and mainly US New and
exciting; 'hip', 'cool'. 1984–. T. KIDDER Bro, that
was fresh! (1989). [A slight shift from the

frame-up frank frat freak freakazoid freckle

freshy noun Also **freshie.** Austral A freshwater crocodile. 1964–. AGE (Melbourne) There are no recorded attacks by 'freshies' on humans (1985). [Shortening.]

fricking adjective and adverb Euphemistic alteration of FRIGGING adjective and adverb or FUCKING adjective and adverb. 1961–. CHICAGO TRIBUNE You could see your own skeleton. . . . Your own fricking bones X-rayed (1987).

fried adjective Drunk. 1926–. N. COWARD After a gay reunion party . . . I retired to bed slightly fried, blissfully happy (1954).

friend noun **a friend of Dorothy** a male homosexual. 1988–. PRIVATE EYE Just because you don't go on holiday with her doesn't mean you're a friend of Dorothy (1990). [From the name, *Dorothy*, of the heroine of L. Frank Baum's *Wizard of Oz* (1900). Judy Garland's performance in this role in the film version (1939) subsequently achieved cult status amongst gays.]

frig mainly euphemistic. verb **1** trans. and intr. **a** = FUCK verb 1. 1598–. MEZZROW & WOLFE *High-pressure romancing* (find 'em, fool 'em, frig 'em and forget 'em) (1946). **b** To masturbate. 1680–. **2** trans. = FUCK verb 2. 1905–. L. MEYNELL 'And what about the rent?' 'Frig the rent' (1970). noun **3** = FUCK noun. *c.*1888–. M. MCCARTHY I don't give a frig about Sinnott's heredity (1955). [Orig sense, to move restlessly; perh. onomatopoeic alteration of obs. *frike* verb, to dance, move briskly.]

frigging adjective and adverb mainly euphemistic = FUCKING adjective and adverb. 1930–. K. WATERHOUSE Take your frigging mucky hands off my pullover (1959).

frightener noun **1 to put the frighteners on** to intimidate. 1958–. A. PRIOR His job had been to put the frighteners on various shopkeepers (1966). **2** A member of a criminal gang employed to intimidate the gang's potential victims. 1962–. DAILY TELEGRAPH Soho 'frighteners'—gangsters who try to extort money from club owners—were told . . . at the Old Bailey . . . that they faced severe punishment (1962).

frippet noun A frivolous or showy young woman. 1908–. E. TAYLOR 'Mistress!' he thought. . . . It was like the swine of a man to use such a word for what he and Edwards would have called a bit of a frippet (1945). [Origin unknown.]

fritz noun orig and mainly US **1 to put on the fritz** (also **to put the fritz on**) to spoil, destroy, put a stop to. 1903–. R. H. R. SMITHIES It's mother's plan to put the fritz on shoplifting (1968). **2 on the fritz** out of order, unsatisfactory. 1924–. GUARDIAN It appeared, for an awful moment, that a cue had failed, that the teleprompter was on the fritz (1962). [Origin unknown.]

Fritz noun mainly derog A German, esp. a German soldier of World War I; also, a German shell, aircraft, submarine, etc. 1915–. J. THOMAS I gathered he was more of a *collaborateur* than anything else. He praised you Fritzes up to the skies (1955). [German nickname for *Friedrich*.]

fro noun Also **'fro** US An Afro haircut. 1970–. WASHINGTON POST He . . . goes through countless hairstyles (from Beatles straightened mop top to angry 'fro) (1993). [Shortening of *Afro*.]

frobnitz noun Also **frob** US computing An unnamed or unspecified thing. 1983–. [Prob. a fanciful coinage.]

frog noun Also **Frog.** derog **1** A French person. 1778–. I. MURDOCH Not that I want you to marry a frog, but she sounded quite a nice person (1962). **2** The French language. 1955–. W. FAULKNER Ask him. . . . You can speak Frog (1955). [From French people's reputation for eating frogs.]

froggy Also **Froggy.** derog noun **1** Also **froggee.** = FROG noun 1. 1872–. GUARDIAN A group of stage-type Limeys spend a weekend in France where they mix with a series of stage-type Froggies (1965). adjective **2** French. 1937–. I. MURDOCH What about that froggy girl, the one you met in Singapore? (1962). [From FROG noun + -y.]

frogskin noun **1** US A banknote, usu. spec. a dollar bill. 1902–. MIAMI VICE A deal somewhere in the neighborhood of two hundred million frogskins (1987). **2** Austral dated A pound (note). 1907–. AUSTRALIAN NEW WRITING You come back here tomorrow night . . . and it's two frogskins for you and drinks all round! (1944). [In sense 1, from the colour.]

frog-spawn noun Brit, children's derog Tapioca or sago pudding. 1959–. NEW STATESMAN The well-known fly cemetery and frogspawn are still o.k.-descriptions of currant puddings and tapioca (1963).

front verb intr. orig US To act as a cover for others' illegal or subversive activities. 1932–. N. FREELING To . . . help him out occasionally I have

freshy fricking fried friend frig frigging fritz

fronted for him—a telephone call. And I'm bound to say he helped me (1971).

front burner noun **on the front burner** orig US Of an issue, etc.: in the state of being actively or urgently considered; in the forefront of attention. 1970–. GUARDIAN WEEKLY The most influential man on the labor scene, who for obvious reasons normally keeps the jobs picture on the front burner (1978). [From the use of the front ring, hotplate, etc. on a cooking stove for boiling rather than simmering.] Cf. BACK BURNER noun.

frosh noun N Amer A college freshman; a member of a freshman sports team. Also, freshmen collectively. 1915–. UNIVERSITY OF WATERLOO (Ontario) GAZETTE 'A university is a very special kind of place,' Wright told the 2,000 frosh (1985). [Modified shortening of *freshman*, perh. influenced by German *Frosch* frog, (*dialect*) grammar-school pupil.]

frost noun orig theatrical A failure. 1886–. R. LINDNER Look, Doc. This analysis is a frost, isn't it? (1955). [Perh. from the notion of getting a cool reception.]

frozen limit noun orig and mainly US Something that is more than one can tolerate; the limit. 1916–.

fruit noun **1** dated A person easily deceived; a dupe. 1895–1931. **2** orig US A male homosexual. 1935–. GUARDIAN He is a fruit, which means . . . that he is a queer (1970). See also OLD FRUIT noun.

fruit-cake noun orig US An eccentric or mad person. 1952–. OBSERVER To be considered as a candidate you must first get onto the Panel, which is a sort of index designed mainly to exclude fruitcakes (1982). [Cf. *nutty as a fruitcake* at NUTTY adjective.]

fruit-loop noun US A crazy or eccentric person; also, an effeminate or ostentatiously homosexual man. 1984–. [From *Fruit Loops*, proprietary name of a US brand of breakfast cereal, punning on FRUIT noun 2, FRUIT-CAKE noun, etc.]

fruit salad noun services' A (copious or ostentatious) display of medals, ribbons, or other decorations. 1943–. N. SHUTE A red-faced old gentleman with . . . a fruit salad of medal ribbons on his chest (1955). [From the array of colours presented by assorted medal ribbons.] Cf. SCRAMBLED EGG noun.

fry verb trans. and intr. US To execute or be executed in the electric chair. 1929–.

J. WYNDHAM You'll hang or you'll fry, every one of you (1956). See also FRIED adjective.

fubar /fuːbɑː(r)/ adjective US, euphemistic, orig military Ruined, messed up; also, very drunk. Cf. SNAFU adjective, noun, and verb. 1944–. S. KING This was my grandfather's and it works just fine . . . My wristwatch, on the other hand, is still FUBAR (2001). [Acronym formed from *fucked up beyond all recognition*.]

fuck coarse. verb **1** intr. and trans. To copulate (with). *a*.1503–. INK I don't want to fuck anyone, and I don't want to be fucked either (1971). **2** trans. Used in curses and exclamations, indicating strong dislike, contempt, or rejection. 1922–. F. KING 'Suppose any of the neighbours were to look out and see them.' 'Oh, f– the neighbours!' (1959). **3a: to fuck about** (or **around**) to fool about, mess about. 1929–. **b: to fuck** (someone) **about** (or **around**) to cause trouble or inconvenience to (someone). 1960–. INDEPENDENT ON SUNDAY 'We did it because we just got fucked around all the time,' Slash explains. 'Everyone's taken pot-shots at us and made up stories' (1991). **4 to fuck off** to go away; also as an expression of contemptuous or angry rejection. 1929–. S. BECKETT She wants to know if you're the one in charge. Fuck off, said Lemuel (1958). **5 to fuck** (someone) **over** orig US to treat (someone) harshly or contemptuously; to damage or betray. 1961–. P. MORGAN They responded by handing our scoop to our immediate commercial rival to fuck us over! (2007) **6 to fuck up: a** trans. To make a mess of. 1967–. IT The . . . neatly planned plot to fuck up their transport scene (1969). **b** intr. To blunder, fail. 1971–. ROLLING STONE We fucked up in New York (1977). noun **7** An act of sexual intercourse. 1680–. E. J. HOWARD Eat well, don't smoke, and a fuck was equal to a five-mile walk (1965). **8** A partner in sexual intercourse. 1874–. J. MORRIS She was a good fuck. . . . She was great in bed (1969). **9** The slightest amount. In negative contexts. 1929–. INK We don't give a fuck if we have to stand around all day doing nothing (1971). **10** Various other casual, intensive, etc. uses. 1959–. D. HOLBROOK Driver speed up. Come on, for fuck's sake (1966); G. LORD What the fuck do you think you're doing? (1970). [Origin unknown.]

fuck-all noun coarse (Absolutely) nothing. 1960–. A. LURIE You don't know fuck-all about life (1985).

fuck buddy noun US (Esp. among male homosexuals) a friend or acquaintance with whom a person has sex without expectation of a romantic relationship. 1973–. M. ALBO

We are simply 'fuck buddies' to each other. Casual casual casual (2000).

fucked adjective coarse In a spoiled or ruined condition; inoperative. 1955–. W. GIBSON Your lungs are filling up with fluid, your kidneys aren't working, your heart's fucked (1988).

fucker noun coarse One who copulates; also as a general term of abuse. 1598–. A. WILSON 'We'll get you, you fucker!' Barley was shouting (1961).

fucking adjective and adverb coarse Used as an intensive to express annoyance, etc. 1893–. W. H. AUDEN I'm so bored with the whole fucking crowd of you I could scream! (1969).

fucking A coarse, orig US military. adjective **1** you're fucking A you're completely right. 1948–. J. BRILEY You're fucking A I had to work hard (1969). adverb **2** Completely, absolutely. 1960–. int **3** Showing heartfelt agreement. 1968–. A. MAUPIN 'I don't think any guy's worth begging for.' 'Fuckin' A' (1992). [Perh. suggested by such expressions as 'You're fucking A-number-one right!']

fucking ada int coarse Brit An expression of annoyance or exasperation. 1962–. [ada perh. arbitrarily from the female personal name Ada.]

fuck-me adjective coarse Sexually alluring, seductive; usu. used of clothes, esp. footwear. 1974–. L. LOCHHEAD Moira McVitie . . . shouts out 'Hiya there Verena is that you trying on some fuck-me shoes for your man gettin back' (1985).

fuck-off noun coarse, orig US military A lazy or apathetic person, a shirker. 1948–. J. BIRMINGHAM Another house full of fuck-offs and misfits and perennial students (1994).

fuck-up noun coarse A mess, muddle. 1958–. M. RICHLER I'm sorry about this fuck-up, Mr Griffin (1968).

fuckwit noun coarse, orig Austral An idiot. 1969–. M. STEEL You cloth-eared brainless overpaid legal fuckwit (2001). Hence **fuckwitted** adjective coarse 1973–. [Perh. modelled on *dimwit* noun and NITWIT noun.]

fud noun orig and mainly US A fuddy-duddy; often as **old fud**. 1942–. NEW YORKER Steve Martin playing straight man to his fud, they're a manic-depression team (1984). [Shortened from *fuddy-duddy* noun, but cf. the name of Elmer Fudd, character in Bugs Bunny cartoons from c.1939.]

fudge factor noun An estimated or speculative quantity included in a calculation, etc., esp. to compensate for the absence of accurate information. 1977–. FINANCIAL TIMES The market soon recognised the fudge factor—half a point tacked on for the drought effect (1989). [From *fudge* verb, to prevaricate + *factor* noun.]

fugly orig Austral military. noun **1** A very ugly person, esp. a woman. *a.*1970–. COSMOPOLITAN 33% of women have dated someone 'as ugly as sin' because he made them laugh. Here's to all the fuglies! (2005). adjective **2** Very ugly. 1988–. [From *f(ucking* + *ugly*.]

full adjective **1** Austral and NZ **a** Drunk. *c.*1848–. C. LEE We were all pretty well full when the van rolled into Mittagong (1980). **b: as full as a tick** (also **as full as a boot, bull, egg, fart, goog**, etc.): drunk. 1892–. D. M. DAVIN Wasn't he in here this afternoon and as full as a tick? (1949). **2 full of beans** full of energy and in high spirits. 1854–. J. ELDER We start off—oh, full of beans—and then we stop (1927).

full monty noun Brit **1** The full amount or complement, everything. 1985–. Popularized by the 1997 film *The Full Monty*. GUARDIAN When conducting a funeral he wears the full monty; frock coat, top hat and a Victorian cane with metal tip (1995). **2 to do** (or **go**) **the Full Monty** to strip, do a striptease; used esp. of men. 1997–. EVENING CHRONICLE (Newcastle) Bingo boys do the Full Monty—Cheeky callers in sponsored strip for charity calendar [headline] (2001). [Origin uncertain: of the many possibilities put forward, the likeliest is that the original reference was to a full suit of men's clothes as supplied by the firm of Montague Burton. In sense 2, from the film *The Full Monty* (see above), in which some unemployed Sheffield steelworkers become strippers to earn some money.]

full whack noun Brit = TOP WHACK noun. MONEY OBSERVER Payments then rise by 5.0 per cent a year, so you pay the full whack after eight or nine years (1989).

fully verb trans. dated To commit (a person) for trial. 1849–1936. J. CURTIS They'll fully me to the Old Bailey, I reckon (1936). [From *fully* adverb, in phr. 'fully committed for trial'.]

fundi noun Also **fundie, fundy**. A fundamentalist, esp. **(a)** a believer in the literal truth of Scripture, and **(b)** a member of the radical left wing of the German Green Party. 1982–. DAILY TELEGRAPH The fundies are the purists who believe the only way to save the Earth is to dismantle industry (1989). [Shortened from *fundamentalist* + *-i(e)*, *-y*.]

fucked fucker fucking A fucking ada full monty

fungus

fungus noun jocular A beard or other facial hair. 1925–. R. CROMPTON 'Is it to be me or that ass with the fungus on his cheeks?' demanded Richard belligerently (1937). See also FACE-FUNGUS noun.

funk¹ noun **1** A strong smell, usually unpleasant; an oppressively thick atmosphere, esp. full of tobacco smoke. 1623–. M. AMIS The darts contest took place, not in the Foaming Quart proper (with its stained glass and heavy drapes and crepuscular funk), but in an adjoining hall (1989). **2** orig US Funky music. 1959–. MAKING MUSIC The bass rhythm is an extension of the pattern that dominated funk in the mid seventies (1987). [From obs. *funk* verb, to blow smoke on, perh. from French dialect *funkier*, from Latin *fūmicare, fūmigāre* to smoke.]

funk² noun **1** Fear, panic. 1743–. J. I. M. STEWART One oughtn't to let funk be catching. Tony was admitting funk—but perhaps not as much as he had actually been feeling (1974). **2** A coward. 1860–. verb Brit **3** intr. To flinch, shrink, show cowardice. 1737–. **4** trans. To be afraid of. 1836–. **5** To try to evade (an undertaking), shirk. 1857–. TIMES Mrs Margaret Thatcher is said to be as firmly committed as ever . . . , despite accusations . . . yesterday that she would 'funk it' (1986). [Orig apparently Oxford University slang; perh. from FUNK¹ noun in obs. sense, tobacco smoke.] See also BLUE FUNK noun.

funk-hole noun mainly derog A place to which one can go to avoid danger, evade an unpleasant duty, etc. 1900–. J. D. CLARK Deep, dark caves were never occupied except very occasionally as refuges or 'funk holes' [From FUNK² noun; cf. *fox-hole* noun.]

funkstick noun dated, orig hunting A coward. 1889–. A. E. W. MASON She thought of William Mardyke and his timidities. 'He'll never do that. What did you call him?' 'A funkstick' (1930). [From earlier sense, a huntsman who baulks at difficult fences, from FUNK verb + *sticks* fence.]

funky¹ adjective **1** now only US Having a strong smell, usually unpleasant. 1784–. J. BALDWIN They knew why his hair was nappy, his armpits funky (1962). **2** orig US Of jazz or rock music: earthy, bluesy, with a heavy rhythmical beat. 1954–. FRENDZ *Brown Sugar* and *Bitch* are Jagger at his foxy, dirty, funky best (1971). **3** orig US Fashionable. 1969–. HOLIDAY WHICH? Once across Broadway from Washington Square, you're in East Village, which is where funky New York is now found (1990). [From FUNK¹ noun + -*y*.]

funky² adjective Frightened, nervous, cowardly. 1837–. [From FUNK² noun + -*y*.]

funny farm noun A mental hospital. 1963–. E. AMBLER *Intercom* was described as 'the Batman of the funny-farm set' and its editor as 'the Lone Ranger of the lunatic fringe' (1969).

funny house noun US = FUNNY FARM noun. 1906–.

funny money noun orig US Money which for some reason is not what it seems to be, esp. **(a)** counterfeit currency; **(b)** assets amassed unscrupulously. 1938–. T. BARLING Sadler's got a name for asset-stripping. . . . It's been whispered Tommy Troy's pulled himself a funny-money man (1976).

furphy /ˈfɜːfɪ/ noun Austral A false report or rumour; an absurd story. 1915–. SYDNEY MORNING HERALD The Premier described the rumours of changes to the legislation as a great furphy that had got out of control (1986). [From the name of a firm, J. Furphy & Sons Pty. Ltd. of Shepparton, Victoria, manufacturing water and sanitary carts used in World War I: the name 'Furphy' appeared on such carts, whose drivers were sources of gossip.] Cf. SCUTTLEBUTT noun.

futz /fʌts/ verb intr. US To loaf, waste time, mess *around*. 1932–. N. BENCHLEY It's bad for your blood pressure to futz around like this (1968). [Perh. alteration of Yiddish *arumfartzen* to fart around.]

fuzz noun orig US **1** The police. 1929–. P. G. WODEHOUSE If the fuzz search my room, I'm sunk (1971). **2** A policeman or detective. 1931–. D. RUNYON A race-track fuzz catches up with him (1938). [Origin unknown.]

fungus funk funk-hole funkstick funky futz fuzz

G noun US Abbreviation of GRAND noun; = GEE[3] noun. 1928–. A. CURRY He'd probably drop me a few G's for the names of the guys in London (1971).

gabfest noun mainly US A gathering for talk; a prolonged conference or conversation. 1897–. SPECTATOR A shambles as big as the Labour gabfest (1960). [From *gab* noun, talk + *fest* noun, meeting for a particular purpose, from German *Fest* celebration.]

gaff[1] noun US Severe treatment, criticism, etc.; in phrs. *to stand, take, give*, etc. *the gaff*. 1896–. W. M. RAINE Just because he shuts his mouth and stands the gaff (1924). [Origin unknown.] See also *to blow the gaff* at BLOW verb.

gaff[2] noun Brit A house, shop, or other building, esp. someone's home. 1932–. J. MACLAREN-ROSS I was keeping an eye on the gaff—seen you going in (1961). [Origin unknown; cf. earlier senses, fair, cheap place of public entertainment.]

gaff verb trans., mainly gamblers' To cheat, hoax. 1934–. H. GOLD I want to play you straight fifty-fifty, not gaff you for fifty-fifty (1965). [From earlier sense, to gamble, toss up.]

gaffer noun Brit A foreman or boss. *a.*1659–. [From earlier use as a term of respect; prob. a contraction of *godfather* noun.]

gag verb intr. **to be gagging for** mainly Brit to be desperately eager for (sexual intercourse, a sexual partner, etc.); in phr. *be gagging for it*. 1990–. H. FIELDING I was going to point out that three potential eligible partners gagging for it plus half the house and the pension schemes wasn't exactly nothing, but I bit my tongue (1996). [From earlier sense, to try desperately to acquire something, esp. to breathe in air.]

gaga /ɡaːɡaː/ adjective **1** Dotty or fatuous, esp. from old age; crazy. 1920–. A. WILSON If Godmanchester was so gaga that he blabbed like this, then our prospects were alarming (1961). noun **2** A senile or crazy person. 1938–. A. KOESTLER Couldn't understand what he said. . . . Disastrous old gaga (1941). [From French *gaga* senile person; senile.]

galah /ɡəˈlaː/ noun Austral A fool, simpleton. 1938–. M. PAICE A bloke feels a galah being laid up like this (1978). [From earlier sense, rose-breasted cockatoo; from Aboriginal (Yuwaalaraay and related languages) *gilaa*.]

galoot /ɡəˈluːt/ noun orig US A clumsy or foolish person. 1866–. D. MCCLEAN I've just thought of something that will interest Ian. What a galoot I am not to think of it sooner

(1960). [Origin unknown; cf. earlier sense, inept or stupid soldier or marine.]

gamahuche /ɡæməhuːʃ/ verb trans. and intr. dated To perform fellatio or cunnilingus (on). 1865–. E. SELLON 'Quick, quick, Blanche!' cried Cerise, 'come and gamahuche the gentleman' (1865). [From French slang *gamahucher* in the same sense.]

game noun **on the game** mainly Brit **a** dated Actively engaged in burglary. 1739–. **b** Working as a prostitute. 1898–. T. PARKER Betty's on the game, isn't she? Has she got you at it too? (1969). [In sense b, cf. Shakespeare's Set them down for sluttish spoils of opportunity, and daughters of the game, TROILUS & CRESSIDA (1606).]

gammon Brit, dated. noun **1** Insincere or nonsensical talk intended to deceive or flatter; humbug, rubbish. 1805–. verb trans. **2** To deceive with insincere or flattering talk. 1812–. G. HEYER He added, as a clincher, that Mr. Christopher need not try to gammon him into believing that he wasn't in the habit of wearing full evening-dress (1963). [Prob. from the 18th- and 19th-cent. thieves' slang expressions *to give someone gammon*, *keep someone in gammon* distract someone's attention while an accomplice robs him, which may be an application of the backgammon term *gammon* complete victory achieved before one's opponent has removed any of his pieces.]

gammy adjective Brit Of a part of the body, esp. the leg: disabled by injury or pain. 1879–. D. M. DAVIN That gammy foot of mine (1947). [Dialectal derivative of *game* lame, crippled, perh. from French *gambi* crooked.]

gamp noun Brit, dated An umbrella, esp. one tied in a loose, untidy way. 1864–. [From the name of Sarah Gamp, a nurse in Dickens's *Martin Chuzzlewit* (1844), who owned such an umbrella.]

G gabfest gaff gaffer gag gaga galah gamahuche

gander verb intr. **1** Now mainly US To look, esp. in a foolishly inquisitive way. 1887–. noun **2** orig US An act of looking at something; esp. in phr. *to have* (or *take*) *a gander at* (something). 1914–. SCIENTIFIC AMERICAN Take a gander at the see-through door below (1971). [From the resemblance between a goose and an inquisitive person stretching out the neck to look.]

gandy dancer noun orig US A railway maintenance worker or section-hand. 1923–. F. MCKENNA Footplatemen have great regard for gandy dancers, the men who keep the railway safe for the train to run over (1970). [Of uncertain origin; perh. from a tool called a *gandy* used for tamping down gravel round the rail, and operated by pushing with the foot.]

gang-bang orig US. noun **1** An act of or occasion for multiple intercourse, esp. one in which several men in succession have sex with the same woman. c.1945–. Also **gangshag.** 1927–. **2** Something undertaken or experienced by a group of people, esp. a situation or activity characterized by high stress, intensity, or confusion. 1953–. M. BEAUMONT Pinki has asked me to remind you that the creative gangbang starts in five in the boardroom (2000). verb **3** intr. and trans. Of males: to engage in multiple successive intercourse (with). 1965–. GUARDIAN A pretty 18-year-old girl . . . used to 'stuff' herself with heroin and let herself be 'gang-banged' all the time (1969). **4** intr. To belong to a street gang; esp. to engage in gang violence. 1969–. GOLDMAN & FULLER War ain't no big deal . . . Be like gang-bangin' on the block (1983). Hence **gang-banger** noun. 1969–.

gangbuster noun (and adjective) orig and mainly US **1** An officer of a law-enforcement agency noted for its successful (and often aggressive) methods in dealing with organized crime. Also attrib or as adjective. 1936–. WASHINGTON POST In his floppy banana trench coat and fabulous matching fedora, Warren Beatty looks more like the fashion police than a gangbuster (1990). **2a: like gangbusters** with great speed, force, or success. Also as adjective phr. 1942–. G. MANDEL Nothing can hold me down. 'Cause I'm like Gangbusters. Watch me come on (1952). **b: to go** (or **do**) **gangbusters** to perform or proceed with unusual vigour or (usu. commercial) success. 1975–. **3** Someone or something outstandingly successful, powerful, etc., esp. in commercial performance. Also attrib or as adjective. 1946–. NEWSDAY He predicted the investment will return an average of 8 percent over the first 15 years, 'but the second fifteen years will be gangbusters' (1989). [From *gang* noun + *-buster*, popularized by the long-running US radio serial *Gang Busters* (1936–57).]

ganja noun Also **ganga.** Cannabis. 1800–. GUARDIAN The telltale smell of ganja assails your nostrils as soon as you enter (1992). [From Hindi *gānjhā*.]

gannet noun orig naval A greedy person. 1929–. P. TEMPEST The bet may be on how many plates of porridge one 'gannet' can put away at a sitting (1950). [From the name of the seabird, renowned as a great eater.]

gaolbait variant of JAILBAIT noun.

gaper noun cricket A simple catch, esp. one that is dropped; a 'dolly'. 1903–. TIMES Certain of the younger members of the side were dropping some regular 'gapers' (1963). [Prob. from the notion that something which 'gapes' open offers easy success.]

garbo noun Austral A dustman. 1953–. GUARDIAN Australian garbos probably could not compete with English dustmen in the length and scale of their strikes (1971). [From *garb(age* + the Austral colloquial suffix *-o*.]

gargle noun An alcoholic drink. 1889–. GUARDIAN 'Copy of the Boss's Wit and Wisdom, old boy,' he said, presenting a neatly typed replica of the non-election address. 'Come and have a gargle' (1987).

garmento noun US fashion industry, sometimes derog A person who works in the fashion industry, esp. in a field regarded as unglamorous. 1985–. [From *garment* noun + *-o*.]

garn verb imperative (Used in writing to represent) a Cockney pronunciation of the exclamation *go on!*, denoting disbelief or derision. 1886–. A. HOLDEN 'Garn!' called out someone, 'tell us something we don't know!' (1968).

Garnet noun **(all) Sir Garnet** Brit, dated Completely satisfactory; all right. 1894–. A. GILBERT She'd been knocked out . . . and her heart being not quite Sir Garnet did the rest

> **all Sir Garnet**
> completely satisfactory; all right

(1958). [From the name of Sir *Garnet Wolseley* (1833–1913), British field-marshal and commander-in-chief of the British Army 1895–9, who was famous for having led several successful military expeditions in the Sudan and elsewhere.]

gas noun **1a: all is gas and gaiters** everything is satisfactory. 1839–. A. CHRISTIE I've only got to get hold of dear old Stylptitch's Reminiscences . . . and all will be gas and gaiters (1925). **b: (all) gas and gaiters** pomposity, verbosity. 1923–. G. B. SHAW Shelley's Epipsychidion is, in comparison, literary gas and gaiters (1932). **2** Lengthy but empty talk. 1847–. C. DAY LEWIS The sisters would sit on the tiny patch of lawn at the back of the house, shelling peas and having a great old gas (1960). **3a** Anglo-Irish Fun; a joke. 1914–. E. O'BRIEN 'Let's do it for gas,' Baba said (1962). **b** orig US Something that gives enormous fun and excitement. 1957–. FRENDZ The Stones . . . were a screaming, speeding, sexy gas (1971). Cf. GASSER noun. verb **4** intr. To talk at length, esp. boringly or pompously. 1852–. **5** trans. orig US To excite, thrill. 1949–. CRESCENDO A . . . cadenza at the end of 'Watermelon man' which really gassed me (1967). See also *to cook with gas* at COOK verb.

gasbag noun A person who talks too much. 1889–. G. KEILLOR One gasbag after another climbed up on the platform (1986).

gas guzzler noun orig US A large car with excessively high fuel consumption. 1973–. WASHINGTON POST The big American family sedan may be a gas-guzzler. But it can also be an insurance bargain (1985). So **gas-guzzling,** adjective Making inefficient use of fuel. 1968–.

gash¹ noun coarse **1** The vulva; the female genitals. 1893–. **2** derog A woman; a prostitute. 1914–. L. GOULD I asked him if I could borrow *The Sun Also Rises*, and he said, 'I never lend books to any gash' (1974). [From earlier sense, cut; cf. SLIT noun.]

gash² noun **1** Austral A second helping of food. 1943–. W. WATKINS He didn't have to beg the cook for left over scran—gash, the crew called it (1972). **2** Brit, mainly naval and military Something superfluous; waste, rubbish. 1945–. TIMES A disgusted stoker is emptying a bottle of the best Demerara down the gash-shute (1960). adjective **3** Brit Surplus to requirements; extra, superfluous. 1945–. M. RUSSELL Cop-shop's stuffed with gash CID apprentices (1971). [Prob. short for earlier *gashion* extras, which may be related to English dialect *gaishen* skeleton, silly-looking person, obstacle.]

gasper noun Brit, dated A cigarette, esp. a cheap or inferior one. 1914–. LISTENER 'Gasper' commercials are with us still at every peak viewing hour (1965). [From their effect on the smoker.]

gassed adjective Brit Drunk. 1925–. DAILY MAIL When I'm with people they laugh so much . . . they figure I'm 'gassed'. But I'm not. I don't drink (1960).

gasser noun orig US Something that gives enormous fun and excitement; = GAS noun 3b. 1944–. SUNDAY TRUTH (Brisbane): Ron's Friday night show . . . was a gasser (1970).

gassy adjective (Habitually) talking excessively or vacuously; characterized by such talk. 1863–.

gat noun Also **gatt**. dated, orig US A revolver or pistol. 1904–. P. G. WODEHOUSE He produced the gat . . . and poised it in an unsteady but resolute grasp. 'Hands up!' he said (1931). [Short for *Gatling (gun)*, a type of automatic machine gun invented by R. J. Gatling (1818–1903).]

gate noun **1 to give someone** (or **get**) **the gate** mainly US To sack someone (or to be sacked). 1918–. SATURDAY EVENING POST There's no reason why he shouldn't be fired . . . or given the gate (1951). **2** Brit The mouth. 1937–. B. NAUGHTON Shut your big ugly gate at once (1966). **3** US A jazz musician; also broadly, a person. Often as a term of address. 1937–. COLLIER'S You've handicapped your tunes with stuff no gate wants to play (1939). [In sense 3, perh. short for 'gate-mouth', a nickname given to the US jazz trumpeter Louis Armstrong, or alternatively a shortening of *alligator*.]

gate-post noun **between you** (**and**) **me and the gate-post** in strict confidence. 1871–. P. H. JOHNSON Strictly between you and me and the gatepost, Colonel, I don't care for them (1959). [Variant of earlier *between you* (*and*) *me and the bed-post* 1830–82, *between you* (*and*) *me and the post* 1838–73.]

'gator noun Also **gator, gater.** orig US Abbreviation of 'alligator'. 1844–.

Gawd noun Also **gaw, gawd.** Representing a vulgar pronunciation of 'God'. 1877–. L. WHITE Gawd knows I got enough problems (1967).

Gawd-forbid variant of GOD-FORBID noun.

Gawd-help-us noun Also **Gawdelpus.** mainly jocular A helpless or exasperating person. 1912–. P. G. WODEHOUSE A pot-bellied baggy-trousered Gawd-help-us (1961). [From

gas gasbag gas guzzler gash gasper gassed gat

the ironically deprecatory exclamation *God* (or *Gawd*) *help us.*]

gay adjective orig US Foolish, stupid, socially inappropriate or disapproved of; 'lame'. 1978–. CREEM CLOSE-UP PRESENTS Your so-stupid-they're-funny captions are gay. Get into some [real] humor (1987). [Apparently from *gay* adjective homosexual.]

gay-cat noun US A young or inexperienced tramp, esp. one who has a homosexual relationship with an older tramp; a hobo who accepts occasional work. 1897–.

gaydar noun An ability, attributed esp. to homosexual people, to identify a (fellow) homosexual person by intuition or by interpreting signals conveyed by his or her appearance, interests, etc. 1982–. [From *gay* adjective and noun homosexual + (ra)*dar*.]

gay deceivers noun pl. dated False breasts. 1942–62. D. POWELL Her pink sweater . . . clung properly to the seductive curves of her Gay Deceivers (1942). [Cf. earlier sing. sense, a deceitful rake or dissolute person.]

gazabo /gəˈzeɪbəʊ/ noun orig and mainly US, often derog A fellow, guy. 1896–. H. MILLER But there was one thing he seldom did, queer gazabo that he was—he seldom asked questions (1953). [Perh. from Spanish *gazapo* sly fellow.]

gazob /gəˈzɒb/ noun Austral, dated A fool, blunderer. 1906–66. [Perh. from GAZABO noun.]

gazook /gəˈzuːk/ noun dated A stupid or unpleasant person. 1928–36. B. PENTON Look at that poor gazook, Sambo. He'd call you old man God Almighty even if he starved him to death (1936). [Origin unknown, but cf. GAZABO noun and GAZOB noun.]

gazump /gəˈzʌmp/ Also **gasumph, gazoomph, gazumph, gezumph.** Brit verb trans. **1** To swindle. 1928–. DAILY MAIL M.P.s admitted that they had been 'gazoomphed' by fast-talking racketeers (1961). **2** trans. and intr. Of a seller: to raise the price of a property after having accepted an offer by (an intending buyer). 1971–. noun **3** A swindle. 1932–. [Origin unknown.]

gazunder /gəˈzʌndə(r)/ verb trans. and intr. Brit Of a buyer: to lower the amount of an offer made to (the seller) for a property, esp. just before exchange of contracts; often as **gazundering,** noun; also **gazunderer,** noun. 1988–. INDEPENDENT Gazumping, gazundering and all manner of noxious debilitations are blamed on slothful solicitors (1990). [Blend of GAZUMP verb

and *under* adverb. In a buyer's market the unwelcome ploy puts pressure on the vendor to sell at the lower price or risk losing the deal.]

gear Brit dated. noun **1** that's (or it's) the gear an expression of approval. 1925–. GUARDIAN The Liverpool Sound . . . put expressions like 'it's the gear' into the mouths of debs (1963). adjective **2** Great, fabulous. 1951–. TODAY They're gear! The Beatles leave for London after their triumphant tour of Sweden (1963).

gee[1] /dʒiː/ noun The accomplice of a salesman or showman, whose job is to arouse the crowd's enthusiasm. Also **gee man.** 1898–. NEWS CHRONICLE Strategically placed in the crowd, the 'gee men' started the bidding going (1959). [Origin unknown; cf. next.]

gee[2] /dʒiː/ noun US A guy, fellow. 1921–. S. CHALLIS 'Just a minute, this ain't O'Brien.' 'No. This is some other gee' (1968). [From the pronunciation of the initial letter of *guy* noun.]

gee[3] /dʒiː/ noun US A thousand dollars; = G noun. 1936–. M. TAYLOR There's a hundred gees at stake (1946). [From the pronunciation of the initial letter of GRAND noun.]

gee[4] /giː, dʒiː/ noun orig US Opium or a similar drug. 1936–. [Origin uncertain; perh. from *ghee* noun, semifluid Indian butter.] Hence **geed-up,** adjective Drugged. 1938–.

gee /dʒiː/ verb trans. To urge or encourage to greater activity; mainly with *up*. 1932–. R. FULLER The directors of the company must be gee'd up (1956). [From earlier sense, to direct a horse by the call of 'gee'.]

geegee /dʒiːdʒiː/ noun A racehorse. Often in pl.; somewhat euphemistic in the context of betting. 1941–. CLEESE & BOOTH Had a little bit of luck on the gee-gees (1979). [From earlier children's use, a horse, reduplicated from *gee* a command to a horse to go faster (cf. GEE verb).]

geek[1] noun **1** orig Brit, dialect A foolish, undesirable, or contemptible person; esp., in recent use, a person who is excessively studious or obsessed with technical matters, esp. to the extent of being socially awkward. 1876–. BARR & POPPY When I looked in the mirror, I saw a fuzzy-haired geek with a silly smile (1987). **2** US A fairground freak. 1954–. [Variant of earlier *geck* in same sense, apparently from Low German *geck* noun.] Hence **geek** verb orig and mainly US **1 to geek it** Also **to geek out** to give up, to back down; to lose one's nerve. 1935–. A. GREELEY He was a physically strong man, capable . . . of decisive action, personal heroism and spectacular

gay gay-cat gaydar gay deceivers gazabo gazob

performance in bed. Why had he geeked out? (1986). **2 to geek** (someone) **up** to excite or stimulate (someone); to make nervous or jittery. 1984–. VIBE When I have the opportunity to combine the music with the words with the scenery behind it, it kinda geeks me up (1994). **3 to geek out** to behave like a geek, esp. (computing) to engage (temporarily and inappropriately) in technical discussions, perform a technically complicated task, etc. 1990–. NEW YORK TIMES Not to geek out on you . . . but back in 1980 a standard work station cost $65,000, plus $34,000 for the software . . . Now you can get 10 times the power in a $7,000 computer (2000). So **geeked** adj US **1** Stimulated; nervous, jumpy. 1989–. NEW YORK TIMES MAGAZINE There's a fine line between staying stoked and what Fielder calls 'getting too geeked' (1992). **2 geeked out** made (fully) characteristic of a geek. 1993–. ENTERTAINMENT WEEKLY Legions of Trekkers, geeked out head to toe in full Federation regalia (1996). Also **geeky** adjective Characteristic of a geek; obnoxious, foolish, socially awkward. 1981–.

geek² noun Austral A look. 1919–. D. O'GRADY We had a geek at the stuff (1968). [From Brit dialect *geek* verb, to peep, look.]

geewhillikins /dʒiːˈwɪlɪkɪnz/ int orig US A mild expression of surprise. Also **ge-, je-, -whil(l)iken(s), -whit(t)aker(s)** /-ˈwɪtəkəz/. 1851–. C. S. FORESTER 'Geewhillikins, sir,' said Hubbard; the dark mobile face lengthened in surprise (1941). [Perh. a fanciful substitute for *Jerusalem!*, but cf. next.]

gee whiz(z) int orig US A mild expression of surprise. Also **gee whitz, gee wiz,** and with hyphen. 1885–. J. D. SALINGER Well, gee whizz. I'm only trying to make polite bathroom talk (1957). [Prob. an alteration of prec. as a euphemism for *Jesus!*; cf. *gee* int, perh. short for *Jesus!*, and JEEZ int.]

Geez int Also **Geeze** = JEEZ int.

geezer noun Also **geeser, geyser.** A person, esp. an old man. 1885–. NEW STATESMAN I have my hands full with his china who is a big geezer of about 14 stone (1965). [Dialectal pronunciation of *guiser* noun, mummer.]

gelt noun Money. *a.*1529–. C. DRUMMOND 'The gelt?' said Reed. . . . 'Four thousand dollars,' said Miss Pocket (1968). [From German, Dutch *geld* money; in early use often with reference to the pay of a (German) army.]

gen /dʒen/ Brit, orig services'. noun **1** Information. 1940–. DAILY TELEGRAPH A vast amount of 'gen' is included, and this will be invaluable for settling arguments (1970). verb **2** trans. and intr. To provide with or obtain information; almost always followed by *up*. 1943–. E. HYAMS He wanted information. I had it. I was in a position to, as we said then, gen him up. I genned him up (1958). [Perh. abbreviation of *general* in the official phrase 'for the general information of all ranks', or possibly from part of the words *genuine* or *intelligence*.]

gendarme /ʒ̃ãdarm, dʒenˈdaːm/ noun A policeman. 1906–. H. CRANE I am to sail to *Mexico* (damn the gendarmes!) next Saturday (1931). [From French *gendarme* (French) policeman.] Cf. JOHNDARM noun.

gender-bender noun A person (esp. a pop singer or follower of a pop cult) who deliberately affects an androgynous appearance by wearing sexually ambiguous clothing, make-up, etc. Also **gender-blender.** 1980–. Hence **gender-bending, gender-blending,** noun.

George noun Brit The automatic pilot of an aircraft. 1931–. [From earlier services' slang sense, airman.]

Geronimo /dʒəˈrɒnɪməʊ/ int orig US A battle-cry shouted by US paratroops when going into action; hence, an exclamation uttered esp. when making a great leap through the air. 1942–. TIGER 'Geronimo!' 'He's done it! He's done it!' 'Eddie's broken the world ski-jump record' (1983). [The name of an Apache Indian chief (1829–1909).]

gertcha /ˈɡɜːtʃə/ int Also **gercha, gertcher.** Brit Alteration of *get away* (or *along*) *with you*, etc., used esp. as a derisive expression of disbelief. 1937–. G. CARR 'Gertcha!' The orator . . . elbowed him away (1963).

get noun **1** orig Scottish and N English A bastard; hence as a general term of abuse: a fool, idiot. 1508–. H. CALVIN Put something on him, the stupid get! (1967). Cf. GIT noun. **2** Austral and NZ A getaway; a quick retreat; in phr. *to do* (or *make*) *a get.* 1898–. A. UPFIELD Musta done a get after bashing up his wife (1963). verb **3** intr. orig US (Often in form *git.*) To go away, clear out. 1864–. K. GILES Anybody in a room either gets or pays for another twenty-four hours (1967). **4 to get at: a** To (try to) influence, esp. dishonestly, by bribery, drugs, intimidation, etc. 1865–. W. SPROTT We are all 'propaganda conscious' in the sense that we put up a resistance if we feel we are being 'got at' (1952). **b** To make annoying insinuations about; to criticize. 1891–. J. OSBORNE Don't look hurt. I'm not getting at you. I love you very much (1957). **5 to get it** to be punished or in

geek geewhillikins gee whiz(z) Geez geezer gelt

trouble. Also **to get it hot, to get it in the neck.** 1872–. **6 to get outside (of)** to eat or drink. 1886–. D. CAMPBELL It takes me half an hour to get outside the mixed grill and the ice-cream and coffee (1967). **7 to get into** to have sexual intercourse with (a woman). *c.*1888–. J. KEROUAC I've just got to get into her sister Mary tonight (1957). **8** trans. and intr. US To understand (a person or statement). 1907–. I. BROMIGE Fiona broke into peals of laughter and became quite helpless for a few moments. 'Don't get it,' said Julian (1956); M. INNES Okay, okay. I get. Norval. My name is Norval (1966). **9 to get his (hers, theirs,** etc.): to be killed. *a.*1910–. N. MAILER He was going to get his, come two three four hours. That was all right, of course, you didn't live forever (1959). **10 to have got it bad(ly)** to have fallen deeply in love; to be infatuated. 1911–. WEBSTER & ELLINGTON (song-title) I got it bad and that ain't good (1941). **11 to get off with** to become acquainted with (someone) with a view to sexual intercourse. 1915–. F. LONSDALE What fun it would be if one of us could get off with him (1925). **12 to get off: a** US Of a jazz musician: to improvise skilfully. 1933–. **b** Used usu. in the imperative as an exclamation expressing impatience or incredulity. 1958–. **c** orig US To get high on drugs; usu. followed by *on.* 1969–. A. KUKLA Did you get off on that acid you took last night? (1980). **13 as all get out** US Very, extremely. 1941–. S. PARETSKY He felt guilty as all get-out when I told him who the doctor was and how bad she'd been hurt (1992). **14 to get lost** to go away, clear out; usu. in imperative. 1947–. H. CALVIN The last time Carabine came in I told him to get lost (1962). **15** trans. To notice, look at (a person, esp. one who is conceited or laughable); usu. as imperative with a pronoun as object. 1958–. NEWS CHRONICLE If he is conceited the girls mutter get *yew!* (1958). **16 to get (someone) at it** to make fun of (someone). 1958–. F. NORMAN He had half sused that the boggie was getting him at it (1958). **17 to get off on: a** To achieve sexual satisfaction or experience an orgasm by means of. 1973–. N. THORNBURG And the shrink getting off on it all, sitting there with one hand stuck in his fly (1977). Cf. *to get one's rocks off* at ROCK noun. **b** To enjoy or be turned on by. 1973–. TIME I really get off on dancing. It's a high (1977). [In sense 1, from earlier sense, that which is begotten, offspring.]

ghetto-blaster noun orig US A large portable radio, esp. used to play loud pop music. 1983–. CHRISTIAN SCIENCE MONITOR Six feet tall, 16 years old, and carrying a 'ghetto blaster' (1983). [From its use in the Black quarter of

American cities; the term was orig used in the early 1980s as the name of a US rock group.]

Gib noun Gibraltar. 1869–. [Abbreviation.]

G.I. can noun dated A German artillery shell. 1928–30. [From earlier sense, galvanized-iron can; from its resemblance in shape.]

giggle adjective Austral, services' Denoting often badly fitting items of clothing of the type issued to Australian service personnel in World War II. 1940–. S. O'LEARY Chrysalis soldiers in their ill-fitting giggle suits and floppy cloth hats (1975). [From their supposedly amusing appearance.]

giggle-house noun Austral and NZ A mental hospital. 1919–. WEEKEND AUSTRALIAN MAGAZINE (Sydney): The classic story of that beautiful poet, John Clare, who had himself locked up in the giggle-house for nearly a quarter of a century (1982). Cf. FUNNY FARM noun.

giggle-water noun Intoxicating drink. 1929–.

gig-lamps noun dated Glasses, spectacles. 1853–. [From earlier sense, lamp at the side of a gig.]

gimme /gɪmɪ/ noun orig US **1** Acquisitiveness, greed. 1927–. C. MORRIS One could only write him off as a victim of our acquisitive, thrusting, philosophy of get and 'gimme' (1963). **2a** golf A short putt conceded to one's opponent. 1929–. **b** Something very easily accomplished. 1986–. [Contraction of *give me.*]

gimp[1] noun Courage, guts. 1901–. J. POTTS She didn't even have the gimp to make the break herself (1962). [Origin unknown.]

gimp[2] orig US. noun **1** A lame person or leg. 1925–. NEW YORKER He'd just kick a gimp in the good leg and leave him lay (1929). verb intr. **2** To limp, hobble. 1961–. P. CRAIG I gimped back on deck (1969). [Origin uncertain; perh. an alteration of GAMMY adjective.] So **gimpy,** noun A cripple; adjective Lame, crippled. 1925–.

gimp[3] noun orig US A stupid or contemptible person. 1924–. RADIO TIMES [He is] a complete gimp. He's quite well-intentioned but manages to irritate everyone around him (1993). [Perh. from German *Gimpel* simpleton.]

ginger-beer noun and adjective (A) homosexual. Also **ginger.** 1959–. A. WILLIAMS

ghetto-blaster Gib G.I. can giggle giggle-house

'Unless you prefer ginger.' 'Ginger?' 'Beer, dear.' . . . 'You ever meet an Aussie who was queer?' (1968). [Rhyming slang for 'queer'.]

gink noun orig US, mainly derog A fellow; a man. 1910–. A. DRAPER George wasn't the most talkative gink alive (1970). [Origin unknown.]

ginormous /dʒarnɔ:məs/ adjective Brit Stupendously large. 1948–. SUNDAY EXPRESS Since Brands Hatch, doors have opened and it's possible to make ginormous money (1986). [From gi(gantic adjective + e)normous adjective.]

ginzo noun US, derog A person of Italian extraction. Also **guinzo**. 1931–. W. MARKFIELD I have a boss, a ginzo—though he speaks a great Jewish (1964). [Perh. from GUINEA noun.]

gippo¹ /dʒɪpəʊ/ noun Often with capital initial. Also **gypo, gyppo**. **1** A gipsy. 1902–. D. THOMAS Ducking under the gippo's clothespegs (1953). **2** An Egyptian, esp. a native Egyptian soldier. 1916–. E. WAUGH 'What's to stop him coming round the other side?' asked Tommy. 'According to plan—the Gyppos,' said the Brigadier (1955). [From gip(sy noun + -o, influenced by Egyptian adjective.]

gippo² /dʒɪpəʊ/ noun dated, mainly services'. Any greasy gravy or sauce. Also **gippy, gyp(p)o, gypoo**. 1914–25. [Variant of dialect jipper noun, gravy, dripping, stew.]

gippy /dʒɪpɪ/ noun Also **gyppie, gyppy**. **1a** = GIPPO¹ noun 2. Also as adjective a.1889–. C. MACKENZIE A captain of the Gyppy Army with a pleasant oblong face (1929). **b** An Egyptian cigarette. 1920–. W. S. MAUGHAM When you once get the taste for them, you prefer them to gippies (1926). **2** = GIPPO¹ noun 1. 1913–. [As GIPPO¹ noun + -y.]

gippy tummy noun Also **gyppy tummy**. Diarrhoea suffered by visitors to hot countries. 1943–. G. EGMONT Always take . . . whatever is your favourite antidote to gippy tummy when you go abroad (1961). [See GIPPY noun 1a.] Cf. DELHI BELLY noun.

gipsy noun Also **gypsy**. US An independently operated truck; also, the driver of such a truck. 1942–. BOSTON SUNDAY GLOBE The primary violators among truck drivers are the so-called 'gypsies' who operate independently (1967).

gism variant of JISM noun.

gismo /gɪzməʊ/ noun Also **gizmo**. orig and mainly US A gadget, thingumajig. 1943–. NEW YORKER Every gismo that made use of a clothes hanger will be demonstrated by its inventor (1970). [Origin unknown.]

git noun Brit A silly or contemptible person. 1946–. OBSERVER The girl scarcely turned her head: 'Shutup yerself yer senseless git!' (1967). [Variant of GET noun 1.]

give verb **1 to give** (a person) **beans** orig US To deal severely with (a person), to punish heavily. 1835–. P. G. WODEHOUSE He wanted to give me beans, but Florence wouldn't let him. She said 'Father you are not to touch him. It was a pure misunderstanding' (1946). **2a** trans. To tell (a person); to offer for acceptance; esp. to tell or offer (a person) something incredible or unacceptable. 1883–. N. HILLARD He drew down the corners of his mouth. 'Don't give me that' (1960). **b** intr. as imperative, speak! tell me! 1956–. P. HOBSON 'Come on. Give.' 'That ruddy policeman went digging things up and he found out I'd written my own testimonials' (1968). **3** trans. To punish (a person) for (doing something), often with reference back to what the person has just said. 1906–. D. H. LAWRENCE Hark at her clicking the flower-pots, shifting the plants. He'd give her shift the plants! He'd show her! (a.1930). **4** intr. orig US To play music, esp. jazz, excitingly or enthusiastically; also with out. 1936–. WOMAN'S OWN You feel that you're in a real jam session with everybody giving, the joint jumping (1958). **5** orig US **a: what gives?** what is happening? (often as a question or merely as a form of greeting). 1940–. F. ROBB George, whistle those lubbers again and ask them what gives (1953). **b: what gives with . . .** what is happening to (someone or something); what is he (she, etc.) doing? 1963–. PRIVATE EYE What gives with this sheilah? (1969). **6 to give** (something) **away** Austral To abandon, give up, or stop (something). 1948–. P. BARTON It just wouldn't work. . . . The lunch gong sounded and everyone gave it away (1981). **7 to give it up** orig US to offer enthusiastic applause or praise; usu. imperative. 1990–. BRAINFRIEZE.NET Give it up for The Dixie Chicks. We're big fans of The Dixie Chicks around our house (2007). [In sense 5, cf. German was gibt's? what is happening? (literally, what gives there?).]

glad eye noun **the glad eye** an amorous glance. 1911–. A. HUXLEY I do see her giving the glad eye to Pete (1939). Hence **glad-eye,** verb trans. To give (someone) the glad eye. 1935–.

glad hand noun **the glad hand** orig US (often used rather ironically) a cordial handshake or greeting; a welcome. 1895–. NEW STATESMAN Crude economic reasons do not explain why Mikoyan should have been given the glad hand (1959). Hence **glad-hand,** verb trans. and intr. To greet (someone) cordially,

gink   ginormous   ginzo   gippo   gippy   gippy tummy

glad rags

to welcome, to please. 1903–; **glad-hander,** noun One who acts cordially towards everyone. 1929–.

glad rags noun orig US One's best clothes; spec. formal evening dress. 1902–. H. B. HERMON-HODGE We all turned out in our glad rags to join in the procession (1922).

glam verb trans. and intr. **1** To make (oneself) glamorous, to tart (oneself) *up.* 1937–. J. OSBORNE Get yourself glammed up, and we'll hit the town (1957). noun **2** Glamour. *c.*1940–. adjective **3** Glamorous. 1963–. SUNDAY TIMES Tonight sees the climax of the 60th Cannes film festival. It looks, at this distance, almost unspeakably glam (2007).

glamour boy noun Brit, dated A member of the RAF. 1941–. [From the glamorous reputation of World War II RAF pilots in World War II; cf. earlier sense, glamorous young man.]

glamour puss noun A glamorous person. 1952–. C. MACINNES 'Now listen, glamour puss,' I said, flicking his bottom with my towel (1959).

Glasgow kiss noun Brit A head-butt. 1982–. [From *Glasgow* name of a city in west central Scotland + *kiss* noun; from the reputation for violence enjoyed by some parts of the city.]

glass-house noun Brit A military prison. 1925–. J. BERTRAM Someone with a lengthy 'crime sheet'—perhaps . . . a notorious frequenter of the glasshouse (1947). [From the name given to the detention barracks at the Aldershot Command at Woking, which had a glass roof; cf. earlier sense, building with glass walls and roof.]

glitch noun A sudden brief irregularity or malfunction (of equipment, etc., esp. orig in a spacecraft); also, something causing this. 1962–. PRODUCT ENGINEERING It generated digital transients that caused the abort guidance to send false signals. Phillips said it took an inordinately long time to find this glitch (1969). [Origin unknown.]

glitterati noun orig US The fashionable set of literary or show-business people. 1956–. TIMES One member of the glitterati . . . offered to send her own hairdresser to Billie's hotel (1984). [Punningly from *glitter* noun + pl. suffix *-ati* as in *literati* noun.]

glitz noun orig US Extravagant but superficial display; show-business glamour. 1977–. TORONTO LIFE There was too much Third-

World esoterica and not enough Hollywood glitz (1985). [Back-formation from GLITZY adjective.]

glitzy adjective orig US Extravagant, ostentatious; tawdry, gaudy. 1966–. LISTENER The Oscars are the high point of the Western film industry's year—a glitzy, vulgar affirmation that they're getting things right (1985). [Perh. blend of *glitter* noun and *ritzy* adjective; but cf. German *glitzerig* glittering.]

glob noun A mass or lump of some liquid or semi-liquid substance. 1900–. NEW SCIENTIST [The fuel] is probably floating around the half-empty fuel tank in globs (1962). [Prob. blend of *blob* noun and *gob* noun, mass, lump.]

glom verb trans. and intr. US To steal; to grab, seize; intr. usu. followed by *on to.* 1907–. C. ARMSTRONG Trust Lily Eden, though, to glom on to a customer (1969). [Variant of Scottish *glaum* verb, to snatch, of unknown origin.]

glop noun US A sticky or liquid mess, esp. inedible food. 1945–. J. POTTS A cheap, soiled cosmetic case crammed with little bottles of glop (1962). [Of imitative origin; cf. obs. *glop* verb, to swallow greedily.]

gnat's piss noun Also **gnats' piss.** derog A weak or insipid beverage, such as beer, tea, etc. 1959–. B. S. JOHNSON Where'd you get this gnatspiss from, Maurie? . . . I can get you gnatspiss as good as this gnatspiss for sixteen bob a bottle (1963). Cf. PANTHER('S) PISS noun.

go noun **1** (**all** or **quite**) **the go** dated The height of fashion; all the rage. 1793–. SUNDAY MAIL MAGAZINE (Brisbane): In Brisbane, Aroma's in Savoir Faire in Park Road is all the go, too. That one's a ton of fun, with a clientele to match (1988). **2** dated A turn of events; a proceeding; usu. with adjective as **a queer, rum go.** 1796–. **3** (**it's**) **no go** (it's) impossible, hopeless. 1825–. **4** dated An agreement, a deal; esp. in phr. *it's a go.* 1878–1936. P. G. WODEHOUSE 'Then say no more,' I said. 'It's a go' (1936). **5** (**a**) (**fair**) **go** Austral and NZ A fair chance, a square deal. 1904–. ADVERTISER (Adelaide): Stop whingeing and give a bloke a go, mates (1969). verb **6 to go on** orig US To care for, concern oneself about; esp. in phr. *not to go much on.* 1824–. N. SHUTE Jo says she wants to live in Tahiti, but I don't go much on that myself (1960). **7 to go through: a** to search and rob; also, to search (a person). 1861–. R. W. SERVICE The girls were 'going through' a drunken sailor (1945). **b** Austral To desert, decamp, abscond; also, to

glad rags glam glamour boy glamour puss glitch

stop, give up. 1943–. B. SCOTT The first few times she went through on him nearly broke his heart (1977). **8** trans. To eat or drink (something specified); esp. in phr. *I, you,* etc. *could go* (a drink, etc.). *c*.1882–. D. BALLANTYNE I could go a good feed of eels just now (1948). **9 to go down: a** To be sent to prison. 1906–. M. ALLINGHAM He went down for eighteen months and is now in Italy pulling his weight, I believe. He's a crook, but not a traitor (1945). **b** orig US To perform fellatio or cunnilingus; usu. followed by *on.* 1916–. K. MILLETT I do not want her body. Do not want to see it, caress it, go down on it (1974). **c** orig US To happen. 1946–. IT If everyone was aware of what went down in these organisations perhaps there would be enough response to keep them from petrifying and dying (1970). **10** intr., euphemistic To urinate or defecate. 1926–. TIME I took off all my clothes but my drawers and—well—I had to go (1935). **11 to go off** To have an orgasm. 1928–. H. MILLER Bango! I went off like a whale (1949). Cf. *to come off* at COME verb 1. **12 to go** US Used of cooked food sold in a restaurant or shop, to denote that it is to be taken away and eaten elsewhere. 1946–. A. BEATTIE Can I have a bagel and a coffee to go? (1980). **13 to go . . . on** (someone): to adopt a particular mode of behaviour towards or affecting (someone). 1963–. NEW SOCIETY (*headline*): Amis goes serious on us (1966). **14** trans. orig US To say; used mainly in the historic present, in reporting speech. 1967–. M. ROSEN So I go, 'Time for the cream, Eddie.' And he goes, 'No cream' (1983). adjective **15** dated, orig US Fashionable, with-it. 1962–4. TIME Beatniks, whose heavy black turtleneck sweaters had never looked particularly go with white tennis socks (1963).

goat noun **1 to get** (a person's) **goat** to irritate or annoy (a person). 1910–. B. KEATON What got my goat was that when I finally did get knocked off . . . it was due to an accident outside the theatre (1960). **2** A fool; a dupe. 1916–. K. TENNANT 'Don't be a goat.' Silly young fools, all three of them (1947).

gob[1] noun mainly Brit The mouth. *a*.1550–. J. O'FAOLAIN Would you be up to that? Just to try to get her to keep her gob shut? (1980). [Perh. from Gaelic and Irish *gob* beak, mouth, or from *gab* noun, talk.]

gob[2] Brit. noun **1** A lump of slimy matter. 1555–. verb trans. and intr. **2** To spit. 1881–. D. THOMAS And they thank God, and gob at a gull for luck (1953). [Middle English, from Old French *go(u)be* mouthful.]

gob[3] noun orig US An American sailor or ordinary seaman. 1915–. T. RATTIGAN Can

you beat that—an earl being a gob (1944). [Cf. GOBBY noun.]

gobby noun A coastguard, or an American sailor. 1890–1929. [Perh. from GOB[2] noun, from the notion of a typically pipe-smoking, spitting sailor.]

gobdaw noun Anglo-Irish A foolish or gullible person; a pretentious fool. *a*.1966–. M. BINCHY All kinds of old gobdaws much worse-looking than you, look terrific when they're dolled up (1982). [Prob. from GOB[1] + *daw* foolish or lazy person; cf. *gabhdán* container, gullible person.]

gobshite noun An unpleasant or despicable person. 1948–. GUARDIAN 'Trust me,' I say. 'You know I'm a regular guy. Whenever have I tried to schmooze you? Haven't I always come across?' 'Gobshite,' she says over her shoulder, and is gone (1992). [Cf. earlier US slang sense, spat-out wad of chewing tobacco; ultimately from GOB[1] noun + SHITE noun excrement.]

gob-smacked adjective Brit Flabbergasted, astounded; speechless or incoherent with amazement. 1985–. OBSERVER NoW staff described themselves as 'gob-smacked' by the shock news (this is the tabloid way of saying 'very surprised') (1988). [From GOB[1] noun + *smacked* adjective, hit, struck: perh. from the shock effect of being struck in the face or from the theatrical gesture of clapping a hand over the mouth as a sign of intense surprise.]

gob-stick noun jazz, dated A clarinet. 1936–. D. THOMAS The double-bed is a swing-band with coffin, oompah, slush-pump, gob-stick (1938). [From GOB[1] noun; cf. earlier dialect sense, spoon.]

gob-stopper noun Brit A very large, hard, usu. spherical sweet. 1928–. [From GOB[1] noun; from its speech-inhibiting size.]

gob-struck adjective Brit = GOB-SMACKED adjective. 1988–. GUARDIAN 'I looked in the mirror and saw this emu.' 'How fast were you going?' 'About 50 mph. . . . I was gobstruck' (1990). [From GOB[1] noun + *struck* adjective, hit.]

God-awful adjective Also **God awful, Godawful.** orig US Extremely unpleasant, nasty, etc. 1878–. P. MCCUTCHAN I heard the most God-awful racket above my head (1959).

God-botherer noun orig services' A parson, chaplain; more generally, any religious-minded person, esp. one who vigorously promotes Christian ideals. Hence

goat gob gobby gobdaw gobshite gob-smacked

God-bothering, adjective. 1937–. K. AMIS 'What do you think of the padre, Max?' . . . 'Not a bad chap for a God-botherer' (1966).

God-box noun A church or other place of worship. 1928–. NEW STATESMAN A ring-a-ding God-box that will go over big with the flat-bottomed latitudinarians (1962).

god-damn adjective and adverb Also **god-dam, god-damned.** Accursed, damnable. 1918–. W. C. WOODS Now you men knock off the goddam chatter in there and listen up (1970). [From the imprecation *God damn (me, you,* etc.).] Cf. GOLDARN verb, adjective, and adverb.

God forbid noun Also **Gawd forbid.** 1 A child. 1909–. M. ALLINGHAM You take 'Er Ladyship and the Gawd-ferbid to the party (1955). 2 A hat. 1936–. J. CURTIS Why don't you take off your gawd-forbid? We're passing the Cenotaph (1936). 3 derog and offensive A Jew. 1960–. 3 orig US [Rhyming slang: in sense 1, for 'kid'; in sense 2, for 'lid'; in sense 3, for 'Yid'.]

Godfrey int US Used as an exclamation of strong feeling or surprise. 1904–. W. FAULKNER They hadn't even cast the dogs yet when Uncle Buck roared, 'Gone away! I godfrey, he broke cover then!' (1942). [Euphemistic assimilation of *God* to the name *Godfrey*.]

God's gift noun mainly ironic A godsend; spec. a man irresistible to women. 1938–. H. CLEVELY It may do him a bit of good to find out he isn't God's gift to women walking the earth (1953).

God slot noun A period in a broadcasting schedule regularly reserved for religious programmes. 1972–.

God squad noun derog, orig US colleges' (The members of) a religious organization, esp. an evangelical Christian group. 1969–. OBSERVER BBC executives . . . said: 'Beware the unexpected—and keep tabs on the God squad' (1983).

gofer noun Also **go-fer, gopher.** orig and mainly US 1 **gopher.** baseball A pitch that can be scored from, esp. one hit for a home run. Also **gopher ball.** 1932–. R. COOVER Partridge was throwing gopher balls and his . . . teammates were fielding like a bunch of bush-leaguers (1970). 2 A person who runs errands, esp. on a film set or in an office; a general dogsbody. 1967–. LISTENER Burt Lancaster plays Lou, an ex-bodyguard and gofer for the mob, still running the bedraggled tail of the numbers racket (1981). [From the verbal phr. *to go for*: in sense 1, because the batter 'goes for' runs,

or the ball 'goes for' a homer; in sense 2, because the person goes and fetches things; influenced by *gopher* noun, small mammal.]

goggle-box noun Brit A television set. 1959–. TIMES Mr. Wilson was . . . so good at television appearances, that he had convinced himself that he, single-handed, could win elections 'with the help of the goggle box' (1967).

going-over noun Also **going over.** 1 orig US A scolding. 1872–. E. BLISHEN Sir, don't give me a going over—but this desk's too small for me. Honest! (1969). 2 orig US An inspection or overhaul. 1919–. H. PINTER How do you think the place is looking? I gave it a good going over (1960). 3 orig US A beating; a thrashing. 1942–. A. ROSS 'Got a going over, did you?' 'Not much, I got a going over. Want to see the bruises?' (1970).

goldarn verb, adjective, and adverb Also **goldarn, goldurn,** etc. US (To) damn. 1832–. MRS. L. B. JOHNSON Well, I'll be goldurned—the salesman that sold it to me said it was Harry Truman (1964). [Euphemistic substitution for GOD-DAMN.] So **goldarned,** adjective. 1856–.

gold-brick noun 1 orig US A thing with only a surface appearance of value; a sham or fraud; esp. in phr. *to sell* (someone) *a gold-brick,* to swindle. 1889–. CHICAGO DAILY NEWS It used to be the city slicker who sold gold bricks to the hick from the country (1947). 2 US A lazy person; a shirker. 1914–. J. STEINBECK In the ranks, billeted with the stinking, cheating, foul-mouthed goldbricks, there were true heroes (1958). verb orig and mainly US 3 trans. To cheat, swindle, defraud. 1902–. 4 intr. To have an easy time, to shirk. 1926–. M. MCCARTHY Students with applied art or science majors tended to gold-brick on their reading courses (1952). [From the practice of passing off an ingot of base metal as gold.] Hence **gold-bricker,** noun A shirker, a swindler. 1932–.

gold-dig verb trans. derog, orig US Of a woman: to attach oneself to (a man) for monetary gain. 1926–. J. STEINBECK I'll bet she just gold-dug Eddie (1947). [Back-formation from GOLD-DIGGER noun.]

gold-digger noun derog, orig US A woman who wheedles money out of men. 1920–. J. BRAINE It was expensive; that appealed to Lois. Not that she was a gold-digger; but once she started going around with her there were more withdrawals than deposits in his Post Office savings book (1959). [From earlier sense, one who digs for gold.]

God-box god-damn God forbid Godfrey God's gift

gomer noun 1 orig and mainly US military **a** An inept or stupid colleague, esp. a trainee; also, a member of the US Marine Corps. 1967-. **b** An enemy soldier, esp. a North Vietnamese soldier in the Vietnam War. 1978-. **2** US medical A difficult or disagreeable patient, esp. an elderly one. 1972-. [From the name of *Gomer* Pyle, a comic yokel character who originally appeared on US television in 1963 (in *The Andy Griffith Show*).]

gonce noun Also **gons**. Austral dated Money. 1899-. J. S. LITCHFIELD Old dad can't spare any time for frills, but he's got the gonce all right. He's worth more than most of the first-class travellers on this boat (1930). [Origin uncertain; perh. from German *Ganze* whole.]

gone adjective **1** Pregnant (for a specified time). 1747-. N. MITCHISON My mother found she was six months gone (1935). **2 gone on** infatuated with. 1885-. S. BELLOW I was gone on her and . . . gave her a real embrace (1978). **3 gone a million** Austral and NZ completely defeated. 1913-. NEW ZEALAND LISTENER We scraped in in that game, only because Elvidge scored his usual try . . . Otherwise, we were gone a million (1958). **4** orig US, jazz musicians'; esp. in phr. *real gone* **a** Completely enthralled or entranced, esp. by rhythmic music, drugs, etc. 1946-. NEWS CHRONICLE The jazz-loving 'hep-cat' who claims that the music 'sends' him until he is 'gone' (1959). **b** Extremely satisfying; excellent. 1946-. L. J. BROWN This is a real gone pad . . . it's what the clients expect (1967).

gone goose noun orig US A person or thing beyond hope; a dead duck. Also **gone gosling**. 1830-. J. & W. HAWKINS If my luck won't hold . . . I'm a gone goose anyway (1958).

goner noun A person or thing that is doomed, ended, irrevocably lost, etc.; spec. a dead person. 1850-. BOYS' MAGAZINE When I found the car burnt out I thought you were a 'goner' (1933). [From *gone* adjective + *-er*.]

gong noun **1** US A narcotic drug, esp. opium. 1915-. J. STEINBECK Let the gong alone for a couple of weeks (1952). **2** Brit A medal or other decoration. 1925-. M. DICKENS Other people came out of the war with Mentions and worthwhile gongs that tacked letters after their names (1958). **3** dated A warning bell on a police car. 1938-. verb trans. and intr. **4** dated Of traffic police: to get (a driver) to stop by sounding a bell. 1934-. T. WISDOM He will then have to 'gong' you into the side on a busy trunk road (1966). [In sense 1, perh. a different word; in sense 2, from its shape.]

gonger noun US Opium; an opium pipe. 1914-. [Prob. from GONG noun 1.]

gongerine noun US An opium pipe. 1914-. [From GONGER noun + diminutive suffix *-ine*.]

gongoozler noun A person who stares idly or protractedly at something, orig at activity on a canal. 1904-. NEW YORKER I stopped off in the Galeana sports park . . . to watch a game on one of three huge outdoor screens that the city had supplied for gongoozlers like me (1986). [Origin uncertain, but cf. Lincolnshire dialect *gawn* verb, to stare vacantly or curiously, and *gooze(n)* verb, to stare aimlessly, gape.]

gonna Representing a casual pronuciation of 'going to'. 1913-. M. SHULMAN I'm gonna keep on yelling till you let me out (1967).

gonzo orig and mainly US. adjective **1** Of or being a type of committed, subjective journalism characterized by factual distortion and exaggerated rhetorical style. 1971-. **2** Bizarre, crazy; far-fetched. 1974-. NEW YORKER He has a small, weird triumph with his gonzo psycho docudrama (1985). noun **3** (A writer of) gonzo journalism. 1972-. **4** A crazy person, a fool. 1977-. CUSTOM CAR To make sure I wouldn't make too big a gonzo of myself . . . I was connected by intercom to the commander who was perched up in the turret (1977). [Prob. from Italian *gonzo* fool(ish) (perh. from Italian *Borgonzone* Burgundian) or Spanish *ganso* goose, fool.]

good buddy noun mainly US A term of address among users of a Citizens' Band or similar radio system; another CB user. 1976-. M. MACHLIN What's your handle, Good Buddy? (1976).

good oil noun Austral Reliable information. 1916-. AUSTRALIAN ROADSPORTS & DRAG RACING NEWS This week's good oil . . . on what is being built is . . . a new Chevy-powered Datsun (1979). [Cf. OIL noun 2.]

goods noun **1 the goods** the stolen articles found in the possession of a thief; unmistakable evidence or proof positive of guilt. 1900-. R. D. PAINE You have caught me with the goods, Wyman. It was my way of getting a slant on you (1923). **2 the goods** the real thing; the genuine article. 1904-. A. WILSON He *was* the most awful old fraud himself, you know. Oh, not as an historian, you always said he was the goods (1956). **3 to have (got) the goods on** to have the advantage of; to have knowledge or information giving one a hold over (another). 1913-. M. MCCARTHY He had a

gomer gonce gone gone goose goner gong gonger

sudden inkling that they would have liked to get the goods on Mulcahy (1952).

goof noun **1** A foolish or stupid person. 1916–. HAY & KING-HALL Have you stopped to think what is happening to that poor old goof in the day-cabin? (1930). **2** A mistake. Also **goof-up** 1955–. DAILY TELEGRAPH I believe they have made a goof (1970). verb **3** intr. mainly US To spend time idly or foolishly; to dawdle; to skive; often followed by *off*. 1932–. NEW YORKER If you ever feel like goofing off sometime, I'll be glad to keep the old ball game going and fill in for you here (1968). **4** intr. To blunder, make a mistake. 1941–. DAILY TELEGRAPH The Census Bureau has admitted that it 'goofed' when it wrote it off as a ghost town (1971). **5** trans. To take a stupefying dose of (a drug); often used in the past participle as an adjective, followed by *up*. 1944–. GUARDIAN Thousands of youths openly . . . 'goofed' amphetamines (1970). **6** trans. To bungle, mess up; usu. followed by *up*. 1960–. LIFE Now, it's hard to goof up pictures (1969). [Variant of dialect *goof* from French *goofe* from Italian *goffo* from medieval Latin *gufus* coarse.]

goof ball noun **1** Also **goof pill**. (A tablet of) any of various drugs, spec. marijuana; a barbiturate tablet or drug. 1938–. NEW SCIENTIST The heroin addict nowadays never knows whether his supply [of heroin] is secure, so he supplements it with the more easily available 'goof-balls' (1966). **2** = GOOF noun 1. 1959–.

goofus noun orig and mainly US A fool. 1917–. VARIETY A mustachioed goofus who thinks he's much hipper than he is (2002). [Origin uncertain; cf. GOOF noun and DOOFUS noun.]

goofy adjective Stupid, daft. 1921–. OBSERVER Commercial television has brought a boom in animation, with comic men and goofy animals bouncing out from everywhere (1958). [From GOOF noun + -*y*.]

goog /guɡ/ noun Austral An egg. 1941–. P. BARTON We half filled the tub with water, chucked in a handful of soap powder, and gingerly tipped in about 120 googs (1981). [Abbreviation of GOOGIE noun.] See also *as full as a goog* at FULL adjective.

googie /guɡɪ/ noun Austral An egg. Also **googie egg, googy (egg)**. 1903–. B. DICKINS Two holy eggcups . . . that once supported my daddy's googy egg when he was a tin-lid (1981). [From Scottish dialect *goggie* child's word for an egg.]

goo-goo adjective derog Of the eyes or glances: (sentimentally) amorous. 1900–.

J. THURBER There was so much spooning and goo-goo eyes (1959). [Perh. connected with *goggle* verb and adjective.]

gook /ɡuːk, ɡʊk/ noun derog, orig and mainly US A foreigner; spec. a coloured person from S.E. or E. Asia. 1935–. GUARDIAN The Gooks [i.e. Viet Cong] hit from bunkers and the Marines had to carry half the company back (1968). [Origin unknown.]

goolie noun Also **gooly**. Austral A stone, pebble. 1924–. D. IRELAND Garn, get out of it, before I let fly with a goolie (1960). [Prob. from a N.S.W. Aboriginal language.]

goolies noun pl. The testicles. 1937–. GUARDIAN To get a performance out of them [i.e. actors] . . . it is sometimes necessary to kick them in the goolies (1971). [Apparently of Indian origin; cf. Hindustani *golí* bullet, ball, pill.]

goom noun Austral Methylated spirit (as a drink). 1967–. [Origin uncertain; perh. from Aboriginal (Jagara and neighbouring languages) *guŋ* fresh water.] Hence **goomy** noun Also **goomee** Austral A drinker of alcohol, a drunkard. 1973–.

goombah noun Also **goomba, gumbah**. US A member of a gang of organized criminals; spec. a Mafioso; also, a gangland godfather. Hence, an associate or crony. 1969–. L. ESTLEMAN 'I guess you two were pretty close.' 'He was my goombah. I was a long time getting over it' (1984). [From Italian dialect pronunciation of Italian *compare* godfather, friend, accomplice.]

goon noun **1** orig US A foolish or dull person. 1921–. S. CLARK There, you goon. You'll bump into them if you don't watch out (1959). **2** orig US A person hired by racketeers, etc. to terrorize political or industrial opponents; a thug. 1938–. IT Heath orders Habershon of Barnet CID to 'turn London over'. And he does exactly that . . . with 500 goons and a score of specially trained dogs (1971). **3** A nickname given by British and US prisoners of war to their German guards during World War II. 1945–. TIMES 'Goon-baiting', which was the favourite occupation of the prisoners (1962). [Perh. from dialect *gooney* noun, simpleton; influenced by the subhuman cartoon character called Alice the *Goon* created by E. C. Segar (1894–1938), American cartoonist.]

goop noun orig US A stupid or fatuous person. 1900–. PUNCH I am very jealous of my position as chairman of *Juke Box Jury* . . . and I

goof goof ball goofus goofy goog googie goo-goo

gramp

don't believe one can be a placid smiling goop all the time (1966). [Cf. GOOF noun.] So **goopy,** adjective Stupid, fatuous. 1926–.

goorie /ˈɡuəri/ noun Also **goory, goori.** NZ A (mongrel) dog. Hence as a term of abuse. 1937–. NEW ZEALAND LISTENER 'Are you going to marry her?' I said. 'Why should I? Let go of me, you goorie,' he said (1970). [Alteration of Maori *kuri*.]

goose verb trans. **1** theatrical To hiss, to express disapproval of (a person or play) by hissing. 1838–. **2** To poke (a person) in the bottom, esp. between the buttocks. 1879–. I. WALLACH Eliot . . . lightly kissed the top of her head. It would be vulgar to say that she leaped as though goosed, but truth can survive anything including vulgarity (1960). **3 to be goosed** to be finished, ruined. 1928–. J. WELCOME If I've guessed wrong and Jason has found out right, then we're goosed (1959). [In sense 2, perh. from a supposed resemblance between a goose's extended neck and the upturned thumb used for poking.]

goosegog noun A gooseberry. 1823–. [Alteration (-*gog* is an alteration of *gob* lump).]

gopher variant of GOFER noun.

gorblimey Also **gaw-, -blime, -blimy.** Brit int **1** An expression of surprise, indignation, etc. 1896–. noun dated **2** A soft service cap. 1919–56. adjective **3** Vulgar. 1958–. LISTENER She offered a gorblimey cheerfulness (1962). [Corruption of *God blind me!*; cf. BLIMEY int, COR BLIMEY int.]

Gordon Bennett int euphemistic An exclamation of astonishment or exasperation. 1937–. [Alteration of COR BLIMEY int, presumably after the name of James *Gordon Bennett* (1841–1918), after whom several motor and aeronautical events were named, or his father James (1795–1872), a celebrated newspaper editor and publisher.]

gotcha Also **gotcher.** Representing a casual or non-standard pronunciation of (*I have*) *got you*, esp. in the senses 'seize' and 'understand'. 1932–. H. WAUGH 'Give her background a once-over on your way to Springfield. . . . You might try for a record of her blood type first. She claims it's O but she doesn't carry any card.' Wilks sighed. 'I gotcha' (1966).

gotta Representing a casual pronunciation of (*I have*) *got a* or (*have*) *got to*. 1924–. A. DIMENT Sorry, can't stay, gotta rush (1968).

gourd noun US The head or mind; often in phr. *off* or *out of* (*one's*) *gourd*. a.1844–. C. MCFADDEN She was still stoned out of her gourd (1977). [From earlier sense, (large) fleshy fruit or its dried shell used as a container.]

governor noun **1** = GUVNER noun. 1802–. **2** dated One's father. 1827–.

grab noun **1 up for grabs** orig US Easily obtainable; inviting capture. 1945–. FINANCIAL MAIL (Johannesburg): So the hotel reservations set-up looks up for grabs (1971). verb trans. **2** To attract the attention of, impress. 1966–. POST (Cape edition): Elton John is big but if his music doesn't grab you then it just doesn't grab you (1971).

gracing noun Brit, dated Contraction of 'greyhound racing'. 1928–35.

graft¹ noun **1** (Hard) work. 1853–. TIMES This view is that salvation . . . is to be won by long, hard graft by industrial management (1968). verb intr. **2** To work (hard). 1859–. A. PRIOR The great mass of mugs were law-abiding . . . doing as they were told, working, grafting (1966). [Perh. a transferred use of obs. *graft* depth of earth lifted by a spade, in its original sense 'digging'.]

graft² orig US. verb intr. **1** To make money by shady or dishonest means. 1859–. J. MORGAN They used to graft together . . . they pulled one or two big capers (1967). noun **2** (Practices, esp. bribery, used to secure) illicit gains in politics or business. 1865–. DAILY TELEGRAPH Victims in a wave of graft, corruption and fear were making regular payments for protection (1970). [Origin unknown.] Cf. GRIFT noun and verb.

grafter¹ noun orig US **1** A politician, official, etc. who uses his or her position in order to obtain dishonest gain or advantage. 1896–. A. J. CRONIN They've always been a set of grafters down there; local government has been one long sweet laugh (1958). **2** One who makes money by shady or dishonest means. 1899–. J. MORGAN She's a straight bird . . . not a grafter (1967). [From GRAFT² verb + -*er*.]

grafter² noun A (hard) worker. 1900–. TIMES He is a grafter rather than a fluent striker, with little back-lift, plenty of concentration, and a willingness to use his feet (1959). [From GRAFT¹ verb + -*er*.]

gramp noun Also **gramps.** Shortened forms of *grandpapa*. 1898–. L. LANE That ther kid's ther dead spit of 'is gramp (1966).

goorie goose goosegog gopher gorblimey gotcha

grand noun orig US A thousand dollars; also, occasionally, a thousand pounds. 1921–. AMERICAN MERCURY I don't know how much it is, but I suppose around ten, twelve, fifteen grand (1932). Cf. G noun, GEE noun.

gran(d)daddy noun Something large, notable, etc. of its kind; followed by *of*. 1956–. M. BEADLE The granddaddy of all electrical storms dumped a cloudburst (1961). [From earlier sense, grandfather.]

grass noun **1 on the grass** Austral out of prison. 1885–. **2** Brit A police informer. 1932–. J. CURTIS Tell you the details and then you'll do the gaff on your jack . . . or else turn grass (1936). **3** orig US Marijuana. 1943–. A. DIMENT Pure Grass cigarettes, at two dollars a pack and none of your watering down with tobacco (1968). verb Brit **4** trans. To betray, esp. to the police; often followed by *up*. 1936–. F. NORMAN What is more he didn't grass anyone else (1958). **5** intr. To inform the police; often followed by *on*. 1938–. J. PORTER It won't come out! Not unless you start grassing (1965). [In sense 2, perh. short for *grasshopper*, rhyming slang for 'shopper' (cf. SHOP verb 3) or 'copper' (Cf. GRASSHOPPER noun 1).]

grasser noun Brit = GRASS noun 1. 1950–. P. ALDING Five minutes alone with you and he'll be babbling like a grasser (1968). [From GRASS verb + *-er*.]

grasshopper noun **1** dated A policeman. 1893–. **2** US A light military aircraft used for observation, liaison, etc. 1942–. [In sense 1, rhyming slang for COPPER noun.]

gravel-crusher noun dated, services' An infantry soldier; also, a drill instructor. 1889–1948. [From the effect of service boots on parade-ground gravel.]

gravy noun Unearned or unexpected money. 1910–. GLOBE & MAIL (Toronto): In the past 10 years, the Manitoba Government has reaped about $8-million from the Downs. . . . This revenue is almost pure gravy (1968). [From the notion of gravy as a pleasing addition (to meat).]

gravy train noun A source of easy unearned financial profit. Also **gravy boat**. 1927–. M. MCCARTHY There was a moment in the spring when the whole Jocelyn sideshow seemed to be boarding the gravy train, on to

fatter triumphs of platitude and mediocrity (1952). [From GRAVY noun.]

grease noun Flattery, wheedling. 1877–. N. MAILER You should have seen the grease job I gave to Carter. I'm dumb, but man, he's dumber (1959).

grease-ball noun US, derog A foreigner, esp. one of Mediterranean or Latin American origin. 1934–. S. ELLIN A certain Mr Garcia—some greaseball who runs a lunch stand (1958). [From the association of oil with the cuisine and other cultural aspects of such countries.] Cf. GREASER noun 1.

grease monkey noun A mechanic. 1928–. TIMES LITERARY SUPPLEMENT In Australia he was impressed by the 'grease-monkey' at Broken Hill who could afford to run a racing stable (1959).

greaser noun **1** US, derog A Mexican or Spanish-American. 1849–. R. MAY & J. ROSA Mexicans . . . and . . . Latin temperaments . . . did not always sit well with Texans who were open in their dislike of 'greasers' (1980). **2** An objectionable person; a sycophant. 1900–. SPECTATOR The dismissive contempt the little greaser had so richly earned (1958). **3** orig US A member of a gang of youths with long hair and riding motor cycles. 1964–. **4** A smooth landing in an aircraft. 1980–. AMATEUR PHOTOGRAPHER The undercarriage structure was intact and . . . the plane could make a 'greaser' (1980). [From *grease* verb + *-er*: in sense 1, cf. GREASE-BALL noun; in sense 3, prob. from the grease they use on their hair and on their bikes; in sense 4, cf. the earlier phr. *to grease* (a plane) *in*, to land smoothly.]

greasy spoon noun orig US A cheap and inferior eating-place. 1925–. TIME They [i.e. the Marx brothers] . . . ate in coffee pots and greasy spoons (1951).

green noun **1** pl. Sexual activity, esp. intercourse. 1889–. G. GREENE Why not go after the girl? . . . She's not getting what I believe is vulgarly called her greens (1967). **2** Also pl. orig US Money. 1925–. R. CRAWFORD When finally we did lay our mitts on a nice pile of green, Arthur simply knuckled under to luxury (1971). **3 on the green** on stage. 1940–. TIMES LITERARY SUPPLEMENT If a modern producer asks his stage-manager to summon down a man from the flies, we might well hear the cry: 'Bill, come down on

> 'She's not getting what I believe is vulgarly called her greens.'

the green a minute' (1957). **4** orig US **Marijuana** of poor quality. 1957–. [In sense 1, perh. from the notion that sexual intercourse is as beneficial as eating one's greens (i.e. cabbages and other green vegetables); in sense 2, from the colour of dollar bills; in sense 3, abbreviation of GREENGAGE noun 1; in sense 4, from the colour of uncured marijuana.]

green-ass adjective US Inexperienced. 1949–.

greenback noun **1** US A dollar bill. 1870–. NEW YORKER We observe him on his way to Mexico with a suitcase full of green-backs (1966). **2** surfing = GREENIE noun. 1965–. [In sense 1, from a name orig applied to a non-convertible US currency note first issued in 1862, during the Civil War, which had a green design on its back.]

greengage noun **1** Rhyming slang for 'stage'. 1931–. **2** pl. Rhyming slang for 'wages'. 1931–. GUARDIAN The money? Greengages we call it, greengages— wages. You'll be surprised. In a lot of places it's a fiver a night (1964).

greenhouse noun RAF A cockpit canopy. 1941–7. W. H. AUDEN 'Why have They killed me?' wondered Bert, our Greenhouse gunner (1947).

greenie noun surfing A large wave before it breaks. 1962–. Cf. GREENBACK noun 2.

green pea noun US An inexperienced person, a beginner. 1912–.

gremlin noun **1** orig RAF A mischievous sprite imagined as the cause of mechanical faults, orig in aircraft. 1941–. TIMES The King said that on his way back from Italy they thought they heard a gremlin in the royal aircraft (1944). **2** surfing **a** A young surfer. 1961–. INTERNATIONAL SURFING There is really a lot of talent running around these days in the form of young gremlins (1967). **b** A trouble- maker who frequents the beaches but does not surf. 1967–. [Origin unknown, but prob. formed by analogy with *goblin* noun].

gremmie noun Also **gremmy.** surfing = GREMLIN noun 2. 1962–. SURFER MAGAZINE He worked all morning with several beach gremmies piling 12-foot sections of plywood and rocks into a small reef on the wet sand (1968). [Shortened form of GREMLIN noun.]

grey US, African-American. noun **1** A white-skinned person. 1960–. O. HARRINGTON The year was 1936, a bad year in most everybody's book. Ellis the cabdriver used to say that even the grays

downtown were having it rough (1965). adjective **2** Of a person: white-skinned. 1962–. E. LACY Funny thing with grey chicks. . . . They're always so sure their white skin is the sexiest ever (1965).

gricer /ˈɡraɪsə(r)/ noun A railway enthusiast, esp. one who assiduously seeks out and photographs unusual trains; loosely, a train-spotter. Also **gricing,** noun and (as a back-formation) **grice,** verb intr. 1968–. NEW SCIENTIST Some of the gricers, earnest fresh-faced young men . . . who had cut their milk teeth on Hornby trains, had booked on this train two years ago (1981). [Origin uncertain: variously associated with grouse-shooting (likened to train-spotting), *Gricer* as a surname, etc., but no suggestion has yet been proven.]

grid noun A bicycle. 1922–. COAST TO COAST 1942 'I'll walk and wheel the bike, and if my dad's home he can drive out in the car to meet me.' 'Gosh, no!' you said. 'Here, you go on, on my grid, an' I'll do the walking' (1943).

grief noun Trouble, hardship; unpleasantness; often in phr. *to give* (*make, have,* etc.) *grief.* 1929–. FACE Marm has had grief from snobby film critics and from the censorship lobby (1989).

griff noun A tip; news; reliable information. 1891–. J. WAINWRIGHT The informant was saying: 'It's griff, guv. The real thing' (1968). [Shortened form of GRIFFIN noun.]

griffin noun A tip (in betting, etc.); a signal, hint. 1889–. F. SHAW ET AL. Let's give de fellers de griffin (1966). [Origin unknown.] Cf. GRIFF noun.

grift noun and verb US = GRAFT[2] noun and verb. 1914–. R. CHANDLER Hell, I thought he sold reefers. With the right protection. But hell, that's a small-time racket. A peanut grift (1940). [Perh. alteration of GRAFT[2] noun.] So **grifter,** noun = GRAFTER[1] noun. 1915–. R. O'CONNOR He lived off the horoscope trade until the World Fair of 1893 suggested a move to Chicago, as it did to thousands of other . . . grifters (1965).

grill noun Austral derog A Greek or other southern European. 1957–. [From a perceived abundance in Australia of Greeks and other southern Europeans as proprietors of cafés.]

grind verb **1** intr. and trans. To have sexual intercourse (with). 1647–. I. JEFFERIES Rob, what do you think about grinding . . . ? I know it's time-wasting but it's so difficult to do without it (1966). **2** intr. orig US To dance erotically by gyrating or rotating the hips. 1942–. M. MACHLIN Deirde began to grind very hard and very close

green-ass greenback greengage greenhouse grey

to him (1976). noun **3** US college, dated A hard-working student. 1893-. s. LEWIS He told himself that, with this conceited grind, there was no merit in even a boarding-house courtesy (1951). **4** (An act of) sexual intercourse. 1893-. J. WAINWRIGHT A grind with a cheap scrubber? (1969). **5** A dancer's suggestive rotary movement of the hips. 1946-. PUNCH Sing a song . . . and do a bump-and-grind routine (1964). Cf. BUMP noun.

grind house noun orig US, dated A small cinema showing short films of low quality or dubious artistic merit; also, a strip club. 1925-. [Perh. from *grind* noun laborious task + *house* noun.]

gringo /grɪŋgəʊ/ noun derog An English person or Anglo-American: used by Spanish Americans. 1849-. A. HUXLEY Annoying foreigners and especially white Gringoes is a national sport in Honduras (1933). [From Mexican Spanish *gringo* gibberish.]

grody /grəʊdɪ/ adjective Also **groady, groddy** /grɒdɪ/, **groaty,** etc. US Disgusting, revolting, 'gross'; slovenly, unhygienic, squalid; esp. in phr. *grody to the max*, unspeakably awful. 1967-. LOS ANGELES TIMES Moon Zappa calls her toenails '*Grody* to the *max*', which means disgusting beyond belief (1982). [From *grod-, groat-* (altered forms of *grot(esque)* + *-y*; cf. GROTTY adjective.]

grog noun Austral and NZ Alcoholic liquor, esp. beer. 1832-. CENTRALIAN ADVOCATE (Alice Springs): Mr Forrester agreed that the main 'grog problem' on the town camps was caused by the licensed stores (1986). [From the earlier sense, a drink of rum (or other spirits) and water.]

grog blossom noun Redness of the nose caused by excessive drinking. 1796-.

groin noun dated A ring. 1931-. J. CURTIS There was one [woman] with three groins on her fingers (1936). [Prob. from the curve of an architectural groin.]

groise Also **groize.** Brit, public schools'. noun **1** A hard worker, a swot; one who curries favour; also, hard work. 1913-. M. MARPLES A corps groize is one who tries to gain favour by his efficiency in the O.T.C. (1940). verb intr. **2** To work hard, to swot; to curry favour. 1913-. [Perh. alteration of GREASE noun.]

grok verb trans. and intr. Also **grock.** US To empathize or communicate sympathetically (with). 1961-. NEW YORKER I was thinking we ought to get together somewhere, Mr. Zzyzbyzynsky, and grok about our problems

(1969). [Arbitrary formation by Robert A. Heinlein in his science-fiction novel *Stranger in a Strange Land*.]

grommet noun Also **grommit.** An enthusiastic young surfer or skateboarder. 1986-. WAVELENGTH SURFING If you want the city surf life of Sydney, sharing each wave with a hoard of surf-crazed young grommits, then Manly is definitely the place for you (1986). [Origin uncertain; cf. *grummit* ship's boy, ring or wreath of rope (esp. in nautical contexts).]

groove orig US. noun **1 in the** (or **a**) **groove** Playing jazz or similar music with fluent inspiration, or in the stated manner; hence, doing or performing well; fashionable. 1932-. HOT NEWS The Boswells are not in the hot groove (1935). **2** A session at which jazz or similar music is played, esp. well or with inspiration. 1954-. JIVE JUNGLE The all-night 'grooves' began (1954). **3** Something one enjoys or appreciates very much. 1958-. MELODY MAKER This is what makes the Indian one such a groove for me (1967). verb **4** intr. or trans. To play (jazz or similar music) with swing; to dance or listen to such music with great pleasure. 1935-. MELODY MAKER The rhythm section . . . grooves along in true Basie manner (1967). **5** trans. To give pleasure to (someone). 1959-. ESQUIRE Her singing grooved me (1959). **6** intr. To make good progress or co-operate; to get on well with someone; to make love. 1967-. NEW YORKER Sad Arthur put away his boots and helmet . . . to stay in Nutley and groove with the fair Lambie (1970). [From the *groove* cut in a gramophone record.]

groovy adjective orig US **1** Playing, or capable of playing, jazz or similar music with fluent inspiration. 1937-. MEZZROW & WOLFE When he was groovy . . . he'd begin to play the blues on a beat-up guitar (1946). **2** Fashionable and exciting; enjoyable, excellent. 1944-. LISTENER There are a lot of guys going round with groovy hair-styles (1968). [From GROOVE noun + *-y*.]

grope verb trans. derog To fondle or attempt to fondle (a person's) sexual organs or (a woman's) breasts. *c.*1250-.

Groper noun Austral A West Australian, esp. (a descendant of) an early settler. 1899-. [Short for SAND-GROPER noun.]

gross orig and mainly US. adjective **1** Extremely unpleasant, disgusting, repulsive, obnoxious. 1959-. J. HYAMS 'She really thinks he's gross, huh?' . . . 'The pits,' said Freda (1978). verb **2 to gross** (someone) **out** To disgust, repel; to shock or horrify. 1968-. C. MCFADDEN

grind house gringo grody grog grog blossom groin

I can dig it. They're grossing me out too, you know? (1977). [In sense 1, from earlier sense, coarse, unrefined (of behaviour, etc.).]

gross-out US. noun **1** A person or thing that disgusts or shocks, esp. (a scene from) a gory horror film. 1966–. NEW YORKER Heads splatter and drip . . . . It's just a gross-out (1984). adjective **2** Disgusting, repellent; shocking. Also, wild, uncontrolled. 1973–. [From *to gross out* (see GROSS verb).]

grot adjective **1** = GROTTY adjective. 1967–. TIMES A new film can be 'totally brilliant' or 'totally grot' (1985). noun **2** An unpleasant or despicable person; a 'nerd'. 1970–. COURIER-MAIL (Brisbane): If you look like a grot, you'll never get a flat (1980). **3** Revolting or grimy stuff, rubbish, dirt, 'gunge'; also, filthiness, 'grottiness'. 1971–. J. WAIN This place, the tawdriness, the awful mound of grot it all is, stands between me and feeling anything (1982). [Back-formation from GROTTY adjective.]

grotty adjective Unpleasant, dirty, shabby, unattractive. 1964–. TIMES 'I don't like the grotty old pub,' says Miss McCormick (1970). [Shortened form of *grotesque* adjective + -y.]

grouch-bag noun US A hidden pocket or a (draw-string) purse carried in a concealed place, for keeping one's money safe; also, money saved and kept hidden. 1908–. TELEGRAPH (Brisbane): Groucho . . . earned his nickname in poker games because he always carried his money in a 'grouch bag' (1969). [From *grouch* noun, grumbling.]

ground-hog noun US A worker who operates at ground level. 1926–. [From earlier sense, American marmot.]

groupie noun **1** RAF A group captain. 1943–. I. LAMBOT Groupie's a devil for the girls (1968). **2** Also **groupy**. An ardent follower of a touring pop group, esp. a girl who tries to have sex with them. 1967–. TIMES His defence described the sisters as 'groupies', girls who deliberately provoke sexual relations with pop stars (1970).

grouse adjective Austral and NZ Excellent, very good. 1941–. D. R. STUART She's a grouse sort of a joint, this bloody Ceylon; do me (1979). [Origin unknown.]

grouter noun Austral An unfair advantage; esp. in phr. *to come in on the grouter*, to win a bet, to gain an unfair advantage. 1902–. R. BEILBY By coming in on the grouter he had augmented the remaining pound of the two Whiteside had given him (1977). [Origin unknown.]

grub noun Food. 1659–. E. TAYLOR We're here, madam. Grub up! (1957). [Perh. from the notion of grubs (larvae) as birds' food.]

grumble noun Brit Women regarded as objects of sexual attraction. 1962–. MELODY MAKER American visitors are invariably delighted by references to birds, scrubbers, grumble (1966). [Shortened from *grumble and grunt*, rhyming slang for *cunt*.]

grunge noun US Something or someone repugnant or odious, unpleasant, or dull; also, dirt, grime. 1965–. WASHINGTON POST Most bands would fall headlong into cliche when dishing out the sort of overdriven guitar grunge served up in 'Don't You Go Walking' (1986). [Prob. back-formation from GRUNGY adjective.]

grungy adjective mainly US Grimy, dirty; hence, of poor quality, unappealing; unpleasant, bad; untidy. 1965–. DIRT BIKE I would like to know who made those blasted white pants so popular—mine are splattered with oil specks and other grungy stains (1985). [Apparently arbitrary formation, after *grubby*, *dingy*, etc.; cf. GUNGE noun.]

grunt noun **1** orig and mainly US An unskilled worker, labourer; a general dogsbody. Orig a ground worker in the construction of power lines. 1926–. DAILY TELEGRAPH Better by far not to attempt to be over-smart (or too clever) by using new words like . . . 'grunt' for a guy who does the dirty work (1986). **2** N Amer An infantry soldier, esp. in the Vietnam war. 1969–. I. KEMP The sound of . . . engines, among the most welcome of all music to the average infantryman—or 'grunt', as we were impolitely called—in Vietnam (1969).

grunt work noun US Unskilled or manual work. Also **grunt job, labour**. 1977–. LOS ANGELES TIMES The Hollywood Park chef . . . did much of the grunt work in construction of the cake base (1989). [See GRUNT noun 1.]

gubbins noun Brit **1** A foolish person. 1916–. J. OSBORNE Have you been on the batter, you old gubbins! (1957). **2** A set of equipment or paraphernalia. 1925–. NEW SCIENTIST Behind that again is the engine and propeller, the fuel tank and various bits of 'gubbins' (1968). **3** Something of little value, nonsense. 1925–. **4** A gadget. 1944–. I. BROWN You can save more petrol by how you drive than with all the gubbinses now floating around (1958). [From earlier sense, fragments, from obs. *gobbon* noun; perh. related to *gobbet* noun.]

guernsey noun **to get a (or the) guernsey** Austral **a** To be selected for a football team.

gross-out grot grotty grouch-bag ground-hog grub

1918–. **b** To gain recognition or selection. 1959–. BULLETIN (Sydney): Doug was the next man on the NSW Liberal Country Party ticket . . . and if everything goes according to the rules . . . then he should be the one to get the guernsey for Canberra (1975). [From *guernsey* sleeveless shirt worn by Australian Rules footballers, from earlier sense, thick shirt worn by seamen; ultimately from *Guernsey*, the name of one of the Channel Islands.]

guff noun orig US Empty talk; nonsense. 1888–. CRESCENDO The sleeve-notes give us a lot of guff about getting with it and so on and tell us nothing constructive (1966). [From earlier sense, puff, whiff; of imitative origin.]

guido noun US A socially unsophisticated person, esp. one whose attire and behaviour are viewed as typically lower-class suburban. Also, spec., an Italian-American man, esp. one who is aggressively masculine and vain about his appearance and possessions. 1986–. MUSIC PAPER All the cool bands play in The City . . . Nothing on Long Island but guidos and meatheads (1991). [From the Italian male forename *Guido*.]

guinea noun Also **ginny, guinny.** US derog, dated An immigrant of Italian or Spanish origin. 1896–. J. O'HARA Tony Murascho, who up to that time had been known only as a tough little guinny, was matched to fight a preliminary bout at McGovern's Hall (1934). [From *Guinea*, the name of part of the West Coast of Africa, presumably with reference to such people's dark skin.]

guinea-pig noun Brit, dated An evacuee or billetee during World War II. 1939–41. [Apparently from the fact that the billeting allowance was one guinea (£1 5p).]

guinzo noun = GINZO noun.

gump¹ noun Also **gumph.** dialect and US, dated A fool. 1825–. A. GILBERT She might do her best to attract attention—any girl who wasn't a complete gumph would (1945). [Origin unknown.]

gump² noun US A chicken. 1914–. AMERICAN BALLADS & FOLK SONGS Not even a shack to beg for a lump, Or a hen-house to frisk for a single gump (1934). [Perh. the same word as GUMP¹ noun.]

gumshoe noun US A detective. 1906–. D. HAMMETT He . . . looked me up and down, growled: 'So you're a lousy gum-shoe' (1927). [From the notion of someone who walks around stealthily wearing 'gumshoes' or galoshes: *gumshoe* from *gum* rubbery material + *shoe*.]

gumsucker noun Austral derog A person from the state of Victoria; also, more broadly, any native-born, non-aboriginal Australian. 1855–. W. LAWSON Some men . . . called them 'gumsuckers', and a few other things (1936). [From the notion of sucking the juice of gum trees.]

gum-tree noun **up a gum-tree** in difficulties. 1926–. ENCOUNTER Until somebody solves the problem of an English idiom we're going to be up a gum-tree (1959). [Cf. earlier Austral *up a gum-tree* in another place, and US *up a tree* trapped, in difficulties.]

gun verb **1 to gun for** to go in search of with a gun; hence, to seek out in order to attack or rebuke. 1888–. C. DAY LEWIS I felt that 'They' were gunning for me again (1960). **2** trans. = *to give* (*her, it, etc.*) *the gun.* 1930–. P. DURST He gunned the Volkswagen and fell in behind (1968). noun **3** US A hypodermic syringe used by drug addicts. 1904–. **4** pl., naval A gunnery officer. 1916–. **5 to give** (**her, it,** etc.) **the gun** orig US To cause (a vehicle) to accelerate; to open the throttle of (an engine). 1917–. G. BAGBY She slid behind the wheel, gave her hearse the gun, swung it around (1968). **6** surfing A large heavy surfboard used for riding big waves. 1963–. SURF '70 While in Hawaii I had two boards. They were an 8ft 9in 'hot-dog' and a 9ft 6in tracker type gun (1970).

gun-fire noun army, dated An early morning cup of tea served to troops before going on first parade. 1912–. GUN BUSTER 'Dawn just breaking, sir,' he affirmed, shoving into my hand a mug of hot 'gunfire' (1940). [From the firing of the morning gun at the start of the day.]

gunge Brit, derog. noun **1** Sticky or viscous matter, esp. when messy or unidentifiable. 1969–. LISTENER Adam and Eve emerge from a transportable saucer of murky gunge (1985). verb trans. and intr. **2** To clog or become clogged with a sticky or messy substance; usu. followed by *up*. 1976–. SOUNDS A few academic 'experts' know *something* about the short-term effects of sniffing, but aren't too sure about exactly *how* it gunges up the body (1977). [Origin uncertain; perh. associated with *goo* noun, GRUNGE noun, GUNK noun, etc.]

gung ho adjective orig US Eager, enthusiastic. 1955–. I. KEMP He . . . was one of the most 'gung-ho' (exceptionally keen to be personally involved in combat) characters I ever met (1969). [From earlier services' slang sense, dedicated to teamwork and effort; orig adopted as a slogan during World War II

guff guido guinea guinea-pig guinzo gump gun

gutser

by the US Marines under Lt. Col. Evans F. Carlson, from Chinese *kung-ho* Industrial Co-operatives, mistakenly taken in its literal meaning 'work together', from *kung* work and *ho* peace, harmony.]

gungy adjective Also **gungey.** Brit, derog Sticky, messy; also, second-rate, spoilt. 1962–. SPECTATOR If you're in the mood for something gungey, there's certainly something here for you: chicken stuffed with lamb served with a port sauce (1985).

gunk noun derog, orig US **1** Viscous or liquid material. 1949–. C. HENRY Too much eye gunk and lipstick—that sort of girl (1966). **2** A person. 1964–. J. D. MACDONALD It was a drag to listen big-eyed to that tired gunk and say Oh and Ahh (1968). [From the proprietary name of a detergent, registered in 1932.]

gun moll noun US A female thief; an armed woman. 1908–. A. KOESTLER Fierce-looking Yemenite gun-molls, Sephardi beauties (1949). Cf. MOLL noun.

gunsel /ˈɡʌnsəl/ noun Also **gonsil, gunshel, gun(t)zel.** US **1** dated A (naïve) youth; a tramp's young companion, male lover; a homosexual youth. 1914–. **2** An informer, a criminal, a gunman. 1950–. W. MARKFIELD After all, didn't Ben Gurion himself hand her a blank cheque, she should have what to hire a couple of gunsels? (1964). [From Yiddish *genzel*, from German *Gänslein* gosling; in sense 2, as if from *gun* noun.]

gun-slinger noun mainly US A gunman. 1953–. BOSTON SUNDAY HERALD The gunslinger . . . comes to town, cigar between teeth, his prowess with a gun for sale (1967).

guntz /ɡʌnts/ noun The whole lot, everything. 1958–. J. MORGAN You don't want a pay-day, you boys are asking for the guntz (1967). [Perh. from Yiddish *gants* whole, from German *Ganze* whole, entirety.]

gup noun Silly talk, nonsense. 1924–. PUNCH Need I give the jury any more of this gup? (1927). [From earlier Anglo-Indian sense, gossip; from Hindustani *gup*; cf. GUFF noun.]

guppie noun mainly jocular or derog **1** A homosexual yuppie. 1984–. **2** A yuppie concerned about the environment and ecological issues. 1985–. DAILY TELEGRAPH The magazine claims that . . . her fellow thinkers, whom it derides as green yuppies or 'guppies',

have 'delivered the green movement into the lap of the industrialist' (1989). [In sense 1, blend of *gay* and YUPPIE; in sense 2, blend of *green* and YUPPIE noun.]

gurgler noun Austral A plughole or drain; often in phr. *to go down the gurgler*, (esp. of a business or other venture) to deteriorate or fail, 'go down the drain'. 1981–. COURIER-MAIL (Brisbane): Channel 7 is making a big comeback locally but Channel O is going down the proverbial gurgler (1988).

gurk Brit. verb intr. **1** To belch. 1923–. NEW STATESMAN They grunted and gurked with an unconcern that amazed me (1966). noun **2** A belch. 1932–. [Echoic.]

gussy up verb trans. To smarten up, esp. to dress smartly. 1952–. M. G. EBERHART 'You're really all gussied up. . . . Coast slang for dressed up,' she explained (1970). [Origin uncertain; cf. obs. Austral slang *gussie* noun, effeminate man, from the diminutive form of the name *Augusta*, and obs. Brit Public School slang *gussy* adjective, over-dressed.]

gut-bucket noun orig US A primitive, unsophisticated style of jazz. 1929–. [Perh. from a type of improvised double bass used in such music, made from a washtub and a catgut string.]

gutful noun As much as one can bear; an excess. 1923–. DAILY TELEGRAPH Lately, we have had a 'gutful' of the permissiveness that seems to tolerate violence against the police (1970).

gut-rot noun **1** Unwholesome or unpalatable liquor or food. 1916–. F. SARGESON The garish-looking sweet stuff he made his living from. . . . 'I make a dishonest living by trading in gutrot' (1965). Cf. ROT-GUT noun. **2** Stomach-ache. 1979–. INDEPENDENT Next day I developed gut rot, so I can't say I gave Puerto Rica a fair chance (1989).

guts verb intr. To eat greedily. 1903–. K. TENNANT 'Gutsing again, Briscoe?' she reproved (1943). [From *guts* noun belly.]

gutser noun Also **gutzer.** Austral and NZ **1** A heavy fall. 1918–. B. SCOTT Smashes were known colloquially as 'gutzers', and it was a lucky and skilful driver who did not have at least one a week (1979). **2 to come a gutser** to come a cropper, to fail. 1918–. CANBERRA TIMES 'The

gungy gunk gun moll gunsel gun-slinger guntz

Opposition', raged Mr Dawkins during Wednesday's Question Time in the House of Representatives, 'has come an absolute gutser on this one!' (1983). [From *guts* noun, belly + *-er*.]

gutted adjective Brit Devastated, shattered; utterly fed up. 1981–. sun I've heard nothing for four months. I'm gutted because I still love him (1991). [From earlier sense, *having the guts removed*.]

gutty adjective jazz Earthy, primitive. 1939–. esquire You feel it in a beat, in jazzy . . . or a good gutty rock number (1958). [From *gut* noun + *-y*; cf. earlier sense, pot-bellied.]

guv noun Short for GUVNER noun. 1890–. n. wallington The Guv was seated at his desk (1974).

guvner noun Also **guv'ner, guvnor, guv'nor.** Brit **1** One's superior, an employer. 1802–. observer Sometimes the peterman finds his own jobs and acts as guvnor of his own team (1960). **2** Used as a term of address to a man. 1852–. listener You can be sure that if somebody calls you 'mister' on the railways he doesn't like you. The term of endearment is 'guv'nor' (1968). See GOVERNOR noun.

guy verb intr. **1** To run away, to do a bunk. 1879–. times Hurry up, I have had to do a chap, we will have to guy out of here (1963). noun **2 to do a guy** to run away, to do a bunk. 1897–. [Origin uncertain.]

guzzle verb trans. dated, orig dialect To seize by the throat, choke, throttle; to strangle, kill. 1885–. d. runyon He will be safe from being guzzled by some of Black Mike's or

Benny's guys (1931). [Cf. obs. *guzzle* noun, throat.]

guzzle-guts noun Brit A greedy person. 1959–.

gynae noun **1** Also **gynie** Gynaecology. 1933–. g. l. cohen 'We didn't come across any horrors,' said Dr. Duncum . . . 'unless you count adolescent girls in gynae wards' (1964). **2** A gynaecologist. 1982–. barr & york Sloanes who aren't producing will go to their sweet gynae, who will tell them to stand on their heads afterwards (1982). [Shortening.]

gyp¹ /dʒɪp/ orig US. verb trans. **1** To cheat, swindle. 1889–. punch If he . . . thinks the conductor is trying to gyp him . . . he . . . need only look at the fares table (1962). noun **2** An act of cheating; a swindle. 1914–. [Perh. from *gyp* noun, college servant at Cambridge or Durham, itself perh. from obs. *gippo* noun, scullion, orig a man's short tunic, from obs. French *jupeau* noun; or perh. shortened from *gipsy*.]

gyp² /dʒɪp/ noun Also **gip. to give (someone) gyp: a** To scold (someone). 1893–. **b** To cause (someone) pain or severe discomfort. 1910–. i. jefferies I should think his tum is giving him gip (1966). [Prob. from *gee-up*.]

gyver /ˈɡaɪvə(r)/ noun Also **givo, givor, guiver, guyver.** mainly Austral and NZ Affected speech or behaviour; esp. in phr. *to put on the gyver*. 1864–. d. stuart Pity they can't find something better to do than all this guiver (1977). [Origin unknown.]

gutty guv guvner guy guzzle guzzle-guts gynae

H noun Abbreviation of 'heroin'. 1926–.
K. ORVIS Suppose I . . . ask you where to connect for H? (1962). Cf. HORSE noun.

habdabs noun Also **abdabs**. Great anxiety, the heebie-jeebies; esp. in phr. *to give* (someone) *the screaming habdabs*. 1946–.
SPECTATOR *Treasure Island* gives pleasure and excitement to some and the screaming habdabs to others (1962). [Origin unknown.]

hack verb trans. orig US To manage, cope with; to tolerate; esp. in phr. *to hack it*. 1955–.
NEWSWEEK I had proved to the world during my four years in the Senate . . . that I can hack it (1972).

hack noun Brit A journalist, esp. a staff newspaper writer. 1810–. ARENA 'Good story'. The other hacks had seen bodies float by: we were the first to see them being fished out (1988). [A slight development from the earlier sense, literary scribbler. The term is often applied jocularly by journalists to themselves.]

hackette noun Brit A female journalist or 'hack'. 1984–. TIMES The worlds of newspapers and publishing are unbuttoned, and hackettes can wear pretty well anything (1987). [From HACK noun + *-ette*.]

hackie noun Also **hacky**. US A taxi-driver. 1937–. M. NEVILLE And now . . . unearth some other blasted hacky that drove me there (1959). [From US *hack* noun, taxi, abbreviation of *hackney* (*carriage*) + *-ie*, *-y*.]

hair noun **to keep one's hair on** to remain calm. 1883–. J. GASH 'Have you seen my car keys?' 'Have I hell!' she screamed, rummaging under the divan for her shoes. 'Keep your hair on' (1977).

hairy adjective **1** Difficult. 1848–. W. COOPER The problem was of the kind that Mike described in his up-to-date slang as 'hairy' (1966). **2 hairy at** (**about, in, round**) **the heel**(**s**) dated Ill-bred. So **hairy-heeled**, adjective, and simple **hairy,** in the same sense. 1890–. N. MARSH I always say that when people start fussing about family and all that, it's because they're a bit hairy round the heels themselves (1962). **3** Out-of-date, passé. 1950–. **4** Frightening, hair-raising. 1966–. Lord Snowdon said during a break for an orange juice: 'I was a bit frightened. Some bends are a bit hairy' (1972).

hairy eyeball noun orig and mainly US A look given with narrowed eyes, esp. indicating hostility or disapproval; esp. in phr. *to give the hairy eyeball*. 1961–. M. AZERRAD A gauntlet of bad-ass mohawked punks lined the edge of the stage, giving the band a massive hairy eyeball (2001).

half adverb **1 not half: a** not at all, the reverse of. 1828–. V. WOOLF I could live on fifteen shillings a week. . . . It wouldn't be half bad (1919). **b** To a considerable degree. 1953–.
PARKER & ALLERTON It doesn't half nark them (1962). noun **2 and a half** of an exceptional kind. 1832–. M. M. KAYE Roaring Rory must have been a hell-raiser and a half in his day (1959). **3** Brit, dated The sum of ten shillings (50p). 1931–. G. GREENE She's just a buer [= (loose) woman]—he gave her a half (1938). [In sense 3, from ten shillings being half of one pound sterling.]

half-arsed adjective Also **half-ass**, **half-assed**. orig US Ineffectual, inadequate, mediocre; stupid, inexperienced. 1932–.
OBSERVER The sort of half-arsed dottiness they dish out in West End comedies (1972).

half-cut adjective Brit Fairly drunk. 1893–. RADIO TIMES Inebriation . . . is the sport of all ranks. How many executives can work reasonably effectively unless they are half-cut? (1971).

half-inch verb trans. To steal. 1925–. TIMES If people are going to go around half-inching planets the situation is pretty serious (1972). [Rhyming slang for 'pinch'.]

half-pie adjective NZ Halfway towards, imperfect, mediocre. c.1926–. LANDFALL He hadn't been a real officer, only a half-pie one (1955). [Perh. from Maori *pai* good.]

half-shot adjective orig US Fairly drunk. 1838–. J. M. CAIN Stuff for guys in college to gag about when they were half shot with beer (1948).

ham noun **1a** An inexpert performer, esp. an actor who overacts. 1882–. TIMES 'He thought I was an old ham,' says Miss Seyler indulgently (1958). **b** An inexpert or over-theatrical performance. 1942–. LISTENER The mummer who thinks that all acting before his time was 'ham' (1959). **2** US An incompetent boxer or fighter. 1888–. SATURDAY EVENING POST They want me to slug with this big ham (1929). verb intr. and trans. **3** To overact; to act or treat emotionally or sentimentally; usu. followed by *up*. 1933–. LISTENER Marie Bell . . . hams it up in a smugly self-conscious cameo portrayal (1965). adjective **4** Clumsy, ineffective, incompetent. 1941–. TIMES LITERARY SUPPLEMENT Nothing he hated more than 'ham' writing and 'prefabricated' characters (1963). [In sense 1, prob. short for obs. US slang *hamfatter* ineffective performer; in senses 2 and 4, partly from *ham-fisted*, *handed* adjectives.] See also HAMBONE noun 1 and HAMMY adjective.

ham and beef noun The chief warder in a prison. 1941–62. [Rhyming slang for 'chief'.]

ham-bone noun **1** US An inferior or amateur actor, esp. one who speaks in a spurious Black accent; a mediocre musician. 1893–. B. KEATON Because I was also a born hambone, I ignored any bumps . . . I may have got at first on hearing audiences gasp (1960). **2** Naval A sextant. 1938–. [In sense 2, from its shape.]

hammy adjective Being or characteristic of a ham actor or ham acting. 1929–. D. JORDAN Condon raised an eyebrow in a hammy attempt to be supercilious (1973). [From HAM noun 1 + -*y*.]

Hampstead Heath noun Brit Rhyming slang for 'teeth'. Also **Hampsteads.** 1887–. R. COOK The rot had set in something horrible with her hampsteads and scotches (1962). [From the name of a district in north London.]

handful noun A five years' prison sentence. 1930–. M. GILBERT He's had a two-stretch . . . He'll collect a handful next time (1953). [From the five fingers of the hand.]

hand-job noun An act of masturbation, esp. of a man by a woman. Cf. BLOW JOB noun. 1969–. D. LEAVITT First he had been satisfied with the films alone; then a quick hand-job in the back row (1986).

handle noun **1** An honorific title or similar distinction attached to a personal name (as *the Honourable, MP*, etc.). 1832–. NEWS OF THE WORLD 'I get very angry if people call me Lord David.' David . . . hates the sort of questions people ask once they find out about his 'handle' (1977). **2** orig US A person's name; a nickname. 1870–. C. F. BURKE One night Jesus met a guy named Nicodemus. How's that for a handle?

(1969). [In sense 1, from the phr. *a handle to one's name* a title attached to one's name.]

hang verb **1 to hang out** to reside or be often present. 1811–. P. G. WODEHOUSE The head of the family has always hung out at the castle (1936). **2 to hang one on** (someone): to hit (someone). 1908–. PUNCH There are moments when most of us have felt the desire to hang one on the boss's chin and walk out (1966). **3 to hang tough** orig and mainly US To remain steadfast, refuse to give up. 1936–. NEW YORK POST That's how the Mets have won four of their last five games. Somehow. They're hanging tough (1972). **4** intr. orig and mainly US To pass time idly or aimlessly; to associate or socialize informally, esp. with one's peers. 1941–. PLAYBOY When I'm not on a football field, I hang with whoever I want to hang with (1969). **5 to hang (a) left or right** orig and mainly US To make a left or right turn, esp. in motoring and skiing; similarly, *to hang a Louie* (*Lilly, Ralph*, etc.). 1966–. SUNDAY TELEGRAPH Hang a right on Santa Monica Freeway, hang a left on Harbour and another right on Sixth Street (1984). **6 to hang in** mainly US To persevere resolutely; often *imperative* and with *there*. 1969–. J. ARCHER 'No, no,' said Simon. 'I'll hang in there now that I've waited this long' (1984). **7 to let it all hang out** orig US To be uninhibited or relaxed; to be candidly truthful. 1970–. VILLAGE VOICE (New York): No names, of course, will be used; he doesn't expect everyone will be as willing as he is to let it all hang out (1972). See also HUNG UP adjective.

hang-out noun A place one lives in or frequently visits. 1893–. GLOBE & MAIL MAGAZINE (Toronto): It is 3 a.m. in a steam bath known as an after-midnight homosexual hangout (1968). [From *to hang out* (see HANG verb 1).]

hang-up noun An emotional problem or inhibition. 1959–. BLACK WORLD Depressing piece about pushers, junkies, whores and their hang-ups (1973). [Prob. from HUNG UP adjective.]

hanky-panky noun **1** Dishonest dealing; trickery. 1841–. **2** Surreptitious sexual activity. 1938–. NEW YORKER They were still 'courting', still occupying separate quarters in Dr. Rounds' boarding house . . . where, according to Lunt, no 'hanky-panky' was permitted (1986). [An arbitrary formation, prob. related to *hocus pocus*; cf. obs. sense, sleight of hand, jugglery.]

happening adjective orig US Currently in vogue, trendy. 1977–. JACKIE POP SPECIAL Some people must really go trainspotting because they think it's the happening thing to do (1989).

happy adjective **as happy as Larry** orig Austral Extremely happy. 1905–.

happy dust noun Cocaine. 1922–. E. ST. V. MILLAY Your head's So full of dope, so full of happy-dust . . . you're just a drug Addict (1937). [From its powdery form and its supposed effect on the user.]

happy pill noun A tranquilliser. 1956–. I. ASIMOV You've got that tranquilliser gleam in your eye, doctor. I don't need any happy pills (1966).

happy slapping noun Brit A type of assault in which someone, esp. a child, is attacked and beaten by a gang, who record the incident on video-phone and transmit it to others. 2005–.

hard noun Brit Hard labour. 1890–. J. BRAINE 'Oh my,' Roy said, 'strap me to the mast, said Ulysses. Almost worth ten years hard, isn't she?' (1957).

hard-ass US. noun **1** A tough, uncompromising person. 1962–. J. WELCH It would have been funny, Hartpence the hardass snitching, if Jack hadn't got stabbed (1990). adjective **2** = HARD-ASSED adjective. 1967–. G. BENFORD You Hiruko guys so hard-ass let's see you corner it (1983).

hard-assed adjective orig and mainly US Having firm buttocks; hence tough, uncompromising, resolute. 1962–. C. S. MURRAY Canadian customs are notoriously hard-assed about drugs (1989).

hardball US. noun **1** Uncompromising methods or dealings, esp. in politics; esp. in phr. *to play hardball*. 1973–. FORTUNE If anyone wants to play hardball, Cub can operate in the 5% to 6% range and still be profitable, because its costs are so lean (1983). verb trans. **2** To pressure or coerce politically. 1984–. OBSERVER She rebelled occasionally, hard-balling O'Neill into attaching to a Bill an Amendment that would help her District, by threatening to kill a million dollar pork-barrel destined for his (1984). [From earlier sense, baseball (as opposed to softball).]

hard case noun orig US A person aggressively difficult to deal with. 1836–. R. KIPLING It [i.e. a school] . . . had been made up . . . by drafts from Haileybury . . . and, I think, a percentage of 'hard cases' from other schools (a.1936).

hard cheese noun Brit Bad luck. Also **hard cheddar**. 1876–. J. I. M. STEWART It was hard cheese on him coming up against another top-class specimen (1973).

hard nut noun A hard or uncompromising person. 1888–. J. GASH While he ordered at the bar I glanced at him. This bloke was a hard nut and no mistake (1981).

hard-on noun An erection of the penis. Also **hard**. 1893–. SCREW Billy and I talked down our hardons and . . . went downstairs to load the truck (1972).

hard tail noun US A mule, esp. an old one. 1917–. [From the imperviousness of their rear ends to the driver's whip.]

hard ticket noun orig US A difficult or unscrupulous person, a 'tough customer'. 1903–.

hard word noun **to put the hard word on** (someone): Austral and NZ To ask a favour, esp. sexual or financial, of (someone). 1918–. NEW ZEALAND LISTENER 'Don't you think hitching's a little dangerous for females?' 'Well, some sheilas I know have had the hard word put on them' (1970).

harness bull noun US A uniformed policeman. Also **harness cop**. 1903–. J. GODEY The cops. From the chief on down to the harness bulls (1972).

harp noun US An Irish person. 1904–. J. DOS PASSOS The foreman was a big loudmouthed harp (1936). [From the harp as a symbol of Ireland.]

Harriet Lane noun dated, mainly nautical Preserved meat, esp. Australian tinned meat. 1896–. W. E. DEXTER On Sunday we were allowed 1 lb. of preserved meat, known as 'Harriet Lane' (1938). [From the name of a famous murder victim; cf. FANNY ADAMS noun.]

Harry noun Brit, mainly nautical Used arbitrarily for expressive or intensive effect before adjectives, nouns, etc., which are typically suffixed with *-ers* (see -ER). 1925–. C. GRAVES Fortunately, the sea has dropped and it is Harry Flatters. Harry Flatters means flat calm (1941); LANCET Get in there, and strip off Harry Nuders (1946); GUARDIAN In the old Imperial Aircraft days . . . the engineer would bring the old kite down harry plonkers on the grass (1969). [From the male personal name *Harry*.]

Harry Tate noun Brit, dated **1** Used attributively or in the possessive to designate something incompetent or disorderly. 1925–35. BRITISH JOURNAL OF PSYCHOLOGY Native courts have been established [in Uganda]. . . . Their methods have been described as 'Harry Tate' procedure; but they are generally successful at arriving at the facts (1935). **2** A

happy happy dust happy pill happy slapping hard

condition of nervous excitement or irritability. 1932. [From the stage-name of R. M. Hutchison (1872–1940), British music-hall comedian; in sense 2, rhyming slang for 'state'.]

Harvey Smith noun A V-sign as a gesture of defiance or contempt; any gesture denoting this. 1973–. TELEGRAPH & ARGUS (Bradford): Centuries from now, people may still refer to a two-fingered gesture as a 'Harvey Smith' (1985). [From the name of Robert *Harvey Smith* (b. 1938), British show-jumper, with reference to a gesture made during a televised event in 1971. Explained by Harvey Smith as a Victory sign.]

hash¹ noun **to settle** (a person's) **hash** to deal with and subdue (a person). 1803–. C. ST. J. SPRIGG What are you going to do? Settle his hash and drop him overboard? (1933). [Cf. earlier sense, dish of recooked meat.]

hash² noun Abbreviation of 'hashish'. 1959–. P. DICKINSON 'It's morphine she's been on?' said Pibble. But Tony shook her head. 'Just grass. Hash' (1972).

hasher noun US A waiter or waitress in a restaurant. 1916–. LISTENER When it came to making an impression on the 'hashers' in the railroad 'beaneries', the boomers really let themselves go (1960).

hash-joint noun US A cheap eating-place, boarding-house, etc. 1895–. J. DOS PASSOS Passing the same Chink hashjoint for the third time (1930). [From HASH¹ noun, dish of recooked meat.]

hash-mark noun US A military service stripe. 1909–. [Apparently from the notion that each stripe (representing a year's service) signifies a year's free 'hash' or food provided by the government.]

hash-slinger noun US, dated = HASHER noun. 1868–. AMERICAN SPEECH The cooks and 'hashslingers' of former years went off to war or to the shipyards (1946).

hash-up noun **1** derog Something concocted afresh from existing material; a reworking. 1895–. TIMES A style perilously close to certain Colour Supplement hash-ups and clearly aligned for Over-ground consumption (1970). **2** A hastily cooked meal. 1902–. [From *hash (up)* verb, to make a dish of recooked meat, to rework.]

hatch noun **down the hatch** (as a drinking toast) drink up, cheers! 1931–.

hatchet job noun A fierce verbal attack on someone, esp. in print. Also **hatchet work**. 1944–. GUARDIAN One critic was the meanest son of a bitch that ever lived. His criticism was a hatchet job on every book (1959).

hatchet man noun **1** A hired killer, orig spec. a hired Chinese assassin in the US. 1880–. P. FRANK He was a hatchet man for the NKVD.He may have delivered Beria over to Malenkov and Krushchev (1957). **2** Someone employed to carry out a hatchet job. 1952–. NEWS CHRONICLE The Kennedy family went into action with a commando team of political hatchetmen (1960).

hate noun Brit, dated In World War I, a bombardment. 1915–. D. REEMAN I'm going to turn in, Sub. I want a couple of hours before the night's hate gets going (1968). [From the German 'Hymn of Hate', which was ridiculed in *Punch* 24 February 1915, p. 150, in the caption of a cartoon, 'Study of a Prussian household having its morning hate'.]

hat-rack noun **1** A scraggy animal. 1935–. R. CAMPBELL One trick is to deprive a hatrack of an old horse of water, and let him have a good lick of salt (1957). **2** The head. 1942–. L. HAIRSTON If you spent half as much time tryin' to put something *inside* that worthless hat-rack as you did having your brains fried (1964). [In sense 1, from the resemblance of the protruding ribs and other bones to the pegs of a hat-rack.]

have verb trans. **1** To have sex with. 1594–. PRIVATE EYE He's had more sheilas than you've had spaghetti breakfasts (1970). **2** To cheat, deceive. 1805–. NEW YORKER You've just been had, dummy (1987). **3 to have** (someone) **on** orig dialect To deceive (someone) playfully; to pull someone's leg. 1867–. L. P. HARTLEY 'Of course,' said Dickie, when the boy had gone off with his *mancia*, whistling, 'he's having us on' (1951). **4 not having any** refusing assent. 1902–. A.L. ROWSE Lady Mary Hastings was thought of for promotion to the bed of Ivan the Terrible. She was not having any (1955). **5 to have it off** (or **away**) (**with**) Brit To have sex (with). 1937–. A. WILSON Having it off may make you feel very good but a diamond bracelet lasts for ever (1967). **6 to have it away** criminals' To escape from prison or custody. 1958–. T. PARKER After I'd had it away three times, they decided it was no use bothering with me in these open places (1969).

have-on noun A swindle, deception. 1931–. LISTENER Puns, tropes, polyglot have-ons,

Harvey Smith hash hasher hash-joint hash-up

batty new coinings (1967). [From *to have on* (see HAVE verb 3).]

hawk verb **to hawk one's mutton** derog Of a woman: to seek a lover, to solicit. 1937–. J. PATRICK They're aw cows hawkin' their mutton (1973). [From obs. slang *mutton* female genitals.]

haybag noun A woman, esp. an unattractive one. 1851–. SPECTATOR The weary certainty that one more stranger has paused to inspect her casually and to depart calling her a haybag (1967).

hay burner noun US and Austral dated jocular A horse. 1920–. [From the notion of hay as the horse's 'fuel'.]

haymaker noun A swinging blow or punch. 1912–. E. LATHEN Rising from a collision, he had thrown off his glove and landed a haymaker (1972). [From the resemblance to the swinging action of someone wielding a haymaking fork.]

head noun **1 off one's head** out of one's mind; crazy. Also **out of one's head.** 1825–. D. LEAVITT They'd sit at the table together . . . both of them secretly bored out of their heads (1989). **2 to do something (standing) on one's head** to do something easily. 1896–. J. M. WHITE The climb he wanted me to attempt was a simple one. At Cambridge I could have done it standing on my head (1968). **3** A drug addict, esp. one who habitually takes the stated drug. 1911–. OBSERVER You've been to the delicatessen, of course, that's where the acid-heads and pot-heads assemble (1966). Cf. ACID HEAD noun, HOPHEAD noun 1, POT-HEAD noun. **4 to give head** orig US to perform fellatio or cunnilingus. 1941–. **5 to do (someone's) head in** Brit to upset, annoy, or exasperate someone, to drive someone to distraction. 1989–. S. VICKERS Everyone started this 'no smoke without fire' stuff. I couldn't stand it—it really did my head in (2000).

head-banger noun **1** A young person shaking violently to the rhythm of pop music. 1979–. **2** A crazy or eccentric person. 1983–. OBSERVER In the European Parliament, they sit alone with a few Spanish and Danish head-bangers, while the main conservative grouping excludes them (1989).

head case noun mainly Brit A person who is mentally deranged; hence, someone whose behaviour is violent and unpredictable; = NUT-CASE noun. 1966–. J. KELMAN Wee Danny could pot a ball with a headcase at his back all ready to set about his skull with a hatchet if he missed (1983).

headless chicken noun A person who has lost composure. 1993–. SUN The players saw the tough side of Taylor as he let fly, accusing them of being headless chickens, of forgetting everything they had worked for and conceding a Sunday parks goal (1993). [From such phrases as *run around like a headless chicken*, from the notion of a decapitated chicken running around aimlessly without a brain to control its movements.]

head shop noun orig N Amer A shop selling paraphernalia associated with recreational drug use. 1967–.

head-shrinker noun orig US A psychiatrist. 1950–. NEW SCIENTIST Dr. Louis West . . . may eventually be taking the caviare out of headshrinkers' mouths with his development of the robot psychiatrist (1968). Cf. SHRINK noun.

heap noun **1** A slovenly woman. 1806–. J. FRAME I may be *forced* to [sell out], if that lazy heap doesn't help me (1957). **2** A battered old motor vehicle; hence, anything old and dilapidated. 1926–. C. F. BURKE You will be like a guy who paid no attention to his heap and it broke down in the traffic (1969).

heat noun **1** US A state of intoxication caused by alcohol or drugs; esp. in phr. *to have a heat on.* 1912–. **2** orig US **a** Intensive pressure or pursuit, e.g. by the police. 1928–. LISTENER The moment seemed opportune to 'turn the heat' on Turkey (1957). **b** A police officer; the police. 1937–. NEW YORKER Out the door comes this great big porcine member of the heat, all belts and bullets and pistols and keys (1969). **3** orig US = HEATER noun. 1929–. R. CHANDLER Then he leaned back . . . and held the Colt on his knee. 'Don't kid yourself I won't use this heat, if I have to' (1939).

heater noun orig US A gun. 1929–. P. G. WODEHOUSE And Dolly, drop the heater and leave that jewel case where it is, I don't want any unpleasantness (1972).

heave-ho noun orig US A snub or dismissal. 1944–. GUARDIAN Mr Heath's prices and income package was given the old heave-ho by . . . the TUC Economic Committee (1973). [From the earlier sense, sailors' cry when raising the anchor.]

heavy noun **1** Scottish A particular type of bitter beer. 1823–. INDEPENDENT Bob Sutherland swigs his fifth pint of 'heavy', knocks it back with a rum chaser (1991). adjective **2** orig in jazz and pop music, used in various senses to designate something profound, serious, etc.

hawk haybag hay burner haymaker head case

1937–. BLESH & JANIS *Victory Rag*, a 'heavy' number of great difficulty, went on the market in 1921 (1958); IT The Bournemouth drug squad (reputed to be one of the heaviest squads in the country) (1971).

heavy sugar noun US dated A large amount of money. 1926–. FLYNN'S Johns with heavy sugar (1928). [From obs. slang *sugar* noun, money.]

heebie-jeebies noun Also **heebies, heeby-jeebies**, etc. orig US **1** A state of nervous depression or anxiety. 1923–. J. FLEMING You've given me the heeby jeebies. . . . It'll be the end of me (1959). **2** dated A type of dance. 1926–7. [Origin unknown.]

heel noun orig US **1** criminals', dated A double-crosser, a sneak-thief. 1914–29. **2** A despicable person. 1932–. TIMES LITERARY SUPPLEMENT John Augustus Grimshawe was a heel about money and women. [Prob. from *heel* noun, back part of the foot.]

heeled adjective orig US **1** Equipped; armed, esp. with a revolver. 1866–. E. MCBAIN 'Were you heeled when they pulled you in?' . . . 'We didn't even have a water pistol between us' (1956). **2** Provided with money; now usu. preceded by *well*. 1880–. DAILY TELEGRAPH Though the million and a quarter left by his grandfather has been spread among a large family he is still well-heeled enough (1968). [From obs. US slang *heel* verb, to provide, arm.]

heifer noun derog A woman. 1835–. BLACK WORLD That heifer that been trying to get next to my man Lucky since the year one (1973). [From earlier sense, young cow, female calf.]

heifer dust noun dated Nonsense. 1927–41.

heifer paddock noun Austral A girls' school. 1835–. N. PULLIAM Basketball here is mainly an indoor game. Mostly it's just played in the heifer paddocks—oh, pardon me, I mean in the girls' schools (1955).

Heinie¹ /ˈhaɪnɪ/ noun Also **Heine, Hiney.** N Amer A German (soldier). 1904–. LISTENER It's not the Russians we should be congratulating . . . but the Heinies. Sure, we got Von Braun, but the Russians grabbed all the rest of the German rocket guys (1961). [From the German male personal name *Heinrich*.]

Heinie² /ˈhaɪnɪ/ noun Also **hiney.** US The backside, buttocks. 1922–. NEW YORKER I could tell how tight that girl's shorts were. I could see her heinie clear across the square (1985). [Perh. from *behind*, influenced by HEINIE¹ noun.]

heist /haɪst/ orig US. noun **1** A hold-up, a robbery. 1930–. E. TREVOR A heist was when you took a motor with the idea of doing a repaint and flogging it with a bent log-book you'd got from a breaker (1968). verb trans. **2** To hold up, rob. 1931–. PUNCH Six years ago Jim Tempest was one of a bunch of tearaways heisting cars round the North Circular (1965). [Representing a local US pronunciation of HOIST verb and noun.]

hell noun **1** Used in or as a curse or expression of impatience or irritation. 1596–. LANDFALL Why in hell didn't you get John to build it for you? (1968). **2: a** (or **the, one**) **hell of a** an extremely or excessively bad, great, loud, etc. 1776–. NEW YORKER His forehand is a hell of a weapon (1969). **3 hell on wheels** something or someone extremely troublesome or annoying. 1843–. S. CHALLIS You don't pull any imitation disease over the immigration doctors. Those guys are hell on wheels (1968). **4 to give** (a person) (or **get**) **hell** to give someone (or get) a hard time. 1851–. N. MARSH Gabriel would give me hell and we would both get rather angry with each other (1940). **5 what the hell?** what does it matter?, who cares? 1872–. R. LEHMANN As if she'd decided to say at last, 'Oh, what the hell! Let them rip' (1936). **6 to get the** (or **to**) **hell out** to leave quickly. *a.*1911–. P. G. WODEHOUSE You ought to be in bed. Get the hell out of here, Bodkin (1972). **7 hell's bells** an expression of anger or annoyance. Also **hell's teeth.** 1912–. M. HASTINGS Hell's bells! You talk and I'll spill the beans (1959). **8** Used in expressions such as *like hell* and *will I hell* to indicate strong disagreement. 1925–. H. MACINNES 'I've quite enjoyed it here.' Like hell I have, she added under her breath (1941); SUNDAY EXPRESS Am I dressed for ease and comfort? Am I *hell*? (1962). See also **merry hell** at MERRY adjective, **to play hell (with)** at PLAY verb. verb intr. **9 to hell around** derog To go around or live one's life at a fast pace; to racket around. 1897–. E. LATHEN 'If he did any helling around, it wasn't here,' the janitor continued (1969).

hella adverb N Amer Very, exceedingly; very impressively or extraordinarily. 1987–. ORANGE

heifer paddock
a girls' school

COUNTY REGISTER Come on! That's hella funny! (2001) [Perh. shortening of HELLUVA adjective.]

hellacious /heˈleɪʃəs/ adjective US Tremendous, formidable; terrific; hence, terrible, awful. 1942–. A. MAUPIN We were camped in this canyon, and there was this hellacious hailstorm which knocked down our tents (1987). [From *hell* noun + *-acious*; cf. BODACIOUS adjective.]

heller noun US A person who 'hells around'. 1895–. LISTENER Jack Harrick, the old hillbilly satyr or 'heller' (1959). [From HELL verb + *-er*.]

hell-hole noun A very unpleasant place. 1866–. J. B. PRIESTLEY Go and drudge in some hell-hole of an office (1945). [From earlier sense, the pit of hell.]

hellishing adjective and adverb mainly Austral and NZ Used as an intensive. Also **hellishun.** 1931–. E. MCGIRR I don't know that anybody . . . has any knowledge of how hellishing thorough we are (1968). [From *hellish* adjective and adverb.]

helluva adjective Representing a casual pronunciation of 'hell of a'. 1910–. TIMES It's very unfortunate looking like him: he must have a helluva life (1968).

hen-fruit noun dated, mainly US Eggs. 1854–1942.

hep adjective dated, orig US Variant of HIP adjective. 1908–. GUARDIAN Not even its bitterest critics could accuse the Labour party of being 'hep' (1960); CAPE TIMES Are you hep to what the Beatles are saying? (1970).

hep-cat noun dated, orig US An enthusiast for jazz, swing music, etc.; a hep person. Cf. HIP-CAT noun. 1938–. TIMES Mr. Louis Armstrong and his fellow hepcats (1961).

hepster noun dated, orig US = HIP-CAT noun 1938–. [From HEP adjective + *-ster*.] Cf. HIPSTER noun.

herbert noun Also **Herbert.** Brit Someone considered stupid or ridiculous. 1960–. T. BARLING A dozen baby-brained herberts looking to face me off just to say they squared up to Kosher Kramer before the cobbles came up a bit smartish (1986). [Arbitrary use of the male forename; cf. '*Erb*, wag, funny fellow (Edward Fraser & John Gibbons, *Soldier and Sailor Words and Phrases* 1925).]

her indoors noun Also **'er indoors.** Brit One's wife (or girlfriend); hence in extended use applied to any domineering woman. 1984–. BOARDROOM How many punters, one

wonders, soften the blow to 'her indoors' concerning the purchase of a new Corniche by also bringing home a snappy little Lotus in her favourite colour! (1989). [Popularized by the Thames television series *Minder* (1979–94).]

herring-choker noun 1 Canadian A native or inhabitant of the Maritime Provinces. 1899–. 2 US A Scandinavian. 1944–. [From their supposed predilection for herrings.]

hey Rube /ruːb/ noun N Amer A fight, dispute, orig between circus workers and the general public. 1935–. DAILY COLONIST (Victoria, British Columbia): There . . . could be a very interesting hey Rube between incumbent Frances Elford and Ald. Brian Smith (1973). [From a cry used by circus people; *Rube* short for the personal name *Reuben*, often applied in N Amer to a country bumpkin (see REUB noun).]

hick noun 1 now mainly US A country bumpkin; a provincial person. 1565–. J. HANSEN He was killed . . . . They just stopped playing him. As though we was such hicks we didn't know there's such a thing as tapes these days (1970). adjective 2 mainly US Unsophisticated, provincial. 1920–. LISTENER Telly was still rather a hick affair back in 1951 (1967). [Pet-form of the personal name *Richard*.]

hickey noun Also **hickie.** 1 mainly US A gadget. 1909–. ATLANTIC MONTHLY We have little hickeys beside our seats to regulate the amount of air admitted through a slot in each window (1932). Cf. DOOHICKEY noun. 2 US A pimple. 1934–. H. GOLD A woman is not just soul and hickie-squeezing (1956). 3 US A love-bite. 1956–. GOOD HOUSEKEEPING A recent letter . . . reports a case of catching herpes from a love bite or, as it's known in the USA, a hickey (1987). [Origin unknown.]

high adjective 1 Drunk; now esp. in phr. *as high as a kite*. 1627–. M. ALLINGHAM He . . . gave them a champagne lunch in a marquee . . . and held a sale. By then everyone was as high as a kite (a.1966). 2 Under the influence of drugs. 1932–. NEW SCIENTIST It is far safer to drive a car when high on marijuana than when drunk (1969). 3 US Highly interested in, keen *on*. 1942–. GUARDIAN 'I am not high on the Thieu brand of Government,' he [i.e. McGovern] said, noting that 40,000 people had been executed . . . by it (1972). noun 4 A euphoric state, esp. one induced by taking drugs. 1953–. TIMES The two cigarettes smoked by each subject were intended to produce a 'normal social cannabis high' (1969).

highball verb intr. and trans. US To go or drive at high speed. 1935–. SATURDAY EVENING POST Everyone else had highballed . . . out of there (1946). [From earlier sense, to signal a train driver to proceed, from *highball* noun, signal to proceed orig given by hoisting a ball.]

high-binder noun US A swindler, esp. a fraudulent politician. 1890–. WENTWORTH & FLEXNER The winter meeting of the grand inner circle of high-binders at Miami Beach (1952). [Cf. earlier senses, a rowdy, a member of a secret Chinese gang.]

high-five orig US. noun **1** A gesture of celebration or greeting in which two people slap each other's hands with arms extended above eye level. 1980–. verb intr. and trans. **2** To exchange or greet with high-fives. 1981–. [From *high* adjective + *five* noun (with reference to the five fingers of the hand).]

high-hat noun orig US A snob. 1923–. G. B. STERN That hot-tempered young high-hat (1931). [From earlier sense, top hat, from the notion that such hats are worn by snobbish or pretentious people.]

high-muck-a-muck noun Also **high-you-muck-a-muck**. N Amer A self-important person. 1856–. TIME Not all the Liberal high muckamucks were as warmly defended as Favreau (1965). [Apparently from Chinook Jargon *hiu* plenty + *mucka-muck* food.]

high-roller noun orig US A person who gambles large sums or spends freely. 1881–. [Prob. from the notion of rolling dice.]

hike verb trans. **1** To lift or convey forcibly or laboriously. 1867–. BLACKWOOD'S MAGAZINE We flitted across the road like ghosts in the moonlight, hiking our equipage, and deposited same at the door of a wooden inn (1927). **2** orig US To increase. 1904–. OBSERVER The Bank of England hiked its minimum lending rate . . . to 9 per cent (1973). noun **3** orig US An increase. 1931–. ECONOMIST A wave of spending at the end of last year in anticipation of hikes in indirect taxes (1966). [Origin uncertain; cf. earlier sense, to walk (vigorously).]

hill noun **a hill of beans** orig US A thing of little value. 1863–. D. H. LAWRENCE Saying my say and seeing other people sup it up doesn't amount to a hill o' beans, as far as I go (1926).

hincty adjective Also **hinkty**. US Conceited, snobbish, stuck-up. 1924–. C. HIMES All those hincty bitches fell on those whitey-babies like they were sugar candy (1969). [Origin uncertain; perh. from a clipped form of

handkerchief-head an Uncle Tom African-American.

hinky adjective Also **hinkey**. US orig African-American and police **1** mainly police Nervous, uneasy. 1956–. P. CORNWELL If the hairs turn out to be Chandonne's, then I'm gonna have to entertain the idea she let him stay out there, and that's why she got all hinky about it (2000). **2** Suspect, questionable; also, unreliable, not working properly. 1961–. C. WHITEHEAD Compass needles spin wildly, act hinky when asked to draw a bead on true north (2003). [Prob. a variant of HINCTY adjective.]

hip orig US. adjective **1** Fully informed or aware; often followed by *to.* 1904–. SPECTATOR Audiences there are hip to the latest gossip (1959). **2** Stylish, trendy. 1951–. V. FERDINAND We sometimes . . . go in for that kind of living thinking it's hip (1972). verb trans. **3** To make 'hip', to inform; often followed by *to.* 1932–. BLACK WORLD I had just about decided to find some way to hip her to contraceptives (1973). [Origin unknown.] Cf. HEP adjective, HIPPED adjective.

hip-cat noun orig US = HEP-CAT noun. 1944–.

hipe noun army A rifle. 1917–. N. SHUTE It was full of muckin' Jerries. All loosing off their hipes at Bert and me (1942). [Representing a pronunciation of *arms* in commands such as 'Slope arms!']

hipped adjective orig US Obsessed, infatuated; usu. followed by *on.* 1920–. SPECTATOR Betjeman is absolutely hipped on his subject (1962). [From HIP verb.]

hippie Also **hippy**. dated, orig US. noun **1** = HIPSTER noun. 1953–. D. WALLOP Man, I really get a bellyful of these would be hippies (1953). adjective **2** Characteristic of hipsters. 1959–. VILLAGE VOICE Imagine coming on so jaded, . . . so hippie, . . . and fed up (1959). [From HIP adjective + *-ie*; cf. later sense, person leading an unconventional life, taking hallucinogenic drugs, etc.]

hipster noun dated, orig US A person who is 'hip'; a hep-cat. 1941–. NEW STATESMAN The anthology is valuable for a speculative essay by Norman Mailer on 'beat' or hipster culture (1958). [From HIP adjective + *-ster.*] Cf. HEPSTER noun.

hit verb trans. **1 to hit the road** (US **trail**, dated **grit**): to leave. 1873–. CHRISTIAN SCIENCE MONITOR These two hit the road together, modern pilgrims making very little progress (1973). **2 to hit the booze, bottle, jug, pot** orig US To drink to excess. 1889–. LANDFALL Everyone knew he'd turn out a flop. . . . Hit the booze and got

hoity-toity

T.B. (1957). **3 to hit the hay** (or **sack**) orig US To go to bed. 1912–. A. MILLER Well, I don't know about you educated people, but us ignorant folks got to hit the sack (1961). **4 to hit** (a person) **up for** US and NZ To ask (someone) for. 1917–. M. J. BOSSE She hit me up for bread (1972). **5 to hit the bricks** US **a** To be set free, esp. from prison. 1931–. **b** To go on strike. 1946–. **6** orig US To give a narcotic drug to. 1953–. NEW YORK TIMES How did he become an addict? 'You mean, who hit me first? My friend, Johnny' (1970). **7** orig US To kill; to rob. 1955–. PUBLISHERS WEEKLY A professional killer who has 'hit' 38 victims (1973). noun **8** orig US A dose of a narcotic drug; the act of obtaining or giving such a dose. 1951–. SOUTHERLY Somebody hands me a joint and I take a hit and hand it to Marlene who takes a hit (1972). **9** orig US A killing; a robbery. 1970–. D. MACKENZIE I got scared and called the whole thing off. Someone else must have made the hit (1971).

hitch noun mainly US A period of service, e.g. in the armed forces. 1835–. LISTENER Newspapermen who did a hitch in Britain during the war (1959).

hitched adjective orig US Married; sometimes followed by *up*. 1857–. J. H. FULLARTON That's the fifth o the old gang to get hitched up in five months (1944).

hit list noun **1** A list of people to be killed. 1976–. **2** A list of targets against which some action is planned. 1977–. TIMES EDUCATIONAL SUPPLEMENT By the time talks resume . . . the Government's 'hit list' of rate-capped authorities in 1986 to 1987 would be published (1985).

hit-man noun A hired killer. 1970–. DAILY TELEGRAPH Bryant is alleged to have been a 'hit man' (assassin) for drug traffickers and to have carried out a 'contract' to kill Finley (1973).

ho noun orig US African-American **1** A prostitute. 1958–. **2** A sexually promiscuous woman; hence, more generally, a woman, spec. a man's sexual partner. 1964–. WIRE In the next verse . . . there was a lot of stuff about beating the shit out of your ho if she hasn't got a meal waiting for you when you get home (1995). [Representing a pronunciation of *whore*.]

ho bag noun N Amer derog A sexually promiscuous woman. 1989–. TORONTO STAR I was still a virgin. Regardless, as far as gossips at my school were concerned, I was a ho-bag (2004). [From HO noun + *bag* noun, perh. inspired by HOSEBAG noun.]

Hobson's choice noun Brit Rhyming slang for 'voice'. Also **Hobson's**. 1937–. NEW STATESMAN The landlady, Queenie Watts, throws her Hobsons . . . so hard that on a clear night you could hear it in Canning Town (1961).

hock mainly US. noun **1 in hock: a** In prison. 1860–. **b** In pawn. 1883–. **c** In debt. 1926–. COLLIER'S My cash was gone, and I was in hock for the next three years (1929). verb trans. **2** To pawn. 1878–. C. F. BURKE Then he went and he took everything he had—his automobile—and he hocked them (1969). [From Dutch *hok* hutch, prison, debt.]

hock-shop noun A pawnshop. 1871–. C. IRVING He had previously pawned one of the Matisse oils . . . to the Mont de Piété, the French national hockshop (1969).

hodad /ˈhəʊdæd/ noun derog, surfing A non-surfer who hangs around surfing beaches. 1962–. [Origin unknown.]

hoe verb intr. **to hoe in** Austral and NZ To begin a task energetically, esp. to eat eagerly. 1935–. I. L. IDRIESS The local cow . . . took a lick; fancied the salty taste and hoed in for breakfast (1939).

hog noun US A large, often old, car or motor-cycle. 1967–. P. L. CAVE Pulling away, he swung the hog round in a wide U-turn and went after Ethel (1971).

hogwash noun Nonsense, rubbish. 1712–. SPECTATOR The whole of the artistic world has been debauched by the hogwash of the do-it-yourself vogue (1965). [From earlier sense, kitchen swill, etc. for pigs.]

hoick verb trans. Also **hoik** To lift or convey forcibly or laboriously. 1898–. COUNTRY LIFE Is there anything conceivably related to the art of fly fishing in hoicking out trout that have had no chance to live a natural life? (1972) [Perh. a local variant of HIKE verb.]

hoist criminals'. verb trans. **1** To steal, rob. 1708–. COAST TO COAST **1961–2** 'I know where we can hoist a car,' Mick said. 'We'll carry the stuff in it' (1962). noun **2** Shoplifting. *a*.1790–. F. NORMAN My old woman's still out on the hoist now (1958). [From the earlier senses, housebreaking, to break into a house; from the notion of hoisting an accomplice up to a window for the purpose of breaking into a building.] Cf. HEIST noun and verb.

hoity-toity adjective Conceited, pretentious, snobbish. 1713–. SUNDAY TIMES She [i.e. Anne Diamond] wasn't the least bit hoity-toity. She was always having me back to her

hoke

place for a bit of cheese on toast (1993). [Cf. earlier obs. sense, frolicsome; ultimately a reduplication of obs. *hoit* to behave boisterously (of unknown origin).]

hoke verb trans. orig US To play (a part) in a hokey manner; often followed by *up*. 1935–. M. BABSON Just *try* it straight . . . it's a mistake to hoke it up (1971). [Back-formation from *hokum* noun, sentimental or melodramatic material in a play or film.]

hokey adjective Also **hokie, hoky.** orig US Sentimental, melodramatic, artificial. 1945–. ROLLING STONE A closing piece [on a record], 'Sometimes', is embarrassingly hokey (1971). [From HOKE verb or *hokum* noun + -*y*.]

hold verb intr. US To be in possession of drugs for sale. 1935–. R. RUSSELL He was holding, just as Red had said. Santa had the sweets (1961).

hole noun **1** The mouth, the anus, or the female external genitals. Cf. CAKE-HOLE noun. 1607–. I. & P. OPIE Habitual grumblers in London's East End receive the poetic injunction: 'Oo, shut yer moanin' 'ole' (1959); L. COHEN Don't give me this all diamond shit, shove it up your occult hole (1966). **2 to put** (a person) **in the hole** dated To defraud (a person). 1812–1926. J. BLACK I thought you put me in the hole for some coin, but I found out that the people lost just what you both said (1926). **3 like a hole in the head,** esp. in phr. *to need* (something) *like a hole in the head*: applied to something not wanted at all or something useless. 1951–. D. CREED He needed Petersen about as much as he needed a hole in the head (1971). verb **4 to hole up** orig US To take or go into hiding. 1875–. N. BLAKE I bet you Elmer's holed up in Harwich, or somewhere near it (1954). [In sense 3, cf. Yiddish *ich darf es vi a loch in kop*.]

holler verb intr. and trans., mainly US To shout. 1699–. TIMES When Colonel Aldrin jumped off the last step of the moon ladder . . . everyone in the Aldrin home was whooping and hollering (1969). [A variant of *hollo* to cry out, and related to *hallo*.]

hols noun pl., mainly Brit Holidays, esp. from school or college. 1905–. SUNDAY TIMES July and August tends to be the party season (our university hols and the Aussie winter) (1993). [Shortening.]

holy adjective Used in various trivial exclamations, e.g. *holy cow!, holy mackerel!, holy Moses!, holy shit!, holy smoke!* 1855–. J. WAINWRIGHT Holy cow! I forgot to

switch the bloody immersion heater off (1973).

holy Joe noun orig nautical **1** A clergyman. 1874–. **2** derog A pious person. 1889–. J. D. SALINGER They all have these Holy Joe voices when they start giving their sermons (1951).

holy Willie noun derog = HOLY JOE noun 2. 1916–. J. A. LEE The Holy Willies would throw a party. 'Come to our Sunday School?' (1934).

homeboy noun orig and mainly US A person from one's home town (orig African-American); hence, a friend, peer; a member of one's own gang or set. More generally, a member of a teenage gang, a street kid. Similarly **homegirl.** 1934–. FACE He's . . . cultivated a market in accessories for the Jags and Mercedes of the flashiest homeboys (1989). [Cf. the earlier senses, boy fond of staying at home, and one brought up in an orphanage or similar institution.]

homer noun Austral and NZ In World War II: a wound sufficiently serious to warrant repatriation. 1942–. R. BIELBY She's apples. Now you just lie back an' take it easy. Ya got a homer, mate, you arsey bastard (1977). Cf. BLIGHTY noun 2.

homework noun **1** US dated Petting, snogging. 1942. **2: a bit** (or **piece**) **of homework** a woman considered as sexually desirable, esp. a man's girlfriend. 1945–. J. SYMONS He produced a dog-eared snap of a girl in a bikini. 'How's that for a piece of homework?' (1968).

homey noun Also **homie.** NZ A British immigrant, esp. one newly arrived. 1927–. D. M. DAVIN An English accent. How hard it was to remember that it was as natural to a homey as your own accent was to you (1970). [From *home* noun + -*y*.]

homie noun orig and mainly African-American A person from one's home town or neighbourhood; a member of one's peer group or gang; also, a member of the hip-hop subculture. 1944–. LOS ANGELES TIMES Then one of them screamed, 'Homie, he ain't got a gun' (1985). [From *home* noun (as in HOMEBOY noun) + -*ie*.]

homo /ˈhəʊməʊ/ noun and adjective mainly derog (A) homosexual. 1929–. LISTENER Sally's breathless confession to Dr Dale about hubby being a homo must have caused many a benighted bigot's heart to stop (1967). [Abbreviation.]

hoke hokey hold hole holler hols holy holy Joe

honcho US. noun **1** A leader or manager, the person in charge, the boss. 1947–. NEW YORKER I was the first employee who was not one of the honchos (1973). verb trans. **2** To be in charge of, oversee. 1964–. [From Japanese *han'chō* group leader.]

honest Injun int orig US An assertion of the truth of what one says. 1876–. L. A. G. STRONG 'You've invented him.' 'Which I never, sir, . . . ' 'Honest Injun?' (1950). [Perh. from an assurance of good faith extracted from Native Americans; *Injun* representing a casual pronunciation of *Indian*.]

honey noun **1** orig US Anyone or anything good of its kind. 1888–. GLOBE & MAIL (Toronto): A real honey, automatic power steering, power brakes, radio (1968). **2** US Anyone or anything difficult, annoying, etc. 1934–. [From the earlier use as a term of endearment.]

honey-baby noun A sweetheart, darling; used as a term of endearment. Also **honey-bun, honey-bunch.** 1904–. R. TASHKENT I'm sorry, honeybun—sorry. Guess I'm a little upset (1969).

honey-bucket noun N Amer A container for excrement. 1931–. BEAVER (Winnipeg, Manitoba): A woman taxi driver tells me most houses have honey-buckets (1969).

honey-pot noun The external female sex organs. 1719–. G. GREER If a woman is food, her sex organ is for consumption also, in the form of *honey-pot* (1970).

honker noun A nose, esp. a large one. 1942–. R. PARK It's yer own fault for having such a God-forgotten honker [i.e. a large nose] (1948). [Prob. from the sound made by blowing the nose.]

honkers adjective Drunk. 1957–. C. WOOD Roll on Wednesday week and we'll all get honkers on champers (1970). [Origin unknown.]

Honkers noun Hong Kong. 1987–. GUARDIAN In describing . . . the attitudes of pink-faced young westerners in Hong Kong, he writes as follows. ' . . . They take these Cathay Pacific stewardesses (known in the local argot as LBFMs, little brown fucking machines) to the discotheques . . . ' Word of this broke in Honkers. Cathay Pacific, seething, politely turned the author away at the departure gate (1992). [From *Hong K(ong + -ers*, perh. subliminally influenced by HONKERS adjective.]

honky noun Also **honkey, honkie.** US Black English, derog A white person; white people collectively. 1967–. B. MALAMUD Mary forcefully

shoved him away. 'Split, honky, you smell' (1971). [Origin unknown.]

honky-tonk orig US noun **1** A tawdry drinking-saloon, dance-hall, or gambling-house; a cheap night-club. 1894–. W. FAULKNER Its master whose anonymous dust lay with that of his blood and of the progenitors of saxophone players in Harlem honky-tonks (1940). adjective **2** Associated with rag-time music or jazz of a type played in honky-tonks, esp. on the piano. 1933–. DRIVE Happy, beery men thumping honky-tonk pianos (1972). [Origin unknown.]

honyock noun = HUNYAK noun.

hooch noun Also **hootch.** orig and mainly N Amer Alcoholic liquor, esp. inferior or illicit whisky. 1897–. NEW YORKER The people of the city were prepared to swallow any old hootch under the rule of some wild thirst (1969). [Abbreviation of Alaskan *Hoochinoo* noun, name of a liquor-making tribe.]

hoochie¹ noun Also **hooch, hoochy, hootch.** military A shelter or dwelling, esp. one that is insubstantial or temporary. 1952–. FREMDSPRACHEN A stereo set was blaring in an enlisted men's hootch shortly after midnight (1971). [Perh. from Japanese *uchi* dwelling.]

hoochie² noun Also **hoochy** and, more fully, **hoochie mama.** orig African-American A young woman, esp. a promiscuous one or one who dresses or behaves in a sexually provocative way. 1989–. [Perh. from *hootchy-kootchy* noun, the name of an erotic dance similar to the belly dance, of unknown origin.]

hood¹ noun US A gangster or gunman. 1930–. P. G. WODEHOUSE The hood was beating the tar out of me (1966). [Abbreviation of *hoodlum* noun.]

hood² noun mainly US, esp. African-American A neighbourhood or community, usu. one's own; *esp.* an inner-city area inhabited predominantly by non-whites; esp. in phr. *boys* (or *boyz*) *in the hood* young men in such an area (popularized by the 1991 film *Boyz N the Hood*). 1969–. NEW YORK TIMES The boys in the 'hood are killing each other (1992). [Shortening of *neighbourhood* noun.]

hoodie noun Brit A hooded sweatshirt, fleece, or other garment; also, a young person wearing such as garment, esp. regarded as being potentially violent, criminal, or otherwise antisocial. 1990–. DAILY TELEGRAPH Members of this demographic wear the dodginess of their surroundings as a badge of

honcho   honest Injun   honey   honey-baby   honker

honour on their Marks & Spencer hoodies (2005). OBSERVER Until recently, Cameron wanted to hug hoodies; now he wants to string 'em up (2007). [From *hood* noun + *-ie*.]

hooey noun and int orig US Nonsense, rubbish. 1924–. G. GREER The horse between a girl's legs is supposed to be a giant penis. What hooey! (1970). [Origin unknown.] Cf. PHOOEY int, noun, and adjective.

hoof verb intr. orig US To dance; also with *it*. 1925–. A. GILBERT A pretty nifty dancer himself in his young days and still able to hoof it quite neatly (1958). Hence **hoofer,** noun A (professional) dancer. 1923–. SUNDAY EXPRESS She was impressed by one of the male dancers . . . . The one-time hoofer ended up by working for her for 40 years (1973).

hoo-ha noun Also hoo-hah, hou-ha. A commotion, a row; uproar, trouble. 1931–. COUNTRY LIFE Some of these lovely irises may . . . be grown . . . successfully without much hoo-ha (1971). [Origin unknown.]

hook noun **1 on one's own hook** on one's own account. 1812–. F. YERBY I'm not going out of this house with you on my own hook (1952). **2 off the hooks** dated Dead. 1840–. J. GALSWORTHY Old Timothy; he might go off the hooks at any moment. I suppose he's made his Will (1921). **3** A thief, a pickpocket. 1863–. G. J. BARRETT We've nothing on him. But then we've nothing on half the hooks in Eastport (1968). **4 to get one's hooks on** or **into** to get hold of. 1926–. J. POTTS Maybe he's eloped with that fat Lang dame. She's been trying to get her hooks into him all winter (1954). verb **5 to hook it** to make off, run away. 1851–. X. HERBERT Pack your traps and get ready to hook it first thing mornin' time (1939). **6** intr. To work as a prostitute. 1959–. DISCH & SLADEK Bessie's girls didn't have to go out hooking in hotel lobbies or honkytonks, no indeedy (1969). [In sense 6, back-formation from HOOKER noun.] See also HOOKED adjective, *to sling one's hook* at SLING verb.

hooked adjective Captivated, addicted; usu. followed by *on*. 1925–. DAILY TELEGRAPH Hundreds of domestic pets die each year after becoming 'hooked' on slug bait (1970).

hooker noun A prostitute. 1845–. J. DOS PASSOS Ain't you got the sense to tell a good girl from a hooker? (1932).

hook-shop noun A brothel. 1889–. J. STEINBECK This kid could be pure murder in a hook-shop (1954).

hooky adjective Brit Illegally acquired or produced; stolen or counterfeit. 1985–. GUARDIAN Does a fake Renoir matter any more than a hooky Rolex? (1996) [Prob. from *hook* adjective (from the notion of not being straight— cf. *bent, crooked*) + *-y*; cf. obs. *hooky-crooky*.]

hoon noun Austral A lout, a rough; a crazy person; a ponce. 1938–. R. BEILBY That bastard ran ya down, the bloody hoon! (1977). [Origin unknown.]

hoople noun US A foolish person, an idiot. 1928–. [Perh. from Major *Hoople*, the name of a US cartoon character created *c*.1923 by Gene Ahern.]

> 'Until recently, Cameron wanted to hug hoodies; now he wants to string 'em up.'

hooptie noun US orig African-American A car, esp. an old or dilapidated one. 1968–. SIERRA You'd do better keeping your mid-1980s hooptie on the road (1997). [Origin unknown.]

hooray int Austral and NZ Goodbye. 1898–. NEW ZEALAND LISTENER Best of luck on the lake. Hooray! (1965) [From earlier use as an exclamation of pleasure.]

Hooray Henry noun Brit, derog A loud, rich, rather ineffectual or foolish young society man; now spec. a fashionable, extroverted, but conventional upper-class young man. Also **Hooray.** 1936–. BARR & YORK Hooray Henrys are the tip of the Sloane iceberg, visible and audible for miles (1982); EXPRESSION! A blanket or rug is also a good idea (tartans for hoorays; kilims for aesthetes) (1986). [From *hooray* int + *Henry* man's personal name.]

hooroo int = HURROO int.

hoosegow /huːsgaʊ/ noun US A prison. 1911–. D. RAMSAY I'm not going to answer any questions. . . . Okay. Off we go to the hoosegow (1973). [From American Spanish *juzgao*, Spanish *juzgado* tribunal, from Latin *judicatum*, neuter past participle of *judicare* to judge.]

hoosh noun dated A kind of thick soup. 1905–22. [Origin unknown.]

hoosier noun US An unsophisticated person from a remote place. 1836–.

horse

[From earlier sense, inhabitant of Indiana; ultimate origin uncertain.]

hoot¹ noun NZ Money, esp. orig as paid in recompense. Also **hootoo, hout, hutu,** etc. 1820–. K. GILES I got the idea of starting a chain of those places . . . for blokes without much hoot and wanting a clean bed (1967). [From Maori *utu* recompense.]

hoot² noun Anything at all. Also **two hoots.** 1878–. LISTENER Winston Churchill was idiosyncratic in that he did not care a hoot about being thought a gentleman (1966). [Prob. the same word as *hoot* loud exclamation; cf. obs. US slang *hooter* noun, anything at all.]

hootch variant of HOOCH noun.

hooter noun The nose. 1958–. TIMES Derek Griffiths is a young coloured comedian with a face like crushed rubber . . . and a hooter to rival Cyrano de Bergerac (1972). [Prob. from the sound made by blowing the nose.]

hop verb **1 to hop the twig** (or **stick**): **a** To die. 1797–. **b** To depart suddenly. 1828–. P. MCCUTCHEON You've not asked yourself why he hopped the twig. . . . Did a disappearing act (1986). **2 to hop it** Brit To go away quickly, get lost. 1914–. T. S. ELIOT The commission bloke on the door looks at us and says: ''op it!' (1934).

hop noun **1** US A narcotic drug; spec. opium. 1887–. US SENATE HEARINGS Opium in the underworld is referred to [as] . . . 'hop' (1955). **2** mainly Austral and NZ Beer; usu. in pl. 1929–. J. HIBBERD I was in a sad state . . . all psychological . . . the hops were having their desired effect (1972). [From the earlier sense, climbing plant used for flavouring beer.]

Hop noun Austral A policeman. 1916–. BULLETIN (Sydney): The Hops were taking the shattered body out of the water (1933). [Abbreviation of JOHN HOP noun.]

hophead noun **1** US A drug addict. 1911–. H. NIELSEN I'll mail the letter to that hophead lawyer (1973). **2** Austral and NZ A drunkard. 1942–. E. NORTH Rat-hole shelters for the plonk merchants and hopheads (1960). [In sense 1, from HOP noun 1 + HEAD noun 3; in sense 2, from HOP noun 2.]

hop-over noun army, dated mainly Austral An assault. 1918–. E. PARTRIDGE In the hop-over, many hoped for and some got a wound sufficiently serious to cause them to be sent 'home' (1933). [From the notion of 'hopping' over the parapet of a trench to make an assault.]

hopped-up adjective US **1** Excited, enthusiastic. 1923–. 'I. DRUMMOND' A hopped-up son with anarchist-pacifist connections (1973). **2** Under the influence of a narcotic drug. Also **hopped.** 1924–. GUARDIAN Chuck Berry don't drink either but he gets hopped (1973). **3** Of a motor vehicle: having its engine altered to give improved performance; souped-up. 1945–. ISLANDER (Victoria, British Columbia): At the urge of the hopped-up motor in seconds they were tearing up Nanaimo Street (1971). [From HOP noun 1.]

hoppy US. noun **1** An opium addict. 1922–. B. HECHT A lush, a prosty, a hoppy, and a pain in the neck, say the police (1941). adjective **2** Of or characterized by drug-taking. 1942–. MEZZROW & WOLFE Detroit is really a hoppy town—people must order their opium along with their groceries (1946). [From HOP noun 1.]

hop toy noun US, dated A container used for smoking opium. 1881–1955. [From HOP noun 1.]

horn noun **1** An erect penis; an erection. 1785–. GUARDIAN Dirty old goat. . . . He only bows his head to get his horn up (1972). **2** jazz **a** A trumpet. 1935–. G. AVAKIAN Each of these trio cuttings ends with Bix picking up his horn to play the coda (1959). **b** Any wind instrument. 1937–. CRESCENDO If I'm happy with the horn I've got, the mouthpiece, the set-up, the reed and everything (1966). verb intr. **3 to horn in** orig US To intrude or interfere. 1912–. AIRMAN'S GAZETTE The lesson for today chicks is how to horn in on the radio racket (1939).

horn-mad adjective = HORNY adjective. 1893–. R. CAMPBELL The evil-minded and horn-mad levantine (1951). [From HORN noun 1.]

hornswoggle verb trans. orig US To cheat, hoax. 1829–. SUNDAY TIMES The Americans look for value; you can't . . . hornswoggle them (1970). [Origin unknown.]

horny noun **1** Also **horney.** dated A policeman. 1753–1922. **2** Austral A bullock. 1901–. C. D. MILLS Nugget gave me a spell after smoke-oh, and I went to the crush to deal with the 'hornies' (1976). adjective **3** Sexually excited, lecherous. 1889–. BLACK WORLD Ain't that the horny bitch that was grindin with the blind dude (1971). [In sense 2, from Scottish dialect *horny* noun, cow; in sense 3, from HORN noun 1.]

horse noun orig US Heroin. 1950–. DAILY TELEGRAPH He had seen the effects of an overdose of 'horse' before (1969). [Perh. from the

hoot   hootch   hooter   hop   hophead   hop-over   horn

shared initial and the horse's power.] Cf.
H noun.

horse feathers noun US Nonsense,
rubbish. 1928–. J. GARDNER Mostyn pointed out
that . . . they could court-martial him *in
camera* . . . . On reflection, Boysie realised that
this was all a load of horse feathers (1967).
[From the incongruity of the notion of
a horse having feathers.]

horse opera noun orig US A 'Western'
film or television series. 1927–. [From the
prominent role of horses in such
productions.]

horse shit noun US Nonsense, rubbish.
1955–. IT 'This is definitely the weekend of
the big bust!' 'Horseshit! You've said the
same thing for the past six weekends!' (1970).
Cf. BULLSHIT noun.

hosebag noun US derog A sexually
promiscuous woman. 1974–. J. GRISHAM What
about that hosebag who ditched you? What's
her name? . . . Yeah, Vicki. I hated that bitch
even at your wedding (2002).

hoser noun Canadian A stupid,
unsophisticated, or loutish person, esp. one
regarded as typically Canadian. 1981–. [Perh.
from *hose* noun.]

hostie noun Austral A female flight
attendant; a stewardess, air hostess. 1960–.
SYDNEY MORNING HERALD The hosties . . . are not
concerned about Qantas picking up passengers
here and there (1981). [Shortened from *air
hostess*.]

hot adjective **1** Full of sexual desire, lustful.
1500–. W. HANLEY 'I'm hot as a firecracker is what
I am,' she said demurely (1971). Cf. HOT PANTS
noun. **2a** Of goods: stolen, esp. easily
identifiable and therefore difficult to dispose
of. 1925–. H. L. LAWRENCE You come here, in a hot
car . . . . And the police know (1960). **b** Of a
person: wanted by the police. 1931–. P. MOYES
Griselda was 'hot'. Griselda had to disappear
(1973). **3 hot to trot** orig US A ready and
willing, eager, esp. for sexual activity. 1950–.
WASHINGTON POST We're supposed to respect
Valerie because she isn't quite as hot to trot as
her homely friend Thelma (1978). **b** very keen
or enthusiastic. 1980–. CANADIAN BUSINESS Right
now, everybody is hot to trot on small-
capitalization stocks (1995). noun **4 the hots** orig
US Strong sexual desire. 1947–. TIMES LITERARY
SUPPLEMENT It is Blodgett who has the hots for
Smackenfelt's mother-in-law (1973).

hot bed noun US A bed in a flop-house
which is used continuously by different

people throughout the day; also, a flop-house
containing such beds. 1945–.

hot beef int Brit, dated Rhyming slang for
'Stop thief!' 1879–. G. BUTLER 'Hot beef, hot
beef,' cried the schoolboys. 'Catch him . . . '
(1973).

hotcha adjective mainly US Of jazz or swing
music: having a strong beat and a high
emotional charge. 1937–. C. RAY There
are hotcha gramophone records (1960).
[Cf. earlier use, in combination with
the traditional interjection *hey nonny
nonny* (1932–); orig a fanciful extension of *hot*
adjective.]

hot diggety dog int US Also **hot
diggety.** = HOT DOG int. 1924–. M. R. RINEHART Hot
diggety dog! Ain't that something! (1952).

hot dog noun **1** N Amer A highly skilled
person, esp. one who is boastful or flashy.
1900–. HOCKEY NEWS (Montreal): Critics label him a
'hot dog' and a 'show-off' and several
unprintable things (1974). **2** surfing A type
of small surfboard. 1963–. int **3** US Expressing
delight or strong approval. 1906–. T. RATTIGAN
Hot dog! There's some Scotch (1944).

hot pants noun US **1 to have** (or **get**) **hot
pants** to be (or become) aroused with sexual
desire. 1927–. S. PRICE You've got the hot-pants
for some good-looking piece (1961). **2** A highly
sexed (young) woman. 1966–. K. AMIS It would
help to hold off little hot-pants, and might
distract him from the thought of what he was so
very soon going to be doing to her (1968).

hot pot noun Austral A horse strongly
fancied or backed to win a race. 1904–.
SPORTING GLOBE (Melbourne): A southern 'hot-
pot'—Lord Setay—dismally let his supporters
down at Albion Park last Saturday night (1969).

hot rod noun orig US Also **rod. 1** A motor
vehicle modified to have extra power
and speed. 1945–. **2** = HOT RODDER noun.
1959–. Hence **hot-rodding,** noun Racing such
vehicles. 1949–.

hot rodder noun orig US The driver of
a hot rod; = RODDER noun. 1949–.

hot seat noun US The electric chair. Also
hot chair, hot squat. 1925–. R. CHANDLER That
scene at the end where the girl visits him in the
condemned cell a few hours before he gets the
hot squat! (1952).

hot-shot noun **1** orig US An important or
exceptionally able person. 1933–. J. HELLER How
about getting us a hotel-room if you're such a

hotshot (1961). **2** US A dose of poison given to a drug addict in place of a drug. 1953–.

hot-stuff verb trans. army, dated To scrounge, steal. 1914–50. [Prob. from *hot stuff* stolen goods (cf. HOT adjective 2a).]

hotsy-totsy adjective orig US Comfortable, satisfactory, just right. 1926–. J. MANN What the law allows me, is mine . . . . So that's all hotsy totsy (1973). [Apparently coined by Billie De Beck, US cartoonist.]

hottie noun Also **hotty.** orig US A sexually attractive person. 1987–. NEWWITCH She has two extremely smart daughters and a very open-minded hottie of a husband (2003). [From HOT adjective + -ie.]

hotting noun Brit Joyriding in stolen, high-performance cars, esp. dangerously and for display. Also **hotter,** noun One who engages in 'hotting'. 1991–. OBSERVER What started as a campaign against 'hotting'— displays of high-speed handbrake turns in stolen cars—has turned into a dispute over territory (1991). [From HOT adjective 2a, perh. reinforced by HOT-WIRE verb.]

hot-wire verb trans. N Amer To bypass the ignition system of (a motor vehicle) as a preliminary to stealing the vehicle. 1966–.

house noun **in the house** orig US, esp. rappers' excellent, wonderful; fashionable; COOL 3. 1989–.

houseman noun US dated A burglar. 1904–24.

House of Lords noun Brit, euphemistic or jocular A lavatory. 1961–. LISTENER When you need the House of Lords, it's through there (1967).

how's your father noun Brit jocular, euphemistic. Sexual intercourse. 1983–. Q 'The Princess and The Pea Brain', as one paper 'dubbed' them, usurped Hugh Grant and Devine Brown as the premier concern of the nation's gossipmongers. Naturally, both parties strenuously denied any how's-your-father (1996). [From earlier more general use as a word for something unnamed or whose name has been forgotten.]

hubba-hubba int US Used to express approval, excitement, or enthusiasm. Also as noun, **nonsense, ballyhoo.** Also **haba-haba.** 1944–. S. STERLING I suppose you think that's a lot of hubba-hubba (1946). [Origin unknown.]

huff verb trans. military, dated To kill. 1919–33.

Hughie noun Austral and NZ The 'god' of weather, esp. in phr. *send her down, Hughie!* 1912–. K. S. PRICHARD Miners and prospectors would turn out and yell to a dull, dirty sky clouded with red dust: 'Send her down! Send her down, Hughie!' (1946). [Diminutive of the male personal name *Hugh*.]

hum[1] verb intr. and noun (To make) a bad smell. 1902–. DAILY TELEGRAPH When the wind drops this stuff really hums (1970).

hum[2] Austral verb trans. and intr. **1** To cadge, scrounge. 1913–. X. HERBERT Gertch—you old blowbag! You're only humming for a drink. Nick off home (1938). noun **2** A cadger, scrounger. 1915–. WHITE & HALLIWELL Two professional hums . . . took an oath at Bendigo no more work they would do (1983). [Short for *humbug* verb and noun.]

humdinger noun orig US An excellent or remarkable person or thing. 1905–. TIMES The last set was a humdinger, to use a transatlantic expression (1958). [Origin unknown.]

hummer noun mainly US **1** = HUMDINGER noun. 1907–. N. SCANLAN When the new car was swung out on to the wharf, Mike walked round it and touched it lovingly. 'She's a hummer, Dad' (1934). **2** False or mistaken arrest. 1932–.

humongous /hjuːˈmɒŋɡəs, -ˈmʌŋ-/ adjective Also **humungous.** orig US Extremely large, huge. 1970–. SUNDAY TIMES His wife went the whole hog and ordered a 'combo Mexicano' ('for those with a humongous appetite') which consisted of a chicken taco, a beef enchilada and a cheese enchilada (1992). [Origin uncertain; perh. based on *huge* and *monstrous*.]

hump noun **1** Brit A fit of annoyance or depression; now always preceded by *the*. 1727–. T. S. ELIOT You seem to be wanting to give us all the hump. I must say, this isn't cheerful for Amy's birthday (1939). **2 to get a hump on** US To hurry. 1892–. W. E. WILSON 'Let's git a hump on, Allen,' Abe said; and the two boys dipped their oars deeper into the brown water (1940). **3** Sexual intercourse; also, a woman considered for her part in sexual intercourse. 1931–. P. ROTH Now you want to treat me as if I'm nothing but some hump (1969). **4** Austral A camel. 1935–. D. STUART I see old Dotty Stanley once . . . with a pair o' camels; it was the first time he'd ever had humps, an' he wasn't too sure of 'em (1978). verb **5** trans. and intr. To have sex (with). 1785–. M. BRADBURY Story is he humped the faculty wives in alphabetical order (1965). **6** refl dated, orig and mainly US To exert oneself, make an effort. 1835–. SAPPER That

hot-stuff hotsy-totsy hottie hotting hot-wire huff

finger will connect with the trigger and the result will connect with you. So, hump yourself (1928). **7 to hump one's swag (bluey, drum, knot, Matilda)** Austral To travel on foot carrying a bundle of possessions, esp. on one's back. 1851–. B. NORMAN He was unable to get a lift home so he decided to hump his bluey the sixty miles to the mission (1976).

Hun noun **1** derog A German, esp. a German soldier of World War I. 1902–. TIMES 'Supposed' statements . . . of American 'advisers' . . . simply smell of Hun propaganda (1918). **2** Air Force A flying cadet during World War I. 1916–25. E. M. ROBERTS Every pilot is a Hun until he has received his wings (1918). [In sense 1, from the earlier sense, member of a warlike Asian tribe; the application was inspired by a speech delivered by Wilhelm II to German troops about to leave for China on 27 July 1900, exhorting them to be as fierce as Huns.]

hung adjective Suffering the after-effects of drinking alcohol (or taking drugs); hung-over. 1958–. H. SLESAR I know you're hung, Mr. Drew (1963). [Prob. short for *hung-over* adjective.] See also HUNG UP adjective, WELL-HUNG adjective.

hung up adjective **1** Confused, bewildered, mixed-up. 1945–. B. MALAMUD He was more than a little hung up, stupid from lack of sleep, worried about his work (1971). **2** Obsessed, preoccupied; followed by *on*. 1957–. NEW SCIENTIST Roszak is very hung up on the power that science grants (1971). [Perh. from verbal phr. *to hang up* to delay, detain.] Cf. HANG-UP noun.

hunk adjective **to get hunk (with)** US To get even (with). 1845–. BOSTON GLOBE Suppose I show you how to get hunk with the cheapskates? (1949). [From earlier sense, safe, all right, from noun, goal or home in children's games, from Dutch *honk* noun.]

hunk¹ noun N Amer, derog An immigrant to the United States from east-central Europe. Also **hunkey, hunkie, hunky.** 1896–. MACLEAN'S MAGAZINE I don't know if I should get mad if someone insults the Irish, or makes cracks about Polacks or Hunkies (1971). [Cf. BOHUNK noun.]

hunk² noun orig US A sexually attractive man. 1968–. MANDY I'm not losing my chance with a hunk like Douglas, for any boring old vow (1989). [From earlier sense, very large person.]

hunky¹ adjective US dated = HUNKY-DORY adjective. 1861–1926. BULLETIN I'll be all hunky.

Nurse Dainton tends me like I was made of glass (1926). [From *hunk* adjective, safe, all right (see HUNK adjective) + -*y*.]

hunky² adjective orig US Of a man: ruggedly handsome and sexually attractive; virile. 1978–. SUN Sheer escapism for all the family with hunky Harrison Ford (1986). [From HUNK² noun + -*y*.]

hunky-dory adjective Also **hunky-dorey.** mainly US Excellent, fine. 1866–. J. GARDNER Everythink's 'unky dorey' ere. No problem (1969). [From HUNKY adjective + unknown second element.]

hunyak noun Also **honyock** US derog An immigrant to the United States from east-central Europe. 1911–. P. FRANK She cooked a Hungarian goulash better than any he'd tasted at a hunyak table (1957). [Alteration of *Hungarian* based on POLACK noun.]

hurroo int Also **hooroo.** Austral and NZ Goodbye. 1906–. COAST TO COAST 1967–68 The others have, one by one, . . . lurched off— 'Hooroo!' 'Seeya, mate!' (1969) [Alteration of HOORAY int.]

hustle verb **1** trans. **a** US To obtain by forceful action; sometimes followed by *up*. 1840–. W. BURROUGHS 'Do you want to score?' he asked. 'I'm due to score in a few minutes. I've been trying to hustle the dough' (1953). **b** N Amer To sell or serve (goods, etc.), esp. in an aggressive, pushing manner. Also, to swindle. 1887–. BLACK WORLD He hustled the watch to a barber for 35 bills (1973). **2** intr. orig US To engage in prostitution. 1930–. LISTENER She . . . revolted in revenge against her family, 'hustled' in Piccadilly, hated men as clients, took a ponce (1959). Cf. HUSTLER noun 3. noun **3** orig US A swindle, racket; a source of income. 1963–. MALCOLM X Each of the military services had their civilian-dress eyes and ears picking up anything of interest to them, such as hustles being used to avoid the draft . . . or hustles that were being worked on servicemen (1965).

hustler noun **1** A person who lives by stealing or other dishonest means; a thief, pimp, etc. 1825–. C. MACINNES They's wreckage of jazz musicians . . . , ponces, and other hustlers like myself. . . . I pimp around the town, picking the pounds up where I can (1957). **2** orig US An aggressively active or enterprising person. 1882–. BLACK WORLD He pulls in £1,500 some weeks, and he's a *small-time* hustler (1971). **3** A prostitute. 1924–. J. STEINBECK They would think she was just a buzzed old hustler (1952). [From HUSTLE verb + -*er*.]

Hun hung hung up hunk hunky-dory hunyak

Hymie noun Also **hymie**. US, derog and offensive A Jew. 1984–. T. WOLFE Yo, Goldberg! You, Goldberg! You, Hymie! (1987). [Pet-form of *Hyman*, anglicization of the popular Jewish male forename *Chaim*.]

hype¹ orig US. noun Also **hyp**. **1** A drug-addict. 1924–. J. WAMBAUGH They were dumb strung-out hypes (1972). **2** A hypodermic needle or injection. 1929–. verb trans. **3** To stimulate (as if) by an injection of drugs; usu. followed by *up*; usu. as past participial adjective 1938–. TIME As he works, Mitchell has at times been so hyped up that Martha once asked his doctor to prescribe medication to slow him down (1973). [Abbreviation of *hypodermic*.]

hype² orig US. noun **1** dated An instance of short-changing, esp. done on purpose to deceive; someone who does this. 1926–. **2** Cheating; a trick. 1962–. L. SANDERS He's been on the con or hustling his ass or pulling paper hypes (1970). **3** Extravagant or intensive publicity promotion. 1967–. LISTENER All the 'hype' and conning that goes into the establishment of every star (1969). verb trans. **4** To short-change, to cheat. 1926–. **5** To promote with extravagant publicity. 1968–. LISTENER Bogus alternatives are hyped into prominence and fortune with appalling ease (1971). [Origin unknown.]

hyper adjective orig and mainly US Extraordinarily active or energetic; excitable, highly-strung. 1942–. DIRT BIKE Andre Malherbe never hopped from sponsor to sponsor like a hyper bumblebee in search of a bit more honey (1985). [Abbreviation of *hyperactive* adjective.]

hypo orig US. noun **1** = HYPE¹ noun. 1904–. J. WAINWRIGHT The night medic . . . held the loaded hypo (1973). verb intr. and trans. **2** To administer a hypodermic injection (to). 1925–. TIME Because of continuing hypo-ing, his arms and legs become abscessed (1960). [Abbreviation of *hypodermic*.]

hurroo hustle hustler Hymie hype hyper hypo

Ii

I am noun derog A (self-)important person. 1926–. N. GULBENKIAN Cyril Radcliffe . . . did not take the short-cut favoured by so many of his colleagues who say . . . : 'I am the great I am, Queen's Counsel' (1965). [From the earlier sense, the Lord Jehovah, from Exodus iii. 14 'And God said unto Moses, I am that I am: And he said, Thus shalt thou say unto the children of Israel, I AM hath sent me unto you'.]

ice noun 1 orig US Diamonds; jewellery. 1906–. H. HOWARD Prager caught sight of five hundred grand in cracked ice (1972). 2 US Profit from the illegal sale of theatre, cinema, etc., tickets. 1927–. ECONOMIST Kick-backs—'ice' as it is called on Broadway —on theatre tickets whose prices are marked up illegally (1964). 3 Protection money. 1948–. ECONOMIST Gross . . . who had confessed to paying this sum in 'ice' for the protection that made it possible for him to earn $100,000 a year (1951). 4 A crystalline form of the drug methamphetamine or 'speed', inhaled or smoked (illegally) as a stimulant. 1989–. COURIER-MAIL (Brisbane): Once ice was something one simply dropped into drinks. Now it could be the latest and most dangerous designer drug being smoked in salons from Beverly Hills to Bronx ghettoes (1989). verb trans. 5 US To kill. 1969–. GUARDIAN A would-be assassin who considers it his mission to 'ice the fascist pig police' (1973). [In sense 4, from the drug's colourless, crystalline appearance (like crushed ice) during the manufacturing process.]

ick int (and noun) orig US An exclamation of distaste, disgust, horror, etc; 'yuck'. 1948–. J. IRVING Blood, people leaking stuff out of their bodies—ick (1985). [Back-formation from ICKY adjective.]

icky Also **ikky.** adjective 1 US, jazz Ignorant (of true swinging jazz and liking the 'sweet' kind). 1935–. 2 Sweet, sickly, sentimental; hence a general term of disapproval: nasty,

repulsive, sticky, etc.; also, ill, sick. 1939–. H. HUNTER She wears the most *fright*-ful cardigans. Always some sort of *ikky* colour—to go with everything, I suppose (1967); M. WOODHOUSE / showed *him* . . . lots of gore, you know, and he went all green and icky and dashed off (1972). noun 3 US, jazz A person who is ignorant of true swinging jazz and likes the 'sweet' kind. 1937–. [Origin uncertain; perh. a baby-talk alteration of *sticky* or *sickly*.]

icky-boo adjective Ill. Also **icky-poo.** 1920–. B. MATHER Call the airline office . . . and tell 'em you're feeling an icksy bit icky-boo and want a stopover (1970). [Prob. a fanciful extension of ICKY adjective.]

idiot board noun A board displaying a television script to a speaker. Also **idiot card, idiot sheet.** 1952–.

idiot box noun derog A television set. 1959–. P. FLOWER I thought you spent all your time with the idiot box (1972). Cf. GOGGLE-BOX noun.

idiot stick noun US A shovel. 1942–.

iffy adjective orig US Uncertain, doubtful. 1937–. E. FENWICK We knew this was rather an iffy tenant, morally speaking, before we rented (1971). [From *if* conj + *-y*.]

ikey /ˈaɪkɪ/ Also **ike, iky.** derog and offensive, dated. noun 1 A Jew. 1835–. 2 A (Jewish) receiver or moneylender. 1864–. 3 A tip, information. 1936–. adjective 4 Having a good opinion of oneself, stuck-up. 1887–. T. PRENTIS Sez as I'm as ikey as the Dook of Boocle-oo (1927). 5 Artful, crafty. 1889–. verb trans. 6 US To lower (a price) by haggling; to cheat. 1932–. [Abbreviated form of the male personal name *Isaac*.]

ikeymo /ˈaɪkɪmoʊ/ noun derog and offensive, dated. = IKEY noun 1,2. 1922–. J. SYMONS I'm a Hackney Jew, Dave. At school they called us Ikeymoes and Jewboys (1954). [From IKEY noun + *Mo*(ses).]

illegit noun An illegitimate child. 1913–. C. CARNAC Somerset House . . . registers the illegits . . . as carefully as the rest (1958). [Abbreviation of *illegitimate*.]

illywhacker noun Austral A professional trickster. 1941–. [Origin unknown.]

imbo noun Austral A gullible person, esp. the victim of a criminal. 1953–. [From *imb*(*ecile* + *-o*.]

impot noun schoolchildren's dated, mainly Brit A task assigned as a punishment. 1899–.

I am ice ick icky icky-boo idiot board idiot box

R. MASSEY Mr Luce succeeded in ruining our handwriting. He used to hand out 'impositions' by handfuls. These 'impots' were enormous multiplication sums, ten figures by ten figures, or fifty or a hundred lines. They would be done after school hours (1976). [Shortening of *imposition*.]

imshi int Also **imshee, imshy.** services' Go away! 1916–. [From colloquial (Egyptian) Arabic *imshi*.] Imshee and what not (1966).

in noun 1 orig US An introduction to someone of power, fame, or authority; influence with such a person. 1929–. J. B. PRIESTLEY I have an *in* with a couple of the directors (1966). adjective 2 Fashionable, sophisticated. 1960–. O. NORTON It *is* the in place. You'd be surprised who you meet there (1970).

Indian hay noun US Marijuana. 1939–.

indie noun orig US An independent theatre, film, or record company. 1942–. [Abbreviation of *independent*.]

info noun Abbreviation of 'information'. 1913–. NEW SCIENTIST (heading): Generating info for schools (1971).

inked adjective Austral Drunk. 1898–. P. ADAM SMITH Driver found well and truly inked and lying down to it (1969). [Apparently from an equation of ink with alcoholic liquor; cf. RED INK noun.]

innards noun 1 Intestines. 1825–. J. T. FARRELL His innards made slight noises, as they diligently furthered the process of digesting a juicy beefsteak (1932). 2 The inner workings of something. 1921–. LISTENER The whole thing [i.e. the jury system] can only live so long as we are not allowed to see its innards (1962). [Dialect pronunciation of *inwards* intestines, from noun use of *inward* adjective, internal.]

inside adverb In prison. 1888–. C. DRUMMOND Over the years she had been convicted three times, spending in all four years 'inside' (1972).

inside job noun A crime committed by or with the connivance of someone living or working in the place where it took place. 1908–. D. L. SAYERS You seem convinced that the murder of Victor Dean was an inside job (1933).

inside man noun US A person involved in any of various special roles in a confidence trick or robbery. 1935–.

inside stand noun The placing of a gang member incognito as one of the staff of a place to be robbed, in order to facilitate the robbery. 1932–.

into prep Interested or involved in; knowledgeable about. 1969–. LISTENER Margaret is 'into' astrology, and consults the *I-Ching* each morning (1973).

Irish confetti noun Stones, bricks, etc., esp. when used as weapons. 1935–. OBSERVER An American friend in Amsterdam, describing last week's riots there, said: 'There's just a lot of Irish confetti around' (1966).

Irish jig noun Also **Irish.** A wig. 1983–. [Rhyming slang.]

Irishman's hurricane noun Also **Irish hurricane.** A flat calm. 1827–.

Irishman's rise noun A reduction in pay. 1889–. TIMES For many low-paid workers with children, an extra £2 a week may be no more than an 'Irishman's rise' (1972).

Irish pennant noun nautical A frayed end of a rope blown by the wind. 1883–.

irk variant of ERK noun.

iron noun 1 Money. 1785–. C. ROUGVIE He was earning a bit of iron (1966). Cf. IRON-MAN noun. 2 pl. mainly services' Eating utensils. 1905–. 3 orig US An old motor vehicle. 1935–. M. REYNOLDS Well, it would mean being able to maintain a decent hovercar rather than the . . . four wheel iron he was currently driving (1967). 4 A homosexual. 1936–. E. PARTRIDGE Gorblimey, 'e's an *iron*, did'n yeh know? (1961). 5 A jemmy used in housebreaking. 1941–. 6 theatrical A metal safety curtain. 1951–. [In sense 4, short for *iron hoof*, rhyming slang for 'poof'; in sense 6, short for *iron curtain*.]

iron man noun 1 US A dollar. 1908–. E. R. JOHNSON An ounce should bring a street pusher about two thousand iron men (1970). 2 orig Austral A pound. 1959–. J. WAINWRIGHT Ten thousand iron men. . . . We're talking bank-notes (1974). Cf. IRON noun 1.

iron mike noun The automatic steering device of a ship. 1926–.

ironmongery noun Firearms. 1902–. J. WAINWRIGHT Shove it. You are only here for the

inked
Australian
drunk

ride. If you hadn't been so damned handy with the ironmongery—(1973).

it pron **1** Sexual intercourse. 1611–. F. WARNER He doesn't even know I'm overdue. And he hasn't had it for a week (1972). **2** dated **Sex appeal.** 1904–. L. P. BACHMANN She really had 'It', as it was called (1972).

item noun orig US A pair of lovers regarded (esp. socially acknowledged) as a couple. 1970–. K. VONNEGUT I hadn't realized that he and she had been an item when they were both at Tarkington, but I guess they were (1990).

itsy-bitsy adjective Very small. 1938–. H. HOWARD If Frankie was here he'd break you into itsy-bitsy pieces (1972). [Baby-form of *little* adjective+ BITSY.]

itty-bitty adjective Very small. 1938–. L. KENNEDY I felt, here I am in this itty-bitty tropical village, a tremendous long ways from anywhere (1969). [Baby-form of *little* adjective + BITTY.]

Ivan noun A Russian, esp. a Russian soldier. 1925–. B. MATHER We'd knocked off quite a few of their side so far, and even dedicated Ivans could be expected to show a little exacerbation under the circumstances (1968). [From the Russian male personal name *Ivan.*]

ivory noun **1** dated The teeth; usu. pl. 1782–. **2** The keys of a piano or other instrument; usu. pl. 1818–. TIMES Its cover portrays the Prime Minister, seated at the organ, tinkling one lot of ivories and flashing the other lot (1974). [In sense 2, from the keys being made of ivory.]

jack noun **1** A policeman or detective; a military policeman. 1889–. J. WAINWRIGHT These county coppers . . . couldn't get their minds unhooked from the words 'New Scotland Yard'— as if every jack in the Metropolitan Police District worked from *there* (1971). **2** orig US Money. 1890–. A. PRIOR I asked him . . . to think of the new suits he could get . . . when the jack came in (1960). **3 I'm all right, Jack** a saying typifying selfish complacency. 1910–. JOHN & HUMPHRY Right now it is, as I said before, dog eat dog. . . . I'm all right, Jack, damn you (1971). **4 on one's jack.** Also **on one's Jack Jones** on one's own. 1925–. Cf. PAT (MALONE) noun. A. DRAPER You're on your Jack Jones. Ben's deserted you (1972); R. PARKES I thought I could go sneaking in there all on my jack and bring out the evidence (1973). **5** Five pounds; a five-pound note. Also **jacks, jax.** 1958–. GUARDIAN 'That one,' says the dealer from Islington, 'that one we *know* she died in; so it'll cost you a jax.' . . . Five quid for a shroud; cheap at the price (1968). **6** A tablet of heroin. 1967–. R. BUSBY He's been cranking up on horse [i.e. heroin]. His last jack is wearing off, and he's grovelling on the floor for another pill (1971). adjective **7** Austral Fed up, disenchanted; usu. followed by *of*. 1889–. AUSTRALIAN GEOGRAPHIC 'The missus might get jack of it and clear out for the city,' observed one miner, 'but most of them come back' (1986). verb **8 to jack off: a** To go away. 1935–. G. ORWELL Flo and Charlie would probably 'jack off' if they got the chance of a lift (1935). **b** To masturbate. 1959–. R. A. CARTER You miserable little queer. . . . You can jack off in Llewellyn's best hat for all I care (1971). **9 to jack (something) up** NZ To arrange, organize, fix up; to put right, spruce up. 1942–. NEW ZEALAND LISTENER I'll see you right at a boardin' place until you get jacked up (1971). **10 to jack (something) in** to stop doing (something), give up, leave off; esp. in phr. *to jack it in.* 1948–. K. ROYCE I'm beginning to wonder if it's worth it. . . . Let me jack it in (1972). [In sense 4, from *Jack Jones*, rhyming slang for 'alone'; in sense 5, short for *Jack's alive*, obs. rhyming slang for 'five'; in sense 7, from *to jack up* to give up.]

jack verb trans. orig and mainly US To take illegally, steal (esp. a car or something from a car); to rob, burgle. 1930–. J. FAVREUR Who would jack your fuckin K-car? (1994). [Shortening of *hijack* verb.]

Jack ashore noun A drunkard. 1909–. E. MCGIRR Jack Ashore does not check bills (1970). [From the notion of a *Jack* (sailor) getting drunk on shore-leave.]

jackass brandy noun US, dated Home-made brandy. 1920–3.

Jack Dusty noun nautical A ship's steward's assistant. *c.*1931–.

jack-leg noun and adjective US (Someone, esp. a lawyer or preacher, who is) incompetent or unscrupulous. 1850–. P. OLIVER The wandering evangelists, and 'Jack-leg' preachers (1958). [From *Jack* + *-leg* as in *blackleg* noun, swindler, strike-breaker.]

Jacko noun Austral A kookaburra. 1907–. [From *Jack* noun kookaburra (short for *laughing jackass* noun kookaburra) + *-o*.]

Jack shalloo noun nautical An (excessively) easy-going officer. Also **Jack Shilloo.** 1904–. [Apparently an alteration of *Jack Chellew*, the name of such an officer in the Royal Navy.]

Jack Strop noun nautical An opinionated or bumptious man. 1945–.

jacksy noun Also **jacksie, jaxey, jaxie.** The backside, arse. Also **jacksy-pardo, jacksy-pardy.** 1896–. A. DRAPER The amount of love in our house you could stick up a dog's jacksie and he wouldn't even yelp (1970). [From *Jack* + *-sy.*]

Jack-the-Lad noun Brit (A nickname for) a troublemaker or rogue, esp. one regarded with both admiration and mistrust, a popular villain; also, a wanted criminal. 1981–. DAILY TELEGRAPH EastEnders . . . with its cast of old gorblimey Cockneys, Supplementary Benefit sub-class, Jack-the-Lad chancers and invading yuppies (1987). [App. the nickname of Jack Sheppard, a celebrated 18th-cent. thief.]

Jacky noun Austral, derog Also **Jacky-Jacky.** (A nickname for) an Aboriginal. 1845–. K. J. GILBERT As the blacks are quick to point out, you don't get to be a councillor unless you are a good jacky who is totally under the manager's thumb (1973).

jack Jack ashore jackass brandy Jack Dusty Jacko

Jacky Howe noun Also **Jackie Howe**.
Austral and NZ A sleeveless vest worn esp.
by sheep-shearers and other rural workers.
1930–. [From the name of *John* Robert *Howe*
(?1861–1920), a noted Queensland
sheep-shearer.]

jag¹ noun **1** A drinking bout; a spree. 1891–.
LISTENER Sid Chaplin's *Saturday Saga*, the
account of two miners on a memorable jag
(1966). **2** orig US A period of indulgence in
a particular activity, emotion, etc. 1913–. NEW
YORKER A neurotic habit . . . may be overt, like a
temper tantrum or a crying jag (1972). [From
earlier sense, as much drink as one can take,
from original sense, load for one horse;
origin unknown.] Cf. JAGGED adjective.

Jag² noun Abbreviation of 'Jaguar' (the
proprietary name of a make of car). 1959–.
T. ALLBEURY They've bought a car. A Jag—
secondhand (1974).

jagged /dʒægd/ adjective mainly US **1** dated
Drunk. 1737–. **2** Under the influence of
drugs. Also with *up*. 1938–. BOYD & PARKES
Solange is—was—God help her, a heroin addict.
When we first met, she was all jagged up. She
was a reject on the junk heap (1973). [From
JAG¹ noun + -*ed*.]

jail-bait noun orig US A girl who is too
young to have sex with legally. 1934–.
J. BRAINE I'm not interested in little girls.
Particularly not in jail-bait like that one (1957).
[From the fact that sexual intercourse with
such a girl may result in imprisonment.]

jake adjective orig US, now Austral and NZ All
right; satisfactory. 1914–. NEW ZEALAND LISTENER
Long as there's plenty of beer, she'll be jake
(1970). [Origin unknown.]

jake noun orig US Methylated spirits used as
an alcoholic drink. 1932–. J. STEINBECK He
would drink jake or whisky until he was a shaken
paralytic (1939). [From earlier sense, alcoholic
drink made from Jamaica ginger;
abbreviated form of *Jamaica*.]

jakeloo /dʒeɪkəluː/ adjective Also **jakealoo,
jakerloo**. Austral and NZ All right, satisfactory.
1919–. S. GORE The least you could do now is
give some sorta guarantee that me and me
Mum and Dad'll be jakealoo, when the invasion
starts (1968). [From JAKE adjective + jocular
suffix -(*a*)*loo*.]

jakes noun A lavatory or toilet; a privy.
1538–. J. JOYCE He kicked open the crazy door of
the jakes (1922). [Origin uncertain; perh. from
the male forenames *Jacques* or *Jack*.]

jalopy /dʒəˈlɒpi/ noun Also **gillopy, jalapa,
jollopy, jallopy, jaloppi(e)**. orig US A
dilapidated old motor vehicle. 1929–.
M. E. B. BANKS Perhaps a succession of broken
down jalopies has impaired my faith in the
internal combustion engine (1955). [Origin
unknown.]

jam noun Austral Affected manners; self-
importance; esp. in phr. *to lay* (or *put*) *on jam*.
1882–. D. STIVENS Sadie put a bit of jam on when
she talked, but not too much (1951). [From the
notion of jam being a luxury foodstuff.]

jam jar noun Brit A car. 1934–. R. COOK
Parking this dreadful great orange-and-cream
jamjar . . . slap under a no-parking sign (1962).
[Rhyming slang.]

jammy adjective mainly Brit Lucky. 1915–.
'TREVANIAN' 'I almost always win. Isn't that odd?'
The Sergeant regarded the slim body . . . 'I'd say
you were bloody jammy' (1973). [Cf. earlier
sense, excellent.]

jam-rag noun A sanitary towel. *a.*1966–.
VIZ The new Vispre Shadow jam rag is designed
to suit your lifestyle, with a wrap-a-round gusset
flap to keep the blood off your knicker elastic
(1992). [Cf. RAG noun 5.]

jam sandwich noun Brit A police car.
1987–. B. WHITEHEAD 'Look, there's a jam
sandwich,' said Ann . . . 'Jam sandwich. Police
car painted white and red. Don't they teach you
colloquial English at your Swedish schools?'
(1992). [From the car's colour: white
bodywork with a horizontal red stripe.]

jane noun orig US A woman, girl, girlfriend.
1906–. E. S. GARDNER 'Who was this jane?
Anybody I know?' 'No one you know. . . . She
had been a nurse in San Francisco' (1967).
[From the female personal name *Jane*.]

jankers noun services' Punishment for
offenders. 1916–. J. PORTER I pulled her leg about
it a bit, you know, said something about having
her put on jankers if she was late again (1965).
[Origin unknown.]

janky adjective US, mainly African-American Of
poor quality, bad; untrustworthy, suspicious.
1993–. CRIMINOLOGY You be watchin' the guy all
the time . . . seein' how he's actin', seein' if he be
reachin' for something suspicious or if he be
actin' all janky (1996). [Origin unknown.]

JAP noun US A young American Jewish
woman. 1972–. [Acronym from Jewish-
American Princess.]

jap verb trans. US, dated To make a sneak
attack on. 1957–8. H. E. SALISBURY An uncertain

Jacky Howe jag jagged jail-bait jake jankers

area where one side or another may at any sudden moment 'jap' an unwary alien (1958). [From *Jap* noun, abbreviation of *Japanese*; apparently with reference to the Japanese surprise attack on Pearl Harbor, 1941.]

jar noun A glass of beer. 1925–. OBSERVER The painter, Raymond Piper, took us for a jar at his local (1972).

jarhead noun US **1a** dialect and military A mule. 1916–. **b** A stupid person. 1942–. WASHINGTON POST The mathclass jarhead who threw up with anxiety at the sight of long division (1987). **2** military **a** A member of the US Army. 1931–. **b** A member of the US Marine Corps. 1944–. [In sense 2a, from the mule mascot of US Army football teams (with reference to sense 1a).]

jasper noun US, mainly derog A person, fellow; spec. a country bumpkin. NEW YORKER What's with those jaspers? (1970). [From the male personal name *Jasper*.]

jaunty noun nautical The master-at-arms on board ship. Also **jaundy, jonty.** 1902–. WEEKLY DISPATCH The sailor spun a yarn that would make the hardest-hearted jonty (master-at-arms) weep (1928). [Apparently from a nautical pronunciation of *gendarme* noun.]

java noun Coffee. 1907–. H. GOLD Lots a guys come in for chatter and java, friend (1956). [From earlier sense, Javan coffee.]

jaw noun **1** (A) conversation, talk. 1748–. J. R. ACKERLEY He invited the two of us into the billiard-room of Grafton House . . . for a 'jaw' (1968). TIMES LITERARY SUPPLEMENT Without these things, committee work is just endless jaw and empty substitute (1972). **2** dated Impudent talk. 1846–. verb **3** intr. To talk, esp. tediously or at too great length. 1748–. W. CHURCHILL To jaw-jaw is always better than to war-war (1954). **4** trans. dated To admonish, scold. 1810–.

jaw-bone noun N Amer (orig Canadian) Deferred payment, credit. 1862–. NEW YORKER A young Canadian . . . started this film on a small grant . . . and apparently finished it on jawbone and by deferring processing costs (1970).

jawboning noun US A policy, first associated with the administration of US President Lyndon Johnson (1963–9), of urging management and union leaders to accept price- and wage-restraint. 1966–.

jazz noun **1** Pretentious talk or behaviour, nonsensical stuff. 1918–. B. MALAMUD I read all about that formalism jazz in the library and it's bullshit (1971). **2** Sexual intercourse. 1924–.

A. LOMAX Winding Boy is a bit on the vulgar side. Let's see—how could I put it—means a fellow that makes good jazz with the women (1950). **3 and all that jazz** and all that sort of thing; et cetera. 1959–. J. PORTER Come to identify the body . . . and all that jazz (1972). verb trans. and intr. **4** To have sexual intercourse (with). 1927–. H. MACLENNAN My sister was being jazzed by half the neighbourhood cats by the time she was fifteen (1948).

jazzbo noun Also **jasbo.** US **1** A vaudeville act featuring low comedy. 1917–. **2** A person; spec. an African-American. 1923–. J. KEROUAC He dodged a mule wagon; in it sat an old Negro plodding along . . . . He slowed down the car for all of us to turn and look at the old jazzbo moaning along (1957). [Origin unknown; perh. an alteration of the name *Jasper*; cf JAZZ noun.]

jazzing noun US, orig African-American = JAZZ noun 2. 1958–. MURTAGH & HARRIS She asked if I wanted to do a little jazzing . . . I said, 'How much?' 'Two dollars,' she said (1958).

jeepers int orig US A mild expression of surprise, delight, etc. Also **jeepers-creepers.** 1929–. J. AIKEN Jeepers, Fernand, we had a bullfight . . . . It was real great! (1972). [Alteration of JESUS int.]

Jeez int Also **Jeeze, Geez(e), Jese, Jez,** and with lower-case initial. orig US A mild expression of surprise, discovery, annoyance, etc. 1923–. PRIVATE EYE Jeez, that's nice of you to say so (1970). [Abbreviation of JESUS int.]

jeff noun US, derog A man, esp. a yokel or a bore; used esp. by African-Americans of white men. Also **Jeff Davis.** 1870–. [From *Jefferson Davis* (1808–89), president of the Confederate States 1861–5.]

jelly¹ noun dated A pretty girl; a girlfriend. 1889–. W. FAULKNER Gowan goes to Oxford a lot. . . . He's got a jelly there (1931). [Apparently from the wobbliness associated with buxom women.]

jelly² noun Also **gelly.** Gelignite. 1941–. GUARDIAN Stolen 'gelly' found (1971). [Shortening of the pronunciation of noun *gelignite*, influenced by the substance's jelly-like appearance.]

jelly bean noun orig US An unpleasant, weak, or dishonest person; spec. a pimp. 1919–. W. FAULKNER Are you hiding out in the woods with one of those damn slick-headed jellybeans? (1929). [From earlier sense, jelly-like bean-shaped sweet.]

jelly-belly noun derog A fat person. 1896–. L. A. G. STRONG If ever I want a ginger-chinned jelly-belly's advice . . . I'll ask for it (1935). Hence **jelly-bellied**, adjective. 1899–.

jelly roll noun US, mainly African-American 1 Sexual intercourse. 1927–. 2 The female genitals; the vagina. 1927–. [From earlier sense, cylindrical cake containing jelly or jam.]

jerk noun 1 orig US A fool; a contemptible person. 1935–. L. MCINTOSH Julian sounds a dismal little jerk when you sum him up like that (1956). verb trans. and intr. 2 to jerk off to masturbate. 1937–. P. ROTH She will jerk off one guy, but only with his pants on (1969). [In sense 1, perh. influenced by JERKWATER adjective.]

jerk-off adjective 1 Erotic; encouraging masturbation. c.1957–. NEW SOCIETY It would prove Screeches was not a 'jerk-off' press but was serious (1965). noun 2 = JERK noun 1. 1968–. W. SHEED You know perfectly well that the jerk-offs do all the talking at meetings (1973). [In sense 1, from verbal phr. to jerk off (see JERK verb 2); in sense 2, prob. from adjective, but cf. JERK noun 1.]

jerkwater adjective US Small, insignificant, inferior. 1897–. R. LOCKRIDGE It won't be easy for him to get another job if he's fired . . . Maybe at some jerkwater college at half what he's getting now (1970). [From earlier application to a train operating on a branch line, from the notion of a locomotive with a small boiler that had to be replenished with water 'jerked' (i.e. pulled up) from track-side streams in a bucket.]

jerry¹ noun Brit A chamber-pot. 1859–. G. ORWELL A bed not yet made and a jerry under the bed (1939). [Prob. abbreviation of jeroboam noun, very large wine bottle, from the name of Jeroboam king of northern Israel, described in the Bible (1 Kings xi. 28) as 'a mighty man of valour'; cf. W. MAGINN The naval officer . . . came into the Clarendon for a Jerry [= jeroboam] of punch (1827).]

jerry² verb intr. and trans. 1 mainly Austral and NZ To understand, realize, tumble; often followed by to. 1894–. BULLETIN (Sydney): I should've jerried when the guy gave me the tug (1975). adjective 2 to be (or get) jerry (on, on to, to): US, dated To be aware (of); to get wise (to). 1908–. FLYNN'S I know that th' fly was jerry because he gave me th' once over as I was comin' out (1926). noun 3 to take a jerry (to) Austral and NZ To investigate and understand (something); to tumble to (something). 1919–. X. HERBERT 'Use y' bit o' brains,' he says, 'an take a jerry to y'self' (1938). [Origin unknown.]

Jerry³ noun and adjective Brit, orig military (A) German; spec a German soldier or aircraft; also, the Germans or German soldiers collectively. 1919–. W. VAUGHAN-THOMAS They almost felt a sympathy for the Jerries under that merciless rain of explosions (1961). [Prob. alteration of German.]

Jesse noun Also **jesse, jessie, jessy.** US, dated Severe treatment; a beating; in the phrs. to give (a person), catch, or get Jesse. 1839–. [Perh. from a jocular interpretation of 'There shall come a rod out of the stem of Jesse' (Isaiah xi. 1).]

Jessie noun Also **Jessy,** and with lower-case initial. derog A cowardly or effeminate man; a male homosexual. 1923–. G. SIMS Duff had been scathing about 'soft jessies who couldn't get their fat heads down' (1971). [From the female personal name.]

Jesus int Used as (part of) an oath or as a strong exclamation of surprise, disbelief, dismay, anger, etc.; also in various phrases, such as by Jesus, Jesus (H.) Christ, Jesus wept. 1377–. B. HEALEY Jesus! It's murder out there (1968).

Jew noun 1 derog and offensive A person who is parsimonious or drives hard bargains. 1606–. T. R. G. LYELL Why waste your time asking him for a subscription? He's a perfect Jew where money's concerned (1931). 2 nautical A ship's tailor. 1916–. verb trans. Also **jew.** 3 derog and offensive To get a financial advantage over; to cheat. 1833–. W. G. HAMMOND Both here and at the mountain top we were unmercifully jewed for all the refreshments (1946). 4 to jew down derog and offensive To beat down in price. 1848–. HARPER'S MAGAZINE Jew the fruitman down for his last Christmas tree (1972).

Jew boy noun derog and offensive A Jewish male. 1796–. OBSERVER Mrs Lane Fox dismisses what she calls the country set, who call their children 'the brats', talk about 'thrashing them into shape', support Enoch Powell and still refer to 'jew boys' (1972).

Jewing-bloke noun nautical = JEW noun 2. 1945–. TACKLINE The 'Jewing-bloke' had a rather ancient Singer sewing machine, bought when ashore at Alexandria with . . . pay in his pocket (1945).

jig¹ noun **1 the jig is up** it is all over, the game is up. 1800–. NATURE The weight of opinion seems to be that the jig is up for the map's supporters (1974). **2 in jig-time** mainly US In a short space of time. 1916–. L. W. ROBINSON If I was you, I'd see Grace Hutchinson. . . . She'd solve your problem in jig time (1968). [In sense 1, from earlier meaning, a game, trifle.]

jig² noun US derog and offensive A black person. 1924–. E. HEMINGWAY This jig we call Othello falls in love with this girl (1935). [Origin unknown; perh. the same word as JIG¹ noun.]

jigaboo noun Also **jiggabo, jijjiboo, zigabo**, etc. US derog and offensive = JIG² noun. 1909–. L. SANDERS The tall one . . . was a jigaboo (1970). [Related to JIG² noun, after *bugaboo* noun.]

jig-a-jig noun Sexual intercourse. Also **jig-jig**. 1932–. A. BARON He put his hand on her knee. 'You like jig-a-jig?' (1953). [From earlier sense, jerking movement; of imitative origin.]

jigger noun A gadget; a thingumajig. 1874–. [Of uncertain origin.]

jigger verb trans. To break, destroy, ruin; often followed by *up*. 1923–. TELEGRAPH (Brisbane): The firing pin's jiggered and the sights are sloppy (1969). [From earlier sense, to tire out.]

jiggered adjective Used in mild oaths, esp. *I'll be jiggered* and *I'm jiggered*. 1837–. [Perh. a euphemistic alteration of *buggered* adjective.]

jiggery-pokery noun Brit Deceitful or dishonest dealing, trickery. 1893–. G. MITCHELL Business reasons could make any alliance respectable . . . so long as there was no jiggery-pokery (1973). [Cf. Scottish *joukery-pawkery* noun, clever trickery, from *jouk* verb, to dodge, skulk.]

jildi Also **jeldi, jildy, juldie**, etc. military, orig Anglo-Indian. noun **1** Haste, as in phrases *on the jildi*, in a hurry, and *to do* or *move a jildi*. 1890–1948. adjective, adverb, and int **2** Quick(ly). 1919–. M. K. JOSEPH Hey, Antonio, where's me rooty [= bread]? And make it juldy, see? (1957). [From Hindustani *jaldi* quickness.]

jills noun Used with a possessive adjective: *my jills* = 'I', *his jills* = 'he', etc. 1906–. [Shelta.]

jim noun Austral, dated A pound. 1889–. A. E. YARRA The racehorse they have just bought in Bourke for fifty jim (1930). [Short for JIMMY O´GOBLIN noun.]

jim-jams noun **1** Delirium tremens. 1885–. **2** A fit of depression or nervousness. 1896–. D. JOHNSON We're both . . . drained by constant fear, the unrelieved jimjams (1986). [A fanciful reduplication.]

Jim Johnson noun = JOHNSON noun. SCREW So I went to take my turn with the hopes of somehow getting my Jim Johnson wet (1972).

jimmies noun = JIM-JAMS noun. 1900–. P. WHITE She was not accustomed to see the grey light sprawling on an empty bed; it gave her the jimmies (1961).

Jimmy Britts noun Also **the jimmies, the Britts**. Austral Fear, panic; used in such phrases as *to have the jimmies, to have the Britts up* to be afraid. 1945–. [From earlier sense, diarrhoea, from rhyming slang for *shits*, from the name of *Jimmy Britt* (1879–1940), US boxer; *jimmies* influenced by earlier *jimmies* delirium tremens.]

Jimmy Grant noun Also **jimmygrant**. Austral, NZ, and S Afr Rhyming slang for 'immigrant' or 'emigrant'. 1845–. F. CLUNE More and more Crown land was taken up by the ever-arriving 'jimmygrants' who had government help and favour (1948).

Jimmy O'Goblin noun Also **jimmy o'goblin, jimmy**. A pound. 1899–. TIMES He . . . had made a profit of some six million jimmy-o-goblins (1973). [Rhyming slang for 'sovereign'.]

Jimmy Riddle noun Also **jimmy**. Rhyming slang for 'piddle'. 1937–. D. CLARK Mrs D. was in there having a jimmy (1971).

Jimmy the One noun Also **Jimmy.** nautical First Lieutenant. 1916–. GUARDIAN Smith told Petty Officer David Lewis, 'We are going to have a sit-in and give the ''Jimmy'' a hard time' (1970).

Jimmy Woodser noun Also **Jimmy Wood(s)**. Austral and NZ A solitary drinker; a drink taken on one's own. 1892–. N.Z.E.F. TIMES You'll find me lonesome in a Naafi, a-drinkin' to me sins, A-sippin' like a Jimmy Woodser (1942). [From *Jimmy Wood*, the name of a character in a poem of that name (1892) by B. H. Boake, and perh. the name of an actual person.]

Jimmy Woodser
a solitary drinker

jig jigaboo jig-a-jig jigger jiggered Jimmy Britts

jingle noun Austral, dated **Money in small coins, change.** 1906–. BULLETIN (Sydney): If he is a youngish man, his pockets are lined with coin, oof, dough, sugar or hay. If he is getting on in years his pockets will hold jingle (1958). [From the sound of coins.]

jingling Johnny noun Austral and NZ **1** One who shears sheep by hand. 1934–. **2** pl. Hand shears. 1941–.

jism /dʒɪz(ə)m/ noun Also **chism, gism, jizz,** etc. **1** Energy, strength. 1842–. S. BECKETT A week will be ample, a week in spring, that puts the jizz in you (1967). **2** Semen. 1899–. SCREW At last I felt my gism rushing up like electricity and I . . . felt the love bolt burst out of my cock into her vacuum-sucking mouth (1972). [Origin unknown.]

jit noun US, derog A Black person. 1931–. [Origin unknown.]

jitney noun US A five-cent piece, a nickel. 1903–. W. SAROYAN Call that money? A jitney? A nickel? (1947). [Origin unknown.]

jitterbug noun dated **1** A jittery or nervous person; an alarmist. 1934–. E. H. JONES Sir Samuel Hoare denounced the 'jitterbugs' who feared war (1966). **2** A jazz musician or fan. 1937–. [From *jitter* verb, to move agitatedly + *bug* noun, person with an obsession; cf. later sense, popular dance of the 1940s.]

jive orig US. noun **1** Talk or conversation; spec. misleading, untrue, empty, or pretentious talk; hence, anything false, worthless, or unpleasant. 1928–. BLACK WORLD Everything that we do must be aimed toward the total liberation, unification and empowerment of Afrika. . . . Anything short of that is jive (1973). **2** (A cigarette containing) marijuana. 1938–. NEW YORK TIMES So Diane smoked jive, pod, and tea (1952). verb **3** trans. To mislead, kid; to taunt or sneer at. 1928–. W. THURMAN But I jived her along, so she ditched him, and gave me her address (1929). **4** intr. To talk nonsense, to act foolishly. 1938–. MEZZROW & WOLFE Monkey wasn't jiving about that bartender (1946). **5** intr. To make sense; to fit in. 1943–. W. GADDIS His analyst says he's in love with her for all the neurotic reasons in the book. It don't jive, man (1955). adjective **6** mainly Black English Deceiving, pretentious. 1971–. E. BULLINS Kiss ma ass ya jive mathafukker! (1973). [Origin unknown; cf. later senses, type of popular dance, slang used by African-Americans.]

jive-ass noun US A deceitful or pretentious person; also, a person who loves fun or

excitement. 1964–. C. BROWN 'You jiveass nigger,' Reb said, laughing. 'No, I'm telling the truth' (1969). [From JIVE noun + ASS noun.]

jivey adjective Also **jivy.** mainly US **1** Jazzy, lively. 1944–. **2** Misleading, phoney, pretentious. 1972–. M. J. BOSSE I'm not sure I would have accepted that sort of jivey explanation, but Mrs. Halliday did (1972). [From JIVE noun + *-y.*]

Jixi noun Also **Jixie.** Brit, dated A two-seater taxi licensed in 1926. 1926–7. [From *Jix,* nickname of Sir William Joynson-Hicks (1865–1932), Home Secretary in 1926 + *-i,* after *taxi.*]

joanna noun Also **joano, johanna,** etc. Rhyming slang for 'piano'. 1846–. LISTENER The old Jo-anna intrudes its amateurish thumpings (1972).

job noun **1** A crime, esp. a robbery. 1722–. DAILY EXPRESS Bird asked Edwards: 'Can you do a job on my old woman?' Edwards is said to have replied: 'No sweat.' The trial continues (1984). **2 on the job** engaged in sexual intercourse. 1966–. DAILY TELEGRAPH 'Why the hell did you play Eric Clapton's *Easy Now?* . . . . Didn't you realise it was all about some guy on the job?' And I said 'Yeah. How many songs aren't?' (1972). verb trans. **3** orig US To swindle; to frame. 1903–. K. GILES You want to watch or they'll job you on that (1973).

Jock¹ noun A Scotsman; a Scottish soldier; often as a nickname. 1788–. NEW STATESMAN Why can't the Jocks support their team without dressing up like that? (1965). [Scottish form of the name *Jack.*]

jock² noun The male genitals. *a.*1790–. J. CROSS Sprigs clattering on the floor, knees, jocks, backsides and shouting as everybody dressed (1960). [Origin unknown; perh. from an old slang word *jockum, -am* penis.]

jock³ noun **1** A jockey. 1826–. **2** A disc-jockey. 1952–. BLUES & SOUL He may be the top radio jock in the land as far as our music's concerned . . . but he should realise that he's no expert on all manner of other things (1987). [Abbreviation.]

jock⁴ noun orig dialect Food. 1879–. P. WRIGHT Food becomes . . . *jock* . . . and contrasts oddly with officialese (1974). [Origin unknown.]

jock⁵ noun N Amer **1** A jock-strap. 1952–. W. MCCARTHY He found the beretta . . . as well as the jock strap. He quickly took off his trousers, put on the jock (1973). **2** A male athlete, esp. at university. 1963–. TIME Rocks for jocks, elementary geology course popular among athletes at Pennsylvania (1972). [Abbreviation; in sense 2, from the wearing of jock-straps by athletes.]

jocker noun N Amer **1** A tramp who is accompanied by a youth who begs for him or is his homosexual partner. 1893–. **2** A male homosexual. 1935–. [From JOCK² noun + -er.]

Joe¹ noun **1** Also **joe**. A fellow, chap, guy. 1846–. PUBLISHERS WEEKLY The average Joe probably thinks that cyclists . . . are eccentric folk (1973). **2** Canadian A French-Canadian. 1963–. [From the male personal name *Joe*.]

joe² noun N Amer Coffee. 1941–. E. MCBAIN 'Would you like some coffee?' Carella asked. 'Is there some?' 'Sure. . . . Can we get two cups of joe?' (1963). [Origin unknown.]

Joe Blake noun Austral Rhyming slang for 'snake'. 1905–. SUNDAY MAIL MAGAZINE (Brisbane): We've camped . . . with the Joe Blakes, the goannas, the flies, and 4000 skinny jumbucks (1970).

Joe Bloggs noun Brit A hypothetical average man. 1969–. DAILY TELEGRAPH In too many cases these forms arrive on the desk of a busy executive who concludes that Joe Bloggs down the corridor must have signed the order (1971).

Joe Blow noun US = JOE BLOGGS noun. *c.*1941–. B. HOLIDAY But just let me walk out of the club one night with a young white boy of my age, whether it was John Roosevelt, the President's son, or Joe Blow (1956).

Joe Doakes noun Also **Joe Dokes**. = JOE BLOGGS noun. 1943–. JAZZ MONTHLY All these items are essentially jazz-tinged versions of Joe Doakes's favourite melodies (1968).

Joe Public noun orig US, theatre Often somewhat derog (A member of) the audience; hence, the general public or the typical member of this. 1942–. D. NORDEN We've really got to provide Joe Public with some sort of ongoing visual reference-point (1978). [From JOE noun 1 + *public* noun.]

joes noun Austral A fit of depression; the blues. 1910–. V. PALMER What I saw in the sugar country gave me the joes (1957). [Origin unknown.]

Joe Soap noun A foolish or gullible person, a mug; also, more generally, = JOE BLOGGS noun. 1943–. J. BROWN Who do you think I am, moosh? Joe Soap? (1972).

Joey noun Also **joey**. A former twelve-sided British coin of nickel-brass worth three 'old' pence; a threepenny bit. 1936–. [From the male personal name *Joey*; cf. earlier sense, fourpenny piece.]

john¹ noun Also **John**. A policeman. 1898–. Also with suffixed quasi-surnames, such as **John Dunn** (Austral), JOHN HOP (Austral and NZ), **John Law** (US). R. HALL He took possession of the book. . . . The johns'll get it if we leave it here (1982). [Abbreviation of JOHNDARM noun; in Austral, NZ, and US perh. shortened directly from JOHN HOP noun and *John Law*.] Cf. JOHNNY¹ noun.

john² noun **1** Also **John**. orig US A prostitute's client. 1928–. NEW YORK Many working girls, when they are new in the city, spend at least a few months with a madam to meet the better johns (1972). **2** mainly US A lavatory. 1932–. C. MACINNES 'You poor old bastard,' I said to the Hoplite, as he sat there on my john (1959). **3** Also **John**. The penis. 1934–. D. BALLANTYNE How often did the nurse find him with his old john lying limply? (1948). [From the male personal name *John*; in sense 2, cf. earlier *cuzjohn* lavatory (1735); in sense 3, short for JOHN THOMAS noun.]

johndarm noun dated A policeman. 1858–. H. HODGE A policeman is the usual cockney 'Grass' . . . Or sometimes 'Johndarm'—thus proving we know French (1939). [From French *gendarme* policeman.]

John Hancock noun US A signature. Also **John Henry**. 1903–. LISTENER Even today an American handing you a contract is apt to say: 'And now if you will just give us your John Hancock' (1972). [From the name of *John Hancock* (1737–93), the first signatory of the American Declaration of Independence (1776).]

John Hop noun Austral and NZ A policeman. 1905–. G. CROSS A couple of John-Hops arrived to investigate the accident (1981). [Rhyming slang for *cop* noun.] Cf. JONNOP noun.

Johnny¹ noun Also **Johnnie**. dated A policeman. *a.*1852–1935. [From the male personal name; cf. JOHN¹ noun.]

johnny² noun **1** mainly US = JOHN² noun 2. 1932–. D. CONOVER Why, oh, why, do little boys . . . rush to a johnny when nature provides opportunity everywhere? (1971). **2** Brit A contraceptive sheath, condom. 1963–. See also RUBBER JOHNNY noun. TIMES EDUCATIONAL SUPPLEMENT [A mark of] 100 . . . , my informant wrote, 'is rightly reserved for full intercourse

jocker Joe Blake Joe Bloggs Joe Blow Joe Doakes

without a johnny' (1970). [From the male personal name *Johnny*.]

Johnny Foreigner noun Brit usu. derog (A personification of) a foreign person; usu. used with ironic reference to British xenophobia. 1990– (first recorded in 1990 but in use earlier). SUNDAY TIMES When Moore was arrested on a trumped-up charge in Bogota just before the 1970 World Cup, we all knew that it was a dastardly ruse by Johnny Foreigner, and so it proved (1993).

John Roscoe noun US A gun. 1938–. A. S. NEILL The USA . . . , where anyone can carry a gun, or, to be more topical, should I say a Betsy or a John Roscoe? (1973). See also ROSCOE noun.

Johnson noun Also **Jim Johnson**. now mainly African-American The penis. 1863–. I. REED Old Sam whips out his 'Johnson,' as they say (1973). [Arbitrary use of the surname *Johnson*.]

John Thomas noun The penis. 1879–. TIMES LITERARY SUPPLEMENT The grotesquely coy accounts of sex, during which Tony tells us that his 'John Thomas' was 'up and raring to go' (1972).

joint noun 1 mainly US A place, a building; spec. a place of meeting for people engaged in some illicit activity, such as drinking or drug-taking. 1821–. Cf. CLIP-JOINT noun. 2 fairground orig US A stall, tent, etc. in a circus or fair; a concession stand. 1927–. 3 dated Hypodermic equipment used by drug addicts. 1935–8. 4 A marijuana cigarette. 1952–. DAILY TELEGRAPH The making of the joint seemed to be as much a part of the ritual as smoking it (1972). 5 US Prison. 1953–. J. WAMBAUGH He was a no-good asshole and belonged in the joint (1972). 6 orig US The product of an artist, esp. a film or recording. 1991–. KNOWLEDGE Featuring rarities and brand-new joints, this is a must for Punk-Rock fans (2002). [In sense 6, perh. from phr. *a Spike Lee joint*, used by the US film director Spike Lee (b. 1957) as a subtitle for his films.]

joker noun mainly Austral and NZ A fellow, chap. 1810–. G. H. FEARNSIDE You think us married jokers have got no lives of our own (1965). [From earlier sense, one who jokes.]

jollo noun Austral A spree, a party. 1907–. N. PULLIAM My mother used to ask some of the chappies in for a little week-end jollo (1955). [From *joll(ity* or *jolli(fication* + Austral suffix *-o.*] Cf. JOLLY noun.

jollop noun 1 (A drink of) strong liquor. 1920–. 2 A purgative, a medicine. 1955–. D. NILAND He nutted out some jollop for her

cough (1955). [Alteration of *jalap* noun, type of purgative obtained from a Mexican plant, ultimately from *Jalapa*, *Xalapa* name of a city in Mexico, from Aztec *Xalapan* sand by the water.]

jolly noun 1 A spree, a party, an entertainment. Also **jolly-up**. 1905–. E. WAUGH Why can't the silly mutt go off home and leave us to have a jolly up (1932). 2 A thrill of enjoyment or excitement; mainly in pl. esp. in phr. *to get one's jollies*. 1957–. SURFER MAGAZINE The announcer acted like this is where all of the surfers go after dark to get their jollies (1968). [Short for *jollification* noun.] Cf. JOLLO noun.

jolly d adjective Brit dated Excellent, highly satisfactory; often used as an exclamation. 1949–. N. FAIRBROTHER I say. Jolly d. It's exactly what I want (1960). [*d* abbreviation of *decent*.]

jolt noun 1 mainly US A drink of liquor. 1904–. R. THOMAS She took two green plastic glasses. . . . I poured a generous jolt into both of them (1973). 2 orig US A prison sentence. 1912–. D. HUME They are only too ready to turn King's evidence . . . you'd take a very stiff jolt (1936). 3 mainly US A quantity of a drug in the form of a cigarette, tablet, etc. 1916–. K. PLATT Her LSD cap would cost about two dollars and fifty cents for the jolt (1970).

jones noun Also **Jones**. US 1 Withdrawal symptoms from drug addiction. 1965–. 2 A drug addict's habit; hence, any intense craving. 1968–. BLACK WORLD I don't have a long jones. I ain't been on it too long (1971). verb intr. 3 To suffer withdrawal symptoms. 1971–. [Prob. from the surname *Jones*.]

jonnop noun Austral A policeman. 1938–. A. LUBBOCK He's not a bad sort for a jonnop (1963). [Contraction of JOHN HOP noun.]

josser noun 1 Brit A fool. 1886–. 2 Austral = JOSS-MAN noun. 1887–. G. ROSE The old josser, all black robe and beard and upside-down hat and silver cross, addressed himself to me (1973). 3 Brit, derog A fellow, chap. 1890–. V. PALMER We've no call to worry about the big jossers putting the screw on us; we've the legal titles to our leases and can get our price for them (1948). [From *joss* noun (see JOSS-MAN noun) + *-er*.]

joss-man noun A priest; a padre. 1913–. NAVY NEWS I was watch aboard and tried to get a sub, but no joy. I asked the Jossman if I could go ashore, and he told me to go (1964). [From *joss* noun, Chinese idol, perh. from Portuguese *deos* god.]

journo noun orig Austral A journalist, esp. a newspaper journalist. 1967–. TIMES Journos who work with the written word are seldom at ease with spoken English (1985). [Shortened from *journalist* + *-o*.]

joy-house noun A brothel. 1940–. B. MATHER All right—so you're a sailor in a joy-house with a sore foot (1970).

joy-juice noun US Alcoholic drink. 1960–. BLACK WORLD He could hear the others as in a dream, laughing, telling dirty jokes, playing cards and swizzling joy-juice (1974).

joy-popper noun orig US An occasional taker of illegal drugs. 1936–. J. BROWN The weekend ravers and joy-poppers . . . for whom smoke and amphetamines alone were not enough (1972). Hence **joy-pop,** noun (An injection or inhalation of) a drug. 1939–. K. ORVIS I take a joy-pop once in a while (1962). [Cf. POP verb 3.]

judy noun A woman. 1885–. GUARDIAN During a strike a man whose judy is working is obviously better off than the man with a wife and three kids about the house (1973). [From the female personal name; cf. earlier sense, ridiculous or contemptible woman, perh. from the name of the wife of Punch.]

jug noun 1 orig US Prison. 1815–. D. FRANCIS Just out of jug, he is (1981). 2 A bank. 1845–. OBSERVER If a villain had seriously suggested screwing a jug (breaking into a bank) (1960). 3 pl. orig US A woman's breasts. 1957–. T. WOLFE She must allow him the precious currency he had earned, which is youth and beauty and juicy jugs and loamy loins (1987). verb trans. 4 orig US To imprison. 1841–. S. BELLOW The hotel could jug him for trespassin' (1978). [In sense 1, short for obs. *stone-jug* noun, a prison, esp. Newgate.]

juggins noun Brit, dated A fool, simpleton. 1882–. I. MURDOCH You are a juggins, you shouldn't walk in those high-heeled shoes (1985). [Perh. from the surname *Juggins*, or alternatively a fanciful derivative of MUG noun (cf. MUGGINS noun).]

juice noun 1 mainly US Alcoholic liquor. 1828–. R. RUSSELL 'Nuthin' at all like juice, either,' Hassan said. 'No hangover' (1961). 2 Electricity, electric current. 1896–. J. M. CAIN They got neon signs, they show up better, and they don't burn as much juice (1934). 3 Petrol. 1909–. K. WEATHERLY The Rover had him worried. If she ran out of juice . . . she had to walk in (1968). 4 A drug or drugs. 1957–. H. C. RAE I wasn't interested in him. I mean, when you shoot juice, you lose the other thing (1972). verb trans. 5 To liven *up.* 1964–.

juiced adjective Drunk; often followed by *up*. 1946–. S. RANSOME He was sitting at the bar brooding over a drink—not making any trouble, not getting juiced up (1971).

juicer noun 1 An electrician. 1928–. V. J. KEHOE He directs the . . . juicers to place the lights in the most effective positions (1957). 2 US An alcoholic. 1967–. [From JUICE noun + *-er*.]

ju-ju noun A marijuana cigarette. 1940–. N. FREELING 'He had juju cigarettes too; like Russians, with a big mouth piece and pretty loose . . . ' 'The jujus are—you feel very clever' (1963). [Reduplication of *mari)ju(ana* noun.]

juke Also **jook, jouk.** orig US. noun 1 A brothel or roadhouse; spec. a cheap roadside establishment providing food and drink, and music for dancing. Also juke-house, juke-joint. 1935–. BLACK WORLD Had done sent Lueta and Carol Ann to every juke joint in Greenwood askin bout you (1971). verb intr. 2 To dance, esp. at a juke or to the music of a jukebox. 1937–. T. WILLIAMS I'd like to go out jooking with you tonight (1958). [Prob. from Gullah *juke, jooq* disorderly, wicked.]

Jumble noun African-American A white man. 1957–. M. DICKENS Get all you can out of the Jumbles (1961). [Alteration of *John Bull*.]

jumbuck noun Austral A sheep. 1824–. BULLETIN (Sydney) With a board of 16 shearers a jumbuck-barbering firm this season cut out 105,000 sheep (1926). [Orig Austral pidgin, but the ultimate origin is unknown.]

jump noun 1 **to have** (or **get**) **the jump on** orig US To have an advantage over (someone), put (someone) in a disadvantageous position. 1912–. REAL ESTATE REVIEW Each of these new developers hopes to get the jump on the other by adding more square footage to the units and giving more in amenities (1972). 2 orig US A journey, trip. 1923–. B. HOLIDAY A six-hundred-mile jump overnight was standard (1956). 3 An act of sexual intercourse. 1934–. G. GREER A wank was as good as a jump in those days (1970).

jumper noun Brit, dated A ticket inspector. 1900–. [From the notion of 'jumping' on to or boarding a bus, tram, etc. to inspect tickets.]

jungle noun orig US A camp for tramps, hoboes, etc. 1914–. ISLANDER (Victoria, British Columbia): During the depression in the 1930s gangs of youths ranged across the country, riding the rails and sleeping in jungles, and caused us concern (1971).

jungle bunny noun derog and offensive
A person of a dark-skinned race of
tropical origin. 1966-. NEW SOCIETY White South
Africans who wanted to gamble, buy
Playboy . . . and go to bed with a 'jungle bunny'
(1974).

jungle juice noun jocular, orig Austral
Alcoholic liquor, esp. powerful or illegally
produced spirits. 1942-. G. DUTTON The
Americans had two bottles of bourbon
and one of jungle juice made from
fermented coconut milk and surgical alcohol
(1968).

junk noun orig US A narcotic drug, esp.
heroin. 1925-. J. BROWN You do anything for
junk. . . . Cheat. Lie. Steal (1972).

junker noun US A drug-addict; a drug-
pusher. 1922-. J. EVANS No slim-waisted junker
with a snapbrim hat and a deck of nose candy
for sale to the right guy (1949). [From JUNK
noun + -er.]

junkie noun orig US A drug-addict. 1923-.
J. BROWN Lacerated hands, the hands of
junkies, scarred where needles had searched
for veins (1972). [From JUNK noun + -ie.]

juvie noun Also **juvey.** US **1** A juvenile or
juvenile delinquent. 1941-. P. STADLEY Just
where would you take me, little juvie? To a
drive-in movie? (1970). **2** A detention centre
or court for juvenile delinquents. 1967-.
[Abbreviation of *juvenile* noun.]

K¹ noun Brit Abbreviation of 'knighthood'. 1910–. LISTENER A 'K' isn't certain any more, even if you're a civil servant (1968).

K² noun Also **k.** A thousand (pounds, etc.); used esp. with reference to salaries offered in job advertisements. 1968–. [From its use in computing to represent 1,000; orig from its use as an abbreviation of *kilo-*.]

kaffir /ˈkæfə(r)/ adjective Also **Kaffir.** S Afr, offensive Bad, unreliable. 1934–. SPECTATOR 'That was a real Kaffir shot' (1961). [From *Kaffir* noun, used disparagingly of a black South African.]

kagg variant of CAG noun.

kale noun N Amer, dated Money. 1912–. FLYNN'S The Kale is cut up and th' biggest corner goes to th' brains (1926). [From the crinkly green leaves' resemblance to dollar bills.]

kaput /kəˈpʊt/ adjective Broken, ruined; done for. 1895–. J. SYMONS Sherlock Holmes is finished. Finito. Kaput (1975). [From German *kaputt*, from French *capot* without tricks in the card-game of piquet.]

kark verb = CARK verb.

karzy noun Also **carsey, carsy, karsey, karzey.** Brit A lavatory. 1961–. G. F. NEWMAN Visits to the karsey (1970). [Alteration of Italian *casa* house.]

Kate and Sidney noun Brit Steak and kidney (pudding or pie). 1914–. M. STEEN Beefsteak pudding? Phew! A pity Johnny's not here, Ma! Remember how he used to go for your Kate and Sidney? (1949) [Rhyming slang (and partial spoonerism).]

Kathleen Mavourneen noun Austral and NZ A prison sentence of indeterminate length. 1910–. H. C. BAKER The judge declared him an 'habitual criminal' and gave him a 'Kathleen Mavourneen' (1978). [An allusion to the song 'Kathleen Mavourneen', in which the refrain runs 'It may be for years, it may be for ever'.]

kaylied /ˈkeɪlɪd, -laɪd/ adjective Also **kailed, kalied.** Extremely drunk. 1937–. J. GASH He offered to brew up but my stomach turned. That left me free to slosh out a gill of gin. Dandy was permanently kaylied (1978). [Origin unknown.]

kayo int O.K. 1923–. P. G. WODEHOUSE If you think it's kayo, it's all right by me (1928). [Reversal of the pronunciation of O.K. under the influence of K.O. knock out.]

kecks noun pl. Also **keks.** Brit Trousers; also, underpants, knickers. 1961–. I. WELSH The last thing Renton wanted to hear, hungover, in a strange place, wearing only his keks, was a male voice (1993). [Prob. a dialect variant of obs. *kicks* trousers.]

kegger noun US **1** A party or similar occasion at which beer is served, esp. one that is wild, raucous, or large. 1968–. VILLAGE VOICE You do get to speed around L.A., competing against opponents whose artificial intelligence sometimes resembles that of a 17-year-old weaving home from a kegger (2003). **2** A keg of beer. 1980–. [From *keg* noun + -*er*.]

keister /ˈkiːstə(r), ˈkaɪstə(r)/ noun Also **keester, keyster.** US **1** A suitcase, satchel; a handbag; a burglar's tool-case; a salesman's sample-case, etc. 1882–. H. E. GOLDIN Ditch the keister. It draws heat (attracts police attention) (1950). **2** A strong-box; a safe. 1913–. AMERICAN SPEECH Can we use a can-opener on this keister? (1931). **3** The buttocks. 1931–. NEW YORKER Just put your keyster in the chair and shut your mouth (1985). [Origin unknown.]

keks noun pl. = KECKS noun pl.

kelch noun Also **kelt, -tch, keltz.** derog A white person. 1912–. C. HIMES Then he met a high-yellah gal, a three-quarter keltz, from down Harlem way (1938). [Origin unknown.]

kelly¹ noun = DERBY KELLY noun. 1970–. A. DRAPER My old kelly was rumbling and I fancied a pie and chips (1970). [Cf. NED KELLY noun.]

kelly² noun Also **Kelly. 1** mainly US A man's hat; spec. a derby hat. 1915–. LAIT & MORTIMER Some of the larger clubs reap up to $50,000 a year for the privilege of checking your kellys (1948). **2** oil industry A rod attached to the top of the drill column. 1934–. [Prob. from the name *Kelly*, a common Irish surname; in sense 1, perh. from DERBY KELLY noun.]

Kelly's eye noun (In the game of bingo and its forerunners) the number one. 1925–.

K kaffir kagg kale kaput kark karzy kaylied

kettle noun dated, mainly criminals' A watch. 1889–. J. CURTIS Next buckshee kettle that comes my way I'll just stick to it (1936).

key noun US A kilogram of a drug. 1968–. J. WAMBAUGH On her coffee table she had at least half a key and that's a pound of pot and that's trouble (1972). [Respelling of *ki-* in *kilo*.]

Keystone noun A policeman. 1935–. A. HUNTER The local Keystones move in demanding alibis (1971). [From the 'Keystone Cops', policemen featured in a series of US slapstick comedy films produced by the Keystone film company, formed by 'Mack Sennett' in 1912.]

Khyber Pass noun Brit Rhyming slang for 'arse'. Also **Khyber**. 1943–. CRESCENDO If we sit on our Khybers, we will miss out on all the things that make our lives the richer (1968). [From the name of the chief pass in the Hindu Kush mountains between Afghanistan and north-west Pakistan.]

kibosh /ˈkaɪbɒʃ/ Also **kybosh**. noun **1 to put the kibosh on** to put an end to, finish off, do for. 1834–. SUNDAY POST (Glasgow): She'd been looking forward to some salmon fishing, but the heatwave's put the kybosh on that (1975). verb trans. **2** To finish off, do for. 1884–. LISTENER What a pity that the stipend has not kept pace . . . with the fall in the value of money (and it even comes to you less PAYE, thus kiboshing manoeuvrability in the field of expenses!) (1969). [Origin uncertain: perh. from obs. costermongers' slang *kye* noun, eighteen pence (from Yiddish *kye* eighteen) + obs. slang *bosh* noun, pence, the underlying notion perh. being a 'derisory sum' (cf. *to give someone a fourpenny one*).]

kick noun **1** dated The fashion, the newest style. *a.*1700–1942. **2** dated A sixpence. *c.*1700–. **3** A pocket. 1851–. SUNDAY TRUTH (Brisbane): One of Luke's jobs was to see that the money was banked every week. Luke put it in his own kick (1968). **4** pl. orig US Shoes. 1904–. BLACK WORLD My terrible blue-and-white kicks (1973). **5** An interest, enthusiasm, fad; esp. in phr. *on the—kick* = doing, or enthusiastic about, the stated thing. 1946–. TIMES LITERARY SUPPLEMENT Somewhere behind the cumulative high, the peace-kick, the good vibes, efficient entrepreneurs . . . were smiling their mean smiles all the way to the bank (1971). verb **6 to kick the bucket** to die. 1785–. S. RUSHDIE

Pinkie was a widow; old Marshal Aurangzeb had kicked the bucket at last (1983). **7 to kick in: a** trans. and intr. orig US To contribute (money, etc.); to pay (one's share). 1908–. FORTUNE Hillard Elkins, producer of *Oh! Calcutta!* asked him to help back his productions of two Ibsen plays; Lufkin kicked in $10,000 (1972). **b** trans. US To break into (a building). 1926–. DETECTIVE FICTION WEEKLY Harold G. Slater's big jewelry store safe had been 'kicked in' and robbed of twelve thousand dollars (1931). **8 to kick off** orig US To die. 1921–. R. LOWELL The old bitches Live into their hundreds, while I'll kick off tomorrow (1970). **9** trans. and intr. US To give up or overcome (a habit, esp. drug-taking). 1936–. BLACK WORLD I'll help you, man, cuz I know you want to kick (1971). TIMES In a moment of weakness, I watched an episode of this [television serial] after having kicked the habit for more than 12 months (1972). **10 to kick ass** orig and mainly US To behave roughly or aggressively, to assert oneself. Also **kick-ass**, adjective Characterized by such behaviour; rough, uncompromising. 1976–. T. MORRISON Kicking ass at Con Edison offices, barking orders in the record companies (1981).

kidvid a television or video programme made for children

kicking adjective Exciting, terrific. 1988–.

kiddo noun A kid; used esp. as a familiar form of address to a man or woman. 1896–. N. FREELING 'How long do I have to stay?' . . . 'Just as long as we thinks right, kiddo' (1974). [From *kid* noun + *-o*.]

kidlet noun A small child. 1889–. [From *kid* noun + *-let*.]

kidstakes noun Also **kidsteaks**. Austral and NZ Nonsense, pretence. 1912–. A. KIMMINS This isn't kid-stakes. . . . This is deadly serious (1960). [Prob. from *kid* noun, nonsense, kidding, as in *no kid*.]

kidvid noun orig US A television or video programme made for children; hence, children's broadcasting. 1955–. FORTUNE She's bringing a new, nonviolent, Disney-created cartoon series to NBC's kidvid schedule (1985). [From *kid* noun + *vid(eo-*.]

kike noun derog and offensive, mainly US A Jew. 1904–. SPECTATOR He knocks down Stern's wife, calls her a kike (1963). [Said to be an alteration of *-ki* (or *-ky*), a common ending of the personal names of Eastern European Jews who emigrated to the US in the late 19th and early 20th centuries.]

killer orig US. noun **1** An impressive, formidable, or excellent person or thing. 1937–. MELODY MAKER George Khan has a solo on the up-tempo passage of the same track which is an absolute killer (1970). adjective **2** Excellent, sensational. 1979–. CITY LIMITS Sometimes James Brown's albums stank, but there was always one killer track (1986). [From *kill* verb, to amuse, delight, etc. greatly + *-er*.]

killer-diller noun and adjective orig US Rhyming reduplication of KILLER noun and adjective. 1938–. W. C. HANDY My old friend Wilbur Sweatman—a killer-diller and a jazz pioneer (1957). [Cf. DILLY noun.]

killick noun Brit, nautical A leading seaman's badge; hence, a leading seaman. 1915–. [From earlier sense, small anchor, from the fact that the badge of a leading seaman in the Royal Navy bears the symbol of an anchor; origin unknown.]

killing adjective Very funny or amusing. 1844–. M. SPARK 'That's exactly what I expected you to say,' Marlene said. 'I think you're killing' (1960). [From the notion of 'dying' with laughter.]

kinder noun Austral A kindergarten. 1955–. M. LURIE Little Norbert and little Hermione and little all the rest of them, are all tucked nicely away in their kinders and creches and day-care centres (1983). [Shortening.]

kindy noun Also **kindie**. Austral = KINDER noun. 1959–. DAILY NEWS (Perth) Lorrelle Holman (5), of Mt Pleasant, is learning pots about the animal kingdom, thanks to her local kindy (1980). [From *kind(ergarten* + *-y*.]

king-fish noun US A leader, chief, boss; often used as a nickname for a particular person, notably for Huey Long (1893–1935), Governor and Senator from Louisiana. 1933–. RICHMOND (Virginia) TIMES DISPATCH Mr. Brown . . . is sometimes referred to as the 'kingfish' of City Council (1946). [From earlier sense, type of large fish.]

king-hit Austral. noun **1** A knock-out punch, esp. an unfair one. 1912–. verb trans. **2** To punch suddenly and hard, often unfairly. 1959–.

King Kong noun **1** US dated Cheap alcohol. 1946–50. **2** Used as a nickname for anyone of outstanding size or strength. 1955–. GUARDIAN Finn MacCool was a legendary Irish giant, a King Kong with a generous heart

(1974). [Name of the ape-like monster featured in the film *King Kong* (1933).]

kink noun **1** dated US, derog and offensive A black person. 1865–. **2** US A criminal. 1914–. **3** A sexually abnormal person; loosely, an eccentric, a person wearing noticeably unusual clothes, behaving in a startling manner, etc. 1965–. J. RIPLEY I have known queers. I have known kinks (1972). [From earlier sense, twist; in sense 1, in allusion to black people's tightly curled hair.] Cf. KINKY adjective.

kinky noun **1** US dated A person with tightly curled hair; spec. a black person. 1926–. Cf. KINK noun 1. **2** criminals' Something dishonestly obtained. 1927–. AMERICAN MERCURY The titles of every car Joe sold could be searched clear back to the factory. . . . Yet the cars were strictly kinkies (1941). **3** A sexually abnormal or perverted person. 1959–. A. DIMENT Porny photos, various drugs and birds for kinkies at Oxford (1967). adjective **4** criminals' Dishonestly acquired, tampered with, etc.; crooked, bent. 1927–. W. R & F. K SIMPSON Canfield . . . was never accused . . . of having 'kinky' gambling paraphernalia. By that I mean dice and cards and roulette wheels that gave the house an unfair advantage (1954). **5** Of people: having unusual or non-normal sexual tastes; spec. homosexual. Of things or situations: suggestive of sexual perversion, as of certain items or styles of dress (e.g. *kinky boots*); in weakened sense, bizarre. 1959–. F. WARNER Kinky sex makes them feel inadequate (1972).

kip Brit noun **1** dated A brothel. Also **kip-house, kip-shop.** 1766–. **2** A bed. 1879–. L. GRIFFITHS Half of the time they're tucked up in their kip reading the *Mirror* and drinking cups of tea (1985). **3** A cheap lodging-house. Also **kip-house, kip-shop.** 1883–. OBSERVER Dossers at a London kip-house (1962). **4** A sleep or nap. 1893–. B. W ALDISS I had to stay with the captain . . . while the other lucky sods settled down for a brief kip (1971). verb intr. **5** To go to bed, sleep; also, to lie *down*. 1889–. WEEKLY NEWS (Glasgow): A driver whose van broke down near Bristol, decided to kip down in the driver's seat (1973). [Cf. Danish *kippe* mean hut, low alehouse; *horekippe* brothel.]

kipper noun **1** A person, esp. a young or small person, a child. 1905–. **2** Austral An English person, spec. an English immigrant in Australia. 1943–. K. GILES You kippers—no guts and two faces—are only strong under the armpits (1967). **3** nautical A torpedo. 1953–. G. JENKINS I evaluate its firing power at eighteen torpedoes—I think kipper is a distressing piece

killer killer-diller killick killing kinder kindy

of naval slang—in thirty minutes (1959). [In sense 2, from a popular Australian association of kippers with the English.]

kishke /ˈkɪʃkə/ noun Also **kishka, kishkeh, kishker.** In sing. and pl. The guts. 1959–. L. ROSTEN I laughed until my *kishkas* were sore (1968). [From earlier sense, sausage made with beef intestine; from Yiddish.]

kiss verb **1** to kiss (someone's) **arse** (or **ass**): **a** As imperative, esp. in phr. *kiss my arse*: used as an angry or contemptuous rejoinder. 1705–. FAIRBANKS (Alaska) DAILY NEWS-MINER McGovern had told an airport antagonist to 'kiss my a . . . ' (1972). **b** To act obsequiously towards (someone). 1749–. H. MILLER If it weren't that I had learned to take the boss's ass, I would have been fired (1934). **2 to kiss off: a** trans. To dismiss, get rid of. 1935–. M. & G. GORDON The same FBI agents . . . getting tough. Well, kiss them off (1973). **b** intr. To go away, die, desist. 1945–. W. MCCARTHY 'I thought you had stopped smoking.' 'Kiss off, I just started again' (1973).

kisser noun orig boxing The mouth; the face. 1860–. J. WAINWRIGHT Open that sweet little, lying little, kisser of yours, and start saying something that makes sense (1973). [= that which kisses, from earlier sense, one who kisses.]

kit noun mainly Brit Clothes; often used in the context of undressing. 1985–. SUNDAY TIMES Fiona Pitt-Kethley has agreed to get her kit off to appear on Channel 4's forthcoming Naked Chat Show (1993). [From earlier sense, set of matching garments worn for a sporting or military activity.]

kitchen noun musicians' The percussion section of an orchestra or band. 1931–. [Prob. from the fanciful resemblance of the timpani (kettledrums) and other percussion instruments to kitchen implements and vessels.]

kite noun **1** criminals' A letter or note, esp. one that is illicit or surreptitious; spec. a letter or message smuggled into or out of prison. 1859–. H. BRYAN Having settled on the girl, one would send her a 'kite', or love letter (1953). **2** Brit, mainly services' An aeroplane. 1917–. M. TRIPP The Squadron hasn't lost a single kite in the last three raids (1952). **3** A cheque, esp. a blank, dud, or forged cheque. 1927–. T. PARKER He's in for what they call 'kites', dud cheques, you know (1969). verb trans. **4** To smuggle (a letter or message) into or out of a prison. 1925–. DETECTIVE FICTION WEEKLY A letter which I had 'kited' out of the prison (1936). **5** To write or cash (a dud or temporarily unbacked cheque). 1934–. E. LATHEN If it had been a

question of . . . kiting a cheque—well, that wouldn't surprise you at all. Clyde cut corners all his life (1969). [In sense 2, prob. from *box-kite* noun, a term used for an early type of biplane, but recorded earlier (1838, 1909) prob. with direct reference to *kite* flying toy; in sense 3, from earlier sense, fraudulent bill of exchange, from phr. *to fly a kite* to issue such a bill, from the notion of a toy kite as something insubstantial that floats in the air temporarily.]

kitten noun **to have kittens** orig US To lose one's composure; to get into a flap. 1900–. A. GILBERT Gertrude was going to have kittens when she discovered that extravagance (1959).

kiwi noun Also **Kiwi.** A non-flying member of an air force. 1918–. [From the kiwi's flightlessness.]

ki-yi /kaɪˈjaɪ/ noun US dated A dog, esp. a small noisy one. 1895–1914. BUFFALO EXPRESS (New York) A butcher in Brussels made sausage of the carcass of a zoo elephant which had been killed. Doubtless the Brussels kiyis yelped for joy (1904). [From earlier sense, howl or yelp of a dog.]

klepto noun Abbreviation of 'kleptomaniac'. 1958–. E. V. CUNNINGHAM You got it . . . right out of Helen Sarbine's purse . . . . What are you—some kind of nut or klepto? (1964).

klick noun Also **click, klik.** N Amer, orig military A kilometre. 1967–. J. SAVARIN They're gone sixty miles by now. Nearly a hundred klicks, if you prefer (1982). [Of uncertain origin: used by US servicemen during the Vietnam war.]

kludge /kluːdʒ/ Also **kluge.** orig US. noun **1** An ill-assorted collection of poorly matching parts. 1962–. **2** computing A machine, system, or program that has been improvised or badly put together. 1976–. WHICH MICRO? The QL is at last available . . . and without 'kludges' tacked on to make it work (1984). verb trans. **3** To improvise with a kludge. 1962–. QL USER Its history was most unfortunate to start with: production delays, 'kludged' machines, extra ROMs hanging off the back (1984). [Coined by J. W. Granholm with ironic reference to German *klug* clever; cf. *bodge* verb, *fudge* verb.]

klunk noun Also **clunk.** US A foolish or contemptible person. 1942–. NEW YORK HERALD-TRIBUNE Mr. Wagner has been a remarkably good mayor, and the klunks who don't realize this . . . understand neither the Mayor himself nor the nature of his responsibilities (1964). [Origin unknown.]

klutz /klʌts/ noun Also **klotz, kluhtz.** US A clumsy, awkward person, esp. one who is socially inept; a fool. 1968–. E.-J. BAHR Janet is an utter klotz (1973). [From Yiddish, from German *Klotz* wooden block.]

knacker verb trans. To exhaust, wear out; often as past participial adjective **knackered.** 1946–. TIMES I kept thinking I should whip up the pace and then I'd think 'I'm knackered, I'll leave it for another lap' (1971). [From earlier senses, to kill, to castrate, from *knacker* noun, horse-slaughterer or KNACKERS noun.]

knackers noun pl. The testicles. 1866–. G. GREENE I may regret him for a while tonight. His knackers were superb (1969). [From earlier sense, castanets, from *knack* verb, to make a sharp cracking noise.]

knee-trembler noun An act of sexual intercourse between people standing up. 1896–. B. W ALDISS Afterwards Nelson would get her against our back wall for a knee-trembler . . . . He claimed that knee-tremblers were the most exhausting way of having sex (1971).

knickers Brit noun **1 to get one's knickers in a twist** jocular To become unduly agitated or angry. 1971–. BRAND NEW YORK There is no reason to get one's knickers in a twist and believe the revolution is nigh (1982). int **2** An expression of contempt, exasperation, etc. 1971–. PACIFIST This is where the revolution's happening, man, and knickers to the metropolis! (1974).

knitting noun sailors' A girl or girls. 1943–. [From the stereotypical view of knitting as a woman's occupation.]

knob noun **1 with knobs on** Brit (That) and more (used in emphatic agreement, as a retort to an insult, etc.) 1930–. A. PRICE If the A.S. 12 was the answer to Egypt's Russian missile boats, the A.S. 15 was the answer with knobs on (1970). **2** The penis. 1971–. MELODY MAKER *No* pictures of pop stars' knobs this week due to a bit of 'Spycatcher' type censorship round these parts (1987).

knobhead noun A fool, idiot. 1926–. [From KNOB noun 2 + *head* noun.]

knock verb **1** trans. Brit To have sex with; also, to make pregnant. 1598–. D. PINNER I've knocked some girls in my time but I've never had such a rabbiter as you (1967). **2** trans., criminals' To rob (esp. a safe or till). 1767–. TIMES The appellant had been asked if he had told someone in the 'Norfolk' that he had got the money by safe breaking. The appellant had replied: 'Aye but you will never prove that I got it by knocking a safe' (1963). **3 to knock up** US

To make pregnant. 1813–. H. C. RAE He screwed her, knocked her up first go and . . . married her . . . before she could even contemplate abortion (1971). **4 to knock down: a** trans. Austral and NZ To spend (one's available resources) in a spree or drinking bout. 1845–. J. H. TRAVERS After they made payment, they would book up another three months' supply, and then knock the balance down at the local pub (1976). **b** trans. and intr. US To steal or embezzle (esp. passengers' fares). a.1854–. J. EVANS Some . . . clerk who was knocking down on the till (1949). **5 to knock out** To earn. 1871–. BULLETIN (Sydney): What about the school-teacher, the young computer programmer or plumber knocking out about $200 a week (1975). **6 to knock off** trans. **a: to knock it off** to stop what one is doing; mainly as imperative. 1902–. J. HELLER 'Hey, knock it off down there,' a voice rang out from the far end of the ward. 'Can't you see we're trying to nap?' (1961). **b** To steal, to rob. 1919–. A. HUNTER Just met a bloke . . . in the nick . . . . Him what was in there for knocking-off cars (1973). Cf. KNOCK-OFF noun. **c** orig US To kill, to murder. 1919–. **d** criminals' To arrest (a person); to raid (an establishment). 1926–. R. V. BESTE You're the sort who'd knock off his mother because she hadn't got a lamp on her bike five minutes after lighting up time (1969). **e** Brit To have sex with, to seduce (a woman). 1952–. TIMES LITERARY SUPPLEMENT Knocking off his best friend's busty wife during boozy sprees on leave in Soho (1974). **7 to knock rotten** Austral To kill or stun. 1919–. **8 to knock over** criminals' To rob, burgle. 1928–. ILLUSTRATED LONDON NEWS The job looks easy enough—a big hotel at Tropico Springs that any fool could 'knock over' (1940). noun **9** (An act of) sexual intercourse; so **on the knock,** working as a prostitute. 1933–. D. BAGLEY Maybe she was on the knock (1969).

knock-down noun US, Austral, and NZ An introduction to a person. 1865–. SUN-HERALD (Sydney): That's a grouse-looking little sheila over there, Sal. Any chance of a knockdown to her later on? (1981).

knockers noun pl. A woman's breasts. 1941–. M. J. BOSSE I'm jealous. She has those big knockers, and I'm afraid you like them (1972).

knocking-shop noun A brothel. 1860–. L. KENNEDY Yes, it seems that some of the girls are running a knocking-shop on the side (1969). [From KNOCK verb 1.]

knock-off noun **1 on the knock-off** engaged in stealing. 1936–. J. CURTIS They [i.e.

gloves] . . . gave away the fact that he was still on the knock-off (1936). **2** Stolen goods. 1963–. **3** A robbery. 1969–. J. GARDNER The really profitable knock-off, like the Train Robbery (1969). [From the verbal phr. *to knock off* (see KNOCK verb 6b).]

knotted adjective **get knotted!** an expression of disbelief, annoyance, etc. 1963–. G. LYALL 'I'll lend you a good book about security.' 'Get knotted, Major' (1972). [From *knot* verb, to tie in a knot.]

know verb trans. **1 not to know beans** US not to know something, to be not well informed. 1833–. Cf. (*to know*) *how many beans make five* at BEAN noun. **2 to know one's onions** to understand a subject fully, to be extremely competent. 1922–. J. CANNAN Shakespeare knew his onions, didn't he? (1958). **3 not to know one's arse from one's elbow** (and similar phrases): used to suggest complete ignorance or innocence. 1930–. N. SHUTE I wish I'd had a crowd like that for my first crew. We none of us knew arse from elbow when they pushed me off (1944). **4 (not) to know from nothing** US To be totally ignorant (about something). 1936–. ENCOUNTER He knows from nuthin' (1968).

knuckle noun **to go the knuckle** Austral To punch, to fight. 1944–. NORTHERN TERRITORY NEWS (Darwin): Katherine went the knuckle against Banks in the NT Football Association—and paid the price (1984).

knucklehead noun orig and mainly US A slow-witted or stupid person. 1944–. R. PARKES What I'm trying to get across to you knuckleheads is that it was *not* murder! (1971).

knuckle sandwich noun A punch in the mouth. 1973–. A. BUZO He tried to hang one on me at Leichhardt Oval once, so I administered a knuckle sandwich to him (1973).

konk[1,2] verb = CONK[1,2] verb.

kook /kuːk/ noun US **1** A crazy or eccentric person. 1960–. PUBLISHERS WEEKLY A bona fide kook who is never quite able to get in gear till he finally dies paddling his canoe across the Atlantic

(1973). **2** A novice or inexpert surfer. 1961–. [Prob. from *cuckoo* noun or adjective.]

kooky /ˈkuːkɪ/ adjective Also **kookie.** Crazy, eccentric. 1959–. NATION REVIEW (Melbourne): 'No Sex Please, We're British!' The funniest, kookiest night of your life (1973). [From KOOK noun + *-y.*]

kosher /ˈkəʊʃə(r)/ adjective Correct, genuine, legitimate. 1896–. L. GRIBBLE 'No financial irregularities?' 'Strictly kosher . . . . It's so good it stinks' (1961). [From earlier sense, in accordance with Jewish law; ultimately from Hebrew *kāshēr* right.]

kozzer noun = COZZER noun.

Kraut noun derog A German, esp. a German soldier. 1918–. T. PYNCHON Maybe . . . he should have been in a war, Japs in trees, Krauts in Tiger tanks (1966). [Abbreviation of *sauerkraut* noun, from its prevalence in the German diet.]

kriegie /ˈkriːgɪ/ noun An Allied prisoner of war in Germany during World War II. 1944–. D. M. DAVIN But there I was, a bloody kriegie for the rest of the war (1956). [Abbreviation of German *Kriegsgefangener* prisoner of war.]

kvell verb intr. US To boast; to feel proud or happy; to gloat. 1967–. L. M. FEINSILVER You've got reason to kvell (1970). [From Yiddish *kveln,* from German *quellen* to gush, well up.]

kvetch Also **kvetsch.** US. noun **1** An annoying or contemptible person; spec. a person who complains a lot, a fault-finder. 1964–. L. ROSTEN It will take forever, he's such a kvetch (1968). verb intr. **2** To complain, to whinge. 1965–. ATLANTIC MONTHLY He is an amiable one, not given to angry kvetching (1968). [noun from Yiddish *kvetsh,* from German *Quetsche* crusher, presser; verb from Yiddish *kvetshn.*]

kye noun nautical **1** A contemptible person, esp. one who is mean with money. 1929–46. **2** Cocoa or drinking chocolate. 1943–. TIMES Kye, as the service names drinking chocolate, is to end (1968). [Origin unknown, but cf. English dialect *kyish* dirty.]

lad noun Brit **1 the lads** A group of male friends. 1896–. INDEPENDENT 'I wasn't one of the lads,' he said. 'I didn't mix with the sporting types and . . . I'm still not very interested in sport' (1991). **2** A lively (young) man, esp. a highly sexed one; esp. in phr. *a bit of a lad* and *quite a lad*. 1913–. H. CARMICHAEL Bit of a lad is Mr. Alan Clark . . . running round fancy-free for years (1960). [From earlier, more general sense, boy, young man.]

laddish adjective Like a lad, esp. exhibiting the typical behaviour of young men in groups. 1907–. SUNDAY TIMES They could talk Shakespeare and football, be sensitive then brutal. Sure, David Baddiel and Frank Skinner were laddish together, but there was never anything vulgar (1996). [From LAD noun + *-ish*.]

ladette noun Brit A young woman who exhibits the typical behaviour of young men in groups. 1995–. SCOTSMAN The TV and radio presenter was undoubtedly the archetypal ladette, single-handedly taking the bad-girl behaviour to hitherto unimagined heights (2001). [From LAD noun + *-ette*.]

la-di-da adjective Also **la-di-dah, lah-di-da(h)**. **1** Snobbish, pretentious. 1895–. GUARDIAN He was . . . the American air-force sergeant with whom a duke's daughter, Anna Neagle, falls in love, his pleasant American baritone providing welcome relief from the lah-di-dah accents (1991). noun **2** Brit A cigar. 1977–. SUNDAY TIMES MAGAZINE Nerves take over, so a puff or two on a Lusitania cigar. Being too poor to bet or have women, . . . a la-di-dah is my one luxury (1996). [From earlier obs. noun use, snobbish or pretentious person; imitative of a supposed typical utterance of such people; in sense 2, rhyming slang.]

lady noun **lady of the evening** (or **night**) euphemistic A prostitute. 1925–. GAINESVILLE (Florida) SUN Around Subic Bay in the Philippines, the U.S. military men outnumber the licensed ladies of the night by 20,000 to 8,000 (1984).

Lady Muck noun A pompous self-opinionated condescending woman. 1957–. I. CROSS She sat there, sipping away at her tea like Lady Muck (1957). Cf. LORD MUCK noun.

lag noun **1** A convict, prisoner; esp. in phr. *old lag*, an ex-convict or habitual convict. 1812–. SUNDAY MAIL MAGAZINE (Brisbane): The old lags inhabiting Queensland's prisons in 1885 must have been disappointed when the colony's official flogger, John Hutton, retired (1989). **2** dated A term of imprisonment or transportation. 1821–. verb trans. dated **3** To send to prison or transport. 1812–. **4** To

arrest. 1847–. [Origin unknown; cf. obs. *lag* verb, to carry off, steal.]

lager lout noun Brit A youth (usu. one of a group) who typically drinks large amounts of lager or beer, and behaves in an offensive, boorish manner. 1988–. PRIVATE EYE It's a clever wheeze dreamed up by a bunch of lager louts with a GCSE in Spanish (1989).

laid-back adjective Of music: mellow, subdued; of a person, etc.: casually unperturbed, relaxed. 1969–. NEW SOCIETY It's all cheerfully grotty and relaxed in the usual laid-back Montreal style (1974).

lair Also **lare**. Austral. noun **1** A youth or man who dresses flashily or shows off. 1923–. T. A. G. HUNGERFORD He used to wear gold cuff-links in the coat sleeves of his blue serge suit: I suppose he was what we used to call a lair (1983). verb intr. **2** To behave or dress like a lair; often followed by *up*. 1928–. A. F. HOWELLS Earning something in the vicinity of three pounds ten shillings a week . . . I could still afford to lair up a bit, get on the scoot occasionally with my mates (1983). [Back-formation from LAIRY adjective.]

lairy adjective Also **lary**. **1** Cockney Knowing, fly, conceited. 1846–. B. NAUGHTON We'll have to keep an eye on him. Spivs are lary perishers. Anything goes wrong they'll never risk their own skin (1945). **2** Also **leary, leery**. Austral Flashily dressed; vulgar. 1898–. B. MARTYN He was a stout fleshy chap wearing a dazzling tie and fancy waistcoat. He was popularly described as a 'bit lairy' (1979). [Alteration of LEERY adjective.]

lakes adjective Also **Lakes o'Killarney**. Of a person: mad, crazy. Also as noun, a mad person. 1934–. M. ALLINGHAM Which is not like a bloke who's done a killing unless he's lakes (1955). [Shortened from *Lakes of Killarney*, rhyming slang for 'barmy'.]

lad laddish ladette la-di-da lady Lady Muck lag

lallapaloosa /ˌlæləpəˈluːsə, -zə/ noun Also **lala-, lolla-, -palooser, -paloozer.** US Something outstandingly good of its kind. 1904–. s. j. perelman All agreed that Luba Pneumatic was a lollapaloosa, the Eighth Wonder of the World (1970). [Fanciful formation.]

lallygag verb intr. Also **lollygag.** US **1** To fool around; to dawdle. 1862–. springfield (Massachusetts) union The Dow Jones average of 30 industrials, which lollygagged most of the day, gained strongly in afternoon trading (1973). **2** dated To cuddle amorously. 1868–. [Origin unknown.]

lam US. verb intr. **1** To run off, escape, beat it; often followed by out. 1886–. m. macintosh The time of death . . . [was] four days before Fisher lammed out (1973). noun **2** Escape, flight; esp. in phr. on the lam, on the run, to take it on the lam, to run away. 1897–. g. baxt Were you stalling for time while your Brunhilde takes it on the lam? (1972). [Perh. from lam verb, to beat.]

lame US. adjective **1** Naïve, socially inept. 1942–. washington post Posers are really lame (1986). noun **2** mainly African-American A socially unsophisticated person; one who does not fit in with a particular social group. 1959–. j. wambaugh They're a couple of lames trying to groove with the Kids. They're nothing (1972).

lame-brain noun mainly US A stupid person. 1929–. times literary supplement We have finished feeling indulgent towards the disaffected lamebrains who turn this kind of stuff out (1972). [From lame adjective + brain noun.]

lamer noun orig and mainly US A dull, stupid, inept, or contemptible person. 1961–. d. verton They thought too highly of themselves to waste their time mentoring lamers and other wannabes (2002). [From LAME adjective + -er.]

lamp¹ verb trans. Brit, orig northern dialect To hit, beat, thrash. 1808–. guardian How long . . . before one player takes things that one stage further than bat-waving and bad-mouthing and slots another. Lamps him one (2007). [Origin uncertain: perh. an alteration of lam verb, to beat.]

lamp² verb trans. orig US To see, look at, recognize, watch. 1916–. r. busby I'd like to know how the coppers got on to us. They couldn't have lamped us on the road (1969). [Cf. LAMPS noun.]

lamps noun pl. dated **1** orig poetical The eyes. 1590–. Cf. GIG-LAMPS noun. f. d. sharpe He had his lamps on the copper (1938). **2** naval A nickname for a sailor responsible for looking after the lamps on board ship. 1866–1933. e. o'neill Fetch a light, Lamps, that's a good boy (1919).

lance-jack noun Brit, services' A lance-corporal or lance-bombardier. 1912–. l. deighton You're not looking too good, Colonel, if you don't mind an ex-lance-jack saying so (1971). [From lance-(corporal noun + obs. jack noun, chap, fellow or the male personal name Jack.]

langer noun coarse, Irish English A penis; also, a fool. 1983–. sunday times My ambition at the end of the festival is that . . . in Cork they won't be calling me a langer (2005). [Origin unknown.]

lard-ass noun mainly N Amer, orig nautical (Someone with) large buttocks; a fat person. Also **lard-assed,** adjective. 1946–. r. a. hill All they do is eat and sit around on their lard asses around the guns (1959).

lark noun Brit A type of activity, affair, etc. 1934–. g. f. fiennes I am up to my ears in this bloody diesel lark (1967). [From earlier sense, amusing activity.]

larn verb trans. To teach (someone) better behaviour; used as a threat of punishment. 1902–. c. blackstock That'll larn you, you so-and-sos (1956). [From earlier sense, to teach, from dialect form of learn verb.]

lash noun Austral and NZ An attempt; esp. in phr. to have a lash, to have a go. 1894–. k. tennant If things get any tougher, I guess I'll have a lash at it (1953). [From earlier sense, sudden blow.]

lat noun Abbreviation of 'latrine'; usu. in pl. 1927–. j. i. m. stewart Turk says that conscientious objectors have to clean out the lats in lunatic asylums (1957).

latrine rumour noun services', dated A baseless rumour believed to originate in gossip in the latrines. Also **latrine.** 1918–50.

> 'Luba Pneumatic was a lollapaloosa, the Eighth Wonder of the World.'

lallapaloosa lallygag lam lame lame-brain lamer

lead

latrinogram noun services' = LATRINE RUMOUR noun. 1944–. D. M. DAVIN According to current latrino-gram we were going to be given a rest (1947). [From *latrin(e + -o + -gram*.]

laugh verb **1 to be laughing** to be in a fortunate or successful position. 1930–. M. STANIER So long as you're a jump ahead you're laughing (1975). **2 to laugh all the way to the bank** used to denote a relishing of one's profits. 1969–. NATIONAL TRUST The taxpayer may be called in to 'save' it [i.e. a great house] for the nation. Then the owner laughs all the way to the bank, and the devil can take his conscience (1985). noun **3** Something or someone very funny or amusing; often used ironically. 1930–. J. WAIN 'Your friends paid for it.' That was a laugh. My friends . . . were a one-way valve for drinks, cigarettes and loans (1960). [In sense 2, alteration of an original (ironic) *to cry all the way to the bank* to deplore one's undeserved profits, attributed to the US pianist Liberace (1919–87).]

laugher noun US **1** baseball An easily won game, walkover. 1964–. **2** Something amusing or ridiculous. 1973–. WASHINGTON POST The voice belongs to . . . the engineer-producer for this laugher of a recording session (1977). [In sense 1, from the notion of victory being laughably easy to achieve.]

laughing-sides noun pl. Austral jocular Elastic-sided boots. 1937–. [Supposedly orig an Aboriginal malapropism.]

launder verb trans. **1** To change (illegally) in order to render acceptable or legitimate. *a.*1961–. NEW YORK TIMES Unscrupulous dealers . . . 'launder' the mileage of cars (1976). **2** To transfer (funds), esp. to a foreign bank account, in order to conceal a dubious or illegal origin. 1973–. GLOBE & MAIL (Toronto): Kerr concedes U.S. criminals 'launder' money in Ontario (1974). [From earlier sense, to wash linen; the use in sense 2 arose from the Watergate inquiry in the United States in 1973–4.]

lav noun Brit Abbreviation for 'lavatory'. 1913–. J. THOMSON Gilbert Leacock went out to the lav. . . . I heard the chain being pulled (1973).

lavvy noun Brit = LAV noun. 1961–. GUARDIAN A house where the lavvy is behind an arras (1971).

law noun orig US The police; also, a policeman, sheriff, or other representative of the law. 1929–. W. BURROUGHS We were in the third precinct about three hours and then the laws put us in the wagon and took us to Parish Prison (1953); TIMES I inquired of the law where I might cash a cheque (1972).

lawk int dated = Lord! Also **lawks, lawk-a-mercy (-mussy)** = Lord have mercy! 1768–. B. L. K. HENDERSON Lawkamercy, lad, what's that? (1927). [Alteration of *lack* noun or of *lord* noun.]

lay verb **1 to lay an egg: a** Of an aircraft: to drop a bomb. 1918–. **b** Of a performer or performance: to flop. 1929–. L. FEATHER The singer had been laying eggs at the Zanzibar . . . and Shaw was undecided what to do with him (1949). **2** orig US **a** trans. To have sex with. 1934–. P. ROTH All I know is I got laid, *twice* (1969). **b** intr. Of a woman: to have or be willing to have sex; often with *for*. 1955–. J. UPDIKE You've laid for Harrison, haven't you? (1960). **3 to lay (something) on** (a person): US To give (something) to (someone). 1942–. IT Of course you can't lay advice on someone (1970). **4 to lay pipe** US Of a man: to have sex; to copulate, esp. vigorously. 1967–. A. HAILEY It made him horny just to look at her, and he laid pipe, sometimes three times a night (1971). noun **5** orig US **a** A person, esp. a woman, considered as a partner in sexual intercourse. 1932–. W. GADDIS She's the girl you used to go around with in college? She's a good lay (1955). **b** An act of sexual intercourse. 1936–. B. MALAMUD Tonight an unexpected party, possibly a lay with a little luck (1971).

lay-down noun **1** orig US A virtual certainty; a sure thing, cinch. 1935–. TIMES A prize will go to the best-dressed trainer of the meeting. It sounds like a lay-down for Henry Cecil (1984). **2** Brit, police and criminals' A remand in custody; also, a remand prisoner. 1938–.

lazy dog noun US, military A type of fragmentation bomb designed to explode in mid-air and scatter steel pellets at high velocity over the target area. 1965–.

lead /led/ noun **lead in one's pencil** male sexual potency or vigour. 1941–. D. LEES The couscous is supposed to put lead in your pencil but with Daria I needed neither a talking point nor an aphrodisiac (1972). See also **to swing the lead** at SWING verb.

lead /liːd/ verb **to lead with one's chin** orig boxing To stick one's neck out, leave oneself unprotected. 1949–. A. MACVICAR Don't go leading with your chin, Bruce (1973). [From *to lead*, to make the first punch of an attack in boxing.]

latrinogram laugh laugher laughing-sides lavvy

lead balloon /led-/ noun A failure, a flop.
1960–. L. DEIGHTON With this boy it went over like a lead balloon (1962).

lead-pipe /led-/ adjective US **a lead-pipe cinch** a complete certainty. 1898–. NEW YORK TIMES To be sure, speculation in gold is not a lead-pipe cinch; its price can go up as well as down (1973).

leaf noun services' Also **leef**. Leave of absence. 1846–. J. IRVING A sailor goes 'on leaf' and *never* on furlough (1946). [Variant of *leave* noun.]

leak verb intr. **1** To urinate. 1596–. J. KEROUAC The prowl car came by and the cop got out to leak (1957). noun **2** An act of urinating; esp. in phr. *to have* (or *take*) *a leak*. 1934–. G. GREENE All these hours of standing without taking a leak (1969).

leather-neck noun **1** nautical **a** dated A soldier. 1890–1916. **b** US A marine. 1914–. R. WEST The U.S. Marine Corps. These legendary troops, nicknamed 'leathernecks' (1968). **2** Austral, dated An unskilled farm labourer, esp. on a sheep station. 1898–1945. [In sense 1a, from the leather neck-piece formerly worn by soldiers.]

leave verb **to leave it out** Brit To stop doing or saying something, to 'give over', 'cut it out'; usu. in imperative. 1969–. P. THEROUX No—leave it out! He had been wrong (1986).

leccer noun Also **lecker, lekker**. Brit, dated A lecture. 1899–1928. DAILY EXPRESS A . . . dilapidated basket filled with gay-coloured 'lekker' notebooks (1928). [Alteration of *lecture* noun.]

lech /letʃ/ Also **letch**. noun **1** A strong desire, esp. sexual. 1796–. SUNDAY TIMES Many so-called platonic friendships . . . are merely one-way leches (1972). **2** A lecher. 1943–. GUARDIAN A rich man can have a beautiful young wife even if he is a gropy old letch! (1970). verb intr. **3** To feel lecherous; to behave lecherously. 1911–. GUARDIAN A fortyish factory worker . . . lives with . . . an obsessively nubile sister whom he obviously leches after (1973). [Back-formation from *lecher* noun.]

leery adjective orig US Wary, suspicious; usu. followed by *of*. 1896–. TUCSON (Arizona) DAILY CITIZEN The Braunlichs will also tell you that . . . middle America is leery of things it gets for free (1973). [From earlier sense, knowing, fly; perh. from obs. *leer* noun, looking askance, from *leer* verb.] Cf. LAIRY adjective.

left field noun mainly US A position away from the centre of interest, the sidelines;

a state of ignorance, confusion, or dissociation from reality; often in phr. *out of* (or *from*) *left field*. Also as adjective. 1959–. S. BELLOW The only answer I could make came from left field. I said, 'Before the First World War, Europe was governed by a royalty of cousins' (1984). [From baseball sense, the part of the outfield to the left of the batter as he stands at the plate.]

left-footer noun derog A Roman Catholic. 1944–. J. H. FULLARTON 'What about the R.C.s?' 'Oh, yes. Leave the left-footers behind as gun-picquets' (1944).

leg noun **to get** (**have**, etc.) **one's leg over** of a man, to have sex with a woman. 1975–. D. KARTUN Daft, spending like that on a tart like her. Half the garrison have had their leg over (1987). [Cf. 18th-cent. *to lift a leg over* (someone) in same sense.]

legal noun Brit, mainly taxi-drivers' (A passenger who pays) the exact fare without any tip. 1923–. H. HODGE Some 'legals' are simply mean, and give excuses instead of a tip (1939).

leg art noun orig US = CHEESECAKE noun. 1940–. SPECTATOR The Cameo Royal, the leg-art cinema by London's Leicester Square (1958).

legit /lɪˈdʒɪt/ noun **1** A legitimate actor, child, etc. 1897–. E. BOWEN Left no children—anyway, no legits (1955). **2 on the legit** within the law. 1931–. adjective **3** Abbreviation of 'legitimate'. 1908–. H. HOWARD This dough isn't strictly legit (1973).

legless adjective Drunk, esp. too drunk to stand. 1976–. DAILY TELEGRAPH I must have had well over half a bottle. . . . In the end I was legless and couldn't talk (1986).

leg-over noun Brit (An act of) sexual intercourse. 1975–. [From *to get one's leg over* (see LEG noun).]

lemon noun **1** A gullible or foolish person; a simpleton. 1908–. A. HALL They'd sent me down to show me something and they knew I couldn't see it and I felt a bit of a lemon (1973). **2** orig US Something unsatisfactory or undesirable; esp. a substandard or defective car. 1909–. SYDNEY MORNING HERALD The effect of this on consumers is too many lemons or part lemons coupled with near impossibility of obtaining redress from the manufacturer (1972). **3** The head. 1923–. COAST TO COAST If you had any brains in that big lemon you'd wipe me (1952). **4** US An informer, one who turns State's evidence. 1931–.

lemon-game noun US A type of confidence trick which involves defrauding a gullible player in a game of pool. Also **lemon**. 1908–37.

lemony adjective Austral and NZ Irritated, angry; esp. in phr. *to go lemony at* (or *on*), to become angry with. 1941–. s. GORE Oh, blimey, they went real lemony on 'im (1968).

length noun A penis; sexual intercourse. 1968–. H. C. RAE Beefy, randy-arsed wives crying out for a length (1968). See also **to slip someone a length** at SLIP verb.

les /lez/ adjective and noun Also **les(s)ie, lessy, lez(z), lezzy,** and with upper-case initial. Abbreviation of 'lesbian'. 1929–. NEW SOCIETY I reckon she's a les you know (1972).

lesbo noun Also **lesbie** and with upper-case initial. A lesbian. 1940–. C. HIMES 'One was a man; a good-looking man at that.' 'Man my ass, they were lesbos' (1969). [From *lesb(ian + -o*.]

leso noun Also **lezo, lezzo** Austral = LESBO noun. 1945–. NATIONAL TIMES (Sydney) And *Gay*! What an insult to the poofs and lezzos who made this country what it is today! (1983). [From *les(bian + -o*.]

lettuce noun orig US Money. 1929–. P. G. WODEHOUSE How are you fixed for lettuce, Hank? . . . Dough. Cash. Glue . . . Money (1967). [From the crinkliness and greenish-white colour of dollar bills.]

letty noun A bed, a lodging. 1846–. J. OSBORNE *Jean*: We can't all spend our time nailing our suitcases to the floor, and shin out of the window. *Archie*: Scarper the letty (1957). [From Italian *letto* bed.]

level verb intr. orig US To be frank or honest; usu. followed by *with*. 1920–. L. DEIGHTON I'd better level with you, son . . . . From now on, control is through me (1974).

liberate verb trans. euphemistic or jocular To loot, to steal. 1944–. G. MELLY He . . . wore a sombrero liberated, I suspect, from the wardrobe of some Latin-American group he had worked with in the past (1965).

lick noun **1a** US, Austral, and NZ A spurt at racing, a short brisk spin; a spell of work. 1809–. **b** Speed. 1847–. P. RUELL Caroline contrived to be first down the gangway and set off along the quay at a good lick. **2** pl. US Criticism, censure. 1971–. TIME Barbara Streisand's A Star is Born does not deserve the licks it has got from Jay Cocks (1977). [In sense 2, from earlier sense, beating, blow.]

lickety-split adverb Also **lickerty-, licketty-, -ity-, -oty-, -spit**. US At full speed; headlong. 1859–. LAST WHOLE EARTH CATALOG Just like that. Stopped in here a few minutes, then took off up that creek lickety-split (1972). [Fanciful coinage.]

lid noun **1** A hat or cap; esp. a soldier's steel helmet or a motorcyclist's crash-helmet. Cf. SKID-LID noun. 1896–. P. G. WODEHOUSE It is almost as foul as Uncle Tom's Sherlock Holmes deerstalker, which has frightened more crows than any other lid in Worcestershire (1960). **2** One ounce of marijuana. 1967–. J. D. MACDONALD We had almost two lids of Acapulco Gold (1968).

lifer noun **1** A prisoner serving a life sentence (or earlier, someone sentenced to transportation for life). 1830–. D. A. DYE The swagger, clearly visible chevrons and pissed-off set to the man's jaw all spelled 'Lifer' (1986). **2** A life-peer. 1959–. SUNDAY TELEGRAPH I will not . . . turn out for Lifers (1969). [From *life* noun + -*er*.]

lift verb trans. **1** To steal. 1526–. J. WAINWRIGHT Lift a bleedin' gun from somewhere (1973). **2** To plagiarize. 1892–. A. CROSS Fran has lifted the perfect phrase for the occasion from a recent Iris Murdoch novel: *Sic biscuitus disintegrat*: that's how the cookie crumbles (1981).

lig verb intr. **1** To loaf about. 1960–. IT It's a time for ligging in the streets and doing your thing, man (1969). **2** To freeload, esp. by gatecrashing parties. 1981–. RADIO TIMES [I] suddenly twigged what ligging was all about when I got my first job as a researcher on *Aquarius* I found . . . I could get free tickets for everything, everywhere (1985). [From a dialectal variant of *lie* verb, to repose.]

ligger noun One who gatecrashes parties, a freeloader. 1977–. OBSERVER I went to a party on Wednesday that was a liggers' delight (1985). [From LIG verb + -*er*.]

lightning noun mainly US Gin; also, any strong, often low-quality alcoholic spirit. 1781–. L. VAN DER POST The fiery Cape brandy known to us children as 'Blitz' or Lightning (1958).

Limey noun derog **1** mainly Austral, NZ, and S Afr A British immigrant. 1888–. J. BERTRAM I can remember scores of fights among the 'Limeys' (1947). **2** US A British person (orig a sailor) or ship. 1918–. J. STEINBECK Fights in the bar-rooms with the goddam Limeys (1952). [Abbreviation of obs. *lime-juicer* noun, from the former

limo

enforced consumption of lime-juice as an antiscorbutic in the British Navy.]

limo /ˈlɪməʊ/ noun US Abbreviation of 'limousine'. 1968–. R. MOORE The company should be sending a limo for me (1973).

line noun A dose of cocaine or other powdered drug taken by inhalation. 1980–.

linen-draper noun Brit Rhyming slang for 'newspaper'. 1857–.

lingo noun A foreign language; hence also, the jargon of a particular group. 1660–. INDEPENDENT 'Chatty-Catty' and friends were era-typical, smart-alecky dolls which . . . talked back at you in up-to-the-minute kid lingo (1991). [Prob. from Portuguese lingoa language.]

lip noun 1 Impudent talk. 1821–. 2 US, dated A lawyer, esp. a criminal lawyer. 1929–50. AMERICAN MERCURY Get a lip for a writ an' I'll lam (1930). verb trans. 3 To be impudent to, to insult. 1898–. A. DRAPER If anyone lips you, just swallow it (1972). Hence **lippy**, adjective Insolent, impertinent; talkative. 1875–. R. THOMAS It might learn them not to be so goddamned lippy (1971).

lippy noun Also **lippie**. orig Austral Lipstick. 1940–. D. HEWETT Just a wee dab of lippy, dear. Look at that, a picture no artist could paint (1976). [From lip(stick + -y.]

liquefied adjective Under the influence of drink, intoxicated. 1939–.

liquid lunch noun often jocular A midday meal at which rather more alcoholic drink than food is consumed. 1970–. B. EVERITT He . . . refused all offers of liquid lunches and bore me off . . . for a great deal of solid pasta (1972).

liquorice-stick noun jazz A clarinet. 1935–.

lit adjective Drunk or under the influence of a drug; often followed by up. 1914–. E. HYAMS Some of the lads a bit lit, eh? (1949).

littley noun Austral A child. 1965–. K. DENTON Mum used to tell me that when I was a littley I wouldn't hold anyone's hand (1976). [From little small, young + -y.]

live stock noun Fleas, body lice, etc. 1785–.

Lizzie noun Also **lizzie**. 1 A lesbian. Also, an effeminate young man; also **lizzie boy**. 1905–. J. SYMONS You'd never have thought I was a lizzie, would you? And butch at that (1970). 2 = TIN LIZZIE noun. 1913–. J. TICKELL These special

duty 'Lizzies' had to be stripped of all guns, armour and wireless equipment . . . in order to allow room for the passengers (1956). 3 dated Lisbon wine. 1934–6. M. ELLISON She drinks 'Lizzie' and methylated spirit (1934). [In sense 1, prob. alteration of lesbian (cf. lezzy at LES adjective and noun), assimilated to the female personal name Lizzie; in sense 2, from the female personal name Lizzie, abbreviation of Elizabeth.]

load noun 1 A large amount of alcohol drunk; esp. in phr. to get (or have) a load on. 1598–. V. PALMER We're not to blame if men get a load on and begin to fight (1948). 2 to get a load of orig US To look at or listen to attentively; to notice. 1929–. D. BLOODWORTH Get a load of that chick over there (1972). 3 A dose of venereal infection. 1937–. F. SARGESON They displayed their rubber goods, and . . . were doubly protected against finding themselves landed with either biological consequences or a load (1965).

loaded adjective 1 Drunk. 1890–. 2 US Under the influence of drugs. 1923–. W. BURROUGHS He was loaded on H and goof-balls (1953). 3 Very rich. 1948–. D. O'CONNOR Adriana's a very popular girl and there are guys here who are absolutely loaded (1971).

loadsa adjective Brit A large amount or number of. 1988–. SPORT It [i.e. Clare Short's bill to outlaw certain sorts of pornography] stands no chance and would deprive loadsa people—men and women—of a lot of pleasure (1988). [Contraction of loads of.]

loaf noun 1 The head, esp. as a source of common sense; esp. in phr. to use one's loaf. 1925–. JEWISH CHRONICLE Use your loaf. Didn't Sir Jack Cohen of Tesco . . . start the same way? (1973). 2 loaf o(f) bread rhyming slang for 'dead'. 1930–. AUDEN & ISHERWOOD O how I cried when Alice died The day we were to have wed! We never had our Roasted Duck And now she's a Loaf of Bread (1935). [In sense 1, prob. from loaf of bread, rhyming slang for 'head'.]

lob verb intr. Austral To arrive, esp. unceremoniously; often followed by in. 1911–. AGE (Melbourne): The Chinese Noodle Shop Restaurant seemed the logical choice, so three of us lobbed there at 8 o'clock (1984). [Prob. from earlier sense, to move heavily or clumsily.]

lobby-gow /ˈlɒbɪɡaʊ/ noun US An errand-boy, messenger; a hanger-on, underling, esp. in an opium den or in the Chinese quarter of a town. 1906–. T. BETTS He flung away fortunes

limo line linen-draper lingo lip lippy liquefied

in grubstakes to bums, heels, and lobby-gows (1956). [Origin unknown.]

locie /ˈləʊkɪ/ noun Also **loci, lokey,** etc. N Amer and NZ Abbreviation of 'locomotive'. 1942–. A. P. GASKELL She often saw wisps of smoke rising against the bush on the hills at the back.... Sometimes she heard a lokey puffing (1947).

loco /ˈləʊkəʊ/ adjective orig US Mad, crazy. 1887–. D. FRANCIS He'd been quietly going loco and making hopeless decisions (1965). [From Spanish *loco* mad.]

loco weed noun Marijuana. 1935–. SUNDAY SUN (Brisbane): Detectives from the CIB Drug Squad in Brisbane are becoming quite familiar now with words like . . . rope and locoweed (1972). [From earlier sense, type of plant that causes brain disease in cattle eating it, from Spanish *loco* (see LOCO adjective).]

lofty noun A nickname for a very tall (or *ironically*, very short) person. 1933–.

loid Also **'loid.** criminals'. noun **1** A celluloid or plastic strip used by thieves to force locks open. 1958–. B. TURNER 'Have you got keys to all Creedy's places?' 'Beatty has. I use a loid myself' (1968). verb trans. **2** To break open (a lock) with a loid; to let (oneself) in with this method. 1968–. [Shortened from *cellu)loid* noun.]

loiner noun An inhabitant of Leeds, West Yorkshire. 1950–. P. RYAN I ran through the ranks of rumbling loiners and out into the eternal, grey twilight of Leeds (1967). [Origin uncertain.]

lolly noun Money. 1943–. G. MOFFAT There's only one person bringing in the lolly in that house (1973). [From earlier sense, lollipop, apparently with reference to the notion of the Government giving away money 'like lollipops'.]

lollygag variant of LALLYGAG verb.

long adjective **as long as one's arm** very long. 1846–. M. ALLINGHAM Jock has a record as long as your arm (1938).

long green noun US Dollar bills, money. 1896–. S. NEWTON We'll be there tomorrow afternoon with Napoleon and the long green (1946). [From the colour of US dollar bills.] Cf. GREEN noun 2.

long-sleever noun Austral (A drink contained in) a tall glass. 1879–. X. HERBERT The priest got out the whisky bottle. Sims had a long-sleever (1975).

loo noun Brit A lavatory. 1940–. P. WILDEBLOOD The loo's on the landing, if you want to spend a

penny (1957). [Origin uncertain; perh. from *Waterloo*.]

looey noun Also **looie, louie.** N Amer A lieutenant. 1916–. I. A. BARAKA Jimmy Lassiter, first looie (1967). [Shortened from N Amer pronunciation of *lieu(tenant* + -y.] Cf. LOOT[1] noun.

loogan noun US, dated A fool. 1929–. P. CAIN There's Rose, with his syndicate behind him, and all the loogans he's imported from back East (1933). [Origin unknown.]

looker noun orig US An attractive person, esp. a woman. 1909–. R. PARKES Bit of a looker.... Otherwise . . . a ranking detective on a priority case, would hardly have bothered driving her home (1971). [From earlier *good looker*.]

look-see noun An inspection, a survey or look. 1883–. A. DIMENT I took a long looksee through my . . . binoculars (1968). [Pidgin-like formation from *look* noun or verb + *see* verb.]

looky-loo noun Also **looky-lou, lookie-loo, lookie-lou.** orig and mainly US **1** A person who views something for sale with no genuine intention to make a purchase. 1977–. R. & T. ADAMS You'll face constant interruption from looky-loos who have no intention of buying your products (2003). **2** A person who comes or stops to look at something out of mere curiosity. 1980–. [From *look* + -y + a partial reduplication of *look*.]

loon noun A crazy person; a simpleton. 1885–. COAST TO COAST **1944** There we were, bottled up in camp because the loon in charge couldn't get the order signed for the trucks to leave (1945). [From earlier sense, type of water bird.]

loon verb intr. To pass time in pleasurable activities. 1966–. IT Children and the younger adults alike looning about in wonderful costumes (1971). [Origin unknown.]

loons noun pl., dated Casual trousers widely flared from the knees to the ankles. Also **loon pants, loon trousers.** 1971–. [From LOON verb.]

loony Also **looney.** adjective **1** Mad, crazy. 1872–. WILCOX & RANTZEN She had lost her place in the television 'record book' of loony pets (1981). **2** politics Unacceptably radical or extreme. 1977–. CITY LIMITS The press has branded Deirdre Wood a 'loony lefty' (1987). noun **3** A mad person. 1884–. L. CODY The man was clearly a loony and she wondered how Mr Brierly would

locie loco loco weed lofty loid loiner lolly lollygag

deal with him (1982). [Shortened form of *lunatic* + *-y*.]

loony bin noun A mental hospital. 1919–. J. SYMONDS Yes, Aunt Marion. She's locked up, you know, in the looney bin (1962). Cf. BIN noun.

loony-doctor noun A psychiatrist. 1925–. P. G. WODEHOUSE She's browsing with Sir Roderick Glossop, the loony-doctor (1960).

looped adjective mainly US Drunk. 1934–. R. MACDONALD The message . . . didn't come through too clear. She talked as if she was slightly looped (1973).

loopy adjective Crazy. 1925–. NEW YORKER The wife . . . is mad neither in the sense of loopy nor in the sense of furious (1970).

loose adjective orig US Relaxed, calm, uninhibited; esp. in phr. *to hang* (or *stay*) *loose*. 1968–. C. MCFADDEN 'And remember,' he told him, waving, 'stay loose' (1977).

loot[1] noun US, military A lieutenant. 1898–. J. G. COZZENS Don't thank the loot! (1948). [Shortened from N Amer pronunciation of *lieut(enant)*.] Cf. LOOEY noun.

loot[2] noun Money. 1943–. J. SANGSTER When you've got his sort of loot I don't suppose it matters (1968). [From earlier sense, goods plundered; ultimately from Hindi *lūṭ* spoils, plunder.]

lor int Also **lor'**. Brit An exclamation of dismay or surprise. 1835–. [Abbreviation of *lord*.]

Lord Muck noun A pompous self-opinionated condescending man. 1937–. J. THOMAS Hey, Lord Muck! May we have the honour of introducing ourselves! (1955). Cf. LADY MUCK noun.

loser noun US A convicted criminal, a person who has been in prison. So **two-time** (or **three-time**, etc.) **loser**, a person who has been in prison twice (or three, etc., times). 1912–. HOUSTON (Texas) CHRONICLE Bob, a three-time loser with a long line of busts and drug abuse . . . was sick of his life (1973).

lotsa Contraction of 'lots of'. 1927–. IT The Notting Hill Carnival was lotsa fun for seven days and nights (1971).

lotta Also **lotter**. Contraction of 'lot of'. 1906–. BLACK WORLD Lotta big talk, but when you get there nothin is happenin (1971).

lounge lizard noun derog A man who frequents fashionable parties, bars, etc., esp. in search of a wealthy patroness. 1918–. TIMES The £50 a week contract which . . . lets her keep her lounge lizard husband, Queckett, in the manner to which he is accustomed, lacks conviction (1973).

louse noun 1 A contemptible or unpleasant person. 1633–. T. MORRISON What a louse Valerian was (1981). verb trans. 2 **to louse up** orig US To make a mess of. 1934–. HUMAN WORLD If . . . he tries to sabotage his actions—he louses up a machine he is purporting to work (1972).

lousy adjective orig US Well supplied, teeming; followed by *with*. 1843–. R. BRADDON The town was lousy with Germans, she noted (1956).

love noun **for the love of Mike** for goodness sake. 1922–. A. MACNAB For the love of Mike, let's hope he's brave (1957).

love juice noun A sexual secretion. 1965–. PUSSYCAT I could feel his lovejuice so hot, trickling down into the start of my stomach (1972).

lovely jubbly Brit 1 noun Money, wealth. 1990–. NON-LEAGUE FOOTBALL TODAY The FA might get a bit upset as well without all that lovely jubbly clinking in at the till (1993). 2 adjective and int Wonderful, great. 1997–. [Orig, in the 1950s, an advertising slogan for an orange drink called 'Jubbly'. The later usage was popularized by the BBC television sitcom *Only Fools and Horses* (1981–93).]

lover boy noun orig US A lover, an attractive man, a woman-chaser; also used as a form of address. Also **lover man**. 1952–. F. WARNER Out on the prowl tonight, lover-boy? (1972).

loverly adjective Representing a Cockney pronunciation of 'lovely'. 1907–. J. WAINWRIGHT He 'ad the ackers—believe me—wiv a car like that. . . . A loverly job, it was (1968).

love-up noun An act of caressing, hugging, etc. 1953–. M. ALLWRIGHT He looked so beaten by the world that I wanted to gather him in my arms on the spot and give him a good love-up (1968).

low-down noun orig US The relevant information, the inside story; often followed by *on*. 1915–. M. MACKINTOSH One of his minions

> ### Lord Muck
> a pompous self-opinionated condescending man

loony bin   loony-doctor   looped   loopy   loose   loot will . . . give me the official low-down on Fisher. Possible police record, etc. (1973).

low-five mainly US. noun **1** A gesture of celebration or greeting in which two people slap each other's hands with arms extended at or below waist level. 1982-. verb intr. **2** To exchange low-fives. 1990-. ROLLING STONE In between takes the women exchange sly jokes . . . She and her band-mates low-five, crackling (1994). [Modelled on HIGH-FIVE noun.]

low-heel noun Austral derog A promiscuous woman. 1939-. [Perh. from the notion of being unsteady on the feet, and hence readily agreeing to lie down for sexual intercourse; cf. ROUND HEELS noun.]

lowie noun Also **lowey**. Austral derog A promiscuous woman. 1953-. SYDNEY MORNING HERALD Harkins points out the 'rev heads' (fast driving teenage yobos) and the 'loweys' (equally fast young girls) he knows lolling about outside the Commercial Hotel (1979). [From LOW(-HEEL noun + -ie.]

low-rider noun orig and mainly US **1** orig African-American A lover or pimp, esp. an itinerant, inconstant, or unreliable one. 1931-. **2** A person who drives in a vehicle with customized hydraulics that lower the chassis close to the ground, or who participates in the culture associated with this; also, such a vehicle. 1968-.

lubricated adjective Inebriated, drunk. 1927-. [Cf. earlier slang *lubricate* verb, to (ply with) drink.]

luck verb **1 to luck out** US To achieve success or advantage by good luck. 1954-. J. WAMBAUGH I started making inquiries . . . and damned if I didn't luck out and get steered into a good job (1972). **2 to luck into** orig US To acquire by good fortune. 1959-.

lug noun **1** The ear. 1507-. **2 to put** (or **pile**) **on lugs** US, dated To put on airs. 1889-1920. S. LEWIS Oh, the lugs he puts on—belted coat, and piqué collar (1920). **3** US A demand for money; esp. in phr. *to put the lug on*, to extort, to put pressure on. 1929-. **4** mainly N Amer A lout; a sponger; a stupid person. 1931-. B. MATHER Any other names you can come up with? . . . You don't owe these lugs anything (1973). [From earlier sense, flap of a cap, etc., covering the ears, perh. of Scandinavian origin.]

lughole noun The ear; the earhole. 1895-. TIMES A session with *Hello, Cheeky* is like being exposed to some noisy, rude and unstoppable urchin who wins you round or at least averts a skull-shattering clout about the lughole simply because he will go on regardless (1973). [From LUG noun 1 + *hole* noun.]

lulu noun orig US, often ironic A remarkable or excellent person or thing. 1886-. EVENING NEWS (Edinburgh): There are some parts of a new book on spying that aren't fit to be printed. . . . This one is a lulu. As long as two years ago, legal proceedings were initiated (1974). [Perh. from *Lulu*, pet form of the female personal name *Louise*.]

lumber¹ Brit noun **1** dated A house or room; spec. one where stolen property is hidden; a house used by criminals. 1753-1950. **2 to be in lumber: a** To be in prison. 1812-. J. PRESCOT My poor old dad was in and out of lumber all his life (1963). **b** To be in trouble. 1965-. L. HENDERSON I've got to keep at it. Break my bloody leg or something stupid like that and I'm in lumber (1972). verb trans. **3** To imprison, arrest. 1812-. M. KENYON We're pros—twice in twelve years I've been lumbered. . . . Only twice in twelve years screwing (1970). [From earlier sense, pawnbroking establishment; variant of obs. *Lombard* noun, pawnbroking establishment, bank, etc., from the traditional role of natives of Lombardy as bankers and pawnbrokers.]

lumber² Scottish. verb trans. and intr. **1** Of a man: to court or chat up (a woman); to make sexual advances towards. 1960-. A. GRAY 'Last Friday I saw her being lumbered by a hardman up a close near the Denistoun Palais.' 'Lumbered?' 'Groped. Felt' (1981). noun **2** A woman courted, esp. one picked up at a party, etc. Also, **a bit of lumber,** a 'bit of stuff'. 1966-. [Origin uncertain; perh. related to *lumber* noun, useless odds and ends, verb, to encumber.]

lumme /lʌmi/ int Also **lummy**. Brit An expression of surprise or interest. 1898-. TIMES A pitch which has evoked from Trueman the classic comment: 'Lumme! A green dusty' (1963). [Contraction of (Lord) *love me*.]

lump noun **1** dated The workhouse. 1874-. **2** US A parcel of food given to a tramp. 1912-. K. ALLSOP I met a husky burly taking of his rest And he flagged me with a big lump and a can (1967).

lunar noun **to take a lunar** dated To take a look. 1906-50. J. GUTHRIE Charles took a lunar (1950). [From earlier sense, observation of the moon.]

lunatic soup noun Austral and NZ Alcoholic drink of poor quality. 1933-. TRANSAIR They

low-five low-heel lowie low-rider lubricated luck

went about destroying themselves with the lunatic soup crippling their larynx as surely as if they'd downed an economy size tin of paint stripper (1986).

lunch noun **out to lunch** orig US Out of touch with reality; crazy. 1955–. MELODY MAKER I think he's out to lunch. He's blown out—completely (1974).

lunchbox noun Brit A man's genitalia, esp. as made more apparent by tightly fitting trousers. 1992–. GUARDIAN 'What is Linford Christie's lunchbox?' Mr Justice Popplewell . . . asked the Olympic gold medallist in bemusement. 'They are making a reference to my genitals, your honour,' replied the agitated athlete (1998).

lunk noun orig US A slow-witted, unintelligent person. 1867–. NEW YORKER He looks incredulous, as if he couldn't figure out how he got turned into such a lunk (1975). [Abbreviation of LUNKHEAD noun.]

lunker noun N Amer An animal, esp. a fish, which is an exceptionally large example of its species; a whopper. 1912–. SPORTS AFIELD A bronzed lunker came out of the shadowy depths and smashed the pigskin (1947). [Origin unknown.]

lunkhead noun orig US = LUNK noun. 1884–. PUNCH The poor lunkhead's concerns soon get lost under all the modelling and backlighting (1966). [Perh. alteration of *lump* noun.]

lurgy noun Also **lurgi**. Brit jocular A (fictitious) highly infectious disease; usu. in phr. *the dreaded lurgy*. 1954–. H. MACINNES I was beginning to feel weak and knew that I had caught the dreaded swamp lurgy (1974). [Coined (perh. on the model of *allergy*) by Spike Milligan and Larry Stephens, writers of *The Goon Show*, British radio comedy programme first broadcast in 1951.]

lurk noun **1** mainly Austral and NZ A profitable stratagem; a scheme or dodge. 1891–. B. ST. A. SMITH I told him once t' try the Repat. for war-nerves. I told 'im what a terrible good lurk it

was (1978). **2** A hiding-place; a hang-out. 1906–. J. GARDNER I met her in a servant's lurk (1974). **3** Austral and NZ A job. 1916–. R. STOW 'What's your lurk, mate?' 'Me? Stockman on a mission' (1958). [From *lurk* verb; in sense 1, from earlier obs. slang sense, a method of fraud.]

lurk verb intr. computing To read communications to an electronic network without actively contributing or making one's presence known. 1983.NET The few US newsgroups I'd lurked on in the past had always been unbearably tedious (1995). Hence **lurker** noun. 1984–.

lurked adjective dated Defeated in a game of chance. 1917–46. C. MORGAN Four straight aces. Good enough? You're lurked, Sandford (1938). [Perh. connected with *lurch* verb, to beat in a game of skill, to leave in the lurch.]

lurkman noun Austral A person who lives by sharp practice. 1945–. L. HORSPHOL I felt strangely sorry for the old man. Lurkman he might have been (1978). [From LURK noun 1 + *man* noun.]

lush mainly US. noun **1** An alcoholic; a drunkard. 1890–. D. DELMAN He's drunk, ain't he? . . . He's a lush. And a lush is a lousy security risk (1972). verb **2 to lush up: a** intr. To get drunk. 1926–. **b** trans. To ply with drink; to make drunk. 1927–. R. GANT By that time Andy Mendoza had got himself lushed up and started careening around the set playing a slow drag (1959). [From earlier sense, alcoholic drink; perh. a jocular use of *lush* adjective, luxuriant.]

lushy noun Also **lushie**. US A drunkard. 1944–. MEZZROW & WOLFE The lushies didn't even play good music (1946). [From obs. *lushy* adjective, drunk, from LUSH noun + *-y*.]

luvvy noun Brit, jocular and mildly derog An actor or actress. 1990–. [An alteration of *lovey*, taken as a typically effusive and affectionate thespian term of address.]

lunch lunchbox lunk lunker lunkhead lurgy lurk

ma noun Used as a title or form of address for an older (married) woman. 1951-. P. G. WODEHOUSE 'Did Ma Purkiss make a speech?' 'Yes, Mrs. Purkiss spoke' (1966). [From earlier sense, mother; shortening of *mamma*.] See also MA STATE noun.

mac noun Also **mack**. Used as a form of address to a man whose name is not known. 1918-. J. WAINWRIGHT The bouncer . . . tapped him on the shoulder and said: 'Hey, mac' (1973). [From earlier sense, person whose name contains the Gaelic prefix *Mac*.]

macaroni noun **1** An Italian. 1845-. D. HAMSON They dropped us practically on to the Italian garrison at Karpenisi. . . . Doug was playing hidey-ho with a couple of macaronis, taking potshots round bushes at each other (1946). **2** mainly Austral Nonsense, rubbish. 1924-. J. VON STERNBERG What is flashed from the projector overhead will be the same old macaroni (1965). [In sense 1, from the Italian origin of the foodstuff macaroni; in sense 2, rhyming slang for *baloney*.]

McCoy noun In the phr. *the real McCoy* (or *Mackay, McKie*): the 'genuine article'; the real thing. 1856-. GUARDIAN Sadler's Wells is playing host to the regal offspring Royal Ballet, and not, please note, a second eleven but the real Macoy [sic] (1972). [Origin uncertain; amongst the suggested derivations are that in its original form, *the real Mackay*, it refers to the true chieftain of the clan Mackay, a much disputed position, and that the variant *the real McCoy* (first recorded in 1922) refers to Kid *McCoy*, the professional name of US boxer Norman Selby (1873-1940), who was nicknamed 'the real McCoy' to distinguish him from other boxers who tried to use his name.]

macher noun In Jewish usage, a person of influence or importance, a fixer. 1928-. [From Yiddish *makher* maker, leader.]

mack noun Also **mac**. A pimp. 1894-. WASHINGTON POST Now comes 'The Mack', a movie about the rise and fall of a sweet pimp named Goldie (1973). **2** US, mainly African-American **a** A deceptive and convincing speaker; also, flattering talk, esp. aimed at seduction. 1973-. **b** A successful, respected, or influential person, spec. a man who is sexually successful with women; a playboy. 1990-. P. MUNRO Tom Cruise is a mack—every girl I know would die to go out with him (1997). verb **3** intr. To be or act as a pimp. 1987-. **4** US **a** intr. To speak flatteringly or deceivingly, esp. with a view to seduction; also, to flirt. 1987-.

b trans. To speak seductively to, flirt with. 1993-. URB Oakland ain't just about mobbin' in your ride, mackin' hoes and getting ya scrilla on (1995). [Short for obs. *mackerel* noun, pimp, from Old French *maquerel* pimp, of uncertain origin.]

mack daddy noun Also **MacDaddy, McDaddy.** US, orig African-American **1** A successful pimp or criminal, esp. one who dresses or behaves in a way characteristic of such a person. 1964-. **2** = MACK noun 2b. 1991-. **3** A supreme or model example of something. 1993-. JOE WEIDER'S MUSCLE & FITNESS Squats, the exercise I consider the mack daddy of mass-building motions (2001). [Prob. from MACK noun + DADDY noun 1, influenced by the surname prefix *Mac*-.]

macker noun Also **macca.** Austral military A new recruit, newcomer. 1944-. J. WYNNUM Only a macca in the outfit, too. Only been in half as long as us (1965). [Prob. from Austral naval slang *mac(aroon* new recruit + *-er*.]

macnoon adjective = MAGNOON adjective.

Maconochie /məˈkɒnəkɪ/ noun Brit, services', dated **1** Meat stewed with vegetables and tinned, esp. as supplied to soldiers on active service. 1901-54. GUN BUSTER He manages to scrape together two tins of Maconochie (stew), a tin of cold potatoes, . . . and some 'issue biscuits' (1940). **2** jocular The stomach. 1919-25. [From the name of the makers of the tinned stew, *Maconochie* Brothers, of London.]

mac out verb intr. Also **mack out.** orig US To consume food, esp. in large quantities; hence, more broadly, to indulge oneself avidly. 1989-. PROFILE.MYSPACE.COM Heterosexual, but VERY comfortable with sexuality—meaning, I'll totally mac out on other guys (2007). [*mac* from a shortening of *McDonald's*, the name of a US-based international chain of hamburger

ma mac macaroni McCoy macher mack macker

restaurants, or from *Big Mac*, the proprietary name of a type of hamburger sold by them.]

mad noun US Madness, fury, anger. 1834–. M. & G. GORDON Well, thanks a lot! I go through hell for you and you take your mad out on me (1973). [From *mad* adjective.]

madam noun Untrue, misleading, or flattering talk; nonsense. 1927–. J. WAINWRIGHT It was not the sort of place conducive to putting over a spot of old madam. The normal glib flannel tended to stick in his throat and the guff and eye-wash hadn't enough elbow-room to...sound...feasible (1973).

made adjective orig and mainly US Initiated into the Mafia. 1969–. C. SIFAKIS Jack Dragma...presided over the Weasel's initiation as a made man in the Los Angeles crime family (1987).

mad mick noun orig Austral A pickaxe. 1919–. F. HUELIN Well, I won't buy drinks f'r any bloody ganger, just f'r a chance to swing a mad mick (1973). [Rhyming slang for *pick* noun.]

mad minute noun military A minute of rapid rifle-fire or frenzied bayonet-practice. 1917–.

mad money noun Money for use in an emergency; spec money taken by a woman on a date in case her escort abandons her and she has to make her own way home. 1922–. D. SHANNON I haven't even a dime of mad money with me, hope I don't need it (1970).

Maggie Ann noun Also **Maggy Anne**. Margarine. Also **maggy**. 1931–. D. LEES Sam never paid him enough to put maggy on his bread (1971). [From the female personal names *Maggie* (familiar form of *Margaret*) and *Ann*, from their phonetic similarity to *margarine* (older pronunciation /mɑːgəriːn/).]

magic mushroom noun orig US Any of several types of mushroom with hallucinogenic properties, esp. one containing psilocybin. 1957–.

maginnis noun **to put** (or **clap**) **the maginnis on** Austral dated to coerce. 1901–41. [Prob. from the name of a wrestler called *McGinnis*.]

magnoon adjective Also **macnoon, magnune, mangoon**. Austral, orig services' Mad. 1917–. R. BEILBY She could be a bit magnoon in the head. Women are funny like that (1970). [From Arabic.]

magsman noun **1** orig Brit, now Austral A confidence trickster. 1822–. BULLETIN (Sydney): My mate was a top-shelf magsman on the phone and could mimic the tone of gruff arrogance so characteristic of the cop in my day (1975). **2** Austral A raconteur. 1924–. TELEGRAPH (Brisbane): Hardy...became the official yarn-spinning champion of Australia today. He won the magsman's championship in Darwin (1967). [From *mag* noun, chatter + *man* noun.]

mahogany flat noun A bed-bug. 1864–. B. J. BANFILL Until two months ago we had only a log shanty. Somehow the Mahogany Flats took over and we had to burn it (1967). [*mahogany* from the bed-bug's colour, *flat* from the shape of its abdomen when empty.]

main verb trans. US = MAIN-LINE verb. 1952–. TIME All my friends were on heroin. I snorted a couple of times, skinned a lot, and after that I mained it (1970).

main line noun orig US A large or principal vein, into which drugs can easily be injected; hence, an intravenous injection of drugs; the act or habit of making such an injection. 1931–. J. WELCOME What about the purple hearts? Gone on main line yet? (1968). [From earlier sense, principal route.]

main-line orig US. verb trans. and intr. **1** To inject (a drug) intravenously. 1934–. Compare SKIN-POP verb. M. PEREIRA He made himself a fix...and he mainlined it (1972). **2** To consume avidly or insatiably; to resort to frequently or cravenly. 1971–. TIMES The one thing that will wreck this satisfactory move...is if someone gets Mrs Parker Bowles mainlining on publicity (1997). So **main-liner,** noun 1934–; **main-lining,** noun 1951–. adjective **3** Of or characterized by the intravenous injection of drugs. 1938–. G. JENKINS Started smoking grass. Grew the stuff...in a potty in his cottage.... He's on to mainline stuff now (1974). [From MAIN LINE noun.]

main man noun US A person's best male friend. 1967–.

main squeeze noun US **1** dated An important person. 1896–. D. HAMMETT Vance seems to be the main squeeze (1927). **2** A man's principal woman friend. 1926–.

main stem noun US The principal street of a town. 1931–.

majat noun S Afr Marijuana, esp. of an inferior grade. 1956–. [Perh. from Malay *madat* raw opium or Urdu *madat, madad* mixture of opium and betel for chewing, both from Arabic *madad* help.]

mad   madam   made   mad mick   mad minute

majita noun S Afr In urban speech, esp. of the townships: a chap, guy, spec. a black youth or black adult male. 1963–. [From Isicamtho (an urban youth argot combining many languages spoken in South Africa) *majita*, apparently an alteration of *majika* magic (as in the name of the film *The Magic Garden* (1951), which depicts the life of a black South African petty thief).]

make noun 1 **on the make** orig US **a** Intent on gain. 1863–. R. ADAMS Insinuating, dandified with the manners, at once familiar and obsequious, of a presuming servant on the make (1974). **b** Looking for sexual partners. 1929–. **2** orig US A (sexual) conquest; spec. an easily seduced woman. 1942–. LANDFALL 'A widow's an easy make,' He said, 'you pedal and let her steer' (1951). **3** orig US An identification of, or information about, a person or thing from police records, fingerprints, etc. 1950–. R. K. SMITH We got a make on the Chevvy.... Stolen last week (1972). verb **4** trans. US, criminals' To recognize or identify (a person, etc.). 1906–. D. SHANNON 'Have you made the gun?' 'Right off. It's a Hi-Standard revolver' (1973). **5** trans. orig US To make successful advances to (a member of the opposite sex); spec. to have or succeed in having sex with. 1918–. E. GOFFMAN James Bond makes the acquaintance of an unattainable girl and then rapidly makes the girl (1969). **6 to make time** N Amer To court or flirt *with*; to have or succeed in having sex *with*. 1934–. D. HUGHES Which I'll bet he did if wanted to make time with her, eh? (1973). **7 to make out** orig US To have or succeed in having sex *with*. 1939–. TIMES The detailed accounts of how he 'made out' sexually and emotionally with some sixteen different girls (1961). **8 to make with** orig US To supply; to perform; to use; to proceed with. 1940–. D. LEES When people like Zodiac make with the dreams you have to listen (1972). **9 to make it** to have sex *with*. 1957–. TIMES LITERARY SUPPLEMENT He finally makes it with long-desired Rachel (1973). [In sense 8, translation of Yiddish *mach mit*.]

makee- combining form Brit, mainly naval Forming nouns denoting an action or a person performing an action, esp. **makee-learn** trainee. 1903–. JOURNAL OF THE ROYAL NAVAL MEDICAL SERVICE The chief cook was sitting on a stool in an opium coma and his 'makee learn' was doing all the work (1981). [From Pidgin English *makee* make.]

malarkey /məˈlɑːkɪ/ noun Also **malaky, malarky, mullarkey.** orig US Nonsense, foolishness. 1924–. OBSERVER Tall stories ... of rattlesnakes bringing up a nestful of baby robins, ... or some such malarkey (1973). [Origin unknown.]

malf noun mainly aeronautical A malfunction. 1986–. B. STERLING Pretty soon they're gonna tell me there's some kind of terrible software malf in this aircraft? (1994) [Shortening.]

malky Scottish. noun **1** A weapon, esp. an open razor used as a weapon. 1973–. verb trans. **2** To wound with an open razor. 1973–. M. MUNRO Tell the crapbag Big Ronnie's on his way roun tae malky him (1996). [Perh. a shortening of *Malcolm Fraser* (or *Frazer*), unrecorded rhyming slang for *razor*.]

mallrat noun orig and mainly US A young person who frequents a shopping mall for social purposes, usu. in a large group or gang. 1982–. OBSERVER Mall rats wage an almost gleeful war on mall security, winding up the rent-a-cops (1994).

mamma noun Also **mama, momma. 1** orig and mainly US A sexually attractive or promiscuous woman. Cf. RED-HOT MOMMA noun. 1916–. TIMES She denied ever being present at an impromptu or organized gathering where there was a 'mama' present, someone available to the whole group for sexual intercourse (1980). **2** US A girlfriend or female lover; a wife. 1926–.

mamzer noun Also **momser, momza, momzer.** Pl. **mamzerim.** A bastard; also in extended uses as a term of abuse or familiarity. 1562–. W. MARKFIELD That mass man, that totalitarian type, that *momza* (1964). [From late Latin *mamzēr*, a Hebrew word (*mamzēr*) adopted by the Vulgate in Deuteronomy xxiii. 2 (where it appears with the gloss 'id est de scorto natus', that is, born of a prostitute), and hence frequently used in the Middle Ages.]

man noun **1 the man,** also **the Man** US A person or people in authority. 1918–. spec. **a** African-American White people. 1931–. GUARDIAN Rus is not Uncle Tomming it around Harlem with 'the Man.' He has brought a foreign visitor (1972). **b** The police. 1962–. **2** Used as a general form of address to both men and women, esp. among African Americans, jazz musicians, hippies, etc. and in Caribbean English. 1933–. BLACK WORLD Hey, only the squares, man, only the squares have it to keep (1971). **3 (little) man in the boat** euphemistic the clitoris. 1979–.

man-eater noun A sexually voracious woman. 1906–. D. GRAY 'She's pretty, you

majita make makee- malarkey malf malky man

said?' . . . 'Very, sir.' 'And a man-eater?' 'I'd say
so, yes, sir' (1968).

mang verb intr. and trans. To beg, cadge.
1811–. P. O'SHAUGNESSY Mang him for a flim [i.e.
a £5 note] (1979). [From Angloromani *mong*,
from Romani *mang* to want, beg.]

mangoon adjective = MAGNOON adjective.

manky adjective Also **mankey**. Brit Bad,
inferior, defective; dirty. 1958–. B. W. ALDISS
Have you chucked out that dirty manky beer you
poisoned me with last time you came? (1971).
[From obs. *mank* adjective, defective (from Old
French *manc, manque*, from Latin *mancus*
maimed) + *-y*; perh. influenced by French
manqué.]

manor noun Brit **1** A police district or
similar administrative area.
1924–. R. COOK 'Then they
whipped him down to the nick
on the hurry-up.' 'Which
manor?' 'The local nick'
(1962). **2** One's home
ground, one's own
particular territory. 1959–.

mantee noun US dated A
lesbian with a masculine
manner, a butch. 1937–.
[Perh. from *Duke Mantee*, the name of a
swaggering gangster in Robert Sherwood's
play *The Petrified Forest* (1934).]

Maori P.T. noun NZ Taking it easy and
doing nothing. 1961–. [From the Maoris'
alleged relaxed attitude to life.]

map noun The face. 1899–. J. CURTIS What
d'you want to sit there staring at me for? I'm not
a bloody oil-painting. You ought to know my
map by now (1936).

marble noun **1** pl. The testicles. 1865–. **2 to
make** (or **keep**) **one's marble good** Austral and
NZ To ingratiate oneself. 1898–. D. CRICK Take my
tip, if you wanter make your marble good: say
nothing (1963). **3** pl. orig N Amer One's mental
faculties; one's sanity. 1902–. OTTAWA JOURNAL 'I
still have most of my marbles,' he said cheerfully
(1973). **4 to pass** (**chuck**, etc.) **in one's marble**
Austral To die, to give up. 1908–. J. HIBBERD What if
I pass in my marble like this? (1972). [In sense 1
prob. from earlier sense, small glass ball, but
latterly rationalized as a shortening of
rhyming slang *marble halls* balls.]

marble orchard noun US A cemetery.
1929–. B. BROADFOOT A couple more punches and it
would have been the marble orchard for him

(1973). [From the marble used for the
headstones.]

marble town noun US = MARBLE ORCHARD
noun. 1945–.

mare noun derog A woman. 1303–. C. W. OGLE
Forgot her keys! Bah! These mares give me the
creeps (1953).

Marge noun US A lesbian who takes the
role of the passive or submissive partner.
1957–. [From the female personal name
Marge, a pet-form of *Margery* and *Margaret*.]

Margery noun **1** An effeminate or
homosexual man. *c*.1850–. A. HOLLINGHURST Made
up like a Regent Street margery (1988).
2 A lesbian who takes the role of the passive
or submissive partner. 1936–. [From the
female personal name
Margery.]

mark noun **1** Austral
A person who is an
object of attention; esp.
in phr. *a good* or *bad
mark*, referring esp. to
the person's financial
probity. 1835–. S. HICKEY
They were usually
long-winded and
otherwise bad marks, through trying to make
one pound do the work of ten (1951). **2** orig US
The intended victim of a swindler,
confidence trickster, etc.; esp. in phr. *a soft* or
easy mark. 1883–. E. MCGIRR In the twenties it was
the Yanks who was the suckers, but now . . . it's
us who are the marks (1973). verb trans. **3 to
mark** (someone's) **card** Brit To tip (someone)
off; to put (someone) right. 1961–. G. F. NEWMAN
The third was to phone the insurance assessor
and mark his card (1970). [In sense 3, from the
annotation of someone's racecard with a tip
for the winning horse.]

marker noun US A promissory note; an
IOU. 1887–. D. RUNYON He is willing to take
Charley's marker for a million if necessary to get
Charley out (1931).

market noun **to go to market** Austral and
NZ To lose one's temper; to behave angrily or
excitably. *a*.1925–. F. J. HARDY I have me
instructions, so it's no use going to market on
me (1950).

marv adjective mainly US Wonderful,
outstanding. 1964–. NEW YORK At Sahara East,
the moussaka's marv (1994). [Back-formation
from *marvellous* adjective.]

Maori P.T.
taking it easy and
doing nothing

marvy adjective mainly US Wonderful, outstanding. 1932–. DAILY NEWS (Los Angeles) Here's an eclectic mishmash of nifty noshes and marvy meals in the middle of horsey land (1999). [From *marv(ellous* + *-y*.]

Mary¹ noun Also **mary**. Austral **1** An Aboriginal woman or other non-white woman. 1830–. COAST TO COAST **1961–2** Some of the older marys did not remove frayed or dirty skirts (1962). **2** A white woman; esp. in phr. *white Mary*. 1853–. N. CATO They made their usual inquiries, saying they were investigating the death of a 'white mary' at the coast (1974). [From the female personal name *Mary*.]

mary² noun Marijuana; also, a marijuana cigarette. 1940–. R.A. SPEARS Max pulled a little packet of Mary out of his pocket (1991). [Shortening of MARY JANE noun, or perh. an independent alteration of *marijuana*.]

Mary Ann noun **1** An effeminate man, esp. a male homosexual; a man who helps with domestic chores; also **Mary**. 1868–. G. ORWELL The woman continues to do all the household. . . . The man would lose his manhood if, merely because he was out of work, he became a 'Mary Ann' (1936). **2** = MARY JANE noun. 1925–. [In sense 2, fanciful alteration of *marijuana*.]

Mary Jane noun Also **Mary J**, **maryjane**. Marijuana; also, a marijuana cigarette. 1928–. D. SHANNON 'What did they buy?' asked Mendoza. 'Oh, Mary Jane. Twenty reefers,' said Callaghan (1970). [Fanciful alteration of *marijuana*.]

Mary Warner noun = MARY JANE noun. 1933–. [Fanciful alteration of *marijuana*.]

mashed adjective Drunk; also, under the influence of drugs. 1942–. A. WARNER 'Ah want to hit the shops fore am too lagered.' 'Aye, shopping when yur mashed is dangerous' (1998).

masher noun orig and mainly US A womanizer; a man who makes indecent advances to women, esp. in public places. 1904–. J. IRVING He was . . . the son of a woman who'd slashed a masher at a movie in Boston (1978). [From earlier sense, dandy.]

mash note noun dated A love-letter. 1890–. NEW YORKER A pen that roared through the Twenties and Thirties writing checks, letters, autographs . . . jazz and mash notes (1970). [From obs. *mash* noun, infatuation, orig US, of unknown origin.]

massive noun Brit, orig Caribbean and in Afro-Caribbean usage A group or gang of young people from a particular place, esp. followers of a particular type of (dance) music. 1989–. M8 DJs from England and abroad such as Carl Cox and Bass Generator, became firm favourites amongst the Scottish massive (1996).

Ma State noun Austral New South Wales. Also **Ma**. 1906–. BULLETIN (Sydney): South Australia . . . missed a great opportunity by not bunging a few million over to the Ma State (1954). [From *ma* noun, mother; from the fact that New South Wales was the earliest Australian colony.]

mat verb trans. Brit To reprimand severely; to admonish or 'carpet'. 1948–. W. HAGGARD The interviewer had been matted and now he was uncertain (1969).

matelot /ˈmætləʊ/ noun Also **matlow**, **matlo**. Brit A sailor. *a*.1847–. LISTENER Our screen matelots . . . should be as reticent as . . . *Captain Horatio Hornblower* (1974). [From French *matelot* sailor.]

matey noun Brit Used as a term of address to a man. 1859–. J. DRUMMOND Right, matey, 'oo told you? (1973). [From *mate* + *-y*.]

Matilda noun Also **matilda**. Austral An itinerant worker's bundle or pack; a swag. 1892–. MARSHALL & DRYSDALE We unrolled our Matildas between the dunes (1962). [From the female personal name *Matilda*; the reason for the application is unknown.] See also *to waltz Matilda* at WALTZ verb.

matman noun A wrestler. 1923–. SOVIET WEEKLY A popular group exercise among the matmen (1971). [From *mat* noun, floor-covering used in wrestling.]

mauler noun A hand; a fist. 1820–. J. ROSSITER You keep your big maulers off this (1973). [Cf. earlier sense, one who mauls; also obs. slang *mauley* noun, hand, prob. from *maul* verb, but perh. connected with Shelta *malya*, said to be a transposition of Gaelic *lamh* hand.]

mau-mau /ˈmaʊmaʊ/ verb trans. US To threaten, terrorize. 1970–. HARPER'S The English Department of Columbia University had been mau-maued by that termagant of Women's Lib (1971). [From *Mau Mau*, the name of a secret society fighting for Kenyan independence, from Kikuyu; the verbal usage was apparently coined by the US writer Tom Wolfe (1931–).]

max verb US **1** trans. To execute, achieve, etc. to the maximum degree of excellence; also

marvy Mary Mary Ann Mary Jane Mary Warner

refl, to reach one's full potential. 1871–.
WASHINGTON POST Scott has just finished maxing
the push-up test at 68, where he was ordered
to stop (1982). **2** intr. To perform excellently
or to the limit of one's capacity, etc.; spec.
to complete a maximum prison sentence;
usu. followed by *out*. 1930–. [From *max*
noun, colloquial shortening from *maximum*
noun.]

mazoola noun orig and mainly US Money.
1951–. **NATIONAL REVIEW** New Ageism . . . just results
in a separation of wallet from Mazoola (1987).
[Blend of MAZUMA noun and MOOLA noun.]

mazuma /məˈzuːmə/ noun Also **mazume**.
US Money, cash. 1900–. **TIMES LITERARY SUPPLEMENT**
Likewise piling up its mazuma by legerdemain
(1972). [Yiddish.]

MCP noun Abbreviation of 'male chauvinist
pig'. 1971–.

mean adjective orig US Skilful, excellent,
formidable. 1918–. **LISTENER** Jack Palance smokes
a mean cigar in *Oklahoma Crude* (1973).

me-and-you noun jocular A menu. 1932–.
N. MARSH Come on, Beautiful! Let's have a slant at
the me-and-you (1943). [Adaptation of
colloquial pronunciation /miːˈnjuː/ of *menu*.]

meany noun Also **meanie**. A mean person.
1927–. **J.B. PRIESTLEY** He was at heart, she felt, a
cunning old meanie (1951). [From *mean* + *-y*.]

measly adjective Disappointingly small in
amount or number. 1864–. **SUNDAY TELEGRAPH**
A spineless exhibition by the early Yorkshire
batting—they have mustered only a measly five
batting points all season—put them on the rack
yet again (1974). [From earlier sense, spotty
(as if) with measles.]

meat noun **1** The penis. 1595–. **BLACK SCHOLAR**
She was in his arms . . . and grabbing his erect
meat (1971). **2** The female genitals. 1611–.
G. GREER It would be unbearable, but less so, if it
were only the vagina that was belittled by terms
like *meat* (1970). See also *to beat one's meat* at
BEAT verb.

meat-head noun mainly US A stupid
person. 1863–. **NEWSWEEK** Archie Bunker, the
middle American hero of 'All in the
Family' . . . sees himself menaced by a rising tide
of spades, . . . meat-heads, . . . fags and four-eyes
(1971). Hence **meat-headed**, adjective 1949–.

meat-hook noun An arm or hand. 1919–.

meat-house noun A brothel. 1896–.
[From obs. slang *meat* noun, prostitute.]

meat-market noun A place or area
where prostitutes ply their trade; also, a
place frequented by people (heterosexuals or
homosexuals) in search of sexual partners.
1896–. **J. OSBORNE** Every tart and pansy boy in the
district are in that place. . . . It's just a meat-
market (1957). [From obs. slang *meat* noun,
prostitute.]

meat rack noun = MEAT-MARKET noun.
1962–.

meat ticket noun military An identity disc.
1919–.

meat tool noun The penis. 1971–.
B. MALAMUD What do you do . . . with your
meat tool? You got no girl, who do you
fuck other than your hand? (1971).

meat-wagon noun mainly US **1** An
ambulance. 1925–. **H. HOWARD** She hadn't
deserved to become a parcel of broken flesh and
bone in the meat wagon (1973). **2** A hearse.
1942–. **S. LONGSTREET** The band would march out
behind the meat-wagon, black plumes on the
hearse horses (1956). **3** A police van, black
Maria. 1954–. **LISTENER** The bogeys . . . bundle us
into the back of a meat-wagon (1964).

mech /mek/ noun Abbreviation of
'mechanic'. 1918–. **A. HUNTER** Hanson called over
a mech. The mech started it for us and drove it
out (1973).

mechanic noun **1** US and Austral A person
who cheats at gambling games, esp. cards.
1897–. **DAILY TELEGRAPH** As croupier . . . always on
guard for the sharps—the mechanics (1966).
2 A hired killer, 'hit man'. 1973–. **J. GARDNER**
Bernie Brazier was Britain's top mechanic
(1986).

medic noun = MEDICO; in standard use in
the 17th century, and revived in US college
slang. 1823–. **EVENING STANDARD** Dr Brian Warren,
Mr Heath's personal physician, called to see him
at Downing Street—but as a friend, not as a
medic (1974). [From Latin *medicus* medical
person.]

medico noun A medical practitioner or
student. 1689–. **NATURE** The twenty thousand
or so scientists, engineers, medicos and so on
on the staff of British universities (1973). [From
Italian *medico* physician.]

meeja /ˈmiːdʒə/ noun Also **meejah, meejer**.
jocular or derog The media, esp. the popular
press; journalists and media people
collectively; usu. with *the*. 1983–. **J. NEEL** We
aren't middle-class poor anymore, you know.
I am part of the rich *meeja* (1988). [Respelling

mazoola   mazuma   MCP   mean   me-and-you   meat

of *media*, representing a common informal pronunciation of the word.]

meemies noun pl. Drunkenness; hysterics; hysterical people; esp. in phr. *screaming meemies*. 1927–. GAGNON & SIMON We've got a nice circle of friends that aren't a bunch of screaming meemies (1973). [Origin unknown.]

meet noun A meeting; an assignation or appointment, esp. with a supplier of drugs; a meeting-place, esp. of criminals. 1879–. G. F. NEWMAN Manso was considering trying to make a meet with you (1970).

mega /megə/ adjective orig US Of enormous size, importance, etc.; great, large. 1968–. INVESTORS CHRONICLE The insurance companies helped promote the industry as a whole with their mega launches and promotions (1988). [From *mega-* (Greek μέγας great, as in *megastar, mega-millionaire*, etc.]

megabuck noun orig US A million dollars; also more generally, in pl., an enormous amount of money. 1946–. AMERICAN ANTHROPOLOGIST He certainly had no megabuck research grant (1968).

Megillah /məgɪlə/ noun A long, tedious, or complicated story; esp. in phr. *a whole Megillah*. 1943–. S. SHELDON 'Do you know the most peculiar thing about this whole megillah?' queried Moody thoughtfully (1970). [From *Megillah* any of five books of the Old Testament: Song of Solomon, Ruth, Lamentations, Ecclesiastes, and Esther (from Hebrew *megillah* roll, scroll), in allusion to the length of the books; *a whole Megillah* translated from Yiddish *a gantse Megillah*.]

MEGO noun US, esp. journalists' A boring subject or story; a feeling or episode of boredom. 1977–. NEW YORK TIMES Brady has begun to worry about overkill. 'We don't want to turn this into a MEGO' (1981). [Acronym from *my eyes glaze over*.]

Melba noun **to do a Melba** Austral To make several farewell performances or comebacks. 1971–. SYDNEY MORNING HERALD It has been intensified by talk from Sir Robert that he is under pressure to stay on, thus giving rise to speculation that he is planning to 'do a Melba' (1974). [From the name of Dame Nellie *Melba* (stage name of Helen Mitchell) (1861–1931), Australian soprano, who was famous for being unable to retire conclusively.]

mellow US. adjective **1** Satisfying, attractive, skilful, pleasant. 1938–. D. BURLEY The whole town's copping the mellow jive (1944). noun **2** orig and mainly African-American

A close friend; a lover. 1967–. BEASTIE BOYS Adam Yauch grab the mic 'cause you know you're my mellow (1994). verb **3 to mellow out** to become mellow or relaxed, esp. under the influence of a drug. 1974–. C. MCFADDEN How about we all smoke a little dope and mellow out, okay? (1977).

mellow yellow noun US Banana peel used as an intoxicant. 1967–.

melon noun **1** Large profits to be shared among a number of people; esp. in phr. *to cut the melon*. 1908–. AURORA (Illinois) BEACON NEWS This year, a record number of your friends and neighbours will split a record 'melon' in our 1948 savings clubs (1948). **2** pl. orig US A woman's breasts; esp., large breasts. 1957–. PUSSYCAT Her full and shapely melons swung and swayed . . . as she moved (1972).

melvin noun US, orig college students' **1** An annoyingly uncharismatic or fuddyduddyish person. 1954–. **2** An act of pulling the cloth of a person's underwear, trousers, etc. tightly between the buttocks, esp. as a practical joke. 1989–. [From the male forename *Melvin*, regarded as being geeky.]

member noun US A black person. 1962–. L. HAIRSTON Three more, one of 'em a member, . . . sailed over (1964).

mensch /mentʃ/ noun Also **mensh**. A person of integrity; one who is morally just, honest, or honourable. 1930–. NEW STATESMAN Nixon is seen as an essentially decent man, . . . but not as a *mensch* on the scale of Roosevelt, Eisenhower, Kennedy (1970). [Yiddish, from German *Mensch* person.]

mensh /mentʃ/ noun and verb Also **mench**. Abbreviation of 'mention'; esp. in phr. *don't mensh*, = don't mention it. 1928–. F. NOLAN 'Thanks, Lucky.' 'Don't mensh, don't mensh,' Luciano said (1974).

mental noun **1** A mentally ill person; a mental patient. 1913–. F. DE FELITTA 'What's to prevent him from going?' 'He is a mental' (1973). adjective **2** Insane, crazy. 1927–. J. PATRICK They must be mental . . . . Shit-bags the lot 'o them (1973).

Merc¹ /mɜːk/ noun Brit A Mercedes car. 1933–. J. WAINWRIGHT There is a pale blue Merc parked not far from the club entrance (1974). [Shortened from *Mercedes*, the brand name of a type of luxury car.]

merc² noun A mercenary soldier. 1967–. T. WILLIS I'm a merc, a hired gunman . . . . If I'm

meemies   meet   mega   megabuck   Megillah   MEGO

merchant

merchant noun mainly derog A person with a partiality for the specified activity, practice, attitude, etc. 1914–. RAILWAY MAGAZINE One wonders how many drivers, other than the confirmed speed merchants, will even attempt to run the 8.20 a.m. from Kings Cross from Hitchin to Huntingdon in 24 min (1957); G. SIMS Sorry to be such a gloom merchant. But . . . we're broke, you see (1971). [From earlier sense, fellow, chap.]

Merkin noun mainly US An American; also, American English. 1990–. SUN SENTINEL (Fort Lauderdale, Florida) L.A. is only marginally American. It's a modern-day Babel, where it's the 'real merkins' who must feel linguistically and culturally alienated (1999). [From a casual pronunciation of *American*, perh. punning on *merkin* noun female pubic-hair wig.]

merry hell noun Great disturbance or upheaval; severe pain. 1911–. M. DUGGAN Watching mum with a shoehorn wedging nines into sevens and suffering merry hell (1963).

meshuga /mrʃʊgə/ adjective Also **meshugga(h,) meshuger, mash-, mish-,** etc.; also, when preceding a noun, **meshugener, meshugenah,** etc. Mad, crazy; stupid. 1885–. SUNDAY TIMES (Johannesburg): Going steady! . . . What kind of a meshugenah idea is this? (1971). [From Yiddish *meshuge*, from Hebrew *mĕshuggā*, participle of *shāgag*, to go astray, wander.]

Mespot noun Also **Mess-pot.** dated Abbreviation of 'Mesopotamia'. 1917–43.

mess noun An objectionable, ineffectual, or stupid person. 1936–. M. SPARK These were lapsed Jews, lapsed Arabs, lapsed citizens, runaway Englishmen, dancing prostitutes, international messes (1965).

meter noun US, orig African-American Twenty-five cents; a quarter. 1940–. [From the use of a twenty-five cent coin to operate gas meters.]

meth noun orig US Abbreviation of 'methamphetamine' and 'Methedrine' (a proprietary name for methamphetamine), taken as a stimulant drug; a tablet of this. 1967–. J. WAMBAUGH She's a meth head and an ex-con (1972).

metho¹ noun Austral and NZ **1** Methylated spirit. 1933–. B. DIXON Old Jimmy Taylor had gone a little bit in the mind, from drinking too much beer and metho (1984). **2** A person addicted to drinking methylated spirit. 1933–. J. ALARD The

old metho snored on (1968). [From *meth(ylated spirit* + *-o*.]

Metho² noun and adjective Austral Abbreviation of 'Methodist'. 1940–. P. WHITE Arch and me are Methoes, except we don't go; life is too short (1961).

metrosexual noun A heterosexual male whose attention to his appearance is likened to that of a homosexual. 1994–.

Mex noun US, forces' Foreign currency, esp. that of the Philippines. 1898–. T. CRUSE The rent was $100 a month 'Mex', which translated as $50 in gold (1941). [From earlier sense, Mexican (money); abbreviation of *Mexican*.]

Mexican overdrive noun US, jocular The putting of the gears of a vehicle, esp. a truck, into neutral while coasting downhill. 1955–.

Mexican stand-off noun orig and mainly US No chance to benefit (or spec to defend oneself); hence, a general stalemate. 1891–. D. MACKENZIE As things stood it was a Mexican standoff. He couldn't go to the law but . . . nor could the Koreans (1979).

mezz noun Marijuana. 1937–. [From the name of *Mezz* Mezzrow (1890–1972), US jazz clarinettist and drug addict.]

Michael noun **1** US = MICKEY FINN noun 1932–. B. BUCKINGHAM He only pretended to trust me and just slipped me a Michael in my drink. I passed out in the car a few minutes after leaving the bar (1957). **2 to take the Michael (out of)** = *to take the micky (out of)* (see at MICKEY¹ noun). 1959–. L. DAVIDSON Jesus, did we take the Michael! We used to chat 'em up, these old bats out looking for prospects (1966). [From the male personal name *Michael*.]

Mick noun Also **mick.** derog and offensive **1** An Irishman. 1850–. M. KENYON Where's Ireland, huh? Who needs Micks? (1970). **2** A Roman Catholic. Also **Mickey.** 1902–. N. SHUTE Stanley and Phyllis went to Church of England schools . . . but all the rest of us are micks (1956). [From the supposed commonness of the male personal name *Mick* in Ireland and amongst Roman Catholics.]

mick¹ noun Austral The reverse side of a coin; the tail. 1918–. T. A. G. HUNGERFORD 'Ten bob he tails 'em!' he intoned. . . . ' I got ten bob to say he tails 'em—ten bob the micks!' (1953). [Origin unknown.]

mick² noun nautical A hammock. 1929–. [Origin unknown.]

merchant Merkin merry hell meshuga Mespot

milko

mickey¹ noun Also **micky. 1** Austral A young wild bull. 1876–. H. G. LAMOND Mickeys roamed through the camping cattle (1954). **2** The penis. 1922–. J. JOYCE Ill put on my best shift and drawers let him have a good eyeful out of that to make his micky stand for him (1922). **3 to take the mickey (out of)** to tease, mock, ridicule. 1948–. B. W. ALDISS Geordie looked anxiously at me, in case I thought he was taking the micky too hard (1971). Hence **mickey-take,** noun and verb, **mickey-taking,** adjective and noun. [From the male personal name *Mick(e)y*; in sense 3, *mickey* perh. shortened from *Mickey Bliss*, rhyming slang for *piss*.]

mickey² noun Also **micky, mick. to do a mickey,** etc.: to go away, to clear off. 1937–. S. CHAPLIN I laid the ring on the notepaper and did a mickey as soon as I heard the front doorbell go (1961). [*mick* variant of MIKE¹ noun, reinterpreted as a proper name.]

Mickey noun US A type of radar-assisted bombsight. 1944–. [From MICKEY MOUSE noun.]

Mickey Finn noun Also **Mickey Flynn** and elliptically **Mickey.** orig US A strong alcoholic drink, esp. one secretly adulterated with a narcotic and given to someone to render them unconscious; also, the adulterant itself. 1928–. D. BAGLEY Meyrick was probably knocked out by a Mickey Finn in his nightly Ovaltine (1973). Hence **mickey-finn,** verb trans. To adulterate or stupefy with a Mickey Finn. 1934–. C. FRANKLIN Two men . . . had mickey-finned his drink (1971). [Origin unknown.]

Mickey Mouse adjective **1** Small, insignificant, or worthless. 1931–. GLOBE & MAIL (Toronto): The titles kept the modern broadcast media from thinking 'it was such a Mickey Mouse operation' (1974). noun **2** air force A type of electrical bomb-release. 1941–3. [From the name of a mouse-like cartoon character created by Walt Disney (1901–66), US cartoonist.]

midder noun Midwifery. 1909–. M. POLLAND Although he . . . did his medicine in Edinburgh, he came here to the Rotunda for his midder (1965). [From *mid(wifery* + *-er.*]

middle leg noun The penis. 1896–. D. THOMAS Men should be two tooled and a poet's middle leg is his pencil (1935).

middy noun Austral A medium-sized measure of beer, or a similar quantity of another drink. 1945–. K. COOK 'Middy of rum, Mick,' said the youth. . . . Ten ounces of rum

sold over the bar cost four dollars (1974). [From *mid* noun, middle + *-y.*]

mierda int Esp. among Spanish-speakers: an exclamation of annoyance or disgust. 1970–. GUARDIAN She'd just dipped it in a cup of her urine . . . In the middle of the stick we could see a faint pink circle. 'Mierda,' she said. 'I am' (1993). [From Spanish *mierda* excrement.]

mifky-pifky noun US Sexual activity, flirting. 1985–. NEW YORK TIMES BOOK REVIEW With a few incidents of mifky-pifky in Clinton's Oval Office . . . Clinton handed them so much ammunition (2000). [Origin unknown.]

mike¹ Brit noun **1** A period of idleness or shirking. 1825–. TIMES The day of the cheerful veteran forward, gratefully relying upon opportunities for a mild 'mike', may be coming to an end (1958). verb intr. **2** To hang around idly, shirk work. 1859–. P. EVETT [He would] spy on us as we worked, and then . . . thunder at any one he thought was miking (1974). [Origin unknown; cf. British dialect *mitch* verb, to skulk, play truant, apparently from Old French *muchier, mucier* to hide, lurk.]

mike² noun **to take the mike (out of)** = to take the micky (out of) (see at MICKEY¹ noun). 1935–. B. MATHER Watch it. . . . The Swami don't dig taking the mike out of the gods (1973).

mike³ noun A microgram, spec. of LSD. 1967–. J. WOOD They wanted me to tell where I got the mikes. . . . The acid, see? (1973). [Abbreviation of *microgram.*]

mike⁴ noun US, orig and mainly military A minute. 1986–. G. A. LINDERER A pair of gunships would be heading out in zero-five mikes (1991). [From *Mike* communications code word for *M*, standing for *minute.*]

Mike Mike noun US military Esp. in the Vietnam war, a weapon, or ammunition, calibrated in millimetres. 1969–. J. R. ELTING Eight-one-mike-mike mortar (1984). [Reduplication of *Mike* communications code word for *M*, after *mm* millimetres.]

milkie noun **1** mainly Brit A milkman. 1886–. NEWS OF THE WORLD Milkies are charging for 'free' pintas (1990). **2** An opaque playing marble. 1908–. [From *milk* + *-ie.*]

milko noun Also **milk-oh.** orig Austral A milkman. 1905–. CANBERRA CHRONICLE He has spent a fair bit of time in banking and an oil company business, but also doubled as a pretty

mickey Mickey Finn Mickey Mouse midder mike

good milko (1985). [From the call *milk O!* used by milkmen.]

milky noun **1** Also **milkie**. A milkman. 1886–. adjective **2** Cowardly. 1936–. H. CARVIC 'Getting milky?' scoffed Doris (1969). [From *milk* noun + *-y*; in sense 2, from the association of milk with mildness or weakness.]

mill verb trans. **1** To hit, strike, fight; also, intr., to box. 1612–. LONDON DAILY NEWS He was an ageing journeyman boxer who had spent years milling in small halls, and then got a chance to make it big (1987). noun **2** dated A prison or guard-house. 1851–. J. JONES 'You were here when one of the old ones was in the mill, weren't you, Jack?' 'Two,' Malloy said. 'Both of them during my first stretch' (1951). **3** US, dated A typewriter. 1911–. H. L. MENCKEN Writer's cramp was cured . . . on the advent of the *mill*, i.e., the typewriter (1948). **4** The engine of an aircraft or a hot-rod racing car. 1918–. B. GARFIELD This was an old car but it must have had a souped-up mill (1975). [In sense 2, from earlier meaning 'treadmill'.]

gone a million
done for,
completely
defeated

million noun **gone a million** Austral and NZ Done for, completely defeated. 1913–. AUSTRALIAN (Sydney): Gough's gone. Gone a million. He's had it. I'd give him inside two weeks before we get his resignation (1976).

mill tog noun dated A shirt, esp. one made or worn by prisoners. 1821–. [Prob. from Shelta *miltŏg* shirt, sheet.]

mince noun = MINCE-PIE noun; usu. in pl. 1937–. R. COOK A general look of dislike in the minces, which tremble a bit in their sockets (1962).

mincemeat noun **to make mincemeat of** to destroy, to annihilate. Also, to beat decisively or easily in a contest. 1876–. TIMES Thames R.C. made mincemeat of all their opponents in the Grand Eights (1955). [From earlier sense, chop into small pieces.]

mince-pie noun Rhyming slang for 'eye'; usu. in pl. 1857–. J. JOYCE Got a prime pair of mincepies, no kid (1922).

mind-blowing adjective That blows one's mind (see BLOW verb 9); incredible, fantastic. 1966–. H. MCCLOY A mind-blowing mustard yellow for the woodwork and on the walls a psychedelic splash of magenta and orchid and lime (1974). Also **mind-blower**, noun. 1968–.

mind-boggling adjective = MIND-BLOWING adjective. 1964–. C. BONNINGTON A monstrous bergschrund, a huge, mind-boggling chasm about fifteen feet across (1973).

minder noun A bodyguard, esp. one employed to protect a criminal; a thief's assistant. 1896–. E. MCGIRR Comes of a whole family of wrong 'uns. . . . A high class 'minder' around the big gambling set (1973).

minge noun The female genitals. 1903–. NEW DIRECTION They've all . . . scented and talced their minges (1974). [Origin unknown.]

minger noun Brit An ugly person. 1992–. [Prob. from MING(ING adjective + *-er*.]

minging adjective Brit, orig Scottish Bad-smelling, stinking; more generally, unpleasant. Also, very drunk. 1970–. R. JOLLY Jus' two beers an' the boy was mingin' (1989). [From Scottish English *ming* noun bad smell (orig. sense excrement) + *-ing*.]

mingy /mɪndʒɪ/ adjective Mean, niggardly; disappointingly small. 1911–. E. V. LUCAS It's dear, but we're not going to be mingy (1930). [Perh. from *m(ean* adjective + *st)ingy* adjective, or a blend of *mangy* adjective and *stingy* adjective.]

Minnie noun Also **minnie, minny**. A German trench-mortar, or the bomb discharged by it. 1917–. G. WILSON That bloody moaning Minnie. . . . It's a hell of a weapon (1950). [Abbreviation of German *Minenwerfer* trench-mortar.]

minstrel noun A capsule containing an amphetamine and a sedative. 1966–. [From its black-and-white colour, with reference to the *Black and White Minstrels*, a troupe of British variety entertainers of the 1960s and '70s.]

misery guts noun derog A person who is always gloomy and complaining. 1974–. GUARDIAN If I hadn't been sitting next to old misery guts, I wouldn't have bothered (1992).

misper noun Brit A missing person. Used esp. by the police. 1994–.

miss noun A miscarriage. 1897–. D. SHANNON She had a miss, that time, lost the baby (1971). [Shortening.]

Miss Ann noun Also **Miss Anne, Miss Annie** US, African-American A white woman. 1926–.

missis noun Also **missus**. **1** A wife. 1823–. DAILY MIRROR If you fancy taking the missus for a day out, you take her virtually free (1975). **2** A form of address to a woman. 1823–. J. CARTWRIGHT Last orders everybody . . . Did you drink all them yourself Missus? Bloody hell you can come again you can (1991). [Alteration of *mistress*; cf. MRS. noun.]

mistake noun **and no mistake** used to emphasize a preceding statement. 1818–. NEW ZEALAND GEOGRAPHER He was a tough old dag, and no mistake (1945).

mister noun A form of address to a man. 1734–. E. LEONARD Mister, gimme a dollar (1987). [From the earlier use as a title prefixed to a man's name.]

mitt orig US. noun **1** A hand. 1893–. R. CHANDLER 'Freeze the mitts on the bar.' The barman and I put our hands on the bar (1940). **2** A welcome or reception of the stated sort; in the phrs. *the glad mitt* a friendly welcome, *the frozen* (or *icy*) *mitt* an unfriendly welcome. 1903–. A. PRIOR She'd have taken it and then handed me the frozen mitt (1960). verb **3** trans. To greet or congratulate with a handshake. 1908–. **4** intr. and trans., boxing To acknowledge (spectators) by raising the hands above the head, esp. as a gesture of triumph. 1930–. WASHINGTON POST [The boxers] blew kisses, bowed and mitted the crowd (2000). [From the earlier sense, mitten.]

mitt camp noun US A palmist's or fortuneteller's establishment. Also **mitt joint.** 1923–.

mittens noun pl. **1** Handcuffs. 1598–. **2** Boxing gloves. 1859–. [From the earlier sense, type of glove.]

mitt-reader noun US A palmist or fortuneteller. 1928–.

mivvy noun A person who is adept at something. 1906–. O. MILLS He's a mivvy with anything like that (1959). [Cf. the earlier obs. senses (perh. not the same word), a marble, (derog) a woman; ultimate origin unknown.]

mix verb **1 to mix it** to fight or quarrel; to start fighting. 1905–. D. LEES These lads don't want to fight for nothing. If they can get away without mixing it they will (1973). **2 to mix in** to start or join in a fight. 1912–.

P. G. WODEHOUSE If you see any more gnats headed in her direction, hold their coats and wish them luck, but restrain the impulse to mix in (1971).

mixer noun A trouble-maker. 1938–. A. E. LINDOP I knew what a mixer she was, and I knew she was not capable of keeping a secret (1966). [Perh. from *to mix it* to quarrel (see MIX verb 1).]

mizzle verb intr. Brit To run away; to decamp. 1781–. R. LLEWELLYN There was a girl with him. . . . He fell behind the table, and she mizzled (1970). [Origin uncertain; cf. Shelta *misli* to go.]

mo[1] noun Austral and NZ Abbreviation of 'moustache'. 1894–. K. GARVEY His mo he paused to wipe (1981). See also *to curl the mo* at CURL verb.

mo[2] noun Also **mo'**. Abbreviation of 'moment'; esp. in phr. *half a mo*: (wait for) a short time. 1896–. T. S. ELIOT 'Arf a mo', 'arf a mo'. It's lucky for you two as you've got someone what's done a bit o' lookin' into things to keep you in line (1934).

mo[3] noun US derog, mainly students' An effeminate male; a homosexual. 1968–. [Shortening of HOMO noun.]

m.o. noun Abbreviation of 'modus operandi'. 1955–. R. EDWARDS His m.o. was to pull two or three jobs in a line and then fade from the scene (1974).

Moab noun dated **1** A type of hat shaped like a turban. 1864–1960. **2** mainly Brit public schools' A tub or other container for washing in. 1865–. [Alluding to Psalms 60:8 'Moab is my washpot'.]

moaning minnie noun Also **moaning Minnie, Moaning Minnie.** **1** = MINNIE noun. 1941–. **2** derog A person who is pessimistic and always complaining. 1962–. NEW ZEALAND NEWS I don't want to give the impression of being a moaning Minnie but may I . . . make a special plea to the railmen to . . . get back to work (1972). [In sense 1, from the noise made by the projectile in flight.]

mob noun **1** An associated group of people. 1688–. S. ASHTON-WARNER I know one girl from another, course you do in my mob anyway (1960). **2** services' A military unit. 1916–. M. PUGH You must have heard of Sharjah and the Trucial Oman Scouts. This mob is modelled on them (1972). **3** US An organization of violent criminals, spec. the Mafia. 1927–. GUARDIAN The Mob from its Chicago headquarters runs the

Miss Ann missis mistake mister mitt mitt camp

mob-handed

subcontinent (1969). [Abbreviation of *mobile*, short for Latin *mobile vulgus* excitable crowd.]

mob-handed adjective As or accompanied by a large gang. 1934–. A. PRIOR Mo and his brother had returned home penniless to find the police mob-handed (1966).

mobilize verb trans. US Esp. in Jewish usage, to administer a beating to. 1923–. B. APPEL Bastids! We'll mobilize yuh! (1977) [Perh. from Yiddish *mapel* (in *mapel zayn* to abort) + *-ize*.]

mobster noun orig US A gangster. 1917–. D. E. WESTLAKE I was afraid to think about Vigano and his mobsters (1972). [From MOB noun + *-ster*.]

moby noun Also **mobie**. Brit A mobile phone. 1997–. C. HALL Get her on the old mobie! (1997). [From *mob(ile* + *-y*.]

mock¹ noun **to put the** (or **a**) **mock(s) on** Austral = *to put the mockers on* (see at MOCKER¹ noun). 1911–. W. G. GROUT I hope I am not 'putting the mock' on Norm because my feelings are the same as the rest of the Australian Test players: When O'Neill is a doubtful Test starter the job always looks grimmer (1965).

mock² noun US derog and offensive = MOCKY noun. 1967–. [Shortening.]

mocker¹ noun orig Austral A jinx; esp in phr. *to put the mocker(s) on*, to put a jinx on, to put a stop to; to ruin. 1922–. BULLETIN (Sydney): The double loss put the mockers on everything. Lake Macquarie is not the place to live without wheels (1983). [Cf. earlier sense, one who mocks or derides.]

mocker² noun Also **mokker**. Austral and NZ Clothes; a dress. 1939–. AUSTRALIAN SHORT STORIES Just wear ordinary mokker (1984). So **mockered-up**, adjective, dressed up. 1938–. [Origin unknown.]

mocky noun Also **mockey, mockie**. US derog and offensive A Jew. 1931–. I. WOLFERT Love thy neighbor if he's not . . . a mockie or a slicked-up greaseball from the Argentine (1943). [From Yiddish *make* sore, plague (often used in curses).]

modoc /ˈməʊdɒk/ noun Also **modock**. US derog A man who becomes a pilot for the sake of pilots' glamorous image. 1931–60. [Origin unknown.]

moffie noun Also **mophy**. mainly S Afr An effeminate man. 1960–. POST (S. Afr.): The life

of Edward Shadi—described as a beautiful, sexy moffie with a sweet soprano voice—was a strange affair (1971). [Perh. a shortening and alteration of *hermaphrodite*; cf. Afrikaans *moffiedaai*, dialectal variant of *hermafrodiet*.]

mofo noun US = MOTHER-FUCKER noun. 1967–. W. L. H. MOON Excuse my language, but for all the good he does this side of the bayou, he's one useless black mofo (1982). [Shortening and alteration of MOTHER-FUCKER noun.]

mog noun Brit **1** A cat. 1926–. P. HESELTINE Such lovely mogs you can't imagine—including the best cat in the world, surely (1934). **2** A fur coat. 1950–. E. PARTRIDGE Annuvver 'orse comes up, an' it's . . . a new mog fer the missus (1950). [Abbreviation of MOGGIE noun.]

moggadored adjective Also **mogodored**. dated Confused, at a loss. 1936–45. B. NAUGHTON He got some of these blokes moggadored: didn't know what to think, or do (1945). [Origin uncertain; perh. connected with Irish *magadh* mock, jeer.]

moggie noun Also **moggy**. Brit A cat. 1911–. PEOPLE'S JOURNAL Oh, and before I leave this topic of pussies, my neighbour across the lane also had a good laugh from the moggie next door to her (1973). [Cf. earlier dialect senses, a calf, cow, an untidy woman; perh. a variant of *Maggie*, pet form of the female personal name *Margaret*.]

mojo /ˈməʊdʒəʊ/ noun US An addictive drug, esp. morphine. 1939–. [Origin uncertain; perh. from Spanish *mojar* to celebrate by drinking.]

moke noun **1** Brit A donkey. 1848–. **2** Austral A horse, esp. an inferior one. 1863–. C. D. MILLS 'How's my horse?' . . . 'Your old moke's alright,' laughed the Boss (1976). [Origin unknown.]

mokker noun US The head of a criminal organization; a gang boss. 1929–. [From Yiddish *makher* maker, leader.]

mokus US. noun **1** Loneliness, depression; also, drunkenness, alcoholic drink. 1927–. adjective **2** Drunk; also, depressed. 1960–. M. GATTZDEN I'm mokus. Canned. Don't know nothing (1970). [Origin unknown.]

mole noun Austral, usu. derog A woman. 1965–. R. D. JONES Give us a hand you lazy mole! (1979) [Perh. a variant of MOLL noun.]

moley noun Brit A gangland weapon consisting of a potato with razor-blades inserted into it. 1950–. SPECTATOR I suppose if I go on criticising him I shall end up by having

mob-handed mobilize mobster moby mock mog

the boys with the moleys call on me one dark
night (1959). [Origin unknown.]

moll noun **1** A prostitute. 1604–. **2** A
criminal's or gangster's female companion.
1823–. N. MARSH I can see you're in a fever lest
slick Ben and his moll should get back . . . before
you make your getaway (1962). **3** US A female
pickpocket or thief. 1955–. [Pet form of the
female personal name *Mary*.]

mollock verb intr. To engage in sexual
dalliance or intercourse. 1932–. W. BAWDEN And
yet, here they were, not more than a foot away,
bedhead to bedhead, merrily mollocking (1983).
[Apparently invented by Stella Gibbons (*Cold
Comfort Farm*), and perh. influenced by MOLL
noun.]

molly-dook noun Also **molly-dooker,
molly-duke.** Austral A left-handed person.
1941–. NORTHERN DAILY LEADER (Tamworth): Five of
the top seven batsmen doing battle for Australia
are left-handers. Kepler Wessels, Wayne Phillips,
[etc.] . . . are all molly dookers (1983). [Prob.
from obs. slang *molly* noun, effeminate man,
from the female personal name *Molly*, a pet
form of *Mary* + *dook*, variant of DUKE noun,
hand; cf. earlier Austral *mauldy* adjective,
left-handed, *molly-hander* noun, left-hander.]

molly the monk adjective Austral Drunk.
1966–. KING'S CROSS WHISPER (Sydney) Ophelia was
more than a little bit Molly the Monk after
Parkinson had been loosening her up a bit with
three bottles of Quelltaler hock (1973).
[Rhyming slang.]

molo adjective Also **mowlow.** Austral Drunk.
1916–. D. R. STUART By the time he ran us down to
the wharf to catch the boat back, we were
nicely molo (1979). [Origin unknown.]

momma variant of MAMMA noun.

momo noun US A stupid person, idiot.
1953–. R. PRICE La Donna would be sitting
there with some big momo from Duluth
front row center (1978). [Origin uncertain;
perh. a reduplication of the first syllable
of *moron*, or from Italian dialect *màmo*
foolish.]

momser variant of MAMZER noun.

Monday-morning quarterback
noun US One who engages in criticism of
something (spec. orig. of the play in an
American football game) only with the
benefit of hindsight. 1931–.

mondo adjective orig and mainly US **1** As an
intensifier: considerable, ultimate, huge.
Also as adverb, very, extremely. 1968–. PEOPLE

The freshly painted mural on the side of the
Hollywood Plaza apartment building marks the
apogee of mondo ego publicity (1987). **2** As a
term of approbation: excellent, admirable,
'cool'. 1986–. [From Italian *mondo* noun,
world.]

mong[1] /mʌŋ/ noun Austral Abbreviation of
'mongrel'. 1903–. J. WRIGHT Gor' on, ya bloody
mong. Git ta buggery. Ya probably lousy with
fleas (1980).

mong[2] /mɒŋ/ noun Brit A fool, idiot; a
mentally slow or backward person. 1980–. R.
RAY 'Well, it's not clear,' I said. 'I can see
that . . . I'm not a fucking mong' (1998).
[Shortening of *mongol* person with Down's
syndrome.]

monged adjective Also **monged-out** Brit
Incapacitated, or very intoxicated, by drugs.
1991–. ECHOES Let's all get blunted, skunked, and
generally monged (1995). [From MONG[2] noun
+ -ed.]

moniker noun Also **monicker, monniker,
monica, monekeer,** etc. A name or nickname. 1851–. TIMES LITERARY SUPPLEMENT Henry
Handel Richardson herself . . . was able to hide
behind the male signature on her books (her
maiden name wedded to two favourite family
monikers) (1959). Hence **monikered,
monickered** adjective Having a (particular)
name or nickname. 1979–. Q Welsh
Rarebit . . . Haughtily monickered brunch staple
reveals itself to be no more than cheese on toast
(1996). [Origin unknown.]

monkey noun **1 to make a monkey (out)
of** orig US To make a fool of (someone);
to deceive, dupe; to ridicule. 1767–.
M. INNES The plain fact was that Bulkington
had . . . made a monkey of her. It was all very
mortifying (1973). **2** Brit £500; US $500. 1832–.
Cf. PONY noun 1. TIMES It looks like you are going
to be roped into that theft from the pub but it
will be all right. It will cost you a monkey (£500)
(1973). **3a** mainly US and Austral The external
female genitals. 1863–. **b** orig and mainly US The
penis; esp. in phr. *to spank the monkey* to
masturbate. 1978–. EMPIRE Keanu Reeves
reassures Garry about excessive monkey
spanking (1999). **4** orig US Addiction to drugs;
esp. in phr. *to have a monkey on one's back*, to
be a drug addict. 1938–. E. R. JOHNSON An addict's
greatest worry would not be his, since Vito
would feed his monkey (1970). **5 not to give
(or care) a monkey's (fuck,** etc.): to be
completely indifferent or unconcerned.
1960–. J. WAINWRIGHT 'Not', snarled Sugden, 'that

moll   mollock   molly-dook   molly the monk   molo

I give a solitary monkey's toss what you wear'
(1975). See also BRASS MONKEY noun.

monkey-hurdler noun US An organist.
1936–. W. MORUM Nelson's a monkey
hurdler. . . . He plays one of those Wurlitzer
organs at the talkies (1951). [Perh. from the
traditional organ-grinder's monkey.]

monkey island noun Also **monkey's
island**. nautical A small bridge above the pilot-
house. 1912–. P. J. ABRAHAM Up on the monkey
island he had realized there would be no power
for the lights (1963).

monkey-man noun US A weak and
servile husband. 1924–.

monkey parade noun Also **monkey's
parade, monkeys' parade.** Brit derog, dated
A promenade of young men and women
in search of sexual partners. 1910–. Hence
monkey-parading, noun and adjective. 1934–.
J. B. PRIESTLEY A Sabbatarian town of this kind,
which could offer its young folk nothing on
Sunday night but a choice between monkey
parading and dubious pubs (1934).

monkey-shines noun pl. US Mischievous,
foolish, or underhanded tricks or acts; also
sing. c.1832–. H. HOWARD Why all the
monkeyshines to get rid of Lucy? He'd been
divorced before and he could be divorced
again (1973).

monkey suit noun orig US A uniform; a
formal dress suit, evening dress. 1914–.
A. FOWLES He could . . . hire one of those monkey-
suits from Moss Bros. (1974).

monster verb trans. orig Austral **1** To attack,
harrass, pester. 1967–. **2** To criticize harshly
or savagely; to disparage. 1976–. INDEPENDENT
She is regularly monstered by the Home Office,
lionised by Woman's Hour and warily admired
by the teaching profession (1998).

monstro adjective orig and mainly US Huge,
monstrous. 1970–. NEW YORKER I have Nile
and Carol to take care of—in the face of recent
monstro financial reverses (1998). [From
monstr(ous + -o.]

Montezuma's revenge noun jocular
Diarrhoea suffered by visitors to Mexico.
1960–. TIMES England's World Cup football squad
suffered their first casualty in Mexico
on Wednesday, when 20-year-old Brian Kidd
was struck down by what is known as
'Montezuma's Revenge'—a stomach complaint
(1970). [From the name of Montezuma II
(1466–1520), Aztec ruler at the time of the
Spanish conquest of Mexico.]

monty noun Also **monte** /ˈmɒntɪ/ Austral and
NZ A certainty; used esp. of a horse considered
certain to win a race. 1894–. J. WYNNUM I was given
the drum . . . that if I put my name to the dotted line,
I'd be a monty to get drafted to the U.S. destroyer
(1965). [Prob. from US monte noun, game of
chance played with cards, from Spanish monte
mountain.]

moo[1] noun Abbreviation of MOOLA noun.
1941–. D. BLOODWORTH Most of my nurses . . . don't
work for moo . . . . But local stuff I pay (1975).

moo[2] noun Brit derog A woman; esp. in phr.
silly moo. 1967–. FUNNY FORTNIGHTLY It was rustling
you heard all right—I'm a rustler! And I've
rustled you, silly moo! Hey! Gerroff! (1989).
[From the earlier sense, cow, in allusion to
cow noun 1.]

mooch verb trans. **1** To beg, cadge,
scrounge. 1865–. D. MORRELL First thing I know, a
bunch of your friends will show up, mooching
food, maybe stealing, maybe pushing drugs
(1972). noun **2** = MOOCHER noun. 1914–.
W. BURROUGHS Cash was a junk mooch on wheels.
He made it difficult to refuse (1953). [In sense 1,
from earlier senses, to loiter, to steal.]

moocher noun A beggar, a cadger. 1853–.
K. ORVIS You moocher, you—don't you respect a
lady's natural curiosity? Be nice to me. After all,
I'm paying for this party (1962). [From MOOCH
verb + -er.]

mooching noun Begging, sponging,
scrounging. 1895–. L. DERWENT The tramps were
adepts at mooching, and never refused any cast-
off (1979).

moody Brit noun **1** Persuasive talk, flannel;
nonsense, rubbish. 1934–. R. BUSBY The same
old moody he'd heard a thousand times before
(1970). **2** A moody temper or period; a fit of
sulks. Also **to pull the moody,** to sulk. 1969–.
T. BARLING I gave you Ollie, so lay off the moody then
(1986). adjective **3** criminals' False, counterfeit;
fake. 1958–. N. J. CRISP 'I don't have to tell you,'
Kenyon went on, 'how easy it is to plant moody
information about a copper' (1978). verb **4** To
bluff or deceive by means of flattery, etc.
1934–. R. COOK Trying to moody through to the
royal enclosure on the knock (1962). [In sense
1, prob. from moody adjective, but some
connection has been suggested with Moody
and Sankey rhyming slang for 'hanky-panky'
(from the names of two US hymn writers,
Dwight L. Moody (1837–99) and Ira D. Sankey
(1840–1908)); in sense 3, apparently from
earlier sense, gloomy, sullen.]

monkey-hurdler monkey island monkey-man moo

mooey noun Also **moey, mooe.** dated
A mouth; a face. 1859–1955. P. WILDEBLOOD
All nylons and high-heeled shoes and paint an
inch thick on their mooeys (1955). [From
Romany *mooi* mouth, face.]

moola noun Also **moolah.** orig US Money.
1939–. J. SYMONS Then the only thing to be settled
is the lolly, the moolah (1975). [Origin
unknown.]

moolie noun US offensive In Italian-American
usage, a black person. 1988–. DAILY NEWS (New
York) 'Hey, moolie,' the white kid said. 'What's
a yom doing on our bus!' (1997). [From
MOOL(INYAN noun + *-ie*.]

moolinyan noun Also **moulinyan.** US
offensive In Italian-American usage, a black
person. 1969–. [From Italian (Calabrian
dialect) *mulignana* aubergine.]

moon noun 1 dated The buttocks. (Used in
sing. and pl.) 1756–. S. BECKETT Placing her hands
upon her moons, plump and plain (1938).
2 A month's imprisonment. 1830–. K. TENNANT
I got a twelve moon (1953). 3 US Illicitly
distilled liquor, esp. whisky. 1928–. SATURDAY
EVENING POST I would buy a couple of pints of
moon (1950). verb intr. and trans. 4 To expose
one's buttocks to (someone). 1968–. NEWS
& REPORTER (Chester, S. Carolina): Fannie has
assured us that she didn't 'moon' anybody
(1974). [In sense 2, from the earlier
meaning, period of one month; in sense
3, short for *moonshine* noun, illicitly distilled
liquor.]

moon-eyed adjective US Drunk. 1737–.
AMERICAN SPEECH Sid gits moon-eyed every Saturday
night (1940).

moonlight verb intr. 1 orig US To have
other paid employment, esp. at night,
in addition to one's regular job. 1957–.
P. CARLON You think I moonlight? Believe me, one
job's enough (1970). noun 2 US = MOONLIGHT
FLIT noun. 1958–. R. PARKES It's no good him trying
to find 'em. . . . Done a moonlight, they did
(1971).

moonlighter noun 1 One who does a
moonlight flit. 1903–. SUNDAY MAIL (Brisbane):
Brisbane flat owners . . . estimate that
moonlighters . . . are costing them £100,000
a year (1964). 2 One who moonlights. 1957–.
C. EGLETON I employ a lot of moonlighters, blokes
who take a second job at nights (1973).

moonlight flit noun A hurried departure
by night, esp. to avoid paying a debt. 1824–.
[Cf. earlier obs. *moonlight flitting* noun.]

moose noun US, forces' A young Japanese or
Korean woman; esp. the wife or mistress of
a serviceman stationed in Japan or Korea.
1953–. AMERICAN SPEECH Signs urging
Americans . . . to meet the best mooses in Kyoto
(1954). [From Japanese *musume* daughter,
girl.]

mootah /ˈmuːtə/ noun Also **mooter, moota,
mootie, mota, muta,** etc. US Marijuana.
1926–. E. McBAIN One of the guys was on mootah.
So he got a little high (1956). [Origin
unknown.]

mop noun and int US A final cadence of
three triplets at the end of a jazz number;
also used as an exclamation of surprise.
1944–. VILLAGE VOICE I wait a while, eyes closed,
and I look, mop! I'm in the bathtub, all
alone (1959). [Imitative; cf. *bop* noun, type
of jazz.]

moral noun now mainly Austral A certainty.
1861–. CANBERRA TIMES The senior puisne judge
(who is an absolute moral for the Chief
Justiceship come February next year) . . . is almost
certainly among the ranks of the deeply
concerned (1986). [Short for *moral certainty*.]

Moreton Bay noun Austral An informer.
1953–. BULLETIN (Sydney): Fifty percent of the
Drug Squad's arrests are based on information
received and woebetide a user, supplier or
anyone else who becomes a dog, a gig or, as
the police term it, a Moreton Bay (1984). [Short
for *Moreton Bay fig*, rhyming slang for FIZGIG
noun.]

morning-glory noun US Something
(e.g. a racehorse) which fails to maintain its
early achievement. 1904–38. [Cf. the earlier
sense, type of climbing plant.]

morph noun US Abbreviation of
'morphine'. 1906–. H. GOLD No morph, no!
I had really kicked that one, and would do my
own traveling from now on (1956).

morphodite noun US A homosexual.
1935–. [Alteration of *hermaphrodite* noun.]

mort noun A girl or woman. Also **mot.**
1567–. J. BLACKBURN 'Look at them two mots,
Fergus.' Dan pointed at two mini-skirted girls
(1969). [Origin unknown.]

moscow verb trans. Austral 1 To pawn.
1910–. C. DREW Do you know where a man
can 'moscow' a couple of snakes? (1917). noun
2 Pawn; latterly mainly in phr. *in Moscow,
gone to Moscow* in pawn. 1910–. [Alteration
(influenced by *Moscow* capital of Russia) of
obs. Brit slang *moskeneer* to pawn an article

moola   moolie   moolinyan   moon   moon-eyed   moral

for more than it is worth, of Yiddish origin, from modern Hebrew *mashkōn* a pledge.]

mosey verb intr. orig US To walk or go in a leisurely or aimless manner. 1870-. D. RAMSAY I thought I'd mosey on over to the liquor store (1974). [From earlier sense, to go away quickly.]

moss-back noun US Someone attached to old-fashioned ideas or ways; an extreme conservative; a fogey. 1878-. TREVANIAN The moss-backs of the National Gallery had pulled off quite a coup in securing the Martini Horse for a one-day exhibition (1973). [From the earlier sense, large old fish so sluggish that it has a growth of algae on its back.]

mossie noun Also **mozzie.** orig Austral A mosquito. 1936-. SHOOTING TIMES & COUNTRY MAGAZINE If it has chosen unwisely, then the newly-hatched mossies rise triumphantly from the surface only to hit their heads on the caterpillars' safety net and fall back into the liquid (1973). [From *mos(quito + -ie.]*

mossy adjective US Extremely conservative or reactionary. 1904-. [From the notion of moss growing on old things; cf. MOSS-BACK noun.]

most noun **the most** orig US The best of all. 1953-. LISTENER I would infinitely prefer to listen to the Kenny Everett programme—'the show that's the most with your tea and toast,' as that masterly DJ himself puts it (1968).

mostest adjective, noun, and adverb dialect and jocular Most; esp. in phr. *the hostess with the mostest,* the perfect hostess. 1882-. DAILY HERALD Here's the hostess with the mostest.... Her guests all agreed Sophia was pretty good ... well, pretty, anyway (1968).

mother noun US Short for MOTHER-FUCKER noun. 1955-. NEW YORK TIMES 'You mothers! I ain't been out five minutes and I just got *outta* the pen this morning!' Her name is Judy, and although she is white, she talks black jive (1975).

Mother Bunch noun A fat or untidy old woman. 1847-. GUARDIAN She no more looks like a Mother Bunch than sounds like one ... a fairly plump but elegant, well-dressed woman (1964). [From the name of a noted fat woman of Elizabethan times.]

mother-fucker noun Also **muthafucka.** coarse, orig and mainly US A despicable person; someone or something very unpleasant.

1918-. BLACK PANTHER We will kill any motherfucker that stands in the way of our freedom (1973). Also **mother-fucking,** adjective Despicable, unpleasant. 1889-. S. ELLIN 'You motherfucking black clown,' Harvey says without heat, 'nothing is changed' (1974).

mothering adjective US = MOTHER-FUCKING adjective. 1951-. NEW YORKER I'm out there cutting that mothering grass all day! (1975).

motherless adverb **1** Austral Completely; esp. in phr. *motherless broke.* 1898-. K. S. PRICHARD 'But I know what it is to be hard up, don't forget,' he said. 'Stony, motherless broke, like I was in Sydney' (1946). **2** adjective Austral Without money; broke. 1916-. B. BENNETT He let half-a-dozen others out at the same time. The motherless hooer (1976). **3** S Afr Drunk. 1988-. [In sense 3, from a translation of Afrikaans *moederloos dronk,* itself prob. an alteration of *moedeloos dronk* hopelessly drunk.]

mother-loving adjective US = MOTHER-FUCKING adjective. 1964-. J. MORRIS Get her out of that mother-lovin' joint an' into the cab (1969).

mother-raper noun coarse, US = MOTHER-FUCKER noun. 1959-. Also **mother-raping,** adjective = MOTHER-FUCKING adjective. 1932-. C. HIMES Mother-raping cocksucking turdeating bastard, are you blind? (1969).

mother's ruin noun Gin. 1933-. P. JONES I have been to a party, darling.... What would you like? 'Mother's ruin'? (1955).

motorhead noun US **1** A car or motorcycle enthusiast. 1974-. **2** An idiot, fool. 1979-. RECORD (Bergen County, New Jersey) Two motorheads named Beavis and Butt-Head who play 'ball' with a live frog, bludgeon a poodle and hum heavy metal tunes (1992). [From *motor* noun + HEAD noun 3.]

motor mouth noun orig US A person who talks incessantly and trivially. 1963-. NATIONAL OBSERVER The increasing number of 'motor mouths' posing as sports broadcasters, ... statisticians and whatever (1977).

motser noun Also **motsa, motza, motzer.** Austral **1** A certainty. 1936-. R. BEILBY You better let that bugger get well ahead ... The Stuka'll be a motsa to have a go at him (1970). **2** A large amount of money, esp. as won in gambling.

> **Mother Bunch**
> a fat or
> untidy old
> woman

mosey   moss-back   mossie   mossy   most   mostest

1943–. BULLETIN (Sydney): Canberra might have cost a motza but it's worth every cent (1985). [Prob. from Yiddish *matse* bread.]

mouldy adjective **1** dated Wretched, boring, depressing, sick. 1876–. A. HUXLEY One feels a bit low and mouldy after those bouts of flu (1956). **2** Used as a general term of disparagement. 1896–. SATURDAY REVIEW The average cabby is a moldy old fascist (1972).

mouldy noun naval and RAF A torpedo. 1916–43. [Origin unknown.]

mouse noun A lump or discoloured bruise, esp. a black eye. 1854–. S. MOODY Touched the mouse under her eye. She just hoped a *Vogue* photog wasn't going to show up (1985).

mousetrap noun Inferior or unpalatable cheese. 1947–. OBSERVER Although sometimes dismissed as 'mousetrap', Cheddar is much the most popular cheese in Britain (1975). [From the use of such cheese to bait mousetraps.]

mouth noun orig US Extravagant, insolent, or boastful talk; empty bragging, impudence; esp. in phr. *to be all mouth*. 1891–. G. F. NEWMAN The youth . . . for all his mouth and supposed cleverness was easily tricked (1970).

mouth-breather noun N Amer A stupid person. 1985–. ESQUIRE Three dateless chuckleheads in mullet cuts—short on top, shoulder length behind; mouth breathers, unibrows, stooges (1998). [From earlier sense, person who breathes through the mouth (rather than the nose).]

mouthful noun orig US Something important or noteworthy. 1916–. P. G. WODEHOUSE 'Nice nurse?' 'Ah, there you have said a mouthful, Pickering. I have a Grade A nurse' (1973).

mouthpiece noun A solicitor, barrister, etc. 1857–. P. B. YUILL The Abreys would get legal aid. The state would fix them up with a good mouthpiece (1974).

mouthy adjective Loquacious and often also boastful or impudent. 1589–. GUARDIAN His mouthy confidence has no limits. Sure of his place in the England side for years to come, Catt was outspoken on the subject of payments for the lads (1997). [From *mouth* + *-y*.]

mowlow adjective = MOLO adjective.

moxie noun US Courage, energy. 1930–. DAILY COLONIST (Victoria, British Columbia): I was very impressed with his all-round moxie. He could snap back at any of them, news reporters,

police, and me (1975). [From the name of an American soft drink.]

moz Also **mozz**. Austral noun **1 to put the moz on** to inconvenience; to jinx. 1924–. K. STACKPOLE She felt she put the moz on him . . . . She couldn't bear to go in case she was a jinx (1974). verb trans. **2** To hinder, interrupt. 1941–. J. POWERS Don't let him mozz you, Monk. You've made it through the first week—that's the hard one (1973). [Abbreviation of dated Austral slang *mozzle* noun, luck, from Hebrew *mazzā* luck.]

Mozart and Liszt /ˌməʊtzɑːt ənd ˈlɪst/ adjective Brit Drunk, intoxicated. Cf. BRAHMS AND LISZT adjective. 1979–. R. BARKER Everybody thought I was *Mozart and Liszt*, falling flat on my *Khyber Pass* like that (1979). [Rhyming slang for PISSED adjective 1; arbitrary use of the names of two composers, Wolfgang Amadeus *Mozart* (1756–91) and Franz *Liszt* (see BRAHMS AND LISZT adjective).]

mozzie noun = MOSSIE noun.

Mr. Big noun The head of an organization of criminals; also, any important man. 1940–. OBSERVER He was just one of a number of the country's Mr Bigs who have laid the foundations for a gang culture that has left a series of deep scars across Britain (2007).

Mr. Clean noun An honourable or incorruptible politician. 1964–. GUARDIAN Mr Shultz himself had never been touched by Watergate. . . . His reputation as a 'Mr Clean' . . . has led him . . . to voice a growing sense of unease (1974).

Mrs. noun = MISSIS noun 1. 1920–. PHILADELPHIA INQUIRER You know, when I go home, the Mrs. says to me: 'Well, what happened tonight, night clerk?' (1973).

mu noun US Marijuana; a marijuana cigarette. 1936–. [Shortening of MOOTAH noun.]

much adverb **1 not much** certainly not, 'not likely'; also (ironically) certainly, 'not half'. 1886–. A. ROSS 'Got a going over, did you?' 'Not much, I got a going over. Want to see the bruises?' (1970). pron **2 too much** orig US Excellent, first-rate. 1937–. G. LEA I want to make it to the City . . . Man, like the City is too much—and that's where I want to be (1958).

mucho /ˈmuːtʃəʊ, ˈmʌtʃəʊ/ adjective Much, many; a lot of (something). Also as adverb, very, a lot. 1870–. MAKING MUSIC Warm valve distortion sound, plus mucho volume, make this an amp worthy of its chart placing (1986).

mouldy   mouse   mousetrap   mouth   mouth-breather

mucker

[From Spanish *mucho* adjective, much, many; adverb, very.]

mucker[1] noun Brit A heavy fall; esp. in phr. *to come* (or *go*) *a mucker*, to come a cropper, to come to grief. 1851–. G. MITCHELL I like old Jimmy boy and I wouldn't want to see him come a mucker (1974). [From *muck* noun, dung, dirt + *-er*; from the notion of falling into muck.]

mucker[2] noun US A coarse, vulgar person. 1884–. F. SCOTT FITZGERALD Why is it that the pick of young Englishmen from Oxford and Cambridge go into politics and in the USA we leave it to the muckers (1920). [Perh. from German *Mucker* sulky person, gloomy fanatic or hypocrite (cf. obs. US sense, fanatic or hypocrite).]

mucker[3] noun Brit A friend, companion, mate. 1947–. M. WOODHOUSE 'Is that my old mucker?' said Bottle. 'None other,' I said (1972). [Prob. from *to muck in* to share tasks, etc. equally.]

mucking adjective and adverb Euphemistic alteration of FUCKING adjective and adverb. 1929–. R. ADAMS You'd better lend him a hand . . . We'll be 'alf the mucking night else (1974).

mucky-muck noun N Amer A (self-)important person. 1968–. GLOBE & MAIL (Toronto): Orpen was always let out at the members' enclosure, but he never sat with the mucky-mucks (1968). [Alteration of *muck-a-muck*, short for HIGH-MUCK-A-MUCK noun.]

mud noun 1 US Opium; in later use, heroin. 1852–. FLYNN'S Some stiffs uses mud but coke don't need any jabbin', cookin' or flops (1926). 2 Coffee. 1855–. N. CULOTTA Got another cuppa mud, Joe? (1957).

mudder noun orig and mainly US 1 A horse which runs well on a wet or muddy racecourse. 1903–. COURIER-MAIL (Brisbane): Chance for 'mudders' . . . after last night's flash storm in Brisbane (1969). 2 A sportsman or team similarly proficient. 1942–. [From MUD noun + *-er*.]

mud-hook noun dated 1 An anchor. 1827–1960. 2 A hand or foot. 1850–1952.

mud kicker noun US derog A street prostitute. 1934–.

mudlark noun 1 dated A pig. 1785–1923. 2 = MUDDER noun. 1906–. SUNDAY TELEGRAPH (Sydney): Born Star a Mudlark. Born Star . . . yesterday outclassed the field at Sandown in his first start on a rain-affected track (1975). [From MUD noun + *lark* noun; in sense 1,

from the notion that pigs like wallowing in mud.]

muff noun 1 The female genitals. 1699–. H. MILLER The local bookie's got Polaroids of her flashing her muff (1973). 2 orig US A girl or woman, esp. a sexually accommodating one; a prostitute. 1914–. H. C. RAE Flappin' about a muff they found up in the woods (1965). [In sense 1, from the supposed resemblance between the pubic hair and a fur muff.]

muff-diver noun A person who practises cunnilingus. 1930–.

mug[1] noun 1a The face. 1708–. L. CODY What! Miss a chance to get your ugly mug in the papers! (1986). b = MUG SHOT noun. 1887–. R. CHANDLER Nulty turned over a photo . . . and handed it to me. It was a police mug, front and profile (1940). 2 dated The act of throttling or strangling someone; esp. in phr. *to put the mug on* (someone). 1862–1955. verb 3 intr. and trans. mainly Austral and NZ To kiss; to snog; often followed by *up*. 1822–. I. CROSS You think there is something funny about them mugging up each other like that? (1957). T. A. G. HUNGERFORD You been mugging up with the postie (1977). 4 intr. To make faces; esp. before an audience, a camera, etc. 1855–. TIMES Grimaces and gestures straight out of silent films, properly deserving the name 'mugging' (1961). 5 trans. US To photograph (a person), esp. for police records. 1899–. G. V. HIGGINS We brought him up to the marshal's office and mugged him and printed him (1972). [In sense 1a, perh. from the drinking mugs made with a grotesque representation of the human face that were common in the 18th century.]

mug[2] noun 1 Brit a A fool, simpleton; a gullible person. 1857–. L. GRIFFITHS I see mugs all around me. I see opportunities, possibilities, expectations and bargains and deals (1985). b criminals' A person who is not part of the underworld. 1938–. OBSERVER There were recognised prop-men or putters up of jobs, what the mugs called master minds (1960). 2 US A hoodlum or thug. 1890–. adjective 3 Stupid; easily duped or defeated. 1922–. SUNDAY AUSTRALIAN Let's just say I'm a good average mug golfer (1971).

mug[3] verb trans. Brit To buy a drink for. 1807–. P. MOLONEY If ye say to them 'scouse, Mug us dem on de house,' Yerl make Birty and Girty all shirty (1966). [From *mug* noun, drinking vessel.]

mug[4] verb trans. and intr. **to mug** (something) **up, to mug up on** (something): To learn (a subject) by concentrated study. 1848–.

mucker   mucking   mucky-muck   mud kicker

by muggin' up history (1940). [Origin unknown.]

mug[5] verb intr. **to mug up** mainly Canadian and nautical To have a large meal; also, to have a snack, a meal, or a hot drink. 1897–. L. HANCOCK. We . . . mugged up on boiled eggs, toast, jam, and coffee (1972). Cf. MUG-UP noun.

mug book noun US **1** A book containing photographs and potted biographies of (would-be) prominent people, paid for by themselves. 1902–. **2** A book kept by the police containing photographs of criminals. 1938–. [From MUG[1] noun 1a.]

mug-faker noun dated A street photographer. 1933–. M. ALLINGHAM These old photographers—mugfakers we call 'em—in the street (1952). [From MUG[1] noun 1a.]

muggins noun **1** A fool, simpleton. 1705–. DAILY TELEGRAPH The letter bomb was not meant for me personally. I was just the muggins who opened it (1973). **2** Used to refer self-deprecatingly to oneself as someone easily fooled or imposed on. 1973–. E. LEMARCHAND 'In a nutshell,' Michael said,' . . . Muggins [i.e. himself] has agreed to be in charge' (1973). [Perh. from the surname *Muggins*, with allusion to MUG[2] noun 1a.]

muggle noun orig US **1** pl. Marijuana. 1926–. MEZZROW & WOLFE 'Ever smoke any muggles?' (1946). **2** A marijuana cigarette. 1946–. A. ARENT Offer our guest a muggle (1969). So **muggler**, noun A marijuana addict. 1938–. [Origin unknown.]

mug shot noun orig US A photograph of a person, esp. in police records. 1950–. R. JEFFRIES Check through the mug shots and see if you can find him (1970). [From MUG[1] noun 1a.]

mug-up noun mainly Canadian and nautical A snack, a meal, or a drink. 1909–. R. PRICE Occasionally they stopped for mug-up (1970). [From MUG[5] verb.]

mule US. noun **1** Someone employed as a courier to smuggle illegal drugs into a country and often to pass them on to a buyer. 1922–. E. MCBAIN I bought from him a coupla times. He was a mule, Dad. That means he pushed to other kids (1959). verb trans. and intr. **2** To smuggle as a drug mule. 1978–. S. KING All dope was nasty stuff . . . After you muled a few loads of that shit, you could wipe your ass with gold toilet-paper (1990). [From the role of the mule as a beast of burden.]

mulga wire /ˈmʌlgə/ noun Austral The bush telegraph; the grapevine. Also **mulga**. 1899–. K. S. PRICHARD The troops've had it all by mulga. They've heard too (1950). M. DURACK Local gossip flourished through a word-of-mouth medium referred to as 'the bushman's mulga wire' (1983). [From Austral. *mulga* the outback, from earlier sense, type of acacia tree, from Aboriginal (Yuwaalaraay) *malga* + *wire* telegraph.]

muller verb trans. Brit To ruin, wreck, destroy; also, in sport, to defeat comprehensively. 1990–. SUNDAY MIRROR If we were getting mullered every week I would be worried, but we're not. We've lost five on the bounce but three of them have been one-nil (2001). [Origin unknown.]

mullered adjective Brit Extremely drunk. 1995–. MIRROR Stella got pregnant after we both got seriously mullered at some work do and slept together (2000). [Prob. from MULLER verb + -ed.]

mullet noun A man's hairstyle in which the hair is cut short at the front and sides and long at the back. 1994–. [Origin uncertain; perh. from MULLET-HEAD noun; popularized by the US hip-hop group the Beastie Boys.]

mullet-head noun US A stupid person. 1890–. Z. N. HURSTON Hey, you mullet heads! Get out de way (1935). [From earlier sense, type of freshwater fish; cf. Brit. dialect *mull-head* stupid person.]

Mulligan noun Golf An extra stroke awarded after a poor shot, not counted on the score card. 1938–. [Prob. from the surname *Mulligan*.]

multiculti often derog. adjective **1** A rhyming alteration of *multicultural*. 1989–. SIGHT & SOUND Those kids were either emblems of the multi-culti melting pot or racist creeps (1995). noun **2** Multiculturalism or a multiculturalist. 1989–. NATIONAL REVIEW [headline] Gore as multiculti (2000).

mum adjective **1** Saying nothing; silent. c.1530–. **2** **mum's the word** say nothing. 1663–. [Imitative of closed lips.]

mumper noun A beggar. a.1652–. COUNTRYMAN Beside the gypsies there are many other pickers—tramps, mumpers, all sorts (1972). [From obs. *mump* verb, to beg + -er.]

mumping noun Brit The acceptance by the police of small gifts or bribes from

mug mug book mug-faker muggins muggle mum

tradespeople. 1970–. [From obs. *mump* verb, to beg.]

munchie noun **1** Food. 1917–. **2** pl. US Hunger caused by taking marijuana; also, a snack eaten to satisfy this hunger. 1971–. [From *munch* verb + *-ie*.]

mung verb trans. orig US To spoil, ruin; esp. to damage or destroy (computer data). 1969–. UNIX REVIEW Mail messages can indeed be transferred readily between UUCP and SMTP MTAs without munging the message (1993). [Origin uncertain; often explained as an acronym from *mash until no good*.]

munga /ˈmʌŋgə/ noun Also **manga, munger, mungey, mungy.** Austral, NZ, and services' Food. 1907–. SYDNEY MORNING HERALD There were odd complaints about the food . . . from mouths that nonetheless wrapped themselves gleefully around the free munga and booze (1982). [Abbreviation of MUNGAREE noun.]

mungaree /mənˈdʒɑːrɪ/ noun Also **mungar(er), munjari.** dated Food. 1846–. C. BARRETT Chameleons are insectivorous and get their own mungaree (food) (1942). [From Italian *mangiare* to eat.]

munjon noun Austral An Australian Aborigine who has little experience of white society and its customs. 1945–. [From Yindjibarndi (Western Australia) *manjaŋ* stranger.]

munt noun S Afr, derog and offensive A Black African. 1948–. NEW STATESMAN The old 'munt', as the African is still widely and insultingly termed (1962). [Bantu *umuntu* person.]

murder noun **1** US dated An excellent or marvellous person or thing. 1927–. M. SHULMAN We got on the dance floor just as a Benny Goodman record started to play. 'Oh. B.G.!' cried Noblesse . . . . 'Man, he's murder, Jack' (1943). See also BLUE MURDER noun. verb **2 could murder** would desperately like to have (esp. an item of food or drink). 1935–. GUARDIAN Alec McCowen as the . . . Englishman who contains reserves of hidden passion behind statements like 'I could murder a cup of tea' (1992).

murder one noun US (A charge of) first-degree murder. 1966–.

Murphy Also **murphy.** noun **1** A potato. 1811–. **2** US A confidence trick in which the victim is duped by unfulfilled promises of money, sex, etc. Also **Murphy game.** 1957–. NEW YORK TIMES Everybody should have a car . . . . How are you going to get it? . . . You know, you can get it playing the Murphy (1966). verb trans. **3** US To deceive or swindle by means of the Murphy game. 1965–. J. MILLS I thought he was a complainant . . . some school kid who'd been Murpheyed (1972). [From the Irish surname *Murphy*; in sense 1, from the former prominence of the potato in the Irish diet.]

Murphy's law noun orig US = SOD'S LAW noun. 1955–. NEW YORK TIMES MAGAZINE 'If anything can go wrong, it will,' says Murphy's Law (1974). [App. developed from a remark of Captain E. *Murphy*, of the Wright Field-Aircraft Laboratory in 1949.]

muscle orig US, criminals'. verb **1** trans. To coerce by violence or by economic or political pressure. 1929–. TIME The old Union Pacific and Central Pacific railroads had once muscled each other (1958). **2** intr. To force oneself on others; to intrude by forceful means; usu. followed by *in* or *in on*. 1928–. J. WAINWRIGHT 'The Ponderosa' was his spread and no cheap, jumped-up, fiddle-foot was gonna muscle in (1973). noun **3** A person employed to use or threaten violence; often used as a collective pl. 1942–. H. NIELSEN The muscle on the trucks . . . were free-lancers (1973).

muscle boy noun US **1** = MUSCLE MAN noun 1. 1940–. **2** A fit athletic young man, esp. a young male homosexual; a bodybuilder. 1979–.

musclehead noun A brawny person, esp. a bodybuilder or muscular athlete. 1923–.

muscle man noun orig US **1** A muscular man employed to intimidate others with (threats of) violence. 1929–. P. OLIVER With the considerable returns accruing from operating policy wheels the racket came under the control of syndicates with muscle-men and hired gunmen ensuring that their 'rights' were protected (1968). **2** A paragon of powerful male physique. 1952–. TIMES Auditions for 'the muscle man with a voice like a bird' [i.e. Tarzan] will start soon (1975).

mush¹ /mʊʃ/; in sense 5 /mʌʃ/ noun **1** Also **moosh.** Brit The mouth or face. 1859–. T. BARLING A big grin all over his ugly mush (1974). **2** Also **moosh.** dated, military A guardroom or cell; a military prison. 1917–43. ATHENAEUM When a man was 'run in' the guardroom he was in 'clink' or in 'moosh' (1919). **3** Also **moosh.** Brit A man, chap; now used mainly as a form of address. 1936–. J. BROWN Look, moosh, you'll strip off or I'll take them off you (1972). **4** Also **moosh.** Austral Prison food, esp. porridge.

1945–. L. NEWCOMBE 'What's mush?'
I asked. . . . 'Breakfast, kid,' said George. 'A dixie
full of lumpy, gluey, wevilled wheat' (1979).
5 surfing The foam produced when a wave
breaks. 1969–. SURF '70 If there is any flat mush
the board tends to stop and lose its turning
ability (1970). verb intr. **6** To kiss; to cuddle or
'neck'. 1939–. S. BELLOW There's plenty of honest
kids to choose from, the kind who'd never let
you stick around till one a.m. mushing with
them on the steps (1953). [Perh. not all the
same word: in senses 1 and 5 from earlier
sense, soft matter, in sense 1 apparently
with reference to the soft flesh of the face; in
sense 2, perh. from obs. dialect *mush* verb, to
crush; in sense 3, perh. from Romany *moosh*
man; in sense 4, perh. from earlier US sense,
type of porridge; in sense 6, from sense 1 of
the noun.]

mush² /mʌʃ/ noun A moustache. 1967–.
K. GILES He read one of these Service ads. . . . You
know, a young bloke with a mush telling troops
to go plunging into the jungle (1969).
[Shortening and alteration of *moustache*,
mustache noun.]

mush-head /mʌʃ-/ noun US A weak or
indecisive person. 1890–. SCREENLAND She has
married the poor little mush-head that had been
wished upon her (1932). [From *mush* noun, soft
matter + *head* noun.]

muso /mjuːzəʊ/ noun orig Austral A musician,
esp. a professional one. 1967–. K. GILBERT I used
to be a muso and a hustler from the city but I'm
a tribal man too (1977). [From *mus(ician* + *-o*.]

mustang noun An officer in the US forces
who has been promoted from the ranks.
1847–. NEW YORK TIMES MAGAZINE The most
decorated enlisted man in the Korean War—the
mustang everybody thought was the perfect
combat commander (1971).

mutha /mʌðə/ noun orig US Abbreviation of
MUTHAFUCKA noun. 1974–. T. N. MURARI 'I'll jam
your head in the fan belt of this fancy car.' 'You
were always a mutha' (1984).

muthafucka, muthafukka variants
of MOTHERFUCKER noun. 1969–.

mutie noun, esp. science fiction A mutant.
1941–. G. BENFORD They got another flock in late
morning, surprising muties in a gully, but then
the mutants ran and got in among the regular
scooters (1983). [From *mut(ant* + *-ie*.]

mutt noun orig US **1** An ignorant, stupid, or
blundering person. 1900–. D. MAY The poor
mutt must have driven it along the bank (1973).
2 derog A dog, esp. a mongrel. 1900–. SATURDAY
EVENING POST That cat! That mutt! they fight it out
And back and forth they shuttle (1949).
[Abbreviation of MUTTON-HEAD noun.]

mutt adjective Brit Deaf. 1973–. J. MEADES You
gone mutt 'ave you Stobey? (1982) [From MUTT
AND JEFF adjective 3.]

Mutt and Jeff noun **1** A stupid pair of
men, esp. one tall and one short. 1917–.
D. SEAMAN He silently named them Mutt and Jeff.
One [man] stood well over six feet . . . while the
other barely reached to his mate's armpits
(1974). **2** dated, Brit, forces' A particular pair of
medals worn together, esp. the 1914–18
British War Medal and Victory Medal.
1937–. adjective **3** Rhyming slang for 'deaf'.
1960–. [From the names of two characters
called *Mutt* (see MUTT noun) and *Jeff*, one tall
and the other short, in a popular cartoon
series by H. C. Fisher (1884–1954), American
cartoonist.]

mutton adjective Brit Deaf. 1983–. GUARDIAN
You will have to speak up, I'm a bit mutton
(1991). [Shortening and alteration of MUTT
AND JEFF adjective 3, punning on *mutton*
sheep meat.]

mutton-head noun orig US A dull, stupid
person. 1803–. J. & E. BONETT Bone-heads, that's
what you are. Mutton-heads. Idiots (1972).
Also **mutton-headed,** adjective Dull, stupid.
1768–.

mystery noun A girl newly arrived in a
town or city; a girl with no fixed address;
a young or inexperienced prostitute. 1937–.
G. F. NEWMAN Instead of calling a couple of
mysteries, he called a cab (1974).

mush   mush-head   muso   mustang   mutha   mutie

'naff off' (1982). Hence **naffing** adjective Used as an intensive to express annoyance, etc. 1959–. CLEMENT & LA FRENAIS Stealing your tin of naffing pineapple chunks? Not even my favourite fruit (1976). [Origin uncertain; perh. from EFF verb, with the addition of the final -n of a preceding word (as in the noun phr. *an eff*); cf. also obs. backslang *naf = fan* female genitals (see FANNY¹ noun 1).]

naff adjective mainly Brit **1** Unfashionable; vulgar; socially awkward. 1966–. SUNDAY TELEGRAPH It is naff to call your house The Gables, Mon Repos, or Dunroamin' (1983). TIMES Gaultier had turned everything that fashion most despises, what English youth calls 'naff', into high style (1985). **2** Worthless, rubbishy, faulty. 1969–. RECORD MIRROR A really naff song that wouldn't get anywhere without Ringo's name on it (1977). [Origin unknown; cf. northern Eng. dialect *naffhead, naffin, naffy* idiot; *niffy-naffy* stupid; Scottish *nyaff* unpleasant person.]

Naffy noun The NAAFI. 1937–. M. AINSWORTH Best if I drop you at the Naffy (1959). [Phonetic spelling, the Navy, Army, and Air Force Institutes, an organization providing canteens, shops, etc. for British forces personnel.]

nag noun An old, slow, or broken-down horse; also, jocular, a racehorse. 1840–. T. WOLFE They . . . heard . . . the two back wheels . . . of an ancient buggy, the lifting hooves of an old boneyard nag, that slowly turned away from the road's centre (1935). [From earlier sense, small riding horse.]

nah¹ adverb Also **na**. Representing a colloquial or vulgar pronunciation of *now*. 1720–. B. KOPS Na Davey, what can I say to you? (1959).

nah² adverb Representing a colloquial or vulgar pronunciation of *no*. 1920–. NEW SOCIETY The waiter knows better. 'Nah, you don't want herrings, I'm gonna give you the soup' (1966).

nail verb trans. **1** To succeed in catching or getting hold of; spec. to arrest. 1760–. C. F. BURKE The cops . . . nail Ben for havin' the cup (1969). **2** mainly boxing To succeed in hitting with a punch or shot; to strike forcefully. 1785–. J. DEMPSEY He . . . is in a position to be nailed on the chin (1950). **3** US Usu. of a man: to have sex with (often with implication of aggression); = SCREW verb 1. 1960–. R. GROSSBACH Who would you rather marry, then—the publishing cupcake in the Florsheims

nab verb trans. **1** To arrest; to catch in wrongdoing. 1933–. BOSTON SUNDAY HERALD Town marshall is slain and a former lawman nabs the killer (1967). **2** To catch, seize, grab. a.1700–. noun **3** A policeman. 1813–. J. WAINWRIGHT All the nabs in the world were in the downstairs front (1971). [Origin uncertain; cf. obs. slang *nap* to seize, preserved in *kidnap*.]

nabe noun US A neighbourhood; spec. a local cinema. Often in pl. 1933–. NEW YORKER They picked an aging star, slapped together a moldy script, and sent the results out to the nabes (1970). [From the pronunciation of *neighb(ourhood* noun.]

nadgers noun pl. Brit jocular **1** A non-specific affliction or illness. 1956–. SCOTLAND ON SUNDAY But we know we get the screaming nadgers if deprived of tobacco for too long (1996). **2** Testicles. 1967–. N. GRIFFITHS Running through Prenton in the nuddy with hatpins through me nadgers (2000). [An invented word, apparently coined by Spike Milligan and Larry Stephens for the 1950s BBC radio comedy programme *The Goon Show*; in sense 2, introduced (with deliberately obscure meaning, but prob. exploiting a similarity to KNACKERS noun, NADS noun, and TODGER noun) as part of the vocabulary of 'Rambling Sid Rumpo' in the 1960s BBC radio comedy programme *Round the Horne*, written by Barry Took and Marty Feldman.]

nads noun pl. orig US **1** Testicles. 1964–. **2** Courage, nerve. 1976–. SPORTS WEEKLY [He] has all the 'nads of a jelly Danish (1998). [Shortening of *gonads* noun pl. testicles.]

naff verb intr. and trans. Brit Used as a euphemistic substitution for FUCK verb, esp. in phr. *to naff off*, to go away (usu. in imperative). 1959–. CUSTOM CAR Go and get yourself naffed, you chauvinistic, capitalistic leper (1977); SUNDAY TIMES Princess Anne . . . lost her temper with persistent photographers and told them to who nailed you on the couch and then fired you? (1979). [From earlier sense, to fix with a nail.]

nailer noun dated A policeman or detective. c.1863–1935. [From NAIL verb + -er.]

nails adjective Of a person: tough, strong. 1974–. VIZ My favourite film is that one with Clint Eastwood when he shoots people with a big gun. He's nails (1990). [From the phr. as hard as nails.]

Nam /næm, nɑːm/ noun Also 'Nam. US Abbreviation of 'Vietnam'; used esp. in the context of the Vietnam War. 1962–. J. DI MONA [We] were a unit in 'Nam (1973).

name noun one's name (and number) is on (something, esp. a bullet, shell, etc.): one is doomed to be killed by. 1917–. D. FRANCIS The bomb probably had my name on it in the first place (1973). Cf. one's number is on at NUMBER noun 4.

nana /nɑːnə/ noun orig Austral 1 A foolish person; a fool. 1941–. TIMES A frank admission that he had made a nana of himself (1974). 2 to do (or lose) one's nana to lose one's temper. 1966–. TELEGRAPH (Brisbane): The baby started crying again. I did my nana and hit him (1974). 3 off one's nana mentally deranged. 1975–. AUSTRALIAN 'We've all learned to laugh at ourselves and our predicament,' Trevor England said. 'If we hadn't we'd all be off our nanas' (1975). [Perh. from banana noun; cf. BANANAS adjective.]

nance noun derog = NANCY noun. 1910–. F. FORSYTH We're looking for a fellow who screwed the arse off a Baroness . . . not a couple of raving nances (1971).

nancy noun derog An effeminate man or boy; a male homosexual. Also **nancy-boy.** 1888–. L. DURRELL I can't stand that Toto fellow. He's an open nancy-boy (1958). Hence **nancified**, adjective. 1918–. K. GILES Beautiful smooth dark rum, not like that nancified white stuff you poms put in your coke (1967). [From obs. slang Miss Nancy noun, effeminate man, from pet-form of the female personal name Ann.]

nanny-goat noun 1 to get (a person's) **nanny-goat** to get a person's goat (see at GOAT noun). Also **to get** (a person's) **nanny.** 1914–. J. MINIFIE Take it easy, old boy . . . . Don't let them get your nanny (1972). 2 A totalisator. 1961–. DAILY MAIL The poor old

ailing Tote—the Nanny Goat, as they call it (1970). [In sense 2, rhyming slang for tote.]

nante adjective and adverb Also **nanti.** 1 No; not any. 1846–. B. RODGERS That chip-and-dale of his is nanti bonar, luv (1972). 2 **nante polari** be quiet; shut up. 1846–. noun 3 Nothing. 1938–. [From Polari, from Italian niente no, nothing.]

nap noun Austral Blankets or other covering used by a person sleeping in the open air; a bed-roll. 1892–. COAST TO COAST 1944 If you carry enough nap, you goes hungry; if you carry enough tucker you sleeps cold (1945). [Prob. from knapsack noun.]

napoo /nɑːˈpuː/ Also **na poo, napooh.** dated verb trans. 1 To finish, kill, or destroy. 1915–25. int 2 Finished; gone; done for. 1915–. adjective 3 Finished; good for nothing; dead. 1917–. W. DEEPING A man's phrase—a war-phrase—seemed to trickle into his head. Everything was na poo, a wash-out. His marriage—(1927). [Alteration of French (il n'y e)n a plus there is no more.]

> 'A frank admission that he had made a nana of himself.'

napper noun Brit The head. 1924–. G. M. WILSON If anyone ever asked for an orangeade bottle on his napper, Fruity did (1959). [Origin unknown.]

narc noun Also **nark.** US A member of a federal, state, or local drug squad. 1966–. NEW YORKER Bo, a rookie detective, . . . is so confused by the Department's manipulations that he doesn't guess that she is an undercover narc (1975). [Abbreviation of narcotics agent.]

narco adjective and noun US Abbreviation of 'narcotic' and 'narcotics'; also = NARC noun. 1954–. D. SHANNON The pedigrees varied from burglary to narco dealing to rape (1971).

nark noun 1 mainly Austral and NZ **a** An annoying, unpleasant, obstructive, or quarrelsome person. 1846–. V. PALMER 'Oh, don't be a nark, Miss Byrne,' he coaxes her (1928). **b** An annoying or unpleasant thing or situation; a source of astonishment or annoyance. 1918–. R. ALLEY Typhoid, malaria, and all the narks (1948). 2 Brit **a** A police informer or decoy. 1859–. TIMES If it was thought we were coppers' narks it could endanger the lives of our film crews (1975). **b** A policeman. 1891–. M. ALLINGHAM I've 'appened on a little something wot the official narks' 'aven't cottoned to yet (*a*.1966). verb **3** trans. To annoy, exasperate; often in passive. 1888–. DAILY TELEGRAPH If you feel especially narked about something, you can turn it into a theory of human development (1973). **4** trans. To stop; mainly in imperative in the phr. *nark it*. 1889–. N. GRAHAM 'Nark it,' I said. 'I want a little bit of information from you' (1973). **5** trans. Austral To thwart. 1891–. R. BEILBY Ya'd do anything to nark me, anything to put me down, wouldn't ya? (1975). **6** intr. To complain, grumble. 1916–. TIMES LITERARY SUPPLEMENT This naturally brings out the worst in their opponents and in the resultant narking and name-calling the 'legitimate contention' is lost sight of (1958). [From Romany *nāk* nose.]

narker noun An informer; a policeman; one who complains or disparages. 1932–. DAILY TELEGRAPH His motto will be to celebrate not denigrate, and I commend this to the legion of glib narkers who tend to monopolise the screen (1971). [From NARK verb + *-er*.]

narks noun Nitrogen narcosis, common amongst divers, and induced by breathing air under pressure; the bends. 1962–. J. PALMER It's lucky the ship lies in such shallow water. We shan't get the 'narks' (1967). [From *narc(osis* + *-s*.]

narky adjective Bad-tempered, irritable; sarcastic. 1895–. IRISH TIMES My husband is narky in the house. If I was to bring heaven down it would not satisfy him (1973). [From NARK noun + *-y*.]

Nar Nar Goon noun Austral Used as the name of any small, remote, and insignificant town. 1918–. AGE (Melbourne) Television football commentaries generally tend to be about as rewarding as a night game at Nar Nar Goon football ground in a power strike (1981). [From the name of a small town southeast of Melbourne.]

nash verb and noun = NOSH verb and noun.

nasho /ˈnæʃəʊ/ noun Austral Compulsory military training; also, one who undergoes this. 1962–. Q. WILD One of the worst things . . . was something that happened in nasho . . . before there was any fighting or anything (1981). [From *nat(ional* (as in 'national service') + *-o*.]

nasty adjective **something nasty in the woodshed** a traumatic experience or concealed unpleasantness in a person's background. 1959–. [From the passage 'When you were very small . . . you had seen something

nasty in the woodshed' in Stella Gibbons, *Cold Comfort* (*Farm* 1932).]

natch adverb orig US Abbreviation of 'naturally'. 1945–. A. DIMENT They blamed you, natch (1971).

natch noun **on the natch** US not on drugs, without taking narcotics; hence, more generally, without artificial help. 1969–. DRUG FORUM An almost invariable return to 'sex on the natch' (natural) is described (1973). [From *natural*.]

natty Rastafarian. adjective **1** Of the hair: knotty, matted, as in dreadlocks; of a person: wearing dreadlocks. Also, characteristic of Rastafarian culture. 1974–. noun **2** A person who wears dreadlocks, a Rastafarian. 1976–. [From the Jamaican pronunciation of *knotty*.]

natural noun One's life. 1891–. J. PORTER I couldn't stay like that for the rest of my natural (1967). [Short for *natural life*.]

naughty mainly Austral and NZ. noun **1** (An act of) sexual intercourse. 1959–. R. BEILBY It was also the opinion of the platoon, privately expressed, that Peppie had enjoyed more thoughties than naughties (1977). verb trans. **2** To have sex with. 1961–. C. KLEIN He didn't want to dob the hard word on her, last thing he had on his mind was to try and naughty her (1977).

nav noun Also **nav.** (with point). mainly RAF Abbreviation of 'navigator'. 1961–. AVIATION NEWS Before long, the student 'nav' could attempt to identify ground features using fine scale maps (1986).

N.B.G. adjective Also **n.b.g.** Euphemistic abbreviation of *no bloody good*. 1903–. G. MITCHELL Bang goes our reason for coming here . . . She said it was N.B.G. and that seems to be just about right (1973).

neat adjective mainly US Good, pleasing, satisfactory. 1806–. D. WESTHEIMER 'I could drive you on into Idyllwild if you want . . . ' 'That would be neat' (1972).

neatnik noun mainly US One who is neat in his or her personal habits (orig as contrasted with a beatnik). 1959–. SEARS CATALOG A new look in Rally-back Jeans that can be worn by Neatniks of any age (1969). [From *neat* adjective + *-nik* as in *beatnik* noun.]

neato adjective mainly US = NEAT adjective. 1951–. MORE (New Zealand): Those were the days when Beaver used to . . . have what she calls 'a neato free time' (1986). [From NEAT adjective + *-o*.]

narker narks narky Nar Nar Goon nash nasho

nebbich /ˈnebɪʃ/ Also **nebbish, nebbishe, nebbisher, nebish.** noun **1** A nobody, a nonentity. 1936–. adjective **2** Innocuous, ineffectual, luckless, hapless, etc. 1941–. ATLANTIC MONTHLY Paranoid psychopaths who, after nebbish lives, suddenly feel themselves invulnerable in the certain wooing of sweet death (1969). [Yiddish.]

neck verb **1** trans. orig Brit To drink, to swallow. 1515–. V. ROUTLEDGE She could easily save a hundred quid in a week just by not being at home necking endless vodka cranberries (2000). **2** intr. and trans. To kiss and caress amorously. 1825–. J. LE CARRÉ A loving couple necking in the back of a Rover (1974). noun **3** Impudence, cheek. 1894–. L. A. G. STRONG And then you have the sheer neck, the bloody effrontery to say you think there's more in life than I do (1942).

neck-oil noun Alcoholic drink, esp. beer. 1860–. PRIVATE EYE A chance encounter . . . leads Barry to consume a lot of nice neck-oil (1970).

necktie party noun orig and mainly US A lynching or hanging. 1882–. LISTENER A drunk or a loud-mouth could wind up like a rustler—the victim of a neck-tie party (1973).

ned noun Scottish A hooligan, thug, petty criminal; also used as a general term of disapproval. 1910–. P. MALLOCH He was a ned. You could always spot them. There was something about them that no trained policeman would ever miss (1973). [Perh. from *Ned*, a familiar abbreviation of the name *Edward*; cf. TED noun.]

neddy noun Austral A horse, esp. a racehorse. 1887–. BULLETIN (Sydney): Needing extra money for the neddies, he'd let it be known that guests were expected to cough up (1981). [From the earlier sense, donkey.]

Ned Kelly noun Austral Rhyming slang for 'belly'. 1945–. B. HUMPHRIES If I don't get a drop of hard stuff up me old Ned Kelly there's a good chance I may chunder in the channel (1970). [From the name of *Ned Kelly* (1857–80), Australian bushranger. Cf. KELLY¹ noun.]

needle noun **1 the needle** a fit of irritation. 1874–. G. F. NEWMAN He's got the needle with you. You've got to go very careful (1970). **2** orig US A hypodermic needle used for injecting drugs; the use of, or addiction to, injected drugs; esp. in phr. *on the needle*, (addicted to) injecting drugs. 1903–. LISTENER Middle Britain thinks . . . one puff on the joint leads to the needle (1973). verb trans. **3** dated US To inject

alcohol or ether into (a drink, esp. beer) to make it more powerful. 1929–31.

needle and pin noun Rhyming slang for 'gin'. 1937–.

needle and thread noun dated Rhyming slang for 'bread'. 1859–1935.

needle beer noun dated US Beer spiked with alcohol or ether. 1928–. [From the use of a needle to add the alcohol, etc.; cf. NEEDLE verb.]

needle man noun US A drug addict, esp. one who is addicted to injecting drugs. 1925–.

nelly noun Also **Nelly, Nellie, nellie.**
1 A silly or effeminate person; a homosexual. 1931–. T. WELLS You don't suppose it could have anything to do with that Strangler business, do you? Not that I'm a nervous Nelly type (1967) K. PLATT He . . . puffed daintily on a long cigarette as he watched the nellies cruising to the 'tearoom' (1970). See also *to sit next to Nelly* at SIT verb. **2** Austral Cheap wine. Also **Nelly's death.** 1935–. KINGS CROSS WHISPER (Sydney): You've got to get up very early in the morning to catch them sober and then you can't always be sure on account of their habit of keeping a flagon of nellie by the bed (1973). **3** not on your Nelly not on your life, not likely. 1941–. GLOBE & MAIL (Toronto): I appear to be giving away most of the plot? Not on your nelly. That's only the beginning (1974). [From the female personal name *Nelly*, familiar form of *Helen* or *Eleanor*; in sense 3, from rhyming slang *Nelly Duff* = *puff* = (breath of) life.]

nembie noun US A capsule of Nembutal. Also **nebbie, nemish, nemmie, nimby.** 1950–. W. BURROUGHS Next day I was worse and could not get out of bed. So I stayed in bed taking nembies at intervals (1953). [Contraction of *Nembutal* noun.]

nerd noun Also **nurd.** mainly US A foolish, feeble, or uninteresting person; also, a studious but socially inept person. 1951–. M. HOWARD He feels . . . like a total nerd in his gentleman's coat with the velvet collar (1986). Hence **nerdy** adjective Characteristic of a nerd. 1960–. Also **nerdish** adjective. 1980–. [Origin uncertain; sometimes taken as a euphemistic alteration of *turd*, though perh. simply derived from the name of a character in the children's book *If I Ran the Zoo* (1950) by 'Dr. Seuss'.]

nerk noun Brit Someone foolish, objectionable, or insignificant; a jerk. 1955–. A. PRIOR 'Slow it down, you nerk, the girl has to

nebbich   neck   neck-oil   necktie party   ned   neddy

get in,' he yelled (1966). [Origin uncertain; prob. a blend of NERD noun and JERK noun.]

nerts int US Representing a colloquial or euphemistic pronunciation of NUTS int. 1931–. E. HEMINGWAY Oh, nerts to you (1937).

never noun nautical **to do a never** to shirk; to loaf. 1946–61.

never-never noun Brit Hire purchase. 1926–. J. WILSON They've still not paid off their mortgage, you know, and I wouldn't mind betting that Rover of theirs is on the never-never (1973). [From the notion of the indefinite postponement of full payment; cf. earlier Austral *on the never* at no cost to oneself (1882–).]

neves /nevɪs/ noun Also **nevis**. Seven years' hard labour. 1901–. Cf. ROUF noun. F. NORMAN Your f-ing lucky, I'm doing a bleeding neves (1958). [Back-slang for *seven*.]

newbie noun orig US military A person new to some activity, a tyro; recently, esp. a new user of computer technology, esp. the Internet. 1970–. WIRED The first 30 pages of *Net Guide* contain how-to instructions, so even newbies can jump in (1993). [Origin uncertain; perh. an alteration of *newie* noun something or someone new.]

newsie noun Also **newsy**. mainly US and Austral A newspaper seller or a boy who delivers newspapers. 1875–. JOHN O' LONDON'S To be polite the newsie took a couple of swigs of it (1962). [From *news* noun + *-ie*, *-y*.]

newspaper noun dated, criminals' A thirty-day prison sentence. 1926–49. [From the time supposedly taken by a convict to read a newspaper.]

next adjective **to get** (or **be**) **next** (**to** or **on**) US To get acquainted with; to find out about, to understand. Also **to put next** (**to**) to acquaint (someone) (with). 1896–. BLACK WORLD If he can't get next to what we're about, we'll just have to school him (1973).

nibble noun Also **nybble**. computing Half a byte; four bits. 1967–. [Humorously, after *byte*.]

nibs noun **his** (or **her**) **nibs** a mock title used for an important or self-important person. 1821–. A. HUNTER Since when were you on first-name terms with His Nibs? (1973). [Origin unknown; cf. earlier *nabs* with same meaning.]

Nick noun Usu. **Old Nick**. A nickname for the Devil. Cf. SCRATCH noun. *a.*1643–. [Perh. a

shortening of *iniquity*, assimilated to the abbreviated form of the name *Nicholas*.]

nick verb **1** trans. **a** To arrest; to imprison. 1806–. J. WAINWRIGHT I am talking to you, copper . . . either nick me . . . or close that bloody door (1973). **b** To steal. 1869–. COURIER MAIL (Brisbane): Nicking toys from chain stores (1973). **2** intr. Austral **a** To go quickly or unobtrusively. 1896–. SYDNEY MORNING HERALD There is no lavatory so the Labor candidate . . . and his helpers nick across the road to use Ansett's (1981). **b: to nick off** to go away hurriedly; often used in imperative. 1901–. P. BARTON I was in this spot first . . . so nick off (1981). noun **3a** A prison. 1882–. IT At the moment, there are over a hundred of our kids in nick as a result of the busts at 144 Piccadilly & Endell Street (1969). **b** A police station. 1957–. J. LOCK Back at the nick the station officer was very cross (1968). **4** Condition of the stated sort. 1890–. F. CLIFFORD Reports are that he's in fair enough nick (1971). [From earlier senses, to catch, to take unawares; in sense 2, perh. a different word (cf. *nip* verb in same sense).]

nickel noun US Five dollars' worth of marijuana. 1963–. Cf. NICKEL BAG noun. [From NICKEL NOTE noun.]

nickel and dime noun Rhyming slang for 'time'. 1935–60.

nickel bag noun US A bag containing, or a measure of, five dollars' worth of a drug, esp. heroin or marijuana. 1963–. BLACK WORLD If . . . he gets high and blurts it out to a stranger in some bar that he got his nickel bag from Joe, the pusher, then Joe's livelihood is endangered (1973). Cf. NICKEL noun.

nickel note noun US A five-dollar bill. 1926–. [From US *nickel* five-cent coin.]

nickel nurser noun US A miser. 1926–. [From US, *nickel* five-cent coin.]

nicker noun Brit A pound sterling. 1871–. J. SYMONS Who said there'd be trouble? Anyway, it's a hundred nicker (1975). [Origin unknown.]

niff Brit verb intr. **1** To smell, stink. 1900–. P. G. WODEHOUSE 'Nasty slinking-looking bleeder.' . . . 'He don't half niff' (1974). noun **2** A smell, esp. an unpleasant one. 1903–. D. FEARON It wouldn't be nice for Rachel if some niff of ancient scandal caught up with her poor papa (1960). Hence **niffy** adjective Having a strong or unpleasant smell. 1903–. BARON CORVO The niffy silted-up little Rio della Croxe (1934). [Perh. from *sniff* verb.]

nerts   never   never-never   neves   newbie   newsie

nifty adjective orig US **1** Smart, stylish. 1868–. J. CANNAN I . . . got the niftiest white overalls (1958). **2** Clever, adroit. 1889–. OBSERVER Duncan was nifty on occasions, indeed scored an immaculate goal, but was at other times rather daintily ineffective (1975). [Origin uncertain; a connection with *magnificent* has been suggested.]

nig noun derog and offensive A black person. c.1832–. R. GADNEY Judd read National Front puts Britain First. Someone had scribbled Nigs Out (1974). [Abbreviation of NIGGER noun.]

nigger noun **1** now mainly derog and offensive when used by white people, but neutral or approving in Black English. A black person. 1574–. L. HUGHES A klansman said, 'Nigger, Look me in the face—And tell me you believe in The great white race' (1964). **2** cinema A screen used to mask studio lights or create special lighting effects. 1925–. [Alteration of obs. *neger* black person, from French *nègre*.]

niggergram noun Caribbean, esp. Trinidad, often jocular (but offensive outside its Afro-Caribbean context) A rumour, piece of gossip. 1957–. [Blend of NIGGER noun 1 and *telegram*.]

nigger heaven noun US, dated, now offensive The top gallery in a theatre. 1878–.

nigger shooter noun US, dated, now offensive A catapult. 1876–.

nigger-stick noun US, offensive A baton or club carried by policemen, prison warders, etc. 1971–. BLACK PANTHER They were attacked and brutally beaten by 50 to 60 guards armed with tear gas, plexiglass shields and four-foot long 'nigger sticks' (1973).

nig-nog[1] noun Brit A foolish person; hence, a raw and unskilled recruit. 1953–. A. WESKER A straight line, you heaving nig-nogs, a straight line (1962). [Cf. NING-NONG noun and obs. *nigmenog* noun, fool.]

nig-nog[2] noun derog and offensive A black person. 1959–. J. SYMONS He wanted to send the nig nogs and the Pakis back where they belong, in the jungle (1975). [Reduplicated shortened form of NIGGER noun.]

nigra /ˈnɪɡrə/ noun Also **nigrah** /ˈnɪɡrɑː/ mainly Southern US, now mainly derog and offensive A black person. 1944–. F. RICHARDS Pretty little thing, as nigras go, Mrs. Prender said (1969). [From a regional pronunciation of *Negro* noun.]

NIMBY Also **Nimby, nimby.** orig US. **1** An acronym formed from 'not in my backyard', used as a slogan objecting to the siting of something considered unpleasant, such as nuclear waste, in one's own locality. 1980–. noun **2** Someone who makes such objections; an adamant objector to local development, esp. building. 1980–. WEEKEND AUSTRALIAN A true Nimby—and consequently the most dedicated—is one whose property is directly threatened either financially or in terms of safety (1988).

nin noun Liverpool Grandmother. 1958–. P. MOLONEY Every true wacker has three relations, viz. 'Me Mar, Me Nin, an me Anti-Mury' (1966). [From Welsh *nain* grandmother.]

nincompoop noun A fool. 1678–. V. WOOLF Never could she understand how he cared. But those Indian women did presumably—silly, pretty, flimsy nincompoops (1925). [Origin uncertain; perh. from the male forename *Nicholas* or *Nicodemus* (cf. French *nicodème* simpleton) with -*n*- due to association with NINNY noun + obs. *poop* deceive, cheat, befool.]

nineteenth hole noun orig US The bar room in a golf club-house. 1901–. [From its use by golfers after playing the eighteen holes of the course.]

ninety-day wonder noun US, services' A graduate of a ninety-day officers' training course; an inexperienced, newly-commissioned officer. 1917–. W. C. WOODS A pale punk kid to run my company, another ninety day wonder (1970). [Humorously, after *nine-day wonder*.]

ning-nong noun Austral A fool, a stupid person. Cf. NONG noun. 1957–. E. MACKIE The trainee Aussie must not go to King's Cross—it's only for the tourists, ningnongs and geezers all the way from Woop Woop (1977). [From obs. Brit dialect *ning-nang* noun fool; cf. NIG-NOG[1] noun.]

ninny noun A fool. 1593–. COSMOPOLITAN If women are made to look like ninnies by agencies, why do magazines like Cosmo run the ads? (1992). [Origin uncertain; perh. from *innocent* with prefixed *n*- (as in *an innocent*).]

nip[1] verb trans. **1** now US To steal, snatch. 1567–. **2** US To defeat narrowly (in a sporting contest). 1893–. NEW YORK TIMES The Pirates nipped the Reds, 3–2 (1966). **3** mainly Austral To cadge (something) from (someone). 1919–. H. C. BAKER No chance of nippin' the bricky for a smoke—he don't smoke (1978). noun **4 to put the nips in** (or **into**) Austral and NZ To cadge (from). 1917–. R. BEILBY 'I'm putting the bite on you,' Gunner explained gently, 'Putting the nips in, touching you for a loan' (1977).

Nip² noun and adjective mainly derog and offensive (A) Japanese. 1942–. J. OSBORNE Few little Nips popping away with cameras (1971). [Abbreviation of *Nipponese* Japanese.]

nip³ noun orig US A nipple. 1970–. COURIER MAGAZINE (Aberystwyth University Students' Union) Fun as it is, Under that skirt, Convinced I am, Your nips are pert (2001). [Shortening.]

nipper noun **1** pl. Handcuffs. 1821–. FORTUNE One of the detectives put nippers on the prisoner's wrist (1939). **2** mainly Brit A young child. 1859–. TIMES When I was a nipper at school in Glasgow [etc.] (1972). [From *nip* verb + *-er*; in sense 2, cf. earlier obs. senses, a boy who assists a costermonger, carter, or workman, a thief or pickpocket.]

Nippy noun Brit dated A waitress in any of the restaurants of J. Lyons & Co. Ltd. in London; hence, any waitress. 1925–. C. V. GALWEY His hands stuck out in front of him like a Nippy carrying a tray (1948). [From *nippy* quick.]

nit¹ noun Brit A stupid person. 1598–. P. CLEIFE If you think . . . I would be willing to allow you . . . to board my aircraft . . . then you must be a nit (1972). [From earlier sense, egg of a body-louse, and latterly prob. influenced by NITWIT noun.]

nit² noun **to keep nit** Austral To keep watch; to act as guard. 1900–. B. SCOTT They'd pick a couple of the mob to keep nit then they'd hoe into the corn (1977). [From earlier obs. use as a warning that someone is coming; perh. a variant of *nix* noun, used to warn of someone's approach.]

nitchie noun Canadian usu. derog A Native American. 1850–. R. D. SYMONS 'Quick, you fellows,' he said, 'them Nitchies are crawling up all around' (1973). [From Ojibwa *ni:či:* friend.]

nitery noun Also **niterie**. US A night club. 1934–. BOSTON SUNDAY HERALD Our story begins in a narrow strip of niteries on 52nd Street (1967). [From *nite* noun, arbitrary respelling of *night* + *-ery*.]

nitro noun Abbreviation of 'nitroglycerine'. 1916–. J. GODEY They had an old-time safe. . . . I hit it with a fat charge of nitro (1972).

nitto verb intr. criminals' To keep quiet; to desist. 1959–. D. WARNER You guys better nitto. The Sparrow's got a line to your run-in (1962). [Cf. NIT² noun.]

nitty-gritty noun orig US The realities or practical details of a matter. 1952–. LISTENER

The Animals were already into the nitty-gritty of blues history (1969). [Origin unknown.]

nitwit noun A stupid person. 1914–. J. DRUMMOND For God's sake, Beryl, don't be such a nitwit (1975). [Perh. from *nit* noun, egg or young form of a body-louse (cf. NIT¹ noun) + *wit* noun.]

nix noun **1** Nothing; nobody. 1781–. A. CONAN DOYLE If I pull down fifty bucks a week it's not for nix (1929). **2 nix on** enough of, away with. 1902–. R. D. PAINE Camp Stuart at ten o'clock. Nix on that kid stuff (1923). adverb **3** No; not possibly. 1862–. D. L. SAYERS As for getting an experienced actor and giving him a show in the part—nix! (1937). verb trans. **4** To cancel, forbid, reject. 1903–. TUCSON (Arizona) DAILY CITIZEN Nude bathing nixed (1973). adjective **5** No; none, not any. 1906–. DAILY TELEGRAPH Oh, I just said battery kaput, nix lights, nix motor. . . . And we fix (1971). [From German and Dutch *nix*, colloquial variant of *nichts* nothing.]

Noah's Ark noun **1** orig Austral Rhyming slang for NARK noun 1. 1898–. J. ALARD Ya knows Bill, yer gettin' to be a real Noah's Ark (1968). **2** Austral Rhyming slang for 'shark'. Also **Noah.** 1945–. BULLETIN (Sydney): 'I'll tell you what's worse than the Noahs,' said Edgar. 'What about those bloody dragon-flies?' (1982).

nob¹ noun The head; latterly (now dated) esp. in phr. *bob a nob*, a shilling a head, a shilling each. 1699–. DAILY TELEGRAPH A shilling-a-head subscription, popularly known as the 'bob-a-nob', for some form of testimonial was launched to-day (1959). [Perh. a variant of *knob* noun.]

nob² noun Brit A person of wealth or high social position. 1809–. [Variant of earlier Scottish *knabb*, *nab*; ultimate origin unknown.]

nobbins noun Brit Money, esp. coins collected by a performer after an entertainment. 1846–. DAILY STAR It's rare to get a 'nobbins' fight these days where the crowd stand on their feet and toss coins into the ring (2001). [Alteration of the pl. of obs. *nobbing* collecting money, from *nob* to seek contributions of money, of uncertain origin.]

nobble verb trans. **1** To drug, lame, etc. (a racehorse) to prevent its winning. 1847–. NEWS CHRONICLE Lord Rosebery confirms today that his horse which was nobbled was Snap (1951). **2** To get (a person) over on to one's own side or to reduce (a person's) efficiency, esp. by underhand means; spec. to induce (a jury) to return a corrupt verdict. 1856–. M. UNDERWOOD

                          noodle

What about the rest of the delegation? . . . No chance of nobbling one of them? (1973). **3** To get for oneself, seize, grab. 1877–. **M. WOODHOUSE** We've got this Shackleton we've nobbled off Coastal Command (1968). [From earlier, obs. sense, to hit; prob. = Brit dialect *knobble, knubble* verb, to knock, hit, from *knob* noun.]

nobbler noun Austral A glass or drink of spirits. 1842–. **WALKABOUT** Whisky costs around 300 rupiahs, or some 75 cents, for a generous nobbler (1971). [From NOBBLE verb 1 or obs. *nobble* verb, to hit + *-er*.]

noble noun dated US A leader or protector of men hired to replace striking workers. 1930–60.

nod noun A state of drowsiness brought on by narcotic drugs; esp. in phr. *on the nod*. 1937–. **K. ORVIS** While I was on the nod (1962).

noddle noun **1** The head. 1507–. **2** The rational faculties. 1579–. [Origin unknown.]

noddy bike noun Also **noddy**. Brit A lightweight police motor-cycle. 1964–. **POLICE REVIEW** Making its debut appearance yesterday was the probable successor to the Noddy (1972). [Perh. an allusion to *Noddy*, a small elf-like boy in children's stories by Enid Blyton (1897–1968), from the toy-like characteristics of the motor-cycle (although said to be due to the rider's inability to salute safely, which necessitates nodding to acknowledge a superior officer).]

noddy suit noun Brit, orig army A protective suit for use in nuclear, chemical, or biological attacks. 1972–. [Perh. an allusion to Enid Blyton's *Noddy* (see NODDY BIKE noun).]

nog noun Austral derog A North Vietnamese or Vietcong soldier. 1969–. **W. NAGLE** 'We suspect that there are about twenty or thirty nogs dug in . . . ' 'VC or NVA?' asks Harry (1975). [Shortening of NIG-NOG² noun.]

noggin noun orig boxing and mainly US The head. 1769–. **P. G. WINSLOW** A rap on the back of the noggin that knocked her out (1975). [From earlier sense, small mug.]

noggy noun Austral derog or offensive An Asian immigrant to Australia; also, a NOG. 1954–. **CANBERRA TIMES** I guess you blokes know why I am around . . . looking for 'noggies'

and 'dapto dogs' (1982). [From NIG)NOG² noun + *-y*.]

no-goodnik noun US A worthless person. 1936–. **NEW YORK TIMES** Lew Archer's job is to find a 17-year-old girl who has run off with a 19-year-old no-goodnik (1968). [From *no-good* adjective, useless, valueless + *-nik*.]

no-hoper noun **1** Austral A racehorse with no chance of winning; a rank outsider. 1943–. **2** orig Austral A useless or incompetent person. 1944–. **R. HALL** That no-hoper! . . . If you turn out like him I shan't go on lettin you buy me a beer (1982).

nonce noun Brit, prisoners' A sexual deviant; one convicted of a sexual offence, esp. child-molesting. 1971–. **SUNDAY TELEGRAPH** As what prisoners call a 'nonce', he now faces years of solitary confinement and regular assaults from fellow inmates (1986). [Origin uncertain; perh. from NANCY noun, but cf. Brit dialect *nonce* noun, good-for-nothing fellow.]

noncy adjective Brit Pretentious, affected. 1989–. **SUNDAY MIRROR** Now, as a native of Newcastle I will not have noncy London magazines casting aspersions on our menfolk (2001). [Perh. a blend of NONCE noun and PONCEY adjective.]

nong noun Austral A fool; a stupid person. Also **nong-nong**. 1944–. **BULLETIN** (Sydney): Rod Cavalier has . . . turned himself into a ridiculous nong (1986). [Cf. NING-NONG noun.]

no-no noun orig US Something that must not be done, used, etc.; something forbidden, impossible, or not acceptable; a failure. 1942–. **SUNDAY ADVOCATE-NEWS** (Barbados): Plants that require a great deal of moisture are no-noes unless you have your own well (1975). [Reduplication of *no* noun.]

noodge mainly US. verb trans. **1** To pester, nag *at*; also, intr., to complain persistently. 1960–. **S. TERKEL** I'll always noodge him for some currency or another (1967). noun **2** A person who complains or nags; pest. 1967–. Hence **noodgy** adjective Fussy, nagging, fretful. 1964–. **ENTERTAINMENT WEEKLY** Stephanie Plum is a big-haired Trenton chick who's juggling two men, a pet hamster, noodgy parents, [etc.] (2001). [From Yiddish *nudyen* to bore, pester.]

noodle noun **1** A simpleton, a foolish person. 1720–. **2** The head. 1762–. **M. TRIST** Take

noddy suit
protective suit for use in nuclear, chemical or biological attacks

nobbler noble nod noddle noddy bike noddy suit

no notice. . . . She's off her noodle (1945). [Origin unknown.]

noogie noun **to give** (someone) **noogies** (or **a noogie**) mainly US schools' and colleges' to give someone a hard poke or grind with the knuckles, esp. on the head. 1978–. [Origin unknown.]

nookie-bookie noun A pimp or madam. 1943–.

nooky /ˈnʊkɪ/ noun Also **nookie**. Sexual intercourse. 1928–. A. WEST Still nooky was nooky he told himself, and who cares what the woman was like if the lay was good (1960). [Perh. from *nook* noun, secluded corner + *-y*.]

nooner noun orig and mainly US **1** An alcoholic drink taken in the middle of the day. 1936–. **2** Sexual intercourse in the daytime, esp. at lunchtime. 1973–. B. RASKIN He looks like the kind of man who prefers nooners to nocturnal sex (1990). **3** An event or activity in the middle of the day. 1980–. [From *noon* noun + *-er*.]

noov /nuːv/ noun Also **noove**. Brit A member of the *nouveaux riches*. 1983–. TIMES The pupils: 45 per cent sons of Old Etonians. . . . Also largish element of noovs to keep up academic standards and/or provide useful business contacts (1986). [Shortened from *nouveau riche*.]

nope adverb orig US Extended form of 'no'. 1888–. H. C. RAE 'Anybody asking for me?' 'Nope' (1971).

nork noun Austral A woman's breast; usu. in pl. 1962–. AUSTRALIAN (Sydney): The minimum requirement is an 'Aw, whacko, cop the norks!' followed by at least a six decibel wolf whistle (1984). [Origin uncertain; perh. from the name of the *Norco* Co-operative Ltd., a butter manufacturer in New South Wales.]

Norm noun Austral A person who spends leisure time passively or idly, esp. watching sport on television. 1980–. AUSTRALIAN For most 'Norms' it [i.e. daylight-saving time] means an extra hour in the pub (1981). [From the name of a cartoon character created in 1975 by Alex Stitt (b. 1937).]

Norski noun Also **Norskie**. US jocular or mildly derog A Scandinavian person, esp. a Norwegian. 1929–. [Prob. alteration of earlier *Norsk* Norwegian, from Norwegian *Norsk* Norwegian, as if from *Nor(wegian* + *-ski*.]

north and south noun Rhyming slang for 'mouth'. 1858–. F. NORMAN Dust floating about in the air, which gets in your north and south (1958).

nose noun **1** A spy or informer; one who gives information to the police. 1789–. R. EDWARDS He knew that CID men are allowed to drink on duty because much of their time is spent with 'noses' or informants (1974). **2 on the nose: a** US Precise(ly). 1883–. N. MAILER Malcolm Cowley was right on the nose when he wrote that *The Deer Park* was a far more difficult book to write than *The Naked and the Dead* (1959). **b** Austral Offensive, annoying; smelly. 1941–. B. HUMPHRIES Excuse I not shakin' hands sport but me *mits* are pretty much on the nose (1971). **3 to keep one's nose clean** to stay out of trouble, behave properly. 1887–. A. ROSS Denis Fitzgerald . . . a known associate of villains, but managed to keep his own nose clean (1974). **4 to get up someone's nose** to annoy someone. 1951–. DAILY MAIL The implication that granny was a little winning knockout with a system that couldn't be bettered . . . does, I'm afraid, get rather up my nose (1975). verb intr. **5** criminals' To inform. 1811–. E. WALLACE You come down 'ere an' expect us to 'nose' for you, and everybody in the court knows we're 'nosing' (1930).

nose-bag noun **1 to put on the nose-bag** to eat; hence *nose-bag* = food, provisions. 1874–. P. G. WODEHOUSE I must rush. I'm putting on the nosebag with a popsy (1973). **2** dated A gas-mask. 1915–40.

nose candy noun US A drug that is inhaled (illegally); spec. cocaine. 1925–. GLOBE & MAIL (Toronto): The movie omitted the morphine and left the cocaine because nose candy is the trendy drug (1974).

nose paint noun jocular Intoxicating drink; also, a reddening of the nose ascribed to habitual drinking. 1880–. AMERICAN SPEECH He drinks . . . *nose paint* instead of 'whiskey' (1968).

Nosey Parker noun Also **nosey parker, nosy parker**. mainly Brit An inquisitive person. 1907–. D. CRAIG All nosey parkers in this street (1974). [Said to have been applied originally as a nickname to a man who spied on courting couples in Hyde Park, London.]

nosh noun Also **nash 1** Food, a meal. 1873–. C. DRUMMOND Burglars go for plain, healthy English nosh (1972). **2** A restaurant; a snack-bar. Also **nosh bar, nosh-house.** 1917–. C. MACINNES After a quick bite at a Nosh, and two strong black coffees, I felt up to the ordeal (1959). **3** mainly US A snack. *a.*1941–. verb trans. and intr. **4** US To eat between meals; to snack. 1957–. TIME The politician, equipped with a trowel and the Fixed Smile, gobs mortar on a cornerstone, or

number

noshes his way along the campaign trail (1970). **5** To practise fellatio (on). 1961–. **6** To eat. 1962–. c. DRUMMOND The Sergeant . . . morosely noshed the veal-and-ham pie (1972). Hence **nosher** noun An eater. 1917–. SUNDAY TIMES Gourmet foods to salivate the palates of jaded British noshers (1974). [From Yiddish; cf. German *naschen* to nibble, eat on the sly.]

noshery noun A restaurant; a snack-bar. 1952–. K. O'HARA The place I'm thinking of for lunch . . . has the reputation of a very superior noshery (1972). [From NOSH verb + -*ery*.]

nosh-up noun Brit A large meal. 1963–. A. DRAPER Like most birds she didn't want to lose out on a nosh-up (1970).

no siree /-sɔˈriː/ adverb Also **no sirree.** mainly US No indeed; certainly not. Cf. YES SIREE adverb. 1845–. J. DI MONA The senator wouldn't protect him. No siree (1973). [*Siree* prob. from obs. dialect *sirry*, from *sir* noun.]

notch-house noun A brothel. 1926–. H. GOLD Nancy ran a notch-house for travelers who loved to see things (1956). [*Notch* perh. an alteration of *nautch* noun, dancing (girl), from Urdu *nāch*.]

no-tell motel noun US A motel used for illicit sexual assignations; also, more generally, a cheap, disreputable, or run-down motel. 1976–.

nothing orig US. int **1** Not at all; in no respect. 1883–. T. BARLING 'It just slipped out.' 'Slipped nothing. You couldn't resist' (1974). noun **2 nothing doing** an announcement of refusal of a request or offer, failure in an attempt, etc. 1910–. PEOPLE It was suggested that she should come incognito. Nothing doing (1947).

no way int orig US **1** It is impossible; it can't be done. 1968–. NEW YORKER He said he wouldn't start up a gang today—no way (1975). **2 no way, José** definitely not. 1979–. NEW YORKER Stand up and trade punches with Tyson? No way, José (1988).

nowhere adjective Insignificant, dreary. 1940–. MELODY MAKER We all thought it was the most nowhere record we'd made (1966).

nozzer noun Brit, nautical A new recruit; a novice sailor. 1912–. [Perh. an alteration of *No, sir.*]

nuddy noun Also **nuddie.** jocular, orig Austral **in the nuddy:** in the nude, naked. 1953–. S. WELLER Quick—ring her back—she's in the

nuddy—give her a scare (1976). [From *nudd*-, jocular alteration of *nude* + -*y*.]

nudnik noun Also **noodnik, noodnick.** US In Jewish usage, a pestering, nagging, or irritating person, a bore. 1925–. [From Yiddish, from *nudyen* to bore, pester.]

nuffin noun Representing a colloquial or dialectal pronunciation of 'nothing'. Also **nuffink.** 1837–. A. GILBERT We don't know nuffin about the dear departed (1974).

nuff said int orig US An indication that nothing more need be said on a particular topic. Also **nuf(f) ced, nuf(f) sed,** abbreviations **N.C., N.S.** 1840–. J. AITKEN 'He and Steinherz knew one another at university before they were here.' 'Nuff said, I suppose' (1971). [*Nuff*, abbreviation and alteration of *enough* noun; cf. SURE 'NUFF int.]

nuke Also (US) **nook.** orig US. noun **1** A nuclear weapon, submarine, installation, etc. 1958–. PUBLISHERS WEEKLY They hijack a liner at sea and sink it with a baby nuke (1973). **2** A nuclear power station. 1969–. FORTUNE Finished nukes . . . can be a boon to investors (1983). verb trans. **3** To bomb or destroy with nuclear weapons. 1962–. JAPAN TIMES WEEKLY I asked how he could be sure that the Soviet Union would nuke us if we nuked China (1972). **4** mainly US To cook or heat (food) in a microwave oven. 1984–. M. MULLER After microwaving a couple of burritos (or 'nuking' them, as my nephew calls it), I left the house (1989). [Abbreviation of *nuclear*.]

nully noun A fool. 1973–. R. PARKES He's a sick, junked-up, pathetic old nully (1973). [Perh. from *null* adjective, of no value; cf. Scottish *nullion* noun, stupid fellow.]

number noun **1 to get (take, have) someone's number** to understand a person's real motives, character, etc. 1853–. TIMES LITERARY SUPPLEMENT Field-Marshal Lord Montgomery . . . had [Augustus] John's number right away. 'Who is this chap?' he demanded to know. 'He drinks, he's dirty, and I know there are women in the background!' (1975). **2** A person or thing, esp. **a** A garment. 1894–. M. STEEN Petula Wimbleby's solution turned out to be an exquisite but throat-high 'little number' redeemed by lumps of jade (1953). **b** A person, esp. a woman, usu. of the stated type. 1919–. W. GADDIS Have you seen a little blond number named Adeline? (1955). **c** An occupation, job assignment. 1928–. LISTENER Transferred to what was described as a 'cushy number' with the Commandos (1968). **3 one's number is up** one is finished or doomed to die. 1899–. J. AIKEN

noshery   nosh-up   no siree   notch-house   nowhere

He'd got leukaemia. He knew his number was up (1975). **4 one's number is on** (something) = one's name (and number) is on (something) (see NAME noun). 1917–. C. FREMLIN I'm as safe here as . . . any where . . . if it's got your number on it, you'll get it, no matter *where* you are (1974). **5 to make one's number** to report one's arrival; to make oneself known. 1942–. D. SEAMAN 'Will you go to the conference site today?' 'Might as well make my number with the R. U. C.' (1974). **6 to do a number on** US To speak or write of with contempt, disparage; to deceive. 1967–. S. BELLOW They did a number on Ridpath. They printed damaging statements (1982).

number one noun **1** Oneself. 1705–. **2** A children's word or euphemism for 'urine' and 'urination'. 1902–. A. WILSON This little ginger [kitten] is going to do a number one if we're not careful (1967).

number two noun A children's word or euphemism for 'faeces' and 'defecation'. 1902–. M. MCCARTHY When I had done Number Two, you always washed them out yourself before sending them to the diaper service (1971).

nummy adjective US Delicious, scrumptious. 1989–. [Prob. imitative of the sound of contented eating, after YUMMY adjective.]

nump noun A fool. 1955–. CALGARY SUN So it stands to reason: if those numps on The Lofters can have a TV station all their own, so can you (2001). [Prob. back-formation from earlier *numps* fool, perh. from a pet-form of the male personal name *Humphrey*.]

numpty Brit, orig Scottish English. noun **1** A fool. 1988–. GUARDIAN No, the problem were the vets. What a bunch of numpties (2001). adjective **2** Foolish, idiotic. 1992–. [Origin uncertain; perh. an alteration of NUMP noun or of NUMSKULL noun, with the ending remodelled after *Humpty-Dumpty*.]

numskull noun Also **numbskull**. A fool. 1724–. [From *numb* adjective + *skull* noun.]

nuppence noun dated No money. 1886–. OBSERVER Living on nuppence. (1964). [Blend of *no* adjective and *tuppence* noun.]

nurd variant of NERD noun.

nut noun **1a** The head. 1841–. **b off one's nut** out of one's mind, insane. 1858–. **c to do one's nut** to be extremely angry or agitated. 1919–. J. BROWN I thought what Grace would say, that she'd do her nut maybe. But she didn't

blink an eyelid (1972). **2** pl. **a** The testicles. 1863–. R. BUSBY Russell got a boot in the nuts (1973). **b to get one's nuts off** to obtain sexual release by copulation and ejaculation. c.1932–. Cf. ROCK. noun **3** orig US **a** A madman; a crank. 1903–. NATION REVIEW (Melbourne): The Worker Student Alliance, a bunch of nuts in Melbourne (1973). **b** An enthusiast or aficionado, a 'buff'; often with qualifying noun. 1915–. L. GOULD If you're such a health nut, how come you take all those pills (1974). **4** dated A fashionable or showy young man of affected elegance. 1904–23. R. MACAULAY He always looked the same, calm, unruffled, tidy, the exquisite nut (1920). **5** US The amount of money needed for a venture; overhead costs; hence, any sum of money. 1909–. PUBLISHERS WEEKLY He submitted a strong script that led Fox to substitute color film and wide screen for black-and-white and the conventional small-screen ratio, and to raise the nut to $400,000 (1972). **6 the nuts** US An excellent person or thing. 1917–. W. GADDIS Get a little cross with mirrors in it, that would be the nuts if you want to suffer your way (1955). verb trans. **7** To consider, think, work out; often followed by *out* or *up*. 1919–. R. DENTRY I've been nutting the whole thing out. . . . There's no future in it for you (1971). **8** To butt with the head; to hit on the head. 1937–. J. MANDELKAU He took it off and as I was getting out of mine he nutted me in the head (1971). **9** To kill; usu. in passive. Also followed by *off*. 1974–. E. FAIRWEATHER He's hated so much he knows he'd be nutted straight away (1984).

nut-case noun A crazy or foolish person. 1959–. LISTENER You nut-case, you ought to be locked up (1969). [Cf. NUT noun 1a, b, 2, NUTS adjective 2.]

nut college noun US = NUT-HOUSE noun. c.1906–.

nut factory noun US = NUT-HOUSE noun. 1900–. J. H. CHASE Johnnie was a rummy. . . . Drink had rotted him, and he was only two jumps ahead of the nut-factory (1939).

nut-house noun A mental hospital. 1906–. RADIO TIMES Clothing for the Government, prisons and nut-'ouses—what is it they call 'em now? (1974).

nut job noun orig US A mad or crazy person. 1975–. MUZIK 'Electric Chicken' . . . is a vinyl-only bucket of weird beat Hot Wings, featuring international nut jobs like Japan's Himuro . . . and Solar X from Russia (2001).

nutmeg Brit association football. noun **1** The act of kicking the ball between the legs of an

number one number two nummy nump numpty

nutty

opposing player (and retaining possession of it afterwards); a ball played in this way. 1968–. TIMES Woodcock . . . could include successive 'nutmegs' on Donachie and Booth among his contributions (1977). verb trans. **2** To confound or outsmart (an opponent) by playing a 'nutmeg'. 1975–. [Perh. from earlier slang *nutmegs* testicles.]

nuts adjective **1** Very enthusiastic; very fond; followed by *about* or *on*. 1785–. NEW YORKER You're nuts about me, right? (1975). **2** Crazy, mad, eccentric. 1908–. N. SHUTE 'Gee,' said Wing Commander Dewar, 'this thing'll drive me nuts' (1953). int **3** An expression of contempt or derision. 1910–. D. FRANCIS 'I'll give you a hundred.' 'Nuts.' 'A hundred and fifty' (1974). [In sense 2, cf. NUT noun 1a, b, 2; in sense 3, from NUT noun 5.]

nutso mainly US. noun **1** A crazy person; a madman, 'nut'. Often as a (usu. insulting or provocative) form of address. 1975–. NEW YORK TIMES Hey, nutso, you're not gonna do that, are you? Bug off! (1986). adjective **2** Crazy, mad. Also as quasi-adverb, esp. in phr. *to go nutso*.

1975–. TIME He swore off meat about this time and took up vegetarianism 'in my typically nutso way' (1983). [From NUTS adjective + -*o*; cf. NUTSY adjective.]

nutsy adjective Also **nutsey**. Crazy, insane. 1923–. GUARDIAN Gee, it was nutsy (1962). [From NUTS adjective 2 + -*y*.]

nutter noun Brit A crazy person; a violent and deranged person. 1958–. A. GARVE I reckon Chris was right, Rosie—King's a nutter. I reckon he'll go on killin' till there ain't no one left (1963). [From NUT noun 2 + -*er*.]

nuttery noun US A mental hospital. 1915–. [From NUT noun 2 + -*ery*.]

nutty adjective **1** Crazy, mad, eccentric; often in phr. *nutty as a fruit-cake*. 1892–. P. G. WODEHOUSE 'He doesn't strike me as unbalanced.' 'On his special subject he's as nutty as a fruit cake' (1967). noun **2** naval Chocolate, sweets. 1947–. J. HALE Their Christmas presents and their nutty and cigarette rations (1964). [From NUT noun 2 + -*y*.]

nutmeg nuts nutso nutsy nutter nuttery nutty

oaf noun A large, clumsy fellow; a stupid or boorish fellow. 1781–. W. GOLDING Running in panic lest I should be grabbed by some enormous oaf from the scrum (1984). [From earlier senses, child stolen by the fairies, idiot child; variant of obs. *auf*, from Old Norse *álfr* elf.]

oafo noun = OAF noun; a lout or hooligan. 1959–. R. COOK The middle classes . . . the working classes . . . not to mention the oafos (1962). [From OAF noun + -o.]

OAO noun services', orig US Abbreviation of 'one and only'; one's sweetheart; anything unique of its kind. 1928–. EVERYBODY'S MAGAZINE (Australia): All would refer to a special girlfriend as their OAO—one and only. Probably, the OAO was met on skirt patrol (1967).

oater noun mainly US = HORSE OPERA noun. 1946–. [From the earlier OATS OPERA noun.]

oath noun **my (colonial, etc.) oath** Austral and NZ A mild expletive or exclamation: 'upon my word', 'of course', etc. 1859–. N. MARSH 'And that's when your headache really sets in, is it, Fred?' 'My oath! Well, take a look at it.' (1974).

oats noun pl. **(to have, get,** etc.**) one's oats** (to obtain) sexual gratification. Rather coarse, and usu. with the woman as obj. 1923–. J. WAINWRIGHT This wife he was lumbered with. Okay—he loved her . . . . But, even *he* wanted his oats, occasionally. He was human (1978).

oats opera noun US, dated Also **oat opera**. = HORSE OPERA noun. 1942–7. [See OATER noun .]

obbo noun Also **obo**. **1** military Abbreviation of 'observation balloon'. 1925–40.
2 Abbreviation of 'observation', esp. (*Police*), keeping a person, building, etc., under surveillance. 1933–. BUSBY & HOLTHAM Now I got a fix on the place I got to do some obo first (1968).

obit /ˈɒbɪt, ˈəʊbɪt/ noun mainly journalists' Abbreviation of 'obituary (notice)'. 1874–. [Earlier non-slang use in the 15th–17th cent. derived directly from Old French *obit* death.]

obs noun Abbreviation of 'observation'. 1943–. See OBBO noun.

ocean wave noun Rhyming slang for 'shave'. 1928–34. JOHN O' LONDON'S I 'as my ocean wave an' when I've got my mince pies open I goes down the apples and pears (1934).

ocker Also **Ocker**. Austral **1** A nickname for an Australian man. 1916–. **2** A typically rough or aggressively boorish Australian; also as adjective 1968–. TELEGRAPH (Brisbane): It is no use telling Australians to wake up; it is not in the ocker character (1976). Hence **ockerish** adjective. 1978–. Also **ockerdom, ockerism,** noun. 1974–. [In sense 2, the name of a character devised and played by Ron Frazer (1924–83) in the Australian television series *The Mavis Bramston Show* (1965–8).]

ocky noun Austral An octopus. 1968–. CANBERRA CHRONICLE Watch out for the ockies that roam all over the sand flats (1984). [From *oc(topus* + -*y*.]

O.D. orig US. noun **1** Abbreviation of 'overdose'; a (fatal) overdose of drugs. 1959–. BLACK WORLD An O.D. takes him, he loses a battle of several years—the 'stuff' wins (1971). verb intr. **2** To take an overdose; **O.D.'d,** adjective overdosed (on drugs). 1965–. **3** To indulge in something to an excessive degree; usu. followed by *on*. 1974–. A. CALCUTT Britain's middle-class late-twentysomethings OD'ed on Habitat furnishing (2000).

oddball noun and adjective orig US An eccentric or unconventional person. Also as adjective. Cf. SCREWBALL noun. 1948–. M. TRUMAN Earlier in 1946 an oddball broke into the National Gallery and cut a hole in Dad's portrait (1973).

odd bod noun An eccentric person. 1955–. J. ROFFMAN Anyone would, except you who have an inborn bias toward the odd bods in society (1976). [*bod* short for *body*.]

odds verb trans. To evade or escape (a situation). 1958–. G. F. NEWMAN I can't odds being mixed up in crime (1970).

odds and sods noun pl. orig services' Forces' personnel (or others) assigned to miscellaneous tasks or not regularly classified; now a general substitute for *odds and ends*. 1930–. E. WAUGH They left me behind with the other odds and sods (1955).

oaf oafo OAO oater oath oats oats opera obbo

O.D.V. noun Joking alteration of 'eau-de-vie', esp. = brandy. 1839–.

ofay /ˈəʊfeɪ/ noun US derog, mainly African-American A white person. Also as adjective. 1899–. **B. HOLIDAY** Most of the ofays, the white people, who came to Harlem those nights were looking for atmosphere (1956). [Of unknown origin, but probably African.]

off verb **1 to off it** to die. 1899–. **2** trans. mainly US African-American To kill (a person). 1967–. **R. B. PARKER** There were various recommendations about pigs [= policemen] being offed scrawled on the sidewalk (1974).

office noun **1** dated A signal or hint, esp. in phr. *to give* (or *take*) *the office*. 1803–. **2** flying An aeroplane's cockpit. 1917–. **V. M. YEATES** He put his head in the office and flew by the instruments (1934).

office copy noun naval, jocular A second or return drink. 1946–.

office hours noun US, forces' A disciplinary session. 1922–. **A. DUBUS** He committed the offense, he was brought in to office hours (1967).

og(g) noun Austral and NZ dated A shilling. 1908–78. [From the older slang *hog* a shilling, (US) a dime.]

oggin noun naval The sea. 1944–. **D. LEES** No one told the two gunners that the sub was about to crash-dive and they had to run like hell to avoid being left in the oggin (1973).[Origin uncertain; perh. from *noggin* a drink (cf. DRINK noun).]

oggy noun West Country and naval A Cornish pasty, esp. one containing half meat and vegetables and half fruit. 1948–. [Prob. alteration of Cornish *hoggan* pasty, pie, perh. related to Welsh *chwiogen* muffin, simnel cake.]

oick noun Also **oik**. A contemptuous term for an unpleasant, uncultured, or obnoxious person; a fool or 'clot'. Orig among schoolboys, a member of another school; an unpopular fellow-pupil. 1925–. **N. BLAKE** Smithers is such an oick (1935). [Of uncertain origin, though possibly from (h)oick verb, to spit. Apparently used derisorily in similar senses in the late nineteenth cent.]

oil verb **1 to oil the knocker** dated Brit To bribe or tip a doorman. 1870–. noun **2** US Money, esp. for bribery and corruption. 1885–. **3** Austral and NZ Information, news. Cf. DINKUM OIL noun, GOOD OIL noun. 1915–.

4 Nonsense; lies, glib falsehood. 1917–. **P. G. WODEHOUSE** Coo to him, and give him the old oil (1940). **5 no oil painting** euphemistic An ugly person. 1930–. **LISTENER** Mr Tillett was no oil painting, but he was a gentlemanly sort of man (1973). [In sense 1, perh. from a translation of French 'on n'entre point chez lui sans graisser le marteau,' (Racine, *Les plaideurs*); in sense 4, from earlier sense, smooth talk.]

oil-burner noun Any run-down vehicle which uses too much engine oil. 1938–.

oil can noun A British Army term for a German trench-mortar in World War I. 1917. **E. A. MACKINTOSH** Look out, sirr, . . . oil can coming over (1917).

oiled adjective (Mildly) intoxicated; drunk. Usu. **well oiled**. 1701–. **E. WALLACE** He'll come out in a minute, oiled to the world (1926).

oily wad noun naval **1** A torpedo boat which burned fuel-oil. 1925. **2** Any seaman with no special skill. 1929–63. [In sense 2, 'from the amount of time they have to spend cleaning brass-work with oily wads' (Frank Bowen, *Sea Slang* 1929).]

oink a couple with no children, living on a single income

oink noun Also **OINK**. jocular A couple with no children, living on a single (esp. large) salary. 1987–. **NEWSWEEK** In the 1980s cable has penetrated urban areas with more upscale viewers like dinks . . . , oinks . . . and the standard-issue Yuppie (1987). [Acronym from *one income, no kids*, after DINK noun.]

O.K. Also **OK**, **ok.** orig US. adjective **1** All right, satisfactory, good. Also as adverb See also — *rule(s) O.K.* at RULE verb. 1839–. **D. H. LAWRENCE** At first Joe thought the job O.K. (1922). **2** Fashionable; socially (or culturally) acceptable; stylish. 1869–. **S. POTTER** The word 'diathesis' . . . is now on the O.K. list for conversation men (1950). noun **3** An endorsement or approval. Also as int, giving assent, agreement, etc. 1829–. verb trans. **4** To endorse or sanction, as by marking with the letters O.K. 1888–. **R. S. WORDSWORTH** Not that Freud would OK our account of dreams up to this point (1921). [Abbreviation of 'orl korrect', used in 1839 by the Boston smart set (see A. W. Read in *American Speech* (1963) and subsequent discussions). The term was picked up or developed independently as a political slogan (1840) by the supporters of

okay

'Old Kinderhook', Martin van Buren, born at Kinderhook, NY.]

okay Also **okey.** orig US. adjective **1** = O.K. adjective 1. Also as adverb. 1919–. E. WAUGH 'Don't let on to anyone that we've made a nonsense of the morning.' 'Okey, Ryder.' (1945). **2** = O.K. adjective 2. 1958–. G. GREER The secretary had . . . moved out of Haight Ashbury when it ceased to be okay to live there (1970). noun **3** = O.K. noun 3. 1925–. verb trans. **4** = O.K. verb 4. 1930–.

oke /əʊk/ adjective orig US = O.K. adjective 1. 1928–. L. HART I like the free, fresh wind in my hair, Life without care. I'm broke—it's oke (1937).

okey-doke /ˌəʊkɪˈdəʊk/ adjective orig US Also **okey-dokey,** etc. = O.K. adjective. 1932–. D. POWELL He saw that tiresome red-faced fellow . . . , the man who knew everybody and said 'okie-dokie' to everything (1936).

O.K. yah Also **okay yah.** Brit. int **1** (In representations or imitations of upper- or upper-middle-class speech, orig. esp. of Sloane Rangers) yes. 1985–. adjective **2** Upper-class, posh, Sloanie. 1985–. SCOTSMAN Come on, then, you OK-yah, sherry-swilling members of the hunting community. Have a go at a bonxie [i.e. a skua]—if you think you're hard enough (2000).

old bean noun dated, Brit A familiar form of address, esp. to a man. 1917–. J. THOMAS I say, old bean, let's stick together (1955).

Old Bill noun Brit (A member of) the police force. 1958–. GUARDIAN He observed a couple of men supping nearby who looked suspiciously like plainclothes men. Coulson asked the landlord. 'Oh no,' he said, 'they're drinking pints. Old Bills only drink halves.' (1967). [Origin uncertain: perh. from the cartoon character Old Bill, created by Bruce Bairnsfather (1888–1959), and portrayed as a grumbling old soldier with a large moustache.]

old boot noun derog A woman or wife. 1958–. F. NORMAN What about the ironing said Soapey? Well what about it said the old boot (1958).

Old Dart noun Austral and NZ The mother country, Great Britain; England. 1889–. [Dart is apparently an alteration of dirt.]

old fruit noun dated, Brit = OLD BEAN noun. 1928–. T. RATTIGAN You don't mind me asking, did you, old fruit? (1951).

oldie noun Also **oldy. 1** An old person. 1874–. J. BROWN We've got our rights, haven't we, same as the oldies (1972). **2** orig US An old (but

familiar) song, tune, film, etc.; esp. in phr. *golden oldie.* 1940–. LISTENER Dragging up old revue skits . . . patter songs . . . golden oldies ('These Foolish Things'), one-liners and sketches (1975). [From *old* + -*ie*.]

old lady noun A girl or woman; a familiar term for one's wife or mother. 1599–.

old man noun **1** One's employer or boss. 1668–. CASTLE & HAILEY Is that you, Dave? Harry. Surprise for you—the Old Man is on the line (1958). **2** A familiar term for one's husband or father. 1673–. **3a** naval A ship's captain. 1821–. TAFFRAIL Having a sherry-and-bitters with the 'old man' (1916). **b** services' A commanding officer. 1830–. **4** The penis. 1902–.

old pot noun mainly Austral One's father. 1916–. [Short for 'old pot and pan': see POT AND PAN noun (rhyming slang for 'old man').]

old ral noun US dated Syphilis. 1878–. [Punning alteration of *neuralgia* noun.]

old rope noun dated, services' Strong, evil-smelling tobacco. 1943–6.

old ship noun dated, naval An old shipmate. 1849–1989.

old soldier noun dated, US **1** The discarded butt of a cigar; a quid of chewed tobacco. 1834–1936. **2** An empty bottle of liquor. Cf. DEAD SOLDIER noun. 1877–1936.

Old Sparky noun US jocular, euphemistic The electric chair. 1923–. NEW YORK TIMES Speed Graphic portrayals of an uncontrollable crime wave of mad-dog felons fairly begged Old Sparky denouements, if only in the interests of popular entertainment (1994).

old sweat noun An old soldier. 1919–.

old thing noun Brit dated A familiar form of address. 1864–. J. DRUMMOND Don't worry, old thing. It may not be as bad as it sounds (1975).

old woman noun **1** derog A timid or fussy man. 1722–. B. WOOD He didn't want Marvin on guard against him . . . 'Give it some time, Marvin . . . Maybe I'm being a bit of an old woman' (1975). **2** A familiar term for one's wife or mother. 1775–. J. O'CONNOR If you went home and found someone indoors with your old woman, what would you do? (1976).

olive oil int A joking substitution for 'au revoir'. Cf. AU RESERVOIR int. 1906–. E. PARTRIDGE For 'good-bye', the boys at Dulwich already in 1906 used . . . *olive oil* (au revoir) (1933).

okay oke okey-doke O.K. yah old bean Old Bill

Oliver noun dated The moon. ?1747–1935. [Despite references to Oliver Cromwell (the last refuge of a lexicographer), no definite origin can be given.]

omee /ˈəʊmɪ/ noun Also **omie**. A man; a landlord or itinerant actor. 1859–. N. MARSH 'A lot of omies the others were then. . . . 'Ted means they were bad actors doing worse shows in one-eyed towns up and down the provinces' (1937). [Showman's corruption of Italian *uomo* man.]

on adverb **1** US Aware of (the situation); alert to or knowledgeable about (something). 1885–. G. ADE The Preacher didn't know what all this meant, . . . but you can rest easy that the Pew-Holders were On in a minute (1900). **2** US On drugs; addicted to or taking drugs. 1938–. W. GADDIS She's high right now, can't you see it? She's been on for three days (1955).

oncer /ˈwʌnsə(r)/ noun A one-pound note. 1931–. M. KENYON They gave you an 'undred quid in oncers to see things their way (1978). [From earlier senses, something that happens only once, a person who only achieves something once (1892).]

one-arm joint noun US A cheap restaurant in which customers support their plates on a widened chair-arm. 1915–. [Earlier, *one-arm lunch room* (1912).]

one-arm(ed) bandit noun orig US A fruit-machine (worked by pulling a single lever at the side). 1936–. D. FRANCIS There's more cars parked along the streets down there than one-armed bandits in Nevada (1972).

one-lunger noun A single-cylinder engine; a vehicle driven by this. 1908–. [Equivalent to 'something with (only) one lung'.]

one-night stand noun A brief sexual liaison or 'affair'. 1956–. [From earlier sense, a single theatrical performance (1880).]

one-pipper noun services' A second lieutenant. 1919–. [From the single star on a second lieutenant's uniform.]

oner /ˈwʌnə(r)/ noun One pound sterling; also, one hundred pounds. Cf. ONCER noun. 1889–.

one-way pockets noun pl. Jokingly, the kinds of pockets maintained by a miserly or tight-fisted person. 1926–. P. G. WODEHOUSE His one-way pockets are a by-word all over England (1961).

onion¹ noun The head, esp. in phr. *off one's onion*, 'off one's head'; mad, crazy. 1881–. H. G. WELLS He came home one day saying Tono-Bungay till I thought he was clean off his onion (1909). See also *to know one's onions* at KNOW verb.

onion² noun Austral, mainly motorcycle gangs' An occasion when several men have sexual intercourse one after another with the same woman; also, the woman involved. 1969–. WEEKEND AUSTRALIAN Woodhouse told the man the girl was to be the 'onion' for the night (1978). [Origin uncertain; perh. from *onion* the vegetable.]

onkus adjective dated **1** NZ Good, pleasant. 1910–44. **2** Austral Unpleasant. 1918–. D. MCLEAN All this yabber about Danny is onkus (1962). [Origin unknown.]

oo-er int Also **ooo-er**. An exclamation of alarm. 1912–. C. MACKENZIE 'Oo-er!' cried Jenny. 'We aren't going to sleep in the dark?' (1912).

oof /uːf/ noun Also **ooftish**. dated Money, cash. 1885–. RIDER HAGGARD Living like a fighting-cock and rolling in 'oof' (1888). Hence **oofy**, adjective Rich, wealthy. 1896–. [From Yiddish *ooftisch*, from German *auf dem Tische* on the table (of gambling stakes).]

oojah /ˈuːdʒɑː/ noun Also **oojar**, etc. dated **1** A what's-it or thingummy. 1917–. B. W. ALDISS I've seen blokes in hot countries go clean round the oojar because of the perverted practices of native women (1971). **2** Also in various comical extensions: **oojah-capivvy, oojah-ka-piv, oojah-ma-flip,** etc. 1925–. [Origin uncertain.]

oojah-cum-spiff adjective Brit Fine, all right. 1930–. OBSERVER For the first couple of centuries all was oojah-cum-spiff (1993). [Origin uncertain; perh. an alteration of *OOJAH-CAPIVVY* (see OOJAH noun) influenced by *cum* with and *spiff* smart (cf. SPIFFY adjective).]

oojiboo /ˈuːdʒɪbuː/ noun dated, services' = OOJAH noun. 1918–.

ook /ʊk/ noun Something shiny or sticky; an unpleasant substance, 'muck'. Also **ooky**, adjective. 1964–. [Origin uncertain.]

oomph /uːmf, ʊmf/ noun Sex appeal, attractiveness; energy, 'go', enthusiasm. 1937–. SAN FRANCISCO EXAMINER All old World War II types will remember when Annie S. was the 'The oomph girl' (1974). Hence **oomphy**, adjective orig US Strong, powerful; (esp. of a woman) sexy, glamorous. 1955–. NEW YORK POST

Oliver omee on oncer one-arm joint oojiboo

Past . . . spots had her looking oomphy in skimpy garb (1980).[Imitative.]

oonchook /uːnʃuːk, ˈʊn-/ noun Irish and Newfoundland Also **oonshick,** etc. A fool or simpleton, a 'clot'. 1825–. F. O'BRIEN The divil himself is in the hearts of that Corporation ownshucks (1961). [From Irish *áinseach* foolish woman, clown.]

oont noun Also **unt.** Indian English and Austral A camel. 1862–. BULLETIN (Sydney) Hell! what a lot of calculation had to go into piloting a couple of smelly oonts! (1933). [From Hindi and Urdu *ūnṭ* camel.]

op noun **1** Abbreviation of 'operation'. **a** A military operation. Often. in pl. 1916–. **b** A surgical operation. 1925–. **2** Abbreviation of 'operative', 'operator'. **a** A radio or telegraph operator. 1921–. **b** A (private) detective. 1924–.

open slather noun Austral and NZ Freedom to operate without impediment, a free rein; a free-for-all. 1919–. B. SCOTT The bloke who finished first was to have open slather with Maria (1977). [*Slather* from Brit dialect and US *slather* verb, to use in large quantities, to squander.]

O.P.M. noun US Abbreviation of 'other people's money'. 1901–. J. FLYNT It cost me nothing to play the game, because I was playing with O.P.M. (1901).

oppo noun orig, services' Abbreviation of 'opposite number'. 1932–. D. REEMAN Me an' the kid is oppos, see? (1967).

orderly noun services' **1 orderly buff** an orderly sergeant, the sergeant acting as officer of the day. 1925–48. **2 orderly dog** an orderly corporal, a corporal attending an officer to carry orders or messages. 1925–48. V. M. YEATES Grey . . . was censoring the men's letters, being orderly dog for the day (1934). **3 orderly pig** an orderly officer, the officer of the day. 1943–48. [According to Partridge, 'the non-regular Army . . . used all three phrases indiscriminately' (*A Dictionary of Forces' Slang* 1948).]

ordie noun US naval An ordnance handler on a ship. 1988–. [From *ord*(*nance* + *-ie*.]

Oreo /ɔːrɪəʊ/ noun Also **oreo.** US A black despised (esp. by other blacks) for appearing or seeking to integrate with the white establishment; an 'Uncle Tom'. 1969–. ['The term comes from a standard commercially prepared cookie which has two disc-shaped chocolate wafers separated by sugar cream

filling. An 'oreo' is thus brown outside but white inside' (Alan Dundes, *Mother Wit from the Laughing Barrel* 1973).]

organ noun euphemistic The penis; often in phr. *male organ.* 1833–. M. CAMPBELL He had the largest organ that anyone had ever seen. It was a truncheon (1967).

ork noun mainly US Abbreviation of 'orchestra', esp. a jazz or dance band. 1936–. C. MACINNES The Dickie Hodfodder ork, led by Richard H. in person, playing away merrily (1959).

orphan noun A discontinued model of motor vehicle. 1942–. Also **orphaned,** adjective. 1920.

ort noun Austral The anus; also, the buttocks. 1952–. J. WYNNUM Take it from me, there's more ways of killin' a cat than fillin' its ort with sand (1962). [Origin unknown.]

orthopod noun An orthopaedic surgeon. 1960–. D. FRANCIS I telephoned to the orthopod who regularly patched me up after falls (1969). [Alteration of *orthopaedic*.]

oscar¹ noun Austral and NZ Also **Oscar,** and in full **Oscar Asche.** Money, cash. 1905– (1917– in shortened form). D. NILAND If you'd been fighting all those blokes in the ring you'd have more oscar in your kick now than the Prime Minister himself (1959). [Rhyming slang from the name of the Australian actor, Oscar Asche (1871–1936).]

Oscar² noun US dated A fellow, guy; a foolish or ignorant man. 1918–. T. GORDON I could have killed that dumb Oscar (1929). [Prob. from the male personal name *Oscar*.]

otaku noun, pl. **otaku** or **otakus.** Orig in Japan, someone extraordinarily knowledgeable about the minute details of a hobby, esp. a solitary or minority one; a nerd. 1992–. [From Japanese, literally 'your house, your home' (orig used by manga and anime fans in the early 1980s as an affectedly formal way of addressing fellow insiders).]

other adjective **1 the other thing** sexual activity. 1846–. J. JOYCE Besides there was absolution so long as you didn't do the other thing before being married (1922). **2 the other side** Austral and NZ The other side of Australia. 1827–. **3 the other half** orig naval A second or return drink. 1922–. noun **4** Sexual activity or intercourse. 1922–. Z. SMITH The men . . . don't like to think they're wanting a bit of the other when they're sitting down to a company dinner with their lady wives (2000).

OTT adjective Brit Abbreviation of 'over the top'; (esp. of behaviour or appearance) outrageous, over-exaggerated, extreme; mad, crazy. Also as adverb phr. 1982–. SUN The Bill continues to go from strength to strength because all the bobbies are completely O.T.T. (1988).

ou /əʊ/ noun S Afr, pl. **ouens, ous.** A fellow or chap; a bloke. 1949–. J. MCCLURE You better not tell Willie that! He wants to murder the *ou!* (1976). [From Afrikaans.]

out verb trans. **1** boxing To knock (one's opponent) unconscious; more generally, to knock out or kill by a blow; to murder. 1898–. **2** orig US To reveal publicly or expose the homosexuality of (someone, esp. a well-known figure), usu. as a political move by gay rights activists; cf. *to come out of the closet* at CLOSET noun. Also **outing,** noun The act or result of doing this. 1990–. LOS ANGELES TIMES Instead of . . . outing this congressman, I . . . called to his attention the hypocrisy that he had been legislating against gays (1990). noun **3** orig US A way out; an excuse or alibi. 1919–. G. F. NEWMAN He wanted an out, a plausible story that would extricate his head from the chopping block (1970). adverb **4 out of it** US Drunk; under the influence of drugs. 1963–.

outasight adjective Modification of OUT-OF-SIGHT adjective. 1893–.

outer noun Austral The part of a racecourse outside the enclosure; similarly, the uncovered area for non-members at a sports ground. Also fig. and **on the outer,** destitute, out of favour. 1915–.

outfit noun **1** mainly US, usu derog A person, a 'chap'. 1867–. **2** The apparatus with which a drug addict takes drugs. 1881–. W. BURROUGHS She keeps outfits in glasses of alcohol so the junkie can fix in the joint and walk out clean (1953). **3** services' A regiment or other group of servicemen. 1909–.

out-of-sight adjective Marvellous, excellent, 'terrific', 'fantastic'; exciting. 1891–. J. D. CORROTHERS 'Out o' sight!' yelled a dozen voices as the poem was concluded (1902).

outside prep **1 to get outside** to eat or drink; to consume fully. 1886–. D. CAMPBELL It takes me half an hour to get outside the mixed grill and the ice-cream and coffee (1967). noun **2** The world outside prison, or out of Army life. 1903–. adverb **3** Out of prison; in civilian

life. 1919–. W. LANG You got to 'ave some bloody religion in the Navy. Now, wot Church did you go to outside? (1919). **4** surfing Out at sea beyond the breaking waves. 1962–.

outside job noun A crime committed by someone not otherwise associated with the household, building, etc., concerned. 1925–. A. CHRISTIE The police are quite certain that this is not what they call an 'outside job'—I mean, it wasn't a burglary. The broken open window was faked (1931).

outside man noun US One who assists in staging a confidence trick or robbery. 1917–.

out the monk adjective NZ **1** Done for, finished. 1939–. **2** Unconscious, esp. as a result of drinking alcohol; asleep. 1945–. R. H. MORRIESON It's Jack Voot, real shickered. Looks like he's out the monk (1976). **3** Disabled by illness; not in working order. 1946–. [Origin uncertain; *monk* perh. from unrecorded rhyming slang for *drunk*.]

oven noun A woman's womb. ?1510–. Mainly in phr. *to have a bun (pudding, something) in the oven,* to be pregnant: see BUN noun 1, PUDDING noun.

over prep **all over** displaying great or excessive admiration or affection for. 1912–. A. CHRISTIE 'Were they friendly?' 'The lady was . . . All over him, as you might say' (1931).

overamp verb US intr. To overdose, esp. on amphetamines; also, trans., to administer an overdose to. 1968–. J. WAMBAUGH Look, he was a doper! He woulda over-amped anyways. Overdosed, I mean (1990). [From *over-* + AMP verb, on the model of *overdose* verb.]

overhung adjective Suffering from a hang-over; 'hung-over'. 1964–. I. FLEMING He was considerably overhung. The hard blue eyes were veined with blood (1964).

overjolt noun US A drug overdose. 1959–. J. ELLROY Terry Lux told him Loftis used to cop H for Claire; Marty Goines was snuffed by a heroin overjolt (1988). [From *over-* + JOLT noun, on the model of *overdose* noun.]

owner noun The captain of a ship, boat, or other vessel (also, of an aircraft). 1903–.

Owsley acid noun High-quality LSD. 1968–. [From the name of Augustus *Owsley* Stanley III (b. 1935), an illegal manufacturer of such drugs.]

OTT ou out outasight outer outfit out-of-sight

Oxford scholar

208

Oxford scholar noun Rhyming slang for 'dollar' (Austral and NZ); also, a crown, five shillings. 1937–.

oyster adjective Austral Saying nothing; silent. 1910–. H. ANDERSON The boy was dragged off to the police station where he remained 'oyster' (1971). [From the proverbial uncommunicativeness of the oyster.]

Oz orig Austral noun **1** Australia. 1908–. PRIVATE EYE If they guess I'm from Oz the shit will really hit the fan (1970). **2** An Australian. 1974–. adjective **3** Australian. 1971–. SUNDAY TELEGRAPH These Oz intellectuals fell over themselves in a desperate parade of learning heavily-worn (1989). [Alteration of initial element of *Australia(n)*; cf. *Aussie.*]

ozoner noun US A drive-in cinema. 1948–.

Ozzie noun and adjective orig Austral (An) Australian. 1918–. NATION REVIEW (Melbourne): Femme, 27, bored by ozzie ockers and oedipal neurotics (1973). [From oz noun and adjective + -*ie.*]

overhung Oxford scholar oyster Oz ozoner Ozzie

pace noun **off the pace** orig US In horse-racing, slower than the leading horses, esp. in the early part of a race; hence, behind the leader or 'below par' in any race or contest. 1911–. RALLY SPORT The best two-wheel drive car was in 20th place, seven seconds per mile off the pace (1987).

pack verb **1** trans. To be armed with. 1902–. R. CHANDLER Don't you pack no rod? (1940). **2** intr. To be armed with a gun. 1953–. PREMIER I worked with rappers who pack guns . . . As long as he ain't packin', I'm straight (2001). [From earlier sense, to carry with one.]

package noun mainly US **1** criminals' A kidnap victim; a dead body. 1933–. **2** A pretty girl or young woman. 1934–.

packet noun **1** mainly military A bullet or other projectile; trouble or misfortune. Esp. in phrs. *to cop* (*stop*, etc.) *a packet*, to be killed or wounded; to get into trouble. 1917–. H. CARMICHAEL Frank Mitchell copped a packet on the river bank (1960). **2** A large amount of money. 1922–. P. G. WODEHOUSE 'Get in on the short end,' said Aurelia earnestly, 'and you'll make a packet' (1928).

pad noun **1** A bed; lodging, somewhere to sleep; one's residence or house. Also, a room used by drug-takers. 1703–. E. MCBAIN 'If Ordiz is a junkie, what's he doing on Whore Street?' 'He's blind in some broad's pad' (1956). **2** US A gambling saloon, etc., which provides police with regular pay-offs. Also, of a policeman: **on the pad.** 1970–. [In sense 1, from earlier sense, straw to lie on.]

paddlefoot noun US **1** An infantryman. 1946–. **2** An airforce ground-crew member. 1948–.

paddy noun **1** often derog A nickname for an Irishman. 1714–. How dar you call me Paddy? (1907). **2** A fit of bad temper; = PADDYWHACK noun 2. 1894–. O. MILLS I used to get into the biggest paddies when I was a kiddie (1959). **3** Black English A White person. 1945–. [From the common Irish name *Padraig*, Patrick.]

Paddy Doyle noun dated, services' Confinement in a cell; detention. Usu. in phr. *to do a Paddy Doyle.* 1919–48.

paddy wagon noun orig US A police van; a police car. 1909–. CHICAGO TRIBUNE He was informed by the pink faced lockup keeper that all Chicago's 'paddy wagons' are motor driven (1932).

Paddy Wester noun dated An inefficient or novice seaman. 1892–1938. W. E. DEXTER They had a pack of fake seamen sailing on dead men's discharges—a crew of 'Paddy Westers' (1938).

paddywhack noun **1** A beating, a blow. 1898–. **2** A rage or fit of temper; = PADDY noun 2. 1899–. [In 19th cent. = an Irishman: see PADDY noun.]

padre /pɑːdreɪ/ noun orig services' A chaplain; a minister of the church. 1836–. DAILY NEWS The 'fighting padre' is by no means an unknown figure in British wars (1898). [Italian, Spanish, Portuguese, = 'father'.]

paedo noun A paedophile. 1993–. OBSERVER Chips, late in life, is supplied with a young wife, so that he doesn't appear a closet paedo (1997). [Shortening.]

pain noun **pain in the arse** (etc.): a person or thing particularly annoying or tiresome. Also, **to give** (someone) **a pain in the arse.** 1972–. E. MCBAIN Homicide cops . . . were pains in the ass to detectives actually . . . trying to solve cases (1973). [Developed from the informal *pain in the neck*.]

Paki /pækɪ/ noun Also **Pak.** derog or offensive A Pakistani, esp. an immigrant from Pakistan. Also, more broadly, a person of South Asian birth or descent. 1964–. Hence, **Paki-bashing,** noun (**-basher,** noun, etc.) Racist assault of Pakistani immigrants. 1970–.

Paki shop noun Brit A corner shop owned or staffed by people of Pakistani or South Asian birth or descent. 1985–.

pal noun Used as a term of address to a man (early vocative uses are difficult to distinguish from the primary sense 'friend'; neutral and hostile uses are a recent development). 1681–. NEW YORK TIMES Kramden's mantra, uttered whenever he was frightened or embarrassed or ashamed, is 'humenahumenahumena'. Gleason, no longer capable of being any of these things, simply said, 'Just wing it, pal' (1992).

palarey, palare, palari variants of POLARI noun.

pale-face noun US, African-American, derog A white person. 1945–.

palone /pəˈləʊn/ noun Also **polone, polony, -i.** A young woman (dismissive); also, an effeminate man. 1934–. P. ALLINGHAM Charlie was not a lady's man, and by 'palones' he meant girls (1934). [Origin unknown.]

palooka /pəˈluːkə/ noun mainly US An unexceptional prizefighter; a foolish or mediocre person. 1920–. A. LOMAX You won't kick me in the ass, because I can beat this palooka (1950). [Origin unknown.]

pan verb trans. **1** To criticize (esp. a play or film) severely. 1908–. N. BLAKE The lurid headline, 'Famous Woman Explorer Pans Domesticity' (1939). **2** To hit or strike (a person); to punch; to knock (some sense) into. 1942–.

pan noun **1 on the pan** US Being reprimanded or criticized. 1899–. **2** The face. 1920–. E. LINKLATER I never want to see that pan of yours again (1931). **3 down the pan** thrown to waste, tossed carelessly away, lost. 1961–. [In sense 1, cf. *dead-pan*; in sense 3, from *pan* = lavatory bowl.]

panhandle verb trans. and intr. mainly US To beg (from) in the street; to steal. Often as **panhandling,** noun and adjective. 1890–. [See next.]

panhandler noun orig US A street beggar. 1893–. E. MCBAIN Don't . . . start screaming if a panhandler taps you on the shoulder. He may only want a quarter for a drink (1973). [Humorously alluding to the beggar's bowl.]

panic verb trans. US To thrill or amuse (an audience, etc.); to make enthusiastic. 1920–. F. ASTAIRE After a while they were saying 'Oompah-Oompah-Oompah' with the music. . . . Adele absolutely panicked 'em (1960).

pannikin noun mainly Austral The head; in phr. *off one's pannikin,* 'off one's head'. 1894–. C. J. DENNIS Per'aps I'm orf me pannikin wiv' sittin' in the sun (1916). [From earlier sense, metal drinking-vessel.]

pansy mainly derog. noun **1** An effeminate man; a male homosexual. Also **pansy-boy.**

1926–. J. BETJEMAN There Bignose plays the organ And the pansies all sing flat (1960). adjective **2** Of a man: effeminate, homosexual. 1929–. E. CRISPIN I'd want her to be walking out with a decent lad, not a pansy little foreign gramophone-record (1951).

pansy verb trans. derog To dress or adorn affectedly or effeminately; often with *up.* 1946–.

panther juice noun mainly US Strong drink, usu. spirits distilled illicitly or locally. Also **panther('s) piss, sweat.** 1929–. W. GADDIS Yeah? Well did you ever drink panther piss? the liquid fuel out of torpedoes? (1955).

pants noun **1 with one's pants down** orig US In an embarrassing situation, unprepared; esp. in *to be caught with one's pants down.* 1922–. **2 to bore (talk,** etc.) **the pants off** (someone), i.e. to a state of terminal rigidity. 1925–. **3** Brit Nonsense, rubbish; esp. in phr. *a pile* (or load) *of pants.* 1994–. TOTAL FILM Then again, Mike says he's pleasantly surprised by our acting. I think he thought we were going to be absolute pants (1997).

'I think he thought we were going to be absolute pants.'

pantsing noun US The action of pulling down or removing someone's trousers (and sometimes underpants), esp. as a practical joke. 1943–.

pants rabbit noun US, mainly military A body louse. 1918–37. J. STEINBECK What the hell kind of bed you giving us, anyways? We don't want no pants rabbits (1937).

papa noun US A woman's husband or lover. 1896–.

Pape noun Scottish/Ulster, derog A Roman Catholic. 1927–. J. BRAINE Adam's a good Catholic. . . . It's smart to be a Pape now (1968). [From *Pope,* or shortening of *papist.*]

paper noun **1** Free admission tickets to the theatre or other entertainment; a free entry pass. 1859–. J. TEY Johnny Garson can tell you how much paper there is in the house (1951). **2a** US A playing-card. 1842–. **b** Card-sharpers' marked cards. 1894–.

paper verb **1** trans. To fill (a theatre, etc.) by means of free passes. Hence **papered,** adjective, etc. 1879–. **2** intr. and trans. To pass forged cheques; to defraud by doing so. 1925–.

paper-hanger noun orig US One who passes forged or fraudulent cheques. Also **paper-hanging**, noun. 1914–. J. G. BRANDON 'Paper-hanger,' McCarthy echoed. 'That's a new one on me, William.' 'Passin' the snide, sir,' Withers informed him. 'Passing flash paper. Bank of Elegance stuff' (1941).

para noun A paratrooper. 1958–. J. CARTWRIGHT Right, paras get ready to jump (1977). [Shortening.]

paralysed adjective mainly US Incapacitated by drink or its after-effects. Cf. PARALYTIC adjective. 1890–. E. WAUGH The only time I got tight I was paralysed all the next day (1945).

paralytic adjective Blind drunk. 1909–. DAILY EXPRESS *Woman at the Thames Court*: I was not drunk. I was suffering from paralysis. *Mr. Cairns*: I have heard being drunk called being paralytic (1927).

parchment noun mainly naval A certificate. 1851–. W. GRANVILLE *Parchment*, naval rating's service certificate on which his character and abilities are assessed by the commanding officer of each ship on which he has served (1962).

parlour-house noun mainly US An expensive type of brothel. 1872–.

parlour-jumper noun A common housebreaker. 1860–.

parlour pink noun derog A person whose professed left-wing principles are insincere or not matched by their lifestyle. 1929–. NEWS CHRONICLE A wonderfully reactionary view of country life, it makes John Buchan look like a 'parlour pink' (1960). [From *parlour* used to characterize people of comfortable or prosperous support, usu. non-participatory, for radical, extreme, or revolutionary political movements + *pink* liberal socialist.]

part verb **to part brass-rags** orig nautical To quarrel. 1898–. ECONOMIST He seems to have finally parted brass rags with the Arab nationalists and President Nasser (1959). [Cf. RAGGIE noun.]

partied-out adjective orig US Exhausted from celebrating, drinking alcohol, etc.; hung over; tired of parties. 1979–.

party noun services' A military engagement; an attack or fight; (the unit engaged in) an operation. 1918–. B. J. ELLAN I just fired when something came into my sights and then turned like hell as something fired at me! What a party! (1942).

party pooper noun US Someone who throws a pall of gloom over a party or other social engagement. 1954–.

pash noun An infatuation; a schoolgirl's 'crush'. 1891–. G. GREENE When you've got a pash for someone like I have, anybody's better than nothing (1934). [Short for *passion*.]

passer noun Someone who 'passes' counterfeit money. 1795–.

passion-killers noun pl. Sturdy, practical, and unromantic ladies' knickers, orig those issued to female Service personnel. 1943–.

passion wagon noun A truck taking servicemen on short leave to a town or other place of entertainment; any old jalopy suitable for petting, etc., in. a.1943–.

passman noun A prisoner allowed to leave his cell in order to enjoy certain privileges. 1965–.

paste verb trans. To beat or thrash (someone); to bomb or shell heavily; (Cricket), to hit (the ball or bowling) hard. Also **pasting**, noun. 1846–. HUTCHINSON'S PICTORIAL HISTORY OF THE WAR The Whirlwind has been used with much success for 'pasting' enemy aerodromes (1942).

pasties /ˈpeɪstɪz/ noun pl. A covering or coverings worn over the nipples of a showgirl's or topless dancer's breasts (esp. to comply with legal requirements for entertainers). ?1954–. SUNDAY TRUTH (Brisbane): Stripper Sharon was promoting a Valley nightclub, wearing nothing on top but a couple of pasties to keep her modest (1969). [From *paste* verb + *-y*.]

Pat noun A nickname for an Irishman. Cf. PADDY noun 1. 1806–.

patch noun Brit, prison Any of a number of cloth pieces sewn on to a uniform in order to identify a prisoner as an escapee. 1958–. S. MCCONVILLE He would be put on the *E*(scape) *list* and compelled to wear an easily identifiable uniform; this is known as *being in patches* (1980).

Pat (Malone) noun mainly Austral Rhyming slang for 'own', usu. in phr. *on one's Pat*, alone. 1908–. N. MARSH We're dopey if we let that bloke go off on his Pat (1943).

patha patha noun S Afr = PHATA PHATA noun.

patoot noun US mainly euphemistic and jocular
= PATOOTIE 2. 1942–. NEWSWEEK If the point of this
exercise is, as some wags suggest, to give Bill the
swift kick in the patoot he so richly deserves,
you've chosen the wrong issue (2000). [Prob.
shortening of PATOOTIE.]

patootie /pəˈtuːtɪ/ noun US A sweetheart or
girl-friend; a pretty girl, esp. in phr. *hot patootie*
and *sweet patootie*. 1918–. NEW YORKER She was,
successively, . . . the wife and/or sweet patootie of
the quartet (1977). **2** mainly euphemistic and jocular
The buttocks, rectum. 1959–. ATLANTA JOURNAL-
CONSTITUTION Mangoes are truly one of the most
wondrous of fruits, but they certainly are a pain
in the patootie to eat (2002). [Prob. alteration of
potato.]

patsy noun orig US Someone who is the
object of ridicule, deceit, or other
victimization. 1899–. [Perh. from Italian
pazzo fool.]

patsy adjective US All right, fine;
satisfactory. 1930–50.

patzer noun chess A weak player. 1948–.
DAILY TELEGRAPH So Fischer after beating off a
ferocious attack . . . 'played like a patzer,' said
one American Grandmaster (1972). [Origin
uncertain; cf. German *patzen* to bungle.]

pavement princess noun citizens' band
A prostitute who touts for business over the
radio network. 1976–.

pax noun A schoolchildren's truce-word.
1843–. R. KIPLING Pax, Turkey. I'm the ass (1899).
[Latin 'peace'.]

Pay noun services', etc. The paymaster. 1878–.
TAFFRAIL Cashley, the fleet pay, was vainly
endeavouring to get up a four at auction
bridge (1916).

paybob noun sailors' The paymaster. Cf. PAY
noun. 1916–.

pay-off noun Also **payoff**. **1** The money
'paid off' to the winners in gambling; the
payment of this. 1905–. **2** criminals'
A confidence trick in which the victim loses
a large sum of money trying to follow the
apparent good luck of the trickster.
1915–. G. BRONSON-HOWARD Specialists in check-
raising, wireless wire-tapping, 'the match', 'the
pay-off', and cards (1915). **3** The share-out
after a robbery. 1927–. **4** The payment of
bribes; graft; money given as a bribe. 1930–.
D. LAMSON Witnesses, juries, pay-off, fixin's—don't
matter what it is . . . There ain't nothing he
won't do, long as you got the potatoes (1935).

pay-off man noun A confidence
trickster; the cashier in a criminal gang.
1927–.

payola noun orig US A bribe or other secret
payment to induce someone to use his or her
influence to promote a commercial product,
etc., esp. one made to a disc-jockey for
'plugging' a record. 1938–. T. PYNCHON They got
the contracts. All drawn up in most kosher
fashion, Manfred. If there was payola in there,
I doubt it got written down (1966). [-ola,
commercial suffix, after *pianola*, etc., used
in *Victrola* and other products.]

P.B.I. noun Abbreviation of 'Poor Bloody
Infantry(man)'. 1916–. B.E.F. TIMES So here's to
the lads of the P.B.I., Who live in a ditch That
never is dry (1916).

PDQ adverb phr Also **pdq**. Abbreviation of
'pretty damn quick'. 1875–. R. KIPLING He went
as his instructions advised p.d.q.—which means
'with speed' (1891).

pea noun mainly Austral A favourite; a horse
tipped to win; someone in a favourable
position, esp. in authority. 1888–. F. HARDY I've
got the tip about it. Old Dapper Dan earwigged
at the track. Swordsman is the pea (1958).
[Perh. from the phr. *this is the pea I choose* in
thimble-rigging.]

pea-brained adjective Having a brain
apparently the size of a pea; dull-witted,
stupid. 1942–. R. GUY That thickheaded
pea-brained two-faced thug (1987). Hence
pea-brain, noun (Someone with) a brain of
this magnitude. 1959–.

peach noun A person or thing of
exceptional merit, or particularly desirable;
a pretty young woman. 1710–. R. CROMPTON Now
would you think that a peach like her would fall
for a fat-headed chump like that? (1930).

peacherino /piːtʃəˈriːnəʊ/ noun mainly
US = PEACH noun. Also **peacherine, peacheroo**.
1900–. C. ROUGVIE When I was his age, they were
hauling them out from under me . . . And all
young peacherinos, too (1967). [Playful
extension of PEACH noun.]

peachy adjective Attractive; marvellous,
fantastic. 1900–. W. TREVOR I'd call her an eyeful,
Kate. Peachy (1976). [From PEACH noun.]

peachy-keen adjective US Fine, excellent.
1951–.

peanut noun **1** Someone small or
unimportant. 1864–. **2** pl. orig US Something
small or trivial; an insignificant amount
of money, an inadequate payment. 1930–.

J. B. PRIESTLEY 'How was the poker game?' 'Peanuts. All I got was about twenty-five dollars and a headache' (1946).

peanut gallery noun US The upper gallery in a theatre. 1888–.

peanut head noun orig US **1** A stupid or foolish person. 1891–. **2** (A person with) an unusually small head. 1906–.

pearl-diver noun orig US Someone who works as a dishwasher in a café or restaurant. Also **pearl-diving,** noun. 1907–.

pearler variant of PURLER noun.

pearly noun **1** pl. Teeth. See sense 3 below. 1914–. T. PYNCHON Secretaries . . . shiver with the winter cold . . . their typewriter keys chattering as their pearlies (1973). **2 the pearlies** musicians' An uncontrollable nervous shaking of the bowing arm sometimes experienced by violinists, etc. before a performance. Cf. YIPS noun. 1960–. adjective **3 pearly whites** teeth. 1935–. [In sense 2, perh. shortened from unrecorded *pearly whites* (= frights).]

pear-shaped adjective Brit, orig RAF **go pear-shaped** To go wrong, go amiss. 1983–. [Prob. from the idea of the shape assumed by a sphere when deflated.]

peasant noun derog Someone remarkable for their ignorance, stupidity, or awkwardness. 1943–. G. LYALL Alone? Of course I'm not alone, you—peasant. Do you think I'd drive myself? (1964).

pea-soup noun N Amer A French Canadian; the French language spoken in Canada. 1866–.

pea-souper noun **1** A dense yellow fog (formerly in London and other cities). 1890–. **2** A 'pea-soup' or French Canadian. 1930–.

peb noun Austral Abbreviation of PEBBLE noun. 1903–. C. J. DENNIS They wus pebs, they wus norks, they wus reel naughty boys (1916).

pebble noun **1** mainly Austral A troublesome person or animal. 1829–. **2** Austral A stayer; often in phr. *as game as a pebble*. Hence, as a term of affection. 1863–. [In early Austral use, a reprobate convict.]

peck noun US, African-American Abbreviation of PECKERWOOD noun. 1924–. C. BROWN A poor white peck will cuss worse'n a nigger (1969).

pecker noun mainly US The penis. 1902–. N. LEVINE Ground sunflower seeds. . . . This will make your pecker stand up to no end of punishment (1958).

peckerhead noun US Someone aggressively objectionable. 1945–.

peckerwood noun US A (poor) white person. 1928–. W. FAULKNER Even a Delta peckerwood would look after a draggle-tail better than that (1942).

Peckham rye noun Rhyming slang for 'tie'; a necktie. 1925–.

peck horn noun jazz A mellophone, saxophone, or other similar instrument. 1936–. SUNDAY TIMES Straight band singers were unknown in the Twenties—everyone, even Bing Crosby, had an instrument to hold. 'I had a peckhorn, like a flugel horn' (1975). [Origin unknown.]

Peck's bad boy noun US dated A wild, unmanageable, or mischievous boy. 1883–. [The name of a fictional character created by G. W. *Peck* (1840–1916).]

pecs noun pl. N Amer Short for 'pectoral muscles'. 1949–. L. COHEN I saw you with massive lower pecs and horseshoe triceps, with bulk and definition simultaneously (1966).

ped noun now mainly US Abbreviation of 'pedestrian'. 1863–.

pedigree noun A criminal record. Also **pedigreed,** adjective. 1911–. D. SHANNON Dorothy had a little pedigree for shoplifting (1964).

pee verb **1** intr. To urinate. 1825–. M. MCCARTHY 'My God,' you yell . . . can't a man pee in his own house?' (1948). **2** trans. **a** To wet by urinating. 1788–. **b** To wet (oneself) by urinating; hence (chiefly metaphorically), **to pee oneself laughing.** 1946–. noun **3** An act of urination. 1880–. **4** Urine. 1957–. [From the sound of the first letter of *piss*.]

peel verb intr. To undress; usu. followed by *off* (orig used in boxing slang, referring to contestants getting stripped ready to fight). 1785–. VARIETY The gals are peelin' in 23 clubs through Los Angeles County (1950).

peep noun **1** Something said; usu. used in negative contexts. 1903–. PICTURE POST 'One more peep out of you, Mister, and I'll get the boys to push you and your b— stall in the oggin', which was a nearby canal (1954). verb intr. **2** To betray an associate to the police or other authority. 1911–. [From earlier sense, cheep, squeak.]

peepers noun pl. Eyes. *a.*1700–. OBSERVER Or is it Liz Hurley? So hard to tell now the old Pendennis peepers have started to fail

peanut gallery   peanut head   pearl-diver   pearler

spectacularly (1997). [From earlier sense, one who peeps.]

peeps noun pl. People; esp. one's own close friends or associates. 1951–. D. ADEBAYO I ain't really doin' no full-blown interviews right now . . . I came to hang with my peeps (2000). [From a respelling of *peop(le* + -s.]

pee-wee noun mainly children's An act of urination. 1909–. S. RAVEN Don't forget the little dears do a pee-wee before they go to bed (1962). [Reduplicated form of PEE noun; see also WEE noun.]

peg noun **1** A tooth, esp. a child's tooth. 1598–. **2** A leg; a wooden or other artificial leg. 1833–. **3** mainly Anglo-Indian A drink, esp. of brandy and soda. 1860–. G. TREVELYAN Brandy and belattee pawnee, a beverage which goes by the name of a 'peg' (according to the favourite derivation, because each draught is a 'peg' in your coffin) (1864). **4** cricket A stump. 1865–. R. ROBINSON Cunis swung one so late and so far that it hit Gandotra's leg peg (1972). **5** military A charge; **on the peg** on a charge, under arrest. 1888–. **6** US A strong or vigorous throw, esp. in baseball. 1906–. NEW YORKER Martinez took a peg from the outfield (1985). **7** A railway semaphore signal. 1911–. verb **8 to peg out** to die; to be ruined. 1852–. **9** trans. US, mainly baseball To throw (the ball) long and low. 1862–. L. B. SMEDES You will hardly ever get them before the catcher pegs the ball to the first baseman (1986). [In sense 3, actually from the pegs or markers in a drinking-vessel; in sense 8, apparently from reaching the end of a game of cribbage.]

peggy noun naval A sailor assigned to menial tasks; a mess-steward. 1902–. S. WATERS I was initiated into the mysteries of acting as 'Peggy'. As the name implies this menial does all the domestic chores (1967). [From the female name *Peggy*.]

peggy-work noun naval The chores to which a 'peggy' is assigned. 1920–.

peg-house noun **1** A public house. Cf. PEG noun 3. 1922. **2** US A brothel; a meeting-place for male homosexuals. 1931–.

pego /piːɡəʊ/ noun The penis. 1663–. [Of unknown origin.]

pen[1] noun orig US A prison; a prison cell. 1845–. NEW YORK EVENING JOURNAL A panic was caused among the prisoners in the pen of the Ewen Street Court jail (1904).

pen[2] noun US Short for 'penitentiary'. 1881–.

pen (and ink) verb (phr) Rhyming slang for 'stink'. 1892–. G. F. NEWMAN 'I don't mind, provided he takes a bath.' 'Yeah, he does pen a bit' (1972).

pencil noun **1** The penis. 1916–. D. FRANCIS That Purple Emperor strain is as soft as an old man's pencil (1967). **2 to have the pencil put on one** criminals' To be reported to the police authorities. 1929–34.

pencil neck noun derog orig US **1** A long thin neck. 1968–. **2** A scrawny, effete, or excessively studious person. 1968–. MUSCLEMAG Society has jobs for strong-men, just as it has jobs for pencil-necks (1991). Hence **pencil-necked**, adjective. Having a pencil neck; scrawny, effete, or excessively studious. 1982–.

penguin noun air force A low-powered machine incapable of flight, used to train airmen; also, an aircraft ground-crewman or other non-flying personnel member. 1915–. ATHENAEUM Members of the W.R.A.F. were called 'Penguins' because they were 'flappers' who did not fly (1919).

penguin suit noun **1** A man's evening-dress suit. 1967–. K. M. PEYTON Geoff'd better go home for his penguin suit. I'll go up and get my tails (1979). **2** A type of tight-fitting suit worn by astronauts. 1971.

penman noun criminals' A forger. 1865–. H. MCLEAVE You'll need a passport. . . . I've got a penman who can doctor it (1974).

pen-mate noun Austral and NZ A shearer who catches sheep out of the same pen as another shearer. 1895–.

pennyweighter noun US dated, criminals' A jewellery-thief; one who takes precious stones or metals. 1886–.

penwiper noun dated A handkerchief. 1902–42.

peola /piːˈəʊlə/ noun US, African-American A light-skinned African-American, esp. a girl. 1938–. Z. N. HURSTON Dat broad you with wasn't no pe-ola (1942). [Origin uncertain; prob. from the name of *Peola* Johnson, a light-skinned African-American woman who attempts to pass as white in Fannie Hurst's novel *Imitation of Life* (1933) and the 1934 film adaptation of the same name.]

pep orig US. noun **1** Vigour; energy or 'go'; spirit. 1908–. P. G. WODEHOUSE He can chafe all right, but there he stops. He's lost his pep. He's got no dash (1923). verb **2 to pep up** to instil with vigour; to enliven or cheer up. 1923–. [Abbreviation of *pepper*.]

pep-pill noun orig US A pill containing a stimulant drug. 1917–. SCIENCE NEWS LETTER Amphetamine, or Benzadrine, known as 'pep pills', . . . is most likely to produce pleasant sensations in normal persons (1955). [See PEP noun and verb.]

per boot adverb Austral jocular On foot, walking. 1895–. BULLETIN (Sydney) Touring Grippsland per boot, Mat was hailed . . . by a dog-tired cocky (1941).

percolator noun mainly US **1** A carburettor. 1942–. **2** A rent party; also, any party. 1946–. S. LONGSTREET You could always . . . get together . . . and charge a few coins and have . . . a percolator (1956).

Percy noun **1** derog A weak or effeminate man; esp. (in World War I) a conscientious objector. 1916–. **2** military, derog An educated man; an officer. 1961–. B. MATHER Most of the young Percies in our mob had to take their boots off to count up to twenty (1974). **3 to point Percy at the porcelain** Brit and Austral (of a man) to urinate. 1965–. [From the male personal name.]

perisher noun **1** A term of contempt (also with suggestion of pity) for a person; someone tiresome or annoying, often of a child. 1896–. P. G. WODEHOUSE If you ask me, they don't learn the little perishers nothing (1935). **2** naval A periscope; hence, a qualifying course for submarine commanders. 1925–.

perishing adjective Annoying, troublesome; 'confounded'. 1847–.

perp noun US The perpetrator of a crime. 1981–. T. N. MURARI Yolande had testified. The perp got twenty-five to life (1984). [Abbreviation of *perpetrator*.]

perv mainly Austral Also **perve**. verb **1** intr. To act as a sexual pervert; to indulge in eroticism; with *at, on*: to ogle. 1941–. I. HAMILTON She's a cheap thrill machine for the boys to stare at and perve on (1972). noun **2** A sexual pervert. Also **perv(y)** adjective. 1942–. [Short for *pervert*.]

pervo adjective **1** Sexually perverted. 1970–. I. KNIGHT What do I get? An absolute pervo smut-freak of a house-mate: a man who lies there dirty-talking himself (2002). noun **2** A pervert. 1978–. [From *perv(ert* or *perv(erted* + *-o*.]

Pete noun Used in oaths, esp. *for Pete's sake* and *for the love of Pete*, as a euphemistic substitute for *pity* (itself used in place of *God* and *Christ*). 1924–. W. GOLDING Marry me, Taffy,

for Pete's sake marry me (1959). [From the male personal name, a pet-form of *Peter*.]

pete noun **1** A safe. Also **pete-box**. Cf. PETER noun 2. 1909–. D. RUNYON This is a very soft pete. It is old-fashioned, and you can open it with a toothpick (1938). **2** Nitroglycerine, used for safe-breaking. 1931–48. [See PETER noun.]

pete-man noun A safe-breaker. 1907–.

peter Also **Peter**. noun **1** A portmanteau, a trunk; any bundle or piece of luggage. 1667–. A. ARMSTRONG 'Peters' are pieces of luggage,—a threepenny extra for the driver (1930). **2** A safe or cash-box; a cash register. 1827–. M. SHADBOLT 'Did he tickle the peter?' . . . 'To the tune of two thousand quid' (1965). **3** The penis. 1870–. J. WAMBAUGH If you look very closely you can see a gerbil's dick, but not a parakeet's peter (1977). **4** US An incapacitating or 'knock-out' drug. 1899–. **5** orig Austral A prison cell, a cell in a police station, etc. 1890–. D. NILAND They could throw you in the peter stone-cold sober (1955). verb **6** intr. To take a stupefying drug. 1925–. **7** trans. To blow open (a safe). 1925–. [From the proper name.]

peterman noun **1** dated Someone who administers 'knock-out' drops in order to commit a robbery. Cf. PETER noun 4. 1897–1908. **2** A safe-blower. 1900–. J. G. BRANDON Your flash 'peterman' is as gentle-natured as the average curate (1936). [Cf. earlier slang sense, one who steals trunks or luggage.]

petrol bowsers noun pl. Also **petrols**. Austral Trousers. 1971–. [Rhyming slang, from *petrol bowser* petrol pump, petrol tanker.]

petrolhead noun orig Austral A car enthusiast. 1980–. LEICESTER MERCURY It's that fast, furious, foot-to-the-floor, V8-powered action that's brought crowds of petrolheads flocking to the new 52,000-seater Rockingham Motor Speedway Course (2003). [From *petrol* noun + HEAD noun 3.]

pew noun A seat; **take a pew** sit down, be seated. 1898–.

P.F.C. noun US, services' Also **pfc**. Abbreviation of 'Private 1st Class'; 'poor foolish (forlorn, etc.) civilian'. 1941–.

phat adjective orig US African-American A term of general or sexual commendation. 1963–. THE FACE They're just really distinctive—a London crew with a really phat funk sound (1992). [Prob. a respelling of *fat*.]

phata phata noun Also **patha patha**. S Afr Sexual intercourse. 1977–. A. P. BRINK 'Others

pep-pill   per boot   percolator   Percy   perisher   perp looking for phata-phata'—illustrated by pushing his thumb through the two fingers in the immemorial sign (1979). [From earlier sense, type of sensual dance; ultimately from Xhosa and Zulu *phatha phatha*, literally 'touch touch'.]

phenom noun US Something remarkable or 'phenomenal', esp. an unusually gifted person, prodigy. 1881–. NEW YORKER He has a series of run-ins with a militant black rookie phenom (1986). [Shortened from *phenomenon*.]

Philly noun Also **Phillie**. US Abbreviation of 'Philadelphia'. 1869–.

phishing noun Getting people's details, esp. credit card details, through fake websites or e-mails. 1996–. [A respelling of *fishing*.]

phiz noun now archaic or jocular A face or countenance; one's look. 1687–. [Shortened from *physiognomy*.]

phizgig noun Austral = FIZGIG noun; a police informer. Also as verb intr., to act as an informer. 1941–.

phizog noun now archaic, or jocular = PHIZ noun. 1811–. RADIO TIMES The phizog is definitely familiar. . . . 'I get recognized wherever I go' (1980). [As PHIZ noun.]

phizzer noun Austral = FIZZER[2] noun; a police informer. 1974–.

phoney verb trans. and intr. Also **phony**. **to phoney up** mainly US To make phoney; to falsify or counterfeit. 1940–.

phoney baloney mainly US, noun and int **1** Nonsense, humbug. 1933–. A. GIRÓN Ha! Ha! Phoney baloney. Said this bomb was going to rip us wide open. Don't pay no mind to that crap (1989). **2** adjective Insincere, fake; also, foolish. 1936–.

phooey int, noun, and adjective An expression of strong disagreement with some remark (also as adjective); 'nonsense', 'rubbish', 'baloney'. 1919–. J. B. PRIESTLEY Oh phooey, Benny. . . . This doesn't count as a drink (1951).

phut noun **to go phut** to become inoperative, go awry. 1888–. DAILY TELEGRAPH The kids had broken a window, and the colour television had gone phut (1972). [Origin uncertain; either imitative of the sound of a dull impact, or from Hindi *phaṭ* crack, sound

of a slap (first recorded in English in the writings of Rudyard Kipling, who was born in India).]

phwoar int orig and mainly Brit Expressing enthusiastic or esp. lubricious approval. 1976–. SNOOP Phwoaar!!! Sexy stars from yesteryear who still give us the horn (2003). [Imitative, and perh. partly modelled on COR int.]

phy noun Abbreviation of 'Physeptone', a proprietary name for the drug methadone hydrochloride. 1971–.

physical torture noun Physical training; fitness training. 1900–. W. C. ANDERSON The physical torture progam . . . started promptly at 0630 every morning at Eglin Air Force Base (1968).

'Phwoaar!!! Sexy stars from yesteryear who still give us the horn.'

pi /paɪ/ adjective dated Pious, sanctimonious. Cf. PI-JAW noun. 1891–. BROADCAST 'Blue Peter', though never pi or holier than thou, is always on the side of the . . . decencies (1978). [Short for *pious*: recorded as a noun ('pious exhortation') around 1870.]

pianist noun A radio operator. 1955–.

piccolo noun US A juke-box. 1938–. NEW YORK AMSTERDAM NEWS The Harlem Hamfats grind out the tune on myriad Harlem piccolos (1938).

piccy noun Also **picky**. A photograph. 1968–. HOT CAR The end result of fitting these packages on your Ford can be, if the piccies are anything to go by, rather on the eye-catching side (1977). [From *pic(ture* + *-y*.]

pick verb **to pick up: a** dated To steal or rob; to swindle. 1770–1928. **b** orig US To arrest or apprehend (a person). 1871–. ALBUQUERQUE JOURNAL 'Stormy' . . . was picked up last year on prostitution charges (1993).

pick noun US A pickpocket. 1907–. [Shortening.]

pickled adjective Drunk. 1842–. D. THOMAS On Sundays, and when pickled, he sang high tenor, and had won many cups (1953).

pick-up noun Brit Robbery or theft; often as adjective. Cf. **to pick up** at PICK verb. 1846–.

pick-up man noun **1** A thief, esp. one who takes luggage. 1938. **2** US Someone who collects (and pays out) money wagered with bookmakers. 1944–.

piddle¹ verb intr. **1** To urinate. 1784–.
R. ADAMS I have no idea what portents he
employs— possibly the bear piddles on the floor
and he observes portents in the steaming whatnot (1974). noun **2** Urine; an act of urinating.
1870–. [Perh. from PISS verb + *puddle* verb
(cf. WIDDLE verb and noun); prob. not the same
word as earlier PIDDLE² verb.]

piddle² verb **to piddle about (or around)**
To fool or mess about; to potter. 1545–. SOUNDS
He returned to New York and 'piddled around'
doing Public Relations (1977). [Origin
uncertain: perh. an alteration of *peddle* to sell
small wares, busy oneself with trifling
matters, by association with Low German
piddeln; in modern use identified with
PIDDLE¹ (cf. *piss about*), which may not
historically be the same word.]

piddling adjective Trivial, insignificant.
1559–. MACLEAN'S MAGAZINE In plain words, I found
out what my job was. No piddling assignment
either. What it amounted to was saving the
country (1971).

pie noun orig US Something easily achieved,
a 'cinch' or 'doddle'; esp. in phr. *as easy
(simple, etc.) as pie.* 1886–. P. G. WODEHOUSE This kid
Mitchell was looked on as a coming champ in
those days. . . . I guess I looked pie to him (1929).

pie adjective **to be pie on** NZ To be good at
(something). 1941–. [From Maori *pai* good.]

pie-card noun US **1** dated A meal ticket;
someone who begs for a meal. 1895–. **2** (One
who holds) a union card. 1931–. C. RUBIN All of
them phony, pie-card officials who sit on their
big fat asses and twiddle their thumbs (1973).

piece noun **1** A share (in some enterprise); a
financial interest in a business, etc.; often in
phr. *a piece of the action.* 1900–. **2** mainly US A
hand-gun. 1930–. L. SANDERS You're a good
shot. . . . But you've never carried a piece on a
job (1970). [Common in standard use from
the 16th cent.] **3** US An ounce of an illegal
drug, esp. morphine or heroin. 1935–.
4 a piece of cake something easy or pleasant.
1936–. T. MCLEAN They took the field against
Canterbury as if the match were 'a piece of
cake' (1960). **5 a piece of ass (tail,** etc.): mainly
US A woman, thought of as an object of
sexual intercourse; intercourse itself. Also,
piece. 1942–. G. V. HIGGINS Him and four buddies
want a little dough to get a high class piece of
tail (1972). **6 a piece of piss** = a piece of cake.
1949–. OBSERVER John Lines, who has a tough
fight defending his seat in Bartley Green ward,
snorted when asked if his task would be easier
under a Labour government and answered

bluntly: 'Piece of piss' (1996). **7** orig US A
spray-painted graffiti mural. 1980–.

pie-eater noun Austral Someone
insignificant, a 'small-timer'; also, a
simpleton. Also **pie-biter,** noun, **pie-eating,**
adjective. 1911–. K. TENNANT He's one of those big
he-men that go sneaking around the park
waiting to snatch some chromo's handbag.
Just a pie-eater. (1953).

pie-eyed adjective orig US Drunk. 1904–.
DAILY EXPRESS Personally I didn't care if the whole
band was pie-eyed, I wanted them to be busy
playing good dance music (1937). [Cf. *pied*
jumbled, confused, and hence unable to
focus correctly.]

pie-face noun US Someone with a round
or expressionless face; a fool. 1891–. [From
the earlier *pie-faced* adjective.]

pie-hole noun US The mouth. 1983–. ESQUIRE
You still squeeze it [i.e. toothpaste] from the
tube onto your brush and jam it into your pie
hole (2000).

pie-wagon noun US dated A police van;
a Black Maria. 1904–.

pig noun **1a** Applied contemptuously to
a person; someone obstinate, annoying,
greedy, etc. 1546–. P. G. WINSLOW I had some
beautiful birds in London, but I had to stay on
the good side of that pig, or she might have
noticed more than was good for her (1977).
b Similarly, applied to a thing; something
difficult or frustrating, etc. 1923–. F. MULLALLY
Watch out for the potholes. It's a pig of a road
(1978). **2** A police officer. 1811–. D. LODGE Any
pig roughs you up, make sure you get his
number (1975). **3** Any of various types of
vehicle: a locomotive, truck, aeroplane, etc.
1898–. TIMES The Pig, the armoured vehicle most
used in Belfast (1978). **4 pigs in blankets** US
Formerly, oysters wrapped in bacon; now,
a sausage-roll or frankfurter sandwich, etc.
1902–. **5 pigs (to you)** Austral A derisive retort.
1906–. N. CULOTTA 'She's worn out.' 'Pigs she is.
There's a lot of life in 'er yet' (1957). **6 in pig**
of a woman, pregnant. 1945–. [In sense
6, from the standard use, of a sow.]

pig verb **to pig out** orig and mainly US To over-
indulge or 'make a pig of oneself' by over-
eating (*on*). Cf. PIG-OUT noun. 1978–. J. FONDA
Troy and Vanessa . . . pig out for days on leftover
Halloween candy (1981).

pig boat noun US, mainly military
A submarine. 1921–.

piddle   piddling   pie   pie-card   piece   pie-eater

pigeon noun **1** Someone easily fooled or swindled; a simpleton. ?1525–. **B. HOLIDAY** So they handed me a white paper to sign. . . . I signed. . . . The rest was up to them. I was just a pigeon (1956). **2** A stool pigeon. 1847–.

pigeon-drop noun US, criminals' A confidence trick, esp. one which starts with a wallet dropped in front of the victim or 'pigeon'. 1937–. **HARNEY & CROSS** Sometimes it was the 'pigeon-drop'. A purse or billfold containing a considerable amount of money was dropped. The 'sucker' was allowed to find it right along with a member of the mob (1961). Also **pigeon-dropper,** noun. 1961–, **-dropping,** noun. 1850–.

pigging adjective and adverb Brit Used as a euphemistic intensifier: flipping, blinking. 1970–. **D. MITCHELL** What an utter, pigging, mess (1999).

pig-ignorant adjective derog Crassly ignorant. 1972–. **T. HEALD** Those press johnnies . . . would never twig. Too gullible and too pig ignorant (1976).

Pig Island noun Also **pig island.** Austral and NZ New Zealand. 1888–. **F. SARGESON** 'Young man,' he said, 'it is my advice that you get off back to England. . . . Pig Island is no place for the likes of you' (1967). Also **Pig Islander,** noun. [Named after the introduction of pigs there by Captain Cook. The pigs reverted to a wild state.]

pig-jump verb intr. Austral Of a horse, etc.: to jump awkwardly (for the rider) from all four feet, without bringing them together as in bucking. 1884–. Also as noun and **pig-jumper,** noun.

pig-out noun orig US A bout of excessive eating; a binge, feast. 1978–. **CHICAGO TRIBUNE** Favorite pigout food: Turkey. In fact, I love the whole Thanksgiving dinner (1989). [From *to pig out* (see PIG verb).]

pig's ear noun **1** Rhyming slang for 'beer'. 1880–. **J. CURTIS** But the most of the fiver would go in the old pig's ear (1936). **2 to make a pig's ear of** Brit to botch, ruin, make a mess of. 1954–. **D. ADAMS** What use is your life to anyone? When I think of what you've made of it the phrase 'pig's ear' comes irresistibly to mind (1979).

pigskin noun **1** dated A saddle. 1839–. **2** US A football. 1894–. **ANDERSON** (S. Carolina) **INDEPENDENT** He carried the pigskin on the end around 11 times for 73 yards (1974).

pig-sticker noun **1** A bayonet, knife, or other sharp weapon. 1867–. **A. MELVILLE-ROSS** Trelawney crossed to the far wall, yanked the knife from it. . . . 'You'll hand over that pig-sticker and come home with uncle' (1978). **2** regional A pork butcher. 1872–.

pi-jaw /paɪ-/ noun dated A sanctimonious, long, moral lecture, as delivered by a schoolteacher or parent. Also as verb trans. and **pi-jawing,** noun. 1891–. [See PI adjective.]

piker noun orig US A cautious gambler; someone who shies away from risk; a shirker or lounger. 1859–. **H. L. WILSON** 'I says to myself the other day: "I bet a cookie he'd like to be like me!" ' Homer was a piker, even when he made bets with himself (1919). [From *pike* verb, perh. in the earlier sense, to depart + *-er*.]

pikey noun also dialect A gypsy or traveller; also, a lower-class person, regarded as coarse or disreputable; also, as adjective, characteristic of pikeys; squalid, disreputable, vulgar. 1847–. **P. WILDEBLOOD** My family's all Pikeys, but we ain't on the road no more! (1955). [From *pike* noun, turnpike.]

piking adjective also dialect Cheating, thieving. 1893–. **W. GADDIS** The Father of his Country was crumpled, folded, and offered in the most piking and meretricious traffic millions of times a day (1955). [Perh. from *pike*, pick (as in *pickpocket*).]

pill noun **1** pl. **a** The testicles. 1608–. **b** Nonsense, rubbish. 1935–. **I. MILLER** I explained to him about the prayers . . . 'Awful pills,' I whispered; 'but it can't be helped' (1935). **2** A bullet or shell; a bomb, a handgrenade; spec. an atomic bomb. 1618–. **P. G. HART** When I got over the town I let my pills go (1939). **3a** dated A pellet of opium for smoking. 1786–. **b** A cigarette. 1914–. **D. HAMMETT** Those pills you smoke are terrible (1927). **c** A tablet of barbiturate or amphetamine. 1963–. **4** A doctor; a (member of) the Royal Army Medical Corps. 1835–. **5** Someone disliked or held in contempt. 1865–. **B. GARFIELD** 'Do you love your wife?' . . . 'You're a pill. Yes, I love her' (1977). **6** A ball: in Football, Golf, and other sports. 1896–. [In sense 2, earliest with the meaning 'cannon-ball'.]

pill verb trans. dated To fail (an examination candidate). 1908–25. [From earlier sense, to blackball.]

pill-head noun A drug addict. 1962–.

pillock noun A fool or half-wit; also as a general term of contempt. 1967–. [From the older word *pillicock* the penis.]

pill-pusher noun A doctor or chemist. 1879–. Also **pill-peddler** (1855–), **-roller, -shooter.** J. CURTIS He was damned if he let a lousy pill-roller know just how bad he felt (1936).

pimp noun **1** orig US, now Austral and NZ An informer or sneak. 1791–. AGE (Melbourne): You fat pimp! The standard response to 'I'm going to tell on you' (1974). **2** US A male prostitute. 1942–. verb intr. **3** To act as a pander or procurer for prostitutes. 1636–. **4** orig US, now Austral and NZ To tell tales or inform *on* (someone). 1865–. [Slang use of *pimp* someone who manages a prostitute or group of prostitutes.]

pimpmobile noun US A large, flashy car used by a pimp. 1971–. DAILY MAIL The pimpmobiles—the long, long Cadillacs with a Rolls front—no longer cruise everywhere. They are finding it less profitable to keep girls here (1975).

pin noun **1** A leg; usu. in pl. 1530–. **2** N Amer A coupling-pin on a railway carriage, trailer, etc., esp. in phr. *to pull the pin*, to loose the coupling-pin, to uncouple; also fig. 1860–. J. WAMBAUGH An old man that should have pulled the pin years ago. Now he'd been here too long. He couldn't leave or he'd die (1972). verb **3** trans. Austral To cheat or cause trouble for. 1934–41.

pinch verb trans. **1** To steal (something). 1632–. **2** To arrest (a person). 1789–. TIMES He explained that Heard gave him the tobacco and then put in another officer to 'pinch' him (1955). noun **3a** An act of theft (or plagiarism). 1757–. MELODY MAKER A pleasant selection of Italian-sung numbers—including what sounds like a Latin pinch from Presley (1966). **b** orig US An arrest or charge; imprisonment. 1900–. H. CARMICHAEL. Before I make a pinch I like to be reasonably sure that the charge will stick (1960).

pineapple noun **1** A bomb; a hand-grenade or light trench mortar. Also **pineapple bomb.** 1916–. SUN (Baltimore): There was a crossfire of ten grenades before one of his pineapples destroyed a position with four enemy soldiers in it (1944). **2 the pineapple** unemployment benefit or 'dole'. 1937–.

pine drape noun US A coffin. 1945–. [US *drape* = curtain. Earlier also *pine overcoat* (cf. WOODEN OVERCOAT noun).]

pine-top noun US Cheap or illicit whisky. 1858–. [From its originally being flavoured with new shoots from pine trees.]

ping(er) noun naval An Asdic (= Anti- Submarine Detection Investigation

Committee) officer or rating. Also **ping-man.** 1946–.

pink¹ adjective **1** dated Violent, extreme; also, utter, as in *the pink limit.* 1896–1946. DAILY EXPRESS The master of the house flies into a pink rage because his chop is not done (1901). noun **2** US, African-American A white person. Also **pink-chaser,** a derog term for an African American who deliberately cultivates friendship with white people. 1926–. C. VAN VECHTEN Funny thing about those pink-chasers the ofays never seem to have any use for them (1926). See also *strike me pink!* at strike verb.

Pink² noun US Abbreviation of 'Pinkerton'; a member of the Pinkerton detective agency. 1913–.

pink button noun Stock Exchange A jobber's clerk. 1973–.

pinkers noun Brit, mainly naval Pink gin. 1961–. D. CLARK 'It was well known that Middleton was the only one who drank pink gin.' . . . 'Rubbish. There were two newcomers. . . . Who knew they didn't drink pinkers?' (1978).

pink-eye noun mainly Austral and Canad Cheap whisky or red wine; someone who drinks this. Cf. PINKY¹ noun 1. 1900–. COAST TO COAST Better put that bottle away . . . If the trooper comes round somebody'll be getting into trouble for selling Charlie pinkeye again (1941).

pink lady noun US **1** A cocktail of gin, grenadine, egg white, etc. 1929–. **2** A barbiturate (tablet). 1954–. M. J. BOSSE There they were, the little pills, the Red Devils, Yellow Jackets, Christmas Trees, and Pink Ladies (1972).

pinko adjective **1** Drunk, esp. on methylated spirits. 1917–. **2** mainly US Politically 'pink' or mildly Communist. 1925–. TRANSATLANTIC REVIEW It's the number three song in China, sir. Saw it in one of those magazines my pinko parents subscribe to (1977). noun **3** One who holds left-of-centre (or mildly Communist) views. 1930–.

pink toe(s) noun US, African-American A light-skinned African-American woman; a white girl. 1930–. C. HIMES *Word* whispered it about that even the great Mamie Mason had lost her own black Joe to a young Pinktoe (1965).

Pink 'Un noun A nickname for a newspaper printed on pink paper, esp. the *Sporting Times* and the *Financial Times.* 1884–. GUARDIAN Today . . . the first Financial Times will hit Wall Street. . . . But for all the . . . computer setting . . . the new international Pink 'un

pill-pusher pimp pimpmobile pin pinch pineapple

depends very much for its birth on the weather (1979). [= 'pink one'.]

pinky[1] noun Also **pinkie**. mainly N Amer (and Scottish Dialect) Anything small, esp. the little finger. 1808–. w. h. auden O lift your pin-kie, and touch the win-ter sky (1962).

pinky[2] noun Also **pinkie**. **1** mainly Austral Cheap red wine (or methylated spirits). Cf. pink-eye noun. 1897–. d. hewett He'd drink anything, they reckoned, plonk, pinkie, straight metho (1959). **2** African-American A white person. 1935–. **3** Someone politically 'pink'; = pinko noun 3. 1946–.

pin-party noun naval A gang of flight-deck workers on an aircraft-carrier who prepare aircraft for take-off. 1942–6.

pin-splitter noun golf **1** A fine golfer. 1916–. **2** An accurate shot to the pin; a club used for this. 1961–.

pip[1] noun A fit of disgust, annoyance, or ill health; esp. in phrs. *to have* (*give someone*, etc.) *the pip*. 1881–. j. b. priestley A proper old Jonah you're turning into! You give me the pip, Dad, you honestly do (1930).

pip[2] noun military Used for the letter *p* in telephone and code messages, esp. in *pip emma* = p.m. 1898–. c. mccullough The second hand was just sweeping up to 9:40 pip-emma (1977).

pip[3] noun orig and mainly US Something remarkably good. 1900–. new yorker He has written a pip of a meeting between Jerry and the therapist in an empty house (1987). [From *pip* the seed of an apple, etc.]

pip[4] noun military A star worn on the epaulette as a mark of rank; spec. one of up to three such stars. 1917–. r. kipling I wrote the usual trimmin's . . . an' what his captain had said about Bert bein' recommended for a pip (1924).

pipe noun **1** orig US A pipe for smoking opium or (in recent use) crack cocaine; an opium addict; also in phr. *on the pipe*, *hit the pipe*, and *pipe-fiend*. 1779–. **2** pl. naval A nickname for a boatswain. 1818–. **3** US Something easily accomplished; a 'cinch'. 1902–. p. g. wodehouse This show's a pipe, and any bird that comes in is going to make plenty (1952). See also *to lay pipe* at lay verb.

pipe verb **1** trans. and intr. To see or look (at); to observe or trail (someone). Also with *off*. 1946–. h. j. parker During the daytime wandering about the area, 'pipe-ing', looking over a car, became a regular practice (1974). **2** noun A look, glance, 1865–. j. mcvicar Have a pipe at her . . . I

just might give her a pull (1980). [Origin uncertain; perh. from *peep* verb to look.]

piped adjective US Drunk or under the influence of drugs. 1906–.

pipe-line noun surfing (The hollow part of) a large wave; the coastal area where these waves occur. 1963–. nz listener The achievement by which the champion surfers are judged is their ability to ride the Hawaiian pipeline. . . . The pipeline breaks less than 50 yards from the beach over a coral reef (1965).

pipped[1] adjective dated Angry, annoyed. 1914–. sunday star-times (Auckland) A devastated Peter Doig said last night credit cards, cash, and a mobile phone were stolen . . . 'We're a bit pipped about it to say the least' (2002). [Cf. *to have* (etc.) *the pip* at pip[1] noun.]

pipped[2] adjective dated Drunk, tipsy. 1911–29.

pipperoo noun US = pip[3] noun. 1934–. [From pip[3] noun + *-eroo*.]

pippin noun orig US Someone (or something) excellent; a beauty. 1897–. j. dos passos He . . . got a book from a man at the hotel. Gosh it was a pippin (1930). [From the name of the apple.]

pip-pip int dated 'Good-bye'. 1920–. g. sims The nine-day 'British Week' had ended. . . . Fisherman's Wharf had been buzzing with 'Cheerio, pip pip and smashin' voices (1973). [From the sound of a motor-horn at departure.]

pipsqueak noun **1** Someone (or something) contemptible or insignificant. 1910–. **2** dated military A small high-velocity shell. 1915–. a. g. empey Pip Squeak, Tommy's term for a small German shell which makes a 'pip' and then a 'squeak', when it comes over (1917). **3** A short, high-pitched sound; (the noise of) a car- or bicycle-horn. 1927–63. **4** dated military A radio transmitter used to establish an aeroplane's position. 1943–.

Pip, Squeak, and Wilfred noun phr. Any three persons or things; spec., the three British First World War medals 1914–15 Star, War Medal, and Victory Medal. 1937–. [From the names of three animal characters in a *Daily Mirror* children's comic strip.]

pirate Austral. verb trans. **1** To form a casual friendship with (someone) with a view to sexual intercourse. 1927–. n. keesing Who but a woman would complain that a man is a 'linen lifter', or is 'trying to pirate me' (1982). noun **2 on the pirate** looking for sexual partners.

pinky   pin-party   pin-splitter   pip   pipe   pippin

1946–. G. GELBIN They are on the pirate. We goes round St. Kilda and tries a few but we want three together (1964).

pisher noun US Someone who wets the bed; hence, a youth, a youngster; a mild term of abuse or contempt. Also as adjective. 1941–. J. CAINE First, they didn't wait to call you *pisher*; they just filled you up with bullet-holes like a matzo (1972). [From Yiddish *pisher*, one who urinates, from Middle High German *pissen*.]

piss verb **1a** intr. To urinate *c*.1300–. **b** To rain heavily; to pour *down*. 1948–. J. THOMSON Tucker wouldn't come . . . not with it pissing down with rain (1977). **c: to piss in** (someone's) **pocket** Austral To ingratiate oneself or be friendly with. 1967. **2 to piss away** to squander or fritter away (money, etc.). 1628–. P. KNAPP Dinty had built up a 'pretty good roll'. But as he now says with a shrug, 'I pissed it all away in Paris' (1972). **3 to piss oneself** to wet oneself; fig. to amuse oneself at another's expense; also, to show extreme annoyance. 1670–. N. COHN The Twist ballooned almost instantaneously from a fad to an industry. The papers pissed themselves. Big money got invested (1969). **4 to piss off: a** intr. To go away or leave (often in the imperative: *piss off!* 1922–. B. W. ALDISS I'll have a drink when I feel like it, and not before. You two piss off if you're so bloody thirsty! (1971) **b** trans. To annoy or irritate; to depress. Cf. PISSED adjective 2. 1945–. **5 to piss up** to spoil or ruin. Cf. PISS-UP noun 1. 1937–. **6 to piss about** (or **around**) to fool or mess about; to potter; also, to cause unnecessary problems for (someone). 1943–. [Ultimately (through French and Latin) from the sound.]

piss noun **1** Urine. 1386–. **2** The act(ion) of urinating. 1916–. **3 piss and wind** wild, blustering talk. 1922–. **4 piss and vinegar** energy, aggression. 1942–. **5 on the piss** on a bout of heavy drinking. 1942–. HORIZON Buggered if I know when he'll be back. Gone on the piss, I shouldn't wonder (1942). **6 to take the piss (out of)** to make fun of, 'take the mickey'. 1945–. R. HILL When Hope replied 'He's a Hungarian' he thought at first he was taking the piss. Wield seemed prepared to accept this as a serious contribution, however (1978). **7** As adverb (**piss-poor, piss-wet**, etc.), extremely (poor, etc.). 1940–. J. ANTOINE 'Here we are,' I said to Joe. 'On a piss-wet cliff and there's no bloody water for a brew!' (1974).

pissabed noun A bed-wetter. 1643–. R. FULLER He beat me at the beginning of term for peeing my bed. . . . Now he thinks of me as a pissabed (1959). [The word existed earlier

as a name for the dandelion, so called after its diuretic properties.]

piss-ant noun **1** Something (or someone) insignificant; also, as a term of abuse. 1935–. **2 drunk as a piss-ant** mainly Austral Extremely drunk. 1930–. **3 game as a piss-ant** mainly Austral Very brave or courageous. 1945–. verb intr. **4** Austral To mess *around*. 1945–. [Literally 'an ant', but influenced by PISS verb and noun.]

piss artist noun A drunkard; an extrovert or loud-mouthed fool, someone who messes about. 1974–. CUSTOM CAR I refer to the auto/ driver self-destruct mechanism known as 'booze'. A piss-artist behind the wheel of a 1935 Austin Seven was a killer (1977).

piss-cutter noun N Amer Someone (or something) excellent; a clever or crafty person. 1935–.

pissed adjective **1** Drunk, intoxicated. Also *pissed up*. 1889–. K. AMIS An uncle of mine went there a year or two ago and was pissed all the time on about ten bob a day (1958). **2** Annoyed; depressed. Usually *pissed off*. 1943–. **3 as pissed as a newt** extremely drunk. 1957–. R. MASON Christ, I'm pissed. I'm pissed as a newt (1957).

piss elegant adjective Extremely elegant; used ironically. 1991–. J. KEENAN 'What's he supposed to be like?' asked one. 'Very piss elegant,' said the young mimic. 'Stuck-up British chintz queen' (1991).

pisser noun **1** coarse The penis; also, the urethra; in phr. *to pull* (someone's) *pisser*, to pull (their) leg. 1901–. **2** orig US Someone (or something) extraordinary; a difficult or distasteful event, etc. Also simply, a bloke or fellow. 1918–.

piss-head noun A drunkard. 1946–.

piss-hole noun Somewhere unpleasant. 1966–.

pissing adjective **1** Insignificant, slight. 1937–. adverb **2** Extremely, 'bloody' (as an intensifier). 1951–. P. WAY 'Pissing awful weather,' said Don (1979).

pissing contest noun A competition to see who can urinate the furthest or highest; hence, more broadly, any futile or purposeless contest, esp. one aggressively pursued. 1961–. CULT TIMES By half way into the show's second season, there's still a bit of a pissing contest going on between Captain Hunt and himself (2002).

pisher   piss   pissabed   piss-ant   piss artist   pissed

piss-take noun A 'send-up' or parody; an instance of 'taking the mickey'. Also **piss-taker,** noun, etc. Cf. PISS noun 6. 1976–.

piss-up noun **1** A mess-up; a bungle or confusion. Cf. *to piss up* at PISS verb 2. 1950–69. **2** A bout of heavy drinking; also in phr. *(he) couldn't organize a piss-up in a brewery*, i.e. has feeble organizational abilities. 1950–.

pissy adjective coarse Of urine; fig. inferior, of poor quality, rubbishy. 1922–. M. AMIS You'll probably say this is rather . . . pissy, but babies are the only things women can have that men can't (1973).

pistol noun US Someone remarkable, esp. for reliability or strength of character; a 'brick'. 1935–. J. PHILLIPS What a pistol she was—still working at the dress shop then, hard as nails and took no truck from anyone (1984).

pit noun **1** A pocket. 1811–. D. W. MAURER The most important pocket in the coat from the pickpocket's point of view is the *coat pit*, or the inside breast pocket. . . . This is often shortened to *pit* (1955). **2** orig services' A bed, a bunk. 1948–. D. TINKER In our pits at night we always get rattled around a bit (1982). **3 the pits** orig US The worst or most despicable example of something. 1953–. OBSERVER I've never been fined for saying something obscene. It's always been for saying 'You're the pits,' or something.—John McEnroe (1981); J. FULLER Hey, give me a little comfort here. This weather is the pits (1985).

pixilated adjective orig US dialect Mildly insane or whimsical; confused; hence, intoxicated, tipsy. 1848–. C. NESBITT We were both ever so slightly inebriated, no not even that, pixilated, to use the lovely movie euphemism (1975). [From *pixy* and *-lated* as in *elated*, etc. (or perh. from *pixy-led*, led astray by pixies).]

pizzazz noun orig US Zest, vitality, or liveliness; showiness. 1937–. G. V. HIGGINS Maybe some guy that could recruit more troops and out-fund us gets involved in a bloodletting with another guy who has some pizzazz, and . . . they knock each other off (1975). [Origin unknown.]

place noun A lavatory. 1901–. J. JOYCE They did right to put him up over a urinal . . . Ought to be places for women (1922).

placer¹ noun Someone who deals in stolen goods; a fence. 1928–.

placer² noun Austral and NZ A sheep which remains in one place. 1921–. S. J. BAKER *Placers* are often lambs whose mothers have died and who have transferred their affection to some object, such as a bush or stone (1941).

plank-owner noun naval mainly US One of the original crew of a ship; a long-serving marine. 1901–. M. DIBNER He became her first gunnery officer as a 'plank-owner' . . . at her commissioning (1967).

plant verb trans. **1** To bury (a corpse). 1600–. J. GALSWORTHY 'Is he to be planted here?' 'I expect in the Cathedral, but father will know' (1931). **2a** To post as a spy. 1693–. **b** To hide (stolen goods, etc.) in order to mislead or incriminate the person who discovers them. 1699–. TIMES LITERARY SUPPLEMENT The nephew . . . sought to clinch the available, and misleading, evidence by planting the victim's dental plate on the spot (1930). noun **3a** A hoard of stolen goods; a hiding-place for people or goods; the objects hidden; spec. (a hiding-place for) the drugs or equipment used by an addict. 1785–. **b** Something 'planted' (see verb 2b), esp. to mislead or incriminate. 1916–. G. VAUGHAN 'Heroin!' the detective shouted. . . . Yardley had never seen the package before. . . . He said: 'That stuff's plant' (1978). **4** A carefully planned swindle or burglary. 1825–.

plaster verb trans. To bomb or shell heavily. 1914–. E. WAUGH The bombers were not aiming at any particular target; they were plastering the ground in front of their cars (1942).

plastered adjective Drunk; highly intoxicated. 1912–. N. MARSH He's overdone it tonight. Flat out in the old bar parlour . . . he was plastered (1964).

plate noun **1** pl. = PLATES OF MEAT noun. Feet. 1896–. P. BRANCH He . . . took off his shoes. 'Heaven!' he sighed. 'My plates have been quite, quite killing me' (1951). **2** US A gramophone record. Cf. PLATTER noun 2. 1935–. verb trans. and intr. **3** To practise fellatio or cunnilingus (on). Also **plating** noun. 1961–. K. LETTE I watched, immobilised by disgust, as he plated her (1987). [In sense 3, shortened from *plate of ham*,

> ## pixilated
> ### mildly insane or whimsical; confused; intoxicated, tipsy

piss-take piss-up pissy pistol pit pixilated place

rhyming slang for *gam*, a shortening of
GAMAHUCHE verb.]

plates of meat noun pl. Rhyming slang
for 'feet'. Cf. PLATE noun 1. 1887–. C. DAY LEWIS
'Your clodhopping feet.' 'Plates of meat,'
murmured Dick Cozzens, who is an expert in
slang (1948).

platter noun 1 pl. = PLATTERS OF MEAT noun.
1945–. 2 mainly US A gramophone record.
Cf. PLATE noun 2. 1926–. T. WELLS I went into
Fink Roth's pad and found treasures. Good
old platters and stamps. I sold them. Got a good
price for the records. The stamps were only
so-so (1967).

platters of meat noun pl. Rhyming
slang for 'feet'; less frequent than PLATES OF
MEAT noun. 1923–.

play verb 1 **to play hell with** to upset,
confuse; to alter for the worse. 1803–. LISTENER
Wingate and his Chindits would play hell with
the Japanese communications (1959). 2 **to play
ball** (**with**) to act fairly; to co-operate. 1903–.
L. A. G. STRONG You play ball with me, and I'll see
you don't regret it (1944). 3 **to play pussy** air
force To fly under cover in order to avoid
detection by another aircraft, etc. 1942–. 4 **to
play silly buggers** (or **bleeders, b-s**): to fool
about, to mess around. 1961–. GUARDIAN We
don't want people jeopardising our position by
playing silly bs (1979). noun orig US 5 **to make a
play for** to seek to acquire, esp. by a venture
or stratagem. 1905–. 6 Attention, publicity;
a show of interest. 1929–. J. O'HARA The Apollo
[hotel] got a big play from salesmen who had
their swindle sheets to think of (1935). [In sense
5, from the US sporting *play* manoeuvre.]

pleb noun One of the common people or
riff-raff; someone regarded contemptuously
as awkward or inferior. 1795–. A. HUXLEY 'A bit
of a pleb, wasn't he?' put in the military friend
(1928). Hence **plebby** adjective Also **plebbie**.
1962–. J. MCCLURE Portland Bill . . . all coach parties
and orange peel . . . It does tend to be a bit
plebbie (1977). [Abbreviation of *plebeian*.]

pledge noun US, colleges' A student who
has pledged to join a fraternity (or sorority).
1901–.

pleep noun military An enemy pilot who
refuses aerial combat. 1942–8. [Perhaps
onomatopoeic; 'echoic of a timorous young
bird' (E. Partridge, *A Dictionary of Forces' Slang*
1948).]

plenty adjective mainly US Excellent, fine.
1933–. R. P. SMITH When they want to say a man's

good, they say he plays plenty sax or plenty
drums (1941).

pling verb intr. and trans. US dated To beg
(from), to 'panhandle'. Also **plinging;
plinger,** noun A street-beggar. 1904–31.
[Of unknown origin.]

plink noun Austral Very low-quality wine.
1943–. HEPWORTH & HINDLE Plink is defined as being
cheap plonk (1980). [Jocular alteration of
PLONK[1] noun.]

plinker noun An airgun or other cheap,
low-calibre firearm. 1982–. SURVIVAL WEAPONRY
Lightweight back garden 'plinker' (1985). [From
plink to make a high-pitched sound + *-er*.]

plod noun Brit 1 Also **P.C. Plod**. A police
officer. 1977–. MAIL ON SUNDAY I might well have
pulled out the big hammer at the thought of
that distinguished plod, John Stalker, leading
a team consisting of Loyd Grossman, Fred
Housego and Peter Stringfellow in the
investigation of dodgy customer practices
(1991). 2 The police. 1986–. L. BRADLEY So far
so Miami Vice . . . until the plod learns that the
cartel's Mr. Big now enjoys US government
approval and is therefore untouchable (1993).
[Alluding to Mr *Plod* the Policeman in Enid
Blyton's *Noddy* stories for children.]

plonk[1] noun orig Austral Cheap or inferior
wine. 1933–. N. SHUTE He asked me if I would
drink tea or beer or plonk. 'Plonk?' I asked. 'Red
wine,' he said (1950). [Prob. from *blanc* in
French *vin blanc* white wine, though *plonk*
is perh. more commonly applied now to
red wine.]

plonk[2] noun RAF dated An aircraftman
second class. 1941–. [Of unknown origin.]

plonk[3] noun Brit, police derog A female police
officer. 1983–. [Origin uncertain; perh.
shortened from PLONKER noun.]

plonked adjective Drunk, intoxicated.
1943–. LIFE A few badly plonked soldiers blearily
unaware of just where they were (1943). [From
PLONK[1] noun.]

plonker noun 1 Austral, services' An explosive
shell. 1918–. 2 mainly Brit and Austral **a** A penis;
hence, **to pull** (someone's) **plonker**
to deceive someone humorously or playfully.
1949–. EMPIRE Mr. Jobsworth realises I'm pulling
his plonker and suggests I 'leave' (1995).
b A fool or half-wit. 1966–. H. SIMPSON You're
going to look a right plonker when the end of
the world *doesn't* come, aren't you? (2000).
[From the earlier dialect sense, anything
large or substantial of its kind.]

plates of meat   platter   platters of meat   play   pleb

plonko noun Austral Someone with a taste for 'plonk' or cheap (also poor) wine. 1963–.

ploot noun = PLUTE noun.

plot noun RAF A group of enemy aircraft as seen on a radar screen. 1943–59.

plotz verb intr. US **1** To burst; esp. fig. to 'explode' with frustration, etc. *c*.1920–. J. KRANTZ She came back to pick them up today and *plotzed* for joy all over the studio (1978). **2** To sit down wearily; to slouch or lounge (*around*). Also trans. 1941–. J. KIRKWOOD He just kind of plotzed around waiting to fall into some sort of a cushy job (1960). [From Yiddish *platsen*, from Middle High German *platzen* to burst, in sense 2 influenced by German *Platz* seat.]

plotzed adjective Drunk, intoxicated. 1962–. [Apparently from PLOTZ verb.]

plough verb trans. **1** Esp. of a man: to have sexual intercourse with. 1664–. J. PEARL Isn't that the broad Charlie Larkin plowed? (1964). **2** To fail (a candidate) in an examination; to fail (an exam). 1854–.

ploughed adjective Also **plowed.** mainly US Drunk. 1853–. G. V. HIGGINS I did not get drunk. . . . You and Frank did. You got absolutely plowed (1985).

pluck verb **to pluck a rose** dated, euphemistic Of a woman: to go to the lavatory; to urinate or defecate. 1613–.

pluck noun US, African-American Wine. 1904–. BLACK WORLD We was gittin away from the broke pluck bottles (1973). [From earlier sense, courage (cf. *Dutch courage* alcohol-fuelled courage).]

plug verb trans. **1** To shoot (a person). 1833–. G. GREENE Don't say a word or I'll plug you (1936). **2** To strike or hit; to punch. 1847–. P. G. WODEHOUSE Sidcup got a black eye. Somebody plugged him with a potato (1971). **3** To copulate with (a woman). 1888–. noun **4** mainly US **a** A poor or worn-out horse, a nag. 1860–. **b** A hopeless or incompetent person; also, a bloke, fellow. 1848–. **5** A book that sells badly. 1889–. PUBLISHER'S CIRCULAR Out of the vast number of publications issued, some must, indeed, turn out to be plugs (1928).

plug-ugly noun orig US A street ruffian; someone who adopts violent, intimidatory methods. Also as adjective. 1856–. PUNCH Readers who have led sheltered lives will think of plug-uglies, and I hope the cleaner kinds of plug-ugly will think of baths (1935). [Perh. from PLUG verb 4 and *ugly*.]

plumber noun **1** services' An armourer or engineering officer. 1941–. NAVY NEWS It would be a great help in this project if, among your readers, there were a few ex-Keyham 'plumbers' who would be prepared to turn out their photographs of those times for us to borrow (1979). **2** mainly US A person employed to investigate or prevent 'leaks' of information from a government office, department, etc. (orig applied to members of a White House special unit during the administration of Richard Nixon which investigated leaks of government secrets, and which was found to have been guilty of illegal practices, including bugging with concealed microphones). 1972–.

plum-pudding noun military A type of trench mortar shell. 1900–33.

plunk verb trans. **1** orig US To hit, shoot; to wound. 1888–. D. & H. TEILHET I wish you'd killed Jeff instead of plunking him in the leg (1937). noun **2** dated US A dollar. 1885–1940. P. G. WODEHOUSE Dere's a loidy here . . . dat's got a necklace of jools what's worth a hundred t'ousand plunks (1929). [*Plunk*, to pluck (a string), to propel suddenly, etc.]

pluperfect adjective Used euphemistically as an intensifier in oaths, etc. 1889–. E. CALDWELL What in the pluperfect hell have you boys got to fight about so much, anyhow? (1933). [Earlier sense 'more than perfect'.]

plurry /ˈplʌrɪ/ adjective Austral and NZ = BLOODY adjective. Cf. BLERRY adjective, PY KORRY int. 1900–. R. D. FINLAYSON It's right for Pakeha's to spout about Maori art but it won't help me to get manure for my plurry cow farm (1938). [Maori alteration of *bloody*.]

plute /pluːt/ noun Also **ploot.** mainly US Abbreviation of 'plutocrat'. Also **plutish** adjective. 1894–. DAILY MAIL 'The plutes', as he [Henry Ford] humorously nicknames the financial and industrial interests of the country, would never permit his nomination (1923).

po noun A chamber-pot. 1880–. [From French *pot* (*de chambre*).]

pocket billiards noun orig schoolboys' Playing with the testicles (cf. BALLS noun 1) with one's hands in one's trouser pockets, for masturbatory stimulation; often in phr. *to play pocket billiards.* 1940–. [From the earlier sense, a variety of snooker or pool.]

pocketbook noun US The female genitals. 1942–. M. ANGELOU Momma had drilled into my head: 'Keep your legs closed, and don't let nobody see your pocketbook' (1969).

plonko ploot plot plotz plotzed plough ploughed

pod noun **1** in pod pregnant. 1890–.
2 Marijuana. Cf. POT[2] noun. 1952–. W. BURROUGHS
A square wants to come on hip . . . Talks about
'pod', and smokes it now and then (1959).

poena /piːnə/ noun dated, schoolchildren's
An exercise given as punishment; an
imposition. 1842–1941. L. A. G. STRONG If you
were in disgrace he . . . helped you with your
poena and shooed you out of the empty
classroom (1941). [From Latin poena penalty.]

po-faced adjective Having a solemn or
humourless expression; poker-faced. 1934–.
[Prob. from PO noun, influenced by POKER-
FACED adjective.]

pogey /pəʊgɪ/ noun dated, N Amer **1** A hostel
or poor-house; a welfare office. 1891–.
2 Welfare relief for the needy;
unemployment benefit. 1954–. TIME Said
a jobless Hamilton steelworker, father of six
children: 'Why should I sweat for $40 a
week? I'm getting more than that from the
pogey, the welfare and the baby bonus (1961).
[Of unknown origin.]

pogey bait noun US Sweets, candy; a
snack. 1918–. [Perh. from pogy a North
American herring.]

poggle(d) adjective mainly military Crazy,
mad; also, drunk. Also **puggle(d).** 1923–. B. W.
ALDISS A woman in this bloody dump? You're
going puggle, Page, that's your trouble! Too
much tropical sun (1971). [From Hindustani
pāgal, paglā madman.]

pogo noun Austral An ineffectual or
incompetent man. 1972–. J. J. COE 'We're on
road clearing again . . . ' 'What about bloody
7 section doing it . . . ?' 'Yeah, bloody pogos'
(1982). [Shortened from pogo stick, rhyming
slang for PRICK noun 2.]

pogue[1] /pəʊg/ noun A bag or purse;
a wallet; also, money. 1819–. M. CRICHTON It was
the stickman's job to take the pogue once Teddy
had snaffled it, thus leaving Teddy clean,
should . . . a constable stop him (1975). [Perh.
related to pough, an old word for 'bag';
cf. also POKE[2] noun.]

pogue[2] noun US, military derog **1** A
non-combatant soldier, esp. one assigned
administrative and supply duties. 1952–.
2 A (young) male homosexual, esp. one
who takes the passive role in a sexual
relationship. 1953–. A. THEROUX A 'green
boy' for homosexuals, is a pretty boy, a pogue,
candy pants, a young brat (1996). [Origin
uncertain; perh. from POGEY BAIT noun.]

poilu /pwaːluː/ noun A French soldier,
esp. in World War I. 1914–. J. DOS PASSOS
The Boche . . . scattered a few salvoes of
artillery . . . just to keep the poilus on their toes
(1966). [French, = 'hairy, virile'.]

poindexter noun US An over-industrious
student, esp. a socially inept one; a swot or
nerd. 1981–. [From a character so named
in the US television animated-cartoon series
Felix the Cat (1959), who was a genius but
spoke impenetrable jargon; he in turn is said
to have been based on Emmett Poindexter,
attorney for the creator of the series.]

pointy-head noun US, derog An
intellectual or 'boffin'; an expert. Also
pointy-headed, adjective. 1968–.

poison noun orig US Alcoholic liquor; an
alcoholic drink; esp. in phrs. to name one's
poison and What's your poison? 1805–. M. TWAIN
In Washoe, when you are . . . invited to take
'your regular poison', etiquette admonishes you
to touch glasses (1866).

poisoner noun Austral and NZ, jocular A cook,
esp. on a sheep (cattle, etc.) station. 1905–.
L. HADOW I'm not much good at cooking but I'll
try.' 'Never you mind about that. Up north
we've got the best poisoners in the country'
(1969).

poke[1] noun **1a** A punch or blow with the
fist, esp. in phr. to take a poke at. 1690–.
**b: better than a poke in the eye with
a burnt stick** (etc.): i.e. just desirable. 1852–.
G. ELIOT 'Then,' he said . . . 'Here are those "Letters
from Ireland" which I hope will be something
better than a poke in the eye' (1852). **2** An
act of sexual intercourse; a woman considered
as an object of this. 1902–. H. C. RAE 'Caroline',
said Derek . . . 'wouldn't make a good poke for
a blind hunchback' (1968). **3** Power, esp.
horsepower. 1965–. verb trans. **4** Of a man:
to copulate with (a woman). Also intr. and
poking, noun. 1868–. J. BRAINE I wanted to poke
Lucy so I poked her (1962). **5** To communicate
with (someone not personally known to you)
on an internet social network in order to
gain their attention. 2007–. GUARDIAN If you
haven't been poked or written on someone's
wall today, then the chances are you are not on
Facebook (2007).

poke[2] noun **1** N Amer A purse or wallet.
1859–. **2** A roll of bank-notes, money. 1926–.
L. J. CUNLIFFE It's a very satisfying feeling knowing
you can put your finger on a bit of poke. (Which
is more slang for money: get it, poke, loot,
poppy—any of them will do!) (1965). [Earlier

pod poena po-faced pogey pogey bait poggle pogo

(esp. in dialect) a bag or small sack, as in *to buy a pig in a poke*.]

poke-out noun A bag of food given to a beggar. 1894–.

poker-faced adjective = PO-FACED adjective. 1915–. [From the expressionless or inscrutable face characteristic of a poker-player.]

pokey[1] noun mainly US A prison or gaol. 1919–. NATIONAL OBSERVER Were it possible to prosecute an actor for stealing scenes, *The Missouri Breaks* (United Artists) would land Marlon Brando in the pokey for life (1976). [From POGEY noun, perh. influenced by *poky* cramped, confined.]

pokey[2] noun Also **pokie**. Austral A 'poker-machine'; a one-armed bandit with card symbols. 1965–.

pol noun N Amer Abbreviation of 'politician'. 1907–. J. CARROLL What had he become? A two-bit pol, flashing about other people's corridors, waiting for his break (1978).

Polack /ˈpəʊlək, -læk, -lɑːk/ noun mainly derog A Polish immigrant; someone of Polish descent. Also as adjective. 1898–. [Ultimately from Polish *Polak* a Pole.]

polari noun Also **polare, palarey, palare, palari.** orig and mainly Brit **1** Talk, chatter. 1846–. K. WILLIAMS We walked right into Dennis 'My dear I know Danny La Rue terribly well . . . & introduced Tennessee Williams to loads of trade' etc. etc. & so we got landed with the round of drinks and the polari (1967). verb intr. **2** To talk, esp. in Polari (an argot of male homosexuals, derived from the maritime Lingua Franca of the Mediterranean) or slang. 1846–. GAY NEWS In the bar we could stand around polarying with our sisters (1977). [From Italian *parlare* to speak.]

pole noun **1** up the (also **a**) **pole** in trouble or difficulty; drunk, crazy; pregnant (and unmarried). 1896–. J. JOYCE That red Carlisle girl, Lily . . . Spooning with him last night on the pier. The father is rotto with money.—Is she up the pole?—Better ask Seymour that (1922). verb intr. **2** Austral To take advantage of someone; to impose or sponge *on*. 1906–.

poler noun Austral A cadger or sponger; someone who shirks work. 1938–. [See POLE verb 2.]

polis /pɒlɪs, ˈpəʊlɪs/ noun mainly Irish and Scottish The police; a member (or members) of the police force. 1833–. H. CALVIN 'But I'll have to get on to the police,' I protested,

and Jumbo . . . pointed to Eddie Bone and said: 'He's a polis. Get on to him' (1967). [Represents regional pronunciation of *police*.]

politricks noun mainly Jamaican English Politics, regarded as being characterized by dishonesty or self-interest. 1908–. [Blend of *politics* and *trick*.]

polluted adjective orig US Drunk; under the influence of drugs. 1900–. P. G. WODEHOUSE I was helping a pal to celebrate the happy conclusion of love's young dream, and it might be that I became a mite polluted (1974).

Polly[1] noun dated Abbreviation of 'Apollinaris', an effervescent mineral water from Apollinarisburg in the Rhineland; a bottle or glass of this. 1878–. D. KYLE 'Soda? Apollinaris?' 'Whisky and Polly. . . . I haven't had one in years.' 'It becomes increasingly difficult to come by' (1973).

polly[2] noun US and Austral Abbreviation of 'politician'. Cf. POL noun. 1932–.

polone, polony variants of PALONE noun.

pom noun and adjective Also **Pom.** mainly Austral and NZ Abbreviation of POMMY noun and adjective 1912–. A. LUBBOCK Be seein' yer soon in England . . . Good on yer, Pom (1963).

pommy Also **Pommie, pommie, Pommy.** Austral and NZ, but well-known generally. noun **1** A somewhat derogatory term for a British person, esp. a recent immigrant. 1913–. J. GALSWORTHY They call us Pommies and treat us as if we'd took a liberty in coming to their blooming country (1926). adjective **2** British, English. Often (at times affectionately) in phr. *Pommy bastard.* 1913–. [An alteration of *pomegranate* after *immigrant* (an intermediate form is JIMMY GRANT noun): see also POM noun and adjective.]

Pompey noun A nickname for the town and dockyards at Portsmouth, and specifically for Portsmouth Football Club. 1899–. C. S. FORESTER The grim wife he had in Pompey (1943). [Alteration of *Portsmouth*, perh. influenced by the name of the Roman general.]

pom-pom noun US, orig military Sexual intercourse, esp. with a prostitute; also in phr. *to make pom-pom.* Also, the female genitalia. 1945–. Q There's nough pom-pom for everybody tonight. It's going to be raining sex I can smell it (1997). [Perh. from a Pidgin English word for 'sexual intercourse' derived from an Austronesian language.]

poke-out   poker-faced   pokey   pol   Polack   polari

pooh

ponce noun **1** A man who lives off prostitutes' earnings; a pimp. 1859–. G. GREER The role of the ponce . . . is too established for us to suppose that prostitutes have found a self-regulating lifestyle (1970). **2** A male homosexual; a lazy or effeminate man. Now often just a vague term of abuse. 1932–. K. AMIS As if I'd have said a word in front of that little ponce (1953). verb **3** intr. To act or behave like a ponce; also figuratively, to sponge (on) or take advantage (of); usu. *to ponce on* or *off* (someone). 1932–. C. MACINNES Best of all . . . is poncing on some woman (1957). **4 to ponce about** to act in an effeminate manner; to fool about. 1947–. **5 to ponce up** to make effeminate, to 'tart' up. 1953–. Hence **poncey, poncy**, adjective Like a ponce, effete, homosexual. 1958–. M. AMIS You haven't half got ponce mates (1973). [Perh. derived from to *pounce* or spring upon someone. This is at least supported by the spelling of an early related word in Mayhew's *London Labour* (1861): The 'pounceys', (the class I have alluded to as fancy-men, called 'pounceys' by my present informant). Webster's dictionary (1961) marks 'ponce' as Brit slang.]

pond noun now mainly US The sea, esp. the North Atlantic Ocean; **on this** (or **the other**) **side of the pond** in Great Britain, or North America. Also, **the big pond** (see also PUDDLE noun). 1612– (and particularly as slang since the early 19th cent.). H. D. THOREAU It is but a step from the glassy surface of the Herring Pond to the big Atlantic Pond where the waves never cease to break (1864).

Pong noun Austral, derog and offensive A Chinese person. 1906–. B. MATHER I'm the only Pong I know who wouldn't say Charling Closs (1970). [Prob. a mixture of *pong* 'stink' with Chinese surnames such as *Wong*.]

pongo /ˈpɒŋgəʊ/ noun **1** naval A sailor; also, a soldier. 1917–. DAILY MAIL Fourteen youths . . . went out looking for soldiers to beat up. . . . Favourite expressions of the gang were 'squaddy bashing' and 'pongo bashing' (1977). **2** Austral and NZ An Englishman. 1942–. **3** military An Army officer. 1943–.

pontoon noun mainly criminals' A prison sentence of twenty-one months. 1948–. E. CRISPIN He had been put away three times . . . the third for a pontoon (1977). [From the name of the card-game *pontoon* or vingt-et-un (French for 'twenty-one').]

pony noun **1** A small glass or measure of alcoholic liquor. 1709–. G. HAMILTON Os pulled a beer each for me and Tommy, and a pony for

himself (1959). **2** Twenty-five pounds sterling. 1797–. J. O'CONNOR 'Bet you the next three guys that come by do that,' he said. 'Make it a pony (£25),' said Charlie (1976). **3** A schoolboy's crib, esp. for classical translation. 1827–. **4** mainly US A racehorse; usu. in pl. 1900–. **5** Brit **a** Faeces; also, an act of defecating. 1931–. **b** Nonsense, rubbish. 1956–. J. SULLIVAN You're not gonna believe all that old pony are you? (1989). verb intr. and trans. **6 to pony up** to pay or settle up. 1824–. NEW REPUBLIC The State Department and White House again pressured the Agriculture Department to pony up the other half (1992). **7** To prepare (a lesson, text, etc.) by means of a pony or crib; also, to memorize, plagiarize. 1847–. [In sense 2, perh. because (like a pony to a horse) it is small compared with £50, etc.; in sense 5, short for *pony and trap*, rhyming slang for 'crap'.]

pooch noun orig US A dog, a mongrel. 1908–. [Of unknown origin.]

poodle-faker noun mainly services' Someone who cultivates female society, esp. for professional advancement; a lady's man; also, a new, young officer. Also **poodle-faking**, noun and adjective. 1902–. J. PORTER There's some blooming Parisian couturier coming to see her. . . . To hear her talk you'd think a bunch of corn slicers and foreign poodle-fakers was more important than solving the crime of the century (1977). [From the idea of fawning to be petted, like a poodle or lap-dog.]

poof /pʊf, puːf/ Also **pouf(f)**, etc., and **poove** /puːv/. noun **1** An effeminate person; a male homosexual, someone who acts like one. ?1855–. A. RICHARDS A young man . . . had been heard in the showers to refer to Elgar as 'a bit of a pouf' (1976). Hence **poufy**, adjective. verb intr. **2** To act like a poof. Also **poofed-up, pooved-up**, adjective. 1964–. [Prob. alteration of *puff* braggart.]

poofter /ˈpʊftə(r), ˈpuːftə(r)/ noun Also **pooftah**, etc. mainly Austral A homosexual or 'poof'; an effeminate man; also as a general term of abuse. Also **poofteroo**. 1889–. I. FLEMING 'You pommy poofter.' . . . Bond smiled mildly, 'What's a poofter?' 'What you'd call a pansy' (1964). [Extension of POOF noun.]

poofter rorter noun Austral A homosexual's pimp or procurer. 1945–.

pooh noun Also **poo. in the pooh** in a difficult situation, in trouble. 1961–. J. MCCLURE 'But what . . . if someone . . . gave him the money and support he needed?' 'We might be right in the poo' (1976). [From children's use of *pooh* = excrement.]

ponce   pond   Pong   pongo   pontoon   pony   pooch   poof

pool verb trans. Austral To implicate or involve (a person) against his will; to inform on. 1907–. K. TENNANT A man thought he'd do the decent thing and tide a girl over a patch of trouble, and she pools him every time. You can't prove it isn't your kid (1967).

poon¹ /puːn/ noun mainly Austral Someone foolish, a simpleton; esp. someone living alone in the outback. 1940–. D. WILLIAMSON What possessed Keren to shack up with a poon like you? (1974). [Of unknown origin.]

poon² /puːn/ noun Abbreviation of POONTANG noun. 1947–.

poon /puːn/ verb trans. **to poon up** Austral To dress, esp. showily or flashily. 1943–.

poontang /puːntæŋ/ noun Sexual intercourse; women (or a woman) as objects of this. 1927–. R. CONDON Every now and then I think about you coming all the way to Korea from New Jersey to get your first piece of poontang (1959). [Prob. from French *putain* prostitute.]

poop¹ noun orig children's An act of breaking wind or of defecation; faeces. 1888–.

poop² noun Someone foolish or ineffectual; a bore. 1893–. R. DENTRY Those bloody stupid Yankee poops blew the panic whistle and the whole shebang went sky-high (1971). [Perh. abbreviation of *nincompoop*.]

poop³ noun mainly US Up-to-date information; 'gen', 'low-down'. 1911–. [Of unknown origin.]

poop verb orig US **1** intr. Of a machine, etc.: to break down. 1927–. **2** To tire or exhaust; often with *out*. Mainly as **pooped,** adjective. 1931–.

pooper-scooper noun Also **poop-scoop.** A small shovel carried to clear up (a dog's) faeces from the street, etc. 1956–.

poop-ornament noun dated, naval A ship's apprentice. 1902–34.

poop-sheet noun mainly US A written notice, report, etc. 1928–. M. ALLEN He sends in a report—straight facts, no frills, and a minimum use of adjectives. What he says is included in the mimeographed poop sheet the organization sends out every month (1974). [See POOP³ noun.]

poopsie noun Also **poopsy.** US A term of endearment for a sweetheart, baby, or small child; also, a girlfriend. 1937–. S. KAUFFMANN

Perry finished and hung up. 'Hiya, poopsie,' he called. 'Have a hotsy-totsy week-end?' (1952). [Cf. POPSY noun.]

poop-stick noun dated A fool; someone ineffectual. 1930–2. P. MACDONALD 'You make me sick!' he said. 'Let a little poop-stick like that walk all over you!' (1932).

poopy¹ adjective mainly US Resembling a 'poop'; stuffy, fuddy-duddy; ineffectual. 1957–. WASHINGTON POST My first serve is hard when it goes in, but my second one is so poopy Granny could return it (1980). [From POOP² noun + -y.]

poopy² noun **1** Also **poopie.** mainly children's. Excrement. Also int, expressing mild annoyance. 1970–. SUNDAY MAIL MAGAZINE (Brisbane): 'You can't kill me, I'm your best friend.' 'Oh poopies' (1987). adjective **2** Frightened, nervous; cf. SHIT-SCARED adjective. 1963–. A. FUGARD Come on. Confess. You were scared, hey! A little bit poopy (1963). **3** US Soiled with excrement. 1983–. [From POOP¹ noun + -y.]

pooper-scooper
a small shovel
carried to clear
up a dog's
faeces

poopy suit noun US military A one-piece garment providing protection for the whole body against the cold, wet, etc. 1953–. [Prob. from POOPY² adjective, perh. alluding to the smell when the garment has been worn for a long time, or to the noises made when removing it.]

poove noun and verb = POOF noun and verb.

pop verb **1** trans. To pawn (an article); to put in pledge. 1731–. **2 to pop off** intr. To die; also trans., to kill or destroy, and without *off*. 1764–. G. S. GORDON I have joined the Defence Volunteers, and hope to pop a parachutist before the business ends (1940). **3** intr. US To pay (for a meal, etc.). 1947–. **4** trans. To take (a narcotic drug); to inject a drug into (the bloodstream); also intr. 1952–. M. WOODHOUSE For him the day . . . started when he swallowed the first pill or popped the first vein (1968). noun **5** The act of pawning something; **in pop,** in pledge. 1819–. **6** An injection of a narcotic drug. 1935–. N. MARSH I'm not hooked. Just the odd pop. Only a fun thing (1970).

poppa stoppa noun US, African-American An elderly man, esp. one who is smart or effective. 1944–. [Rhyming form on *poppa* father.]

pool   poon   poontang   poop   poop-sheet   poove

popped adjective US Arrested or caught by the police. 1960–.

popper noun **1** One who takes drugs, esp. in pill form. 1967–. **2** orig US A capsule of amyl or (iso)butyl nitrite, taken esp. as a stimulant; also, a container of the drug. 1967–. R. SILVERBERG She closed the door behind him and looked about for something to offer him, a drink, a popper, anything to calm him (1985). [From POP verb 4 + -er. The capsule in sense 2 is typically crushed or 'popped', and the drug taken by inhalation.]

poppy noun **1** Opium. 1935–. **2** Money. 1943–. AUTOCAR A good many British families which run their own cars must spend at least 13 per cent of the family poppy on that (1963). [In sense 1, a revival of an older non-slang use.]

poppycock noun orig US Nonsense, 'rubbish', 'balderdash'. 1852–. [From Dutch dialect *pappekak* soft excrement.]

pops noun **1** A father. 1928–. S. HARVESTER Me a defenceless girl . . . without my Mom and Pops (1976). **2** orig jazz musicians' A term of address to a man. 1944–. R.D. BOYER The other card players looked over and in succession asked, 'How's it going, Pops?' 'Getting anywhere, Sandhead?' and 'You sending 'em, Fatso?' (1944). [A variant of *pop* noun father.]

pop-shop noun A pawn-shop. Cf. POP verb 1. 1772–. P. G. WODEHOUSE This makes me feel like a pawnbroker. . . . As if you had brought it in to the old pop shop and were asking me what I could spring on it (1942).

popskull noun N Amer A strong or poor liquor; inferior whisky. 1865–.

popsy noun Also **popsie**. (A term of endearment for) a young woman or girl; a girl-friend. 1855–. C. LITHGOW Chase me, you fast women; ginger yourselves up, you slow 'uns! . . . Lord, but I *like* a good popsy (1931).

pork noun US Federal funds obtained through political influence. Cf. PORK BARREL noun. 1879–.

pork verb orig US **1** intr. **a: to pork up** to gain weight. 1967–. **b: to pork out** to eat gluttonously, gorge oneself. 1979–. J. COPE We porked out on home-made chocolate chip cookies and sweet apple pies (1999). **2** intr. and trans. To have sexual intercourse (with). 1968–. TOTAL FILM Getting in lots of brawls, swashing buckles and porking chambermaids (2002). **3** trans. **to pork up** US politics to load (a federal spending bill, etc.) with usu.

unnecessary items intended to direct funds towards favoured districts or causes. 1987–. [In sense 3, from PORK noun.] Hence **porking**, noun (An act or instance of) sexual intercourse. 1988–. M. AMIS The rough stuff shrinks to insignificance compared to the five-star porking he gave her earlier (2003).

pork barrel noun mainly US The state's financial resources for regional expenditure; esp. (US) funds obtained by political influence. 1873–.

pork chop noun US An African-American who accepts a position of inferiority to whites. 1968–. [From the notion of pork as a food eaten by non-Muslims.]

pork-chopper noun US A full-time union official (esp. used derogatorily by rank-and-file members). 1946–.

pork pie noun Brit Rhyming slang for 'lie'. Also **porkie, porky**. 1973–. OBSERVER The word 'porkie' was deemed unparliamentary last week. and thus no longer a proper word to be used in the Commons (1992).

pornie noun A pornographic film. 1965–.

porny adjective Of or relating to pornography; pornographic. 1961–.

porpoise noun services' A steep dive by a submarine, esp. in phr. *doing a porpoise*; also, a bumpy sea-landing by an aeroplane. 1929–.

porridge noun Brit A prison sentence or term of imprisonment. 1950–. E. CRISPIN His emotions at the prospect . . . of yet another dose of porridge were such that he was . . . incapable of thinking clearly (1977). [Perh. influenced (punningly) by the earlier STIR noun, and by conventional prison food.]

Portuguese parliament noun naval A noisy discussion when 'everybody talks and nobody listens' (W. Granville, *A Dictionary of Sailors' Slang* 1962); a hubbub. 1897–.

posh adjective **1** Smart, classy; stylish, first-rate; also, socially superior (rather derog). 1918–. K. AMIS This railway . . . though posher and faster, had often reminded him of the tram-like train (1958). verb trans. **2 to posh up** to smarten up or make 'posh'. 1919–. [Perh. related to the older noun *posh* money, a dandy: apparently nothing to do with 'port out, starboard home', of cabins on the sea-passage between England and India.]

popped popper poppy poppycock pops pop-shop pork

posse /pɒsiː/ noun orig Jamaican English A gang of black (esp. Jamaican) youths involved in organized or violent crime, often drug-related. 1986–. BOSTON Enforcement agents blame Jamaican posses for some 500 homicides and . . . gun-running (1987). [From earlier sense, body of men summoned by a sheriff, etc. to enforce the law.]

possie /pɒzi/ noun Also **pozzy,** etc. mainly Austral and NZ A position or location, esp. a military position; an occupation or appointment. 1915–. D. M. DAVIN 'I've brought a picnic,' he said. 'So you watch out for a nice little pozzy while a good husband keeps his eyes on the road' (1956). [Abbreviation of *position*.]

possum noun Austral A person of the stated sort; also used as a term of address. 1894–. R. HALL Goodness what an ugly little possum you've turned into (1982). [From earlier sense, small marsupial.]

post noun Abbreviation of 'post-mortem'; an autopsy. As verb trans., to perform an autopsy on (someone). 1942–.

postal adjective **to go postal** US to behave violently or frenziedly, esp. as a result of stress; hence, more broadly, to get very angry, fly into a rage. 1993–. NEW YORKER A man two seats away 'went postal' when the battery on his cell phone gave out. A heavyset passenger had to sit on the man until the train finally pulled into Grand Central (1999). [Inspired by several incidents in which employees of the U.S. Postal Service shot at colleagues.]

postie noun Also **posty.** A postman. 1871–. TAFFRAIL The marine postman . . . was delayed. . . . ''Ere, posty!' shouted some one, 'got my *Dispatch?*' (1916).

postil(l)ion verb trans. To stimulate (a sexual partner) anally with the finger. 1880–.

post office noun Someone who passes on or holds for collection information, esp. in espionage; a safe hiding-place for secret information left for collection, a 'drop'. 1885–. D. WILLIAMS It became evident in 1911 that the hairdresser's shop of Karl Gustav Ernst was being used as a 'post office' or clearing-house for German espionage agents in this country (1965).

pot[1] noun **1 to put** (someone's) **pot on** Austral and NZ To inform against or tell tales about; to ruin (someone's) chances. 1864–. DAVISON & NICHOLLS He saw some blacks . . . standing on the platform under guard of a policeman. 'Hullo, what's up?' One of them replied, 'Aw,

somebody's been putting our pot on' (1935). **2** A prize or trophy. 1885–. **3** mainly services' An aircraft cylinder; a carburettor. 1941–. verb trans. **4** Austral To hand (someone) over for trial; to inform on. 1911–. See also **shit or get off the pot** at SHIT verb.

pot[2] noun Marijuana. 1938–. T. PYNCHON 'But we don't repeat what we hear,' said another girl. 'None of us smoke Beaconfields anyway. We're all on pot' (1966). [Prob. from Mexican Spanish *potiguaya* marijuana leaves.]

pot and pan noun Rhyming slang for 'old man', one's father or husband. 1906–.

potato noun **1** dated The real thing; something correct or excellent; often in phr. *not (quite) the clean potato*. 1822–. M. FRANKLIN She was the only great-granddaughter of old Larry Healey of Little River, none so clean a potato, if rumour was correct (1931). **2** pl. US Money; also, dollars, or pounds. 1931–. **3** Austral A girl or woman. 1957–. G. GREER Terms . . . often extended to the female herself. . . . Who likes to be called . . . a *potato*? (1970). [In sense 3, short for *potato peeler*, rhyming slang for 'sheila'.] See also COUCH POTATO noun.

pot-head noun A habitual pot-smoker; someone addicted to smoking marijuana. Cf. POT[2] noun. 1957–.

potsy noun North-eastern US The badge of office worn by a policeman or fireman. 1932–. NEW YORK HERALD TRIBUNE This boniface has been wearing his potsy as house dick for only a brief time (1952). [From (the name of a squashed tin thrown instead of a stone in) a game similar to hopscotch.]

potted adjective **1** N Amer Drunk, intoxicated. 1922–. **2** US Under the influence of 'pot' or marijuana. 1959–.

POTUS noun Also **Potus.** US The President of the United States. 1903–. NEW SCIENTIST The Potus showed up, spoke, no one threw up or passed out, and all the NIH officials clapped themselves on the back for a job well done (1999). [Acronym.]

potzer variant of PATZER noun.

poule /puːl/ noun A (promiscuous) young woman or girl; **poule-de-luxe** /-də luːks/, a prostitute. 1926–. J. B. PRIESTLEY He is probably amusing himself somewhere with that little brown poule of his (1949). [French, 'hen'.]

poultice noun Austral **1** A (large) sum of money; a bribe. 1902–. **2** A mortgage. 1932–. K. S. PRICHARD Mick Mallane . . . sayin' if the bank wanted his farm, poultice or no poultice, it'd have to go out and take it from him, and he'd be waitin' for 'm with his gun loaded (1932).

pound verb **to pound (one's) ear** orig US To sleep. 1894–1947. M. WALSH 'Only just awakened,' I admitted . . . 'and how are my comrades in misfortune?' . . . 'Still pounding their ears, no doubt' (1926).

pound noun **1** dated, naval **pound and pint** a sailor's ration (according to Board of Trade regulations); **pound and pinter** a ship on which this was served. 1865–. **2** US A sum of five dollars; a five-dollar bill. 1928–.

pounder noun **1** US A policeman or detective; a patrolman. 1919–. **2** surfing A large breaker. 1927–.

pound-noteish adjective Affected or pompous. 1936–. W. H. AUDEN When we get pound-noteish . . . send us some deflating Image (1966).

pour verb **to pour (on) the coal** to cause an aircraft to accelerate; to pilot an aircraft at high speed; hence, to drive very fast. 1937–. J. M. FOSTER He poured the coal to his plane and banked to avoid passing too close (1961).

pow int orig US Representing the sound of a punch, blow, shot, etc.; also used to denote the impact of an emotion or idea. 1881–. G. GREER Perhaps they will not fall in love all at once but feel a tenderness growing until one day *pow!* that amazing kiss (1970). [Imitative.]

powder noun **to take a powder** mainly US To depart hastily, to abscond. 1916–.

pox noun **1** Venereal disease, esp. syphilis. 1503–. J. O'CONNOR Wally . . . strangled a prostitute for giving him a dose of the pox (1976). verb **2** To infect with venereal disease. Also fig, to spoil or affect adversely; to ruin, etc. 1601–. G. F. NEWMAN The car became expedient. He was poxed with running for trains, missing trains, and worse, catching trains crowded with sickly commuters (1970). [Altered plural of *pock*, spot or pustule.]

pox-doctor noun A doctor specializing in venereal diseases; esp. fig in phr. *got up like a pox-doctor's clerk*, etc.: i.e. overdressed, smartly but in bad taste. 1680–. E. LAMBERT They was all dressed like they was at Buckingham Palace and Foran was done up like a pox doctor's clerk (1965).

poxy adjective Infected with pox; fig. worthless. Also as a general term of abuse. *a.*1758–. M. PEAKE Every poxy sunrise of the year, eh, that you burst out of the decent darkness in that plucked way? (1950).

prad noun now Austral A horse. 1703–. [By metathesis from Dutch *paard*.]

prang orig RAF. verb **1** trans. **a** To crash(-land) (an aircraft); to damage (part of a plane) during a crash-landing. 1941–. N. SHUTE After so many operations it was an acute personal grief to him that he had pranged his Wimpey (1944). **b** To bomb (a target) successfully from the air. 1941–. **c** To crash (a road vehicle, etc.); to collide with. 1952–. A. MANN Most of them don't drive. . . . If they prang a car, there's always plenty of witnesses to say it's the priest's fault (1973). **2** intr. To crash(-land) an aircraft. 1943–. **3** trans. To break, to smash into; to damage, injure. 1942–. NEW YORKER There was a new tear, with a smeary stain, in one knee of his trousers. 'Pranged my leg,' Burgess said (1995). noun **4** A crash-landing; an accident or 'smash-up'. 1942–. J. LE FANU My problem may be due to damage . . . following a slight prang in the car (2001). **5** A bombing-raid; often in phr. *wizard prang* (often used as a general expression of enthusiastic approval). 1943–. [Of uncertain origin; perh. from the sound of a crash.]

prat noun **1** orig criminals' The backside; formerly in pl., a buttock. 1567–. D. DELMAN I'm a *shmo* about tennis, so if I fall on my prat a time or two you have to bear with me (1972). **2** US, criminals' A hip-pocket. 1908–. **3** A fool or 'jerk'. 1968–. verb **4** intr. To fool *about*; to act in a silly or annoying way. 1961–. [Of unknown origin.]

prat digger noun US A pick-pocket. Also **prat-digging**, noun. 1908–55.

pratfall mainly N Amer. noun **1** theatrical A comedy fall (on to the buttocks). 1939–. **2** An unfortunate set-back; a humiliating failure. 1941–. D. KARP That gentleman is in for a rude surprise some morning soon. I understand he handles government contracts. Another pratfall soon (1956). verb intr. **3** To fall on to the buttocks. 1940–. [From PRAT noun 1.]

prat kick noun dated, US A hip-pocket. 1896–1955. [See KICK noun 3.]

prat leather noun dated, US A wallet kept in the hip-pocket. Also **prat poke**. 1908–39.

prawn noun Austral A fool; also as a generalized term of contempt. 1893–. L. GLOSSOP What an odious prawn this Anderson is, I thought (1944). See also RAW PRAWN noun.

prayer noun **not to have (got) a prayer** To have no chance at all. 1924–. A. ROSS He went for me. . . . He was a big lad, and strong, but he didn't have a prayer. An amateur up against a professional almost never does (1973).

preem US. noun **1** A theatrical premiere; a first showing of a film, etc. 1936–. VARIETY The mother-daughter act . . . has been bought by ABC and set for an Oct. 4 preem (1948). verb **2** To premiere (a play, film, etc.). 1937–.

preemie noun Also **premie, premy.** N Amer A premature birth; a baby born prematurely. 1927–.

preg adjective Abbreviation of 'Pregnant'. 1927–. E. O'BRIEN Are you preg? . . . 'Cos if you are, you won't be able to cycle (1962).

preggers adjective Brit Pregnant. 1942–. M. DICKENS Let anyone mention in her hearing that they felt sick, and it would be all over the hospital that they were 'preggers' (1942). [Abbreviation of pregnant, + -ers, as in bonkers, crackers, etc.]

preggo adjective Austral = PREGGERS adjective. Also as noun, a pregnant woman. 1951–. P. WHITE 'Can't resist the bananas.' 'Yeah. They say you go for them like one thing when you're preggo' (1965).

preggy adjective = PREGGERS adjective. 1938–.

prejudice noun US, espionage In phr. to terminate (dismiss, etc.) with extreme prejudice: to kill or assassinate (someone). 1969–.

prep verb **1** trans. orig US To prepare (a person or thing); esp. to train (a race-horse) or to prime (a witness); also, to prepare (a patient) for an operation. 1894–. BOSTON SUNDAY HERALD Anyone planning to enter greyhound racing should know it costs close to $600 to prep each dog for the races (1967). **2** intr. US To prepare oneself for an event, etc., esp. in sport. 1900–. [The noun prep is used colloquially in the senses 'preparatory school-work', 'homework', 'a preparatory horse-race', etc.]

prepper noun **1** US (A member of) a preparatory sports team. 1922–. **2** A preparatory or 'prep' school. 1956–. R. GORDON 'Actually, I'm a stinks beak in a prepper,' he confessed (1962).

preppy US. adjective **1** (Characteristic) of a student in a preparatory school; immature. Esp. of clothes, etc.: fashionably smart, like a student's uniform. 1900–. noun **2** A pupil at a preparatory school; someone who dresses in a 'preppy' style. 1956–.

press verb **to press the flesh** orig US To greet by physical contact; spec to shake hands. 1918–. TIME Aides had to coax him into playing

fewer tennis matches with celebrities . . . and spending more time pressing the flesh (1977).

pretty-boy noun An effeminate man, a male homosexual. Ironically, a thing. Also as adjective. 1835–. P. DE VRIES You're not cross-eyed . . . and your ears are pasted on straight. Not any pretty-boy, but probably photogenic (1974).

pretzel noun jazz A French horn. Also **pretzel-bender,** noun Someone who plays a French horn. 1923–. [Pretzel knot-shaped savoury biscuit.]

previous noun criminals' Previous criminal convictions. 1935–. G. F. NEWMAN 'Neither had any previous, Terry,' Burgess said. 'I thought perhaps the fella might have had a bit,' he shrugged (1970). [Elliptical use of the adjective.]

Prex(y) noun US The President of a college, etc. 1828–. VARIETY 'It's going to be a weird transitional year,' says Focus co-prexy and Berlin regular David Linde (2005). [Altered form of president.]

prick noun **1** The penis. c.1555–. E. MCBAIN Jocko had . . . a very small pecker. . . . Blood on the bulging pectorals, tiny contradictory prick (1976). **2** A term of contempt or abuse for a man; a fool or 'jerk'. 1822–. E. TREVOR We don't like bein' pushed around by an incompetent prick of a commanding officer (1967). **3 a spare prick (at a wedding)** Brit A person who is conspicuously and esp. embarrassingly out of place or superfluous in a particular situation. 1961–.

pricker noun **to get** (or **have**) **the pricker** Austral and NZ To be(come) angry. 1945–.

prick-farrier noun services' A medical officer. 1961–.

prick-sucker noun A fellator or 'cock-sucker'. 1868–.

prick-teaser noun = COCK-TEASER noun. Also **prick-teasing,** noun and adjective, etc. 1939–.

primo /priːˈməʊ/ adjective orig and mainly US First-class, first-rate. 1973–. AMERICAN FILM The Taylor murder had all the elements of a primo Hollywood thriller (1986). [From Italian primo first.]

prior noun US A prior conviction; usu. in pl. Cf. PREVIOUS noun. 1886–. J. WAMBAUGH Burglary . . . rarely drew a state prison term, unless you had a lot of priors (1978).

private business noun Eton College Extra tuition. 1868–. D. NEWSOME Half-an-hour's

preem preemie preg preggers preggo preggy prep

preparation for his Private Business lecture on Napoleon (1979).

privates noun pl. Genitalia; first recorded as a pun on the sense 'intimate friends' in Shakespeare *Hamlet* 2 ii: In the middle of her favour . . . her privates, we. 1602–. [Shortened from earlier *private parts*.]

pro noun Abbreviation of '(professional) prostitute'. 1937–. E. MCBAIN Benny already had himself two girls . . . experienced pros who were bringing in enough cash every week to keep him living pretty good (1976).

prob noun **1** A problem. 1934–. CORNISHMAN Parking's a bit of a prob, but you could fill in a bit at the back of the pier for a car-park (2003). **2 no probs** (or **prob**) Fine, OK, no problem. 1983–. ADVENTURE TRAVEL You could be back at your desk for 9am Monday no probs (2002). [Shortening.]

Prod noun and adjective mainly Irish and Scottish English Anglo-Irish abbreviation of 'Protestant'. Cf. PROT noun and adjective. 1837–. P. CARTER Most of the kids were in tough Prod gangs, like the Tartans. . . . They always seemed to . . . tell if you were as hard-line Prod as they were (1977).

Proddy adjective and noun mainly Irish English Protestant. 1954–.

Proddy-Dog noun Irish English, mainly derog A Protestant, as opposed to a Catholic (a 'Cat'). Also **Proddy-hopper, Proddy-woddy**. 1954–.

prodnose noun **1** An inquisitive person, a nosey parker; hence, a detective. 1934–. verb intr. **2** To stick one's nose into other people's business; to pry. Also **prodnosing**, noun. 1954–. [From the name of a character invented by the writer J. B. Morton ('Beachcomber') (1893–1975).]

profesh /prəˈfeʃ/ noun Abbreviation of 'profession', esp. applied to the theatre; US, the community of professional tramps. 1871–. E. PUGH 'Mr. Alexander, . . . being a hartist in his profesh, which there's only one thing as keeps him off the London stage at this present moment, and that is—' 'Eggs!' (1914).

prog¹ noun **1** A proctor (university official) at Oxford and Cambridge. Also **proggins**. 1890–. verb trans. **2** To subject (a student) to the proctor's authority. 1892–. [*Proggins* from *proctor* + *-gins* (as in JUGGINS noun, MUGGINS noun).]

prog² noun Abbreviation of *programme*; a broadcast radio or television programme. 1946–.

prog³ adjective and noun Abbreviation of 'progressive', esp. of apparent social or political views. 1958–.

promote verb trans. orig US To borrow or obtain (usu. illicitly); to exploit. 1918–. Z. N. HURSTON You skillets is trying to promote a meal on me (1942).

prong noun A penis. 1927–. M. AMIS This old prong has been sutured and stitched together in a state-of-the-art cosmetics lab (1984).

pronk noun Brit Someone weak or effeminate; a fool. 1959–. C. MACINNES No one is going to . . . try to blackmail me with that crazy old mixture of threats and congratulations that a pronk like you falls for (1959). [Of uncertain origin; cf. Dutch *pronker* fop.]

prop noun A diamond or valuable piece of jewellery. 1914–. [Earlier slang = scarf pin; cf. Dutch *prop* skewer.]

propellerhead noun orig US Someone with an obsessive interest in computers or other technology. 1983–. Hence **propellerheaded**, adjective 1987–. [From the wearing of a 'beanie' hat (a small often brimless cap) with a small propeller on top.]

proper adverb Completely, fully, utterly; recorded in standard use in the 15th century. 1816–. NORTHERN ECHO Alan Milburn, Darlington's NHS conscious Labour candidate, has been proper poorly (1992).

prop game noun A fraud racket by which householders are coaxed (by a *prop man*) into paying heavily for unnecessary repairs. 1966–. [Abbreviation of *property*.]

propho /ˈprɒfəʊ/ noun orig US Prophylaxis of venereal disease. 1919–. J. DOS PASSOS That's one thing you guys are lucky in, don't have to worry about propho (1921).

pross noun Also **pros**. Abbreviation of 'prostitute'. 1901–. J. SEABROOK She's been hanging round the Cherry Tree—that's the pub where all the old prosses go—and she's been going down there since she was thirteen (1973).

prossie /ˈprɒsɪ, -zɪ/ noun Also **prossy, prozzy**. orig Austral = PROSS noun. 1901–. F. RAPHAEL A shipmate of mine had this gag . . . 'What's in a prossie's telegram?' Answer, 'Come at once' (1971).

prosty /ˈprɒstɪ/ noun Also **prostie**. US Abbreviation of 'prostitute'. 1926–.

privates pro prob Prod Proddy Proddy-Dog prog

Prot

234

Prot noun and adjective Abbreviation of 'Protestant' (often contemptuously, opposed to *Catholic*). Cf. PROD noun and adjective. 1725–.

provo /prəʊvəʊ/ noun A member of the Provisional IRA. Also as adjective. 1971–. [Abbreviation of *provisional*.]

prowl verb trans. US, criminals' To inspect or search (a place, etc.), esp. before a robbery; to rob. 1914–. R. CHANDLER I went back to the kitchen and prowled the open shelves above and behind the sink (1943).

prune noun **1** orig US Someone unpleasant, disagreeable, or foolish. 1895–. N. SHUTE He wished . . . that he knew what it was that worried her, whether it was some prune that she had left at her last station (1944). **2** RAF A personification of stupidity and incompetence, esp. as *P.O. Prune*. 1942–.

prune-picker noun dated Someone from California. 1918–29.

pruno noun US prisoners' An improvised alcoholic drink made by fermenting a mixture of fruit, water, sugar, etc. 1936–. [From *prune* noun + -o.]

prushun /prʌʃən/ noun US A tramp's boy. 1893–1927. DIALECT NOTES The tramp lives in idleness while the boy goes about begging food for both. Many continue as *prushuns* until middle life, and when their master dies are left helpless (1927). [Of unknown origin.]

psych /saɪk/ verb **1** trans. To psychoanalyse. 1917–. **2** trans. mainly US To excite or stimulate (psychologically); to get (oneself, etc.) into a state of mental preparedness; often with *up*. 1957–. **3 to psych out: a** trans. To gain a psychological advantage over. 1963–. **b** intr. To become confused or (mentally) deranged. 1970–. [The colloquial noun *psych* = psychology, psychiatry, dates from 1895.]

psycho /saɪkəʊ/ noun Abbreviation of 'psychopath'. 1942–. C. MACINNES Wiz has for all oldies . . . the same kind of hatred psychos have for Jews or foreigners or coloureds (1959).

pubes noun pl. The pubic hair; first recorded in the late 16th century as a two-syllable word adopted from Latin *pubes* pubic hair; the slang usage, pronounced /pjuːbz/, is a comparatively recent development. INTERNATIONAL H & E MONTHLY If I did shave my pubes I would end up sporting lots of elastoplast in all the places where I had cut myself (1990).

puckeroo /pʌkəruː/ Also **buckeroo, pukeru,** etc. NZ. verb trans. **1** To ruin or break. Mainly as **puckerooed,** adjective. 1885–. S. T. OLLIVIER I come to see if you've got a spare shovel. Mine's puckerooed and I got a cow in the drain (1965). adjective **2** Broken, useless. 1925–. [From Maori *pakaru* broken; to break.]

puckerow /pʌkərəʊ/ verb trans. Also **puckero,** etc. dated, mainly services' To take hold of or seize. 1866–1931. W. KIRK Not all the legislators, robbing poor and rich today, can puckarow my talisman—the Badge of Cabar Feidh (1931). [From Hindustani *pakro* (imperative) seize.]

pud /pʊd/ noun **1** US Something easily accomplished, esp. an easy college course. 1938–. **2** The penis. Cf. PUDDING noun 1 and **to pull one's pudding** at PULL verb. 1939–. [Abbreviation of *pudding*.]

pudding noun **1** The penis. Cf. PUD noun 2 and **to pull one's pudding** at PULL verb. 1719–. **2** US = PUD noun 1. 1887–. **3a** A foetus; an unborn child. In phr. *a pudding in the oven,* etc.: a child conceived but not yet born. 1937–. J. PORTER 'None of us ever suspected that she'd got a pudding in the oven.' 'She was going to have a baby?' asked Dover (1965). **b:** in the pudding club = *in the club* (see CLUB noun). 1890–. L DAVIDSON 'Was she in the pudding club?' . . . 'Probably. They aren't saying' (1978).

puddle noun The sea, esp. the Atlantic Ocean; esp. in phr. *on this* (etc.) *side of the puddle.* Cf. POND noun. 1889–.

puddle-jumper noun US A fast, manoeuvrable vehicle, esp. a light plane. 1932–.

puff noun **1** A male homosexual or effeminate man. Cf. POOF noun 1. 1902–. H. W. SUTHERLAND He'd be a puff boy, this Magnie, and God knows what entertainment he laid on for Arthur (1967). **2** criminals', orig US Gunpowder or other explosive used to blow open a safe. 1904–26. **3** Life, span of existence; esp. in phr. *in (all) one's puff* and variants, in all one's life. 1890–. A. ARMSTRONG Here's me actually going to dial nine-nine-nine! Never in all me puff would

Prot provo prowl prune prune-picker pruno pud

I've thought it! (1972). **4** Marijuana for smoking. 1989–. GUARDIAN In George's book, a drink, a few lines, a bit of puff is okay but those E's and stuff like acid turns people into wrong uns (1992).

pug noun dated Abbreviation of 'pugilist'; a boxer or prize-fighter. 1858–. J. BUCHAN The man had been in the ring, and not so very long ago, I wondered at Medina's choice, for a pug is not the kind of servant I would choose myself (1924).

puggle(d) adjective = POGGLE(D) adjective.

puke /pju:k/ verb **1** intr. To vomit. 1600–. **2** trans. To vomit (food). Also with *up*. 1601–. noun **3** An act of vomiting. 1737–. [Prob. imitative.]

pukka adjective Brit Excellent, of the highest quality; fashionable. 1991–. OBSERVER Girls mug girls for jewellery or pukka clothes (1998). [From earlier sense, genuine.]

puku /pʊkʊ/ noun NZ The stomach. 1941–. [Maori.]

pull verb **1 to pull a boner,** etc. US To make a foolish mistake. 1913–. **2 to pull** (oneself, etc.) **off** to cause to ejaculate by masturbation. 1922–. **3 to pull one's pudding** or **wire** to masturbate. 1944–. **4 to pull** (someone's) **coat** US, Black English To give someone information, to tip someone off. 1946–. B. MALAMUD The black . . . said: 'Lesser, I have to pull your coat about a certain matter' (1971). **5** trans. To pick up (a sexual partner); to copulate with. 1965–. BOYD & PARKES Five years ago you did the big male-menopause bit, didn't you? Skulking off to Paris to prove you could still pull the birds (1973). **6 to pull a train,** to have sexual intercourse with a succession of partners. 1965–. noun **7** A woman picked up as a sexual partner. 1969–. **8 to give** (someone) **a pull** to pick (someone) up as a sexual partner. 1975–. **9 on the pull** looking for sexual partners. 1990–. GUARDIAN It's easier to pick up four grand simply by smiling when Chris asks if you and Trevor ever go out on the pull (1996).

pulpit noun RAF The cockpit of an aeroplane. 1933–42.

pump verb **1** intr. and trans. To have sexual intercourse (with). 1730–. J. PATRICK Skidmarks had come by her name through the boys' practice of kicking her naked behind after they had 'pumped' her (1973). **2 to pump ship** orig nautical To urinate. 1788–. D. RUTHERFORD A couple of men had come in to pump ship at the stand-up urinals (1973).

punch verb intr. **to punch out** to eject from an aircraft. 1970–.

punch-board noun A woman who is sexually promiscuous. 1963–. G. GREER Girls who pride themselves on their monogamous instincts . . . speak of the 'campus punchboard' (1970).

punk noun **1** dated Bread; also **punk and plaster,** bread and butter. 1891–. **2** mainly US **a** A passive male homosexual; a tramp's young companion. 1904–. **b** A worthless or insignificant person; a hooligan or small-time criminal. 1917–. **c** show business A novice; a young circus animal. 1923–. **3** Short for 'punk rock(er)'. 1974–. EVENING NEWS London's growing army of punks have developed a powerful animosity for teds. . . . For the uninitiated, punks . . . are the ones who match short, ragged hair with short ragged leather jackets (1977). verb intr. **4 to punk out** US To back out or quit. H. SALISBURY The Chimp, unfortunately, has a tendency to 'punk out' when the fighting gets tough (1959). [From the earlier sense of *punk*, rotten wood.]

punk-ass adjective US Of a person: good-for-nothing. 1972–.

punt verb intr. police To patrol; followed by *around*. Also as noun, **to have a punt around.** 1970–.

punter noun **1** Any of a number of different types of criminal, esp. one who assists as a confederate. 1891–. S. J. BAKER We have also acquired [this century] some underworld slang of our own: . . . *punter,* an assistant of a pickpocket who diverts the victim's attention while robbery is committed (1941). **2** Someone who is swindled. 1934–. G. F. NEWMAN They were three card tricksters. Their patter never changed, but still punters stood for it (1974). **3** A customer or client, esp. of a prostitute; a spectator. 1965–. OBSERVER Irene, a 19-year-old prostitute, was giving the glad eye to prospecting punters on the sidestreets of Chapeltown, Leeds (1978). [*Punt* verb, to lay a stake against the bank; to bet on a horse.]

pup noun US A four-wheeled trailer drawn by a tractor or other road vehicle. 1951–.

puppy foot noun US The ace of clubs; any club card. 1907–. [From the shape of a small paw-print.]

puppy-hole noun Eton College A pupil-room, in which pupils work with their tutors. 1922–40.

pug puggle(d) puke pukka puku pull pulpit pup

pure merino noun Austral A (descendant of a) voluntary settler in Australia (as opposed to a transported convict); one who finds in this a basis for social pretension. 1826–. DAILY MAIL (Sydney): Will pure merino progressives invade city fold? (1922). [From *merino* noun, type of sheep introduced into Australia in the early years of settlement.]

purler noun Also **pearler.** mainly Austral Something excellent or outstanding; a beauty. 1935–. L. MANTELL Never thought he'd ever get round to having any [children], then they produce a purler like that . . . a real little darling (1980). [From earlier sense, a knock-down blow.]

purple noun = PURPLE HEART noun; also, = LSD. See next. 1968–.

purple haze noun The drug LSD. 1967–. J. HENDRIX Purple haze is in my brain lately things don't seem the same (1967).

purple heart noun A tablet of the stimulant drug Drinamyl, an amphetamine. 1961–. N. STACEY They became more responsible, they took more interest in life, they stopped taking purple hearts and they settled down in their homes, their schools and their jobs (1971). [From the shape and colour of the tablets.]

push noun 1 mainly Austral A gang of thieves or ruffians; any throng or crowd. 1884–. C. MACKENZIE Presently there burst into the room half a dozen of the rowing 'push' (1964). verb 2 **to push up (the) daisies** to be dead and buried. *a.*1918–. GUARDIAN In ten years time I think I should be pushing up daisies (1970). 3 trans. To peddle (illegal drugs). 1938–.

pusher noun 1 A young woman; a prostitute. 1923–. B. W. ALDISS Nelson and his pusher took the chance to sneak away, and I managed to manoeuvre Sylvia as far as the kitchen (1971). 2 orig US Someone who peddles illegal drugs. 1935–.

push money noun US Commission on items sold. 1939–60.

puss¹ noun = PUSSY noun; the vulva. 1902–.

puss² noun mainly US A miserable or ugly face; the face or mouth (esp. when hit by a blow). 1890–. C. MCCULLERS When you looked at the picture I didn't like the look on your puss (1961). [From Irish *pus* lip, mouth.]

pussy noun 1 The vulva; the external female sexual organs; also, sexual intercourse, or women considered sexually. Cf. **to eat pussy** at EAT verb. 1880–. MACLEAN'S MAGAZINE As one blonde in a black leather coat bluntly replied, 'I sell pussy, not opinions' (1979). 2 criminals' A fur garment. 1937–. J. WAINWRIGHT The coat. . . . Ten to one, a fur coat, and there was always somebody ready to lift a pussy (1972). 3 An effeminate boy or man; a male homosexual. 1942–. See also *to play pussy* at PLAY verb.

pussy posse noun The vice squad. 1963–.

pussy-whip verb trans., mainly in passive To hen-peck (a man). 1963–.

put verb 1 trans. **to put** (someone) **in** to frame or have convicted; to send to prison. 2 intr. **to put out** of a woman: to offer oneself for sexual intercourse (*for* a man). 1947–. D. LODGE If she won't put out the men will accuse her of being bourgeois and uptight (1975).

puta /ˈpuːtaː/ noun A whore or slut. 1967–. [Spanish.]

putty noun naval A ship's painter. 1946–61.

putty medal noun An appropriately worthless reward for insignificant service. 1898–. GUARDIAN Putty medal blues. . . . The Americans are busy mounting a major public inquest on their showing at Munich and on the Olympic Games (1972).

putz /pʊts, pʌts/ noun mainly US 1 The penis. 1934–. P. ROTH He simply cannot—*will* not—control the fires in his putz, the fevers in his brain (1969). 2 A fool; someone obnoxious. 1964–. J. KRANTZ 'You,' she said, enunciating clearly, 'are a putz, a schmekel, a schmuck, a schlong, and a shvantz. And a WASP putz, at that' (1978). [Yiddish, from Middle High German *Putz* ornaments.]

Pygmalion quasi-adverb In phr. *not Pygmalion likely*, a euphemism for 'not bloody likely'. 1949–. G. FALLON 'Are you thinking of joining in?' 'Not Pygmalion likely,' Bland returned brusquely (1967). [The original phrase occurs in Shaw's *Pygmalion* (1914) and caused a sensation at the time of the play's first London production.]

py korry /paɪ ˈkɒrɪ/ int NZ Maori corruption of 'by golly!'. Cf. PLURRY adjective. 1938–.

pyro noun Abbreviation of 'pyromaniac'. 1977–. M. BRINGLE A pyro grateful for rain. . . . Now I've heard everything (1987).

Q.B.I. adjective and noun RAF Abbreviation of 'quite bloody impossible' (flying conditions). 1938–42. TIMES Instructions . . . as to height and position to be kept when flying in controlled areas during 'Q.B.I.' conditions (1938).

q.t. noun Abbreviation of 'quiet'; secret, confidential; usu. in phr. (*strictly*) *on the q.t.*, 'on the quiet'. 1884–. A. BENNETT This is strictly q.t.! Nobody knows a word about it, nobody! (1910).

quack noun orig Austral and NZ A doctor; also military, a medical officer. 1919–. J. IGGULDEN I'll get the quack at the Bush Hospital to have a look at it in the morning (1960). [From earlier sense, an unqualified doctor, a charlatan.]

quail noun US A young woman or girl. 1859–. TIME A less active sport is 'piping the flock', when Cal males watch Cal 'quails' preening in the sun on the steps of Wheeler Hall (1947).

quaiss kitir /kwaɪs kɪtɪə(r)/ int (Spellings vary.) 'Very good!', 'fine!', 'O.K.!'. 1898–. W. H. CANAWAY 'They'll take us off to Germany and make us have not but sausages and beer.' Sergeant Entwistle said, 'Sausages and beer, kwais ketir, I wish I had some now instead of this muck' (1967). [From Egyptian Arabic.]

qualified adjective dated Euphemistic substitute for 'bloody', 'damned', etc. 1886–1949. E. C. R. LORAC I . . . knocked my head on those qualified rocks (1949).

quandong /kwɒndɒŋ/ noun Austral Someone who looks after his or her own interests, esp. disreputably. 1939–. [The name of two species of Australian tree and their fruit; according to Sidney Baker, 'because the fruit is soft, but with a hard centre' (letter to Eric Partridge, quoted in his *Dictionary of Slang and Unconventional English*).]

quarter-bloke noun services' A quartermaster(-sergeant). 1919–50. GEN Nickly overstepped the mark when he suggested to the quarter-bloke . . . that he was flogging the rations (1944).

quean noun An effeminate male homosexual; = QUEEN noun 2. 1935–. [The original sense of *quean* is 'woman', and it was generally used as a term of abuse, 'strumpet, harlot, etc.' It is not clear whether QUEEN noun 2 represents the older form (it is certainly the commoner spelling), and whether *quean* is just a purist's respelling.]

queen noun 1 A pretty woman; a girlfriend. 1900–. P. SILLITOE Both gangs used hatchets, swords, and sharpened bicycle chains . . . and these were conveyed to the scenes of their battles by their 'queens' (1955). 2 A male homosexual, esp. one who is passive or effeminate; see QUEAN noun. 1924–. E. WAUGH 'Now what may *you* want, my Italian queen?' said Lottie as the waiter came in with a tray (1930).

queenie noun Also **queeny**. An effeminate man; a male homosexual, esp. as a term of address. 1933–.

Queen Mary noun dated A long, low-loading road trailer. 1943–68. [After the Cunard passenger liner, the Queen Mary.]

queeny adjective Effeminate. Cf. QUEEN noun 2.

queer[1] dated. adjective 1 Of coins or banknotes: counterfeit or forged. 1740–1941. R. CHANDLER If it was discovered to be queer money, as you say, it would be very difficult to trace the source of it (1941). 2a Counterfeit money; also, forged banknotes or bonds. 1812–. b: **on the queer** (living) by dishonest means, esp. by counterfeiting. 1905–42. [The earlier sense, 'bad, worthless', dates from the 16th cent., when the word was spelled *quire*, *quyre*, etc. More recently, it has tended to be identified with QUEER[2] adjective and noun, because of the rough similarity of meaning.]

queer[2] adjective 1 Homosexual. Also in phr. *as queer as a coot*. 1922–. A. WHITE 'I say, Peter, you're not turning *queer* by any chance, are you?' (1976). noun 2 A homosexual, esp. a male homosexual. 1935–.

queer-bashing noun Unprovoked assault on homosexuals. Also **queer-basher**, noun. 1970–.

queerie noun Someone queer or peculiar; esp. a homosexual. 1938–. NEW YORK JOURNAL-AMERICAN Why then does he want to get his hands on these millions? To pay the wages of a lot of queeries in the State Department? (1951).

Queer Street noun **in Queer Street** in difficulty or trouble; in debt. 1811–. A. WILSON He enjoys a little flutter . . . and if he finds himself in Queer Street now and again, I'm sure no one would grudge him his bit of fun (1952).

quid noun **1** The sum of one pound sterling; also, a sovereign; a note or coin of this amount. 1688–. W. P. RIDGE Milton received only ten quid for the first edition of 'Paradise Lost' (1929). **2 quids in** in luck or money; up on a deal, in profit. 1919–. **3** (**not**) **the full quid** Austral and NZ (Not) in full possession of one's faculties. 1944. [Prob. from *quid* the nature of something, from Latin *quid* what.]

quiff[1] noun mainly naval A clever dodge, a neat trick. 1881–. J. MASEFIELD It was young Mr. Abbott worked that quiff on you, sir (1933).

quiff[2] noun A young woman, a prostitute or 'tart'. 1923–. L. SNELLING If only there was some other quiff about I might be able to deal with her indifference (1973).

quim noun **1** The vulva or vagina. 1735–. **2** A woman; women. 1935–. SATURDAY NIGHT (Toronto): The key to success in this contest is a flashy car; and if the car is both expensive and impressive 'you have to beat the quim off with a hockey stick' (1974). [Of uncertain origin; perh. related to the old word *queme* pleasant.]

quince noun **to get on** (someone's) **quince** Austral To annoy or exasperate (a person). 1941–. A. E. FARRELL These bloody trees are getting on me quince (1963).

quirk noun dated, RAF **1** An inexperienced airman. 1916–31. C. F. S. GAMBLE The pilot, a very harmless, innocent 'quirk', hardly fledged, straight from Chingford (1928). **2** A type of slow, steady aeroplane; one used to train novice pilots; also, any peculiar plane. 1917–25. [Perh. from *quirk* eccentricity, oddity, but cf. ERK noun.]

quirley noun dated, US and Austral A cigarette, esp. one which is hand-rolled. 1932–55. [From *querl* to twist or coil.]

quis? pron Brit schoolchildren's dated 'Who wants this?': the first person to answer '*Ego*' (= 'I do') gets the object on offer. 1913–. E. WAUGH Who wants it? Quis? Would you like it, Cara? No, of course you would not. Cordelia? (1945). [Latin = 'who?'] See EGO pron.

quod noun **1** Prison; often in phr. *in quod*, in prison. 1700–. LISTENER Now, one of this chap's maternal uncles . . . has got to pay a 50 quid debt or go to quod (1968). verb trans. **2** dated To put in prison. 1812–1930. [Of unknown origin.]

quoit noun Also **coit** Austral The buttocks. 1941–. J. BAILEY 'I think he needs a good kick up the coit,' says Cromwell (1972). [From earlier sense, rope ring, in allusion to the anus.]

rabbit noun **1a** dated, Austral Alcoholic drink; a bottle of beer. In phr. *to run the rabbit*, to take drink (illegally) from a public house, esp. after hours. 1895–1955. **b** naval and Austral Something smuggled or stolen. 1929–. **2** A poor player; a novice. 1904–. PEOPLE Engines roar and the four 'rabbits' get away as best they can, but definitely not in the style of champions (1947). **3** A conversation or talk; lingo. 1941–. verb **4** trans. dated, naval and Austral To borrow or steal. See sense 1b. 1943–55. K. TENNANT Why were Australian Navy men better at 'rabbiting' little valuable articles than Americans? (1953). **5** intr. To talk or gabble (on). See sense 3. 1950–. J. BINGHAM You go into a pub with a short-back-and-sides and people stop rabbiting and stare at you (1976). [In senses 3 and 5, short for RABBIT-AND-PORK noun and verb.]

rabbit-and-pork verb intr. Rhyming slang for 'talk'. Mainly shortened to RABBIT noun 3, verb 5. 1941–.

rabbit-o noun Also **rabbit-oh**. Austral A travelling seller of rabbit-meat. 1902–. K. TENNANT Mrs. Drew knew all about her neighbours from the butcher and the grocer and the rabbit-o (1945).

race verb trans. **to race off** Austral To seduce (a woman); to take away in order to seduce. 1965–. M. WILDING Perhaps Peter thought he would try to race her . . . off. He relished the phrase, race off. He had not heard it in England (1967).

racket noun A dodge or scheme, a line of business; a criminal scheme for extorting money, etc. (esp. in organized crime). 1812–. TIMES Ulster by the middle of 1974 was suffering from rackets and violent crime on a scale equal to some of Europe's most notorious cities (1977).

rad adjective N Amer Admirably up to date, fantastic, 'cool'. 1982–. NEW YORKER I jam on the taboos, but my sister was rad (1985). [Abbreviation of RADICAL adjective.]

radge orig dialect, now mainly Scottish English. adjective **1** Extremely angry; wild, crazy. 1857–. I. WELSH They're radge, the Doyles, every fucker in the scheme kens that (1994). noun **2** A mad or violent person; an idiot. 1990–. [Origin uncertain; perh. an alteration of *rage* noun.]

radgie adjective orig dialect, now mainly Scottish English = RADGE 1 adjective. 1904–.

radical adjective orig surfers' At or exceeding the limits of safety; hence, remarkable, amazing, 'far out', 'cool'. 1968–. E. LOCHHEAD The Young Mothers' Meeting we had there was Really Radical (1985).

Rafferty('s) rules noun Austral and NZ No rules at all, esp. in boxing. 1918–. H. P. TRITTON The Show adjourned at noon for the races. They seemed to be run on the 'Rafferty rules' principle, but I heard no complaints (1964). [*Rafferty*, alteration of *refractory*, or simply as the Irish surname; cf. *Queensberry rules.*]

rag noun **1** A newspaper, esp. one of poor quality. 1734–. **2** Paper money; a note or bill. 1817–. D. W. MAURER The working stiff had over two C's in rag on him (1955). **3** **the Rag (and Famish)**: the Army and Navy Club in London. 1858–. NEVILL & JERNINGHAM The familiar name of the 'Rag', by which it is generally known, was invented by Captain William Duff, of the 23rd Fusiliers. . . . Coming into supper late one night, the refreshment obtained appeared so meagre that he nicknamed the club the 'Rag and Famish' (1908). **4 to get one's rag out** to make or become angry. Also **to lose one's rag** and **on the rag** (angry or irritable). 1914–. L. COOPER Roger was definitely shirty about that. . . . He really got his rag out (1960). **5** A sanitary towel. 1948–.

rag-bag noun A woman who is sloppily dressed, a slattern. Also, a general term of contempt for a woman. 1888–. [From the metaphorical sense, a motley collection.]

rag-chewing noun mainly US Talk, discussion, or argument, esp. when long-winded or protracted. Cf. **to chew the rag** at CHEW verb. 1885–.

rage Austral and NZ. verb intr. **1** To have a good time, to party, 1979–. SUN (Sydney): 'Over Christmas, I'll probably be drinking too much and raging too much,' said the . . . breakfast Bimbo (1986). noun **2** A party, a good time.

1980–. Also **rager,** noun A fun-lover, a dedicated party-goer. 1972–.

raggedy-ass(ed) adjective US, orig military Of a person: raw; new and inexperienced. Also applied to things. 1930–. J. A. MCPHERSON Who taught you the moves when you were just a raggedy-ass waiter? (1969). [See ASS noun.]

raggie noun naval A close friend or colleague (esp. on board ship). 1912–. TAFFRAIL Men who are friendly with each other are 'raggies', because they have the free run of each others' polishing paste and rags; but if their friendship terminates they are said to have 'parted brass-rags' (1916).

rag-head noun N Amer, offensive Someone who wears a turban or similar head-dress. 1921–. CANADIAN MAGAZINE East Indians are called 'rag-heads' if they continue to wear the traditional turban of the Sikh religion (1975).

rag-top noun US A convertible (car) with a soft roof or hood. 1955–. SPRINGFIELD (Mass.) DAILY NEWS The last U. S. built convertible, a Cadillac Eldorado, rolls along the assembly at the General Motors' plant in Detroit Wednesday. It ended an era for ragtops that began 74 years ago (1976).

rag-trade noun The business of manufacturing and selling ladies' garments. 1890–. J. COATES I know that line. It's going to be fashionable. . . . Forgive the digression but I'm in the rag trade (1957).

rah rah noun orig US A shout of support or encouragement for a college sports team, etc. Also as adjective, of a college or its students: collegiate, that generates enthusiasm or excitement, as in cheer-leading. 1911–.

rainbow noun orig US A capsule of the barbiturates Amytral and Seconal, of which one end is blue and the other red. Cf. RED BIRD noun. 1970–. J. WAMBAUGH One lousy time I dropped a red devil and a rainbow with some guys at school, and that's all the dope I ever took (1972).

raise verb **to raise Cain** to get very angry and make a fuss. 1840–. J. B. PRIESTLEY If we stand here talking another minute the mistress'll be raising Cain the way she'll say she's destroyed with the draught (1930). [Perh. from the

equation of Cain (who killed his brother Abel) with the Devil.]

rake-off noun orig US A share or portion of the proceeds (of gambling, etc.); a commission or 'cut'. 1888–. J. CARY I didn't say fifty to you. Sorry. But the agency would give me a rake off on reprints (1959).

ralph /rælf, rɑʊf/ verb intr. and trans. Also **Ralph.** orig and mainly US To vomit or gag; often followed by *up*. 1967–. VILLAGE VOICE He ralphs up the downers and the quarts of beer (1974). [Apparently a use of the personal name, but perh. imitative of the sound of vomiting.]

ram¹ noun **1** Eton College 'After scoring a rouge the attackers could gain an extra point by charging in column and bundling their opponents and the ball into the goal. The column was known as a ram, which was also the name given to the twin columns of Colleger and Oppidan sixth-formers, as they processed into Chapel' (A. J. Ayer, 1977). **2** A virile or sexually aggressive man; a lecher. 1935–. PENGUIN NEW WRITING 'Yes, it's the Chalk all right,' Willie said. 'The old ram!' he added, happily (1946).

ram² orig and mainly Austral. noun **1** An accomplice in petty crime; a confederate or decoy. 1941–. S. BAKER The ram would say, 'Give the old boy a fair go; he's nearly too old to spin them!' (1966). verb intr. **2** To act as a 'ram'. 1952–. [Origin uncertain; perh. simply a transferred use of *ram* male sheep.]

rammies noun pl. Austral and S Afr Trousers. 1906–. BULLETIN (Sydney): Old Bill watched the youngest jackeroo disrobing. . . . 'If I was you, young feller,' he said, 'I'd leave them rammies on' (1933). [Shortened form of ROUND-THE-HOUSES noun (rhyming slang).]

rammy noun Scottish A fight or brawl, esp. between gangs. 1935–. EVENING STANDARD (Glasgow): Gallaher had the body, he was Irish, he laid out two slops in the last rammy (1938). [Perh. from Scottish dialect *rammle* a row or uproar.]

ramp noun **1** A swindle or racket, esp. by charging exorbitant prices. 1812–. R. MACAULEY If I had my way, you would sign a paper . . . confessing that your whole business is a ramp and a fraud (1934). verb trans. **2** To

rammies
Australian and South African
trousers

raggedy-ass(ed) raggie rag-head rag-top rah rah

swindle (a person). 1812–. [Prob. from an older sense, to snatch or pluck.]

rampsman noun Someone who commits robbery with violence. 1859–. H. WALPOLE The perils of London—the cracksmen, the rampsmen, the snorrers and thimble-screwers (1932).

ram-raiding noun Brit The perpetration of a smash-and-grab raid in which access to the goods is obtained by ramming a vehicle into the shopfront. Also **ram-raider,** noun One who participates in this activity. 1991–. DAILY TELEGRAPH The ram-raiding started about five years ago, they say, going first for soft targets like tobacconists and off-licences, then later for television shops and jewellers (1991).

ramrod noun An erect penis. 1902–. A. SILLITOE I'd undone my belt and zip on our way across, and fell onto her with my ramrod already out (1979).

ram-sammy noun orig dialect A fight or scrap; a family quarrel; a noisy gathering. 1891–. [Of unknown origin.]

Randlord noun Someone who owns or manages a gold-field on the South African Rand. 1904–. R. J. M. GOOLD-ADAMS The black man may . . . die a premature death, but that—so the Rand-lords say—is not the fault of the mines in which he worked (1936). [After landlord.]

randy-arsed adjective Lustful. 1968–. H. C. RAE Beefy, randy-arsed wives crying out for a length (1968).

rank verb trans. US, African-American To insult or put down (a person), esp. within one's social group. Also **ranking,** noun. 1958–. C. MITCHELL-KERNAN 'Barbara was trying to rank Mary', to put her down by typing her (1971).

rap¹ noun A small amount, the least bit; esp. in phr. not to care a rap. 1834–. [From earlier sense, an Irish counterfeit coin of the 18th century, abbreviation of Irish ropaire.]

rap² noun 1 A rebuke: blame or criticism. 1777–. A. ROLLS It's up to us to keep a damn sharp look-out, my boy. . . . We've had a bit of a rap over it, between you and me (1932). **2a** mainly US A criminal accusation or charge. 1903–. R. D. ABRAHAMS I was standing on the corner, wasn't even shooting crap, When a policeman came by, picked me up on a lame rap (1970). **b** An identification, esp. of a criminal in an identity parade. 1914–26. **c** A prison sentence. 1927–56. **3** (In various phrases, mainly after sense 2.) **a: to get the rap** to receive the blame; to take a rebuke. 1865–.

b: to beat the rap mainly US To escape punishment (esp. a prison sentence). 1927–. W. BURROUGHS At the time, he was out on bail, but expected to beat the rap on the grounds of illegal seizure (1953). **c: to take the rap** to accept responsibility and punishment, esp. for a crime. 1930–. **d: to hang (pin,** etc.) **the rap on** to make a charge 'stick' on (someone). 1932–. **4** orig African-American A style of talking or singing, esp. as impromptu repartee. 1967–. verb **5** trans. To charge or prosecute (a person). 1904–. **6** intr. To talk or chat, esp. casually and at length. Also, (orig African-American) to talk or sing in the style of the 'rap' (sense 4). 1929–. S. HENDERSON The younger poet will usually rap or declaim or sing, but if he wants to create a Black character . . . he usually turns to drama or the short story (1973).

rapper noun **1** US A complainant or plaintiff; a prosecutor. See RAP verb 5. 1904–55. **2** orig US Someone who talks or chats; one who speaks in the style of the 'rap': see RAP² verb 6. 1971–. C. MILNER He is recognized as among the best talkers or 'rappers' in the hustling world (1973).

rap sheet noun A police record. 1960–. G. V. HIGGINS He was convicted. . . . Two charges . . . were dismissed, but remained on his rap sheet as having been brought (1976). [See RAP² noun 2.]

raspberry noun Also (N Amer) **razzberry. 1** A sound, gesture, etc. expressing derision or disapproval; the contemptuous noise made by forcing air out of the mouth with the tongue held limply under the lower lip. 1890–. G. DURRELL To my complete astonishment Minnie responded by . . . giving a prolonged raspberry of the juiciest variety (1960). **2** A refusal or reprimand; dismissal. 1920–. M. SPARK The security officer mutters all the way to the compound about what a raspberry the police are going to get because of this, a raspberry in these days being already an outdated expression meaning a reprimand (1973). [Abbreviation of earlier raspberry tart, rhyming slang for 'fart'.]

rass Jamaican. noun **1** The buttocks or arse. Also fig. 1790–. BOOT & THOMAS If he gave them any rass they'd hit from all sides with a gale of maniacal rhetoric that would reduce the poor man to blubber (1976). verb **2** In coarse expletives: rass you, etc. I. FLEMING 'Rass, man! Ah doan talk wid buckra.' The expression 'rass' is Jamaican for 'shove it' (1965). [By metathesis of arse.]

rampsman ram-raiding ramrod ram-sammy rap

rat

rat noun **1** Someone unpleasant or contemptible. 1594–. **2 rats** orig US An expression of incredulity, annoyance, disgust, etc. 1886–. J. CORNISH 'I don't kiss girls,' I said hurriedly. 'I never kiss girls. Never.' 'Oh, rats!' (1951). **3** A police informer, a 'nark'. Cf. sense 6b. 1902–. G. JACKSON You see every time a rat does get put away, the prison authorities always release a different reason for the attack, never that he was an informer (1970). **4 to get** (or **have**) **a rat** (or **rats**) Austral and NZ To be eccentric or crazy. 1894–1955. MIXER 'Lend us a quid!' 'Lend you a what! Blime, have you got a rat?' (1926). **5 rats and mice** rhyming slang for 'dice'; a game of dice. 1932–8. F. D. SHARPE We used to play dice with them. . . . Rats and Mice the game was called (1938). verb **6** intr. **a** To desert one's party, cause, etc. Also with *on*. 1812–. **b** criminals' To inform (*on* someone). 1932–. **7** trans. mainly Austral and NZ To search (a person, etc.) with intent to steal; to rob or steal. 1898–. V. PALMER 'Look here, you slinking cur!' he began. 'You've been ratting other people's property for months' (1931).

rat-arsed adjective Brit Intoxicated or incapacitated by drink; drunk. Cf. RATTED adjective. 1984–. GUARDIAN Guillaume Apollinaire talks of distillation, of reality cyphered through shimmery experience. Not a mention of being a rat-arsed French git (1990). [Cf. earlier *as drunk as a rat*.]

ratbag noun orig Austral and NZ Someone foolish, eccentric, or unpleasant; a trouble-maker or rogue. Also as adjective, stupid, uncouth. 1890–. B. CRUMP This'd be the best scrapper among you bunch of ratbags, wouldn't it? (1961).

rat fink noun mainly US Someone obnoxious or contemptible, esp. an informer or traitor. 1964–. C. BURKE His name was Judas and he was a rat fink. So this dirty rat fink he says to the pres of the gang, Caiaphas, 'What's in it for me if I put the finger on him?' (1969).

rat house noun Austral and NZ A mental hospital. 1900–. V. PALMER Hadn't it been plain all along that there was a streak of madness in the old boy? . . . He had done a spell in the rat-house and was only out on sufferance (1948).

ration noun **to come up with** (or **be given**) **the rations** derog, military To be awarded a service or other medal not earned in combat. 1925–. J. BRAINE Lampton had no decorations apart from those which all servicemen who served his length of time were given, as they say, with the rations (1957).

rat pack noun orig US A disorderly mob of youths. 1951–.

ratted adjective Brit Drunk; = RAT-ARSED adjective. 1983–. DAILY TELEGRAPH He zipped up his anorak and went out to get ratted with the rest of the ice hockey team (1987).

rattle verb **to rattle one's dags** Austral and NZ To hurry up. 1968–. S. THORNE Hurry up! Get down there 'n bleed him! Rattle your dags! (1980). [*Dag* a lump of matted wool and excrement on a sheep's behind.]

raunch noun orig US Shabbiness, grubbiness; hence, crudeness, vulgarity; earthiness. See RAUNCHY adjective. 1964–. GUARDIAN Her co-producer wanted to raise the raunch-quotient by having her perform in a garter belt (1979).

raunchy adjective orig US **1** Incompetent, sloppy; disreputable, grubby. 1939–. D. E. WESTLAKE I suddenly felt raunchy. Still in the same slacks I'd been wearing when this thing started (1965). **2** Boisterous, earthy; sexually provocative, suggestive; also, bawdy, salacious. 1967–. D. ANTHONY If you mean *Couplings*, I liked it. . . . I happen to like raunchy films (1977). [Origin unknown.]

rave noun **1** An infatuation; a passionate liking for somebody or something, a 'craze'; also, one who or that which excites such a feeling. 1902–. L. DAVIDSON T. L. had been having at the time one of his not uncommon raves; on this occasion for the multi-disciplinary benefits of a classical language (1962). **2** orig US A highly enthusiastic review of a book, film, etc.; often as adjective. 1926–. P. G. WODEHOUSE Of course he can open the safe. He's an expert. You should have read what the papers said of him at the time of the trial. He got rave notices (1951). **3** A lively party or rowdy gathering. Also **rave-up**. 1960–. H. MILLER Phyllis McBain is invited to an old-style rave-up, knickers and husbands optional (1973). verb intr. **4** To have a good time, to 'live it up'. 1961–.

raver noun Someone who is passionately enthusiastic about a particular thing, cause, etc.; a fanatic. Also, one who 'lives it up' or has a wild time, esp. sexually. 1959–. BUSBY & HOLTHAM There's a bloke I know makes his own LSD. Some of the ravers are giving it a try (1968).

ravers adjective dated Raving mad or delirious; also, furious, angry. Used predicatively. 1938–. N. MARSH Jeremy . . . will probably go stark ravers if they're sold out of the country (1967). [From *raving*; cf. *crackers*, *bonkers*, etc.]

raw prawn noun Austral **1** An act of deception; something unfair or 'difficult to swallow'. 1940–. **2 to come the raw prawn** (**over, with,** etc.): to try to deceive (someone). 1942–.

razoo[1] /rəˈzuː/ noun N Amer Ridicule, provocation; also, a contemptuous noise, a 'raspberry'. 1890–1959. [Prob. from RASPBERRY noun 2.]

razoo[2] /raːˈzuː, raːˈzuː/ noun Austral and NZ An imaginary coin of little value, a 'farthing'. Also **brass razoo**. In negative contexts only. 1919–. R. CLAPPERTON He isn't rolling in the stuff—he hasn't got two brass razoos to rub together (1968). [Origin unknown.]

razor-back noun US, circuses' A circus hand; someone who (un)loads the wagons. [From earlier sense, a poor or scraggy animal.]

razz noun **1** orig US = RASPBERRY noun 2. 1919–. S. LEWIS The Red Swede got the grand razz handed to him (1920). verb trans. **2** To hiss or deride; to make fun of. 1921–. B. HOLIDAY When I came to work the other girls used to razz me, call me 'Duchess' and say, 'Look at her, she thinks she's a lady' (1956). [Abbreviation.]

razzle noun A spree, a 'good time'. Usu. in phr. *on the razzle*. 1908–. J. LE CARRÉ Your wife was in England, and you went on the razzle with Leo (1968). [Short for RAZZLE-DAZZLE noun.]

razzle-dazzle noun **1** Excitement or bustle; also, deception, fraud; noisy publicity. 1889–. **2** A type of fairground ride. 1891–. D. BRAITHWAITE Four years before his death in 1897, Savage patented the 'Razzle Dazzle', otherwise known as 'Whirligig' or 'Aerial Novelty' (1968). [Rhyming formation on *dazzle*.]

razzmatazz noun Also **razzamatazz**. orig US Rag-time or early jazz; old-fashioned, 'straight', jazz; hence, sentimental jazz, and (by an unfortunate decline) stuff, rubbish. Still worse: noisy, showy publicity or display; fuss, commotion. 1894–. J. WAIN The enormous selling bonanza that was going on about him, in its astonishing flood of genuine goodwill, even a grain here and there of genuine piety, with unscrupulous salesman's razzmatazz, heightened his sense of living in a dream (1959). [Of unknown origin: perh. after RAZZLE-DAZZLE noun.]

razzo noun dated The nose. 1899–. J. CURTIS If the queer fellow tried to come any acid he would get hit right on the razzo (1936). [Origin uncertain; perh. an alteration of *raspberry* noun.]

reach verb trans. US To bribe. 1906–. L. KATCHER It is impossible . . . to open a big, notorious gambling operation without buying off public officials. . . . This does not necessarily mean a sheriff or District Attorney or a chief of police is being reached (1967).

read verb intr. **you wouldn't read about it** Austral and NZ expressing astonishment, usu. with an element of incredulity or disgust. 1950–. H. WILLIAMS You wouldn't read about it. A bloke his missus reckons was a doctor of philosophy, whatever that was, and just about the biggest dill you could meet (1973).

reader noun US, criminals' A circular notifying police officers of a suspected criminal to be arrested. 1920–55.

ready noun **1a** Ready money or cash. 1688–. **b** pl. Bank notes. 1937–. D. FRANCIS He sort of winks at me and gives me a thousand quid in readies (1974). adjective **2** US Excellent; very competent or mature; mainly of music or musicians. 1938–. N. E. WILLIAMS When an individual or a piece of music is high class or greatly admired, we indicate it by saying, 'He's ready!' or 'That's ready!' (1938). **3** US, Black English Street-wise; alert or receptive, 'hip'. 1967–.

ready-up noun Austral A conspiracy or swindle; a fake. 1924–. H. R. F. KEATING I don't accept all the pretences and ready-ups you people put out (1961).

ream verb trans. US **1** To cheat or swindle. 1914–52. S. KAUFFMANN Yeah, I smell the rat. Joe Bass's new relatives. Well, palsy, they're liable to ream you yet (1952). **2** US To have anal sex with. 1942–. T. WOLFE The man reams him so hard the pain brings him to his knees (1979). **3** To reprimand; usu. followed by *out*. 1950–. A. HAILEY A half-wit in my department has been sitting on the thing all morning. I'll ream her out later (1979).

rear noun orig school and university A water-closet or latrine; a lavatory; often pl. 1902–. B. MARSHALL And now let's raid the rears and rout out any of the other new swine that are hiding there (1946). [Perh. from their position behind a building.]

rear gunner noun Brit derog A male homosexual. 2006–. DAILY STAR Ashley Cole: I'm not a rear gunner (2006). [From earlier sense, machine-gunner stationed at the aft end of an aircraft; from the implication of anal sexual intercouse.]

rec noun Abbreviation of *recreation* (*area*, *ground*, etc.). 1929–.

raw prawn razoo razor-back razz razzle razzo

recce

recce /ˈrekɪ/ orig military. noun **1** Short for *reconnaissance*. Cf. RECCO. noun 1941–. A. HAILEY I sometimes think about two guys in Korea, close buddies of mine. We were on a recce patrol near the Yalu river (1979). verb trans. and intr. **2** To reconnoitre (a place, etc.). 1943–.

recco noun military Abbreviation of *reconnaissance*; = RECCE noun. 1917–. W. SIMPSON This was the last 'recco.' flight we made, and for months we had to content ourselves with mock air battles (1942).

recess noun criminals' A prison lavatory; usu. pl. 1950–. OBSERVER Locked in their cells at 5.30, with one opening later to go to the recesses (lavatories) and to have a hot drink (1974).

recon /ˈriːkɒn/ US military. noun **1** Abbreviation of *reconnaissance*; = RECCE noun 1. Often as adjective, *recon unit*, etc. 1918–. verb trans. and intr. **2** Abbreviation of *reconnoitre*. 1966–. I. KEMP Our orders were to recon only, and avoid all contact with the enemy whatsoever (1969).

red noun **1** An anarchist or republican; a Russian Bolshevik, a communist or extreme socialist. Often in phr. *reds under the bed*, indicating an excessive fear of the creeping influence or presence of communists, etc. 1851–. J. LE CARRÉ There's a story that you people had some local Russian embassy link. . . . Any Reds under your bed . . . if I may ask? (1977). **2** = RED BIRD noun. 1967–. J. WAMBAUGH What've you got, boy? Bennies or reds? Or maybe you're an acid freak? (1972).

red-arse noun military A recruit. 1946–7.

red ball noun US A fast goods train or lorry; priority freight. 1927–. NEW YORK TIMES It was assumed that bullets and butter, and gasoline as important as either, would be delivered. It was—once the Red Ball got rolling (1944).

red band noun criminals' A privileged prisoner, allowed to carry out special duties. 1950–.

red biddy noun Cheap red wine; a drink of meths and poor red wine. 1928–. C. WILLOCK Any idea where we could get any of the hard stuff? This flipping red biddy's burning a hole in my stomach (1961).

red bird noun The drug secobarbital (Seconal); a red coloured tablet of this. 1969–.

red board noun US **1** A railway stop signal. 1929–. **2** The board on which the official winners of a horse-race are declared. 1935–.

red cap noun military Brit A military policeman. 1919–. J. O'CONNOR She used to take me to nightclubs tucked away which no officers or redcaps knew about (1976).

red cent noun orig US A cent; an insignificant amount of money (in negative expressions). 1839–. T. SHARPE 'I'll alimony you for all the money you've got.' 'Fat chance. You won't get a red cent' (1976). [From the copper of which cents were made.]

red devil noun **1** A type of Italian hand grenade. 1944–. **2** = RED BIRD noun. 1967–. D. SHANNON Quite a collection of the pills . . . The Blue Angels and the Red Devils and the Yellow Submarines (1971).

red duster noun The red ensign. 1925–. DAILY EXPRESS His papers have not yet come through allowing him to fly the White Ensign, so, meanwhile, the Vita sails under the 'red duster' (1928).

red-eye noun **1a** US Rough, strong whisky. 1819–. A. HYND Barrow put down a slug of red eye and walked up to her (1949). **b** Canadian A drink of beer mixed with tomato juice. 1973–. **2** US Tomato ketchup. 1927–. **3** As adjective applied to aeroplane flights on which passengers are unable to get enough sleep because of differences in time-zones between the place of departure and arrival, etc. 1968–. NATIONAL OBSERVER (US): Schweiker . . . and Newhall took the red-eye special back to Washington that same night. Newhall just wanted to sleep, but Schweiker was, in Newhall's words, 'euphoric' (1976).

red hat noun military A staff officer. 1916–. A. WAUGH A number of very high-ranking officers were invited. . . . The visiting red hats were not impressed (1978).

red horse noun orig military Corned beef. 1864–1941.

red-hot adjective **1** Sexy, passionate; lively. 1887–. J. WAINWRIGHT It was jive and blues; either red-hot or smoochy (1977). **2** Austral Unfair, unreasonable. 1896–. noun **3** US A frankfurter or hot dog. 1892–. B. MALAMUD I got this redhot with mustard on it (1971).

red-hot momma noun **1** An earthy woman jazz-singer. 1926–. **2** A female lover or girlfriend. 1936–.

red ink noun mainly US Cheap red wine. 1919–. E. O'NEILL You'd lie awake . . . with . . . the wine of passion poets blab about, a sour aftertaste in your mouth of Dago red ink! (1952).

recce recco recess recon red red-arse red ball

Redland noun orig US, dated The Soviet Union. Cf. RED noun 1. 1942–. W. GARNER Morton picked up the camera. . . . He said, 'Exacta. Made in Dresden. East Germany. A favourite with Redland agents' (1969).

red lead /-led/ noun naval **1** Tomato ketchup. 1918–59. **2** Tinned tomatoes. 1919–45. TACKLINE Everything went into a pot-mess—meat, spuds, peas, beans, rice, oxo, 'red-lead' (tinned tomatoes)—and the result was invariably good (1945).

red legs noun pl. US, military An artilleryman. 1900–. S. N. SPETZ Anyway, you'll get a chance to cool it down there, just guarding a bunch of Red Legs (1969).

redneck noun orig US A Southern rural white; hence, a reactionary. 1830–.

Red Ned noun Austral and NZ Cheap wine or other similar drink. 1941–. I. HAMILTON Jo clutched the glass of Red Ned that I had thrust at him (1972).

red-ragger noun Austral derog A Communist or socialist. 1916–. N. MEDCALF Bluey was considered a bit of a red-ragger (1985). [From the red flag that symbolizes the Communist movement.]

Red Sea pedestrian noun jocular, offensive A Jew. 1984–. [From the crossing of the Red Sea by the children of Israel on foot after God created a passage through the water (Exodus 14:21–2).]

red steer noun Austral A fire; a bush-fire. 1936–. F. HARDY Like the bushfires: hadn't he patented the special extinguisher to end the blight of the red steer for all time? (1971).

red 'un noun dated A sovereign. 1890–. A. HEWINS I don't think much o' that stone you got. I'll give you a red un for it (1981).

reef verb trans. **1** criminals' To pull up (a pocket-lining) to steal the contents, to pick (a pocket); also, to steal or obtain dishonestly. 1903–. TIMES As the talent suckers chummy, the wire reefs his leather. . . . A slick pickpocket team has a private language for its dirty work (1977). **2** coarse To feel (a person's) genitals. 1962–.

reefer noun **1** orig US A marijuana cigarette; (someone who smokes) marijuana. 1931–. CHICAGO DEFENDER The humble 'reefer', 'the weed', the marijuana, or what have you by way of a name for a doped cigarette have moved to Park Ave. from Harlem (1933). **2** criminals' A pickpocket; a pickpocket's accomplice. See REEF verb. 1935–41. [In sense 1, from

earlier sense, something rolled (from naval use), or perh. from Mexican Spanish *grifo* marijuana.]

reffo noun Austral A European refugee, esp. one who left Germany or German-occupied Europe before World War II. 1941–. P. WHITE He was . . . a blasted foreigner, and bloody reffo, and should have been glad he was allowed to exist at all (1961). [Abbreviation of *refugee* + *-o*.]

reg noun Brit Motor-vehicle registration. 1969–. DAILY MAIL At midnight, a businessman and his female companion took a drive to the beach in his H-reg Mercedes (1991). [Abbreviation.]

rego /ˈredʒəʊ/ noun Also **reggo**. Austral Motor-vehicle registration. 1967–. R. HALL If the cops catch us they'll have us cold: no rego, one headlamp, baldy tyres (1982). [Abbreviation of *registration* + *-o*.]

rehab /ˈriːhæb/ noun **1** Austral, NZ, and Canadian Retraining after military service; the rebuilding of an industry, etc., after a war. 1945–. G. W. TURNER A house may be bought with a rehab loan or a State advances loan (1966). **2** US The rehabilitation of a criminal, disabled person, etc. to some degree of normal life. 1961–. **3** US Restoration of something to its previous state or condition. 1975–. [Abbreviation of *rehabilitation*.]

rent noun **1** Money, esp. as criminal gain or in return for homosexual favours. Also as adjective of a person. 1828–. GAY NEWS A word of warning about the Strand Bar in Hope Street. . . . It's rough and some of the people there are rent (1977). verb trans. **2** To obtain money from (a person) by criminal means, or for homosexual favours. 1898–.

rent-boy noun A young male homosexual prostitute. See RENT noun and verb. 1969–. DEAKIN & WILLIS Between the ages of fifteen and twenty he had been a rent boy, a boy prostitute living and working in the West End (1976).

renter noun A male prostitute. See RENT-BOY noun. 1893–.

repple depple noun US, military A replacement depot in a theatre of war. 1945–. J. A. MICHENER He was sent to Korea, not with a formed unit but to a replacement depot, a repple depple he explained to his parents (1978). [Modified abbreviation of *replacement depot*.]

retard /ˈriːtɑːd, rɪˈtɑːd/ noun US A mentally-retarded person. 1970–.

Redland red lead red legs redneck Red Ned reef

retread noun **1** military, mainly US, Austral, and NZ A retired soldier recalled for service; also, a worker who undergoes retraining. 1941–. **D. BEATY** A diplomat with thirty years experience . . . not the retread given a job with other unwanted Civil Servants (1977). verb trans. **2** US To retrain (a person), esp. after a period of retirement. 1963–.

Reub /ruːb/ noun Also **Rube, rube**. N Amer = REUBEN noun. 1896–. **J. GORES** The rube who wanders into the pool hall and loses a few games. . . . Then the bets get bigger and he . . . starts clearing tables (1973). [Abbreviation of REUBEN noun.]

Reuben noun N Amer A bumpkin; a farmer or country fellow. See REUB noun. 1804–1953. [From the personal name.]

re-up /riːˈʌp/ US services'. verb intr. **1** To re-enlist for service. 1906–. **E. COLBY** When enlisting and being sworn in, a man is said to 'hold up his right hand' for three years. So when he does it after being discharged, he 're-ups' (1942). noun **2** Someone who re-enlists. 1955–. [From re- again and up verb.]

revusical noun orig US A musical revue. 1931–. **AMERICAN SPEECH** Pardon Us Please, 'presenting thirty-five stars in person', advertises itself in newspapers as a Revusical (1941). [Blend of revue and musical.]

rhino noun dated Money. 1688–. **F. MARRYAT** Now that I see you look so sharp after the rhino, it's my idea that you're some poor devil of a Scotchman (1834). [Origin unknown.]

rhubarb noun **1** orig theatre The word 'rhubarb' repeated to give the impression of the murmur of conversation, etc. 1934–. **J. BETJEMAN** And in the next-door room is heard the tramp And 'rhubarb, rhubarb' as the crowd rehearse A one-act play in verse (1960). **2** military A low-level strafing raid. 1943–56. **3** US A noisy dispute or row; (orig baseball) a ruckus on the field of play. 1943–. **TIMES** 'Rhubarbs', the name used for noisy arguments that break out on the field, started when a Yankee batter, after missing a Perry special, yelled 'spitter' at him (1973). **4** Nonsense, rubbish. 1963–. verb intr. **5** orig theatre To repeat 'rhubarb', as in crowd noises; also trans. with direct speech. 1958–.

rib verb trans. orig US To fool or make fun of; to tease. Also absol. and **ribbing**, noun. 1930–.

L. P. HARTLEY When the chaps rib her she doesn't quite know how to act up (1955). [From the dialect sense, to beat (someone) on the ribs.]

ribby adjective Shabby, seedy, run-down; nasty. 1936–. **P. ALEXANDER** She lived at the ribby end of Maida Vale (1976).

rib-joint noun US A brothel. 1943–.

Richard noun Also **richard**. **1** mainly US A detective or 'dick'. 1914–. **E. MCGIRR** A surprisingly high proportion of well-to-do murderers hire private richards to delve into the demise of the victim (1974). **2** A girl or woman. 1950–. [In sense 2, abbreviation of rhyming slang 'Richard the Third' = 'bird'.]

richie noun Also **richy**. orig and mainly US A wealthy person. 1966–. **CAMBRIDGE CHRONICLE** (Massachusetts) Her only chance of going to the prom is her budding relationship with Blaine, . . . a 'richie' (1986). [From rich adjective + -ie.]

ride the lightning
to be executed in the electric chair

rick noun A swindler's accomplice planted in the crowd (to start the bidding, etc.). 1928–. **P. ALLINGHAM** On . . . occasions the worker has a rick, that is to say, a confederate planted in the crowd, whom he could always choose as the first bidder (1934). [Of unknown origin.]

ricket noun A mistake or blunder. 1958–.

ricky-tick noun **1** A simple, repetitive rhythm, as in early 'straight' jazz; ragtime, old-fashioned jazz. 1938–. adjective **2** Of music or tempo: repetitive, dull, 'corny'. Also **ricky-ticky**, adjective. 1942–. [Imitative.]

ride verb **1** trans. To have sexual intercourse with (a woman); to mount or copulate with. 1520–. **S. ALLAN** She mounted him and rode him, until they climaxed together (1978). **2** intr. jazz To play with an easy-flowing rhythm. 1929–. **J. WAINWRIGHT** When Ellington opens on an eight-bar piano intro . . . you know that . . . when the full outfit starts leaning back and riding, you are going to be lifted cloud-high (1973). **3 to ride the lightning** US To be executed in the electric chair. 1935–. noun **4a: to take for a ride** orig US To take (someone) in a car to murder or kidnap them. 1927–. **E. S. GARDNER** These persons whispered that some day Carr would mysteriously disappear, and no one would ever know whether he had quietly faded into voluntary oblivion or had been 'taken for a ride' (1944). **b** N Amer A motor vehicle. 1930–. **5** jazz An easy, swinging rhythm or passage. 1930–. **6** An act of sex. 1937–. J. STURROCK He reckons to have a ride on her . . . even if he has to marry her to get it (1981). [In sense 1, formerly also used intr., since the Middle Ages.]

rideman noun US jazz Someone who improvises with a pronounced rhythm. 1935–. [See RIDE noun 5.]

rideout noun jazz A final chorus. 1939–. NEW YORKER 'On the Other Side of the Tracks' . . . has an ebullient and remarkable rideout section (1977).

ridge adjective Austral All right, good; genuine. 1938–. D. IRELAND I convinced her the whole thing was ridge! (1971). [From an obsolete word for 'gold'.]

ridge-runner noun US A Southern mountain farmer; a hillbilly; (African-American) a white person. 1933–.

ridgy-didge adjective. Austral = RIDGE adjective 1953–. [Elaboration of *ridgy*, from RIDGE adjective.]

ridiculous adjective orig jazz Excellent, outstanding. 1959–.

rig noun The penis. 1964–. M. AMIS All weekend I cried, . . . thought of ways of committing suicide, . . . considered lopping off my rig with a razor-blade (1973).

right adjective **1** criminals' Reliable or trustworthy. 1856–. **2 too right** Austral and NZ Expressing strong agreement. 1919–. ZIGZAG Something better change—too right mate! (1977). adverb **3 right on** orig US Expressing approval, encouragement, etc. 1925–.

right croaker noun dated, criminals' A doctor who will treat criminals without informing, or supply drugs. 1929–51.

righteous adjective US, mainly African-American Fine, excellent; esp. as *righteous moss* (i.e. hair). 1942–. T. PYNCHON 'She's up there' Matilda said, with a smile for everybody, even musicians with a headful of righteous moss, who were making money and drove sports cars (1963).

rigmo noun Shortening of 'rigor mortis'. 1966–.

Riley noun Also **Reilly**. In phr. *the life of Riley*, an enjoyable, carefree existence. 1919–. J. B. PRIESTLEY The life of Reilly, which some people imagine me to lead, has been further away than a fading dream (1949). [From the common

Irish surname: the phrase is said to come from one of a number of late 19th-cent. songs, but it was popularized by H. Pease's *My Name is Kelly* (1919).]

rim noun **1** US The outer edge of a semicircular or horseshoe-shaped newspaper subeditors' desk. 1923–. verb trans. **2** coarse, orig US To lick the anus of, esp. before sexual intercourse. 1959–. **3** N Amer To cheat or swindle (someone). 1945–. D. HUGHES Ten bucks? For that old thing? I'd be rimming you, Charles (1973). [Prob. a variant of *ream*.]

rind noun Cheek or effrontery. 1903–. P. G. WODEHOUSE You have the immortal rind to suppose that I will stand being nagged and bullied (1915).

ring¹ verb trans. **1** To substitute fraudulently; to 'switch'. 1812–. **2** To change the identity of (a motor car) fraudulently. 1967–. A. HUNTER The Parry brothers . . . copped three years apiece for ringing cars (1977). noun **3 the dead ring (of)** Austral and NZ An exact likeness (to); a 'spitting image'. 1899–. [From *ring*, the sound (of a bell, etc.).]

ring² verb trans. Austral To beat (other shearers in a shed). 1894–. [Back-formation from RINGER¹ noun 2.]

ring³ noun The anus. 1949–. [From *ring*, a band of precious metal, etc.]

ringer¹ noun **1** Austral Someone who excels at an activity, etc.; an expert. 1848–. **2** Austral and NZ The fastest shearer in a shed. 1871–. T. WOOD He can shear a hundred a day; a hundred and twenty, a hundred and fifty; two hundred— even three hundred and twenty, at times, if he is a Ringer—that is the quickest of the team (1934). [From Brit dialect *ringer* anything supremely good.]

ringer² noun **1** orig US A horse, player, etc. fraudulently substituted in a competition to boost the chances of winning. 1890–. TIMES The Crown claimed that the horse had been switched and that the winner was in fact a 'ringer', a more successful stablemate called Cobblers March (1980). **2 to be a (dead) ringer for** (or **of**) orig US To be an exact likeness or counterpart of. 1891–. **3** US An outsider or intruder; an imposter, esp. in a political or other group. 1896–. **4** A false registration plate on a stolen vehicle; someone who uses these. 1962–. P. LAURIE All the ringer has to do is buy a [car] key, come along as innocent as pie, open the door and drive off to wherever he does his ringing (1970). [From RING¹ verb.]

rideman rideout ridge ridge-runner ridgy-didge

ringie noun Austral and NZ The ring-keeper in the game of two-up. 1917–.

ring-in noun Austral A fraudulent substitution or 'switch', esp. in a race. 1918–. [See RING[1] verb 1.]

ring-tail noun US Someone worthless; a tramp. 1926–.

ring-worm noun US Someone who regularly attends boxing-matches. 1929–54.

ringy adjective N Amer Irritable, angry. 1932–.

rinky-dink mainly US. noun **1** Something worn out or antiquated; a cheap place of entertainment. In phr. *to give* (someone) *the rinky-dink*, etc., to cheat or swindle. 1912–. NEW YORKER *Red Garter* . . . eighteen–nineties rinky-dink, complete with fire engine, but the banjo band is above average (1969). adjective **2** Worthless or worn out; outmoded. 1913–. [Of unknown origin: cf. RICKY-TICK noun and adjective.]

rinky-tink adjective mainly US Of a jazz or ragtime piano on which simple, repetitive tunes are played; jangling. 1962–. [Imitative; see RINKY-DINK noun and adjective, and cf. *tink*.]

rip verb trans. **1** To steal. 1904–. **2** Austral To exasperate; usu. in the expression *wouldn't it rip you!* Also, *get ripped!*, 'get lost!' 1941–. **3** to rip off orig US **a** to steal or embezzle. 1967–. A. CROSS Soldiers are always ripping things off, from their own outfit, from the enemy, everything (1981). **b** To cheat or defraud; to rob, deceive. 1971–. **c** To burgle or steal from (a shop, etc.). 1972–. **d** To copy or plagiarize. 1975–. noun **4** US, police A fine (of so many days' pay) imposed for breaking police regulations. 1939–58.

ripe adjective **1** Drunk. 1823–1925. **2** Fine, excellent (often ironically); excessive. 1923–. J. FRASER 'What the bloody hell are you playing at?' 'That's ripe considering you just near broke my arm' (1969).

rip-off noun orig US **1** A thief. 1970–. **2** A fraud or swindle; an instance of exploitation. 1970–. **3** An imitation or plagiarism. 1971–. **4** **rip-off artist** or **merchant** someone who perpetrates a 'rip-off'. 1971–.

ripped adjective US High on drugs. 1971–.

ripper noun **1** now mainly Austral Someone (or something) outstanding, esp. an attractive young woman. 1838–. **2** criminals' A tool for opening safes, etc. 1889–.

rip-snorter noun orig US Someone or something remarkable (in appearance, strength, etc.), esp. a storm or gale. 1842–. LAST WHOLE EARTH CATALOG This is Gurney Norman the author speaking, bringing you the end of this folk tale, and it's a rip-snorter (1972).

rip-snorting adjective orig US Rip-roaring. 1846–.

rise noun An erection of the penis; usu. in phr. *to get a rise*. 1949–.

river hog noun N Amer Someone who guides logs downstream. 1902–.

River Ouse noun Also **River Ooze**. Rhyming slang for 'booze'. 1931–.

river pip noun N Amer = RIVER HOG noun. 1921–47.

rivets noun pl. dated Money or coins. 1846–1937. J. CURTIS 'So you got a bit of rivets to speculate?' 'I ain't said so. All I said as I could put up a bit' (1937).

roach noun mainly US **1** A cockroach. 1848–. E. PAUL Her failure to get results kept her hopping like a roach in a skillet (1942). **2** US An unpleasant or despicable person; spec. a woman considered unattractive or licentious. 1930–. T. MORRISON They watched her far more closely than they watched any other roach or bitch in the town (1974). **3** A policeman. 1932–. **4** A cigarette-butt, esp. of a marijuana cigarette. 1938–. T. PYNCHON Holding up the glowing roaches of their cigarettes . . . to spell out alternate S's and O's (1966). [In sense 4, perh. a different word.]

road apples noun pl. N Amer Horse droppings. 1942–. J. H. GRAY The best pucks were always those supplied by passing horses, 'road apples' we called them (1970).

roader noun taxi-drivers' A long-distance fare or journey. 1939–.

road hog noun An inconsiderate (usu. obstructive) driver or cyclist. 1891–. K. BONFIGLIOLI 'Lost my temper. . . . Bloody road hog.' 'He might easily have done us a mischief,' I agreed (1972).

roadie noun Someone who organizes and supervises a touring pop group, etc.; also, an assistant who helps with this. 1969–.

road kid noun A young tramp or 'hobo'. 1970–.

road rash noun Cuts and grazing caused by falling off a skateboard. 1970–.

ringie   ring-in   ring-tail   ring-worm   ringy   ripe

roadwork noun criminals' The work of a travelling thief. 1925–55.

roar verb trans. **to roar up** mainly Austral To abuse or reprimand (someone). 1917–. N. LINDSAY Bill was able to roar him up, anyway, for having the blinkin' cheek to come shoving his nose into Bill's affairs (1947).

roaring forties noun pl. '*Roaring forties*, rough seas in 40–50 degrees south latitude, hence, a slang name for certain taut-handed lieut-commanders in their forties, who are always roaring up the hands' (W. Granville *A Dictionary of Sailors' Slang* 1962). 1942–62.

robbo noun Austral A horse and trap, or its driver; a poor horse; hence, anything of a low standard. 1897–1956. [Short for the name *Robinson*, apparently the name of a local proprietor of a shabby horse-and-trap business.]

rock noun **1a** US A piece of money; a dollar. 1840–. **b** orig US A precious stone; a diamond. 1908–. A. DIMENT He . . . listened to my vague replies like my advice was worth its weight in sparkling rocks (1968). **2 on the rocks** in a destitute situation; (of a marriage) on the point of breaking down; finished. 1889–. **3** orig US, usu. pl. An ice-cube or crushed ice served in a drink; **on the rocks** of spirituous liquor, served with ice. 1946–. **4** US, baseball An error, esp. in phr. *to pull a rock*, to make a mistake. 1939–. **5** pl. The testicles; in the coarse phr. *to get one's rocks off*, to achieve sexual satisfaction; to ejaculate; also, to enjoy oneself. 1948–.

rocker noun **off one's rocker** mad, crazy. 1897–. P. G. WODEHOUSE The Duke is off his rocker (1923). [From *rocker* curved bar on which something rocks.]

rocket noun **1 off one's rocket** mad, 'off one's rocker'. 1925–59. **2** orig military A sharp reprimand. 1941–. N. BLAKE Your Superintendent gave me a rocket yesterday about 'harbouring her', as he put it (1949). verb trans. **3** orig military To give (someone) a stern reprimand. 1948–.

rocket fuel noun orig US The drug phencyclidine. 1977–. SUNDAY TIMES PCP or 'angel dust', a strong anaesthetic which came after LSD in 1960s drug fashions . . . has recently emerged anew. Now they call it 'rocket fuel' in Chicago and mix it with peanut butter (1985).

rock-happy adjective US, military Mentally unhinged from serving too long on a (Pacific) island. 1945–6.

rock of ages noun Rhyming slang for 'wages'. 1937–.

rock pile noun US A pile of stones; hence, a gaol or prison (from the convicts' task of breaking stones). Also fig. 1888–.

rocky noun naval A recruit in the RNVR or another naval division. 1919–. KERR & GRANVILLE The active-service men labelled them a 'rocky' lot—'rocky' being an oblique reference to unstable sea-legs and the waved tapes in their blue jean collars (1957).

rod noun **1** The (erect) penis. 1902–. E. POUND His rod hath made god in my belly (1934). **2** mainly US A gun; a pistol or revolver. 1903–. J. CARROLL I ain't getting my ass blown off because you're stupid. You won't get near Zorelli with a rod anyways (1978). **3** N Amer The draw-rod of a railway coach or truck. 1904–. D. STIFF We beat it on the run. . . . Some rode the rods on passengers, While some blew out on freights (1931). **4** mainly US = HOT ROD noun. 1945–. J. GORES A two-bit Mission District auto and accessory dealer who specialized in old cars for conversion to dune buggies, drag cars, rods, and the like (1972). verb intr. **5 to rod up** US To arm oneself with a gun or guns. 1929–.

rodder noun mainly US = HOT RODDER noun; someone who converts production cars into 'hot rods'. 1949–.

rodman noun mainly US A gunman. 1929–.

roger verb trans. Also **rodger.** To copulate or have sexual intercourse with (a woman). 1711–. A. WILSON I'm not at all sure about the Empress Theodora. I fancy she was rogered by an ape more than once in her circus acts (1961). [Apparently a metaphorical use of the personal name. The noun *roger* 'the penis', is now obsolete (1700–1863).]

rogue and villain noun dated Rhyming slang for 'shilling'. 1859–.

roll noun **1a** US and Austral A collection of bills or notes rolled together; one's money. 1846–. J. BLACK No Missouri dip would take his roll, extract two fifty dollar bills, and put the rest back in his pocket (1926). **b: a roll Jack Rice couldn't jump over** Austral A large amount of money. 1945–. **2 go and have a roll** go away, 'get lost'. 1941–59. verb **3** trans. To rob (someone, esp. one who is asleep, drunk, or otherwise incapacitated). 1873–. R. CHANDLER Here we are with a guy who . . . has fifteen grand in his pants. . . . Somebody rolls him for it and rolls him too hard, so they have to take him out in the desert and plant him among the cactuses (1939). **4 to roll the bones** US To play

roadwork   roar   roaring forties   robbo   rock   rocker

dice. 1929–. **5** intr. and trans. To start moving, esp. as a command to start cameras filming (*roll 'em*). 1939–.

roller noun **1** mainly N Amer A thief, esp. someone who robs drunks; a prostitute (who steals from her clients). 1915–. **2** US A policeman. 1964–. c. & r. milner Look, for a roller (policeman) to come to this door—he's insane, he's gotta be a nut (1973).

rollicking noun A sharp reprimand. See bollocking noun. 1932–. m. k. joseph Someone's dropped a clanger. Someone's going to get a rollicking (1958). [From earlier sense, boisterous play.]

rollocks noun pl. A euphemistic alteration of 'bollocks'; rubbish. 1961–.

roll-up noun orig prisoners' A hand-rolled cigarette. 1950–.

Roman Candle noun **1** A Roman Catholic. 1941–. p. haines She said: 'I've noticed you lots—you're a Roman Candle, aren't you?' 'What?' . . . 'R.C., silly' (1974). **2** A parachute jump in which the parachute fails to open; the parachute involved; also, a bad landing by an aeroplane. 1943–. e. waugh The first thing the commandant asked when I reported Crouchback's accident. 'A Roman Candle?' he asked (1961).

roo noun Austral A kangaroo. 1898–. caravan world (Australia) The river had brought emus and 'roos close to the road (1977). [Shortening.]

rook verb trans. To cheat or swindle (someone); to charge extortionately. 1590–. [From the old noun = 'a swindler', after the gloomy-looking bird.]

rook noun US Abbreviation of rookie noun. 1901–42.

rookie noun mainly N Amer A raw recruit, esp. in the army or the police; a novice in a sports team. Also as adjective. 1892–. h. a. franck From the lieutenant to the newest uniformless 'rookie' every member of the police was swarming in and out of the building (1913). [Prob. a modified alteration of *recruit*.]

Roosky noun and adjective = rusky noun and adjective.

root noun **1** The penis. 1846–. **2** orig schools' A forceful kick. Also **root about**. 1900–. n. scanlan Matt gave him 'a root in the gear' and told him not to talk like a stable boy (1934). **3** Austral An act of sexual intercourse; a (female) sexual partner. 1959–. d. ireland Johnny Bickel . . . thought she'd be an easy root

and began to take notice of her (1976). verb **4** trans. mainly schools' To kick, esp. in the backside. 1890–. **5** trans. Austral To outwit, exhaust, or confound (someone); to ruin; esp. in phr. *wouldn't it root you!* and *get rooted!* 1944–. telegraph (Brisbane): Mr. Whitlam later admitted having said in an aside: 'It is what he put in his guts that rooted him' (1973). **6** trans. and intr. Austral To copulate (with): usu. of a man. Also in phr. *to root like a rattlesnake* (i.e. vigorously). 1958–. k. cook We found this bloody little poofter down on the beach fiddling with a bird. . . . Couldn't even root her (1974).

rooty noun military Bread. 1883–. [From Urdu, Hindi *roti*.]

rooty gong noun military A medal formerly awarded to members of the British Army in India. 1925–48. f. richards The Good Conduct medal or 'Rooty Gong' . . . was so called because it was a regular ration-issue, like bread or meat or boots (1936). [See rooty noun and gong noun.]

rope noun **1** US A cigar. 1934–. h. wouk Carter Aster was smoking a long brown Havana tonight. That meant his spirits were high; otherwise he consumed vile gray Philippine ropes (1978). **2** mainly US Marijuana. 1944–.

ropeable adjective Austral and NZ Angry, annoyed. 1874–. j. cantwell She was going to have my kid, but she dropped it when another bloke put the acid on. I got ropeable and did her (1963). [From earlier sense, (of an animal) that needs to be roped; intractable.]

rope-yarn noun mainly naval Applied to a day given as (half-)holiday. 1886–. e. n. rogers Rope-yarn Sunday is the seaman's Monday. Actually, it is a half day off and comes on a Wednesday afternoon (1956).

rort verb **1** intr. and trans. Austral To engage in dishonest practices, to defraud. 1919–. **2** intr. To shout or complain loudly; to call the odds at a race-meeting. 1931–. noun **3** Austral A dishonest or sharp practice, a trick. 1926–. j. delaveny The cockies are supposed to pay this retention money into the bank . . . but normally they don't pay it in. . . . It's the greatest rort ever (1936). **4** Austral A crowd; a wild party. 1941–. g. johnston I am not, strictly, a true devotee of the wild Australian 'rort' and always remorseful in my hangovers (1969). [From rorty adjective.]

rorty adjective Fine, jolly; also, boisterous, noisy; coarse or earthy; crudely comic. 1882–. w. tute The rorty brigadier must have a taste for lean stringy meat, though of course

roller   rollicking   rollocks   roll-up   Roman Candle

rough-up

she had been a baronet's daughter and that made up for a lot (1969). [Of unknown origin.]

Rory O'More noun Also **rory**. Rhyming slang for: (*a*) the floor; (*b*) a door. 1857–. J. CURTIS Some lousy berk must have been snooping around the place and found that rory open (1936). [The name of a legendary Irish rebel.]

roscoe noun US A gun, esp. a pistol or revolver. 1914–. E. NEWMAN 'You'll shoot me if I don't sell?' . . . His hand went to the bulge again. 'Is that what they call a 'roscoe'? (1979). [From the surname *Roscoe*.]

rose noun **to pluck a rose** see at PLUCK verb.

rosin-back noun circuses' A horse used by a bareback rider or acrobat; a bareback rider. 1923–. C. B. COCHRAN A 'rosin-back' is a ring-horse used by bareback riders. . . . Rosin is rubbed into the horse's back to help the rider get a firm footing as he jumps from the ring on to the horse (1945). [From *rosin* resin, with which the horse's back was rubbed for a firmer seat.]

rosiner noun Irish and Austral A drink of spirits; a stiff drink. 1932–. D. STUART There's no harm in a bit of rosiner after a hard day's travel, just once in a while (1973). [From *rosin* resin.]

rosy adjective **1** Drunk, tipsy. 1905–. D. BAGLEY Sure, there was drinking. Some of the boys . . . got pretty smashed. . . . I was a bit rosy myself (1975). noun **2** naval A ship's rubbish-bin. 1937–.

Rosy Lee noun Also **Rosie** (**Lee**) and with small *r* (and *l*). Rhyming slang for 'tea'. 1925–. A. PRIOR This is the best cup of rosy I get all day, Janey (1964).

rot noun **1** Rubbish, nonsense. Also as int. See TOMMY-ROT. 1848–. C. MCCULLOUGH 'What if it isn't the Eyetie girl?' . . . 'Rot!' said Paddy scornfully (1977). verb trans. **2** To assail with banter; to abuse or denigrate; also absol, to talk nonsense, to joke. 1890–1934. **3** To spoil or ruin. Also with *up*. 1908–. A. BRIDGE I've got a complex about the whole business, and you know why. Well, that might rot it all up, at any moment (1932).

rot-gut noun Adulterated or poor liquid, esp. inferior whisky. Also as adjective. 1633–. E. O'NEILL That isn't Phil's rotgut. That's real, honest-to-God bonded Bourbon (1952).

rotten adjective **1** Austral Drunk. 1864–. J. FAMECHON A reporter from one of the Sydney papers—he was the last to leave, rotten

(1971). **2** Disagreeable, beastly; bad, poor, as in *rotten luck*, *shame*, etc. Also as adverb. 1880–.

rouf /raʊf/ adjective and noun Also **roaf, rofe, roof,** etc. Backslang (mainly criminals') for 'four', esp. four shillings or pounds; a four-year prison sentence. 1851–. K. ROYCE From under a pottery sugar jar . . . protruded two jacks. . . . I found a roof under them (1972).

rough adjective **1 rough as bags, guts,** etc. mainly Austral and NZ Coarse or uncouth. 1919–. F. HARDY The old Territorian is a good bloke, rough as guts but his heart's in the right place (1968). verb trans. **2 to rough up** to treat roughly, manhandle, assault. See ROUGH-UP noun. 1942–. M. BRAITHWAITE They began to rough us up and we kicked and pulled and yelled about what our dads would do if they didn't leave us alone (1970).

rough house noun **1** An uproar or disturbance; horseplay. Also as adjective. 1887–. E. BOWEN Mr. Bursely was shoved against the bookcase by Wallace Parker shoving, that rude way. . . . I didn't like him to see us so rough house (1938). verb **2** intr. To make a disturbance or row; to act boisterously or fight (*with*). 1900–. **3** trans. To treat violently. 1902–52.

roughie noun **1** A rough; a brawler or hooligan. 1905–. P. DRISCOLL I know a roughie when I see one. . . . He's just one of those blokes who can't stay away from trouble (1971). **2** Austral An outsider (in a horse- or dog-race). 1922–.

rough neck noun orig US **1** A rough; someone uncultivated or of a quarrelsome disposition; also as adjective. 1836–. D. HASTON Jimmy was twenty-eight, and already a qualified architect; we were seventeen- year-old roughnecks (1972). **2** An oil-rig worker, esp. a labourer on the rig-floor. 1917–.

rough spin noun Austral A misfortune or piece of bad luck. 1924–.

rough trade noun The tough or sadistic element among male homosexuals; male homosexual prostitute practices, or someone 'picked up' for these. 1935–. PLAYBOY The gay boys call us 'rough trade'! We're the ones they date. . . . We're the ones they buy presents for (1965).

rough-up noun **1** An informal encounter or contest. 1889–1951. E. RICKMAN This one may be fit enough in a week or two to be given a 'rough-up' (a good gallop with companions but not a formal trial) (1951). **2** A fight or brawl. 1896–.

Rory O'More   roscoe   rose   rosin-back   rosiner   rosy

rounder noun US A transient railway worker. 1908–. LISTENER His was a six-pipe job whose moans sent every coloured 'rounder' from Chicago to New Orleans into ecstasies (1961).

roundeye noun A European person (as opposed to a *slant-eye*, etc.). 1967–.

round heels noun mainly US (Implying unsteadiness on one's feet, esp. of a poor boxer or loose woman.) Also **round-heeled,** adjective and **round-heeler,** noun. 1926–. R. CHANDLER You'd think . . . I'd . . . picked me a change in types at least. But little roundheels over there ain't even that (1944).

roundhouse noun orig US A heavy blow delivered with a wide sweep of the arm. 1920–. J. KEROUAC Damion's girl suddenly socked Damion on the jaw with a roundhouse right (1958).

round-the-houses noun Rhyming slang for 'trousers'. 1857–.

roust N Amer, orig criminals'. verb trans. **1** To jostle; to harass or rough up. 1904–. N. THORNBURG He ran into Sergeant Verdugo, one of the detectives who had rousted him the night of the murder (1976). noun **2** An act of jostling or harassment. 1942–. [Earlier senses (stir, etc.) suggest derivation from *rouse*.]

row /rəʊ/ verb **to row in** to conspire. 1897–. P. ALLINGHAM I think these boys had better row in with us. . . . We may as well stick together (1934).

Roy noun Austral A smart, fashionable, or 'smooth' man. 1960–. NATION (Australia) Middle-class 'Roys' in sports cars and yachting jackets (1965). [From the male personal name.]

roz noun Abbreviation of ROZZER noun. 1971–.

rozzer noun A policeman or detective. 1893–. A. M. BINSTEAD He . . . nearly knocked down the rozzer in the mackintosh suit who was regulating the traffic from the middle of the road (1903). [Of unknown origin.]

rub verb **1 to rub up: a** trans. To stimulate sexually by rubbing or stroking. 1656–. **b** intr. To masturbate. 1937–. C. MACKENZIE Just as I was going down the steps into our area B- asked me if I ever rubbed up. . . . In bed that night I tried the experiment recommended by B- (1963).

2 to rub out orig US To kill or murder; to destroy. Cf. RUB-OUT noun. 1848–. A. LOMAX The gangsters . . . had promised to rub him out if he didn't stop trying to hire away their star New Orleans side-men (1950). noun **3** naval A loan *of* (earlier also *at*) money, etc. 1914–. W. LANG 'Innyone as hasn't had a letter can have a rub of mines,' says Moriarty, the big Irishman, generously (1919).

rub-a-dub(-dub) noun Austral and NZ Alteration of RUBBEDY noun. 1926–.

rubbedy noun Also **rubberdy, rubbity (-dub),** etc. Austral Rhyming slang for 'pub'; a hotel. 1898–. D. NILAND How about a gargle? Down to the rubberdy, come on (1957).

rubber noun A condom. 1947–. W. GADDIS What are you reading? . . . Malthus, for Christ sake. . . . The next thing, you'll be peddling rubbers in the street (1955).

'He . . . nearly knocked down the rozzer'

rubber johnny noun = RUBBER noun. 1980–.

rubbish verb trans. orig and mainly Austral and NZ To speak or write critically or disparagingly of; to criticize adversely. 1953–. OBSERVER His plight, and that of the cricketers, have both been latched on to as a chance, not to be missed, of rubbishing the Poms (1975). [From *rubbish* worthless material.]

rube variant of REUB noun.

rub-out noun orig US A murder or assassination, esp. in gang warfare. Cf. **to rub out** at RUB verb. 1927–. WASHINGTON POST Two hoodlums were gunned to death on Chicago's West Side today and police said at least one of the executions was probably a crime syndicate 'rubout' (1959).

ruby-dazzler noun Austral and NZ Something particularly fine. Cf. BOBBY-DAZZLER noun. 1941–.

Ruby Murray noun Brit A curry. 1983–. [Rhyming slang, from the name of the Northern Irish popular singer Ruby Murray (1935–96).]

Ruby Queen noun dated, services' An attractive young nurse. 1925–34. E. BLUNDEN With Ruby Queens We once crowned feeds of pork and beans (1934).

run

ruck verb **1** trans. To take to task; to reprimand or scold. 1936–. noun **2** A row or quarrel. 1958–. P. B. YUILL 'I heard him and her having a ruck about Nicholas, that's all.' 'What kind of a row?' (1976). [In sense 1, alteration of *rux* vb. (1899), of uncertain origin; in sense 2, perh. from *ruction* or RUCKUS noun.]

ruckus noun Also **rukus**, etc. mainly US A commotion or disturbance; an uproar, quarrel. 1890–. F. BLAKE With this Kiowa-'Rapaho ruckus and these picture-book soldiers that just showed up, we don't want anything more on our hands (1948). [Prob. from *ruction* and *rumpus*.]

ruddy adjective and adverb Euphemistic alteration of BLOODY adjective and adverb; damned, confounded. 1914–. J. JOYCE Lay you two to one Jenatzy licks him ruddy well hollow (1922).

rug noun **1** US A wig. 1940–. W. & M. MORRIS Advertisements for men's wigs invariably refer to them as *hair pieces*, but in the trade a wig may be a *doily*, a *divot* or a *rug* (1967). **2** Pubic hair, esp. of women. 1966–.

rug-cutter noun US An expert or enthusiastic dancer. Also **rug-cutting**, noun. 1938–. N. MAILER He seemed full of strength and merriment. He would clap two geishas to him, and call across . . . to another soldier. 'Hey, Brown,' he would shout, 'ain't this a rug-cutter!' (1959).

rugger bugger noun orig S Afr A boorish, chauvinistic, excessively masculine (young) man who is fanatical about sport, esp. rugby, and habitually participates in drunken, boisterous social gatherings. 1970–.

rug-muncher noun derog and offensive A lesbian; also, a man who performs cunnilingus. 1989–. Cf. CARPET MUNCHER noun. [From RUG noun 2.]

rug-rat noun N Amer A child. 1968–.

rule verb intr. –**rule(s) OK?** a slogan or graffito aggressively demanding assent. 1975–. SUNDAY EXPRESS When he left the train . . . he gave . . . a look which said: 'First Class Rules—O.K.?' (1976).

rum adjective Strange, odd; queer. Also, bad, spurious. 1774–. G. B. SHAW He must have been a rum old bird. . . . Not rum enough to be noticed (1930). [An application of *rum* = fine, splendid (1567–), as in *rum cove*.]

rumble verb **1** trans. To understand fully or see through; to grasp or recognize (something intentionally concealed from

another). 1886–. E. NEWMAN 'Have you any influence with him?' 'He'd rumble that. He'd think I was your agent' (1979). **2** intr. mainly US To take part in a gang-fight. 1959–. S. GREENLEE The teenage gangs . . . haven't a lot of latent hostility to get rid of (1969). noun **3** criminals' An interruption in the course of a crime; a tip-off. 1911–57. LIFE The boys slip into town. You wouldn't think they would be noticed. But some busybody catches on and puts in a rumble (1957). **4** mainly US A gang-fight. 1946–. [In senses 1 and 3, perh. a different word.]

rum-hound noun dated A heavy drinker. Cf. RUMMY noun 1. 1918–51.

rum-jar noun dated A type of German trench-mortar shell. 1916–.

rummy noun **1** mainly US An alcoholic; a drunkard. 1851–. G. B. SHAW Your Rummies of the tamest respectability pretending to a past of reckless and dazzling vice (1907). **2** dated US A fool; a sucker. 1912–37.

rumpo noun Brit = RUMPY-PUMPY noun. 1986–. EMPIRE Borrowing her hubbie's new car, Mrs Spong stops off for some rumpo. They get stuck together mid book (1999). [Prob. a variant of RUMPY-PUMPY noun, perh. inspired by the name of Rambling Sid *Rumpo*, character much given to sexual innuendo in the BBC radio comedy programme *Round the Horne* (1965–9).]

rum-pot noun N Amer = RUM-HOUND noun. 1930–. T. H. RADDALL I had him moved in there as soon as that rumpot of a doctor was off tae the toon (1966).

Rumpty[1] noun A nickname for the Farman training aeroplane, used in World War I. 1917–. V. M. YEATES Tom told them the first time he went up was in a Rumpty, that was to say, a Maurice Farman Shorthorn, a queer sort of bus like an assemblage of birdcages (1934). [From *rump*, after *bumpety*.]

rumpty[2] noun and adjective dated, Austral and NZ (Something) excellent or fine. 1941–6.

rumpy-pumpy noun Brit Sexual intercourse; also = HANKY-PANKY noun 2. Also **rumpty-tumpty**. 1986–. [Prob. elaborated from *rump* noun or a derivative.]

run verb **1** to run (someone) **in** to arrest (and imprison). 1859–. **2** trans. dated To report or surrender (something) to the police, etc.; (military) to bring a charge against. 1909–35. G. INGRAM Was any of you monkeying with the cocoa last night? . . . If I find out who it was,

ruck ruckus ruddy rug rug-cutter rugger bugger

rundown

I'll run 'im and make it' 'ot for him (1933).
3 US **a: to run off at the mouth** to talk excessively; to talk nonsense. 1909–. NATIONAL OBSERVER The man they simply ran off at the mouth about here, Jimmy Carter (1976). **b: to run one's mouth** mainly Black English To talk profusely or excessively; to chatter; to complain. Cf. *to shoot off one's mouth* at SHOOT verb 1. 1940–. TIME All there is to real estate is running your mouth a bit, knocking on doors and asking people if they want to sell their house (1977). **4** trans. mainly Austral To drive through or 'jump' (a red traffic light). 1935–. **5 to run down: a** trans. US To rehearse or perform (music); to recite (verse). 1948–. R. RUSSELL Bernie struck off a rich chord and began running the tune down in his immaculate post-Teddy Wilson style (1961). **b: to run it down** US To explain a situation in full or truthfully. 1964–.

rundown noun **1** dated, US, horse-racing A list of entries and betting odds. Mainly attrib 1935–51. **2** orig US A catalogue of information, facts, etc.; a short description. 1945–. T. PYNCHON John Nefastis . . . brought out his Machine . . . 'You know how this works?' 'Stanley gave me a kind of rundown' (1966).

run-in noun criminals' A hiding-place for stolen goods. 1959–. D. WARNER Just waiting to hear that the lorry reached the run-in. It's late (1962).

runner noun **1** mainly US Someone who trafficks in prohibited liquor, etc. 1930–. **2 to do a runner** Brit to depart hurriedly, esp. orig. to escape quickly from the police or other authority. 1981–. MORE! They sense you want something else, but they're so scared of whatever it might be that they do a runner (1992).

running jump noun **to take a running jump (at oneself)** used as an expression of contempt, hostility, or indifference. 1933–. LANDFALL If you think I'm subsidizing you . . . you can take a running jump at yourself (1968).

run-off noun An act of urination. 1961–.

runs noun pl. euphemistic Diarrhoea. 1962–. B. MALAMUD Sam Clemence, a witness from Harlem U.S.A., despite a bad case of the runs.., stands up for his friend Willie (1971). [From the notion of having to run to the lavatory.]

ruptured duck noun US, forces' **1** dated A damaged aeroplane. 1930. **2** A button given on discharge from the Services. 1945–. W. FAULKNER The ex-soldier or -sailor or -marine with his ruptured duck pushing the perambulator with one hand (1959). [In sense 2, from its eagle design.]

rush verb trans. To charge (a customer) an exorbitant price; to cheat or defraud. 1887–. N. W. SCHUR 'How much did they rush you for that sherry?' To rush is to charge, with the distinct implication that the price was too high (1973).

rushee /rʌˈʃiː/ noun US, colleges' Someone 'rushed' or entertained to assess their suitability for membership of a fraternity or sorority; a candidate for membership. 1916–. AMERICAN SPEECH The girl rushee who does not have 'tights-omania' will be blackballed in short order (1960).

Rusky noun and adjective Also **Russky, Roosky,** etc. (A) Russian or Soviet. 1858–. C. MACINNES We've got to produce our own variety, and not imitate the Americans—or the Ruskis, or anybody (1959).

rust-bucket noun **1** N Amer An old, rusty ship. 1945–. **2** mainly Austral An old, rust-ridden car. 1965–.

rux noun dated, naval A disturbance or uproar. 1918–31. R. KIPLING The nastiest rux I ever saw, when a boy, began with 'All hands to skylark.' / don't hold with it (1931). [See RUCK verb and noun.]

rye noun dated A man; a gentleman. Also **rye-mort,** noun A lady; **rye must,** noun A gentleman. 1851–1939. J. CURTIS Anyone taking a quick look at her might think she was on the up-and-up. She would give that impression too, to anyone who heard her talk and saw her act. Though . . . she would have to give up that rye mort touch. (1936). [From Romany *rai* gentleman.]

ryebuck Also **ribuck,** etc. dated, mainly Austral. adjective **1** Good, excellent, genuine. Also as adverb. 1859–. R. H. KNYVETT They even knew our slang, for there was 'The "Fair Dinkum" Store', and across the way 'Ribuck Goods' (1918). int **2** An expression of agreement or assent. 1859–. C. J. DENNIS We kin get an intro, if we've luck. 'E sez, 'Ribuck' (1916). [Of uncertain origin: cf. German *Reibach* profit.]

rundown   run-in   runner   running jump   run-off

S.A. noun Also **s.a.** Abbreviation of 'sex appeal'. 1926–. E. MCGIRR I saw you and the dame go into her apartment. . . . I expected you to take longer. Losing the old s.a., Piron? (1974).

sac noun Also **sacch.** (A tablet of) saccharine. 1961–. E. TREVOR Sacchs. You couldn't get them down there (1968). [Shortening.]

sack noun **1** Dismissal from service or employment; mainly in phr. *to get* (or *give* someone) *the sack*. 1825–. **2** mainly US **a** orig naval A hammock or bunk. 1829–. D. DEVINE The first time I came on board you were lying in your goddam sack (1950). **b** A bed; esp. in phrs. *to hit the sack*, to go to (or collapse into) bed; (*to be good*, etc.) *in the sack* (with reference to sexual intercourse). 1943–. J. UPDIKE Women with that superheated skin are usually fantastic in the sack (1968). **3** US A bag of paper or other material. 1904–. B. HOLIDAY I got so tired of scenes in crummy roadside restaurants over getting served, I used to . . . sit on the bus and rest—and let them bring me out something in a sack (1956). **4** N Amer, football A tackle on the quarterback behind the scrimmage line before he can make a pass; the act of tackling in this way. 1972–. DETROIT FREE PRESS Other changes have been made, this year and in recent years, to put juice into the offence, the feeling being that people come to see touchdowns and not quarterback sacks (1978). verb **5** trans. To dismiss (someone) from service or employment. See SACK noun 1. 1841–. **6 to sack in** orig US To go to bed; to lie in. 1946–. T. WELLS Benedict's call, at about nine o'clock, woke me up. . . . I'd planned to sack in till about eleven (1967). **7 to sack out** mainly US To go to bed; to sleep. 1946–. DAILY TELEGRAPH Many young travellers . . . are faced with the choice of curling up in a doorway or 'sacking out' in some of London's parks (1971). **8 to sack down** to go to bed. 1956–. E. V. CUNNINGHAM I lost a night's sleep. . . . How about I sack down for a few hours? (1978). **9** N Amer, football trans. To tackle (the quarterback) behind the line of scrimmage before he can make a pass. 1969–. WASHINGTON POST Kilmer . . . was sacked early in the second quarter by Bears tackle Ron Rydalch (1976). [In sense 1, equivalent phrases recorded in French, Dutch, etc., though the precise derivation is not clear: perh. the bag of tools returned to an apprentice on dismissal.]

sack drill noun US, naval Sleep, or time spent in bed. Also **sack duty**. 1946–.

sacker noun N Amer, baseball A baseman; a fieldsman who guards a base. Usu. as **first sacker** (= first baseman), etc. 1914–. H. E. WEST Wally Pipp became the Yankee first sacker in 1915, and Lou Gehrig succeeded him ten years later and is still going strong (1938).

sack rat noun US A person who spends too much time in bed; a shirker. 1978–. H. WOUK A perfect solution, you young sack rat (1978).

sack time noun orig US, services' Time spent in bed. Cf. SACK DRILL noun. 1944–. ALFRED HITCHCOCK'S MYSTERY MAGAZINE Last night, when I was just getting eyes for some sack time, this bear falls up to my pad, a type looking to score for free (1959).

sacré bleu /ˌsækreɪ ˈblɜː/ int A French oath. 1869–. M. TWAIN 'Is, ah—is he dead?' 'Oh, *sacre bleu*, been dead three thousan' year!' (1869). [Literally 'sacred blue', euphemism for *sacré Dieu* 'sacred God'.]

sad-ass adjective N Amer Poor, contemptible: as a term of abuse. Also **sad-assed**. 1971–. BLACK WORLD How is Philadelphia? . . . Thats one sad-ass city . . . bout to sink into the ground (1971). [*ass = arse*.]

saddle tramp noun N Amer A vagrant who travels on horseback. 1942–. RADIO TIMES Kirk Douglas back on the range for King Vidor, in the one about the saddle tramp up against the barbed wire (1979).

saddling paddock noun Austral A bar at the Theatre Royal, Melbourne (a favourite rendezvous for prostitutes in the 19th cent.); a similar bar or place of rendezvous elsewhere. 1876–. G. CASEY The ribald, popular name of the enclosure round the Government Dam was 'the saddling paddock' (1958).

saddo noun A socially inadequate, unfashionable, or otherwise contemptible person. 1992–. NET He actually met his wife through CompuServe, but is not a saddo in spite of this (1994).

S.A. sac sack sack drill sacker sack rat sack time

sad sack noun mainly US A stupid, blundering serviceman; someone who is inept or unfortunate. 1943–. M. MCLUHAN Model mother saddled with a sad sack and a dope (1951). [A cartoon character created by the US cartoonist G. Baker.]

safe noun A contraceptive sheath or condom. 1897–. E. KOCH Just in time he remembered his safe. He took it out of his pants pocket (1979).

safe adjective orig S Afr Good, excellent; OK, fine. 1970–. A. WHEATLE 'Yeah. I have to go back inside for a pen so I can write down my phone number.' 'Yeah, safe' (1999).

sag verb intr. and trans. Merseyside To play truant (from). 1959–. WOMAN I re-visit childhood haunts in Liverpool, meet the next generation in the Cathedral grounds where we used to 'sag'— that is, play truant (1965). [From *sag*, sink or hang down (with intermediate Naval sense, to drift off course).]

sailor's blessing noun naval A curse. 1876–.

sailor's farewell noun A parting curse. 1937–.

sainted adjective **my sainted aunt** (formerly also **mother**)!: a mild expletive. 1869–. P. G. WODEHOUSE 'Oh, my aunt! Don't tell me she's changed her mind and wants the stuff after all?' . . . 'Exactly.' 'Oh, my sainted bally aunt!' (1939).

sake noun In various mild oaths, such as **for Pete's sake** (1924–) [after **for pity's** (**God's, goodness**) **sake,** dating from the Middle Ages.] W. GOLDING Marry me, Taffy, for Pete's sake marry me (1959).

salaud /sælǝʊ/ noun A French term of abuse: 'swine', 'bastard'. 1962–. D. LESSING Jules said he would only pay me three hundred dollars for it. Salaud! (1962). [French, from *sale* dirty.]

sale Boche /ˌsæl ˈbɒʃ/ noun A French term of abuse for a German. 1919–. D. L. SAYERS A man . . . called him *sale Boche*—but Jean knocked him down (1934). [From French *sale* (see SALAUD noun) and *Boche* (orig = rascal, applied esp. to Germans in World War I).]

Sally noun **1a** The Salvation Army. 1915–. **b** A member of this; in pl. the Salvation Army. 1936–. D. NILAND The woman that runs it, she used to be some sort of high-up with the Sallies down in Sydney (1957). **2** A Salvation Army hostel. 1931–. NEW STATESMAN Julie Felix sang against the Salvation Army—and we were . . . miles away from the sad Sally where the

methdrinkers are deloused (1966). [Alteration of *Salvation* (*Army*); cf. SALVO noun.]

Sally Ann(e) noun Also **Sally Army.** The Salvation Army; a Salvation Army hostel. 1927–. W. A. HAGELUND Now you go see the Major at the Johnson Street Sally Anne about some meal tickets and beds (1961). [See SALLY noun.]

salt verb trans. **1 to salt away, down** to put by (money, etc.); to store away, esp. in order to conceal profits. 1849–. KANSAS CITY (Missouri) STAR It is a well known fact that all gamblers salt away their ill-gotten gains and die inordinately rich (1931). **2** To misrepresent the value of (a mine) by introducing ore from elsewhere; also fig. 1852–. **3** To misrepresent the contents of (an account), by adding ghost entries, falsifying details, etc. 1882–.

Saltash luck noun A miserable task that involves getting wet through. Also **Saltash chance.** 1914–. BARTIMEUS One of the securing chains wants tautening. . . . 'Saltash Luck' for some one! (1914). [Supposedly from the lucklessness of the fishermen of Saltash, a port in Cornwall.]

salt chuck noun N Amer A west Canadian and north-western US term for the sea; the ocean. 1868–. G. CASH Unless you are camped near a long dump—which means where a logging company is dumping logs into the salt chuck—you have quite a time gathering enough (1938). [Chinook jargon, from *salt* + *chuck* (= water).]

salt horse noun naval **1** Salted beef. 1836–. **2** An officer with general duties. 1914–. TAFFRAIL Next came Lieutenant Hinckson, the senior 'salt horse', two and a half striped Lieutenant (1917).

salty adjective US **1** naval Of a sailor: tough, aggressive. 1920–41. M. GOODRICH The consensus was that Delilah's men now, for some reason, thought they were 'salty' and were looking for trouble (1941). **2** Angry; hostile; **to jump salty** to change one's mood suddenly; to become annoyed. 1938–.

Salvo noun Austral A member of the Salvation Army; in pl. the Salvation Army. Also as adjective. 1891–. R. MCKIE When workers everywhere got their notices and the slump showed every sign of lasting, the Salvos decided to open a doss house (1978). [As SALLY noun, with Austral. colloquial suffix -o, as in *arvo*, etc.]

sambie noun Also **sammie.** mainly Austral and NZ A sandwich. 1976–. B. HUMPHRIES Some exciting sambies . . . an increasingly popular diminutive for 'sandwiches' (1976). [From *samb-*, representing the pronunciation of *sand(wich*, + *-ie*; cf. SARNIE noun.]

Sambo¹ noun A nickname and, more recently, an (offensive) derogatory name for a black person. 1704–. [Origin uncertain; perh. from Spanish, person of mixed race, or from an African language (e.g. Foulah, uncle).]

sambo² noun Austral A sandwich. 1984–. SUNDAY MORNING HERALD The last sprig of parsley disappeared from the final platter of sambos (1984). [From SAMB(IE + -o.]

Sam Hill noun N Amer A euphemism for 'Hell', esp. in *what in* (or *the*) *Sam Hill . . . !* 1839–. M. E. FREEMAN What in Sam Hill made you treat him so durned mean fur? (1918). [Origin unknown, except for the alteration of *hell* to *hill*.]

Sammy noun Brit World War I term for an American soldier. 1917–21. [From *Uncle Sam*, personification of the US federal government.]

sand verb trans. **to sand and canvas** orig naval To clean thoroughly. Also fig. 1912–33.

sandbag verb orig and mainly US **1** trans. To coerce or bully; to criticize. 1901–. **2a** intr. and trans. poker To hold off from raising at the first opportunity in the hope of raising by a greater amount later. 1940–. D. ANTHONY He fondled his stack of blue chips. He was sandbagging me. I gave him the same dose of silence (1977). **b** intr. More generally, to underperform in a race or other competition in order to gain an unfair handicap or other advantage. 1985–. Also **sandbagger,** noun. 1893–; **sandbagging,** noun. 1940–. [From earlier sense, to fell with a blow from a sandbag.]

sand-groper noun Austral A non-Aboriginal person, native to or resident in Western Australia. Cf. GROPER noun. 1896–.

san fairy ann(e) phr An expression of indifference or resigned acceptance. 1919–. L. BRIAN 'I wish you'd thought of my ulcer before you—' he began, and then broke off. 'Oh, san fairy anne!' (1965). [Humorous alteration of French *ça ne fait rien* it doesn't matter.]

sanger noun Also **sango**. Austral A sandwich. 1943–. SUNDAY MAIL (Brisbane) A colleague went to order a chicken 'sanger' and decided to ask the serving lady why they seemed 'a little thin of late' (1980). [From alteration of *san(dwich* + *-er*, *-o*.]

sanguinary adjective A euphemistic or humorous substitute for 'bloody', in oaths, etc. 1890–. G. B. SHAW The inhabitants raise up their voices and call one another sanguinary liars (1910).

sanno (man) noun Also **sano (man)**. Austral A man who collects excrement from unsewered areas. 1959–. L. FOX Mother sympathised with the Sanno man's job; she always greeted him (1977). [From *san(itary* + *-o*.]

sap¹ noun A fool or simpleton. 1815–. I. & P. OPIE The word 'sap' . . . the children define as meaning a sissy or a softy ('soft' in that he does not do anything wrong), and suggest other moist alternatives, as 'milksop', 'soppy date', a 'wet', or a 'drip' (1959). [Abbreviation of earlier *sapskull*, in the same sense.]

sap² US. noun **1** A club or short staff. 1899–. R. CHANDLER He had the sap out this time, a nice little tool about five inches long, covered with woven brown leather (1940). verb **2** trans. To hit with a club or 'sap'. Also with *up* and (intr.) *up on* (someone). 1926–. J. BLACK The posse fell upon the convention and 'sapped up' on those therein assembled and ran them . . . out of town (1926). [In sense 1, from *sap* vital juice, in sense 'sapwood', soft wood between the heart and the bark.]

sapristi /sæˈprɪstɪ/ int An exclamation of astonishment, exasperation, etc. 1839–. A. CHRISTIE Ah *Sapristi!* That must be a woman—undoubtedly a woman (1966). [French, alteration of *sacristi!*]

sarbut /ˈsaːbət/ noun Also **sarbot**. Birmingham A police informer. 1897–. R. BUSBY Your sarbut's story wasn't good enough. . . . We were fooled (1969). [Apparently a proper name.]

sarky adjective Brit Sarcastic, mocking. 1912–. DIARY OF A PUBLIC SCHOOL GIRL Made some currant buns. Bob very sarky about them (1930). [From *sarc(astic* + *-y*.]

sarnie noun A sandwich. 1961–. [From colloquial and northern pronunciation of *sand(wich*); cf. SAMMIE noun.]

sass US. noun **1** Also **sas**. Impudent talk. 1835–. P. WELLES Is this what we get? Sass? No gratitude (1967). verb trans. and intr. **2** To speak rudely (to). 1856–. W. FAULKNER Don't you sass me, nigger boy (1929). [Alteration of *sauce* noun and verb.]

Saturday night noun In various expressions, as: **1 Saturday night palsy** (or **paralysis**) (mainly US), temporary local

sambo Sam Hill sambie Sammy sand sandbag

paralysis of the arm, usu. as a result of sleeping on it after hard drinking. 1927–. E. PAUL Berthe was suffering from what is known in the United States as Saturday-night paralysis, . . . when drunken men go to sleep in gutters, with one arm across a sharp kerbstone (1951). **2 Saturday night pistol (or special)**, a cheap handgun of the type used by petty criminals. 1929–. **3 Saturday night soldier**, a volunteer soldier, a Territorial. 1917–. [From *Saturday night*, the traditional evening for enjoying oneself or taking some other occupation than that usual during the week.]

sauce noun orig US Alcoholic drink. 1940–. W. TREVOR 'You often get loonies in joints like that,' he remarked on the street. 'They drink the sauce and it softens their brains for them' (1976).

saucepan lid noun Rhyming slang for: **1** A pound or 'quid'. 1951–. **2** A child or 'kid'. 1960–.

sausage noun **1** A German. 1890–1929. **2** A type of German trench-mortar. 1915–26. **3 not a sausage** nothing at all. 1938–. TIMES Mr Healey said the press did not print Labour's actual policies. 'Not a sausage' (1981). **4** Austral The penis; mainly in the jocular phr. *to hide the sausage* to have sexual intercourse. 1944–. D. WILLIAMSON Raylene's a hell of a nice girl but the word is she's not a great one for hiding the sausage (1977). [In sense 2, from its shape.]

sausage balloon noun services' A kite balloon used for observation. 1916–30. SAPPER A row of sausage balloons like a barber's rash adorned the sky (1917). [From earlier sense, an elongated air-balloon (1874–).]

sav noun A saveloy. 1936–. C. DRUMMOND Some home-made savs—not the shop kind (1969). [Shortening.]

savvy Also **savee, savey**. verb **1** trans. and intr. To know or understand: in a question (e.g. 'Do you savvy?'), following an explanation esp. to a foreigner or someone thought slow-witted. 1785–. M. LOWRY Let's have two starboard lights. Savee starboard lights? (1933). noun **2** Intelligence, understanding, 'gumption'. 1785–. W. R. TITTERTON Which idea . . . Armstrong actively disliked because, having more savvy than I had, he saw it meant death to his doctrine (1936). adjective **3** Of a person, etc.: knowing, quick-witted; wise (*to

something). 1905–. [From Black or pidgin English, after Spanish *sabe usted* 'you know'.]

saw verb **1 to saw gourds** US To snore. 1870–. **2 to saw a chunk** (etc.) **off** to copulate. 1961–. J. WAINWRIGHT The act is . . . known, in polite circles, as 'copulation'. Known, in less polite circles, as . . . 'sawing a length off snoring' (1977). [In sense 1, from the sound of snoring.]

sawbones noun A surgeon or doctor. 1837–. R. HAGGARD I found her the affianced bride of a parish sawbones (1898).

sawbuck noun US **1** Ten dollars, a ten-dollar bill. 1850–. J. WAMBAUGH I gave him a ten, which was just like folding up a sawbuck and sticking it in his arm. He'd be in the same shape twelve hours from now (1973). **2** A ten-year prison sentence. 1925–50. Cf. DOUBLE SAWBUCK noun. [In sense 1, from the x-shaped end (Roman X = 10) of a sawyer's horse or 'buck'.]

saw gourds
to snore

sawn noun Austral Abbreviation of SAWNEY noun 1953–. K. TENNANT I'm always getting into trouble through sawns (1953).

sawney noun A fool or simpleton. 1700–. [Perh. a variant of the proper name *Sandy*, as in the earlier sense *sawney* a Scotsman.]

scab noun **1** A term of contempt for a person; a rascal, scoundrel. 1590–. **2** derog A worker who refuses to join a trade union or association; a blackleg or strike-breaker. 1777–. SOCIALIST WORKER 180 women walked out. But 70 stayed in. . . . The scabs soon found out what it was like to be hated (1974). verb intr. **3** derog To refuse to join a trade-union or association; to act as a blackleg, to strike-break. 1806–. [From the literal sense of the noun, a dry, rough incrustation formed over a wound or sore.]

scads noun pl. mainly US A large amount or number. 1869–. Also **scad** noun. 1950–. WASHINGTON POST In addition to King, scads of other veteran players should contend (1993). [From *scad* dollar, hence (in pl.) money; ultimate origin unknown.]

scag noun orig US Also **skag. 1** A cigarette (stub). 1915–36. **2** Heroin. 1967–. N. ADAM I'm no junkie myself, never touched the scag, never even used the White Dragon Pearl (1977). [Of unknown origin.]

scale noun **1** US A coin; money. 1872–1929. verb trans. and intr. **2** Austral and NZ To avoid paying what is due (esp. one's fare); to cheat or defraud (someone); to steal (something). Esp. in phr. *to scale a train* (*tram*, etc.), to ride on public transport without paying. 1904–. SYDNEY MORNING HERALD The tram guards . . . were generally much admired by little boys, even though we did our best to outwit them by 'scaling' a ride, crouching unseen on the footboard on the other side of the tram (1984). [From the noun, overlapping protective plate on a fish, and the verb, to remove (this).]

scaler noun Austral and NZ A fraudster or cheat; someone who 'scales' a train or tram. 1915–. G. CROSS The Tramway is very down on scalers, and brings a court action whenever possible . . . against people who try to swindle His Majesty's government (1981). [From SCALE verb.]

scally noun Brit In Liverpool and Manchester: a rogue or 'chancer'. 1986–. INDEPENDENT I think McCartney has the philosophy that he was one of four scallys who did it all with no assistance (1990). [Shortened from *scallywag* noun.]

scalp verb trans. orig US To sell (stock, tickets, etc.), esp. below the official rates. Also intr. 1886–. SUN (Baltimore): The Stadium attendants told me they are the same men . . . who scalp at other games, . . . selling 60-cent tickets for $1 (1948).

scalper noun orig US Someone who sells tickets, etc., esp. below the official rates; spec. a spectator who touts tickets for a show, lottery, etc. at inflated prices. 1869–. G. VIDAL One-third of the tickets for the rally . . . are now in the hands of scalpers who are selling the most desirable seats . . . for as high as one thousand dollars a-piece (1978). [See SCALP verb.]

scam orig US. noun **1** A trick or ruse; a swindle, a racket (spec. a fraudulent bankruptcy). 1963–. M. PUZO The bribe-taking scam had been going on for nearly two years without any kind of hitch (1978). **2** A story or rumour; information. 1964–. verb intr. and trans. **3** To defraud or cheat; to trick, swindle. 1963–. NEW YORKER Local citizens . . . try to avoid being scammed by the familiar tergiversations of city politicians (1977). [Of unknown origin.]

scammer noun Also **skammer.** orig US A criminal, esp. a petty crook or swindler. 1972–. L. SANDERS 'You're good,' he said, 'but not *that* good. Never try to scam a scammer' (1980). [From SCAM verb + -er.]

scarecrow noun services' A manoeuvre, weapon, etc. used for its deterrent effect. 1943–66. M. TRIPP Two daylight attacks on Solingen. . . . Gigantic blobs of oily smoke hung in the sky. . . . It was their first experience of the German terror weapon, the scarecrow (1952).

scarf US. noun **1** Food. 1932–. L. SNELLING How's for a bit of scarf, my tummy's anguished (1973). verb trans. and intr. **2** To eat, scoff. Also with *up*, *down*. 1960–. [Variant of *scoff*.]

scarfing noun Brit The practice of auto-asphyxiation for sexual stimulation. 1994–.

scarper verb intr. **1** To depart quickly; to run away or escape. 1846–. E. CRISPIN He's downstairs now with the others—and they're keeping a sharp eye on him; he won't have a chance to scarper again (1977). noun **2 to do a scarper** to run away, 'do a bunk'. 1958–. [Prob. from Italian *scappare* to escape or get away, reinforced (at the time of World War I) by rhyming slang *Scapa Flow* 'go'.]

scat[1] noun US Whisky. 1914–55. PUBLICATIONS OF THE AMERICAN DIALECT SOCIETY Peter men don't punch much guff as a rule, but sometimes the scat will loosen them up for some good yarns (1955).

scat[2] noun Heroin. 1970–. D. E. WESTLAKE You're dealing in machismo, man, just like I'm dealing in scat (1972). [From earlier sense, dung, (pl.) animal droppings, from the Greek *skat-, skōr* dung. Cf. SHIT noun.]

schiz /skɪts/ mainly N Amer noun **1** A schizophrenic person; esp. someone who experiences drug-induced hallucinations. 1955–. A. LURIE How can you tell what a schiz like her is going to do? (1967). adjective **2** Schizophrenic. 1960–. [Abbreviation of *schizophrenic*; cf. SCHIZO noun and adjective.]

schizo /ˈskɪtsəʊ/ noun **1** A schizophrenic person. 1945–. J. I. M. STEWART He might have been a schizo . . . for all the tie-up there seemed to be between the Phil of this rational conversation and the Phil who wanted Jean Caraway (1961). adjective **2** Schizophrenic. 1957–. [Abbreviation of *schizophrenic*; cf. SCHIZ noun and adjective.]

schlemiel /ʃləˈmiːl/ noun mainly US An awkward, clumsy person; a 'born loser', someone foolish or unprepossessing. 1892–. B. SCHULBERG Don't talk like a schlemiel, you schlemiel. Sounds like you're letting them push you around (1941). [Yiddish.]

schlenter /ˈʃlentə(r)/ noun **1** Also **slanter, slinter,** etc. Austral and NZ A trick. 1864–.

scale scaler scally scalp scalper scam scammer

F. J. HARDY One rider was prepared to make a sworn statement that the race had been rigged. . . . Cycling enthusiasts became convinced that Austral had been a 'slanter' (1950). **2** S Afr Something counterfeit, esp. a fake diamond. 1892–. J. M. WHITE The best Schlenters in South West are made from the marbles in the necks of the lemonade or mineral-water bottles that can be found in dozens in the old German diggings (1969). adjective **3** Austral, NZ, and S Afr Counterfeit; fake. 1889–. C. J. DENNIS The slanter game I'd played wiv my Doreen— . . . I seen wot made me feel fair rotten mean (1916). [From Afrikaans, Dutch *slenter* knavery, or a trick.]

schlep /ʃlep/ Also **schlepp, shlep**. mainly US. verb **1** trans. To drag or carry. Also transf and fig. 1922–. R. H. RIMMER Merle schleps cocktails at the Persian Room in the Sheraton between six and midnight (1975). **2** intr. To toil or slave; to go with effort, to traipse. 1963–. D. E. WESTLAKE We don't both have to hang around. Why don't you shlep back to the station (1972). noun **3** = SCHLEPPER noun. 1939–. **4** Something difficult or troublesome; hard work. 1964–. [Yiddish *shlepn*, from German *schleppen* to drag.]

schlepper /ʃlepə(r)/ noun mainly US Someone contemptuous; a fool or beggar. 1934–. G. MARX The paupers, or schlepper crowd, still hang on to their portable radios, but unfortunately they're not the ones who buy Chryslers (1950). [See SCHLEP verb.]

schlimazel /ʃlɪmɒz(ə)l/ noun Also **shlemazl**, etc. mainly US Someone consistently unlucky or accident-prone. 1948–. ENCOUNTER If the *schlimazl* went into the hat business, babies would be born without heads (1960). [Yiddish, from Middle High German *slim* crooked and Hebrew *mazzāl* luck.]

schlock /ʃlɒk/ noun and adjective Also **shlock**. mainly N Amer Cheap, shoddy, or defective goods; rubbish, junk (esp. applied to inferior art or entertainment). 1915–. Hence **schlocky,** adjective Shoddy, trashy, or of inferior standard. 1968–. [Yiddish, apparently from *slogn* to strike.]

schlong /ʃlɒŋ/ noun Also **shlong**. US A penis; also applied contemptuously to a person. 1969–. T. BOYLE He's stark naked and he's got about the longest schlong I ever seen on a white man (1985). [From Yiddish *shlang*, from Middle High German *slange* serpent.]

schlub /ʃlʌb/ noun Also **shlub**. US Someone foolish or worthless; an oaf. 1964–. E. MCBAIN 'Kaplowitz,' I say, 'are you a janitor or a schlub?' 'I'm a janitor. . . . And such a dirty basement I can't stand' (1964). [Yiddish, perh. from Polish *żłób* a blockhead.]

schlump /ʃlʊmp/ noun Also **schloomp, shlump**. orig and mainly US A dull-witted or slovenly person; a slob, fool. Also in affectionate abuse. 1948–. J. HELLER Kissinger would not be recalled in history as a Bismarck . . . but as an odious *shlump* who made war gladly (1979). [Prob. from Yiddish; cf. Yiddish *schlumperdik* dowdy, German *Schlumpe* slattern.]

schm- prefix Also **shm-**. Added to or replacing the beginning of a word, which then follows the original word, to form a doublet indicating contempt, derision, etc., as 'Oedipus, Schmoedipus'. 1929–. I. GOLLER 'I know he made Davy go to the Palace to-day with the idea of hastening on the crisis in his illness.' . . . '*Crisis-schmisis*!' mocked Barnett disparagingly (1929). [In imitation of the many Yiddish words beginning with this letter-sequence.]

schmaltz /ʃmɒlts, ʃmælts/ Also **shmaltz**, etc. orig US. noun **1** Sentimentality; writing, music, etc. which is considered sentimental or 'sugary'. 1935–. verb trans. **2** To give a sentimental or 'sugary' aspect to; to play (music) in this way; often followed by up. 1936–. D. SKIRROW She was like the white light of early morning, before the hot sun schmalzes up the scene (1966). [From German and Yiddish *schmalz* fat, dripping, also used in English (1931–) in the sense 'melted chicken fat'.]

schmaltzy /ʃmɒltsɪ, ʃmæltsɪ/ adjective orig US Sentimentalized, 'corny'. 1935–. [See SCHMALTZ noun.]

schmatte /ʃmætə/ noun Also **shmatte**, etc. US A rag or ragged garment; hence, any item of clothing. 1970–. [Yiddish, from Polish *szmata*: see SCHMUTTER noun.]

schmeck /ʃmek/ noun mainly US A drug, esp. heroin. Cf. SMACK noun. 1932–. M. CALPAN 'He was always wild. . . . Anything for kicks. . . . In the end it was schmeck.' 'Heroin?' 'Yes. Hooked' (1967). [From Yiddish *schmeck* sniff.]

schmecker /ʃmekə(r)/ noun Also **shmecker**, etc. US A drug-addict, esp. someone who takes heroin. 1953–. W. BURROUGHS He went on talking about some old acquaintances who got their start in junk and later turned respectable. 'Now they say, "Don't have anything to do with Sol. He's a *schmecker*" ' (1953). [From SCHMECK noun.]

schlep schlepper schlimazel schlock schlong schm-

schmeer /ʃmɪə(r)/ Also **schmere, shmeer,** etc. N Amer. verb trans. and intr. **1** To flatter; to bribe. 1930–. noun **2** Bribery or corruption; flattery. 1961–. **3** In phr. *the whole schmeer*, everything, the 'whole thing'. 1969–. **H. KEMELMAN** Some special kind of prayer maybe where you could ask for the success of an enterprise ... especially the financing, but I was thinking of the whole *shmeer* (1972). [From Yiddish *schmirn* to smear, grease, or flatter.]

schmegeggy /ʃməˈgegɪ/ noun Also **shmegegge,** etc. US **1** A contemptible person; a fool or idiot. 1964–. **OBSERVER** He says he's a schlemiel which is ... better than being a schmagogy ... Schlemiels ... drop things and ... they drop on schmagogys (1971). **2** Rubbish, nonsense. [Apparently Yiddish: of uncertain ulterior derivation.]

schmendrik /ʃmendrɪk/ noun Also **shmendrik,** etc. US Someone foolish, immature, or contemptible; an upstart or 'sucker'. 1944–. [From the name of a character in an operetta by Abraham Goldfaden (1840–1908).]

schmo /ʃməʊ/ noun Also **shmo,** etc. mainly US A fool or idiot. 1948–. **D. FRANCIS** 'Who,' he said crossly, 'is going to give that schmo a thousand quid for breaking his ankle? (1970). [Shortened from SCHMUCK noun.]

schmooze /ʃmuːz, ʃmuːs/ Also **schmoos(e),** verb intr. **1** To chat or gossip; to engage in a long, intimate conversation. 1897–. **H. KEMELMAN** On Friday nights or Saturdays, don't we stand around after the services and *schmoos* a while? (1966). noun **2** (A) chat or gossip; a long, intimate conversation. 1939–. [From Yiddish *shmuesn* to talk or chat, *schmues* (noun), from Hebrew *shěmū'ah* rumour.]

schmuck /ʃmʌk/ noun Also **shmuck,** etc. mainly US Someone objectionable or contemptible; an idiot. Also **schmucky,** adjective. 1892–. [From Yiddish (orig a taboo-word for 'penis').]

schmutter /ʃmʌtə(r)/ noun Also **shmutter,** etc. mainly US Clothing, rags. Often attrib, as **schmutter trade,** etc. Also fig, rubbish. 1959–. **G. SIMS** They said it was like Buck House but it was a right load of old schmutter! You see, everyone's an antique dealer today (1967). [From Yiddish *schmatte*: see SCHMATTE noun.]

schmutz /ʃmʊts/ noun Also **shmutz,** etc. mainly US Filth, dirt; rubbish. 1967–. **M. RICHLER** 'Of my son's ability there is no question.' '—and, em, the contents of your son's novel. You see—' '*Shmutz*,' Daniels shouted at Katansky.

'Pardon?' 'Filth. Today nothing sells like filth' (1968). [From Yiddish or German *schmutz*.]

schnockered /ʃnɒkəd/ adjective US Humorous alteration of SNOCKERED adjective, drunk. 1955–. **B. GARFIELD** Bradleigh took the empty glass. 'That's probably enough. You don't want to get schnockered' (1977).

schnook /ʃnʊk/ noun Also **shnook,** etc. US A dupe or simpleton; a poor wretch. 1948–. **N. MAILER** I'd be making a stinking seven hundred and fifty a week now like all those poor exploited schnooks (1955). [Apparently Yiddish (cf. Yiddish *shnut* snout or German *Schnucke* small sheep).]

schnorr /ʃnɔː(r)/ verb trans. and intr. Also **shnoor.** US To obtain by begging; to beg or sponge (*off*). 1892–. [See SCHNORRER noun.]

schnorrer /ʃnɒrə(r)/ noun Also **shnorrer.** US A beggar or scrounger; a layabout. 1892–. **J. D. SALINGER** I had lunch with him one day a couple of weeks ago. A real schnorrer, but sort of likable (1962). [From Yiddish, from German *Schnurrer* (*schnurren* to go begging).]

schnozz /ʃnɒz/ noun Also **schnoz.** US **1** The nose; a nostril. 1942–. **R. HAYES** 'You remember what our boy looks like?' 'Gray hair, widow's peak, big schnozz, red ski parka and no luggage' (1973). **2** (**right**) **on the schnozz** precisely, exactly; on the dot. 1949–. [Apparently Yiddish (cf. German *Schnauze* snout): see SCHNOZZLE noun.]

schnozzle /ʃnɒz(ə)l/ noun Also **schnozzola.** US The nose (esp. as a nickname for the entertainer Jimmy Durante (1893–1980)). 1930–. [Pseudo-Yiddish: see SCHNOZZ noun.]

schoolie noun naval A classroom instructor. 1946–. **J. HALE** The schoolies began to ... brace themselves for another day of ramming drill and P.T. ... into the minds and bodies of eight divisions of apprentices (1964). [From earlier sense (esp. Austral), school-teacher.]

school-ma'am noun N Amer A tree which has forked into two main trunks. 1939–.

schooner on the rocks noun naval A joint of meat roasted on potatoes (or in batter). 1916–.

schvartze(r) /ʃvaːtsə(r)/ noun Also **schwartze(r),** etc. mainly US, rather derog A black person, esp. a black maid. 1961–. [From Yiddish, from *shvarts* (German *schwarz*) black: the forms in final -*r* should represent the masculine, but the sexual distinction is commonly confused.]

schmeer schmegeggy schmendrik schmo schmooze

schwein(e)hund /ˈʃvaɪn(ə)hʊnt/ noun Also **schwine-**, etc. A German term of abuse: 'swine', 'bastard'. 1941–. [German, from *Schwein* pig and *Hund* dog.]

scissor(s)-bill noun mainly US An idler; someone foolish, incompetent, talkative, or otherwise objectionable. 1871–. R. P. HOBSON The hell you did, you big scissorbill, you stepped on my bum leg and my hand both (1961). [From earlier sense, a type of bird (the skimmer or shearwater).]

scone noun 1 Austral and NZ The head. 1942–. D. NILAND I can just see you running a house. I'd give you a week before you went off your scone (1957). 2 **to do one's scone** NZ To lose one's temper or self-control. Also **scone-doer**, noun, etc. 1942–.

scone-hot adjective **to go** (someone) **scone-hot** Austral To reprimand sharply; to lose one's temper with. 1927–. [See SCONE noun.]

scoot¹ noun Austral and NZ A drunken bout or spree; esp. in phr. *on the scoot*. 1916–. S. GORE Make mine a glass this time, seein' I have to go on the scoot with you booze artists to-night (1962). [From earlier sense, an act of scooting or going hastily.]

scoot² noun A motor-cycle or motor-car; also (US), a fast train. 1943–. [Abbreviation of SCOOTER noun.]

scooter noun mainly US A fast vehicle, esp. a train or car. 1917–. J. EVANS 'We'll use your scooter, Mac. . . . Where's she parked?' . . . I wondered how they knew I had a car (1948).

scope verb **to scope out** US To investigate or assess (a person, situation, etc.); to examine, check out. 1977–. R. B. PARKER I leaned against the front wall . . . and scoped things out (1986). [From *scope* range, extent.]

scorcher noun 1 A very hot day. 1874–. 2 A very attractive girl or woman. 1881–. P. G. WODEHOUSE When I'd had a look at the young lady next door and seen what a scorcher she is (1935). 3 An extremely hard shot or hit. 1900–. BELFAST TELEGRAPH He . . . diverted a scorcher from Pat Spence later in the game (1977). 4 Something licentious or risqué, esp. a book or play. 1942–. P. CAVE Then he produced a scorcher which managed to get itself banned by the country's leading booksellers and nominated for public prosecution at the Old Bailey (1974).

score noun **1a** criminals' The money or goods obtained by a successful crime. 1914–.

H. KURNITZ He's just a few months out of the jug and he hasn't turned a trick or made a score anywhere (1956). **b** orig US The act (or process) of obtaining illegal drugs; a supplier of these. 1951–. **c** A prostitute's client; also in homosexuals' use. 1961–. G. BAXT I got my hot tail out of there. I heard the score yelling (1972). **2** criminals' **a** US Twenty dollars; a twenty-dollar bill. 1929–. **b** Twenty pounds sterling (esp. in banknotes). 1933–. F. NORMAN When they turned me over I had about a score on me (1958). verb intr. or trans. **3** orig US To commit a crime; to steal or filch (esp. from an open counter). 1914–. D. MACKENZIE 'Where did you get it [the newspaper]?' . . . 'Nicked it. . . . It was too early to score any milk' (1977). **4** orig US To obtain (an illegal drug). 1935–. W. BURROUGHS Junk wins by default. I tried it as a matter of curiosity. I drifted along taking shots when I could score (1953). **5** orig US Of a man: to have or achieve sexual intercourse with (a woman). 1960–. G. GREER The boys used to go to the local dance halls and stand around . . . until the . . . sexual urge prompted them to *score a chick* (1970).

scorp noun services' Abbreviation of SCORPION noun. 1912–. W. TUTE Perks and privileges for the ruling classes. Fifteen in a room for the poor quality 'Scorps' whose rock it was (1957).

scorpion noun services' A civilian inhabitant of Gibraltar. 1845–. [Earlier *rock scorpion* in same sense.]

scotty adjective orig and mainly Austral Angry. 1872–. N. KEESING Getting a bit wild was called getting 'scotty' . . . 'Be good now. I'm a bit scotty with you' (1982). [From the supposed irritability of the Scots.]

Scouse noun 1 An inhabitant (or native) of Liverpool. 1945–. TIMES A roly-poly, amiable Liverpudlian, with the Scouse's seemingly god-given gift of being able to send up an overblown . . . occasion (1980). 2 The dialect of English spoken in Liverpool. 1963–. adjective 3 Liverpudlian; typical of the Scouse. 1960–. GUARDIAN Scouse House was the tongue-in-cheek name given to the Merseyside Development Office (1973). [Abbreviation of *lobscouse* a sailors' meat stew.]

Scouser noun = SCOUSE noun 1. 1959–. LIVERPOOL ECHO It's pretty well established that where there's a ship there you'll find a Scouser (1976).

scout noun A fellow or chap; often as *good scout* and as a term of address. 1912–. A. WILSON

schwein(e)hund   scissor(s)-bill   scone   scone-hot

She had only two roles with men—tomboy and good scout (1950).

scrag verb trans. **1** To manhandle or treat roughly. 1835–. ɪ. & ᴘ. ᴏᴘɪᴇ One boy makes the distinction: To scrag is a more gentle way of having a kind of hurtful revenge (1959). **2** US To kill or murder. 1930–. [From earlier sense, to hang (on a gallows) or garotte, from the noun, a lean animal, hence (by 1829), the neck.]

scram verb intr. orig US To depart quickly or rush off; often as an imperative. 1928–. ᴘ. ɢ. ᴡᴏᴅᴇʜᴏᴜsᴇ 'Go away, boy!' he boomed. 'You mean "Scram!", don't you, chum?' said George, who liked to get these things right (1962). [Prob. abbreviation of *scramble*.]

scramble military. noun **1** A rapid (or operational) take-off by a group of aircraft. 1940–. verb **2a** intr. Of an aircraft (esp. a fighter plane) or its crew: to effect such a take-off. 1940–. ʙʀᴇɴɴᴀɴ & ʜᴇssᴇʟʏɴ The signal to scramble came at about eleven o'clock. . . . We rushed to our aircraft and in less than two minutes were off the ground (1942). **b** trans. To cause (a plane) to take off quickly. 1940–.

scrambled egg noun mainly services' The gold braid or insignia on an officer's dress uniform; hence, an officer. 1943–. ᴍ. ᴅɪᴄᴋᴇɴs I don't care about the scrambled egg, but it may be a bit tough at first, not being an officer (1958).

scran noun naval Food, rations. 1916–. ᴛ. ᴇ. ʟᴀᴡʀᴇɴᴄᴇ 'Scran up!' he called in his sailor's belling tone against my ear (1935). [From earlier general sense, food, provisions; ultimate origin unknown.]

scrap iron noun US An alcoholic drink of poor quality. 1942–. ᴡᴀsʜɪɴɢᴛᴏɴ ᴘᴏsᴛ A trio of investigators warned the drinking public yesterday to beware of a new bootleg concoction, 'scrap iron', noted more for its voltage than vintage (1958).

Scratch¹ noun, usu. **Old Scratch.** A nickname for the Devil. Cf. ɴɪᴄᴋ¹ noun. 1740–. [Cf. earlier sense, hermaphrodite, related to Old Norse *skrat(t)i* goblin, Old High German *scrato* sprite.]

scratch² verb trans. **1** US To forge (banknotes and other papers). 1859–1935. noun **2** orig US Money, esp. paper money. 1914–. ᴅ. ᴀɴᴛʜᴏɴʏ She runs some kind of talent agency. Probably a tax write-off. . . . She doesn't need the scratch (1972).

scratcher noun orig US A forger of banknotes, etc. 1859–1941. [See sᴄʀᴀᴛᴄʜ verb.]

scream noun An irresistibly comical person or thing. 1888–. ʀ. ᴄ. sʜᴇʀʀɪꜰꜰ Oh, skipper, you *are* a scream—and no mistake! (1929).

scream verb intr. To turn informer; to give evidence against one's accomplices. 1903–. ᴊ. ᴍᴏʀɢᴀɴ He never got paid . . . and my information is he's ready to scream (1967). See also *screaming habdabs* at ʜᴀʙᴅᴀʙs noun, *screaming meemies* at ᴍᴇᴇᴍɪᴇs noun.

screamer noun **1** A tale, etc. that raises screams of laughter. 1831–. **2** Something or someone exceptionally large or fine; a splendid specimen. 1837–. **3** An exclamation mark. 1895–. ᴅ. ʟ. sᴀʏᴇʀs 'Waste Nerve-Power!' Capital N, capital P, and screamer. Got that? (1933). **4** sport A very powerful shot, esp. in golf. 1896–. ᴠ. ᴄᴀɴɴɪɴɢ Amadeo hit a screamer, dead straight and slightly left of the middle of the fairway (1963). **5** An informer or tell-tale. Cf. sᴄʀᴇᴀᴍ verb. 1903–. **6** A large headline, a banner. Also **screamer headline.** 1926–. **7** jazz A passage of music containing shrill notes on a woodwind instrument; a note of this kind. 1940–58. **8** A bomb that makes a screaming sound as it falls. 1942–3. **9 the screamers** = the screaming habdabs (see ʜᴀʙᴅᴀʙs noun). 1948–52. ᴍ. ᴛʀɪᴘᴘ 'Cut it out, you two,' said Bergen, 'you give me the screamers' (1952). See also ᴛᴡᴏ-ᴘᴏᴛ sᴄʀᴇᴀᴍᴇʀ noun.

screaming eagle noun US = ʀᴜᴘᴛᴜʀᴇᴅ ᴅᴜᴄᴋ noun. 1946–8.

screech noun Whisky; also any other strong alcoholic liquor (esp. one of poor quality). In Newfoundland, a type of rum; a mixture of rums. 1902–. ᴡ. ʜ. ᴘᴜɢsʟᴇʏ [The rating] gets hold of some bootleg scotch—'high life', they call it on the West Coast, and 'screech' in Newfie—and then he's away to . . . Cells or Detention (1945).

screenager noun orig US A young person who is at ease with and adept at using new technology and media, esp. computers. 1994–. [Blend of *screen* noun and *teenager* noun.]

screw verb **1a** intr. To copulate (*with* someone); trans. usu. of a man: to have sexual intercourse with. 1725–. ᴛ. ᴘʏɴᴄʜᴏɴ Santa's bag is filled with all your dreams come true: Nickel beers that sparkle like champagne, Barmaids who all love to screw (1963). **b: to screw around** orig US To be sexually promiscuous; to sleep around; hence, to mess about.

scrag scram scramble scrambled egg scran screw

1939–. T. HEALD I've been sort of screwing around
a little. . . . I don't want to upset my husband,
but a girl only has one life (1981). **c** As an
equivalent to 'fuck', in curses, exclamations,
etc. 1949–. R. DAHL 'Don't shout. There might be
keepers.' 'Screw the keepers!' he cried (1960).
2 intr. orig US To leave hurriedly; to push *off* or
get *out*. 1896–. D. RICHARDS Now if you don't screw
off out of here, I'll use the phone (1974). **3** trans.
mainly N Amer To defraud (esp. of money); to
cheat or 'rook'. 1900–. **4** trans. and intr. orig
Austral To look at or watch (esp. before a
fight). 1917–. **5a** trans. orig US To spoil or ruin;
to pervert, upset (esp. mentally). 1938–. **b: to
screw up** intr. and trans. orig US To blunder; to
make a mess of, ruin, spoil; to disturb or
upset (esp. mentally). 1942–. J. IRVING He said
that women's lib had screwed up his wife
so much that she divorced him
(1978). noun **6** A prison
warder. 1812–. G. F. NEWMAN
The lights never out, pervy
screws watching every
movement (1970). **7** A salary
or wage. 1858–. T. S. ELIOT He's
offered me the job With a jolly
good screw, and some
pickings in commissions
(1959). **8** A tonic or 'pick-me-
up'. 1877–. **9 the screws** rheumatism. 1897–.
L. BLACK Any rheumatism? An occasional touch of
the screws, she admitted (1976). **10** orig Austral A
look or stare; esp. in phr. *to have a screw at*.
1907–. **11a** An act of sexual intercourse (esp.
of a hasty and casual nature). 1929–. P. L. CAVE
Five or six Angel birds sat around over cold cups
of coffee waiting for a fast ride or a quick screw
(1971). **b** A woman considered as a (good
or bad) sexual partner. 1937–. [In sense
6, from earlier sense, false key; in sense 11,
cf. the older sense, prostitute (from 1725).]

screwball mainly US. noun **1** Someone
eccentric or crazy; a fool. 1933–. P. G. WODEHOUSE
You are going to Blandings Castle now,
no doubt, to inspect some well-connected
screwball (1939). **2** jazz Fast improvisation
or unrestrained swing; often attrib. 1936–47.
R. P. DODGE When inspiration leaves the
player . . . he becomes what is known as a
screw-ball player. I must say that I prefer the
jump style to the screw-ball style (1947). adjective
3 Eccentric; mad, crazy. 1936–. [From the
earlier US sense, a baseball pitched with
reverse spin against the natural curve.]

screwer noun criminals' = SCREWSMAN noun.
1932–47.

screwmatics noun pl. Also **screwmaticks**.
dated jocular Rheumatism. 1895–. E. V. LUCAS Wet,
and rats, . . . and dirt and screwmaticks (1916).
[Blend of SCREW noun 9 and *rheumatics* noun pl.]

screwsman noun A thief or burglar.
1812–. J. PRESCOT What does our imaginary
screwsman do? He gets his hands on the
keys . . . to take impressions (1963). [From *screw*
= false key.]

screwy adjective orig US Mad, crazy;
eccentric, foolish. 1887–. R. H. RIMMER Sheila
was Tom's date and I had Tom's sister, Ruth, for
a date. Sound screwy? (1966).

scrimshank verb intr. orig military To shirk
duty; to malinger. Also **scrimshanker,** noun,
etc. 1890–. E. WAUGH Brigade expects us to clean
up the house for them. I
should have thought
some of those half-
shaven scrimshankers I
see lounging around
Headquarters might have
saved us the trouble
(1945). [Of unknown
origin.]

> 'Don't shout.
> There might be
> keepers.'
> 'Screw the
> keepers!' he cried.

script noun orig US
Shortened from
prescription, esp. one for narcotic drugs.
1951–. J. BROWN You're just like a bloody junkie
I know. Gets his script at mid-day every day,
then works his fixes out (1972).

scrote noun mainly Brit, orig police and prisoners'
A worthless or despicable person. 1975–.
CLEMENT & LA FRENAIS D'you know I was only out the
cell for half an hour, but in that time some
scrote whipped the rest (1975). [Shortening
of *scrotum* pouch of skin containing the
testicles.]

scroucher noun Also **scrowsher,
scrowcher**. Austral An unpleasant or
despicable person. 1901–. D. NILAND Ah, I could
puke. That scrousher, that rough-house annie,
what's she got to get uppety about? (1966)
[Origin uncertain; perh. connected with
dialect *scrouch* to crouch, bend.]

scroungy adjective orig and mainly US Shabby,
dirty; sordid, disreputable; hence, inferior.
1949–. T. PYNCHON One sunburned, scroungy unit
of force preserving the Sheik and the oil money
against any threat from east of the English
Channel (1973). [From *scrounge* verb, sponge,
cadge + *-y*.]

scrub[1] noun **1** A disreputable woman;
a prostitute or 'tart'. 1900–. **2 The Scrubs**
Wormwood Scrubs Prison, in Greater

London. 1923–. A. PRIOR He had . . . taken his medicine, which had turned out to be three years in the Scrubs (1966). verb **3** trans. services', mainly naval To reprimand sharply or punish. 1911–49. **4 to scrub round** orig services' To dispense with or ignore; to drop (a subject). 1943–. J. WAIN 'I just said I didn't want to break the contract we had at present,' I said. 'I felt it was no good trying to scrub round it' (1962).

scrub² noun Something cancelled or abandoned (esp. a flying mission). 1952–.

scrubber noun **1** A prostitute or 'tart'; a disorderly or slatternly woman. 1959–. B. MATHER 'She looked a scrubber. That means—' 'A mare that runs wild in the scrub country, copulating indiscriminately with stray stallions. Derivation Australian' (1973). **2** mainly Austral and NZ In sport, a second-rate player or competitor; one not of professional standard. 1974–. NEW ZEALAND HERALD The three winners . . . have rather enjoyed their reputation as 'scrubbers' since they unexpectedly won their club title (1977). [See quot. (1973), but in sense 1 perh. from *scrubber* one who scrubs hard to clean; with sense 2, cf. earlier sense, inferior horse.]

scruffo noun A scruffy person, a layabout. 1959–. C. MACINNES One of the scruffos turned and looked at his choice companions (1959).

scrummy adjective Delicious. 1915–. GOOD FOOD GUIDE 1997 A man who ate . . . 'scrummy' chocolate marquise was a well-satisfied customer (1996). [From *scrum(ptious* + *-y* or a blend of *scrumptious* and *yummy*.]

scrungy adjective mainly US Dirty, grimy; sleazy, shabby. 1974–. ROLLING STONE As the scrungy taxi passenger, he has driver De Niro stop the cab and look at his wife's lurid silhouette up against a window (1977). [Prob. related to SCROUNGY adjective; cf. GRUNGY adjective.]

scuffer noun mainly Northern A policeman. Also **scufter**. 1860–. P. MOLONEY Scuffer! Scuffer! on the beat, With thy elephantine feet, You can't see the way to go Cos yer 'at comes down too low (1966). [Of uncertain origin; perh. from *scuff* noun, the scruff of the neck (seized for lifting, etc.) or *scuff* verb, to strike.]

scum noun mainly US Semen. 1967–.

scumbag noun coarse, mainly US **1** A condom. 1967–. **2** A despicable person. Also as a vulgar term of abuse. 1971–.

scunge noun Any sticky or messy substance; filth, dirt. 1975–. J. WAIN God, the

scunge of this place (1982). [Prob. from *scum* noun and GUNGE noun, but cf. SCROUNGY adjective.]

scunner noun orig Scottish and Northern A dislike or grudge; esp. in phr. *to take a scunner on* (or *to*, etc.). 1300–. [From *scunner* verb, to shrink back from or flinch, of uncertain origin.]

scupper noun A depreciatory term for a woman; a prostitute. 1935–. F. WARNER 'You were always firm.' . . . 'Your limbs and trunk were in angles of contingency.' 'I was your scupper' (1972). [From naval sense, hole in a ship's side to carry away water.]

scut noun Also **scutt, skut.** Someone beneath contempt. 1873–. J. B. COOPER The likes of them skuts to find fault with my cookin'— 'deed it's more than O'Callaghan himself would dare do (1916). [Perh. ultimately from *scout* verb, to mock, deride, of Scandinavian origin.]

scuttlebutt noun orig US, naval Rumour or gossip. 1901–. SUN (Baltimore): Also a cause for betting was the ultimate destination. In navy slang 'scuttlebutt' was rife and had the ship bound everywhere from China to Murmansk (1943). [Used as the name of a miscellany column in the *Smoking Lamp* (1901–), from the earlier sense, water-butt on deck (around which sailors would gather to exchange gossip).]

scuzz noun Also **scuz.** orig and mainly N Amer Someone or something disgusting and unpleasant. 1968–. M. ATWOOD In the larger picture, we're just a little green scuzz on the surface (1988). [Prob. abbreviation of *disgusting*, but cf. *scum* noun and *fuzz* noun.]

scuzzbag noun orig and mainly N Amer A contemptible or despicable person; also as a general term of abuse. Also **scuzzball**, noun **scuzzbucket**, noun 1983–. [From SCUZZ noun + *bag* noun.]

scuzzy adjective orig and mainly N Amer Disgusting in appearance, behaviour, etc.; dirty, grimy; despicable, sleazy. 1968–. NEW MUSICAL EXPRESS Zeppelin were really dumb: visibly hanging out . . . with the scuzziest groupies in town (1987). Hence **scuzziness**, noun. 1980–. [From SCUZZ noun + *-y*.]

sea-gull noun NZ A casual, non-union dock labourer. c.1926–. G. SLATTER Ended up as a sea-gull on the Wellington wharves loading up the Home boats (1959).

seam-squirrel noun dated US, mainly military A louse. 1899–. C. J. POST There is the gray-back,

scrub scrubber scruffo scrummy scrungy scuffer

or seam-squirrel, from the days of our Civil War (1956).

secko noun Austral A sexual pervert; a sex offender. 1949–. w. dick You look like you'd be the sort a bloke who'd take little kids down a lane and give 'em two bob, yuh bloody secko (1969). [Shortened form of *sex* + *-o*.]

second banana noun US A supporting comedian. 1953–. new york times He [*sc.* Jack Benny] was often the butt of his second bananas, who devastated him with their barbs (1974). Cf. top banana noun.

second-stor(e)y man noun N Amer criminals' A cat-burglar. 1886–. malcolm x Hustlers . . . sold 'reefers', or had just come out of prison, or were 'second-story men' (1965).

Section Eight noun US military Discharge from the Army under section eight of Army Regulations 615–360 on the grounds of insanity or inability to adjust to Army life. 1943–. Hence **section-eight,** verb trans. To discharge from the Army on such grounds. 1945–. e. hemingway You stay in until you are hit badly or killed or go crazy and get section-eighted (1950).

see verb trans. **to see a man about a dog** orig US Used as a jocular or euphemistic excuse for leaving or being absent, esp. when going to the lavatory or going to buy a drink. 1927–. private eye I got to see a man about a dog! (1969).

seg noun **1** US Abbreviation for 'segregationist'. Also **seggie.** 1965–. new yorker Fulbright for the first time openly appealed for black votes, because he believed that he couldn't win without them and that the 'seggies' . . . would vote against him no matter what he did (1970). **2** mainly US An isolation unit for difficult prisoners. 1974–. new society He continued his [hunger] strike simply in order to prevent an early return to 'seg' (1977). [In sense 2, abbreviation of *segregation (unit).*]

sell noun **1** A deception or disappointment. 1838–. verb trans. **2** To cheat, trick, deceive, take in. 1849–.

send verb trans. **1 to send down** orig US To send to prison. 1840–. p. b. yuill 'Is there any chance he *could* go to gaol?' 'You'd like him sent down, would you?' (1976). **2 send her (**or **it) down, Davy** (also **Hughie,** etc.): Austral A phrase expressing a wish for rain to fall. 1919–. Cf. hughie noun. **3** orig US Esp. of popular music: to affect emotionally, put into ecstasy. 1932–. b. holiday Meade Lux Lewis knocked them out; Ammons and Johnson

flipped them . . . Newton's band sent them (1956). Cf. sent adjective.

sender noun orig and mainly US A person (esp. a popular musician) who or thing that enthrals or puts into ecstasy. 1935–. spectator Fabian, the teenagers' sender, indistinguishable from Cliff Richards [sic] (1960). [From send verb 3 + *-er.*]

sent adjective In a state of ecstasy; in a drug-induced stupor. 1940–. spectator The girls wore thick eye-makeup and 'sent' expressions (1958). [From the past participle of send verb 3.]

septic adjective Unpleasant, nasty, rotten. 1914–. g. mitchell Mummy and Daddy have had a row. Isn't it septic of them? (1974).

septic tank noun mainly Austral Rhyming slang for yank noun 1. 1967–. Also **septic.** 1976–. d. stuart Jesus, lover of my soul, if it isn't the Goddams, the Septics themselves! . . . Stick around long enough, I told myself, and . . . you'll see some real live Yanks (1981).

sergeant-major noun Also **sergeant-major's.** Brit, military Strong sweet tea; also, tea with rum. (Usually attrib designating this.) 1925–. j. wainwright This tea . . . it damn near dissolved the spoon. A real 'sergeant- major' brew. The way tea *should* be made (1981). [From the notion that such tea is the prerogative of sergeant-majors; cf. the earlier obs. US military slang sense, coffee with cream and milk or sugar.]

seriously adverb orig US As an intensifier: very, really; substantially; esp. in phr. *seriously rich.* 1981–. washington post He became seriously rich, but in 1977 experienced a mid-wealth crisis (1981).

serve noun **to give (**someone**) a serve** Austral To deal roughly with; to criticize or reprimand sharply. 1967–. woman's day (Sydney): 'Yeah,' he said, 'Oges is set to give the Poms a serve' (1983).

sesh noun orig services' A session or bout, esp. of drinking. 1943–. g. netherwood Empty lager bottles . . . signified that Hans and Fritz also knew the joys of a desert 'sesh' (1944). [Shortened from *session.*]

set noun **1** Austral and NZ A grudge; esp. in phr. *to get (*or *make, take) a set on.* 1866–. tennent creek times I did notice . . . a set against Territorian officialdom (1956). **2** US mainly African-American A meeting of a street gang; also, the place where such a group meets. 1959–. j. mills When junkies and pushers on a particular set learn or suspect a particular agent's identity,

secko   second banana   second-stor(e)y man   send

he has 'taken a burn' (1972). verb **3 to have or get** (a person) **set** Austral and NZ To have a grudge against, have it in for. 1899–. A. RUSSELL It ain't too bad, but when the Jacks get er man set, like they did me over in Melbourne, its got ter slump (1929). **4 to set over** US, criminals' To kill or murder. 1931–. W. R. BURNETT I've been trying to find you ever since you set Doc over (1944). **5 to set up** to lead on in order to fool, cheat, or incriminate; to frame. 1956–. A. PRICE 'You're deliberately using them for bait, for God's sake.' 'Oh no we're not. . . . We didn't set them up' (1979). [In sense 1, from *set* attack, as in *dead set*; in sense 3, from obs. *set* to fix on as a victim; in sense 5, from earlier Boxing sense, to get one's opponent into a position in which he can be knocked down.]

settle verb trans. US To send to prison. 1899–. D. W. MAURER Maybe he will get *settled*, or sent to prison (1955).

set-up noun **1** orig and mainly US An opponent who is easy to defeat; something easily overcome or accomplished; a pushover. 1926–. M. MILLAR I went after him, tooth and nail. It was easy. Ron was a perfect set-up (1957). **2** US The glass, ice, soda, etc. required for mixing a drink, which is served to customers, who supply their own spirits, in unlicensed premises. 1930–. W. MCCARTHY He looked over to the sideboard and saw a complete assortment of liquors, rums and set-ups (1973). **3** US A place-setting at a restaurant. 1934–. J. D. MACDONALD He led us to a corner booth set up for four, whipped away the extra setups (1978). **4** orig US A scheme or trick whereby an innocent person is caused to incriminate himself or a criminal is caught red-handed; a frame-up. 1968–. J. GARDNER Arthur's clean. . . . It was a set-up. . . . I had him checked like you'd check a dodgy engine (1978). [In sense 1, from earlier boxing sense, an opponent put into a position in which he is easily knocked down; cf. **to set up** (SET verb 5).]

seven adjective **1 seven bells** nautical In the phrs. *to knock seven bells out of*, to beat severely; *to scare seven bells out of*, to terrify. 1929–. M. LOWRY He's knocked seven bells out of harder cases than you in his time (1933). verb **2 to seven out** US In the game of craps: to throw a seven and so lose one's bet; also, broadly, to suffer a misfortune, to die. 1934–. S. BELLOW 'Why do you push it, Charlie?' he said. 'At our age one short game is plenty. . . . One of these days you could seven out' (1975). Cf. *to crap out* at CRAP verb 3.

sew verb trans. **to sew up: a** To tire out, exhaust (a person); to outwit, cheat, swindle; to convict. 1837–. D. HAMMETT I expected something like that. That's why I sewed you up. And you are sewed up (1929). **b** To bring to a desired conclusion or condition; to organize or gain control of; spec. to ensure the favourable outcome of (a match). 1904–. NEWS OF THE WORLD Charlton appeared to have the game sewn up (1977). [In sense a, from earlier sense, to sew out a horse.]

sewer /ˈs(j)uːə(r)/ noun Brit A despicable or repulsive person. 1945–. N. MITFORD Who is that sewer with Linda? (1945).

sex noun **1** The genitals. 1938–. H. GOLD His eyes turned to his pants, gaping open, and his sex sick as an overhandled rattler gaping through (1956); T. ALLBEURY The narrow white briefs that barely captured her sex (1977). verb **2 to sex up** to make more sexy; to increase the sexual or sensational content of. 1959–. IRAQDOSSIER.COM As a result of this and other spin doctor interference, the dossier was indeed 'sexed-up', far more than anyone had realised (2007). **3** intr. To have sexual intercourse. 1966–. J. BARNETT Maybe we sex together at yo' place (1980).

sexational adjective Also **sexsational**. orig US Sexually sensational. 1928–. WEST LANCS. EVENING GAZETTE 1st Blackpool showing of the Sexational *Highway Through The Bedroom* (X) (1976). [Blend of *sex* noun and *sensational* adjective.] So **sexationalism**, noun. 1927–.

sexboat noun US = SEXPOT noun. 1962–.

sex-bomb noun = SEXPOT noun. 1963–. P. CAVE Sex-bomb, Sonya Stelling might be. Oscar contender she was not (1976).

sexcapade noun A sexual escapade. 1965–. HONOLULU STAR-BULLETIN A generally less swinging group than the lone men off on sexcapades who helped give tourism a bad name (1976). [Blend of *sex* noun and *escapade* noun.]

sexed-up adjective Sexually aroused. 1969–.

sex kitten noun A young woman who asserts her sex appeal. 1958–. GUARDIAN Brigitte Bardot . . . the original sex kitten with the French charm (1966).

sexpert noun orig US An expert on sexual matters. 1924–. RADIO TIMES Every other interviewed sexpert seemed to come from California where . . . you can graduate in any old spurious subject (1979). [Blend of *sex* noun and *expert* noun.]

settle   set-up   seven   sew   sewer   sexational   sexboat

sexpot noun A sexy person, esp. a woman. 1957–. LONDON MAGAZINE Tough Games Mistress. Rebellious sexpot pupil (pregnant again) (1981).

sez **1** Jocular representation of the pronunciation of 'says', esp. in dialectal or colloquial speech. 1844–. J. STROUD If I make a movement, he sez: 'Oh, don't be disgusting!' he sez (1960). **2 sez you** orig US Used to convey doubt about, or contempt for, the remark of a previous speaker. 1931–. B. GRAEME 'He's . . . not nearly so useful in a rough house.' 'Sez you!' Sanders growled (1973).

S.F.A. noun Abbreviation of *sweet Fanny Adams* (see FANNY ADAMS noun); = nothing at all. 1933–.

shack¹ noun **1** US A room or small building housing radio equipment. 1929–. verb **2 to shack up** (also **to be shacked up**) to cohabit, esp. as lovers; usually followed by *with* or *together*. 1935–. D. LODGE Philip Swallow is shacked up with Melanie at that address (1975).

shack² noun N Amer A brakeman or guard on a train. Also **shacks**. 1899–. D. STIFF A great many hobo writers . . . are full ready to tell the novice how to outwit the brakemen, or shacks (1931). [Origin unknown.]

shack-job noun US = SHACK-UP noun 2. 1946–. W. GADDIS Look, rabbit, I'm looking for a shack-job, see? (1955). [From SHACK verb 2 + *job* noun.]

shackles noun Broth, soup, or stew. 1886–. TELEGRAPH (Brisbane): Mr. Coppard records how one night he stumbled on a field kitchen and enjoyed a wonderful meal of shackles, a soup made up from leftovers (1969). [Prob. from *shackle-bone* noun, knuckle-bone.]

shackle-up noun dated An act of preparing food in a pot. 1935–6. J. CURTIS A spare shirt and a couple o' tins in case they want to have a shackle up (1936). [Origin uncertain; cf. SHACKLES noun.]

shack-up noun **1** (An instance of) cohabitation. 1935–. TIMES LITERARY SUPPLEMENT An affair with David, . . . a shack-up with Colin (1974). **2** A sexual partner. 1969–. E. R. JOHNSON That's not like Angel. She was still Mike's shackup (1969). [From SHACK verb 2.]

shaddup int Representing a colloquial or casual pronunciation of 'shut up!' 1959–. DAILY MIRROR 'Snooker isn't a trifle!' 'Aw, Shaddup!!' (1977).

shades noun orig US Sunglasses. 1958–. G. V. HIGGINS I looked at Emerson, hiding behind his shades and his imported-cigarette smoke (1980).

shaft noun **1** US, dated A human leg. 1935–9. C. MORLEY If anyone showed a good shaft Pop would wink at me (1939). **2** US Harsh or unfair treatment; rejection, 'the push'; esp. in **to give** or **get the shaft**. 1959–. AMERICAN SPEECH She gave him the shaft after he broke their date last weekend (1977). **3** The penis. 1971–. B. W. ALDISS It was never enough merely to lower your trousers—they had to come off, . . . so that you could crouch there naked but for your shirt, frantically rubbing your shaft (1971). verb trans. **4** orig and mainly US To treat harshly or unfairly; to cheat; to take unfair advantage of; to reject. 1959–. M. MACHIN I think how they're shafting us with this whole deal (1976). **5** Of a man: to have sex with; to fuck. 1970–. B. W. ALDISS How sinful he looked, squatting there by the water while his wife was being shafted by some dirty big Mendip only a few feet away! (1971). [In sense 3, cf. obs. *shaft of delight* penis.]

shag¹ coarse. verb trans. and intr. **1** To have sex (with). 1788–. R. ADAMS Well, I 'ope 'e ain't 'angin' around when I'm shaggin' my missus! (1980). **2** Used in curses and exclamations. 1933–. G. PINSENT 'Then shag you!' I shouted, as he swaggered away (1973). noun **3** An act of copulation. 1937–. B. W. ALDISS It was not just a good shag I needed. It was romance (1971). **4** One who copulates; used as a general term of abuse. 1971–. K. AMIS The moustached shag and the flat-chested bint . . . had moved away from the bar with their drinks (1978). [Origin uncertain; perh. from obs. *shag* to shake, waggle.]

shag² verb intr. To wander aimlessly; to traipse; to go away. 1851–. W. H. CANAWAY We'd been shagging around over these mountains for four days now, and we hadn't seen one single musk deer (1976). [Origin unknown.]

shag³ noun **like a shag on a rock** Austral denoting the isolation or unhappiness associated with solitude. 1845–. K. SMITH It was the voice of Godley, in high gear, raised to compete with the noise around him, but suddenly left by itself like a shag on a rock, when everyone else quietened down in response to the gong (1965). [From *shag* type of cormorant.]

shagged adjective Weary, exhausted; often followed by *out*. 1932–. G. W. TARGET The two other-rankers were now sitting in the back of

sexpot sez S.F.A. shack shack-job shackle-up

sharpie

the jeep, with all of 'em looking shagged out (1975). [Origin uncertain; perh. related to SHAG[1] verb.]

shagtastic adjective Very sexually attractive. 1998–. TIMES Retailers who failed to predict the appeal of 'shag-tastic' super-spy Austin Powers are determined not to miss out on next summer's sequel (1998). [Blend of SHAG[1] verb 1 and *fantastic*; orig applied to the fictional Austin Powers (played by Mike Myers), who appeared in such US spy-spoof films as *Austin Powers: International Man of Mystery* (1997) and *Austin Powers: The Spy Who Shagged Me* (1999).]

shake verb **1 more than you can shake a stick at** orig and mainly US A large amount or number. 1818–. E. MCBAIN We get more damn cancellations than you can shake a stick at (1960). **2 to be** (also **get**) **shook on** Austral and NZ To be infatuated with; also, to admire. 1868–. B. SCOTT Those stories you read about in books where two blokes get shook on the same sheila (1977). **3 to shake down** orig and mainly US **a** To extort money from; to blackmail or otherwise pressurize (a person). 1872–. J. ROSS Sickert has been shaken down for protection money (1976). **b** (Esp. of the police, etc.) to search (a person or place). 1915–. D. BAGLEY Once Mayberry had been shaken down the guards were taken from Penny and Gillian (1977). **4 to shake a leg** to hurry. 1904–. P. G. WODEHOUSE 'Clean this place up.' ... 'Yes, sir.' 'And shake a leg' (1952). noun **5 no great shakes** of indifferent quality, skill, etc. 1819–. DAILY MIRROR Sir Richard may not have been particularly great shakes. But he was never given much chance to show his paces (1976). **6 a fair** (or **even, good**) **shake** US A fair deal; also opposite, **an unfair shake.** 1830–. S. TERKEL I'd like to see an America where so much power was not in the hands of the few. Where everybody'd get a fair shake (1980). **7** US A party, esp. a rent party. 1946–. AMERICAN SPEECH There's a shake at Jim's house (1977). [In sense 4, cf. earlier meaning, to dance; in sense 6, perh. in allusion to the shaking of dice.]

shake-down noun orig and mainly US **1** A forced contribution; an instance of extortion. 1902–. S. BRILL While the shakedown was proved, it was never shown that the money went to Presser personally (1978). **2** A search of a person or place. 1914–. LANDFALL But about nine o'clock, without any warning, there was a shake-down [of prisoners] (1958). [From SHAKE verb 3.]

shaky do noun dated, orig RAF A difficult or risky situation; a close shave. 1942–. F. MACLEAN The earth all round was kicked up by a burst from the plane's tail-gunner ... 'This,' said the Australian, 'is going to be a shaky do' (1949).

shambolic adjective Brit Extremely disorganized. 1958–. TIMES The average listener is in the position of anybody who encounters an organization at work for the first time. It may appear shambolic but how much is that because he hasn't yet made sense of it (1975). [From *shamb*(*les* scene of complete disorder + -*olic*.]

shampoo noun Champagne. 1957–. A. SINCLAIR The waiter brings a bottle of champagne. ... Shampoo, Sheila dear? (1959). [Arbitrary alteration.]

shamus /ʃeɪməs/ noun Also **sharmus, shommus.** US A policeman; a private detective. 1925–. NEW YORKER I think my wife is having me tailed by a private shamus (1977). [Origin uncertain; perh. from *shamas* Jewish beadle or sexton (from Yiddish *shames*) or from the Irish personal name *Seamus*.]

shanghai verb trans. **1** nautical, orig US To force to be a sailor on a ship by using drugs or other trickery. 1871–. **2** orig US, military To transfer forcibly or abduct; to put into an awkward situation by trickery. 1919–. J. GIBSON Most of my guests get shanghaied into giving a general knowledge talk to the boys (1976). [From the name of *Shanghai*, city and seaport in China.]

shant /ʃænt/ noun An alcoholic drink. 1960–. A. DRAPER 'So I had a few shants,' I said (1970). [From earlier sense, a (quart) pot of drink; origin uncertain.]

shark noun A person who unscrupulously exploits or swindles others. 1599–. [Orig perh. from German *Schurke* worthless rogue, influenced by *shark* rapacious fish.]

shark bait noun Also **shark-baiter.** Austral A lone or daring swimmer far out from shore. 1912–. AUSTRALIAN ENCYCLOPEDIA Solitary bathers are more often attacked than groups, but the 'shark-baiter' farthest off shore is not necessarily the victim (1965).

sharp adjective orig US Excellent, stylish, smart. 1940–. ARIZONA DAILY STAR The home is sharp with four bedrooms (1979).

sharpie noun **1** orig US **a** A swindler, cheat. 1942–. S. BELLOW He had chosen to be dreamy ... and the sharpies cleaned him out (1964). **b** A person who is or claims to be

shagtastic shake shake-down shaky do shambolic

clever. 1949–. **2** Austral A young person with extreme or provocative style of hair, dress, etc. 1965–. SUNDAY MAIL (Brisbane): Carmel says her mother accepted her being a sharpie—even a punk—till she shaved her hair off (1977). **3** N Amer Something smart or in good condition. 1970–. TUCSON (Arizona) CITIZEN Starter home . . . carpeting, drapes and remodeled kitchen. Call . . . to see this little sharpie (1979). [From *sharp* adjective + *-ie*: in sense 1a, cf. *sharper* noun, swindler; in sense 1b, cf. *sharp* adjective, clever; in sense 3, cf. SHARP adjective.]

sharpish adverb Brit Quickly. T. ALLBEURY They shuffled him back to Moscow pretty sharpish (1975).

shaver noun dated A young male, a boy; esp. in phrs. *young shaver*, *little shaver*. 1854–. NEW YORKER Sometimes I think of your father when he was a little shaver of four or five setting solemnly off (1970). [From earlier sense, fellow, chap.]

shavetail noun orig. US, military An inexperienced person, spec. a newly commissioned officer. 1891–. L. DEIGHTON I was a shavetail, just out of pilot training (1976). [From the earlier sense, untrained pack animal identified by a shaven tail.]

shazam /ʃəˈzæm/ int children's Used as a 'magic' word to introduce an extraordinary deed or story. 1940–. [Invented word, first used in 'Captain Marvel' adventure stories.]

she pron mainly Austral and NZ Used informally in place of 'it'; the present state of affairs. 1863–. NEW ZEALAND LISTENER If you tear the hamstring, in the back of the leg just above the knee, you're gone a million—she's nasty (1958).

shebang /ʃɪˈbæŋ/ noun Also **chebang** (obs), **shee-bang**. N Amer The whole lot, everything; esp. in phr. *the whole shebang*. 1869–. R. E. MEGILL The standard deviation is then calculated by dividing the total number of wells, *N*, into the sum of all the group deviations . . . and then taking the square root of the whole shebang (1977). [From earlier senses, hut, tavern; ultimate origin unknown.]

shedload noun mainly Brit A large amount or number. 1992–. HULL DAILY MAIL 'Course, the banks love it. Property prices rise and they make shedloads more money (2002). [Perh. a euphemistic alteration of SHITLOAD noun.]

sheen noun US A car. 1969–. AMERICAN SPEECH Hey, look down the street pas' that sheen double-parked (1975). [Prob. abbreviation of *machine* noun.]

sheeny noun Also **shen(e)y**, **sheeney**, **-ie.** derog and offensive A Jew. 1816–. HONOLULU STAR-BULLETIN Hey mom, there's a couple of sheenies at our door with a turkey (1976). [Origin uncertain; cf. Russian *zhid*, Polish, Czech *žid* (pronounced /ʒiːd/) a Jew.]

sheepshagger noun Brit, Irish English, Austral and NZ derog One who has sex with a sheep: used as a term of insult, applied orig to members of various Scottish regiments, esp. the Black Watch, and subsequently to people from remote country areas where such sexual diversions are stereotypically rife. 1958–. PRIVATE EYE She is now back and planning a Victory Parade, not to mention her own visit to the reconquered territories [i.e. the Falkland Islands] to receive the homage of the grateful sheepshaggers, all fifty-nine of them (1982).

Hence **sheepshagging** noun. 1958–.

> 'Property prices
> rise and they
> make shedloads
> more money.'

sheet noun **1** A dollar bill (US) or pound note (Brit) 1937–. HOT CAR Maserati air horns [have] . . . a howling, double high-pitched screaming note. . . . This cacophony can be yours . . . for less than ten sheets (1978). **2** US = RAP SHEET noun. 1958–. C. WESTON Somebody scared him into it. Let's take a look at his sheet, I want to know why (1976).

sheila /ˈʃiːlə/ noun Also **sheelah**, **sheilah**, **shelah.** now Austral and NZ A girl or young woman; a girlfriend. 1832–. H. GARNER If I was to fight over every sheila I'd ever fucked there'd be fights from here to bloody Darwin (1985). [Prob. from the generic use of the (originally Irish) female personal name *Sheila*.]

shekels noun pl. Money; often in phr. *to rake in the shekels*, to make money rapidly. 1883–. L. OLIVIER We extended for another four weeks—not so much to rake in the shekels as because I couldn't bear to say farewell to the part I loved doing so much (1982). [From pl. of *shekel* noun, ancient Hebrew coin, from Hebrew *sheqel*.]

shelf Austral. noun **1** An informer. Also **shelfer.** 1916–. W. MOXHAM 'Who's going to split? His word wouldn't carry much weight.' 'I'm no shelf' (1969). verb trans. **2** To inform on. 1936–. v. KELLY 'Is he all right?' . . . 'Of course he's all right. Pat never shelfed a man in his life. The court records show that' (1975). [Prob. from the phr. *on the shelf*, out of the way.]

shell verb **1 to shell out** trans. and intr. To give out (money), to pay up. 1801–. **2** trans. N Amer, baseball To score heavily against (an opposing player or team); often in passive 1942–. **FIRST BASE** Gooden . . . was shelled twice by Boston in the World Series, finishing 0–3 in the post-season (1987). [In sense 1, from the notion of taking seeds out of their pod or shell; in sense 2, from earlier sense, to bombard with (explosive) shells.]

shellac /ʃəˈlæk/ verb trans. US To beat, thrash, defeat. 1930–. TIME Pitcher McArdle was shellacked for . . . six runs in the first inning (1977). Hence **shellacking,** noun US A beating, a thorough defeat. 1931–. H. WOUK The Japs can't recover from the shellacking they took at Midway (1978). [From earlier sense, to varnish with shellac.]

shellacked adjective US, dated Drunk. 1922–48.

shellback noun jocular **1** A sailor, esp. a hardened or experienced one. 1853–. **2** A person of long experience, esp. also with reactionary views. 1943–. LISTENER I have no doubt a lot of right-wing shell-backs are now conceding, with blimpish magnanimity, that there's really something to be said for these young fellows after all (1963).

she-male noun A passive male homosexual or transvestite. 1983–. [From the earlier US colloquial sense, woman.]

shemozzle /ʃəˈmɒz(ə)l/ Also **schemozzle, s(c)hi-, s(c)hlemozzle.** noun **1** A muddle; a brawl or commotion. 1899–. L. MEYNELL There was going to be one hell of an uncomfortable shemozzle in his life if he didn't get his priorities right (1978). verb intr. **2** dated To decamp, scarper. 1903–. W. H. AUDEN He was caught by a common cold and condemned to the whiskey mines, But schemozzled back to the Army (1944). [Origin uncertain; prob. from Yiddish *shlimazl* misfortune, unlucky person (see SCHLIMAZEL noun), with subsequent reduction of *schle-* to *s(c)he-*.]

sherbet noun An alcoholic drink. 1890–. F. ARCHER He had a strident voice and with a few sherbets under his belt you knew he was about (1974). [In earlier use, a cooling drink of Eastern origin.]

shice /ʃaɪs/ noun dated Nothing; counterfeit money; something worthless. 1859–1939. J. B. PRIESTLEY 'I keep tellin' Knocker it's a shice,' said Mickey earnestly (1939). [From German *Scheiss* shit.]

shicer /ˈʃaɪsə(r)/ noun Also **schicer, shiser.** A worthless or despicable person. 1846–. [From German *Scheisser* shitter.]

shick adjective and noun Austral and NZ Abbreviation of SHICKER adjective and noun. 1907–. BULLETIN (Sydney) Men getting 'shick' and coming home and raising hell's delight (1930).

shicker Also **shiker, shikker.** Austral and NZ. adjective **1** Drunk. 1898–. D. STUART She goes crook when he lands home shicker (1977). noun **2** (A drink of) alcoholic liquor; esp. in phr. *on the shicker.* 1901–. KINGS CROSS WHISPER (Sydney): Surfers Paradise beer garden, where everyone got on the shicker (1966). **3** A drunk. 1906–. X. HERBERT He's the biggest shikker in Town. Now nick off, you old sponge (1938). verb intr. **4** To drink alcohol, to get drunk. 1908–. CUSACK & JAMES He'd gamble his shirt off . . . but he doesn't shicker (1951). Hence **shickered,** adjective. Also **shikkered.** Drunk. 1898–. D. STIVENS By five o'clock Metho Bill wasn't the only one shickered (1979). [From Yiddish *shiker* adjective, drunk.]

shift verb **1** trans. To consume (food or drink) hastily or in bulk. 1896–. W. RUSSELL Although his speech is not slurred, we should recognize the voice of a man who shifts a lot of booze (1981). **2** intr. To move quickly, hurry. 1922–. M. KENYON You'll have time for a bite at Murphy's if you shift (1970). **3** trans. To sell. 1976–. CHURCH TIMES He was also hopeful that some £40,000-worth of unsold books would eventually be shifted (1990).

shill mainly N Amer. verb **1** intr. To act as a shill (sense 3 below). 1914–. H. GOLD It's how to get the audience. . . . I shilled for my wife (1965). **2** trans. To entice (a person) as a shill; to act as a shill for (a gambling game, etc.). 1974–. M. PUZO Diane, the blonde that shills baccarat (1978). noun **3** A decoy or accomplice, esp. one posing as an enthusiastic or successful customer to encourage other buyers, gamblers, etc. 1916–. J. GRAY The commonest trap was for a shill to haunt Ninth Avenue disguised as a farm hand (1971). [Prob. abbreviation of SHILLABER noun.]

shillaber /ˈʃɪləbə(r)/ noun dated, mainly N Amer = SHILL noun. 1913–40. [Origin unknown.]

shim criminals', mainly US. noun **1** A strip of plastic used to force open a lock. 1968–. L. EGAN Denny and I went to Nonie's place, and he

shell shellac shellacked shellback she-male shice

used a shim to get us in (1977). verb trans. **2** To open (a lock or door) with a shim 1972–. [From earlier sense, thin slip used to fill up or adjust the space between parts; ultimate origin unknown.]

shine noun US, derog and offensive A black person. 1908–. R. CHANDLER His voice said bitterly: 'Shines. Another shine killing. That's what I rate after eighteen years in this man's police department' (1940).

shiner noun **1** A diamond or other jewel; usu. in pl. 1884–. D. L. SAYERS I never had those shiners (1934). **2** A black eye. 1904–. G. F. FIENNES Out shot a telescopic left, and I had the shiner of all time for weeks (1967). **3** Brit A window-cleaner. 1958–. CENTURYAN There we were, shiners and cleaning ladies, surrounding Fred and Dora on the float by the London Wall (1977).

Shinner noun A member or supporter of Sinn Fein. 1921–. J. JOHNSTON I thought I'd heard it about that you were with the Shinners (1974). [From *Shinn-* representing the pronunciation of *Sinn* + *-er*.]

Shinola /ʃaɪnəʊlə/ noun US In phr. *not to know shit from Shinola*: denoting ignorance or innocence; **neither shit nor Shinola,** neither one thing nor the other; also used euphemistically alone for 'shit'. c.1930–. BOSTON GLOBE Pinhead Ivy League professors who impress the Shinola out of the brightest little boy from Brookline High (1989). [From the proprietary name of a brand of shoe polish.]

shiralee /ʃɪrəliː/ noun Also **shirallee.** Austral A traveller's bundle of blankets and personal belongings, a swag. 1892–. SUNDAY SUN (Brisbane): The fences, the barns, the houses—they're all gone and I'm out on the road with my shiralee (1974). [Origin unknown.]

shirt noun **1** orig US In the phrs. *to keep one's shirt on,* to remain calm, *to get* (someone's) *shirt out,* to make (someone) lose their temper. 1854–. P. THEROUX 'Keep your shirt on,' Father shouted (1981). **2** In the phrs. *to bet one's shirt, to put one's shirt on,* to bet all one's money on (esp. a horse in a race), *to lose one's shirt,* to lose all one's possessions, esp. by gambling or speculation. 1892–. E. B. MANN He hit the market . . . about the time the bottom dropped out of it. He lost his shirt! (1935).

shirtlifter noun Austral, derog A male homosexual. 1966–. B. HUMPHRIES When I first seen them photos of him in his 'Riverina Rig' I took him for an out-of-work ballet dancer or some kind of shirtlifter (1974).

shirty adjective Angry. 1846–. J. RAE All right; all right; there's no need to get shirty about it (1960). [From SHIRT noun 1 + *-y.*]

shit Also **shite.** coarse. verb **1** intr. To defecate. c.1308–. GUARDIAN WEEKLY Shat in his pants with fear (1979). **2** trans. **a** To excrete. a.1382–. T. L. SMITH The planes . . . had shit a neat stream of Day-Glo orange bricks (1978). **b** To defecate in. 1877–. **3** **to shit oneself: a** To make oneself dirty by defecating. 1914–. SUNDAY TIMES I can easily arrange not to be diverted by knowing when a sorry old man shat himself (1980). **b** To be afraid. 1914–. SPARE RIB I was shitting myself before I came, looking for all kinds of excuses (1977). **4** trans. To tease or attempt to deceive. 1934–. C. KILIAN Didja see the wave comin' across the Shelf? . . . There was a wave. I'm not shittin' you (1979). **5** **to shit a brick** or **bricks** to be extremely worried or frightened. 1961–. H. FERGUSON By the time I got back to the hospital they were all shitting bricks (1976). noun **6** Excrement. a.1585–. **7** A contemptible person. 1508–. J. IRVING I never knew what *shits* men were until I became a woman (1978). **8** Anything; esp. in phr. *not to give a shit,* not to care at all. 1922–. K. AMIS An interviewer . . . being very rude to a politician . . . and the politician not giving a shit (1978). **9** An act of defecation. 1928–. **10** Rubbish, trash. 1930–. ROLLING STONE I enjoyed Simmons' logic that Shakespeare is 'shit' simply because he can't understand it (1977). **11** Misfortune, unpleasantness; esp. in phr. *to be in the shit,* to be in trouble. 1937–. B. W. ALDISS We were all in the shit together and it was madness to try and escape it (1971). **12** **up shit creek** in (or into) an unpleasant situation or awkward predicament. 1937–. PRIVATE EYE If they'd followed her this far up shit creek it's a long way to walk back (1981). **13** **no shit** US An emphatic response or asseveration; really, in truth, 'no kidding'. 1939–. SPECTATOR (New Canaan High School, Conn.): I turned to Steve and told him that Cheryl said he looked like a fruit because of his pants. I told him I liked his pants, no shit (1978). **14** **shit out of luck** very unlucky. 1969–. M. PUZO So you see, my dear, you're shit out of luck (1978). **15** **the shits** diarrhoea. 1947–. ZIGZAG 'I've had the shits,' he cried. 'You want to avoid the food' (1977). **16** An intoxicating drug, esp. cannabis, heroin, or marijuana. 1950–. S. WILSON 'Hope it's good shit,' I whispered as he swabbed my arm (1980). **17** **(when) the shit flies** or **hits the fan** (when) a crisis occurs and its repercussions are felt. 1966–. H. FAST Tomorrow, the shit hits the fan (1977). **18** **to beat, kick,** or **knock the shit out of** to

shine shiner Shinner Shinola shiralee shirt shit

thrash or beat severely. 1966–. **B. W. ALDISS** The Japs . . . were meek and respectful. . . . The shit had been knocked out of them (1971). **19 to get one's shit together** US To collect oneself, to manage one's affairs. 1969–. **20 shit happens** orig US bad things are bound to happen, unpleasant situations are unavoidable; also, esp. as a rejoinder, expressing a resigned attitude to any state of affairs or course of events: these things happen, such is life. 1983–. int Also (emphatic) **shee-y-it, she.it. 21** An exclamation of annoyance or disgust. 1920–. **TIME** Aw, she-it, as the street kids say (1977). **22** In trivial use. 1937–. **P. CAVE** 'Aw, shit. It was nothing,' she muttered, writing the matter off casually (1976). Cf. **SHOOT** int 11. [From Old English *scītan*, recorded in past participle *be-sciten*.]

shit-bag noun coarse **1** dated The stomach; in pl., the guts. 1937–. **2** A disgusting or despicable person. 1961–. **J. PATRICK** They must be mental. . . . Shit-bags the lot o' them (1973).

shit-eater noun coarse orig US **1** A contemptible or despicable person. 1937–. **2** A person or animal which eats faeces. 1968–. Hence **shit-eating**, adjective **1 shit-eating grin:** a a broad grin expressing uncontrollable delight or (self-)satisfaction, esp. at having got away with something outrageous or improper. 1957–. **b** an ingratiating, embarrassed, or uncomfortable expression, esp. as exhibited by someone undergoing a humiliating experience; a forced smile. 1990–. **2** Contemptible, despicable. 1960–. **3** Of or engaging in the eating of faeces. 1970–.

shite-hawk noun coarse A despicable person. 1958–. **J. B. HILTON** I liked the man. . . . And yet he was a shite-hawk. He was a journalist (1981). [From earlier Indian English sense, a kite, said to have been in British Army use.]

shitface noun coarse A despicable person; esp. as a term of abusive address. 1937–. **M. AMIS** 'Why,' I wondered, 'did old shitface come round? What was he after?' (1973).

shithead noun coarse A despicable person. 1961–. **P. NIESEWAND** You lying shithead! (1979).

shit-hole noun coarse **1** The anus. 1937–. **2** A disgusting place. 1969–. **ZIGZAG** John went to a Catholic school in Caledonian Road—'a right shit-hole' (1977).

shit-hot adjective coarse Exceptionally talented, knowledgeable, etc.; excellent. 1961–. **M. AMIS** They've elected a new

guy . . . I don't know anything about him. Except that he's shit-hot (1973).

shit-house coarse. noun **1** A building housing a lavatory. 1795–. adjective **2** Disgusting, despicable. 1972–. **ZIGZAG** If you're banned in town A and then banned in town B, well then town C has just got to ban you or it's, 'well what kind of shithouse place are you running there, councillor?' (1977).

shit-kicker noun US, coarse, derog A rustic. 1966–.

shitless adjective coarse In a state of extreme fear or physical distress; esp. in phr. *scared shitless.* 1936–. **NEW MUSICAL EXPRESS** The self-appointed guardians of public morality who campaign against pornography because they're simply scared shitless by it (1976).

shit-list noun coarse A blacklist. 1942–. **R. D. ABRAHAMS** Moynihan had made it onto the black shit-list in spite of his obvious sympathies (1970).

shitload noun orig US A large amount or number. 1962–. **W. MCPHERSON** There was nothing quite like a shitload of money (1987).

shit-scared adjective coarse Extremely frightened. 1958–. **ROLLING STONE** Stewart was 'shit scared' about opening night (1977).

shit-stir verb coarse mainly Brit, Austral, and NZ **1** intr. To make trouble for its own sake. 1984–. **C. AHERNE ET AL.** *Antony.* You fancy her don't you? *Dave.* Stop shit-stirring. *Denise.* Why does he have to cause trouble? (1998) **2** trans. To provoke, aggravate. 1991–. Also **shit-stirrer**, noun An agitator, troublemaker. 1961–. **shit-stirring**, noun Trouble-making. 1974–.

shitter noun coarse A lavatory. 1969–. **BLACK SCHOLAR** He lit a square and sat down on the shitter and tried to collect his thoughts (1971).

shitting adjective coarse Despicable. 1967–. **L. COOPER** That shitting girl looks at me as if I was dirt (1980).

shitty adjective coarse **1** Disgusting, contemptible. 1924–. **SPARE RIB** All the shitty jobs that most women . . . do every day of their lives (1977). **2** Dirty with excrement. 1935–. **C. MCCULLOUGH** If I catch you flaming little twerps touching that doll again I'll brand your shitty little arses (1977). [From **SHIT** noun + -*y.*]

shitwork noun coarse, mainly feminists' Menial or routine work, esp. housework. 1968–.

shlep **shlemazl, shlock, shlong, shlub, shlump, shmaltz, shmatte, shmecker, shmeer, shmegegge, shmendrick, shmo,**

shit-bag shit-eater shite-hawk shitface shithead

shmuck, shmutter, shmutz, shnook, shnoor, variants of SCHLEP verb and noun, SCHLIMAZEL noun, SCHLOCK noun and adjective, SCHLONG noun, SCHLUB noun, SCHLUMP noun, SCHMALTZ noun and verb, SCHMATTE noun, SCHMECKER noun, SCHMEER verb and noun, SCHMEGEGGY noun, SCHMENDRICK noun, SCHMO noun, SCHMUCK noun, SCHMUTTER noun, SCHMUTZ noun, SCHNOOK noun, SCHNOOR verb.

shoddy dropper noun Austral and NZ A pedlar of cheap or falsely described clothing. 1937–. A. BURNETT Cotadabeen was a shoddy dropper—a travelling draper (1973). [From *shoddy* woollen yarn + *dropper* one who delivers goods.]

shoe adjective US Conforming to the dress, behaviour, or attitudes of students at exclusive schools and colleges. 1962–. NEW YORK TIMES Perhaps it is significant that one favourite mode of protest in the fifties was satire. We—a lot of us—were cool, ironic, 'shoe' (1973). [Origin unknown.]

shoey noun Brit A shoeing-smith in a cavalry regiment. 1919–. S. MAYS Shoey . . . Slap some shoes on my new horse (1969). [From *shoe* noun + *-y*.]

shonicker noun Also **shoniker, shonnicker.** US, derog and offensive A Jew. 1914–. J. T. FARRELL Two hooknoses . . . did come along. Andy and Johnny O'Brien . . . stopped the shonickers (1932). [Origin uncertain; perh. from Yiddish *shoniker* itinerant trader.]

shonk[1] noun 1 derog and offensive A Jew. 1938–. W. HAGGARD 'Brighton? . . . It's full of shonks.' . . . 'Which means there are hotels with night clerks' (1981). 2 A (large) nose. 1938–. [Shortened form of SHONIKER noun.]

shonk[2] noun Austral Someone engaged in irregular or illegal business activities, a shark. 1981–. TRUCKIN' LIFE The governments could control the numbers of middle men and stop any 'shonks' from operating (1981). [Back-formation from SHONKY adjective.]

shonky adjective Also **shonkie.** Austral Unreliable, unsound, dishonest. 1970–. AUSTRALIAN (Sydney): The woman . . . was forthright about the cut-price air fares. . . . 'We call these tickets shonky,' she said (1981). [Perh. from SHONK[1] noun or British dialect *shonk* adjective, smart + *-y*.]

shoo-fly noun US A policeman, usu. in plain clothes, whose job is to watch and report on other police officers. 1877–. E. MCBAIN 'You want a beer? . . . Officially I'm still on duty, but fuck it.' 'Shooflies are heavy around

the holidays' (1980). [From *shoo!* int + *fly*, orig popularized by the song 'Shoo! fly! don't bother me!']

shook adjective **shook on** Austral and NZ Infatuated with. 1868–. B. SCOTT Those stories you read about in books where two blokes get shook on the same sheila (1977).

shoot verb 1 **to shoot off one's mouth** (also **to shoot one's mouth off**) orig US To talk too much or indiscreetly. 1864–. W. J. BURLEY With Matthew Eva shooting his mouth off about Peters it could turn ugly (1973). 2 **to shoot the crow** Scottish To leave hurriedly, esp. without paying one's bill; to abscond. 1887–. W. MCILVANNEY There'll only be his mother in the house. His father shot the crow years ago (1977). 3 trans. and intr. orig US To inject esp. oneself with (a drug); often followed by *up*. 1914–. OZ They were using those needles man, they were shooting up (1971). 4 intr. orig US Used in imperative as a demand or invitation to continue, esp. with what one wishes to say; 'fire away'. 1915–. H. WOUK 'Can I pick your brain on one more point?' 'Shoot' (1978). 5 intr. To ejaculate. 1922–. H. C. RAE I wanted him to shoot and get it over (1972). 6 **to shoot the works** mainly US To do something to the fullest extent; spec. to discharge the necessary business; to tell the truth, reveal all. 1922–. W. STEVENS We have people who seem to hand a list of names to a stenographer and tell her to shoot the works (1951). 7 **to shoot the bull** US To talk nonsense. 1930–. MACLEAN'S MAGAZINE 'Writes all my speeches,' he'd say and slap me on the back. 'Smart boy! He can sure shoot the bull' (1972). Cf. BULL noun 1. 8 **to shoot up** RAF Of an aircraft or pilot: to dive over (a person or place) as if or in order to attack; to buzz. 1937–. 9 **to shoot the breeze** US To chat, talk idly. 1941–. R. K. SMITH There were negative signs, too. No one had come by to shoot the breeze, to have a cup of coffee (1971). 10 **to shoot through** Austral and NZ To escape, abscond; to leave. 1947–. BULLETIN (Sydney): Me wife's shot through . . . . Can't get a bird . . . Can't pay the rent (1985). int 11 US An exclamation of disgust, anger, etc. 1934–. R. MOORE 'Oh shoot,' she told Jen, when Jen suggested they'd better write the next batch of boarders not to come (1950). [In sense 11, partially a euphemistic alteration of SHIT int.]

shoot-'em-up noun Also **shoot-em-up, shootemup.** orig US A fast-moving story or film, esp. a Western, of which gun-play is a dominant feature. 1953–. NEW YORK TIMES The new or free-form Western has several choice entries . . . 'Oklahoma Crude,' a splendid

shoddy dropper   shoe   shoey   shonicker   shoo-fly

shootemup about a lady wildcatter in the oilfields (1973).

shooter noun **1** A gun, esp. a revolver. 1840–. G. F. NEWMAN Why did you pull the shooter on the two detectives? (1970). **2** US A measure or drink of spirits, esp. whisky. 1971–. W. MCCARTHY Let's have a shooter and a beer (1973).

shooting gallery noun US A place where illegal drugs can be obtained and injected. 1951–. [Cf. SHOOT verb 3.]

shop noun **1 all over the shop** everywhere, esp. randomly or in a state of untidiness or disarray. 1874–. J. I. M. STEWART At one of Anthea Gender's [parties] one was substantially although not too obtrusively in the presence of grandees drawn from all over the shop (1978). **2** theatrical A period of employment, an engagement. 1885–. G. MITCHELL He was an out-of-work actor and was very anxious to get a shop, as he called it (1978). **3 the Shop: a** Austral The University of Melbourne. 1889–. **b** Brit Army The Royal Military Academy, Woolwich. 1899–. G. M. FRASER We treated each other decently, and weren't one jot more incompetent than this Sandhurst-and-Shop crowd (1978). verb trans. **4** mainly Brit To inform against (a criminal, etc.). 1899–. S. KNIGHT One of the men who is thinking very seriously of 'shopping' Tearle, Oates and the rest of the crew told me, 'One word from me and they go down for a long, long while' (1984). [In sense 4, from earlier sense, to imprison, from obs. slang shop noun, a prison.]

shoppy noun Also **shoppie**. dated A shop assistant. 1909–34. [From shop noun + -y.]

short adjective **1 to get** or **have** (someone) **by the short hairs** to have (someone) completely in one's power. 1888–. Also **to get** or **have** (someone) **by the short and curlies**. 1948–. SAYERS & EUSTACE She's evidently got her husband by the short hairs (1930). P. HILL There is no need for kid gloves now, we've got him by the short and curlies (1976). **2 to be caught** or **taken short** to have an urgent need to urinate or defecate. 1890–. J. ASHFORD Simon was in such a terrible state of nerves that he had already been taken short twice and had to rush for the lavatory (1967). **3 (. . .) short of a . . .** Used as a formula to imply (slight) mental instability or eccentricity, as if not having the full complement of mental faculties; the earliest recorded formulation is short of a sheet (US and Austral), but more recent examples (from the mid-1980s) usu. identify individual elements which go to

make up the whole—the commonest are two (etc.) bricks short of a load and a few (etc.) sandwiches short of a picnic, but the variations are almost infinite. 1941–. J. HODGKINS You try to do the right thing by hiring local girls and you discover they can be as thick as fenceposts. There's one in there that's two bricks short of a load, I swear it (1987). S. JOHNSON I'm afraid he's a few sandwiches short of a picnic. Still, he's harmless (1990). POST (Denver): This guy was weird . . . He was a few pickles short of a barrel (1994). noun **4** US A street-car or tram; a car. 1914–. W. MCCARTHY Everybody brings him hot cars . . . shorts, we get up north, he fixes 'em up and then sells 'em (1975). [In sense 1, from the notion of seizing someone by the pubic hairs so that they are immobilized; in sense 4, apparently from the relatively short duration of tram-rides as compared with those on a train.]

short-arm adjective and noun orig and mainly military (Being) an inspection of the penis for venereal disease or other infection. 1919–. M. PUZO Before you go to bed with a guy, give him a short arm. . . . You strip down his penis, you know, like you're masturbating him, and if there's a yellow fluid coming out like a drippage, you know he's infected (1978). [From the notion of the penis as an additional (but shorter) limb.]

short-arse noun Also **short-ass**. derog A short person. 1706–. M. AMIS 'What's her real name?' I implored. 'Jean.' 'Oh. The short-arse? Yeah, she's all right. Boring dress' (1973). Hence **short-arsed**, adjective. Also **short-assed**. 1951–.

short con noun US A small-scale confidence racket. 1932–.

short end noun orig US The inferior part; the losing end; a bad deal. 1904–. TIME Annie went back to Broadway on the short end of a 6–2 score (1977).

shorthorn noun US, dated A new arrival, a greenhorn. 1888–1942.

short-snorter noun US, military A souvenir of countries visited consisting of a set of banknotes autographed by colleagues and acquaintances. 1944–. [Prob. from snorter noun, a length of rope, variant of snotter noun, of unknown origin; from the banknotes being attached to a piece of string.]

short time noun A brief visit to a prostitute; a brief stay in a hotel for sexual purposes. Also attrib. 1937–. GUARDIAN Miles of

shooter   shooting gallery   shop   shoppy   short-arm

girlie bars, short time hotels (1971). [See SHORT-TIMER noun 2.]

short-timer noun **1** US, military A person nearing the end of his military service. 1906–. M. RUSS Being what is known as a short-timer . . . I'm at peace with service life (1952). **2** A person who visits a prostitute or stays briefly at a hotel for sexual purposes. 1923–. G. GREENE The shabby hotel to which 'short timers' come (1939).

shorty noun Also **shortie**. **1** derog or jocular A short person; often with capital initial as a nickname or form of address. 1888–. BARTIMEUS Your middle watch, Shortie? (1914). **2** orig US A drink of spirits, a short. 1931–. FREEDOMWAYS Yarborough . . . yelled, 'Bartender. Give the professor another shorty of gin there' (1963).

shot adjective **1 to be** or **get shot of** to get rid of. 1802–. DAILY TELEGRAPH Advising its members to make haste to get shot of unsuitable employees (1976). **2** mainly US, Austral, and NZ Drunk. 1864–. D. R. STUART Ah well, I got shot, real staggery . . . but that arrack, hell, it's great stuff (1979). **3** mainly US **a** Worn out, ruined, used up. 1933–. G. V. HIGGINS Your boiler is one of those old things. . . . I think it's about shot (1981). **b** Exhausted. 1939–. J. GORES He . . . [was] literally too tired to move. . . . Shot. Utterly shot (1972). noun **4 the shot** Austral What is needed, just the thing. 1953–. C. WALLACE-CRABBE 'Beer, Bob?' Sandstone asked. . . . 'Just the shot, thanks.' Bob was thirsty now (1979).

shouse /ʃaʊs/ noun Also **shoush, sh'touse**. Austral A lavatory. 1941–. T. KENEALLY I'd like some trees out, pines and gums, so you don't have to see your neighbour's shouse first thing each morning (1968). [Syncopated form of SHIT-HOUSE noun.]

shout verb **1** Austral and NZ **a** intr. To buy a round of drinks. 1850–. NATIONAL TIMES (Australia): The tightwad . . . wouldn't shout if a shark bit him (1981). **b** trans. To buy (a drink or other refreshment) for (someone). 1854–. S. T. OLLIVIER 'Mingy old skinflints!' hissed Jane. 'They could have shouted us an ice-cream!' (1965). noun **2** (A turn to pay for) a round of drinks. 1854–. D. BAGLEY Honnister addressed the landlord. 'Hi, Monte: a large scotch and a pint of Director's.' 'My shout,' I said (1977).

shove verb **1** intr. orig US To go away, leave; usu. followed by *off*. 1844–. N FREELING I have to ferry you down to the office. . . . Let's shove,

shall we? (1975); D. ANTHONY My, look at the hour. I'd better shove off (1977). **2 to shove it** used for expressing contemptuous rejection or dismissal. 1941–. L. STEWART If he doesn't like it he can shove it, but don't worry—he won't (1978). noun **3 the shove** dismissal (e.g. from employment); the 'push'. 1899–. J. LE CARRÉ They should never have given old Connie Sachs the shove (1977).

shover /ʃʌvə(r)/ noun Also **shovver, shuv(v)er**. Jocular alteration of 'chauffeur'. 1905–. J. CHARLTON Rabbiting on with the Pritchards' shover (1976).

showboat verb intr. **1** US To perform or behave ostentatiously, to show off. 1951–. R. BUSBY The Europeans are enough of a handful without DEA prima donnas showboating all over the place (1987). noun **2** orig and mainly US An attention-seeker or show-off. 1953–.

shower /ʃaʊə(r)/ noun Brit A contemptible or unpleasant person or group of people. 1942–. P. ALDING 'You're a right shower,' said Welland (1973).

> 'The Celtics shredded the Los Angeles Lakers with a third-quarter explosion.'

show-up noun US A police identification parade. 1929–. SUN (Baltimore): Lyman Brown . . . picked Graham out of a 'showup' of seven jail inmates (1955).

shred verb **1** trans. orig US to defeat comprehensively, esp. in sport; to trounce. 1966–. NEW YORK TIMES The Celtics shredded the Los Angeles Lakers with a third-quarter explosion (1966). **2** trans. and intr. surfing To cut rapidly through (the water, etc.) on a surfboard; hence, to speed along (a route). 1977–.

shrewd-head noun Austral and NZ A cunning person. 1916–. N. HILLIARD Only the shrewd-heads go for that hard stuff: the shysters the takes (1960).

shrimp noun A small or puny person. c.1386–. N. SAHGAL At least one could hold up one's head with a distinguished-looking Kashmiri Brahmin Prime Minister, but here was this shrimp who was a Kayasath as well, and filling up the secretariat with Kayasaths (1985).

shrink noun orig US A psychiatrist. 1966–. TIMES LITERARY SUPPLEMENT It does not take a shrink to see that a man so humanly flawed and artistically inept has got to be a loser (1980). [Shortening of HEAD-SHRINKER noun.]

short-timer   shorty   shot   shouse   shout   shover

shrinker noun. = SHRINK noun. 1967–.
J. B. HILTON It had to be the clinic for her.
Maybe they'd left it too late; or maybe she was
too clever for the shrinkers (1980). [Shortening
of HEAD-SHRINKER noun.]

shroom noun orig and mainly US **1** A
mushroom. 1977–. **2** = MAGIC MUSHROOM noun.
1979–. R. PEFFER Note that mixing shrooms with
alcohol is asking for trouble (2001). [Shortening
of *mushroom* noun.]

shtick noun Also **schtick, schtik, shtik.** US
1 A theatrical routine, gimmick, etc. 1961–.
TIME The former Prime Minister is not at all
apologetic about his Yuletide shtik, pointing out
that he has chosen to write books and sell
records rather than go the David Frost route
(1977). **2** A particular area of activity or
interest; a sphere or scene. 1968–. PUBLISHERS
WEEKLY A husband trying to puzzle out his
woman, women-God-bless-them in general,
and the whole female *shtick* (1976). [From
Yiddish, from German *Stück* piece, play.]

shtook /ʃtʊk/ noun Also **shtook, schtuck,
shtuck,** etc. Trouble; esp. in phr. *in (dead)
shtook.* 1936–. J. GARDNER You know I'm in schtuck
with my bosses (1978). [Origin unknown;
apparently not a Yiddish word.]

shtoom /ʃtʊm/ Also **schtoom, shtum(m),
stumm,** etc. adjective **1** Saying nothing, silent.
1958–. G. MARKSTEIN Keep stumm about how you
heard (1981). verb **2** to **shtoom up** (also **to
shtoom it**) to keep silent, say nothing. 1958–.
J. GASH Shtum it. Sounds carry in this (1982).
[Yiddish, from German *stumm* silent, mute.]

shtup /ʃtʊp/ verb **1** trans. To push. 1968–.
2 trans. and intr. To have sex (with). 1969–.
D. WESTLAKE He'd go on home . . . shtup the
wife . . . then shlep on back here (1974).
[Yiddish; cf. German *stupfen* to nudge, jog.]

shuck noun **1** Nonsense; a deception; sham.
1958–. A. TOFFLER The recently graduated
son . . . proclaims the nine-to-five job a
degrading sham and a shuck (1980). verb
2 trans. and intr. To deceive or defraud
(someone). 1959–. C. WESTON You shucking me,
man, I didn't get rid of nobody! (1976).
3 shucking and jiving US, African-American
Fooling. 1969–. H. L. FOSTER For many blacks,
shuckin' and jivin' is a survival technique to avoid
and stay out of trouble (1974). [In sense 1,
from earlier sense, something of little value
(orig sense, husk, pod).]

shucks int An expression of annoyance or
regret or self-deprecation in response to
praise. 1847–. D. BAGLEY Byrne . . . adopted a
'Shucks, 't'warn't nuthin' ' attitude (1978).
[From plural of *shuck* noun, something of little
value (see SHUCK noun).]

shuddup int Also **shaddup.** Representing
a casual pronunciation of *shut up.* 1940–. DAILY
MIRROR 'Snooker isn't a trifle!' 'Aw, Shaddup!!'
(1977). F. MULLALLY 'Shuddup,' Macdonald
snorted (1978).

shufti /ʃʊftɪ, ʃʌ-/ Also **shufty.** Brit, orig
military. noun **1** A look or glance; esp. in phr.
to have or *take a shufti (at).* 1943–. R. ADAMS Good
idea, old boy. I'm game. Let's 'ave a crafty shufti
round with that in mind, shall we? (1980). verb
intr. **2** dated To look or watch. 1943–7. [From
Arabic *šufti* have you seen?, from *šāf* to see.]

shunt noun A road accident, esp. a collision
of vehicles travelling one close behind
another. 1959–. G. VAUGHAN 'Another bloody
shunt,' Yardley groaned. The Zagreb trunk was
notorious for accidents (1978).

shunt-up noun Brit A multiple road
accident. 1976–. [From SHUNT noun, modelled
on *pile-up.*]

shurrup int Representing a casual
pronunciation of *shut up.* 1893–. J. WAINWRIGHT
Shurrup, Richard, don't show your ignorance
(1978).

shut adjective **1 to be** or **get shut of** = to be
or get shot of (see at SHOT adjective 1). 1575–.
S. BARSTOW 'I haven't *got* her.' 'You're sure well
shut, from all I hear' (1976). verb **2a: to shut
one's face** (or **head** or **mouth** or **trap**) to stop
talking. 1809–. BEST SHORT STORIES 'Shut your
daft grinning face,' growled Arthur (1939).
b: to shut it to stop talking. 1886–. G. MILLAR
'Enough,' cried Boulaya. 'Shut it, Frisé . . . You
know nothing' (1945).

shutter-bug noun An enthusiastic
photographer. 1940–.

Shylock Also **shylock.** derog and offensive.
noun **1** A hard-hearted money-lender. Also,
a pawnbroker; a Jew. 1786–. TURKUS & FEDER
'Sometimes it's as good as 3,000 per cent,' one
of the shylocks . . . explained (1951). verb trans.
2 To force (someone) to repay a debt, esp.
at an extortionate rate of interest. 1930–.
[From the name of the Jewish moneylender
in Shakespeare's *Merchant of Venice.*]

shypoo /ʃaɪpuː, ʃaɾpuː/ noun Also **shipoo.**
Austral Inferior alcoholic drink, esp. beer;
a pub that sells this. 1897–. N. BARTLETT You
could get drunk, at Cossack's other pub, on
Colonial ale or 'shypoo' at sixpence the quart
(1954). [Origin unknown.]

shrinker shroom shtick shtook shtoom shuddup

shyster

shyster /ˈʃaɪstə(r)/ noun orig and mainly US A person, esp. a lawyer, who uses unscrupulous methods. 1844–. J. WAINWRIGHT The shyster lawyers . . . swear blind the client's been manhandled while in police custody (1981). [Origin unknown.]

sick adjective **1a** Mortified, chagrined. 1853–. K. ISHIGURO It's just the way you do things. . . . It makes me sick (1982). **b: sick as a parrot** extremely chagrined. 1979–. PRIVATE EYE The Moggatollah admitted frankly that he was 'sick as a parrot' at the way events had been unfolding (1979). **2** US Suffering drug withdrawal symptoms. 1951–. W. BURROUGHS The usual routine is to grab someone with junk on him, and let him stew in jail until he is good and sick (1953). **3** orig US, now mainly skateboarders' and surfers' Excellent, impressive; risky. 1983–. BMX PLUS! Jeff Harrington has some of the sickest jumping variations we have ever seen (1997). US NEWS & WORLD REPORT 'That's siiiick!' gushes an admiring fan (2002). verb **4** trans. and intr. To vomit; usu. followed by *up*. 1924–. SUNDAY TELEGRAPH She sings *Away in a Manger* . . . and drinks lots of drinks and then she sicks up (1980). noun **5 on the sick** incapacitated by illness, receiving sickness benefit. 1976–. L. THOMAS I took it [an allotment] on . . . but then I was on the sick for months . . . and the council . . . takes it off me (1976).

sickie noun Also **sicky. 1** Austral and NZ A day's sick leave, esp. one taken without valid medical reason. 1953–. COURIER-MAIL (Brisbane): A part-time fireman's sense of duty cost him his job after he answered an emergency call when he was taking a 'sickie' from work (1981). **2** N Amer One who is mentally ill or perverted. 1973–. P. DE VRIES 'Shall I . . . make it clear . . . I'm a sickie?' 'No! . . . this—ailment of yours . . . it's an expression of some deep-seated conflict' (1974). [From SICK adjective + *-ie*.]

sicko noun US = SICKIE noun 2. 1977–. CHICAGO SUN-TIMES Is it asking too much for these sickos to stop bothering decent women? (1982). [From SICK adjective + *-o*.]

siddown int Representing a casual pronunciation of 'sit down'. 1936–. D. BEATY What do you know about it, sonny?. . . . Siddown! Siddown! (1975).

side noun **1** Brit Boastfulness, swagger; often in phr. *to put on side*, to give oneself airs. 1878–. B. MASON But they soon warmed to his lively personality and the sanctifying remark—'He's a good sort; no side about him', was heard three days after he arrived (1980).

2 on the side orig US Secretly or illicitly; often used with reference to extramarital sexual affairs. 1893–. R. L. HUDSON What would some of you say if I told you that I, as a married man, have had three women on the side? (1968). **3** US A recording; a record. 1936–. J. BALDWIN 'How about some sides?' . . . Lorenzo put on something . . . by the Modern Jazz Quartet (1960).

side-door Pullman noun N Amer, dated, mainly tramps' A railway goods wagon with sliding doors in the sides. 1887–1927. [*Pullman* from the name of a luxurious type of railway carriage; from the use of such wagons by tramps.]

sidekick noun **1** orig US A companion or close associate, esp. one in a subordinate position. 1906–. J. MCVEAN It was the White House. . . . And not just some little cotton-tail sidekick either, but counsel to the president (1981). **2** US criminals' A side-pocket. 1916–55. [Back-formation from SIDE-KICKER noun.]

side-kicker noun US, dated = SIDEKICK noun 1. 1903–33.

sidy adjective Also **sidey.** Brit Conceited. 1898–. B. MARSHALL He couldn't very well put himself in first because people might think it rather sidey (1946). [From SIDE noun 1.]

siff variant of SYPH noun.

signify verb intr. US, mainly African-American To boast or brag; to make insulting remarks or insinuations. 1932–. C. MITCHELL I wasn't signifying at her, but . . . if the shoe fits, wear it (1969). Hence **signifier,** noun US, mainly African-American One who boasts or insults. 1962–. H. GOLD When he bragged like any carnie signifier, then I wondered where and why I was going (1965).

silk noun mainly US, air force A parachute; esp. in phr. *to take to* or *hit the silk*, to bale out by parachute. 1933–. N. MARSH Over Germany . . . we got clobbered and I hit the silk (1956). [From the fabric from which parachutes have been made.]

silly billy noun Brit A foolish or feeble-minded person. 1834–. WORDPOWER Mr Healey is a Silly Billy to have waited so long before doing so little of what everyone knew was necessary (1977). [From *Billy*, familiar form of the male personal name *William*; orig used spec. as a nickname of William Frederick, Duke of Gloucester (1776–1834), and of William IV (1765–1837).]

shyster sick sickie sicko siddown side signify

simoleon /sɪˈməʊlɪən/ noun Also **samoleon**. US A dollar. 1896–. D. ANTHONY I bet the limit, five thousand simoleons (1977). [Origin uncertain; perh. modelled on *napoleon* noun, French coin.]

simp noun US A fool, simpleton. 1903–. PUBLISHERS WEEKLY The book's assumption is that single men are simps who don't know the difference between a pepper mill and a can opener (1976). [Abbreviation of *simple* noun, fool or *simpleton* noun.]

Simple Simon noun US, dated Rhyming slang for 'diamond'. 1928–. D. RUNYON I do not see any Simple Simon on your lean and linger [= finger] (1929).

sin noun **as sin** extremely; esp. in phr. *(as) ugly as sin, (as) miserable as sin*. 1821–. N. SHUTE I think it looks ugly as sin, and it's starting to ponk a bit (1944).

sin bin noun A place set aside for offenders. 1982–. DAILY TELEGRAPH It often took several months for an infant who has created chaos to be removed to a special school or a 'sin-bin' (1982). [From earlier sense, enclosure for players who have been sent off in the game of ice hockey.]

sin-bin verb trans. orig Austral To send (a player) to the sin bin; hence, to send away as a punishment; to banish. 1983–. SUNDAY MAIL (Brisbane): A former FBI agent who has been sin-binned to a jerkwater town in America for playing too rough with a prospective witness (1986).

sin bosun noun naval A ship's chaplain. 1948–. NAVY NEWS Well, at least the Sin Bosun doesn't seem too old (1964).

sin city noun often jocular A city of licentiousness and vice. 1973–. A. THACKERAY What's going to happen Chicago? . . . All you want to do is run amok in 'Sin City' (1975).

sing verb intr. now mainly US To turn informer; to confess; often in phr. *to sing like a canary*. 1929–. P. NIESEWAND You don't think they'd sing like canaries? . . . They'll sing, Claud. . . . If they thought it would help them, they'd tell on their mothers (1981). Hence **singer**, noun dated An informer. 1935–.

single noun US A one-dollar bill. 1936–. H. FAST He . . . took out a wad of bills, peeling off two fives and two singles (1977).

single-o US mainly criminals'. noun **1** A crime committed without an accomplice; also, a person, esp. a criminal, who works alone. 1930–. adjective **2** (Done by someone, esp. a criminal) acting alone. 1930–. adverb **3** Alone; without an accomplice. 1948–. K. ORVIS Little Faysy wants to go dream-streeting single-o (1962).

sinker noun dated, orig US A doughy cake, esp. a doughnut; a dumpling. 1870–. E. FERBER The coffee was hot, strong, revivifying; the sinkers crisp and fresh (1926). [Perh. from their sinking into the fat or liquid when cooking.]

sin-shifter noun dated A clergyman. a.1912–66. [Perh. influenced by *scene-shifter*.]

siph variant of SYPH noun.

siphon verb Also **syphon**. **to siphon the python** jocular, orig Austral of a male: to urinate. 1968–. D. BALL Brooks was struck with an overwhelming desire to piss. Syphon the python, he thought (1978). [From the common analogy between the penis and a snake.]

sippers noun Brit, nautical A sip (of rum), esp. taken from another's tot, as a reward for some service or in celebration. 1944–. H. TUNSTALL-BEHRENS A bottle appeared with enough in it to give us all 'sippers' (1956). [From *sip* noun + -ERS suffix.]

sister noun **1** Used as a form of address to a woman, esp. one whose name is not known. 1906–. R. BOYLE Come on, sister. . . . Why won't you stay and talk to me? I'm a nice guy (1976). **2** orig US A fellow homosexual; a male homosexual, esp. one who is a friend rather than a lover. 1941–.

sit verb **to sit next to** (or **by, with**) **Nellie** to learn an occupation on the job by watching how others do it. 1963–. LISTENER Journalists are the casual labourers of the intellectual world. . . . Most training still consists of sitting next to Nellie (1972).

sitch noun orig US A situation, state of affairs. 1989–. COSMOPOLITAN Searching for that perfect phrase to describe your out-of-control crush or recent dating dilemma? This list of lingo will give you the right term for every romantic sitch (2001). [Shortening of *situation* noun.]

sit-down noun N Amer, tramps', dated A free sit-down meal. 1919–36.

site noun US, nautical A job, a situation. 1930–. NEW YORKER Joe, who generally keeps his own counsel, tells me that he is hoping to get a site—a job—on the Sniktaw (1977).

sitter noun US Someone employed to sit in a bar and encourage other patrons to buy drinks. 1938–48.

simoleon simp Simple Simon sin sin bin sin city

six adjective **six feet under** dead and buried. 1942–. J. GERSON In Islay . . . we make sure the dead are stiff and cold and six feet under (1979). Cf. DEEP SIX noun.

six by six noun US, military A six-wheel truck with six-wheel drive. Also **six-by.** 1942–.

sixer noun **1** Six months' hard labour; also, six months' imprisonment. 1849–. D. W. MAURER Maybe he will get off with a *bit* . . . or a *sixer*, which is six months in jail (1955). **2** Six strokes of the cane as a school punishment. 1927–. C. MCCULLOUGH They all got sixers, but Meggie was terribly upset because she thought she ought to have been the only one punished (1977). [From *six* adjective + *-er*.]

sixty-nine noun = SOIXANTE-NEUF noun. Also **69.** 1888–. D. LANG We spent many hours lying on her bed, more or less in the classical 69 position, but motionless (1973).

skag variant of SCAG noun.

skammer variant of SCAMMER noun.

skank noun orig US A person, esp. a woman, regarded as unattractive, sleazy, sexually promiscuous, or immoral. 1964–. PLAYBOY Girl M.B.A.s could slip into gabardine suits and floppy bow ties and feel, if not exactly alluring, at least not like total skanks (1986). Hence **skanky** adjective 1982–. [Origin unknown.]

skate[1] noun **1 to get** or **put one's skates on** Brit, orig military To hurry up. 1895–. W. J. BURLEY I'd better be getting my skates on, I'm catching the night train and I haven't done a thing about getting ready (1976). verb intr. **2** To leave speedily. 1915–. G. FRANKAU When one's happy—well, time simply flies. Me for the hay. Let's get our bill, and skate (1937). **3** US To avoid one's obligations, to shirk. 1945–. OBSERVER I'm not a woman's libber but I don't want to skate (shirk) (1979).

skate[2] noun mainly US **1** A worn-out decrepit horse. 1894–. E. TIDYMAN The man was a gambler. . . . A pony player. Used to bet thousands on the worst-looking skates you've ever seen (1978). **2** A mean or contemptible person. Cf. CHEAPSKATE noun. 1896–. H. PINTER *Aston:* I saw him have a go at you. *Davies:* . . . The filthy skate, an old man like me (1960). [Origin unknown.]

skedaddle verb intr. To run away, depart quickly. 1862–. [Orig US military slang, introduced during the Civil War of 1861–5; prob. a fanciful formation.]

skee noun Austral and NZ Whisky. 1959–. G. JENKIN And for this here quid and a bottle of skee I'm betting at ten to one (1967). [Shortening.]

skeeter noun US and Austral A mosquito. 1839–. J. B. HILTON If a slave broke loose, he would sometimes make a go of it in Florida—if he could survive the 'gators and the skeeters (1982). [Abbreviation of regional pronunciation of *mosquito*.]

skeeve US. verb trans. **1** To disgust, repel; often followed by *out*. 1986–. J. FRIEDMAN I'm terrified to get touched by a floor mop. They skeeve me out (1986). **2** To loathe. 1991–. noun **3** An obnoxious or contemptible person. 1990–. B. WAGNER Of course I'm coming to the bat mitzvah. What am I, a skeeve? (1997). [Back-formation from SKEEVY adjective.]

skeevy adjective US Disgusting, distasteful, or dirty; discomforting; sleazy. 1976–. WALKER & SCHONE I suffered through a few months of late hours at the front desk of a skeevy Vegas motel (2001). [From Italian *schifo* disgusting + *-y.*]

skeezicks /ˈskiːzɪks/ noun Also **skeesicks, -zacks, -zecks.** US, dated A rascal, rogue. 1850–1939. P. A. ROLLINS Hawkins, that ol' skeesicks you met on th' railway train an' liked, is th' feller that's acted as th' owners' agent in sellin' rights to your uncle (1939). [Prob. a fanciful coinage.]

skell noun US In New York City, a homeless person or derelict, esp. one who sleeps in the subway system. 1982–. [Perh. shortened from *skeleton.*]

skepsel /ˈskepsəl/ noun Also **schepsel.** S Afr A creature; often used derogatorily of a Black or Coloured person. 1844–. M. MURRAY How can we bring up our children decently when there are skepsels like that about? (1953). [From Afrikaans *skepsel*, Dutch *schepsel*, from *scheppen* to create.]

skerrick noun now mainly Austral The smallest bit; often in negative contexts. 1825–. D. CLARK 'Any luck?' 'Not a skerrick,' said Green (1969). [Origin unknown.]

sketch noun dated A ridiculous sight, a very amusing person; often in **hot sketch,** a comical or colourful person. 1917–30. J. B. PRIESTLEY You do look a sight, Dad. . . . I never saw such a sketch (1930).

ski bum noun N Amer A skiing enthusiast who works casually at a resort in order to ski. 1960–.

six   six by six   sixer   sixty-nine   skag   skammer

skid-lid noun A motor-cyclist's crash-helmet. Cf. LID noun 1. 1958–. C. WATSON This bird in motor-cycle get-up . . . with that great skid lid hiding half her face (1977).

skidoo /skɪˈduː/ verb intr. N Amer To leave hurriedly. 1905–. B. MALAMUD 'If you skidoo now . . . you'll get spit.' 'Who's skidooing?' (1963). See also TWENTY-THREE SKIDOO int. [Origin uncertain; perh. from SKEDADDLE verb.]

skid row noun mainly N Amer A part of a town frequented by vagrants, alcoholics, etc. 1931–. [Alteration of *skid road* in same sense, from earlier sense, part of a town frequented by loggers (orig sense, track formed by skids along which logs are rolled).]

skilly noun mainly nautical An insipid beverage; tea or coffee. 1927–. J. MASEFIELD A cup of skilly completed the repast (1953). [From earlier sense, thin porridge or soup; abbreviation of obs. slang *skilligalee* noun, thin porridge or soup, prob. a fanciful formation.]

skim verb trans. and intr. US To conceal or divert (some of one's earnings or takings, esp. from gambling) to avoid paying tax on them. 1966–. M. PUZO Gronevelts felt that the hotel owners who skimmed money in the casino counting room were jerks, that the FBI would catch up with them sooner or later (1978).

skimish /ˈskɪmɪʃ/ noun Alcoholic drink. 1908–. J. CURTIS He had been drinking all that skimish without having had a bite to eat (1936). [From Shelta *škimis* to drink, *škimišk* drunk.]

skimmer noun 1 mainly US A broad-brimmed boater. 1830–. P. DE VRIES The thoroughly incompatible straw hat. . . . The brightly banded boater, or 'skimmer' or 'katy' (1974). 2 US A person who skims money (see SKIM verb). 1970–. S. BRILL The cash was being split, some to be counted for taxes and the rest to go to the skimmers (1978).

skin noun 1 criminals', dated A purse or wallet. a.1790–. J. CURTIS Proper jobs I mean. Not nicking skins from blokes what are lit up (1936). 2 dated A horse or mule. 1923–41. 3 US A dollar. 1930–. R. B. PARKER I got a buyer with about a hundred thousand dollars . . . a hundred thousand skins (1976). 4 jazz A drum; usu. pl. 1938–. 5 US, African-American The skin of the palm of the hand, as making contact in shaking or slapping hands in friendship or solidarity; esp. in phrs. *to give (some) skin*, imperative *gimme some skin*. 1942–. H. L. FOSTER The viewer of TV sporting events will often observe black athletes, and whites now too,

giving skin after a home run, a touch-down, or at the start of a basketball game (1974). 6 A tyre. 1954–. HOT CAR The answer is to run at the *same pressure* as the standard tyres, as by dropping the pressure any more than two pounds, you could cause sidewall failure, even in the big American skins (1977). 7 orig US A condom. 1960–. T. SHARPE 'You got those rubbers you use?' he asked suddenly. . . . 'I want those skins' (1976). 8 orig US A paper for rolling (esp. marijuana) cigarettes. 1969–. 9 Brit A skinhead. 1970–. TIMES There are black skins, and there are non-violent skins. . . . Certainly, many of the skins are thugs (1981). verb 10 trans. To fleece or swindle. 1819–. P. G. WODEHOUSE The only thing to do seems to be to get back to the course and try to skin a bookie or two (1930). 11 trans. US To beat or overcome completely. 1862–. VERBATIM Puns ('Eagles *skin* Washington') . . . offer limitless possibilities to the enterprising sports journalist (1981). 12 trans. and intr. To inject (a drug) subcutaneously. 1953–. J. BROWN The bastard, he mained me. I said to skin it, but he mained it. First time (1972). Compare MAIN verb, SKIN-POP verb. [In sense 4, from the earlier sense, a drum-head, from its being made of animal skin.]

skin and blister noun Rhyming slang for 'sister'. 1925–. G. INGRAM I saw your skin and blister last night (1935).

skin-beater noun dated A drummer in a jazz- or dance-band. 1936–. NEW YORK TIMES BOOK REVIEW Red, the reefer-smitten skin beater (1953). [From SKIN noun 4 + *beater* noun.]

skin-flick noun An explicitly pornographic film. 1968–.

skinful noun Enough alcoholic drink to make one drunk. 1788–. B. BEAUMONT I . . . sought suitable solace in the local beer. By closing time I had had a right skinful (1982).

skin game noun US A game, trick, enterprise, etc. intended to swindle. 1868–. E. MCGIRR As a very small [antiques] dealer, I was no opposition. . . . His business is rather a skin game (1973). [From SKIN verb 10 + *game* noun.]

skin house noun US An establishment featuring nude shows, pornographic films, etc. 1970–. HARPER'S MAGAZINE The skin houses were mostly playing short subjects—a girl taking a bath in a sylvan stream, a volley-ball game in a nudist camp (1970).

skinned adjective = SKINT adjective; also with *out*. 1935–. OBSERVER I'm skinned, I know I can always count on someone helpin' me (1958).

skid-lid skidoo skid row skilly skim skimmer

skinner noun **1** Austral A horse that wins a race at very long odds; a betting coup. 1891–. SYDNEY MORNING HERALD Skinner for bookmakers (1974). **2 a skinner** NZ Skint, broke; empty. 1943–. LANDFALL Sure you're a skinner? Not a drop in the place, I mean? (1967). [In sense 1, from earlier sense, one who swindles, from SKIN verb 10.]

skinny-dip verb intr. orig US To swim naked. 1966–. L. BIRNBACH Once every summer, teenagers are caught skinny-dipping after dark (1980). So **skinny-dipper,** noun. 1971–. [From the notion of swimming only in one's skin.]

Skinny Liz noun derog A thin girl or woman. 1959–. N. FITZGERALD She takes no interest in . . . eatin'. That's why she's such a Skinny Liz (1961).

skin-pop verb intr. orig US To inject a drug subcutaneously. 1953–. DAILY TELEGRAPH She had also 'skin-popped' (injected drugs just below the surface of the skin) and taken a vast assortment of pills (1970). Hence **skin-popper,** noun 1953–. Compare MAIN-LINE verb, SKIN verb 12.

skint adjective Brit Having no money left, broke. 1925–. TIMES Are the British really as skint as we like to make out? (1981). [Variant of SKINNED adjective.]

skip noun **1** N Amer A person who absconds, esp. to avoid paying debts. 1915–. DETROIT FREE PRESS Jean Phelan traces all kinds of hard-to-locate 'skips'—the defaulters who have 'skipped' out (1978). verb **2 to skip out** to make off, abscond. 1865–. J. THOMSON Bibby hadn't turned up. He wondered if he had skipped out (1977). **3a: (let's) skip it** orig US An exhortation or command to drop a subject or forget something. 1934–. R. DENTRY At home . . . we cope and never give it a second thought. Out here we—oh, skip it! (1971). **b: to skip it** to leave, esp. hurriedly. 1959–. M. NA GOPALEEN The son turned out to be a very bad bit of work, sold all the furniture to buy drink and then skipped it to America (a.1966).

skipper¹ noun **1** orig curling The captain of a sports team. 1830–. **2** services' A commanding officer in the army; the captain of an aircraft or squadron. 1906–. R.A.F. NEWS The headmaster . . . will join his wartime Whitley skipper, Gp Capt Leonard Cheshire (1977). **3** orig US A police captain or sergeant; a police chief. 1929–. D. BARNES Good

piece of police work. . . . I'll fill the skipper in. I'm sure he'll be pleased (1976). [From earlier sense, ship's captain.]

skipper² noun Brit **1** A sleeping place for a vagrant. 1925–. COUNTRY LIFE He had painfully to learn the rudiments of vagrant survival; to make sure of his 'skipper' or kip before dark (1978). **2** A vagrant; one who sleeps rough. 1925–. GUARDIAN It was the night of the big Government census of the 'skippers'—the people who sleep rough (1965). **3** An act of sleeping rough; esp. in phr. *to do a skipper*. 1935–. OBSERVER There are not enough beds. Many will be turned away and have to do a 'skipper' in station, park or ruin (1962). [From earlier cant sense, a barn, shed, etc. used by vagrants; perh. from Cornish *scíber* or Welsh *ysgubor* a barn.]

skirt noun A woman regarded as an object of sexual desire. 1914–. K. MILLETT The two patriarchs, never tired of chasing twenty-year-old skirts in their old age (1974). See also **bit of skirt** at BIT noun.

skirt-chaser noun derog A man who obsessively pursues women. 1942–. L. PETERS He had always despised . . . the indiscriminate skirt-chaser (1962). Hence **skirt-chase,** verb intr. 1943–.

skirt patrol noun orig US A search for female sexual partners. 1941–. EVERYBODY'S MAGAZINE (Australia): In each war, a new vocabulary is created. Today, in Vietnam, Australians are again catching up on American Army slang . . . All would refer to a special girlfriend as their OAO—one and only. Probably, the OAO was met on skirt patrol (1967).

skite verb intr. **1** Austral and NZ To boast, brag. 1857–. R. HALL That's skiting, if you want to hear me skite. We'd beat the lot of youse, him and me (1982). noun **2** Austral and NZ **a** A boast; boasting; ostentation. 1860–. S. T. OLLIVIER 'Alister Bridgeman says it's mostly skite,' Sarah said breezily (1965). **b** A boaster; a conceited person. 1897–. A. B. FACEY Charlie was a terrific skite and he told everyone about the incident (1981). **3** Scottish A spree, a binge; esp. in phr. *on the skite*. 1869–. N. SMYTHE I was a bit too fond of the old jar. Went on the skite once too often (1972). [Verb perh. from earlier *skite*, to shoot, dart, leave quickly, perh. from Old Norse *skýt*-, umlauted stem of *skóta* to shoot.]

skirt patrol
**a search for
female sexual
partners**

skive Brit orig military. verb intr. **1** To avoid one's work or duty, esp. by absenting oneself; often followed by *off*. 1919–. J. MANN The girls who dig are always glad of an excuse to skive off and have a rest (1973). noun **2** An act of or opportunity for skiving; an easy option. 1958–. J. DITTON He thought the sentry was on the skive. Thought he'd come down . . . for a cup of coffee (1980). Hence **skiver,** noun. 1941–. [Perh. from French *esquiver* to dodge, slink away, or from earlier *skive* to split or cut (leather, rubber, etc.), from Old Norse *skífa*.]

skivvy¹ Also **scivey, skivey.** mainly derog. noun **1** A female domestic servant, esp. a maid-of-all-work. 1902–. verb intr. **2** To work as a skivvy. 1931–. J. THOMSON It wasn't no skivvying job. . . . Mrs King treated me like a friend (1973). [Origin unknown.]

skivvy² noun Also **scivvy, skivie, skivvie.** N Amer, orig nautical **1** A vest, undershirt. Also **skivvy shirt.** 1932–. **2** pl. Underclothes. 1945–. [Origin unknown.]

skosh /skəʊʃ/ noun US, orig services' A small amount; often adverbially in *a skosh*, slightly, somewhat. 1959–. CYCLE WORLD The GSX-R's seat is more comfortable than the Yamaha's thinly padded perch, and its bars are a skosh higher (1988). [From Japanese *sukoshi* a little, somewhat, apparently picked up by US servicemen in the Korean war.]

skull noun **1** US and Austral A leader or chief; also, an expert. 1880–. G. H. JOHNSTON 'Who does he fix the deal with?' 'God knows! D'ye think the skulls tell us that?' (1948). **2 out of one's skull** out of one's mind, crazy. 1968–. G. VIDAL I thought that Kalki was out of his skull (1978). verb trans. **3** mainly US To hit on the head. 1945–. A. BERGMAN My waking came in drugged stages. . . . I had been skulled (1975). [In sense 1, cf. the earlier obsolete sense, the head of an Oxford college or hall.]

skull-buster noun US Something that taxes the mind; a complicated problem; a brain-teaser. 1926–.

skull session noun US A discussion or conference. 1959–. D. JORDAN Joe was ready for skull session (1973).

skunk US. verb trans. **1** To defeat or get the better of. 1843–. D. DELMAN She'll skunk Nell Duncan today, and win (1972). **2a** To fail to pay (a bill or creditor). 1851–. **b** To cheat. 1890–. E. FENWICK I'm beginning to think we skunked you over the price (1971). noun **3** military An unidentified surface craft. 1945–. NEW YORK

TIMES MAGAZINE The cruiser is . . . useful at times for coastal bombardment or to seek out and destroy enemy 'skunks' (surface craft) (1952). **4 (as) drunk as a skunk** extremely drunk. 1981–. T3 It's also got lots of little pointers to work out tack angles and stuff like that—essential for when you're walking home drunk as a skunk (1997). **5** A type of marijuana with a pungent smell; esp., latterly, a very potent variety made from hybrid plants grown under artificial conditions. 1982–. Also **skunkweed.**

skutt variant of SCUT noun.

sky noun **1** Abbreviation of SKY-ROCKET noun. 1890–. P. HILL Said 'ee found it [a gun] on the rattler. Put it in 'is sky when 'ee got off at Leicester Square (1979). verb **2 to sky the wipe** dated Austral, boxing To throw in the towel, give up. 1916–33.

sky bear noun N Amer (An officer in) a police helicopter. 1975–. Cf. SMOKEY BEAR noun.

skyman noun journalists' A paratrooper. 1952–. SUNDAY TELEGRAPH Skymen hit the target (1964).

sky pilot noun A priest or clergyman, esp. a military or naval chaplain. 1883–. B. BROADFOOT At the missions you would get a sermon, say 15 minutes of religion from a sky pilot (1973).

sky-rocket noun **1** US, dated An enthusiastic cheer, raised esp. by college students. 1867–1947. **2** Rhyming slang for 'pocket'. 1879–. B. MATHER Ten trouble-free runs . . . and you're back in England with five thousand quid in your skyrocket (1973).

slack adjective **1** Jamaican Esp. of a woman: promiscuous, 'loose'. 1956–. DAILY TELEGRAPH She claimed the 33-year-old javelin thrower was 'slack' . . . , and added: 'Morals, she had none' (1990). noun **2** A prostitute. 1959–. W. YOUNG The slack is afraid of disease, and afraid of the sex maniac who thinks it'd be fun to strangle her (1965). **3 to give** (or **cut**) (a person) **some slack** US To show (a person) understanding or restraint; to give (one) a chance. 1968–. BLACK WORLD Tradesmen give them no slack in the unfamiliar bargaining processes (1973).

slacker noun orig and mainly US A person regarded as one of a large group or generation of young people (esp. in the 1980s to mid-1990s) characterized by apathy, aimlessness, and lack of ambition. The usage was popularized by the 1991 US film *Slacker*.

skive   skivvy   skosh   skull   skull-buster   sky bear

slag¹ noun criminals', dated A watch-chain or similar decorative chain. 1857–1929. CLUES Then we'll take the hot hoops and slags up to the block dealers (1926). [Prob. from obs. slang *slang*, a watch-chain, perh. from Dutch *slang* snake.]

slag² noun **1a** An objectionable or contemptible person. 1943–. DAILY TELEGRAPH As sentence was announced, the dead boy's father . . . shouted: 'I hope you rot in it, you slag' (1981). **b** A vagrant or petty criminal; also, such people collectively. 1955–. P. LAURIE I could get them up the nick and take their prints with ink, but that's really for slag (1970). **c** A slatternly, promiscuous, or objectionable woman; a prostitute. 1958–. J. SEABROOK I went out with a girl called Angie, who was really a bit of a slag (1973). **2** Worthless matter; rubbish, nonsense. 1948–. NEW YORKER It is very depressing to think about the wonderful . . . letters people used to get . . . and then look at the slag on one's desk (1970). verb trans. **3** To criticize, insult; often followed by *off.* 1971–. DAILY TELEGRAPH He followed me down the street, slagging me off (1981). Hence **slaggy,** adjective. 1943–. R. CONNOLLY He thought about some of the slaggy models he had known (1980). [From earlier sense, waste matter; in sense 1, cf. earlier slang senses, a coward, a thug.]

slam noun US **1** An insult or put-down. 1884–. R. L. DUNCAN I don't take that description as a slam. I was a great piece of ass (1980). **2** Prison; usu. with *the.* Cf. SLAMMER noun. 1960–. J. GORES You're going to the slam for fifteen (1978). verb trans. **3** orig US To criticize severely. 1916–. J. IRVING A long, cocky letter, quoting Marcus Aurelius and slamming Franz Grillparzer (1978).

slammer noun orig US Prison; usu. with *the*; sometimes *the slammers.* Cf. SLAM noun 2. 1952–. D. BAGLEY This one's not for the slammer. He'll go to Broadmoor for sure (1977). [Perh. from the slamming shut of cell doors.]

slant noun US, derog and offensive = SLANT-EYE noun. 1942–. M. MACHLIN And the fuckin' Eskimo slants are tryin' to get the rest of it (1976). Cf. SLOPE noun.

slanter variant of SCHLENTER noun.

slant-eye noun derog and offensive, orig US A slant-eyed person; spec. an Asian. Also **slant-eyes.** 1929–. TIMES LITERARY SUPPLEMENT And those Jap Ph.D.'s, their questionnaires! (Replying 'Sod off, Slant-Eyes' led to friction) (1974).

slap noun **1** Theatrical make-up, as rouge or grease-paint; hence generally, any cosmetic make-up, esp. applied thickly or carelessly. 1860–. J. R. ACKERLEY She was all dolled up, her face thick with slap (1960). verb trans. **2** US To play (a double-bass) without a bow in jazz style, spec. to pull the strings so as to let them snap back on to the fingerboard. 1933–. [In sense 1, from the notion of make-up *slapped* on to the face.]

slap and tickle noun Brit Light-hearted kissing, cuddling, etc. 1928–.

slap-happy noun orig US **1** Dazed, punch-drunk; dizzy (with happiness). 1936–. DETECTIVE TALES He was a little slap-happy from a decade of slug-festing (1940). **2** Cheerfully casual or flippant. 1937–. [From *slap* noun, blow with the hand.]

slaphead noun orig and mainly Brit A bald (or balding) man; someone with a shaven head. 1990–. Hence **slap-headed,** adjective. 1994–. ODDS ON England, cruising earlier in the match, were now level and struggling, and all because of a slap-headed, middle-aged German (1999).

slapper noun Brit A promiscuous woman. 1992–. [Perh. from earlier dialect sense, a large or strapping person.]

slash Brit. noun **1** An act of urinating. 1950–. N. J. CRISP He decided to risk a quick slash, which . . . he needed (1977). verb intr. **2** To urinate. 1973–. M. AMIS If you can slash in my bed . . . don't tell me you can't suck my cock (1973). [Perh. from obs. *slash* noun, a drink, of uncertain origin.]

slather /ˈslæðə(r)/ verb trans. N Amer To thrash, defeat thoroughly, castigate. 1910–. GLOBE & MAIL (Toronto): Canadians can get slathered in Olympic hockey (1968). See also OPEN SLATHER noun. [From the earlier senses, to spill, to squander, to smear; origin unknown.]

slats noun pl., orig and mainly US **1** The ribs. 1898–. **2** The buttocks; usu. in phr. *a kick in the slats.* Also fig. 1935–. BUSINESS WEEK Unless we get a new kick in the slats from inflation next year, I would look for continued relative restraint in the settlements (1975).

slaughter-house noun A cheap brothel. 1928–. W. FAULKNER Both of you get to hell back to that slaughterhouse (1962).

slay verb trans. To overwhelm with delight; to convulse with laughter. 1848–. D. O'SULLIVAN They're fun. . . . They'll slay you! (1975).

sleaze verb intr. **1** To move sleazily. 1964–. WHIG-STANDARD (Kingston, Ontario): When not thumping . . . , they [a rock group] just kind of sleaze along, a little like Lou Reed at his best (1978). noun **2** Squalor; sordidness, sleaziness. 1967–. NATIONAL OBSERVER (US): At home with the sleaze king (1976). **3** A sleazy person. 1976–. TIME Oh God, red nail polish—I look like a sleaze (1977). [Back-formation from *sleazy* adjective.]

sleazebag noun orig US A sleazy, corrupt, disgusting, or repellent person. 1981–. NATIONAL TIMES (Australia): We are not giving away any principles, because we do have a few on this side of the House, unlike the sleazebags over there (1985).

sleazeball noun US = SLEAZEBAG noun. 1983–.

sleazo noun and adjective US (Something) sleazy, (something) pornographic. 1972–. COURIER-MAIL (Brisbane): Norman Mailer said he liked sex movies, especially 'love pornies' and 'the sleazos' (1978). [From *sleazy* adjective + *-o*.]

sleazoid mainly US. adjective **1** Sleazy, disgusting, disreputable, or prurient. 1976–. ESQUIRE It's not like it's some sleazoid club with a bunch of . . . businessmen shoving dollar bills up your crotches (2000). noun **2** A sleazoid person or thing. 1984–. [From *sleazy* adjective + *-oid*.]

sleb noun A celebrity. 1997–. [Shortening.]

sledging noun Austral, cricket Unsportsmanlike attempts by fielders to upset a batsman's concentration by abuse, needling, etc. 1975–. GUARDIAN Howarth says he intends to complain about the amount of swearing, sledging and unchecked short-pitched bowling New Zealand have faced (1983). [From *sledge* noun, a large hammer.]

sleep noun orig US A prison sentence, usu. comparatively short. 1911–. J. PHELAN I wasn't interested myself [in escaping]. Three years was nothing—just a sleep, as you chaps put it (1938).

sleeping dictionary noun A foreign woman with whom a man has a sexual relationship and from whom he learns the rudiments of her language. 1928–.

sleeve noun **to put the sleeve on** (someone): US **a** To arrest. 1930–. **b** To beg or borrow from. 1931–. H. N. ROSE Wait'll I put the sleeve on Joe for some chewin' (1934).

sleigh-ride US. verb intr. **1** To take a narcotic drug. 1915–. noun **2** The taking of a narcotic drug, esp. cocaine; the euphoria resulting from this; esp. in phr. *to take* (or *go on*) *a sleigh-ride*. 1925–. D. SHANNON It was just some dope out on a sleigh-ride (1963). **3** An

implausible or false story; a hoax; esp. in phr. *to take for a sleigh-ride*. 1931–. SUN (Baltimore): House Republicans, charging that the taxpayers are being taken for a 'bureaucratic sleighride' (1950).

slewed adjective **1** Drunk. 1801–. D. LODGE I was somewhat slewed by this time and kept calling him Sparrow (1975). **2** Austral and NZ Lost in the bush. 1879–. TEECE & PIKE That is where I must have got 'slewed' for . . . the sun came out and I could see we were heading into the sun instead of having sundown at our backs (1978). [From the past participle of *slew* verb, to turn round.]

slick noun US A slicker; a cheat or swindler. 1959–. E. BULLINS Dandy's mother had a civil-service job in the city, and the city slick Dandy was from Philly (1971).

slicker noun orig and mainly US A smart and sophisticated person; a plausible rogue; esp. in phr. *a city slicker*. 1900–. X. FIELDING The two city-slickers were travelling on business (1953); MORECAMBE GUARDIAN He becomes a sort of Midnight Cowboy, lost and confused by the slickers around him (1978).

slickster noun US A swindler. 1965–. C. BROWN All the Muslims now felt as though 125th Street was theirs. It used to belong to the hustlers and the slicksters (1965).

slide verb intr. **1** dated, orig US To go away, esp. hurriedly. 1859–. E. WALLACE There's only one word that any sensible man can read in this situation, and that word is—slide! (1932). noun **2** US A trouser pocket. 1932–. I. SLIM How would you like a half a 'G' in your 'slide'? (1967).

slider noun A portion of ice-cream served between two wafers. 1915–.

sling verb **1 to sling one's hook** to go away, clear out. 1874–. **2 to sling off** (**at**) Austral and NZ To jeer (at). 1900–. R. BEILBY I wasn't slinging off at your religion (1977). **3** trans. To abandon, give up; often followed by *in* or *up*. 1902–. K. TENNANT We both slung in our jobs . . . and went off after him (1953). **4 to sling hash** US To wait at tables. 1906–. LIFE She . . . slung hash for a couple of weeks (1949). Cf. HASH-SLINGER noun. **5** intr. Austral To make a gift or pay a bribe. *c.*1907–. F. HARDY On first name terms with every Shire president so long as they didn't forget to sling when backhanders came in (1971). noun **6** Austral A gratuity; a bribe. Also **sling back**. 1948–. CANBERRA TIMES To have a house . . . given to you, is to put it colloquially, a sling of major proportions (1982).

sleazebag   sleazeball   sleazo   sleazoid   sleb   sledging

slinger noun mainly services' Bread soaked in tea; usu. in pl. 1882–.

slinter variant of SCHLENTER noun.

slip verb **1 to slip** (something) **over** (**on**) (someone), 1912–. To hoodwink (someone). 1912–. B. MCCORQUODALE It was something he really wanted to know and was trying to slip it over on her unexpectedly (1960). **2 to slip** (someone) **a length** (of a man) to have sex with (someone). 1949–. C. WOOD Come on, Suggy, you're 'is batman, 'e's never slipped you a crafty length 'as 'e (1970). Cf. LENGTH noun.

slit noun coarse The vulva. 1648–. ROLLING STONE What am I going to call it? Snatch, Twat? Pussy? Puss puss, nice kitty, nice little animal that's so goddam patronizing it's almost as bad as saying 'slit' (1977).

Sloane Ranger noun Brit A fashionable and conventional upper-middle-class young person (usu. female), esp. living in London. Also **Sloane**. 1975–. S. ALLAN She wore a cashmere sweater . . . a Sloane ranger type (1980). Hence **Sloaney**, adjective. [Blend of *Sloane* Square, London, and Lone *Ranger*, a hero of Western stories and films.]

Sloanie noun Brit = SLOANE RANGER noun. Also as adjective. 1982–. BARR & YORK 'A Sloanie has a pony' is . . . ingrained in the Sloanie mind (1982).

slob noun A stupid, careless, coarse, or fat person. 1861–. J. IRVING I think you're an irresponsible slob (1978). Hence **slobby**, adjective. 1967–. W. BURROUGHS Vicki told me that I looked like a slobby bum (1970). [From the earlier (esp. Irish) sense, mud, muddy land.]

slop verb **1 to slop up** US, dated To get drunk. 1899–1926. J. BLACK No use takin' a bunch of thirsty bums along and stealin' money for them to slop up in some saloon the next day (1926). noun **2** US and Austral Beer; usu. in pl. 1904–. AUSTRALASIAN POST Bung me and me mate over a droppa slops, will yer love? (1963).

slope noun US, derog and offensive An Asian; spec. a Vietnamese. 1948–. R. THOMAS All the Chinaman's gotta do is get into Saigon. . . . Once he's in nobody's gonna notice him, because all those slopes look alike (1978). [From Asians' stereotypically slanting eyes; cf. SLANT noun.]

slopehead noun US, derog and offensive = SLOPE noun. 1966–. LISTENER At Can Tho, two years ago, I heard American Air Force men sing a ballad about the Vietnamese, whom they then called 'slopeheads' or 'slopes' (1968).

slopy noun Also **slopey**. US, derog and offensive = SLOPE noun. 1948–.

slosh Brit. verb trans. **1** To hit, esp. heavily. 1890–. J. GASH I've sloshed her . . . sometimes when she'd got me mad (1977). noun **2** A heavy blow. 1936–. DAILY MIRROR I'll give you such a slosh when I get up from here (1977). [From the earlier senses, to splash, to pour liquid.]

sloshed adjective Brit Drunk. 1946–. R. LUDLUM They drank a *great* deal. . . . They appeared quite sloshed (1978). [From *slosh* verb, to splash, to pour liquid.]

slot noun **1** coarse The vulva. 1942–. **2** Austral A prison cell; also, a prison. 1947–. J. ALARD Siddy was in the next slot to Taggy (1968). **3** A slot-machine. 1950–. M. PUZO The slots usually brought in a profit of about a hundred thousand dollars a week (1978). verb trans. **4** Brit Army To kill or injure by shooting. 1987–.

slot man noun US A newspaper's chief subeditor, a news editor. 1928–. [From *slot* noun, the middle of a semi-circular desk at which sub-editors work, occupied by the chief subeditor.]

slough verb trans. dated To lock up, imprison. 1848–1935. J. BLACK They'll . . . haul us over to Martinez . . . an' slough us in the county jail (1926). [From *slough* noun, soft muddy ground.]

slowpoke noun mainly US A slow-coach. 1848–. S. RUSHDIE Come on, slowpoke, you don't want to be late (1981). [From *slow* adjective + obs. US *poke* noun, a lazy person.]

slows noun **the slows** an imaginary disease accounting for slowness. 1843–. D. FRANCIS They might as well send him [a racehorse] to the knackers. Got the slows right and proper, that one has (1970).

slug noun **1** now mainly US A drink of spirits, a tot. 1762–. L. HEREN Their simple niceness was almost as good as a slug of scotch and a cigarette (1978). **2** A contemptible person; a fat person. 1931–. G. & S. LORIMER 'He didn't love me and I felt pretty bad about it!' 'The complete and utter slug!' (1940).

slug verb **to slug it out** to fight it out; to stick it out. 1943–. DETROIT FREE PRESS They'll slug it out, week by week, blow by blow, for all the world to see (1978).

slug-fest noun US A hard-hitting contest, esp. in boxing or baseball. 1916–. ARIZONA DAILY STAR Powers gave up four runs on seven hits, a contrast from the 33-hit slugfest of Friday night

(1979). [From *slug* verb, to hit + *fest* noun, special occasion, festival.]

slugger noun orig and mainly US **1** A hard hitter. Also, in baseball, a hard-hitting batter. 1877–. **2** Ear-to-chin whiskers; usu. in pl. Also **slugger whiskers.** 1898–.

slug-nutty adjective US Punch-drunk. 1933–. E. HEMINGWAY He's been beat up so much he's slug-nutty (1950). [From *slug* verb, to hit + NUTTY adjective.]

slum¹ noun = SLUMGULLION noun 2. 1847–. [Apparently an abbreviation of SLUMGULLION noun.]

slum² noun N Amer **1** Cheap or imitation jewellery. 1914–. K. ORVIS Jewellery. . . . Top stuff. No slum (1962). **2** Cheap prizes at a fair, carnival, etc. 1929–. [Cf. the earlier obs. sense, nonsense, blarney.]

slum burner noun military An army cook. 1930–. M. HARGROVE Oscar of the Waldorf, in the Army, would still be . . . a *slum-burner* (1943). [From SLUM¹ noun + *burner* noun.]

slumgullion noun **1** US A muddy deposit in a mining sluice. 1887–. **2** mainly US A watery stew or hash. 1902–. T. WALKER For want of a better word we called it slumgullion (1976). [Prob. a fanciful formation.]

slum gun noun military A field-kitchen. 1917–. D. RUNYON Our slum-gun busted down (1947). [From SLUM¹ noun + *gun* noun.]

slummy noun Also **slummie.** A slum-dweller. 1934–. J. PATRICK Big Fry . . . tauntingly called out: 'We're the slummies!' (1973). [From *slum* noun, squalid neighbourhood + -*y*.]

slump noun A fat, slovenly person, 'slob'. 1906–. J. ASHFORD D'you reckon we'd waste good bees and honey on a slump like you for nothing? (1960). [From earlier sense, sudden decline.]

slush noun **1** dated Counterfeit paper money. 1924–. D. HUME We've been handling slush lately—ten bobs and quids. Where they were printed doesn't matter to you (1933). **2** Food, esp. of a watery consistency. 1941–. J. THOMAS It was years since he had tasted anything but jail slush (1955).

slush fund noun orig and mainly US **1** naval Money collected from the sale of 'slush' (fat or grease obtained from boiling meat) and used to buy luxuries for the crew. 1839–. **2** A reserve fund used esp. for political bribery. 1874–. [*Slush* refuse fat (see sense 1 above) from earlier sense, watery mud or melting snow.]

slush pump noun US A trombone. 1937–. J. WAINWRIGHT Get Walt to help on the slushpump tryouts. Walt stays first trombone (1977).

slushy noun Also **slushey, slushie.** A ship's cook (spec. as a nickname); also, any cook, any unskilled kitchen or domestic help. 1859–. K. GILES A grey-headed woman was crying in a corner—'The part-time slushy,' said Porterman (1970). [From *slush* noun (cf. SLUSH noun 2) or verb + -*y*.]

sly adjective mainly Austral Illicit, illegal. 1828–. BULLETIN (Sydney): The Board of Works has actually asked people to dob in their neighbours for sly watering (1973).

sly-boots noun mainly jocular A crafty person; one who does things secretively or on the sly. *a*.1700–.

sly grog noun Austral Alcoholic drink as sold by an unlicensed vendor. 1825–. NATIONAL TIMES (Sydney): The family was suspected of being sly grog dealers during the Second World War (1984).

smack noun orig US A drug, spec. heroin. 1942–. P. KINSLEY You're dealing . . . and I'm going to prove it. You're into opium and smack (1980). [Prob. alteration of SCHMECK noun.]

smacker noun **1** A loud kiss. 1775–. **2** orig US A coin or banknote; spec. a dollar or pound. 1920–. L. BLACK 'Gone at twelve thousand pounds.' . . . Twelve thousand smackers for a tray of old coins. Whew! (1979). [From *smack* verb + -*er*.]

smackeroo noun orig and mainly US = SMACKER noun 2. 1940–. E. V. CUNNINGHAM The price is eight thousand pounds, and the pound was five dollars then, so that makes it forty thousand smackeroos (1977). [Blend of SMACKER noun and -*eroo*.]

small potatoes noun orig US Something or someone trivial or insignificant. 1846–. GRAMOPHONE Serenus is small potatoes by CBS or RCA standards but its albums are tastefully produced and carefully annotated (1976).

smart-arse Also (US) **smart-ass.** adjective **1** Ostentatiously or smugly clever. Also **smart-arsed, -assed.** 1960–. GLOBE & MAIL (Toronto): It is tempting to be smart-assed when reviewing a Richard Rohmer novel (1979). noun **2** A smart-arse person, a smart alec. 1965–. J. BARNETT He had indulged in reckless speculation. . . . He was just as much a smart-arse as the Farnham D.I. (1981). verb trans. and intr. **3** To behave in a smart-arse way

slugger   slug-nutty   slum   slum burner   slum gun

(towards). 1970–. F. ROSS 'I guess it's something to do with the generation gap, sir.' 'Don't smart-ass me!' (1978).

smart mouth noun US A person who is cheeky or good at repartee. 1968–. So **smart-mouth**, verb trans. To be cheeky to, to be witty at the expense of. 1976–. J. L. HENSLEY He . . . beat up three kids . . . when one of them smart-mouthed him (1978).

smarts noun pl. US Intelligence, cleverness, acumen; wits. Also **smart**. 1970–. GUARDIAN WEEKLY They complain that the level of intelligence is low and that the soldiers have neither the smarts nor the education to work the complicated weapons of modern warfare (1981).

smarty-pants noun orig US A know-all. 1941–. Also **smarty-boots, smartie-boots**. 1962–. M. DICKENS He jumped right in with his slick talk . . . That smarty pants (1953). J. PORTER He was grateful that smartie-boots MacGregor had overlooked the obvious, too (1965).

smash noun 1 Loose change. 1821–. K. TENNANT Giving her his smash on pay-night so's she can blow it (1953). 2 N Amer An alcoholic drink, esp. wine. 1959–. AMERICAN SPEECH Let's get in the wind and belt some smash (1975). 3 N Amer A party, esp. one that is noisy or unrestrained. 1963–. NEW YORKER Every spring the Thrales gave a party. . . . They called this decorous event 'our smash' (1977). [In sense 1, of uncertain origin; in sense 2, from the earlier sense, mixed drink made of spirits, water, ice, etc.; in sense 3, cf. BASH noun 2, THRASH noun.]

smashed adjective orig US Drunk; under the influence of drugs. 1962–. NEW SOCIETY If you're smashed out of your skull . . . on peyote, then even the bizarre patronage of Marlon Brando must seem tolerable (1977).

smasher noun A (sexually) attractive woman or man. 1948–. C. MCCULLOUGH In a long black wig, tan body paint and my few scraps of metal I look a smasher (1977). [From earlier sense, something unusually excellent.]

smasheroo /smæʃəˈruː/ noun orig and mainly US A great success. 1948–. NEW YORKER Is one going to make the burning a big Broadway smasheroo of a scene? (1975). [From smash noun + -eroo.]

smear verb trans. To thrash or kill; to destroy by bombing. 1935–. P. FRANK We can smear every base, every industrial complex, once and for all (1957).

smeller noun dated A heavy fall; esp. in phr. to come a smeller. Cf. CROPPER noun. 1923–. P. G. WODEHOUSE A man's brain whizzes along for years exceeding the speed limit, and then something suddenly goes wrong with the steering gear and it skids and comes a smeller in the ditch (1934). [Perh. from the notion of 'smelling' the ground.]

smelly adjective Arousing suspicion. 1923–. G. F. NEWMAN Seems a bit smelly, Terry. I should blow him out (1970).

smoke noun 1 the (big, great) Smoke Brit and Austral A big city, esp. London. 1848–. SUNDAY AUSTRALIAN The unhappy pilgrimage from bush to big smoke (1971). 2 US Cheap whisky; a cheap drink based on raw alcohol, methylated spirit, solvent, etc. 1904–. WASHINGTON POST It was the smoke that made Heaton a loner and junk peddler in the demolition jungles of the Southwest area (1959). 3 in(to) smoke mainly Austral In(to) hiding. 1908–. K. S. PRICHARD Meanwhile Tony's got to be kept in smoke? (1967). 4 US derog and offensive A black person. 1913–. L. SANDERS Five men. One's a smoke (1970). verb 5 intr. Austral To make a rapid departure; often followed by off. 1893–. P. WHITE Dubbo had gone all right. Had taken his tin box . . . and smoked off (1961). 6 trans. US To shoot with a firearm. 1926–. DETECTIVE FICTION You didn't figure Tommy and those heels could hold me, did you? I smoked them just like I'm gonna smoke you, Bugs (1942).

smoke-ho
a stoppage of work for a rest and a smoke

smoke-ho noun Also **smoke-oh, smoke-o, smoko**. Austral and NZ 1 A stoppage of work for a rest and a smoke; a tea break. 1865–. SYDNEY MORNING HERALD Restrictive work practices—from heavily subsidised housing to the provision of pink salmon and oysters for workers' 'smoko' breaks (1986). 2 A party at which smoking is allowed. 1918–. [From smoke noun, period of smoking tobacco + -o.]

smoke-pole noun A firearm. 1929–. NEW ZEALAND LISTENER A long time since he'd fired the old smoke-pole, anyway (1970).

smoke-stick noun = SMOKE-POLE noun. 1927–.

smoke-up noun US An official notice that a student's work is not up to the required standard. 1927–. INDIANA DAILY STUDENT Sikes say 56 p.c. of Frosh probably had one Smoke-up (1960).

smoke-wagon noun US = SMOKE-POLE noun. 1891–.

Smokey Bear noun Also **Smoky Bear**. US **1** A type of wide-brimmed hat. 1969–. I. KEMP Sergeants Sullivan, McKane and Rothweiller . . . wore the round, soft-brimmed hats known by Americans as 'Smokey Bear'— similar to those of the Royal Canadian Mounted Police (1969). **2** A state policeman; also, collectively, the state police. Also **Smokey the Bear, Smok(e)y**. 1974–. O. MCNAB That Smoky looking at us? (1979). [From the name of an animal character used in US fire-prevention advertising.]

smooch orig US. verb trans. **1** To kiss and caress, esp. while dancing to slow romantic music. 1932–. L. NKOSI Mary and Gama are sharing a studio couch on which they are smooching quietly (1964). noun **2** A fondling embrace or caress; also, slow close dancing. 1942–. TIME Ethel Merman and Fernando Lamas . . . found that their nightly onstage smooch grated too harshly on their star-crossed sensibilities (1957). [Variant of obs. smouch to kiss, related to German dialect schmutzen to kiss, smile.]

smoothie noun orig US A person who is suave or stylish, often excessively so. 1929–. H. JENKINS I have nothing but contempt for the international art market. It is a racket none the better for being operated by cultivated smoothies (1979). [From smooth adjective + -ie.]

smoush noun Austral A kiss. 1963–. D. IRELAND Reminds me of a widow I knew at Richmond. Whenever I visited her and a plane went over she'd drop whatever she was doing and rush over for a smoush (1971). [Variant of SMOOCH noun.]

smudge noun **1** A photograph, esp. one taken by a street or press photographer. a.1931–. **2** = SMUDGER noun. 1968–. Q Cole is on his way to a photo session with acclaimed French smudge Claude Gassian (1990). [Perh. from the blurring of a hastily taken snapshot, but first applied in prison slang to a picture of a fingerprint.]

smudger noun A photographer, esp. a street or press photographer. 1961–.

smush /smʌʃ/ noun US, dated The mouth. 1930–. D. RUNYON He grabs Miss Amelia Bodkin in his arms and kisses her kerplump on the smush (1935). [Alteration of MUSH noun.]

snack noun Austral Something easy to accomplish, a push-over. 1941–. R. BEILBY 'How could I do that, Harry?' 'Easy. It'll be a snack' (1970).

snafu /snæfuː/ orig US, military. adjective **1** In utter confusion or chaos. 1942–. D. DIVINE Situation Snafu. . . . Send for the Seabees (1950). noun **2** A confusion or mix-up; a hitch. 1943–. B. MASON And Holy Moses, what a snafu! Why foul up poor, harmless, gormless Glad? (1980). verb **3** trans. To mess up, ruin. 1943–. G. MARKSTEIN My arrangements seemed snafued. I guess the lines got crossed (1981). **4** intr. To go wrong. 1975–. J. GRADY Every now and then something snafus and there is one hell of a mess (1975). [Acronym for 'situation normal: all fouled (or fucked) up'.]

snag noun Austral A sausage. 1941–. BULLETIN (Sydney): I make my own snags, my own pies and pasties (1980). [Prob. from Brit dialect snag noun, a morsel.]

snake noun **1** US and Austral Any of various categories of railway worker. 1929–. Cf. SNAKE CHARMER noun. **2** Austral, military A sergeant. 1941–. E. LAMBERT Baxter reckoned the officers and snakes are pinching our beer (1951). Cf. SNAKE-PIT noun.

snake charmer noun Austral A railway maintenance worker. 1937–.

snake eyes noun N Amer A throw of two ones with a pair of dice; also, fig., bad luck. Cf. KELLY´S EYE noun. 1929–. G. VIDAL It's like throwing dice. Let's just hope it won't be snake eyes for Jim Kelly (1978).

snake-headed adjective Austral = SNAKY adjective. 1900–. M. FRANKLIN Everybody is snake-headed about your blooming old book (1946).

snake juice noun mainly Austral Alcoholic liquor, esp. inferior whisky. Cf. JUNGLE JUICE noun. 1890–. SOUTHERLY Ironbark . . . went into the poison shop. Old Nick handed him a glass of snake juice (1962).

snake-pit noun **1** Austral, military A sergeants' mess. Also **snake-pen**. 1941–. S. L. ELLIOTT Andy Edwards has been promoted and moved up to the snake pit with you and the other snakes (1948). **2** A mental hospital. 1947–. A. LASKI They had visited him in the snake-pit (1968). [In sense 2, from the title of a novel by M. J. Ward.]

snake poison noun US and Austral Whisky. 1890–. K. TENNANT If Bee-Bonnet ever again wants

smoke-up   smoke-wagon   Smokey Bear   smoothie

me to sample his snake poison, I'll pour it on him and set it alight (1947).

snaky adjective Austral and NZ Angry, irritable. 1894–. D. WILLIAMSON What are you snaky about this time? (1970).

snap noun **1** mainly N Amer An easy task. 1877–. TECHNOLOGY WEEK Blazing a path to the moon is no snap. Neither is charting a career (1967). **2** pl. Hand-cuffs. 1895–. M. PROCTER Sergeant, we'd better have the snaps on these three (1967). **3** journalists' A short news report, esp. one dispatched or broadcast from the scene; a newsflash, press release. 1937–. L. HEREN Valentine found a telephone . . . , dictated a couple of snaps, and then . . . removed the microphone from the phone thus making it useless for the opposition (1978).

snapper noun **1** pl. Teeth; a set of false teeth. 1924–. LISTENER Do your snappers fit snugly? (1958). **2** A ticket inspector. 1938–. N. CULOTTA 'E doesn't want yer ticket. The snapper's got yer ticket (1957). [In sense 2, from the clipping of tickets.]

snarf verb trans. orig US **1** To eat or drink quickly or greedily. 1963–. J. LEAVY If they behave, they are allowed out to mingle with the glitterati for exactly one half hour and snarf up crudités and crab claws (1990). **2** To grab or snatch, esp. without permission; to take greedily. 1968–. **3** To inhale (a drug in powdered form). 1973–. Hence **snarfer** noun 1973–. [Imitative, perh. influenced by SCARF verb 2.]

snarfle verb US **1** intr. To sniff or snort; to eat noisily. 1985–. **2** trans. To consume or use rapidly or in large amounts; to grab, snatch. 1990–. ANTIGONISH REVIEW Fringe benefits include free rejects, which you'd snarfle without compunction, knowing they'd otherwise just be used . . . to clean streets (1999). [Imitative, or a blend of SNARF verb and *snaffle* or *snuffle*.]

snatch noun The female genitals. 1904–. P. ROTH Know what I did when I was fifteen? Sent a lock of my snatch-hair off in an envelope to Marlon Brando (1961). [Perh. from earlier obs. sense, a brief fondle or act of sexual intercourse.]

snavel /snæv(ə)1/ verb trans. Also **snavvel.** now mainly Austral To steal; to grab. a.1790–. V. PALMER They're booming the notion o' a new township and snavelling all the land within a mile o' it (1948). [Perh. a variant of obs. slang *snabble* to plunder, mug or *snaffle* to seize.]

snazzy adjective orig US Fashionably stylish or smart. 1932–. J. LOCK They've made the plain uniforms look as snazzy as possible with whiter-than-white hat-bands, belts and gaiters (1968). [Origin unknown.]

Sneaky Pete noun Also **sneaky pete.** orig and mainly US An illicit or cheap alcoholic drink. 1949–. J. H. JONES He walked around an unconscious Sneaky Pete drinker (1971).

snide adjective **1** Counterfeit, sham, bogus. Also more widely, inferior, worthless. 1859–. noun **2** A contemptible person; a swindler, cheat. 1874–. L. HENDERSON Tolly's not a snide, he's better than most, and he's been bloody unlucky (1972). **3** Counterfeit jewellery. 1885–. [Origin unknown.]

snidey adjective Also **sniddy, snidy.** dated Bad, contemptible. 1890–. F. HURST 'Fraid! Snidey! Poof! 'Fraid. Poof! Poof! Poof! (1928). [From SNIDE adjective + -*y*.]

sniff verb intr. To inhale cocaine, the fumes of glue or solvents, etc., through the nose. 1925–. E. WALLACE Red, you're . . . a hop-head. . . . We got no room in this outfit for guys who sniff (1931).

sniffer noun **1** The nose. 1858–. R. COOK They'll . . . look down their sniffers at you (1962). **2** orig US One who inhales drugs or toxic substances. 1920–. DAILY TELEGRAPH A self-confessed 'sniffer' denied being unfit to drive through drink or drugs while in charge of a motorcycle (1981).

snifter noun **1** orig US A small drink of alcohol. 1844–. P. G. WODEHOUSE And now, old horse, you may lead me across the street to the Coal Hole for a short snifter (1924). **2a** US A cocaine addict. 1925–. DETECTIVE FICTION WEEKLY A certain cocaine addict, known as Snifter Selton (1929). **b** orig US A small quantity of cocaine inhaled through the nose. 1930–. J. WAINWRIGHT A snifter when the pain's bad. . . . it ain't for kicks. You're no junkie (1974). **3** US A portable radio direction-finder. 1944–. [From dialect *snift* verb, to sniff: see SNIFTY adjective.]

snifty adjective orig and mainly US Haughty, disdainful. 1889–. [From dialect *snift* verb, to sniff, perh. of Scandinavian origin.]

snip noun **1** Something easily obtained; a sure thing, a certainty. a.1890–. N. SHUTE It is a snip; we will get both of them (1945). **2** Brit Something cheaply obtained; a bargain. 1926–. TIMES At a time when Beaujolais prices are soaring it is a snip at £1.90 (1977).

snipe verb trans. and intr. mainly N Amer To steal; to pick up or obtain; *spec.* to prospect for gold. 1909–. NEW YORKER He 'sniped' a lot of

snaky snap snapper snarf snarfle snatch snavel

snorter

his gold—just took it from likely spots without settling down to the formalities of a claim (1977).

snit noun orig and mainly US A state of agitation; a fit of rage; a tantrum or sulk. 1939–. NEW YORK TIMES I was recently . . . put in charge of six other copywriters, two of them men. The men are in a quiet snit (1980). [Origin unknown.] See also SNITTY adjective.

snitch noun **1** The nose. a.1700–. L. MARSHALL I'm not curious. I never had a long nose. . . . Peter . . . had a very long snitch. He had to push it into things that shouldn't have bothered him (1965). **2** An informer. 1785–. S. RIFKIN Lopez was an informant . . . a paragon among snitches (1979). **3 to have** (or **get**) **a snitch on** (someone): NZ To have a grudge against, to dislike. 1943–. G. SLATTER Got a snitch on me and put me in crook with the boss (1959). verb **4** intr. To inform *on*; to turn informer. 1801–. B. SCHULBERG I felt a little guilty about snitching on my neighbor (1941). **5** trans. To steal. 1904–. M. MACHLIN How about the guy who snitched a whole 9-D tractor, brand-new? (1976). [In sense 1, from earlier sense, a blow on the nose; ultimate origin unknown.]

snitty adjective orig and mainly US Bad-tempered, sulky. 1978–. PEOPLE A sixteen-year-old orphan, the child of an affair, who lives with her half-brother . . . and his snooty, snitty wife (1987). [From SNIT noun + -y.]

snockered adjective Drunk. 1961–. GLOBE & MAIL (Toronto): I'll get a bottle of Jack Daniel's for cocktails. Get them snockered on bourbon and they won't know the difference (1980). Cf. SCHNOCKERED adjective. [Perh. an arbitrary alteration of snookered adjective, stymied.]

snodger adjective Austral and NZ Excellent. 1917–. C. J. DENNIS It was a snodger day! . . . The apple trees was white with bloom. All things seemed good to me (1924). [Origin uncertain; cf. Brit dialect snod adjective, sleek, neat.]

snog Brit. verb intr. and trans. **1** To kiss and cuddle. 1945–. A. SAMPSON The cinema has lost its hold—except among unmarried teenagers, two-thirds of whom go at least once a week, perhaps to snog in the doubles (1962). PRIVATE EYE Mirror cartoonist Griffin even put the hapless Parsons in last Friday's cartoon: a line of 'nutters' queueing for a turn to snog the Princess of Wales—an unshaven 'Chucky' at the tail end (1995). noun **2** A period of snogging. 1959–. M. AMIS They were enjoying a kiss—well, more of a snog really (1973). [Origin unknown; perh. related to snug verb and noun.]

snollygoster noun US A shrewd, unprincipled person, esp. a politician. 1846–. A. ROUDYBUSH The deaths of a middle-aged tart and an elderly snollygoster are of little moment (1972). [Origin uncertain; perh. connected with *snallygaster*, name of a monster supposedly found in Maryland, from German *schnelle Geister* quick spirits.]

snoot noun **1** The nose. 1861–. D. M. DAVIN At first I was all for poking the bloke in the snoot (1956). verb trans. **2** US To treat scornfully or disdainfully. 1928–. TIME Cinderella . . . gets snooted by her Stepsisters and gazes sorrowfully into the flames of the scullery fire (1977). [Dialectal variant of *snout* noun.]

snoozer noun orig US A fellow, chap. 1884–. J. JOYCE They had cornered him about until there was not a snoozer among them but was utterly undeceived (1939). [From earlier sense, sleeper, from *snooze* verb, to sleep + -er:]

snore-off noun mainly Austral and NZ A sleep or nap, esp. after drinking. 1950–. D. O'GRADY He surfaced from his plonk-induced snore-off (1968).

snorer noun The nose. 1891–. [Cf. earlier sense, one who snores.]

snork noun Austral and NZ A baby. 1941–. B. PEARSON It's better to knock it on the head at birth, isn't it? Like a snork you don't want (1963). [From earlier sense, young pig, from *snork* verb, to snort or grunt, prob. from Middle Dutch or Middle Low German *snorken*.]

snort[1] orig US. noun **1** A small drink of spirits. 1889–. M. E. ATKINS We'll have another snort . . . C'mon, drink up, I'll fill your glass (1981). **2** An inhaled dose of cocaine, heroin, etc. 1951–. G. VIDAL 'Want a snort?' Bruce produced a cocaine snifter (1978). verb trans. and intr. **3** To inhale (a usu. illegal narcotic drug, esp. cocaine or heroin). 1935–. DAILY TELEGRAPH Mrs Pulitzer's lawyers claim that she started snorting cocaine after being sucked into the vortex of the 'Palm Beach lifestyle' (1982).

snort[2] dated, nautical. noun **1** A snorkel. NEW YORK HERALD TRIBUNE 'Snorts' said to enable vessels to stay under 20 days (1944). verb intr. **2** (Of a submarine) To travel underwater by means of a snort. 1953–. M. HEBDEN They were snorting slowly back up the Solent (1974). [Anglicized alteration of German *Schnorchel*, after *snort* noun, explosive nasal sound.]

snorter noun Something exceptionally remarkable for size, strength, severity, etc. 1859–. J. H. FINGLETON May . . . now hit another

snit snitch snitty snockered snodger snollygoster

'snorter' through the covers (1954). [Cf. earlier sense, one that snorts.]

snot noun **1** Nasal mucus. *c.*1425–. A. HALEY Trying futilely to breathe through nostrils nearly plugged with snot, he gaped open his cracked lips and took a deep breath of sea air (1976). **2** A contemptible or disgusting person. 1809–. J. MELVILLE We've let the boy go home on bail.... Miserable little snot, but no real harm in him (1981). [Prob. from Middle Dutch, Middle Low German *snotte*, Middle High German *snuz*.]

snotnose noun = SNOTTY-NOSE noun. 1941–. Hence **snot-nosed,** adjective = SNOTTY-NOSED adjective. 1941–. M. WOODHOUSE A persuasive manner you picked up at some snot-nosed advertising agency (1972).

snot-rag noun **1** A handkerchief. 1886–. N. MAILER One of them said he was going to take my shirt and use it as a snotrag (1959). **2** = SNOT noun 2. 1973–.

snotty adjective **1** Running with or dirty with nasal mucus. 1570–. I. M. GASKIN A baby can seem snorty and snotty, but sometimes it sounds worse than it is (1978). **2** Contemptible. 1681–. J. C. HEROLD Albertine had slapped the Crown Prince and called him a snotty brat (1958). **3** Supercilious, conceited. 1870–. GLOBE & MAIL MAGAZINE (Toronto): François is not always snotty, thank heaven (1968). noun **4** Brit A midshipman. 1903–. P. DICKINSON A British Naval Party under the command of a snappily saluting little snotty (1974). [From SNOT noun + *-y*; in sense 4, said to be from midshipmen's use of the buttons on their sleeve for wiping their nose.]

snotty-nose noun Someone whose nose is dirty with mucus; hence, a contemptible or supercilious person. 1602–. L. GOLDING A little snotty-nose like that... and he's the [boxing] champion from all the world! (1932).

snotty-nosed adjective Having a nose dirty or running with mucus; hence, contemptible, supercilious. 1610–. N. J. CRISP There's a snotty nosed young DC from the Yard sitting in his car outside (1978).

snout[1] noun Brit mainly prisoners' **1** Tobacco. 1885–. ECONOMIST The 'snout barons'— prisoners who make a profit from the shortage of tobacco within prisons (1964). **2** A cigarette. 1950–. P. MOLONEY Goin down the city fer a booze an a snout (1966). [Origin unknown.]

snout[2] noun **1 to have a snout on** or **against** Austral and NZ To be badly disposed towards. 1905–. **2** A police informer. 1910–.

OBSERVER You may have been 'grassed'...by a 'snout' (1982). verb **3** trans. Austral To harass; to rebuff. 1913–. A. MARSHALL I was sore as a snouted sheila for weeks (1944). **4** intr. To act as a police informer. 1923–. E. WALLACE Dr. Marford knows, but he's not the feller that goes snouting on his patients (1930). [From earlier sense, nose.]

snow noun **1** orig US Cocaine, also occasionally heroin or morphine. 1914–. A. HALL Pangsapa was a narcotics contrabandist and would therefore know people... prepared for a fix of snow (1966). **2** (Silver) money. 1925–. J. CURTIS Count up that snow while I go through the other drawers (1936). verb trans. **3** US To drug, to dope. 1927–. R. CHANDLER She looked snowed, weaved around funny (1934). **4** orig and mainly US To deceive or charm with plausible words. 1945–. N. FREELING I won't get mad. Just don't snow me with any sob-sister business (1963). [In sense 1, from the white powdery appearance of the drug.]

snow-bird noun US **1** dated One who joins or returns to the army in the winter for the sake of food and accommodation. 1905–30. **2** One who sniffs cocaine; broadly, a drug-addict. 1914–. SUNDAY TIMES New York is not... a city overrun by 'snowbirds' jabbing needles into their arms (1952). **3** A Northerner who goes to live or work in the South during the winter. 1923–. [In sense 2, from SNOW noun 1.]

snow bunny noun N Amer An inexperienced usu. female skier; a pretty girl who frequents ski slopes. 1953–.

snowdrop noun US An American military policeman; hence, more broadly, any military policeman. 1944–. [From the white helmets of US military policemen.]

snow job noun orig US A concerted attempt at flattery, deception, or persuasion. 1943–. K. TENNANT He... made a bee-line for the red-head. 'Now for the snow job,' Geechi murmured (1953). Hence **snow-job,** verb trans. To do a snow job on (someone). 1962–.

snow-man noun US One who deceives or charms with plausible words. 1967–. [From SNOW verb 4 + *man* noun.]

snozzle noun orig US = SCHNOZZLE noun. 1930–. D. O'GRADY The poor Old Girl [a truck] was mud from anus to snozzle (1968).

snozzler noun NZ An excellent person or thing. 1941–. [Origin unknown.]

snot   snotnose   snot-rag   snotty   snotty-nose   snow

snubby noun Also **snubbie**. US A small short-barrelled pistol. 1981–. E. LEONARD You want a snubbie. This one, .38 Special, two-inch barrel (1983). [From *snub(-nosed* designating such a gun + *-y*.]

snuff noun **up to snuff: a** Brit Knowing; not easily deceived. 1811–. **b** Up to standard. 1931–. E. B. WHITE The Central Park piece . . . is up to snuff or better (1943). [Apparently from the notion of being old or experienced enough to take snuff.]

snuff verb **1 to snuff it** to die. 1885–. M. GEE I mean, he didn't let the grass grow under his feet, it wasn't much more than a year after the first Mrs. Tatlock snuffed it (1981). **2 to snuff out** to kill, to murder. 1932–. E. BEHR If I cause too much embarrassment, they'll just snuff me out (1980). adjective **3** (Of a pornographic film, photograph, etc.) featuring the actual killing of a person. 1975–. DAILY COLONIST (Victoria, British Columbia): Charged with attempted murder in the making of 'snuff' photographic stills (1977).

snuggle-pup noun US, dated An attractive young girl. Also **snuggle-pupper, snuggle-puppy.** 1922–. FORUM & CENTURY I glimmed him with a snuggle-puppy (1930).

snurge noun An informer; a toady; broadly, an obnoxious person. 1933–. M. GILBERT He's such a little snurge. . . . He's so bogus (1955). [Origin unknown.]

so adjective dated, orig euphemistic Homosexual. 1937–. J. R. ACKERLEY A young 'so' man, picked up by Arthur in a Hyde Park urinal (1968).

soak verb **1** intr. To drink persistently, booze. 1687–. **2** trans. Brit To pawn. 1882–. **3** US, dated **a: to soak it to** = *to sock it to* (see SOCK verb 2). 1892–. **b** trans. To punish, hit hard, criticize. 1896–. **4** trans. orig US To extract money from by extortionate charges, taxation, etc. 1895–. M. FRENCH Roger wanted the divorce, and she was angry, so she really soaked him. She asked for fifteen thousand a year (1977). noun **5** A drunkard. 1820–. J. FENTON Old soaks from farmers poets' pubs And after-hours drinking clubs (1982). Hence **soaked,** adjective Drunk; often as the second element of a compound. 1737–. E. O'NEILL Like a rum-soaked trooper, brawling before a brothel on a Saturday night (*a*.1953). **soaker,** noun = SOAK noun 5. 1593–. G. M. TREVELYAN The upper class got drunk . . . on ale and . . . on wine. It is hard to say whether men of fashion or the rural gentry were the worst soakers (1946).

soap[1] noun **1** Flattery. Cf. SOFT SOAP noun. 1854–. W. FAULKNER 'The pattern,' Uncle Gavin said. 'First the soap, then the threat, then the bribe' (1957). **2 no soap** orig and mainly US An announcement of refusal of a request or offer, failure in an attempt, etc.; 'nothing doing'. 1926–. E. CRISPIN 'The police tried to trace the handkerchief, I take it?' 'They did, but no soap' (1977). Hence **soapy,** adjective Ingratiating, unctuous. 1854–. R. BOLT Steward (*to audience, soapy*): Lady Margaret, my master's daughter, lovely; lovely lovely (1960).

soap[2] noun espionage The truth drug sodium pentothal (or a mixture of this and amphetamines). 1975–. J. GARDNER Soap—as the Service called it—would sometimes produce spectacular results (1980). [From the initial letters of *sodium pentothal,* humorously respelled after *soap,* the cleaning agent.]

soap-dodger noun Brit A scruffy or dirty person. 1990–. INDEPENDENT They are neither 'crusties'—the dog-on-a-string brigade (or soap-dodgers as the tabloids call them)— nor style fetishists (1992).

sob noun Brit A pound. 1970–. K. ROYCE Norman could have back his fifty sobs; when I failed I didn't want compensation (1973). [Prob. alteration of SOV noun.]

S.O.B. noun Also **s.o.b.** mainly US Abbreviation of SON OF A BITCH noun; also of silly old bastard, etc. 1918–. C. STEAD That s.o.b. Montagu got me the job 'ere, you know (1934).

sob sister noun orig US A female journalist who writes sentimental articles; a writer of sob stories; hence in various metaphorical uses, esp. an actress who plays sentimental roles; a sentimental, impractical person, a do-gooder; an agony-column writer. 1912–. SUN (Baltimore): Forecasting opposition to his plan by 'sob-sisters' Goodwin said 'it wouldn't do any harm to give these sob-sisters a couple of wallops too' (1939).

sock[1] verb trans. **1** To hit forcefully. *a*.1700–. B. CHATWIN The porter had socked him on the jaw, and he now lay, face down on the paving (1982). **2 to sock it to** (someone) orig and mainly US To hit (someone) forcefully; to let (someone) have it; hence in the catch phrase **sock it to me** (**them,** etc.)**!,** used to express encouragement, sexual invitation, etc. 1877–. S. SHELDON She reached between his legs and stroked him, whispering, 'Go, baby. Sock it to me' (1970). **3** jazz To perform (music) in a swinging manner; esp. in phr. *to sock it* (*out*). 1927–. RADIO TIMES He's spent his evenings singing

snubby snuff snuggle-pup snurge so soap-dodger

in pubs . . . 'socking' out the rhythm and blues (1968). **4** US To impose something onerous (e.g. a heavy charge) on. 1939–. DETROIT FREE PRESS The township socked the company with a building permit violation (1978). noun **5** A hard blow. a.1700–. **6** US A strong impact, emphasis, a 'kick'. 1936–. ARIZONA DAILY STAR I figure we have enough speed and sock in our lineup to score runs (1979). [Origin unknown.]

sock² noun **1 to knock (or beat, rot) the socks off** US To beat thoroughly, to trounce. 1845–. ARIZONA DAILY STAR 'Trucks have been beating our socks off,' said . . . a spokesman for the Atchison, Topeka & Santa Fe Railway in Chicago. 'But now we have a chance to get some of the business back' (1979). **2 to put a sock in it** Brit To be quiet, shut up; usu. imperative. 1919–. N. SHUTE 'For Christ's sake put a sock in it,' he had said . . . 'and tell them I want an ambulance down here' (1944).

sockeroo /ˌsɒkəˈruː/ noun orig US Something with an overwhelming impact, a 'smash'. 1942–. SPECTATOR This latest box-office sockeroo also provides a modest example of the industry's throat-cutting activities (1964). [From SOCK¹ noun + -eroo.]

socko orig and mainly US. int **1** Imitative of the sound of a violent blow. 1924–. L. COHEN We're fat, F.—Smack! Wham! Pow!—Fat.—Socko! Sok! Bash! (1966). noun **2** A success, a hit. 1937–. P. G. WODEHOUSE Triumph or disaster, socko or flop, he went on forever like one of those permanent officials at the Foreign Office (1973). adjective **3** Stunningly effective or successful. 1939–. UNDERGROUND GRAMMARIAN Their latest brochure starts *right off* with this absolutely socko bit of dialog (1981). [From SOCK¹ noun 5 + -o.]

SOCO noun Also **Soco.** Brit A police officer trained to examine scenes of crime for forensic evidence or clues. 1980–. D. SIMPSON The SOCOs had finished with the body (1986). [Acronym from scene(s) of crime officer.]

sod noun **1a** A despicable or contemptible person, typically male. 1818–. J. BRAINE It's time he was dead. . . . If you want to destroy the sod, Frank, I'll give you absolutely all the dirt (1968). **b** A fellow, chap (often used affectionately or in commiseration). 1931–. D. WALLACE That's a shame, the poor little dawg, but if that was moine I'd hev that put down. That can't help but make no end o' work, the poor little sod

(1969). **2** A person who practises sodomy; a male homosexual. c.1855–. P. WYNDHAM LEWIS When you come to write your book . . . I should put in the sods. Sartre has shown what a superb figure of comedy a homo can be (1949). **3** Something difficult; a great nuisance. 1936–. HOT CAR The finish will be a nice satin which is a sod to keep clean (1977). **4 not to give a sod** not to care at all. 1961–. D. STOREY I don't give a sod for any of them, Phil (1973). See also **odds and sods** at ODDS noun. verb **5** trans. Used as a more forceful alternative to 'damn' in various expressions. 1904–. P. SCOTT At seven-fifteen they had to go out to dinner. Sod it (1953). **6 to sod off** to go away; usu. in imperative, expressing contempt, rejection, etc. 1960–. OBSERVER I am simply waiting for the day when I can say 'sod off' to your institution (1977). [Abbreviation of *sodomite* noun.]

SOCO

a police officer trained to examine scenes of crime for forensic evidence

soda noun Austral Something easy to do, a pushover. 1917–. G. H. JOHNSTON 'The Middle East was a soda beside this,' one of them told me (1943). [Perh. from the earlier sense, the deal card in the game of faro.]

sod-all noun and adjective Nothing, no. 1958–. K. AMIS There's been sod-all since (1958); K. BLAKE Here he was in this cold chill room, and two maniacs sitting playing cards at the table and taking sod-all notice of him (1978).

sodding adjective Used to express contempt or anger; often as a simple intensive. 1912–. D. BOGARDE I'll remember this sodding day until the day I die (1980). [From the present participle of SOD verb.]

Sod's law noun The supposed tendency of things to go wrong in a perverse or annoying way; = MURPHY'S LAW noun. 1970–.

soft soap noun orig US Flattery; often attrib. 1830–. SUN (Baltimore): Assailing Governor Lehman for his 'soft soap' manner of campaign, the park commissioner . . . renewed his assault on the Lehman banking family (1934). Hence **soft-soap**, verb trans. To flatter. 1840–.

soft touch noun A person easily manipulated; spec one easily induced to part with money; also, a task or opponent easily handled. Also **easy touch**. 1940–. H. KURNITZ Dorsey's appetite for easy money . . . was honed to a razor edge. . . . He sensed a vast soft touch (1955).

sock sockeroo socko SOCO sod soda soft touch

soixante-neuf /ˌswaːsɒnt ˈnɜːf/ noun
Sexual activity involving mutual oral
stimulation of the genitals. Cf. SIXTY-NINE
noun. 1888–. M. AMIS The other couple were
writhing about still, now seemingly poised for
a session of fully robed soixante-neuf (1973).
[French, literally 'sixty-nine'; from the
position of the couple.]

soldier noun **1** nautical, orig and mainly US
A worthless seaman; a loafer, shirker; often
in phr. old soldier. 1840–. B. HAMILTON He's a bit
of an old soldier, but a first-rate seaman, and a
hundred percent reliable at sea (1958). **2 sod
(etc.) this for a game of soldiers** and
variants: expressing irritation or
exasperation at a situation or (esp. time-
wasting) activity. 1979–. R. M. WILSON Fuck this
for a game of soldiers, you conclude. You've got
to move before you die (1989). See also DEAD
SOLDIER noun.

soldier's farewell noun An abusive
farewell. Cf. SAILOR'S FAREWELL noun. 1909–.
F. D. SHARPE As you pass through the door, you'll
sometimes hear a raspberry. . . . No one wants
to accept responsibility for that soldier's farewell
(1938).

solid adjective **1** Austral and NZ Severe;
difficult. 1916–. R. PARK After all, Auntie Josie's
got all them kids to look after. It must be pretty
well solid for her with Grandma as well (1948). **2**
US orig jazz Excellent, great. 1935–. W. HJORTSBERG
'Park your axe and have a drink.' 'Solid.' He
placed his saxophone case carefully on the table
(1978).

solitary noun Solitary confinement. 1854–.
W. M. RAINE 'He's been in solitary for a week,'
explained the warden (1924).

sollicker noun Also **soliker**. Austral
Something very big, a whopper. 1898–.
FRANKLIN & CUSACK She gave me a sollicker of a dose
out of a blue bottle (1939). Hence **sollicking**,
adjective Very big. 1917–. [Perh. from Brit
dialect sollock noun, impetus, force.]

some adjective **1** orig US A remarkable (. . .);
notably such a.1808–. W. S. CHURCHILL When
I warned them [the French Government] that
Britain would fight on alone whatever they did,
their Generals told their Prime Minister . . . : 'In
three weeks England will have her neck wrung
like a chicken.' Some chicken! Some neck!
(1941). pron **2 to get some** US To have sex; to
succeed in finding a sexual partner. 1889–.
J. KRANTZ Since his last visit she was getting some,
somewhere, he'd bet his life on it (1978). **3 and
then some** mainly US And (plenty) more in
addition. T. E. LAWRENCE It . . . will be 12

guineas and then some! (1931). adverb **4 to
go some** US To go well or fast; to do well;
to work hard. 1911–. H. LIEBERMAN He'd
known the girl for two months; for
Daughtry that was going some (1982).

something pron **1 something else** orig
N Amer Something exceptional. 1909–. O.D. Oh,
wow, these guides are . . . something else man!
(1977). **2 to have something going (with)** to
have a close (sexual) relationship (with).
1971–. PHILADELPHIA INQUIRER Is it true that Sammy
Davis Jr. has something going with Linda
Lovelace? (1973).

sometimey adjective US, African-American and
prisoners' Variable, unstable. 1946–. R. PHARR
She's the evilest and sometime-iest woman I
ever shacked up with (1969).

son of a bitch Also **son-of-a-bitch,
sonofabitch, sonuvabitch,** etc. pl. **sons of
bitches.** now mainly US. noun **1** A despicable
or contemptible man. 1707–. J. D. SALINGER Boy,
I can't stand that sonuvabitch (1951). **2** A
fellow, chap. 1951–. A. HAILEY Besides, the son-
of-a-bitch had guts and was honest (1979). int
3 Used to express anger, disgust, etc. 1953–.
M. MILLAR Sonuvabitch, I don't get it. What's the
matter? What did I do? (1957). Hence **son-of-
a-bitching,** adjective A general epithet of
abuse. 1930–. J. KIRKWOOD The meanest son-
of-a-bitching parrot you could ever run up
against (1960). Cf. S.O.B. noun.

soogee-moogee /ˈsuːdʒiː ˌmuːdʒiː/ noun
Also **soogie-moogie, soojee-moojee,
souji-mouji, sugi-mugi,** etc. nautical
1 A mixture containing caustic soda used for
cleaning paintwork and woodwork on boats.
1882–. **2** A cleaning operation done with
soogee-moogee. 1935–. [Origin unknown.]

sook /sʊk/ noun Austral and NZ A stupid,
cowardly, or timid person. 1933–. G. GREER She
may be reviled as a cissy, a sook (1970). [Perh.
from Brit. dialect suck noun, duffer.]

sool /suːl/ verb trans. Austral and NZ **1** (Of a dog)
to attack or worry (an animal). 1849–.
A. MARSHALL Urged the dog: 'Sool 'im, Bluey! Get
hold of him!' (1946). **2** To urge or goad on.
1889–. P. BARTON The cooking teacher, sooled on
by half a dozen or so by-now-tearful girls, took
to me with a large wooden spoon (1981).
[Variant of Brit dialect sowl verb, to seize
roughly.]

sooner noun mainly Austral An idler, shirker.
1892–. V. PALMER 'The dirty sooners!' he burst out.
'They don't know a man when they find one,
those heads down south' (1948). [Said to be

soixante-neuf soldier soldier's farewell sollicker

soor

from *sooner* adverb, rather, from the notion that such a person would sooner be idle than work.]

soor /suːə(r)/ noun dated Anglo-Indian A contemptible person. 1848–. F. RICHARDS You black soor, when I order you to do a thing I expect it to be done at once (1936). [From Hindi *suār* noun, pig.]

sooty noun offensive and derog, orig US A black person. 1838–. SUNDAY EXPRESS I am not racialist, but I can't bear to watch the sooties any more—it's like Uncle Tom's Cabin (1986).

sore-head noun mainly N Amer A discontented or mean person. 1848–. T. WOLFE We thought the was a man, but he turns out to be just a little sore-head (1939).

sort noun 1 orig Austral A woman, esp. a young and attractive one; a girlfriend. 1933–. N. MEDCALF This sheila . . . is a drack sort (1985). verb 2 **to sort** (someone) **out** to deal with (someone), esp. forcefully; to reprimand. 1941–. TIMES Richards came in to sort Willis out and, although Willis prevailed in the end, it was not before Richards had hit him several times for four (1974).

sort-out noun A fight or dispute. 1937–. C. WILLOCK Beaton himself had a sort-out with a buffalo bull that tried to overturn his Land-Rover (1964).

sounds noun pl. orig US Pop music, esp. records. 1955–. DAILY MIRROR Together cats don't buy records, they buy *sounds*, and they never blow their cool (1968).

soup noun 1 **in the soup** orig US In trouble. 1889–. H. G. WELLS We're in the soup. . . . We've got to do 1914 over again (1939). 2 orig US Nitroglycerine or gelignite, esp. for safe-breaking. 1902–. D. L. SAYERS Sam put the soup in at the 'inges and blowed the 'ole front clean off (1930). 3 The chemicals in which film is developed. 1929–. L. DEIGHTON Any special instructions? Over or under development? Fine grain soup? (1978). 4 surfing The foam of a breaking wave. 1962–. verb trans. 5 To put in difficulties; usu. in passive. 1895–. DAILY TELEGRAPH Admitting that he earned £3,000 a year, Lord Taylor said that if he accepted a junior Ministry he would be 'souped' (1964).

soup-and-fish noun Men's evening dress, a dinner suit. 1918–. H. MCLEAVE Get him to take off his soup-and-fish and show us his scar (1970).

soup gun noun dated US, military A mobile army kitchen. 1918–.

soup-strainer noun jocular A long moustache. 1932–. E. LUCIA A soulfully humming male quartet in soup-strainers and sideburns (1962).

soupy noun Also **soupie**. US, military (A summons to) a meal. 1899–. STARS & STRIPES I say 'Yum yum' when 'soupie' blows (1918). [From SOUP noun + -*y*.]

sourpuss noun orig US A peevish or miserable person. 1937–. LOGOPHILE He had always been henpecked by his wife, a sourpuss with a waspish temper (1980). [From *sour* adjective + PUSS² noun.]

souse noun 1 US A heavy drinking-bout. 1903–. E. O'NEILL Bejees, we'll go on a grand old souse together (1946). 2 orig US A drunkard. 1915–. R. CHANDLER Sylvia is not a souse. When she does get over the edge it's pretty drastic (1953). verb intr. 3 To drink to the point of drunkenness. 1921–. M. WATTS Just as they're middling honest and don't souse (1923).

soused adjective Drunk. 1902–. M. RUSSELL Ralph's a pro. He's soused every night, and I don't recall an edition going astray yet (1976).

souvenir verb trans. orig military To take as a 'souvenir'; to pilfer, steal. 1919–. F. CLUNE I dug up his body, souvenired his false teeth (1944).

sov noun Brit A pound sterling. 1829–. T. BARLING There's more to life than bashing pimps and publicans for a handful of sovs (1988). [Abbreviation of *sovereign* noun, a pound.]

sozzle verb intr. To drink alcohol. 1937–. N. FITZGERALD We can sit here and sozzle gently and enjoy ourselves (1953). [Back-formation from SOZZLED adjective.]

sozzled adjective Drunk. 1886–. N. MARSH 'She'm sozzled,' said Wally, and indeed, it was so (1963). [Past participle of dialect *sozzle* verb, to mix sloppily, prob. imitative.]

space verb intr. **to space out** US To become 'spaced out' (see next). 1968–. NEW YORK Karenga . . . looks like he's going crazy or spacing out on dope (1970).

spaced adjective orig US In a state of euphoria, distraction, or disorientation, esp. from taking drugs; usu. followed by *out*. 1968–. J. MANDELKAU I remember being really spaced out and someone handing me a ladybird—telling me how nice they tasted (1971).

spacy adjective Also **spacey**. mainly US = SPACED adjective. 1968–. J. A. CARVER His head

soor sooty sore-head sort sort-out sounds soup

felt large, and a little spacey, and he felt a heightened sense of geometry, of perspective (1980).

spade noun **1** offensive, orig US A black person. 1928-. N. SAUNDERS On Saturdays try Brixton market—nearly as big, more genuine, lots of spades (1971). **2 in spades** orig US To a high degree, with great force. 1929-. P. G. WODEHOUSE 'It's the law I'm beefing about. You didn't make the law.' 'But I administer it.' 'I'll say you do, in spades' (1964). [In sense 1, from the colour of the playing-card suit; in sense 2, from spades being the highest ranking suit in bridge.]

spag noun Abbreviation of 'spaghetti'. 1948-. SOUTHERLY I'll shout you a plate of steak and spag (1969).

spag bol noun Abbreviation of 'spaghetti Bolognese'. 1970-.

spaggers noun Brit Spaghetti. Also **spadgers.** 1960-. I. MURDOCH 'You said you were tired of spaghetti and potatoes—' 'Spuds and spadgers fill you up at least' (1980). [From *spag(hetti* noun + -ERS suffix.]

spaghetti noun derog and offensive An Italian. 1931-.

spam orig US. noun **1** Unsolicited and unwelcome e-mail messages. 1994-. verb trans. and intr. **2** To flood (a network, newsgroup, or indvidual) with spam; to send spam. 1994-. Hence **spammer** noun One who sends spam. 1994-. [From *Spam* name of a brand of tinned luncheon meat.]

Spam medal noun jocular, military A medal awarded to all members of a force; spec., Brit the 1939-45 star. 1945-. [From the ubiquitousness of Spam as a food during World War II; in spec. sense, perh. also from the resemblance of the colours of the medal ribbon to those of the armbands of waitresses in NAAFI canteens, where Spam was a staple item.]

Spanish tummy noun A stomach upset of a type often suffered by tourists in Spain. 1967-.

spanner noun **a spanner in the works** Brit A drawback or impediment; esp. in phr. *to throw a spanner in the works.* 1934-. NEWS CHRONICLE Mr. Cousins has thrown a spanner into the Labour Party's works (1959).

spare adjective **1 to go spare** Brit To become extremely angry or distraught. 1958-. J. N. SMITH The train had just gone. His lordship nearly went spare (1969). noun **2** An unattached woman, esp. one available

for casual sex; esp. in phr. *a bit of spare.* 1969-. R. BUSBY I . . . got the impression Maurice was . . . on the look-out for a bit of spare. . . . Some of the girls we get in here . . . don't leave much to the imagination (1978).

spare tyre noun A roll of fat around the midriff. 1961-.

spark noun **to get a spark up** NZ To raise one's spirits by drinking alcohol. 1939-.

sparkler noun A diamond or other gem. 1822-. LISTENER Two of her safes contained vast quantities of sparklers and folding stuff (1984).

spark out adjective Unconscious. 1936-. M. ALLINGHAM He's spark out, only just breathin'. Bin like that two days (1952). [From earlier sense, completely extinguished.]

spark-prop noun criminals', dated A diamond pin, a tie-pin. Cf. PROP noun. 1879-1923.

sparks noun One who works with electrical equipment: a radio operator, an electrician, etc. 1914-. LISTENER Lord Sneaker tells his sparks to wrap up the lights (1975).

sparrow-brain noun (A person with) a tiny brain, (a person of) limited intelligence. 1930-. H. FLEETWOOD She didn't actually *care* about her, and even, with her sparrow brain, despised her (1975).

sparrow cop noun US A policeman who is assigned low-grade duties such as patrolling parks. 1896-.

sparrow-fart noun orig dialect Daybreak. 1886-. H. MCLEAVE It was important enough to bring you out here at sparrow fart (1974).

spastic adjective **1** Incompetent; foolish; tiresome. 1981-. SUNDAY TELEGRAPH They never hear folk music, and it takes an exceptional child not to dismiss the classics as 'boring' and 'spastic' (1985). noun **2** An incompetent or foolish person. Cf. SPAZ noun. 1981-. [From earlier sense, (person) affected by spastic paralysis.]

spaz noun Also **spas.** Abbreviation of SPASTIC noun. 1965-. GUARDIAN Come onnnnn— bag your face, you geek, you grody totally shanky spaz (1982).

spazz verb Also **spaz. to spazz out** US To suffer a spasm, lose physical control of oneself; hence, to be overcome by intense emotion. 1957-. P. THEROUX Rooks the toughie . . . spazzing out at the sight of New Jersey! (1986).

spade   spag   spag bol   spaggers   spaghetti   spanner

speak noun US = SPEAKEASY noun. 1930–.
E. O'NEILL There'll be a speak open, and some drunk laughing (1952).

speakeasy noun orig and mainly US An illicit liquor shop or drinking club, esp. during Prohibition. 1889–. S. TRAILL Every cheap speakeasy had its resident piano player (1958). [From *speak* verb + *easy* adverb; from the notion of speaking 'easily' or quietly when ordering illicit goods.]

speako noun US = SPEAKEASY noun. 1931–. J. M. CAIN Making the grand tour of all the speako's he knows (1941). [From SPEAK(EASY noun + -o.]

spear noun **1** Austral Dismissal, the sack; esp. in phr. *to get the spear*. 1897–. D. MCLEAN Danny got the spear from the job (1962). verb **2** Trans. Austral To dismiss from employment. 1911–. A. B. PATERSON Didn't he spear (dismiss) you for cutting a plateful of meat off one of them stud rams? (1936). **3** intr. and trans. US To beg; to obtain by begging. 1912–.

spear-carrier noun orig theatre An actor with a walk-on part; hence, an unimportant participant. 1960–.

spec[1] noun orig US **1** A commercial speculation or venture; a prospect of future success or gain. 1794–. J. FOWLES I was rich, a good spec as a husband now (1963). **2 on spec** in the hope of success; on the off chance. 1832–. B. HINES 'Is he expecting you?' 'No, we just came on spec' (1981). [Abbreviation of *speculation* noun.]

spec[2] noun A detailed working description; often in pl. 1956–. AMATEUR PHOTOGRAPHER The basic specs of these two new OMs remain the same (1979). [Abbreviation of *specification* noun.]

spec[3] noun US An enlisted man in the US army employed on specialized duties. 1958–. [Abbreviation of *specialist* noun.]

spec adjective Of or being someone who puts up buildings without a prior guarantee of sale. 1958–. J. BETJEMAN Spec. builders and advertisement hoardings and litter droppers (1970). [Abbreviation of *speculative* adjective.]

special verb trans. Of a nurse: to attend continuously to (a single patient). 1961–. NURSING TIMES A nurse will have to 'special' the patient to make the necessary observations (1967).

specky adjective mainly Scottish Wearing glasses, bespectacled. 1956–. R. JENKINS The unbraw unlovable puke married to yon specky

gasping smout of a barber (1956). [From SPEC(s noun + -y.]

specs noun pl. Also **specks**. Spectacles, glasses. 1807–. D. DELILLO Peter, her son, . . . reddish hair, wire-frame specs (1982). [Abbreviation.]

speed orig US. noun **1** An amphetamine drug, esp. methamphetamine, often taken intravenously. 1967–. J. SYMONS 'What was he on?' . . . 'Speed mostly. Sometimes acid' (1975). verb intr. **2** To be on the drug 'speed'; esp. in *be speeding*. 1973–. S. GEORGE 'You speeding?' He shrugged. 'Yes. Cancels the alcohol' (1978). [From the drug's stimulant effect; cf. SPEEDBALL noun.]

speedball noun **1** orig US A mixture of cocaine with heroin or morphine. 1909–. W. BURROUGHS A shot of morphine would be nice later when I was ready to sleep, or, better, a speedball, half cocaine, half morphine (1953). **2** US A glass of wine, spec. when strengthened with additional alcohol. 1926–.

speed freak noun orig US Someone addicted to an amphetamine drug. 1967–.

speed king noun orig US A motor-racing champion. 1913–. C. GRAVES German princes, English speed-kings . . . are usually to be found here (1938).

speedo noun Abbreviation of 'speedometer'. 1934–. P. HILL The car [was as] steady as a rock . . . as the speedo reached up towards its limit (1976).

speed shop noun orig US A shop which sells vehicle accessories and spares. 1954–. HOT CAR You can often pick up reasonable headers off the shelf from a good speed shop (1977).

spelunker /sprlʌŋkə(r)/ noun N Amer One who explores caves, esp. as a hobby. 1942–. E. MCBAIN The cave seemed not to be the least bit inviting. He had always considered spelunkers the choicest sorts of maniacs (1980). Hence (as a back-formation) **spelunk**, verb intr. To explore caves as a hobby. 1946–. [From obsolete *spelunk* noun, a cave, from Latin *spelunca*, Old French *spelonque*, *spelunque*.]

spend verb intr. To ejaculate; to have an orgasm. 1662–. R. L. DUNCAN He felt himself spending at the very moment she contracted around him (1980).

spic noun Also **spick, spig, spik**. US derog and offensive **1** A Spanish-speaking person from Central or South America or the Caribbean. 1913–. D. E. WESTLAKE You'd put your kids in a school with a lotta niggers and kikes and wops and spics? (1977). **2** The Spanish language; spec. Spanish-American. 1933–. [Abbreviation and alteration of SPIGGOTY noun.]

spider noun Austral **1** dated A drink usually consisting of brandy mixed with lemonade. 1850–. **2** A soft drink with ice-cream floating on it. 1941–.

spiel /spi:l, ʃpi:l/ orig US. verb **1a** intr. and trans. To gamble. 1859–. W. MANKOWITZ You go to the dog tracks in the evening? Not for me.... Horses? No horses, neither. You must spiel something. Poker, shemmy? (1953). **b** intr. To play music. 1870–. G. S. PERRY Denver's Symphony chooses to spiel only when winter's winds doth blow (1947). **2** intr. To speak glibly; to hold forth. 1894–. MEZZROW & WOLFE One of the funniest things I ever heard was Mac spieling in Yiddish (1946). **3** trans. To reel *off* (patter, etc.); to announce; to perform. 1904–. A. TOFFLER Each participant spieled off his reason for attending (1970). noun **4** A glib speech or story, esp. a salesman's patter. 1896–. LISTENER A long spiel... from a tart about how much horrider Soho has become (1980). **5** A swindle, a dishonest line of business. 1901–. T. A. G. HUNGERFORD This isn't a spiel, Colone.... I know the bloke, and he's on the level (1954). [verb from German *spielen* to play, gamble; noun from German *Spiel* game, play.]

spieler /spi:lə(r), ʃpi:lə(r)/ noun orig US **1** now mainly Austral A gambler; a swindler. 1859–. W. W. AMMON I wouldn't even risk cashing her with you mob of spielers around (1984). **2** One who talks glibly. 1894–. **3** A gambling club. 1931–. J. O'CONNOR A well-known boxing referee who used to run a dirty low-down dive of a spieler (1976). [From German *Spieler* player, gambler.]

spiff verb trans. To smarten *up*. 1877–. ARIZONA DAILY STAR The man doing it was an interior decorator, not an art conservator, and he did what he felt was best—he went in and spiffed up the church (1979). [See SPIFFY adjective.]

spiffing adjective dated **1** Smart, handsome. 1861–. **2** Excellent. 1872–. CLEESE & BOOTH Oh, spiffing! Absolutely spiffing. Well done! Two dead, twenty-five to go (1979). [See SPIFFY adjective.]

spiffy adjective mainly US = SPIFFING adjective 1. 1853–. H. WOUK She's turned into quite the spiffy New York gal (1978). [Origin unknown; cf. obs. dialect *spiff* adjective, smart, obs. slang *spiff* noun, a well-dressed man, a swell, and SPIV noun.]

spiflicated adjective Also **spifflicated.** orig US Drunk. 1906–. H. A. SMITH I do not believe... that I was spifflicated last night (1971). [Past participle of colloquial *spiflicate* verb, to overwhelm, crush, destroy, prob. a fanciful formation.]

spiggoty noun Also **spiggity, spigotti, spigoty.** US, dated = SPIC noun. 1910–. R. STOUT 'He's a dirty spiggoty.' 'No, Archie, Mr Manuel Kimball is an Argentine' (1934). [Perh. an alteration of *spika de*, as in *no spíka de English* '(I do) not speak the English,' supposedly representing a common response of Spanish-Americans to questions in English.]

spike¹ noun **1** Brit A doss-house. 1866–. G. ORWELL D'you come out o' one o' de London spikes (casual wards), eh? (1933). **2 to have** (or **get**) **the spike** to be (or become) angry or offended. 1890–. N. HILLIARD But you don't have to get the spike with me just for that (1960). **3** US A quantity of alcohol, esp. spirits, added to a drink. 1906–. TIMES-PICAYUNE (New Orleans): It's like chips without dips, or punch without the spike (1974). **4** orig US **a** A hypodermic needle for injecting an intoxicating drug. 1934–. P. DRISCOLL This punk kid, shooting amphetamines, can't find enough spikes (1979). **b** An injection, or the drug injected. 1953–. J. WAINWRIGHT It was a mounting yearning. A craving.... He needed a spike—badly! (1974). verb **5** trans. orig US To lace (a drink) with alcohol, a drug, etc. 1889–. G. THOMPSON She made tea, which he spiked with bourbon (1980). **6** intr. and trans. To inject (with) an intoxicating drug. 1935–. GUARDIAN The addicts... 'll sometime try and spike you, try and get you mainlining too (1974). **7** trans. To plant a concealed microphone in (a place); to bug, esp. with a spike microphone. 1974–. D. GETHIN Quittenden's plumbers... were the crack team who could spike a high security building in under an hour (1983). [In sense 7, from *spike microphone*, one that can be driven into a wall to bug an inner chamber.]

spike² Brit, derog. noun **1** An Anglican who advocates or practises Anglo-Catholic ritual and observances. 1902–. A. N. WILSON There were several other effigies of famous spikes, including the legendary Father Tooth (1980). verb trans. **2 to spike up** to make more High Church. 1923–. [Back-formation from SPIKY adjective.]

spike-bozzle verb trans. Also **spike-boozle.** dated, orig military To render (an enemy plane, etc.) unserviceable; to destroy; to upset. 1915–. [From *spike* verb, to render (a gun) unserviceable + perh. *bam)boozle* verb.]

spider spiel spieler spiff spiffing spiffy spiflicated

spiky adjective Brit, derog Extremely ritualistic or High-Church Anglican in character. Cf. SPIKE² noun and verb. 1893–. B. PYM He had been a server at the spikiest Anglo-Catholic church (1977).

spill verb trans. **1** orig US To utter (words); to confess or divulge (facts). 1917–. I. SHAW He picked up the phone to call the Colonel, spill everything (1977). **2 to spill the beans** orig US To divulge information, esp. unintentionally or indiscreetly. 1919–. E. LINKLATER 'Tell me the truth,' she says. 'Spill the beans, Holly, old man!' (1929). **3 to spill one's guts** mainly US To divulge as much as one can, to confess. 1927–. A. HAILEY The kid—he was eighteen, by the way, and not long out of trade school—broke down and spilled his guts (1979).

spin¹ noun Austral and NZ A run of good or bad luck. 1917–. K. S. PRICHARD She married the wrong man, she says, and has had a crook spin ever since (1950). [From the spinning of a coin in the game of two-up.]

spin² noun Austral Abbreviation of SPINNAKER noun. 1941–. S. GORE Backed Sweet Friday for a spin. . . . But it never run a drum (1962).

spin verb trans. Brit, police To search (a person or place), esp. rapidly; to frisk. Often in phr. *to spin the drum* (cf. DRUM noun 1). 1972–. J. BARNETT We iron him to the banisters while we spin the drum from top to bottom (1982).

spinach noun US, dated Nonsense, rubbish. 1929–. A. WOOLLCOTT This . . . reticence . . . will . . . be described by certain temperaments as . . . good taste. . . . I say it's spinach (1934). [Perh. from the phr. *gammon and spinach*, part of the refrain of the song 'A frog he would a-wooing go', in allusion to GAMMON noun 1, nonsense.]

spine-bash verb intr. Austral To rest; to loaf. 1941–. R. ROBINSON They would rather have stayed in the camp to spine-bash or go down to the swy game (1958). Hence **spine-basher,** noun Austral A loafer. 1945–.

spinnaker noun Austral, dated Five pounds; a five-pound note. Cf. SPIN² noun. 1898–. N. PULLIAM I'll bet the first Aussie taker a couple of spinnakers the Snowy Mountains dream comes true (1955). [From earlier sense, large sail.]

spit¹ verb trans. **1 to spit chips** Austral **a** To be extremely thirsty. 1901–. A. MARSHALL I was

spitting chips. God, I was dry! (1946). **b** To be extremely angry. 1947–. I. SOUTHALL Not when I saw Mr Fairhall last. He was spittin' chips because Peter had gone away (1965). **2 to spit blood: a** To be extremely angry. 1963–. L. LANE When I think of it I could spit blood (1966). **b** Of a spy, etc.: to fear exposure. 1963–. L. DEIGHTON A man tailed or suspected is said to be 'spitting blood' (1966). noun **3 to go for the big spit** Austral To vomit. 1960–. A. BUZO Remember the time he got sick at Davo's twenty-first and went for the big spit? (1969).

Spit² noun Abbreviation of 'Spitfire', the name of a British fighter aircraft produced between 1936 and 1947. 1941–.

spitchered adjective orig nautical Broken, ruined, done for. 1920–. P. DICKINSON That damned gadget might . . . be functioning right as rain in thirty seconds, or it might be spitchered for ever (1970). [From Maltese *spiċċa* finished, ended, perh. ultimately from Italian *spezzare* to break into pieces.]

> 'We spivved ourselves up, put on clean shirts, and strolled out of camp.'

Spithead

pheasant noun dated, Brit, nautical A kipper or bloater. 1948–. [*Spithead* from the name of a British naval anchorage off Portsmouth.]

spiv Brit. noun **1** A man, often flashily dressed, who makes a living by illicit or unscrupulous dealings. 1934–. CORNISH GUARDIAN Metrication will be an open invitation for every spiv and racketeer to cheat the British public (1978). verb **2** intr. To make one's living as a spiv. 1947–. TIMES Instead of that brave new Britain all they had left was a land fit for bookies to spiv in (1947). **3** trans. To spruce (oneself) *up*. 1959–. B. W. ALDISS We spivved ourselves up, put on clean shirts, and strolled out of camp (1971). Hence **spiv(v)ery,** noun Behaviour of a spiv; the state of being a spiv. 1948–; **spivvish, spiv(v)y,** adjective Of or like a spiv. 1945–. C. DAY LEWIS Tilting his hat at an even more spivvish angle (1948). [Origin uncertain; perh. from SPIFF verb, SPIFFY adjective.]

splash noun **1** A small quantity of liquid, esp. soda water, to dilute spirits. 1922–. G. GREENE The atmosphere of . . . the week-end jaunt, the whisky and splash (1935). **2** Brit Tea. 1960–. C. DALE Look, I gotta get to work. . . . Give 'er a cup of splash (1964). **3** US Amphetamines. 1969–. [In sense 2, presumably from the sound of tea being poured noisily.]

splendiferous adjective jocular, orig US Remarkably fine; magnificent. 1843–. [Fanciful formation from *splendid* adjective; cf. earlier obs. use (*c.*1460–1546) in sense 'full of splendour', from medieval Latin *splendifer*.]

splib noun US African-American A black person. 1964–. A. YOUNG Nobody want no nice nigger no more . . . They want an angry splib A furious nigrah (1969). [Origin unknown.]

splice verb intr. To get married. 1874–. T. HEALD If the old flapper spliced with the colonel she stood to lose a million dollars (1981).

spliced adjective Married. 1751–. C. BROOKE-ROSE Yes, I worked in an office before I got spliced, didn't you know, solicitors in the Strand (1968).

spliff noun Also **splif.** orig W Indies A cannabis cigarette. 1936–. HIGH TIMES Like Marley, he's a spliff-toking Rastafarian (1975). [Origin unknown.]

split verb **1** intr. To betray secrets; to inform *on*. 1795–. L. CODY If I tell you, and you ever split on me, I'll make you very sorry (1982). **2** intr. and trans. orig US To depart (from); to leave. 1954–. B. HOLIDAY I grabbed him and told him to do something because I had to split for the bathroom again (1956); SUNDAY SUN (Brisbane): When he split the Brisbane scene he left behind documents that could be incriminating to the drug gangsters (1971). noun **3** An informer; a detective; a policeman. 1812–. G. ORWELL He would . . . exclaim 'Fucking toe-rag!' . . . meaning the 'split' who had arrested him (1932). **4** A division or share of the proceeds of a legal or illegal undertaking. 1889–. J. T. FARRELL I wasn't working for a long time, and then I got me this job, and now I'm also lined up with a can-house, and get my split on anybody I bring there (1934). **5** N Amer A girl, a woman. 1935–. GLOBE & MAIL (Toronto): An announcement was posted that the force's first female officer Constable Jacqueline Hall, had been hired. 'He's gone and hired another split, as if we don't have enough whores and splits in the department already,' Mrs. Nesbitt quoted the sergeant as saying (1975).

split-arse Also **split-ass.** dated, services' orig air force. adjective **1** Classy, showy; (of a pilot) reckless, given to performing stunts; (of an aircraft) having good manoeuvrability. 1917–. V. M. YEATES They were sufficiently splitarse and did all the stunts, but there was nothing like

a Camel for lightness of touch (1934). verb intr. **2** To make a sudden turn in an aircraft; to perform stunt flying. 1917–. noun **3** A flying stunt; also, an aircraft performing such a stunt. 1919–.

split beaver noun A pornographic photograph of the female genitals showing the inner labia. 1972–. [Cf. BEAVER noun 1.]

split pea noun dated Rhyming slang for 'tea'. 1857–1931. S. KAYE-SMITH I'll make you a nice cup of split pea (1931).

splitter noun hunting An excellent hunt. 1843–. SHOOTING TIMES & COUNTRY MAGAZINE There was more than a holding scent and . . . we were in for a splitter (1976).

splosh noun Money. 1893–. P. G. WODEHOUSE The jolliness of having all that splosh in the old sock (1950). [From earlier sense, splashing sound.]

spod noun Brit A dull or socially inept person, esp. one who is excessively studious; someone who pursues an unfashionable, technical, or esoteric interest with obsessive dedication. 1989–. OBSERVER Far from being an enclave for spods no one likes, the competition hall is encircled with a ring of well-adjusted confidence (1997). Hence **spoddy** adjective. 1990–. J. TROLLOPE Remember those French boys we had to have at school? They were utterly spoddy (1993). [Origin unknown.]

spondulicks /spɒnˈdjuːlɪks/ noun Also **-ics, -ix; spondoolic(k)s, -ix;** and as quasi-*sing.* **spondulick, spondoolick,** etc. orig US Money; also, a coin. 1857–. PRIVATE EYE No one seemed very anxious to come up with the spondulicks (1980). [A fanciful coinage.]

spook noun orig and mainly US **1** A spy. 1942–. L. PRYOR 'My training was also in espionage at the CIA farm.' . . . 'A spook,' I said in wonder (1979). **2** derog and offensive A Black person. 1945–. E. LEONARD We almost had another riot. . . . The bar-owner . . . shoots a spook in his parking lot (1977). [From earlier sense, ghost.]

spooky adjective **1** surfing Of a wave: dangerous or frightening. 1966–. **2** US Of spies or espionage. 1975–. J. MELVILLE Somebody on the spooky side of the Embassy might have a view (1980).

spoon dated. verb **1a** intr. To behave amorously, esp. in a foolish way. 1831–. H. WILLIAMSON It's like one of the Mecca coffee rooms in the City, where men go to spoon with the waitresses (1957). **b** trans. To woo in a silly or sentimental way. 1877–. noun **2** A silly or

splendiferous splib splice spliced spliff split spod

demonstratively fond lover; an act of spooning; **the spoons,** sentimental or silly fondness. D. H. LAWRENCE Yes, his reputation as a spoon would not belie him. He had lovely lips for kissing (c.1921). [Prob. from obs. noun sense, simpleton, fool.]

sport noun mainly Austral A form of address, esp. among men. 1923–. H. KNORR Don't get y' knickers in a knot, sport! (1982).

spot noun **1** A (small) alcoholic drink. 1885–. P. G. WODEHOUSE May I offer you a spot? . . . I can recommend the Scotch (1936). **2** US A term of imprisonment, esp. of the stated number of years. 1901–. M. BREWER He was serving a three spot for cunning. . . . He got into a row with one of the warders (1966). **3 to put** (someone) **on the spot** US To arrange for the murder of, to kill. 1929–. PUNCH You get rid of inconvenient subordinates . . . by 'putting them on the spot'—that is deliberately sending them to their death (1930). [In sense 2, prob. from earlier senses, pip on a playing card, playing card with the specified number of pips.]

spout noun **1 up the spout: a** dated In pawn. 1812–. **b** Useless, ruined, hopeless. 1829–. L. P. HARTLEY Where would the Knightons be if it wasn't for Mrs. Knighton? Up the spout, down the drain—anywhere but in the position of influence and honour (1955). **c** Pregnant. 1937–. S. TROY Up the spout, isn't she? I thought Michel would have more bloody savvy (1970). **2** A gun barrel; esp. in phr. *up the spout,* of a bullet or cartridge: loaded and ready for firing. 1943–. M. GILBERT I can count six here in the clip. . . . There's probably one up the spout (1969).

sprag verb trans. Austral **1** dated To obstruct, thwart. 1911–. U. R. ELLIS Attempt to sprag New State Referendum (1965). **2** To accost truculently; to pester. 1915–. D. R. STUART This cove, Pommy, all mo. an' buck teeth, he sprags me an' Joey an' nothin'll do but he's gotta buy us grog (1979). [From earlier sense, to stop (a wheel) moving with a bar or chock, from *sprag* noun, such a bar or chock; ultimate origin unknown.]

sprauncy adjective Also **sprauntsy, sproncy.** Brit Smart or showy. 1957–. GUARDIAN The 'sprauntsy' (showy) antique dealers (1969). [Origin uncertain; perh. related to dialect *sprouncey* cheerful.]

sprazer /ˈsprɑːzə(r)/ noun Also **spraser, sprasy, sprazey,** etc. dated, Brit Sixpence; a sixpenny piece. 1931–. J. B. PRIESTLEY See if we can't take another spraser or two from

the punters (1939). Cf. SPROWSIE noun. [From Shelta *sprazi*.]

spring verb **1** trans. and intr. orig US To release or escape from prison. 1900–. K. ORVIS When I sprung . . . Moss was standing by the prison door (1962); SECURITY GAZETTE Those who may be preparing to 'spring' an inmate (1963). **2** intr. Austral and US To pay *for* a treat. 1906–. M. MACHLIN We'll spring for the booze (1976). noun **3** orig US An escape or release from prison. 1901–. F. ROSS Springing some bugger from the Scrubs—O.K. Not easy. . . . You can't pull a spring like that without help on the inside (1977).

springer noun **1** A racehorse on which the betting odds suddenly shorten. 1922–. **2** nautical A physical-training instructor in the navy. 1935–. J. HALE The springers all fancy their chance in the training line (1964).

sprog noun **1** services' A new recruit; a trainee; a novice. Cf. ERK noun. 1941–. J. HILLIER Never mind, Wendy, you sprogs of 'B' flight will learn to fly yet—if you live long enough! (1943). **2** orig nautical A child; a baby. 1945–. D. CLARK I don't think he's been really with us since the sprog came along (1981). [Perh. from obs. *sprag* noun, lively young man.]

sprout noun US A young person, a child. 1934–. VERBATIM The young sprouts and broths of lads who feel their oats and are full of beans (1983).

sprowsie /ˈsprauzɪ/ noun Also **sprouse, sprowser.** dated, Brit Sixpence; a sixpenny piece. 1931–. A. PRIOR Half-Nelson, do me a favour and put a sprouse in there for me. . . . I've got no change (1960). [Prob. variant of SPRAZER noun.]

spruce verb Brit, orig services' **1** intr. To lie; to evade a duty, malinger. 1917–. G. M. WILSON Dr. Meunier's no fool, he'd have known if she was sprucing. . . . Malingering. Faking tummy trouble (1967). **2** trans. To deceive. 1919–. DAILY TELEGRAPH A kipper . . . should cost more than the untreated fish. Who is sprucing whom? (1978). Hence **sprucer,** noun 1917–. [Origin unknown.]

spruik /spruːk/ verb intr. Austral and NZ To speak in public, esp. in order to advertise a show, etc. 1902–. N. BARTLETT Spruiked for a circus in the U.S.A. (1954). Hence **spruiker,** noun Also **sprooker.** A speaker employed to attract custom; an eloquent speaker. 1902–. [Origin unknown.]

spud noun **1** A potato. 1845–. K. WEATHERLY Some sugar, tea and a few spuds and onions formed the rest of their supplies (1968).

2 A hole in a sock, stocking, etc. 1960–.
M. DE LARRABEITI There were huge spuds in the heels
of their socks (1978). [From earlier sense,
small narrow spade.]

spud barber noun jocular A potato peeler.
1935–. G. FOULSER The galley-boy [was] just a
spudbarber after all (1961).

spud-bashing noun Brit, orig services'
(A lengthy spell of) peeling potatoes. 1940–.
TIMES Between dashing home from the
office . . . and having a bath, there is not much
time for spud bashing (1980). [Cf. BASHING noun.]

Spud Islander noun Canadian A native
or inhabitant of Prince Edward Island. 1957–.
[From the island's reputation for fine
potatoes.]

spud line noun in the spud line pregnant.
1937–. H. W. SUTHERLAND It couldn't have been
himself that put Kathleen Ertall in the spud line
(1967).

spunk noun **1** Semen. c.1888–. B. W. ALDISS By
sprawling right back on the seat and ignoring
the stink of the shit-pit below me, I managed in
no time to lob some spurts of spunk over my
stomach (1971). **2** Austral A sexually attractive
person; esp. in phr. *young spunk*. 1978–. SUNDAY
MAIL (Brisbane): No matter how skittish she might
feel, she didn't give 59 mustn't even flutter an
eyelash at a young spunk (1986). [From earlier
sense, courage, spirit.]

squaddie noun Also **squaddy.** Brit, services'
A recruit; a private. 1933–. I. JEFFERIES I had a
motley but effective army of luckless squaddies
who had been selected by orderly sergeants
(1959). [From *squad* noun + -*ie*, perh.
influenced by obs. slang *swaddy* noun, soldier.]

squadrol /ˈskwɒdrəʊl/ noun US A small
police van. 1961–. [From *squad* noun + *pat*)*rol*
noun.]

square verb **1a** trans. To conciliate or
satisfy, esp. by bribery. 1859–. E. BOWEN 'What's
poor Willy going to think of us?' 'I'll square
Willy' (1969). **b: to square** (someone) **off** intr.
and trans. Austral To settle a difference (with);
to placate, conciliate. 1943–. J. POWERS What I
don't twig is how he'll square off with the brass?
(1973). noun **2** military A parade ground. 1915–.
3 derog, orig US, jazz A conventional or old-
fashioned person. 1944–. H. HOBSON The odd fifty
million citizens who don't dig them are dead-
beats—squares (1959). **4** US, mainly African-
American A cigarette containing tobacco
(rather than marijuana). 1970–. BLACK WORLD
Light me up a square, baby (1974). adjective **5**
derog, orig US, jazz Conventional or old-

fashioned, unsophisticated, conservative.
1946–. F. RAPHAEL You know books. Those things
with pages very square people still
occasionally read (1965).

square-bashing noun Brit, military Drill on
a barrack-square. 1943–. G. BLACK Attached
to a Malay regiment, supervising weapon
training and square bashing (1975). Hence
square-basher, noun. 1959–. [Cf. BASHING
noun.]

squarehead noun **1** now Austral An honest
person; one with no criminal convictions.
1890–. BULLETIN (Sydney): He was a one-off
offender, a 'squarehead' (1984). **2** derog A
foreigner of Germanic extraction, esp. a
German (spec. military slang in World War I) or
Scandinavian. H. C. WITWER The English call 'em
'Uns . . . we call 'em squareheads (1918).

square John noun N Amer An upright
respectable person; spec. one who is not a
drug-addict. 1934–. K. ORVIS I played it even safer
with those uptown Square Johns (1962).

square-pushing noun and present participle,
dated, Brit Courting, love-making. 1918–30.
J. B. PRIESTLEY 'E wouldn't bother, though, too busy
square-pushing, taking the girls out, see (1930).
[From the practice of suitors accompanying
nursemaids while they pushed prams round
town squares.]

square-rig noun nautical The uniform of
a naval rating. 1951–. N. COWARD Attired as they
were in the usual 'Square-Rig' of British Ordinary
Seamen, they caused a mild sensation (1951).
[From earlier sense, rig in which sails are
suspended from horizontal yards.]

square-shooter noun orig and mainly US
An honest dependable person. 1914–.
P. WYNDHAM LEWIS My friend . . . was somehow
treacherous and not at all the good sport and
'square-shooter' I had supposed him to be (1937).

squaresville noun Also **squareville.** derog
orig US A conventional place or institution;
also used adjectivally to denote
conventionality. 1956–. E. MCBAIN This guy is
from Squaresville, fellas, I'm telling you. He
wouldn't know a .45 from a cement mixer
(1956). LISTENER And they went away, more than
ever convinced that the war between the
generations was for real. And through the
window there floated a querulous, puzzled
voice. 'A queer fish, real squaresville' (1966).
[From SQUARE noun 3 + -VILLE comb. form.]

squarie noun Also **squarey** Austral A female
partner or companion. 1917–. ROYAL AUSTRALIAN
NAVY NEWS You bloody beaut . . . we'll be back

spud barber spud-bashing Spud Islander spud line

outside with our squaries! (1970). [From obs. Austral. slang *square* (of a woman) respectable + *-ie*.]

squashed fly noun Also **squashed fly biscuit.** Brit A garibaldi biscuit. 1900–. [From the appearance of the currants in the biscuits.]

squat noun US Nothing at all; (following a negative construction) anything. 1967–. P. BENCHLEY It'll be another forecast-of-Armageddon cover that won't amount to squat (1979).

squawk verb **1** intr. US = SQUEAL verb. 1872–. TIMES LITERARY SUPPLEMENT The thief who 'squawks' is expelled as professionally infamous; his occupation's gone (1937). **2** trans. orig US Of an aircraft, etc.: to transmit (an identification signal), enabling its position to be located by radar. 1956–. J. GARDNER His eyes remained on the huge radarscope. . . . The indicator numbers 12—'squawked' by the Boeing's transponder—flicked off and changed (1982). noun **3** An identification signal given out by an aircraft. 1975–.

squawk-box noun US **1** A loudspeaker or public-address system. 1945–. **2** An intercom. 1954–.

squeak verb intr. **1** = SQUEAL verb. 1690–. E. AMADI All I want you to do is swear to secrecy. I have assured them that you will not squeak when once you promise (1986). noun **2** A piece of incriminating information given to the police; esp. in phr. *to put in the* (or a) *squeak,* to inform *against.* 1922–. A. HUNTER I can see another villain putting a squeak in but knocking off Freddie would be just stupid (1973).

squeaker noun **1** = SQUEALER noun. 1903–. OBSERVER The recent attempt to murder him . . . was not due to . . . the impulse to remove rivals or 'squeakers' (1930). **2** N Amer A game won by a very narrow margin. 1961–. GLOBE & MAIL (Toronto): Ottawa Rough Riders . . . lost a squeaker to Montreal (1970). [In sense 2, from the phr. *a narrow squeak* a success barely attained.]

squeaky clean adjective Above criticism, beyond reproach. 1975–. GUARDIAN WEEKLY The [Ford Motor] company has denied making any illegal payments, claiming that it is 'squeaky clean' in this area (1978). [Cf. literal sense, washed and rinsed so clean as to squeak (1976–).]

squeal verb intr. **1** To turn informer, to 'grass'. 1846–. T. TRYON Initiation into the club required a sacred oath, sworn in

blood . . . never to squeal on a fellow member, and never to break the code of silence (1989). noun **2** An act of informing on someone. 1872–. **3** police A call for police assistance or investigation; a report of a case investigated by the police. 1949–. E. MCBAIN Parker's on the prowl, Hernandez is answering a squeal (1960).

squealer noun An informer, a 'grass'. 1865–. J. WAINWRIGHT The vengeance of the Clan upon squealers . . . would be both hard and painful (1976).

squeeze noun **1** An impression of an object made for criminal purposes. 1882–. G. D. H. & M. COLE Where did the dummy keys . . . come from? . . . If they were forgeries it would be simpler, for Sir Hiram might remember if anyone had handled his keys long enough to take a squeeze (1930). **2** *to put the squeeze on* orig US To coerce or pressure (someone). 1941–. S. BRILL Spilotto's army of enforcers . . . put the squeeze on hard-pressed loan-shark victims (1978). **3** mainly US A close friend, esp. a girlfriend or lover. 1980–. R. FORD I would love to grill him about his little seminary squeeze, but he would be indignant (1986). [In sense 3, shortened from MAIN SQUEEZE noun 2.]

squeeze-box noun An accordion or concertina. 1936–. [From its being played by pushing the two parts together; cf. earlier obsolete Nautical sense, a ship's harmonium.]

squeeze-pidgin noun A bribe. 1946–.

squeeze-play noun mainly US An act of coercion or pressurizing. 1916–. D. WECTER You perhaps mentioned the fact that Hitler was putting the squeeze play on Hindenburg a few years later (1944). [From earlier baseball sense, a tactic involving bunting or hitting the ball softly so that the runner at third base can reach home.]

squib noun **1** now Austral A small, thin, or insignificant person. 1586–. COURIER-MAIL (Brisbane): We have numerous utility expressions for people such as . . . sparrow squib, nugget and streak, for men of varying sizes (1979). **2** Austral A horse lacking stamina. 1915–. SUN-HERALD (Sydney): It has to be said . . . that the Golden Slipper is a race for speedy squibs (1984). **3** Austral A spineless person, a coward. 1945–. J. ALARD 'I'm no squib,' he thought, 'I'll show them' (1968). verb Austral **4** trans. To evade (a difficulty or responsibility), to shirk. 1918–. D. NILAND The rough-and-tumble doesn't worry me. I'm not squibbing the issue (1955). **5** intr. **a** To fail to act; to back down; to give up.

squashed fly squat squawk squawk-box squeak

stag

1934–. SYDNEY MORNING HERALD The Treasury-types'
eternal search for 'a politician with some guts' is
futile. Mr Fraser looked tough enough at the
time, but he squibbed (1984). **b to squib on** to
betray or let down. 1954–. COAST TO COAST He
could finish on a good wicket in anything. And
never squib on a bloke (1962).

squidge noun US A person who performs
troublesome duties for another; a factotum.
1907–. G. ADE When Mr. and Mrs. Al Laflin and
I traveled in distant countries, we always hired
a 'squidge' the moment we arrived in a new
town (1942). [Origin unknown.]

squiffed adjective Drunk. 1890–. B. GARFIELD
I'm already a little squiffed. Ought to go on the
wagon (1977). [Variant of SQUIFFY adjective.]

squiffy adjective mainly Brit **1** Drunk. 1855–.
D. POTTER 'There's another bottle,' said Helen.
'Good! I feel like getting a bit squiffy' (1988).
2 Askew, skew-whiff. 1941–. G. MELLY I never
associated it with an orgy, a term I felt to imply
a Roman profusion of grapes, wine, buttocks,
breasts, marble *chaises-longues*, and squiffy
laurel crowns (1977). [Origin unknown.]

squillion noun **1** A very large number of
millions; an enormous number. Often as
adjective, **multi-million**. 1943–. INDEPENDENT The
Prime Minister intends to fill the gap between
the Queen's Christmas broadcast and the Boxing
Day walk by reading Sir Frank Layfield's
squillion-word report on Sizewell (1986).
2 A very large amount of money. 1986–.
[Arbitrary alteration of *million, billion*, etc.;
cf. ZILLION noun.]

squillionaire noun Someone
extraordinarily wealthy; a multi- millionaire.
1979–. PRIVATE EYE Several of the squillionaires at
the back start shouting abusive remarks about
the morality of queue-barging (1989). [From
SQUILLION noun (and adjective) + *-aire*, after
millionaire, etc.]

squire noun Brit A form of address to a man.
1959–. TIMES Tell you what, squire—keep the
pension and I'll take the cash! (1982).

squirt noun **1** orig US An insignificant but
presumptuous person; also, a child, a young
person. 1848–. N. BLAKE It's about time that squirt
Wemyss was suppressed (1935). **2** dated, air force
A jet aircraft. 1945–8.

squit noun Brit **1** A small or insignificant
person. *a*.1825–. E. COXHEAD It's impossible,
darling. That—that little squit—and Peggy
Jacques! (1947). **2** Nonsense. 1893–. A. WESKER
Love? I don't believe in any of that squit—we

just got married (1959). [Perh. related to obs.
dialectal *squit* verb, to squirt.]

squits noun Brit Diarrhoea. 1841–. D. LODGE
'Olive oil doesn't agree with me.' 'Gives you the
squits, does it?' (1988). [From obs. dialectal
squit verb, to squirt.]

squitters noun = SQUITS noun. 1664–. LORD
HAREWOOD We went incessantly to those over-
public latrines. . . . My squitters were at their
worst (1981). [From obs. *squitter* verb, to squirt,
to have diarrhoea, prob. of imitative origin.]

squiz Also **squizz**. Austral and NZ. noun
1 A look, an inspection. 1913–. K. SMITH Hey,
youse blokes! Come over here and take a squiz
at *this*! (1965). verb trans. and intr. **2** To look
(at). 1941–. C. B. MAXWELL He only wanted to squiz at
the beach from the best vantage point of all
(1949). [Prob. blend of *squint* and *quiz*.]

squizzed adjective US Drunk. 1845–. SATURDAY
REVIEW OF LITERATURE A judge of good whiskey, who
is, for the purpose of this narrative, slightly
squizzed (1941). [Origin unknown.]

stable noun A group of prostitutes working
for the same person or organization. Cf.
STRING noun 3. 1937–. J. CRAD He . . . now runs a
'stable' of white women for coloured seamen
in Cardiff (1940).

stach verb = STASH[1] verb.

stack verb intr. **to stack up** mainly US To
present oneself or itself, to measure up;
to arise, build up. 1911–. M. MCLUHAN See how
you stack up with your fellow men on the
following issues (1951). [From earlier sense, to
pile up one's chips at poker.]

stacked adjective orig US Having large
breasts; used as a term of male approval.
Also **stacked up, well stacked**. 1942–.
D. SHANNON A cute little blond chick . . . really
stacked (1981).

staff-wallah noun Brit, derog
A noncombatant army officer. 1951–.

stag verb **1** trans. and intr. To observe, watch;
to keep watch. 1796–. **2** intr. US To attend
a social occasion unaccompanied. 1900–.
LEBENDE SPRACHEN He had planned to stag at the
class dance (1973). noun **3** N Amer **a** A party,
dinner, etc. for men only. 1904–. R. LEWIS He's
getting married tomorrow. Tonight he's holding
his stag, and most of the men from the dam are
going along (1971). **b** A man who attends
such a party, etc. 1905–. R. L. DUNCAN They're not
going to let you in by yourself. They have a rule
against stags (1980). **4** A spell of duty. 1931–.
R. STOREY There's seven stags in the hours o'

squidge squiffed squillion squillionaire squitters

darkness and only five of you to do 'em. Somebody has to do two (1958).

stage noun A period of imprisonment during which privileges are allowed. 1932–. F. NORMAN My punishment was three days bread and water . . . and twenty eight days stage (1958).

stage-door Johnny noun mainly US A (young) man who frequents stage doors for the company of actresses. 1912–.

stagger noun theatre and broadcasting A preliminary rehearsal or run-through of a play, television programme, etc. Also **stagger-through**. 1964–.

stagger juice noun jocular orig Austral Alcoholic drink. 1896–. J. WYNNUM 'These two bowls of punch look exciting.' . . . 'Well now, that one . . . is our customary Stagger Juice' (1962).

stair dancer noun A thief who steals from open buildings. 1958–. [Cf. DANCER noun.]

stake noun N Amer An amount of money earned or saved. 1853–. J. UPDIKE I worked in that oil town in the Rift . . . and when I had a little stake I hitched back to Istiqlal (1978). [From earlier slang sense, amount won at gambling.]

stake verb trans. orig US **1 to stake out** to place under surveillance. 1942–. L. DEIGHTON When . . . the French police staked out the courier routes, they found . . . 50,000 dollars of forged signed travellers' cheques (1962). **2 to be staked out** to be placed so as to maintain surveillance. 1951–. H. KISSINGER David Bruce . . . came to the Embassy through the front door where the press was staked out (1979).

stake-out noun orig US A period of (esp. police) surveillance. 1942–. R. CHANDLER Somebody stood behind that green curtain . . . as silently as only a cop on a stake-out knows how to stand (1943).

stakey adjective Also **staky.** mainly Canadian Having a lot of money, flush. 1919–. B. BROADFOOT Why, we were making 15 cents a glass. . . . Both of us were getting stakey as hell (1973). [From STAKE noun + -y.]

stalk noun A penis, esp. an erect one. 1961–. A. WHITE I had a stalk on me as long as my arm. A right handful, that one (1976).

stall verb trans. and intr. criminals', dated To surround, decoy, jostle, or distract (someone whose pocket is being picked). 1592–. Hence **staller**, noun A pickpocket's confederate. 1812–. [From obs. *stall* noun, decoy-bird.]

stand noun **1** = COCK-STAND noun. 1867–. verb **2 stand on me** Brit Rely on me, believe me. 1933–. F. NEWMAN You'll be all right, stand on me (1970). **3 to stand over** (someone) Austral To intimidate or threaten; to extort money from. 1939–. F. HARDY We'll have to stand over them to get our money (1958).

standover man noun Austral One who uses intimidatory tactics. Also **standover merchant.** 1939–. CUSACK & JAMES It was Joe's bodyguard, Curly—stand-over man as well, they said (1951). [From *stand over*, to intimidate (see STAND verb 3).]

stand-up noun US A police identification parade. 1935–. PHILADELPHIA EVENING BULLETIN Jackson was brought to City Hall last night to take a look at Norman in a police standup, but he could not positively identify the prisoner (1949).

star noun Brit A convict serving a first prison sentence. 1903–. A. MILLER Several . . . said that if that was what one-time Stars became, they were cured of returning (1976). [From the star-shaped badge formerly worn by first offenders in prison.]

star-back noun An expensive, reserved seat at a circus. 1931–.

starch verb trans. N Amer, boxing To defeat (one's opponent) by a knockout; to floor. 1975–. LOS ANGELES TIMES A promotional video cassette sent out to the boxing media showing scenes of Pazienza starching inferior opponents (1990). [From the notion of rendering stiff or rigid on the canvas.]

starkers adjective Brit **1** Stark naked. 1923–. GUARDIAN There was no stripping. . . . The girls were starkers all the time (1963). **2** Stark raving mad. 1962–. L. P. DAVIES You belted out of that room. . . . They thought you were starkers (1972). [From *stark* adverb + -*ers*.]

starko adjective Brit = STARKERS adjective 1. 1923–. B. MARSHALL Doing a bundle means getting dressed from starko in five minutes (1946). [From *stark* adverb + -*o*.]

> 'There was no stripping . . . The girls were starkers all the time.'

stem

starrer noun A film or play with a leading star in a principal role. 1951–. M. PUZO A Kellino starrer would get the studio's two million back (1978). [From *star* noun + *-er*.]

starve verb **starve the crows** Austral = stone the crows (see STONE verb). Also **starve the lizards, starve the rats.** 1908–. F. B. VICKERS 'Well, starve the bloody crows,' he exclaimed, stopping to eye me off (1977).

starver noun dated Austral A saveloy. 1941–. D. NILAND I know what the things I eat cost me. Starvers, crumpets, stale cakes, speckled fruit, pies (1959). [Apparently from their use as a cheap food by the hungry and destitute during the Depression.]

stash¹ Also **stach**. orig criminals'. verb trans.
1 dated To bring (a matter, a practice) to an end; to leave (a place); often imperative. **to stash up** to bring to an abrupt end. 1794–. **2** To conceal, put in a safe or hidden place; to stow, store. 1797–. D. RUNYON She must have some scratch of her own stashed away somewhere (1937). noun **3a** Something hidden; a cache. 1914–. DAILY TELEGRAPH Chief Insp. Newark said he was satisfied Barnes had no stashes of money hidden away (1979). **b** A cache or quantity of an (illegal) drug; the drug itself. 1942–. GUARDIAN The hairy young man in Lee Cooper jeans ... asking 'Anyone seen my stash?' (1982). **4** A hiding-place; a rendezvous; a 'pad'. 1927–. MEZZROW & WOLFE No Hotel Ritz for us this time; our stash was over some kind of feed store (1946). [Origin unknown.]

stash² noun US A moustache. 1940–. TIME Sandy is a superannuated swinger, complete with stash, burns and a 17-year-old hippie on his arm (1971). [Abbreviation; cf. TASH noun.]

statie noun US A state trooper or policeman. 1934–. R. BANKS Study at the trooper academy down in Concord and become a statie (1989). [From *state* (*trooper*, etc.) + *-ie*.]

steal noun orig US A bargain. 1942–. NEW YORK HERALD-TRIBUNE The asking price is $45,000, but I'm pretty sure you could get it for 43,000, and at that price it's a steal (1951). [From earlier sense, an act of theft.]

steam noun Austral and NZ Cheap wine laced with methylated spirits; methylated spirits used as an intoxicant. 1941–. T. A. G. HUNGERFORD I've got a bottle of steam in my room—I think I'll have a snort and turn in (1953).

steam verb Brit **1 to steam in** to start or join in a fight. 1961–. NEW STATESMAN As the

underworld put it, 'He steamed in like a slag and roughed them up as he topped them' (1961). **2a** intr. Of a gang: to rush through a public place, train, etc., robbing anyone in one's path. Cf. STEAMING noun. 1987–. TIMES Several members of a mob of young robbers who 'steamed' through crowds at the Notting Hill Carnival in 1987 were jailed yesterday (1989). **b** trans. To subject (a place or those in it) to 'steaming'. 1987–. [From the notion of proceeding like a train 'at full steam'.]

steamed adjective Drunk; usu. followed by *up*. 1929–. LANDFALL Little Spike is six foot two and has a reputation for being a hard case when he is steamed-up (1950).

steamer noun **1** A foolish or gullible person, a mug. 1932–. M. PUZO The third player at the table was a 'steamer', a bad gambler who chased losing bets (1978). **2** A male homosexual, esp. one who seeks passive partners. 1958–. **3** surfing A wetsuit. 1982–. **4** Brit A member of a gang engaged in 'steaming'. 1987–. SUNDAY TIMES Last November, steamers ... hit crowds outside a rock concert at Hammersmith Odeon (1988). [In sense 1, abbreviation of *steam tug*, rhyming slang for 'mug'.]

steaming adjective Used as an intensifier. 1962–. A. GARNER Roland! You great steaming chudd! Come back! (1965).

steaming noun Brit The action of a gang rushing through a public place, train, etc. robbing bystanders or passengers by force of numbers. 1987–. TIMES Four youths were acquitted yesterday ... of conspiring to commit robbery during the 'steaming' of a London Underground train (1988). [See STEAM verb.]

steen adjective Also **'steen**. US An indefinite (but fairly large) number of; umpteen. 1886–. S. LEWIS 'I've told you lots of times about building a really first-class inn,' said Myron. ... 'Yes, sure, steen thousand times,' said Effie (1934). [Shortened from *sixteen*.]

steenth Also **'steenth**. US. adjective **1** Sixteenth; hence, latest in an indefinitely long series. 1895–. B. REYNOLDS For the steenth time, you ride in a Chandle car (1927). noun **2** A sixteenth part. 1981–. [Shortened from *sixteenth*; cf. STEEN adjective.]

stem noun **1** pl. The legs. 1860–. **2** US **a** A street, esp. one frequented by beggars and tramps. 1914–. D. STIFF The hobo also damns the hash houses along the stem (1931). **b** An act of begging. 1929–. **3** US A pipe used for smoking opium or crack. 1925–. VILLAGE VOICE Now the

starrer starve starver stash statie steal steamed

johns drive up, they don't even say hello. They just go, 'Hey, you got a stem on you?' (1990).

stemming noun US Begging on the streets. 1924–. [From STEM noun 2.]

stem-winder noun US A forceful energetic person, esp. one who makes vigorous rabble-rousing speeches; also, such a speech. 1892–. T. H. WHITE After . . . a stemwinder in the old tradition from Hubert Humphrey . . . Sargent Shriver was formally nominated for Vice-President (1973). [From earlier sense, a keyless watch.]

steno noun orig and mainly US A (female) shorthand-typist. 1906–. MOTION PICTURE Frances Dee . . . skyrockets to new importance with an amazingly fine performance as a small town steno who wins a five-thousand-dollar lottery (1935). [Shortening of *stenographer*.]

step verb intr. **1 to step on it** orig US To go faster, esp. in a motor vehicle. Also **to step on the gas**. 1920–. G. GREENE 'Step on it, Joe.' They ricocheted down the rough path (1939). **2 to step out** RAF To parachute out of a (disabled) aircraft. 1942–. noun **3 to go up the steps** Brit To be committed or appear for trial at a higher court, esp. the Old Bailey. Cf. *to send down* at SEND verb 1. 1931–. J. HENRY They think it's wonderful 'to go up the steps'— to be sent for trial at the Old Bailey (1952).

sterks noun Also **sturks**. Austral A fit of depression or exasperation. 1941–. N. MILES 'Wouldn't it give you the sturks?' complained Bill (1972). [Perh. from *stercoraceous* adjective, of excrement.]

stew noun US An air stewardess. 1970–. S. BARLAY I'm Mara. I used to be a stew myself (1979). [Abbreviation of *stewardess* noun.]

stew-bum noun dated US A tramp; spec. one who is habitually drunk. 1902–. B. HARWIN How come you to be a drunk damn' stew-bum when I found you? (1952). [Cf. BUM noun 1 and STEWED adjective.]

stewed adjective orig US Drunk; also in phr. *stewed to the ears* (*eyebrows, gills*, etc.). 1737–. J. DOS PASSOS They're a bunch o bums and hypocrates, stewed to the ears most of em already (1930).

stick¹ noun **1** criminals' A jemmy or crowbar. 1879–. P. SAVAGE I's a fair cop. I'll go quiet, and here's my stick (jemmy). (1934). **2 the sticks** orig US Remote rural areas; esp. in phr. *in the sticks*. 1905–. WHITEMAN & MCBRIDE They had . . . all the real New Yorker's prejudice against 'the sticks' (1926). **3** pl., naval A drummer. 1909–.

4 A cigarette or cigar; spec. **a marijuana cigarette**; also **stick of tea, weed.** 1919–. C. MACINNES 'I'll roll you a stick.' . . . I lit up. . . . 'Good stuff. And what do they make you pay for a stick here?' (1957). **5** US = SHILL noun. 1926–. G. IRWIN The stick never has enough of his employer's money to make it worth his while to decamp (1931). **6 up the stick** pregnant. 1941–. R. LAIT Mary up the stick; funny how everyone counts the months (1968). **7** Severe treatment; heavy punishment or criticism. 1942–. J. BURKE He went out on the booze. . . . She didn't half give him some stick when she found out (1967). **8** pl. Football goal-posts; esp. in phr. *between the sticks*, usu. with reference to the position of the goalkeeper. 1950–. SPORT Good news for Reading fans is that goalkeeper George Marks is expected to be back between the Elm Park sticks at the start of season 1950–1951 (1950).

Stick² noun = STICKIE noun. 1978–. AN PHOBLACHT The Sticks' chairman in South Antrim, Kevin Smyth, accused the IRA of 'gross sectarianism' in bombing the Lisburn premises (1979).

stick verb **1a: to stick up** orig Austral To rob or threaten with a gun. 1846–. S. BRILL They had served time for sticking up a variety store in Akron, Ohio (1978). Cf. STICK-UP noun. **b: stick 'em up** orig US An (armed) robber's order to raise the hands above the head. 1931–. G. GREENE The children were scouting among the rubble with pistols from Woolworth's. . . . Someone said in a high treble: 'Stick 'em up' (1938). **2** trans. Used in various phrs. expressing contemptuous rejection, usu. with the underlying idea of inserting an object into the anus. 1922–. P. DRISCOLL If you do earn your thousand pounds you can stick it, d'you hear? Stick it right up where it belongs. I don't want a penny of it (1971). **3 to stick one** (or **it**) **on** (someone): to strike forcefully, to hit. 1960–. MAKING MUSIC I could have fallen through the floor—I thought he was there to stick one on me (1986). See also STUCK adjective.

Stickie noun Also **Sticky**. A member of the official IRA or Sinn Fein. Cf. STICK² noun. 1972–. D. MURPHY Her son . . . was 'executed' last year as a punishment for deserting from the Stickies (1978). [From *stick* verb + *-ie*; perh. from the use of an adhesive Easter Lily badge by the official IRA, in contrast to the pin used by the Provisionals.]

stickout US. noun **1** A horse that seems a certain winner. 1937–. SUN (Baltimore): A 'stickout' on paper, Nokomis was in front most of the way along the six-furlong route (1949). **2** An outstanding sportsman

sting

or -woman. 1942–. WASHINGTON POST As for third base, ball players and fans alike have no range of choice. Frank Malzone of the Red Sox is a stickout (1958). adjective **3** Outstanding. 1948–. DAILY PROGRESS (Charlottesville, Virginia): After that, you have to scratch your head to think of another stickout box office attraction (1948).

stick-up noun orig Austral, now mainly US An armed robbery. 1887–. SUN (Baltimore): The bank manager told police that the bandit . . . drew a gun and said: 'This is a stickup' (1944). [From to stick up (see STICK verb 1a).]

sticky noun Something sticky, spec. (a) an adhesive material; (b) a sticky wicket. 1859–. DAILY MAIL As well as cash, the thieves took 'stickies'—the slang term for postage, national insurance and TV licence stamps (1975). [From sticky adjective.]

stickybeak Austral and NZ. noun **1** An inquisitive person, a Nosey Parker. 1920–. R. HALL Disguised as a mobile heap of blankets in case some stickybeak might be awake and prying (1982). verb intr. **2** To pry, to snoop. 1933–. L. GLASSOP You deny me the right to think as I like. . . . You must prod, and pry, and stickybeak (1945).

sticky dog noun cricket, dated A wicket made difficult to bat on by rain and hot sun; a sticky wicket. 1925–.

sticky-fingered adjective Apt to steal, light-fingered. 1890–. DAILY TELEGRAPH Mr Steel announced menacingly that a list of sticky fingered policeman had been made available (1982).

stiff adjective **1** US Drunk. 1737–. G. V. HIGGINS I always got stiff on the Fourth because it was the only way I could listen to all that crap (1975). **2** Austral and NZ Unlucky. 1918–. R. BOYD I recall . . . a waiter . . . responding to my circumspect enquiry about the possibility of a glass of wine with the succinct phrase: 'I think you'll be stiff, mate' (1960). noun **3** A corpse. 1859–. T. PYNCHON Ten thousand stiffs humped under the snow in the Ardennes take on the sunny Disneyfied look of numbered babies under white wool blankets (1973). **4** orig US A foolish, useless, or disagreeable person. 1882–. SUN A bad customer . . . a stiff who orders the table d'hote and nothing to drink (1967). **5** orig US A poor competitor, a certain loser; spec. a racehorse which is unlikely (or not intended) to win. a.1890–. SUN (Baltimore): We either get shut out or find we are on a stiff which won't run (1944). **6** dated Money. 1897–. H. BELLOC He wrang his hands, exclaiming, 'If I only had a bit of Stiff How different would be my

life!' (1930). **7** A penniless man; a tramp; a migratory or unskilled worker. 1899–. E. WARD The driver . . . reached out to pull Burnett into the dusty cab. Construction stiff. A wandering freemasonry (1976). **8** A drunkard. 1907–. N. THORNBURG It had taken a good part of the day just to locate the poor stiff (1976). **9** orig US A commercial venture (esp. in the entertainment business) which merits or meets with public indifference; a flop. 1937–. AMERICAN WEEKLY Juggy listened to the tune and was disheartened. 'It's a stiff,' he said—meaning that it was no good (1949). **10** football A member of the reserve team; usu. in pl. 1950–. SUN Gunners sign Metchick for stiffs (1970). **11** An erection of the penis. 1980–. verb trans. **12** orig and mainly US To cheat; to refuse to pay or tip. 1950–. WASHINGTON POST Instead of stiffing his servers, McCarthy should be stiffing their employers (1982). **13** To kill, to murder. 1974–. C. EGLETON Did he blow their cover too? Is that how they got stiffed in Prague? (1978). See also WORKING STIFF noun.

stiff-arsed adjective Also **stiff-assed.** Reserved, supercilious, stand-offish. 1937–. B. MALAMUD If you think you . . . are going to be stiffassed and uptight by what I say, maybe we ought to call it off before we start? (1971).

stiffen verb **stiffen the crows** Austral and NZ = stone the crows (see STONE verb). Also **stiffen the lizards.** 1932–. M. RAYMOND Stone the crows and stiffen the lizards (1959).

stiffener noun orig Austral A fortifying or reviving drink, spec. an alcoholic one. 1864–. G. MITCHELL I'll buy you a stiffener in the bar (1973).

stiffy noun US **1** A beggar who pretends to be paralysed. 1917–. S. HARRIS Red Bill was the best stiffy in New York (1956). **2** A naïve or stupid person. 1965–. C. KEIL Negro artists who find their way into white concert halls still find it necessary to 'hip' those 'stiffies' in the audience who insist on clapping their hands in a martial manner (1966). **3** Brit A formal invitation card. 1980–. DAILY TELEGRAPH Nigel [Lawson] had in hand a gilt-edged stiffy for a banquet at the Stock Exchange (1987). **4** also **stiffie.** An erection of the penis. 1983–. A. MAUPIN Her hot Cuban lover with the permanent stiffie (1987). [In sense 3, from the thick cardboard of which it is made.]

sting verb trans. orig US **1** to sting (someone) for (something): to extort (esp. money) from (someone) exploitatively. 1903–. N. MARSH We hope to sting Uncle G. for two thousand [pounds] (1940). **2** To swindle, overcharge.

stick-up   sticky   stickybeak   sticky dog   stiff-arsed

1905–. LONDON MAGAZINE I've no idea how much her son pays her. . . . I like to think she's really stinging her son (1981). noun **3** Austral **a** A strong drink. 1927–. J. DE HOOG You can share a bottle of sting (methylated spirit) down a lane (1972). **b** A drug, spec. one illegally injected into a racehorse. 1949–. F. HARDY The 'smarties' soon found stings that didn't show on a swab (1958). **4** mainly US, orig criminals' **a** A burglary or other act of theft, fraud, etc., esp. a complex and meticulously planned one carried out quickly. 1930–. COURIER-MAIL (Brisbane): A transaction between a jewellery salesman and a professional buyer with $230,000 in his pocket was intercepted yesterday by a cab driver who made off with the cash. Investigators believe the theft was a set-up 'sting' (1975). **b** A police undercover operation to catch criminals. 1976–. OBSERVER His second reaction was to inform the American authorities and get their approval for an elaborate and costly 'sting' (1983). [In sense 3, prob. from *stingo* noun, strong beer.]

stingo /ˈsɪŋɡəʊ/ noun dated Vigour, energy. 1927–. OBSERVER Some shanties, sung by Raymond Newell and a chorus, are full of stingo (1928). [From earlier sense, strong beer.]

stink noun **1** A row or fuss; a furore; esp. in phrs. *to cause* (*kick up, make, raise*) *a stink*. 1812–. M. CRONIN The first thing he'd do when he got back was to see his M.P. and kick up a stink (1959). **2** pl. Brit Chemistry as a school or university subject. 1869–. A. WILSON Eventually . . . the laboratory work will be on a scale that will make this place look like a school stinks room (1961). **3** like stink furiously, intensely. 1929–. D. DEVINE She wasn't really clever, she just worked like stink (1972). verb intr. **4 to stink of** (or **with**) **money** to be offensively rich. 1877–. I. BROWN We must do our best. He stinks of money. Will you fix up about rooms and for God's sake let's have a decent dinner (1932). **5** To be or seem extremely unpleasant, contemptible, or scandalous. 1934–. TIMES The affairs of Lonrho stunk to high heaven (1973).

stinker noun **1** An unpleasant or contemptible person. 1898–. A. HUXLEY Saying what a stinker he is, both in bed and out (1949). **2** dated A cigarette or cigar, esp. a cheap or foul-smelling one. 1907–. P. G. WODEHOUSE Have you such a thing as a stinker? . . . And a match? (1935). **3** A strongly worded letter. 1912–. L. DURRELL I was afraid . . . that you would write me a stinker calling me a peach fed sod (1945). **4** Something excessively disagreeable, difficult, of low quality, etc. 1917–. LISTENER

Stylistically, the Royal Victoria Hospital is indeed a stinker (1967).

stinkeroo /stɪŋkəˈruː/ noun orig US Something of a very low standard; a very bad performance. 1934–. J. B. PRIESTLEY They've sunk two-and-a-half million dollars in this new stinkeroo that opens tonight (1951). [From STINK noun or verb + -*eroo*.]

stinking adjective **1** Extremely drunk. 1887–. E. WAUGH 'Tight that night?' 'Stinking' (1934). adverb **2** Offensively; used as an intensive, esp. in *stinking drunk, rich*. 1926–. N. MARSH She was in affluent circumstances, stinking rich in fact (1978). Cf. STINK verb 4.

stinkingly adverb = STINKING adverb 2. 1906–. M. KENNEDY He is . . . frightfully good-looking . . . and stinkingly rich (1951).

stinko adjective orig US = STINKING adjective 1. 1927–. D. RAMSAY Jessie's a lush. Stinko most of her waking time (1974). [From STINK verb + -*o*.]

stink-pot noun **1** A disgusting or contemptible person or thing. 1854–. D. BALLANTYNE They can call me a miserable old stinkpot (1948). **2** A vehicle or boat that gives off foul exhaust fumes. 1972–.

stipe noun Also **stip**. **1** A stipendiary magistrate. 1860–. NEW SOCIETY Roberts devoted the remainder of his . . . speech to remembering odd little incidents in the early career of the senior 'stip' (1978). **2** mainly Austral A stipendiary racing steward. 1902–. AUSTRALIAN The racing page screamed Stipes Probe Jockey (1977). [Abbreviation of *stipendiary* adjective and noun.]

stir noun (A) prison; esp. in phr. *in stir*. 1851–. E. CRISPIN You get better conditions than that in stir (1977). [Origin unknown.]

stir-crazy adjective mainly US Mentally deranged (as if) from long imprisonment. Also **stir-nuts, stir-simple**. 1908–. WASHINGTON POST A Democratic President would go 'stir crazy' without a depression or war to occupy his time (1960).

stitch verb trans. **to stitch** (someone) **up: a** To cause to be wrongfully arrested, convicted, etc., esp. by informing, fabricating evidence, etc. 1970–. NEW SOCIETY Both Sheila and Gary have many stories of being 'stitched up' by the police or fleeced. Gary says the Dip Squad—the special police patrol looking for pickpockets—are 'a bunch of wankers' (1977). **b** To swindle; to overcharge. 1977–. WOMAN After shelling out £1.50 for a fold-up version [of an umbrella] she found that she'd been stitched up. . . . Two spokes were broken (1977).

stocious /stəʊʃəs/ adjective Also **stotious.** mainly Anglo-Irish Drunk. CARIBBEAN QUARTERLY Since when you become so damn stocious? (1952). [Origin unknown.]

stoke verb trans. mainly surfing To excite, thrill, elate. 1963–. SOUTH AFRICAN SURFER Your magazine stoked me out of my mind (1965). Hence **stoked,** adjective Excited; hooked on. 1963–. SUNDAY MAIL (Brisbane): I'm stoked on Chinese food (1969).

stompers noun orig US Shoes or boots; spec. large heavy shoes. 1899–. K. MILLETT The Left wears its jeans and stompers (1974). Cf. WAFFLE STOMPER noun.

stompie noun S African A cigarette end; also, a partially smoked cigarette, esp. one stubbed out and kept for relighting later. 1947–. J. MEIRING She pulled a stompie out of her pocket and lighted it (1959). [From Afrikaans, diminutive of *stomp* stump.]

stone noun **1** A testicle; mainly pl. orig in general use, but now coarse 1154–. **2** criminals' A diamond. 1904–. verb **3a: stone the crows** orig Austral An exclamation of surprise or disgust. Cf. *starve the crows* at STARVE verb. and *stiffen the crows* at STIFFEN verb. 1927–. J. C. TRENCH Cor stone the crows, he thought, this could go on till Christmas (1953). **b: stone me** = stone the crows. 1961–. J. WAINWRIGHT Stone me!—next thing I know I have a . . . hand-grenade here in my pocket (1979). **4** orig US **a** intr. To become intoxicated with drink or drugs; usu. followed by out. 1952–. G. MANDEL I'd rather stay with the tea. It's great pod. I don't want to stone out (1952). **b** trans. To make drunk or ecstatic. 1959–. J. BROWN You smoke Egyptian Black, that will stone you out of your head (1972). See STONED adjective.

stoned adjective orig US **1** Drunk. 1952–. J. KEROUAC I had finished the wine . . . and I was proper stoned (1957). **2** Under the influence of drugs, high. 1953–. D. HALLIDAY They're all lying around in there wearing beads and stoned out of their skulls on French Blues (1971).

stone frigate noun nautical A naval shore establishment or barracks. 1917–. MARINER'S MIRROR H.M.S. *Thunderer* (our title as a 'stone frigate') has since prospered. . . . It is planned . . . to produce a book on the history of the college (1979).

stone ginger noun A certainty, a 'sure thing'. 1936–. [From the name of a celebrated New Zealand racehorse.]

stonk military. noun **1** A concentrated artillery bombardment. 1944–. D. M. DAVIN I wasn't so crackers I wasn't still listening for that bloody stonk to come screaming down on us (1947). verb trans. **2** To bombard with concentrated artillery fire. 1944–. [From earlier sense, (stake in) a game of marbles; perh. imitative.]

stonker verb trans. mainly Austral and NZ To kill; to defeat; to outwit. 1918–. T. DAVIES A teacher guaranteed to stonker any student with ideas above his ability (1978). Hence **stonkered,** adjective **1** Exhausted. 1918–. **2** (Very) drunk. 1924–. SOUTHERLY 'Tastes absolutely bonzer. . . . ' 'I'm out to get stonkered good and proper' (1946). [Prob. from STONK noun + -*er*.]

stonking adjective Excellent, great, fantastic. Also as adverb, very, extremely. 1980–. INDEPENDENT When they've got their dosh, they go out and have a stonking good time (1990). Hence **stonker** noun Something large or excellent of its type. 1987–. OBSERVER FOOD MONTHLY There's not a whole heap of Sangiovese Down Under . . . But this is a stonker (2007). [From STONK verb + -*ing*.]

stony adjective Also **stoney.** Short for STONY-BROKE adjective. 1886–. E. GILL The Guild is very hard up, and Hilary is at the very bottom of his fortunes & Joseph . . . is stony as can be too (1923).

stony-broke adjective Completely without money. Also **stone-broke.** 1886–. BULLETIN (Sydney): There was a hardy war-time story of a stonebroke Digger (1933).

stooge orig US. noun **1a** A stage hand; a stage assistant, esp. one who acts as the butt or foil for a leading character or comedian; the assistant of a conjuror or similar performer. 1913–. **b** A subordinate, esp. for routine or unpleasant work; a compliant person, a puppet. 1937–. DETROIT FREE PRESS Joshua Nkomo and Robert Mugabe . . . branded the moderate African leaders as 'sworn stooges of Premier (Ian) Smith' (1978). **2** A newcomer, esp. a new prisoner or first offender. 1930–. **3** RAF A flight during which one does not expect to meet the enemy. 1942–. M. TRIPP At one stage we saw a Fortress orbiting slowly, presumably on a stooge with a team of W/Ops jamming enemy frequencies (1952). verb intr. **4** To act as a 'stooge' (sense 1) (for). 1939–. SCIENTIFIC AMERICAN That Strang often stooged for Geller is well established (1979). **5a** RAF To fly without any fixed purpose or target. 1941–. M. K. JOSEPH Been in 691 Squadron,

stocious   stoke   stompers   stompie   stoned   stonker

stooging around the Channel ports all winter (1958). **b** To move randomly or aimlessly. 1953–. J. WYNDHAM The streets became . . . full of crowds stooging around (1956). [Origin unknown; the possibility that it represents an altered form of *student* has been suggested (students having frequently been employed as stage assistants).]

stool noun US A police informer. 1906–. B. COBB He said he wasn't a stool, he wasn't giving anyone away (1962). [Short for *stool-pigeon*, from earlier senses, pigeon fastened to a stool as a decoy, person employed as a decoy.]

stoolie noun US = STOOL noun. 1924–. E. MCBAIN The policeman trusted the stoolie's information (1958).

stop verb trans. **1** orig military To be hit by (a bullet, etc.), to receive (a blow); in phrs. *to stop one*, to be hit or killed; *to stop a packet*, to be killed or wounded. 1901–. H. S. WALPOLE Maurice stood there wishing that he might 'stop one' before he had to go over the top (1933). **2** Austral To drink; esp. in phr. *to stop one*, to have an alcoholic drink. 1924–. L. MANN But if he should recognise any one, he could scarcely avoid asking: 'Could you stop a pint?'

stoppo noun criminals' An escape, a get-away; now esp. attrib with reference to a quick get-away by car from the scene of a crime. 1935–. M. KENYON Walk, then, to the stoppo car . . . And wait. . . . Till Slicker comes (1975). [From *stop* noun or verb + -o.]

stork verb trans. US To make pregnant. 1936–. R. STOUT 'Didn't she stop because she was pregnant?' . . . 'Yes,' he said. 'She was storked' (1968). [From *stork* noun, with reference to the nursery fiction that babies are brought by the stork.]

stormer noun Brit Something of remarkable size, power, or excellence. 1978–.

storming adjective mainly sport Displaying outstanding power, speed, or skill. 1961–.

stoush /staʊʃ/ Also **stouch**. Austral and NZ. noun **1** Fighting; a brawl, punch-up; a punch. 1893–. BULLETIN (Sydney): Hayden . . . is prepared to take risks, even a stoush with the left if necessary (1986). verb **2** trans. To punch or strike. 1893–. E. LAMBERT There was no mistaking that voice. 'Get out of that bloody car while I

stoush yer!' (1965). **3** intr. To fight; to struggle. 1909–. J. E. MACDONNELL He was in a position to stoush with the local larrikins (1954). [Prob. from British dialect *stashie*, an uproar, quarrel.]

stove-up adjective N Amer Run-down, exhausted; worn out. 1901–. R. HOBSON You look stove-up, boy, what's the trouble with that hind leg of yours? (1955). [*stove* from irregular past participle of *stave* verb, to crush inwards.]

stow verb trans. dated To desist from, stop; esp. in phr. *stow it!* 1676–. K. AMIS No use telling her to stow it or cheese it or come off it because she really believes it (1984).

straddle-bug noun US dated A politician who is non-committal or who equivocates. 1872–. SATURDAY EVENING POST I will not support either a conservative or a straddlebug (1948). [From earlier sense, the name of a type of beetle; from the notion of 'straddling' or being equivocal about an issue.]

'No use telling her how to stow it or cheese it or come off it.'

straight adjective **1** Law-abiding, not criminal. 1864–. Cf. GO STRAIGHT at STRAIGHT adverb 4. J. WAINWRIGHT Inky was straight. . . . Ten years ago, Inky had walked away from prison . . . and, since that day, he hadn't put a foot wrong (1977). **2** orig US a Heterosexual. 1941–. SAN FRANCISCO EXAMINER A lot of us have 'straight' friends (1965). **b** Not using or under the influence of drugs. 1959–. V. MARTIN I wish I had some dope. I haven't been straight this long in years (1978). **c** Conventional, respectable. 1960–. NEW YORK TIMES BOOK REVIEW A fastidiously distant man without the hint of a sex life, straight or otherwise (1975). **3** US Of a drug-user: drugged, high. 1946–. LIFE Once the addict has had his shot and is 'straight' he may become admirably, though briefly, industrious (1965). adverb **4 to go straight: a** To reform, to stop being a criminal. 1940–. R. SIMONS I'm goin' straight. Last time I was done was two years ago, and I ain't been tapped on the shoulder since (1968). **b** To conform to social conventions, spec. by renouncing drugs or homosexuality. 1973–. D. E. WESTLAKE 'He's a fag.' . . . Well, maybe he's trying to go straight (1977). noun **5** A cigarette, esp. one containing tobacco as opposed to marijuana. 1959–. **6** orig US A conventional or respectable person. 1967–. DAILY MIRROR Straights prefer 'mums and dads' type pop music made by bands

stool   stoolie   stop   stoppo   stork   stormer   storming like Boomtown Rats, Blondie and, more recently, Police (1980). **b** One who does not take drugs. 1967–. **c** A heterosexual. *c.*1971–. GAY NEWS It was a campaign shared and supported by a number of gays—even straights (1977).

straight arrow noun N Amer An honest or genuine person. 1969–. C. MCFADDEN I keep trying to tell you, I'm really a straight arrow (1977).

straighten verb orig US **1 to straighten up** To adopt an honest way of life, to 'go straight'. 1907–. **2** trans. To bribe or corrupt; often followed by *out.* 1923–. J. O'CONNOR I didn't fancy being in the hands of the Wiltshire police. I couldn't straighten them, but I had one in London straightened (1976).

straight goods noun US, dated The truth; an honest person. 1892–. E. O'NEILL Is all dat straight goods? (1922).

straight leg noun US, military A member of the ground staff as opposed to one of the flying personnel. 1951–.

straight shooter noun mainly US An honest person. 1928–.

straight-up adjective **1** Exact, complete; true, trustworthy. 1936–. R. HILL You looked honest to me . . . and you sounded like a straight-up guy (1982). adverb **2** Truthfully, honestly. 1963–. W. J. BURLEY I don't know where he is, Mr Gill, straight up, I don't (1973).

strain verb **to strain the potatoes (or spuds)** Austral jocular of a male: to urinate. 1965–. P. BURGESS Keep Ted's chair for him. He's only gone out to strain the spuds (1982).

strap-hanger noun A passenger in a bus, train, etc. who has to stand, holding on to an overhead support, because all the seats on the vehicle are taken; hence, a commuter on public transport. 1905–. TIMES Washington . . . commuters . . . are not strap-hangers like New Yorkers, Londoners and Parisians (1981). Hence **strap-hang,** verb intr. 1908–.

strapped adjective orig US Subject to a shortage, esp. of money; usu. followed by *for.* 1857–. M. FRANKLIN Also she was strapped for ready money (1936).

strawberry noun **1** N Amer, dated A graze on the skin. 1921–. **2** A red nose, esp. as caused by drinking alcohol. 1949–. C. SMITH His nose . . . had turned . . . to the characteristic boozer's strawberry (1980).

streak noun **1** derog, orig Austral A tall thin person; esp. in phr. *a long streak.* 1937–.

J. J. FAHEY O.K., you long streak. You can try that again after the game (1946). **2** orig US An act of 'streaking' (see sense 3). 1974–. verb intr. **3** orig US To run naked in a public place as a stunt. 1973–. Hence **streaker,** noun One who 'streaks'. 1973–. J. IRVING A young woman had reported that she was approached by an exhibitionist—at least, by a streaker (1978).

street cred noun Familiarity with fashionable urban subculture. 1981–. INTERNATIONAL MUSICIAN I know that walking down main street with an oboe in hand does nothing for the street cred (1985). [Short for *street credibility* noun.]

streetman noun US A petty criminal who works on the city streets, esp. as a pickpocket or drug pedlar. 1908–. PUBLISHERS WEEKLY He is playing partner to the pusher whose street man is keeping the girl hooked (1974).

stretch noun **1** A period of imprisonment. 1821–. P. BRANCH He's in Joe Gurr again. He got nicked in Cardiff on a snout gaff. . . . It's only a two stretch and a lot of the Boys had their collars felt (1951). verb trans. **2** To kill. 1902–. M. GILBERT Once . . . Annie had a husband. She got tired of him, so she 'stretched him with a bottle' (1953).

strewth int Also **streuth, 'strewth, 'strooth, 'struth, struth.** Used as a mild oath. 1892–. P. G. WINSLOW Strewth, they've made a mess of this office (1975). [Short for *God's truth.*]

strides noun pl. now mainly Austral Trousers. 1889–. N. SHUTE Could you get into a pair of my strides? (1950).

strike verb trans. **1** Used in phrs. such as *strike me blind (dead, pink)* as an exclamation, esp. of surprise. Also (Austral and NZ) **strike (me)**. 1696–. D. NILAND Strike me pink, Mac, you're not leaving? (1955); B. CRUMP Strike, he went crook! Who the hell was responsible? Had we been blasting fish? (1960). **2 strike a light** Brit, Austral, and NZ Used as a mild oath. 1936–. I. CROSS 'Strike a light,' he hissed. . . . 'Get over here, quick,' he said. 'Have a bloody look, man' (1960).

string verb **1** trans. now mainly US To fool, deceive, 1812–. H. ENGEL I guess I don't have any reason to believe they'd string me (1982). **2 to string out** US To be under the influence of a drug. Cf. STRUNG OUT adjective. 1967–. SUNDAY TELEGRAPH How long did you string out? (1970). noun **3** US A group of prostitutes working for the same person or organization. Cf. STABLE noun. 1913–. L. BLOCK She wants out of my string of girls (1982).

straight arrow   straighten   straight goods   strain

string-bean noun US A tall thin person. 1936–.

striper noun An officer in the Royal Navy or the US Navy of a rank designated by the stated number of stripes on the uniform; in the army, a lance-corporal (**one-striper**), corporal (**two-striper**), or sergeant (**three-striper**). 1917–. G. HACKFORTH-JONES It made me remember how I felt when some pompous four-striper came slumming or snooping on board my submarine (1950).

stripes noun US A prison uniform. 1887–. P. STURGES He's going to be in jail, Trudy, for a long time. He can't do you any good in stripes, honey (1943). [From the stripes patterning such uniforms.]

stripey noun Brit, naval A long-service able seaman; one with good-conduct stripes. 1942–. TACKLINE Stripey was a small, middle-aged A.B. (1945). [From *stripe* noun + *-y*.]

stroke noun Brit An underhand trick; esp. in phr. *to pull a stroke*, to play such a trick. 1970–. J. MCVICAR It would be wrong to let Charlie go. . . . He's pulled too many strokes (1974).

stroll verb In the phr. *stroll on!*, expressing incredulity at the preceding remark. 1959–. P. TINNISWOOD 'Excuse me, but do you by any chance suffer from hay fever?' 'No,' said Brenda Woodhead. 'Why?' 'Well, your eyes are all puffy and you've got a red nose.'—Bloody rotate, Carter. Bloody stroll on (1985). [The implication is that hearers should carry on as if no remark had been made.]

strong noun **1 the strong of** Austral The point or meaning of; the truth about. 1915–. B. DAWE H-hey fellers. . . . What's the strong of this—empty glasses? C'mon it's my shout. What're we having? (1983). verb trans. **2 to strong it** Brit To behave excessively; to exaggerate. 1964–. G. F. NEWMAN Don't you think that's stronging it (1970).

strongers /ˈstrɒŋəz/ noun nautical = SOOGEE-MOOGEE noun. 1929–. [From *strong* adjective + *-ers* suffix.]

stroppy adjective Brit Bad-tempered, angry, rebellious, awkward. 1951–. A. DIMENT Should the shit hit the fan and the Swedes come over stroppy, he could say . . . 'weren't nothing to do with us, son!' (1968). [Perh. abbreviation of *obstreperous* adjective with altered stem-vowel.]

struggle-buggy noun US, dated A motor vehicle; spec. an old and battered one. 1925–.

strung out adjective orig and mainly US Weak or ill, esp. as a result of drug addiction;

hence, addicted to, using, or high *on* drugs. Cf. STRING verb 2. 1959–. GUARDIAN WEEKLY Young people get strung out on heroin (1977).

strut verb **to strut one's stuff** US To display one's ability. 1926–. SUN (Baltimore): Rain today made the prospect for off-going for the first card, thus giving the 'mudders' an opportunity to strut their stuff (1941).

stubble-jumper noun mainly Canadian A prairie farmer. 1961–.

stubby noun Also **stubbie**. Austral **1** A dumpy beer bottle. 1957–. G. MORLEY Phil opened the freezer and pulled out four stubbies (1972). **2** pl. A proprietary name for a brand of shorts. 1973–.

stuck adjective **1 stuck on** orig US Infatuated with. 1886–. A. HUXLEY You'd say she was kind of stuck on the fellow (1939). **2 to get stuck in (to)** orig Austral To begin in earnest or with gusto. 1941–. MIRAGE Noticed old J.D. was getting stuck into a feed in the Flight kitchen yesterday (1966).

stud noun **1** A man of (reputedly) great sexual prowess; a womanizer. 1895–. S. RUSHDIE A notorious seducer; a ladies'-man; a cuckolder of the rich; in short, a stud (1981). **2** US, mainly African-American A man, a fellow, esp. one who is well informed; a youth. 1929–. D. BURLEY If you're a hipped stud, you'll latch on (1944). adjective mainly US **3** Displaying a masculine sexual character. 1944–. BLACK SCHOLAR He had learned the stories about stud broads . . . but he knew Christine 'used' to be a stud broad (1971). **4** Fine, excellent. 1969–. [From earlier sense, horse kept for breeding.]

student noun US An inexperienced user of illegal drugs; spec. one who takes small or occasional doses. 1936–. N. ALGREN You're not a student any more. . . . Junkie—you're *hooked* (1949).

stud muffin noun orig US A sexually attractive young man. 1986–. GUARDIAN But to me he'll always be Tony Manero, white-suit-wearer and studmuffin (1998). [From STUD noun 1 + *muffin* noun (cf. dated Canadian slang *muffin* young woman who is regularly partnered by a particular man; also *-cake* as in BEEFCAKE noun and CHEESECAKE noun).]

stuff verb trans. **1** Of a male: to have sex with. 1598–. SUNDAY TIMES He was sacked from Eton for stuffing the boys' maids (1983). Cf. STUFFED adjective. **2** To dispose of as unwanted; used in various expressions of contemptuous rejection, esp. **stuff it,** with the underlying notion of insertion in the anus. 1955–.

string-bean striper stripes stripey stroke stroll

T. HINDE 'Stuff you,' I said (1965); J. PORTER He should have taken a stronger line. . . . Told old Crouch to stuff it (1973). noun **3** dated **Money**; usu. preceded by *the*. 1775–. P. G. WODEHOUSE I presumed Uncle Tom would brass up if given the green light, he having the stuff in heaping sackfuls (1971). **4** orig US **Drugs, dope**; esp. in phr. *on the stuff*, on drugs. 1929–. L. HELLMAN Years before she had told me her son was on the stuff (1973). **5 no stuff** US Used to express sincerity or truthfulness; no kidding. 1946–70. **6 not to give a stuff** mainly Austral and NZ Not to care at all. 1974–. B. MASON I don't give a stuff if it was or not (1980). See also **bit of stuff** at BIT noun 1.

stuffed adjective **get stuffed** an exclamation of dismissal, contempt, etc. 1952–. R. RENDELL Who're you giving orders to? You can get stuffed (1979). Cf. STUFF verb 1,2.

stumblebum noun orig and mainly US A clumsy or inept person. 1932–. A. LA BERN These stumble-bums may have stumbled across the main culprit (1966). [From *stumble* verb + BUM noun.]

stumer /stjuːmə(r)/ noun Also **stumor**. **1** Something worthless, a failure, flop. 1886–. TIMES Eclecticism guarantees that in a period like this the [Tate] collection will come to include a fair proportion of stumers (1976). **2** A worthless cheque; a counterfeit coin or note. 1890–. F. M. FORD Two [were] awaiting court-martial for giving stumer cheques (1926). **3** dated Austral Also **stoomer**. A penniless person; in phr. *to come a stumer*, to lose one's money. 1898–1941. **4** Also **stuma**. A state of agitation. 1932–. [Origin unknown.]

stump noun **up a stump** dated, orig and mainly US In difficulties. Cf. *up a gum-tree* at GUM-TREE noun. 1829–. J. GALSWORTHY Look here, Uncle Soames, I'm up a stump (1924).

stung adjective Austral Drunk. 1913–. T. A. G. HUNGERFORD Jerry's nice and stung today— the third in a row (1953).

stunned adjective **1** dated Austral and NZ Drunk. 1919–. P. CADEY I'm afraid I got a bit stunned. . . . I had one over the odd (1933). **2 like a stunned mullet** Austral Dull, stupefied. 1953–.

stupe /stjuːp/ noun orig dialect A stupid person. 1762–. T. WELLS His assistant, a big stupe called Jersey Eng (1967). [Shortened from *stupid* adjective and noun.]

sturks variant of STERKS noun.

sub Brit. noun **1** An advance payment of wages or salary. Also more generally, an advance of money. 1866–. verb trans. **2** To pay (someone) (a 'sub'). Also (intr.) **to sub up** to pay up or subscribe. 1874–. G. MITCHELL 'Wasn't that rather expensive?' . . . 'I believe Tony Biancini subbed up' (1958). [Short for *subsist* (*payment*), itself short for *subsistence* (*payment*).]

sub-cheese /ˈsʌbtʃiːz/ noun Also **sub-cheeze, -chiz.** dated, military, orig Anglo-Indian Everything, the whole lot; also in phr. *the whole sub-cheese*. 1874–. B. W. ALDISS Of course we were lugging our ammo, machine-guns, mortars, and the whole *subcheeze* with us (1971). [From Hindustani *sab* all + *chiz* thing.]

sub-deb noun dated, mainly US A girl who will soon 'come out' as a débutante; hence, broadly, a girl in her mid-teens. 1917–. TIME The season's debutantes danced their way into society, while eager sub-debs looked on (1947).

submarine verb trans. US To put out of action in an underhand way; to sabotage. 1978–. NEWSDAY Charles Hyner, now Brooklyn district attorney, doesn't call Dinkins the way he used to ever since he was submarined by a report by the Dinkins team (1990).

subway alumni noun pl. US City-dwelling supporters of a college football team who, though not graduates of the college, attend games or follow the results. 1947–.

suck verb **1 to suck up** to behave obsequiously, esp. for one's own advantage; usu. followed by *to*. 1860–. M. MITCHELL We hear how you suck up to the Yankees . . . to get money out of them (1936). **2a** intr. To practise fellatio or cunnilingus. 1928–. E. HANNON White chicks dig suckin, that's a fact. That's cause suckin's sophisticated (1975). **b: to suck off** to bring to orgasm by fellatio or cunnilingus. 1928–. GUARDIAN One American GI is forcing a Vietnamese woman to suck him off (1971). **3 to suck (a)round** orig and mainly US To go about behaving obsequiously. 1931–. G. ADE As for the Landis party . . . I have had no invitation but maybe I could suck around and get one (1934). **4** intr. To be contemptible or disgusting. 1971–. M. GORDON All the hotels have the same pictures. The last one, the food sucked (1978). noun **5** A sycophant; esp. a schoolchild who curries favour with teachers. 1900–. W. GADDIS The shade of the boy whom he had not seen since they were boys together (Martin was Father Joseph's 'suck') lived on the air as though

stuffed stumblebum stumer stump stung stupe

they had parted only minutes before (1955).
6 Canadian A worthless or contemptible
person. 1974–. CITIZEN (Ottawa): Lots of people
used to call him a suck. . . . He didn't do much
socially or in the way of sports (1975).

sucker noun orig N Amer **1** A gullible or easily
deceived person. 1838–. A. CONAN DOYLE I'll see
this sucker and fill him up with a bogus
confession (1927). **2** A person especially
susceptible to something; followed by *for*.
1957–. ESSAYS IN CRITICISM I confess to being a
sucker myself, if not for Malory, for Welsh
legend (1957). **3** orig and mainly US In
generalized, neutral use: any object or thing
(as specified by context). 1978–. SPORTS
ILLUSTRATED One day David said, 'Never fear, I'll
shut that sucker off.' And he grabbed it and
gave it a huge twist (1982). verb trans. **4** orig and
mainly US To cheat, to trick. 1939–. J. & W. HAWKINS
We are going to sucker the killer out in the open
(1958).

suck-hole verb intr. **1** orig and mainly Canadian
To curry favour. 1961–. J. METCALF Can't even fix
yourself a sandwich without suckholing round
that man (1972). noun **2** Canadian and Austral
= SUCK noun 6. 1966–. GLOBE MAGAZINE (Toronto):
No matter how strong I could become there was
still someone in this city of 470,000 who
thought I was a suckhole (1970).

sucks int An expression of derision, used
esp. by children; often in phrs. *sucks to you;
yah, boo, sucks*. 1913–. LISTENER The council
treated the urbane Mr Cook to the politician's
equivalent of 'Yah, boo, sucks' (1983).

suds noun orig and mainly US Beer. 1904–.
C. L. SONNICHSEN The bear . . . was still consuming
his free bottle of suds (1943).

sudser noun US, derog A soap opera. 1968–.
WASHINGTON POST Clooney's autobiography . . . has
been turned into another drably shabby TV
sudser (1982). [From *suds* noun + *-er*.]

suey pow /suːɪ paʊ/ noun Also **sueypow,
sui pow.** dated US A sponge or rag used for
cleaning or cooling an opium bowl.
1914–. [Origin unknown.]

sug verb trans. Brit To (attempt to) sell
(someone) a product under the guise of
conducting market research. Also **sugging,**
noun. 1980–. WHICH? If someone tries to 'sug' you,
write to the Market Research Society (1988).
[Acronym from *sell*(*ing*) *under guise*.]

sugar noun orig US **1** A term of endearment;
also in compounds, such as **sugar-babe,
-baby, -pie,** etc. 1930–. J. CURTIS When am
I going to see you again, sugar? (1936). **2a** A

narcotic drug, esp. heroin. Cf. BROWN SUGAR
noun. 1935–. H. GOLD You'll dream about the
sugar yet. You'll wake up hot for it. No joy-
popping, hear? Stay off, kid (1956). **b** LSD
taken on a lump of sugar. 1967–.

sugar daddy noun orig US An elderly man
who lavishes gifts on a young woman. 1926–.
TIMES Norma Levy, a prostitute, had a 'sugar
daddy' called Bunny who paid her rent and gave
her a Mercedes car (1973).

suicide blonde noun jocular A woman
with hair dyed blonde, esp. rather inexpertly
or garishly. 1942–. A. SILLITOE The snow-white
hair of a suicide-blonde flashed around: 'Hey up,
Margaret' (1973).

suit noun derog, orig US Anyone who wears
a business suit at work; a business executive.
1979–. TV WEEK (Melbourne): A kid . . . eager to
propel himself out of the mail-room, where he
has a menial job, into the executive ranks . . . of
those who are called 'suits' (1987).

sumbitch noun US Contraction of SON OF
A BITCH noun. 1975–. P. MALLORY The sumbitch has
sure got him a way with the womenfolk (1981).

Sunday punch noun US A knock-out
punch. 1929–. [Prob. from the notion that
the victim does not come round until
Sunday (or 'the middle of next week').]

sunshine noun Brit A form of address,
esp. to someone whose name is not known.
1972–. P. CAVE I turned back to the ticket man.
'OK now, sunshine?' (1976).

super verb **1** intr. theatre To appear in a play
or film as an extra. 1889–. NEW YORKER Chance
for man to super in new Met production of Aida
(1976). **2** trans. dated, Brit, schools' To remove (a
pupil) from a school or form on account of
age. 1902–. T. RATTIGAN He was super'd from Eton
(1945). [In sense 1, from *super* noun, extra,
short for *supernumerary*; in sense 2, short for
superannuate verb.]

supercool adjective orig US Very cool,
relaxed, fine, etc. 1970–. HOT CAR They were
super-cool amongst the sixties surfing set in the
USA (1978).

superfly US. adjective **1** Esp. of a drug:
excellent, the best. 1971–. R. WOODLEY 'That,'
he said in crisp, sure tones, 'is top-shelf coke.
Super-fly' (1971). **2** Also **Superfly.** Typical
of the character Super Fly, a cocaine dealer
in a 1972 US film of the same name.
1974–. noun **3** A drug pusher. 1973–. [From
super- + FLY adjective; in sense 3, from the title
of the film—see sense 2 of the adjective above.]

sure adverb **sure 'nuff** US, mainly African-American Sure enough; used for emphasis, esp. in demonstrating a point. Also **sho' nuff.** 1880–. J. D. CARR He's sho' nuff in good shape and ought to thank you (1971).

surf verb intr. and trans. To joyride on the roof or outside of (a railway train, car, etc.). 1985–. DAILY TELEGRAPH A verdict of misadventure was recorded yesterday on an 18-year-old student who fell to his death ... while 'surfing' on a 70mph Tube train (1988).

surf-bum noun A surfing enthusiast who frequents beaches suitable for surfing. 1958–.

surfie noun Also **surfy.** orig and mainly Austral = SURF-BUM noun; also, one who frequents surfing beaches but does little or no surfing. 1962–. [From *surf* noun + *-ie*.]

sus Also **suss.** noun 1 Suspicion of having committed a crime; suspicious behaviour; often in phr. *on sus*. 1936–. G. F. NEWMAN Chance nickings in the street, from anything on sus, to indecent exposure (1970). 2 A suspected person; a police suspect. 1936–. K. GILES Sorry, old man, they found your chief sus. with his neck broken (1967). adjective 3 Suspect, suspicious; of questionable legality or provenance. Also as adverb, in a suspicious manner. 1958–. AGE (Melbourne): [The coat] was a bit sus so I washed it and then soaked it for a week before I went near it (1983). [In sense 1, abbreviation of *suspicion* noun or *suspicious* adjective; in sense 2, abbreviation of *suspect* noun or *suspected* adjective; in sense 3, abbreviation of *suspect* adjective or *suspicious* adjective.]

suss verb trans. Also **sus.** Brit **1a** To suspect of a crime. 1953–. D. WEBB He turned to Hodge and said, 'Who's sussed for this job?' (1953). **b** To suspect, surmise, consider likely. 1958–. PUNCH I sussed that all the dodgy bookshops would soon be skint (1960). **2** Usu. followed by *out*. **a** To work out; to grasp, understand, realize. 1966–. DAILY TELEGRAPH 'If ever my members sussed out that I can't read, I'd be a gonner,' he said (1975). **b** To investigate, inspect. 1969–. DAILY MIRROR It took me about half a day to suss out the industry and realise how easy it would be to move in (1977). [Abbreviation of *suspect* verb.]

sussed adjective Brit Well-informed, in the know, *au fait*. 1984–. GAY TIMES I butt in—'Em, em'—in my most sussed manner! (1990).

susso noun Austral, dated **1** State-government unemployment benefit, esp. as paid during the Depression; also in phr. *on (the) susso*. 1941–. **2** Someone paid such benefit. 1947–. F. HARDY The very thought ... of the contempt the respectable held for the sussos changed his mood to defiance (1963). [From *sus(tenance* noun + *-o*.]

sussy adjective Brit Suspicious; suspected. 1965–. G. F. NEWMAN Sneed's questions were becoming more accusing; there was something sussy about Roger Dawes (1974). [From *sus(picious* adjective or *sus(pected* adjective + *-y*.]

swacked adjective US Drunk. 1932–. H. KANE I'm slightly swacked on champagne (1965). [From Scottish *swack* verb, to gulp, swill, of imitative origin.]

swag noun **1** The stolen goods carried away by a burglar, loot; broadly, any illicit gains. 1794–. J. FENTON And there were villains enough, but none of them slipped away with the swag (1982). **2** Now mainly Austral and NZ A large quantity *of* something. 1812–. NEW JOURNALIST (Australia): It is cheaper to buy a swag of aged situation comedies ... than to produce even the simplest studio-bound program in Australia (1973). verb trans. **3** To shove; to take or snatch away roughly. 1958–. J. BARNETT The object is to see if the Commissioner was swagged away by anyone during the demo (1978).

SWAK orig forces' Abbreviation of 'sealed with a kiss' (used on envelopes). Cf. SWALK. 1925–.

SWALK orig forces' Abbreviation of 'sealed with a loving kiss' (used on envelopes). Cf. SWAK. 1948–. D. HALLIDAY I posted him a long letter with SWALK on it to make him laugh (1973).

swallow noun A woman employed by the Soviet intelligence service to seduce men for the purposes of espionage. 1972–. M. BARAK I need a swallow in America. One ... who is sexually skilled and expert in obtaining information (1976).

swamp verb intr. Austral To obtain a lift; to travel as a driver's assistant. 1897–. W. W. AMMON ET AL. He promised that if I gave him a hand to load the big wagon I could swamp up with him for as far as I wanted to go (1984). [Back-formation from SWAMPER noun 2.]

swamper noun **1** orig US An assistant to the driver of horses, mules, or bullocks. 1870–. K. S. PRICHARD Red Burke shouted to the bullocks. ... His swamper yelled and danced (1926). **2** Austral One who travels on foot but has his swag carried on a wagon; hence, one who obtains a lift. 1894–. T. RONAN My ... fellow

sure   surf   surf-bum   surfie   sus   suss   sussed   susso swamper tossed his swag off [the mailman's truck] here; he was home (1966). **3** N Amer The assistant to the driver of a lorry. 1929–. E. IGLAUER We don't have swampers, a second man on the truck, the way the oil-field men have (1975).

swan orig military. verb intr. **1** To move freely or aimlessly; to wander. 1942–. D. BOGARDE She swanned about at the party like the Queen Mother (1980). noun **2** A period or occasion of swanning; an aimless journey. 1946–. D. CLARK 'Reed and I may have to go to London for the day.' . . . 'It's not just a swan is it?' (1979).

Swanee noun **to go down the Swanee** to be lost or wasted; to become ruined or bankrupt. 1977–. OBSERVER A senior Leyland convener . . . called on the Government to give Leyland 'latitude' in settling its pay problems. Without that, he said, the company 'would go down the Swanee' (1977). [From the name of a river in Georgia and Florida, USA; cf. *down the river* finished, done for.]

swankpot noun Brit An ostentatious or boastful person. 1914–. PICTURE FUN Brimstone . . . and Billy kept the old swankpot nicely on the run (1914). [From *swank* noun + *pot* noun, as in *fusspot*, etc.]

sweat verb **1** trans. To interrogate closely, often with (threats of) violence. 1764–. J. LE CARRÉ Probably Mikhel intercepted and read it. . . . We could sweat him, but I doubt if it would help (1979). **2 to sweat one's guts out** to work very hard. 1890–. R. JEFFRIES You sweated your guts out for months and finished your book, then the public looked the other way (1961). **3 to sweat blood: a** To do one's utmost; to work very hard. 1911–. J. TEY I expect he sweats blood over his writing. He has no imagination (1950). **b** To be terrified. 1924–. W. M. DUNCAN I was sitting there sweating blood when those damned cops arrived (1973). **4** orig military **a: to sweat on** (something): to await anxiously. 1917–. **b: to sweat on the top-line** to be in a state of anxious expectation. 1919–. **5 don't sweat it** US Don't worry. 1963–. N. THORNBURG Cutter reached over and covered her hand with his own, patted it. 'Don't sweat it, kid,' he said. 'It's nothing' (1976). **6** intr. To be anxious or uneasy. 1973–. D. DEVINE No point in being early. Let him sweat (1978). noun **7** Brit, public schools' A long training run. 1916–. W. BLUNT Long melancholy 'sweats' (runs) over the downs [at Marlborough] (1983).

8 no sweat orig US No trouble, no bother. 1955–. K. GILES No sweat, mate. . . . We're not looking for trouble (1973). See also OLD SWEAT noun. [In sense 4b, from the notion of waiting for a number to be called at bingo that will complete the top line of one's card.]

sweat-hog noun US A difficult student singled out in school or college for special instruction. 1976–. SENIOR SCHOLASTIC John Travolta . . . [is] back in the classroom . . . as the leader of the sweathogs in ABC's *Welcome Back, Kotter* (1976).

swede-basher noun jocular, derog A farm worker; hence, a rustic. 1943–. J. GRENFELL I tried to sing a song appropriate for the swedebashers from Lincolnshire (1976). So **swede-bashing,** adjective. 1936–.

sweat on the top-line
to be in a state of anxious expectation

Sweeney noun Also **Sweeny.** Brit (A member of) a police flying squad. 1936–. N. LUCAS By the way, don't bother to call the Sweeny (1967). [Short for *Sweeney Todd*, rhyming slang for 'flying squad'; from the name of a London barber who murdered his customers, the central character of a play by George Dibdin Pitt (1799–1855).]

sweet adjective **1** Austral Fine, in order, ready; esp. in phr. *she's sweet*, all is well. 1898–. K. TENNANT 'Everything O.K.?' 'Yep,' said the scrawny man beneath us. 'She's sweet' (1964). **2** Used as an intensifier in certain phrases meaning 'nothing at all'. See also SWEET F.A. noun, *sweet Fanny Adams* at FANNY ADAMS noun. 1958–. B. BROADFOOT The government provided sweet bugger all. Absolutely sweet bugger all (1973).

sweetback noun US A woman's lover, a ladies' man; a pimp. Also **sweetback man.** 1929–. BLESH & JANIS The dapper, foppish 'macks' or 'sweet-back men' . . . got their gambling stakes from the girls (1950).

sweet F.A. noun Nothing at all. Cf. S.F.A. noun. 1930–. J. GARDNER The small industrial organisation whose own security officers know sweet FA (1967). [Abbreviation of *sweet Fanny Adams* (see FANNY ADAMS noun); cf. SWEET adjective 2.]

sweetie-pie noun A lovable person; also as a term of endearment. 1928–. E. HYAMS 'I think they're all perfect sweetie-pies,' Barbara said (1957).

swan Swanee swankpot sweat sweat-hog sweet

sweet man noun US = SWEETBACK noun. 1942–. J. MARYLAND Damn, Rev., that's some real cruel shit, suggesting a sweet man be iced (1972).

sweetmouth verb trans. mainly US, African-American To flatter. 1948–. J. JONES He went on sweetmouthing me, with his slippery mean eyes (1973).

sweets noun pl. US Drugs, esp. amphetamines. 1961–.

swey, swi variants of SWY noun.

swiftie noun Also **swifty**. **1** One who thinks or acts quickly. 1945–. **2** Austral A deceptive trick, a 'fast one'; esp. in phr. to pull a swiftie. 1945–. NORTHERN TERRITORY NEWS (Darwin): Not many opportunities for pulling a swifty you'd think (1962). [From swift adjective + -ie.]

swill noun Austral and NZ The rapid consumption of drink in a pub just before closing time (formerly six p.m.); esp. in phr. six o'clock swill. 1945–. G. COTTERELL You ought to see the swill hour in New Zealand, five o'clock to six (1958).

swindle sheet noun mainly US, jocular A document containing fraudulent claims, spec. on an expense account. 1923–. H. L. LAWRENCE The fare's ten bob. . . . Put it on the swindle sheet (1960).

swine noun **1** A contemptible or despicable person; as a term of abuse. 1842–. **2** = PIG noun 1b. 1933–. H. MACINNES This car's . . . a swine to drive at slow speeds (1976). [In sense 1, from earlier more specific sense, a sensual, degraded, or coarse person.]

swing verb **1** intr. To be executed by hanging. 1542–. A. GILBERT She'd have let you swing, sugar, don't make any mistake about that (1956). **2 to swing the gate** Austral and NZ To be the fastest shearer in a shearing shed. 1898–. **3 to swing the lead** Brit To malinger; to shirk one's duty. 1917–. DAILY EXPRESS He said he . . . had been 'swinging the lead' for the purpose of getting a permanent pension (1927). **4** intr. To be lively or up to date; also, to enjoy oneself. 1957–. D. LODGE Jane Austen and the Theory of Fiction. Professor Morris J. Zapp. . . . ' He makes Austen swing,' was one comment (1975). **5** intr. **a** To be promiscuous; spec. to engage in group sex, partner-swapping, etc. 1964–. E. M. BRECHER If only one-tenth of one percent of married couples . . . swing, however, the total still adds up to some 45,000 swinging American couples (1970). **b: to swing both ways** to be bisexual. 1972–. noun **6** US A

worker's rest period; a shift system which incorporates such breaks; also, time off work. 1917–. J. MILLS I went on my swing after that (1972).

swinger noun **1** A sexually promiscuous person; spec. one who engages in group sex, partner-swapping, etc. 1964–. T. PYNCHON I had a date last night with an eight-year-old. And she's a swinger just like me (1966). **2** A lively, fashionable, or with-it person. 1965–. M. FRENCH I'd meet some middle-aged swinger with a deep tan and sideburns (1977).

swinging adjective **1** dated Lively; up to date; excellent. 1958–. N. VAUGHAN When people ask me how I feel about the months ahead, I tell them: 'Sometimes it's a bit dodgy, but most of the time it's swinging!' (1964). **2** Sexually promiscuous. 1964–. BULLETIN (Sydney): 'Swinging couples' are no longer addicted to square dancing but to the less innocuous pastime of wife-swapping (1978).

swingle noun N Amer A promiscuous single person; spec. one in search of a sexual partner. 1967–. [Blend of SWINGING adjective and single noun.]

swing man noun **1** US, sports A versatile player who can play effectively in different positions. 1969–. **2** A drug pusher. 1972–. J. WAINWRIGHT Tell us about all the dope he pushed. . . . He was taking from his swingman (1973).

swingster noun A musician who plays jazz with a swing. 1937–. [From swing noun + -ster.]

swipe verb trans. **1** orig US To steal, take. 1889–. S. RUSSELL Is there another drink going before you swipe the lot? (1946). noun **2** US A groom or stableboy. 1929–. **3** An objectionable person; also, such people collectively. 1929–. R. PARK His tormentors leapt off him. . . . 'Bloody little swipes!' said Mr Mate Solivich (1951). **4** US, African-American The penis. 1967–. [From earlier sense, to hit; perh. orig a variant of sweep.]

swish noun US A male homosexual; an effeminate man. 1941–. J. F. BURKE [He] dresses mod, and he talks like some kind of a swish (1975). Hence **swishy**, adjective Effeminate. 1941–. C. ISHERWOOD You thought it meant a swishy little boy with peroxided hair, dressed in a picture hat and a feather boa, pretending to be Marlene Dietrich? Yes, in queer circles, they call that camping (1954).

Swiss itch noun US A method of drinking spirits, esp. tequila, involving licking salt

sweet man   sweetmouth   sweets   swey, swi   swiftie

from the back of the hand, taking a drink, and then biting a slice of lime. 1959–.

switch noun A substitution which involves criminal deception. 1938–. w. GADDIS Somebody pulled the old twenty-dollar-bill switch on her, Ellery said looking up from his magazine (1955).

switched-on adjective Fashionable; up to date; aware of what is going on. 1964–. D. DEVINE Her mother wasn't switched on, she knew nothing of modern fashion (1970).

switcheroo /swɪtʃəˈruː/ noun mainly US A change, reversal, or exchange, esp. a surprising or deceptive one; spec. an unexpected twist in a story. 1933–. C. M. KORNBLUTH Two strapping girls . . . began to tear *his* clothes off, laughing at their switcheroo on the year's big gag (1953). [From switch noun + -eroo.]

switch-hitter noun US A bisexual person. Cf. *to swing both ways* at SWING verb. 1960–. [From earlier sense, ambidextrous baseball batter.]

swizz noun Also **swiz**. Brit, mainly schoolchildren's Something unfair or disappointing; also, a swindle. 1915–. R. FULLER He's given him not out. What a sodding swiz (1959). [Shortened from SWIZZLE noun.]

swizzle noun Brit, mainly schoolchildren's = SWIZZ noun. 1913–. A. BUCKERIDGE It was a rotten swizzle, sir, because we flew through low cloud and we couldn't see a thing (1950). [Prob. alteration of *swindle* noun.]

swizzled adjective Drunk. 1843–. AMERICAN SPECTATOR The editors of *The American Spectator* got somewhat swizzled one night last week and didn't feel so good the next day (1934). [From *swizzle* noun, any of various frothy alcoholic drinks; ultimate origin unknown.]

swy /swaɪ/ noun Also **swey, swi, zwei**. Austral 1 The game of two-up. Also **swy-up**. 1913–. ACTION FRONT His income from 'Swi' will be a thing of the past (1941). 2 dated A two-shilling coin. 1941–. J. DUFFY 'Here's a swy,' he said, ringing it down on the table. 'Buy yourself one on me' (1963). [From German *zwei* two.]

Sydney noun **Sydney or the bush** Austral All or nothing. 1915–. T. A. G. HUNGERFORD 'Spin for five,' Murdoch suggested to Novikowsky. 'Sydney or the bush!' (1953). [From the name of the capital of New South Wales.]

syph /sɪf/ noun Also **siph, siff**. Abbreviation of 'syphilis'. 1914–. C. WILLINGHAM Why don't you tell us about that time you got siff from your nigger maid? (1947).

syrup of figs noun Also **syrup** Brit A wig. 1981–. [Rhyming slang.]

sysop /ˈsɪsɒp/ noun computing, orig US A person responsible for (assisting in) the day-to-day running of a computer system; a system operator. 1983–. TELELINK Operational initially for 20 hours a day . . . the board will eventually feature up to 16 sub-boards, each run by separate sysops (1986). [Abbreviation of *system operator*.

ta int Brit Thank you. 1772–. D. CLARK 'You know your way, don't you?' 'Ta, love' (1981). [Baby-talk alteration of *thank you*.]

tab¹ noun **1** orig dialect An ear. 1866–. NEW STATESMAN Dad was sitting by the fire, behind his paper with one tab lifted (1959). **2** orig Northern dialect A cigarette. 1934–. C. ROSS 'Tab?' Duncan looked blank. 'Cigarette?' he said. Duncan accepted (1980). **3** A tablet or pill, spec. one containing LSD or another illicit drug. 1961–. M. WALKER An order for two tabs of acid (1978). [In sense 3 perh. a different word, short for *tablet*.]

tab² noun **1** An elderly woman. 1909–. R. RENDELL We've got some old tab coming here.... Pal of my ma-in-law's (1971). **2** dated Austral A (young) woman. 1918–. H. SIMPSON We pay our tabs ... when we want 'em, and tell 'em to get to hell out of it when we don't (1932). [Abbreviation of TABBY noun (in sense 1, from earlier meaning, older woman).]

Tab³ noun dated, Brit, university A member of Cambridge University. 1914–30. [Short for *Cantab*.]

tab verb intr. Brit, military Esp. in the Parachute Regiment: = YOMP verb. Also **tabbing** noun, and **tab** noun, a forced march with heavy kit. 1982–. [Origin uncertain.]

tabby noun An (attractive) young woman or girl. 1916–. J. WAIN 'I said, is it true what Joe says that you've got yourself fitted out with a tabby?' 'My humble roof,' said Robert ... 'is shared by a distinguished actress' (1958). [From earlier sense, (catty) older woman.]

table noun (**to put**, etc.) **under the table** (to make) drunk to the point of insensibility. 1921–. V. W. BROOKS He was far from sober, or would have been if two tumblers of brandy had been enough to put him under the table (1936).

tabnab noun nautical A cake, bun, or pastry; a savoury snack. 1933–. K. BONFIGLIOLI My favourite 'tabnab' was ... a little fried potato-cake with a morsel of kari'd mutton inside (1978). [Origin unknown.]

tab show noun US A short version of a musical, esp. one performed by a travelling company. 1951–. [From *tab*(*loid* adjective, condensed + *show* noun.]

tadger noun Brit, orig N England A penis. 1949–. [Origin unknown.]

Taff noun Abbreviation of TAFFY¹ noun. 1929–. LISTENER Taffs and Geordies and Scouses who were barely intelligible (1977).

Taffia noun Also **Tafia**. jocular Any supposed network of prominent or influential Welsh people, esp. one which is strongly nationalistic. 1980–. T. HEALD I heard murmurings from the London Welsh network (otherwise known as the 'Tafia') on the subject of Sir Geoffrey's repudiation of true Welshness (1983). [Blend of TAFFY¹ noun and *Mafia* noun.]

Taffy¹ noun often offensive A Welsh person, esp. a man. *a*.1700–. B. BEHAN 'Welsh are the most honest of the lot,' murmured Knowlesy, 'you never see a Taffy in for knocking off' (1958). [Representing a supposed Welsh pronunciation of the name *Davy* = *David* (Welsh *Dafydd*).]

taffy² noun N Amer Insincere flattery. 1878–. DAILY COLONIST (Victoria, British Columbia): A little 'taffy' doesn't hurt anybody and it makes the world sweeter (1926). [From earlier sense, toffee.]

tag¹ noun **1** N Amer A vehicle licence plate. 1935–. BILLINGS (Montana) GAZETTE [They] observed a Thunderbird with Louisiana tags circling the block (1976). **2** orig US A nickname or other (often elaborately decorative) identifying mark written as the signature of a graffiti artist. 1980–. TIMES Gang members ... used coloured paints and red pencils to deface hundreds of buses in Birmingham with their nicknames, or 'tags' (1987). verb trans. and intr. **3** To decorate with a graffiti tag. 1980–. NEW MUSICAL EXPRESS Rap Kids don't drink much and were once inclined to tag previously paint-free walls (1990). Hence **tagger,** noun A tag artist. 1986–. **tagging,** noun Decorating with graffiti tags; also, graffiti tags collectively. 1984–.

tag² verb trans. orig US, boxing To strike (an opponent). 1940–. RING If I tag him the way I tagged Shufford, he'll go down (1986). [From earlier sense, to touch or hit (as in the game of tag).]

ta   tab   tabby   table   tabnab   tab show   tadger

Taig /teɪg, tiːg/ noun Also **Teague**. offensive (In Northern Ireland) a Protestant name for a Catholic. 1971–. OBSERVER This week a new slogan appeared along the Shankill Road, the backbone of Protestant West Belfast. It read: 'All Taigs are targets' (1982). [Anglicized spelling of the Irish name *Tadhg*, a nickname for an Irish person.]

tail noun **1a** now mainly US The buttocks, bottom; now mainly in figurative phrases, such as *to work one's tail off*. 1303–. W. FAULKNER This is the first time you've had your tail out of that kitchen since we got here except to chop a little wood (1942). **b** A woman's buttocks and genital area, regarded as an object of sexual desire. 1972–. TRANSATLANTIC REVIEW He had been after her tail for months, but Judy, being an old-fashioned girl, declined his advances (1977). **2** Women regarded collectively (by men) as means of sexual gratification; sexual intercourse; esp. in phrs. *a piece* (or *bit*) *of tail*. 1933–. J. D. SALINGER Innarested in a little tail t'night? (1951); R. GORDON Even if it was deciding whether to go out on the booze at night or have a bit of tail off of the wife (1976). verb trans. **3** To have sex with (a woman). 1778–. J. WAINWRIGHT So, I tailed his wife. . . . So what? (1973).

tail-end Charlie noun **1** RAF a rear-gunner; also, the last aircraft in a flying formation. 1941–. P. SCOTT My brother . . . was killed in the war. . . . A tail-end Charlie (1956). **2** One who comes last or behind. 1962–. OUTDOOR LIFE I found myself on a hillside where the birds were flushing below, but then there was one tail-end Charlie who went up the hill (1980).

tailgate verb intr. orig US To drive too close behind another vehicle. 1951–. GOOD MORNING In the dangerous sphere of motorway driving, for example, they would not tailgate at speeds where if the man in front stopped suddenly they could not . . . help but stop in exactly the same place on the road (1976). [From US *tailgate* noun tail-board on a lorry, etc.]

tailor-made noun orig US A ready-made (as opposed to hand-rolled) cigarette. 1924–. N. FREELING Martin stayed quiet after distributing his last tailormades (1962).

take noun **1** mainly US Money acquired by theft or fraud. 1888–. C. F. COE After the stick-up . . . Carrots . . . can watch the take till I send the porter over after it (1927). **2 on the take** orig US Taking bribes. 1930–. BOSTON SUNDAY GLOBE In an unguarded public moment . . . [he] said, 'Half the people in Philadelphia are on the take' (1967). **3** Austral and NZ A crook; a swindler or confidence trickster. 1945–. N. HILLIARD Only the

shrewd-heads go for that hard stuff: the shysters, the takes (1960). verb **4 to take to** (someone) NZ To attack, esp. with the fists. 1911–. N. HILLIARD When we got home he really took to me. That was when I lost a lot of my teeth (1960). **5** trans. criminals' To rob. 1926–. D. RUNYON Someone takes a jewellery store in the town (1930). **6** trans. To swindle, cheat, or deprive of money by extortion; often followed by *for*. 1927–. E. LATHEN 'I told Mary to take them for every penny she could get,' he said stoutly (1982). **7** trans. To confront, attack; to defeat; to kill. 1939–. E. BERCOVICI The man who tried to take me was Martinez. . . . Next time I am going to kill him (1979). **8 to take** (someone or something) **out** to kill or murder; to destroy or obliterate (a specific target). 1939–. DAILY TELEGRAPH For several hours, as a commanding officer and his officers tried to 'take out' the sniper with machine gun, rifle and artillery fire, his bullets ricochetted off rocks above our heads (1982). **9 to take** (someone) **in** to take into custody, arrest. 1942–. J. VAN DE WETERING You're not taking me in, sheriff (1979). **10 to take** (someone or something) **off** US, African-American To rob or burgle; to hold up. 1970–. BLACK WORLD He and Cecil B were to take off a supermarket in San Jose (1973).

take-down noun Austral A deceiver, cheat, or thief. 1905–. BULLETIN (Sydney): I could learn something from a cool-headed young take-down like you (1934).

talent noun **1** Austral (Members of) the criminal underworld. 1879–. D. CUSACK He'd learn responsibility quicker married than he would knocking about the ports with the rest of the talent (1953). **2** Members of the opposite sex judged in terms of potential sexual availability; esp. in phr. *local talent*. 1947–. SUNDAY TIMES You can take a turn on the [sea-]front and see what the talent is like (1963).

talk verb **1 to talk turkey** orig N Amer To talk frankly and straightforwardly; to get down to business. Also (dated) **to talk cold turkey**. 1903–. A. CHRISTIE Send for a high powered lawyer and tell him you're willing to talk turkey. Then he fixes . . . the amount of alimony (1967). **2** intr. To disclose secret or confidential information, esp. to the police. 1924–. M. ALLINGHAM They've been through it today, but they're not talking. Why should they? (1952).

tallow pot noun dated, US and Austral A fireman on a locomotive. 1914–.

tan verb **to tan** (someone's) **hide**, also simply **to tan** (a person, their backside, etc.): to thrash soundly, esp. on the buttocks, esp.

as a punishment. *c.*1670–. M. GEE If you lock this door I'll tan your bum (1985).

tank¹ verb **1 to tank up** to drink heavily; to get drunk. 1902–. I. HUNTER Behan arrived for the interview 'somewhat full' and proceeded to tank up further in the BBC hospitality room (1980). Cf. TANKED adjective. **2** intr. In tennis, to lose deliberately, to default. 1976–. GUARDIAN But it is ironic that Connors, a player generally considered too honest to 'tank' to anyone, should be the one to suffer (1979). noun **3** US A cell in a police station, spec one in which several prisoners (esp. drunks) are held. 1912–. L. DEIGHTON And then tossed into the drunk tank like a common criminal (1981).

tank² noun The amount held by a drinking glass; hence loosely, a drink (esp. of beer). 1936–. SPECTATOR Their carousals over a few friendly tanks at the neighbouring Whitehall milk bar (1958). [Prob. abbreviation of *tankard* noun, but cf. *to tank up* at TANK verb 1 and TANKED adjective.]

tank buster noun An aircraft or other device designed to combat tanks. 1941–.

tanked adjective mainly Brit Drunk; also, drugged; often followed by *up*; also in phr. *tanked to the wide.* Cf. *to tank up* at TANK verb 1. 1893–. H. SIMPSON Dawlish wrote poetry, and when caused acute discomfort by reciting it aloud . . . he was tanked up (1932).

tanker noun A heavy drinker. 1932–. J. O'HARA But the rest of them! God, what a gang of tankers they were (1935). [From *tank* verb + *-er*; cf. *to tank up* at TANK verb 1.]

tank town noun US A small unimportant town at which trains stop to take on water; hence, a remote place. 1906–.

tanky noun Also **tankie**. **1** nautical The navigator's assistant; the captain of the hold. 1909–. H. TUNSTALL-BEHRENS The sharp-witted Amigo had the job of Mate's Tanky (1956). **2** A member of the former British Communist Party who supported hardline (esp. interventionist) Soviet policies; usu. in pl. 1985–. GUARDIAN The New Communist Party of Britain . . . has issued this guidance to the world's press. 'Please do not describe the NCP as ''Stalinists'' or ''Tankies'' ' (1988). [From *tank* noun + *-y*; in sense 1, apparently from the care of the freshwater tanks, which was part of the tanky's duties; in sense 2, from the use of Soviet tanks to put down uprisings.]

tanner noun Brit, dated A sixpence (6*d.*). 1811–. J. JOYCE You look like a fellow that had lost a bob and found a tanner (1922). [Origin

uncertain; suggested sources include Romany *tawno* young (hence, small) and Latin *tener* young.]

tap verb **1a** trans. To extract money or elicit information from, esp. by cadging. 1840–. TUCSON (Arizona) MAGAZINE Many of the big plush resorts that tap you for $80 to $100 a day (1979). **b** intr. To beg. 1935–. G. ORWELL They were begging . . . 'tapping' at every . . . likely-looking cottage (1935). **2** trans. To rob, burgle. 1879–. T. HORSLEY We'll tap these mansions (1931). noun **3 on the tap** cadging, making requests for loans. 1932–. P. CARTER She was a real moaner and always on the tap, borrowing sugar and milk (1977).

tape noun Army and RAF A chevron indicating rank, a stripe. 1943–. R.A.F. JOURNAL I wouldn't leave this unit for three tapes (1944).

tapper noun A cadger, beggar. 1930–. J. WORBY I didn't have time to light a cigarette before I was accosted by a tapper (1939). [From TAP verb 1 + *-er.*]

tar noun **1** A sailor. 1676–. E. JONG Whereupon Lancelot started for the Deck with Horatio and his Black Pyrates trailing him, after which the Officers and Tars of the *Hopewell* also follow'd with great Whoops of Delight (1980). **2 to beat (knock,** etc.) **the tar out of** US To beat unmercifully. 1884–. **3** US **a** dated Opium, taken as an intoxicant or stimulant drug. 1935–. **b** Heroin, esp. in a potent black form (**black tar**). 1986–. TIMES A cheap but often deadly form of heroin is being smuggled over the Mexican border into the United States . . . known as 'tar' or 'black tar' because of its colour and texture (1986). [In sense 1, prob. abbreviation of obsolete slang *tarpaulin* noun, sailor.]

tarantula-juice noun US Inferior whisky. 1861–.

tarnation noun mainly US Damnation. 1790–. M. K. RAWLINGS Git away, you blasted bacon-thieves! . . . Git to tarnation! (1938). [Alteration of *damnation* noun, apparently influenced by obs. US slang *tarnal* adjective, damned, an alteration of *eternal* adjective.]

tart noun **1** A girl or woman, spec someone's girlfriend or wife. 1864–. T. RONAN Hangin' around my tart? (1977). **2** A promiscuous woman; a prostitute; also loosely, as a term of abuse for any girl or woman. 1887–. G. GREENE A woman policeman kept an eye on the tarts at the corner (1936). **3** The young homosexual companion of an older man; also loosely, a male prostitute. 1935–. TIMES LITERARY SUPPLEMENT

tank   tank buster   tanked   tanker   tank   town

The boys that Isherwood and his friends picked up were not professional tarts only out for what they could get (1977). verb mainly Brit **4** Usu. followed by *up*. **a** trans. To smarten up, esp. flashily or gaudily. 1938–. J. WILSON You won't be able to tart yourself up like a teenager much longer, Rose (1972). **b** intr. To dress up, make oneself up, etc. gaudily; to titivate oneself. 1961–. J. COOPER They were tarting up in the Ladies (1976). **5** intr. Of a girl or woman: to behave promiscuously; often followed by (*a*) *round*. 1948–. J. WAINWRIGHT Her mother was tarting around with this other bloke (1983). [Prob. short for *raspberry tart*, rhyming slang for 'sweetheart'.]

tash noun Also **tache**. Abbreviation of 'moustache'. Cf. STASH noun, TAZ noun. 1893–. R. SIMONS 'E 'ad a little tash, just under 'is nose (1965).

Tassie noun Also **Tassey, Tassy**. Austral **1** Tasmania. 1892–. HERALD (Melbourne): Come to 'Tassie' the Casino State (1977). **2** A Tasmanian. 1899–. S. WELLER You know I can always pick a Tassy (1976). [From *Tas(mania)* and *Tas(manian)* noun + *-ie*.]

taste noun US An alcoholic drink; alcohol. 1919–. NEW YORKER He said, 'Take me for a taste.' We went into a bar, and I thought he'd settle down for a few, but he only had two shots (1976).

tasty adjective **1** Attractive, esp. sexually; pleasant. 1796–. R. THOMAS One of the women, a new actress with hopes of a plum part, turned to the other. 'Tasty guy, wouldn't you say, Dinah?' (1984). **2** Brit Having a criminal record. 1975–. DAILY MAIL A 'tasty villain' (a known criminal) (1980).

tat noun Also **tatt**. **1** A shabby person, a slut. 1936–. N. MARSH Do they think it's any catch living in a mausoleum with a couple of old tats? (1947). **2** Rubbish, junk. 1951–. TIMES LITERARY SUPPLEMENT New ways of getting the johns to spend their money on previously unsellable old tat (1981). [From earlier sense, a rag; ultimate origin uncertain.]

tater noun Also **tatie, tato, tator, tattie, tatur, taty**. A potato. 1759–. F. THOMPSON Mother spent hours boiling up the 'little taturs' (1939). [Orig dialectal variants of 'potato'.]

tats noun pl. Also **tatts**. mainly Austral Teeth; spec false teeth. 1906–. R. PARK He heard her calling after him, 'Hey, you forgot yer tats! Don't

you want yer teeth?' (1949). [From earlier sense, dice; ultimate origin unknown.]

tatty-bye int Brit Goodbye. 1971–. M. BABSON I'll say tatty-bye for now then . . . And we'll see you soon. You know the way, don't you? (1974) [From *tatty* (a fanciful alteration of *ta-ta* goodbye) + *good*(*bye*).]

taxi noun US A prison sentence of between five and fifteen years. 1930–. D. SHANNON Whalen had done a five-to-fifteen year stretch—that's a taxi (1962). [From the fares (in cents) displayed in New York taxis.]

taz noun = TASH noun. 1951–. M. DUFFY He was proud of his little toothbrush taz and element white raincoat (1969).

tats
teeth;
specifically
false teeth

T.B. noun Also **t.b., tb**. US A confidence trickster. 1930–. C. HIMES Men . . . of all stages of deterioration—drifters and hopheads and tb's and beggars and bums and bindle-stiffs and big sisters (1942). [From the notion of the common element 'con-' in 'consumption' ('tuberculosis' or 'T.B.') and 'confidence'.]

tea noun **1** orig US Marijuana; spec marijuana brewed in hot water to make a drink. 1935–. SAN FRANCISCO CHRONICLE A couple of years ago she started blowing tea (1950). **2 to go (out) for one's tea** N Irish To go out on a dangerous mission, or to be taken outside to be punished. 1978–. [In sense 1, cf. earlier sense, spirituous or intoxicating liquor.]

teach noun Abbreviation of 'teacher'. 1958–. A. HILL 'I always suspected it, Hill,' Teach had called across the classroom (1976).

teaed adjective Also **tea-d**. US In a euphoric state caused by alcohol or marijuana; often followed by *up*. 1928–. C. HIMES The driver was teaed to the gills and on a livewire edge (1966). [From TEA noun 1 + *-ed*.]

Teague variant of TAIG noun.

tea-head noun orig US A habitual user of marijuana. 1953–. [From TEA noun 1 + HEAD noun 3.]

tea-leaf noun Rhyming slang for 'thief'. Also **tea-leafing**, noun Thieving. 1899–. D. CLARK A tea-leaf wouldn't find the key on your person if he broke in (1977).

tash Tassie taste tasty tat tater tats tatty-bye

team noun mainly criminals' A gang. 1950–.
P. LAURIE We had a whisper about a team going to
do a certain pay van (1970).

teaman noun US One who smokes or sells
marijuana. 1938–. [From TEA noun 1 + *man*
noun.]

tea pad noun US A place where one can
buy and smoke marijuana. 1938–. [From TEA
noun 1 + PAD noun 1.]

tea party noun US A gathering at which
marijuana is smoked. 1944–. J. SYMONS Used to
give tea parties—marihuana (1956). [From TEA
noun 1 + *party* noun.]

tear /teə(r)/ noun 1 US A spree; (in Sport),
a successful run, a winning streak; esp. in
phr. **on a tear.** 1869–. CHICAGO TRIBUNE In the fifth,
Mitch Webster, who has been on a tear, hustled
his second single of the night into a double
(1988). verb trans. **2 to tear it** Brit To spoil one's
chances, ruin one's plans; esp. in phr. *that's
torn it.* 1909–. M. PROCTER He looked at his watch.
'That's torn it,' he said (1954). **3 to tear it** (or
things) **up** US mainly jazz To perform, behave,
etc. with unrestrained excitement. 1932–. Cf.
TEAR-UP noun. LISTENER The trumpeter Wild Bill
Davison who 'tore it up' with admirable
primitivity and sensuality (1963). **4 to tear off a
bit** (or **piece**) orig Austral To have sex with a
woman. 1941–. CUSTOM CAR Italian wives must
sit and suffer if the men tear off a bit on the
sly (1977).

tear-arse /teər-/ Also (US) **tear-ass.** noun 1 A
very active, busy person. 1923–. J. FRASER You'll
need to settle down. You can't be a teararse all
your life (1976). verb intr. **2** To drive recklessly,
rush *around* wildly and rowdily. 1942–.
J. WAINWRIGHT We're the . . . killjoys. The miserable
bastards who won't let 'em tear-arse around the
town at sixty miles an hour (1968).

tea room noun US A public lavatory used
as a meeting-place by homosexuals. Cf.
COTTAGE noun. 1970–.

tear-up /teər-/ noun orig US 1 jazz A period or
passage of wild and inspired playing. 1958–.
LISTENER The music is not the tear-up associated
with jazz at the Phil (1983). **2** A spell of wild
destructive behaviour. 1964–. NEW SOCIETY
We've had a tear-up with the police (1982). [Cf.
to tear it up (TEAR verb 3).]

tec noun Also **'tec. 1** A detective. 1879–.
DAILY MIRROR Porn tec admits bribe plot (1977). **2** A
detective story. 1934–. R. CHANDLER The mystery
and 'tec are on the wane (1949). [Abbreviation
of *detective* noun.]

technicolor yawn noun Also
technicolour yawn. Austral An act of
vomiting. 1964–. BULLETIN (Sydney): The
sick-making sequences will probably have less
impact in this country because we've all been
well initiated with Bazza McKenzie and his
technicolor yawns (1974).

Ted noun Also **ted.** Brit Abbreviation of
'Teddy boy'. 1956–. NEW SCIENTIST The gangs [of
baboons] appeared to carry out his orders,
roaming through the troupe like a bunch of
leather-jacketed teds (1968).

teddy bear noun **1** US A fur-lined high-
altitude flying suit. 1917–. C. CODMAN We issued
forth . . . clad in fur-lined Teddy Bears and fleece-
lined overshoes (1937). **2** Austral Rhyming slang
for LAIR noun 1. 1953–.

tee verb **1 to tee off on** US To hit out at,
attack, criticize severely. 1955–. BILLINGS
(Montana) GAZETTE Our country is not at war.
Despite all the sabre rattling . . . the nation is not
about to tee off on another nation, large or
small (1976). **2 to tee (someone) off** N Amer To
annoy, irritate. 1961–. NEW YORKER Frankly, it just
tees me off. I consider them to be a god-damned
curse (1977). Hence **teed-off,** adjective
Annoyed, disgruntled. 1955–. G. V. HIGGINS He is
kind of teed off. . . . I mean, this man is *angry*
(1981). [From earlier sense, to hit a golf ball
off the tee; in sense 2, prob. euphemistic
substitution for *peed off* = *pissed off* annoyed
(see PISSED adjective 2).]

teeny-bopper noun A young teenager,
typically a girl, who keenly follows the latest
fashions in clothes, pop music, etc. Cf.
WEENY-BOPPER noun. 1966–. Hence **teenybop,**
adjective Of or being teeny- boppers. 1967–.
[From *teen* noun or *teen(ager* noun + *bopper* noun,
dancer to or fan of pop music; influenced by
teeny adjective, small.]

tell verb trans. **1 tell it** (or **that**) **to the
marines** a dismissive expression of
incredulity. Also (dated) **tell it to the horse
marines.** 1806–. D. FRANCIS 'When this is over you
can sleep for a fortnight.' 'Yeah?' he said
sarcastically. 'Tell it to the marines' (1967). **2 to
tell it like it is** orig US, African-American To give
the facts of a matter realistically or honestly,
holding nothing back. 1964–. L. LOKOS The
crowd responded fervently with 'Amen, amen,'
and 'Tell it like it is' (1969). [In sense 1,
apparently from marines' reputation among
sailors for being credulous.]

tenderloin noun US A district of a city
where vice and corruption are rife. 1887–.
[From earlier sense, undercut of a sirloin

steak; orig applied specifically to a district of New York City, from the notion that the proceeds from corruption made it a 'juicy' morsel for the local police.]

ten-four Also **10-4.** orig and mainly US. int **1** A radio code phrase signifying 'message received'; used loosely as a message of affirmation. 1962-. verb intr. **2** To understand a message. 1962-. [One of a set of code phrases, all beginning with the number ten, used orig in radio communication by the police in the US and later adopted by Citizens' Band radio operators.]

terp theatre. noun **1** A stage dancer, esp. a chorus girl; also, a ballroom dancer. 1937-. verb intr. **2** To dance. 1942-. SPARTANBURG (S. Carolina) HERALD Donna McKechnie is the best dancer in the musical comedy theater (one dance critic tripped over his typewriter when he suggested Donna can't terp) (1974). [Abbreviation of *terpsechorean* adjective, of dancing.]

terr /tɜː(r)/ noun Rhodesian In Rhodesia (now Zimbabwe) before independence, a guerrilla fighting to overthrow the White minority government; usu. in pl. 1976-. TIMES Infiltration over the Zambesi River by 'terrs'—or terrorists/ freedom fighters, depending on your politics (1980). [Abbreviation of *terrorist* noun.]

terrier noun Brit A member of the Territorial Army. 1908-. TIMES More Terriers. The strength of the Territorial Army on December 31 last year was just under 62,000 (1980). [From *terrier* small dog, punning on the resemblance to *Territorial*.]

TEWT /tjuːt/ noun Also **Tewt, tewt,** etc. army An acronym formed from the initial letters of tactical *e*xercise *w*ithout *t*roops, an exercise used in the training of junior officers. 1942-. E. WAUGH Leonard improvised 'No more TEWTS and no more drill, No night ops to cause a chill' (1952).

that demonstrative pron **that there** Brit, euphemistic Used for referring to sexual activity, esp. in catch-phrase *you can't do that there 'ere*. 1819-. EVENING NEWS The British Government gives vent to a 'John-Bullism', and says, after the abduction of a Hindu girl from within the border, 'You can't do that there 'ere!' (1937). [The catch-phrase derives from a popular song by Squiers and Wark, published in *Feldman's 41st Song and Dance Album* (1933).]

thatch noun A mass or growth of female pubic hair. 1933-. C. MCKAY Looking to the stand

where the girls were, Tack, indicating Rita, said, 'And tha's a finer piece a beauty than thisere. Man! Man! Oh, how I'd love to get under her thatch' (1933).

there adverb **in there** US Excellent, superb (esp. of a jazz musician's performance); well-informed, au fait. 1944-. DOWN BEAT A guy playing a horn has . . . gotta get in there (1962). See also **all there** at ALL pron, **that there** at THAT demonstrative pron.

thick adjective **1** Stupid. *a.*1800-. G. HONEYCOMBE 'He must be as thick as two planks,' said Nick (1974). **2** Brit Unreasonable or intolerable; esp. in phr. *a bit thick*. 1902-. W. E. JOHNS The way you snaffled my Hun! I call that a bit thick. . . . He was my meat, absolutely, yes by Jingo (1942). noun **3** orig schoolchildren's A stupid person. 1857-. G. LORD Some of those thicks in Earls Court would do it just for the kicks (1970). **4** A drink of thick or heavy consistency. 1887-. W. DE LA MARE The mugs of thick proved to be cocoa (1947).

thick ear noun Brit An ear swollen by a blow; esp. in phr *to give* (someone) *a thick ear*, to hit someone hard (on the ear). 1909-.

thickie noun = THICK noun 3. 1968-. TIMES Teachers still think that engineering is a subject for 'thickies' (1983). [From THICK adjective and noun + *-ie*.]

thicko noun = THICK noun 3. 1976-. P. THEROUX Where's the camp store, thicko? (1981). [From THICK adjective and noun + *-o*.]

thick 'un noun Also **thick one.** dated Brit A gold sovereign; also, a crown or five-shilling piece. 1848-. SAPPER Done with you, your Graces; a thick 'un it is (1926).

Thiefrow noun A nickname for London's Heathrow Airport, after its reputation for lax security, luggage theft, etc. 1973-. E. WARD Jewel couriers are hired for . . . security and insurance. Special air freight is available but London Airport is still called Thief Row (1981). [Alteration of *Heathrow*, after *thief*.]

thing noun **1** euphemistic The external sex organs, esp. the penis. *c.*1386-. J. P. DONLEAVY Men wagging their things at you from doorways. Disgusting (1955). **2** One's own particular interests or inclinations; esp. in phr. *to do one's own thing*. 1841-. E. BULLINS Anything that anybody wants to do is groovy with me. . . . Go ahead and do your thing, champ (1970). **3** A love affair; esp. in phr. *to have a thing (with* someone). 1967-. R. LEWIS I know Sandy Kyle, had a thing going with her (1978).

ten-four terp terr terrier TEWT that thick ear

third-rail adjective dated, US Of an alcoholic drink: highly intoxicating. 1916–. J. CALLAHAN A shot of the third-rail booze that the Silver Alley joints peddled (1929). [From earlier sense, rail providing electric current to a train.]

thirty US. noun **1** mainly journalists' The end; death. 1895–. G. VIDAL 'When we know those two things, it's fat thirty time.' Bruce had obviously been impressed by journalism school (1978). adjective **2 like thirty cents** dated Cheap, worthless. 1896–. T. TOBIN Feeling 'like thirty cents' and 'the cold gray down of the morning after' became part of the American idiom (1973). [In sense 1, from the use of the figure 30 to mark the end of a piece of journalist's copy.]

thou /θaʊ/ noun **1** A thousand; spec. a thousand pounds or dollars. 1867–. NEW YORKER The gesture cost me a cool ten thou, but I didn't begrudge it (1965). **2** One thousandth. 1902–. [Abbreviation.]

thousand-miler noun nautical A dark shirt that does not show the dirt. 1929–. [From its only needing to be washed after a thousand miles of voyaging.]

thrash noun A party, esp. a lavish one. 1957–. K. AMIS No quiet family party at all, it had turned out, but a twenty-cover thrash (1968). [From earlier sense, act of thrashing.]

threads noun pl. orig and mainly US Clothes. 1926–. J. GARDNER Load it and get in on under that set of executive threads (1978).

throne noun A lavatory seat and bowl. 1922–. F. THOMPSON The commode turned out to be a kind of throne with carpeted steps and a lid which opened (1941).

throw verb **1 to throw up** to vomit. 1793–. A. E. FISHER Ogy got drunk and threw up in the backyard (1980). **2** trans. orig US To lose (a contest, race, etc.) deliberately. 1868–. MANCHESTER GUARDIAN WEEKLY Baseball games had been 'thrown' by bribed players (1951). noun **3 a throw** orig US Each; per item. 1898–. AUTHOR The cost of research. . . . The BBC Archives charge £2 a throw (1975).

thugged out adjective US, esp. African-American Like a thug in behaviour or dress; tough-looking; also (approving), tough, hard. 1996–. ATLANTA JOURNAL & CONSTITUTION Some want to be a little hard and thugged out. It's OK to be a little sensitive (2001).

thump-up noun A fight, punch-up. 1967–.

thunder-box noun A portable commode; hence, any lavatory. 1939–. E. WAUGH 'If you

must know, it's my thunderbox.' . . . He . . . dragged out the treasure, a brass-bound, oak cube. . . . On the inside of the lid was a plaque bearing the embossed title *Connolly's Chemical Closet* (1952).

thunder-mug noun A chamber pot. 1890–.

tich noun Also **Tich, titch**. A small person; a child. 1934–. D. ABSE I vowed to work harder. To make more money. For you and the titch (1960). Cf. TITCHY adjective. [From Little *Tich*, stage name of the diminutive English music-hall comedian Harry Relph (1868– 1928), who was given the nickname as a child because of a resemblance to the so-called 'Tichborne claimant' (Arthur Orton (1834–98), who claimed to be the long-lost Roger Tichborne, heir to an English baronetcy).]

tick¹ noun **1** An unpleasant and despicable person. 1631–. R. FULFORD How often in those early days did I hear those ominous words 'that awful little tick Waugh' (1973). **2 as full (or tight) as a tick** very drunk. 1678–. M. LOWRY He was tight as a tick so couldn't tell the difference (1933). [From earlier sense, parasitic insect-like creature.]

tick² noun **1** Credit; esp. in phr. *on tick*. 1642–. J. WAINWRIGHT Three of the others are already inside, anyway . . . and they were damn near living on tick (1976). verb trans. **2** To leave (an amount) owing to be entered to one's debit. 1674–. J. HACKSTON Going on the slate and ticking up a few rounds of drinks (1966). [Prob. an abbreviation of *ticket* noun, in phr. *on the ticket*.]

tick³ noun mainly Brit A moment, instant. 1879–. E. REVELEY Just wait a tick while I tell George where we'll be (1983). [From the notion of the time between two ticks of the clock.]

tick⁴ verb **1 to tick (someone) off: a** orig services' To reprimand. 1915–. LISTENER 'Ticked off' by one of the boys for leaving his car unlocked and complete with ignition key (1957). **b** US To annoy; to dispirit. Also **ticked-off,** adjective. 1959–. R. L. SIMON Shit, it ticks me off I spent all the money on this tour and look what happens (1979). **2** intr. orig services' To grumble, complain. 1925–. B. W. ALDISS Certainly there was always something to tick about. Our manoeuvres were pure hell (1971). [From earlier sense, to mark off with a tick.]

ticker noun **1** orig US The heart. 1930–. J. CARTWRIGHT Put something at the bottom about your heart. Say, 'The ticker seems to be a little dodgy at the moment' (1980). **2** US and Austral Courage, guts. 1935–. SUNDAY SUN (Brisbane): The lady has ticker. . . . She didn't opt for the soft life (1979). [From the resemblance of the beating of the heart to the steady ticking of a clock.]

ticket noun **1 the ticket** what is correct or needed. 1838–. G. SWIFT But sweetness and innocence were never really the ticket, were they? (1988). **2 to have tickets on** Austral To have a high opinion of; esp. *to have tickets on oneself,* to be conceited. 1908–. J. HIBBERD You're the bastard that's always been smug and had tickets on himself (1970). **3** A (counterfeit) pass or passport. 1969–. G. M. FRASER Russia—where everyone has to show his damned ticket every few miles (1973). [In sense 1, perh. from earlier sense, list of election candidates, or from the notion of the winning ticket in a lottery.]

tickety-boo /ˌtɪkətɪ ˈbuː/ adjective Also **ticketty-boo, tiggity-boo,** etc. dated, Brit All right; in order. 1939–. S. RUSHDIE Everything's in fine fettle, don't you agree? Tickety-boo, we used to say (1981). [Origin uncertain: perh. from Hindi *ṭhík hai* all right; cf. also TICKET noun 1.]

tickle verb trans. **1 tickled pink** (or **to death**) extremely amused or pleased. 1907–. P. G. WODEHOUSE Your view, then, is that he is tickled pink to be freed from his obligations (1950). **2** criminals' mainly Austral and NZ To rob or burgle; esp. in phr. *to tickle the peter,* to rob a till or cash box. 1945–. F. GREENLAND Get a Portuguese villain to tickle the place (1976). noun **3** criminals' A successful deal or crime. 1938–. D. WEBB If there is a good tickle, say for as much as £10,000, which is as much as anyone got from any job, it soon goes to the birds, . . . the bookmakers, the hangers-on (1955).

tickler noun **1** nautical A hand-rolled cigarette or the tobacco from which it is made. 1929–. J. HALE Brooks rolls and lights a tickler (1964). **2** A pianist. 1948–. J. MCCLURE Me? I'm the tickler. Pianist. Y'know (1975). [In sense 2, from the phr. *to tickle the ivories* to play the piano.]

tick-off noun Fortune-telling; a fortune-teller; **to work the tick-off,** to tell fortunes. 1934–. PUNCH No palmists, tick-offs, character readers, mock auctions, pick-a-straw (1966).

Tico /ˈtiːkəʊ/ noun and adjective mainly US (A) Costa Rican. 1905–. [From American Spanish *Tico,* apparently after the frequent use of the diminutive *-tico* in Costa Rican Spanish.]

tiddly Also **tiddley,** (obs) **titley.** noun **1** Dated (Alcoholic) drink. 1859–. E. V. LUCAS It wasn't oysters that she really wanted, but . . . tiddly (1930). adjective Also **tiddled. 2** Drunk. 1905–. J. SCOTT Yvonne giggled. 'I do believe I'm tiddly,' she said (1979). [Origin uncertain; cf. obsolete rhyming slang *tiddlywink* drink.]

tiddy oggy noun West Country and naval A Cornish pasty. 1942–. [From *tiddy* a West Country variant of *tatie* potato (see TATER noun) + OGGY noun.]

tie verb trans. **1 tie that bull outside** (or **to another ashcan**) US Used to express incredulity. 1921–. E. O'NEILL Aw say, you fresh kid, tie that bull outside! (1933). **2 to tie a can to** (or **on**) to reject or dismiss (a person); to stop (an activity). 1926–. P. G. WODEHOUSE I'm warning you to kiss her goodbye and tie a can to her. Never marry anyone who makes conditions (1972). **3 to tie one on** mainly US To get drunk. 1951–. A. MATHER He had . . . tied one on, if you know what I mean (1982).

tiger noun **1** Austral A menial labourer, esp. a sheep shearer. 1865–. F. B. VICKERS Those tigers (he meant the shearers) will make you dance (1956). **2** nautical A captain's personal steward. 1929–. TIMES Captain Jackson's 'tiger'—the merchant navy equivalent of a batman . . . was married after the weekend (1982).

tight adjective **1** Mean, stingy. 1805–. J. GASKELL When I was on the cabs . . . who'd give you a grand-hearted tip, never tight, but all the brass? (1969). **2** Drunk. 1830–. D. LODGE Among the other guests was Mrs Zapp, extremely tight, and in a highly aggressive mood (1975). **3** US Of a person: tough, unyielding; also, aggressive, stroppy. 1928–. L. BUCKLEY He was a hard, tight, tough Cat (1960).

tight-ass noun Also **tight-arse.** orig and mainly US An inhibited or strait-laced person; also, a stingy person. 1969–. J. SHERWOOD As though any policeman in his senses would pocket cash . . . with a virgin-faced tight-arse like Verney looking on (1982). [Back-formation from TIGHT-ASSED adjective.]

tight-assed adjective Also **tight-arsed.** Full of inhibitions, unable to relax and enjoy oneself; also, stingy. 1961–. J. ORTON I hate this tight-assed civilization (1967).

tightwad noun orig and mainly US A mean, stingy person. 1906–. SUNDAY TELEGRAPH Bleeding tightwad! You'd think with all that cash he'd take a taxi (1977). [From *tight* adjective + *wad* noun, bundle of banknotes.]

tile noun **1** dated A hat. 1813–. P. FITZGERALD Willis . . . had not been able to lay hands on his waterproof 'tile', but made do with a deep-crowned felt hat (1979). **2 on the tiles** having a spree. 1887–. C. MCCULLOUGH They all went out on the tiles. . . . It was some night (1977). [In sense 2, from the nocturnal activities of cats.]

Tim noun Scottish A Protestant nickname for a Roman Catholic, esp. a supporter of Glasgow Celtic football club. 1958–. [Diminutive form of the personal name *Timothy*.]

timbers noun pl. cricket The stumps, the wicket. 1876–. TIMES It must have interested elder listeners when they recently heard one of the B.B.C.'s fluent commentators on Test match cricket call the wickets the timbers (1963). [From the stumps being made of wood, and falling when hit.]

time noun A prison sentence; esp. in phr. *to do time*. Cf. BIRD noun 4, BIRD-LIME noun. 1837–. E. ST. JOHNSTON The Queen was much interested and amused for I don't expect she often lunches with someone who has 'done time' (1978).

tin noun **1** Money. 1836–. V. NABOKOV He could always let me have as much cash as I might require—I think he used the word 'tin', though I am not sure (1941). **2** US A policeman's badge or shield. 1949–. S. MARLOWE Mason Reed flashed the tin. 'Police officer. March right out of here' (1975).

tin-arsed adjective Austral and NZ Very lucky. 1937–.

tin back noun Austral An unusually lucky person. Also **tin arse, tin bum.** 1897–. D. NILAND I come up with a stone worth five hundred quid. . . . Tin-bum, they call me (1955). [See TIN-ARSED adjective.]

tincture noun An alcoholic drink, a snifter. 1914–. INGRAMS & WELLS Rough diamond, especially after a tincture or two (1980).

tin ear noun **1** An ear swollen by blows. 1923–. YOUNG & WILLMOTT A man with skill as a boxer, and a 'tin ear' (cauliflower ear) to prove it, had . . . prestige (1962). **2** Tone-deafness. 1935–. TIMES Manson had a tin ear but . . . the Beach Boys recorded at least one of his songs (1975).

tin fish noun nautical A torpedo; also, a submarine. 1925–. R. HARLING They do say the old QM's had a tin-fish under her tail (1946). Cf. FISH noun 3.

tin hare noun mainly Austral An electric hare used in greyhound racing. 1927–.

tin hat noun **1** A military steel helmet. 1903–. **2** dated Used after a verb, usu. in pl.: drunk. 1909–19. **3 to put the tin hat on** to bring to a (usu. unwelcome) close or climax. 1919–. C. DICKSON Next . . . came the point that put the tin hat on it (1943).

tinhorn orig and mainly US. adjective **1** Inferior, cheap, pretentious. 1886–. R. STOUT 'You tinhorn Casanova,' she said. . . . 'Hinting to me that you had her, and I knew all the time you didn't' (1959). noun **2** A pretentious but unimpressive person. 1887–. S. LEWIS I'll bet I make a whole lot more money than some of those tin-horns that spend all they got on dress-suits (1922). [Shortened from TINHORN GAMBLER noun.]

tinhorn gambler noun US A cheap gambler, esp. one who acts showily. 1885–. [Perh. from the use by such gamblers of a small tin container for shaking their dice.]

tinhorn sport noun US A contemptible person. 1906–. R. DAVIES Swifty Dealer, the village tin-horn sport (1975).

tinker's cuss noun Also **tinker's damn.** A trivial or insignificant amount; in such phr. as *not worth a tinker's cuss, not matter a tinker's cuss,* and *not give* (or *care*) *a tinker's cuss.* 1824–. O. SITWELL The human being who is not worth a tinker's cuss,—or, in a more elegant simile, two hoots—does not exist (1942). JEWISH CHRONICLE It doesn't matter a tinker's cuss whether you amend the constitution to call the chairman president, macher or grand panjandrum (1973). [From the former reputation of tinkers for profanity.]

tinkle verb intr. **1** orig US To urinate. 1960–. E. MCBAIN I'm looking for the loo. . . . I really have to tinkle (1976). noun **2** An act of urinating. 1965–. E. BRAWLEY And went over and had a tinkle (1974).

tin lid noun Austral A child. 1905–. B. DICKINS What are the things of light that made me bawl as a tinlid? (1981). [Rhyming slang for *kid* noun.]

tin Lizzie noun An old or decrepit car. 1915–. D. M. DAVIN The pace they drove their old tin lizzies (1949). [*Lizzie* from the female forename, an abbreviation of *Elizabeth*: orig applied to an early model of Ford car.]

tinned dog noun Austral Tinned meat. 1895–. R. ELLIS Another frugal meal of 'tinned dog', a couple of flats to mend, and straight into our swags (1982).

tile Tim timbers time tin tin-arsed tin Lizzie

tinny adjective **1** Austral and NZ Lucky. 1918–. Cf. TIN-ARSED adjective. O. WHITE You'll have to be pretty tinny to pin down those blokes (1978). noun **2** Also **tinnie**. Austral A can of beer. 1964–. CANBERRA TIMES A tinnie or two may be good for you (1986). [In sense 1, from TIN BACK noun.]

Tinseltown noun Hollywood; often used in allusion to the supposedly glittering world of Hollywood cinema. 1975–. TIMES When a filmmaker starts cherishing the natural roar of traffic on the soundtrack . . . you know she believes in Tinseltown (1987).

tip¹ verb **to tip (someone) the wink** to give someone private information, esp. discreetly. 1676–. A. CARTER She tipped the young reporter a huge wink in the ambiguity of the mirror (1984).

tip² verb trans. **1 to tip (someone) off: a** To give information to (someone), esp. about criminal activity. 1891–. T. ALLBEURY Was there any mileage in tipping them off? Experience said that tippers-off always got their hands caught in the machinery (1975). **b** dated To dispose of or kill. 1920–. EVENING NEWS Jake's sort o' done me a good turn, getting himself tipped off (1928). **2 to tip one's hand(s) (or mitt)** orig and mainly US To disclose one's intentions inadvertently. 1917–. ECONOMIST Mr Hunt will not tip his hand on the price at which he will buy more bullion (1979).

tip noun An untidy or disorderly place (esp. a room). 1983–. P. BARKER She was anything but pleased: the living-room was a tip (1984). [From earlier sense, a place where coal, waste, etc. is tipped for storage or disposal.]

tip-off noun A piece of information, esp. about criminal activity. 1901–. OBSERVER There was a tip-off available about when it [i.e. a bank] was going to be stacked up with cash (1960).

tip-slinger noun Austral A racecourse tipster. 1915–. BULLETIN (Sydney): By their conversation most of them were tipslingers or urgers (1934).

tired and emotional adjective euphemistic Drunk. 1981–. DAILY TELEGRAPH Sensing that Penrose's efforts might have left him tired and emotional, the four Eye men called at the Mirror building (1986). [Cf. earlier tired and overwrought in same sense: PRIVATE EYE Mr Brown had been tired and overwrought on many occasions (1967).]

tiswas /ˈtɪzwɒz/ noun Also **tis-was**, **tizz-wozz**. A state of nervous agitation or confusion. 1960–. M. CECIL Gets you all of a tiswas, when he's up the wall (1960). [Perh. a fanciful enlargement of tiz(z) noun, state of nervous agitation.]

tit¹ noun dated, derog A woman. 1599–. E. R. EDDISON The Demons, . . . since they had a strong loathing for such ugly tits and stale old trots, would no doubt hang her up or disembowel her (1922). [Cf. earlier sense, small horse; apparently an onomatopoeic formation, as a term for something small.]

tit² noun **1a** pl. A woman's breasts; also in sing. 1928–. OZ Mary Anne Shelley, with the best tits off-off-Broadway (1969). **b: to get on one's tits** to irritate one intensely. 1945–. J. WILSON This Sherlock Holmes act of yours gets right on my tits (1977). **c: tit(s) and ass (or arse)** crude female sexuality, esp. as displayed on stage, in films, newspapers, magazines, etc. Also **tits and bums**. 1972–. SUNDAY TIMES Ugly George, America's prime TV porn artist (who invites women to undress for his video camera), with his 'tit n' ass' cable channel (1982). **2** orig services' A push-button, esp. one used to fire a gun or release a bomb. 1942–. A. PRICE They've built this mock-up in the Museum. . . . You press the tit, and the lights go out (1972). [Variant of teat noun.]

> 'You press the tit, and the lights go out.'

tit³ noun A foolish or ineffectual person. 1947–. S. WILSON We always took a gun, and it kept me quite alert, not wishing to make a tit of myself in front of the laird (1978). [Origin uncertain; perh. from TIT² noun 1.]

titchy adjective Brit Very small. 1950–. SPECTATOR Towering six foot three inches over a titchy Laertes (1958). [From titch, variant of TICH noun + -y.]

titfer noun Also **titfa**, **titfor**. Brit A hat. 1930–. J. B. PRIESTLEY I'll see Billy Fitt, with me titfer in me and (1939). [Short for tit for tat, rhyming slang.]

titter noun dated A young woman or girl. 1812–1953. LANDFALL Boys, she's a larky little titter (1953). [Origin uncertain; cf. TIT¹ noun, TIT² noun.]

titty noun orig dialect = TIT² noun 1. 1746–. SCREW Man, those firm nice buttocks and titties filled that bikini to overflowing (1972). See also **tough titty** at TOUGH adjective.

tizzy noun Also **tizzey, tissey**. dated Brit
A sixpenny-piece. 1804–1946. [Origin unknown.]

toadskin noun US A banknote, usu. spec.
a dollar bill. 1912–. FLYNN'S Still I can flash a
toad-skin now and then, and have a few iron
men planted where th' berries grow (1926).
[Cf. earlier obs. sense, postage stamp, and cf.
also FROGSKIN noun.]

toad-stabber noun mainly US A large
pocket-knife or jack-knife. 1885–.

toad-sticker noun US A large knife.
1858–. J. S. PENNELL I must have picked up this old
toadsticker (1944).

toast noun **to have** (someone) **on toast** to
have someone where one wants them, esp.
at a disadvantage; to cause someone anxiety.
1889–. R. CROMPTON Well, let's have 'em on toast
for a bit wonderin' what's happened to him
(1942).

tobacco baron noun A prisoner who
controls the supply of cigarettes to other
prisoners, and so dominates them. 1964–.

tober /ˈtəʊbə(r)/ noun Also **tobur**. showmen's
The site occupied by a circus, fair, or market.
1890–. E. SEAGO How can I walk about the tober
without me trousers, I'd be askin' ye? (1933).
[From Shelta *tobar* road.]

toboggan noun US A rapid decline; esp.
in phr. *on the toboggan*. 1910–. J. DEMPSEY
A veteran of thirty or thirty-one who is on the
'toboggan' (1950).

toby noun Austral A stick of ochre used for
marking sheep which have not been shorn
to the owner's satisfaction. 1912–. [From the
forename *Toby*.]

toc emma noun Also **tock** (and **toch**)
emma. dated, military A trench mortar.
1916–31. R. C. SHERRIFF Can't have men out there
while the toch-emmas are blowing holes in the
Boche wire (1928). [From *toc* and *emma*, the
communications code-words for *t* and *m*,
representing T.M., abbreviation of 'trench
mortar'.]

tochus /ˈtəʊxəs, ˈtɒxəs/ noun Also **tochas,
tochess, tuchus, tuchas, tokus** /ˈtəʊkəs/,
tocus, etc. mainly N Amer The bottom,
buttocks; the anus. 1914–. W. R. BURNETT I
was . . . getting my tokus pinched all over the
place (1952). [From Yiddish *tokhes*, from
Hebrew *taḥat* beneath.]

toco /ˈtəʊkəʊ/ noun Also **toko**. dated
A beating, a hiding. 1823–. J. CARY You'd better
tell people how I took your trousers down last
time and gave you toko (1941). [From Hindi
ṭhōko, imperative of *ṭhoknā* to beat, thrash.]

tod noun **on one's tod** Brit Alone. Cf. PAT
(MALONE) noun. 1934–. G. GAUNT Maybe they don't
want your company. . . . Never seen you on your
tod before (1981). [Short for *Tod* Sloan, name
of a US jockey (1874–1933), used as rhyming
slang for 'own' in the phr. *on one's own*.]

todger noun Brit A penis. 1986–. [Variant of
TADGER noun.]

toe noun **1** Austral and NZ Strength, speed.
1889–. SUN-HERALD (Sydney): In Lawson and Hogg
we have two penetrating fast bowlers who have
enough 'toe' to keep any batsman honest
(1983). **2 to have it on one's toes** to run
away. 1958–. P. B. YUILL I had it across the road on
my toes (1976). See also **to turn one's toes up**
at TURN verb.

toe-cover noun A cheap and useless
present. 1948–. LISTENER Gifts are given, not only
the completely useless trivia or 'toe-covers'
which litter the surgery, but more substantial
gifts, such as briefcases (1983).

toe-jam noun Dirt that accumulates
between the toes. 1934–. BLACK WORLD If you miss
nose Picking time Then you collect Three and
one half milograms Of toejam And give it to
barbara's cat (1973).

toe-rag noun Brit A contemptible or
worthless person. 1912–. H. CALVIN Move, ya
useless big toerag! (1971). [From earlier sense,
tramp, vagrant, from the rag wound round a
tramp's foot in place of a sock.]

toe-ragger noun Austral A tramp, a down-
and-out. 1891–. [From TOE-RAG noun in earlier
sense, tramp.]

toey /ˈtəʊi/ adjective mainly Austral Restive,
anxious, touchy. 1930–. NATIONAL TIMES
(Australia): Dallas Jongs . . . had a hotel bouncer
friend who could get as toey as a Roman sandle
(1981). [Perh. from the notion of a nervous
animal pawing the ground with its toes.]

toff Brit. noun **1** An upper-class,
distinguished, or well-dressed person, a
'nob'. 1851–. W. GOLDING The mantelpiece or
overmantel as the toffs say (1984). **2** An
admirable or excellent person. 1898–. verb
trans. **3** To dress *up* like a toff. 1914–. EAST END
STAR Notice the perfect stillness when the 'lovely
lidy all toffed up' sings (1928). [Perh. an
alteration of *tuft* noun, titled undergraduate at

toadskin   toad-stabber   toad-sticker   toast   tochus

Oxford and Cambridge, from the gold tassel formerly worn on the cap.]

toffee noun **not for toffee** not at all; used to denote incompetence, esp. after *cannot*. 1914–. M. KENNEDY Those dreary girls you get in every Drama School who can't act for toffee (1951).

toffee-nosed adjective mainly Brit Snobbish, pretentious. 1925–. T. E. LAWRENCE A premature 'life' will do more to disgust the select and superior people (the R.A.F. call them the 'toffee-nosed') than anything (1928). Hence **toffee-nose**, noun A toffee-nosed person. 1943–. WOMAN People thought I was a bit of a toffee-nose for the first few months because I didn't speak to them (1958).

together adjective Fashionable, up to date; hence used as a general term of approval. 1968–. JAMAICAN WEEKLY GLEANER I read in the Miami Herald that conditions in the women's jails [are] not so together (1971).

togs noun pl. **1** Clothes. 1779–. **2** Austral and NZ A swimming-costume. 1918–. [From pl. of earlier vagabonds' slang tog noun, coat, apparently a shortening of *togeman(s), togman* noun, cloak or loose coat, from French *toge* or Latin *toga* toga + cant suffix -*man(s)*.]

Tojo /ˈtəʊdʒəʊ/ noun services' A Japanese serviceman; Japanese forces collectively. 1942–. J. BINNING The monotone of the bombers is easing. Tojo is on his way out and now it is safe to get up (1943). [From the name of Hideki *Tojo*, Japanese minister of war and prime minister during World War II.]

toke¹ noun dated (A piece of) bread. 1843–. M. KENDON Dripping . . . spread on 'tokes' was eaten for eleven o'clock lunch by schoolgirls for well nigh forty years (1963). [Origin unknown.]

toke² US. verb intr. and trans. **1** To smoke (a marijuana cigarette). 1952–. N. MAILER He had been over at a friend of his selling drugs, a little crystal, some speed, toked a couple, got blasted (1979). noun **2** A drag on a cigarette or pipe containing marijuana or other narcotic substance. 1968–. [Origin unknown.]

toke³ noun N Amer A gratuity or tip. 1971–. MIAMI HERALD They have just gone in and hassled people on tips and tokes (1981). [Origin uncertain; perh. an abbreviation of *token* noun.]

tom¹ noun Also **Tom**. **1** Austral A girl or woman; a girlfriend. 1906–. N. LINDSAY Who's yer tom? She must be yer sweetheart. Why don't yer up an' kiss her (1933). **2** Brit A

prostitute. 1941–. M. HASTINGS I'll bet she's holding out on us. We know these toms, sir (1955). **3** US = UNCLE TOM noun. 1959–. PUBLISHERS WEEKLY By installing 'American Nigger Toms' as the Third World élite, the US has controlled the angry hunger of the poor populace (1975). verb intr. **4** US derog To behave ingratiatingly and servilely to someone of another (esp. white) race; also **to tom it** (**up**). 1963–. M. J. BOSSE Virgil just smiled, Tomming it up (1972). **5** To be a prostitute; to have sex promiscuously or as a prostitute; also **to tom** (**it**) **around**. 1964–. J. ROSSITER This woman . . . Is she tomming it around with the local villains? (1973). [From the male forename *Tom*; in sense 1, short for obs. Austral. *Tomtart*, rhyming slang for 'sweetheart'.]

tom² noun Jewellery. 1955–. G. F. NEWMAN What d'you do with the tom and money you had out of Manor Gardens this afternoon? (1970). [Abbreviation of TOMFOOLERY noun.]

tomato noun orig US An attractive girl. 1929–. H. FAST This tomato is twenty-three years old and she's a virgin (1977).

tomato sauce noun Austral Rhyming slang for 'horse'. 1905–. J. ALARD 'Nice weak tomato sauce ta be puttin' money on,' said the Wrecker (1968).

tom-cat verb intr. US To pursue women promiscuously for the sake of sexual gratification; often followed by *around*. 1927–. G. THOMPSON A man who's been tomcatting around with three women all day long (1980). [From the reputation of male cats for sexual voraciousness.]

tomfoolery noun = TOM² noun. 1931–. [Rhyming slang for *jewellery* noun.]

Tommy noun Brit, dated A British private soldier. 1884–. [Short for *Tommy Atkins*, familiar form of *Thomas Atkins*, a name used in specimens of completed official forms.]

tommy-rot noun Nonsense, rubbish. 1884–.

Tom Thumb noun orig Austral Rhyming slang for 'rum'. 1905–. [From the name of a legendary diminutive character.]

tom-tit noun Rhyming slang for 'shit'. 1943–. C. WOOD Perhaps 'e stopped for a tomtit (1970).

ton noun mainly Brit **1** A score of one hundred in a game, spec. in cricket and darts. 1936–. PUNCH I got a ton in the Freshman's Match of 1941 (1958). **2** A hundred pounds. 1946–. P. TURNBULL The old man would charge three ton

toffee toffee-nosed together togs Tojo tomfoolery

for this but me and the boys will do it for half-price (1981). **3** A speed of one hundred miles an hour, esp. on a motor cycle; esp. in phr. *to do the* (or *a*) *ton*. 1954–. HANSARD LORDS In that case you must have been doing a 'ton', if very few cars passed you (1973). Cf. TON-UP noun and adjective.

tonicked adjective Austral Drunk. 1911–. F. LEECHMAN But the wicked old lout had been 'tonic'd' as they call it and had wandered about bushed for twenty-four hours (1961). [From *tonic* invigorating drink.]

tonk verb trans. Brit, mainly sport To hit hard. 1910–. A. ROSS Our spinners have been tonked about yet again by uncouth country batsmen (1963). [Imitative.]

tonk noun mainly Austral **1** A fool. 1943–. R. BEILBY You're a good bloke, Turk, but sometimes you talk like a tonk (1970). **2** A male homosexual. 1943–. G. JOHNSTON He'll either pick up a dose, or he'll get her up the duff . . . Either that or he'll end up a tonk (1964). **3** The penis. 1970–. J. CAREY Most of his boyhood was spent worrying about the size of his 'tonk' (as he disarmingly dubs it) (1980). [Origin unknown.]

tonto noun and adjective orig US (Someone who is) foolish or crazy. 1973–. TIMES LITERARY SUPPLEMENT You compile a dossier on the habits and rituals of those around you. This is all much more interesting than going tonto at home (1988). [From Spanish *tonto*.]

ton-up Brit. noun **1** = TON noun 3; also, a motorcyclist who achieves this. 1961–. NEW STATESMAN Many made a point of . . . assuring me that the ton-ups weren't as black as they thought I'd painted them (1964). adjective **2** (Of a motorcyclist) achieving one hundred miles an hour, esp. habitually and recklessly. 1961–. G. MCINNES The Ton-Up kids on the M1 had nothing on him (1965). **3** Achieving a speed or score of 100 in other contexts. 1967–. NEWS OF THE WORLD 'Ton-up' Taylor—he landed 100 winners last season for the first time (1977).

toodle-oo int Also **tootle-oo**. Brit, dated Goodbye. Also **toodle-**, **tootle-pip**. 1907–. STANDARD Toodlepip to the poor British Exec (1983). [Origin unknown; perh. from *toot* noun, short blast on a horn.]

toofer variant of TWOFER noun.

tool noun **1** The penis. 1553–. L. COHEN You uncovered his nakedness!—You peeked at his tool! (1966). **2** criminals' A weapon. 1938–. J. MANDELKAU We grabbed our tools and by then the Mods were at the bottom of the street (1971). verb intr. **3** To go or drive, esp. in a

casual or leisurely manner. 1862–. E. WAUGH Tool off to Headquarters and get the gen about tonight's do (1955); D. ANTHONY I tooled down the Coast Highway to Sunset (1977). **4** To play *around*; to behave aimlessly or irresponsibly. 1932–. A. HALL We were tooling around in Malta on a friendly visit (1973). **5 to tool up** to arm oneself. 1959–. J. MANDELKAU We tooled up with pieces of wood and iron bars and hiked over towards their main camp (1971). Hence **tooled up**, adjective Armed. 1959–. J. BARNETT Smith brandished the shotgun . . . to let the minder know he was tooled up (1982).

tool-man noun A lock-picker or (US) safe-breaker. 1949–.

toomler variant of TUMMLER noun.

toot¹ /tuːt/ US. verb trans. **1** To inhale (cocaine). 1975–. HIGH TIMES You'll feel better knowing that what you toot is cut with the original Italian Mannite Conoscenti (1979). noun **2** (A 'snort' of) cocaine. 1977–. DAILY NEWS (New York): Each man dipped a spoon into the white powder and got his toot (1979). [Cf. earlier slang sense, (to go on) a drunken spree.]

toot² /tʊt/ noun Austral A lavatory. 1965–. J. ROWE Waldon added over his shoulder, 'Gobind's in the toot. He'll be right out' (1978). [Prob. from British dialect *tut* noun, a small seat or hassock.]

tooting /ˈtuːtɪŋ/ adjective and adverb US Used as an intensifier, usu. with a preceding adjective or adverb 1932–. B. MALAMUD You're plumb tootin' crazy (1952).

toots /tʊts/ noun orig and mainly US = TOOTSY noun 2. NEW YORKER 'Hi, toots,' Ducky said in Donald's voice a few minutes later to a tiny girl (1975). [Prob. abbreviation of TOOTSY noun.]

tootsy /ˈtʊtsɪ/ noun Also **tootsie, tootsy-wootsy, tootsie-wootsie**, etc. **1** mainly jocular A foot. 1854–. M. WESLEY You can rest your tootsies while I listen to music (1983). **2** mainly US A woman, girl; a girlfriend; also, a male lover; often as a familiar form of address. 1895–. B. WOLFE 'What's the matter, tootsie?' she whispered (1952). [Alteration of *foot* noun + diminutive suffix -*sy*.]

top verb trans. **1a** To execute, esp. by hanging; to kill. 1718–. M. LITCHFIELD That shooter . . . wasn't used to top Frost (1984). **b** To kill (oneself). 1958–. LISTENER I have to try and get a key to it all, otherwise I'll just top myself (1983). noun **2** US, military = TOP SERGEANT noun. 1898–. W. JUST Don't worry, Top (1970).

tonicked   tonk   tonto   ton-up   toodle-oo   toofer   tool

top banana noun orig US, theatre The leading comic in a burlesque entertainment; hence, the leading or most powerful person, etc. Cf. SECOND BANANA noun. 1953–. TIME Dentsu Advertising Ltd . . . had become the new top banana of world-wide advertising (1974).

top dog noun The most important or highest-ranking person; the person in charge. 1900–. ECONOMIST Joint ventures often fall apart because one partner insists on being top dog (1988).

top-off noun Austral An informer. Also **top-off man, top-off merchant.** 1941–. H. C. BAKER 'Don't have much to say to that bloke,' he advised, 'he's a top-off' (1978). [Prob. alteration of *tip-off* noun.]

topper noun US, military = TOP SERGEANT noun. 1918–. [From *top* noun + *-er*.]

topping adjective Excellent. 1822–. K. VONNEGUT That was a really fine performance . . . really topping, really first rate (1987). [From earlier sense, superior, pre-eminent.]

tops noun pl. **1** orig US The best. 1935–. PUNCH Cooney's Cassocks stand the test, Choosy Churchmen say they're best. Sure-fire sermons, never flops; Cooney's Cassocks are the tops (1958). adverb **2** orig and mainly US At the most. 1956–. D. MAMET I find the combination fifteen minutes, tops (1977).

top sergeant noun US, military First sergeant. Also **top, top cutter, top kick, top kicker, topper, top soldier.** 1898–.

torch verb trans. **1** orig and mainly US To set fire to, spec. in order to claim insurance money. 1931–. TIME Griffith relied on an arsonist turned informant . . . who worked as a 'broker' for landlords eager to torch their property (1977). noun **2** US An arsonist. 1938–.

torp noun Abbreviation of 'torpedo' and TORPEDO JUICE noun. 1929–.

torpedo noun **1** US A professional gunman. 1929–. R. CHANDLER There's yellow cops and there's yellow torpedoes (1940). **2** A tablet or capsule of a narcotic drug. 1971–. M. RUSSELL He tried to estimate how long . . . it took a couple of the torpedoes to send him off (1978).

torpedo juice noun Intoxicating drink extracted from torpedo fuel; any strong home-made alcoholic liquor. 1946–.

torqued /tɔːkt/ adjective US Upset, angry; excited, worked up; often followed by *up*.

1967–. M. MILLAR Can't I even ask a question without you getting all torqued up? (1979).

torso-tosser noun dated A female erotic dancer. 1927–. F. P. KEYES Barbara Villiers, a torsotosser who got to be no less than the Duchess of Cleveland (1954).

tosh[1] noun Rubbish, nonsense. 1892–. J. MORRIS Anna Novochka also denies it: pure tosh, she says (1985). [Origin unknown.]

tosh[2] noun Abbreviation of TOSHEROON noun. Also used *broadly* for two shillings, money. Also **tush.** 1912–. J. MACLAREN-ROSS Here's a tosh to buy yourself some beer (1961).

tosh[3] noun Brit Used as a form of address to a person, esp. a man, of unknown name. 1954–. M. KENYON 'Sortin' you out for a start, tosh!' came a voice (1978). [Origin uncertain; perh. from Scottish *tosh* adjective, neat, agreeable, friendly.]

tosheroon /tɒʃəˈruːn/ noun dated A half-crown. Also **tusheroon.** 1859–. G. ORWELL A tosheroon (half a crown) for the coat, two 'ogs for the trousers (1933). [Origin unknown.]

toss verb **1** to toss off trans. and intr. Brit To masturbate. 1879–. D. KAVANAGH Would you like me to toss you off? . . . It's ten if you're worried about the price (1981). **2** trans. US To search (a building or person) in the course of a police investigation. 1939–. E. MCBAIN We ought to try for an order to toss his apartment (1980). **3 to toss it in** NZ To finish, give up. 1956–. noun **4 not give** (or **care**) **a toss** to be indifferent; not care. 1876–. TIME OUT I don't give a toss whether he's black, white or purple (1973). **5** US A search of a building or person carried out by the police. 1970–.

tosser noun A contemptible or disgusting person. 1977–. P. INCHBALD It's a right pig's job. . . . Poor little tosser. As if he wasn't suffering enough already (1983). [Prob. from TOSS verb 1 + *-er*.]

toss-up noun Something dependent on chance. 1809–. WALL STREET JOURNAL Some said it's a toss-up whether oil prices go up or down (1989). [From the notion of tossing a coin.]

tot Brit. noun **1** An article collected from refuse. 1873–. verb intr. **2** To collect saleable items from refuse as an occupation. 1884–. M. RUSSELL I could earn as much, totting for the corporation (1976). Hence **totter,** noun A rag-and-bone collector. 1891–. [Origin unknown.]

total verb trans. mainly N Amer To wreck (esp. a car) completely. 1954–. GUARDIAN Daddy's BMW

top banana   top dog   top-off   topper   topping   tops

which she can drive any time she wants as long as she doesn't total it (1982).

totally adverb orig US As a simple intensive before an adjective: = really; utterly, completely. Often as **totally awesome, tubular,** etc. 1972–. WASHINGTON POST Scott Wallace is padded and pumped. . . . Awesome, man, totally awesome (1981).

tothersider noun Austral A person from one of the eastern states of Australia. c.1872–. SYDNEY MORNING HERALD Kalgoorlie was a huge seat with a big population of radical T'Othersider miners (1983). [From *tother* the other + *-sider*; from these states being viewed as on 'the other side' of the continent from Western Australia.]

toto /ˈtəʊtəʊ/ noun dated military A louse. 1918–29. RADIATOR Dr. Kent Hagler . . . saw no evidence of flea or toto (1918). [From French military slang *toto*.]

totty noun Brit **1** A girl or woman, esp. a sexually promiscuous one. 1890–. C. WATSON Showing off. Certainly, why not? There were a couple of totties just behind (1977). **2** People, esp. women, collectively regarded as objects of sexual desire; esp. in phr. *a bit of totty*. 1985–. S. INGHAM Clever me, I've scored the most glorious bit of totty (2000). [From earlier sense, a small child.]

touch verb trans. **1** To succeed in getting money from, esp. by borrowing; often followed by *for*. 1760–. G. GREENE 'If you would lend me a pound.' . . . Had she 'touched' Henry once too often? (1951). **2 to touch with (the end of) a barge-pole** to have anything to do with. 1893–. **3 to touch up** to touch or stroke (a person) in the area of the sex organs, as a sexual advance. 1903–. C. EGLETON Good-looking tart. . . . I wouldn't have minded her touching me up (1973). noun **4** An act of getting money from someone, esp. by persuasion or glib talk. 1914–. C. CHAPLIN It seemed obvious from the tone of the letter that it was all leading up to a 'touch'. So I thought I would take along $500 (1964). Hence **toucher**, noun A person who tries to get gifts or loans of money. 1919–. See also SOFT TOUCH noun.

tough adjective **1 tough shit** orig US Bad luck; usu. used ironically. Also **tough titty**. 1934–. A. BURGESS [I got] robbed and rumpled.— Tough titty she said with little sympathy (1971); J. CARROLL Tough shit, Lady! Morning wears to evening and hearts break (1978). **2** US, orig African-American Great, fine. 1937–. J. HUDSON Now my singing ain't none too tough, but I can sell some dope (1972).

toup /tuːp/ noun Abbreviation of 'toupee'. 1959–. P. BULL 'Say, Padre, is that a toup?' he naïvely enquires (1959).

towel verb trans. To beat, thrash; in Austral, usu. followed by *up*. 1705–. CUSACK & JAMES I think you deserve the V.C. for the way you towelled old Mole up (1951).

towelhead noun derog and offensive = RAG-HEAD noun. 1985–. OBSERVER If you did a brain scan of the British racist mentality, you find that, on the whole, we reckon the 'towelheads' have a pretty rough time of it (1991).

town clown noun US A policeman working in a village or small town. 1927–.

toy noun US A small tin or jar containing opium; the quantity of opium held in such a container. 1934–.

toy boy noun A woman's much younger male lover. 1981–. NEWS OF THE WORLD At 48 she is like a teenage girl again—raving it up with four different lovers including a toyboy of 27! (1987).

track verb **1 to track with** Austral To go out with (a member of the opposite sex); to court. 1910–. D. STUART Maybe some married couple'll move in with a daughter for you to track with (1978). noun **2** US A ballroom or dancehall. 1945–. MALCOLM X I dig your holding this all-originals scene at the track (1965). **3** A line on the skin made by repeated injections of an addictive drug; usu. in pl. 1964–. J. MILLS Whaddya mean, lemme see your tracks? I'm a pros, man, I shoot up in my thighs (1972).

trade noun **1 the trade: a** Prostitution. 1680–. **b** Brit The Submarine Service of the Royal Navy. 1916–. A. MELVILLE-ROSS It had been tacitly established in 'The Trade' that you did not mourn friends (1982). **c** The Secret Service. 1966–. **2** A prostitute or pick-up used by a homosexual; a homosexual partner; also, such people collectively. See also ROUGH TRADE noun. 1935–. JEREMY These are men who because they are too old, or unattractive, cannot pick up free 'trade' (1969). **3** services', orig RAF Aerial combat; enemy aircraft, esp. those engaged or lost in combat. 1942–. R. JOLLY Hello Silver Leader—we have trade for you at ninety miles to the north (1989).

train smash noun nautical Cooked tinned tomatoes, usu. with bacon. 1941–.

tramp noun **1** US A sexually promiscuous woman. 1922–. J. WELCOME You can usually tell . . . the nice girls from the tramps (1959). verb trans. **2** Austral To dismiss from employment. 1941–. M. WATTONE I went to the surface and

totally tothersider toto totty touch tough toup

immediately was tramped (sacked) (1982). [In sense 2, from earlier sense, to stamp on.]

trank noun Also **tranq**. Abbreviation of 'tranquillizer'. 1967–. A. SKINNER We'll have to go back to slipping tranks into his coffee (1980). Hence **tranked**, adjective Drugged by tranquillizers. 1972–. OBSERVER Lulling drugs are prescribed; tots shamble eerily about, tranked (1974).

trannie noun A transvestite. 1983–. GAY TIMES By 11pm they seem drunkenly immune to the influx of trannies, trendies, and other creatures of the night (1990). [From abbreviation of *transvestite + -ie*.]

tranny¹ noun Also **trannie**. mainly Brit A transistor radio. 1969–. LISTENER The Controller surely had her tranny in the shed with her (1976). [From abbreviation of *transistor + -y*.]

tranny² noun orig and mainly US The transmission of a motor vehicle (esp. of a truck or van). 1970–. BILLINGS (Montana) GAZETTE That was $1,500 or $1,700 damage to the tranny and the guy in the coffee pot cost $150 (1976). [From abbreviation of *transmission + -y*.]

trap noun **1** Now only Austral An officer of the law, esp. a policeman or detective. 1705–. K. GARVEY Muldoon heads for town and gets the traps (1978). **2** The mouth; esp. in phr. *to shut one's trap*, to keep silent. 1776–. M. DUFFY If Emily should open her great trap and spill the lot she could find herself deep in trouble (1981). **3** US, mainly criminals' A concealed compartment; a hiding-place for stolen, etc. goods, a stash. 1930–. TIME Other mobsters keep their escape money in bank safe-deposit boxes or hiding places called 'traps' (1977).

traps noun pl. orig US In a jazz or dance band, percussion instruments or devices (e.g. wood-blocks, whistles) used to produce a variety of special effects; these together with the standard jazz or dance band drum-kit. 1903–. [Origin uncertain; prob. some slang application of *trap* device or arrangement for capturing.]

trash noun **1** A worthless or disreputable person; now, usually, such people collectively; esp. in **white trash,** the poor white population in the Southern States of America, also (derog) white people in general. 1604–. SUNDAY TIMES He said that all the

Australians were white trash (1973). verb trans. **2** mainly US To vandalize (property or goods), esp. as a means of protest. 1970–. S. MARLOWE The room . . . had been trashed . . . by either the patrons . . . or by the police (1975). **3** US To injure seriously, destroy, or kill. 1973–. C. MCFADDEN Harvey threatened Spenser with grievous bodily harm. . . . 'Whaddaya wanna trash me for?' (1977). **4** mainly US To reduce or impair the quality of (a work of art, etc.); to expose the worthless nature of (something), to deprecate. 1975–. LONDON REVIEW OF BOOKS She writes . . . yet another trashing of radical chic. This might be more gripping had she herself not trashed radical chic already (1981).

trashed adjective mainly US Bungled, spoiled; ill-treated or injured; run-down. Often followed by an adverb. 1926–. TUCSON (Arizona) CITIZEN 'I've sat through this movie three times.' . . . 'In this trashed-out theater? The picture's that good?' 'It's a lousy picture! I can't get my feet unstuck from the floor!' (1979).

treff a secret rendezvous, esp. for the transfer of goods or information

tratt noun Also **trat**. Abbreviation of 'trattoria'. 1969–. GUARDIAN Mostly I mean the white-tiled tratts of SW 1, 3 and 7 (1970).

travel verb intr. To move quickly. 1884–. M. KENYON Mercy, the lorry's travelling. Foot down (1970).

treatment noun **the (full) treatment** the most complete or elaborate way of dealing with something; also, rough or aggressive handling. Cf. *the (whole) works* at WORK noun. 1950–. R. HILL I'm really getting the treatment, thought Pascoe. What does he expect from me? (1973).

tree noun **out of one's tree** US Irrational, mad. 1966–. N. THORNBURG 'We is duh [= the] loanees.' 'You're out of your tree' (1976).

treff noun espionage, orig US A secret rendezvous, esp. for the transfer of goods or information. 1943–. W. GARNER Make a list . . . of all the drops, pick-ups and treffs (1983). [From German *Treff* meeting(-place); cf. *Treffpunkt* rendezvous.]

trey noun Also **tray**. The number three, in various connections; a set of three; spec. a three-year period of imprisonment, (US) a three-dollar packet of a narcotic drug. 1887–. A. BURGESS 'I know all about you. You did a tray on the moor.' . . . 'It wasn't a tray . . . it was only a stretch' (1960); J. MILLS She wants to buy two treys, $3 bags of heroin (1972). [From earlier sense, the three at dice or cards, from Old French and Anglo-Norman *treis, trei* three (modern French *trois*).]

trick noun 1 US A robbery, theft; esp. in phr. *to turn a trick*, to commit a successful robbery. 1865–. D. MACKENZIE Campbell's claim was that he hadn't turned a trick in a year but the money had to be coming from somewhere (1979). 2 orig and mainly US a An act of sexual intercourse, spec. a prostitute's session with a client; esp. in phr. *to turn a trick*, to have sex with a casual partner, typically for money. 1926–. TIME Some of the young prostitutes live at home and turn tricks merely for pocket money (1977). b A casual sexual partner, spec. a prostitute's client. 1925–. B. TURNER I doubt there's one trick in twenty who isn't a married man (1968). 3 US A term of service on a ship; also, a term of imprisonment. 1933–. J. GORES He got caught . . . and did a little trick at Quentin (1975). adjective 4 orig US Stylish, fancy, 'neat'; smart, ingenious. 1951–. DIRT BIKES This new RM is more trick than ever. It's faster, sharper, it even handles better than before (1985). verb intr. 5 US To have casual sex *with*, esp. for money. 1965–. J. WAMBAUGH He tricked with a whore the night before in the Orchid Hotel (1973).

trick cyclist noun jocular A psychiatrist. 1930–. LISTENER Is neurotic, inadequate, unhappy . . . is up in Harley Street being sorted out by a trick cyclist (1977). [Alteration of *psychiatrist* noun.]

trickeration noun US, African-American A trick or stratagem. 1940–. [From *tricker(y + -ation*.]

trigger man noun mainly US A gunman; a hired thug or bodyguard. 1930–.

trim noun US A woman; sexual intercourse with a woman. 1955–. E. LACY The broad isn't worth it, no trim is (1962).

trip orig US. noun 1 A hallucinatory experience caused by a drug, esp. LSD. 1959–. SCIENTIFIC AMERICAN One of the volunteers had a bad trip, entering a panicky and nearly psychotic state (1971). 2 An experience, esp. a stimulating one. 1966–. MELODY MAKER The drums are bright shiny cab yellow by the way. It's a trip (1974). 3 An activity, attitude, or state of mind, esp. one that is delusory or self-indulgent. 1967–. R. L. SIMON I shouldn't bother—politics was a sixties trip (1979). verb intr. 4 To experience drug-induced hallucinations; sometimes followed by *out*. 1966–. J. SCOTT

Some of the people here were tripping already. Seemed a pity not to bust 'em (1980). Hence **tripper**, noun One who experiences hallucinatory effects of a drug. 1966–. B. MALAMUD One of the swamis there, a secret acid tripper, got on my nerves (1979). **trippy**, adjective Of or like a drug-induced hallucination. 1969–. NEW AGE Trippy music for meditation, massage, free-form movement, tantric loving, and a relaxing environment (1980). See also TRIPPED-OUT adjective.

tripe noun 1 Something of inferior quality. 1902–. W. H. CANAWAY The group of girls who were watching some tripe on television (1973). 2 Nonsense. 1935–. CHURCH TIMES Bomber Harris, who initially said, 'The idea is tripe', could be said to have been proved right (1993). [From earlier sense, stomach tissue used as food.]

tripe-hound noun derog 1 An unpleasant or contemptible person; also spec. a newspaper reporter or an informer. 1923–. N. MARSH You damned little tripe-hound (1937). 2 A dog; spec. (Austral and NZ), a sheep-dog. 1933–.

triple-A noun military, orig US Anti-aircraft artillery. 1983–. TIMES With triple A coming at you, it concentrates the mind wonderfully. It was the longest minute of my life (1991). [From earlier *AAA*.]

tripped-out adjective Under the influence of a hallucinogenic drug, esp. LSD. 1973–. [See TRIP noun and verb.]

trizzie noun Also **trizzy.** dated Austral A threepenny piece. 1941–. ACK ACK NEWS (Melbourne): Speaking of Christmas pudding, a certain very high ranker left behind nine-pence in trizzies in the pud (1942). [Prob. alteration of TREY noun.]

trog noun 1 An obnoxious person, a lout, a hooligan. 1956–. GRANTA The scowling vandals, bus-stop boogies, and soccer trogs malevolently lining the streets (1983). 2 NZ A large overhanging rock that offers shelter. 1958–. NEW ZEALAND LISTENER They found a possie in a bit of a trog and boiled-up (1971). [Abbreviation of *troglodyte* noun, cave-dweller.]

trog verb intr., Brit To proceed heavily or laboriously; to plod, trudge; also to walk casually, stroll. 1984–. MIZZ Upset-the-apple-cart *Uranus* trogs over your love-planet Venus this year, and there are more ups and downs to come (1989). [Origin uncertain; perh. influenced by *trudge, traipse, slog, jog,* etc.]

troll verb intr. Of a homosexual: to walk the streets, or 'cruise', in search of a sexual encounter. 1967–. A. WILSON At first . . . I just got

trolley

myself picked up. . . . But later I started trolling (1967). [From earlier sense, to saunter; cf. also the earlier sense, to fish, angle.]

trolley noun **off one's trolley** crazy. 1896–. N. R. NASH If you suspect Patty, you're off your trolley! (1949).

trolleyed adjective Brit Very drunk. 1992–. G. HILLS Didn't mind him lying trolleyed on my lap (1997). [Origin uncertain; cf. *off one's trolley* at TROLLEY noun.]

trollies noun Also **trolleys**. Brit, mainly schoolgirls' Women's underpants. 1934–. B. PYM I bought a peach coloured vest and trollies to match (1934). [Perh. from *trolly* noun, type of lace.]

trombenik noun Also **trombenick**. US A boaster, braggart; any idle, dissolute, or conceited person. 1931–. J. HELLER The gaudy militarism of the portly *trombenik* was more Germanic than Jewish (1979). [From Yiddish, from *tromba* trumpet, horn + *-nik*, suffix denoting a person associated with a specified thing or quality.]

troppo adjective Austral Mentally ill, esp. from exposure to a tropical climate; esp. in phr. *to go troppo*. 1941–. B. HUMPHRIES Am I going troppo? Mum's gettin' hitched again? (1979). [From *trop(ic* or *trop(ical* + *-o.*]

trot¹ noun **1** US A literal translation of a text used by students. 1891–. TIMES LITERARY SUPPLEMENT The translations are rarely better than lame trots (1984). **2 the trots** diarrhoea. 1904–. C. MCCULLOUGH 'Go easy on the water at first,' he advised. 'Beer won't give you the trots' (1977). verb trans. **3** NZ To go out with (a woman), to court. 1946–. B. CRUMP I didn't know she was going steady with you. . . . If I'd known you were trotting her [etc.] (1964). [In sense 3, from earlier British *to trot out*, to escort, to court.]

Trot² noun and adjective mainly derog Abbreviation of 'Trotskyist, Trotskyite'. 1962–. J. LE CARRÉ Some kind of loony Trot splinter group (1983).

trouble and strife noun Rhyming slang for 'wife'. 1908–. G. FISHER It's the old trouble and strife—wife. I want to see her all right (1977).

trousers noun **(to catch) with one's trousers down** in a state of embarrassing unpreparedness. 1966–. J. GARDNER A job. . . . Took us by surprise: with the trousers down (1980).

trout noun derog A woman, esp. an old or bad-tempered one; esp. in phr. *old trout.*

1897–. S. GIBBONS 'Serve her right, the old trout,' muttered Flora (1932).

truck verb intr. US **1** To proceed; to go, stroll. 1925–. UNITED STATES **1980/81** You'll still find plenty of people trucking through the streets in flannel shirts, blue jeans, cowboy hats, and boots (1979). **2 to keep on trucking** to persevere: a phrase of encouragement. 1972–. NEW YORKER Feels like I frosted the ends of my toes a bit, but they're far from my heart, so I'll keep on truckin (1977). [In sense 1, from earlier sense, to go in a truck.]

trump noun Austral and NZ A person in authority. 1925–. SUN (Sydney): Officers are trumps, and reinforcements reos (1942). [From earlier sense, card belonging to a suit which ranks above others.]

Trustafarian noun Brit A young person from a wealthy background who affects the attitudes and lifestyle of the inner-city ghetto. 1992–. [Blend of *trust (fund)* and *rastafarian.*]

try verb **to try it on** to try to outwit or deceive someone; also, to test someone's patience. 1811–. MANDY Huh! Thought you'd try it on, eh? Beat it, the pair of you—I've seen that trick before (1989).

try-on noun Brit An act of 'trying it on'; an attempt to deceive. 1874–. P. TOWNEND It was only a try-on, to see if I would react (1959).

T.S. noun and int US services' Abbreviation of *tough shit* (see TOUGH adjective 1). 1944–.

T.T.F.N. dated Brit Abbreviation for 'ta-ta for now' (a catch-phrase popularized by the 1940s BBC radio programme *Itma*). 1948–. OBSERVER JY [i.e. Jimmy Young] said TTFN to Mr Healey (1976).

tub noun mainly criminals' A bus; **to work the tubs,** to pick pockets on buses or at bus-stops. 1929–.

tube noun **1** A cigarette. 1946–. HIGH TIMES Filter tipped tubes a smoother smoke to the very end (1975). **2 the tube** orig and mainly US Television. See also BOOB TUBE noun. 1959–. SUNDAY NEWS (New York): She . . . is making a name for herself as a singer on the tube (1965). **3 down the tube(s)** lost, finished, in trouble; esp. in phr. *to go down the tube(s).* 1963–. LISTENER The smile on Sir Freddie's face the week before it was revealed that he was down the tubes to the extent of something over £270 million was that of a consummate actor (1982). **4** Austral A can (or sometimes a bottle) of beer. 1964–. J. POWERS You can just sit back an'

trolley trolleyed trollies trombenik troppo trout

suck on your tube an' watch (1973). **5** pl. The Fallopian tubes; often in phr. *to have one's tubes tied*, etc., to undergo sterilization by tubal ligation. 1970–. K. MILLETT Too old to have more children, afraid of pregnancy and now tying her tubes (1974). verb trans. and intr. **6** US To fail, to perform badly (in). 1966–.

tube steak noun US A hot dog, a frankfurter. 1963–.

tubular adjective orig and mainly US Often in phr. *totally tubular*. **1** surfing Of a wave: hollow and well-curved, and so excellent for riding. 1982–. **2** Wonderful, amazing; fantastic. 1982–. HERBECK & ROSS Donatello was at a loss. His brothers continued to top each other: 'Tubular!' 'Radical!' 'Dynamite!' (1990).

tuchas, tuchus variants of TOCHUS noun.

tucker verb trans. US To tire, weary; esp. as **tuckered out** adjective, exhausted. *c.*1840–. [From *tuck* verb, to put tucks in.]

tucker noun Austral and NZ Food. 1850–. S. LOCKE ELLIOTT We've all been off our tucker with the worry (1977). Hence **tuckerless**, adjective Without food. 1910–. [From earlier obs. sense, a meal, from *tuck* verb, to consume (as in *to tuck away*, *to tuck in*).]

tug[1] Brit public schools'. noun **1** At Eton, a student on the foundation, a colleger as opposed to an oppidan; in wider use, a studious or academic pupil, a swot. 1864–. adjective **2** (Esp. at Winchester) ordinary, commonplace. 1890–. C. P. SNOW No one on earth could call Jago tug. . . . He's the least commonplace of men (1951). [Origin uncertain; adjective perh. not the same word.]

tug[2] noun Austral, dated A rogue or sharper; also, an uncouth or rowdy fellow, a larrikin. 1896–. A. REID So that chaps could know why a top-notch tug Can work 'his' ramps in a card-room snug (1933). [Origin uncertain; perh. related to *tug* verb, to pull or move by pulling.]

tumble verb **1** trans. To have sex with. 1602–. R. LEWIS Tommy Elias had tumbled the schoolgirl in the ferns (1976). **2a** intr. To grasp the meaning or hidden implication of an idea, circumstance, etc.; often followed by *to*, *that*. 1846–. NEW STATESMAN By the time you tumble that your drum has been turned over, we're miles away (1962). **b** trans. To detect, see through. 1901–. J. BARNETT Have to have words with Simonson, in case he has tumbled the tattoo (1981). noun **3a: to take a tumble (to oneself)** orig US To realize the facts of one's situation. 1877–. M. GEE After a while I give up,

and I take a tumble to what's happening. I'm getting the bum's rush (1959). **b** US A sign of recognition or acknowledgement, a response; esp. in phr. *to give a tumble*. 1921–. NEW YORK TIMES BOOK REVIEW If the right boy won't give you [i.e. a girl] a tumble, you've got a problem (1953). **5** An act of sexual intercourse; esp. in phr. *to give a tumble*. 1903–. J. TRENCH He was . . . giving la Vitrey a tumble somewhere (1954).

tummler /ˈtʊmlə(r)/ noun Also **toomler, tumeler**. orig and mainly US A jokester, someone who plays the fool; spec. a person responsible for entertaining the patrons at a hotel or the like. 1966–. L. M. FEINSILVER Danny Kaye and other entertainers got their starts as tumelers in the Catskills (1970). [Yiddish, from German *tummeln* verb, to stir.]

tuneage noun orig US Music. 1985–. D. COUPLAND Extremely torrid tuneage from London beckoned—songs about money written by machines (1992).

tunket /ˈtʊŋkɪt/ noun Also **tunkett**. US orig dialect Euphemistic substitution for *hell*, esp. in phr. *who* (*what, why*, etc.) *in tunket*. 1871–. E. GRAHAM 'And why not, in tunket?' she says (1951). [Origin unknown.]

tup verb trans. Of a man: to copulate with (a woman). 1970–. R. JEFFRIES You wouldn't tup her? . . . Neither of us cut out for adultery (1976). [From earlier sense, of a ram, to copulate with (a ewe).]

turd noun A contemptible person. 1936–. HOWARD & WEST A purple-faced steward went up to a scrawny, pale heckler and yelled, 'Shut up, you ignorant turd!' (1965). [From earlier sense, a piece of excrement.]

turf noun **1 on the turf** working as a prostitute. 1860–. J. O'DONOGHUE 'I might have been one of Ma Dolma's brasses for all you know.' . . . 'Come off it. You've never been on the turf' (1984). **2** orig and mainly US **a** The streets controlled by a juvenile street gang and regarded by them as territory. 1953–. H. SALISBURY These blocks constituted the 'turf' of a well-known street-gang (1959). **b** The part of a city or other area in which a criminal, detective, etc. operates. 1962–. D. BENNETT Special Branch would not want to be involved in a killing so far from their own turf (1976). **c** A person's sphere of influence or activity. 1970–. E. LATHEN They think that, on their own turf, they can overawe Ackerman and Werzel (1982).

tube steak tubular tuchas, tuchus tucker tunket

Turk noun Also **turk.** mainly US, usu derog
A person of Irish birth or descent. 1914–.
OBSERVER Their backs are to the wall in a desperate
tyre-chain feudal war to protect the integrity of
their declining manor against the invasions of
'bubbles and squeaks' (Greeks and Cypriots),
'turks' (Irish) and 'spades' (coloureds) (1959).
[Perh. from Irish *torc* noun, boar, hog,
influenced by *Turk* noun, Turkish person; but
cf. TURKEY noun 3.]

turkey noun **1** N Amer and Austral A bundle
or holdall carried by itinerant workers,
vagrants, etc. 1893–. R. SYMONS The cowboys'
'turkeys'—as they called their bedrolls, in which
were wrapped their personal possessions such as
tobacco—when the outfit was on the move
(1963). **2** US An inferior or unsuccessful film
or theatrical production, a flop; hence,
anything disappointing or of inferior value.
1927–. H. FAST 'Have you ever thought of selling
the place?' Jake asked . . . 'Oh? And who the hell
would buy this turkey?' (1977). **3** US = TURK
noun; spec. an Irish immigrant in the US.
1932–. **4** US A stupid, slow, inept, or
otherwise worthless person. 1951–. TAMPA
(Florida) TRIBUNE I decided I had had enough of
that turkey (1984). See also COLD TURKEY noun,
to talk turkey at TALK verb.

turkey shoot noun US A military
engagement in which the enemy are easily
routed; a usage brought to prominence in
the Gulf War (1991). 1947–. NEW YORKER The
Administration was . . . coming under substantial
fire for engaging in 'overkill': Kuwait had been
liberated; tens of thousands of Iraqi soldiers had
surrendered; and it was clearly no contest. Even
American soldiers were expressing some
revulsion at being engaged in a 'turkey shoot'
(1991). [From the fact that the turkey, a
cumbersome bird, often presents a sitting
target.]

turn verb **1 to turn** (something or someone)
up trans. **a** To give (something) up, discard,
abandon; now only in imperative phr. *turn it
up!*, stop it! 1621–. J. B. PRIESTLEY Turn it up, will
you. . . . You're arguing with yourself (1945).
b To cause (someone) to vomit; to nauseate.
S. GIBBONS Turns you up, don't it, seein' terday's
dinner come in 'anging around someone's neck
(1932). **2 to turn up one's toes** to die. 1851–.
3 to turn (something or someone) **over** trans.
a to search (a person); to ransack (a place),
usu. in order to commit robbery. 1859–.
L. MEYNELL What about that girl's bedroom that
got turned over? (1981). **b** To distress
(someone) greatly, upset, affect with nausea.
1865–. NEW SOCIETY Escalope I had, though what

they do to those calves turns me over (1972).
4 to turn (someone) **on** orig US **a** trans. To
excite; to stimulate the interest of, esp.
sexually. 1903–. NEWS OF THE WORLD Dinner jacket,
wing collar, and bow tie may not sound the sort
of gear to turn on a teeny bopper (1976). **b** trans.
and intr. To intoxicate or become intoxicated
with drugs. 1953–. R. JAFFE She walked in while I
was turning on so I offered her some [marijuana]
(1979). Cf. TURN-ON noun. **5 to turn** (someone)
off trans. To repel; to cause to lose interest.
1965–. DAILY TELEGRAPH [He] is kinky for short-
back-and-sides and turned off by long-haired
television performers (1972). Cf. TURN-OFF noun.

turn-off noun Something that repels or
disgusts one. 1975–. NEW YORK TIMES Patrons
dined on cervelle Grenobloise. 'Sounds better in
French,' said the chef. . . . 'Brains is a turn-off'
(1975). [From *to turn off* (see TURN verb 5).]

turn-on noun The act or an instance of
turning someone on; a drug-taker's 'trip';
something which or someone who arouses
interest, enthusiasm, or sexual response.
1969–. D. HOCKNEY A medieval city is unstimulating
to me, whereas to others it might be a great
turn-on (1982). [From *to turn on* (see TURN
verb 4).]

turps noun Austral Alcoholic drink, esp.
beer; esp. in phr. *on the turps*. 1865–. S. THORNE
Dan was a good bloke, but a terror on the turps.
Once he started on rum—look out! (1980).
[From earlier sense, turpentine.]

turtle noun = TURTLE-DOVE noun; usu. pl.
1893–. J. CURTIS Got any turtles? The Gilt Kid,
having no gloves, answered: 'No, but I'll buy
a pair' (1936).

turtle-dove noun Rhyming slang for
'glove'; usu. pl. 1857–.

tush /tʊʃ/ noun mainly N Amer The bottom,
backside. Also **tushie, -y.** 1962–. PIX (Australia):
Pretty young girls who walk around with . . . their
tushes out there asking for it (1970).
[Abbreviation or diminutive of TOCHUS noun.]

TV noun orig and mainly N Amer Abbreviation of
'transvestite'. 1965–. THE MAGAZINE We get a lot
of TVs in and a few of the leather boys of course
(1983).

twang noun dated, Austral Opium. 1898–.
T. RONAN The honest Chinese limits himself to his
one pipe of 'Twang' per night (1945). [Prob.
back-formation from *Twankay* noun, a variety
of green tea.]

twat /twɒt, twæt/ noun Also **twot(t).** **1** The
female genitals. 1656–. P. WHITE This young

thing with the swinging hair and partially revealed twat (1973). **2** A despicable or foolish person. 1929–. P. ROTH Here comes another dumb and stupid remark out of that brainless twat (1969). [Origin unknown.]

tweedle criminals'. noun **1** A counterfeit ring; hence, a swindle (involving counterfeit goods), a fiddle, a racket. 1890–. NEW SOCIETY Then it was back to the shop for the 'tweedle'—for the switch (1982). verb intr. **2** To swindle, practise confidence tricks. 1925–. Hence **tweedler,** noun A swindler, confidence trickster. 1925–. [Prob. variant of *twiddle* verb, to twist.]

twenty noun Citizens' Band Radio, orig and mainly US (One's) location or position. 1975–. CITIZENS' BAND Thank you Silver Fox for your excellent work in what is a very important area, with . . . all the fender-benders that occur around that twenty (1985). [Shortened from *10–20* in the 'ten-code', a police (and subsequently CB) communication code.]

twenty-three skiddoo int dated US Go away, scram. 1926–. [Origin unknown; cf. SKIDOO verb.]

twerp noun Also **twirp**. A stupid or objectionable person. 1874–. S. BARSTOW If she turns me down I'll look more of a twerp than ever (1960). [Origin unknown; the suggestion that it is from the name of T. W. Earp, an early 20th-cent. Oxford undergraduate, is refuted by evidence of its late 19th-cent. use.]

twicer noun A crook, liar, cheat; a deceitful or cunning person. 1924–. E. WINGFIELD-STRATFORD The recent dismissal . . . of that elderly twicer, Sir Harry Vane (1949). [From earlier sense, one who does something twice; perh. from the notion of duplicity.]

twig verb **1** trans. To perceive, catch sight of; to recognize. 1796–. **2** trans. and intr. To understand, to realize the true significance (of). 1815–. [From earlier sense, to watch; ultimate origin unknown.]

twinkie noun Also **twinky**. US A male homosexual; an effeminate man. Also **twink**. 1963–. [Prob. related to *twink* verb and *twinkle* verb, though popularly associated with the proprietary *Twinkie*, a brand of cupcake with a creamy filling.]

twirl noun **1** criminals' A skeleton key. 1879–. P. KINSLEY She scarcely heard him open the old lock . . . with the set of 'twirls' (1980). **2** A prison warder. 1891–. JOHN O' LONDON'S Prison officers . . . are sometimes referred to as *twirls*

(1962). [Semantic development analogous to SCREW noun.]

twirler noun = TWIRL noun 1. 1921–. J. ASHFORD Weir, who was an expert with the twirlers, forced the lock in six seconds (1974).

twist¹ verb trans. **1** To cheat, to defraud. 1914–. PEOPLE Don't imagine that all the boys in the trade are out to twist you (1956). noun **2 the twist** criminals' Cheating, dishonesty; treachery; also in phrs. *on, at the twist.* 1933–. J. WAINWRIGHT Silver-smiths, . . . one of 'em on the twist (1977). **3 round the twist** Brit Crazy. 1960–. D. BAGLEY I swear Ogilvie thought I was going round the twist (1977). See also **to get one's knickers in a twist** at KNICKERS noun.

twist² noun mainly US, often derog Short for TWIST-AND-TWIRL noun. 1926–. R. MACDONALD I hate to see it happen to a pretty little twist like Fern (1953).

twist-and-twirl noun mainly US, often derog A young woman. 1924–. [Rhyming slang for *girl* noun.]

twister noun **1** Brit A swindler; a dishonest person. 1897–. J. B. PRIESTLEY If you ask me, he looks a rotten twister—bit of a crook or something (1930). **2** US A key. 1940–. **3** US **a** A spasm experienced by a drug-taker as a withdrawal symptom. 1936–. **b** An intravenous injection of esp. a mixture of drugs. 1938–.

twit noun mainly Brit A silly or foolish person. 1934–. F. RAPHAEL Don't be a twit, Sid (1960). [Perh. from *twit* verb, to reproach, taunt.]

twitched adjective Irritable, rattled. 1959–. S. JACKMAN The C.O.'s in there and he's a bit twitched (1981).

two adjective **in two ups** Austral In a very short time, immediately. 1934–. J. MORRISON Too close to dark now, Mister, but we'll have you out of that in two ups in the morning (1967).

two and eight noun Brit An agitated, distressed, dishevelled, etc. condition. 1938–. M. CECIL Poor old Clinker! Bet she's in a proper two-and-eight! (1960). [Rhyming slang for *state* noun.]

two-bit adjective US Cheap, petty, insignificant. 1932–. T. WILLIS Some other two-bit General will try shooting us up (1978). [From *two bits* twenty-five cents or two-eighths of a dollar.]

twoc verb Brit To steal (a car). 1990–. Hence **twocker** noun. 1990–. Also **twocking** noun.

tweedle twenty twenty-three skiddoo twerp twicer

1991–. [From the initial letters of *take without (the) owner's consent*.]

twofer noun Also **too-, -fah, -for, -fur**. US
1 A cigar sold at two for a quarter; hence, any cheap cigar. *a*.1911–. P. G. WODEHOUSE I found him . . . lying on the bed with his feet on the rail, smoking a toofah (1923). **2** A coupon that entitles someone to buy two tickets for a theatre show for the price of one. 1948–.
3 A black woman appointed to a post, the appointment being seen as evidence of both racial and sexual equality of opportunity. 1977–. DAILY TELEGRAPH Personnel departments [in the United States] are told always to try and hire a 'toofer' (1979). [From *two* + (representation of) *for* prep.]

twopenny /tʌpənɪ/ noun Also **tuppenny**. **1** dated The head. 1859–. C. E. MONTAGUE 'Into it, Jemmy,' I yelled. 'Into the sewer and tuck in your tuppenny' (1928). adjective **2 not give** (or **care**) **a twopenny damn** Brit to be completely indifferent to something; not care. 1897–. D. K. CAMERON It was rich in its lairds, men who . . . gave not a tuppenny damn . . . for anybody (1980). [In sense 1, from *twopenny loaf* = *loaf of bread*, rhyming slang for *head*: cf. LOAF noun 1.]

twopenny upright noun A prostitute. 1958–. MALEDICTA At the turn of the century, an Iowa woman was awarded $200 for being called a 'whore' while in England, at about the same time, a woman was denied any award for being called a 'two-penny upright' (1978). [From the amount charged for an act of sexual intercourse standing up out of doors.]

two-pot screamer
someone who becomes easily drunk

two-pot screamer noun Austral
Someone who becomes easily drunk. 1959–.
J. DE HOGG It says experienced and sober, ya bloody two-part screamer (1972).

two-time verb trans. orig US **1** To deceive or be unfaithful to (esp. a partner or lover). 1924–. SUNDAY TIMES Judith Exner . . . two-timed the late President John Kennedy with a leader of organised crime (1981). **2** To swindle, double-cross. 1959–.

tyee /taɪi/ noun Also **tyhee**. N Amer A chief; a person of distinction. 1792–. H. MARRIOTT The agricultural tyees in both Canada and the United States have taken a wise view (1966). [From Chinook jargon.]

tyke noun **1** Brit A person from Yorkshire. *a*.1700–. P. RYAN The Yorkshire terrier seems fitter mate for a volatile Taffy than for a taciturn Tyke (1967). **2** Austral and NZ derog and offensive A Roman Catholic. 1902–. D. WHITTINGTON Too many bloody tykes in the Labor Party (1957). [From earlier sense, dog, from Old Norse *tík* noun, bitch; in sense 2, assimilated from TAIG noun.]

type noun A person, esp. of the stated sort or belonging to the stated organization. 1922–. D. E. WESTLAKE I was not alone in the room. Three army types were there . . . tall, fat, khaki-uniformed (1971).

typewriter noun A machine-gun or sub-machine-gun. Cf. WOODPECKER noun. 1915–. P. EVANS Al Capone['s] . . . torpedoes . . . were mean with a Thompson 'type-writer' (1973). [From the sound of its rapid and often irregular firing.]

U-ey /ˈjuːiː/ noun Also **uy, youee.** Austral A U-turn. 1973–. TRUCKIN' LIFE The turning circle is 15.2 m. . . . Not natural U-ey material but adequate for a six tonner (1983). [From U(-*turn* + −*y*.]

uglies noun **the uglies: a** Depression, bad temper. 1846–. N. LAST A gloom seems over us all. I've shaken off my fit of the uglies, but I felt I'd just like to crawl into a hole (1939). **b** Nitrogen narcosis affecting deep-sea divers. 1974–.

umbrella noun US, military A parachute. 1933–. J. DITTON It takes ages to come down on an umbrella. . . . Then you have to get rid of the chute (1980).

ump noun mainly US Abbreviation of 'umpire', spec. in baseball. Also **umps.** 1915–. ARIZONA DAILY STAR A few bad calls by the rookie umps will no doubt be cause for more outcries from the baseball world (1979).

umpty adjective Unpleasant. 1948–. C. FREMLIN This rather umpty friend of his (1980). [Apparently from obs. military slang *umpty iddy* unwell, from *umpty* and *iddy*, fanciful verbal representations of respectively the dash and the dot in Morse code.]

uncle noun **1** A pawnbroker. In early usage, usu. preceded by a possessive adjective. 1756–. TIMES 'Uncle' is changing his image. His clients may still be in dire financial straits, but they are no longer the traditional working class (1988). **2** cap, US (**The members of**) a federal agency. 1849–. W. BURROUGHS 'He belongs to Uncle, now,' said the [police] captain to my wife as they left the house (1953). **3 to say** (**cry, holler,** etc.) **uncle** N Amer To acknowledge defeat, to cry for mercy. 1918–. D. DELMAN 'Stop it, darling, please.' 'Say uncle.' 'Uncle' (1972). [In sense 2, short for *Uncle Sam* the US; in sense 3, perh. from Irish *anacol* deliverance, mercy, assimilated to English *uncle* parent's brother.]

Uncle Ned noun **1** Rhyming slang for 'bed'. Also **uncle.** 1925–. J. SCOTT You did right, shoving him back in his uncle (1982). **2** Rhyming slang for 'head'. 1955–. LISTENER I have spent an hour fixing the big, loose curls on top of my Uncle Ned (1964).

Uncle Tom derog, orig US. noun **1** A black man considered to be servile, cringing, etc. 1922–. NEW YORKER Pryor goes through his part pop-eyed, playing Uncle Tom for Uncle Toms (1977). verb intr. **2** To act like an Uncle Tom. 1947–. PUNCH An obligation . . . applies constantly to all underdog groups, constantly tempted by rewards to uncle-tom, to pull the forelock

(1967). [From the name of the hero of the novel *Uncle Tom's Cabin* (1851–2), by Harriet Beecher Stowe.]

uncool adjective Unrelaxed; unpleasant; (of jazz) not 'cool'. Cf. COOL adjective. 1953–. IT The whole place [i.e. Turkey] is very very uncool. The Turks seem to be ready to turn with malicious vengeance on young Europeans for the least (often no) provocation (1968).

undercart noun An aircraft's undercarriage. 1934–. N. SHUTE Honey had ruined a Reindeer at Gander by pulling up its undercart (1948).

undercover noun An undercover agent. 1962–. J. MILLS She was a very good detective. She was a narcotics undercover (1972).

underfug noun Brit, public schools' An undervest; also, underpants. 1924–. B. MARSHALL The matron kept everybody's spare shirts, underfugs and towels and dished clean ones out once a week (1946). [From *under-* + *fug* noun, stuffy atmosphere.]

underground mutton noun Austral A rabbit; rabbit meat. 1919–.

uni /ˈjuːniː/ noun mainly Austral and NZ Abbreviation of 'university'. 1898–. AUSTRALIAN (Sydney): Unis look to industry for more funds (1984).

unreal adjective **a** mainly US and Austral So good or impressive as to seem incredible; remarkable, amazing, fantastic. 1965–. TRUCKIN' LIFE I reckon your magazine is unreal. I've never missed an issue for the last four years (1986). **b** US In a negative sense: bizarre, unbelievably difficult or awful. 1966–. NEW YORKER In the summer the dust and the flies are unreal (1986).

unshirted hell noun US Serious trouble; 'a bad time'. 1932–. H. KISSINGER I've been catching unshirted hell every half-hour from the

President who says we're not tough enough (1979).

unstick verb intr. **1** To leave the ground, take off. 1912–. J. GARDNER The British Airways Trident unstuck from the cold stressed-concrete (1977). noun **2** The moment of take-off. 1926–.

unstuck adjective **1** to come unstuck to come to grief, to fail. 1911–. LISTENER This is where the theory comes unstuck (1958). **2** to get, come, etc., unstuck to get into the air, to take off. 1913–.

unt variant of OONT noun.

untogether adjective Poorly co-ordinated; not in full control of one's faculties. 1969–. J. COOPER She felt staggeringly untogether . . . She had a blinding headache (1976).

up prep **1** Of a man: having sex with. 1937–. J. PATRICK We've aw been up her (1973). **2 up yours** an exclamation of contemptuous rejection (often accompanied by a rude gesture). Also **up you.** 1956–. J. SYMONS She made a V sign at the audience, said distinctly 'Up yours' (1975). noun **3** US A prospective customer. 1942–. NEW YORK TIMES The hottest salesman who ever turned a looker into an up (1949). **4** = UPPER² noun 1. 1969–. P. G. WINSLOW 'She did take pills, ups, if you get me.' Capricorn understood her to mean amphetamines (1978). [In sense 2, shortened from *up your arse* and similar expressions; in sense 3, perh. from the sales assistant having to stand 'up' to go and serve a customer.]

up-and-downer noun A fight or violent quarrel. Also **up-and-a-downer, upper and downer.** 1927–. P. MACDONALD I 'appened to hear them in a proper up-and-downer (1932). [From obs. *up-and-down* adjective, applied to violent, brawling fights + *-er*.]

upchuck verb intr. US To vomit. 1960–. T. WELLS Anyway, Natalie had to upchuck, it's that kind of bug (1967). [Cf. *to throw up* (THROW verb 1).]

upfront Also **up-front, up front.** adverb **1** At the front, in front. 1937–. **2** Of payments: in advance, initially. Also, openly, frankly. 1972–. S. WILSON 'How much cash did you have in mind?' 'Five thousand, up front.' 'I beg your pardon?' 'In advance' (1982). adjective **3** That is in the forefront; honest, open, frank; (of money) paid in advance. 1967–.

upper¹ noun **1** Brit, public schools' A pupil of the upper school. 1929–. **2** An upper-class person. 1955–. ECONOMIST The genuine uppers'

genuine feeling of superiority (1968). [From *upper* adjective.]

upper² noun **1** A drug, esp. an amphetamine, often in the form of a pill, which has a stimulant or euphoric effect. 1968–. D. SHANNON I want all your pills, man, all the uppers and downers you got (1981). **2** Something that stimulates or energizes. 1973–. TIME Singing is a real upper. It makes me feel dizzy and energetic (1977). [From *up* verb + *-er*.]

upper storey noun The head as the repository of sanity or intelligence. 1885–. I. & P. OPIE A person who is 'wanting in the upper storey' is . . . daffy (1959).

uppie noun = UPPER² noun 1. 1966–. J. F. BURKE There's nothing in the box but a few uppies. I haven't got a regular subscription (1975). [From *up* verb + *-ie*.]

upstairs adverb Mentally, 'in the head'; mainly in phrases indicating weak mental capacity. 1932–. G. W. BRACE He just ain't right upstairs (1952).

upstate adverb US In prison. 1934–. E. MCBAIN She got married while I was upstate doing time (1977). [From the earlier sense, remote from centres of population; from the placement of prisons in areas remote from large cities.]

upter adjective Also **upta.** Austral Bad, hopeless, no good. 1918–. J. CLEARY 'How you going?' 'Upta. I've lost on every race so far' (1947). [From the Austral. phr. *up to putty* in a mess.]

uptight adjective orig US **1a** Nervously tense or angry. 1934–. C. YOUNG He looked worried. Really worried. As the kids say, he was up-tight (1969). **b** Rigidly conventional. 1969–. E. M. BRECHER They tended to swing in the same socially correct, formal, 'up-tight' style they followed in their other activities (1970). **2** Excellent, fine. 1962–. COURIER-MAIL (Brisbane): Disc jockeys . . . talk in a kind of sub-English . . . as in 'All right baby sock-it-to-me it's allright uptight yeah' (1969). **3** Having little or no money; broke. 1967–.

upya int Also **upyer.** mainly Austral Expressing contemptuous rejection. 1941–. D. NILAND No, he said, I won't truckle to you. Upya for the rent (1955). [Alteration of *up you* (see *up yours* at UP prep 2).]

urger noun Austral Someone who obtains money illegally or by deceit, esp. as a tipster

unstick unstuck unt untogether up-and-downer

at a racecourse. 1919–. BULLETIN (Sydney): He was a tout or an urger, I gathered. 'Mixed up in racecourses,' was the way she put it (1934).

use verb **1** intr. To take drugs. 1953–. K. ORVIS Almost twenty-four hours . . . since I've had a fix. . . . Are you the only one? . . . You forget I use, too (1962). **2 could use** would be glad to have; would be improved by having. 1956–. R. GODDEN 'I could use a gin,' said Bella (1961). Hence **user,** noun One who takes drugs

regularly. 1935–. EASYRIDERS No boozers or heavy users (1983).

U.S. of A. noun Abbreviation of 'United States of America'. 1973–.

ute /juːt/ noun mainly Austral and NZ A small truck for carrying light loads. 1943–. NZ FARMER Now Nissan has followed it with a tough new 4 × ute, known at this stage just as the 720 (1984). [Abbreviation of *utility* noun, as in *utility truck* or *vehicle*.]

upter   uptight   upya   urger   use   U.S. of A.   ute

vac noun Brit A vacation, esp. a university vacation. 1709–. CATHOLIC WEEKLY Others lectured to working men in the vacs (1906). [Shortening.]

vag Austral and N Amer. noun **1** Abbreviation of: **a** 'vagrancy'; phr. **on the vag**, on a charge of vagrancy. 1859–. K. S. PRICHARD Was you on the game, love? Or did they get you on the vag? (1959). **b** 'vagrant'. 1868–. M. RUTHERFORD The vag waited but the policeman just walked past him to a car (1979). verb trans. **2** To charge with vagrancy. 1876–. P. READ I walked into town . . . and I got vagged. . . . Got ten days out of it (1984).

vamoose /vævmuːs/ verb intr. orig and mainly US To depart hurriedly; often in imperative. 1834–. J. REEVES 'See anyone?' asked Winston. 'Not a soul. Whoever it was has vamoosed' (1958). [From Spanish vamos let us go.]

vapourware noun computing, orig US A piece of software or other product which is publicized or marketed before it has been developed commercially (or at all). 1984–. SAN JOSE (California) MERCURY Perhaps the most heralded piece of 'vaporware' in recent history is vapor no longer. As of now you can buy Lotus Development Corp's 1-2-3/G (1990). [Humorously from vapour, because the product is only a misty presence as yet, + -ware (as in hardware, software, etc.).]

Vatican roulette noun jocular The rhythm method of birth control, as permitted by the Roman Catholic Church. 1962–. [By analogy from Russian roulette; from the method's unpredictable efficacy.]

veddy adverb Representing a childish, affected, or (US) British pronunciation of very. 1859–. PUBLISHER'S WEEKLY Note humorous anachronism as Dylan's fish-girl pours him tea from a bone china teapot—veddy British! (1975)

veejay noun Also **VJ.** mainly US One who presents a programme of (pop music) videos, esp. on television. 1982–. [From the pronunciation of the initial letters of video jockey, after DJ (= disc jockey).]

veeno variant of VINO noun.

veep noun US A vice-president. 1949–. FORTUNE His Makati business club constituents would be happy to nominate E.Z. for veep (1983). [Shortened from the pronunciation of the initial letters V.P.]

veg /vedʒ/ verb intr. Also **vedge.** orig and mainly US Usu. with out. To 'vegetate' or pass the time in mindless or vacuous inactivity (esp. by watching television). Also **vegged(-out)** adjective. 1980–.

veggie /ˈvedʒɪ/ adjective Also **veggy.** Sometimes derog Shortened from 'vegetarian'. 1975–. CITY LIMITS Built on a solid base of traditional veggie dishes like nut roasts . . . it doesn't seem to be living up to its reputation (1986).

velvet noun Gain, profit, winnings. 1901–. AMERICAN SPEECH I have been taking in plenty of velvet these days working the Fair (1942).

vent noun theatre Abbreviation of 'ventriloquist'. 1893–. NATIONAL OBSERVER We've got magicians here . . . We've got jugglers, mentalists, clowns, and vents (1976).

ventilate verb trans. To shoot with a gun, usu. to kill. 1875–. C. EGLETON You'd just better pray he doesn't kill somebody . . . because he's talking about ventilating people (1979). [From the hole made by the bullet.]

verbal noun **1** A verbal statement, spec. a damaging admission alleged to have been made by a suspected criminal and offered in evidence against him at a trial; often in pl. 1963–. M. UNDERWOOD 'Have a look through the police evidence.' . . . 'At least, they haven't put in any verbals' (1974). **2** Abuse, an insult; esp. in phr. to give (someone) the verbal. 1973–. OBSERVER Each 'ball' consisted of a distinctly lethargic head-high bouncer . . . followed by a rousing collection of verbals (money will be paid to lip-reading viewers for translation) (1982). verb trans. **3** To attribute a damaging statement to (an arrested or suspected person); often followed by up. 1963–. C. ROSS 'He's made no statement yet either.' 'But you verballed him?' . . . The police officer said nothing (1981).

versatile adjective euphemistic Bisexual. Cf. to swing both ways at SWING verb. 1959–.

M. SPARK Dougal was probably pansy. 'I don't think so . . . He's got a girl somewhere.' 'Might be versatile' (1960).

vet noun A medical doctor. 1925–. **A. POWELL** Saw my vet last week. Said he'd never inspected a fitter man of my age (1975). [From earlier sense, veterinary surgeon.]

vibe verb **1** intr. Of a place: to be lively, busy, or exciting. 1968–. **TIME OUT** Danny Delta and Cyrus welcome DJ Bias to help keep the loft room vibing with their breaks, reggae, hip hop and funk guns (2004). **2** trans. To transmit (a feeling, etc.) in the form of 'vibes'; to affect in this way. 1971–. **J. GASH** Kurack smouldered his way to the Rolls, vibing pure hate in my direction (1983). **3** intr. Of people: to interact (well), 'click'. 1986–. **COSMOPOLITAN** I was vibing with this chick at a bar, but she seemed blasé about everything (2004).

vibes noun pl. **1** A vibraphone. 1940–. **2** Feelings or atmosphere communicated; often in phr. *bad vibes.* Sometimes sing. 1967–. **E. ROSSITER** The damned thing's got bad vibes. . . . Throw it in the lake (1983). [Abbreviation, in sense 2 of *vibrations.*]

Victor Charlie noun US, services' = CHARLIE noun 4. 1966–. **SATURDAY NIGHT** (Toronto): [Westmoreland's] men say they have to get them one 'Victor Charlie' (1968). [From the communications code-names for the initial letters of *Viet Cong.*]

vidiot noun derog, orig and mainly US A habitual and undiscriminating watcher of television or player of video games. 1949–. **WASHINGTON TIMES** They are eyeballing the Federal Communications Commission as carefully as any youthful vidiot ever did the Teenage Mutant Ninja Turtles (1991). [Blend of *video* and *idiot.*]

viff noun **1** Viffing; the ability to viff. 1972–. verb intr. **2** Of an aircraft: to change direction abruptly as a result of a change in the direction of thrust of the engine(s). 1981–. **TIMES LITERARY SUPPLEMENT** The VSTOL Harrier with its swivelable jets and ability to 'viff' (1983). [From the initial letters of *vectoring in forward flight.*]

vig noun US = VIGORISH noun. 1968–.

vigorish noun Also **viggerish,** etc. US The percentage deducted by the organizers of a game from the winnings of a gambler; also, the rate of interest on a usurious loan. 1912–. **E. MCBAIN** 'Was he taking a house vigorish?' 'Nope.' 'What do you mean? He wasn't taking a cut?' (1964). [Prob. from Yiddish, from Russian *vyigrysh* gain, winnings.]

villain noun Brit A professional criminal. 1960–. **L. DEIGHTON** The villain is doing a nice Cabinet Minister's home (1963).

ville¹ noun now US A town or village. 1837–. **M. HERR** Once we fanned over a little ville that had just been airstruck (1977). [From French *ville* town.]

'University? Man, that's just dragsville.'

Ville² noun Also **'Ville, (')ville.** Brit **the Ville** Pentonville Prison in London. 1903–. **L. HENDERSON** Yeah, that's right, he was in the 'Ville (1972).

-ville comb form Forming the name of fictitious places with reference to a particular (often unpleasant) quality. 1843–. **J. AITKIN** University? Man, that's just dragsville (1967). [From French *ville* town, as in many American town names.]

vine noun US A suit of clothes; pl., clothing. 1932–. **L. HAIRSTON** I . . . laid out my vine, a clean shirt and things on my bed (1964). [From the notion of clothes clinging to the body.]

vino noun Also **veeno.** Wine, esp. of an inferior kind. 1919–. **L. DURRELL** I bear up very well under the stacks of local vino I am forced to consume (1935). [From Spanish and Italian *vino,* wine.]

violate verb trans. US To accuse or find (a prisoner on parole) guilty of violating the conditions of parole. (1971). **E. BRAWLEY** My parole officer violated me on another phony beef and I wound up in the Joint again (1974).

virgin noun dated A cigarette made of Virginia tobacco. 1923–. **C. BROOKS** You gave me a virgin; I hadn't smoked one for nearly a fortnight (1935). [Abbreviation of *Virginia,* assimilated to *virgin* person who has not had sex, perh. in allusion to the mildness of Virginia tobacco.]

vet vibe vibes Victor Charlie vidiot viff villain

vis /viz/ noun Also **vis.** (with point). orig military Abbreviation of 'visibility'. 1943-. PILOT The weather forecast we received assured good VFR conditions but mentioned local reduced vis around Villahermosa (1990).

visiting fireman noun US A visitor given especially cordial treatment. 1926-. H. S. TRUMAN Naturally got pointed out as the visiting fireman and had a kind of reception between acts and afterwards (1945). [From the notion of one set of fire-fighters visiting another station and receiving a cordial welcome.]

visitor noun euphemistic A menstrual discharge. 1980-. NEW YORKER Girls used to say they had the curse. Or they had a visitor (1984). [Cf. obsolete *visit* noun in same sense.]

vino violate virgin vis visiting fireman visitor

W noun A lavatory. 1953–. E. MALPASS A small garden of weeds, with a cinder path leading to a W (1978). [Abbreviation of *W.C.*]

wack noun **1** Also **whack**. orig US A crazy or eccentric person. 1938–. G. F. NEWMAN The cop shrugged. 'Some wack with a grudge' (1982). adjective **2** US Esp. with reference to (use of) the drug 'crack': bad, harmful. 1986–. ATLANTIC Crack is wack. You use crack today, tomorrow you be bumming (1989). [In sense 1, prob. back-formation from WACKY adjective; in sense 2, prob. shortened from WACKY adjective or WACKO adjective, the implication being that it is crazy to get involved with drug-taking.]

wacko int variant of WHACKO int.

wacko Also **whacko**. orig and mainly US. adjective **1** = WACKY adjective. 1977–. D. UHNAK She's gone slightly wacko politically (1981). noun **2** = WACK noun. 1977–. [From WACK(Y adjective + -o.]

wacky adjective Also **whacky**. orig US Crazy, odd, eccentric. 1935–. OBSERVER She plays the wacky mother of Debra Winger (1984). [From earlier dialect sense, left-handed; from *whack* noun + -y.]

wad noun Brit, orig services' A bun, sandwich, etc. 1919–. G. KERSH I'm in a caff, getting a tea 'n' a wad (1942).

waddy /ˈwɒdɪ/ noun Also **waddie**. US A cattle rustler; a cowboy, esp. a temporary cowhand. 1897–. [Origin unknown.]

waffle stomper noun US A boot or shoe with a heavy, ridged sole. 1974–. Cf. STOMPERS noun.

wag noun Brit The female partner of a male celebrity, esp. a sportsman. 2004–. MAIL ON SUNDAY She [i.e. Victoria Beckham] accepted the Football Association's offer of accommodation with the other Wags (2004). [Back-formation from *wags*, acronym from *wives and girlfriends*.]

Wagga /ˈwɒɡə/ noun Austral An improvised covering, esp. of sacking. Also **Wagga blanket, rug**. 1900–. L HADOW 'Take your wagga, then.' 'No, it's too heavy' (1969). [Abbreviation of *Wagga Wagga*, name of a town in New South Wales.]

wagger noun orig Oxford University A waste-paper basket. Also **wagger-pagger, wagger-pagger-bagger**. 1903–. [Addition of the arbitrary jocular suffix *-agger* to the initial letters of *waste(-paper basket)*; cf. -ER suffix.]

wagon noun **on the wagon** teetotal. 1906–. L. HELLMAN A few years ago I'd go on the wagon twice a year. Now . . . I don't care (1951). [From earlier phr. *on the water-wagon*.] See also *to fix (someone's) wagon* at FIX verb.

wahine /wɑːˈhiːnɪ/ noun surfing A girl surfer. 1963–. [From earlier sense, Maori woman; from Maori, Hawaiian, and other Polynesian languages.]

wail verb intr. US, orig and mainly jazz To perform very well, with great feeling, etc. 1955–. SHAPIRO & HENTOFF I revered the amazing Fats Waller, who had lately made a splash wailing on organ at the Lincoln (1955).

wake-up noun Austral and NZ An alert and resourceful person; esp. in phr. *to be a (full) wake-up (to)*, to be alert (to) or aware of the intentions (of). 1916–. D. WHITINGTON I should have been a wake up to you. I should have known you for the bastard you are (1957). [Perh. from *awake* adjective.]

wake-up pill noun A pep-pill. Also **wake-up**. 1969–.

wakey-wakey Also **wakee-wakee, waky-waky**. orig services'. noun **1** Reveille. 1941–. int **2** Wake up! Often combined with phr. *rise and shine*. 1945–. M. WOODHOUSE 'Wakey-wakey,' he said. 'Stand by your beds' (1968). [Reduplicated arbitrary extension of *wake* verb.]

waler variant of WHALER noun.

walk verb **1** trans. To win easily. 1937–. TIMES I went to the British [championship] thinking I'd walk it. . . . This was a mistake. . . . It was a close shave (1976). **2** intr. US To escape legal custody as a result of being released from suspicion or from a charge. 1958–. F. KELLERMAN They plea bargained him down to the lesser charge . . . in exchange for the names of his friends. Old Cory's going to walk (1986).

walk-back noun US A rear apartment. 1945-.

wall noun **1 over the wall** escaped from prison. 1935-. G. BEARE He's out. Over the wall (1973). **2 off the wall** US Unorthodox, unconventional. 1968-. NATIONAL REVIEW Brian knows how to startle the over-interviewed with off-the-wall questions that get surprising answers: Ever see a ghost? (1974).

wallah /wɒlə/ noun Also **wal(l)a** orig Anglo-Indian **1** A person concerned with or in charge of a usu. specified thing, business, etc. 1785-. J. I. M. STEWART It's marvellous what these ambulance wallas can do at a pinch (1977). **2** derog A person doing a routine administrative job; a bureaucrat. 1965-. COURIER-MAIL (Brisbane): Some wallahs in Canberra are sitting in air-conditioned offices telling us what has been flooded and what hasn't (1974). [From Hindi -wālā suffix, = '-er'.]

wallflower noun A neglected or socially awkward person, esp. a woman sitting out at a dance for lack of partners. 1820-. TV TIMES I used to go to dances when I was young but I was always the wall-flower, always the shy one (1990). [From such women sitting along the wall of the room in which dancing is taking place.]

wallop noun Beer or other alcoholic drink. 1933-. L. LAMB Mrs Tyler could do nothing to improve the wallop she served at the Hurdlemakers (1972). [Perh. from earlier sense, bubbling of boiling liquid.]

walloper noun Austral A policeman. 1945-. A. F. HOWELLS The two wallopers dragged him to his feet and tried to frog-march him off (1983). [From *wallop* verb, to hit + *-er*.]

wally noun Brit A foolish or inept person. Cf. WOLLY noun. 1969-. DAILY TELEGRAPH 'They looked a right load of wallies,' said an eye-witness (1984). [Origin uncertain; perh. a use of the male forename *Wally* (cf. CHARLIE noun), a familiar form of *Walter*, but cf. also Scottish *wallydrag*, *wallydraigle* noun, a feeble or worthless person.]

waltz verb **to waltz Matilda** Austral to carry one's swag; to travel the road. 1893-. J. DEVANNY Nowadays they waltz Matilda on bikes (1945). [Cf. MATILDA noun.]

wang variant of WHANG noun.

wangle orig printers'. verb trans. **1** To obtain by devious means. 1888-. P. WYNDHAM LEWIS In the last war like yourself I joined the army, instead of wangling myself into some safe job in London (1942). noun **2** An act of wangling. 1915-. P. DICKINSON I worked a wangle. I got a line on the Minister of Tourism (1977). [Origin unknown.]

wank noun **1** An act of (male) masturbation. 1948-. SNIFFIN' GLUE Behind that door are you thinkin' readin' or just havin' a wank (1977). **2** = WANKER noun 2; also, an objectionable thing. 1970-. NATION REVIEW (Melbourne): Kenneth S. Jaffrey, that naturopathic scientific wank (1973). verb intr. and trans. **3** To masturbate; often followed by *off*. 1950-. W. MCILVANNEY You've been wankin' . . . That's no' nice in public places (1977); J. BARNES I saw a monkey in the street jump on a donkey and try to wank him off (1984). [Origin unknown.]

wanker noun **1** A (male) masturbator. 1950-. B. W. ALDISS Failed fucker, failed wanker was an inglorious double billing (1971). **2** An objectionable or contemptible person, esp. male; spec. an incompetent, pretentious, or ostentatious person. 1972-. P. NIESEWAND They're such a bunch of wankers. . . . You can't trust any of them to do anything properly (1981). [From WANK verb + *-er*.]

wanking pit noun A bed. Also **wanking couch**. 1951-.

wanky adjective Objectionable, contemptible; masturbatory. 1972-. ZIGZAG We loved that, 'cos it's such a wanky plastic paper and they thought by slagging us early they'd be in first (1977). [From WANK noun or verb + *-y*.]

wannabe noun Also **wannabee** orig US A person who wishes to emulate someone else. 1988-. AUSTRALASIAN POST Scores of Samantha Fox and Linda Lusardi wannabees raided British lingerie shops for skimpy lace and satin undies recently (1988). [Respelling of *want to be*.]

warb /wɔːb/ noun Also **waub, worb**. Austral An idle, unkempt, or disreputable person. See also WARBY adjective. 1933-. PARK & NILAND Alongside this masterpiece he felt the warbiest of the warbs, the shabbiest of the shabs (1956). [Prob. from *warble* noun, the maggot of a warble-fly.]

war baby noun **1** A young or inexperienced officer. 1917-. **2** US A bond or the like which is sold during a war, or which increases in value because of a war. 1917-.

War Box noun Brit The War Office. Cf. WAR HOUSE noun. 1952-. M. PUGH I flit between Downing Street and the War Box and the Ministry of Defence (1969).

walk-back wall wallah wallflower wallop walloper

warby /ˈwɔːbi/ adjective Austral Shabby, decrepit. 1923–. R. H. CONQUEST They're old police boots, a bit worn down in the heels and warby in the soles (1978). [Cf. WARB noun.]

warehouse noun **1** US A large and impersonal institution providing accommodation for mental patients, old people, or poor people. 1970–. verb trans. **2** Stock Exchange To buy (shares) as a nominee of another trader, with a view to a take-over. 1971–. **3** To place (a person, esp. a mental patient) in a large and impersonal institution. 1972–. CHICAGO SUN-TIMES Warehousing became the new 'thing'. Forget about making men better, the theory ran (1983).

warez /ˈweəz/ noun pl. computing Illegal copies of commercial software, pornographic images, etc., distributed through computer bulletin boards or Internet sites; a counter-culture centred on the distribtion of such software, and the online discussion of such activities. 1987–. [Prob. alteration of *wares*.]

War House noun Brit The War Office. Cf. WAR BOX noun. 1925–. SAPPER They thought I was mad at the War House (1926).

wart noun **1** An obnoxious or objectionable person. 1896–. NEW YORK TIMES BOOK REVIEW What! . . . is the old wart going to go on some more about reading? (1984). **2** naval A junior midshipman or naval cadet. 1916–.

wash verb trans. **1 to wash out** dated, air force To kill (a pilot) in a crash; to crash (an aircraft). Usu. in passive. 1918–. F. H. JOSEPH Three planes were washed out completely, others damaged (1942). **2 to wash up** US To bring to a conclusion; to end or finish. Cf. WASHED UP adjective. 1925–. D. DELMAN The man washed himself up with me because he couldn't keep his big, fat, fairy's mouth shut (1972). **3** To murder. 1941–. E. MCBAIN 'This Alfredo Kid, he not sush a bad guy.' 'He's getting washed and that's it' (1960). **4** = LAUNDER verb. 1973–. R. THOMAS What was their payoff for washing the money? (1981).

washed up adjective orig and mainly US Defeated, exhausted, finished; having failed. 1923–. C. WILLIAMS I'm washed up as a writer (1958).

waste verb trans. orig and mainly US To beat up, kill, murder; to devastate. 1964–. C. WESTON They wasted Barrett because he blew their deal (1975).

wasted adjective orig US Intoxicated (from drink or drugs). 1968–.

watering hole noun A place where alcoholic refreshment is available. 1975–. GAINESVILLE (Florida) SUN In a simpler time, players and fans mingled at local watering holes, drinking beers together and becoming friends (1984).

waterworks noun pl. **1** mainly jocular The shedding of tears, or the capacity for this. 1647–. **2** Brit euphemistic The urinary system. 1902–. W. HILDICK I'd been plagued for a long time . . . by—well—let's call it waterworks trouble (1977).

Wavy Navy noun Brit The Royal Naval Volunteer Reserve. 1918–. [From the wavy braid worn by officers on their sleeves before 1956.]

wax¹ noun dated A fit of anger. 1854–. B. DUFFY Giggling and swallowing his hiccups, acting the part of Caliban, that professional guest and sporadic author Lytton Strachey called back, Oh, O. Don't be in a wax now (1987). Hence **waxy,** adjective Brit Angry, quick-tempered. 1853–. [Origin uncertain; perh. from phr. *to wax wroth, angry*, etc., to become angry.]

wax² verb trans. US **1** To beat, thrash; to defeat thoroughly. 1884–. **2** orig military To kill, murder. 1968–. L. BLOCK A whole family gets waxed because somebody burned somebody else in a coke deal (1982). [Origin unknown.]

wax³ mainly US. noun **1** A gramophone record; **on wax,** on a gramophone record. 1932–. W. C. HANDY Recording companies . . . made them available on wax (1941). verb trans. **2** To record for the gramophone. 1935–. DAILY TIMES (Lagos): Another new LP Record waxed by the Celestial Church of Christ Choir (1976). [From the 'wax' discs in which the recording stylus cuts its groove.]

way noun **1 (to put) in the** (or **a, that**) **way** euphemistic (To make) pregnant. 1742–. J. ROSE She suspected herself of being pregnant, 'in the way' as she called it (1980). **2 to go all the way, the whole way** euphemistic To have sexual intercourse (*with* someone), as opposed to engaging only in kissing or foreplay. 1924–. W. J. BURLEY The things we found in her room! I mean it was obvious she was going all the way and her not fifteen! (1970). **3 that way** euphemistic Homosexual. a.1960–. J. R. ACKERLEY I divined that he was homosexual, or as we put it, 'one of us,' 'that way,' 'so,' or 'queer' (a.1967). adverb **4** As an intensifier: very, really. 1988–. NEW MUSICAL EXPRESS When we recorded it originally I doubled up the drums and it sounded way Gary Glitter, way Clash (1990).

way-in adjective Conventional; fashionable, sophisticated. 1960–. PUNCH There's a real way-in guy looking like how a guy on *The Times Saturday Review* ought to look like (1967). [From *way* adverb + *in* adverb, after WAY-OUT adjective.]

way-out adjective Unusual, eccentric, unconventional; avant-garde, progressive. 1959–. LIFE The way-out world of micro-electronics (1961). [From *way* adverb + *out* adverb.]

wazoo noun orig and mainly US **1** The buttocks; esp. as a euphemistic substitute for *ass* in various phrs. 1961–. SAN FRANCISCO CHRONICLE Dating is a real pain in the wazoo (1975). **2 up** (or **out**) **the wazoo** in abundance; to excess. 1981–. L. BLOCK There'd be security up the wazoo, cops and Secret Service agents a mile deep (2003). [Origin unknown.]

wazz Brit. verb intr. **1** To urinate. 1984–. INDEPENDENT ON SUNDAY Max, that's me dog, he only came on and wazzed on it (1995). noun **2** An act of urination. 1994–. C. GLAZEBROOK Oh God, oh God, he saw me having a wazz (2001). [Origin uncertain; perh. an alteration of WHIZZ verb 3.]

wazzed adjective Brit Drunk. 1990–. B. GRAHAM We used to knock off early on Fridays and just neck loads of 'em [i.e. wine gums], walk into town fuckin' wazzed (1997). [From WAZZ verb, on the model of PISSED adjective 1.]

wazzock /ˈwæzək/ noun Brit A stupid, clumsy, or incompetent person; a fool, 'jerk'. 1983–. INDEPENDENT A plot . . . which boasted that hilarious device in which the hero says 'I need to find a right wazzock' (1991). [Origin uncertain; perh. dialectal.]

weakie noun Also **weaky**. **1** mainly Austral Someone weak in constitution or ability; a weakling. 1959–. D. HEWETT 'Don't overdo it son. Leave it go for a while. It's too damned hot out.' 'What d'ya think I am . . . a weaky' (1959). **2** spec. in *Chess*, a poor player. 1962–. GUARDIAN WEEKLY Tony opted for a conservative approach drawing briefly with the favourites and beating the weakies (1977). [From *weak* adjective + *-ie*.]

weapon noun The penis. *a*.1000–. H. & R. GREENWALD This sexual thrill still comes over me whenever I see a horse flashing his weapon (1972).

weasel verb intr. **to weasel out** to avoid an obligation, esp. dishonourably; also used

with *one's* way. 1962–. M. PUZO A real fucking claim agent weaseling out of his obligations (1978).

weave verb **to get weaving** orig RAF To begin action; hurry. 1942–. B. W. ALDISS Pack your night things in a small pack and get weaving, while I lay on transport (1971). [From *weave* to move repeatedly from side to side, in RAF usage, to fly a devious course, esp. in avoiding or escaping danger.]

wedge noun Brit, orig criminals' A wad of bank notes; hence, (a significant amount of) money. 1977–. MELODY MAKER Don't part with your hard earned wedge until you've seen it (1987). [From the notion of a thick pile of bank notes; cf. *wodge* noun and earlier slang sense, silver plate, silver money (1725–).]

wedgie noun orig US An act of pulling the cloth of a person's underwear, trousers, etc. tightly between the buttocks, esp. as a practical joke. 1977–.

wee verb intr. and noun euphemistic = WEE-WEE verb and noun 1. 1934–. P. PURSER Hurry up, I want to do a wee (1971). [Imitative.]

weed noun **1** Tobacco. 1606–. **2** Marijuana; a marijuana cigarette. 1929–. J. KEROUAC They could smell tea, weed, I mean marijuana, floating in the air (1955).

weedhead noun mainly US A habitual marijuana smoker. 1952–. [From WEED noun 2 + HEAD noun 3.]

weekender noun orig US Someone who indulges in occasional drug-taking, esp. at weekends. 1955–. TIMES 'Weekenders' . . . who needed 'speed' to get through school and personal crises (1970).

weeny[1] noun Also **weeney**, **weenie**. US = WIENIE noun. 1906–.

weeny[2] noun US **1a** A girl. 1929–. **b** An effeminate man. 1963–. **2** An objectionable person. 1964–. [From earlier sense, very young child, from *weeny* adjective, small.]

weeny-bopper noun A very young (female) pop fan (sometimes notionally of a younger age than a teeny-bopper, but the two terms are often interchangeable). 1972–. [From *weeny* adjective, small, after TEENY-BOPPER noun.]

weeping willow noun Brit, dated Rhyming slang for 'pillow'. 1880–. N. STREATFIELD Time young Holly was in bed. . . . Hannah wants your head on your weeping willow, pillow to you (1944).

way-in way-out wazoo wazz wazzed wazzock

wee-wee euphemistic. verb intr. **1** To urinate. 1930–. D. ABSE I suddenly rushed into the sea . . . and wee-weed in the water for a joke (1954). noun **2** Urine; an act of urination. 1937–. J. SCOTT When he needed a wee-wee he did it in the corner of the hut (1982). **3** A penis. 1964–. SCREW [The] self-righteous defender of what he thought to be his threatened wee wee, could not contain his machismo (1977). [Imitative; often as a child's word.]

weigh verb trans. **to weigh off** orig military, now mainly criminals' To punish; to convict or sentence. 1925–. B. NORMAN Another was in custody . . . waiting to be weighed off (1978).

weight noun A measure of an illegal drug; hence, the drug. 1971–. S. WILSON Neil was taking colossal risks, there'd be up to thirty weights sitting in the flat at one time (1978).

weirdie noun Also **weirdy**. = WEIRDO noun. 1894–. DAILY TELEGRAPH There was not an unwashed bearded weirdie in sight (1966). [From *weird* adjective + *-ie*.]

weirdo noun **1** An odd or eccentric person. 1955–. MELODY MAKER This record is for the real weirdos (1984). adjective **2** Bizarre, eccentric, odd. 1962–. C. BURKE About halfway through the party a real weirdo thing happened (1969). [From *weird* adjective + *-o*.]

well adverb **1a** Used after an intensive adverb or adjective, as in *bloody well*, *damned well*, etc. 1884–. L. R. BANKS Because actually, as a matter of fact, don't y'know, I'm not sodding well coming (1962). **b** As an intensifier: very, extremely (esp. approvingly). 1986–. FACE A city where Walters is 'well sound' and Led Zeppelin are 'a better buzz'. This is Liverpool in 1988 (1989). **2 well away** fast asleep or drunk. 1927–. A. CARTER The Colonel . . . overcomes his resistance to vodka to such an extent he is soon well away and sings songs of Old Kentucky (1984).

well-hung adjective Of a man: having large genitals. 1868–. D. WILES Hey, man. . . . You sure is well hung for a priest (1977).

welly Also **wellie**. Brit. verb trans. **1** To kick hard. 1966–. noun **2** A forceful kick; acceleration. 1977–. D. GETHIN 'When I say go, give it some welly. . . . Go.' . . . Explosions sounded (1983). [From earlier sense, wellington boot; abbreviation of *wellington*.]

Welshy noun Also **Welshie**. A Welshman or Welshwoman. 1951–. [From *Welsh* adjective + *-y*.]

west adverb **to go west** to be killed, destroyed, lost, etc. 1915–. J. B. MORTON 'All the Lewis guns gone west,' someone said (1919). [Perh. from the notion of the sun setting in the west.]

wet noun **1** A drink. 1719–. **2** An act of urinating; urine. 1925–. J. CLEARY The children want to wet. . . . Come on, love. Have your wet (1975). **3** US = WETBACK noun. 1973–. G. SWARTHOUT Why doesn't this [system] detect every wet who puts a toe across the line? (1979). **4** motor-racing, etc. A wet-weather tyre. 1977–. GRAND PRIX INTERNATIONAL There was little chance that the track was going to dry out. . . . Everybody fitted wets apart from Boutsen (1986). **5** Brit, derog A Conservative politician with liberal or middle-of-the-road views (often applied to those opposed to the monetarist policies of Margaret Thatcher). Cf. DRY noun **4**. 1980–. adjective **6** Austral Irritable, exasperated; esp. in phr. *to get wet*. 1898–. B. SCOTT Naturally, Grandad was wet as hell. Pushing a pumper home eleven miles on a Friday night didn't make him too happy (1977). **7 all wet** orig and mainly US Mistaken, completely wrong. 1923–. A. BARON You're all wet if you think I'm giving up that easy (1951). **8 to get (someone) wet** NZ to gain the upper hand over; to have at one's mercy. c.1926–. F. SARGESON Now we've got 'em wet (1945). **9** Of or being an activity of intelligence organizations, esp. the KGB, involving assassination. 1972–. J. GARDNER He had seen men killed: and killed them himself: he had directed 'wet operations', as they used to be called (1980). **10** Brit, derog Being or characteristic of a political 'wet' (see sense 5). 1981–. LISTENER In considering the promotion of wet (or wettish) Ministers, she will tell herself that Pope was right (1982). verb **11 to wet oneself: a** To urinate involuntarily. 1922–. **b** To become excited or upset (as if to the extent of involuntarily urinating). Also **to wet one's pants**. 1970–. M. UNDERWOOD There are quite a few people who'll wet their pants if I get sent down (1979). **12** intr. To urinate. 1925–. V. WOOLF The marmoset is just about to wet on my shoulder (1935).

weeny-bopper
a very young
(female) pop fan

wetback noun US An illegal immigrant from Mexico to the US; hence, any illegal immigrant. 1929–. [From the practice of swimming the Rio Grande to reach the US.]

wet leg noun A self-pitying person. 1922–. TIMES LITERARY SUPPLEMENT We know how much Auden hated wet-legs, how constantly he repeated his many litanies of his own good fortune (1981).

wet smack noun orig US A spoilsport. 1927–. P. G. WODEHOUSE The man is beyond question a flat tyre and a wet smack (1929).

whack¹ noun 1 A share, portion. 1785–. M. BINCHY They still had to pay a huge whack of the wedding reception cost, and the cake, and the limousines (1988). 2 orig and mainly US A chance; a turn or attempt, a 'go'; esp. in phr. *to have* (or *take*) *a whack* (*at*). 1884–. MUSCULAR DEVELOPMENT Hydrostatic weighing or skinfold techniques . . . can become expensive at $25–$40 a whack (1988). 3 out of whack mainly US Out of order, malfunctioning. 1885–. M. AMIS Everything is out of whack at Appleseed Rectory; its rooms are without bearing and without certainty (1975). 4 top (or full) whack Brit A very high (esp. the highest) price or rate. 1978–. MONEY OBSERVER Payments then rise by 5.0 per cent a year, so you pay the full whack after eight or nine years (1989). verb 5 trans. To share, divide; often followed by *up*. 1812–. COAST TO COAST I'll whack up the breakfast, then, and see how poor bloody Bill's getting on (1961). 6 to whack off intr. US To masturbate. Cf. *to toss off* at TOSS verb 1. 1969–. TRANSATLANTIC REVIEW 'What-in-hell you do for sex anyway?' he asked the boy one night. 'Whack off into the tin pot where they keep the mashed potatoes?' (1977).

whack² noun Variant of WACK noun.

whacked adjective 1 mainly Brit Tired out, exhausted. 1919–. J. A. SNOW I was whacked when I arrived back in England from the MCC tour (1976). 2 whacked out US Mad, crazy; spec. intoxicated with drugs. Cf. WACKY adjective. 1969–.

whacko int Also **wacko**. Expressing delight or enjoyment. 1941–. L. DAVIDSON After all it was only two days to—whacko!—Monday (1978).

whacko adjective and noun variant of WACKO adjective and noun.

whacky variant of WACKY adjective.

whaler noun Also **waler**. Austral A tramp, orig one whose route followed the course of a river. 1878–. C. BARRETT I've been a whaler . . . since I was a nipper, mostly on the Murray (1941). [From their catching 'whales' (a type of freshwater fish) in the rivers they lived by.]

whales noun pl. school and university, dated Anchovies on toast. 1890–. M. COX They were held at 9.45–10p.m. on Saturdays at the rooms of the readers of the paper, who provided coffee, a cup, and *whales* (1983).

wham bam int Also **wham bang. wham, bam, thank you ma'am** used with reference to sexual intercourse done quickly and without tenderness. 1971–. PLAYGIRL Not all men are 'wham bam thank you ma'am' types (1977).

whammy noun US An evil or unlucky influence; from the 1950s, often with reference to the comic strip Li'l Abner, in which the character Evil-Eye Fleegle exerts the *double whammy* or double evil eye; hence, an intense or powerful look, something effective, upsetting, problematic, etc. 1940–. C. JAMES Holmes was a noncomformist in a conformist age, yet still won all the conformist awards. It was a double whammy (1979). [Origin unknown.]

whang noun Also **wang**. orig and mainly US The penis. 1935–. G. HAMMOND Maybe you're not as ready with your whang as you were, or maybe you couldn't keep it up (1981). [From earlier sense, thong.]

whangdoodle noun N Amer Something unspecified, a thingummy. Also **whangydoodle**. 1931–. GLOBE & MAIL (Toronto): A new company sprang to the fore in Quebec. . . . PQ Productions claimed to have invented the whangdoodle (1979). [A fanciful formation; cf. earlier sense, an imaginary creature.]

whanger noun Also **wanger** US = WHANG noun. 1939–. M. MACHLIN She didn't get the idea so fast, so he whipped the old whanger out of his union suit and laid it on the table in front of her (1976).

wharfie noun Austral and NZ A wharf-labourer; a stevedore or docker. 1911–. [From *wharf* noun + *-ie*.]

whassit /wɒsɪt/ noun US = WHATSIT noun. 1931–.

what pron 1 and (I don't know) what all and various other (unknown or unspecified) things. 1702–. A. LURIE That old Mr Higginson. . . . Got his house full of bird dirt and what-all

(1962). **2 what for** a severe reprimand or punishment. 1873–. J. WILSON She deserves to have her bottom smacked . . . and I shall give young Alice what for too (1972). **3 what's with . . . ?** orig and mainly US What's the matter with . . . ?, what has happened to . . . ?, what's the reason for . . . ? 1940–. E. MCBAIN 'What's with this kosher bit?' he asked. 'Get me some butter' (1960).

whatchamacallit /wɒtʃəməkɔːlɪt/ noun mainly US = WHATSIT noun. 1942–. R. B. PARKER A pet whatchamacallit. . . . Guinea pig (1974). [Representing a pronunciation of *what you may call it.*]

whatnot noun = WHATSIT noun. 1964–. M. RILEY She said . . . tapping the Cellophane-covered éclairs, 'I don't know about you but these always put me in mind of nignogs' whatnots' (1977). [From earlier sense, *anything whatever.*]

whatsisface /wɒtsɪzfeɪs/ noun orig and mainly US Used as a substitute for a name that is not known or not remembered. 1967–. J. WAMBAUGH They're having another Save Harry Whatzisface party there today (1977). [Representing a pronunciation of *what's-his-face*, alteration of earlier *what's-his-name.*]

whatsit noun A thing or person whose name is not known or not remembered, or which the speaker does not wish to name. *a.*1882–. P. FRANKAU I couldn't even walk along the passage to the whatsit (1954). [Representing a casual pronunciation of *what is it.*]

what-the-hell adjective Casual, insouciant. 1968–. TIME The only real stumbling block is fear of failure. In cooking you've got to have a what-the-hell attitude (1977).

wheel noun **1 to be on someone's wheel** mainly Austral To hound someone, put pressure on someone. 1922–. O. WHITE The inspector's been on my wheel to trace him (1969). **2** US orig criminals' A leg; mainly in pl. 1927–. E. MCBAIN Big blonde job, maybe five-nine, five-ten. Blue eyes. Tits out to here. Wheels like Betty Grable (1985). **3** orig and mainly US = BIG WHEEL noun. 1933–. A. FOX Some Pentagon wheel's flying in and Don feels he has to travel up there with him (1980). **4** pl. orig US A car. 1959–. G. LYALL 'Did you find me some wheels?' . . . 'Yep: a Renault 16TX' (1982).

wheelie noun **1** orig US **a** The stunt of riding a bicycle or motor cycle for a short distance with the front wheel off the ground. 1966–. DAILY MAIL That's the bike seen on TV with crashhatted kids doing wheelies (1985). **b** In

skateboarding, the stunt of riding on only one pair of wheels. 1976–. **2** orig Austral A sharp U-turn made by a motor vehicle, causing skidding of the wheels. 1973–. **3** Austral A person in or confined to a wheelchair. 1977–. SUNDAY MAIL (Brisbane): So many places and things are inaccessible to the 'wheelie' (1978). [From *wheel* noun + *-ie.*]

wheelman noun orig US A driver; spec. (criminals') the driver of a getaway vehicle. 1935–. K. ORVIS Later on, . . . he began driving a cab. Also being a wheel-man for the mobs (1962).

wheeze noun Brit A clever scheme. 1903–. J. CURRAN His precarious lifestyle of climber, writer, . . . lecturer and gentleman of leisure was always something of a balancing act and his constant 'wheezes', as he called them, to achieve wealth through brilliant ideas but a minimum of work were usually doomed to failure (1987). [From earlier theatrical slang sense, *interpolated joke.*]

Wheneye /wenaɪ/ noun Also **Whennie.** derog Someone (esp. a visitor or foreigner) who exasperates listeners by continually recounting tales of his or her former exploits. 1982–. DAILY MIRROR The islanders now call members of HM Forces 'Whennies'. The reason for this? '*When* I stormed Goose Green', '*When* I took Tumbledown', '*When* I entered Stanley' . . . And so on (1983). [Respelling of phr. '*When I (was . . .)*'.]

where adverb **where it's (he's, she's) at** orig US The true state of affairs; a place of central or fashionable activity. 1965–. MELODY MAKER The musicians frequently became frustrated . . . not really believing their own bands were where it was at (1971).

whiff US. verb **1a** intr. Of a batter in baseball or a golfer: to miss the ball. 1913–. **b** trans. Of a baseball pitcher: to cause (a batter) to strike out. 1914–. NEBRASKA STATE JOURNAL Hurler whiffs 20 (1941). noun **2** A failure to hit the ball. 1952–. [From earlier senses, to blow or puff lightly, a puff or breath of air.]

whiffled adjective Drunk. 1927–. J. D. CARR Helen . . . was much too clear-headed . . . ever to let herself get whiffled (1956). [Origin unknown.]

whifflow noun nautical A device or gadget whose name is forgotten or not known. 1961–. A. BURGESS The cabin was still a mess of smashed and battered whifflows (1971). [Fanciful formation.]

whatchamacallit   whatnot   whatsisface   whatsit

whinge Austral. verb intr. **1** To complain peevishly. 1946–. SUNDAY TIMES 'What sort of people do Australians hate most?' 'The whingeing Pom . . . Poms that come over and do nothing but whinge' (1983). noun **2** A peevish complaint. 1947–. TIMES In my one-but-last whinge I was going on about the burdensome duties of The Talk (1985). Hence **whinger**, noun. 1934–. [From Irish, Scottish, and northern dialect, from earlier sense 'whine'; ultimately from a northern form of Old English *hwinsian* whine.]

whip verb trans. Also (US dialect) **whup** /wʌp, wʊp/ **1** Now US To defeat, overcome; to surpass. 1571–. PUNCH The Matt Dillon urge to 'whup' the Commies (1968). **2 to whip the cat** Austral and NZ To suffer remorse; to complain. 1847–. AIR FORCE NEWS (Melbourne): He, the— sucker . . . must stay and whip the cat (1941). **3** Brit, orig criminals' To steal. 1859–. M. K. JOSEPH 'Where's your hat, Barnett?' . . . 'Dunno, someone musta whipped it' (1958).

whipped adjective US Exhausted, tired out. Also with *up*. 1940–. G. LEA 'Oh sure.' He pulled in his feet, hugged his knees, yawned. 'I'm whipped' (1958).

whip-saw verb trans. and intr. US To cheat or be cheated in two ways at once or by the joint action of two others. 1873–. D. BAGLEY 'Okay, so you've whipsawed me,' said Follet sourly (1969).

whirl noun orig US An attempt; in such phr. as *give it a whirl*. 1884–. TIMES John Syer came to me and said he could help . . . So I thought I would give it a whirl (1985).

whirlybird noun orig US A helicopter. 1951–.

whisker noun **to have** (or **have grown**) **whiskers** of news, a story, etc.: to be no longer novel or fresh. 1935–. D. O'SULLIVAN 'Did I ever tell you the one about the Scotsman and the octopus?' . . . 'It has whiskers' (1977).

whistle verb intr. **to whistle for** (something) to want (something) in vain. 1605–. GUARDIAN A remarkable point about the report was the number of women who were prepared to give Tuohy phials of their blood. I mean, I've nothing against the man but he can whistle for mine (1992).

whistle and flute noun Rhyming slang for 'suit' (of clothes). Also **whistle**. 1931–. J. GASH Him with the fancy whistle (1980).

whistled adjective Drunk. 1938–. PRIVATE EYE We all sidled off to a very nice little snug at the Golden Goose, where . . . all of us got faintly whistled (1979). [Origin uncertain; cf. 'He was indeed, according to the vulgar Phrase, whistled drunk,' Henry Fielding, *Tom Jones* 1749.]

white noun **1a** Morphine. 1914–. N. ADAM By 1965 they were growing poppies for half the world's white (1977). **b** An amphetamine tablet. 1967–. H. C. RAE He had anticipated a rash of arrests for possession of brown drugs and amphetamines—but not this, not a straight leap into the lethal whites (1972). **2** Money. 1960–. OBSERVER The white, crinkle, cabbage, poppy, lolly, in other words cash (1960). [In sense 2, from earlier slang sense, silver coin.]

white ants noun Austral Failing sanity or intelligence; esp. in phr. *to have white ants*, to be eccentric or dotty. 1908–. I. L. IDRIESS A hardened old nor'-wester can develop a few 'white ants', as well as the veriest new-chum (1937). [From the destructiveness of termites or white ants.]

white-arsed adjective Contemptible, despicable. 1922–. DAILY COLONIST (Victoria, British Columbia): Delegates . . . sat in shocked silence when an Indian leader accused them of being 'white-arsed Liberals' (1975).

Whitehall Warrior noun Brit A civil servant; an officer in the armed forces employed in administration rather than on active service. 1973–. P. O'DONNELL Roger was a Whitehall Warrior until he retired (1978). [From *Whitehall*, name of a street in London in which several principal government offices are situated.]

white hat noun **1** US naval An enlisted man. 1956–. **2** orig US A good man; a hero. 1975–. GUARDIAN WEEKLY His judgments of the men he dealt with. . . . The white hats are Truman [etc.]. A prime villain is Britain's postwar foreign secretary (1978). [In sense 2, from the white hats traditionally worn by the 'goodies' in Western films.]

white knight noun Stock Exchange A company that comes to the aid of another facing an unwelcome take-over bid. 1981–. [From earlier sense, a hero or champion.]

white lady noun Austral A drink of or including methylated spirits. 1935–. [Cf. earlier sense, cocktail made of gin, orange liqueur, and lemon juice.]

white lightning noun Orig US **1** Inferior or illegally distilled whisky. 1921–. **2** A kind of LSD. 1972–.

white line noun dated US Alcohol as a drink; also, a drinker of alcohol. 1908–. FLYNN'S All we could glom was a shot of white line (1926).

white meat noun mainly US White women considered as sexual conquests or partners. 1940–. M. MAGUIRE I'm off white meat. I have a good thing going with a negro film editor (1976).

white mule noun US A potent colourless alcoholic drink; spec. illegally distilled whisky. 1889–.

white nigger noun derog and offensive, orig US **1** A black person who defers to white people or accepts a role prescribed by them. 1837–. **2** A white person who does menial work. 1871–.

white-shoe adjective mainly US Effeminate, immature. 1957–. G. JENKINS What sort of white-shoe captain are you? (1974).

white stuff noun mainly US Morphine, heroin, or cocaine. 1908–. N. LUCAS Luckier still not to have graduated from pep pills to . . . 'The White Stuff' . . . heroin (1967). Cf. WHITE noun 1.

Whitey noun Also **Whitie.** derog, mainly African-American A white person; also, white people collectively. 1942–. C. DRUMMOND Get to hell away from me! You Whities stink! (1967). [From white adjective + -y.]

whizz Also **whiz.** noun **1** orig and mainly US The practice of picking pockets (esp. in phr. on the whizz); a pickpocket. 1925–. J. CURTIS They might pinch him for being on the whizz (1936). **2** An act of urinating. 1971–. verb intr. **3** To urinate. 1929–. R. B. PARKER I wondered if anyone had whizzed on Allan Pinkerton's shoe (1976).

whizz-boy noun A pickpocket. Also **whizz-man.** 1931–.

whizzer noun **1** Something or someone extraordinary or wonderful. 1888–. ZIGZAG 'She's long' features Bill's best guitar solo (despite many other whizzers) (1976). **2 on a whizzer** dated, N Amer On a drinking spree. 1910–. **3** A pickpocket. 1925–. R. EDWARDS It was also a right place for 'whizzers'— pickpockets (1974).

whizz-mob noun A gang of pickpockets. 1929–.

whizzo Also **wizzo.** int **1** An exclamation of delight. 1905–. D. AMES 'It's really a little surprise for the kiddies.' 'Whizzo!' cried Anna, grabbing it (1954). adjective **2** Excellent, wonderful. 1948–. M. ALLINGHAM I wanted to look

at some wizzo lettering on . . . the Tomb (1955). noun **3** A highly talented person. 1977–. SYDNEY MIRROR Electronics Wizzo Dick Smith . . . aims to become the taxman's friend in another way (1981). [From whizz noun + -o.]

whizzy adjective **1** Technologically innovative or advanced; up to date, modern. 1977–. MAKING MUSIC A whizzy Roland-style alpha wheel for modifying your sounds (1986). **2** Of a person: exceptionally talented or successful; often in superlative. 1979–. [From whizz noun + -y; in sense 2, after whiz-kid noun.]

whoop-de-do noun Also **whoop-de-doo.** US Fuss, palaver, to-do. 1929–. VERBATIM There was many an angry powwow and much whoop-de-do, but in the end, of course, the bigwigs won (1981). [Fanciful extension of the verb whoop or the interjection whoops.]

whoopsie noun A piece of excrement; often in pl. Esp. in phr. to do a whoopsie (or whoopsies), to defecate. 1973–. PUNCH The dog's done a whoopsie on the carpet (1986). [From whoopsie int; popularized by the BBC TV programme Some mothers do 'ave 'em.]

whoop-up noun mainly N Amer A noisy celebration or party. 1913–. D. HEFFRON I thought it quite . . . sensible of Big Point to have one great annual public whoop-up in which to give a little exercise to the witch and devil of one's soul (1976). [From whoop it up to have a noisy good time.]

whore noun A promiscuous or unprincipled person; as a term of abuse. 1906–. E. GAINES 'You hear me whore?' 'I might be a whore, but I'm not a merciless killer,' he said (1968). [From earlier senses, female prostitute, promiscuous woman.]

whore-shop noun A brothel. 1938–. A. MACVICAR I hate the Golden Venus. . . . It's just a whoreshop (1972).

whosis /huːzɪs/ noun Also **whoosis.** Used for referring to someone whose name is not known or remembered; often following a title. 1923–. I. FLEMING Don't forget one thing, Mister Whoosis. I rile mighty easy (1965). [Representing a casual pronunciation of 'who is this?']

whosit /huːzɪt/ noun Also **whoosit, whoozit, whozit.** = WHOSIS noun. 1948–. J. TEY Someone, say, insists that Lady Whoosit never had a child (1951). [Representing a casual pronunciation of 'who is it?']

wick noun **to get on (someone's) wick** Brit To annoy someone, to get on someone's

white line   white meat   white mule   white nigger

nerves. 1945–. B. FRANCIS Gets on my wick, she do (1984). [Said to be from (*Hampton*) *Wick* (name of a locality in SW London), rhyming slang for *prick* noun, penis.] See also **to dip one's wick** at DIP verb.

wicked adjective orig US Excellent, remarkable. Cf. BAD adjective 2. 1920–. AUTOBLOG. COM 2009 Lotus Esprit will be wicked (2007).

widdle noun **1** An act of urination. 1954–. verb intr. **2** To urinate. 1968–. W. HARRISS He headed straight for me. . . . I damn near widdled (1983). [Imitative; cf. PIDDLE verb and noun, WEE verb and noun.]

wide adjective **1** Brit Shrewd; skilled in sharp practice. See also WIDE BOY noun. 1879–. F. D. SHARPE Underworld men and women . . . refer to themselves as 'wide people' or 'one of us'. They're a colourful, rascally lot these 'wide 'uns' (1938). noun **2 to the wide** entirely, utterly; in phrs. *blind* (*broke*, *dead*, *out*, etc.) *to the wide.* 1915–. L. LEE Wake up, lamb. . . . He's wacked to the wide. Let's try and carry him (1959).

wide boy noun Brit A man who lives by his wits, often dishonestly; a spiv or petty criminal. 1937–. V. GIELGUD Blackmailed—for the murder? Not even the widest of the local wide-boys could have got on to it (1960).

widgie noun Austral and NZ Applied to the Australasian equivalent of the Teddy-girl. 1950–. Cf. BODGIE. TIMES Gang delinquency . . . has made its mark around the world . . . in Australia the bodgies and widgies (1977). [Origin unknown.]

widow noun **the widow** champagne; in later use associated with *Veuve* (= widow) *Clicquot* name of a brand of champagne. 1781–. G. BOOTHBY A good luncheon and a pint of the Widow to wash it down (1899).

wienie /wiːniː/ noun N Amer A type of smoked pork or beef sausage. 1911–. [From *wiener* noun, such a sausage (short for *wienerwurst*, from German *Wienerwurst* Viennese sausage) + *-ie*.]

wife noun The passive member of a homosexual partnership. 1883–. J. HYAMS The group's leader [a homosexual] . . . made his 'wife' head of production (1978).

wig verb intr. **to wig out** US To be overcome by extreme emotion; to go mad, freak out. 1955–. J. GORES Kearney was going to wig out when the expense voucher for $100 worth of cocaine came in (1978). Cf. WIGGY adjective.

wigger noun Also **wigga.** orig and mainly US, often derog or offensive A white or other

non-black person who identifies with aspects of urban African-American culture, esp. hip-hop, and behaves or is perceived to behave in a way associated with those cultural forms. 1988–. PHILADELPHIA If you're white, don't try to be black. There's nothing more insulting to black people than a wigger (2003). [Blend of *white* and NIGGER noun 1.]

wigging noun A severe rebuke, a scolding. 1813–. [From obs. slang *wig* noun, rebuke (perh. as administered by a BIGWIG noun) + *-ing*.]

wiggle noun **to get a wiggle on** orig US To hurry up. 1896–. NEWSWEEK If Americans don't get a wiggle on . . . they may forfeit their place in the vanguard of the human future that will be lived outside the cradle of Earth (1990).

wiggy adjective US Mad, crazy, freaky. 1963–. LAST WHOLE EARTH CATALOG Traditionally considerations such as his—economics, organizations, the future—turn a prophet's soul terrible and dark or at least partially wiggy (1972). [From *to wig out* (see WIG verb) + *-y*.]

wig-picker noun US A psychiatrist. 1961–. M. MCCARTHY Was I afraid of what a wig-picker might say? (1971).

wilco int Also **willco.** orig military Abbreviation of 'will comply', used to express acceptance of instructions, esp. those received by radio or telephone. 1946–. D. BEATY 'Please clear the runway quickly for the President's Starjet!' . . . 'Wilco,' he said (1977).

wild adjective US Remarkable, unusual, exciting. 1955–. LISTENER Los Angeles is so wild they should just let it swing and see what happens (1968).

wilding noun US Rampaging by a gang of youths through a public place, attacking or mugging people along the way; an instance of this. 1989–. NEW YORK TIMES There has been little response by the city government to the widespread concern over wilding in general (1990). [Prob. from *wild* adjective + *-ing*; first associated with an incident in New York City's Central Park in April 1989.]

William noun Also **william.** dated, US A dollar bill. 1865–. C. A. SIRINGO Mr. Myers wrote me . . . to buy a suit of clothes with the twenty-dollar 'william' (1927). [From punning association of *bill* noun, banknote and *Bill*, familiar form of the male forename *William*.]

willies noun pl. orig US Nervous discomfort; esp. in phrs. *to give* (or *get*) *the willies.* 1896–. G. KERSH It *can* give you the willies when, in broad

wicked widdle wide wide boy widgie widow wienie

daylight, you hear a rifle go off (1942). [Origin unknown.]

willy noun Also **willie**. Brit The penis. 1905–. P. ANGADI We used to hold each other's willies. . . . We didn't know about sex then (1985). [From a familiar form of the male forename *William*.]

wimp[1] noun **1** orig US A feeble or ineffectual person. 1920–. SHE Masseur! Huh! He sounds a right little wimp (1985). As adjective = WIMPISH adjective. 1979–. WINE AND SPIRITS This is no wimp wine. It's Paul Bunyon, overalls and all (1991). verb **2 to wimp out** US To demonstrate one's feebleness by failing to act or by withdrawing from an undertaking; to 'chicken out' or renege *on* in this way. 1981–. NEW ENGLAND MONTHLY One of the women suggested the night had already been very full and rewarding and she wasn't sure she needed to continue it. 'Hey, are you wimping out?' Patti asked (1990). Hence **wimpish**, adjective 1925–; **wimpy**, adjective 1967–. [Origin uncertain; perh. from *whimper* verb.]

wimp[2] noun A woman or girl. 1923–. [Origin uncertain; perh. an abbreviated alteration of *woman*.]

Wimpey noun Also **Wimpy**. A Vickers Wellington, a British bomber aeroplane of World War II. 1941–. N. SHUTE There was a Wimpey running up one engine, somewhere away out in the middle distance of the aerodrome (1944). [From J. Wellington *Wimpy*, name of a character in the 'Popeye' cartoons.]

wind /wɪnd/ noun In phrs. *to get the wind up*, to be alarmed, *to put the wind up*, to alarm. 1916–. C. ALINGTON I tell you you've absolutely put the wind up Uncle Bob and Peter! They're scared to death of your finding them out (1922). See also WIND-UP[1] noun.

wind /waɪnd/ verb **to wind (someone) up** Brit To irritate or provoke someone to the point of anger; to pull someone's leg. 1979–. MATCH All he kept saying was 'boss, you're kidding me, boss, you're winding me up' (1987). See also WIND-UP[2] noun.

windbag noun **1** A person who talks a lot but says little of value. 1827–. ATLANTIC CITY You'll be stopped dead by a posse of venomous old windbags (1991). **2** nautical A sailing ship or windjammer. 1924–. W. MCFEE He had been cook

in a windbag and a sailor before the mast (1946).

window-pane noun dated A monocle. 1923–. P. G. WODEHOUSE Freddie no longer wore the monocle. . . . His father-in-law had happened to ask him one day would he please remove that damned window-pane from his eye (1966).

wind-up[1] /wɪndʌp/ noun A state of nervous anxiety or fear. 1917–. A. PRICE Bit of nerves . . . the old wind-up (1980). [From phr. *to get the wind up* (see WIND noun).]

wind-up[2] /waɪndʌp/ noun Brit An attempt to irritate or hoax someone or to pull someone's leg. 1984–. TIMES My recollection of this is quite clear. I thought it was a wind-up to be honest with you (1984). [From phr. *to wind someone up* (see WIND verb).]

wine-dot
a habitual
drinker of
cheap wine

windy /wɪndɪ/ adjective **1** Nervous, frightened. 1916–. D. CLARK 'Are you feeling windy?' 'Do I look as if I am?' (1985). **2** dated, services' Frightening, nerve-wracking. 1919–. T. E. LAWRENCE Such performances require a manner to carry them off. . . . A windy business (1928). [From WIND noun + -*y*; cf. *to get* (or *put*) *the wind up* (see WIND noun).]

Windy City noun US Chicago. 1887–.

wine dot noun Austral A habitual drinker of cheap wine. 1940–. T. A. G. HUNGERFORD 'Is he a wine-dot?' 'Is he hell! . . . He's never off it' (1953). [Pun on *Wyandotte*, name of a breed of chicken.]

wing noun **1** An arm. 1823–. SUN (Baltimore): He came up with a bad arm during the season, and had been troubled before with it. If the big man's wing behaves this year he should be of considerable value (1947). **2 a wing and a prayer** used jocularly for referring to an emergency landing by an aircraft. 1943–. W. MARSHALL The co-pilot brought it in. . . . Wing and a prayer! (1977). verb **3 to wing it** orig and mainly US To improvise. 1970–. GLOBE & MAIL (Toronto): Mr. Trudeau came without notes, choosing to wing it, and struggled . . . unsuccessfully to establish Mr. Leger's resemblance to an owl (1979). [In sense 2, from the name of the song *Comin' in on a Wing & a Prayer* (1943) by H. Adamson; in sense 3, from earlier theatrical sense, to

willy wimp Wimpey wind windbag window-pane

learn lines in the wings having undertaken a role at short notice.]

Wingco noun Also **Winco, Winko.** RAF Abbreviation of 'Wing Commander'. 1941–. F. PARRISH There was a pub . . . taken over by a retired Wing Commander. . . . The Winco, as he liked to be called, was a ready market (1982).

wingding noun **1** US A drug addict's real or feigned seizure; esp. in phr. *to throw a wingding*. 1927–. P. TAMONY It assigned . . . Winifred Sweet . . . to throw a wing-ding . . . in Market Street (1965). **2** orig and mainly US A wild party; a celebration or social gathering. 1949–. A. HAILEY How are you, Nim? Don't see you often at these Jewish wingdings (1979). [Reduplication of *wing* noun.]

winger noun Brit, nautical **1** A steward. 1929–. **2** mainly services' A comrade or friend. 1943–. PENGUIN NEW WRITING He had seen his 'winger', his best friend, decapitated (1943). [Cf. earlier sense, cask stored in the wing of a ship's hold.]

wingy noun A one-armed man. 1880–. D. STIFF Missions are very anxious to recruit the 'wingies' and 'armies', or the one-armed hobos (1931). [From WING noun 1 + -*y*.]

winkle noun The penis (of a young boy). 1951–. T. HUGHES O do not chop his winkle off His Mammy cried (1970). [From earlier sense, small mollusc.]

winkle-pin noun military A bayonet. 1924–.

winkler noun One who assists in the eviction of tenants. 1970–. WHIG-STANDARD (Kingston, Ontario): The tenants said the agents aided by middlemen called 'winklers', had bribed and harassed them to get them to move (1977). [From *to winkle out* to extract.]

wino noun orig US A habitual excessive drinker of cheap wine or other alcohol, esp. one who is destitute. 1915–. J. MARKS That sonuvabitch Dean Martin . . . that lousy wino wop! (1973). [From *wine* noun + -*o*.]

wipe verb **1 to wipe the floor with** orig US To inflict a humiliating defeat on. 1887–. G. A. BIRMINGHAM He was so infernally certain that the Emperor would wipe the floor with us (1918). **2** Austral and NZ To dismiss, discard, disown. 1941–. P. WHITE Suspended once—but they didn't wipe me (1983). **3 to wipe out: a** trans. or intr., surfing To knock or be knocked off a surfboard. 1962–. SURFER MAGAZINE Frye misjudged one of his turns high in the curl and wiped-out in the white water (1968). **b** trans. orig US Of drink, etc.: to render intoxicated or

senseless. Also fig, to overwhelm. 1971–. YEAGER & JANOS Dad grew some tobacco for his smoking; I tried chewing some and it wiped me out (1985). **4** trans. To murder, kill; often followed by *out*. 1968–. J. MCCLURE Someone tried to wipe Bradshaw. . . . The shot caught him here in the collar-bone (1980).

wiped adjective Mainly with *out*. **1** orig US Exhausted, tired out. 1958–. M. ATWOOD 'Christ, am I wiped,' he says. 'Somebody break me out a beer' (1972). **2** mainly US Intoxicated or incapacitated by drugs or alcohol. 1966–. HARPER'S MAGAZINE The dining-car waiters were vying with each other as to how wiped-out they were (1991). **3** Financially ruined, penniless. 1977–. J. BLUME I am almost wiped out financially, but maybe I can pick up a babysitting job over the holidays (1981).

wipe-out noun **1** surfing A fall from one's surfboard as a result of a collision with another surfboard or a wave. 1962–. **2** orig US Destruction, annihilation; a killing; a crushing defeat; an overwhelming experience. 1968–. M. HEBDEN Think it was a gang wipe-out, Patron? (1984). [From *to wipe out* (see WIPE verb 3, 4).]

Wipers noun services' A nickname for the Flemish town of *Ypres*, the site of three significant battles involving great loss of life in World War I. 1914–. N. MITFORD We'd like to see old Wipers again. . . . We had the time of our lives in those trenches when we were young (1960). [Representing the anglicized pronunciation of *Ypres* adopted by servicemen.]

wired adjective **1 to have (got) it,** etc. **wired** orig US To be in an enviable situation, have it 'made'. 1955–. DIRT BIKE All he had to do was stay on time—maybe even drop a few more points, and he still had it wired (1985). **2** mainly US Under the influence of drugs or alcohol; intoxicated, 'high'. Also with *up*. 1977–. FORTUNE I worked on both Chrysler refinancings, and by the second one, I was wired most of the time (1985). **3** orig and mainly US In a state of nervous excitement; tense, anxious, edgy. Also with *up*. 1982–. E. PIZZEY He's really wired up. It's fun to see him do the jumping for a change (1983).

wise adjective **1** orig US Aware, informed; esp. in phrs. *to get* (or *put*) *wise*. 1896–. M. GILBERT I suppose Bill had just about got wise to you (1955). verb **2 to wise up** trans. and intr. orig and mainly US To put or get wise. 1905–. WALL STREET JOURNAL Antique dealers are wising up to the growing demand for old radios (1971). **3 to wise off** intr. To make wisecracks *at* someone 1943–. P. MALLORY He's a real meanie. I wouldn't be wising off at him if I were you (1981).

wise-ass noun and adjective US = SMART-ARSE adjective and noun. 1971–. J. IRVING Benny Potter from New York—a *born* wise-ass (1978). Also **wise-assed**, adjective = SMART-ARSED adjective. 1967–.

wise guy noun orig US A know-all. 1896–. B. SCHULBERG Listen, wise guy . . . if you found something wrong . . . why didn't you come and tell me? (1941).

wisenheimer /ˈwaɪzənhaɪmə(r)/ noun Also **weisen-, wise-.** US = WISE GUY noun. 1904–. WASHINGTON POST Then some wisenheimer from the agency decided we needed a trailer (1959). [From *wise* adjective + *-enheimer*, as in German names such as *Oppenheimer*.]

wish book noun N Amer A mail-order catalogue. 1933–.

witch-doctor noun military A psychiatrist. 1966–. D. ANTHONY That sounds like one of your witch doctors at the Retreat (1979).

with it adjective orig US **1** Fashionable, up to date. 1931–. DAILY MAIL Horne made a strong attempt to get with it. Result: the stronger emphasis on fashionwear (1971). **2** Mentally alert. 1961–. W. J. BURLEY There's an old man, living in a home. . . . He's quite with it—I mean he's mentally alert (1985).

wizard adjective mainly Brit Wonderful, excellent. 1922–. TIMES 'How wizard!' they said. . . . 'How absolutely super!' (1974).

wizzo variant of WHIZZO int, adjective, and noun.

wobbler noun orig US = WOBBLY noun; esp. in phr. *to throw a wobbler*. 1942–. LOOKS Mum throws a wobbler with three weeks to go (1989).

wobbly noun A fit of annoyance, temper, panic, etc.; esp. in phr. *to throw a wobbly*. 1977–. D. NORDEN Not only did she throw a wobbly at the slightest murmur of tango rhythms, even the sight of a piano-accordion brought her out in hives (1978). [From *wobbly* adjective.]

wog[1] noun derog and offensive **1** A foreigner, esp. a non-white one. 1929–. TIMES LITERARY SUPPLEMENT We have travelled some distance from the days when Wogs began at Calais (1958). **2** The Arabic language. 1977–.

W. HAGGARD 'I've picked up a few words of wog, sir.' . . . The driver spoke terrible barrack-room Arabic (1982). [Origin unknown; often said to be an acronym (e.g. 'worthy Oriental gentleman'), but this is not supported by early evidence.]

wog[2] noun Austral **1** An insect, esp. a predatory or disagreeable one. 1938–. NORTHERN TERRITORY NEWS (Darwin): Mr Wilson of the City Council was present also and answered questions on treatment of grubs and 'wogs' on foliage (1960). **2** A microbe or germ, a bug. 1941–. C. GREEN A 'flu wog' struck, and several families of children were absent with . . . 'terrible hackin' coffs' (1978). [Origin unknown.]

wog verb trans. To steal, pinch. 1971–. P. FERGUSON A new acquisition, no less, and one smuggled out of the shop under the assistant's very nose; one snaffled, pocketed, pinched, wogged, nicked (1985). [Origin unknown.]

wolf noun **1** A sexually aggressive man, a habitual would-be seducer of women. 1847–. S. LEWIS She was innocent, but this Roskinen was a wolf (1945). **2** orig US A male homosexual seducer or one who adopts an active role with a partner. 1917–. K. J. DOVER In prisons the 'wolf' is the active homosexual, and does not reverse roles with his partners (1978).

wolly noun Also **wally.** Brit A uniformed policeman, esp. a constable. 1970–. J. B. HILTON These traffic Wollies make sure it all goes down, once they've licked their pencils (1983). [Origin unknown; perh. the same word as WALLY noun.]

wonga noun Brit Money. 1984–. CORRESPONDENT MAGAZINE He hopes the book will make him loads of wonga (1989). [From British Romani *wongar* coal, money, from Romani *angar* coal.]

wonk noun derog **1** nautical An inexperienced or inefficient person, esp. a cadet or midshipman. 1929–. **2** Austral **a** A white (i.e. non-Aboriginal) person. 1938–. E. WEBB Sometimes whites would get out of cars along the road and walk over to the Camp and peer inside the humpies, or rough bough shelters, curious to see how the abos lived. . . . One of the boys nailed a board up on a tree near the road with '*wonks*—keep out!' on it (1959). **b** An effeminate or homosexual man. 1945–. P. WHITE I'd have to have a chauffeur to drive me about—with a good body—just for show, though. I wouldn't mind if the chauffeur was a wonk (1970). **c** Used as a

wise-ass wise guy wisenheimer wish book with it

general term of abuse. 1967–. R. DONALDSON 'Good on y', y' fat-gutted wonk.' 'An you, Elephant-belly' (1967). **3** US A studious or hard-working person. 1962–. E. SEGAL Who could Jenny be talking to that was worth appropriating moments set aside for a date with me? Some musical wonk? (1970). [Perh. from *wonky* adjective, unsteady, unsound.]

wood noun **1 to have the wood on** (someone): Austral and NZ To have an advantage over, to have a hold on. 1926–. N. MANNING We've got the wood on Wilkie and McKenzie. . . . I caught them smoking pot in the out-of-bounds area (1977). **2** orig Brit The penis, esp. (now) an erection of the penis; esp. in phr. *to get wood*. 1985–. GUARDIAN Will . . . [he] be able to get it up or, to use the porn industry term, 'get wood'? (1996). [In sense 1, perh. in allusion to WOODEN verb.]

wood-and-water joey noun Austral An odd-job man. 1882–. D. STUART You might consider taking a job here with me, wood-and-water joey, general rouseabout (1978). [From *wood-and-water*, in allusion to 'hewers of wood and drawers of water' (*Joshua* xi. 21) + obs. Austral *joey* noun, a recent arrival on a goldfield, an inexperienced miner.]

Woodbine noun dated, Austral An English person, esp. a soldier. 1919–. E. HILL Bagtown became 'Woodbine Ave' . . . so-called from the number of English settlers in residence (1937). [From the proprietary name of a British brand of cigarettes.]

woodchuck noun US An unsophisticated rustic, yokel, 'hick'; also as a term of mild contempt. 1931–. R. BANKS He could go to weddings or funerals . . . and not look like a hick, a woodchuck (1989). [From earlier sense, species of N. American marmot.]

wooden verb trans. Austral and NZ To hit; to knock unconscious. 1904–. A. UPFIELD Got woodened with something wot wasn't a bike chain (1959). Also **woodener,** noun A staggering blow, a knock-out punch. 1899–. [From *wooden* adjective, perh. after STIFFEN verb, to kill.]

wooden cross noun military A wooden cross on a serviceman's grave; hence, death in action regarded ironically as an award of merit. 1917–.

wooden kimono noun = WOODEN OVERCOAT noun. 1926–. MEZZROW & WILSON I expected the man to turn up . . . with his tape

measure to outfit me with a wooden kimono (1946).

wooden nickel noun US A worthless or counterfeit coin; esp. in phr. *to take a wooden nickel*, to be swindled or fooled. Also **wooden money.** 1915–. L. HELLMAN Luis and I got to Madrid. He said I was not to take any wooden nickels (1937).

wooden overcoat noun A coffin. 1903–. GUARDIAN The paratroops were edgy and the one who let me through the barricade reckoned I would come out in a wooden overcoat (1971).

wooden suit noun = WOODEN OVERCOAT noun. 1968–.

woodentop noun Brit **1** A uniformed policeman. 1981–. J. WAINWRIGHT I'm a copper. An ordinary flatfoot. . . . A real old woodentop (1981). **2** A slow-witted person. 1983–. A. BEEVOR They've even got the bleeding Army out. . . . Bunch of woodentops from Chelsea barracks (1983). [In sense 1, from the notion that uniformed policemen have 'wooden tops' (i.e. are slow-witted), in contrast with the mental acuteness of detectives; prob. a reapplication of *Woodentops*, the name of a BBC television children's puppet programme first broadcast in 1955.]

woodpecker noun US and Austral, military A machine-gun. Cf. TYPEWRITER noun. 1898–. YANK The Japs opened up with what sounded like dual-purpose 75s, 20mm pompoms and woodpeckers (1945).

woodpile noun musicians' A xylophone. 1936–. TIME Red Norvo kept salting his half-hour stands with such tunes as . . . he used to rap out on his 'woodpile' (xylophone) with Paul Whiteman's band 20 years ago (1951). [From its tuned wooden bars.]

woodshed noun **1 to take into the woodshed** N Amer To reprimand or punish. 1907–. CHICAGO SUN-TIMES Assuming the Fed is traditionally pliant, why does not Reagan simply take Volcker to the woodshed and tell him to ease up? (1983). **2** musicians' A place where a musician may, or should, practise in private. 1946–. ROLLING STONE Leavell's playing won't scare many jazz pianists into the woodshed (1977). verb trans. and intr. **3** musicians' To play or rehearse, esp. privately. 1936–. MEZZROW & WOLFE I'll have to woodshed this thing awhile so I can get straight with you all (1946). See also **something nasty in the woodshed** at NASTY adjective. [In sense 1, from the former practice of spanking a child in

wood   wood-and-water joey   Woodbine   woodchuck

world

the woodshed, i.e. not in the presence of others.]

woodwork noun **1** The frame of soccer goalposts. 1960–. GRIMSBY EVENING TELEGRAPH Twice in the first half, Scunthorpe hit the Bradford woodwork (1977). **2 out of the woodwork** out of obscurity into (unwelcome) prominence. 1964–. CURRENT AFFAIRS BULLETIN (Sydney): They are the new Australian playwrights and they are coming out of the woodwork everywhere (1973).

woody noun Also **woodie.** orig surfers', mainly US An estate car with timber-framed sides. 1961–. [From *wood* noun + *-y*.]

woof verb **1** intr. and trans., US, African-American To talk (to) or say ostentatiously or aggressively. 1934–. J. WAMBAUGH He was woofing me, because he winked at the blond kid (1972). **2** trans. orig Air Force To eat ravenously, 'wolf'. Also with *down*. 1943–. C. H. D. TODD In every case the six dogs at once 'woofed' the tripe (1961). Hence **woofer,** noun 1935–. [From earlier sense, to bark gruffly.]

woofits noun An unwell feeling, esp. in the head; moody depression. 1918–. N. SHUTE Getting the woofits now, because I don't sleep so well (1958). [Origin unknown.]

woofter noun Also **wooftah.** derog. A male homosexual. 1977–. A. N. WILSON The two young woofters in the pub (1980). [Fanciful alteration of POOFTER noun.]

woolly noun A uniformed policeman. 1965–. PRIVATE EYE A small army of 'Woollies'—CID slang for uniformed officers—were summoned (1984). [Cf. WOLLY noun.]

woolly bear noun dated, military A type of German high-explosive shell. 1915–.

woopie noun Also **woopy.** orig N Amer A 'well-off older person', able to enjoy an affluent and active lifestyle in retirement; often in pl. 1986–. DAILY TELEGRAPH We are in the age of the 'woopy' . . . and it is about time we all recognised that fact, planned for our own future and helped them to enjoy theirs (1988). [Acronym from *well-off old(er) person* + *-ie*, after YUPPIE noun.]

Woop Woop /wʊp wʊp/ noun Austral **1** An imaginary town in the remote outback, supposedly backward. 1918–. SYDNEY MORNING HERALD It was like council night in Woop Woop—Federal Parliament on Tuesday, that is (1986). **2 the woop-woops** remote country. 1950–. [Jocular formation, prob. influenced by the

use of reduplication in Aboriginal languages to indicate plurality or intensity.]

wop[1] derog and offensive orig US. noun **1** An Italian or other southern European. 1914–. E. HEMINGWAY Wops, said Boyle, I can tell wops a mile off (1924). **2** The Italian language. 1937–. A. MELVILLE-ROSS There's a lot of chat in Wop which I doesn't understand (1982). adjective **3** Italian. 1938–. E. WAUGH You'll find her full of wop prisoners (1955). [Origin uncertain; perh. from Italian *guappo* bold, showy, from Spanish *guapo* dandy, from Latin *vappa*, sour wine, worthless fellow.]

wop[2] noun RAF A radio operator. 1939–. R. BARKER Wireless operator/air gunners . . . most of the wop/A.G.s . . . came straight from gunnery school (1957). [Acronym from *w(ireless) op(erator).*]

worb variant of WARB noun.

word verb trans. Austral To speak to, accost; to tell, pass word to; also, to rebuke or tell off. 1905–. J. MURRAY The 'donahs' would grimace and giggle, and the boys would 'word' 'em (1973).

work noun **1 the (whole) works** orig US The whole lot, everything; esp. in phr. *to give* (someone) *the works*, to give or tell someone everything, to treat someone harshly, to kill someone. Cf. *the (full) treatment* at TREATMENT noun. 1899–. P. G. WODEHOUSE Heave a couple of sighs. Grab her hand. And give her the works (1934); L. KALLEN I have uncovered a sensational story that is crying to be written. . . . Best-seller list, movie, the works (1979). **2** pl. US A drug addict's equipment for taking drugs. 1934–. W. BURROUGHS I went into the bathroom to get my works. Needle, dropper, and a piece of cotton (1953). verb **3 to work** (someone) **over** to treat with violence, beat up. 1927–. R. PERRY Alan held me and Bernard worked me over (1978).

working girl noun euphemistic, orig US A prostitute. 1968–. CHICAGO SUN-TIMES U.S. Prostitutes has estimated that thousands of 'working girls' will travel to San Francisco for business generated by the convention (1984).

working stiff noun orig US An ordinary working man. 1930–. GUARDIAN WEEKLY The idea of two young working stiffs [i.e. Bernstein and Woodward] carrying off the prize is irresistible to youngsters with their careers before them (1977).

world noun **the world** US, military The territorial United States, 'home'; esp. in phr. *to go (get, etc.) back to the world* (i.e. after active

woodwork woody woof woofits woofter woolly woopie

service overseas). 1971–. D. A. DYE You'll kill boo-coo gooks before you go on back to the World (1987).

worry-guts noun A person who habitually worries unduly. Also (mainly US) **worry-wart.** 1932–. O. NORTON He laughed. 'Worryguts!' 'I wasn't worried. I was just trying to be efficient' (1966).

wot pron and adjective Brit **1** Non-standard written form of 'what'. 1829–. H. CARMICHAEL He's going to have a tough job convincing the police he wasn't the one who done it (1972). **2 wot no—?** orig a World War II catchphrase protesting against shortages, written as the caption accompanying a drawing of the imaginary character Mr. Chad; later also in extended humorous use. 1945–. K. CONLON Joanna sent a postcard which said, 'Wot no tulle and confetti?' (1979).

wotcher int Also **wotcha.** Brit A form of casual greeting. 1894–. J. GASH 'Hello, Lovejoy.' 'Wotcher, love' (1980). [Alteration of *what cheer*?]

would verb **wouldn't it?** Austral and NZ An exclamation of annoyance and disgust or (less usually) amusement. 1940–. J. O'GRADY The barmaid's sigh was greatly exaggerated. She said to the audience, 'Wouldn't it? It's just not my day' (1972). [Short for such catchphrases as *wouldn't it rock you?*, *wouldn't it root you?*, etc.]

wow orig US. noun **1** A sensational success. 1920–. V. CONNAUGHT From that moment forward, she was a wow with every Australian in the land (1962). adjective **2** Exciting or expressing admiration and delight. 1921–. JOHN O' LONDON'S A chorus of wow reviews from international critics (1962). verb trans. **3** To impress or excite greatly. 1924–. DAILY TELEGRAPH Mr Macdonald, who supplied the off-screen commentary for this year's Channel 4 coverage of the SDP conference, had the bright notion of training up a novice speaker who would wow them at Buxton (1984). [From *wow* int, expressing surprise, admiration, etc.; orig Scottish.]

wowee int An exclamation of surprise or astonishment. 1921–. MAD MAGAZINE Boy! Wow-wee! That's quite an exciting evening line-up! (1963). [From *wow* int + arbitrary suffix *-ee*; orig spelt *wowey*.]

wowser /waʊzə(r)/ noun Austral and NZ **1** dated An obnoxious or disruptive person. 1899–. **2** An excessively puritanical or prudish person. 1900–. BULLETIN (Sydney): Victoria's publicans seem utterly to have lost their marbles.

They have made common cause with the wowsers (1986). [Origin uncertain; perh. from Brit. dialect *wow* verb, to howl, grumble; claimed by John Norton (*c*.1858–1916), editor of the Sydney *Truth*, as his coinage.]

Wrac /ræk/ noun A member of the Women's Royal Army Corps, the former women's corps of the British Army. 1956–. [From the initial letters of the corps' name.]

Wraf /ræf/ noun A member of the Women's Royal Air Force, the women's corps of the Royal Air Force. 1921–. [From the initial letters of the corps' name.]

wrap verb **1 to wrap up** to be quiet, stop talking; often as imperative 1943–. O. MILLS 'Geoff, wrap up about the jigsaws,' Charles entreated him (1959). **2 to wrap** (something) **(a)round** (something): to crash a vehicle into a stationary object. 1950–. TIMES The men towing the boat from one training venue to another wrapped it round a traffic light (1984).

wrecked adjective US Drunk or under the influence of drugs. 1968–. D. LANG I could not get it on, could not get it *on*, not unless I was, one: totally wrecked; and, two: had to have a gun in my hand (1973).

Wren[1] noun Also **wren.** A member of the Women's Royal Naval Service, the women's service of the Royal Navy. 1918–. [From three of the initial letters of the service's name, assimilated to *wren* noun, small bird.]

wren[2] noun US A woman, esp. a young woman. 1920–. A. CONAN DOYLE Scanlan has . . . married his wren in Philadelphia (1929). [From earlier sense, small bird.]

Wrennery noun jocular, services' A building used to accommodate Wrens. 1943–. NAVY NEWS The work included . . . the building of a Wrennery to accommodate 200 Wrens (1964). [From WREN[1] noun + *-ery*.]

wriggler noun Austral A snake. 1927–. W. WATKINS 'Let's go in here and get the wriggler.' 'The men will be home soon.' 'Bugger the men . . . The snake will have gone by then' (1972).

wringer noun **to put through the wringer** orig US To subject to severe treatment, esp. interrogation. 1942–. TIMES Not since the controversial Bishop of Durham . . . has an episcopal appointee been put through the wringer in this fashion (1984).

worry-guts wot wotcher would wow wowee wowser

wrinkly noun Also **wrinklie**. An old or middle-aged person. Cf. CRUMBLY noun. 1972–. CHURCH TIMES I am a wrinkly whose monthly cheque from the Church Commissioners is labelled 'Diocesan Dignitary' (1983). [From *wrinkle* noun + -*y*; from older people's wrinkled skin.]

wrong adjective criminals' Untrustworthy, unreliable; not sympathetic to or cooperative with criminals. 1908–. D. W. MAURER He was what thieves call a *wrong copper*, that is, he did not take the *fix* (1955).

wrongo /ˈrɒŋəʊ, ˈrɒŋɡəʊ/ noun Also **wronggo**. mainly US = WRONG 'UN noun 2; also, a counterfeit coin. 1937–. D. RAYMOND I've had my eyes on both of you . . . and you look like a couple of wrongos to me (1985). [From *wrong* adjective + -*o*.]

wrong 'un noun 1 A racehorse held in check so that it loses the race. 1889–. H. SPRING Hansford had never been known to tip a wrong 'un (1935). **2** A person of bad character. 1892–. J. B. HILTON It seemed quite a hobby with her—Teds, and dropouts and wrong 'uns (1978). [Contraction of *wrong one*.]

wump /wʌmp/ noun dated A foolish or feeble person. 1908–34. R. NICHOLS Hail to thee, thou much sniffed at by superior Persons and all wowsers, wumps and knock-knees (1934). [Origin unknown.]

wuss noun, orig US An ineffectual person. 1984–. [Prob. a back-formation from *wussy* ineffectual, of unknown origin.]

wrinkly   wrong   wrongo   wrong 'un   wump   wuss

WOMAN For once the place will be free of giggles and girlish yakitty-yak (1959).

yah adverb Yes; orig dialect, but now (also **ya**, **yar**) used mainly in representations of the speech of 'Sloane Rangers'. 1863–. **TELEGRAPH SUNDAY MAGAZINE** 'Can I tempt you with a crouton?' 'Yar, absolutely' (1986). [Variant of *yea* adverb or *yes* adverb.]

yah boo int Also **ya(a) boo**. orig childrens' Expressing scorn or derision. Also **yah boo sucks**. 1921–. **A. CHRISTIE** Two small boys arrived . . . preparing as usual to say, 'Yah. Boo. Shan't go' (*a*.1976). [From *yah* int, in same sense + *boo* int.]

Yahudi /jəˈhuːdɪ/ Also **Yehudi**. mainly US. noun **1** A Jew; Jews. 1900–. **I. JEFFERIES** As far as the Yehudis were concerned I knew the dirt that was being done (1959). adjective **2** Jewish. 1977–. **WASHINGTON POST** I see the hate in your eyes, you Yahudi (Jewish) whore, and when we go to work on you, you'll be sorry (1977). [From Arabic *yahudi*, Hebrew *yehūdī*, Jew; in earlier non-slang English use (1823–) referring to Jews in Arabic-speaking or Muslim countries.]

yakka noun Also **yacca, yacka, yacker, yakker**. Austral (Strenuous) work; esp. in phr. *hard yakka*. 1888–. **NATIONAL TIMES** (Sydney): Child care remains women's responsibility . . . There's no evidence that men are taking part in the hard yakka (1986). [From dated Austral *yakker* verb, to work, from Aboriginal (Jagara) *yaga*.]

Yank noun **1** Often derog An inhabitant of the US; an American. Also as adjective. 1778– (in early use, applied to New Englanders or inhabitants of the northern states generally). **J. TROLLOPE** They give me vast tips, especially the Yanks who love it that I'm titled (1989). **2** An American car. 1959–. [Abbreviation of *Yankee* noun, New Englander, American, perh. from Dutch *Janke*, diminutive of *Jan* John.]

yap verb intr. **1** To talk idly, chatter. 1886–. **A. T. ELLIS** They end up writing books about it and yapping away on the television (1985). noun **2** US The mouth. 1900–. **H. FAST** They know that if they open their yaps, we'll close them down (1977). **3** Idle talk; chatter. 1907–. **K. WEATHERLY** Never mind that yap. Where's the tucker? (1968). **4** A chat. 1930–. **R. LAWLER** Real ear-basher he is, always on for a yap (1957). [From earlier sense, to bark sharply.]

Yard[1] noun Brit Short for 'Scotland Yard'. 1888–.

yard[2] noun US One hundred dollars; one thousand dollars. 1926–. **V. PATRICK** You throw a

---

Y noun mainly US Abbreviation of 'YMCA' or 'YWCA'. 1915–. **NEW YORKER** Rose . . . did not yet have a place to live; she was staying at the Y (1977).

yack Also **yak**. derog. verb intr. **1** To engage in trivial or unduly persistent conversation; to chatter. 1950–. **J. TRENHAILE** Those two will yak all day (1981). noun **2** Persistent trivial talk. Also **yak-yak**. 1958–. **N. FREELING** The sudden head-down butt jabbed into someone's face, is a highly effective way of putting a stop to his yack (1983). [Imitative.]

yacker[1] Also **yakker**. derog. noun **1** Austral Talk, chatter. 1882–. **P. WHITE** Couldn't get on with me work—not with all the yakker that was goin' on in 'ere (1973). verb intr. **2** = YACK verb. 1961–. **FINANCIAL TIMES** 'Yellow Polka-Dot Bikini'—one of the scratchy 78s . . . —yackers melodiously while the characters gallivant through daytime Calcutta (1982). [Imitative.]

yacker[2] noun Also **yakker**. derog One who yacks; a chatterbox or gossip. 1959–. **NEW YORK TIMES** She just brought the parrot along for the ride. . . . He was quite a yacker (1984). [From YACK verb + -*er*.]

yacket verb intr. derog = YACK verb. 1958–. **NEW YORKER** We warn them, we yacket away day and night . . . but they never learn (1969). [Back-formation from YACKETY int.]

yackety int Also **yackity, yaketty, yakkety, yakkity**. derog Expressing the sound of incessant chatter; usu. reduplicated or followed by *ya(c)k*. 1953–. **D. BAGLEY** The Sergeant . . . only talks when he has something to say. Everybody else goes yacketty-yack all the time (1982). [Imitative.]

yackety-yack Also **yackety-yacket(y)**. derog. verb intr. **1** = YACK verb. 1953–. **M. DICKENS** Our laundry's full of yackety-yacketing women this morning (1953). noun **2** = YACK noun. 1958–.

Y   yack   yacker   yacket   yackety   yackety-yack

yet

hundred to the guy who makes the loan. . . . He writes the loan for thirteen hundred, you take twelve, and a yard goes south to him (1979).

yardbird noun US **1** A new military recruit; also, a serviceman under discipline for a misdemeanour; one assigned to menial tasks. 1941–. c. brown For the next two weeks, K. B. was Claiborne's yardbird. He had to go everywhere Claiborne went from morning till night. He even had to ask Claiborne when he wanted to go to the bathroom (1965). **2** A convict. 1956–. **3** A worker in a yard. 1963–. t. pynchon 'Yardbirds are the same all over,' Pappy said. . . . The dock workers fled by, jostling them (1963). [From *yard* noun, enclosed area + *bird* noun, perh. after *jailbird* noun.]

yardie noun orig West Indies A member of any of a number of West Indian (esp. Jamaican) gangs engaged in usu. drug-related organized crime; more generally, a Jamaican. Often as adjective. 1986–. financial times The so-called Godfather of Britain's Yardie gangs . . . was deported to Jamaica, for questioning about murders (1988). [From *yard* (esp. in West Indian sense, dwelling, home (including land attached)) + *-ie*.]

yarra adjective Austral Mad. 1943–. sydney morning herald Kingston Town is a good horse . . . but in my opinion he would not have lived with Phar Lap. I know a lot of my people will say I'm 'Yarra'; but that's my belief (1980). [From the name of a mental hospital at *Yarra* Bend, Victoria.]

yatter verb intr. and noun derog, orig Scottish dialect = yack verb and noun. 1825–. j. n. harris This dear old Betty was yattering at me on Sunday morning when I was hung over to the eyeballs (1963). [Imitative, perh. after *yammer* verb + *chatter* verb.]

yay /jeɪ/ adverb Also **yea**. US **yay big** (or **high**) this big (or high). 1960–. t. kochman Jeff fired on him. He came back and all this was swelled up bout yay big, you know (1972). [Prob. from *yea* adverb, yes.]

yay /jeɪ/ int An exclamation of triumph, approval, or encouragement. 1963–. new wave magazine The Slits won the argument (Yay!) but we didn't get the interview (Boo!) (1977). [Origin uncertain; perh. from yay adverb or *yeah* adverb.]

yech /jek, jex/ int Also **yecch, yeck**. US = yuck int. 1969–. a. hailey As for the food there—yech! (1979). Hence **yec(c)hy,** adjective US = yucky adjective. 1969–. [Imitative.]

yekke /jekə/ noun Also **Yekke** and (anglicized) **Yekkie**. derog and offensive A German Jew; hence, a pedant. 1950–. h. kemelman The bunch of Anglo-Saxons and Yekkies that run Hadassah and your hospital, too, you call them real Israelis? (1972). [From Yiddish, of uncertain origin; cf. German *Geck* fool, idiot.]

yell noun Someone or something extremely funny; a scream. 1926–. e. coxhead All these doctors and their ecologists—what a yell (1949).

yellow-belly noun orig US A coward. 1930–. j. steinbeck I'm a cowardly yellow-belly (1952). Hence **yellow-bellied,** adjective orig US Cowardly. 1924–. m. hebden I'm . . . a yellow-bellied, lily-livered coward (1979). [From *yellow* adjective, cowardly + *belly* noun.]

yellow jack noun dated Yellow fever. 1836–.

yellow jacket noun US A pentobarbitone tablet. 1953–.

yellow peril noun The political or military threat regarded as emanating from Asian peoples, esp. the Chinese. 1900–.

yenta noun Also **yente**. US A gossip or busybody; a noisy, vulgar person; a nagging woman. 1923–. b. hecht Jesus God, you talk like a typical *yenta* (1931). [Yiddish, orig a personal name.]

yentz verb trans. US To cheat, swindle. 1930–. j. krantz 'I don't *yentz* them,' Maggie explained, Coca-Cola-coloured eyes all innocence, 'they just yentz themselves and I try not to run out of tape' (1978). [Yiddish, from *yentzen* to copulate.]

yen-yen noun dated US A craving for opium, opium addiction. 1886–. j. black He [i.e. an old Chinese man] was shaking with the 'yen yen', the hop habit (1926). [Prob. from Chinese (Cantonese) *yīnyán* craving for opium, from *yīn* opium + *yán* craving.]

yes siree /-səriː/ adverb Also **yes sirree**. mainly US Yes indeed; certainly. 1846–. b. holiday Yes siree bob, life is just a bowl of cherries (1956). Cf. no siree adverb. [*Siree* prob. from obs. dialect *sirry*, from *sir* noun.]

yet adverb orig US Used as an ironic intensive at the end of a sentence, clause, etc. (imitating the use of Yiddish *noch*). 1936–. oxford times The tracks include . . . 'To Know Him is to Love Him' (with David Bowie on saxophone, yet!) (1980).

yardbird yardie yarra yatter yay yech yekke yet

Yid noun derog and offensive A Jew. 1874–.
V. NABOKOV Then she went and married a yid
(1963). [Back-formation from *Yiddish* noun and
adjective.]

yike noun Austral A quarrel, fight. 1941–.
BUSINESS REVIEW WEEKLY (Sydney): We have had a
couple of small yikes, mainly on things like
contract prices (1984). [Origin unknown.]

yikes int Expressing astonishment. 1971–.
DETROIT FREE PRESS Yikes! Even Paul Newman loses
the woman in this new breed of movies (1978).
[Origin unknown, but cf. *yoicks* int used by
huntsmen.]

yips noun A state of nervousness which
causes a golfer to miss an easy putt. 1963–.
[Origin unknown.]

yo int orig and mainly US An exclamation used
as a greeting, to express excitement, to
attract attention, or as a general sign of
familiarity (originating among young
African-Americans). 1966–. A. TYLER 'Fresco?' he
called. 'Yo,' Fresco said from the rear (1980).

yob noun Brit A lout, hooligan. 1927–. TIMES I
would not want anybody looking at me to think
this man is a thick, stupid, illiterate yob (1984).
Hence **yobbery**, noun Hooliganism. 1974–.
yobbish, adjective 1972–. **yobby,** adjective
1955–. [From earlier sense, boy; backslang
for *boy* noun.]

yobbo noun Also **yobo**. Brit = YOB noun.
1938–. NEWS CHRONICLE The local Teddies and
yobbos swing their dubious weight behind the
strike (1960). [From YOB noun + -o.]

yock Also **yok**. theatrical, mainly US. noun
1 A laugh. 1938–. NEW YORKER A chuckle or even a
short, muted yock is acceptable from time to
time (1965). verb intr. 2 To laugh. 1938–.
[Cf. English dialect *yocha* to laugh.]

yok noun derog A non-Jew, a Gentile. 1923–.
R. SAMUEL There were five Jewish boys in the
gang—I was the only 'Yok' (1981). [Yiddish, *goy*
noun 'non-Jew' reversed with unvoicing of
final consonant.]

yomp verb Brit, military 1 intr. To march with
heavy equipment over difficult terrain.
1982–. SUNDAY TIMES So the sweaty soldier
yomping into battle ends up with blisters and a
pool of water inside the boot (1984). 2 trans. To
cover (a certain distance) in this way. 1983–.
[Origin uncertain; cf. YUMP verb.]

yonks noun A long time; esp. in phr. *for
yonks*. 1968–. A. BLOND Nicholas Bagnall and David
Holloway have run the *Telegraph's* book pages
for yonks (1985). [Origin unknown.]

yonnie noun Austral A small stone, a pebble.
1941–. [Perh. from a Victorian Aboriginal
language.]

youee variant of U-EY noun.

yow noun **to keep yow** Austral To keep a
look-out, esp. in order to conceal some
criminal activity. 1942–. G. MCINNES Molly kept a
look out ('kept yow', as we used to say) (1965).
[Origin unknown.]

yo-yo noun US A fool. 1970–. V. BUGLIOSI I've
got enough problems without some punk yo-yo
threatening me (1978). [From earlier sense,
toy that goes up and down.]

yuck¹ noun orig US A fool; a disagreeable or
despicable person. 1943–. J. WAINWRIGHT Three
no-good yucks had felt like playing footsie with
the law (1979). [Origin unknown.]

yuck² Also **yuk**. int 1 Expressing strong
distaste or disgust. 1966–. D. SIMPSON It was the
way he talked about her. . . . 'You know what
older women are, wink, wink.' . . . Yuk! (1983).
noun 2 Messy, unpleasant, or disgusting
material. 1966–. M. E. ATKINS One of those
syndicated advice columns. . . . All noble
sentiments and romantic yuk (1981). adjective
3 = YUCKY adjective. 1971–. P. DICKINSON She's got
a really yuck family, even worse than mine
(1973). [Imitative.]

yuck³ Also **yuk**. Mainly N Amer. verb 1 **to yuck
it up** to fool around. 1964–. 2 intr. To laugh.
1974–. TIME OUT Pryor has them yukking at whitey
one moment and at themselves the next (1975).
noun 3 A laugh. 1971–. NATIONAL OBSERVER The
biggest yuck of the night was when Mr. T. called
Mrs. Llewelyn 'Mrs. Rreweryn' (1976). [Origin
unknown.]

yucky adjective Also **yukky**. 1 Nasty,
unpleasant; sickly sentimental. 1970–.
M. GORDON It's only bats, I say . . . 'They're weird,'
says Linda. 'Yucky' (1981). 2 Messy, gooey.
1975–. J. WILSON Let's get these yucky things
off and get you washed (1977). [From YUCK²
noun + -y.]

yump verb intr. 1 Of a rally car or its driver:
to leave the ground while taking a crest at
speed. 1962–. noun 2 An instance of yumping.
1975–. [Alteration of *jump* verb, representing
the supposed pronunciation of it by Swedish
speakers or the Norwegian *jump* noun, jump,
jumpe verb, jump (Scandinavians being
leading ralliers).]

yumpie noun Also **yump**. orig US = YUPPIE
noun. 1984–. [From the initial letters of young
upwardly mobile people + -ie.]

Yid yike yikes yips yo yob yobbo yock yok yomp

yum-yum noun **1** Pleasurable activity, esp. love-making. 1885–. A. HUXLEY Enjoying what she called 'a bit of yum-yum' (1939). **2** naval Love-letters. 1943–. [Reduplication of *yum* int expressing pleasurable anticipation.]

yum-yum girl noun euphemistic A prostitute. Also **yum-yum tart.** 1960–. A. BUCHWALD Don't let her kid you. All her girls are really yum-yum girls from the dance halls (1962).

yup noun orig and mainly US Abbreviation of YUPPIE noun. Also as adjective. 1984–. CHICAGO TRIBUNE One group of yups asked the conference information desk: 'Where's the spouses' volleyball game?' (1990).

yuppie noun Also **yuppy.** orig US A member of a socio-economic group comprising young professional people working in cities. Also as adjective. Cf. BUPPIE noun, GUPPIE noun, YUMPIE noun. 1984–. [Orig. from the initial letters of young urban professional; now also often interpreted as young upwardly mobile professional (or person, people).]

yuppify verb trans. orig US, often derog To change (an area, building, clothing, etc.) so as to be characteristic of or suitable to yuppies. Hence **yuppification,** noun 1984–. OBSERVER Their 'bashers' (shacks) will be forcibly removed by police to make way for developers who want to 'yuppify' the Charing Cross area (1987). [From YUPPIE noun + -fy.]

yow yum-yum yum-yum girl yup yuppie yuppify

Zz

z noun **to catch** (or **get, bag,** etc.) **some z's** /zi:z/: US To get some sleep. 1963–. A. DUNDES Got to go . . . cop me some z's (1973). Cf. zizz noun 1 and verb. [From the use of z (usually repeated) to represent the sound of snoring.]

za /za:/ noun US Abbreviation of 'pizza'. 1968–. VERBATIM One of the boys called up and asked the parlor to *bag the za* (meaning 'cancel the pizza') (1983).

zac noun Also **zack, zak.** Austral A sixpence; also, a trifling sum of money. 1898–. NATIONAL TIMES (Sydney): No wonder Paul Keating has angrily refused to give the ABC another zac (1986). [Prob. from Scottish dialect *saxpence*.]

zaftig adjective Also **zoftig, zofti(c)k.** US Of a woman: plump, curvaceous, sexy. 1937–. GOSSIP Zaftig Dolly Parton . . . once described herself as looking like a 'hooker with a heart of gold' (1981). [Yiddish, from German *saftig* juicy.]

zambuk /ˈzæmbʌk/ noun Also **zambuc, -buck.** Austral and NZ A first-aider, a St. John Ambulance man or woman, esp. at a sporting occasion. 1918–. [From the proprietary name of a brand of antiseptic ointment.]

zap orig US. int **1** Representing the sound of a ray gun, laser, bullet, etc.; also, expressing any sudden or dramatic event. 1929–. PARADE MAGAZINE A staff meeting will be Wick just shooting out those things one after another— zap, zap, zap (1985). verb **2** trans. **a** To kill, esp. with a gun; to deal a sudden blow to. 1942–. N. FREELING Unbureaucratically, any bugger who shoots, you zap (1982). **b** To put an end to, do away with. 1976–. SUNDAY SUN-TIMES (Chicago): Atari seeks to zap X-rated video games (1982). **3** trans. To fail (someone) in a test, course, etc.; to punish. 1961–. **4** trans. To overwhelm emotionally. 1967–. THEOLOGY A well-known evangelist invited the undergraduates of Oxford to allow themselves to be 'zapped by the Holy Spirit' (1983). **5** trans. To send, put, or hit forcefully. 1967–. D. DELMAN I nosed the car out of town and on to 118, where I zapped it into high (1972). **6** intr. To move quickly and vigorously. 1968–. TIMES Several smaller craft zap past (1985). **7** trans. To make more powerful, exciting, etc.; to enliven, spice *up*. 1979–. FAMILY CIRCLE How to find shoes, hats, accessories that zap last year's clothes to look like new (1986). **8** trans. computing To erase or change (an item in a program). 1982–. **80** MICROCOMPUTING On DRS 304, RB 2C you will find the byte to be 20H. Zap this to 18H (1983). **9** intr. To fast-forward a video recorder so as to go quickly *through* the advertisements in a recorded television programme; to switch *through* other channels during advertisements when watching programmes off-air. 1983–. noun **10** Liveliness, energy, power; also, a strong emotional effect. 1968–. NEW YORKER He gives the film a manic zap (1984). **11** US A charge or bolt (of electricity, etc.); a beam of radiation (from a laser, etc.); a burst or blast. 1979–. DISCOVER When Alvarez published his theories, people snapped them up because they explained everything in one great iridium zap (1991). **12** Computing A change in a program. 1983–. Hence **zappy,** adjective Lively, amusing, energetic; striking. 1969–. LISTENER The company felt the need for a zappier profile (1984). [Imitative.]

zapper noun orig US A remote-control unit for an electronic device, esp. a television or video recorder. 1981–. LOS ANGELES TIMES Hit the zapper, Maude. Maybe there's some bowling on another channel (1987). [From ZAP verb + -er.]

zatch noun The female genitals; the buttocks; an act of sexual intercourse. 1950–. J. KRANTZ You're going to take her home and give her a zatch (1980). [Perh. alteration of *satchel* noun in similar slang sense.]

zazzy adjective mainly US Flashy, colourful, vivid; stylish, strikingly novel. 1961–. A. HAILEY *The Chicago Sun-Times* conceded. 'Yessir! This one's zazzy' (1971). [Origin uncertain; perh. from PIZ(ZAZZ noun + -y, but cf. also *jazzy*, *sassy*, and *snazzy*.]

zero verb trans. To eliminate or delete, to omit. Also with *out*. 1965–. TENNIS 'Zero Screen 311!' he bellowed (1990).

zhoosh /ʒʊʃ, ʒu:ʃ/ verb trans. Orig among homosexual men: to make more stylish or smart; to enliven; often followed by *up*. 1977–. GAY TIMES In 1815 the Prince had employed John Nash . . . to zhoosh up his rather plain and classical farmhouse by the sea (1990). [From Polari, prob. of imitative origin.]

ziff noun Austral and NZ A beard. 1917–. G. KELLY 'Better get rid of that ziff,' she said pointing to his embryonic beard (1981). [Origin unknown.]

zigabo variant of JIGABOO noun.

ziggety int Also **ziggedy, ziggetty, ziggity.** orig and mainly US Used in exclamations preceded by *hot* and usu. followed by *dog* or another monosyllable. 1924–. NEW YORKER Mr. Deforest entered with his face bright, his hands folded behind him. 'Well, hot ziggetty, a holiday for me. What have we got going here?' (1984). [Prob. alteration of *diggety*, as in *hot diggety dog*.]

zig-zag adjective dated, mainly US Drunk. 1918–. E. PAUL He groped and floundered . . . not completely 'zigzag' (1923). [From the uncertain course typically taken by drunks.]

zig-zig noun US military = JIG-A-JIG noun. 1918–. W. ROBINSON 'Allo, baybee! Comment alley vooz—zigzig? (1962).

zilch noun **1** orig and mainly US Nothing. 1966–. SOUNDS Three further 45s ensued in 1979 and '80, plus an album which didn't sell. After that, zilch (1984). verb trans. **2** US In Sport, to prevent (the opposition) from scoring; to defeat. Also transf. = ZERO verb. 1969–. HUNTING ANNUAL There is no going out later using a scoped rifle after getting zilched with a smokepole (1980). [Origin unknown.]

zillion noun mainly US A very large but indefinite number. Cf. SQUILLION noun. 1944–. SUNDAY TELEGRAPH Broken Hill Proprietary . . . is Australia's biggest company and a zillion times bigger than his own (1983). Hence **zillionth,** adjective and noun 1972–. [From *z* (representing the last in a long sequence) + m)*illion* noun.]

zillionaire noun An extremely rich person. 1946–. I. FLEMING He's a zillionaire himself. . . . He's crawling with money (1959). [From ZILLION noun + *-aire*.]

zinger noun US **1** Something outstandingly good of its kind. 1955–. R. ADAMS My private collection was becoming what an American friend . . . described as a 'zinger' (1980). **2a** A wisecrack; a punch-line. 1970–. HOMEMAKER'S MAGAZINE The Vancouver Status of Women is planning to put out a booklet of useful zingers. . . . Sometimes you need just one

sharp line to show you mean business (1975). **b** A surprise question; an unexpected turn of events, e.g. in a plot. 1973–. PUBLISHERS WEEKLY There's a zinger toward the end, in which the nominal hit man gets hit, but it doesn't really compensate for the tedium the reader's gone through (1976). [From *zing* verb + *-er*.]

zip noun orig and mainly US Nothing, nought, zero. 1900–. J. KRANTZ No launch, no commercials, no nothing. Zip! Finished! Over! (1980). [From earlier sense, light fast sound or movement.]

zipless adjective Denoting a brief and passionate sexual encounter. 1973–. G. VIDAL Girls who feared flying tended to race blindly through zipless fucks (1978). [Coined by Erica Jong, 'because when you came together zippers fell away like petals'.]

> '**No launch,
> no commercials
> no nothing. Zip!**'

zit noun mainly N Amer A pimple; an acne spot. 1966–. COURIER-MAIL (Brisbane): You know playing with teenagers will give you zits (1980). [Origin unknown.]

zizz noun **1** Also **ziz.** A short sleep, a nap. 1941–. M. TABOR Philip's having a zizz. He can't stay awake (1979). **2** Gaiety, liveliness, sparkle. 1942–. TIMES The Queensgate centre lacks, perhaps, finesse and a touch of zizz (1983). verb intr. **3** To doze or sleep. 1942–. D. MOORE Reckon this sector's safe. Might as well zizz (1961). [From earlier sense, buzzing sound; in senses 1 and 3, with reference to the sound of snoring; cf. z noun.]

zizzy adjective Showy, spectacular; lively, uninhibited. 1966–. GUARDIAN WEEKLY Zizzy little TV charts (1983). [From ZIZZ noun 2 + *-y*.]

zob noun dated, US A weak or contemptible person; a fool. 1911–. S. LEWIS It's a mighty beneficial thing for the poor zob that hasn't got any will-power (1922). [Origin unknown.]

zoftig, zofti(c)k variants of ZAFTIG adjective.

zombie noun **1** A dull, apathetic, or slow-witted person. 1936–. GUARDIAN Mr. Dawson describes the committee as a parliament of zombies (1981). **2** Canadian, military, derog In World War II, a man conscripted for home defence. 1943–. [From earlier sense, re-animated corpse.]

zonk verb **1** trans. To hit, knock. 1950–. I. CROSS She zonked me again on the head with

ziff   zigabo   ziggety   zig-zag   zilch   zillion   zipless this hairbrush (1960). **2** intr. To fail; to lose consciousness, to die. 1968–. LISTENER If Johnny zonked, it would be bad for my book (1968). **3 to zonk out: a** intr. To fall heavily asleep. 1970–. NEW YORK NEWS MAGAZINE If mothers zonk out at three in the afternoon every day, they may continue that pattern after it's no longer necessary (1984). **b** trans. To overcome, overwhelm, knock out. 1973–. TELEGRAPH (Brisbane): It's J.R.'s power that zonks women out (1980). int and noun **4** (Representing the sound of) a blow or heavy impact, used to indicate finality. 1958–. R. BLYTHE He was a man with a catapult. He'd knock a pheasant down— *zonk!* (1979). [Imitative.]

zonked adjective **1** Intoxicated by alcohol or drugs; often followed by *out*. 1959–. DAILY TELEGRAPH A . . . Caucasian woman obviously zonked out . . . and a tracery of leaves resembling cannabis (1979). **2** Exhausted, tired *out*. 1972–. [From ZONK verb + *-ed*.]

zonking adjective and adverb Impressively (large or great). 1958–. TIMES Rather than play three zonking great parts . . . I will try to find some dazzling little cameo roles (1976). [From ZONK verb + *-ing*.]

zonky adjective Also **zonkey**. Odd, weird, freaky. 1972–. TIMES His book is really a study in ideas—or to coin an appropriately zonkey term—*weirdology* (1980). [From ZONK(ED adjective + *-y*.]

zoot suit noun orig US A man's suit with a long loose jacket and high-waisted tapering trousers, popular esp. in the 1940s (orig. worn by African-Americans). Also **zoot.** 1942–. T. PYNCHON Where'd you get that zoot you're wearing, there? (1973). [Reduplicated rhyming formation on *suit* noun.]

zooty adjective (Strikingly) fashionable, sharp. 1946–. S. BELLOW Her lover, too, with long jaws and zooty sideburns (1964). [From ZOOT noun + *-y*.]

zowie /zaʊiː, zaʊiː/ int US Expressing astonishment and often also admiration. *c.*1913–. P. G. WODEHOUSE He gets out and *zowie* a gang of thugs come jumping out of the bushes, and next thing you know they're off with your jewel case (1972). [Perh. blend of ZAP int and POW int + *-ie*.]

zob zonked zonking zonky zoot suit zooty zowie

Index

This index is arranged by subject matter, enabling users to home in on particular themes (such as knives, or anger) and see at a glance the slang vocabulary that relates to that area. To follow up on a particular item, simply refer to its alphabetical place in the dictionary.

The body and its functions

1. The body and its parts

Head bean; block; bonce; chump; cruet; filbert; hat-rack; lemon; napper; nob; noddle; noggin; nut; twopenny; Uncle Ned

Head as repository of sanity and source of common sense barnet; crumpet; loaf; noodle; onion; pannikin; scone

Hair barnet

Hair colour bluey

Bald person slaphead

Face boat; boat-race; chivvy; clock; dial; kisser; map; mooey; mug; mush; pan; phiz; phizog; puss

Eyes lamps; mince-pies; peepers

Ear earhole; lug; tab

Ear swollen by blows thick ear; tin ear

Nose beezer; boko; conk; honker; hooter; razzo; schnozz; schnozzle; shonk; sniffer; snitch; snoot; snorer

Mouth cake-hole; gash; gate; gob; hole; kisser; mooey; mush; north and south; pie-hole; smuch; trap; yap

Teeth choppers; Hampstead Heath; ivories; pearlies; pegs; snappers; tats

Men's facial hair bum fluff; face-fungus

Beard ziff

Moustache cookie-duster; mo; mush; soup-strainer; stash; tash; taz

Whiskers sluggers

Shave ocean wave

Bearded person beardie

Neck pencil neck

Arm wing

Hand duke; flipper; mauler; meat-hook; mitt; mud-hook

Left-handed person molly-dook

Finger pinkie

Breasts bazongas; bazookas; bazooms; bristols; charlies; dingleberries; jugs; knockers; melons; norks; titties

Large-breasted stacked

Nipples nips

Ribs slats

Abdomen amidships; beer belly; bingy; bread-basket; Derby kelly; Maconochie; Ned Kelly; puku

Navel belly button

Heart ticker

Intestines innards; kishke; shitbags

Womb oven

Pubic hair bush; carpet; pubes; thatch

Genitalia privates; sex; thing

Male genitals crown jewels; family jewels; jock; lunchbox

Penis bell end; chopper; cock; dick; ding; ding-a-ling; dingus; dipstick; dong; dork; Johnson; John Thomas; knob; langer; meat; meat tool; mickey; middle leg; old man; organ; pecker; pego; pencil; peter; plonker; prick; prong; pudding; putz; rig; rod; root; sausage; shaft; stalk; swipe; tadger; todger; tonk; tool; weapon; wee-wee; whang; willy; winkle

An erection of the penis boner; cock-stand; hard-on; horn; ramrod; rise; stiff; stiffie; wood

Testicles balls; bollocks; cobblers; cojones; goolies; knackers; marbles; nadgers; nads; nuts; pills; rocks; stones

Female genitals box; cunt; fanny; gash; hole; honey-pot; jelly roll; meat; minge; muff; pocketbook; pussy; quim; slit; snatch; zatch

Clitoris clit; (little) man in the boat

Buttocks acre; arse; backside; batty; beam; behind; bim; booty; botty; bronze; builder's bum; bum; buns; butt; can; chuff; duff; fanny; heinie; jacksy; keister; Khyber Pass; moon; patoot; patootie; prat; quoit; rass; slats; tail; tochus; tush; wazoo; zatch

Anus arsehole; bronze; freckle; hole; ort; ring; shithole

Rectum back passage

Legs benders; pegs; pins; stems; wheels

Shortness of legs duck's disease

Feet beetle-crushers; dogs; mud-hooks; plates of meat; tootsies

2. Nakedness

Naked bollock-naked; in the altogether; in the nuddy; starkers; starko

The bare skin the buff

To undress do the Full Monty; peel

To go naked skinny-dip; streak

3. Physique

Fat jelly-bellied

Fat person fatso; fatty; flop; lard-ass; Mother Bunch; slob; slug; slump

Fatness spare tyre

Muscular; massive beef to the heels

Thin person or animal beanpole; Skinny Liz; streak; string-bean

4. Sight, vision

A look, a glance bo-peep; butcher's; Captain Cook; decko; double O; gander; geek; look-see; pipe; shufti; squint; squiz

To look (at) clock; eyeball; gander; get a load; lamp; pipe; screw; shufti; squiz; take a lunar; twig

To keep watch, be observant keep nit; keep yow; stag; stake out

Observation obbo; obs; stake-out

To catch sight of, spot twig

A person who looks gongoozler

Glasses bins; cheaters; gig-lamps; specs

Sunglasses shades

A monocle window-pane

Wearing glasses specky

A bespectacled person four-eyes

Visually impaired boss-eyed

Visibility vis

5. Hearing

To listen, hear earhole; earwig; get a load of

Deaf cloth-eared; mutt; Mutt and Jeff; mutton

Impaired hearing cloth ears

A deaf person cloth ears; dummy

6. Smell

A smell funk; hum; niff

To smell unpleasantly hum; niff; pen and ink; whiff

Smelly funky; minging; niffy; on the nose

7. Bodily functions

To urinate or defecate do it; go

An unintentional act of urinating or defecating accident

To have an urgent need to urinate or defecate be caught short

Urination Jimmy Riddle; leak; number one; pee; pee-wee; piddle; piss; run-off; slash; tinkle; wazz; wee-wee; wet; whizz; widdle

To urinate leak; pee; piddle; piss; pluck a rose; point Percy at the porcelain; pump ship; strain the potatoes; syphon the python; tinkle; wazz; wee-wee; wet; whizz; widdle

Urine pee; piddle; piss; wee-wee; wet

The urinary system water-works

A bed-wetter pissabed

Defecation biggies; crap; dump; number two; shit; tom-tit

To defecate crap; dump; poop; shit

Excrement crap; dingleberry; do; doings; doo-doo; dooky; pony; poop; poopy; road apples; shit

Diarrhoea Aztec hop; Delhi belly; gippy tummy; Montezuma's revenge; runs; shits; squits; squitters; trots

A lavatory bog; can; crapper; dunny; dyke; House of Lords; jakes; john; karzy; lat; lav; lavvy; loo; place; rear; recess; shit-house; shouse; toot; W

A lavatory pan or other receptacle article; honey-bucket; jerry; po; pooperscooper; shitter; throne; thunder-box; thunder-mug

To vomit barf; chunder; go for the big spit; puke; ralph; sick up; turn up; upchuck; whip the cat

Vomiting chunder; technicolor yawn

A fart breezer

To belch gurk

To spit gob

Nasal mucus bogy; snot

Sexual secretions come; love juice; scum

To ejaculate shoot

Menstruation curse; jam-rag; rag; visitor

8. Pregnancy and childbirth

Pregnant gone; in pig; in pod; in the club; in the spud line; in the way; preg; preggers; preggo; preggy; up the creek; up the duff; up the pole; up the spout; up the stick

To make pregnant knock up; stork

A conceived child in the womb a bun in the oven; a pudding in the oven

Unplanned pregnancy accident; afterthought

A miscarriage miss

A premature birth or baby preemie

A Caesarian section Caesar

Midwifery; a midwifery case midder

Contraception Vatican roulette

9. Tiredness

Tired all in; beat; buggered; bushed; creased; euchred; knackered; like death warmed up; rooted; shagged; shot; stonkered; stove-up; tuckered; whacked; whipped; wiped; zonked

Tiredness bonk

To tire, exhaust do in; knacker; poop; sew up; tucker

10. Sleep

(A period of) sleep kip; nod; sack time; skipper

A short sleep caulk; snooze; snore-off; zizz

A rest sit-down

To sleep kip; pound one's ear; zizz

To go to bed crash; doss; hit the hay; kip down; sack down; sack out

To go to sleep zonk out

To snore saw gourds

Waking up wakey-wakey

To remain in bed late in the morning sack in

A place to sleep crash pad; doss; doss-house; flop; flop-house; kip; letty; skipper; spike

Bed flea-bag; hot bed; kip; mick; pit; sack; Uncle Ned; wanking pit

Sleeping soundly well away

Bedding nap; weeping willow

Sleepy dopey

11. Illness

Ill all-overish; butcher's hook; crook; dicky; icky-boo; like death warmed up; on the sick

An illness crud; lurgy; nadgers; woofits

To suffer illness come over

To injure do in

Bruising mouse; shiner

Cancer big C

Cramp Charley-horse

Diarrhoea Aztec hop; Delhi belly; gippy tummy; Montezuma's revenge; runs; shits; squits; squitters; trots

Dizzy slap-happy; slug-nutty

To have a fit spazz out

Nitrogen narcosis narks

Paralysis Saturday night palsy

Rheumatism screwmatics; screws

A spot, pimple hickey; zit

Stomach pain gut-rot

Tropical diseases yellow jack

Unconscious spark out

Venereal diseases clap; dose; load; old ral; pox; syph

Protection against venereal disease propho

Wounds homer; road rash; strawberry

Lame gammy; gimpy

A disabled person basket case; gimp; wheelie; wingy

Germs wog

Sick leave sickie

Medical practitioners and nurses medic; medico; prick-farrier; zambuck

Doctors croaker; pill; pill-peddler; quack; right croaker; vet

Surgeons gynae; orthopod; sawbones

Medicine jollop

Hospital in/out of dock

Ambulance blood wagon; meat wagon

Medical examination short-arm

Surgery op

Gynaecology gynae

Nursing special

Autopsy post

12. Death

Death big sleep; chop; curtains; deep-six; thirty; wooden cross

Dead brown bread; bung; loaf of bread; napoo; off the hooks

(To be) dead and buried push up the daisies; six feet under; under the daisies

To die buy the farm; cark; cash in; croak; get; go for a Burton; go west; hand in one's dinner-pail; hop the twig; kick off; kick the bucket; kiss off; off it; pass in one's chips; peg out; pop off; snuff it; stop; turn up one's toes

Doomed to die one's number is up

Someone who has died floater; goner; stiff

A **coffin** box; pine drape; wooden overcoat

A **cemetery** marble orchard

A **hearse** meat-wagon

To **bury** plant

Rigor mortis rigmo

People and society

1. Ethnic and national groups

English people choom; homey; kipper; Limey; loiner; pommy; pongo; Scouse; Scouser; tyke; Woodbine

French people Frenchy; frog; froggy

Germans Boche; Dutchy; Erich; Fritz; Heinie; Hun; Jerry; Kraut; sale Boche; sausage; squarehead

Gibraltarians scorpion

Greeks bubble and squeak

Irish people bog-trotter; harp; Mick; Paddy; Pat; turk; turkey

Italians Eyetie; ginzo; macaroni; spaghetti; wop

Poles Polack

Russians Ivan; Rusky

Scandinavians herring-choker; Norski; squarehead

Scots Jock

Welsh people Taffia; Taffy; Welshy

Southern Europeans; people of the western Mediterranean dago; grease-ball; grill; guinea

Central and Southeastern Europeans bohunk; hunk; hunyak

Egyptians gippy

Chinese Chink; Chinkey; chow; Pong

Japanese Charlie; Nip; Tojo

Pakistanis Paki

Vietnamese Charlie; dink; gomer; nog; Victor Charlie

East Asians dothead; gook; moose; noggy; slant; slant-eye; slope; slopehead; yellow peril

Americans; the US bean-eater; cugine; guido; Merkin; prune picker; Sammy; septic tank; snow-bird

Canadians Canuck; herring-choker; Joe; pea-soup; Spud Islander

Native Americans nitchie

Latin Americans grease-ball; greaser; spic; spiggoty; wetback

Argentinians Argie

Costa Ricans Tico

Mexicans beaner; chili-eater

Australians Alf; Aussie; Bananalander; Barcoo salute; cornstalk; dig; digger; Groper; gumsucker; ocker; Oz; Ozzie; pure merino; sand-groper; Tassie; tothersider

Aboriginals abo; binghi; boong; Jacky; Mary; munjon

Arabs and other Middle Eastern peoples Abdul; camel jockey

Jews bagel; five-to-two; four-by-two; God forbid; Hymie; ikey; ikeymo; JAP; Jew boy; kike; mocky; Red Sea pedestrian; sheeny; shoniker; shonk; Yahudi; yekke; Yid

Gentiles yok

White people Amerika; Babylon; Charlie; combo; grey; gringo; honky; jeff; jumble; kelch; man; Mary; Miss Ann; Mr Charlie; ofay; pale-face; peck; peckerwood; pink; pink toe; ridge-runner; roundeye; white meat; white nigger; Whitey; wigger; wonk

Coloured people black velvet; boong; darky; jungle bunny; skepsel; wog

Black people boogie; boot; buppie; coon; dinge; jazzbo; jig; jigaboo; jit; kink; member; moolie; munt; nig; nigger; nig-nog; nigra; peola; pink toe; Sambo; schvartzer; shine; smoke; sooty; spade; splib; spook

A subservient black person coconut; oreo; pink chaser; pork chop; tom; Uncle Tom; white nigger

Gipsies didicoi; gippo

Foreigners dago; gook; Johnny Foreigner; wog

An immigrant ethno; Jimmy Grant

A person who wears a turban rag-head; towelhead

A supporter of racial segregation seg

2. People

A person animal; article; artist; beggar; bleeder; bod; cookie; egg; face; fish; gunk; merchant; outfit; perisher; possum; scout; sort; type; whatsit; whosis; whosit

Oneself ego; jills; number one; one's arse

A male person; a fellow bastard; bimbo; bird; blighter; blokie; bugger; cat; cove; dog; dude; fella; feller; gazebo; gee; geezer; gink; gunsel; jasper; Joe; Joe Bloggs; Joe Blow; Joe Doakes; Joe Public; Joe Soap; joker; josser; lad; majita; omee; ou; outfit; pisser; plug; rye; snoozer; sod; son-of-a-bitch; stud; whatsisface

Typical of a man blokeish; laddish

A woman Betty; biddy; bim; bimbo; bint; bird; bit; bride; broad; buer; chapess; chick; chicklet; chippy; dame; dona; faggot; femme; frail; frippet; gash; girls; heifer; jane; judy; knitting; ladette; mole; mort; mot; muff; mystery; number; palone; popsy; potato; poule; quiff; quim; Richard; rye mort; sheila; sort; split; sub-deb; tab; tabby; tit; titter; tom; toots; tootsy; totty; twist-and-twirl; wimp; wren

A female partner or companion best girl; dinah; frat; jelly; mamma; moll; patootie; queen; red-hot mamma; squarie; tart; wag

A domineering woman battleaxe

A stupid woman bimbette; bimbo; dumb Dora

3. Children

A child ankle-biter; chavvy; God forbid; juvie; kiddo; kidlet; littley; nipper; rug-rat; saucepan lid; shaver; sprog; sprout; squirt; tin lid

A mischievous child Peck's bad boy; perisher

An illegitimate/legitimate child illegit; legit

A baby chavvy; snork

A teenager teeny-bopper; weeny-bopper

A person who has a sexual affair with someone much younger baby-snatcher; cradle-snatcher

4. Relations

Father governor; old man

Mother old girl; old lady; old woman

Husband monkey man; old man; old pot; papa; pot and pan

Wife ball and chain; dutch; her indoors; missus; Mrs; old lady; old woman; trouble and strife

Brother bro

Sister skin and blister

Grandfather gramp

Grandmother nin

A former spouse or lover ex

To marry, get married splice

Married hitched; spliced

5. Terms of address

Used to address a male big boy; bo; bro; bub; buster; chummy; cobber; cock; cocker; dad; daddy; guv; mac; matey; mister; mush; old bean; pal; pops; squire; sport; sunshine; tosh

Used to address a female duchess; girls; ma; missis; sister

Unisex darl; duck; face; face-ache; fatso; fatty; four-eyes; honey-baby; kiddo; man; old thing; poopsie; sugar

6. Groups

A group of people crew; crush; flash mob; massive; mob; posse; push; rat pack; team

A group of things or people Pip, Squeak, and Wilfred

As a group mob-handed

To act in a group; conspire row in

Acting as a group in cahoots

7. Status

Status, reputation cred; street cred

That which is important nitty-gritty

An important statement mouthful

A high-ranking or important person big boy; big brass; big bug; big cheese; big daddy; big enchilada; big fish; biggie; big gun; big noise; big shot; big wheel; bigwig; brass; brass-hat; tyee; wheel

The most important or highest-ranking person; the person in charge bloke; chiefy; gaffer; guv; guvner; honcho; king-fish; macher; main squeeze; man; Mr Big; old man; owner; pea; prex; skipper; skull; top banana; top dog; trump

Someone unimportant spear-carrier

A title handle; K

A titled person lifer

Service ranks buck-ass; buck general; buck private; buck sergeant; butterbar; chicken colonel; chiefy; corp; erk; groupie; Jimmy the One; killick; lance-jack; looey; loot; one-pipper; P.F.C.; plonk; quarter-bloke; snake; snotty; spec; striper; top; topper; top sergeant; wingco

A badge or other insignia of rank hash-mark; killick; pip; scrambled egg; tape

The upper classes Hooray Henry; nob; Sloane Ranger; Sloanie; toff; upper

Of or characteristic of the upper classes; socially superior posh

A snob high-hat; pure merino; toffee-nose

Snobbish, pretentious hoity-toity; la-di-da; toffee-nosed

A self-important person I am

A lower-class person chav; pikey; pleb

Of or characteristic of the lower classes; ill-bred chavvy; hairy; hairy at the heels; plebby

8. Social categories

Lifestyle buppie; chuppie; dink; dinky; empty nester; guppie; oink; woopie; yump; yup; yuppie

To change in lifestyle yuppify

Youth groups bodgie; duck-tail; hoodie; sharpie; skin; ted; widgie

9. Conventionality

Conventional, conservative, respectable corn-fed; square; straight; way-in

A conventional person cube; mossback; shellback; square; square John

A conventional place or institution auntie; cubesville; squaresville

Unconventional, avant-garde far out; way out

10. Friends

A friend ace boon coon; china; cobber; good buddy; goombah; homeboy; homie; lads; main man; main squeeze; matey; mellow; mucker; OAO; oppo; peeps; raggie; sidekick; side-kicker; squeeze; winger

Having a friendly relationship; friendly matey

To form a friendship cobber up

An introduction to a person knock-down

11. Solitude

On one's own like a shag on a rock; on one's Jack Jones; on one's Pat Malone; on one's tod; single-o

Someone on their own wallflower

To act alone do one's own thing; stag

12. Sex

Sexual desire bedroom eyes; glad eye; hot pants; hots; lech

Feeling sexual desire, lustful horn-mad; horny; hot; hot to trot; randy-arsed; red-hot; sexed up

To experience sexual desire lech

To ogle perv

Infatuated cunt-struck; gone on; shook on; stuck on

To be infatuated with have a case on

An infatuation pash; spoons; thing

A glance indicative of infatuation goo-goo eyes

To flirt, woo, court be all over; chat; frat; groove; mack; make time; pirate; pull; race off; spoon; track with; trot

A person who flirts or courts cock-teaser; debs' delight; prick-teaser; spoon

Courtship monkey parade; sexcapade

Looking for sexual partners gagging for; on the make; on the pirate; on the pull

A promiscuous person raver; skank; swinger; swingle

A promiscuous man chaser; lech; lounge lizard; lover boy; poodle-faker; ram; skirt-chaser; wolf

A promiscuous woman alley cat; bike; chippy; floozie; groupie; ho; hobag; hoochie; hosebag; hot pants; low-heel; lowie; mamma; man-eater; punch-board; puta; roach; round-heels; scrub; scupper; slag; slapper; tart; totty; tramp

To behave promiscuously cruise; hawk one's mutton; pull a train; put out; screw around; swing; tom-cat

A city characterized by licentiousness and vice sin city

Sex appeal it; oomph; S.A.

A sexually attractive person babe; corker; cracker; cutie; cutie-pie; dish; dream-boat; eyeful; glamour puss; hottie; (little) bit of all right; looker; peach; peacherino; ripper; scorcher; sexboat; sex-bomb; sexpot; smasher; spunk; sweetie-pie

A sexually attractive man beefcake; God's gift; hunk; stud; stud muffin

A sexually attractive woman cheesecake; cookie; cutie; doll; dolly; dolly-bird; fox; jelly; package; patootie; queen; Ruby Queen; sex kitten; snuggle-pup; tomato

A sexually attractive person or thing turn-on

Sexually attractive babelicious; bootylicious; buff; dishy; dreamy; fit; foxy; glam; hunky; peachy; phat; sexational; shagtastic; tasty

To attract or stimulate sexually turn on

A person considered as an object of sexual desire or availability crumpet; homework; make; talent

A female sex object ass; beaver; bit of fluff; brush; crackling; grumble; piece of ass; poontang; pussy; quim; skirt; spare; tail; totty

A sexual partner or partner in sexual intercourse cliner; easy rider; fancy man; ho; lover boy; main squeeze; OAO; papa; patootie; pull; shack-job; shack-up; squeeze; sweetback; sweet man; trick; wag

A person considered solely as a partner in sexual intercourse fuck; hump; lay; poke; root; screw

An older sexual partner baby-snatcher; cradle-snatcher; daddy; dirty old man; DOM

A younger sexual partner jail-bait; toy boy

A kiss banger; smoush

A love-bite hickey

Caressing, foreplay canoodle; feel; footie; grope; lallygag; love-up; lumber; mush; neck; reef; slap and tickle; smooch; snog

Sexual activity, sexual intercourse ass; bang; bonk; booty; frig; fuck; greens; hanky-panky; how's your father; hump; it; jazz; jelly roll; jig-a-jig; jump; knee-trembler; lay; length; mifky-pifky; naughty; nooky; nooner; oats; one-night stand; other; other thing; phata phata; poke; pom-pom; poontang; pussy; root; rumpy-pumpy; screw; shag; tail; that there; trick; trim; tumble; wham, bam, thank you ma'am; yum-yum; zatch; zig-zig; zipless

Simulated sexual intercourse dry fuck

To have sex (with), copulate (with) ball; bang; boff; bonk; cop off; diddle; dip one's wick; do; do over; frig; fuck; get into; get one's end away; get one's leg over; get one's nuts off; get one's rocks off; get some; have; have it off; hump; jazz; knock; knock off; lay; lay pipe; make; make it; make out; make time; mollock; nail; naughty; plug; poke; pump; ride; roger; root; saw a chunk off; score; screw; sex; shaft; shag; shtup; slip someone a length; stuff; tail; tear off a bit; trick; tumble; tup

Having sex on the job; up

To achieve orgasm come; get off on; go off; spend

Multiple sex clusterfuck; daisy chain; dogging; gang-bang; gang-shag; onion

To perform oral sex (on) eat; felch; French; gamahuche; give head; go down; plate; suck

Oral sex French; sixty-nine; soixante-neuf

To perform cunnilingus eat pussy

A cunnilinguist muff-diver

To fellate blow; nosh

Fellatio blow job

A fellator or fellatrix cock-sucker; prick-sucker

Someone with unconventional sexual tastes kink; kinky; nonce; paedo; perv; pervo; secko; sheepshagger

Sado-masochism fladge

Anal sex fist-fuck; fisting; postilion; ream; rim

To expose one's genitals as a means of sexual gratification flash

Autoeroticism scarfing

To masturbate beat the meat; diddle; frig; jack off; jerk off; pull off; pull one's pudding; rub up; toss off; wank; whack off

Masturbation hand-job; pocket billiards; wank

Contraceptives fish skin; French letter; frog; johnny; rubber; rubber johnny; safe; scumbag; skin

Pornographic, erotic adult; beaver; feelthy; fuck-me; jerk-off; naughty; porny; raunchy; sexational; split beaver; tits and ass

Pornography leg art; pornie; schmutz

To make more sexy sex up

Virginity cherry

Virility lead in one's pencil

Relationships bach; item; sleeping dictionary

To have a sexual relationship carry on; shack up

An expert on sexual matters sexpert

13. Sexual orientation

Homosexual bent; queer; so; that way

A homosexual ginger-beer; guppie; homo; morphodite; queer

A male homosexual arse bandit; batty boy; battyman; booty bandit; bufu; bum-boy; fag; faggot; fairy; flit; friend of Dorothy; fruit; fruit-loop; fuck buddy; gunsel; iron; jessie; jocker; lizzie; Margery; Mary Ann; mo; moffie; nance; nancy; nancy-boy; nelly; palone; pansy; ponce; poncey; poof; poofter; pretty boy; puff; punk; pussy; quean; queen; queenie; rear gunner; shirt-lifter; sister; sod; steamer; swish; tart; tonk; trade; twinkie; weeny; white-shoe; wife; wonk; woofter

A female homosexual bulldagger; bull-dyke; butch; carpet muncher; diesel dyke; dyke; femme; les; lesbo; leso; lizzie; mantee; Marge; Margery; rug-muncher

Places of homosexual assignation cottage; tea room

Concealment and revelation closet queen; out

A homosexual's pimp poofter rorter

A woman who habitually consorts with homosexual men fag hag

Assault on homosexuals queer-bashing

(A) heterosexual straight

(A) bisexual AC/DC; ambidextrous; ambisextrous; bi; bi-guy; gender-bender; switch-hitter; versatile

To be bisexual swing both ways

A transvestite drag queen; she-male; trannie; TV

14. Prostitution

Prostitutes bimbo; brass; broad; chippy; chromo; crow; gash; ho; hooker; hustler; lady of the night; moll; mud kicker; muff; mystery; pavement princess; poule-de-luxe; pro; pross; prosty; pusher; quiff; scrubber; scupper; slack; slag; tart; tom; twopenny upright; working girl; yum-yum girl

Male prostitutes bum-boy; pimp; rent; rent-boy; renter; rough trade; trade

Working as a prostitute on the bash; on the game; on the knock; on the turf

To work as a prostitute hawk one's mutton; hook; hustle; tom

Prostitution trade

An assignation with a prostitute business; short time; trick

A prostitute's client john; score; short-timer; sugar daddy; trick

Brothels cat-house; chicken ranch; creep-house; crib; drum; hook-shop; joy-house; juke; kip; knocking shop; meat-house; meat-market; notch-house; parlour-house; peg-house; rib-joint; slaughter-house; whore-shop

Pimps bludger; jelly bean; mack; mack daddy; nookie-bookie; ponce; sweetback

To act as a pimp bludge; mack; pimp

A group of prostitutes working for the same person or organization stable; string

The vice squad pussy posse

15. Crime

Dishonest, corrupt bent; cronk; crook; dodgy; wide

Dishonestly or illegally acquired or produced crooked; hooky; shonky; sly

Not illegal legit

Dishonest or corrupt activity graft; grift; hanky-panky; jiggery-pokery; lurk; mumping; shenanigan

To act dishonestly or corruptly graft; grift; rort; spiv

To put to a dishonest or corrupt use; to induce to behave corruptly bend; nobble

A criminal undertaking caper; frame-up; inside job; job; outside job; scam; single-o; tickle

A dishonest or corrupt person grafter; lurkman; shyster; spiv

A criminal baddy; bail bandit; chummy; crim; grafter; grifter; hustler; inside man; juvie; kink; perp; punk; punter; ram; scammer; slag; streetman; talent; urger; villain; wheelman

A rogue, ne'er-do-well chancer; Jack the Lad; scally; skeezicks; wide boy

A member of a criminal gang goombah; hood; made; mobster; moll; mug; yardie

A criminal gang mob

An armed criminal gun moll; gunsel; gun-slinger; rodman; torpedo

A criminal's equipment dub; iron; loid; ripper; shim; squeeze; twirl

To reconnoitre with a view to commiting a robbery or other crime case; drum; prowl

A criminal's look-out or sentinel cockatoo

An area frequented by criminals Costa del Crime; tenderloin

A victim of crime fly-flat; mark; package

A getaway after committing a crime stoppo

Stealing, theft blag; creep; dip; dragging; five-finger discount; heist; hoist; knock-off; on the game; pick-up; ram-raiding; roadwork; steaming; stick-up; sting; trick; whizz; wilding

To steal; to rob blag; bust; do; dodge; drum; duff; glom; go through; half-inch; heist; hoist; hot-stuff; hot-wire; knock; knock down; knock off; liberate; lift; loid; nick; nip; peter; pick up; pinch; rabbit; rat; reef; rip; roll; score; shim; snavel; snipe; snitch; souvenir; stall; steam; stick up; swipe; take; take off; thieve; tickle; twoc; whip; wog; work the tubs

A thief blagger; cracksman; creep; dancer; dip; drummer; duffer; finger; heel; hook; houseman; klepto; moll; parlour-jumper; pennyweighter; pete-man; peterman; pick; pick-up man; prat-digger; rampsman; ram-raider; reefer; screwer; screwman; second-storey man; stair-dancer; steamer; tea-leaf; tool-man; waddy; whizz; whizzer; whizz-mob

Inclined to steal sticky-fingered; thieving

Stolen bent; hot; kinky

Stolen property goods; kinky; knock-off; rabbit; score; swag; take

16. Killing

17. Reprimanding and punishing

someone up; rocket; ruck; scrub; sort someone out; take someone out to the woodshed; tick someone off; word

Being reprimanded on the carpet; on the pan; on the peg

Punishment book; rap

Corporal punishment cuts; sixer; toco

To punish weigh someone off

To punish by hitting tan someone's hide

To avoid punishment walk

18. The police

A police officer bear; bogy; brown bomber; cop; copper; cozzer; cozzpot; demon; dick; Fed; flat-foot; flatty; fuzz; gangbuster; gendarme; grass; grasshopper; harness bull; Hop; horny; jack; john; johndarm; John Law; Johnny; jonnop; Keystone; law; nab; nailer; narc; Old Bill; pig; plod; polis; pounder; roach; roller; roz; rozzer; scuffer; shamus; shoo-fly; skipper; sky bear; Smokey Bear; sparrow cop; split; statie; trap; walloper; wolly; woodentop

A female police officer Dickless Tracy; plonk

A detective busy; D; dee; demon; dick; eye; fink; gumshoe; jack; op; Pink; Richard; shamus; tec

The police bacon; bill; filth; Five-O; fuzz; heat; law; man; Old Bill; plod; polis; Sweeney

A police station cop-shop; factory; nick

A police district manor

A police vehicle jam sandwich; meat wagon; noddy bike; paddy-wagon; pie-wagon; sky bear; squadrol

A police bell gong

Police action squeal

Police surveillance obbo

Police information reader

Police insignia potsy; tin

19. Prisons

Prison big house; boob; booby hatch; can; choky; clink; cooler; dummy; factory; flowery; glass-house; hoosegow; jug; juvie; mill; mush; nick; pen; peter; pokey; quod; rock pile; slam; slammer; tank

In prison in hock; in lumber; inside; in stir; upstate

Imprisonment; a prison sentence bird; birdlime; bit; carpet; double sawbuck; fall; handful; hard; jolt; Kathleen Mavourneen; lag; moon; neves; newspaper; Paddy Doyle;

pontoon; porridge; rouf; sawbuck; seg; sleep; sixer; solitary; spot; stage; stretch; taxi; time; trey; trick

To send or be sent to prison bang up; dub up; go down; lag; send down; settle; slough

A prisoner con; ex-con; lag; lifer; loser; passman; red band; star; tobacco baron; yardbird

A prisoner-of-war kriegie

Prison staff goon; ham and beef; screw; twirl

Prison uniform patch; stripes

Prison discipline dry bath

Communication inside prison floater; kite

Parole violate

To leave prison have it away; hit the bricks; spring

Leaving prison spring

Out of prison on the grass

Escaped from prison over the wall

The world out of prison outside

20. Vagrancy

A vagrant, tramp, etc. bag lady; bindle man; bum; dingbat; dosser; drummer; dyno; gay-cat; jocker; mumper; pikey; prushun; ring-tail; road kid; saddle tramp; skell; skipper; slag; stew-bum; stiff; swamper; toe-ragger; vag; whaler

Vagrants collectively profesh

Vagrancy vag

A vagrant's possessions, equipment, etc. bindle; bluey; drum; lump; Matilda; nap; shiralee; turkey; Wagga Wagga blanket

To travel as a vagrant, carrying one's possessions hump one's swag; waltz Matilda

A place frequented by vagrants derry; jungle; skid row; stem

21. Politics

Politicians and political activists Commie; Commo; dry; fundi; high-binder; parlour pink; pinko; pinky; pol; polly; prog; red; redneck; red-ragger; shellback; Shinner; snollygoster; Stickie; straddle-bug; tanky; Trot; wet

Administrators veep; Whitehall Warrior

Campaigning press the flesh

Political corruption graft; sleaze

Displaced person reffo

22. Military, maritime, and airforce

Personnel ack emma; ATS; bloke; brass; brass-hat; dug-out; erk; guns; Jack Shalloo; jaunty; kiwi; lamps; mustang; odds and sods; old man; orderly buff; orderly dog; orderly pig; paddlefoot; Pay; paybob; penguin; pill; ping; pin-party; pipes; plank-owner; plumber; pongo; red hat; red legs; retread; salt horse; Saturday night soldier; shoey; staff wallah; straight leg; tanky; terrier; top brass; white hat; Whitehall Warrior; Wrac; Wraf; Wren

Soldiers brown job; choco; dogface; doughboy; doughfoot; gravel-crusher; grunt; jarhead; leather-neck; merc; old sweat; P.B.I.; poilu; pongo; squaddie; Tommy

Sailors farmer; fowl; gob; gobby; Jack-tar; matelot; oily wad; old ship; Paddy Wester; peggy; salt; shellback; soldier; stripey; tar

The Navy Andrew; red duster; Wavy Navy

Marines jarhead; leather-neck

Airmen fly boy; glamour boy; modoc; tail-end charlie

Military police jack; provo; red cap; snowdrop

Batmen and other assistants doggy; dog-robber; Jack Dusty

Units crush; mob; outfit

To join the services re-up

Conscription nasho

A conscript nasho; zombie

Leave of absence leaf

Discharge Section Eight; short-timer

Marching and drill square-bashing; tab; yomp

Discipline AWOL; bullshit; fizzer; glass-house; jankers; mush; on the peg

Navigation angels; Bradshaw; ham-bone; iron mike; nav; pipsqueak

Training boot camp; mad minute; perisher; quirk; Shop; TEWT

Uniform giggle; square rig

Identity discs dog tag; meat ticket

Gas masks nose-bag

Decorations come up with the rations; fruit salad; gong; Mutt and Jeff; Pip, Squeak, and Wilfred; rooty gong; ruptured duck; screaming eagle; Spam medal

Bombs bread-basket; doodlebug; lazy dog; nuke; pill; screamer

Bombing equipment Mickey; Mickey Mouse

Mortars, grenades, etc. moaning minnie; oil can; pill; pineapple; plum-pudding; red devil; rum-jar; sausage; toc emma

Depth charges ash-can; pill

Ammunition ammo; G.I. can; pill; pipsqueak; plonker; woolly bear

Torpedoes fish; kipper; mouldy; torp

Anti-aircraft fire flaming onions; triple-A

Weapon emplacements and defensive structures asparagus-bed; dustbin; elephant

An attack hate; mad minute; op; party; prang; rhubarb; scramble; stonk

To attack attrit; jap; lay an egg; nuke; plaster; prang; scramble; shoot; smear; spike-bozzle; stonk

A parachute brolly; silk; umbrella

A paratrooper para; skyman

A parachute accident cigarette roll; Roman Candle

To jump using a parachute step out

Accommodation and catering bivvy; Naffy; stone frigate; snake-pit; Wrennery

Terrorists terr

Civilians civvy; P.F.C.

Civilian life Civvy Street; outside

Civilian clothes civvies; dog-robbers

Pacifism conchy; Cuthbert

23. Espionage

A spy cut-out; mole; plumber; spook; swallow; undercover

Spy organizations Circus; Company; trade

Communication drop; post office; treff

To equip with hidden microphones spike

Reconnaissance obbo

Assassination wet

24. Religion

An (over)enthusiastically religious person Bible-banger; Bible-pounder; Christer; fundi; God-botherer; God squad; holy Joe

Excessively religious pi

A member of a particular religion Doolan; left-footer; Metho; Pape; Prod; Proddy-dog; Prot; Roman Candle; spike; Taig; Tim; tyke

A priest or clergyman holy Joe; josser; joss-man; padre; sin bosun; sin-shifter; sky pilot

A church God-box

The Salvation Army Sally Anne; Sally Army; Salvo

God Gawd

The Devil Old Scratch

Animals

Birds chook; gump; Jacko

Camels hump; oont

Cats mog; moggie

Cattle horny; mickey

Crocodilians freshy; 'gator

Dogs dawg; goorie; ki-yi; mong; mutt; pooch

Donkeys, mules, etc. donk; hard tail; jarhead; moke; skin

Horses bronk; dog; geegee; hay-burner; moke; mudder; mudlark; nag; neddy; plug; pony; prad; rosin-back; skate; skin; skinner; squib; stickout; tomato sauce

Insects and the like cootie; live stock; mahogany flat; mossie; pants rabbit; seam-squirrel; skeeter; toto; wog

An entomologist bug-hunter

Kangaroos boomer; roo

Octopuses ocky

Pigs mudlark

Sharks Noah's Ark

Sheep jumbuck; placer

Snakes Joe Blake

A large animal lunker

A scraggy animal hat-rack

Sustenance and intoxication

1. Foodstuffs

Food chow; eats; grub; gut-rot; jock; lump; munchie; munchies; munga; mungaree; mush; nosh; poke-out; pound and pint; scarf; scran; slush; stodge; tucker

Bread dodger; door-step; needle and thread; punk; rooty; slinger; toke

Sandwiches BLT; dodger; sambo; sammie; sanger; sarnie; wad

Meat baby's head; Fanny Adams; Harriet Lane; Kate and Sidney; Maconochie; red horse; salt horse; schooner on the rocks; tinned horse; underground mutton

Sausages bags of mystery; banger; frank; red-hot; sav; snag; starver; tube steak; weeny; wienie

Curry Ruby Murray

Fish Spithead pheasant; whales

Sauces gippo; red-eye; red lead

Soup hoosh; shackles; slum; slumgullion

Eggs goog; googie; hen-fruit

Margarine Maggie Ann

Potatoes murphy; spud; tater

Beans and peas bullets

Mushrooms shroom

Gooseberries goosegog

Cakes sinker; tabnab

Biscuit squashed fly

Puddings frog-spawn

Sweets chewy; chutty; gob-stopper; nutty; pogey bait

Miscellaneous oggy; sac; slider; spag; spag bol; spaggers; tiddy oggy; train smash; za

Beverages skilly

Tea char; gun-fire; Rosy (Lee); sergeant-major; splash; split pea

Coffee mud; java; joe

Cocoa, drinking chocolate kye

Soft drinks fizz; Polly; spider

2. Eating and drinking

To consume get outside of; go; guts; hoe in; mac out; mug up; neck; nosh; pig out; put on the nose-bag; scarf; shift; snarf; snarfle; woof

An eater nosher

An overeater dustbin; gannet; guzzle-guts

Dietary preferences veggie

Meals hash-up; mug-up; sit-down; soupy

A large or over-large meal beano; nosh-up; pig-out

Food distribution, preparation, cooking, and serving barbie; Dutching; eighty-six; irons; me-and-you; nuke; rabbit-o; set-up; shackle-up; sling hash; slum-gun; soup gun; spud-bashing; to go

A second helping of food gash

Preparation and serving of drinks drum; drum up; on the rocks; set-up

Cooks bab; babbling brook; cookie; doctor; poisoner; slum burner; slushy; spud barber

Waiting and kitchen staff biscuit-shooter; cookie-pusher; hasher; hash-slinger; Nippy; pearl diver

Eating places and food shops beanery; caff; chippy; greasy spoon; hash-joint; nosh; noshery; one-arm joint; tratt

Hungry could eat a horse
Thirsty spit chips

3. Alcohol

Alcoholic drink alky; booze; electric soup; giggle-water; grog; jollop; joy-juice; juice; jungle juice; neck-oil; nose paint; panther juice; poison; rabbit; River Ouse; sauce; shick; shicker; skimish; smash; stagger juice; wallop; white line

A drink bevvy; chaser; gargle; jar; jolt; middy; nobbler; nooner; other half; peg; pony; rosiner; shant; sherbet; shooter; shorty; sippers; slug; snifter; snort; speedball; spot; stiffener; tank; taste; tincture; wet

Poor-quality drink firewater; gnat's piss; gut-rot; hooch; King Kong; lunatic soup; pink-eye; popskull; rot-gut; scrap iron; screech; shypoo; snake-juice; Sneaky Pete

Illicitly distilled or irregularly concocted drink moon; pruno; sly grog; smoke; torp; torpedo juice

Beer amber fluid; Britney Spears; coldie; heavy; hop; pig's ear; slop; suds; wallop

Brandy jackass brandy; O.D.V.

Champagne Bolly; boy; champers; fizz; shampoo; widow

Gin lightning; mother's ruin; needle and pin

Methylated spirit goom; jake; metho; white lady

Pink gin pinkers

Rum Tom Thumb

Whisky forty-rod whisky; pine-top; red-eye; scat; screech; skee; smoke; snake poison; tarantula-juice; white lightning; white mule

Wine bombo; dago red; fourpenny dark; Lizzie; nelly; pinky; plink; plonk; red biddy; red ink; Red Ned; vino

A container for drink long-sleever; set-up; stubby; tinny

An empty container dead soldier; old soldier

A place where alcohol is sold or drunk beer-off; boozer; crib; dive; drum; nineteenth hole; peg-house; rub-a-dub; rubbity; rubbity-dub; shypoo; speak; speakeasy; speako; watering hole

An employee in such a place B-girl; sitter

To provide or serve with drink mug; shout

A drinking spree bat; beer-up; bender; binge; blind; booze; boozeroo; booze-up; brannigan; drunk; jag; liquid lunch; piss-up; sesh; souse

On a drinking spree on a whizzer; on the bash; on the batter; on the bend; on the piss; on the skite

To drink alcohol (to excess) be on the bottle; bevvy; binge; booze; chug; chugalug; get a spark up; hit the booze; put under the table; shicker; slop up; souse; sozzle; stop; tank up

Drunk Adrian Quist; arseholed; as drunk as a piss-ant; as pissed as a newt; bevvied; binged; bladdered; blasted; blind; blithered; blotto; boiled; bombed; boozed; bottled; Brahms and Liszt; buffy; canned; cock-eyed; corned; crocked; elephant's trunk; fried; full; gassed; half-cut; half-shot; high; honkers; inked; jagged; juiced; kaylied; legless; liquefied; lit; loaded; looped; lubricated; mashed; minging; mokus; molly the monk; molo; moon-eyed; motherless; Mozart and Liszt; mullered; oiled; out of it; out the monk; paralysed; paralytic; pickled; pie-eyed; pinko; piped; pipped; pissed; pixilated; plastered; plonked; plotzed; ploughed; polluted; potted; rat-arsed; ratted; ripe; rosy; rotten; schnockered; shellacked; shicker; shickered; shot; slewed; sloshed; smashed; snockered; soaked; soused; sozzled; spiflicated; squiffed; squiffy; squizzed; steamed; stewed; stiff; stinking; stinko; stocious; stoned; stonkered; stung; stunned; swacked; swizzled; tanked; tiddled; tiddly; tight; tin hats; tired and emotional; tonicked; trashed; trolleyed; up the pole; wasted; wazzed; well away; whiffled; whistled; wiped; wired; wrecked; zig-zag; zonked

A large amount of alcoholic drink load; skinful

The state of being drunk brannigan; bun; edge; heat; mokus

To drink to excess; become drunk feel no pain; (have had) one over the eight; tie one on

A drinker of alcohol; a drunkard alky; boozer; goomy; hophead; Jack ashore; Jimmy Woodser; juicer; lager lout; lush; lushy; metho; piss artist; piss-head; plonko; rum-hound; rummy; rum-pot; shicker; soak; soaker; souse; stiff; tanker; two-pot screamer; white line; wine dot; wino

A cell for an arrested drunk drunk tank

The effects of drinking (too much) alcohol beer belly; beer goggles; brewer's droop; brewer's goitre; D.T.'s; grog blossom; jim-jams; jimmies; nose paint; strawberry

Suffering from the effects of drinking alcohol hung; overhung

A hang-over cure corpse reviver

To adulterate a drink needle; spike

Adulterated drink needle beer

Accompaniments to an alcoholic drink rock; splash

Toasts bung-ho; chin chin; down the hatch

Absence of alcohol dry; dry out; on the wagon

4. Tobacco

Tobacco baccy; old rope; snout; weed

Cigarettes bifter; cancer stick; cig; cigger; ciggy; coffin-nail; doofer; drag; durry; fag; gasper; gippy; pill; quirley; roll-up; scag; snout; square; stick; stinker; straight; tab; tailor-made; tickler; tube; virgin

Cigars la-di-da; rope; twofer

Cigarette ends bumper; dog-end; fag-end; old soldier; scag; stompie

Cigarette paper skin

An act of smoking; a smoke burn; drag

A stoppage of work for a smoke smoke-ho

To smoke a cigarette, etc. burn; drag

5. Drugs

An (illegal) drug dope; French blue; juice; junk; magic mushroom; mellow yellow; Mickey Finn; minstrel; mojo; narco; peter; schmeck; shroom; smack; speedball; sting; stuff; sugar; tab; torpedo

Relating to drugs or drug-users druggy; hoppy

A stimulant drug pep-pill; up; upper; uppie; wake-up pill

A tranquillizing drug down; downer; downie; happy pill; trank

Amphetamine benny; black bomber; dexie; goof ball; ice; meth; pill; purple heart; speed; splash; sweets; white

Amyl nitrate popper

Barbiturates bomber; goof ball; nembie; pill; pink lady; rainbow; red bird; red devil; yellow jacket

Bromide bromo

Cannabis Acapulco gold; bifter; blunt; bomb; bomber; boo; charge; doobie; ganja; goof; grass; green; hash; Indian hay; jive; joint; ju-ju; loco weed; majat; mary; Mary Ann; Mary Jane; Mary Warner; mezz; mootah; muggles; pod; pot; puff; roach; rope; shit; skunk; spliff; stick; tea

Cocaine blow; Charlie; coke; crack; freebase; happy dust; nose candy; snow; toot; white stuff

Heroin black tar; brown sugar; duji; dynamite; H; horse; jack; mud; scag; scat; schmack; shit; smack; white stuff

LSD acid; Owsley acid; purple haze; sugar; white lightning

Methadone phy

Methylene dioxymethamphetamine (MDMA) Adam; E; ecstasy

Morphine mojo; morph; white stuff

Opium gee; hop; mud; pill; poppy; tar; twang

Phencyclidine angel dust; rocket fuel

Sodium pentothal soap

A quantity, portion, or dose of a drug bang; bindie; charge; deck; fix; fix-up; hit; jolt; key; lid; line; mike; nickel; nickel bag; O.D.; piece; pop; snifter; snort; spike; toke; toot; trey; twister; weight

A drug taker or addict acid head; cokie; crackhead; dope; dopester; drugger; druggy; freak; head; hophead; hoppy; hype; joy-popper; junker; junkie; muggler; needle man; pill-head; pipe; popper; pot-head; schmecker; sniffer; snifter; snow-bird; student; tea-head; teaman; weed-head; weekender

A non-addict straight

Addiction jones; monkey; needle; yum-yum

To take drugs blast; bogart; chase the dragon; coke; crank; do; dope; drop; fix; freebase; goof; main; main-line; peter; pop; shoot; skin; sleigh-ride; snarf; sniff; snort; speed; spike; toke; toot

Taking drugs on

Not on drugs on the natch

Equipment for taking drugs gong; gonger; gongerine; gun; hop toy; hype; hypo; joint; needle; outfit; pipe; skin; spike; stem; suey pow; toy; works

To give a drug to dope; hit; hypo; snow

A drugged state acid trip; bummer; flash; heat; high; munchies; nod; sleigh-ride; trip; turn-on; wingding

In a drugged state blasted; bombed; cabbaged; geed-up; high; hopped; jagged; loaded; mashed; monged; out of it; piped; polluted; potted; ripped; smashed; spaced; spacey; stoned; straight; strung out; teaed; tripped-out; wasted; whacked-out; wiped; wired; wrecked; zonked

To (cause to) experience the effect of a drug blow someone's mind; freak; get off; mellow out; O.D.; overamp; space out; stone; string out; trip; turn on

Physical effects of drug taking tracks

Detoxification clean; cold turkey; dry out; kick; sick; twister

To buy or sell drugs connect; deal; hold; push; score

A supplier of drugs connection; junker; mule; pusher; superfly; swing man; teaman

A supply of drugs or place where drugs are available script; shooting gallery; tea pad; tea party

Articles and substances

1. Things

A thing of a particular type animal; sucker

An unnamed or unspecified thing bizzo; dingbat; dingus; doobry; doodad; doodah; doofer; doohickey; doojigger; doover; frobnitz; gismo; gubbins; hickey; jigger; oojah; oojiboo; whangdoodle; whassit; whatchamacallit; whatnot; whatsit; whifflow

Unspecified things, paraphernalia and (I don't know) what all; clobber; doings; gubbins

An object collected from refuse tot

2. Clothing and accessories

Clothing cits; civvies; clobber; dog-robbers; drag; drape; duds; glad rags; kit; mocker; schmutter; threads; togs; vines

A garment number; schmatte; woolly

A pocket kick; pit; side-kicker; sky; sky-rocket; slide

A hole in a garment spud

A hat blocker; God forbid; gorblimey; kelly; lid; skid-lid; skimmer; Smokey Bear; tile; tin hat; titfer

A garment for the upper body boob-tube; cardy; hoodie; Jacky Howe; mill tog; thousand-miler

A coat ben; benny; mog; pussy

A jacket bum-freezer

Trousers bags; kecks; loons; petrol bowsers; rammies; round-the-houses; strides; stubbies

A suit fiddle and flute; monkey suit; penguin suit; soup and fish; vine; whistle and flute; zoot suit

A tie Peckham Rye

A handkerchief penwiper; snot-rag

Swimwear cossie

Protective clothing noddy suit; penguin suit; poopy suit; steamer; teddy bear; tin hat

Underwear chuddies; falsies; gay deceivers; jock; kecks; passion-killers; pasties; skivvy; trolleys; underfug

A loincloth cockrag

Gloves turtle; turtle-dove

Shoes beetle-crusher; bovver boot; brothel-creeper; Claire Rayners; clodhopper; creeper; daisy roots; DMs; kicks; laughing-sides; stomper; waffle stomper

An umbrella brolly; bumbershoot; gamp

Jewellery and similar personal items bling-bling; groin; ice; kettle; prop; rock; shiner; Simple Simon; slag; slum; sparkler; spark-prop; stone; tom; tomfoolery

Bags, luggage keister; peter; pogue; poke

To dress (oneself) dude up; gussy up; poon up; spiv up; toff up

Dressed dressed up like a dog's dinner; dressed up like a pox doctor's clerk; lairy; mockered up; sprauncy

To undress debag; de-pants; peel

The clothing business rag trade

Cosmetics lippy; slap; war paint

Coiffure big hair; D.A.; do; duck's arse; flat top; fro; natty; suicide blonde

To straighten curly hair conk

A wig divot; Irish jig; rug; syrup of figs; toup

3. Tools, implements, and containers

An axe Douglas; kelly

A shovel idiot stick

A pickaxe mad mick

A jemmy, crowbar iron; stick

A key twister

A waste-paper basket wagger

4. Weapons

Weapons equalizer; Mike Mike; tool

Guns Betsy; gat; heat; hipe; ironmongery; piece; rod; roscoe; Saturday night special; shooter; smoke-wagon

A machine-gun chopper; plinker; snubby; typewriter; woodpecker

The barrel of a gun spout

Knives and other cutting weapons chib; chiv; malky; pig-sticker; toad-sticker; winkle-pin

Clubs nigger-stick; sap

Stones Irish confetti

Other weapons moley; nigger shooter

A beggar chugger; dummy; panhandler; plinger; schnorrer; tapper

(An act of) begging stem; stemming

Wages gravy; greengages; Irishman's rise; rock of ages; screw; stake; toke

To earn as wages knock out

Profit bunce; clean-up; gravy; melon; velvet; vig; vigorish

Something profitable earner; gravy train

To make a profit clean up; laugh all the way to the bank

To save money salt away

Money saved stake

In debt; in financial difficulty in hock; in Queer Street

An IOU marker

Cheap as cheap as chips; cheapie; el cheapo

Something cheap cheapie; el cheapo; snip; steal

Free of charge buckshee; freebie

Something free freebie

The (high) cost of something arm and a leg; damage; nut

A bank jug

A cheque kite; stumer

A safe box; keister; pete; peter

A container for money grouch-bag; pogue; poke; skin

Welfare baby bonus; pogey; susso

2. Bribery

A bribe backhander; boodle; bung; drop; dropsy; graft; oil; pay-off; payola; schmeer; sling; squeeze-pidgin

To bribe boodle; bung; oil the knocker; reach; schmeer; sling; square

Acceptance of bribes; corruption mumping

Taking bribes on the take

An establishment that pays bribes pad

3. Work

Work bashing; graft; grunt work; schlep; shitwork; yakka

To work graft; schlep

A worker basher; grafter; wallah

A product of work foreigner

A job or occupation bag; lurk; number; site

To have more than one job moonlight

A building-trade worker brickie; chippy; Chips; putty

A butcher pig-sticker

A cook bab; babbling brook; cookie; doctor; poisoner; slum burner; slushy; spud barber

A delivery worker milko; milky; postie

An electrician juicer; sparks

A farmer backyarder; cockatoo; cocky; cow-spanker; drummer; jingling Johnny; leather-neck; pen-mate; stubble-jumper; swede-basher; tiger; waddy

A fashion-trade worker garmento

A general worker dogsbody; gofer; ground-hog; grunt; lobby-gow; tiger; wood-and-water joey; working stiff; yardbird

A groom swipe

A hairdresser crimper

A mechanic grease monkey; mech

An office worker cookie-pusher; pink button; steno; suit; sysop; wallah

Office work admin

An oil-rig worker rough neck

A publicist flack

A refuse collector binman; bottle-o; garbo; sanno (man); totter

To collect refuse tot

A scientist backroom boy; boff

A servant skivvy; tiger

To do the work of a servant skivvy

A shop-worker counter-jumper; shoppy

A tailor Jew; Jewing-bloke

A transport worker clippie; gandy dancer; hackie; hostie; jumper; river hog; sea-gull; shack; snake; snake charmer; snapper; stew; swamper; tallow pot; wharfie; winger

Waiting and kitchen staff biscuit-shooter; cookie-pusher; hasher; hash-slinger; Nippy; pearl diver

A window-cleaner shiner

A work period dogwatch; hitch; lick; shop; stag; trick

A break from work hols; rope-yarn; smoke-ho; swing; vac

Unemployment benefit buroo; compo; pineapple

To go on strike hit the bricks

A strike-breaker, blackleg scab

A retrained person retread

Equal opportunities twofer

4. Business and commerce

A seller ampster; scalper; shill; shillaber; shoddy dropper; stick

To sell flog; gazump; hustle; scalp; shift; shill; sug

To bargain jew down

To buy gazunder

Mail-order wish book

Mortgages Fannie Mae

Deferred payment, credit cred; jaw-bone; never-never; tick

In pawn in hock; in pop; up the spout

A pawnshop hock-shop; moscow; pop-shop

A pawnbroker uncle

To pawn hock; moscow; pop; soak

Profit clean-up; push money

A dividend divvy

Something profitable earner; skinner

In profit quids in

To make (as) a profit clean up

Loss downer

A customer punter; up

Investment piece; spec

An investor angel; arb; white knight

Stocks and shares Big Bang; churning

Organization admin

A type of business racket

An agreement, a deal go

5. Dismissal

Dismissal air; arse; big E; bird; boot; bullet; bum's rush; chop; chuck; elbow; gate; heave-ho; raspberry; sack; shaft; shove; spear

To dismiss, get rid of be shot of; be shut of; bowler-hat; bust; eighty-six; kiss off; sack; spear; tie a can to; tramp; wipe

To be dismissed flunk out

Behaviour, attitudes, and emotions

1. Behaviour

To behave well or satisfactorily keep one's nose clean

To behave in an unacceptable way act up; carry on; crap around; fart about; piss about; play silly buggers

To behave like come; go … on

A period of indulgence in a particular type of behaviour jag

One's preferred mode of behaviour thing

Affected behaviour or speech gyver

2. Favour and disfavour

Out of favour in bad; in Dutch; in the dog-house; on the outer

(A) favourite fave; fave rave

That which one favours or prefers bag

Favourable opinion or comment Brownie point; rave

To regard favourably, like, enjoy, approve of dig; get off on; go on; have tickets on

To express enthusiastic approval (of) be all over; big up; drool

Showing enthusiastic approval or liking rave; wow

Someone who favours or enjoys something; an enthusiast buff; freak; nut; sucker

Liking, fond of; enthusiastic about big on; high on; hipped on; hot on; into; nuts about; stoked on

In love with gone on

To regard with disfavour have a derry on; have a down on

Exclamations of dislike or distaste ick; yech; yuck

3. Wanting and getting

Wanting could murder; could use; make a play for

Wanting something in vain whistle for

A person who cannot resist a particular thing sucker

That which is wanted or needed shot; ticket

Acquisitiveness gimme

Acquisitive on the make

To seize for oneself; to grab glom

4. Ambition

An ambitious person wannabe

5. Indifference

To be indifferent to something; not care not give a bugger; not give a damn; not give a frig; not give a fuck; not give a hoot; not give a monkey's (fuck); not give a rap; not give a shit; not give a sod; not give a stuff; not give a twopenny damn

Indifferent, insouciant what-the-hell

It doesn't matter; it makes no difference san fairy ann

6. Excellence, remarkableness

Excellent ace; aces; A1; awesome; bad; beaut; bitching; bona; bonzer; bosker; boss;

bottling; brill; cool; corker; corking; crackerjack; cracking; crazy; crucial; crunk; curl-the-mo; cushty; daisy; death; def; dodger; doozy; end; fab; fantabulous; far-out; fresh; gear; gone; groovy; grouse; hunky; hunky-dory; in the house; jolly d; killer; marv; marvy; mean; mondo; onkus; oojah-cum-spiff; outasight; out-of-sight; peachy; peachy-keen; plenty; primo; rad; radical; ready; ridiculous; righteous; rumpty; ryebuck; safe; shit-hot; snodger; socko; solid; spiffing; splendiferous; storming; stud; together; too much; topping; tubular; whizzo; wicked; wizard

An excellent person or thing beaner; beaut; bee's knees; berries; bobby-dazzler; bottler; cat's whiskers; clinker; corker; cracker; crackerjack; dog's bollocks; honey; humdinger; hummer; killer; killer-diller; nuts; peach; peacherino; pip; pipperoo; pippin; piss-cutter; ripper; ruby-dazzler; rumpty; smasher; snozzler; whizzer

An excellent or admirable person diamond; toff; white hat

An excellent thing blinder; daisy; lallapaloosa; purler; splitter; stonker; zinger

To do (something) excellently max; wail

Surpassing (all) others stickout

Someone or something outstanding or surpassing all others daddy; grand-daddy; stickout

The best end; endsville; most; tops

To surpass all others beat the band; beat the Dutch

Delightful deevy; dreamy; ducky; loverly; mellow; neat; neato

Delicious nummy; scrummy

Remarkable, exceptional and a half; bodacious; hellacious; some; unreal

A remarkable or exceptional person or thing dilly; lulu; phenom; rip-snorter

A remarkable or exceptional thing doozer; doozy; scorcher; snorter; sockeroo; something else; stormer

Satisfactory all is gas and gaiters; all-right; (all) Sir Garnet; A-OK; apples; copacetic; not so dusty; hotsy-totsy; jake; jakeloo; kayo; O.K.; oke; okey-doke; patsy; sweet; tickety-boo

Something satisfactory (little) bit of all right

Adequate better than a poke in the eye

7. Beauty and ugliness

A beautiful person or thing beaut; eye candy

To beautify glam

Ugly, unattractive drack; fugly

An ugly person or thing bag; boiler; crow; dogface; drack; fugly; haybag; heap; Mother Bunch; old boot; rag-bag; roach; trout

8. Bad quality

Of low quality; bad; inferior; unsatisfactory bodger; bum; chronic; cheesy; crappy; crook; duff; for the birds; half-arsed; janky; kaffir; manky; mouldy; naff; N.B.G.; not much chop; not much cop; nowhere; piss-poor; pissy; poxy; ribby; rotten; schlock; snide; under the arm; wanky

Something of inferior quality crap; dog; hash-up; scrubber; shit; slum; stinker; stinkeroo; tat; toe-cover; tripe; turkey

Bad advice bum steer

Indifferent half-pie; no great shakes

Notification of bad quality smoke-up

9. Unpleasantness

Unpleasant, deplorable bitching; bloody; Godawful; grotty; grungy; hellacious; like thirty cents; minging; onkus; over the fence; poxy; punk-ass; scroungy; septic; shithouse; shitting; shitty; snotty; umpty; uncool; unreal; upter; wack; white-arsed

Disgusting grody; gross; grotty; grungy; icky; scroungy; scuzzy; skeevy; sleazoid; yechy; yucky

Someone or something unpleasant or unendurable end; pits

An unpleasant or despicable person bad news; blister; crumb; cunt; face-ache; nark; Noah's Ark; pig; pill; roach; scroucher; scunge; whore; wowser

An unpleasant or despicable male person arsehole; b; basket; bastard; bleeder; blighter; booger; bugger; cheap skate; chickenshit; cock-sucker; creep; crud; crut; dickwad; dickweed; erk; fink; four-letter man; fucker; get; git; gobshite; gomer; goorie; grot; heel; jelly bean; jerk; jerk-off; louse; lug; mamzer; mofo; mother; mother-fucker; no-goodnik; oik; peckerhead; piss-artist; ponce; rat; ratbag; rat fink; salaud; scab; schweinhund; scrote; scumbag; scuzz; scuzzbag; sewer; shag; shicer; shit; shit-bag; shite; shite-hawk; shitface; shithead; skate; skeeve; slag; sleazebag; sleazeball; sleazoid; S.O.B.; sod; son-of-a-bitch; stiff; stinker; stinkpot; suck; suck-hole; sumbitch; swine; swipe; toe-rag; tosser; turd; twat; wank; wanker

An unpleasant or despicable female person bitch; cow; mare; moo

Index

Something unpleasant or undesirable bad news; bastard; bitch; bugger; bummer; cow

An unpleasant experience something nasty in the woodshed

Something disgusting gross-out; turn-off

Disgusting material crud; dreck; glop; grot; grunge; gunge; gunk; scuzz

An unpleasant place armpit of …; arsehole of the universe; flea-bag; hell-hole; piss-hole; shit-hole

To be unpleasant stink; suck

To repel gross out; skeeve; turn off

10. Contemptibleness

A contemptible person douche-bag; dweeb; kvetch; kye; pipsqueak; piss-ant; sad sack; schmegeggy; scut; shit-eater; slug; snot; snotnose; snot-rag; snurge; soor; squirt; squit; tick; tinhorn sport; trash; tripe-hound; wart; weeny; wonk; yuck; zob; zombie

Contemptible sad-ass

11. Ineffectualness, incompetence

Ineffectual, incompetent chinless; drippy; drooby; gay; half-arsed; ham; Harry Tate; jack-leg; lame; Mickey Mouse; nebbich; nerdy; poopy; spastic; untogether; wimpish; wimpy

Ineffectually, incompetently not for toffee

An ineffectual or incompetent person anorak; big girl's blouse; dexter; drip; droob; droop; droopy-drawers; dub; duffer; feeb; Gawd-help-us; gazook; geek; ham; lame; lamer; melvin; mess; mush-head; nebbich; nerd; nerk; no-hoper; otaku; palooka; pencil neck; pisher; plug; pogo; poindexter; poop; poop-stick; prick; prune; punk; rabbit; schlemiel; scissor-bill; shower; spastic; spaz; spod; stiff; stumblebum; turkey; wimp; wuss

A clumsy or awkward person clod-hopper

Something ineffectual kludge

12. Sentimentality

Excessively sentimental icky; schmaltzy; yechy; yucky

Excessive sentiment schmaltz

To sentimentalize schmaltz

An excessively sentimental person sob sister

A self-pitying person wet leg

13. Fairness and unfairness

A fair chance, fair treatment fair dinkum; fair go; fair shake

Unfair, unreasonable red-hot

Something disappointingly unfair swizz; swizzle

To treat unfairly do the dirty on; shaft

14. Pleasure, enjoyment

Happy, pleased as happy as Larry; chuffed; tickled pink

Euphorically happy, elated, ecstatic gone; sent

Pleasure, enjoyment, fun crack; jollies; yum-yum

A life of pleasure life of Riley

A euphoric state high

A good time; a spree; a party bash; beanfeast; beano; blast; ding; ding-dong; jollo; jolly; kegger; percolator; rage; rave; rort; shake; smash; tear; thrash; whoop-up; wingding

A drinking spree bat; beer-up; bender; binge; blind; booze; boozeroo; booze-up; brannigan; drunk; jag; liquid lunch; piss-up; sesh; souse

An invitation to a party or other event stiffy

On a spree on the razzle; on the tiles

Someone on a spree heller; rager; raver

To please, delight gas; grab; groove; panic; send; slay; turn on

One that pleases or delights; something enjoyable gas; gasser; groove; sender; turn-on

To enjoy oneself, have a good time, have fun; to go on a spree ball; ball it up; beat it up; bliss out; get one's rocks off; groove; hell around; loon; rage; rave; whoop it up

To relax, take it easy chill out; cool it; let it all hang out; mellow out

Exclamations of delight or exultation cowabunga; Geronimo; good egg; hot diggety dog; hot dog; hubba-hubba; quaiss kitir; right on; whacko; whizzo; yay

15. Laughter and amusement

To laugh crease up; fall about; laugh like a drain; piss oneself; wet oneself; yock; yuck

To cause to laugh break up; crease; fracture; slay

A laugh belly laugh; boffola; yock; yuck

Very funny or amusing killing; ripe

Fun, amusement gas

Something or someone very funny or amusing boffola; laugh; laugher; scream; screamer; yell

An amusing person card

16. Gratitude
Thank you ta

17. Depression
Depressed down; gutted; mokus; mouldy

Depression blahs; hump; joes; mokus; starks; uglies; woofits

Something depressing bummer; downer

A dreary-looking person drear; dreary; face-ache

Weeping waterworks

18. Hopelessness
Hopelessness Buckley's; not a cat (in hell's) chance; not an earthly; not have a prayer

One who is beyond hope dead duck; gone goose; goner

19. Confusion
Confused, bewildered hung up; moggadored

To confuse, bewilder bamboozle; discombobulate

20. Trouble
Trouble, harm, misfortune grief; merry hell; packet; shtook; unshirted hell

(When) trouble occurs (when) the shit hits the fan

Pain gyp; merry hell

In trouble for it; in deep doo-doo; in Dutch; in lumber; in Queer Street; in the cart; in the pooh; in the shit; in the soup; up a gum-tree; up a stump; up shit creek; up the creek; up the spout

In financial trouble in Queer Street; on the rocks

Lost slewed

To be in trouble cop it; get it; get it hot; get it in the neck; have one's ass in a sling

To cause trouble or harm to someone or something bugger about; drop in it; fuck about; play (merry) hell with; soup

To upset, distress turn over

A trouble-maker bolshie; mixer

Something or someone very troublesome or annoying handful; hell on wheels; pain; pain in the arse; peb; pebble; pisser; schlep

21. Excitement
Excited all of a doodah

Exciting wild; wow

(A state or feeling of) excitement; a thrill bang; charge; drive

To excite; cause to lose composure; overwhelm emotionally freak out; psych; stoke; wow; zap

To give way to heightened emotion; lose one's composure flip; flip one's lid; flip one's wig; freak out; plotz; tear it up; wet oneself; wet one's pants

Someone who has lost composure headless chicken

Exclamations of excitement pow; shazam

22. Eagerness, enthusiasm
Eager, enthusiastic gung ho; hot to trot

Enthusiastic support rah rah; sky-rocket

An enthusiast for the stated thing culture vulture; motorhead; petrolhead

An enthusiasm kick

Obsessed hung up

23. Effort
To make one's maximum effort go for broke; go for the doctor; pull one's finger out; sweat blood; sweat one's guts out

An attempt bash; burl; lash; whack; whirl

24. Surprise
To surprise blow away

Surprising, astonishing mind-blowing; mind-boggling

Surprised, astonished gob-smacked; gob-struck

Something surprising zinger

Exclamations of surprise or astonishment begorra; bejabers; bejesus; blimey; blow me tight; coo; coo-er; cor; crikey; cripes; geewhillikins; gee whizz; gorblimey; Gordon Bennett; holy cow; holy mackerel; holy Moses; holy shit; holy smoke; jeepers; jeepers-creepers; Jeez; Jesus; Jesus (H.) Christ; Jesus wept; lawks; lor; lumme; my sainted aunt; sacré bleu; sapristi; starve the crows; starve the lizards; stiffen the crows; stiffen the lizards; stone me; stone the crows; strewth; strike a light; strike me blind; strike me pink; stroll on; wowee; yikes; zowie

25. Boredom and disenchantment
Something or someone boring or tiresome bind; binder; drag; dullsville; fag; grind; MEGO

To bore bind; feed

Boring, dull, tedious blah; drack; draggy; feeding

Bored, fed-up brassed off; browned off; cheesed off; chocker

26. Composure

Composure cool

Composed, relaxed laid-back; loose; slap-happy

To keep one's composure, remain relaxed keep one's hair on; keep one's shirt on

To calm down chill out; cool it

Impassive po-faced; poker-faced

A fuss ballyhoo; bobsy-die; carry-on; hoo-ha; whoop-de-do

27. Anger

(A fit of) anger allovers; bate; eppie; hump; mad; needle; pricker; snit; spike; wax; wobbler; wobbly

Angry arsey; batey; butcher's; crook; crooked; lemony; off one's block; radge; radgie; ravers; ringy; ropeable; salty; scotty; shirty; snake-headed; snaky; torqued; up in the air; waxy; wet

Annoyed and disappointed choked; chuffed; pipped; pissed off; sick; sick as a parrot; teed off

To be or get angry blow one's stack; create; do one's bun; do one's nana; do one's nut; do one's scone; get off one's bike; get one's rag out; go (in) off the deep end; go postal; go spare; go to market; have a cob on; lose one's block; lose one's rag; spit blood; spit chips; wig out

To become angrily agitated or upset get one's knickers in a twist; piss oneself; wet oneself

To annoy or infuriate get; get across; get on someone's quince; get one someone's tits; get on someone's wick; get someone's goat; get someone's nanny-goat; get someone's shirt out; get up someone's nose; give someone the pip; nark; piss someone off; rip; tee someone off; tick someone off

Annoying balls-aching

Something annoying aggro; chizz; nark

A bad temper or fit of sulking moody; paddy; snit

Bad-tempered narky; snitty; spikey; stroppy

A bad-tempered or discontented person sore-head

Exclamations of annoyance drat; fuck; fucking ada; hell; hell's bells; hell's teeth; Jesus; Jesus (H.) Christ; Jesus wept; knickers; rats; shee-y-it; shit; shoot; sod it; son of a bitch; tarnation; wouldn't it

28. Argument, quarrelling

(An) argument, row argy-bargy; barney; blue; bull and cow; cag; ding-dong; donnybrook; dust-up; rhubarb; ruck; run-in; up-and-downer; yike

To argue argy-bargy; barney; cag; part brass-rags

Argumentative, touchy feisty

29. Violence

Fighting; a fight, brawl aggro; bovver; brannigan; hey Rube; rammy; ram-sammy; rough house; rough-up; ruckus; rumble; rux; shemozzle; sort-out; stoush; tear-up; thump-up; up-and-downer

To fight dish it out; go the knuckle; mix in; mix it; rough house; rumble; slug it out; steam in; stoush

To hit bean; belt; biff; bitch-slap; clock; clonk; cream; crown; dong; dot; fan; fetch; hang one on; king-hit; knock someone's block off; lamp; mill; nail; nut; pan; plug; sap; skull; slosh; soak; sock; sock it to; stick one on; stoush; tag; zonk

To hit repeatedly; assault by hitting bash up; beat (the) bejesus out of; beat the shit out of; beat the tar out of; break someone's ass; clobber; do; do over; duff up; dust; fill in; mobilize; paste; rough up; roust; scrag; take to; tan; tan someone's arse; work over

To knock out out; wooden

A blow biff; bitch slap; dinnyhaser; dong; fourpenny one; Glasgow kiss; paddywhack; slosh; sock; woodener

A punch bunch of fives; clock; haymaker; king-hit; knuckle sandwich; poke; roundhouse; stoush; Sunday punch

An act of hitting; a beating-up doing; going-over; happy slapping; Jesse; pasting

To kick put the boot in; root; welly

A kick boot; root; welly

To attack with a sharp instrument; to stab carve; chiv; chivvy; malky

To shoot plug; plunk; smoke; ventilate

To attack or worry an animal sool

A violent person; a thug; a ruffian bovver boy; clogger; droog; enforcer; frightener; goon; hoon; mug; muscle; muscle man; ned; plug-ugly; roughie; rough-neck; trigger man; trog; yob; yobbo

To intimidate get at; mau-mau; put the frighteners on

A black eye shiner

30. Caution

Cautious, wary leery

31. Nervousness, agitation

A state of nervousness or unease all-overs; habdabs; heebie-jeebies; jim-jams; jimmies; screamers; willies; wind; wind-up

Nervous, ill at ease funky; hinky; windy

To be nervous or anxious sweat; sweat on the top line

To await nervously sweat on

A state of agitation or restlessness Harry Tate; stuma; tiswas; two and eight

Agitated, restless antsy; toey; twitched

To be or become agitated flap; have ants in one's pants

Tense up-tight; wired

Trembling pearlies; yips

To behave frenziedly get one's knickers in a twist; go ape; have kittens

A nervous or agitated person jitterbug

A person who worries worry-guts; worry-wart

32. Fear

Fear blue funk; funk; Jimmy Britts; wind-up

Afraid Charlie; funky; poopy; shitless; shit-scared; windy

To be afraid (of) brick it; funk; get the breeze up; get the wind up; shit a brick; shit oneself; spit blood; sweat blood

Frightening hairy; spooky; windy

To frighten buffalo; funk; put the breeze up; put the wind up; spook

A timorous person fraid cat

Exclamations of fear or alarm oo-er; yikes

33. Courage and cowardice

Courage balls; bottle; cojones; gimp; moxie; nads; ticker

Brave ballsy; game as a piss-ant; tight

A coward chicken-shit; dingo; funk; funkstick; pleep; sook; squib; yellow-belly

Cowardly chicken-shit; funky; milky; yellow-bellied

To lose one's nerve, withdraw pusillanimously bottle out; chicken; dingo; funk; punk out; squib; wimp out

A place to which one withdraws out of fear funk-hole

34. Perseverance

To persevere hang in; hang tough; keep on trucking

Someone who perseveres; a resolute person pebble

35. Conceit, boastfulness, ostentation

Conceit jam; side

Conceited chesty; dicty; ditsy; hincty; hoity-toity; ikey; lairy; pound-notish; sidey; smart-arse; snifty; snotty; stiff-arsed; toffee-nosed

A conceited person smart-arse; toffee-nose

A self-important person high-muck-a-muck; his nibs; I am; Jack Strop; Lord Muck; mucky-muck

A swaggering, showy, or boastful person bucko; drug-store cowboy; fancy Dan; fancy pants; Flash Harry; frippet; glitterati; God's gift; hot dog; lair; showboat; signifier; skite; swankpot; teddy boy; trombenik; Wheneye

A suave person smoothie

To be conceited have tickets on oneself

To boast, behave boastfully, self-importantly, or ostentatiously kvell; lair; put on lugs; put on the dog; shoot one's mouth off; signify

Boastful talk; behaviour intended to impress (all) gas and gaiters; buck; line-shoot; mouth; piss and wind; skite; swank

A boastful talker bullshitter

To show off showboat; strut one's stuff

Given to showing off split-arse

36. Audacity and rudeness

Audacity, effrontery brass neck; chutzpah; crust; neck; rind

Impudent talk jaw; lip; sass

Impudent lippy

To speak rudely (to) lip; sass

37. Contempt

To regard or treat with contempt blank; diss; give someone the finger; rank; razz; snoot

A sign of contempt Harvey Smith; raspberry; razoo; razz;

Exclamations of contempt or derision big deal; drop dead; garn; get knotted; get stuffed; kiss my arse; knickers; nerts; nuts; pigs; shove it; sucks; take a running jump; upya; up yours; ya boo

38. Meanness

Mean, ungenerous mingy; tight

A mean person cheap Charlie; cheapskate; Jew; meany; nickel nurser; skate; tightwad

Meanness one-way pockets

39. Honesty

Honest clean; kosher; legit; on the legit; straight; straight-up; upfront

An honest person clean-skin; Mr Clean; straight arrow; straight goods; straight shooter

A reliable person brick; pistol

To be, remain, or become honest go straight; keep one's nose clean; straighten up

The truth dinkum; dinkum oil; strong of; straight; straight goods; where it's at

To tell the truth let it all hang out; level with; shoot the works; tell it like it is

40. Sincerity and insincerity

Obsequious behaviour; toadying arse-licking; ass-kissing; bum-sucking

To behave obsequiously (towards) arse-lick; ass-kiss; brown-nose; bum-suck; kiss someone's arse; piss in someone's pocket; suck around; suck-hole; suck up

An obsequious person; a toady, sycophant apple-polisher; arse-licker; ass-kisser; brown-noser; bum-sucker; greaser; suck

To flatter; to deceive with insincere or flattering talk blag; bullshit; crap; flannel; gammon; schmeer; snow; soap; soft-soap; sweetmouth

Insincere or exaggerated talk intended to flatter or deceive; humbug or flattery ackamarackus; applesauce; blah; borak; B.S.; bull; bull dust; bullshit; bull's wool; bushwa; crock of shit; drip; eyewash; flannel; gammon; grease; jazz; jive; kidstakes; madam; malarkey; moody; oil; schmeer; snow job; soap; spinach; taffy

A flatterer; an exaggerated talker blagger; bullshitter; flannel-mouth; snow-man

Outward show, empty display glitz; razzmatazz

Characterized by outward show; flashy glitzy; zazzy

Insincere in manner, ingratiating soapy

An ingratiating person smoothie

To ingratiate oneself make one's marble good

An instance of insincere behaviour act

Pretentious arty-farty; hokey; noncy

To render something insincere or artificial hoke

A person of integrity mensch

Sincerely honest Injun; no stuff

41. Lying

A lie porkie; pork pie

To lie spruce

42. Deception, cheating

Deception, swindling, fraud bunco; carve-up; con; fast one; fiddle; flanker; gazump; gyp; have-on; hustle; hype; lemon-game; Murphy game; pay-off; pigeon-drop; prop game; ramp; ready-up; rip-off; rort; scam; sell; short con; shucking and jiving; skin game; slanter; spiel; stroke; swiftie; swindle sheet; trickeration; try-on; tweedle; wangle

To deceive, dupe come the raw prawn; con; have; have on; hype; jive; make a monkey (out) of; Murphy; sell; shanghai; shit; shuck; slip something over on; spruce; string; sucker; take for a ride; take for a sleigh-ride; try it on; two-time

To swindle, cheat bunco; burn; carve up; chisel; clean; clip; come it over; diddle; do; fiddle; finagle; gaff; gazump; gold-brick; gyp; hornswoggle; ikey; paper; pin; put someone in the hole; ramp; ream; rim; rip off; rook; rush; scale; scam; screw; sew up; skin; skunk; stiff; sting; stitch up; sug; tweedle; two-time; wangle; whip-saw; yentz

A swindler chiseller; con; con artist; con merchant; forty; four-flusher; gee-man; heel; high-binder; jive-ass; magsman; pigeon-dropper; rick; scaler; scammer; shark; sharpie; shonky; slick; slicker; slickster; snide; spieler; sprucer; take; take-down; T.B.; tug; tweedler; twicer; twister

An establishment where one is swindled clip-joint

43. Betrayal

To betray do the dirty on; dob in; fink; pool; rat; two-time

To betray an associate to the police or other authority; to inform (on); to incriminate finger; grass; have the pencil put on one; nose; peep; pot; rat; scream; shelf; shop; sing; snitch; snout; split; squawk; squeal; talk; turn in

An instance of informing on someone rumble

A traitor; one who is disloyal to associates dog; fink; rat fink

One who betrays associates to the police or other authorities finger; fizgig; fizzer;

grass; grasser; lemon; Moreton Bay; nark; narker; nose; pigeon; pimp; rat; sarbut; screamer; shelf; singer; snitch; snout; split; squeaker; squealer; stool; stoolie; top-off

44. Exploitation

To behave or obtain exploitatively gold-dig; lig; promote; tap

An exploiter gold-digger; ligger; shark

45. Slyness, artfulness

Sly, artful carney; crazy like a fox; ikey

A sly person shrewd-head; sly-boots

46. Secrecy, confidentiality, concealment

Done or kept in secret on the side; q.t.

To conceal or be concealed hole up; lie doggo; stash

A hiding place lurk; stash; trap

Something hidden stash

In or into hiding in(to) smoke

47. Energy, vigour

Energy, vigour, vitality go; jism; moxie; oomph; pep; piss and vinegar; pizzazz; razzle-dazzle; zap; zizz

To instil with vigour, liven up juice up; pep up; zap

To be lively swing

Energetic, vigorous, lively full of beans; hopped up; hyped up; hyper; jivey; rorty; swinging; zappy; zizzy

An energetic or lively person stem-winder; tear-ass

48. Laziness

A lazy person; a shirker beach bum; bench-warmer; bludger; bum; bummer; couch potato; fuck-off; gold-brick; Norm; piker; poler; sack rat; scrimshanker; skiver; soldier; sooner; spine-basher

To be lazy bludge; do a never; dodge the column; dog it; gold-brick; goof; lallygag; lig; mike; piss about; plotz; scrimshank; skate; skive; spine-bash; spruce; swing the lead; veg

Laziness; avoidance of work Maori P.T.

A period of lazy inactivity bludge; mike

Thought and communication

1. Belief and disbelief

To believe Adam-and-Eve; buy

Believe me! stand on me

I don't believe it! Aunt Fanny; bollocks; come off it; dicken; do me a favour; garn; gertcha; get off; hell; phooey; sez you; stroll on; tell it to the marines; tie that bull outside

2. Understanding

To understand or realize the meaning of something be jerry; capisce; click; dig; drop (down) to; get; get next (to); get someone's number; get wise (to); gotcha; jerry (to); rumble; savvy; suss (out); take a jerry (to); take a tumble; tumble; twig; wise up (to)

3. Knowledge and ignorance

Intelligence smarts; upper storey

Good sense common; savvy

Knowledgeable, clever fly; pointy-headed; savvy; smart-arsed; up to snuff; wise-assed

A knowledgeable or clever person brainiac; clever-boots; clever-clogs; clever Dick; clever-sticks; pointy-head; sharpie; smart-arse; smarty-boots; smarty-pants; wise-ass; wise guy; wisenheimer

To be knowledgeable know beans; know one's onions

To behave in a smugly clever way (towards) smart-ass

To lack knowledge ask me another; dunno

To be ignorant (not) know from nothing; not know one's arse from one's elbow; not know shit from Shinola

Ignorant pig-ignorant

4. Skill

A skilled person hot-shot; mivvy; ringer; whizzo

Highly skilled or capable bionic; nifty; pie; shit-hot

A skill-less person rabbit

5. Sanity

Sanity marbles

The head as the repository of sanity upper storey; upstairs

Failing sanity white ants

Sane all there; with it

Mad bananas; barking (mad); blah; bonkers; doolally (tap); lakes; loco; magnoon; mental; nuts; off one's chump; off one's conk; off one's gourd; off one's head; off one's nana; off one's nut; off one's onion; off one's pannikin; off one's rocker; off one's rocket; off one's trolley; out of one's head; out of one's skull; out of one's tree; poggle; ravers; rock-happy; round the bend; round the twist; starkers; stir-crazy; troppo; whacked out; yarra

9. Communication

The voice Hobson's choice

To speak (to) give; jaw; mensh; word

To repeat what one has said come again

Something said dicky-bird; mouthful; peep

To converse chew the fat (or rag); chin-wag; polari; rap; schmooze; shoot the breeze

(A) conversation, talk buck; chin; chin-wag; gabfest; jaw; polari; rabbit; rag-chewing; rhubarb; schmooze; skull session; yap

To say go; sez

Loquacity big mouth; yackety

To talk loquaciously bang on; bash someone's ear; ear-bash; fat-mouth; gas; rabbit; run off at the mouth; run one's mouth off; shoot one's mouth off; yack; yacker; yacket; yackety-yack; yatter

Loquacious talk gas; stem-winder; yack; yacker; yackety-yack; yap

A loquacious talker big-mouth; blatherskite; ear-basher; fat-mouth; gas-bag; motor mouth; rapper; stem-winder; windbag; yacker

To speak frankly talk turkey

To speak revealingly blow; blow the gaff; cough; shoot one's mouth off; spill; spill one's guts; spill the beans; talk; tip one's hand

A revealing speaker blabbermouth

Pretentious or misleading talk blah; jazz; jive; moody

To talk (to) pretentiously or ostentatiously blah; woof

To talk exaggeratedly strong it

Insolent talk lip; mouth

To talk insolently to lip; smart-mouth

An insolent talker smart mouth

Glib or persuasive talk fanny; spiel

To talk to glibly, persuasively, or cajolingly fanny; fat-mouth

To shout cry blue murder; holler; rort

To swear blind; eff

To talk amorously chat (up)

To be, become, or remain silent belt up; button it; button one's lip; clam; dry up; dummy up; kiss off; leave it out; nark it; nitto; put a sock in it; shaddup; shtoom it; shtoom up; shuddup; shurrup; shut one's face; turn it up; wrap up

Saying nothing; silent mum; nuff said; oyster; shtoom

Information dope; drum; gen; good oil; goods; griff; griffin; ikey; info; low-down; oil; poop; poop sheet; reader; rundown; scam; spec; tip-off

To give information drum; gen; hip; mark someone's card; pull someone's coat; tip off; tip the wink; wise up

Informed, aware hip; on; ready; sussed

A person with information dopester

Misleading information, rumour dirt; furphy; latrine rumour; latrinogram; mulga wire; scam; scuttlebutt

Narrative, story-telling Megillah

A storyteller magsman

A letter bluey; kite; mash note; stiffy; stinker; yum-yum

Salutations BOLTOP; SWAK; SWALK

A typewriter mill

The telephone blower; dog and bone; moby

To telephone give someone a bell; give someone a buzz

A signal emma; griffin; office; peg; pip; red board; squawk; ten-four

To signal squawk

Public address squawk-box

Language lingo

10. Greetings and farewells

Hello what gives; wotcher; yo

A handshake or other greeting glad hand; skin

To greet glad-hand; press the flesh

Goodbye Abyssinia; au reservoir; hooray; hurroo; olive oil; pip-pip; see you later, alligator; tatty-bye; toodle-oo; toodle-pip; T.T.F.N.

11. Complaining

To complain beef; belly-ache; bind; bitch; carry on; chew the rag (or fat); kvetch; nark; noodge; raise Cain; tick; whinge; whip the cat

A complaint; an instance of complaining beef; crab; drip; grouch; stink; whinge

A complainer belly-acher; binder; kvetch; moaning minnie; narker; sourpuss; whinger; wowser

12. Criticism

Adverse criticism, disapprobation bad mouth; bird; licks; stick

An instance of adverse criticism hatchet job; rap; slam

To speak or write critically or disparagingly of; to criticize bad-mouth; bag; clobber; do a number on; dump on; get at; give someone a serve; monster; pan; rubbish; sandbag; slag; slam; soak; take to the cleaners; tee off on; trash

To speak sarcastically; to sneer chuck off; sling off

To express derision or disapproval (of); to barrack; to tease chiack; chi-hike; goose

To insult signify

Insults, abuse verbal

Being criticized on the pan

Someone who speaks critically or disparagingly back-seat driver; hatchet man; Monday-morning quarterback

13. Ridicule

To make fun of someone or something; to mock, tease get someone at it; mickey-take; pull someone's pisser; rag; razz; rib; rot; smart-mouth; take the mickey; take the piss; wind up; wise off

Ridicule razoo

An instance of mocking; send-up mickey-take; piss-take; wind-up

Someone who mocks or ridicules piss-taker

Mocking sarky

An object of ridicule sketch

14. Assent and refusal

Expressions of assent, agreement, or acceptance fucking A; natch; not half; not much; OK; okey-doke; right on; ten-four; too right; wilco; yah; yes siree

An endorsement, acceptance, or authorization OK

Permission open slather

To assent to, authorize, endorse OK

Expressions of refusal, denial, or rejection I should cocoa; nah; nix; nope; no siree; no soap; nothing; nothing doing; not much; not on your Nelly; not Pygmalion likely; no way; stick; stuff

Refusing assent not having any

Something that must not be done no-no

To refuse, reject nix

15. Nonsense

Nonsense all my eye (and Betty Martin); balderdash; balls; baloney; blatherskite; bilge; bollocks; bosh; bullshit; bunkum; cobblers; cock; cod; codswallop; crap; crud; crut; drip; drool; eyewash; flapdoodle; guff; gup; heifer dust; hogwash; hooey; horse feathers; horse shit; macaroni; pants; phoney baloney; phooey; pills; pony; poppycock; rhubarb; rollocks; rot; schmegeggy; shit; shuck; squit; tommy-rot; tosh; tripe

16. Emphatic language

Very, extremely all; awful; dead; dirty; hella; mondo; mucho; not half; piss-; real; seriously; stinking; stinkingly; stonking; veddy; way; well; zonking

Extreme in amount, bigness, badness, difficulty, etc. a hell of a; a helluva; and a half; mondo; mucho

Completely, fully, utterly dead; Harry; motherless; proper; tooting; totally

Complete, utter pluperfect; proper; sweet

Cursed, cursedly adjectival; adjective; all-fired; all-firedly; bally; bee; bleeding; blerry; bloody; blooming; chuffing; cotton-picking; dad-blamed; dad-blasted; dad-gasted; dang; doggone; dratted; effing; fecking; flaming; flipping; fricking; frigging; fucking; god-damn; hellishing; mother-fucking; mothering; mucking; naffing; perishing; pigging; plurry; poxy; Pygmalion; qualified; ruddy; sanguinary; sodding; steaming

Reinforcement formulae and how; my oath; no shit; py korry; sure 'nuff

To the maximum extent and no mistake; big-time; in spades; like a hole in the head; like crazy; like hell; like stink; out of one's mind; seven bells out of; the (living) daylights out of; the pants off; to the wide; with knobs on

17. Imprecations

Imprecations bee aitch; bugger; buggery; Chrisake; drat; feck; frig; fuck; fucking ada; Gawd; Godfrey; hell; jiggered; rass; Sam Hill; screw; shag; sod; tarnation; tunket

A curse sailor's blessing; sailor's farewell; soldier's farewell

18. Names

A name handle; moniker; tag

A signature John Hancock; John Henry

A title handle

Pseudonymously aka

The arts, entertainment, and the media

1. Entertainment

Broadcasting; radio and television boob tube; boom box; box; ghetto-blaster; God slot; goggle-box; idiot box; kidvid; pianist;

Horseracing cert; hot pot; jock; mudder; nanny-goat; nobble; no-hoper; outer; pea; red board; roughie; springer; stickout; stiff; stipe; wrong 'un

Running sweat

Skiing ski bum; snow bunny

Surfing greenback; greenie; gremlin; gremmie; grommet; gun; hodad; hot dog; kook; mush; outside; pipe-line; pounder; shred; soup; surf-bum; surfie; wahine; wipe-out

Swimming bogy; shark-bait

Tennis tank

Wrestling matman

5. Cards and gaming

Playing-cards broads; paper; puppy-foot

A card (to be played) ace in the hole

A throw at dice snake eyes

A gambler broadsman; high-roler; mechanic; piker; punter; ringie; spieler; tinhorn gambler

Gambling games bunco; chemmy; rats and mice; swy

Gambling activity action

A gambling establishment pad; spieler

To gamble fade; go for the doctor; roll the bones; sandbag; seven out; spiel

An instance of gambling flutter

Something gambled on springer

A stake shirt

Winnings pay-off; vig; vigorish

Bookmaking pick-up man

A tipster tip-slinger; urger

A fruit-machine one-arm(ed) bandit; pokey

Time and tide

1. Time

Time nickel and dime

A long time dog's age; yonks

A very short time mo; jig-time; tick

Early on early doors

A minute mike

Dawn sparrow-fart

In the morning ack emma

Afternoon after; arvo

In the afternoon/evening pip emma

2. Beginning

To begin get stuck in; get weaving; hoe in; shoot

3. Deferral and stopping

In a state of being deferred or postponed on the back burner

To stop doing something; desist break down; can; cheese; chuck; jack in; kiss off; knock off; leave it out; nark; stash; stow; tie a can to; turn up

Something cancelled scrub

To give (something) up chuck; jack in; toss it in

To dispense with scrub round; skip it

To put a stop to put the fritz on; put the tin hat on; wash up; zap; zero

The end curtains; endsville; thirty

The game is up the jig is up

4. Experience and inexperience

An experienced person old sweat

To gain experience see the elephant

An inexperienced person; a beginner boot; butter-boy; green pea; Hun; macker; nig-nog; ninety-day wonder; nozzer; poodle-faker; poop-ornament; quirk; red-arse; rocky; rook; rookie; shavetail; shorthorn; snotnose; sprog; stooge; war-baby; wart; wonk; yardbird

Inexperienced green-ass; raggedy-ass; white-shoe

5. Fashionableness, stylishness

Fashion fash

Fashionable, up-to-date big; edgy; fash; funky; happening; in; O.K.; switched on; together; way-in; where it's at; with it

(Fashionably) stylish or smart cool; dicty; doggy; fresh; glam; go; groovy; hep; hip; nifty; piss elegant; posh; preppy; rad; radical; sharp; snappy; snazzy; spiffing; spiffy; swinging; whizzy; zooty

That which is fashionable all the go; the kick

A fashionable or stylish person hippie; hipster; nut; Roy; slick; slicker; swinger

Something stylish or smart sharpie

To make or become more stylish or smart glam; posh up; spiff; spiv; zhoosh

Unfashionable, unstylish naff

6. Old

Old age Anno Domini

An old person crock; crumbly; oldie; woopie; wrinkly

An old man buffer; codger; poppa stoppa

An old woman biddy; ma; tab

An (old) person with old-fashioned or reactionary ideas or habits dug-out; fart; fogey; fud; moss-back

Old-fashioned, outdated hairy; mossy

Senile gaga

An old or worn-out thing rinky-dink

An old or worn-out vehicle banger; crock; heap; jalopy; oil-burner; orphan; rust-bucket; struggle-buggy; tin Lizzie

Worn out by long or rough usage or by neglect beat-up; clapped out; shot; stove-up; warby

To be old or worn out have whiskers

A place for old people Costa Geriatrica

7. Weather

Weather Hughie; QBI

Rain piss; send her down, Davy

Wind cock-eye Bob; Irishman's hurricane

Fog pea-souper

8. Temperature

Cold weather brass monkey

Hot weather scorcher

Location and movement

1. Places

A locality hood; nabe; possie; turf; twenty

Everywhere all over the auction

Cities and towns Big Smoke; Smoke

Boston, Massachusetts Bean Town

Chicago Chi; Windy City

Dallas, Texas Big D

Hollywood Tinseltown

New Orleans Big Easy

New York Apple; Big Apple; Big Town

Philadelphia Philly

Portsmouth Pompey

San Francisco Bay City

Ypres Wipers

A city, place, or situation with the stated characteristics city; -ville

Australia Aussie; other side; Oz

Britain Blighty; Old Dart

Hong Kong Honkers

Mesopotamia Mespot

New South Wales Ma State

New Zealand Pig Island

Queensland Bananaland

Soviet Union Redland

Tasmania Tassie

USA Big PX; U.S. of A.; world

Vietnam Nam

Buildings and institutions Ally Pally; Buck House; Rag (and Famish); Thiefrow; Yard

Prisons Big Q; Scrubs; Ville

Roads drag; Main Stem; stem

The sea Big Ditch; big pond; ditch; drink; oggin; pond; puddle; salt chuck

The moon Oliver

The sun currant bun

2. Habitation, territory

A dwelling, a house, a building des res; drum; gaff; hang-out; hoochie; pad; pogey; stash; walk-back; warehouse

A door Rory O'More

The floor Rory O'More

Stairs apples and pears

A dweller guinea-pig; slummy

To reside in or frequent a place hang out

An area for which one has responsibility; territory manor

3. Remoteness and nearness

A remote place back of Bourke; boondock; boonie; Nar Nar Goon; sticks; tank town; Woop Woop

An (unsophisticated) person from a remote place cornball; culchie; dude; hick; hoosier; jasper; redneck; Reub; Reuben; ridge-runner; shit-kicker; swede-basher; woodchuck

Near within (a) cooee of

Distance klick

4. Movement

To go, walk ankle; choof

To go laboriously flog; schlep; trog; yomp

To go aimlessly shag

To go in a particular direction hang (a) left/right

To go casually mosey; waltz

To lift or carry with effort hike; hoick; lug; schlep

To pull with sudden vigour yank

5. Falling

A fall cropper; gutser; mucker; pratfall; smeller; wipe-out

To fall come a cropper; pratfall; wipe out

6. Speed

Rate of speed bat; lick

A speed of one hundred miles an hour ton; ton-up

Fast in two up; jildi; lickety-split; like a bat out of hell; like a dose of salts; like gangbusters; like the clappers; PDQ; sharpish

High speed toe

To go fast ball the jack; beetle; belt; blind; burn; highball; nick; pour (on) the coal; shift; swing the gate; travel; zap

A fast person or thing scooter; swiftie

To accelerate give her the gun; gun; pour (on) the coal; step on the gas

Acceleration welly

To hurry drag ass; get a hump on; get a wiggle on; get one's skates on; haul ass; rattle one's dags; shake a leg; tear ass

Be quick! chop-chop

Slowness slows

A slow person or animal slowpoke

To go slowly drag the chain

7. Arrival

To arrive lob

To arrive eventually in the stated place or condition fetch up

To announce one's arrival make one's number

To approach belly up

A welcome or reception of the stated sort mitt

8. Departure

To go away amscray; beat it; blow; bug off; bug out; bugger off; bunk; buzz off; cut along; cut and run; do a bunk; do a fade; do a get; do a guy; do a mickey; do a runner; do a scarper; drag one's ass; eff off; fuck off; get; get lost; get the hell out; go and have a roll; go fly a kite; go through; guy; have it on one's toes; hit the breeze; hit the road; hook it; hop it; hop the twig; jack off; lam; mizzle; naff off; nick off; piss off; scram; see a man about a dog; shemozzle; shoot the crow; shoot

through; shove; skate; skedaddle; skidoo; skip it; skip out; slide; sling one's hook; smoke; sod off; split; vamoose

To leave the ground, take off get unstuck; scramble; unstick

To leave an aircraft by ejecting punch out

To depart frequently do a Melba

To leave (a place) skip; split; stash; vamoose

Go away! imshi; on your bike; twenty-three skidoo

A departure moonlight; moonlight flit

One who departs fly-by-night; moonlighter; skip

9. Transport

To transport, carry, take cart; schlep

A journey, trip jump

A ticket ducat

Driving and road manoeuvres Mexican overdrive; tailgate; U-ey; wheelie

A driver bikie; cowboy; gipsy; greaser; hackie; road hog

A pilot George

A passenger legal; strap-hanger

A pedestrian ped

Walking per boot

Traffic offences feed the bears; hotting; run

Accidents fender-bender; prang; shunt; shunt-up; wing and a prayer

To crash buy the farm; prang; total; wrap round

Vehicle registration reg; rego; tag

Taxis duck-shoving; Jixi; roader

Railways gandy dancer; gricer; rounder; shack; snake; snake charmer

Flying and air travel greaser; red eye; split-arse; stooger; viff

10. Vehicles

A towed vehicle pup; Queen Mary

A motor vehicle banger; bomb; bus; Chelsea tractor; crate; crummy; drag; flivver; gas guzzler; heap; hog; hooptie; hot rod; iron; jalopy; jam jar; limo; lizzie; oil-burner; one-lunger; orphan; passion wagon; pimpmobile; rag-top; ride; rod; rust-bucket; scoot; scooter; sheen; short; stink-pot; struggle-buggy; wheels; woodie

A lorry artic; gipsy; passion wagon; red ball; six by six; ute

A bus scooter; short; tub

A make of car Beamer; Jag; Merc; Roller

A cycle chopper; grid; hog; scoot

A train crummy; dog-box; drag; locie; red ball; side-door Pullman

A ship, boat crate; fizz-boat; flat-top; pig boat; rust-bucket; skunk; stink-pot; tin fish; windbag

Parts of a ship monkey island; mud-hook; perisher; sharp end

An aircraft bird; bus; crate; duck; flivver; flying boxcar; grasshopper; kite; penguin; puddle-jumper; quirk; ruptured duck; squirt

A helicopter chopper; egg-beater; sky bear

A type of aircraft Rumpty; Spit; Wimpey

Parts of an aircraft greenhouse; office; pulpit; undercart

An engine and its parts cat; mill; one-lunger; percolator; pot; tranny

Given enhanced engine performance hopped-up

Instrumentation speedo

Brakes anchors

A tyre skin

Fuel juice

A mechanical fault gremlin

A shop selling vehicle accessories and spares speed shop

Abstract qualities and states

1. Size

Large corking; ginormous; humongous; mega; monstro; sollicking; zonking

Large one boomer; doozer; doozy; grand(d) addy; King Kong; lunker; sollicker

Long as long as one's arm

A tall person beanpole; lofty

Small bitsy; bitty; itsy-bitsy; itty-bitty; mingy; titchy

Small one peanut; peanuts; pinky; shrimp; squib; tich

Short person short-arse; shorty

2. Quantity

Nothing bugger-all; bupkis; damn-all; Fanny Adams; fuck-all; not a sausage; S.F.A.; sod-all; sweet F.A.; wot no...; zilch

A trivial or insignificant amount or number damn; diddly; diddly-shit; doodly; doodly-squat; hill of beans; hoot; squat; tinker's cuss; two hoots

A small amount or number fat lot; skerrick; skosh

Small in amount measly; mingy

An amount glob; gob; nibble

One Kelly's eye

Three trey

Four rouf

Sixty-six clickety-click

A thousand K; thou

To increase hike; jack up

A large amount (of) bags; loadsa; lotsa; lotta; more than you can shake a stick at; mucho; scads; shedload; shitload; squillion; steen; steenth; swag; zillion

Everything full monty; guntz; shebang; sub-cheese; whole kit and caboodle; whole schmeer; (whole) works

The maximum amount mostest

An excessive amount; as much as one can bear basinful; bellyful; earful; gutful

Having more than is desirable lousy with

Behaviour, an event, etc. that is more than one can tolerate bit thick; frozen limit; OTT

Excessive in quantity dime a dozen

Curbing excess eighty-six on

Calculation yay

3. Fate

Something dependent on chance toss-up

The perverse workings of fate Murphy's law; Sod's law; (that's) how the cookie crumbles

That which is preordained one's name (and number) is on; one's number is on

A run of (good or bad) luck spin

Bad luck hard cheddar; hard cheese; rough spin; Saltash luck; snake eyes; T.S.; tough shit; tough titty

Unlucky shit out of luck; stiff

An unlucky person schlimazel

Lucky arsey; jammy; tin-arsed; tinny

A lucky person tin arse; tin back; tin bum

To enjoy good luck luck into; luck out

4. Possibility, probability, and certainty

A negligible prospect Chinaman's chance; earthly; fat chance; fat show

Something certain cert; lay-down; lead-pipe cinch; monty; moral; motser; stickout; stone ginger

Impossible no go

To be certain betcha; bet one's boots; bet one's bottom dollar; bet one's life

Uncertain on spec

5. Risk

Risky dicey

A risky or dangerous experience or situation shaky do

To do something risky; take a risk ask for it; go for broke; go for one's tea; lead with one's chin

As a speculation; without certainty of success on spec

6. Advantage and disadvantage

An advantage ace in the hole; bulge; catbird seat; grouter

To be in an advantageous situation have it wired

To get an advantage over someone; put someone in a disadvantageous situation catch someone bending; get someone by the balls; get the dead-wood on; get the drop on; have someone by the short and curlies; have someone by the short hairs; have someone on toast; have the goods on; have the jump on; have the wood on

A disadvantageous situation short end

In a disadvantageous situation behind the eight ball; off the pace; with one's pants/trousers down

Lack of advantage; a stalemate Mexican stand-off

7. Easiness

Easy cushy; easy-peasy; no sweat

Something easy to do breeze; doddle; drop-in; duck soup; gaper; gimme; laugher; pie; piece of cake; piece of piss; pipe; pud; pudding; snack; snap; snip; soda; turkey shoot

8. Difficulty

Difficult dodgy; hairy; solid

Something difficult ball-breaker; ball-buster; bastard; bitch; bugger; cow; honey; pig; skull buster; sod; swine

9. Precision, approximation, and correctness

Precise(ly) on the nose; on the schnozz; straight-up

Approximation ballpark

Correct, right fucking A; on the beam

To be correct cook with gas

10. Mistakes

A mistake bish; black; blob; bloomer; blooper; blue; boner; boob; boo-boo; clanger; clink; clinker; floater; flub; fluff; goof; goof-up; ricket; rock; whiff

To make a mistake boob; duff; fuck up; goof; screw up

Mistaken all wet; off (the) beam

11. Success

To succeed, achieve success ace it; bring home the bacon; curl the mo; cut the mustard; get the guernsey

To be achieving success be laughing; cook with gas; go gangbusters

To succeed in doing or dealing with hack

To ensure success in or against sew up

A great success smasheroo; sockeroo; socko; tear; wow

The highest level of success big time

Successful socko

Successfully like gangbusters

A prize pot

12. Spoiling, ruination

To spoil, ruin, botch, make a mess of arse up; ball up; balls up; banjax; bitch; bollix; bugger; cock up; cruel; dish; flub; foozle; fritz; fuck up; goof; jigger; louse up; make a balls of; mung; piss up; pox; puckeroo; screw up; snafu; trash

To put a stop to, thwart kibosh; put the bee on; put the kibosh on; put the mockers on; sprag; stonker

To frustrate someone's purposes banjax; ditch; fix someone's wagon; moz; nark; put the mockers on; put the mock(s) on; put the moz on; put the pot on; root; settle someone's hash; tear it

To go wrong snafu

An instance of spoiling or ruining something; a bungle, botch, mess balls-up; bollix; clusterfuck; cock-up; fuck-up; piss-up; snafu

To be spoiled, ruined, or lost bang goes; go down the Swanee; go west; have had one's chips

To become inoperative; go awry conk; go blooey; poop

In a spoiled or ruined condition; inoperative blooey; buckeroo; buggered; buggered up; bung; down the drain; down the gurgler; down the pan; down the tube(s); finito; fubar; fucked; goosed; hinky; kaput; on the fritz; on the rocks; on the toboggan; out of whack; puckerood; rooted; shot; snafu; spitchered; trashed; washed up

Something that spoils or ruins spanner in the works

A spoilsport party pooper; wet smack; wowser

13. Failure

Something that fails; an unsuccessful person or thing; a fiasco bomb; bosh-shot; boss-shot; dud; duffer; fizzer; flopperoo; frost; lead balloon; morning-glory; no dice; no-no; no soap; pratfall; stiff; stumer; turkey

A failure of function glitch

To be unsuccessful bomb; come a cropper; come a gutser; come a mucker; come unstuck; crap out; duffer; flunk; fuck up; lay an egg

To fail at or in flunk

To designate as failing flunk; pill; plough

14. Defeat and victory

To defeat (heavily) cream; do; donkey-lick; donkey-wallop; dust off; eat someone alive; knock the socks off; make mincemeat of; muller; ring; shellac; shred; skin; skunk; slather; starch; take; wax; whip; whup; wipe the floor with; zilch

To defeat narrowly nip

A heavy defeat shellacking; wipe-out

Completely defeated gone a million; lurked

To admit defeat (and give up) drop one's bundle; say uncle; sky the wipe

To lose deliberately take a dive; throw

To win easily walk

15. Power, influence

Power, influence clout; drag; in

To have in one's power have by the short and curlies; have by the short hairs

16. Coercion

Coercion, pressurizing hardball; heat; squeeze play

To pressurize be on someone's wheel; bogart; gee; hardball; hustle; muscle; put the acid on; put the bite on; put the lug on; put the maginnis on; put the squeeze on; sool; stand over; sweat

Someone who intimidates or coerces others enforcer; muscle; muscle man; standover man

Inducement come-on

17. Organization

Organization, administration, bureaucracy admin; bumf

To organize jack up

To organize one's affairs efficiently get one's act together; get one's shit together

Disorganization couldn't organize a piss-up in a brewery; too many chiefs and not enough Indians

Disorganized shambolic

18. Subservience

Subservient eat crow; pussy-whipped; under the cosh

A subservient person monkey-man; squidge; stooge

To put in a subservient position have by the short and curlies; have by the short hairs; have on toast

19. Genuineness and spuriousness

Genuine actual; dinkum; dinky-die; kosher; ridge; ridgy-didge; ryebuck

Something or someone genuine goods; McCoy

Spurious bodger; duff; moody; phoney baloney; snide

Something or someone spurious dog-and-pony show; duff; gold brick; not the clean potato; shuck

To falsify phoney up

20. Triviality, insignificance

Trivial, insignificant jerkwater; piddling; pissing; two-bit

Something or someone trivial or insignificant pie-eater; pipsqueak; putty medal; small potatoes

21. Similarity

Something or someone similar ring; ringer

22. Strangeness

Strange, odd, eccentric freakazoid; rum; way-out; zonky

Something or someone strange or eccentric card; freakazoid; fruit-loop; oddball; odd bod

23. Severity, oppressiveness

Severe, uncompromising hard-ass; hard-assed; heavy

To deal with severely, harshly, or oppressively clobber; give someone beans; give someone hell; give someone the works; put through the wringer; shaft; sock

Harsh treatment gaff; shaft; stick

A severe, hard, or uncompromising person ball-breaker; ball-buster; hard-ass; hard case; hard nut; hard ticket

24. Searching

To search a person or place shake down; spin; toss

To search a person fan; go through

To search and rob a person or place go through; turn over

To search for in order to harm gun for

To search an area or place punt around; recce; recon

A search of an area punt; recce; recco; recon

To investigate or assess a person, situation, etc. scope out; suss

To search for information grill

25. Intrusion

To intrude crash; get into the act; horn in; prodnose; shit-stir; stickybeak

An intrusive person buttinsky

An inquisitive person looky-loo; nosey parker; prodnose; stickybeak

An impostor ringer

26. Involvement

Involved (in) in on the act; into

Involvement piece of the action

To become involved get into the act

27. Sharing, distribution

A sharing out carve-up

A share given or received chop; cut; rake-off; split; whack

Equally or fairly shared even Stephen

Per item a throw

28. Avoidance

To avoid or evade something dodge Pompey; odds; skip; skip it; skive; weasel out

To avoid at all costs not touch with a barge-pole

A person who avoids things skiver

29. Abandonment

To discard, get rid of chuck it; dice; ditch; sling

To stop attempting, give up on give away

Rid of shot of

Ayto is a freelance lexicographer
itor of *Brewer's Dictionary of*
and Fable.

Simpson is Chief Editor of the
English Dictionary.